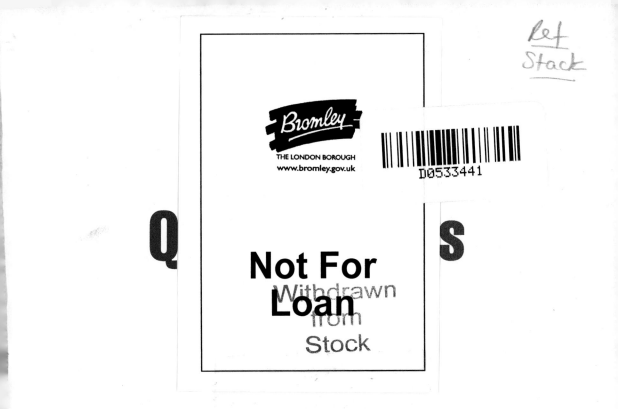

British Qualifications 2018

48TH EDITION

A Complete Guide to Professional,
Vocational & Academic Qualifications
in the United Kingdom

KoganPage

LONDON NEW YORK NEW DELHI

Publisher's note

Every possible effort has been made to ensure that the information contained in this book is accurate at the time of going to press, and the publishers and authors cannot accept responsibility for any errors or omissions, however caused. No responsibility for loss or damage occasioned to any person acting, or refraining from action, as a result of the material in this publication can be accepted by the editor, the publisher or any of the authors.

First published in Great Britain in 1966

Forty-eighth edition published in Great Britain and the United States in 2018 by Kogan Page Limited

2nd Floor, 45 Gee Street	c/o Martin P Hill Consulting	4737/23 Ansari Road
London EC1V 3RS	122 W 27th St, 10th Floor	Daryaganj
United Kingdom	New York NY 10001	New Delhi 110002
www.koganpage.com	USA	India

© Kogan Page, 2018

British Library Cataloguing-in-Publication Data

A CIP record for this book is available from the British Library.

ISBN 978 0 7494 8148 3
E-ISBN 978 0 7494 8147 6
ISSN 0141-5972

Typeset by AMA DataSet Ltd, Preston
Print production managed by Jellyfish
Printed and bound by Ashford Colour Press Ltd

PUBLISHER'S NOTE

This 48th edition of *British Qualifications* has been considerably revised and updated to reflect the many changes in degree, diploma and certificate courses and to take account of legislative reforms affecting the structure of higher and further education over the past year.

The editor and compilers are most grateful to the academic registrars and the secretaries of the many bodies they have contacted for information and advice. Without their cooperation, the revision and updating of *British Qualifications* would not have been possible.

CONTENTS

Contents

Contents

Contents

Contents

Contents

REFERENCES

Association of MBAs (AMBA) (annual) *AMBA – Financial Times Guide to Business Schools*, AMBA, London

Committee of Vice-Chancellors and Principals (CVCP) (annual) *University Entrance: The official guide*, CVCP, London

Department for Education and Skills (DfES) (2003) *The Future of Higher Education*, The Stationery Office, London [online] http://www.dfes.gov.uk/hegateway/strategy/hestrategy/foreword.shtml

DfES (2004) *Five-Year Strategy for Children and Learners*, DfES, London

Qualifications and Curriculum Authority (QCA) (2004) *New Thinking for Reform: A framework for achievement*, QCA, London (July)

HOW TO USE THIS BOOK

You may find these notes helpful when using the book.

Part 1 presents an overview of the further and higher educational systems currently in operation in the United Kingdom, including a discussion of the major reforms that have taken place over the past year and their impact.

Part 2 takes a look at the teaching establishments whose qualifications are listed in Part 4 of the book, offering an explanation of the different types of institution, their place in the overall system and the levels of qualification that they award.

Part 3 presents a detailed description of vocational qualifications awarded by many of the professional associations included in Part 5, including an explanation of validating, examining and awarding bodies.

Part 4 is a directory of qualifications awarded by universities in the United Kingdom (ordered by university name). There is a brief introduction detailing admission to degree courses, degree structure and the various categories of degree available.

Part 5 is a directory of qualifications awarded by professional, trade and specialist associations in the United Kingdom (ordered by profession / discipline), including certificates, diplomas, NVQs and SVQs. A short introduction explains the functions of professional associations and how to gain membership.

Part 6 describes various bodies involved in the accreditation of colleges in the independent sector of further and higher education.

Part 7 is a list of study associations and learned societies.

Also included (at the beginning of the book) is a list of all abbreviations and designatory letters used throughout *British Qualifications*.

INDEX OF ABBREVIATIONS AND DESIGNATORY LETTERS

AAB	Associate of the Association of Book-keepers
AACB	Associate of the Association of Certified Bookkeepers
AACP	Associate of the Association of Computer Professionals
AAFC	Associate of the Association of Financial Controllers and Administrators
AAIA	Associate of the Association of International Accountants
AAMS	Associate of the Association of Medical Secretaries, Practice Managers, Administrators and Receptionists
AASI	Associate of the Ambulance Service Institute
AASW	Advanced Award in Social Work
AAT	Association of Accounting Technicians
ABC	Awarding Body Consortium
ABDO	Associate of the British Dispensing Opticians
ABE	Association of Business Executives
ABEng	Associate Member of the Association of Building Engineers
ABHA	Associate of the British Hypnotherapy Association
ABIAT	Associate Member of the British Institute of Architectural Technologists
ABIPP	Associate of the British Institute of Professional Photography
ABMA	Associate of the Business Management Association
ABPR	Association of British Picture Restorers
ABRSM	Associated Board of the Royal Schools of Music
ABS	Association of Business Schools
ABSSG	Associate of the British Society of Scientific Glassblowers
ACA	Associate of the Institute of Chartered Accountants in England and Wales
ACA	Associate of the Institute of Chartered Accountants in Ireland
ACB	Association of Certified Bookkeepers
ACC	Accredited Clinical Coders
ACCA	Associate of the Association of Chartered Certified Accountants
ACCA	Association of Chartered Certified Accountants
ACE	Association for Conferences and Events
ACEA	Associate of the Institute of Cost and Executive Accountants
ACertCM	Archbishop of Canterbury's Certificate in Church Music
ACGI	Associate of City and Guilds of London Institute
ACIArb	Associate of the Chartered Institute of Arbitrators
ACIB	Associate of the Chartered Institute of Bankers
ACIBS	Associate of the Chartered Institute of Bankers in Scotland
ACIBSE	Associate of the Chartered Institution of Building Services Engineers
ACIH	Associate of the Chartered Institute of Housing
ACII	Associate of the Chartered Insurance Institute
ACILA	Associate of the Chartered Institute of Loss Adjusters
ACIM	Associate of the Chartered Institute of Marketing
ACIOB	Associate of the Chartered Institute of Building
ACIS	Associate of the Institute of Chartered Secretaries and Administrators
ACIT	Advanced Certificate in International Trade
ACLIP	Certified Affiliate of CILIP
ACMA	Associate of the Chartered Institute of Management Accountants
ACP	Association of Child Psychotherapists
ACP	Associate of the College of Preceptors

ACP	Association of Computer Professionals
ACPM	Associate of the Confederation of Professional Management
ACPP	Associate of the College of Pharmacy Practice
ACT	Associate of the College of Teachers
ACYW	Associate of the Community and Youth Work Association
ADCE	Advanced Diploma in Childcare and Education
ADCM	Archbishop of Canterbury's Diploma in Church Music
AdDipEd	Advanced Diploma in Education
ADI	Approved Driving Instructor
AECI	Association Member of the Institute of Employment Consultants
AEWVH	Association for the Education and Welfare of the Visually Handicapped
AFA	Associate of the Faculty of Actuaries
AFA	Associate of the Institute of Financial Accountants
AFBPsS	Associate Fellow of the British Psychological Society
AFCI	Associate of the Faculty of Commerce and Industry Ltd
AffBMA	Affiliate of the Business Management Association
AffIManf	Affiliate of the Institute of Manufacturing
AffIMI	Affiliate of the Institute of the Motor Industry
AffIMS	Affiliate of the Institute of Management Specialists
AffInstM	Affiliate of the Meat Training Council
AffIP	Affiliate of the Institute of Plumbing
AffProfBTM	Affiliate of Professional Business and Technical Management
AFIMA	Associate Fellow of the Institute of Mathematics and its Applications
AFISOL	Aerodrome Flight Information Service Officer's Licence
AFPC	Advanced Financial Planning Certificate
AFRCSEd	Associate Fellow of Royal College of Surgeons of Edinburgh
AGCL	Associate of the Guild of Cleaners and Launderers
AGI	Associate of the Greek Institute
AGSM	Associate of the Guildhall School of Music and Drama
AHCIMA	Associate of the Hotel and Catering International Management Association
AHFS	Associate of the Council of Health Fitness and Sports Therapists
AHRIM	Associate of the Institute of Health Record Information and Management
AIA	Associate of the Institute of Actuaries
AIA	Association of International Accountants
AIAgrE	Associate of the Institution of Agricultural Engineers
AIAT	Associate of the Institute of Asphalt Technology
AIBCM	Associate of the Institute of British Carriage and Automobile Manufacturers
AIBMS	Associate of the Institute of Biomedical Science
AICB	Associate of the Institute of Certified Book-Keepers
AIChor	Associate of the Benesh Institute of Choreology
AICHT	Associate of the International Council of Holistic Therapists
AICM(Cert)	Associate Member of the Institute of Credit Management
AICS	Associate of the Institution of Chartered Shipbrokers
AICSc	Associate of the Institute of Consumer Sciences Incorporating Home Economics
AIDTA	Associate of the International Dance Teachers' Association
AIE	Associate of the Institute of Electrolysis
AIEM	Associate of the Institute of Executives and Managers
AIExpE	Associate of the Institute of Explosive Engineers
AIFA	Associate of the Institute of Field Archaeologists
AIFBQ	Associate of the International Faculty of Business Qualifications
AIFireE	Associate of the Institution of Fire Engineers
AIFP	Associate of the British International Freight Association

AIGD	Associate of the Institute of Grocery Distribution
AIHort	Associate Member of the Institute of Horticulture
AIIMR	Associate of the Institute of Investment Management and Research
AIIRSM	Associate of the International Institute of Risk and Safety Management
AIL	Associate of the Institute of Linguists
AILAM	Associate of the Institute of Leisure and Amenity Management
AIMBM	Associate of the Institute of Maintenance and Building Management
AIMC	Associate of the Institute of Management Consultancy
AIMgt	Associate of the Institute of Management
AIMIS	Associate of the Institute for the Management of Information Systems
AIMM	Associate of the Institute of Massage and Movement
AInstAM	Associate of the Institute of Administrative Management
AInstBA	Associate of the Institute of Business Administration
AInstBCA	Associate of the Institute of Burial and Cremation Administration
AInstBM	Associate of the Institute of Builders' Merchants
AInstCM	Associate of the Institute of Commercial Management
AInstM	Associate of the Meat Training Council
AInstPkg	Associate of the Institute of Packaging
AInstPM	Associate of the Institute of Professional Managers and Administrators
AInstSMM	Associate of the Institute of Sales and Marketing Management
AInstTA	Associate of the Institute of Transport Administration
AInstTT	Associate Member of the Institute of Travel and Tourism
AIOC	Associate of the Institute of Carpenters
AIOFMS	Associate of the Institute of Financial and Management Studies
AIP	Associate of the Institute of Plumbing
AIQA	Associate of the Institute of Quality Assurance
AIS	Accredited Imaging Scientist
AISOB	Associate of the Incorporated Society of Organ Builders
AISTD	Associate of the Imperial Society of Teachers of Dancing
AISTDDip	Associate Diploma of the Imperial Society of Teachers of Dancing
AITSA	Associate of the Institute of Trading Standards Administration
AIVehE	Associate of the Institute of Vehicle Engineers
AIWSc	Associate Member of the Institute of Wood Science
ALCM	Associate of the London College of Music
ALI	Associate of the Landscape Institute
ALS	Associate of the Linnean Society of London
AMA	Associate of the Museums Association
AMABE	Associate Member of the Association of Business Executives
AMAE	Associate Member of the Academy of Experts
AMASI	Associate Member of the Architecture and Surveying Institute
AMBA	Association of MBAs
AMBA	Non-Teacher Associate Member of the British (Theatrical) Arts
AMBCS	Associate Member of the British Computer Society
AMBII	Associate Member of the British Institute of Innkeeping
AmCAM	Associate of the Communication Advertising and Marketing Education Foundation
AMCT	Associate of the Association of Corporate Treasurers
AMCTHCM	Associate Member of the Confederation of Tourism, Hotel and Catering Management
AMI	Association Montessori Internationale
AMIA	Affiliated Member of the Association of International Accountants
AMIAgrE	Associate Member of the Institution of Agricultural Engineers
AMIAP	Associate Member of the Institution of Analysts and Programmers

AMIAT	Associate Member of the Institute of Asphalt Technology
AMIBC	Associate Member of the Institute of Building Control
AMIBCM	Associate Member of the Institute of British Carriage and Automobile Manufacturers
AMIBE	Associate Member of the Institution of British Engineers
AMIBF	Associate Member of the Institute of British Foundrymen
AMICE	Associate Member of the Institution of Civil Engineers
AMIChemE	Associate Member of the Institution of Chemical Engineers
AMIED	Associate Member of the Institution of Engineering Designers
AMIEE	Associate Member of the Institution of Electrical Engineers
AMIEx	Associate Member of the Institute of Export
AMIHIE	Associate Member of the Institute of Highway Incorporated Engineers
AMIHT	Associate Member of the Institution of Highways and Transportation
AMIIE	Associate Member of the Institution of Incorporated Engineers
AMIIExE	Associate Member of the Institution of Incorporated Executive Engineers
AMIIHTM	Associate Member of the International Institute of Hospitality Tourism & Management
AMIISE	Associate Member of the International Institute of Social Economics
AMIM	Associate Member of the Institute of Materials
AMIManf	Member of the Institute of Manufacturing
AMIMechE	Associate Member of the Institution of Mechanical Engineers
AMIMechIE	Associate Member of the Institution of Mechanical Incorporated Engineers
AMIMI	Associate Member of the Institute of the Motor Industry
AMIMinE	Associate of the Institute of Mining Engineers
AMIMM	Associate Member of the Institution of Mining and Metallurgy
AMIMS	Associate Member of the Institute of Management Specialists
AMInstAEA	Associate Member of the Institute of Automotive Engineer Assessors
AMInstBE	Associate Member of the Institution of British Engineers
AMInstE	Associate Member of the Institute of Energy
AMInstR	Associate Member of the Institute of Refrigeration
AMInstTA	Associate Member of the Institute of Transport Administration
AMIPlantE	Associate Member of the Institution of Plant Engineers
AMIPR	Associate Member of the Institute of Public Relations
AMIPRE	Associate Member of the Incorporated Practitioners in Radio and Electronics
AMIQ	Associate Member of the Institute of Quarrying
AMIQA	Associate Member of the Institute of Quality Assurance
AMIRTE	Associate Member of the Institute of Road Transport Engineers
AMISM	Associate Member of the Institute for Supervision & Management
AMIStrutE	Associate Member of the Institution of Structural Engineers
AMITD	Associate Member of the Institute of Training and Development
AMIVehE	Associate Member of the Institute of Vehicle Engineers
AMNI	Associate Member of the Nautical Institute
AMPA	Associate Member of the Master Photographers Association
AMProfBTM	Associate Member of Professional Business and Technical Management
AMRAeS	Associate Member of the Royal Aeronautical Society
AMRSH	Associate Member of the Royal Society for the Promotion of Health
AMS	Associate of the Institute of Management Services
AMS(Aff)	Affiliate of the Association of Medical Secretaries, Practice Managers, Administrators and Receptionists
AMSE	Associate Member of the Society of Engineers (Inc)
AMSPAR	Association of Medical Secretaries, Practice Managers, Administrators and Receptionists

AMusEd	Associate Diploma in Music Education
AMusLCM	Associate in Music of the London College of Music
AMusTCL	Associate in Music of Trinity College of Music
AMWES	Associate Member of the Women's Engineering Society
ANAEA	Associate of the National Association of Estate Agents
ANCA	Advanced National Certificate in Agriculture
AOP	Association of Photographers
AOR	Association of Reflexologists
APA	Accreditation of Prior Experience
APC	Assessment of Professional Competence
APCS	Associate of the Property Consultants Society
APMI	Associate of the Pensions Management Institute
APMP	Association for Project Management Professional
AQA	Assessment & Qualifications Alliance
ARAD	Associate of the Royal Academy of Dancing
ARAM	Associate of the Royal Academy of Music
ARB	Architects Registration Board
ARCM	Associate of Royal College of Music
ARCO	Associate of the Royal College of Organists
ARCS	Associate of the Royal College of Science
AREC	Associate of the Recruitment and Employment Confederation
ARELS	Association of Recognised English Language Services
ARELS-FELCO	Association of Recognised English Language Teaching Establishments in Britain
ARIBA	Associate of the Royal Institute of British Architects
ARICS	Associate of the Royal Institution of Chartered Surveyors
ARIPHH	Associate of the Royal Institute of Public Health and Hygiene
ARPS	Associate of the Royal Photographic Society
ARSC	Associate of the Royal Society of Chemistry
ARSCM	Associate of the Royal School of Church Music
ARSM	Associate of the Royal School of Mines
AS	Advanced Supplementary level
ASCA	Associate of the Institute of Company Accountants
ASCT	Associate of the Society of Claims Technicians
ASDC	Associate of the Society of Dyers and Colourists
ASE	Associate of the Society of Engineers (Inc)
ASI	Ambulance Service Institute
ASI	Architecture and Surveying Institute
ASIAffil	Affiliate of the Ambulance Service Institute
ASIS	Accredited Senior Imaging Scientist
ASLC	Advanced Secretarial Language Certificate
ASMA	Associate of the Society of Sales Management Administrators Ltd
ASNN	Associate of the Society of Nursery Nursing
AssCI	Associate of the Institute of Commerce
AssociateCIPD	Associate of the Chartered Institute of Personnel and Development
AssociateIEEE	Associate of the Institution of Electrical and Electronics Engineers Incorporated
AssociateIIE	Associate of the Institution of Incorporated Engineers
AssocIMechIE	Associate of the Institution of Mechanical Incorporated Engineers
AssocIPD	Associate of the Institute of Personnel & Development
AssocIPHE	Associate of the Institution of Public Health Engineers
AssocMIWM	Associate Member of the Institute of Wastes Management
AssocTechIIE	Associate Technician of the Institution of Incorporated Engineers
ASTA	Associate of the Swimming Teachers' Association

ASVA	Associate of the Incorporated Society of Valuers and Auctioneers
ATC	Art Teacher's Certificate
ATCL	Associate of Trinity College of Music
ATCLicence	Air Traffic Controller's Licence
ATCLTESOL	Associate Diploma in the Teaching of English to Speakers of Other Languages, Trinity College
ATD	Art Teacher's Diploma
ATI	Associate of the Textile Industry
ATII	Associate of the Chartered Institute of Taxation
ATPL	Airline Transport Pilot's Licence
ATSC	Associate of the Oil and Colour Chemists' Association
ATSC	Associate in the Technology of Surface Coatings
ATT	Association of Taxation Technicians
ATT	Member of the Association of Taxation Technicians
ATTA	Association of Therapy Teachers Associate
ATTF	Association of Therapy Teachers Fellow
ATTM	Association of Therapy Teachers Member
AWeldI	Associate of the Welding Institute
BA	Bachelor of Arts
BA(Econ)	Bachelor of Arts in Economics & Social Studies
BA(Ed)	Bachelor of Arts (Education)
BA(Lan)	Bachelor of Languages
BA(Law)	Bachelor of Arts in Law
BA(Music)	Bachelor of Music
BABTAC	British Association of Beauty Therapy and Cosmetology Ltd
BAC	British Accreditation Council for Independent Further and Higher Education
BAC	British Association for Counselling
BAcc	Bachelor of Accountancy
BACP	British Association for Counselling Psychotherapy
BADA	British Antique Dealers' Association
BADN	British Association of Dental Nurses
BAE	British Association of Electrolysists Ltd
BAGMA	British Agricultural and Garden Machinery Association
BAgr	Bachelor of Agriculture
BAO	Bachelor of Obstetrics
BAP	British Association of Psychotherapists
BArch	Bachelor of Architecture
BASELT	British Association in State English Language Teaching
BBO	British Ballet Organisation
BChD	Bachelor of Dental Surgery
BChir	Bachelor of Surgery
BCL	Bachelor of Civil Law
BCom	Bachelor of Commerce
BCombStuds	Bachelor of Combined Studies
BComm	Bachelor of Communications
BCS	Bachelor of Combined Studies
BCS	British Computer Society
BD	Bachelor of Divinity
BDA	British Dietetic Association
BDes	Bachelor of Design
BDS	Bachelor of Dental Surgery
BEconSc	Bachelor of Economics

BECTU	Broadcasting, Entertainment, Cinematograph and Theatre Union
BEd	Bachelor of Education
BEng	Bachelor of Engineering
BEng and Man	Bachelor of Mechanical Engineering, Manufacture and Management
BER	Board for Engineers' Regulation
BFA	Bachelor of Fine Arts
BFin	Bachelor of Finance
BHA	British Hypnotherapy Association
BHI	British Horological Institute Ltd
BHS	British Horse Society
BHSAI	British Horse Society's Assistant Instructor's Certificate
BHSI	British Horse Society's Instructor's Certificate
BHSII	British Horse Society's Intermediate Instructor's Certificate
BHSIntSM	British Horse Society's Intermediate Stable Manager's Certificate
BHSSM	British Horse Society's Stable Manager's Certificate
BIA	Beauty Industry Authority
BIAT	British Institute of Architectural Technologists
BIBA	Bachelor of International Business Administration
BIE	British Institute of Embalmers
BIFA	British International Freight Association
BIPP	British Institute of Professional Photography
BIS	British Interplanetary Society
BKSTS	British Kinematograph Sound and Television Society
BLD	Bachelor of Landscape Design
BLE	Bachelor of Land Economy
BLEng	Bi-Lingual Engineer
BLib	Bachelor of Librarianship
BLing	Bachelor of Linguistics
BLitt	Bachelor of Letters
BLS	Bachelor of Library Studies
BM	Bachelor of Medicine
BMA	British Medical Association
BM, BCh	Conjoint degree of Bachelor of Medicine, Bachelor of Surgery
BM, BS	Conjoint degree of Bachelor of Medicine, Bachelor of Surgery
BMedBiol	Bachelor of Medical Biology
BMedSci	Bachelor of Medical Sciences
BMedSci(Speech)	Bachelor of Medical Sciences (Speech)
BMet	Bachelor of Metallurgy
BMid	Bachelor of Midwifery
BMidwif	Bachelor of Midwifery
BMSc	Bachelor of Medical Sciences
BMus	Bachelor of Music
BN	Bachelor of Nursing
BNNursing	Bachelor of Nursing, Nursing Studies
BNSc	Bachelor of Nursing
BNurs	Bachelor of Nursing
BOptom	Bachelor of Optometry
BPA	Bachelor of Performing Arts
BPharm	Bachelor of Pharmacy
BPhil	Bachelor of Philosophy
BPhil(Ed)	Bachelor of Philosophy (Education)
BPL	Bachelor of Planning

BSc	Bachelor of Science
BSc(Archit)	Bachelor of Science (Architecture)
BSc(DentSci)	Bachelor of Science in Dental Science
BSc(Econ)	Bachelor of Science in Economics
BSc(MedSci)	Bachelor of Science (Medical Science)
BSc(Social Science)	Bachelor of Science (Social Science)
BSc(Town & Regional Planning)	Bachelor of Science (Town & Regional Planning)
BSc(VetSc)	Bachelor of Science (Veterinary Science)
BScAgr	Bachelor of Science in Agriculture
BScEng	Bachelor of Science in Engineering
BScFor	Bachelor of Science in Forestry
BScTech	Bachelor of Technical Science
BSocSc	Bachelor of Social Science
BSSc	Bachelor of Social Science
BSSG	Member of the British Society of Scientific Glassblowers
BTEC	Business and Technology Education Council
BTech	Bachelor of Technology
BTechEd	Bachelor of Technological Education
BTEC HC	Business and Technology Education Council Higher Certificate
BTEC HD	Business and Technology Education Council Higher Diploma
BTEC HNC	Business and Technology Education Council Higher National Certificate
BTEC HND	Business and Technology Education Council Higher National Diploma
BTechS	Bachelor of Technology Studies
BTh	Bachelor of Theology
BTheol	Bachelor of Theology
BTP	Bachelor of Town Planning
BVC	Bar Vocational Course
BVetMed	Bachelor of Veterinary Medicine
BVMS	Bachelor of Veterinary Medicine
BVM&S	Bachelor of Veterinary Medicine
BVSc	Bachelor of Veterinary Science
C&G	City and Guilds
CA	Member of the Institute of Chartered Accountants of Scotland
CAA	Civil Aviation Authority
CABE	Companion of the Association of Business Executives
CACHE	Council for Awards in Children's Care and Education
CAE	Certificated Automotive Engineer
CAE	Companion of the Academy of Experts
CAM	Communication Advertising and Marketing Education Foundation
CAS	Certification of Accountancy Studies
CASS	Certificate of Applied Social Studies
CAT	Certificate for Accounting Technicians
CAT	College of Advanced Technology
CATS	Postgraduate Qualification by Credit Accumulation and Transfer
CBA	Companion of the British (Theatrical) Arts
CBAE	Companion of the British Academy of Experts
CBIM	Companion of the British Institute of Management
CBiol	Chartered Biologist
CBLC	Certificate in Business Language Competence
CBSSG	Craft Member of the British Society of Scientific Glassblowers
CCETSW	Central Council for Education and Training in Social Work

CChem	Chartered Chemist
CCol	Chartered Colourist
CCST	Certificate of Completion of Specialist Training
CDBA	Certified Doctor of Business Administration
CDipAF	Certified Diploma in Accounting and Finance
CEE	Extended European Command Endorsement
CeFA	Certificate for Financial Advisers
CEM	Certificate in Executive Management
CeMAP	Certificate in Mortgage Advice and Practice
CEng	Chartered Engineer
CertAMed	Certificate in Aviation Medicine
CertArb	Certificate in Arboriculture
CertBibKnowl	Certificate of Bible Knowledge
CertCIH	Chartered Institute of Housing recognised Housing Qualification
CertCM	Certificate of Cash Management
CertDesRCA	Certificate of Designer of the Royal College of Art
CertEd	Certificate in Education
CertEPK	Certificate of Essential Pensions Knowledge
CertHE	Certificate of Higher Education
CertHSAP	Certificate in Health Services Administration Practice
CertHSM	Certificate in Health Services Management
CertMFS	Certificate in the Marketing of Financial Services
CertOccHyg	Certificate in Operational Competence in Comprehensive Occupational Hygiene
CertRP	Certificate in Recruitment Practice
CertTEL	Certificate in the Teaching of European Languages
CertTESOL	Certificate of Teaching of English to Speakers of Other Languages
CertTEYL	Certificate of Teaching of English to Young Learners
CertYCW	Certificate in Youth and Community Work
CETHV	Certificate of Education in Training as Health Visitor
CEYA	Council for Early Years Awards
CFS	Certificate in Financial Services
CFSP	Certificate in Financial Services Practice
CGeol	Chartered Geologist
CGLI	City & Guilds of London Institute
CHARM	Centre for Hazard and Risk Management
ChB	Bachelor of Surgery
CHD	Choral-Training Diploma
ChM	Master of Surgery
CHP	Certificate in Hypnosis and Psychology
CHRIM	Certified Member of the Institute of Health Record Information and Management
CIAgrE	Companion of the Institution of Agricultural Engineers
CIArb	Chartered Institute of Arbitrators
CIB	Chartered Institute of Bankers
CIBM	Corporate Member of the Institute of Builders' Merchants
CIBS	Chartered Institute of Bankers in Scotland
CIBSE	Chartered Institution of Building Services Engineers
CIC	Construction Industry Council
CIEx	Companion of the Institute of Export
CIFE	Conference for Independent Further Education
CIH	Chartered Institute of Housing
CII	Chartered Insurance Institute
CILA	Chartered Institute of Loss Adjusters

CILIP	Chartered Institute of Library and Information Professionals
CIM	Chartered Institute of Marketing
CIMA	Chartered Institute of Management Accountants
CIMediE	Companion of the Institution of Mechanical Engineers
CIMgt	Companion of the Institute of Management
CIOB	Chartered Institute of Building
CIP	Certificate of Institute Practice
CIPD	Chartered Institute of Personnel and Development
CIPFA	Chartered Institute of Public Finance & Accounting
CIPS	Chartered Institute of Purchasing and Supply
CISOB	Counsellor of the Incorporated Society of Organ Builders
CIT	Certificate in Information Technology
CIWEM	Chartered Institution of Water and Environmental Management
CL(ABDO)	Diploma in Contact Lens Practice of the Association of British Dispensing Opticians
CLAC	Commercial Language Assistant Certificate
CLAIT	Computer Literacy & Information Technology
CLC	Council for Licensed Conveyancers
CLE	Limited European Command Endorsement
ClinPsyD	Doctorate in Clinical Psychology
CMA	Certificate in Management Accountancy
CMathFIMA	Fellow of the Institute of Mathematics and its Applications
CMBA	Certified Master of Business Administration
CMBHI	Craft Member of the British Horological Institute
CMC	Certified Management Consultants
CMet	Chartered Meteorologist
CMIWSc	Certified Member of the Institute of Wood Science
CMS	Certificate in Management Studies
CNAA	Council for National Academic Awards
COA	Certificate of Accreditation
COBC	Certificate of Basic Competence
CoEA	Certificate of Educational Achievement
COES	Certificate of Educational Studies
CofE	Church of England
CofS	Church of Scotland
CompBCS	Companion of the British Computer Society
CompIAP	Companion of the Institution of Analysts and Programmers
CompIEE	Companion of the Institution of Electrical Engineers
CompIGasE	Companion of the Institution of Gas Engineers
CompIManf	Companion of the Institute of Manufacturing
CompIMS	Companion of the Institute of Management Specialists
CompIP	Companion of the Institute of Plumbing
CorporateIRRV	Corporate Member of the Institute of Revenues, Rating and Valuation
COSCA	Confederation of Scottish Counselling Agencies
CPA	Chartered Patent Agents
CPC	Certificate of Professional Competence, the Institute of Transport Administration
CPD	Continuing Professional Development
CPE	Common Professional Exam
CPEA	Certificate of Practice in Estate Agency
CPFA	Member of Chartered Institute of Public Finance and Accountancy
CPhys	Chartered Physicist of the Institute of Physics
CPIM	Certificate in Production and Inventory Management

CPL	Commercial Pilot's Licence
CPM	Certified Professional Manager
CPP	Certificate of Pre-school Practice
CPR	Chartered Professional Review
CProfBTM	Companion of Professional Business and Technical Management
CPS	Certificate in Pastoral Studies and Applied Theology
CPSC	Certificate of Proficiency in Survival Craft
CPsychol	Chartered Psychologist, British Psychological Society
CPT	Continuing Professional Training
CPVE	Certificate of Pre-Vocational Training
CRAeS	Companion of the Royal Aeronautical Society
CRAH	Central Register of Advanced Hypnotherapists
CRCW	Church Related Community Workers
CRNCM	Companion of the Royal Northern College of Music
CSCT	Central School for Counselling Training
CSD	Chartered Society of Designers
CSE	Certificate of Secondary Education
CSM	Certificate in Safety Management
CSMGSM	Certificate in Stage Management (Guildhall School of Music and Drama)
CStat	Chartered Statistician
CSYS	Certificate of Sixth Year Studies
CTABRSM	Certificate of Teaching of the Associated Board of the Royal School of Music
CTextATI	Associate of the Textile Institute
CTextFTI	Fellow of the Textile Institute
CTHCM	Confederation of Tourism, Hotel and Catering Management
CVA	Certificated Value Analyst
CVM	Certificated Value Manager
CVT	Certified Vehicle Technologist
DA	Diploma in Anaesthetics
DAdmin	Doctor of Administration
DAES	Diploma in Advanced Educational Studies
DArch	Doctor of Architecture
DAvMed	Diploma in Aviation Medicine
DBA	Doctor of Business Administration
DBE	Diploma in Business Engineering
DBO	Diploma of the British Orthoptic Society
DBS	Diploma in Business Studies
DCC	Diploma of Chelsea College
DCDH	Diploma in Child Dental Health
DCE	Dangerous Cargo Endorsements
DCE	Diploma in Childcare and Education
DCG	Diploma in Careers Guidance
DCH	Diploma in Child Health
DChD	Diploma of Dental Surgery
DChM	Diploma in Chiropodial Medicine, Institute of Chiropodists and Podiatrists
DCHT	Diploma in Community Health in Tropical Countries
DCL	Doctor of Civil Law
DCLF	Diploma in Contact Lens Fitting
DClinPsych	Doctor of Clinical Psychiatry
DCLP	Diploma in Contact Lens Practice
DCR(R)or(T)	Diploma of the College of Radiographers
DD	Doctor of Divinity

DDH(Birm)	Diploma in Dental Health, University of Birmingham
DDOrthRCPSGlas	Diploma in Dental Orthopaedics of the Royal College of Physicians and Surgeons of Glasgow
DDPHRCS(Eng)	Diploma in Dental Public Health, Royal College of Surgeons of England
DDS	Doctor of Dental Surgery
DDSc	Doctor of Dental Science
DEBA	Diploma in European Business Administration
DEdPsy	Doctor of Educational Psychiatry
DEM	Diploma in Executive Management
DEng	Doctor of Engineering
DES	Department of Education and Science (now the Department for Education)
DETR	Department of the Environment, Transport and the Regions
DFin	Doctor of Finance
DFSM	Diploma in Financial Services Management
DGA	Diamond Member of the Gemmological Association and Gem Testing Laboratory of Great Britain
DGDPRCSEng	Diploma in General Dental Practice, Royal College of Surgeons of England
DGM	Diploma in Geriatric Medicine
DGO	Diploma in Obstetrics and Gynaecology
DHC	Doctorate in Healthcare
DHE	Diploma in Horticulture, Royal Botanic Garden, Edinburgh
DHMSA	Diploma in the History of Medicine, Society of Apothecaries of London
DHP	Diploma in Hypnosis and Psychotherapy
DIA	Diploma of Industrial Administration
DIB	Diploma in International Business
DIC	Diploma of Membership of Imperial College of Science and Technology, University of London
DIH	Diploma in Industrial Health
DipABRSM	Diploma of the Associated Board of the Royal Schools of Music
DipAD	Diploma in Art and Design
DipAdvHYP	Diploma in Advanced Hypnotherapy
DipAE	Diploma in Adult Education
DipAgrComm	Diploma in Agricultural Communication
DipArb	Diploma in Arbitration
DipArb	Diploma in Arboriculture
DipArch	Diploma in Architecture
DipASE(CofP)	Graduate Level Specialist Diploma in Advanced Study in Education, College of Preceptors
DipASSc	Diploma in Arts and Social Sciences
DipAT	Diploma in Accounting Technology
DipAvMed	Diploma in Aviation Medicine
DipBA	Diploma in Business Administration
DipBldgCons	Diploma in Building Conservation
DipBMA	Diploma in Business Management
DipCAM	Diploma in the Communication Advertising and Marketing Education Foundation
DipCD	Diploma in Community Development
DipCHM	Diploma in Choir Training, Royal College of Organists
DipClinPath	Diploma in Clinical Pathology
DipCOT	Diploma of the College of Occupational Therapists
DipCP	Diploma of the College of Teachers
DipCT	Diploma in Corporate Treasury Management
DipDerm	Diploma in Dermatology

DipEd	Diploma in Education
DipEF	Diploma in Executive Finance
DipEH	Diploma in Environmental Health
DipEM	Diploma in Environmental Management
DipEMA	Diploma in Executive and Management Accountancy
DipEngLit	Diploma in English Literature
DipFD	Diploma in Funeral Directing, National Association of Funeral Directors
DipFS	Diploma in Financial Services
DipGAI	Diploma of the Guild of Architectural Ironmongers
DipGrTrans	Diploma in Greek Translation
DipGSM	Diploma of the Guildhall School of Music and Drama
DipHE	Diploma of Higher Education
DipHS	Diploma of the Heraldry Society
DipIEB	Diploma of the International Employee Benefits
DipISW	Diploma of the Institute of Social Welfare
DipLE	Diploma in Land Economy
DipLP	Diploma in Legal Practice
DipM	Postgraduate Diploma in Marketing
DipMedAc	Diploma in Medical Acupuncture
DipMetEng	Diploma in Meteorological Engineering
DipMFS	Diploma in the Marketing of Financial Services
DipMth	Diploma in Music Therapy
DipOccH	Diploma in Occupational Health
DipOccHyg	Diploma of Professional Competence in Comprehensive Occupational Hygiene
DipPDTC	Diploma in Professional Dancers Teaching Course
DipPharmMed	Diploma in Pharmaceutical Medicine
DipPhil	Diploma in Philosophy
DipProjMan	Diploma in Project Management
DipPropInv	Diploma in Property Investment
DipRAM	Diploma of the Royal Academy of Music
DipRCM	Diploma of the Royal College of Music
DipRMS	Diploma of the Royal Microscopical Society
DipSc	Diploma in Science
DipSM	Diploma in Safety Management
DipSurv	Diploma in Surveying
DipSW	Diploma in Social Work
DipTCL	Diploma of the Trinity College of Music, London
DipTCR	Diploma in Organ Teaching
DipTESOL	Diploma in Teaching of English to Speakers of Other Languages
DipTHP	Diploma in Therapeutic Hypnosis and Psychotherapy
DipTM	Diploma in Training Management, Institute of Personnel and Development
DipTransIoL	Diploma in Translation, Institute of Linguists
DipUniv	Diploma of the University
DipVen	Diploma in Venereology, Society of Apothecaries of London
DipWCF	Diploma of the Worshipful Company of Farriers
DIS	Diploma in Industrial Studies
DLang	Doctor of Language
DLit(t)	Doctor of Letters or Literature
DLO	Diploma of Laryngology and Otology
DLORCSEng	Diploma in Laryngology and Otology, Royal College of Surgeons of England
DLP	Diploma in Legal Practice
DM	Doctor of Medicine

DMedRehab	Diploma in Medical Rehabilitation
DMedSc	Doctor in Medical Science
DMet	Doctor of Metallurgy
DMJ(Clin) or	Diploma in Medical Jurisprudence (Clinical or Pathological), Society of
DMJ(Path)	Apothecaries of London
DMRD	Diploma in Medical Radio-Diagnosis
DMRT	Diploma in Radiotherapy
DMS	Diploma in Management Studies
DMU	Diploma in Medical Ultrasound
DMus	Doctor of Music
DMusCantuar	Archbishop of Canterbury's Doctorate in Music
DNSc	Doctor in Nursing Science
DO	Diploma in Ophthalmology
DO	Diploma in Osteopathy
DocEdPsy	Doctorate in Educational Psychology
DOpt	Diploma in Ophthalmic Optics
DOrth	Diploma in Orthoptics
DOrthRCSEdin	Diploma in Orthodontics, Royal College of Surgeons of Edinburgh
DOrthRCSEng	Diplomate in Orthodontics, Royal College of Surgeons of England
DP	Diploma in Psychotherapy
DPA	Diploma in Public Administration
DpBact	Diploma in Bacteriology
DPD(Dund)	Diploma in Public Dentistry, University of Dundee
DPH	Diploma in Public Health
DPharm	Diploma in Pharmacy
DPhil	Diploma in Philosophy
DPHRCSEng	Diploma in Dental Public Health, Royal College of Surgeons of England
DPM	Diploma in Psychological Medicine
DPodM	Diploma in Podiatric Medicine
DProf	Doctor of Professional Studies
DPS	Diploma in Professional Studies
DPSE	Diploma in Pastoral Studies and Applied Theology
DPsychol	Doctor of Psychology
DrAc	Doctor of Acupuncture
Dr(RCA)	Doctor of the Royal College of Art
DRCOG	Diploma of the Royal College of Obstetricians and Gynaecologists
DRDRCSEd	Diploma in Restorative Dentistry, Royal College of Surgeons of Edinburgh
DRE	Diploma in Remedial Electrolysis, Institute of Electrolysis
DRI	Diploma in Radionuclide Imaging
DRSAMD	Diploma in the Royal Scottish Academy of Music and Drama
DSA	Diploma in Secretarial Administration
DSc	Doctor of Science
DSc(Econ)	Doctor of Science (Economics) or in Economics
DSc(Eng)	Doctor of Science (Engineering)
DSc(Social)	Doctor of Science in the Social Sciences
DScEcon	Doctor in the Faculty of Economics and Social Studies
DSCh(Ox)	Diploma in Surgical Chiropody (Oxon), Oxford School of Chiropody and Podiatry
DScTech	Doctor of Technical Science
DSocSc	Doctor of Social Science
DSSc	Doctor of Social Science
DSTA	Diploma Member of the Swimming Teachers' Association
DTCD	Diploma in Tuberculosis and Chest Diseases

DTech	Doctor of Technology
DTI	Department of Trade and Industry
DTMH	Diploma in Tropical Medicine and Hygiene
DTM&H	Diploma in Tropical Medicine and Hygiene
DTp	Department of Transport
DUniv	Doctor of the University
DVetMed	Doctor of Veterinary Medicine
DVM	Doctor of Veterinary Medicine
DVM&S	Doctor of Veterinary Medicine and Surgery
DVS	Doctor of Veterinary Surgery
DVSc	Doctor of Veterinary Science
ECBL	European Certification Board for Logistics
ECDL	European Computer Driving Licence
ECG	Executive Group Committees (of the Board for Engineers Registration)
EDBA	Executive Diploma in Business Accounting
EdD	Doctor of Education
EDH	Efficient Deck Hand
EdPsyD	Doctor of Educational Psychology
EEAC	European Executive Assistant Certificate
EFB	English for Business
EFL	English as a Foreign Language
EHO	Environmental Health Officer
EIS	Educational Institute of Scotland
EITB	Engineering Industry Training Board
EMBA	European Master of Business Administration
EMBS	European Master of Business Sciences
EMFEC	East Midland Further Education Council
EN	Enrolled Nurse
EN(G)	Enrolled Nurse (General)
EN(M)	Enrolled Nurse (Mental)
EN(MH)	Enrolled Nurse (Mental Handicap)
ENB	English National Board
EngC	Engineering Council
EngD	Doctor of Engineering
EngTech	Engineering Technician
ENS	Electronic Navigational System
ESD	Executive Secretary's Diploma
ESOL	English for Speakers of Other Languages
ESSTL	Engineering Services Training Trust Ltd
EurIng	European Engineer
EuroBiol	European Biologist
FABE	Fellow of the Association of Business Executives
FACB	Fellow of the Association of Certified Bookkeepers
FACP	Fellow of the Association of Computer Professionals
FAE	Fellow of the Academy of Experts
FAFC	Fellow of the Association of Financial Controllers and Administrators
FAIA	Fellow of the Association of International Accountants
FAMS	Fellow of the Association of Medical Secretaries, Practice Managers, Administrators and Receptionists
FAPM	Fellow of the Association for Project Management
FASI	Fellow of the Ambulance Service Institute
FASI	Fellow of the Architecture and Surveying Institute

FASP	Fellow of the Association of Sales Personnel
FBA	Fellow of the British Academy
FBA	Fellow of the British (Theatrical) Arts
FBCS	Fellow of the British Computer Society
FBDO	Fellow of the Association of British Dispensing Opticians
FBDO(Hons)	Fellow of the Association of British Dispensing Opticians with Honours Diploma
FBDO(Hons)CL	Fellow of the Association of British Dispensing Opticians with Honours Diploma and Diploma in Contact Lens Practice
FBEI	Fellow of the Institution of Body Engineers
FBEng	Fellow of the Association of Building Engineers
FBHA	Fellow of the British Hypnotherapy Association
FBHI	Fellow of the British Horological Institute
FBHS	Fellow of the British Horse Society
FBID	Fellow of the British Institute of Interior Design
FBIDST	Fellow of the British Institute of Dental and Surgical Technologists
FBIE	Fellow of the British Institute of Embalmers
FBIPP	Fellow of the British Institute of Professional Photography
FBIS	Fellow of the British Interplanetary Society
FBMA	Fellow of the Business Management Association
FBPsS	Fellow of the British Psychological Society
FCA	Fellow of the Institute of Chartered Accountants in England and Wales
FCAM	Fellow of the Communication Advertising and Marketing Education Foundation
FCB	Fellow of the British Association of Communicators in Business Ltd
FCBSI	Fellow of the Chartered Building Societies Institute
FCCA	Fellow of the Association of Chartered Certified Accountants
FCEA	Fellow of the Institute of Cost and Executive Accountants
FCGI	Fellowship, City & Guilds
FChS	Fellow of the Society of Chiropodists and Podiatrists
FCI	Faculty of Commerce and Industry
FCI	Fellow of the Institute of Commerce
FCIArb	Fellow of the Chartered Institute of Arbitrators
FCIB	Fellow of the Chartered Institute of Bankers
FCIBS	Fellow of the Chartered Institute of Bankers in Scotland
FCIBSE	Fellow of the Chartered Institute of Building Services Engineers
FCIH	Fellow of the Chartered Institute of Housing
FCII	Fellow of the Chartered Insurance Institute
FCIJ	Fellow of the Chartered Institute of Journalists
FCILA	Fellow of the Chartered Institute of Loss Adjusters
FCIM	Fellow of the Chartered Institute of Marketing
FCIOB	Fellow of the Chartered Institute of Building
FCIPD	Fellow of the Chartered Institute of Personnel and Development
FCIPS	Fellow of the Chartered Institute of Purchasing and Supply
FCIS	Fellow of the Institute of Chartered Secretaries and Administrators
FCIT	Fellow of the Chartered Institute of Transport
FCLIP	Chartered Fellow of CILIP
FCLS	First Certificate for Legal Secretaries
FCMA	Fellow of the Chartered Institute of Management Accountants
FCMA	Fellow of the Institute of Cost and Management Accountants
FCMC	Fellow Grade Certified Management Consultants
FCOphth	Fellow of the College of Ophthalmology
FCOptom	Fellow of the College of Optometrists
FCoT	Ordinary Fellow of the College of Teachers

FCPM	Fellow of the Confederation of Professional Management
FCPP	Fellow of the College of Pharmacy Practice
FCSP	Fellow of the Chartered Society of Physiotherapy
FCT	Fellow of the Association of Corporate Treasurers
FCoT	Fellow of the College of Teachers
FCTHCM	Fellow of the Confederation of Tourism, Hotel and Catering Management
FCYW	Fellow of the Community and Youth Work Association
FDSRCPSGlas	Fellow in Dental Surgery of the Royal College of Surgeons of Glasgow
FDSRCSEd	Fellow in Dental Surgery of the Royal College of Physicians and Surgeons of Edinburgh
FDSRCSEng	Fellow in Dental Surgery of the Royal College of Surgeons of England
FE	Further Education
FEANI	Fédération Européene d'Associations Nationales d'Ingénieurs
FECI	Fellow of the Institute of Employment Consultants
FEFC	Further Education Funding Council
FEIS	Fellow of the Educational Institute of Scotland
FFA	Fellow of the Faculty of Actuaries
FFA	Fellow of the Institute of Financial Accountants
FFARCSEng	Fellow of the Faculty of Anaesthetists of the Royal College of Surgeons in England
FFARCSIrel	Fellow of the Faculty of Anaesthetists of the Royal College of Surgeons in Ireland
FFAS	Fellow of the Faculty of Architects and Surveyors (Architects)
FFCA	Fellow of the Association of Financial Controllers and Administrators
FFCI	Fellow of the Faculty of Commerce and Industry
FFCS	Fellow of the Faculty of Secretaries
FFHom	Fellow of the Faculty of Homeopathy
FFPHM	Fellow of the Faculty of Public Health Medicine, Royal College of Physicians of London and Edinburgh and Royal College of Physicians and Surgeons of Glasgow
FFPHMIrel	Fellow of the Faculty of Public Health Medicine, Royal College of Physicians of Ireland
FFRRCSIrel	Fellow of the Faculty of Radiologists, Royal College of Surgeons in Ireland
FFS	Fellow of the Faculty of Architects and Surveyors (Surveyors)
FGA	Fellow of the Gemmological Association and Gem Testing Laboratory of Great Britain
FGCL	Fellow of the Guild of Cleaners and Launderers
FGI	Fellow of the Greek Institute
FGSM	Fellow of the Guildhall School of Music and Drama
FHCIMA	Fellow of the Hotel and Catering International Management Association
FHFS	Fellow of the Council of Health, Fitness and Sports Therapists
FHG	Fellow of the Institute of Heraldic and Genealogical Studies
FHRIM	Fellow of the Institute of Health Record Information and Management
FHS	Fellow of the Heraldry Society
FHSM	Fellow of the Institute of Health Services Management
FHT	Federation of Holistic Therapies
FIA	Fellow of the Institute of Actuaries
FIAB	Fellow of the International Association of Book-keepers
FIAEA	Fellow of the Institute of Automotive Engineer Assessors
FIAgrE	Fellow of the Institution of Agricultural Engineers
FIAP	Fellow of the Institution of Analysts and Programmers
FIAT	Fellow of the Institute of Asphalt Technology
FIBA	Fellow of the Institution of Business Agents
FIBC	Fellow of the Institute of Building Control

FIBCM	Fellow of the Institute of British Carriage and Automobile Manufacturers
FIBCO	Fellow of the Institute of Building Control Officers
FIBE	Fellow of the Institution of British Engineers
FIBF	Fellow of the Institute of British Foundrymen
FIBiol	Fellow of the Institute of Biology
FIBM	Fellow of the Institute of Builders' Merchants
FIBMS	Fellow of the Institute of Biomedical Science
FIBMS	Fellow of the Institute of Medical Laboratory Sciences
FICA	Fellow of the Institute of Company Accountants
FICB	Fellow of the Institute of Certified Book-Keepers
FICE	Fellow of the Institution of Civil Engineers
FIChemE	Fellow of the Institution of Chemical Engineers
FIChor	Fellow of the Benesh Institute of Choreology
FICHT	Fellow of the International Council of Holistic Therapies
FICM	Fellow of the Institute of Credit Management
FICorr	Fellow of the Institute of Corrosion
FICS	Fellow of the Institute of Chartered Shipbrokers
FICW	Fellow of the Institute of Clerks of Works of Great Britain Incorporated
FIDTA	Fellow of the International Dance Teachers' Association
FIED	Fellow of the Institution of Engineering Designers
FIEE	Fellow of the Institution of Electrical Engineers
FIEM	Fellow of the Institute of Executives and Managers
FIEx	Fellow of the Institute of Export
FIExpE	Fellow of the Institute of Explosives Engineers
FIFBQ	Fellow of the International Faculty of Business Qualifications
FIFireE	Fellow of the Institution of Fire Engineers
FIFM	Fellow of the Institute of Fisheries Management
FIFST	Fellow of the Institute of Food Science and Technology
FIGasE	Fellow of the Institution of Gas Engineers
FIGD	Fellow of the Institute of Grocery Distribution
FIGeol	Fellow of the Institute of Geologists
FIHEc	Fellow of the Institute of Home Economics Ltd
FIHIE	Fellow of the Institute of Highway Incorporated Engineers
FIHort	Fellow of the Institute of Horticulture
FIHT	Fellow of the Institution of Highways and Transportation
FIIE	Fellow of the Institution of Incorporated Engineers
FIIHTM	Fellow of the International Institute of Hospitality Tourism & Management
FIIM	Fellow of the International Institute of Management
FIIMR	Fellow of the Institute of Investment Management and Research
FIIRSM	Fellow of the International Institute of Risk and Safety Management
FIISE	Fellow of the International Institute of Social Economics
FIISec	Fellow of the International Institute of Security
FIL	Fellow of the Institute of Linguists
FILAM	Fellow of the Institute of Leisure and Amenity Management
FILT	Fellow of the Institute of Logistics and Transport
FIM	Fellow of the Institute of Materials
FIMA	Fellow of the Institute of Mathematics and its Applications
FIManf	Fellow of the Institute of Manufacturing
FIMarE	Fellow of the Institute of Marine Engineers
FIMatM	Fellow of the Institute of Materials Management
FIMBM	Fellow of the Institute of Maintenance and Building Management
FIMechE	Fellow of the Institute of Mechanical Engineers

FIMechIE	Fellow of the Institute of Mechanical Incorporated Engineers
FIMF	Fellow of the Institute of Metal Finishing
FIMgt	Fellow of the Institute of Management
FIMI	Fellow of the Institute of the Motor Industry
FIMIS	Fellow of the Institute for the Management of Information Systems
FIMM	Fellow of the Institute of Massage and Movement
FIMM	Fellow of the Institution of Mining and Metallurgy
FIMM	International Federation of Manual Medicine
FIMS	Fellow of the Institute of Management Specialists
FIMunE	Fellow of the Institution of Municipal Engineers
FInstAEA	Fellow of the Institute of Automotive Engineer Assessors
FInstAM	Fellow of the Institute of Administrative Management
FInstBA	Fellow of the Institute of Business Administration
FInstBCA	Fellow of the Institute of Burial and Cremation Administration
FInstBM	Fellow of the Institute of Builders' Merchants
FInstBRM	Fellow of the Institute of Baths and Recreation Management
FInstCh	Fellow of the Institute of Chiropodists
FInstCM	Fellow of the Institute of Commercial Management
FInstD	Fellow of the Institute of Directors
FInstE	Fellow of the Institute of Energy
FInstLEx	Fellow of the Institute of Legal Executives
FInstMC	Fellow of the Institute of Measurement and Control
FInstNDT	Fellow of the British Institute of Non-Destructive Testing
FInstP	Fellow of the Institute of Physics
FInstPet	Fellow of the Institute of Petroleum
FInstPkg	Fellow of the Institute of Packaging
FInstPM	Fellow of the Institute of Professional Managers and Administrators
FInstPS	Fellow of the Institute of Purchasing and Supply
FInstR	Fellow of the Institute of Refrigeration
FInstSMM	Fellow of the Institute of Sales and Marketing Management
FInstTA	Fellow of the Institute of Transport Administration
FInstTT	Fellow of the Institute of Travel and Tourism
FInstWM	Fellow of the Institute of Wastes Management
FInstWM	Fellowship of the Institute of Wastes Management
FIntMC	Fellow of International Management Centre
FIOC	Fellow of the Institute of Carpenters
FIOM	Fellow of the Institute of Operations Management
FIOP	Fellow of the Institute of Plumbing
FIOP	Fellow of the Institute of Printing
FIOSH	Fellow of the Institution of Occupational Safety and Health
FIPA	Fellow of the Institute of Practitioners in Advertising
FIPD	Fellow of the Institute of Personnel Development
FIPI	Fellow of the Institute of Professional Investigators
FIPlantE	Fellow of the Institution of Plant Engineers
FIPR	Fellow of the Institute of Public Relations
FIQ	Fellow of the Institute of Quarrying
FIQA	Fellow of the Institute of Quality Assurance
FIR	Fellow of the Institute of Population Registration
FIRSE	Fellow of the Institution of Railway Signal Engineers
FIRTE	Fellow of the Institute of Road Transport Engineers
FIS	Fellow of the Institute of Statisticians
FISM	Fellow of the Institute for Supervision & Management

FISOB	Fellow of the Incorporated Society of Organ Builders
FISTC	Fellow of the Institute of Scientific and Technical Communicators
FISTD	Fellow of the Imperial Society of Teachers of Dancing
FIStrucE	Fellow of the Institution of Structural Engineers
FISW	Fellow of the Institute of Social Welfare
FIT	Foundation Insurance Test
FITD	Fellow of the Institute of Training and Development
FITSA	Fellow of the Institute of Trading Standards Administration
FIVehE	Fellow of the Institute of Vehicle Engineers
FIWM	Fellow of the Institute of Wastes Management
FLAW	Foreign Languages at Work
FLCM	Fellow of the London College of Music
FLCSP	Fellow of the London and Counties Society of Physiologists
FLI	Fellow of the Landscape Institute
FLIC	Foreign Languages for Industry and Commerce
FLS	Fellow of the Linnean Society of London
FMA	Fellow of the Museums Association
FMAAT	Fellow Member of the Association of Accounting Technicians
FMPA	Fellow of the Master Photographers Association
FMR	Fellow of the Association of Health Care Information and Medical Records Officers
FMS	Fellow of the Institute of Management Services
FMusEd	Fellowship in Music Education
FN	Fellow of the Nautical Society
FNAEA	Fellow of the National Association of Estate Agents
FNAEAHon	Honoured Fellow of the National Association of Estate Agents
FNCP	Fellow of the National Council of Psychotherapists
FNI	Fellow of the Nautical Institute
FNIMH	Fellow of the National Institute of Medical Herbalists
FPC	Financial Planning Certificate
FPC	Foundation for Psychotherapy and Counselling
FPCS	Fellow of the Property Consultants Society
FPMI	Fellow of the Pensions Management Institute
FPodS	Fellow of the Surgical Faculty of the College of Podiatrists
FProfBTM	Fellow of Professional Business and Technical Management
FRAeS	Fellow of the Royal Aeronautical Society
FRAS	Fellow of the Royal Astronomical Society
FRCA	Fellow of the Royal College of Anaesthetists
FRCGP	Fellow of the Royal College of General Practitioners
FRCM	Fellow of the Royal College of Music
FRCO	Fellow of the Royal College of Organists
FRCO(CHM)	Fellow of the Royal College of Organists (Choir-training Diploma)
FRCOG	Fellow of the Royal College of Obstetricians and Gynaecologists
FRCP	Fellow of the Royal College of Physicians of London
FRCPath	Fellow of the Royal College of Pathologists
FRCPEdin	Fellow of the Royal College of Physicians of Edinburgh
FRCPsych	Fellow of the Royal College of Psychiatrists
FRCR	Fellow of the Royal College of Radiologists
FRCS(Irel)	Fellow of the Royal College of Surgeons in Ireland
FRCSEd	Fellow of the Royal College of Surgeons of Edinburgh
FRCSEd(C/TH)	Fellow of the Royal College of Surgeons of Edinburgh, specialising in Cardiothoracic Surgery

FRCSEd(Orth)	Fellow of the Royal College of Surgeons of Edinburgh, specialising in Orthopaedic Surgery
FRCSEd(SN)	Fellow of the Royal College of Surgeons of Edinburgh, specialising in Surgical Neurology
FRCSEng	Fellow of the Royal College of Surgeons of England
FRCSEng(Oto)	Fellow of the Royal College of Surgeons of England, with Otolaryngology
FRCSGlasg	Fellow of the Royal College of Physicians and Surgeons of Glasgow
FRCVS	Fellow of the Royal College of Veterinary Surgeons
FREC	Fellow of the Recruitment and Employment Confederation
FRHS	Fellow of the Royal Horticultural Society
FRIBA	Fellow of the Royal Institute of British Architects
FRICS	Fellow of the Royal Institution of Chartered Surveyors
FRIN	Fellow of the Royal Institute of Navigation
FRINA	Fellow of the Royal Institution of Naval Architects
FRIPHH	Fellow of the Royal Institution of Public Health and Hygiene
FRNCM	Fellow of the Royal Northern College of Music
FRPharmS	Fellow of the Royal Pharmaceutical Society of Great Britain
FRPS	Fellow of the Royal Photographic Society
FRS	Fellow of the Royal Society
FRSC	Fellow of the Royal Society of Chemistry
FRSCM	Fellow of the Royal School of Church Music
FRSH	Fellow of the Royal Society for the Promotion of Health
FRTPI	Fellow of the Royal Town Planning Institute
FSAPP	Fellow of the Society of Advanced Psychotherapy Practitioners
FSBP	Fellow of the Society of Business Practitioners
FSBT	Fellow of the Society of Teachers in Business Education
FSCT	Fellow of the Society of Claims Technicians
FSDC	Fellow of the Society of Dyers and Colourists
FSE	Fellow of the Society of Engineers (Inc)
FSElec	Fellow of the Society of Electroscience
FSG	Fellow of the Society of Genealogists
FSG(Hon)	Honorary Fellow of the Society of Genealogists
FSGT	Fellow of the Society of Glass Technology
FSIAD	Fellow of the Society of Industrial Artists and Designers
FSMA	Fellow of the Society of Martial Arts
FSMA	Fellow of the Society of Sales Management Administrators Ltd
FSNN	Fellow of the Society of Nursery Nursing
FSS	Fellow of the Royal Statistical Society
FSSCh	Fellow of the British Chiropody and Podiatry Association
FSSF	Fellow of the Society of Shoe Fitters
FSTA	Fellow of the Swimming Teachers' Association
FSVA	Fellow of the Incorporated Society of Valuers and Auctioneers
FTCL	Fellow of the Trinity College of Music
FTI	Fellow of the Textile Institute
FTII	Fellow of the Chartered Institute of Taxation
FTSC	Fellow of the Oil and Colour Chemists' Association
FTSC	Fellow in the Technology of Surface Coatings
FWeldI	Fellow of the Welding Institute
FYDA	Associate Fellowship of the Youth Development Association
GAGTL	Gemmological Association and Gem Testing Laboratory of Great Britain
GAI	Guild of Architectural Ironmongers
GASI	Graduate Member of the Ambulance Service Institute

GBSM	Graduate of the Birmingham School of Music
GCE	General Certificate of Education
GCE A	General Certificate of Education Advanced Level
GCE O	General Certificate of Education Ordinary Level
GCGI	Graduateship, City & Guilds
GCL	Guild of Cleaners and Launderers
GCSE	General Certificate of Secondary Education
GDC	General Dental Council
GIBCM	Graduate of the Institute of British Carriage and Automobile Manufacturers
GIBiol	Graduate of the Institute of Biology
GIEM	Graduate of the Institute of Executives and Managers
GIMA	Graduate of the Institute of Mathematics and its Applications
GIMI	Graduate of the Institute of the Motor Industry
GInstP	Graduate of the Institute of Physics
GIntMC	Graduate of the International Management Centre
GIS	Graduate Imaging Scientist
GLCM	Graduate Diploma of the London College of Music
GMAT	Graduate Management Admissions Test
GMC	General Medical Council
GMDSS	Global Maritime Distress & Safety System
GMInstM	Graduate Member of the Meat Training Council
GMus	Graduate Diploma in Music
GMusRNCM	Graduate in Music of the Royal Northern College of Music
GNSM	Graduate of the Northern School of Music
GNVQ	General National Vocational Qualifications
GradAES	Graduate of the Royal Aeronautical Society
GradBEng	Graduate Member of the Association of Building Engineers
GradBHI	Graduate of the British Horological Institute
GradDip	Graduate Diploma
GradIAP	Graduate of the Institution of Analysts and Programmers
GradIBE	Graduate of the Institution of British Engineers
GradIElecIE	Graduate of the Institution of Electrical and Electronics Incorporated Engineers
GradIIE	Graduate of the Institution of Incorporated Engineers
GradIISec	Graduate of the International Institute of Security
GradIManf	Graduate of the Institute Manufacturing
GradIMF	Graduate of the Institute of Metal Finishing
GradIMS	Graduate of the Institute of Management Specialists
GradInstNDT	Graduate of the British Institute of Non-Destructive Testing
GradInstP	Graduate of the Institute of Physics
GradInstPS	Graduate of the Institute of Purchasing and Supply
GradIOP	Graduate of the Institute of Printing
GradIPD	Graduate of the Institute of Personnel and Development
GradIS	Graduate of the Institute of Statisticians
GradISCA	Graduate of the Institute of Chartered Secretaries and Administrators
GradMechE	Graduate of the Institution of Mechanical Engineers
GradMIWM	Graduate Member of the Institute of Wastes Management
GradRNCM	Graduate of the Royal Northern College of Music
GradRSC	Graduate of the Royal Society of Chemistry
GradSMA	Graduate of the Society of Martial Arts
GradStat	Graduate Statistician
GraduateCIPD	Graduate of the Chartered Institute of Personnel and Development
GraduateIEIE	Graduate of the Institution of Electrical and Electronics Incorporated Engineers

GradWeldI	Graduate of the Welding Institute
GRC	General Readers Certificate
GRC	Grade Related Criteria
GRIC	Graduate Membership of the Royal Institute of Chemistry
GRSC	Graduate of the Royal Society of Chemistry
GRSM	Graduate Diploma of the Royal Manchester School of Music
GRSM(Hons)	Graduate of the Royal Schools of Music
GSMA	Graduate of the Society of Sales Management Administrators Ltd
GSNN	Graduate of the Society of Nursery Nursing
GTC	General Teaching Council
HABIA	Hairdressing and Beauty Industry Authority
HC	Higher Certificate
HCIMA	Hotel and Catering International Management Association
HD	Higher Diploma
HDCR (R) or (T)	Higher Award in Radiodiagnosis or Radiotherapy, College of Radiographers
HEFCE	Higher Education Funding Council for England
HFInstE	Honorary Fellow of the Institute of Energy
HNC	Higher National Certificate
HND	Higher National Diploma
HonASTA	Honorary Associate of the Swimming Teachers' Association
HonDrRCA	Honorary Doctorate of the Royal College of Art
HonFAE	Honorary Fellow of the Academy of Experts
HonFBID	Honorary Fellow of the British Institute of Interior Design
HonFBIPP	Honorary Fellow of the British Institute of Professional Photography
HonFCP	Charter Fellow of the College of Preceptors
HonFEIS	Honorary Fellow of the Educational Institute of Scotland
HonFHCIMA	Honorary Fellow of the Hotel, Catering and Institutional Management Association
HonFHS	Honorary Fellow of the Heraldry Society
HonFIEE	Honorary Fellow of the Institution of Electrical Engineers
HonFIExpE	Honorary Fellow of the Institute of Explosives Engineers
HonFIGasE	Honorary Fellow of the Institution of Gas Engineers
HonFIMarE	Honorary Fellow of the Institute of Marine Engineers
HonFIMechE	Honorary Fellow of the Institution of Mechanical Engineers
HonFIMM	Honorary Fellow of the Institution of Mining and Metallurgy
HonFInstE	Honorary Fellow of the Institute of Energy
HonFInstMC	Honorary Fellow of the Institute of Measurement and Control
HonFInstNDT	Honorary Fellow of the British Institute of Non-Destructive Testing
HonFIQA	Honorary Fellow of the Institute of Quality Assurance
HonFIRSE	Honorary Fellow of the Institution of Railway Signal Engineers
HonFIRTE	Honorary Fellow of the Institute of Road Transport Engineers
HonFPRI	Honorary Fellow of the Plastics and Rubber Institute
HonFRIN	Honorary Fellow of the Royal Institute of Navigation
HonFRINA	Honorary Fellow of the Royal Institution of Naval Architects
HonFRPS	Honorary Fellow of the Royal Photographic Society
HonFSE	Honorary Fellow of the Society of Engineers (Inc)
HonFSGT	Honorary Fellow of the Society of Glass Technology
HonFWeldI	Honorary Fellow of the Welding Institute
HonGSM	Honorary Member of the Guildhall School of Music and Drama
HonMIFM	Honorary Member of the Institute of Fisheries Management
HonMInstNDT	Honorary Member of the British Institute of Non-Destructive Testing
HonMRIN	Honorary Member of the Royal Institute of Navigation
HonMWES	Honorary Member of the Women's Engineering Society

HonRAM	Honorary Member of the Royal Academy of Music
HonRCM	Honorary Member of the Royal College of Music
HonRNCM	Honorary Member of the Royal Northern College of Music
HonRSCM	Honorary Member of the Royal School of Church Music
HSC	Higher School Certificate
HSE	Health & Safety Executive
HTB	Hairdressing Training Board
HTC	Higher Technical Certificate
IAAP	International Association for Analytic Psychology
IAB	International Association of Book-Keepers
IABC	International Association of Business Computing
IAC	Investment Advice Certificate
IAgrE	Institution of Agricultural Engineers
IAP	Institution of Analysts and Programmers
IAQ	Investment Administration Qualification
IAT	Institute of Asphalt Technology
IBA	Institute of Business Administration
IBC	Institute of Building Control
IBE	Institution of British Engineers
IBF	Institute of British Foundrymen
IBMS	Institute of Biomedical Science
ICAEW	Institute of Chartered Accountants in England and Wales
ICAI	Institute of Chartered Accountants in Ireland
ICAS	Institute of Chartered Accountants of Scotland
ICB	Institute of Certified Book-Keepers
ICE	Institution of Civil Engineers
ICEA	Institute of Cost and Executive Accountants
ICG	Institute of Careers Guidance
IChemE	Institution of Chemical Engineers
ICIOB	Incorporated Member of the Chartered Institute of Building
ICM	Institute of Commercial Management
ICM	Institute of Complementary Medicine
ICM	Institute of Credit Management
ICMQ	International Capital Markets Qualification
ICSA	Institute of Chartered Secretaries and Administrators
ICSF	Intermediate Certificate of the Society of Floristry
IDA	Improvement and Development Agency
IDTA	International Dance Teachers' Association Ltd
IED	Institution of Engineering Designers
IEE	Institution of Electrical Engineers
IEM	Institute of Executives and Managers
IEng	Incorporated Engineer
IETTL	Insulation and Environmental Training Trust Ltd
IEx	Institute of Export
IExpE	Institute of Explosives Engineers
IFA	Institute of Field Archaeologists
IFA	Institute of Financial Accountants
IFA	Insurance Foundation Certificate
IFBQ	International Faculty of Business Qualifications
IFM	Institute of Fisheries Management
IFST	Institute of Food Science and Technology (UK)
IHBC	International Health & Beauty Council

IHIE	Institute of Highway Incorporated Engineers
IHort	Institute of Horticulture
IHT	Institute of Highways and Transportation
IIA	Institute of Internal Auditors
IIE	Institution of Incorporated Engineers
IIExE	Institution of Incorporated Executive Engineers
IIHHT	International Institute of Health & Holistic Therapies
IIHTM	International Institute of Hospitality Tourism & Management
IIRSM	International Institute of Risk and Safety Management
ILAM	Institute of Leisure and Amenity Management
ILE	Institution of Lighting Engineers
ILEX	Institute of Legal Executives
ILT	Institute of Logistics and Transport
IMarE	Institute of Marine Engineers
IMBM	Institute of Maintenance and Building Management
IMC	Institute of Management Consultancy
IMechE	Institution of Mechanical Engineers
IMF	Institute of Metal Finishing
IMI	Institute of the Motor Industry
IMIBC	Incorporated Member of the Institute of Building Control
IMInstAEA	Incorporated Member of the Institute of Automotive Engineer Assessors
IMIS	Institute for the Management of Information Systems
IMM	Institution of Mining and Metallurgy
IMS	Institute of Management Specialists
IncMWeldI	Incorporated Member of the Welding Institute
InstAEA	Institute of Automotive Engineer Assessors
InstAM	Institute of Administrative Management
InstBCA	Institute of Burial and Cremation Administration
InstE	Institute of Energy
InstPet	Institute of Petroleum
IOB	Institute of Brewing
IOC	Institute of Carpenters
IoD	Institute of Directors
IOM	Institute of Operations Management
IOP	Institute of Packaging
IOSH	Institution of Occupational Safety and Health
IOTA	Institute of Transport Administration
IPA	Institute of Practitioners in Advertising
IPD	Initial Professional Development
IPD	Institute of Personnel and Development
IPFA	Member of the Chartered Institute of Public Finance and Accountancy
IPlantE	Institution of Plant Engineers
IPR	Incorporated Professional Review
IPR	Institute of Public Relations
IPSM	Institute of Public Service Management
IQ	Institute of Quarrying
IQA	Institute of Quality Assurance
IRMT	International Register of Massage Therapists
IRRV	Corporate Member of the Institute of Revenues, Rating and Valuation
IRRV	Institute of Revenues, Rating and Valuation
IRSE	Institution of Railway Signal Engineers
IRTE	Institute of Road Transport Engineers

`

ISEB	Information Systems Examinations Board
ISM	Incorporated Society of Musicians
ISM	Institute for Supervision & Management
ISMM	Institute of Sales and Marketing Management
ISRM	Institute of Sport and Recreation Management
ISTD	Imperial Society of Teachers of Dancing
IStructE	Institution of Structural Engineers
ITEC	International Therapy Examination Council
ITIL	IT Infrastructure Library
ITSA	Institute of Trading Standards Administration
IVehE	Institute of the Vehicle Engineers
IVM	Institute of Value Management
IWSc	Institute of Wood Science
JEB	Joint Examination Board
JET	Jewellery, Education and Training
JP	Justice of the Peace
LA	Library Association
LABAC	Licentiate Member of the Association of Business and Administrative Computing
LAE	Licentiate Automotive Engineer
LAEx	Legal Accounts Executive
LAMDA	London Academy of Music and Dramatic Art
LAMRTPI	Legal Associate Member of the Royal Town Planning Institute
LASI	Licentiate of the Ambulance Service Institute
LASI	Licentiate of the Architecture and Surveying Institute
LBEI	Licentiate of the Institution of Body Engineers
LBIDST	Licentiate of the British Institute of Dental and Surgical Technologists
LBIPP	Licentiate of the British Institute of Professional Photography
LCCI	London Chamber of Commerce and Industry
LCCIEB	London Chamber of Commerce and Industry Examinations Board
LCEA	Licentiate of the Association of Cost and Executive Accountants
LCFI	Licentiate of CFI International (Clothing and Footwear Institute)
LCGI	Licentiate, City & Guilds
LCIBSE	Licentiate of the Chartered Institution of Building Services Engineers
LCP	Licentiate of the College of Preceptors
LCSP	London and Counties Society of Physiologists
LCSP(Assoc)	Associate of the London and Counties Society of Physiologists
LCSP(BTh)	Member of the London and Counties Society of Physiologists (Beauty Therapy)
LCSP(Chir)	Member of the London and Counties Society of Physiologists (Chiropody)
LCSP(Phys)	Member of the London and Counties Society of Physiologists (Physical and Manipulative Therapy)
LCT	Licentiate of the College of Teachers
LDS	Licentiate in Dental Surgery
LDSRCPSGlas	Licentiate in Dental Surgery of the Royal College of Physicians and Surgeons of Glasgow
LDSRCSEd	Licentiate in Dental Surgery of the Royal College of Surgeons of Edinburgh
LDSRCSEng	Licentiate in Dental Surgery of the Royal College of Surgeons of England
LFA	Licentiate of the Institute of Financial Accountants
LFCI	Licentiate of the Faculty of Commerce and Industry
LFCS	Licentiate of the Faculty of Secretaries
LFS	Licentiate of the Faculty of Architects and Surveyors (Surveyors)
LGCL	Licentiate of the Guild of Cleaners and Launderers
LGSM	Licentiate of the Guildhall School of Music and Drama

LHCIMA	Licentiate of the Hotel and Catering International Management Association
LHG	Licentiate of the Institute of Heraldic and Genealogical Studies
LI	Landscape Institute
LicentiateCIPD	Licentiate of the Chartered Institute of Personnel and Development
LicIPD	Licentiate of the Institute of Personnel & Development
LicIQA	Licentiate of the Institute of Quality Assurance
LICW	Licentiate of the Institute of Clerks of Works of Great Britain Incorporated
LIDPM	Licentiate of the Institute of Data Processing Management
LIEM	Licentiate of the Institute of Executives and Managers
LIIST	Licentiate of the International Institute of Sports Therapy
LILAM	Licentiate of the Institute of Leisure and Amenity Management
LIM	Licentiate of the Institute of Materials
LIMA	Licentiate of the Institute of Mathematics and its Applications
LIMF	Licentiate of the Institute of Metal Finishing
LIMIS	Licentiate of the Institute for the Management of Information Systems
LInstBCA	Licentiate of the Institute of Burial and Cremation Administration
LInstBM	Licentiate of the Institute of Builders' Merchants
LIOC	Licentiate of the Institute of Carpenters
LIR	Licentiate of the Institute of Population Registration
LISTD	Licentiate of the Imperial Society of Teachers of Dancing
LISTD(Dip)	Licentiate Diploma of the Imperial Society of Teachers of Dancing
LittD	Doctor of Letters
LIWM	Licentiate of the Institute of Wastes Management
LLB	Bachelor of Law
LLCM	Performers Diploma of Licentiateship in Speech, Drama and Public Speaking
LLCM(TD)	Licentiate of the London College of Music and Media (Teachers' Diploma)
LLD	Doctor of Law
LLM	Master of Law
LM	Licentiate in Midwifery
LMIFM	Licentiate Member of the Institute of Fisheries Management
LMInstE	Licentiate Member of the Institute of Energy
LMPA	Licentiate Member of the Master Photographers Association
LMRTPI	Legal Member of the Royal Town Planning Institute
LMSSALond	Licentiate in Medicine, Surgery and Obstetrics & Gynaecology, Society of Apothecaries of London
LMusEd	Licentiate Diploma in Music Education
LMusLCM	Licentiate in Music of the London College of Music
LMusTCL	Licentiate in Music, Trinity College of Music
LNCP	Licentiate of the National Council of Psychotherapists
LPC	Legal Practice Course
LRAD	Licentiate of the Royal Academy of Dancing
LRAM	Licentiate of the Royal Academy of Music
LRCPEdin	Conjoint Diplomas Licentiate of the Royal College of Physicians of Edinburgh
LRCPSGlasg	Conjoint Diplomas Licentiate of the Royal College of Physicians and Surgeons of Glasgow
LRCSEdin	Conjoint Diplomas Licentiate of the Royal College of Surgeons of Edinburgh
LRCSEng	Licentiate of the Royal College of Surgeons in England
LRPS	Licentiate of the Royal Photographic Society
LRSC	Licentiate of the Royal Society of Chemistry
LRSM	Licentiate Diploma of the Royal Schools of Music
LSBP	Licentiate of the Society of Business Practitioners
LSCP(Assoc)	Associate of the London and Counties Society of Physiologists

LTCL	Licentiate of Trinity College of Music
LTh	Licentiate in Theology
LTI	Licentiate of the Textile Industry
LTSC	Licentiate of the Oil and Colour Chemists' Association
LVT	Licentiate Vehicle Technologist
MA	Master of Arts
MA(Architectural)	Master of Arts (Architectural Studies)
MA(Econ)	Master of Arts in Economic and Social Studies
MA(Ed)	Master of Arts in Education
MA(LD)	Master of Arts (Landscape Design)
MA(MUS)	Master of Arts (Music)
MA(RCA)	Master of Arts, Royal College of Art
MA(SocSci)	Master of Arts (Social Science)
MA(Theol)	Master of Arts in Theology
MAAT	Member of the Association of Accounting Technicians
MABAC	Member of the Association of Business and Administrative Computing
MABE	Member of the Association of Business Executives
MAcc	Master of Accountancy
MACP	Member of the Association of Computer Professionals
MAE	Member of the Academy of Experts
MAgr	Master of Agriculture
MAgrSc	Master of Agricultural Science
MAMS	Member of the Association of Medical Secretaries, Practice Managers, Administrators and Receptionists
MAMSA	Managing & Marketing Sales Association Examination Board
MAnimSc	Master of Animal Science
MAO	Master of Obstetrics
MAP	Membership by Assessment of Performance
MAPM	Member of the Association for Project Management
MAppSci	Master of Applied Science
MAQ	Mortgage Advice Qualification
MArAd	Master of Archive Administration
MArb	Master of Arboriculture
MArch	Master of Architecture
MArt/RCA	Master of Arts, Royal College of Art
MasFCI	Master of the Faculty of Commerce and Industry
MASHAM	Management and Administration of Safety and Health at Mines
MASI	Member of the Architecture and Surveying Institute
MBA	Master of Business Administration
MBAE	Member of the British Association of Electrolysists
MB, BCh	Conjoint Degree of Bachelor of Medicine, Bachelor of Surgery
MB, BChir	Conjoint Degree of Bachelor of Medicine, Bachelor of Surgery
MB, BS	Conjoint Degree of Bachelor of Medicine, Bachelor of Surgery
MB, ChB	Conjoint Degree of Bachelor of Medicine, Bachelor of Surgery
MBChA	Member of the British Chiropody and Podiatry Association
MBCO	Member of the British College of Ophthalmic Opticians
MBCS	Member of the British Computer Society
MBEng	Member of the Association of Building Engineers
MBHA	Member of the British Hypnotherapy Association
MBHI	Member of the British Horological Institute
MBIAT	Member of the British Institute of Architectural Technologists
MBID	Member of the British Institute of Interior Design

MBIE	Member of the British Institute of Embalmers
MBII	Member of the British Institute of Innkeeping
MBioc	Master of Biochemistry
MBKS	Member of the British Kinematograph, Sound and Television Society
MBM	Master of Business Management
MBMA	Member of the Business Management Association
MBSc	Master in Business Science
MBSSG	Master of the British Society of Scientific Glassblowers
MCAM	Member of the Communication Advertising and Marketing Education Foundation
MCB	Mastership in Clinical Biochemistry
MCB	Member of the British Association of Communicators in Business
MCBDip	Member of the British Association of Communicators in Business who hold the Association's Certificate and Diploma
MCC	Master of Community Care
MCCDRCS(Eng)	Member of the Royal College of Surgeons of England, Clinical Community Dentistry
MCD	Master of Civic Design
MCDH	Master of Community Dental Health
MCGI	Membership, City & Guilds
MCGPIrel	Member of the Irish College of General Practitioners
MCh	Master of Surgery
MChD	Master of Dental Surgery
MChem	Master of Chemistry
MChemA	Master of Chemical Analysis
MChemPhys	Master of Chemical Physics
MChemPST	Master of Chemistry Polymer Science and Technology
MChir	Master of Surgery
MChOrth	Master of Orthopaedic Surgery
MChS	Member of the Society of Chiropodists and Podiatrists
MCIArb	Member of the Chartered Institute of Arbitrators
MCIBS	Member of the Chartered Institute of Bankers in Scotland
MCIBSE	Member of the Chartered Institution of Building Services Engineers
MCIH	Corporate Member of the Chartered Institute of Housing
MCIJ	Member of the Chartered Institute of Journalists
MCIM	Member of the Chartered Institute of Marketing
MCIOB	Member of the Chartered Institute of Building
MCIPD	Member of the Chartered Institute of Personnel and Development
MCIPS	Member of the Chartered Institute of Purchasing and Supply
MCIT	Member of the Chartered Institute of Transport
MCIWEM	Member of the Chartered Institution of Water and Environmental Management
MCLIP	Chartered Member of CILIP
MCom	Master of Commerce
MCommH	Master of Community Health
MComp	Master of Computer Science
MCOptom	Member of the College of Optometrists
MCoT	Member of the College of Teachers
MCPM	Member of the Confederation of Professional Management
MCPP	Member of the College of Pharmacy Practice
MCQ	Multiple Choice Question paper
MCSD	Member of the Chartered Society of Designers
MCSP	Member of the Chartered Society of Physiotherapy
MCT	Member of the Association of Corporate Treasurers

MCTHCM	Member of the Confederation of Tourism, Hotel and Catering Management
MCYW	Member of the Community and Youth Work Association
MD	Doctor of Medicine
MDA	Master of Defence Administration
MD; ChM	Conjoint Doctorate in Medicine, Doctorate in Surgery
MDCR	Management Diploma of the College of Radiographers
MDent	Master of Dental Science
MDes	Master of Design
MDes(RCA)	Master of Design, Royal College of Art
MDORCPSGlas	Membership of Dental Orthopaedics, Royal College of Physicians and Surgeons of Glasgow
MDra	Master of Drama
MDS	Master of Dental Surgery
MDSc	Master of Dental Science
MEBA	Master of European Business Administration
MECI	Member of the Institute of Employment Consultants
MEd	Master of Education
MEd(EdPsych)	Master of Education (Educational Psychology)
MEdStud	Master of Educational Studies
MEng	Master of Engineering
MEnv	Master of Environmental Studies
MEnvSci	Master of Environmental Science
MESc	Master of Earth Sciences
MFA	Master of Fine Art
MFC	Mastership in Food Control
MFCM	Member of the Faculty of Community Medicine
MFDO	Member of the Faculty of Dispensing Opticians
MFDS	Member of the Faculty of Dental Surgery
MFGDPEng	Membership in General Dental Practice, Royal College of Surgeons of England
MFHom	Member of the Faculty of Homeopathy
MFM	Master of Forensic Medicine
MFPHM	Member of the Faculty of Public Health Medicine, Royal College of Physicians of London and Edinburgh and Royal College of Physicians and Surgeons of Glasgow
MFPHMIrel	Member of the Faculty of Public Health Medicine, Royal College of Physicians of Ireland
MFTCom	Member of the Faculty of Teachers in Commerce
MGDSRCSEd	Membership in General Dental Surgery, Royal College of Surgeons of Edinburgh
MGDSRCSEng	Membership in General Dental Surgery, Royal College of Surgeons of England
MGeog	Master of Geography
MGeol	Master of Geology
MGeophys	Master of Geophysical Sciences
MHCIMA	Member of the Hotel and Catering International Management Association
MHM	Master of Health Management
MHort(RHS)	Master of Horticulture, Royal Horticultural Society
MHSM	Member of the Institute of Health Services Management
MIAB	Member of the International Association of Book-keepers
MIAEA	Member of the Institute of Automotive Engineer Assessors
MIAgrE	Member of the Institution of Agricultural Engineers
MIAP	Member of the Institution of Analysts and Programmers
MIAT	Member of the Institute of Asphalt Technology
MIBC	Member of the Institute of Building Control

MIBCM	Member of the Institute British Carriage and Automobile Manufacturers
MIBCO	Member of the Institution of Building Control Officers
MIBE	Member of the Institution of British Engineers
MIBF	Member of the Institute of British Foundrymen
MIBiol	Member of the Institute of Biology
MIBM	Member of the Institute of Builders' Merchants
MICB	Member of the Institute of Certified Book-Keepers
MICE	Member of the Institute of Civil Engineers
MIChemE	Member of the Institution of Chemical Engineers
MICHT	Member of the International Council for Holistic Therapies
MICM	Member of the Institute of Credit Management
MICM(Grad)	Graduate Member of the Institute of Credit Management
MICorr	Member of the Institute of Corrosion
MICS	Member of the Institute of Chartered Shipbrokers
MICSc	Corporate Member of the Institute of Consumer Sciences Incorporating Home Economics
MICW	Member of the Institute of Clerks of Works of Great Britain Incorporated
MIDTA	Member of the International Dance Teachers' Association
MIED	Member of the Institution of Engineering Designers
MIEE	Member of the Institution of Electrical Engineers
MIEM	Member of the Institute of Executives and Managers
MIEx	Member of the Institute of Export
MIEx(Grad)	Graduate Member of the Institute of Export
MIExpE	Member of the Institute of Explosives Engineers
MIFA	Member of the Institute of Field Archaeologists
MIFireE	Member of the Institution of Fire Engineers
MIFM	Registered Member of the Institute of Fisheries Management
MIFST	Member of the Institute of Food Science and Technology
MIGasE	Member of the Institution of Gas Engineers
MIGD	Member of the Institute of Grocery Distribution
MIHEc	Member of the Institute of Home Economics
MIHIE	Member of the Institute of Highway Incorporated Engineers
MIHM	Member of the Institute of Healthcare Management
MIHort	Member of the Institute of Horticulture
MIHT	Member of the Institution of Highways and Transportation
MIIA	Member of the Institute of Internal Auditors
MIIE	Member of the Institution of Incorporated Engineers
MIIExE	Member of the Institution of Incorporated Executive Engineers
MIIHTM	Member of the International Institute of Hospitality Tourism & Management
MIIM	Member of the Institute of Industrial Managers
MIIM	Member of the International Institute of Management
MIIRSM	Member of the International Institute of Risk and Safety Management
MIISE	Member of the International Institute of Social Economics
MIISec	Member of the International Institute of Security
MIL	Member of the Institute of Linguists
MILAM	Member of the Institute of Leisure and Amenity Management
MILT	Member of the Institute of Logistics and Transport
MIM	Professional Member of the Institute of Materials
MIMA	Member of the Institute of Mathematics and its Applications
MIManf	Member of the Institute of Manufacturing
MIMarE	Member of the Institute of Marine Engineers
MIMatM	Member of the Institute of Materials Management

MIMBM	Member of the Institute of Maintenance and Building Management
MIMC	Member of the Institute of Management Consultancy
MIMechE	Member of the Institution of Mechanical Engineers
MIMechIE	Member of the Institution of Mechanical Incorporated Engineers
MIMF	Member of the Institute of Metal Finishing
MIMI	Member of the Institute of the Motor Industry
MIMinE	Member of the Institution of Mining Engineers
MIMIS	Member of the Institute for the Management of Information Systems
MIMM	Member of the Institute of Massage and Movement
MIMM	Member of the Institution of Mining and Metallurgy
MIMS	Member of the Institute of Management Specialists
MInstAEA	Member of the Institute of Automotive Engineer Assessors
MInstAM	Member of the Institute of Administrative Management
MInstBA	Member of the Institute of Business Administration
MInstBCA	Member of the Institute of Burial and Cremation Administration
MInstBE	Member of the Institution of British Engineers
MInstBM	Member of the Institute of Builders' Merchants
MInstCF	Master Fitter of the National Institute of Carpet and Floorlayers
MInstChP	Member of the Institute of Chiropodists & Podiatrists
MInstCM	Member of the Institute of Commercial Management
MInstD	Member of the Institute of Directors
MInstE	Member of the Institute of Energy
MInstLEx	Member of the Institute of Legal Executives
MInstMC	Member of the Institute of Measurement and Control
MInstNDT	Member of the British Institute of Non-Destructive Testing
MInstP	Member of the Institute of Physics
MInstPet	Member of the Institute of Petroleum
MInstPkg	Member of the Institute of Packaging
MInstPkg(Dip)	Diploma Member of the Institute of Packaging
MInstPM	Member of the Institute of Professional Managers and Administrators
MInstPS	Corporate Member of the Institute of Purchasing and Supply
MInstPSA	Member of the Institute of Public Service Administrators
MInstR	Member of the Institute of Refrigeration
MInstSMM	Member of the Institute of Sales and Marketing Management
MInstTA	Member of the Institute of Transport Administration
MInstTT	Full Member of the Institute of Travel and Tourism
MInstWM	Member of the Institute of Wastes Management
MIOC	Member of the Institute of Carpenters
MIOFMS	Member of the Institute of Financial and Management Studies
MIOM	Member of the Institute of Operations Management
MIOP	Member of the Institute of Printing
MIOSH	Member of the Institution of Occupational Safety and Health
MIP	Member of the Institute of Plumbing
MIPA	Member of the Institute of Practitioners in Advertising
MIPD	Member of the Institute of Personnel and Development
MIPI	Member of the Institute of Professional Investigators
MIPlantE	Member of the Institution of Plant Engineers
MIPR	Member of the Institute of Public Relations
MIPRE	Member of the Incorporated Practitioners in Radio & Electronics
MIQ	Member of the Institute of Quarrying
MIQA	Member of the Institute of Quality Assurance
MIR	Member of the Institute of Population Registration

MIRRV	Member of the Institute of Revenue, Rating and Valuation
MIRSE	Member of the Institution of Railway Signal Engineers
MIRTE	Member of the Institute of Road Transport Engineering
MISM	Member of the Institute for Supervision & Management
MISOB	Member of the Incorporated Society of Organ Builders
MISTC	Member of the Institute of Scientific and Technical Communicators
MIStrucE	Member of the Institution of Structural Engineers
MISW	Member of the Institute of Social Welfare
MITAI	Member of the Institute of Traffic Accident Investigators
MITSA	Member of the Institute of Trading Standards Administration
MIVehE	Member of the Institute of Vehicle Engineers
MIWM	Member of the Institute of Wastes Management
MIWPC	Member of the Institute of Water Pollution Control
MJur	Master of Jurisprudence
MLA	Master of Landscape Architecture
MLang	Master of Languages
MLangEng	Master of Language Engineering
MLD	Master of Landscape Design
MLE	Master of Land Economy
MLI	Member of the Landscape Institute
MLing	Master of Languages
MLitt	Master of Letters
MLPM	Master of Landscape Planning and Management
MLS	Master of Library Science
MM	Master of Midwifery
MMA	Master of Management and Administration
MMAS	Master of Minimal Access Surgery
MMath	Master of Mathematics
MMedE	Master of Medical Education
MMedSci	Master of Medical Science
MMet	Master of Metallurgy
MML	Master of Modern Languages
MMS	Member of the Institute of Management Services
MMSc	Master of Medical Sciences
MMus	Master of Music
MMus(Comp)	Master of Music (Composition)
MMus(Perf)	Master of Music (Performance)
MMus, RCM	Master of Music, Royal College of Music
MMusArt	Master of Musical Arts
MN	Master of Nursing
MNAEA	Member of the National Association of Estate Agents
MNatSc	Master of Natural Science
MNCP	Member of the National Council of Psychotherapists
MNeuro	Master of Neuroscience
MNI	Member of the Nautical Institute
MNIMH	Member of the National Institute of Medical Herbalists
MNRHP	Full Member of the National Register of Hypnotherapists and Psychotherapists
MNRHP(Eqv)	Full Member (Equivalent) of the National Register of Hypnotherapists and Psychotherapists
MNTB	Merchant Navy Training Board
MObstG	Master of Obstetrics and Gynaecology
MOptom	Master of Optometry

MOrthRCSEng	Membership in Orthodontics, Royal College of Surgeons of England
MPA	Master of Public Administration
MPaedDenRCSEng	Membership in Paediatric Dentistry, Royal College of Surgeons of England
MPC	Master of Palliative Care
MPH	Master of Public Health
MPharm	Master of Pharmacy
MPharmSci	Master of Pharmaceutical Science
MPhil	Master of Philosophy
MPhil(Eng)	Master of Philosophy in Engineering
MPhys	Master of Physics
MPhysGeog	Master of Physical Geography
MPlan	Master of Planning
MPPS	Master of Public Policy Studies
MPRI	Member of the Plastics and Rubber Institute
MProf	Master of Professional Studies
MProfBTM	Member of the Professional Business and Technical Management
MPS	Member of the Pharmaceutical Society of Northern Ireland
MPsychMed	Master of Psychological Medicine
MPsychol	Master of Psychology
MQB	Mining Qualifications Board
MRad	Master of Radiology
MRad; MRad(D)	Master of Radiology (Radiodiagnosis) or (Radiotherapy)
MRAeS	Member of the Royal Aeronautical Society
MRCGP	Member of the Royal College of General Practitioners
MRCOG	Member of the Royal College of Obstetricians and Gynaecologists
MRCP	Member of the Royal College of Physicians of London
MRCP(UK)	Member of the Royal College of Physicians of the United Kingdom
MRCPath	Member of the Royal College of Pathologists
MRCPEdin	Member of the Royal College of Physicians of Edinburgh (superceded by MRCP(UK))
MRCPGlasg	Member of the Royal College of Physicians of Glasgow (superceded by MRCP(UK))
MRCPIrel	Member of the Royal College of Physicians of Ireland
MRCPsych	Member of the Royal College of Psychiatrists
MRCSEd	Member of the Royal College of Surgeons of Edinburgh
MRCSEng	Member of the Royal College of Surgeons of England
MRCVS	Member of the Royal College of Veterinary Surgeons
MRDRCS	Membership in Restorative Dentistry, Royal College of Surgeons of England
MREC	Member of the Recruitment and Employment Confederation
MREHIS	Member of the Royal Environmental Health Institute of Scotland
MRes	Master of Research
MRIN	Member of the Royal Institute of Navigation
MRINA	Member of the Royal Institution of Naval Architects
MRIPHH	Member of the Royal Institute of Public Health and Hygiene
MRPharmS	Member of the Pharmaceutical Society of Great Britain
MRSC	Member of the Royal Society of Chemistry
MRSH	Member of the Royal Society for the Promotion of Health
MRSS	Member of the Royal Statistical Society
MRTPI	Member of the Royal Town Planning Institute
MS	Master of Surgery
MSA	Marine Safety Agency
MSAPP	Member of the Society of Advanced Psychotherapy Practitioners

MSBP	Member of the Society of Business Practitioners
MSBT	Member of the Society of Teachers in Business Education
MSc	Master of Science
MSc(Econ)	Master of Science in Economics
MSc(Ed)	Master of Science in Education
MSc(Eng)	Master of Science in Engineering
MSc(Entr)	Master of Entrepreneurship
MSc(Mgt)	Master of Science in Management
MScD	Master of Dental Science
MScEcon	Master in Faculty of Economic and Social Studies
MSCi	Master of Natural Sciences
MScTech	Master of Technical Science
MSE	Member of Society of Engineers (Inc)
MSF	Member of the SMAE Institute
MSFA	Advanced Financial Planning Certificate
MSIAD	Member of the Society of Industrial Artists and Designers
MSMA	Member of the Society of Martial Arts
MSocSc	Master of Social Science
MSSc	Master of Social Science
MSSc	Master of Surgical Science
MSSCh	Member of the British Chiropody and Podiatry Association
MSSF	Member of the Society of Shoe Fitters
MSt	Master of Studies
MSTA	Member of the Swimming Teachers' Association
MSTI	Certificate of Insurance Work
MSurgDentRCSEng	Membership in Surgical Dentistry, Royal College of Surgeons of England
MSW	Master of Social Work
MTCP	Master of Town and Country Planning
MTD	Master of Transport Design
MTech	Master of Technology
MTh	Master of Theology
MTheol	Master of Theology
MTP	Master of Town Planning
MTPI	Master of Town Planning
MTropMed	Master of Tropical Medicine
MTropPaediatrics	Master of Tropical Paediatrics
MUniv	Master of University (Honorary)
MURP	Master of Urban and Regional Planning
MusB	Bachelor of Music
MusD	Doctor of Music
MVC	Management Verification Consortium
MVM	Master of Veterinary Medicine
MVSc	Master of Veterinary Science
MWeldI	Member of the Welding Institute
MWES	Member of the Women's Engineering Society
MYD	Member of the Youth Development Association
NACOS	National Approval Council for Security Systems
NAEA	National Association of Estate Agents
NAG	National Association of Goldsmiths
NAMCW	National Association for Maternal and Child Welfare
NC	National Certificate
NCA	National Certificate in Agriculture

NCC	National Computing Centre
NCC	Navigational Control Course
NCDT	National Council for Drama Training
NCTJ	National Council for the Training of Journalists
NCVQ	National Council for Vocational Qualifications
ND	Diploma in Naturopathy
NDD	National Diploma in Design
NDF	National Diploma in Forestry
NDH	National Diploma in Horticulture
NDSF	National Diploma of the Society of Floristry
NDT	National Diploma in the Science and Practice of Turfculture and Sports Ground Management
NEBOSH	National Examination Board in Occupational Safety and Health
NEBS	National Examining Board for Supervision & Management
NFTS	National Film and Television School
NICCEA	Northern Ireland Council for the Curriculum, Examinations and Assessment
NID	National Intermediate Diploma
NIM	Northern Institute of Massage
NNEB	National Nursery Examination Board
NRHP	National Register of Hypnotherapists and Psychotherapists
NRHP(Affil)	Affiliate of the National Register of Hypnotherapists and Psychotherapists
NRHP(Assoc)	Associate of the National Register of Hypnotherapists and Psychotherapists
N-SHAP	National School of Hypnosis and Psychotherapy
NTTG	National Textile Training Group
NUJ	National Union of Journalists
NVQ	National Vocational Qualifications
NWRAC	North Western Regional Advisory Council for Further Education
OCR	Oxford, Cambridge & RSA Examinations
ODLQC	Open & Distance Learning Quality Council, formerly CACC, Council for Accreditation of Correspondence Colleges
ONC	Ordinary National Certificate
OND	Ordinary National Diploma
OSCE	Objective Structured Clinical Exam
PBTM	Professional Business and Technical Management
PCN	Personnel Certification in Non-Destructive Testing Ltd
PDP	Professional Development Programme
PESD	Private and Executive Secretary's Diploma, London Chamber of Commerce and Industry
PgC	Postgraduate Certificate
PGCE	Postgraduate Certificate in Education
PGCert	Postgraduate Certificate
PgD	Postgraduate Diploma
PGDip	Postgraduate Diploma
PGDip(Comp)	Postgraduate Diploma in Composition
PGDip(LCM)	Postgraduate Diploma of the London College of Music
PGDip(Perf)	Postgraduate Diploma in Performance
PGDip(RCM)	Postgraduate Diploma of the Royal College of Music
PGDipMin	Postgraduate Diploma in Ministry
PGDipMus	Postgraduate Diploma in Music
PhD	Doctor of Philosophy
PhD(RCA)	Doctor of Philosophy (Royal College of Art)
PIC	Professional Investment Certificate

PIFA	Practitioner of the Institute of Field Archaeologists
PIIA	Practitioner of the Institute of Internal Auditors
PInstNDT	Practitioner of the British Institute of Non-Destructive Testing
PJDip	Professional Jewellers' Diploma
PJGemDip	Professional Jewellers' Gemstone Diploma
PJManDip	Professional Jewellers' Management Diploma
PJValDip	Professional Jewellers' Valuation Diploma
PPL	Private Pilot's Licence
PPRNCM	Professional Performance Diploma of the Royal Northern College of Music
PQS	Professional Qualification Structure
PQSW	Post-Qualifying Award in Social Work
PRCA	Public Relations Consultants Association
PSC	Private Secretary's Certificate
PSD	Private Secretary's Diploma
PTA	Pianoforte Tuners' Association
PVM	Professional in Value Management
QC	Queen's Counsel
QCA	Qualifications and Curriculum Authority
QCG	Qualification in Careers Guidance
QDR	Qualified Dispute Resolver
QICA	Qualification in Computer Auditing
QIS	Qualified Imaging Scientist
QPA	Qualification in Pensions Administration
QPSPA	Qualification in Public Sector Pensions Administration
RA	Royal Academician
RAD	Royal Academy of Dancing
RADA	Royal Academy of Dramatic Art
RAM	Royal Academy of Music
RANA	Royal Animal Nursing Auxiliary
RAS	Royal Astronomical Society
RBS	Royal Ballet School
RC	Roman Catholic
RCM	Royal College of Midwives
RCN	Royal College of Nursing
RCSLT	Royal College of Speech and Language Therapists
RCVS	Royal College of Veterinary Surgeons
REA	Regional Examining Body
REC	Recruitment and Employment Confederation
Ret'dABID	Retired Associate of the British Institute of Interior Design
Ret'dFBID	Retired Fellow of the British Institute of Interior Design
Ret'dMBID	Retired Member of the British Institute of Interior Design
RGN	Registered General Nurse
RHS	Royal Horticultural Society
RHV	Registered Health Visitor
RIBA	Royal Institute of British Architects
RICS	Royal Institution of Chartered Surveyors
RINA	Royal Institution of Naval Architects
RJDip	Diploma for Retail Jewellers
RJGemDip	National Association of Goldsmiths Gemstone Diploma
RM	Registered Midwife
RMN	Registered Mental Nurse
RMS	Royal Microscopical Society

RNMH	Registered Nurse for the Mentally Handicapped
RP	Registered Plumber
RPS	Royal Photographic Society
RSA	Royal Society of Arts
RSBEI	Registered Student of the Institution of Body Engineers
RSC	Royal Society of Chemistry
RSCN	Registered Sick Children's Nurse
RSP	Registered Safety Practitioner
RTO	Recognised Training Organisation
RTPI	Royal Town Planning Institute
SA	Salvation Army Management
SBP	Society of Business Practitioners
SCAA	School Curriculum and Assessment Authority
ScD	Doctor of Science
SCE	Scottish Certificate of Education
SCLS	Second Certificate for Legal Secretaries
SCMT	Ship Captain's Medical Training
SCOTVEC	Scottish Vocational Education Council
SCPL	Senior Commercial Pilot's Licence
SE	Society of Engineers
SEE	Society of Environmental Engineers
SEFIC	Spoken English for Industry and Commerce
SenAWeldI	Senior Associate of the Welding Institute
SEng	Qualified Sales Engineer
SenMWeldI	Senior Member of the Welding Institute
SF	Society of Floristry Ltd
SFA	Securities and Futures Authority
SFInstE	Senior Fellow of the Institute of Energy
SG	Society of Genealogists
SGT	Society of Glass Technology
SHNC	Scottish Higher National Certificate
SHND	Scottish Higher National Diploma
SIEDip	Securities Industry Examination Diploma
SInstPet	Student of the Institute of Petroleum
SITO	Security Industry Training Organisation Ltd
SLC	Secretarial Language Certificate
SLD	Secretarial Language Diploma
SNC	Scottish National Certificate
SND	Scottish National Diploma
SNNEB	Scottish Nursery Nurses Examination Board
SPA	Screen Printing Association
SPRINT	Sport Play and Recreation Industries National Training Executive
SQA	Scottish Qualifications Authority
SRD	State Registered Dietician
SRN	State Registered Nurse
SSC	Secretarial Studies Certificate, London Chamber of Commerce and Industry
STA	Specialist Teacher Assistant (CACHE)
STA	Swimming Teachers' Association
STAT	Society of Teachers of the Alexander Technique
StudentIEE	Student of the Institution of Electrical Engineers
StudentIIE	Student of the Institution of Incorporated Engineers
StudentIMechE	Student of the Institution of Mechanical Engineers

StudIAP	Student of the Institution of Analysts and Programmers
StudIManf	Student Member of the Institute of Manufacturing
StudIMS	Student of the Institute of Management Specialists
StudProfBTM	Student of the Professional Business and Technical Management
StudSE	Student of the Society of Engineers (Inc)
StudSElec	Student of the Society of Electroscience
StudWeldI	Student of the Welding Institute
SVQ	Scottish Vocational Qualification
TC	Technician Certificate
TCA	Technician in Costing and Accounting
TCA	Technician of the Institute of Cost and Executive Accountants
TCert	Teacher's Certificate
TD	Technician Diploma
TDCR	Teacher's Diploma of the College of Radiographers
TechICorr	Technician of the Institute of Corrosion
TechMIWM	Technician Member of the Institute of Wastes Management
TechRICS	Technical Surveyor of the Royal Institution of Chartered Surveyors
TechRMS	Technological Qualification in Microscopy, Royal Microscopical Society
TechRTPI	Technical Member of the Royal Town Planning Institute
TechSP	Technician Safety Practitioner
TechWeldI	Technician of the Welding Institute
TEMOL	Training in Energy Management through Open Learning
TI	Textile Institute
TIMBM	Technician of the Institute of Maintenance and Building Management
TMBA	Teacher Member of the British (Theatrical) Arts
TnIMBM	Technicians of the Institute of Maintenance and Building Management
TOEFL	Test of English as a Foreign Language
TPP	Test of Professional Practice
TVM	Trainer in Value Management
UCAS	Universities and Colleges Admissions Service
UCL	University College London
UEB	United Examining Board
UKCC	United Kingdom Central Council
UKCP	United Kingdom Council for Psychotherapy
UMIST	University of Manchester Institute of Science and Technology
URC	United Reformed Church
VetMB	Bachelor of Veterinary Medicine
VTCT	Vocational Training Charitable Trust
WCMD	Welsh College of Music and Drama
WES	Women's Engineering Society
WJEC	Welsh Joint Education Committee
WMAC	West Midlands Advisory Council for Further Education
WSA	West of Scotland Agricultural College
YHAFHE	Yorkshire and Humberside Association for Further and Higher Education
ZSL	Zoological Society of London

Part 1

Introduction

INTRODUCTION

Since its first publication in 1970, *British Qualifications* has charted a number of fundamental changes in further and higher education provision in the UK. Major advances in technology and more flexible delivery and attendance patterns have created different types of learning opportunity, encouraging an ever more diverse student population to access education at all levels. The range of subjects delivered has grown beyond all recognition. New areas of research have been established and developed into major subject specialisms. Employers and professional bodies have collaborated to develop subject areas aligned to changing industry requirements. Flexibility and choice are the hallmarks of today's system, and anyone new to higher education may well be bewildered by the sheer variety of degree pathways available. The capacity to combine and mix modules and subjects has in fact grown beyond anything that could have been imagined in 1970.

Traditional boundaries between academic and vocational pathways continue to break down, and today most degrees have a vocational slant. Extended industry and professional placements, sponsored research projects, practitioner input and field-based assignments are common features in many degrees, and provide an important link into practice at the early stages of learning. Overall, in 20 years universities have doubled in size and the responsibilities they have taken on have expanded considerably. Collaboration between further education (FE) and higher education (HE) institutions has enabled a substantial amount of HE-level provision to be delivered in FE institutions. Clear progression routes have been established for some time. Considerable breadth of provision is now available in FE: not only has the sector grown to accommodate sub-degree provision, it has also continued to deliver a wide range of pre-and post-18 vocational qualifications, which include technical, occupational and professional awards.

Today, certain types of external qualification cross the boundaries between further and higher education. Several higher education institutions (HEIs) – particularly those that gained university status in the 1990s and in 2005 – deliver advanced professional qualifications and higher national diplomas or certificates from awarding bodies like Edexcel, OCR and SQA. At the same time there has been a significant shift towards FE's involvement in delivery of these types of qualification, and a greater input from private sector colleges.

EDUCATION REFORM

The Higher Education Act 2004 introduced in 2006/07 brought new student support and tuition fee arrangements. Following the Browne Review of 2010, universities are able to charge full-time UK and EU undergraduate students up to £9,000 a year as part of a reorganization of HE funding and student finance. You will find further authoritative, official information about universities and colleges in the UK at the Unistats website: http://unistats.direct.gov.uk/. The Unistats website enables you to compare data and information on UK university and college courses, as well as providing useful information on cost and financial support. Information on student finance and how to apply for it can be found at www.gov.uk, and this site also gives information about university and higher education courses.

As well as implementing reforms, the further and higher education sectors contribute to UK economic performance and the delivery of the government's policies on HE. As part of this shared responsibility a great deal of effort is being made to increase access to and participation in education, particularly among individuals who have not had much involvement in the past. The general availability of modular study programmes and related credit recognition of units, and greater use of ICT and e-learning resources, have done a lot to create more flexible methods of delivery and attendance requirements in further and higher education.

Foundation degrees

Foundation degrees (FDs) were established to give people the intermediate technical and profes-sional skills that are in demand from employers, and to provide more flexible and accessible ways of studying. They are a higher-level qualification awarded by universities. A foundation degree is the equivalent of two thirds of a full honours degree and is a fully flexible qualification allowing students to study part-time or full-time to fit their lifestyle. Unlike full degrees, there are no set entry requirements for foundation degrees. The qualification can be 'built up' from a range of relevant learning experiences, to allow for extremely flexible and adaptable qualifications that can be 'tailored' by employers to support their workforce and business development needs. They offer opportunities for employment and career advancement. Progression routes include links with associated professional qualifications and/or direct entry to the final year of a relevant Honours-level degree. FDs are offered by universities, colleges and other providers.

The first FDs in 2001 were studied by 4,000 students. In 2014–15, 2.3% of the higher education qualifications awarded were FDs. There are now hundreds of FD courses available, both full-and part-time.

- Information about FDs can be found on the UCAS website: www.ucas.com/ucas/under-graduate/getting-started/what-study/foundation-degrees
- Information, advice and guidance resources for work-based learners and their advisers are hosted by unionlearn at www.unionlearn.org.uk/higher-learning-work
- Foundation Degree Forward (fdf) offered e-learning resources to support the delivery of work-based higher education in sectors such as retail, travel and low carbon energy but closed at the end of July 2011. The Higher Education Academy hosts publications produced by fdf so that they remain available to the higher education community at www.heacademy.ac.uk/fdf

Policy and regulation

The UK and Scottish parliaments and the Welsh and Northern Ireland assemblies set national priorities for further and higher education. Policy development, planning and implementation rest with the government departments responsible for each national education brief – the Depart-ment for Education (DfE, website: www.gov.uk/government/organisations/department-for-education), the Department for the Economy (DfENI, website: www.economy-ni.gov.uk) for Northern Ireland (covering further and higher education), the Scottish Government (www.gov.scot), and The Department for Education and Skills (DfES, website: http://gov.wales/topics/educationandskills) in Wales.

In England, delivery of FE is subject to external audit and public reporting by the Office for Standards in Education, Children's Services and Schools (Ofsted, website: www.gov.uk/govern-ment/organisations/ofsted).

In Scotland, the Scottish Funding Council (SFC, website: www.sfc.ac.uk) is the national, strategic body that is responsible for funding teaching and learning provision, research and other activities in Scotland's 26 colleges and 19 universities and higher education institutes. Inspection is carried out by Education Scotland (www.educationscotland.gov.uk/inspectionandreview).

DfES is responsible for planning, funding and promotion of all post-16 education in Wales. Estyn (the Welsh-language acronym for Her Majesty's Inspectorate for Education and Training in

Wales, website: www.estyn.gov.uk) is the appointed authority for audit of the quality of provision and related areas.

The Department for the Economy (DfE) is responsible for planning and funding of further education provision in Northern Ireland. The Education and Training Inspectorate (ETI) (www.etini.gov.uk) undertakes inspection and audit on behalf of the Department.

QUALITY ASSURANCE

A degree of convergence exists in the quality assurance of qualifications at level 3 and below. England, Wales and Northern Ireland share a common qualifications system, and the regulators in each country (listed below) work together in regulating qualifications for use across the three countries. Scotland has a separate qualifications system, although there is close correlation across all four countries, particularly in the area of vocational qualifications.

The following four bodies are responsible for the accreditation and standards of external qualifications and for curriculum and assessment for ages 3–16:

- *England*: Office of the Qualifications and Examinations Regulator (Ofqual, website: www.gov.uk/government/organisations/ofqual);
- *Northern Ireland*: Council for Curriculum, Examinations and Assessment (CCEA*, website: http://ccea.org.uk);
- *Scotland*: Scottish Qualifications Authority (SQA**, website: www.sqa.org.uk);
- *Wales*: Qualifications Wales, which was established through the Qualifications Wales Act 2015 (website: http://qualificationswales.org) and is organised to focus on: recognising awarding bodies and approving and designating qualifications; regulating awarding bodies and reviewing qualifications already in existence; developing and commissioning new qualification requirements for Wales; and research to provide the evidence base for regulatory decision-making.

*CCEA is also an Awarding Body for qualifications in Northern Ireland, offering a diverse range of qualifications, such as GCSEs, including the GCSE Double Award specifications in vocational subjects, GCE A and AS levels, Entry Level Qualifications, and Online Language Assessment (OLA). **SQA is also an Awarding Body that develops and validates SQA-branded qualifications including National Qualifications, Skills for Work, Scottish Baccalaureates, National Progression Awards and National Certificates, Higher National Certificates and Diplomas, Scottish Vocational Qualifications and Modern Apprenticeships, and Scottish Professional Development Awards. The Scottish Credit and Qualifications Framework (SCQF) is Scotland's national qualifications framework.

In HE the responsibility for standards and quality rests firmly with each institution. All institutions work with the independent Quality Assurance Agency for Higher Education (QAA) for England, Northern Ireland, Scotland and Wales. Institutional audits and subject-level reviews have been undertaken by QAA since 2001. It publishes its findings on its website (www.qaa.ac.uk) as publicly accessible information.

Given the current scale and diversity of degree provision in the HE sector, there has been a need to clarify what can reasonably be expected from undergraduate and postgraduate programmes. QAA has responded to this requirement and developed the Quality Code for HE providers (www.qaa.ac.uk/assuring-standards-and-quality/the-quality-code), and subject benchmark statements indicating the expected standards of degrees across a range of subjects.

QUALIFICATION FRAMEWORKS

In further response to the breadth and diversity of qualifications available, a number of national qualification frameworks have been introduced. The framework concept is closely associated with greater transparency and comparability between types of qualification, particularly between those that were traditionally classified as academic or vocational. The frameworks allow comparison with qualifications in different countries by grading them into levels based on the learning outcomes.

The framework for Higher Education Qualifications in England, Wales and Northern Ireland (FHEQ) applies to degrees, diplomas, certificates and other academic awards by higher education providers (see Figure 1.1). Further information can be found at www.qaa.ac.uk/assuring-standards-and-quality/the-quality-code/qualifications.

The Scottish Credit and Qualification Framework (SCQF) was developed by SQA, the Scottish Executive, QAA (Scottish Office) and Universities for Scotland. It provides an overview of all levels of national and higher qualifications provision in Scotland (see Figure 1.2). Further information and the database of courses can be found at http://scqf.org.uk

The Regulated Qualifications Framework was introduced in October 2015 (find more information at: https://ofqual.blog.gov.uk/2015/10/01/explaining-the-rqf).It is the new framework for recognizing and accrediting general and vocational qualifications in England and vocational qualifications Northern Ireland. It is intended to act as a simple tool for describing qualifications. Ofqual regulates this framework, and more information can be found at https://www.gov.uk/what-different-qualification-levels-mean and http://register.ofqual.gov.uk/, which is a searchable database of qualifications and organizations.

For current information about qualifications offered in Wales, please go to the Qualifications in Wales website, www.qiw.wales

The European Qualifications Framework (EQF) compares the level of qualifications across Europe to make it easier for employers and educational establishments to compare their value. More information can be found at the website of the European Commission: https://ec.europa.eu/ploteus/en

Part 2

Teaching Establishments

INTRODUCTION

The statutory responsibility for the provision of education in the United Kingdom lies with the Department for Education (DfE) (www.gov.uk/government/organisations/department-for-education) in England, the Welsh Assembly Government's Department for Education and Skills (DfES) (http://gov.wales/topics/educationandskills), the Education Department of the Scottish Government (www.gov.scot/Topics/Education) and the Department of Education (DENI) (www.education-ni.gov.uk) and the Department for the Economy (DfENI) (www.economy-ni.gov.uk/), which is responsible for further and higher education, in Northern Ireland.

In the United Kingdom the statutory system of public education has three progressive stages: primary education (up to the age of 11 or 12), secondary education (up to age 16), and further education (post-16).

The Education and Skills Act 2008 introduced a new requirement that all young people in England must continue in education or training at least part-time until they are 18 years old, and this applies to any person born on or after 1 September 1997. The website www.ucas.com/ucas/after-gcses gives useful information on the options available and the government website www.gov.uk/further-education-courses also gives information on courses and funding.

This section briefly describes further and higher provision and the main types of institution.

FURTHER AND HIGHER EDUCATION

'Higher education' (HE) is a term that broadly defines any course of study leading to a qualification at level 4 and above in the Regulated Qualifications Framework for England, Wales and Northern Ireland, and level 6 and above in the Scottish Credit and Qualifications Framework.

HE incorporates study towards a wide range of qualifications including Foundation, undergraduate and postgraduate degrees, certificates and diplomas awarded by individual universities and other higher education institutions (HEIs) with degree-awarding powers. It can also include study towards general, technical or occupationally-related diplomas and certificates awarded by the large unitary awarding bodies. Unitary awarding bodies are characterized by their breadth of provision, from NVQs and BTEC courses and A levels through to qualifications at level 5 and above in the national frameworks.

The other category that can be characterized as HE, includes post-experience education above level 4 (and level 7 in Scotland). This includes qualifications available from awarding bodies that represent a particular sector, occupation or technical/craft area, and professional institutions that are also approved as awarding bodies.

HE can take place in universities and HE colleges (which continue to provide the majority of undergraduate and postgraduate courses). It can also take place in colleges of further education (FE). A significant number of colleges deliver parts of, and in some cases entire, Foundation and undergraduate degree courses in agreement with a selected university partner that is responsible for quality assurance and final awards.

In general terms, FE is available for students who are over the age of 16 and still in full-time education, and for adults aged 19 and over. FE provision includes GCSEs, A levels and other types of general and vocational qualifications below level 4 (and level 6 in Scotland) in the National Qualifications Frameworks.

All qualifications are awarded by approved external awarding bodies that include AQA, City & Guilds, Edexcel, LCCI, OCR, OCN and SQA in Scotland. This also includes qualifications below level 4 (level 6 in Scotland) that have a craft or technical focus or are related to an occupation/ sector. At the time of writing, readers who want to find out more about approved qualifications below level 4 will find The Register of Regulated Qualifications website informative (http:// register.ofqual.gov.uk). It contains details of all regulated qualifications in England (Ofqual), Wales (Welsh Government) and Northern Ireland (Ofqual and CCEA).

FURTHER AND HIGHER EDUCATION INSTITUTIONS

England and Wales

There is a wide range of further and higher education establishments, including colleges with various titles. There are also a number of independent specialist establishments, like secretarial and correspondence colleges.

In 2016 there were 161 universities and colleges that were allowed to award degrees. All institutions that are recognized as having degree-awarding powers in the UK can be found on the government website (www.gov.uk/check-a-university-is-officially-recognised/recognised-bodies).

There were also over 600 colleges and other institutions that could not award degrees themselves, but provided courses leading to UK degrees. Institutions offering courses leading to a degree from a recognized body can be found at www.gov.uk/check-a-university-is-officially-recognised/listed-bodies. For general information on UK degrees visit www.gov.uk/recognised-uk-degrees.

Courses include those for first and second degrees, certain graduate-equivalent qualifications, and the examinations of the principal professional associations. These institutions also provide courses leading to important qualifications below degree level, such as Foundation degrees, Higher National Diplomas and Certificates, and Diplomas of Higher Education. Most FE colleges specialize in providing courses that lead to qualifications below degree level, such as A levels and BTEC qualifications. Some offer degree courses, including in many cases Foundation degrees.

Students aged 16–18 who have been ordinarily resident in the UK for three years and, while the UK is still part of the European Union, European Economic Area nationals normally have the right to attend a full-time course without paying tuition fees. More detailed information on tuition fees for international students can be found at www.ukcisa.org.uk. Colleges are free to determine fee levels for students who do not qualify for 'home fees'.

Further Education choices can be searched on www.gov.uk/government/statistical-data-sets/ fe-choices-performance-indicators and also http://findfe.com. The 2016 figures show there were 348 FE colleges in England (of which 94 were sixth-form colleges) 19 in Wales, 40 in Scotland and 6 in Northern Ireland.

Scotland

There are 26 FE colleges in Scotland that provide a broad mix of courses, many awarded by the Scottish Qualifications Authority (SQA). Most HE courses at or near degree level and beyond are provided by the 18 universities/HE institutions and The Open University in Scotland (www.universities-scotland.ac.uk; www.studyinscotland.org). These institutions offer a range of vocationally-oriented courses ranging from science, engineering and computing to health care, art and design, music and drama, and teacher training, as well as the more traditional 'academic' courses. The Scottish Funding Council funds all the universities and HE institutions in Scotland.

Northern Ireland

Responsibility for the FE sector in Northern Ireland rests with the Department for the Economy (DfENI) which directly funds colleges. There are six further and higher education colleges, offering a wide range of vocational and non-vocational courses for both full- and part-time students. Details can be found at www.anic.ac.uk

Queen's University Belfast and the University of Ulster receive Quality-related Research (QR) funding from the Department for the Economy. Many of the courses in both universities are designed to suit the needs of industry, commerce and the professions. Agricultural, horticultural and food colleges in Northern Ireland are administered through the Department of Agriculture, Environment and Rural Affairs (DAERA, website: www.daera-ni.gov.uk), which works with the College of Agriculture, Food and Rural Enterprise (CAFRE, website: www.cafre.ac.uk) to offer a range of further and higher education courses.

UNIVERSITIES AND HE COLLEGES

Universities are self-governing bodies, largely financed by the government through the Higher Education Funding Councils in the UK. They generally derive their rights and privileges from Royal Charter or Act of Parliament, and any amendment of their charters or statutes is made by the Crown acting through the Privy Council on the application of the universities themselves. The universities alone decide what degrees they award and the conditions on which they are awarded; they alone decide which students to admit and which staff to appoint. However, government policies have started to influence admission criteria, particularly in terms of widening access and participation in HE. Student fees set by universities are also subject to strict guidelines set by the government.

The Higher Education Funding Council (www.hefce.ac.uk) funds HE, research and related activities in English HE institutions and FE colleges. In 2016–17 it funded 132 HE institutions and 214 FE colleges.

Institutions receiving funding from Higher Education Funding Council for England

The schools and institutes of the University of London which receive funds directly from the HEFCE are marked *.

Anglia Ruskin University; Aston University; University of Bath; Bath Spa University; University of Bedfordshire; Birkbeck College, University of London*; University of Birmingham; Birmingham City University; University College Birmingham; Bishop Grosseteste University; University of Bolton; Arts University Bournemouth; Bournemouth University; University of Bradford; University of Brighton; University of Bristol; British School of Osteopathy; Brunel University; Buckinghamshire New University; University of Cambridge; Institute of Cancer Research*; Canterbury Christ Church University; University of Central Lancashire; University of Chester; University of Chichester; City University, London; Conservatoire for Dance and Drama; Courtauld Institute of Art*; Coventry University; Cranfield University; University for the Creative Arts; University of Cumbria; De Montfort University; University of Derby; University of Durham; University of East Anglia; University of East London; Edge Hill University; University of Essex; University of Exeter; Falmouth University; University of Gloucestershire; Goldsmiths' College, University of London*; University of Greenwich; Guildhall School of Music and Drama; Harper

Adams University; University of Hertfordshire; Heythrop College, University of London*; University of Huddersfield; University of Hull; Imperial College London; Keele University; University of Kent; King's College London*; Kingston University; University of Lancaster; University of Leeds; Leeds College of Art; Leeds Beckett University; Leeds Trinity University; University of Leicester; University of Lincoln; University of Liverpool; Liverpool Hope University; Liverpool Institute for Performing Arts; Liverpool John Moores University; Liverpool School of Tropical Medicine; University of the Arts, London; University of London; London Business School*; London School of Economics and Political Science*; London School of Hygiene and Tropical Medicine*; London Metropolitan University; London South Bank University; Loughborough University; University of Manchester; Manchester Metropolitan University; Middlesex University, London; National Film and Television School; University of Newcastle upon Tyne; Newman University; University of Northampton; University of Northumbria at Newcastle; Norwich University of the Arts; University of Nottingham; Nottingham Trent University; The Open University; University of Oxford; Oxford Brookes University; Plymouth University; Plymouth College of Art; University of Portsmouth; Queen Mary, University of London*; Ravensbourne; University of Reading; Roehampton University; Rose Bruford College; Royal Academy of Music*; Royal Agricultural University; Royal Central School of Speech and Drama*; Royal College of Art; Royal College of Music; Royal Holloway, University of London*; Royal Northern College of Music; Royal Veterinary College*; St George's, University of London*; University of St Mark and St John; St Mary's University, Twickenham; University of Salford; University of Sheffield; Sheffield Hallam University; School of Oriental and African Studies, University of London*; University of Southampton; Southampton Solent University; Staffordshire University; University Campus Suffolk; University of Sunderland; University of Surrey; University of Sussex; Teesside University; Trinity Laban Conservatoire of Music and Dance; University College London (including UCL Institute of Education)*; University of Warwick; University of the West of England, Bristol; University of West London; University of Westminster; University of Winchester; University of Wolverhampton; University of Worcester; Writtle College; University of York; York St John University.

(*Source*: Higher Education Funding Council for England)

Universities receiving funding from the Department for Employment and Learning in Northern Ireland

Queen's University Belfast; University of Ulster.

(*Source*: Higher Education Funding Council for England)

Higher Education Institutions receiving funding from the Scottish Funding Council

University of Aberdeen; Abertay University; University of Dundee; Edinburgh Napier University; University of Edinburgh; Glasgow Caledonian University; Glasgow School of Art; University of Glasgow; Heriot-Watt University; The Open University in Scotland; Queen Margaret University; Robert Gordon University; Royal Conservatoire of Scotland; SRUC; University of St Andrews; University of Stirling; University of Strathclyde; University of the Highlands and Islands; University of the West of Scotland. They also fund 25 colleges.

(*Source*: Scottish Funding Council, www.sfc.ac.uk/funding/funding.aspx)

Institutions receiving funding from the Higher Education Funding Council for Wales

Aberystwyth University; Bangor University; Cardiff University; Cardiff Metropolitan University; The Open University in Wales; University of South Wales; Swansea University; University of Wales; University of Wales Trinity Saint David; Wrexham Glyndwr University.

(*Source*: Higher Education Funding Council for Wales, www.hefcw.ac.uk)

OTHER HE ORGANIZATIONS

There are a number of other organizations involved in shaping the HE sector. You can find a full list of these organizations on the Universities UK website: www.universitiesuk.ac.uk

Part 3

Qualifications

INTRODUCTION

Definition of Common Terms

A number of terms are commonly used as synonyms for qualifications, for example 'examinations' and 'courses'. This can hide important differences of meaning and lead to confusion and misunderstanding. In some contexts it may be important to make these differences explicit to guard against exaggerating or diminishing the level of achievement, which is an essential core of the concept of qualification. It is especially important to clarify the difference in meaning between 'examination', 'course' and 'qualification'.

Examination

An examination is a formal test or assessment. It can focus on one or more of the following: knowledge, understanding, skill or competence. An examination may be set as a written test, an oral test, an aural and oral test (e.g. a foreign language test) or a practical test. In the past, most forms of external assessment in FE were based on a model of examination dominated by the psychometric model, designed to discriminate between individuals – normative referencing – and took the form of written tests. There was considerable variation in different kinds of written examination, including essays, question and answer, and 'multiple response'. Today, largely as a result of the introduction of National Vocational Qualifications (NVQs), the purpose and format of many examinations have been reappraised, and criterion-referenced examinations that focus on achievement (and in the case of NVQs, competence) are increasingly common. Many forms of assessment are now an integral part of the learning process, with a formative as well as a summative function rather than a separate, terminal, summative function.

Course

A course implies an ordered sequence of teaching or learning over a period of time. A course is governed by regulations or requirements, frequently imposed by an external awarding body and sometimes by the institution providing the course. An important distinguishing feature between different courses is the length of time allocated to study: it can vary from a few days to several years. Some courses offer a terminal award on the basis of course completion, and these courses are set for a given period of time. Other 'set period' courses may prescribe examinations; these can include continuous assessment, terminal testing or a combination of both. In other courses, the programme of study may be accomplished at a faster or slower rate; such courses normally enjoin continuous assessment or a terminal examination, or both. Many courses require attendance at an institution, while distance learning, correspondence courses, and various forms of flexible learning courses are usually free of these requirements, although some may require occasional attendance for residential components or face-to-face tutoring. A successful examination result usually confers a qualification or an award.

Qualification

A qualification is normally a certificated endorsement, from a recognized awarding body, that a level or quality of accomplishment has been achieved by an individual. Qualifications are usually conferred on successful completion of an examination, although not all examinations necessarily offer qualifications. An examination may offer an award that is a part-qualification. For example, an NVQ candidate may acquire a unit of competence that is a part-qualification building towards a full statement of competence – an NVQ. A first-year student on an HND course may be required to pass all first-year examinations to be permitted to continue into the second year: in a sense that student is 'qualified' to continue the course but no qualification is awarded. Some award-bearing examinations may be fully recognized and certificated qualifications in themselves (e.g. a BTEC HNC) but only part-qualifications for a profession (e.g. chartered engineer).

Apparent anomalies do exist. Some professional bodies and trade associations award qualifications that are recognized within the profession or association but are not obtained by examination. They are usually awarded on the basis of experience, and payment of a fee, and denote membership or acceptance. When the body also offers an examination route to the same qualification, successful examinees are usually known as 'graduate members'.

There are a number of accreditation authorities that approve qualifications. There are also many specialist and general validating, examining and awarding bodies that are responsible for the design and assessment of qualifications.

ACCREDITING REGULATORY BODIES

England

Sector Skills Councils

Federation for Industry Sector Skills and Standards (FISSS)
Tel: 0300 303 4444 E-mail: info@fisss.org Website: www.fisss.org
The Federation for Industry Sector Skills and Standards, is an organization that supports the network of licensed UK Sector Skills Councils (SSCs). These are employer-led, independent organizations that cover specific work sectors across the UK (currently accounting for approximately 90 per cent of the UK workforce).With the influence granted by licences from the governments of England, Scotland, Wales and Northern Ireland, and with private and public funding, this independent network engages with the education and training supply-side such as universities, colleges, funders and qualifications bodies to increase productivity at all levels in the workforce. There are 20 Sector Skills Councils who work with over 550,000 employers to define skills needs and skills standards in their industry. There are also 19 National Skills Academies. Details of the Sector Skills Councils are listed in the following table.

Table 3.1

Cogent skills *Sector:* Science industries Tel: 01925 515 200 E-mail: info@cogentskills.com Website: www.cogentskills.com	**Creative & Cultural Skills** *Sector:* Craft, cultural heritage, design, literature, music, performing and visual arts Tel: 020 7015 1800 E-mail: info@ccskills.org.uk Website: www.ccskills.org.uk
Construction Skills *Sector:* Construction Tel: 0344 994 4400 E-mail: call.centre@cskills.org Website: www.cskills.org	**Creative Skillset** *Sector:* TV, film, radio, interactive media, animation, computer games, facilities, photo imaging, publishing, advertising and fashion and textiles Tel: 020 7713 9800 E-mail: info@creativeskillset.org Website: www.creativeskillset.org

continued

Table 3.1 *Continued*

Energy & Utility Skills
Sector: Gas, power, waste management and water industries
Tel: 0845 077 9922
E-mail: enquiries@euskills.co.uk
Website: www.euskills.co.uk

ecITB
Sector: Engineering
Tel: 01923 260000
E-mail: ecitb@ecitb.org.uk
Website: www.ecitb.org.uk

Financial Skills Partnership
Sector: Finance, accountancy and financial services
Tel: 0114 261 5800
E-mail: info@financialskillspartnership.org.uk
Website: www.financialskillspartnership.org.uk

IMI The Institute of the Motor Industry
Sector: Retail motor industry
Tel: 01992 519039
E-mail: comms@theimi.org.uk
Website: www.theimi.org.uk

Instructus Group
Sector: Business and administration, customer service, enterprise and business support, human resources and recruitment, industrial relations, leadership and management, marketing and sales
Tel: 0207 091 9620
E-mail: info@skillscfa.org
Website: www.skillscfa.org

Lantra
Sector: Land management and production, animal health and welfare and environmental industries
Tel: 024 7669 6996
E-mail: connect@lantra.co.uk
Website: www.lantra.co.uk

National Skills Academy for Food and Drink
Sector: Food and drink manufacturing and associated supply chains
Tel: 0845 644 0558
E-mail: info@insafd.co.uk
Website: www.nsafd.co.uk

People 1st
Sector: Hospitality, leisure, passenger transport, travel and tourism and retail
Tel: 020 3074 1222
E-mail: info@people1st.co.uk
Website: www.people1st.co.uk

SEMTA
Sector: Science, engineering and manufacturing technologies
Tel: 0845 643 9001
E-mail: customerservices@semta.org.uk
Website: www.semta.org.uk

Skills Active
Sector: Sport, fitness, outdoors, playwork, caravans and hair and beauty
Tel: 0207 840 1900
E-mail: skills@skillsactive.com
Website: www.skillsactive.com

Skills for Care & Development
Sector: Social care, children, early years and young people's workforces in the UK
Tel: 01133 241 1240
E-mail: sscinfo@skillsforcareanddevelopment.org.uk
Website: www.skillsforcareanddevelopment.org.uk

Skills for Health
Sector: UK Health
Tel: 0117 922 1155
E-mail: office@skillsforhealth.org.uk
Website: www.skillsforhealth.org.uk

continued

Table 3.1 *Continued*

Skills for Justice	Summit Skills
Sector: Community Justice, Courts Services, Custodial Care, Fire and Rescue, Forensic Science, Policing and Law Enforcement and Prosecution Services	*Sector:* Building Services Engineering
	Tel: 0207 313 4890
	E-mail: enquiries@summitskills.org.uk
	Website: www.summitskills.org.uk
Tel: 0114 261 1499	**Tech Partnership**
E-mail: info@skillsforjustice.com	*Sector:* Software, internet and web, IT services, telecommunications and business change
Website: www.skillsforjustice.com	
Skills for Security	
Sector: Security	Tel: 020 7963 8920
Tel: 01905 744000	E-mail: info@thetechpartnership.com
E-mail: info@skillsforsecurity.org.uk	Website: www.thetechpartnership.com
Website: www.skillsforsecurity.org.uk	

In October 2013, in response to the Richard Review of Apprenticeships (2012), the government set out its plans to reform Apprenticeships in England by replacing the existing Apprenticeship frameworks with employer-defined standards, putting employers in control and giving them a high degree of freedom to develop these standards to best meet the needs of their occupations and sectors. To support this reform, they established 'trailblazers' – groups led by employers and professional bodies – to develop the first of these new Apprenticeship standards (www.gov.uk/government/publications/future-of-apprenticeships-in-england-guidance-for-trailblazers).

The Government plan to introduce new standards for all occupations by 2017. A number of new Apprenticeship standards have already been government approved with the number growing all the time. Information on the new standards can be found at www.apprenticeships.org.uk/standards. The Federation for Industry Sector Skills and Standards (http://fisss.org) is developing a series of practical tools and guides for employers and employer-led partnerships to support the development of a new Apprenticeship standard and the detail of the implementation requirements which go with it – assessment, training and governance. The Federation currently manages the following certification systems for apprenticeships: ACE (England), ACW (Wales), MA Online v1 (Scotland) and MA Online v2 (Scotland).

The National College for Teaching and Leadership

The National College for Teaching and Leadership (NCTL) is part of the Department for Education and is involved in the exam administration function. The NCTL can be found at www.gov.uk/nctl, General enquiries, Ministerial and Public Communications Division, Department for Education, Piccadilly Gate, Store Street, Manchester, M1 2WD; Tel: 0370 000 2288. Information about the administration of exams can be found at www.gov.uk/exams-administration-information-for-exam-centres. The Department for Education is also a useful source of information, www.gov.uk/government/organisations/department-for-education.

Standards and Testing Agency (STA)

The Standards and Testing Agency is responsible for the development and delivery of all statutory assessments from early years to the end of Key Stage 3; Standards and Testing Agency,

53–55 Butts Road, Earlsdon Park, Coventry, CV1 3BH; National Curriculum assessments helpline: 0300 303 3013; E-mail: assessments@education.gov.uk; Website: www.gov.uk/sta

Ofqual: Office of Qualifications and Examinations Regulation

Contact details for Ofqual are: Ofqual, Spring Place, HeraldAvenue, Coventry, CV5 6UB; Tel: 0300 303 3344; E-mail: public.enquiries@ofqual.gov.uk; Website: www.gov.uk/government/organisa-tions/ ofqual. Vocational qualifications that are only provided in Northern Ireland are regulated by the Council for the Curriculum, Examinations and Assessment, 29 Clarendon Road, Clarendon Dock, Belfast BT1 3BG; Tel: 02890 261200; E-mail: info@ccea.org.uk; Website: http://ccea.org.uk/

Ofqual is the regulator of qualifications, examinations and tests in England and a wide range of vocational qualifications in both England and Northern Ireland. Ofqual also regulates the National Curriculum Assessments in England. It monitors organizations that deliver qualifica-tions and assessments as set out in the Apprenticeship, Skills, Children and Learning Act (2009) and Education Act (2011). Ofqual's role is to ensure all learners get the results they deserve, standards are maintained, and qualifications are correctly valued and understood, now and in the future.

Ofqual is accountable to parliament rather than to government ministers and advises the Government on qualifications and assessment based on their research into these areas.

Scotland

Scottish Qualifications Authority (SQA)

Customer Contact Centre, Tel: 0345 279 1000; Fax: 0345 213 5000; E-mail: customer@sqa.org.uk; Website: www.sqa.org.uk

The Scottish Qualifications Authority (SQA) is the national accreditation and awarding body in Scotland. It is an executive non-departmental public body (NDPB) sponsored by the Scottish Government's Learning Directorate and is fully committed to working with other organizations, agencies and institutions in Scotland to help meet the Scottish Government's National Outcomes, strategies, policies and priorities.

SQA works in partnership with schools, colleges, universities and industry to provide high quality, flexible and relevant qualifications and assessments, embedding industry standards where appropriate. It strives to ensure that SQA qualifications are inclusive and accessible to all, that they provide clear progression pathways, facilitate lifelong learning and recognize candidate achievement. The National Qualifications have been designed to meet the aims, purposes and values of Curriculum for Excellence.

People take SQA qualifications at all stages of their lives – at school, at college, at work and in their leisure time. There are qualifications at all levels of attainment. SQA is responsible for three main types of qualification: units, courses and group awards. Most SQA-awarded qualifications are made up of a combination of units, which can also be used in their own right. Each unit repre-sents approximately 40 hours of teaching with additional study. Units are achieved by passing an assessment.

National Courses

There are seven levels of National Courses – National 1–5, Higher, and Advanced Higher and there are at present four Scottish Baccalaureates, which are awarded at Pass and Distinction.

National Courses are designed to develop skills and knowledge in a specific subject area as well as skills for learning, skills for life and skills for work. Achieving a National Course shows that a learner has demonstrated the specified knowledge and skills in a particular subject at the defined national standard. Some of the new Awards cover work from across different subject areas, are shorter than traditional courses and recognize success at different levels of difficulty, meaning they are suitable for young people of all abilities.

Higher National Courses

Higher Courses provide progression from National 5 and lead on to Advanced Higher and are designed to develop skills and knowledge in a specific subject area. Offered by colleges, some universities and many other training centres, Higher National Certificates (HNCs) and Higher National Diplomas (HNDs) are specially designed to meet the needs of employers. HNCs are usually made up of 12 Higher National Unit credits (one credit represents roughly 40 hours of timetabled learning and 40 hours of self-guided learning and study) and usually take one year to complete; HNDs are made up of 30 credits and usually take two years to complete.

Advanced Higher National Courses

Advanced Higher awards are designed to meet the aims, purposes and values of Curriculum for Excellence, and provide progression from Higher Courses. These courses, which are designed to develop skills and knowledge in a specific subject area, are usually made up of three National Units and an external assessment by means of an examination and a project. Advanced Highers tend to be taken in the sixth year at school or college by students who have normally passed Highers.

Skills for Work

There are also Skills for Work Courses from National 3 to National 5. These are vocational courses for pupils in third and fourth year of secondary school and above. Normally pupils following the Skills for Work courses will spend some of their time at a local college or another training provider or with an employer. The courses are intended to provide progression pathways to further education, training and employment.

Skills for Work courses, National 3, 4 and 5 and Higher are designed to develop skills and knowledge in a broad vocational area, as well as an understanding of: the workplace skills and attitudes for employability, Core Skills, and other transferable skills. They involve a strong element of learning through involvement in practical activities which are directly related to a particular vocational area. National 3 is usually made up of three 40-hour units and National 4, 5 and Higher are usually made up of four 40-hour units.

Other SQA Courses

National Qualification Group Awards – National Certificates (NCs), Higher National Certificates and Diplomas (HNCs and HNDs) and National Progression Awards (NPAs) – are designed to be taken at college; Scottish Vocational Qualifications (SVQs), Professional Development Awards (PDAs), QCF (Qualifications and Credit Framework) registered Awards, Certificates and Diplomas and Functional Skills, and Customized Awards are designed for the workplace. A private company or training provider must become an 'approved centre' to deliver SQA qualifications, or work in partnership with a college or training provider. SQA also offer Modern Apprenticeships.

SQA Qualifications

Higher National Certificates (HNCs) and **Higher National Diplomas** (HNDs) are developed by SQA in partnership with FE colleges, universities, and industry and commerce. They are credible, flexible qualifications that are designed to deliver skills and knowledge to meet the needs of today's businesses. Some HNCs allow direct entry into the second year of a degree programme, and some HNDs allow direct entry to the third year. Higher National qualifications can also give you the knowledge and understanding required for Scottish Vocational Qualifications (SVQs).

National Progression Awards (NPAs) are designed to assess a defined set of skills and knowledge in specialist vocational areas. They are mainly used by colleges for short programmes of study.

National Certificates are primarily aimed at 16–18-year olds and adults in full-time education. They prepare candidates for employment or further study by developing a range of knowledge and skills.

Scottish Vocational Qualifications (SVQs) are based on job competence, and recognize the skills and knowledge people need in employment. SVQs can be attained in most occupations and are available for all types and levels of job. They are primarily delivered to candidates in full-time employment and in the workplace.

Professional Development Awards (PDAs) are qualifications for people who are already in a career and who wish to extend or broaden their skills. In some cases they are designed for people wishing to enter employment. PDAs can be taken at college or the workplace.

Customized Awards are specially designed vocational qualifications at any level to meet an organization's need for skills and expertise and provide recognition and development opportunities for individuals. They can also help a company meet regulatory requirements and demonstrate the competence of its employees to external parties.

Scottish Credit and Qualifications Framework

The SQA is a partner in a 'credit' system called the Scottish Credit and Qualifications Framework (SCQF), which sets out the Scottish qualifications and how they relate to one another by making clear the credit value of each type of qualification available in Scotland. The framework has 12 levels, from Level 1 for very basic education to Level 12 for doctoral degrees.

More information about SQA and its qualifications can be found at its website: www.sqa.org.uk

Validating, examining and awarding bodies/organizations

A large number of external bodies provide qualifications recognized by accrediting and regulatory bodies. Not all qualifications are available across the entire FE sector: some colleges specialize in particular vocational areas while others are involved in more general adult education provision.

The Federation of Awarding Bodies (FAB) is a trade federation and membership organization for vocational awarding bodies. At the time of writing there are around 120 Ofqual-recognized awarding bodies that are full members of FAB. It also has associate members. Find more information at www.awarding.org.uk.

It is important to contact the examining or awarding bodies directly to find which colleges deliver the qualifications desired. However, most colleges deliver courses leading to qualifications awarded by the sample selection of organizations listed below.

ABC Awards

Robins Wood House, Robins Wood Road, Aspley, Nottingham NG8 3NH; Tel: 0115 854 1620; Fax: 0115 854 1617; E-mail: centresupport@abcawards.co.uk; website: www.abcawards.co.uk

ABC Awards is a vocational awarding organization with accredited QCF qualifications in all sectors. It is a registered charity and part of the EMFEC Group. ABC has a portfolio of Ofqual regulated qualifications covering 16 industry sectors as well as functional skills and is designed for all ages and abilities post-14. ABC Awards' qualifications give learners the skills they need to find employment, progress within education and training or enhance their skills within their current job roles.

AQA

Stag Hill House, Guildford, Surrey GU2 7XJ; Tel: 0800 197 7162; Exams Office Support e-mail: eos@aqa.org.uk; website: www.aqa.org.uk

AQA is an independent education charity and the largest of the exam boards, currently setting and marking the papers for around half of all GCSEs and A-levels in England, Wales and Northern Ireland. AQA qualifications are internationally recognized and are taught in 30 countries around the world. As an awarding body AQA offers a broad range of academic qualifications for 14–19-year olds including GCEs, GCSEs, AQA iGCSEs, the Extended Project Qualification and the AQA Baccalaureate.

ASDAN

Wainbrook House, Hudds Vale Road, St George, Bristol BS5 7HY; Tel: 0117 941 1126; e-mail: info@asdan.org.uk; website: www.asdan.org.uk

ASDAN is a curriculum development organization and awarding body, offering programmes and qualifications that explicitly grow skills for learning, for employment and for life. ASDAN is established as a registered charity for the 'advancement of education, by providing opportunities for all learners to develop their personal and social attributes and levels of achievement through ASDAN awards and resources, and the relief of poverty, where poverty inhibits such opportunities for learners'.

ASDAN qualifications contribute towards school/college performance measures and Ofsted requirements. ASDAN offers a range of nationally approved qualifications based around the development of personal, social and employability skills:

- Entry 1, 2 and 3 (Access) qualifications meet the needs of learners working below GCSE (Intermediate) level
- Levels 1 and 2 (Intermediate) qualifications are comparable to GCSEs
- Level 3 (Higher) qualifications are A/AS-level comparable
- Level 4 accreditation represents a Certificate of Higher Education

Ofqual, Qualifications Wales and CCEA approve ASDAN qualifications for pre-and post-16 provision. ASDAN qualifications sit within the Regulated Qualifications Framework (RQF) and the Qualifications and Credit Framework (QCF), and some have approval within the SCQF in Scotland. ASDAN also offers a wide choice of activity-based curriculum programmes that can be used in a variety of educational settings with learners working at a range of levels, offering imaginative ways of developing, recording and certificating young people's personal achievements. Through Customised Accreditation ASDAN also accredits programmes that are already being offered or has been written by another organization.

The following ASDAN qualifications are available:
- Qualifications in Personal Progress: Entry 1
- Personal and Social Development (PSD): Entry 1–3, Levels 1 and 2
- Employability: Entry 2 to Level 3
- Diplomas in Life Skills: Entry 1–3
- Event Volunteering Qualifications: Entry 3 to Level 3
- Wider Key Skills: Levels 1–4
- Certificate of Personal Effectiveness (CoPE): Levels 1–3
- Award of Personal Effectiveness (AoPE) Levels 1–3

City & Guilds

1 Giltspur Street, London EC1A 9DD; Tel: Customers: 0844 543 0000, Main switchboard: 0207 294 2468; e-mail: centresupport@cityandguilds.com; website: www.cityandguilds.com

City & Guilds is a leading vocational educational organization, offering hundreds of work-related qualifications worldwide. City & Guilds' qualifications, which span from basic skills to the highest level of professional achievement, are delivered in more than 80 countries across the world.

With over 130 years of experience, City & Guilds offers a wide range of vocational qualifications, apprenticeships and traineeships from agriculture to engineering; hairdressing to health and social care; IT to tourism; and photography to catering. They are developed with the help of industry experts and are workplace-relevant, so these qualifications equip people for doing a real job – benefiting them and their employer.

City & Guilds qualifications develop both knowledge and practical skills. They are available at nine levels, from Entry Level to Level 8, and are suitable for anyone, whether they are beginners or advanced in their career or area of study. Assessment is based on any combination of examination, projects or coursework. The organizations that offer City & Guilds qualifications include schools, colleges, training organizations, companies and adult education institutes. Depending on the organization, it is possible to study full time, part time or through distance learning.

City and Guilds offer the following qualifications: National Vocational Qualifications (NVQs) and Scottish Vocational Qualifications (SVQs), Functional Skills, Core Skills and Essential Skills, International Vocational Qualifications (IVQs), Single Subject Qualifications, International English Qualifications (IEQs), Institute of Leadership and Management (ILM) qualifications, Professional Recognition Awards, Tech Levels, TechBac, Apprenticeships and Traineeships.

Pearson (Edexcel, BTEC and LCCI)

190 High Holborn, London WC1V 7BH; website: https://qualifications.pearson.com, online contact form for students: http://qualifications.pearson.com/en/support/support-for-you/students/contact-us.html

Edexcel, of Pearson Education Limited, is the UK's largest awarding organization, offering academic and vocational qualifications and testing to schools, colleges, employers and other places of learning in the UK and internationally. Edexcel academic qualifications include GCSE,

GCE (A level) and International GCSE (Edexcel Certificate for UK state schools). Edexcel vocational qualifications include NVQ and BTEC from entry level to Higher National Diplomas.

Pearson acquired EDI, a leading provider of education and training qualifications and assessment services and the EDI qualifications have been rebranded as Pearson material. The qualifications selected from EDI have been redeveloped or reaccredited to be delivered through Pearson's brands including: Pearson Edexcel, Pearson BTEC and Pearson LCCI.

LCCI International Qualifications are widely used in South East Asia and over 100 countries around the world. LCCI International Qualifications, vocational qualifications available as single subjects or diplomas, cover the key areas of business, language and teaching.

NCFE

Q6, Quorum Business Park, Benton Lane, Newcastle upon Tyne NE12 8BT; Tel: 0191 239 8000; e-mail: service@ncfe.org.uk; website: www.ncfe.org.uk

NCFE is a national awarding organization and registered educational charity. It currently offers over 500 nationally accredited qualifications from Entry level up to and including level 4 as well as NVQs, Functional Skills, Apprenticeships and Traineeships. Further qualifications are constantly in development. The NCFE website has a qualifications finder search facility: www.ncfe.org.uk/qualification-search

OCR

1 Hills Road, Cambridge CB1 2EU;
General qualifications: Tel: 01223 553998; e-mail: general.qualifications@ocr.org.uk;
Vocational qualifications: Tel: 02476 851 509; e-mail: vocational. qualifications@ocr.org.uk; website: www.ocr.org.uk

OCR is a leading UK awarding body, committed to providing qualifications that engage learners of all ages at school, college, in work or through part-time learning programmes to achieve their full potential. OCR offers a wide range of general and vocational qualifications, from GCSEs, A levels and Diplomas to OCR Nationals, NVQs and specialist qualifications. You can find a full index of OCR qualifications at: www.ocr.org.uk/qualifications/index.aspx

WJEC

245 Western Avenue, Cardiff CF5 2YX; Tel: 029 2026 5000; e-mail: info@wjec.co.uk; website: www.wjec.co.uk

A registered charity with members from the 22 local authorities in Wales, WJEC is a leading awarding organization providing assessment, training and educational resources in England, Wales, Northern Ireland and elsewhere; WJEC CBAC Ltd is a company limited by guarantee, registered in England and Wales. WJEC offers the following major qualifications: GCSE; Entry Level (EL) and Advanced (A)/Advanced Supplementary (AS) levels and theWelsh Baccalaureate, which is available at different levels and incorporates GCSEs, A Levels and NVQs. In addition, WJEC provides Essential Skills Wales, Project and Extended Project, Pathways QCF, Principal Learning and Wider Key Skills qualifications. The reformed GCSE and GCE qualifications in England are provided via Eduqas, the new brand from WJEC (www.eduqas.co.uk).

Part 4

Qualifications Awarded or Validated by Universities

ADMISSION TO DEGREE COURSES

Higher Education Institutions (HEIs)

Most institutions have a general requirement for admission to a degree course; special requirements may be in force for particular courses. Requirements are usually expressed in terms of subjects passed at GCE A level and the Higher Grade of the SQC. UCAS is the clearing house for the universities and it handles applications for university courses (www.ucas.com).

All intending students who live in the UK may obtain information on application procedures from their schools or colleges, or directly from UCAS. The scheme covers all universities and all medical schools. UCAS also has specialist services: the UCAS Teacher Training www.ucas.com/ucas/teacher-training, the UK Postgraduate Application and Statistical Service (www.ucas.com/ucas/postgraduate) and the UCAS Conservatoires (www.ucas.com/ucas/conservatories). HEIs have specific schemes to encourage access and participation in higher education. These can include partnerships with further education colleges that run access to higher education courses.

The Open University

For admission to most first-degree courses, no formal educational qualifications are necessary. However, students who have successfully completed one or more years of full-time study at the higher education level (or its equivalent in part-time study) may be eligible for exemption from some credit requirements of the BA degree. The Open University handles its own admissions.

Business schools

The degrees awarded by the various university business schools are postgraduate and therefore normally require an Honours degree as part of their entrance qualification.

AWARDS

The awards made by the universities may be separated into the following categories: first degrees; higher degrees; honorary degrees; first diplomas and certificates; higher diplomas and certificates.

First degrees

Nomenclature

Various names are given to first degrees at British universities. At most universities the first degree in Arts is the BA (Bachelor of Arts) and the first degree in Science is the BSc (Bachelor of Science), but at the universities of Oxford and Cambridge and at several new universities, the BA is the first degree gained by students in both arts and science. Although the first degree in most faculties in Scottish universities is a Bachelor's degree, the first degree in Arts in the four 'ancient' universities and Dundee University is MA or Master of Arts. Heriot-Watt University also offers some 'first degree' MAs, but at Honours level only.

There are numerous variations on the bachelor theme, for example BSc (Econ) (Bachelor of Science in Economics), BCom (Bachelor of Commerce), BSocSc (Bachelor of Social Science), BEng (Bachelor of Engineering) and BTech (Bachelor of Technology). The first award in medicine is the joint degrees of MB, ChB (Bachelor of Medicine, Bachelor of Surgery), the designatory letters of which vary from university to university.

Structure of courses

First-degree courses vary considerably in structure, not only between one university and another but also between faculties in a single university. The degree examination is usually in two sections, Part I coming after one or two years of the course and Part II, 'finals, at the end of the course. The first-degree system at some Scottish universities differs substantially from that in English and Welsh universities (see below).

Bachelor degrees

These degrees, sometimes known as 'ordinary' or 'first' degrees, lead to qualifications such as Bachelor of Arts (BA), Bachelor of Science (BSc) or Bachelor of Medicine (MB). Each university decides the form and content of its own degree examinations. These vary from university to university.

The first-degree structure in all British universities is based on the honours degree. Successful candidates in honours degree examinations are placed in different classes according to their performance, first class being the highest. The other classes given vary from university to university, but the classification most often used is: Class I; Class II (Division 1); Class II (Division 2); Class III. Most graduates who go on to higher academic qualifications and those entering, for example, the higher grades in the Civil Service or research, normally have a good class honours degree.

You can find out more about recognized UK degrees at the Government website: www.gov.uk/recognised-uk-degrees.

Number of subjects studied

Excluding medicine and dentistry, the broad subject areas are Arts (or Humanities), Social Science, Pure Science and Applied Science. Most students study one main subject selected from one of these areas. It is possible to distinguish many types of degree course according to the number of subjects studied; these types are a variation on three main categories:

1. Honours course in one to three subjects with or without examinable subsidiary subjects.
2. Pass or ordinary courses in one to three subjects with or without examinable subsidiary subjects.
3. Common studies for pass and Honours in one to three subjects, with or without examinable subsidiary subjects.

Length of degree course

First-degree courses may be preceded by a preliminary year, from which students with the appropriate entry qualifications may be exempted. At most universities Honours and pass courses in arts, social science, pure and applied science last three or four years, but courses in architecture, dentistry and veterinary medicine usually last five years, and complete qualifying courses in medicine up to six years. Courses in fine arts and pharmacy may last four years; four-year courses exist mainly in double Honours schools, especially when they involve foreign languages and a period of study abroad, and in the technological universities where some courses include a period of integrated industrial training (sandwich courses).

The Scottish first degree

Undergraduate Honours degrees in Scotland are usually four years in duration and are structured to ensure a great deal of flexibility during the first two years of study. Most students only confirm their major in the final two years of study, which usually allows the student to choose a variety of subjects. This is different from the English system of undergraduate education, which is normally three years in duration and is more specialized from the beginning. After three years study students can gain a Bachelor or Ordinary degree or obtain the Honours degree by studying for a further year.

The Medicine and Veterinary Medicine degrees and MA Fine Art degree all take five years. In several science and engineering subjects there are opportunities to study for a five-year MChem, MChemPhys, MEng or MPhys degree. These degrees entail in-depth study, often with a research focus, but are undergraduate degrees and not equivalent to postgraduate Master's.

Aegrotat degrees

Candidates who have followed a course for a degree but have been prevented from taking the examinations by illness may be awarded a degree certificate indicating that they were likely to have obtained the degree had they taken the examinations.

Higher degrees

These comprise:

- some Bachelor's degrees: BPhil, BLitt, etc;
- Master's degrees: MA, MSc, etc;
- Doctor of Philosophy: PhD or DPhil;
- Higher Doctorates: DLitt, DSc, etc.

At Oxford and Cambridge the degree of MA is conferred on any BA of the university without any further course of study or examination after a specified number of years and on payment of a fee.

Candidates for a Master's degree at other universities (and at some for the degrees of BPhil, BLitt and BD, which are of equivalent standing) are normally required to have a first degree, although it need not have been obtained in the same university. Master's degrees are taken after one or two years' full-time study. The PhD requires at least two or more – usually three – years of full-time study.

In some universities and faculties students may be selected for a PhD course after an initial year's study or research common to both a PhD and a Master's degree. Candidates for a Master's degree are required either to prepare a thesis for presentation to examiners, who may afterwards question candidates on it orally, or to take written examination papers; they may be required to do both. All PhD students present a thesis; some may be required to take an examination paper as well. MPhil, MSc and similar degrees are usually awarded at the end of a one- or two-year course in a specific topic on the results of a written examination or a thesis. Higher doctorates are designated on a faculty basis, eg DLitt (Doctor of Letters) and DSc (Doctor of Science). Candidates are usually required to have at least a Master's degree of the awarding university. Senior doctorates are conferred on more mature and established people, usually on the basis of published contributions to knowledge.

Foundation degrees

Foundation degrees were established to give people the intermediate technical and professional skills that are in demand from employers and to provide more flexible and accessible ways of studying. Increasing opportunities for employment and career advancement are priorities; Foundation degree content and assessment are therefore designed in consultation with employers. Additional progression routes include links with associated professional qualifications and/or direct entry to the final year of a relevant Honours-level degree. Provision is available across a range of FE colleges and a number of HEIs.

Honorary degrees

Most universities confer honorary degrees on people of distinction in academic and public life, and on others who have rendered service to the university or to the local community. Normally degrees awarded are at least Foundation level.

Diplomas and certificates of higher education

Courses for first diplomas and certificates are relatively simple in structure; they usually reach a level lower than that required for the award of a degree. There is usually a carefully defined course in a specialized or vocational subject, lasting one or two years, followed by all candidates. Most courses are full time.

Postgraduate diplomas and certificates

Diplomas (eg in public health, social administration, medicine and technology) are awarded either on a full-time or, less often, part-time basis according to the subject and the university. Candidates must usually be graduates or hold equivalent qualifications. Diplomas are awarded after formal courses of instruction and success in written examinations. A Certificate or Diploma in Education is awarded to graduates training to become teachers after one year's full-time study and teaching practice.

Postgraduate courses

A number of courses for graduates or people with equivalent qualifications are offered in FE establishments. They include short specialist courses in management and business studies and secretarial courses for graduates.

Business schools

A Master of Business Administration (MBA) is an internationally recognized postgraduate qualification intended to prepare individuals for middle to senior general managerial positions. Most programmes contain as their core a number of subjects considered essential for understanding the operations of any enterprise. These are: accounting and finance, operations management, business policy, economics, human resource management, marketing, information systems and strategic planning.

Unlike any other Master's programme, the MBA is not only postgraduate, it is also strongly postexperience. A minimum of three years' (often more) work experience at an appropriate level of responsibility is generally expected of applicants. The requirement for a first degree (or equivalent) is sometimes waived for those holding an impressive track record of over five years at managerial level. Approximately one-third of MBA students have an engineering or information technology background. Many undertake the qualification to facilitate change from technical or specialist positions to more general ones.

The MBA was conceived originally in the United States at the beginning of the twentieth century. Introduced in the United Kingdom in the late 1960s, it did not grow in popularity until the late 1980s. The popularity of this degree in the United Kingdom can be seen in the rapid expansion in the number of providers.

The Association of MBAs (AMBA) operates a system of accreditation. The accreditation process, which is internationally recognized for all MBA, DBA and Master's in Business and Management (MBM) programmes, measures individual MBA programmes against specific accreditation criteria.

Further information, including a list of accredited MBA programmes, can be obtained from the Association of MBAs, 25 Hosier Lane, London EC1A 9LQ; Tel: 020 7246 2686; e-mail: info@mbaworld.com; website: www.mbaworld.com.

The Chartered Association of Business Schools (CABS)

3rd Floor, 40 Queen Street, London EC4R 1DD; Tel: 020 7236 7678; website: www.associationof-businessschools.org.

The CABS is the representative body for management and business education and all the United Kingdom's leading business schools and acts as a hub for sharing new ideas and developing best practice. The CABS works broadly in three main areas: policy development, promotion and representation, and training and development. The CABS is able to provide general information about the wide range of courses and programmes provided by the United Kingdom's business schools.

First awards

- **BA, BEd, BEng, LLB, BSc, BBA, BMedSci:** with 1st Class, 2nd Class (Divisions 1 and 2), 3rd Class Honours or Pass; or unclassified with or without Distinction.

- **MEng:** awarded to students who successfully complete a course of study that is longer and more demanding than the BEng first degree course in engineering.
- **GMus (Graduate Diploma in Music):** awarded to those students who complete three years' approved full-time study (or equivalent) in music and who demonstrate competence in musical performance.

- **M.Ost (Master of Osteophathy):** M.Ost is an undergraduate degree of four years' full-time study.
- **DipHE (Diploma of Higher Education):** equivalent in standard and often similar in content to the first two years of an Honours degree course.
- **Certificates of Higher Education:** equivalent to the first year of an Honours degree course.

Higher awards

- **MA, MBA, MEd, MSc:** for successful completion of an approved postgraduate course of full-time study of three trimesters duration (or the part-time equivalent).
- **MPhil, PhD:** for successful completion of approved programmes of supervised research.
- **DSc, DLitt, DTech:** for original and important contributions to knowledge and/or its applications.
- **Postgraduate Diploma:** awarded for the successful completion of an approved postgraduate course of study of 30 weeks' duration (or the part-time equivalent).

- **Postgraduate Certificate:** awarded for the successful completion of postgraduate/post-experience courses of 15 weeks' duration (or the part-time equivalent).
- **Postgraduate Certificate in Education (PGCE):** awarded on completion of a one-year full-time course; candidates must be British graduates or hold another recognized qualification.
- **Diploma in Professional Studies:** available in the fields of education and nursing, health visiting, midwifery and sports coaching. Students normally hold an initial professional qualification. A minimum of two years' experience is normally expected.

UNIVERSITY OF ABERDEEN
www.abdn.ac.uk

Aberdeen Business School; www.abdn.ac.uk/business

MA Accountancy and Finance, MA Business Management, MA Economics, MA Real Estate; MBA (Aberdeen), MBA Global, MBA Energy Management; MSc Accounting and Finance, MSc Digital Marketing Leadership, MSc Finance (on-line)(from January 2018), MSc Finance and Investment Management, MSc Finance and Real Estate, MSc International Business and Finance, MSc International Business Management, MSc Marketing Management, MSc Petroleum Energy Economics and Finance, MSc Real Estate; MRes Business Research; PhDs in the areas of accountancy, finance and real estate, business management, economics.

College of Arts and Social Sciences; www.abdn.ac.uk/cass

School of Divinity, History & Philosophy; www.abdn.ac.uk/sdhp

MA Theology and Religious Studies, Bachelor of Theology, Bachelor of Divinity, MA History of Art, MA History, MA Philosophy, MA Philosophy, Politics and Economics, Certificate in Christian Studies, Diploma in Christian Studies, MTh Biblical Studies, MTh Ministry Studies, MTh Systematic Theology, Mth Theological Ethics, MLitt Islamic Studies, MLitt Islamic Studies (distance learning), MLitt Art and Business, MLitt Scandinavian Studies, MLitt in Medieval and Early Modern Studies, MLitt Modern History, MLitt Scottish Heritage (distance learning), MLitt Philosophy by Research; PhDs in the areas of divinity, history, history of art, philosophy, religious studies and Scandinavian studies.

School of Education; www.abdn.ac.uk/education

BA in Childhood Practice, BMus with Honours (Education), MA(Honours) Education, Professional Graduate Diploma in Education (PGDE)

School of Language, Literature, Music and Visual Culture; www.abdn.ac.uk/sll

MA Celtic & Anglo-Saxon Studies, MA Archaeology and Celtic & Anglo-Saxon Studies, MA Celtic & Anglo-Saxon Studies and English, MA Celtic & Anglo-Saxon Studies and Film & Visual Culture,, MA English, MA English and Scottish Literature, MA English with Creative Writing, MA Film & Visual Culture, MA French Studies, MA French Studies (5 years), MA Gaelic Studies, MA German Studies (5 years), MA Language & Linguistics, BMus Music, BMus Music and Communities, BMus Music Education, ADD IN JOINT HONOURS IF NEEDED, MA Spanish & Latin American Studies (5 years); MSc Professional Communication

MSc TESOL(Teaching English as a Second or Other Language), MSc Translation Studies; MLitt in Celtic and Anglo-Saxon Studies, MLitt in Creative Writing, MLitt in English Literary Studies, MLitt in Ethnology and Folklore, MLitt in Irish and Scottish Literature, MLitt in Literature, Science and Medicine, MLitt in Migration and Postcolonial Studies, MLitt in The Novel, MLitt in Film and Visual Culture; MMus in Music, MMus in Sonic Arts, MMus in Vocal Music; PhDs, MPhils and Masters in all of the school's subject areas.

School of Law; www.abdn.ac.uk/law

LLB, LLB with Honours, Law with English Law, with options in French, Gaelic, German and Spanish languages, options in accountancy, economics, management studies and music, and options in Belgian law, French law, German law and Spanish law; Diploma in Professional Legal Practice; online programmes in LL.M. Dispute Resolution, LL.M. International Trade Law, LL.M. International Trade Law and Treaty Negotiation with Professional Skills (Online and Summer School), LL.M. Oil and Gas Law with Dissertation, LL.M. Oil and Gas Law with Professional Skills (Online and Summer School); LL.M. Criminal Justice, LL.M. Human Rights, LL.M. Criminal Justice & Human Rights, LL.M. Human Rights & Criminal Justice, LL.M. International Law, LL.M. Public International Law, LL.M. Private International Law, LL.M. International Law and International Relations, LL.M. International Law and Strategic Studies, LL.M. International Commercial Law with Dissertation, LL.M. International Commercial Law with Professional Skills, LL.M. International Trade Law & Treaty Negotiation with Professional Skills, Graduate Diploma in International Arbitration, LL.M. Energy Law with Dissertation, LL.M. Energy Law with Professional Skills, LL.M. Oil & Gas Law with Dissertation, LL.M. Oil & Gas Law with Professional Skills, LL.M. Energy and Environmental Law with Dissertation, LL.M. Energy and Environmental Law with Professional Skills, LL.M Intellectual Property Law; LLM by research and PhDs.

School of Social Science; www.abdn.ac.uk/socsci/

MA Anthropology, MA Politics and International relations, MA Philosophy, Politics and Economics, MA Sociology; Postgraduate courses in MLitt Museum Studies, MSc in People and Environment, MRes in Social Anthropology, MSc International Political Economy, MSc Energy Politics & Law, MSc in International Relations, MSc in International Relations & International Law, MSC in International Security, MSc in Latin American Studies, MSc Strategic Studies, MSc Strategic Studies and International Law, MSc in Strategic Studies & International Law, MSc in Strategic, & Management, MSc in Strategic Studies and Energy Security, MRes in Political Research, MSc in Comparative European Societies, MSc in Global Conflict & Peace Processes, MSc in Globalization, MSc in Post-Conflict Justice & Peacebuilding, MSc in Religion & Society, MSc in Sex, Gender Violence: Contemporary Critical Approaches, MSc in Sociology, MRes in Social Research

The College of Life Sciences and Medicine; www.abdn.ac.uk/clsm/

The School of Biological Science; www.abdn.ac.uk/biologicalsci

BSc Animal Behaviour, BSc Behavioural Biology, BSc Biological Sciences,, BSc Biology, BSc Conservation Biology, BSc Ecology, BSc Environmental and Forest Management, BSc Environmental Science, BSc Marine Biology, BSc Plant and Soil Science, BSc Zoology, MSci Biological Sciences; Postgraduate courses in MSc Applied Marine and Fisheries Ecology, MSc Ecology and Conservation, MSc Environmental and Forest Management, MSc Environmental and Ecological Sciences, MSc Environmental Management, MSc Environmental Pollution and Remediation, MSc Environmental Science, MSc Marine Conservation, MSc Soil Science

The School of Medicine, Medical Sciences and Nutrition; www.abdn.ac.uk/smmsn/

Medicine (MBChB), BSc/MSci Medical Science, Dentistry (BDS); Postgraduate courses in MSc Biotechnology, Bioinformatics and Bio-business, MSc Genetics, MSc Immunology, MSc Microbiology, MSc Clinical Pharmacology, MSc Drug Discovery and Development, MRes Drug Discovery, Master of Public Health (MPH), MSc Clinical Nutrition (Online), MSc Global Health and Management, MSc Health Psychology, MSc Human Nutrition, MSc Health Economics for Health Professionals (Online), MSc Clinical Education, MSc Physician Associate Studies, PgCert Medical Research Skills, PgCert Research Methods for Health, MSc Medical Imaging, MSc Medical Physics, PhD, MRes, MPhil, MD, ChM

The School of Psychology; www.abdn.ac.uk/psychology/

BSc Psychology, MA Psychology, MA Psychology with Counselling Skills; Postgraduate degrees in MSc Foundations of Clinical Psychology, MSc Psychological Studies, PhD and MRes study

School of Engineering; www.abdn.ac.uk/engineering/

MEng Chemical Engineering, MEng Civil Engineering, MEng Electrical and Electronic Engineering, MEng Mechanical Engineering, MEng Petroleum Engineering; Postgraduate courses in MSc Oil & Gas Engineering, MSc Oil & Gas Structural Engineering MSc Oil & Gas Structural Engineering, MSc Petroleum Engineering, MSc Process Safety, MSc Project Management, MSc Renewable Energy Engineering, MSc Reservoir Engineering, MSc Safety and Reliability Engineering for Oil & Gas, MSc Subsea Engineering, PhD and MRes study

School of Geosciences; www.abdn.ac.uk/geosciences/
Archaeology
Master of Arts in Archaeology (MA), Bachelor of Science in Archaeology (BSc); Postgraduate courses in MSc Archaeology, MSc Archaeology of the North, MSc Archaeology: Vikings in Focus, MSc Osteoarchaeology, PhD study
Geography and the Environment
BSc and MA Geography, Postgraduate courses in MSc Data Analysis, Visualisation and Communication, MSc Environmental Partnership Management, MSc Geographical Information Systems, MSc Land Economy (Rural Surveying), PhD and MRes study
Geology and Petroleum
BSc Geology and Petroleum; MSc Geophysics, MSc Integrated Petroleum Geoscience, MSc Oil & Gas Enterprise Management, MSc Petrophysics and Formation Evaluation, MSc Reservoir Engineering, PhD and research study

The School of Natural and Computing Sciences; www.abdn.ac.uk/ncs/
Chemistry
BSc Chemistry, MChem Chemistry; Postgraduate courses in MSc Environmental Analytical Chemistry, MSc Oil and Gas Chemistry, PhD study
Computing Science
BSc Honours in Computing Science, MA Honours in Computing, MEng in Computing Science, MSci Honours in Computing Science with Industrial Placement, MSci Honours in Information Systems with Industrial Placement, MSci Honours in Computing with Industrial Placement; Postgraduate courses in MSc Artificial Intelligence, MSc Information Technology, PhD study
Mathematical Sciences
MA Mathematics, BSc Mathematics; Postgraduate courses in MSc Financial Mathematics, MSc Mathematics of Computing, PhD study
Physics
Physics (BSc), Physical Sciences (BSc), Physics-Education (BSc); Postgraduate research PhDs

UNIVERSITY OF ABERTAY, DUNDEE
www.abertay.ac.uk

School of Arts, Media & Computer Games; www.abertay.ac.uk/studying/schools/amg

BA(Hons) Game Design and Production Management, BSc(Hons) Computer Games Technology, BA(Hons) Computer Arts, BA(Hons) Sound and Music for Games, BSc(Hons) Computer Games Application Development, BSc(Hons) Ethical Hacking, MSc Ethical Hacking, BSc(Hons) Computing, Postgraduate courses, MSc Computer Games Technology, MProf Games Development,

School of Science, Engineering & Technology; www.abertay.ac.uk/studying/schools/set

BSc(Hons) Forensic Sciences, BSc(Hons) Biomedical Science/BSc(Hons) Applied Biomedical Science, BSc(Hons) Degree in Civil Engineering, BSc(Hons) Environmental Science and Technology, BSc(Hons) Fitness, Nutrition and Health, BSc(Hons) Food and Consumer Sciences, BSc(Hons) Food, Nutrition and Health, MProf Food and Drink Innovation, MSc Energy, Water and Environmental Management

Dundee Business School; www.abertay.ac.uk/studying/schools/dbs

BA(Hons) Business Management, BA(Hons) Business Management, BA(Hons) Marketing and Business, BA(Hons) Marketing and Business, Batchelor of Laws LLB(Hons), MSc/PGDip International Human Resource Management, MSc/PGDip International Human Resource Management, MSc/PGDip International Management, MSc/PGDip International Management

The School of Social & Health Sciences; www.abertay.ac.uk/studying/schools/shs

Undergraduate Courses

BA Accounting and Finance, BSc(Hons) Biomedical Science,BA(Hons) Business and Human resource Management, BA(Hons) Business Management, BEng Civil and environmental Engineering, BSc(Hons) Civil Engineering, BA(Hons) Computer Arts, BSc(Hons) Computer Game Applications, BSc(Hons) Computer Games Technology, BSc (HOns), BA(Hons) Criminology, BSc(Hons) Environmental Science and Technology, BSc(Hons) Ethical Hacking, BSc(Hons) Fitness, Nutrition and Health, BSc(Hons) Food and Consumer Science, BSc(Hons) Food, Nutrition and Health, BSc(Hons) Forensic Sciences, BA(Hons) Games Design and Production Management, BA(Hons) Management and the Games Industry, BA(Hons) Marketing and Business, BSc(Hons) Nursing (Mental Health Nursing), BSc Physical Activity and Health, BSc(Hons) Psychology, BSc (hons) Psychology and Counselling, BSc(Hons) Psychology and Forensic Biology, BSc(Hons) Psychology and Human Resource Management, BA(Hons) Social Science, BA(Hons) Sociology, BA(Hons) Sound and Music for Games, BSc(Hons) Sport and Exercise, BSc(Hons) Sport and Exercise Science, BA(Hons) Sport and Management, BSc(Hons) Sport nad Psychology, BSc(Hons) Sports Development, BSc(Hons) Strength and Conditioning, Llb(Hons) Law; Postgraduate Taught Courses MSc/PGDip Computer Games Technology, MSc Counselling, MSc/PGDip Ethical Hacking and Cyber Security, MSc Food and Drink Innovation, MSc/PGDip International Human Resource Management, MSc/PGDip/PGCert Mental Health, MSc/PGDip Mental Health Nursing (post-registration), MProf Games Development, MSc/PGDip Psychology, Research Masters Degrees (MPhil or MbR) and Doctorates (PhD or DBA) in a range of subjects.

ABERYSTWYTH UNIVERSITY
www.aber.ac.uk

School of Art; www.aber.ac.uk/en/art

Art History (BA, 3 year), Creative Arts (BA, 3 year), Fine Art (BA, 3 year), Liberal Arts (BA, 3 year),

Institute of Biological, Environmental & Rural Sciences; www.aber.ac.uk/en/ibers

Agriculture (BSC, 4 year), Agriculture (BSC, 3 year), Agriculture with Animal Science (BSC, 3 year), Agriculture with Animal Science (BSC, 4 year), Agriculture with Business Studies (BSC, 4 year), Agriculture with Business Studies (BSC, 3 year), Life Sciences (BSC, 4 year), Animal Science (MSC, 1 year), Biotechnology (MSC, 1 year), Environmental Management (MSC, 1 year), Equine Science (MSC, 1 year), Livestock Science (MSC, 1 year), Statistics for Computational Biology (MSC, 1 year), Biological Sciences (PHD, 3 year), Sport and Exercise Science (PHD, 3 year)

Dept of Computer Science; www.aber.ac.uk/en/cs

Artificial Intelligence and Robotics (BSC, 3 year), Artificial Intelligence and Robotics (inc Integrated Industrial and Professional Training) (BSC, 4 year), Business Information Technology (BSC, 3 year), Business Information Technology (inc Integrated Industrial and Professional Training) (BSC, 4 year), Business Information Technology (includes foundation year) (BSC, 4 year), Computer Graphics, Vision and Games (BSC, 3 year), Computer Science (BSC, 3 year), Computer Science (inc Integrated Industrial and Professional Training) (BSC, 4 year), Computer Science (includes foundation year) (BSC, 4 year), Computer Science and Artificial Intelligence (BSC, 3 year), Computer Science and Artificial Intelligence (inc Integrated Industrial and Professional Training) (BSC, 4 year), Data Science (BSC, 3 year), Data Science (inc Integrated Industrial and Professional Training) (BSC, 4 year), Internet Computing and Systems Administration (BSC, 3 year), Internet Computing and Systems Administration (inc Integrated Industrial and Professional Training) (BSC, 4 year), Robotics and Embedded Systems Engineering (BENG, 3 year), Robotics and Embedded Systems Engineering (including integrated year in industry) (BENG, 4 year), Software Engineering (inc Integrated Industrial and Professional Training) (BENG, 4 year), Space Science and Robotics (BSC, 3 year), Computer Science (Software Engineering) (MSC, 1 year), Computer Science Software Engineering (inc Integrated Industrial and Professional Training) (MSC, 2 year), Data Science (MSC, 1 year), Statistics for Computational Biology (MSC, 1 year), Computer Science (PHD, 3 year)

School of Education & Lifelong Learning; www.aber.ac.uk/en/sell

Childhood Studies (BA, 3 year), Education and International Development (BA, 3 year), ICT and Computer Science (PGCE, 1 year), Biology with Balanced Science (PGCE, 1 year), Chemistry with Balanced Science (PGCE, 1 year), Drama (PGCE, 1 year), English (PGCE, 1 year), French (PGCE, 1 year), Geography (PGCE, 1 year), German (PGCE, 1 year), History (PGCE, 1 year), Physics with Balanced Science (PGCE, 1 year), Spanish (PGCE, 1 year), Almaeneg (PGCE, 1 year), Cemeg gyda Gwyddoniaeth Gytbwys (PGCE, 1 year), Drama (Cyfrwng Cymraeg) (PGCE, 1 year), Saesneg (PGCE, 1 year), Welsh (PGCE, 1 year)

Dept of English & Creative Writing; www.aber.ac.uk/en/english

Creative Arts (BA, 3 year), Creative Writing (BA, 3 year), English Literature (BA, 3 year), English Literature and Creative Writing (BA, 3 year), Liberal Arts (BA, 3 year), Liberal Arts (MLIBA, 4 year), Creative Writing (MA, 1 year), Literary Studies (MA, 1 year), Literary Studies (American Studies) (MA, 1 year), Literary Studies (Eighteenth Century Writing and Romanticism) (MA, 1 year), Literary Studies (Medieval and Renaissance Writing) (MA, 1 year), Literary Studies (Post-modern Writing) (MA, 1 year),

Literary Studies (Welsh Writing in English) (MA, 1 year), Literature and Creative Writing (MA, 1 year), Creative Writing (PHD, 3 year), English (PHD, 3 year)

Dept of European Languages; www.aber.ac.uk/en/eurolangs

European Languages (BA, 4 year), French (BA, 4 year), Liberal Arts (BA, 3 year), Modern German Studies (BA, 4 year), Romance Languages (BA, 4 year), Spanish and Latin American Studies (BA, 4 year), European Languages (PHD, 3 year)

Department of Geography & Earth Sciences; www.aber.ac.uk/en/dges/

Environmental Earth Science (BSC, 3 year), Environmental Science (BSC, 3 year), Geography (BSC, 3 year), Geography (with integrated year in industry) (BSC, 4 year), Geography (with integrated year studying abroad) (BSC, 4 year), Human Geography (BA, 3 year), Human Geography (with integrated year in industry) (BA, 4 year), Human Geography (with integrated year studying abroad) (BA, 4 year), Physical Geography (BSC, 3 year), Physical Geography (with integrated year in industry) (BSC, 4 year), Physical Geography (with integrated year studying abroad) (BSC, 4 year), Practising Human Geography (MA, 1 year), Environmental Change, Impact and Adaptation (MSC, 1 year), Glaciology (MSC, 1 year), Remote Sensing and GIS (MSC, 1 year), Geography and Earth Sciences (Science) (PHD, 3 year)

Dept of History & Welsh History; www.aber.ac.uk/en/history

European History (BA, 3 year), History (BA, 3 year), History and Media (BA, 3 year), History and Welsh History (BA, 3 year), International Politics and Military History (BA, 3 year), Liberal Arts (BA, 3 year), Medieval and Early Modern History (BA, 3 year), Modern and Contemporary History (BA, 3 year), Politics and Modern History (BA, 3 year), History and Heritage (MA, 1 year), History of Wales (MA, 1 year), Media History (MA, 1 year), Medieval Britain & Europe (MA, 1 year), Modern History (MA, 1 year), History (PHD, 3 year)

Dept of Information Studies; www.aber.ac.uk/en/dis

Information and Library Studies Single Honours by Distance Learning (BSc), Archive Administration (MA / Diploma), Digital Curation (MSc), Information and Library Studies (MA / Diploma), MPhil and PhD full and part time research

Dept of International Politics; www.aber.ac.uk/en/interpol

International Politics (BA, 3 year), International Politics and Global Development (BA, 3 year), International Politics and Intelligence Studies (BA, 3 year), International Politics and Military History (BA, 3 year), International Politics and Strategic Studies (BA, 3 year), Political Studies (BA, 3 year), Politics and Modern History (BA, 3 year), MA in International Politics, MA Welsh Politics and Society, MA Politics, Media and Performance

Dept of Law and Criminology; www.aber.ac.uk/en/law-criminology

Business Law (LLB, 3 year), Criminal Law (LLB, 3 year), Criminology (BSC, 3 year), Criminology with Applied Psychology (BSC, 3 year), European Law (LLB, 3 year), Human Rights (LLB, 3 year), Law (LLB, 3 year), Law (LLB, 2 year), Law (BA, 3 year), Climate Change and Human Rights (LLM, 1 year), Human Rights and Development (LLM, 1 year), Human Rights and Humanitarian Law (LLM, 1 year), Information Technology Law (LLM, 1 year), International Commercial Law (LLM, 1 year), International Commercial Law and Human Rights (LLM, 1 year), International Commercial Law and the Environment (LLM, 1 year), International Law and Criminology of Armed Conflict (LLM, 1 year), Law (LLM, 1 year), Legal Practice (LLM, 1 year), Research Training (Law) (LLM, 1 year), Law (PHD, 3 year)

School of Management and Business; www.aber.ac.uk/en/smb

Accounting and Finance (BSC, 3 year), Business Finance (BSC, 3 year), Adventure Tourism Management (BSC, 3 year), Agriculture with Business Studies (BSC, 4 year), Agriculture with Business Studies (BSC, 3 year), Business Economics (BSC, 3 year), Business Finance (BSC, 3 year), Business and Management (BSC, 3 year), Tourism Management (BSC, 3 year), Business Economics (BSC, 3 year), Economics (BSC, 3 year), Marketing (BSC, 3 year), Adventure Tourism Management (BSC, 3 year), Tourism Management (BSC, 3 year)

Dept of Mathematics; www.aber.ac.uk/en/maths

Applied Mathematics / Pure Mathematics (BSC, 3 year), Applied Mathematics / Statistics (BSC, 3 year), Data Science (BSC, 3 year), Data Science (inc Integrated Industrial and Professional Training) (BSC, 4 year), Financial Mathematics (BSC, 3 year), Mathematical and Theoretical Physics (BSC, 3 year), Mathematics (BSC, 3 year), Mathematics (includes foundation year) (BSC, 4 year), Pure Mathematics / Statistics (BSC, 3 year), Data Science (MSC, 1 year), Statistics for Computational Biology (MSC, 1 year), Mathematics (PHD, 3 year),

Dept of Physics; www.aber.ac.uk/en/physics

Astrophysics (BSC, 3 year), Astrophysics (BSC, 4 year), Engineering Physics (BENG, 3 year), Engineering Physics (with integrated year in industry) (BENG, 4 year), Mathematical and Theoretical Physics (BSC, 3 year), Physics (BSC, 3 year), Physics (BSC, 4 year), Physics (inc Integrated Industrial and Professional Training) (BSC, 4 year), Physics with Planetary and Space Physics (BSC, 3 year), Space Science and Robotics (BSC, 3 year), PhD study

Dept of Psychology; www.aber.ac.uk/en/psychology

Psychology (BSC, 3 year), Psychology (with integrated year in industry) (BSC, 4 year), Psychology (with integrated year studying abroad) (BSC, 4 year), Psychology (MPhil, 1 year), Psychology (PHD, 3 year)

Dept of Theatre, Film & Television Studies; www.aber.ac.uk/en/tfts

Creative Arts (BA, 3 year), Drama and Theatre Studies (BA, 3 year), Film and Television Studies (BA, 3 year), Film-making (BA, 3 year), History and Media (BA, 3 year), Liberal Arts (BA, 3 year), Media and Communication Studies (BA, 3 year), Scenography and Theatre Design (BA, 3 year), Writing for Broadcasting, Media and Performance (BA, 3 year), Politics, Media and Performance (MA, 1 year), Theatre, Film and Television Studies (PHD, 3 year),

Dept of Welsh; www.aber.ac.uk/en/cymraeg

Celtic Studies (BA, 4 year), Liberal Arts (BA, 3 year), Professional Welsh (BA, 3 year), Welsh (BA, 4 year), Welsh and the Celtic Languages (BA, 3 year), Cymraeg (PHD, 3 year)

ANGLIA RUSKIN UNIVERSITY
www.anglia.ac.uk

Anglia Law School; www.anglia.ac.uk/arts-law-and-social-sciences/anglia-law-school

Undergarduate LLB(Hons) Law; Professional courses PG Dip Legal Practice Course, CILEx Graduate Fast-track Diploma, CILEx Level 6 Single Subject Certificates, Postgraduate taught degrees in LLM Digital Economy, LLM International Law, LLM International Business Law, LLM International Commercial Law, LLM Legal Practice (top-up), LLM Medical Law and Ethics (part-time only); Research degrees MPhil / PhD Laws

Cambridge School of Art; www.anglia.ac.uk/arts-law-and-social-sciences/cambridge-school-of-art

Undergraduate courses in BA(Hons) Computer Games Art, BA(Hons) Digital Media, BA(Hons) Fashion Design, BA(Hons) Film and Television Production, BA(Hons) Fine Art, BA(Hons) Graphic Design, BA(Hons) Illustration, BA(Hons) Illustration and Animation, BA(Hons) Interior Design, BA(Hons) Photography; Postgraduate Taught courses in MA Children's Book Illustration, MA Computer Games Development (Art), MA Fashion Design, MA Film and Television Production, MA Fine Art, MA Graphic Design and Typography, MA Illustration and Book Arts, MA Photography, MA Printmaking; Research Degrees in MPhil/PhD Art and Design, MPhil/PhD Children's Book Illustration, MPhil/PhD Film and Television Production, MPhil/PhD Fine Art, MPhil/PhD Graphic Design and Typography

Department of English and Media; http://www.anglia.ac.uk/arts-law-and-social-sciences/department-of-english-and-media

Undergraduate courses in BA(Hons) Drama and English Literature, BA(Hons) Drama and Film Studies, BA(Hons) English Language and English Language Teaching, BA(Hons) English Language and Linguistics, BA(Hons) English Language, BA(Hons) English Literature, BA(Hons) Film Studies, BA(Hons) Film Studies and Media Studies, BA(Hons) Media Studies, BA(Hons) Philosophy and English Literature, BA(Hons) Writing and English Literature, BA(Hons) Writing and Film Studies; Postgraduate taught courses in MA Applied Linguistics and TESOL, MA Children's Literature, MA Creative Writing, MA Creative Writing and Publishing, MA English Literature, MA Intercultural Communication, MA Publishing, MA Science Fiction and Fantasy, MA TESOL and Materials Development; Postgraduate research in PhD/MPhil Creative Writing, PhD/MPhil English Language and Intercultural Communication, PhD/MPhil English Language and Linguistics, PhD/MPhil English Literature, PhD/MPhil Film Studies and Media Studies, PhD/MPhil Publishing

Department of Humanities and Social Sciences; www.anglia.ac.uk/arts-law-and-social-sciences/department-of-humanities-and-social-sciences

Undergraduate courses in BA(Hons) Criminology, BA(Hons) Criminology and Sociology, BA(Hons) History, BA(Hons) Philosophy, BA(Hons) Philosophy and English Literature, BSc(Hons) Policing and Criminal Justice, BA(Hons) Politics, FdA Public Service, BA(Hons) Public Service, BA(Hons) Public Service (Top-up), BA(Hons) Sociology; Postgraduate taught courses in MA Criminology, MA International Relations, MA Sociology; Postgraduate research in PhD/MPhil Criminology, PhD/MPhil History, PhD/MPhil International Relations, PhD/MPhil Philosophy, PhD/MPhil Sociology

Department of Music and Performing Arts; www.anglia.ac.uk/arts-law-and-social-sciences/department-of-music-and-performing-arts

Undergraduate courses in BA(Hons) Creative Music Technology, BA(Hons) Drama BA(Hons) Drama and English Literature, BA(Hons) Drama and Film Studies, BA(Hons) Music, BA(Hons) Performing Arts, BA(Hons) Popular Music; Postgraduate taught courses in MA Body Psychotherapy (Top-up), MA Dramatherapy, MA Music Therapy; Postgraduate research in PhD/MPhil Dramatherapy, PhD/MPhil Musicology, PhD/MPhil Music Technology, Sonic Arts and Composition, PhD/MPhil Music Therapy, PhD/MPhil Theatre and Performance

Faculty of Health, Social Care and Education; www.anglia.ac.uk/health-social-care-and-education

School of Education and Social Care; www.anglia.ac.uk/health-social-care-and-education/about/school-of-education-and-social-care

Undergraduate courses in Counselling and Psychotherapy (Top-Up) – BA(Hons), Counselling and Psychotherapy (Top-Up) – BA(Hons), Counselling (Child and Young Person) – DipHE, Early Childhood Professional Studies (Top-up) – BA(Hons), Early Childhood Studies – BA(Hons), Early Years, Playwork and Education – FdA, Education – BA(Hons), Education – BA(Hons), Primary Education Studies – BA(Hons), Primary Education Studies – BA(Hons), Social Policy – BA(Hons), Social Policy – BA(Hons), Social Work – BA(Hons), Social Work – BA(Hons); Postgraduate courses in Early Childhood Education – MA, Education – MA, Educational Leadership and Management – MBA, Global Military Veteran and Family Studies – MSc, Higher Education – MA, International Social Welfare and Social Policy – MSc, Learning and Teaching (Higher Education) – PG Cert, Special Educational Needs and Disability – MA, Student Affairs in Higher Education – MA

Lord Ashcroft International Business School; www.anglia.ac.uk/lord-ashcroft-international-business-school

Undergraduate courses in Accounting and Finance – BSc(Hons), Banking and Finance – BSc(Hons), Banking and Finance (Top-Up) – BSc(Hons), Business Administration (Top-Up) – BSc(Hons), Business and Human Resource Management – BSc(Hons), Business Economics – BSc(Hons), Business Management – BSc(Hons), Business Management and Finance – BSc(Hons), Business Management and Leadership – BSc(Hons), Charity and Social Enterprise Management – CertHE, Events Management – BSc(Hons), Finance and Business Analytics – BSc(Hons), Finance and Business Analytics – BSc(Hons), International Business Management (Accelerated) – BSc(Hons), International Business (Top-Up) – BSc(Hons), Management – BA(Hons), Management – FdA, Marketing – BA(Hons), Tourism Management – BSc(Hons); Postgraduate taught courses in Accounting and Finance – MSc, Data Centre Leadership and Management – MA, Human Resource Management – MA, Human Resource Management (CIPD Block Delivery) – PG Dip, Human Resource Management (CIPD – day release) – PG Dip, Human Resource Management MA Stage 3 only (Top-Up) – MA, International Business – MSc, International Hospitality and Tourism Management – MSc, International Project Management – MSc, Management – MSc, Marketing – MSc, Master of Business Administration – MBA, Master of Business Administration – Healthcare – MBA, Master of Business Administration – International – MBA, Supply Chain Management – MSc

Faculty of Medical Science; http://www.anglia.ac.uk/medical-science

Undergraduate courses in Applied Nutritional Science – BSc(Hons), Applied Nutritional Science with Foundation Year – BSc(Hons), Healthcare Science – BSc(Hons), Leadership and Management in Health and Social Care – FdSc, Management and Leadership in Health and Social Care (Top up) – BSc(Hons), Medical Science – BSc(Hons), Medical Science with Foundation Year – BSc(Hons), Medicine – MBChB, Operating Department Practice – BSc(Hons), Osteopathy – MOst, Osteopathy – BOst, Paramedic Science – BSc(Hons), Pharmaceutical Science – BSc(Hons), Pharmaceutical Science with Foundation Year – BSc(Hons), Public Health – BSc(Hons); Postgraduate taught courses in Healthcare Management – MBA, Healthcare Management – MSc, Magnetic Resonance Imaging – MSc, Medical and Healthcare Education – MSc, Minimally Invasive and Robotic Surgery – Master of Surgery (MCh), Out of Hospital Acute Cardiac Care – PG Cert, Out of Hospital Acute Cardiac Care – PG Cert, Physician Associate – MSc, Plastic and Aesthetic Surgery Practice – Master of Surgery (MCh), Public Health – MSc, Surgical Care Practice – MSc, Urology – Master of Surgery (MCh); Research courses in Doctor of Medicine by Research – MD (Res), Medical Science – MPhil – PhD

Facuty of Science and Technology; www.anglia.ac.uk/science-and-technology

Undergraduate courses in Abnormal and Clinical Psychology – BSc(Hons), Animal Behaviour – BSc(Hons), Applied Computer Science – BSc(Hons), Architectural Technology – BSc(Hons), Architecture – BA(Hons), Audio and Music Technology – BSc(Hons), Biomedical Science – BSc(Hons), Biomedical Science with Foundation Year – BSc(Hons), Bioscience – FdSc, Bioscience – BSc(Hons), Building Surveying – BSc(Hons), Building Surveying – BSc(Hons), Business Information Systems –

BSc(Hons), Civil Engineering – BEng(Hons), Civil Engineering – BSc(Hons), Civil Engineering – FdSc, Civil Engineering – MEng(Hons), Civil Engineering – FdSc, Civil Engineering – BEng(Hons), Civil Engineering – BSc(Hons), Coaching for Performance in Football – BSc(Hons), Computer Gaming Technology – BSc(Hons), Computer Gaming Technology with Foundation Year – BSc(Hons), Computer Networks – BSc(Hons), Computer Science – FdSc, Computer Science – BEng(Hons), Computing and Information Systems – BSc(Hons), Computing and Information Systems – FdSc, Computing and Information Systems – BSc(Hons), Construction – FdSc, Construction Management – BSc(Hons), Crime and Investigative Studies – FdSc, Crime and Investigative Studies – BSc(Hons), Crime and Investigative Studies with Foundation Year – BSc(Hons), Cyber Security – BSc(Hons), Electronic Engineering – BEng(Hons), Forensic Science – BSc(Hons), Forensic Science with Foundation Year – BSc(Hons), Hearing Aid Audiology – FdSc, Hearing Sciences (Top-Up) – BSc(Hons), Integrated Engineering (Top-Up) – BEng(Hons), Marine Biology with Biodiversity and Conservation – BSc(Hons), Marine Biology with Biodiversity and Conservation – with Foundation Year – BSc(Hons), Mechanical Engineering – BEng(Hons), Mechanical Engineering – MEng(Hons), Medical Engineering – BEng(Hons), Ophthalmic Dispensing – BSc(Hons), Ophthalmic Dispensing Registerable Award – FdSc, Ophthalmic Dispensing with Foundation Year – BSc(Hons), Optometry – BOptom(Hons), Psychology – BSc(Hons), Psychology and Criminology – BSc(Hons), Quantity Surveying – BSc(Hons), Smart Computing – BSc(Hons), Software Development – BSc(Hons), Sport and Exercise Science – BSc(Hons), Sport and Exercise Science with Foundation Year – BSc(Hons), Sports Coaching and Physical Education – BSc(Hons), Sports Coaching and Physical Education with Foundation Year – BSc(Hons), Veterinary Nursing and Applied Animal Behaviour – BSc(Hons), Veterinary Nursing and Applied Animal Behaviour – FdSc, Zoology – BSc(Hons), Zoology with Foundation Year – BSc(Hons); Postgraduate taught courses in Additive Manufacturing – MSc, Animal Behaviour Applications for Conservation – MSc, Applied Bioscience – MSc, Applied Positive Psychology – MSc, Applied Wildlife Conservation – MSc, Biomedical Science – MSc, Civil Engineering – MSc, Clinical Child Psychology – MSc, Cloud Computing – MSc, Cognitive and Clinical Neuroscience – MSc, Computer Games Development (Computing) – MSc, Computer Science – MSc, Construction Management – MSc, Construction Project Management – MSc, Consumer Psychology – MSc, Cyber Security – MSc, Electronic and Electrical Engineering – MSc, Engineering Management – MSc, Forensic Science – MSc, Foundations in Clinical Psychology – MSc, Information and Communication Technology (Conversion) – MSc, Mechanical Engineering – MSc, Project Management – MSc, Property and Facilities Management – MSc, Research Methods in Psychology – MSc, Sport and Exercise Science – MSc, Sustainability – MSc, Town Planning – MSc; Postgraduate research degrees in Analytical Chemistry – MPhil – PhD, Animal and Environmental Sciences – MPhil – PhD, Audiology and Hearing Disability Research – MPhil – PhD, Biomedical Science – MPhil – PhD, Built Environment – MPhil – PhD, Computer Science – MPhil – PhD, Electronics – MPhil – PhD, Engineering and Tribology – MPhil – PhD, Equine Science – MPhil – PhD, Forensic Science – MPhil – PhD, Mechanical Engineering – MPhil – PhD, Molecular Biology – MPhil – PhD, Optometry and Vision Sciences – MPhil – PhD, Professional Doctorate in Science and Technology – DProf, Psychology – MPhil – PhD, Sound Engineering – MPhil – PhD, Sport and Exercise Sciences – MPhil – PhD, Sustainability – MPhil – PhD, Telecommunications – MPhil – PhD, Zoology – MPhil – PhD

COLCHESTER INSTITUTE
www.colchester.ac.uk

business innovation and applied management, counselling studies, 3D design and craft, art and design with foundation year, creative performance (acting), digital film production, early years, education studies, fashion and textiles, film music and soundtrack production, fine art, graphic design, health and social care, management, music education, musical theatre, photography, popular music, sport management, technical theatre, construction management (commercial management/ site management), IT systems and applications, business administration, construction, management of sport, photography, education, business administration (MBA), project management, reflective management and leadership, business environment, person-centred counselling; BSc(Hons), BA(Hons), CertHE, FD, MA, MBA, DipHE

ASHRIDGE
www.ashridge.org.uk

Open programs in Advanced Coaching for Organization Consultants, Advanced HR Strategy and Impact, Advanced Leadership: Influencing Strategies, Advanced Leadership: Leading on the Edge, Advanced Management Program, Advanced Organization Design, Advanced Strategy: Translating Strategy into Action, Designing Operating Models, Expert Strategy: Driving Growth and Innovation, Financial Foundations, Formulating Strategy, Harnessing Artificial Intelligence, Leadership Foundations: Performance Through People, Leading Change and Growth, Leading Change and Organizational Development, Management Development Program, Personalized Development Program, Senior Executive Program, Strategy Foundations: Strategic Decisions, Strategy Team Seminars, Strategy Tools, Team Coaching, Transformational Senior Leadership, Translating Strategy into Action: Middle East; Masters in Executive Coaching

ASTON UNIVERSITY
www.aston.ac.uk

Aston Business School; http://www.aston.ac.uk/aston-business-school/

Undergraduate courses in BSc Accounting for Management, BSc Business & Management, BSc Business Computing & IT, BSc Business Management & English Language, BSc Economics & Management, BSc Economics & Management, BSc Finance, BSc Human Resource Management, BSc International Business & Economics, BSc International Business & Management, BSc International Business & Management, BSc International Business & Modern Languages (French / German / Spanish), BSc International Business and Economics, BSc International Business and Modern Languages, LLB Law, LLB Law with Management, Marketing; Postgraduate courses in Executive MBA, International Pre-Masters, MSc Accounting & Finance, MSc Accounting & Finance (online), MSc Business & Management, MSc Business & Management (online), MSc Business Analytics, MSc Business Economics & Finance, MSc Entrepreneurship and International Business, MSc Entrepreneurship and International Business, MSc Finance, MSc Human Resource Management & Business, MSc Information Systems & Business Analysis, MSc International Accounting & Finance, MSc International Accounting & Finance, MSc International Accounting & Finance (online), MSc International Accounting & Finance (online), MSc International Business, MSc Investment Analysis, MSc Organisational Behaviour, MSc Services Innovation, MSc Strategic Marketing Management, MSc Strategy and International Business, MSc Supply Chain Management, MSc Work Psychology & Business

Aston Medical School; www.aston.ac.uk/aston-medical-school/mbchb-medicine/

MBChB Medicine; MCh Orthopaedics

School of Engineering & Applied Science; www.aston.ac.uk/eas/

BSc Applied Physics, MPhys Applied Physics, Biomedical Engineering, BEng Biomedical Engineering, BSc Chemistry with Biotechnology, MEng Chemical Engineering, BEng Chemical Engineering, BSc Chemistry, BSc Applied Chemistry, BSc Computer Science, BSc Computer Science with Business, BSc Computer Science and Mathematics, BSc Computer Science with Multimedia, BEng Communications Engineering, MEng Electrical & Electronic Engineering, BEng Electrical & Electronic Engineering, MEng Electronic Engineering & Computer Science, BEng Electronic Engineering & Computer Science, BEng Electrical Power Engineering, BSc Construction Project Management, BSc Business & Supply Chain Management, BSc Logistics with Supply Chain Management, BSc Logistics with Transport Management, BSc Logistics with Purchasing Management, Foundation Programme in Engineering and Applied Science, International Foundation Programme in Engineering and Applied Science, BSc Mathematics, BSc Mathematics with Computing, BSc Business & Maths (Joint honours), BSc Mathematics with

Economics (Joint honours), BSc Mathematics for Industry, MEng Mechanical Engineering, BEng Electromechanical Engineering, BEng Mechanical Engineering, BEng Design Engineering, BSc Transport Product Design, BSc Industrial Product Design, BSc Product Design & Management; Postgraduate courses in MSc by Research (Computational Mathematics and Systems Analytics), MSc by Research (Photonics), MSc by Research (Wireless Communications), MSc Computer Science, MSc Computer Science in Practice (Work-based learning), MSc Electrical Power Engineering and Systems, MSc Engineering Leadership & Management (Work-based learning), MSc Engineering Management, MSc IT Project Management, MSc Mechanical Engineering, MSc Product Design, MSc Professional Engineering (Work-based learning), MSc Professional IT Project Management (Work-based learning), MSc Software Engineering, MSc Supply Chain Leadership and Management (Work-based learning), MSc Supply Chain Management, MSc Telecommunications Systems, MSc Wireless Communications and Networking

School of Languages and Social Sciences
BA French, BA English Language, BA German, BA Politics with International Relations, BA Sociology, BA Spanish, Double MA in Emerging Europe in a Global Perspective, Double MA in Europe & the World, Double MA in Governance and International Politics, Joint MA in Conflict and Security, Joint MA in Multilevel Governance & International Relations, MA in Forensic Linguistics, MA in International Relations and Global Governance, MA in Policy and Social Research, MA in Teaching English to Speakers of other Languages (TESOL), MA in TESOL and Translation Studies, MA in TESOL and Translation

Studies, MA in the European Union & International Relations, MA in Translation in a European Context, MA in Translation Studies

School of Life and Health Sciences; www1.aston.ac.uk/lhs
BSc Healthcare Science (Audiology), BSc Biochemistry, BSc Biological Sciences, BSc Human Biology, MBiol Biological Sciences, BSc Biomedical Science, BEng/ MEng Biomedical Engineering, BSc Neuroscience, BSc Optometry/MOptom, BSc Optometry & Clinical Practice, MPharm Pharmacy, BSc Psychology; Postgraduate courses in Advanced Hearing Therapy Practice – MSc, Clinical Science (Neurosensory Sciences) – MSc, Doctor of Hearing Therapy – Professional Doctorate, Biomedical Science &′ MSc, Stem Cells and Regenerative Medicine &′ MSc, Clinical Neurophysiology Practice – MSc, Clinical Science (Neurosensory Sciences) – MSc, Neurophysiology – PgCert, Neurophysiology &′ PgDip, Clinical Science (Neurosensory Sciences) – MSc, Doctor of Optometry / Doctor of Ophthalmic Science – Professional Doctorate, Graduate Diploma in Optometry – Graduate Diploma, Independent Prescribing for Optometrists – Professional Accreditation, Optometry / Ophthalmic Science &′ MSc, Doctor of Pharmacy (PharmD) – Professional Doctorate, Overseas Pharmacists course (OSPAP) – Full time PgDip / MSc, Pharmacist Independent Prescribing – PgCert, Pharmacy (includes: MSc Pharmaceutical Sciences, MSc Drug Delivery, and MSc Pharmacokinetics) &′ MSc, Psychiatric Pharmacy by Distance Learning and Practice – PgDip, Psychiatric Pharmacy Practice – MSc, Psychiatric Therapeutics by Distance Learning &′ PgCert, Cognitive Neuroscience – MSc, Health Psychology (online) – MSc, Health Psychology (on campus) – MSc

BANGOR UNIVERSITY
www.bangor.ac.uk

College of Arts and Humanities; www.bangor.ac.uk/cah
Creative and Professional Writing BA(Hons) (3 years), Creative Practice MArts (4 years), Creative Studies BA(Hons) (3 years), Film Studies BA(Hons) (3 years), Media Studies BA(Hons) (3 years), Media Studies MArts (4 years), Professional Writing MArts (4 years), Creative and Professional Writing BA(Hons) (3 years), Cymraeg a Llenyddiaeth Saesneg

BA (Cydanrhydedd) (3 years), English Language and English Literature BA (Joint Hons) (3 years), English Language with Creative Writing BA(Hons) (3 years), English Language with English Literature BA(Hons) (3 years), English Literature BA(Hons) (3 years), English Literature and Chinese BA (Joint Hons) (4 years), English Literature and Creative Writing BA(Hons) (3 years), English Literature and Criminology and Criminal Justice BA (Joint Hons) (3 years),

English Literature and Film Studies BA (Joint Hons) (3 years), English Literature and Italian BA(Hons) (4 years), English Literature and Linguistics BA(Hons) (3 years), English Literature and Music BA (Joint Hons) (3 years), English Literature and Spanish BA (Joint Hons) (4 years), English Literature with Creative Writing BA(Hons) (3 years), English Literature with English Language BA(Hons) (3 years), English Literature with Journalism BA(Hons) (3 years), English Literature with Theatre and Performance BA(Hons) (3 years), French and English Literature BA (Joint Hons) (4 years), French with Creative Writing BA(Hons) (4 years), German and English Literature BA (Joint Hons) (4 years), German with Creative Writing BA(Hons) (4 years), History and English Literature BA (Joint Hons) (3 years), Linguistics with English Literature BA(Hons) (3 years), Media Studies and English Literature BA(Hons) (3 years), Philosophy & Religion and English Literature BA (Joint Hons) (3 years), Sociology and English Literature BA (Joint Hons) (3 years), Spanish with Creative Writing BA(Hons) (4 years), Cymdeithaseg a Hanes BA (Cydanrhydedd) (3 years), Cymdeithaseg a Hanes Cymru BA (Cydanrhydedd) (3 years), Cymraeg a Hanes BA (Cydanrhydedd) (3 years), Film Studies and History BA (Joint Hons) (3 years), Hanes Cymru a Chymraeg BA (Cydanrhydedd) (3 years), Hanes gyda Newyddiaduraeth BA(Hons) (3 years), Heritage, Archaeology and History BA(Hons) (3 years), History BA(Hons) (3 years), History MArts (4 years), History and Archaeology BA(Hons) (3 years), History and Criminology and Criminal Justice BA (Joint Hons) (3 years), History and Economics BA(Hons) (3 years), History and English Literature BA (Joint Hons) (3 years), History and French BA (Joint Hons) (4 years), History and German BA (Joint Hons) (4 years), History and Italian BA(Hons) (4 years), History and Music BA (Joint Hons) (3 years), History and Spanish BA (Joint Hons) (4 years), History with Archaeology BA(Hons) (3 years), History with Film Studies BA(Hons) (3 years), History with Journalism BA(Hons) (3 years), Medieval and Early Modern History BA(Hons) (3 years), Modern and Contemporary History BA(Hons) (3 years), Music and History and Welsh History BA (Joint Hons) (3 years), Philosophy & Religion and History BA (Joint Hons) (3 years), Philosophy & Religion and Welsh History BA (Joint Hons) (3 years), Polisi Cymdeithasol a Hanes BA (Cydanrhydedd) (3 years), Polisi Cymdeithasol a Hanes Cymru BA (Cydanrhydedd) (3 years), Social Policy and History BA(Hons) (3 years), Bilingualism MArts (4 years), English Language BA(Hons) (3 years), English Language for TEFL BA(Hons) (3 years), English Language for TEFL MArts (4 years), International English Language for TEFL BA(Hons) (3 years), Linguistics BA(Hons) (3 years), Linguistics MArts (4 years), French BA(Hons) (4 years), German BA(Hons) (4 years), Spanish BA(Hons) (4 years), Creative Studies and Music BA (Joint Hons) (3 years), Cymraeg a Cherddoriaeth BA (Cydanrhydedd) (3 years), Cymraeg Creadigol gyda Cherddoriaeth Boblogaidd BA (Anrhydedd) (3 years), Music BA(Hons) (3 years), Music BMus(Hons) (3 years), Philosophy and Religion BA(Hons) (3 years)

Postgraduate courses: 20th- and 21st-Century Music MA/PgDip/PgCert, Applied Linguistics for TEFL MA, Archaeology PhD/MPhil, Arthurian Literature MA/PgDip, Bilingualism MA, Bilingualism PhD/MPhil, Celtic Archaeology MA/PgDip, Composition / Electroacoustic Composition / Sonic Art MMus/PgDip, Creative and Critical Writing PhD/MPhil, Creative Practice MRes, Creative Writing MA/PgDip, Early Music MA/PgDip/PgCert, English Literature MA/PgDip, English PhD/MPhil, Film Studies MRes, Filmmaking: Concept to Screen MA, Heritage PhD/MPhil, History MA/PgDip, History PhD/MPhil, International Media and Management MSc, Language Acquisition and Development MSc, Linguistics MA, Linguistics PhD/MPhil, Literatures of Wales MA/PgDip, MA European Languages and Cultures, MA in Translation Studies, Media and Practice MRes, Medieval Studies MA/PgDip, Medieval Studies MA/PgDip, Music (MA by Research), Music (MMus by Research), Music (MPhil), Music (PhD), Music MA/PgDip/PgCert, Music with Education MA, Performance MMus/PgDip, Philosophy and Religion PhD/MPhil, Professional Writing MRes, The Celt (MA), The Celts MA/PgDip, Welsh / Celtic Studies (MA/Diploma), Welsh / Celtic Studies (MPhil/PhD), Welsh History MA/PgDip, Welsh History PhD/MPhil, Y Celtiaid MA/PgDip,

English Literature; www.bangor.ac.uk/ english

College of Business, Social Sciences & Law; www.bangor.ac.uk/cbless/

Accounting and Banking BSc(Hons) (3 years), Accounting and Economics BSc(Hons) (3 years), Addysg Gynradd BA(Hons) with QTS (3 years), Astudiaethau Plentyndod ac Ieuenctid a Chymdeithaseg BA (Cydanrhydedd) (3 years), Astudiaethau Plentyndod ac Ieuenctid a Chymdeithaseg

BA (Cydanrhydedd) (3 years), Astudiaethau Plentyndod ac Ieuenctid BA (Cydanrhydedd) (3 years), Business and Law BA(Hons) (3 years), Business Economics BSc(Hons) (3 years), Business Studies BSc(Hons) (3 years), Childhood and Youth Studies and Psychology BA (Joint Hons) (3 years), Childhood and Youth Studies and Social Policy BA (Joint Hons) (3 years), Childhood and Youth Studies and Sociology BA (Joint Hons) (3 years), Childhood and Youth Studies BA(Hons) (3 years), Criminology & Criminal Justice and Italian BA(Hons) (4 years), Criminology and Criminal Justice MSocSci (4 years), Cymdeithaseg a Chymraeg BA (Cydanrhydedd) (3 years), Cymdeithaseg a Gofal Iechyd a Chymdeithasol BA (Cydanrhydedd) (3 years), Cymdeithaseg a Hanes BA (Cydanrhydedd) (3 years), Cymdeithaseg a Hanes Cymru BA (Cydanrhydedd) (3 years), Design and Technology Secondary Education BSc(Hons) with QTS (3 years), Dylunio Cynnyrch BSc (Anrhydedd) (3 years), English Law and French Law LLB (4 years), Financial Economics BSc(Hons) (3 years), Health & Social Care and Social Policy BA(Hons) (3 years), Health and Social Care BA(Hons) (3 years), Health and Social Care MSocSci (4 years), Iechyd a Gofal Cymdeithasol BA (Anrhydedd) (3 years), International Law LLB (3 years), Law (2-Year Degree Scheme) LLB(Hons) (2 years), Law LLB(Hons) (3 years), Law with Accounting and Finance LLB(Hons) (3 years), Law with Business Studies LLB(Hons) (3 years), Law with Contemporary Chinese Studies LLB(Hons) (3 years), Law with Creative Media Writing LLB(Hons) (3 years), Law with Criminology LLB(Hons) (3 years), Law with French (European Experience) LLB(Hons) (4 years), Law with German (European Experience) LLB(Hons) (4 years), Law with History LLB(Hons) (3 years), Law with Italian (European Experience) LLB (4 years), Law with Media Studies LLB(Hons) (3 years), Law with Philosophy and Religion LLB(Hons) (3 years), Law with Social Policy LLB(Hons) (3 years), Law with Spanish (European Experience) LLB(Hons) (4 years), Marketing BSc(Hons) (3 years), Polisi Cymdeithasol a Chymraeg BA (Cydanrhydedd) (3 years), Polisi Cymdeithasol a Gofal Iechyd a Chymdeithasol BA (Cydanrhydedd) (3 years), Polisi Cymdeithasol a Hanes BA (Cydanrhydedd) (3 years), Polisi Cymdeithasol a Hanes Cymru BA (Cydanrhydedd) (3 years), Polisi Cymdeithasol a Throseddeg a Chyfiawnder Troseddol BA (Cydanrhydedd) (3 years), Primary Education BA(Hons) with QTS (3 years), Product Design BSc(Hons) (3 years), Y Gyfraith gydar Gymraeg (Law with Welsh) LLB(Hons) (3 years)

Postgraduate Courses; Law and Banking LLM, Accounting and Banking MSc, Accounting and Finance MSc, Accounting MSc, Banking and Finance (Chartered Banker) MA, Banking and Finance (Chartered Banker) MSc, Banking and Finance MA, Banking and Finance MBA, Banking and Finance MSc, Banking and Law MA, Banking and Law MA, Banking and Law MBA, Business and Marketing MA, Business with Consumer Psychology MA, Business with Consumer Psychology MSc, Chartered Banker MBA, Childhood and Youth MRes, Comparative Criminology and Criminal Justice MA/PgDip/PgCert, Criminology and Criminal Justice PhD/MPhil, Criminology and Law MA, Criminology and Law MA, Criminology and Sociology MA/PgDip/PgCert, Criminology, Criminal Justice, Social Policy, Sociology MARes, Education Doctorate Programme EdD, Education PhD/MPhil, Education Studies (Fulltime) MA/PgDip/PgCert, Education Studies (Parttime) MA/PgDip/PgCert, Environmental Management MBA, Finance MA, Finance MBA, Finance MSc, Information Management MBA, International Banking MSc, International Business MBA, International Climate Change Law and Sustainable Development LLM, International Commercial and Business Law LLM, International Criminal Law and International Human Rights Law LLM, International Finance MSc, International Intellectual Property Law LLM, International Law LLM, International Marketing MBA, International Media and Management MSc, Investment Management MSc, Islamic Banking and Finance MA, Islamic Banking and Finance MBA, Islamic Banking and Finance MSc, Law and Banking LLM, Law and Criminology LLM, Law and Management MBA, Law LLM, Law LLM Res, Law of the Sea LLM, Law PhD/MPhil, Law with Psychology LLM, Leadership for Collaboration PgCert, Management and Finance MA, Management and Finance MSc, Management MBA, Maritime Law LLM, Music with Education MA/PgDip/PgCert, Polisi a Chynllunio Ieithyddol MA, Procurement Law, Strategy and Practice by Blended Learning LLM, Public Procurement Law and Strategy LLM, Research Methodolgy MSc, Social Policy MA/PgDip/PgCert, Social Policy, Sociology PhD/MPhil, Social Work MA, Sociology MA

Bangor University

College of Health and Behavioural Sciences; www.bangor.ac.uk/cohabs/index.php.en

Adult Nursing BN(Hons) (3 years), Biomedical Science BSc(Hons) (3 years), Children's Nursing BN(Hons) (3 years), Diagnostic Radiography BSc(Hons) (3 years), Health and Wellbeing BSc(Hons) (3 years), Health Studies (International Students), Learning Disability Nursing BN(Hons) (3 years), Medical Biology BSc(Hons) (3 years), Medical Biology MBiol (4 years), Medical Sciences BMedSci(Hons) (3 years), Mental Health Nursing BN(Hons) (3 years), Midwifery BM(Hons) (3 years), Neuropsychology degree BSc (Intercalated) (1 years), Psychology degree BSc(Hons) (3 years), Psychology degree MSci (4 years), Psychology with Business degree BSc(Hons) (3 years), Psychology with Clinical and Health Psychology degree BSc(Hons) (3 years), Psychology with Clinical and Health Psychology degree MSci (4 years), Psychology with Law degree BA (3 years), Psychology with Neuropsychology degree BSc(Hons) (3 years), Sport and Exercise Psychology BSc(Hons), Sport Science (Outdoor Activities) BSc(Hons), Sport Science (Outdoor Activities) MSci, Sport Science BSc(Hons), Sport Science MSci, Sport, Health and Exercise Science BSc(Hons), Sport, Health and Exercise Science MSci, Sport, Health and Physical Education BSc(Hons),

Postgraduate courses: Applied Sport and Exercise Physiology MSc, Applied Sport Science MSc, Applied Sport Science and Outdoor Activities MSc, Exercise Rehabilitation MSc, Sport and Exercise Psychology (BPS Accredited) MSc, Chronic Disease Graduate Certificate, Emergency Practitioner Graduate Certificate, General Practice Nursing Graduate Certificate, Advanced Clinical Practice MSc/PgDip/PgCert, Advanced Clinical Practice (AHP) MSc/PgDip/PgCert, Advanced Healthcare Practice MSc/PgDip/PgCert, Applied Health Research MSc/PgDip/PgCert, Dementia Studies MSc/PgDip/PgCert, Leading Quality Improvement MSc/PgDip/PgCert, Midwifery Studies MSc/PgDip/PgCert, Public Health and Health Promotion MSc/PgDip/PgCert, Acute Medical Care PG Cert, Acute Surgical Care PG Cert, Contraception / Associated Health PG Cert, Diabetes Care and Management PG Cert, Examination of the Newborn PG Cert, Intensive Care Nursing PG Cert, Legal and Ethical Concepts in Healthcare PG Cert, Mental Health PG Cert, Optimising Breastfeeding PG Cert, Optimising Childbirth PG Cert, Prudent Healthcare PG Cert, Adult Nursing PG Dip, Clinical Sciences MSc, Medical Molecular Biology with Genetics MSc,

Medical Education Practice PgCert, Physician Associate Studies PGDip, Clinical Psychology DClinPsy, Law with Psychology LLM, Consumer Psychology with Business MA/PGDip/PGCert, Mindfulness-Based Approaches (5 years) MA/PGDip/PGCert, Mindfulness-Based Approaches (Train to be a Mindfulness Teacher and get a Masters degree) MA/PGDip/PGCert, Psychology MA/PGDip/PGCert, Applied Behaviour Analysis MSc/PGDip/PGCert, Clinical and Health Psychology MSc/PGDip/PGCert, Consumer Psychology with Business MSc/PGDip/PGCert, Counselling MSc/PGDip/PGCert, Mindfulness-Based Approaches (5 years) MSc/PGDip/PGCert, Mindfulness-Based Approaches (Train to be a Mindfulness Teacher and get a Masters degree) MSc/PGDip/PGCert, Neuroimaging MSc/PGDip/PGCert, Positive Behaviour Support MSc/PGDip/PGCert, Principles of Clinical Neuropsychology MSc/PGDip/PGCert, Psychological Research MSc/PGDip/PGCert, Psychology MSc/PGDip/PGCert

College of Natural Sciences; www.bangor.ac.uk/cns/

Biology BSc(Hons) (3 years), Applied Marine Biology BSc(Hons) (4 years), Applied Terrestrial and Marine Ecology (with placement year) BSc(Hons) (4 years), Applied Terrestrial and Marine Ecology BSc(Hons) (3 years), Biology MBiol (4 years), Biology with Biotechnology BSc(Hons) (3 years), Biology with Biotechnology MBiol (4 years), Conservation with Forestry (with placement year) BSc(Hons) (4 years), Conservation with Forestry BSc(Hons) (3 years), Environmental Conservation (with placement year) BSc(Hons) (4 years), Environmental Conservation BSc(Hons) (3 years), Environmental Management BSc (3 years), Environmental Management MEnvSci (4 years), Environmental Science BSc(Hons) (3 years), Environmental Science MEnvSci (4 years), Forestry (with placement year) BSc(Hons) (4 years), Forestry BSc(Hons) (3 years), Geography BA(Hons) (3 years), Geography BSc(Hons) (3 years), Geography MGeog (4 years), Geography with Environmental Forestry (with placement year) BSc (4 years), Geography with Environmental Forestry BSc(Hons) (3 years), Geological Oceanography BSc(Hons) (3 years), Geological Oceanography MSci (4 years), Marine Biology and Oceanography BSc(Hons) (3 years), Marine Biology and Oceanography MSci (4 years), Marine Biology and Oceanography MSci (4 years), Marine Biology and Zoology BSc(Hons) (3 years), Marine Biology and Zoology MSci (4 years), Marine Biology BSc(Hons) (3 years), Marine Biology MSci (4 years),

Marine Environmental Studies BSc(Hons) (3 years), Marine Geography BSc(Hons) (3 years), Marine Vertebrate Zoology BSc(Hons) (3 years), Marine Vertebrate Zoology MSci (4 years), Ocean and Geophysics BSc(Hons) (3 years), Ocean Science BSc(Hons) (3 years), Physical Geography and Oceanography BSc(Hons) (3 years), Physical Geography and Oceanography BSc(Hons) (3 years), Physical Oceanography MSci (4 years), Zoology BSc(Hons) (3 years), Zoology MZool (4 years), Zoology with Animal Behaviour BSc(Hons) (3 years), Zoology with Animal Behaviour MZool (Animal Behaviour) (4 years), Zoology with Conservation BSc(Hons) (3 years), Zoology with Conservation MZool (Conservation) (4 years), Zoology with Herpetology BSc(Hons) (3 years), Zoology with Herpetology MZool (Herpetology) (4 years), Zoology with Marine Zoology BSc(Hons) (3 years), Zoology with Marine Zoology MZool (Marine Zoology) (4 years)

Postgraduate courses: Agricultural Systems PhD/MPhil, Agriculture and Environment MRes, Agroforestry MSc, Agroforestry PhD/MPhil, Applied Marine Geoscience MSc, Biodiversity Conservation PhD/MPhil, Biological Sciences MScRes, Biological Sciences PhD/MPhil, Conservation and Land Management MSc, Doctor of Agriculture and Environment DAgEnv, Environmental and Business Management MSc, Environmental and Soil Science PhD/MPhil, Environmental Forestry MSc, Environmental Management MBA, Environmental Sciences MSc by Research, Forest Ecology and Management PhD/MPhil, Forestry and Environmental Management degrees (TRANSFOR-M) MSc, Marine Biology MSc, Marine Environmental Protection MSc, Marine Renewable Energy MSc, Molecular Biology with Biotechnology MSc, Ocean Sciences MSc by Research, Ocean Sciences PhD/MPhil, Physical Oceanography MSc, Renewable Materials PhD/MPhil, Rheolaeth Amgylcheddol Gynaliadwy MSc/MA, Sustainable Forest and Nature Management (SUFONAMA) (Erasmus Mundus course) MSc, Sustainable Tropical Forestry (SUTROFOR) (Erasmus Mundus course) MSc, Tropical Ecosystems PhD/MPhil, Wetland Science and Conservation MSc, Wetland Science for Pollution Control MSc,

School of Environment, Natural Resources, & Geography; www.bangor.ac.uk/senrg

College of Physical and Applied Sciences; www.bangor.ac.uk/copas

Chemistry MChem (4 years), Chemistry BSc(Hons) (3 years), Chemistry with European Experience BSc(Hons) (4 years), Chemistry with Industrial Experience BSc(Hons) (4 years), Chemistry with Industrial Experience MChem (5 years), Computer Information Systems BSc(Hons) (3 years), Computer Information Systems for Business BSc(Hons) (3 years), Computer Science BSc(Hons) (3 years), Computer Science for Business BSc(Hons) (3 years), Computer Systems Engineering BEng(Hons) (3 years), Computer Systems Engineering BSc(Hons) (3 years), Computer Systems Engineering MEng (4 years), Control and Instrumentation Engineering MEng (4 years), Creative Technologies BSc(Hons) (3 years), Critical Safety Engineering MEng(Hons) (4 years), Electronic Engineering and Music BSc (Joint Hons) (3 years), Electronic Engineering BEng(Hons) (3 years), Electronic Engineering BSc(Hons) (3 years), Electronic Engineering MEng (4 years), Music and Electronic Engineering BA (Joint Hons) (3 years)

Postgraduate courses: Analytical Chemistry (MSc), MRes Chemistry, MPhil/PhD Chemistry, Broadband and Optical Communications MSc, Advanced Visualization, Virtual Environments and Computer Animation MRes, Artificial Intelligence and Intelligent Agents PhD/MPhil, Communication Networks and Protocols PhD/MPhil, Computer Science MSc, Computer Science with Visualisation MSc, Electrical Materials Science PhD/MPhil, Electronic Engineering (Bio-Electronics) MRes, Electronic Engineering (Micromachining) MRes, Electronic Engineering (Microwave Devices) MRes, Electronic Engineering (Nanotechnology) MRes, Electronic Engineering (Optical Communications) MRes, Electronic Engineering (Optoelectronics) MRes, Electronic Engineering (Organic Electronics) MRes, Electronic Engineering (Polymer Electronics) MRes, Electronic Engineering (VLSI Design) MRes, Electronic Engineering MRes, Electronic Engineering MSc, Image Processing for Mobile Devices PhD/MPhil, Laser Micromachining and Laboratory-on-a-Chip PhD/MPhil, Medical Visualization and Simulation PhD/MPhil, Nanotechnology and Microfabrication MSc, Optical Communications PhD/MPhil, Optoelectronics PhD/MPhil, Organic Electronics PhD/MPhil, Pattern Recognition/Classifiers PhD/MPhil

UNIVERSITY CAMPUS, BARNSLEY
https://universitycampus.barnsley.ac.uk/

Animal Management Foundation Degree (FdSc), Business Foundation Degree FdA, Early Years BA(Hons), Enterprise and Entrepreneurship BA(Hons), Psychology BSc(Hons), Popular Music BA(Hons), Music Technology and Production BA(Hons), Acting for Touring Theatre BA(Hons), Teacher Training (Lifelong Learning) Pre-Service Certificate in Education, Teacher Training (Lifelong Learning) Pre-Service PGCE

UNIVERSITY OF BATH
www.bath.ac.uk

Faculty of Engineering and Design; www.bath.ac.uk/engineering

Architecture & Civil Engineering; www.bath.ac.uk/ace
BSc(Hons) Architecture, BEng/MEng(Hons) Civil Engineering, MEng(Hons) Civil and Architectural Engineering; Postgraduate courses: MSc Architectural Engineering: Environmental Design, MSc Conservation of Historic Buildings, MSc in Civil Engineering: Innovative Structural Materials, MSc in Modern Building Design, PG Certificate in Professional Practice – RIBA Part 3

Chemical Engineering; www.bath.ac.uk/chem-eng
MEng/BEng Chemical Engineering; Postgraduate courses: Sustainable Chemical Engineering MSc, MRes/PhD

Electronic & Electrical Engineering; www.bath.ac.uk/elec-eng
Aerospace Engineering MEng(Hons), BEng/MEng electrical & electronic/electrical power engineering, BEng/MEng computer systems engineering, BEng/MEng electrical power engineering, BEng/MEng electronic systems engineering, mechatronics, Robotics Engineering MEng, BEng space science & technology; Postgraduate courses: MSc Architectural Engineering: Environmental Design, MSc Automotive Engineering, MSc Conservation of Historic Buildings, MSc Electrical Power Systems, MSc Electronic Systems Design, MSc Engineering Business Management, MSc Engineering Design, MSc in Civil Engineering: Innovative Structural Materials, MSc in Modern Building Design, MSc in Sustainable Chemical Engineering, MSc Innovation and Technology Management (delivered jointly with School of Management), MSc Mechatronics, MSc Robotics and Autonomous Systems (new for 2018), MSc Robotics and Autonomous Systems with three-month placement, PG Certificate in Professional Practice – RIBA Part 3

Mechanical Engineering; www.bath.ac.uk/mech-eng
Aerospace Engineering MEng(Hons), Integrated Design Engineering MEng(Hons), Mechanical Engineering MEng(Hons), Mechanical Engineering with Manufacturing and Management MEng(Hons), Mechanical with Automotive Engineering MEng(Hons); Postgraduate courses: MSc Automotive Engineering, MSc Engineering Design, MSc in Innovation and Technology Management, MSc Mechatronics

Faculty of Humanities and Social Science; www.bath.ac.uk/hss

Dept of Economics; www.bath.ac.uk/economics
BSc(Hons) Economics, BSc(Hons) Economics and Politics, BSc(Hons) Economics and Mathematics; Postgraduate courses: MSc Applied Economics, MSc Economics, MSc Economics & Finance, MRes Economics

Dept of Education; www.bath.ac.uk/education
BA(Hons) Education with Psychology

Dept for Health; www.bath.ac.uk/health
BSc/MSci(Hons) Health and Exercise Science, BSc/MSci(Hons) Sport and Exercise Science, BA(Hons) Sport and Social Sciences, Foundation Degree and BSc(Hons) Sport (Sports Performance), Foundation Degree Addictions Counselling (Franchised); Postgraduate courses: MA Education, MA International

Education and Globalisation, MA Teaching English to Speakers of Other Languages (TESOL), MRes Education

Dept of Politics, Languages & International Studies; www.bath.ac.uk/polis

BSc(Hons) International Management and Modern Languages, BA(Hons) Language and Politics, BA(Hons) Modern Languages and European Studies, BSc(Hons) Politics with Economics, BSc(Hons) Politics and International Relations; Postgraduate courses: MA Contemporary European Studies ('Euromasters' and 'Euromasters with Trans-Atlantic track'), MA International Relations, MA International Relations and European Politics, MA International Security, MA Interpreting & Translating, MA Translation & Professional Language Skills, MA Translation with Business Interpreting (Chinese), MRes Politics and International Studies

Dept of Psychology; www.bath.ac.uk/ psychology

BSc/MSci(Hons) Psychology; Postgraduate courses: MSc Applied Clinical Psychology, MSc Health Psychology, MRes Sustainable Futures, MRes Psychology

Dept of Social & Policy Science; www.bath.ac.uk/sps

BSc(Hons) Sociology, BSc(Hons) Social Policy, BSc(Hons) Social Sciences, BSc(Hons) Sociology and Social Policy, BSc(Hons) Social Work and Applied Social Studies, BSc(Hons) International Development with Economics; Postgraduate courses: MSc International Development, MRes Advanced Quantitative Methods in Social Sciences, MRes European Social Policy, MRes Global Political Economy, MRes International Development, MRes Security, Conflict and Human Rights, MRes Social Policy, MRes Social Work, MRes Sociology

Faculty of Science; www.bath.ac.uk/ science

Dept of Biology & Biochemistry; www.bath.ac.uk/bio-sci

Biochemistry BSc(Hons), Biology BSc(Hons), Biomedical Sciences BSc(Hons); Postgraduate courses: Msc Biosciences, Msc Developmental Biology, Msc Evolutionary and Population Biology, Msc Medical Biosciences, Msc Molecular Microbiology, Msc Molecular Plant Sciences, Msc Protein Structure and Function, MRes and PhD

Dept of Chemistry; www.bath.ac.uk/ chemistry

Chemistry BSc(Hons), Chemistry for Drug Discovery BSc(Hons), Chemistry for Drug Discovery MChem(Hons), Chemistry MChem(Hons), Chemistry with Management BSc(Hons); Postgraduate courses: MSc in Chemistry for Drug Discovery, MRes and PhD

Dept of Computer Science; www.bath.ac.uk/comp-sci

Computer Science BSc(Hons), Computer Science and Mathematics BSc(Hons), Computer Science and Mathematics MComp(Hons), Computer Science MComp(Hons), Computer Science with Business BSc(Hons); Postgraduate courses: MSc Data Science, MSc Software Systems, MSc Human Computer Interaction, MSc Digital Entertainment, MSc Computer Science, MRes and PhD

Dept of Mathematics; www.bath.ac.uk/ math-sci

Mathematical Sciences BSc(Hons), Mathematics BSc(Hons), Mathematics and Statistics BSc(Hons), Mathematics MMath(Hons), Statistics BSc(Hons); Postgraduate courses: MSc Modern Applications of Mathematics, PhD

Dept of Natural Sciences; www.bath.ac.uk/ nat-sci

Natural Sciences BSc(Hons), Natural Sciences MSci(Hons)

Dept of Pharmacy & Pharmacology; www.bath.ac.uk/pharmacy

Pharmacology BSc(Hons), Pharmacology MPharmacol(Hons), Pharmacy MPharm(Hons); MSc, PhD study options

Dept of Physics; www.bath.ac.uk/physics

Mathematics and Physics BSc(Hons), Mathematics and Physics MSci(Hons), Physics BSc(Hons), Physics MPhys(Hons), Physics with Astrophysics BSc(Hons), Physics with Astrophysics MPhys(Hons); PhD study

School of Management; www.bath.ac.uk/management

Accounting and Finance BSc(Hons), Business Administration BSc(Hons), International Management BSc(Hons), Management BSc(Hons), Management with Marketing BSc(Hons); Postgraduate courses: MSc in Accounting & Finance, MSc in Business Analytics, MSc in Entrepreneurship & Management, MSc in Finance, MSc in Finance with Banking, MSc in Finance with Risk Management, MSc in Human

Resource Management & Consulting, MSc in Innovation & Technology Management, MSc in International Management, MSc in Management, MSc in Marketing, MSc in Operations, Logistics & Supply Chain Management, MSc in Sustainability & Management, MBA, PhD research

BATH SPA UNIVERSITY
www.bathspa.ac.uk

Bath School of Art & Design; www.artbathspa.com

BA(Hons) History of Art & Design, BA(Hons) Contemporary Arts Practice, BA(Hons) Creative Arts, BA(Hons) Fashion Design, BA(Hons) Fine Art, BA(Hons) Graphic Communication, BA(Hons) Photography, BA(Hons) Textile Design for Fashion and Interiors, BA(Hons) Three Dimensional Design; Postgraduate courses: MA Fashion Portfolio, MA Design, MA Ceramics, MA Design, Fashion and Textiles, MA Curatorial Practice, MA Fine Art, MA Visual Communication

Institute of Education; www.bathspa.ac.uk/schools/education

Undergraduate BA degrees; early years education, early years education (primary teaching/work-based), education (primary teaching), education studies, international education/primary teaching, youth and community studies

Postgraduate Masters degrees; professional master's, learning and innovation, education studies, education: international education, PMP: specific learning difficulties /dyslexia/PMP: counselling and psychotherapy, professional practice in HE, education: leadership and management, education: early years, education: learning technology, TESOL, national award for special educational needs coordination, early years initial teacher training, subject knowledge enhancement courses mathematics/modern languages/physics, foundation; early years, education studies for teaching assistants; PGCE (primary (3-11)/middle years (7-14)/secondary (11-16); range of subjects), TESOL, international education & global citizenship

School of Liberal Arts; www.bathspa.ac.uk/liberal-arts/

Undergraduate BA degrees; creative arts, creative computing, creative computing (animation/gaming/software development), creative media practice, creative writing, English literature, film and screen studies, film, TV and digital production, heritage, history, media communications, philosophy and ethics, publishing, religion, philosophy and ethics, study of religions; Postgraduate Masters degrees; arts management, creative technologies and enterprise, creative writing, feature filmmaking, heritage management, independent filmmaking, Jane Austen's England, literature, landscape and environment, scriptwriting, travel and nature writing, writing for young people, MPhil/MRes/PhD study

Bath Business School; www.bathspa.ac.uk/bath-business-school/

BA degrees in Business and Management, Business and Management (Accounting), Business and Management (Entrepreneurship), Business and Management (Festivals and Events), Business and Management (Human Resource Management), Business and Management (International Business), Business and Management (Law), Business and Management (Marketing), Business and Management (Tourism Management); Postgraduate Masters degrees in Business and Management, Business and Management (Accounting), Business and Management (Entrepreneurship), Business and Management (International Business), Business and Management (Marketing), Business and Management 15 Month Masters

UNIVERSITY OF BEDFORDSHIRE
www.beds.ac.uk

Faculty of Creative Arts, Technologies & Science; www.beds.ac.uk/howtoapply/ departments/cats

Art & Design

Advertising and Branding Design – Bachelor of Arts with Honours, Animation – Bachelor of Arts with Honours, Animation for Industry – Bachelor of Arts with Honours, Art and Design – Bachelor of Arts with Honours, Contemporary Fine Art Practice – Foundation Degree, Creative and Editorial Photography – Foundation Degree, Fashion and Surface Pattern Design – Foundation Degree, Fashion Design – Bachelor of Arts with Honours, Fashion Design (Top up) – Bachelor of Arts with Honours, Fine Art – Bachelor of Arts with Honours, Graphic Design – Foundation Degree, Graphic Design – Bachelor of Arts with Honours, Graphic Design – Foundation Degree, Graphic Design (with placement) – Bachelor of Arts with Honours, Graphic Design and Advertising – Foundation Degree, Illustration – Foundation Degree, Illustration – Bachelor of Arts with Honours, Interior Architecture – Bachelor of Arts with Honours, Interior Design and Retail Branding – Bachelor of Arts with Honours, Photographic Practices – Bachelor of Arts with Honours, Photography and Video Art – Bachelor of Arts with Honours; Postgraduate courses: Art and Design – Master of Arts, Fashion Design, Styling and Promotion – Master of Arts

Computer Science and Technology

Artificial Intelligence and Robotics – Bachelor of Sciences with Honours, Building Services and Sustainability – Foundation Degree, Building Technology – Foundation Degree of Science, Building Technology (Top up) – Bachelor of Sciences with Honours, Business Information Systems – Bachelor of Sciences with Honours, Computer Animation and Visual Effects – Bachelor of Sciences with Honours, Computer Games Development – Bachelor of Sciences with Honours, Computer Networking – Bachelor of Sciences with Honours, Computer Science – Bachelor of Sciences with Honours, Computer Science (with Placement) – Bachelor of Sciences with Honours, Computer Science and Robotics – Bachelor of Sciences with Honours, Computer Science and Software Engineering – Bachelor of Sciences with Honours, Computer Security and Forensics – Bachelor of Sciences with Honours, Computer Systems Engineering – Bachelor of Engineering with Honours, Computing and Mathematics – Bachelor of Sciences with Honours, Construction Management – Foundation Degree of Science, Construction Management (Top up) – Bachelor of Sciences with Honours, Data Science – Bachelor of Sciences with Honours, Electronic Engineering – Bachelor of Engineering with Honours, Information Systems – Bachelor of Sciences with Honours, Interactive Digital Technologies – Bachelor of Sciences with Honours, Mathematics and Finance – Bachelor of Sciences with Honours, Mathematics and Finance (with Placement) – Bachelor of Sciences with Honours, Network Management – Foundation Degree, Procedural Programming (Python Summer School) – Undergraduate Course, Product Design – Bachelor of Sciences with Honours, Quantity Surveying and Value Engineering – Bachelor of Sciences with Honours, Software Engineering – Bachelor of Sciences with Honours, Sustainable Construction – Foundation Degree, Telecommunications and Network Engineering – Bachelor of Engineering with Honours

Postgraduate; Applied Computing and Information Technology – Master of Science, Applied Computing and Information Technology (15 months) – Master of Science, Computer Networking – Master of Science, Computer Networking (15 month) – Master of Science, Computer Science – Master of Science, Computer Science (15 months) – Master of Science, Computer Security and Forensics – Master of Science, Computer Security and Forensics – Master of Science, Cyber Security – Master of Science, Electronic Engineering – Master of Science, Electronic Engineering – Master of Science, Electronic Engineering (15 months) – Master of Science, Information Security and Digital Forensics – Master of Science, Sensors and Smart Cities – Master of Science, Sensors and Smart Cities (15 months) – Master of Science, Telecommunications Management – Master of Science, Telecommunications Management – Master of Science, Telecommunications Management (15 months) – Master of Science

Culture and Communications

BA degrees in broadcast journalism, creative writing, creative writing & journalism, English literature, journalism, journalism and PR, magazine journalism, media communications, media and PR, radio and audio, sport journalism

Postgraduate courses: MA international journalism, MA mass communications, MA international cinema, MA English literature, MA television production

Life Sciences

Food and Nutrition Science – BSc(Hons), Forensic Science – BSc(Hons), Biological Science – BSc(Hons), Biomedical Science – BSc(Hons), Biochemistry – BSc(Hons), Animal Science (Top Up) – BSc(Hons); Postgraduate courses: MSc Biomedical Engineering, MSc Biochemistry, MSc Pharmacology, MSc Micro-biology in Public Health

Media and Performance

Film and Television Production – Bachelor of Arts with Honours, Acting – Bachelor of Arts with Honours, Dance and Professional Practice – Bachelor of Arts with Honours, Film Production – Bachelor of Arts with Honours, Media Make Up and Character Design Foundation Degree, Media Performance for Film, TV and Theatre – Bachelor of Arts with Honours, Media Production – Bachelor of Arts with Honours, Media Production – Foundation Degree, Media Production (Radio) – Bachelor of Arts with Honours, Music Technology – Bachelor of Arts with Honours, Music Technology – Foundation Degree, Performing Arts – Bachelor of Arts with Honours, Technical Theatre and Stage Management – Foundation Degree of the Arts, Theatre and Professional Practice – Bachelor of Arts with Honours

Postgraduate courses: Creative Digital Film Production – Master of Arts, Digital Film Technologies and Production – Master of Arts, Documentary – Master of Arts, Performing Before the Camera – Postgraduate Certificate, Screen Performance and Communications Techniques – Master of Arts, Dance Performance and Choreography – Master of Arts, Dance Science – Master of Science, Performing Arts: Creative Practice and Leadership – Master of Arts

Psychology

Applied Psychology – Bachelor of Sciences with Honours, Health Psychology – Bachelor of Sciences with Honours, Psychological Studies (Top-Up) – Bachelor of Arts with Honours, Psychology – Bachelor of Sciences with Honours, Psychology and Crime – Foundation Degree, Psychology and Crime – Foundation Degree, Psychology and Criminal Behaviour – Foundation Degree, Psychology and Criminal Behaviour – Bachelor of Sciences with Honours,

Psychology and Criminal Behaviour (Top up) – Bachelor of Arts with Honours, Psychology and Criminal Behaviour (Top up) – Bachelor of Arts with Honours, Psychology and Criminology – Bachelor of Sciences with Honours, Psychology with Languages – Bachelor of Sciences with Honours, Psychology, Counselling and Therapies – Bachelor of Sciences with Honours

Postgraduate courses: Applied Psychology (Conversion) – Master of Science, Forensic Psychology – Master of Science, Health Psychology – Master of Science

Faculty of Education and Sport; www.beds.ac.uk/howtoapply/ departments/es

Education and English Language

Early Childhood Education – BA(Hons), Education Studies – BA(Hons), Education with Psychology – BA(Hons), English Language Teaching – Certificate in English Language Teaching, English Language Teaching – Certificate in English Language Teaching, English Language and Linguistics – BA(Hons), English Language and Teaching English as a Foreign Language – BA(Hons), Special Needs and Inclusive Education – BA(Hons)

Postgraduate courses: Applied Linguistics – MA, Applied Linguistics (TEFL) – MA, Applied Linguistics (TEFL) – MA, Applied Linguistics (Testing and Assessment) & MA, Behavioural Issues in Schools – (PgCert), Difficulties in Literacy Development and Dyslexia – (PgCert), Education – MA, Education (Early Years) – MA, Education (Leadership) – MA, Education (National Award for Special Educational Needs Co-ordination) – (PgCert), Education (Practice) – MA, Education (Social Justice) – MA, Education (Special Educational Needs) – MA, English Language Teaching (Leadership and Management) – MA, International Development & MA

Sport and Physical Activity

Applied Personal Training and Specialist Exercise Instruction – BSc(Hons), Applied Sport Development and Management – BA(Hons), Applied Sport Science and Coaching – BSc(Hons), Applied Sport and Physical Education – BSc(Hons), Football Studies – BA(Hons), Health, Nutrition and Exercise – BSc(Hons), Sport Development and Management – BA(Hons), Sport Science and Coaching – BSc(Hons), Sport Science and Personal Training – BSc(Hons), Sport Science and Physical Education – FD of Science, Sport and Exercise Science – BSc(Hons),

Sport and Physical Education – BSc(Hons), Sport and Physical Education – BA(Hons), Sports Science (Personal Training) – FD of Science, Sports Science (Sports Coaching) – FD of Science, Sports Studies – BA(Hons), Strength and Conditioning – BSc(Hons) Postgraduate courses: Clinical Exercise Physiology – (PgDip), Clinical Exercise Physiology – MSc, Leadership and Management of Sport and Physical Activity, Physical Activity, Nutrition and Health Promotion – MSc, Physical Education and Sport Pedagogy – MA, Strength and Conditioning – MSc,

Teaching and Education

BA degrees in disability studies, early years studies, educational practice, applied disability studies, applied early years studies, applied education studies, mathematics with secondary education (with QTS), PE secondary, with QTS, primary education (with QTS), primary years education, PGCE primary, early years and PE, and numerous secondary subjects, all with QTS, and PGCE early years teaching with EYTS, and PGCE early years birth to 5 with EYTS, post compulsory education, university certificate of continuing professional development in TESOL, continuing professional development in mathematics
Postgraduate courses: PGCerts in a variety of subject specialisms in Education, Primary and Secondary PGCerts, PGCerts in Post-Compulsory Education

Faculty of Health and Social Science; *www.beds.ac.uk/howtoapply/* *departments/healthsciences*

applied social studies, child and adolescent studies, criminology/and sociology, health and social care; BA(Hons), BSc(Hons)

Sports Therapy and Rehabilitation

Sports Therapy – BSc(Hons), MSc Clinical Biomechanics, MSc Health and Ageing

Healthcare Practice

Health Care Practice (Top up) – Bachelor of Sciences with Honours, Healthcare Practice – Foundation Degree of Science, Midwifery: Registered Midwife (2nd Registration) – Bachelor of Sciences with Honours, Midwifery: Registered Midwife (3 Year) – Bachelor of Sciences with Honours, Nursing Associate – Foundation Degree, Nursing Studies (Top up) – Bachelor of Sciences with Honours, Nursing with Registered Nurse: Adult – Bachelor of Sciences with Honours, Nursing with Registered Nurse: Child – Bachelor of Sciences with Honours, Nursing with

Registered Nurse: Mental Health – Bachelor of Sciences with Honours, Operating Department Practice – Bachelor of Sciences with Honours, Paramedic Science – Bachelor of Sciences with Honours
Postgraduate courses: Advanced Clinical Practice (Midwifery) – Master of Science, Advanced Clinical Practice (Nursing) – Master of Science, Advanced Clinical Practice (Paramedic Science) – Master of Science, Advanced Nursing Studies – Master of Science, Dental Education – Postgraduate Certificate, Dental Education – Postgraduate Diploma, Dental Education – Master of Arts, Dental Law and Ethics – Postgraduate Certificate, Dental Law and Ethics – Postgraduate Diploma, Dental Law and Ethics – Master of Arts, Integrated Care – Postgraduate Certificate, Medical Education – Postgraduate Certificate, Medical Education – Postgraduate Diploma, Medical Education – Master of Arts, Medical Simulation – Postgraduate Certificate, Nursing with Registration (Adult) – Master of Science, Nursing with Registration (Mental Health) – Master of Science, Public Health – Master of Science, Specialist Community Public Health Nursing (Health Visiting) – Master of Science, Specialist Community Public Health Nursing (Health Visiting) – Postgraduate Diploma, Specialist Community Public Health Nursing (School Nursing) – Master of Science, Specialist Community Public Health Nursing (School Nursing) – Postgraduate Diploma, Specialist Practitioner Community District Nursing – Postgraduate Diploma, Specialist Practitioner Community District Nursing – Master of Science

Applied Social Studies

Applied Social Studies (Extended) – Bachelor of Arts with Honours, Child and Adolescent Studies – Bachelor of Arts with Honours, Child and Family Studies – Foundation Degree, Child and Family Studies – Foundation Degree, Child and Family Studies – Foundation Degree, Children, Families and Community Health – Foundation Degree, Criminology – Bachelor of Arts with Honours, Criminology and Sociology – Bachelor of Arts with Honours, Health and Social Care – Foundation Degree of the Arts, Health and Social Care – Foundation Degree of the Arts, Health and Social Care – Foundation Degree of the Arts, Health and Social Care – Foundation Degree of the Arts, Health and Social Care – Foundation Degree of the Arts, Health and Social Care – Bachelor of Arts with Honours, Health and Social Care (Top up) – Bachelor of Arts with Honours, Health and Social Care Practice –

Foundation Degree of the Arts, Health and Social Care Practice – Foundation Degree of the Arts, Health and Social Care Practice (Top up) – Bachelor of Arts with Honours, Health and Social Care Practice (Top up) – Bachelor of Arts with Honours, Integrated City Urban Planning & Design – Bachelor of Arts with Honours, Policing and Criminal Investigation – Bachelor of Arts with Honours, Professional Social Work Practice (UCMK) – Bachelor of Sciences with Honours, Social Studies – Bachelor of Arts with Honours, Social Work – Bachelor of Sciences with Honours, Sociology – Bachelor of Arts with Honours, Systemic Practice (Child Focused Practice) – Graduate Certificate, Systemic Practice (Families and Couples) – Graduate Certificate, Youth and Community Work – Bachelor of Arts with Honours

Postgraduate courses: Applied Social Work Practice: Children and Families – Master of Arts, Applied Social Work Practice: Leadership and Management – Master of Arts, Applied Social Work: Practice Education – Master of Arts, Childhood and Youth: Applied Perspectives – Master of Arts, Criminology – Master of Arts, Family and Systemic Psychotherapy – Master of Science, Intermediate Child Focused Systemic Practice – Postgraduate Certificate, Intermediate Systemic Practice with Families and Couples – Postgraduate Certificate, International Social Work and Social Development – Master of Arts, Professional Social Work Practice – Postgraduate Diploma, Social Work – Master of Science, Social Work Practice – Master of Professional Social Work Practice, Systemic Leadership and Organisational Development – Master of Science

University of Bedfordshire Business School; www.beds.ac.uk/howtoapply/departments/businessschool

Accounting BA(Hons), Accounting and Finance BSc(Hons), Business Economics BA(Hons), Business Information Systems BSc(Hons), Business Management BA(Hons), Business Management with Law BSc(Hons), Economics and Finance BSc(Hons), Hospitality and Tourism Management BA(Hons), Human Resource Management BSc(Hons), Integrated City Urban Planning & Design BA(Hons), International Business BA(Hons), Law LLB(Hons), Law with Criminology LLB(Hons), Law with Financial Management LLB(Hons), Law with Psychology LLB(Hons), Marketing BA(Hons), Policing and Criminal Investigation BA(Hons), Travel and Tourism BA(Hons)

Postgraduate courses: Accounting and Business Finance MSc, Business Administration (Finance) MBA, Business Administration (Marketing) MBA, Digital Marketing MSc, Events Management MSc, Financial Economics MSc, Financial Risk Management MSc, International Business Law LLM, International Business with Law MSc, International Commercial and Dispute Resolution Law LLM, International Oil and Gas Law LLM, International Tourism Planning and Management MSc, Management MSc, Marketing MSc, MBA, Purchasing, Logistics and Supply Chain Management MSc

THE QUEEN'S UNIVERSITY OF BELFAST
www.qub.ac.uk

School of Biological Sciences; www.qub.ac.uk/schools/schoolofbiologicalsciences

agricultural technology, biochemistry, biological sciences, food science and security, food quality, safety and nutrition, land use & environmental management, energy, environment and sustainability; marine biology, microbiology, zoology, Postgraduate; microbes and pathogen biology, ecosystem biology and sustainability; BSc(Hons), MSc, PhD, MPhil

School of Chemistry and Chemical Engineering; www.ch.qub.ac.uk

chemistry, chemistry with French/Spanish, medicinal chemistry, chemical engineering, chemical research, chemical technology, pharmaceutical analysis, process engineering, professional studies; BSc(Hons), MSci, BEng, MEng, MSc, PGDip, PhD, MSci

School of Creative Arts; www.qub.ac.uk/schools/SchoolofCreativeArts

arts management, music, music technology/& sonic arts, drama/& English, film studies, film & visual studies, arts management, musicology; BA, MA, BMus, BSc, MPhil, PhD

School of Education; www.qub.ac.uk/schools/schoolofeducation

appl behavioural analysis, autism spectrum disorders, children's rights, initial teacher education (PGCE in wide range of secondary education subjects), educational leadership, Irish medium post primary PGCE, educational studies, inclusion and special needs education, teaching English to speakers of other languages (TESOL), professional development, quantitative methods in educational research; AdvCertEd, DASE, EdD, MA, MEd, MSc, MSSc, PGCE, PGDip/Cert, UnivCert, BA(Hons), EdD(TESOL)

School of Electronics, Electrical Engineering and Computer Science; www.qub.ac.uk/schools/eeecs

business IT, computing and IT, computer science, cyber security, electrical & electronic engineering, electronics, software/engineering & electronic systems engineering, software development; BEng, BSc, MEng, MSc, MPhil, PhD

School of English; www.qub.ac.uk/schools/SchoolofEnglish

English literature and language, English with creative writing, Postgraduate; creative writing, English literary studies, poetry: creativity and criticism, speech and language; BA(Hons), MA, PhD

School of Geography, Archaeology and Palaeoecology; www.qub.ac.uk/schools/gap

geography, geography with extended studies in Europe, archaeology, palaeoecology and geography, archaeology, archaeology jt degrees, archaeology-palaeoecology, archaeology-palaeoecology and geography, Postgraduate; cultural heritage and GIS, human geography: society, space and culture; BA(Hons), BSc(Hons), MSc, PhD, PGDip/Cert, MSci

School of History and Anthropology; www.qub.ac.uk/schools/SchoolofHistoryandAnthropology

history, anthropology, history & archaeology/theology/philosophy/politics/sociology/modern languages, anthropology and languages, history & international studies, history
Postgraduate; history, anthropology, social anthropology, Irish Studies
BA(Hons), GradDip, MA, MPhil, PhD

School of Law; www.law.qub.ac.uk

law, law/with politics/languages, human rights, Postgraduate; human rights, human rights & criminal justice, European law and governance, international business and law, criminal justice, environmental law and governance, international corporate governance, criminal justice and criminology; LlB, LlM, MSSc, MLSc, PGDip, MPhil, PhD, JD, MLaw

Queens University Management School; www.qub.ac.uk/schools/QueensUniversityManagementSchool

accounting/& finance, actuarial science & risk management, business information technology, politics, philosophy & economics, economics
Postgraduate; accounting and finance, finance, computational finance and trading, risk and investment management, economics, management, international business, marketing, HRM, executive/international; MBA, BSc(Hons), MSc, MScs, MBA, PhD, MSSc

School of Mathematics and Physics; www.qub.ac.uk/schools/SchoolofMathematicsandPhysics

mathematics, applied mathematics/& physics, plasma physics, materials science, pure & applied mathematics, applied physics, theoretical physics, mathematics with finance; BSc(Hons), GradDip, MSc, MSci, PhD

School of Mechanical and Aerospace Engineering; www.qub.ac.uk/schools/SchoolofMechanicalandAerospaceEngineering

adv/aerospace engineering, adv/mechanical engineering, product design engineering; BEng, MEng, MSc, PhD

School of Medicine, Dentistry and Biomedical Sciences; www.qub.ac.uk/schools/mdbs

medicine, biomedical science, clinical education, clinical anatomy, dentistry, dental surgery, human biology, surgery, bioinformatics and computational genomics, translational medicine, public health, mental health, obstetrics; BCh, BAO, BSc(Hons), BDS, DAO, MB, MD, MSc, MPH, PGDip/Cert

School of Modern Languages; www.qub.ac.uk/schools/SchoolofModernLanguages

French/Irish/Spanish & Portuguese studies, interpreting & translation, business/law/science with a language, arts & humanities; BA(Hons), MA, PhD

School of Nursing and Midwifery; www.qub.ac.uk/schools/ SchoolofNursingandMidwifery

nursing adult/children/learning disability/mental health/midwifery sciences, caring for children & young people with complex health needs, continuing professional development, clinical practice, neonatal studies, non-medical prescribing, health studies and health & clinical studies, specialist practice in nursing, professional studies in midwifery, enhanced/ neonatal studies, trauma studies, advanced professional practice, advanced professional & clinical practice, practice development, cognitive behaviour therapy, introduction to counselling skills; BSc(Hons), Diploma, MPhil, PhD, DNursingPractice

School of Pharmacy; www.qub.ac.uk/ schools/SchoolofPharmacy

adv pharmaceutical practice, pharmaceutical analysis, clinical pharmacy, community pharmacy, non medical prescribing, pharmaceutical science/biotechnology, adv pharmacy practice; MPharm, MSc, PGCert/Dip, MPhil

School of Planning, Architecture and Civil Engineering; www.qub.ac.uk/schools/ SchoolofPlanningArchitectureand CivilEngineering

architecture, building & regeneration, building information modelling project management, environmental/& civil engineering, construction/ & project management, environmental engineering/planning, environmental & civil engineering, planning and regeneration, planning environment & design, portfolio guidance, urban & rural design, structural engineering with architecture,design & management sustainable practice in the built environment; BSc(Hons), MSc, MArch, MPhil, PhD, PGDip/Cert,MPlan

School of Politics, International Studies and Philosophy; www.qub.ac.uk/schools/ SchoolofPoliticsInternationalStudies andPhilosophy

international relations, politics, philosophy, legislative studies & practice, philosophy, politics & economics, international politics & conflict studies, violence, terrorism and security, public policy; BA(Hons), LlB, MA, MRes, MPhil, PhD

School of Psychology; www.psych.qub.ac.uk

atypical child development, applied psychology (clinical specialism), psychology, educational child & adolescent psychology, political psychology, politics, clinical psychology, psychology of childhood adversity; BSc(Hons), MSc, DocClinPsych, PhD DocEducational

School of Sociology, Social Policy and Social Work; www.qub.ac.uk/schools/ SchoolofSociologySocialPolicySocialWork

applied social studies, criminology, childhood studies, social work, social policy, social research methods, sociology, sociology with quantitative methods, cognitive behavioural therapy; BA(Hons), BSW, MA, MSc, DChild, MRes

UNIVERSITY OF BIRMINGHAM
www.bham.ac.uk

College of Arts and Law; www.birmingham.ac.uk/university/ colleges/artslaw/index.aspx

African Studies
African Studies BA, African Studies with Development BA, Anthropology and African Studies BA, Anthropology and History BA, Anthropology and Political Science BA, Archaeology and Anthropology BA

American and Canadian Studies
American and Canadian Studies BA, American and Canadian Studies with year abroad BA

Archaeology
Ancient History BA, Archaeology & Ancient History and History BA, Archaeology and Ancient History BA, Archaeology and Anthropology BA,

Classics
Ancient History BA, Anthropology and Classical Literature and Civilisation BA, Archaeology & Ancient History and History BA, Archaeology and Ancient History BA, Classical Literature & Civilisation and Philosophy BA, Classical Literature and Civilisation BA, Classics BA, English and Classical Literature & Civilisation BA,

Drama and Theatre Arts
Drama and English BA, Drama and Theatre Arts BA

English Literature
Drama and English BA, English and Classical Literature & Civilisation BA, English and Creative Writing BA, English and Film BA, English and History BA, English and History of Art BA, English and Philosophy BA, English BA, English Language and Literature BA, Modern Languages and English BA; Postgraduate courses: Creative Writing MA, Film and Television: Research and Production MA,

English Language and Applied Linguistics
English and Creative Writing BA, English Language and Linguistics BA, English Language and Literature BA, English Language BA, Modern Languages and English BA; Postgraduate courses: Applied Linguistics MA, Applied Linguistics MA (Distance Learning), Applied Linguistics PgCert (Distance Learning), Applied Linguistics with TESOL MA, Language, Culture and Communication MA, Teaching English to Speakers of Other Languages (TESOL) MA, Teaching English to Speakers of Other Languages (TESOL) MA (distance learning)

History
Ancient and Medieval History BA, Ancient History BA, Anthropology and History BA, Archaeology & Ancient History and History BA, Archaeology and Ancient History BA, Education and History BA(Hons), English and History BA, French Studies and History BA, Geography and History BA, German Studies and History BA, Hispanic Studies and History BA, History and History of Art BA, History and Philosophy BA, History and Political Science BA, History and Russian Studies BA, History and Theology BA, History BA
Postgraduate courses: Colonial and Postcolonial Studies MA, Contemporary History MA, Early Modern History MA, Global History MA, History of Warfare MA, Holocaust and Genocide MA/Diploma/Certificate, Medieval Studies MA, Modern British Studies MA, Social Research (Economic and Social History) MA, West Midlands History MA

History of Art
English and History of Art BA, History and History of Art BA, History of Art BA, Modern Languages and History of Art BA; Postgraduate courses: Art History and Curating MA, History of Art MA

Law
Law LLB, Law with Business Studies LLB, Law with Criminology LLB, Law with French Law LLB, Law with German Law LLB, LLB for Graduates, LLB International Law and Globalisation
Postgraduate courses: Commercial Law LLM, Criminal Law and Criminal Justice LLM, International Commercial Law LLM, International Law LLM: Crime, Justice and Human Rights, International Law, Ethics and Politics MA, LLB for Graduates, LLM (General)

Modern Languages and Cultures
Chemistry with a Modern Language BSc, Chemistry with a Modern Language MSci, Economics with German BSc, Economics with Italian BSc, Economics with Japanese BSc, Economics with Portuguese BSc, Economics with Spanish BSc, French Studies and Geography BA, French Studies and History BA, French Studies and Mathematics BA, Geography and German Studies BA, German Studies and History BA, Hispanic Studies and History BA, History and Russian Studies BA, International Business with Language BSc, International Relations with French BA, International Relations with German BA, International Relations with Spanish BA, Law with French Law LLB, Law with German Law LLB, Modern Languages (University of Birmingham with The Open University pathway) BA, Modern Languages and English BA, Modern Languages and History of Art BA, Modern Languages and Music BA, Modern Languages BA, Modern Languages with Business Management BA, Money, Banking and Finance with German BSc, Money, Banking and Finance with Italian BSc, Money, Banking and Finance with Spanish BSc, Russian Studies and International Relations BA
Postgraduate courses: Colonial and Postcolonial Studies MA, Holocaust and Genocide MA/Diploma/Certificate, Translation Studies MA

Music
Mathematics and Music BA, Modern Languages and Music BA, Music BMus
Postgraduate courses: Music MA: British Music Studies pathway, Music MA: Choral Conducting pathway, Music MA: Critical Musicology pathway, Music MA: Early Music pathway, Music MA: Electroacoustic composition/sonic art pathway, Music MA: Global Popular Musics pathway, Music MA: Instrumental/Vocal Composition pathway, Music MA: Mixed Composition pathway, Music MA: Open Pathway with Performance, Music MA:

Open Pathway without Performance, Music MA: Performance pathway, Music MA: Performance Practice pathway

Philosophy

Classical Literature & Civilisation and Philosophy BA, English and Philosophy BA, History and Philosophy BA, Mathematics and Philosophy BA, Philosophy and Sociology BA, Philosophy BA, Philosophy, Religion and Ethics BA, Political Science and Philosophy BA, Political Science and Philosophy with Year Abroad BA

Postgraduate courses: Global Ethics MSc, Human Values and Human Rights MSc, International Law, Ethics and Politics MA, Philosophy MA, Philosophy of Health and Happiness MA, Philosophy of Mind and Cognitive Science MA, Philosophy of Religion and Ethics MA/Diploma

Theology and Religion

History and Theology BA, Philosophy, Religion and Ethics BA, Politics, Religion and Philosophy BA, Theology and Religion BA

Postgraduate courses: Holocaust and Genocide MA/Diploma/Certificate, Philosophy of Religion and Ethics MA/Diploma, Religion, Politics and Society, Theology and Religion MA

College of Medical and Dental Sciences; www.birmingham.ac.uk/university/colleges/mds/undergraduate/index.aspx

Biomedical Materials Science BMedSc, Biomedical Science BSc, Dental Hygiene and Therapy BSc, Dental Surgery BDS, Medicine and Surgery MBChB, Medicine and Surgery MBChB Graduate Entry Course, Nursing BNurs, Nursing MNurs, Pharmacy MPharm (4 year), Public Health BSc, Clinical Anatomy BSc – Intercalated Degree, Clinical Science BMedSc – Intercalated Degree, Health Management and Leadership – Intercalated Degree, International Health BMedSc – Intercalated Degree, Medical Sciences BMedSc – Intercalated Degree, Psychological Medicine BMedSc – Intercalated Degree, Public Health & Population Sciences BMedSc – Intercalated Degree

Postgraduate courses: Advanced Clinical Practice MSc, Advanced Critical Care Practitioner (ACCP) – Postgraduate Diploma, Advanced General Dental Practice MSc (Distance Learning), Advanced Practice in Healthcare (Global) MSc/PGDip/PGCert, Bioinformatics MSc/Diploma/Certificate, Biomedical Research: Integrative and Translational MRes, Cancer Sciences MRes, Cardiovascular Science MRes, Clinical Health Research MRes, Clinical Neuropsychiatry

MSc/Diploma, Clinical Oncology MSc/Diploma – Full-time, Clinical Oncology MSc/Diploma – Part-time, Clinical Primary and Community Care MSc/Diploma, Clinical Research – Academic Clinical Fellows (ACF) Framework MRes/PGDip/PGCert, Functional and Clinical Anatomy MSc, Genomic Medicine MSc/Diploma/Certificate, Health Economics and Econometrics MSc/Diploma, Health Economics and Health Policy MSc/Diploma, Health Research Methods – MSc/Diploma/Certificate, Immunology and Immunotherapy MSc, Medicine and Surgery MBChB Graduate Entry Course, Multidisciplinary Healthcare Simulation – PGCert, Musculoskeletal Ageing and Health – MSc/Diploma, Occupational Health MSc/Diploma/Certificate, Pharmaceutical Enterprise MSc/Diploma, Physician Associate Studies Diploma, Physician Associate Studies MSc, Physicians Assistant (Anaesthesia) Postgraduate Diploma, Practice Certificate in Independent Prescribing, Professional Doctorate in Pharmacy (DPharm), Public Health – Statement of Extra Accredited Learning (SEAL) MPH, Public Health (Health Technology Assessment) MPH/Diploma/Certificate, Public Health (International) MPH/Diploma/Certificate, Public Health MPH/Diploma/Certificate, Restorative Dentistry MSc/Diploma/Certificate Part-Time (Distance Learning), Trauma Science MSc; PhD and research Applied Health Research – PhD/MSc by Research, Biomedical Sciences – PhD/MSc by Research, Cancer and Genomic Sciences – PhD/MSc by Research, Cardiovascular Sciences – PhD/MSc by Research, Clinical Sciences – PhD/MSc by Research, Dentistry – PhD/MSc by Research, Immunology and Immunotherapy – PhD/MSc by Research, Inflammation and Ageing – PhD/MSc by Research, Metabolism and Systems Research – PhD/MSc by Research, Microbiology and Infection – PhD/MSc by Research, Nursing – PhD/MSc by Research, Pharmacy – PhD/MSc by Research

College of Life and Environmental Sciences; www.birmingham.ac.uk/university/colleges/les/index.aspx

Biosciences

Biochemistry (Genetics) BSc, Biochemistry BSc(Hons), Biochemistry MSci(Hons), Biochemistry with an International Year BSc(Hons), Biochemistry with Professional Placement MSci(Hons), Biochemistry with Study in Continental Europe BSc(Hons), Biological Sciences (Genetics) BSc, Biological Sciences (Zoology) BSc(Hons), Biological Sciences BSc(Hons),

Biological Sciences MSci(Hons), Biological Sciences with an International Year BSc(Hons), Biological Sciences with Professional Placement MSci(Hons), Biological Sciences with Study in Continental Europe BSc(Hons), Human Biology BSc(Hons), Human Biology MSci(Hons), Human Biology with an International Year BSc(Hons), Human Biology with Professional Placement MSci(Hons), Medical Biochemistry BSc(Hons)

Postgraduate courses: Microbiology and Infection MSc, Molecular Biotechnology MSc, Toxicology MSc, PhD study

Earth Sciences (Geology)

Geology and Physical Geography BSc(Hons), Geology and Physical Geography MSci(Hons), Geology and Physical Geography with an International Year MSci(Hons), Geology BSc(Hons), Geology MSci(Hons), Geology with an International Year MSci(Hons), Palaeobiology and Palaeoenvironments BSc(Hons), Palaeobiology and Palaeoenvironments MSci(Hons), Palaeobiology and Palaeoenvironments with an International Year MSci(Hons)

Postgraduate courses: Applied and Petroleum Micropalaeontology MSc, Applied Meteorology and Climatology MSc, Hydrogeology MSc, Science of Occupational Health, Safety and the Environment MSc/Diploma, PhD study

Environmental Science

Environmental Science BSc(Hons), Environmental Science MSci(Hons), Environmental Science with Professional Placement Abroad (Australasia) BSc(Hons), Environmental Science with Year Abroad BSc(Hons)

Air Pollution Management and Control MSc/Diploma, Applied Meteorology and Climatology MSc, Environmental Health MSc, Hydrogeology MSc, Public and Environmental Health Sciences MSc, Science of Occupational Health, Safety and the Environment MSc/Diploma, MRes and PhD study

Geography and Urban Planning

Geography and Urban and Regional Planning BSc(Hons), Geography BA(Hons), Geography BSc(Hons), Geography MSci(Hons), Geography with International Year MSci(Hons), Geography with Year Abroad BA(Hons), Geography with Year Abroad BSc(Hons), Geology and Physical Geography BSc(Hons), Geology and Physical Geography MSci(Hons), Geology and Physical Geography with an International Year MSci(Hons)

Postgraduate courses: Applied Meteorology and Climatology MSc, Hydrogeology MSc, Research in Human Geography MSc, River Environments and their Management MSc, Science of Occupational Health, Safety and the Environment MSc/Diploma, Urban and Regional Planning (with RTPI accreditation) MSc/PG Diploma/Certificate, MRes and PhD

Psychology (including Neuroscience)

Human Neuroscience BSc(Hons), Psychology and Psychological Practice MSci(Hons), Psychology and Psychological Research MSci(Hons), Psychology BSc(Hons)

Postgraduate courses: Brain Imaging and Cognitive Neuroscience MSc, Cognitive Behaviour Therapy High Intensity Postgraduate Diploma, Cognitive Behaviour Therapy Postgraduate Diploma, Compassion Focused Therapy Postgraduate Diploma, Computational Neuroscience and Cognitive Robotics MSc, Psychology MA, Psychology MSc

Sport, Exercise and Rehabilitation Sciences

Applied Golf Management Studies BSc(Hons), Physiotherapy BSc(Hons), Sport and Exercise Sciences BSc(Hons), Sport, Physical Education and Coaching Science BSc(Hons)

Postgraduate courses: Advanced Certificate in Golf Coaching, Advanced Manipulative Physiotherapy MSc/Postgraduate Diploma, Clinical Health Research MRes, Exercise and Sports Medicine (Football) MSc/Postgraduate Diploma, Physical Education and Sport Pedagogy MSc, Physiotherapy (pre-registration) MSc, Sport Coaching PGDip/MSc, MRes and PhD study

College of Engineering and Physical Sciences; www.birmingham.ac.uk/university/colleges/eps/index.aspx

Chemical Engineering

Chemical Engineering (International Study) MEng, Chemical Engineering BEng, Chemical Engineering MEng, Chemical Engineering with Foundation Year, Chemical Engineering with Industrial Study BEng, Chemical Engineering with Industrial Study MEng, Chemical Engineering with International and Industrial Study MEng

Postgraduate courses: Advanced Chemical Engineering Masters/MSc/Diploma, Biochemical Engineering Masters/MSc/Diploma, Efficient Fossil Energy Technologies Masters/MSc, Food Safety, Hygiene and Management Masters/MSc/PG Diploma/PG

Certificate, Industrial Project Management Masters/MSc/Diploma/Certificate, PhD

Chemistry

Chemistry BSc, Chemistry MSci, Chemistry with a Modern Language BSc, Chemistry with a Modern Language MSci, Chemistry with Business Management BSc, Chemistry with Business Management MSci, Chemistry with Foundation Year, Chemistry with Industrial Experience MSci, Chemistry with Pharmacology BSc, Chemistry with Pharmacology MSci, Chemistry with Study Abroad MSci; Physical Sciences for Health (Sci-Phy-4-Health) PhD/Masters/MSc

Civil Engineering

Civil and Railway Engineering BEng, Civil and Railway Engineering MEng, Civil Engineering BEng, Civil Engineering MEng, Civil Engineering with Industrial Experience MEng, Civil Engineering with International Study MEng, Engineering BEng, Engineering Foundation Year, Engineering MEng

Postgraduate courses: Advanced Engineering Management MSc: Construction Management, Civil Engineering and Management Masters/MSc/Diploma/Certificate, Civil Engineering Masters/MSc/Diploma, Geotechnical Engineering and Management Masters/MSc/Diploma/Certificate, Geotechnical Engineering Masters/MSc/Diploma/Certificate, Railway Risk and Safety Management /MSc/Diploma/Certificate, Railway Systems Engineering and Integration Masters/MSc/Diploma/Certificate, Road Management and Engineering Masters/MSc/Diploma, Structural Engineering and Practice Masters/MSc/Diploma

Computer Science

Artificial Intelligence and Computer Science BSc, Artificial Intelligence and Computer Science BSc with a year in industry, Computer Science BSc, Computer Science BSc with a year in industry, Computer Science MSci, Computer Science with an Industrial Year MSci, Computer Science with Digital Technology Partnership, Computer Science with Study Abroad BSc, Computer Science with Study Abroad MSci, Computer Science/Software Engineering MEng, Computer Science/Software Engineering MEng with a year in industry, Mathematics and Computer Science BSc, Mathematics and Computer Science MSci, Mathematics and Computer Science with Industrial Year BSc, Mathematics and Computer Science with Industrial Year MSci, Physical Sciences Foundation Year

Postgraduate courses: Advanced Computer Science Masters/MSc, Computational Neuroscience and Cognitive Robotics MSc, Computer Science Masters/MSc, Cyber Security Masters/MSc, Human Computer Interaction Masters/MSc, Physical Sciences for Health (Sci-Phy-4-Health) PhD/Masters/MSc, Robotics Masters/MSc

Electronic, Electrical and Systems Engineering

Electrical and Railway Engineering BEng, Electrical and Railway Engineering MEng, Electronic and Electrical Engineering BEng, Electronic and Electrical Engineering MEng, Electronic and Electrical Engineering with Industrial Year BEng, Electronic and Electrical Engineering with Industrial Year MEng, Engineering BEng, Engineering Foundation Year, Engineering MEng, Mechatronics and Robotics Engineering BEng, Mechatronics and Robotics Engineering MEng

Postgraduate courses: Communications Engineering and Networks Masters/MSc, Electrical Power Systems Masters/MSc, Electrical Power Systems with Advanced Research Masters/MSc (Two Year), Electronic and Computer Engineering Masters/MSc, Railway Risk and Safety Management /MSc/Diploma/Certificate, Railway Systems Engineering and Integration Masters/MSc/Diploma/Certificate, RF and Microwave Engineering Masters/MSc

Materials Science and Engineering

Aerospace Engineering BEng, Aerospace Engineering MEng, Engineering Foundation Year, Materials Science and Engineering BEng, Materials Science and Engineering MEng, Materials Science and Engineering with Industrial Experience MEng, Mechanical and Materials Engineering BEng, Mechanical and Materials Engineering MEng, Metallurgy BEng, Nuclear Engineering MEng, Nuclear Science and Materials BSc

Mathematics

French Studies and Mathematics BA, Mathematics and Computer Science BSc, Mathematics and Computer Science MSci, Mathematics and Computer Science with Industrial Year BSc, Mathematics and Computer Science with Industrial Year MSci, Mathematics and Music BA, Mathematics and Philosophy BA, Mathematics BSc, Mathematics MSci, Mathematics with a Year in Industry BSc, Mathematics with an International Year BSc, Mathematics with Business Management BSc, Mathematics with Business Management MSci, Mathematics with Study in

Continental Europe BSc, Physical Sciences Foundation Year, Theoretical Physics and Applied Mathematics BSc, Theoretical Physics and Applied Mathematics MSci

Postgraduate courses: Financial Engineering Masters/MSc, Mathematical Finance MSc, Mathematical Modelling MSc, Mathematics, Operational Research, Statistics and Econometrics (MORSE) Masters/MSc, Pre-Masters Certificate in Mathematics

Mechanical Engineering

Aerospace Engineering BEng, Aerospace Engineering MEng, Engineering BEng, Engineering Foundation Year, Engineering MEng, Mechanical and Materials Engineering BEng, Mechanical and Materials Engineering MEng, Mechanical Engineering (Automotive) BEng, Mechanical Engineering (Automotive) MEng, Mechanical Engineering BEng, Mechanical Engineering MEng, Mechanical Engineering with Industrial Year MEng

Postgraduate courses: Advanced Engineering Management MSc, Advanced Engineering Management MSc: Operations Management, Advanced Engineering Management MSc: Project Management, Advanced Engineering Management MSc: Systems Management, Advanced Mechanical Engineering Masters/MSc

Nuclear Engineering

Nuclear Engineering MEng, Nuclear Science and Materials BSc

Physics and Astronomy

Nuclear Engineering MEng, Nuclear Science and Materials BSc, Physical Sciences Foundation Year, Physics (International Study) BSc, Physics (International Study) MSci, Physics and Astrophysics (International Study) BSc, Physics and Astrophysics BSc, Physics and Astrophysics MSci, Physics BSc, Physics MSci, Physics with Particle Physics and Cosmology BSc, Physics with Particle Physics and Cosmology MSci, Theoretical Physics and Applied Mathematics BSc, Theoretical Physics and Applied Mathematics MSci, Theoretical Physics BSc, Theoretical Physics MSci

Postgraduate courses: Nuclear Decommissioning and Waste Management MSc/PG Diploma, Physical Sciences for Health (Sci-Phy-4-Health) PhD/Masters/MSc, Physics and Technology of Nuclear Reactors Masters\MSc, PhD and MRes

College of Social Sciences (CoSS); www.birmingham.ac.uk/university/colleges/socsci/index.aspx

Business

Accounting and Finance (BSc), Business Management (BSc), Economics (BSc), International Business (BSc), Money Banking and Finance (BSc), Mathematical Economics and Statistics (BSc)

Postgraduate courses: Accounting and Finance MSc, Advanced Engineering Management MSc, Economics, Finance and Statistical MSc, Management MSc, Marketing MSc, Online MSc, Graduate Diploma in Business Administration, MBA, PhD

Education

BA(Hons) Education, BA Primary Education, Primary Maths, BA Secondary Education, Schoo Direct Postgraduate study in the fields of autism (adults), autism (children), autism spectrum disorders (webautism), bilingualism in education, education for health professionals, initial teaching education, education (qts), subject knowledge enhancement courses (physics, mathematics), school direct (qts), teaching studies; Postgraduate; autism (adults), autism (children), autism spectrum disorders (webautism), bilingualism in education, character education, education for health professionals, education of learners with multisensory impairment (deafblindness),inclusion and special educational needs, international studies in education, language, literacies and dyslexia, management of special education in developing countries, school improvement and educational leadership, severe, profound and multiple learning difficulties, special educational needs coordination, special educational needs and disabilities, social, emotional and behavioural difficulties, teachers of children with hearing impairment, teaching English as a foreign language TEFL, visual impairment: mandatory and non-mandatory qualification for teachers of children and young people with a visual impairment, educational studies, PhD

Government and Society

International Relations BA, Political Science BA, Political Economy BA

Postgraduate courses: Global Cooperation and Security MSc, Political Psychology of International Relations MSc, Development Management (with specialist pathways) MSc/GDip, Aid Management MSc/GDip, Human Resources and Development Management MSc/GDip, Public Economic Management and Finance MSc/GDip, International Development MSc/

GDip, Environment, Sustainability and Politics MSc/ GDip, Conflict, Security and Development MSc/ GDip, Governance and Statebuilding MSc/GDip, International Political Economy and Development MSc/GDip, Poverty, Inequality and Development MSc/Gdip, Urban Development MSc/GDip, Masters in Public Administration (MPA), Political Science MA/PGDip, British Politics and the State MA/PGDip, Political Theory MA/PGDip, Social and Political Theory MA, Research Methods MA, International Political Economy MA/PGDip, International Relations MA/PGDip, Contemporary Asia Pacific MA/ PGDip, Diplomacy MA/PGDip, Gender MA/PGDip, Global Cooperation and Security MSc, International Peacekeeping MA/PGDip, Political Psychology of International Relations MSc, Security MA/PGDip, Terrorism and Political Violence MA/PGDip, Research Methods MA

Social Policy

Policy, Politics and Economics BA, Social Work BA, Social Policy BA, Sociology BA, Health Management and Leadership BMedSc – Intercalated Degree Postgraduate courses: Health Care Policy and Management MSc/PGCert/PGDip, Migration, Superdiversity and Policy MA/PGDip/PGCert, Policy into Practice MA/PGDip/PGCert, Policy into Practice with Integrated Placement MA/PGDip, Social Policy MA, Social Research (Social Policy) MA, Social Research (Social Work and Professional Practice) MA/PGDip, Social Work MA, Specialist Social Work with Adults MA/PGDip/PGCert, Advanced Child Protection Studies MSc/PGDip/PGCert (online, distance learning)

SCHOOL OF EDUCATION, SELLY OAK
www.education.bham.ac.uk Refer to School of Education in University of Birmingham entry, above

---

UNIVERSITY COLLEGE BIRMINGHAM
www.ucb.ac.uk

applied food and nutrition, aviation and airport management, bakery and confectionery technology, beauty therapy management,business enterprise, childhood studies, culinary arts management/science, digital marketing, events management, food development and innovation, health and social care, hospitality and restaurant management, hospitality and tourism management, hospitality business management, hospitality with events management, international hospitality and tourism management, international tourism/business management, managing in service industries, marketing management, marketing with events management, spa management, specialist hair and media, sport and fitness studies, sports management/therapy,youth, community and families; Postgraduate; culinary arts management, early years initial teacher training, global meetings and events management, hospitality with tourism management,international hospitality management/ tourism business administration, learning and teaching, marketing management for events, hospitality and tourism, PGCE primary QTS (qualified teacher status) (primary 3-7 and primary 5-11 years pathways),PGCE direct pathway (primary 3-7 and primary 5-11 years), tourism destination management, youth/work and community development; BA(Hons), BSc(Hons), FdA, Dip HE, FdSc, MA, MSc, PGCE, PGDip/Cert

BIRMINGHAM CITY UNIVERSITY
www.bcu.ac.uk

Faculty of Arts, Design and Media;
www.bcu.ac.uk/arts-design-and-media

Birmingham School of Architecture and Design; www.bcu.ac.uk/architecture-and-design

BA(Hons) Architecture (RIBA Part 1 Exemption), BA(Hons) Interior Architecture and Design, BA(Hons) Landscape Architecture, BA(Hons) Product and Furniture Design,

Postgraduate courses: PGDip Architectural Practice (RIBA Part 3 Exemption), MArch Architecture (RIBA Part 2 Exemption), MA/PGDip/PGCert Conservation of the Historic Environment, MA Design and Visualisation, MA Design Management, MA Interior Architecture and Design, MA Landscape Architecture, MA Product and Furniture Design

Birmingham School of Art; www.bcu.ac.uk/art

BA(Hons) Art and Design, BA(Hons)/HND Fine Art
Postgraduate courses: MA Art and Design: Interdisciplinary Practices, MA Arts and Education Practices, MA Arts and Project Management, MA Contemporary Arts China, MA Fine Art, MA Innovation and Leadership in Museum Practice

Birmingham Conservatoire; www.bcu.ac.uk/conservatoire

BA(Hons) Acting, BA(Hons) Applied Performance (Community and Education), BMus Jazz, BMus Music/Instrumental and Vocal Performance/Composition/Music Technology, BSc(Hons) Music Technology, BA(Hons) Stage Management
Postgraduate courses: MA/PGDip Acting, MFA Acting (The British Tradition), MMus/PGDip Choral Conducting, MMus/PGCert/PGDip Composition, MMus/PGCert/PGDip Instrumental Performance, MMus/PGCert/PGDip Jazz, MMus/PGCert/PGDip Music Technology, MA Musicology, MMus/PGDip Orchestral Conducting, MMus/PGDip Orchestral Performance (Strings), AdvPGDip Professional Performance, MA/PGDip Professional Voice Practice, MMus/PGCert/PGDip Vocal Performance

School of English; www.bcu.ac.uk/english

BA(Hons) English, BA(Hons) English and Creative Writing, BA(Hons) English and Drama, BA(Hons) English and Journalism, BA(Hons) English Language and Literature, BA(Hons) English Literature

Postgraduate course: MA Creative Writing

School of Fashion and Textiles; www.bcu.ac.uk/fashion-and-textiles

BA(Hons) Costume Design and Practice, BA(Hons) Fashion Branding and Communication, BA(Hons) Fashion Business and Promotion, BA(Hons) Fashion Design, BA(Hons) Garment Technology, BA(Hons) Textile Design
Postgraduate courses: MA Cosmetics Branding and Promotion, MA Fashion Design, MA Fashion Management, MA Fashion Promotion, MA Fashion Styling, MA Garment Technology, MA Luxury Brand Management, MA Textile and Surface Design

School of Jewellery; www.bcu.ac.uk/jewellery

BSc(Hons) Gemmology and Jewellery Studies, BA(Hons) Horology, BA(Hons) International Jewellery Business, BA(Hons) Jewellery and Objects, HND Jewellery and Silversmithing, BA(Hons) Jewellery and Silversmithing – Design for Industry
Postgraduate courses: GradCert/MA Jewellery and Related Products, MA Luxury Jewellery Management

Birmingham School of Media; www.bcu.ac.uk/media

BA(Hons) Digital Marketing, BA(Hons) English and Journalism, BA(Hons) Film Business and Promotion, BA(Hons)/HND Media and Communication, BA(Hons) Media and Communication (Event and Exhibition Industries), BA(Hons) Media and Communication (Journalism), BA(Hons) Media and Communication (Music Industries), BA(Hons) Media and Communication (New Media), BA(Hons) Media and Communication (Public Relations), BA(Hons) Media and Communication (Radio), BA(Hons) Media and Communication (Television), BA(Hons) Video Game Design and Production, BSc(Hons) Video Game Development, BA(Hons) Video Game Digital Art
Postgraduate courses: AdvCert Chartered Institute of Public Relations Advanced Certificate, Dip Chartered Institute of Public Relations Professional PR Diploma, MA Event, Festival and Exhibition Management, PGCert Film Distribution, MA Film Distribution and Marketing, MA/MSc Future Media, MA Global Media Management, MA Media and Cultural Studies, MA Multiplatform and Mobile Journalism,

MA Public Relations, MA/MSc Video Game Development, MSc Video Game Enterprise and Production

School of Visual Communication; www.bcu.ac.uk/visual-communication

BA(Hons) Commercial Photography, BA(Hons) Design for Performance, BA(Hons) Film and Animation, BA(Hons) Graphic Communication, BA(Hons) Illustration, BA(Hons) Photography, BA(Hons) Visual Communication & Graphic Communication
Postgraduate course: MA Visual Communication

Faculty of Business, Law and Social Sciences; www.bcu.ac.uk/business-law-and-social-sciences

Birmingham City Business School; www.bcu.ac.uk/business-school

BSc(Hons) Accountancy, MAcc Accounting and Finance, BSc(Hons) Accounting and Finance, BA(Hons) Business, BA(Hons) Business (Analytics), BA(Hons) Business (Marketing), BA(Hons) Business (Professional Practice), BSc(Hons) Business Accounting, BA(Hons) Business Administration (Top-up), HND Business and Management, BA(Hons) Business Economics, BSc(Hons)/MFin Business Finance, BA(Hons) Business Management, BA(Hons) Business Management (Consultancy), BA(Hons) Business Management (Enterprise), BA(Hons) Business Management (Professional Practice), BA(Hons) Business Management (Supply Chain Management), BA(Hons) Economics
Postgraduate courses: MSc Accounting and Finance, MBA Executive Master of Business Administration, MSc Finance and Investment, MA Innovation Management, MSc Insurance and Risk Management, MSc Internal Audit Management and Consultancy, MA/PGDip International Human Resource Management/Development, MBA International MBA, MSc Management and Entrepreneurship, MSc Management and Finance, MSc Management and International Business, MSc Management and Marketing, MSc Management Consultancy, MBA Master of Business Administration (Online), MSc/PGDip Multi-Unit Leadership and Strategy, MSc Organisation Risk Management

School of Law; www.bcu.ac.uk/law

LLB Law, LLB Law with American Legal Studies, LLB Law with Business, LLB Law with Criminology
Postgraduate courses: LLM International Business Law, LLM International Human Rights, LLM International Law, LPC/LLM Legal Practice, LLM/PGDL/CPE Professional Law, PGDL/CPE Postgraduate Diploma in Law

School of Social Sciences; www.bcu.ac.uk/social-sciences

BA(Hons) Black Studies, BA(Hons) Criminology, BA(Hons) Criminology and Security Studies, BA(Hons) Criminology, Policing and Investigation, BSc(Hons) Psychology, BSc(Hons) Psychology with Business, BSc(Hons) Psychology with Criminology, BA(Hons) Public Sociology, BSc(Hons) Psychology with Marketing, BSc(Hons) Psychology with Sociology, BA(Hons) Sociology, BA(Hons) Sociology and Criminology
Postgraduate courses: MA Criminology, MSc Forensic Psychology, MSc Health Psychology, MSc Psychology, MA Psychology, MA Security Studies

Faculty of Health, Education and Life Sciences; www.bcu.ac.uk/health-education-and-life-sciences

School of Education and Social Work; www.bcu.ac.uk/education-and-social-work

Initial Teacher Training

BA(Hons) Primary Education with QTS, PGCE Primary Education with Specialism in Mathematics with QTS, PGCE Post-Compulsory Education and Training, PGCE Primary and Early Years Education, PGCE Primary Education with Specialism in SEN with QTS, PGCE Secondary Art and Design, PGCE Secondary Computer Science, PGCE Secondary Drama, PGCE Secondary Design and Technology: Food, Textiles and Product Design, PGCE Secondary English, PGCE Secondary Mathematics, PGCE Secondary Modern Foreign Languages, PGCE Secondary Music, PGCE Secondary Religious Education, PGCE Secondary Science: Biology, PGCE Secondary Science: Chemistry, PGCE Secondary Science: Physics, SKE Subject Knowledge Enhancement in Mathematics, SKE Subject Knowledge Enhancement in Chemistry

Education, Childhood and Youth

BA(Hons) Conductive Education, BA(Hons) Early Childhood Studies, FdA Early Years, BA(Hons) Education Studies, BA(Hons) Working with Children, Young People and Families, MA Education, MA Education (International Education), BSc Social Work

Professional Development

MA Education, MA Education (Special Needs Education), MA Education (Global Education Management), MA Education (International Education), PGDip/MTL/MEL Teaching and Learning/Educational Leadership, MA Education (Childhood Studies), MA Education (Early Years Leadership)

School of Health Sciences; www.bcu.ac.uk/allied-and-public-health-professions

BEng/MEng Biomedical Engineering, BSc(Hons) Biomedical Sciences, BSc(Hons) Diagnostic Radiography, BSc(Hons) Food and Nutrition, BSc(Hons) Health Studies (Public Health), BSc(Hons) Medical Ultrasound, DipHE/BSc (Hons Operating Department Practice, BSc(Hons) Physical Education and School Sport, BSc(Hons) Radiotherapy, FdSc Rehabilitation Work (Visual Impairment), BSc(Hons) Specialist Complex Needs Rehabilitation Work (Visual Impairment) Top-Up, BSc(Hons) Speech and Language Therapy, BSc(Hons) Sport and Exercise Nutrition, BSc(Hons) Sport and Exercise Science, BSc(Hons) Sports Therapy

Postgraduate courses: MSc/PGDip/PGCert Advanced Clinical Practice, MSc Advanced Practice, MSc Dietetics (pre-registration), MSc/PGDip/PGCert Medical Ultrasound, PGDip Mental Health, MSc Physiotherapy, MSc/PGDip/PGCert Public Health, MSc/PGDip/PGCert Radiography

School of Nursing and Midwifery; www.bcu.ac.uk/nursing-and-midwifery

BSc(Hons) Midwifery, BSc(Hons) Nursing (Adult), BSc(Hons) Nursing (Child), BSc(Hons) Nursing (Learning Disability), BSc(Hons) Nursing (Mental Health)

Postgraduate courses: MSc Diabetes Care, MSc/PGDip/PGCert Safeguarding, BSc(Hons)/PG Specialist Community Public Health Nurse (HV/SN)

Faculty of Computing, Engineering and the Built Environment; www.bcu.ac.uk/computing-engineering-and-the-built-environment

School of the Built Environment; www.bcu.ac.uk/built-environment

BSc(Hons) Architectural Technology, BSc(Hons) Building Surveying, BEng/MEng Civil Engineering,

BSc(Hons) Construction Management, BSc(Hons)/MPlan Property Development and planning, BSc(Hons) Quantity Surveying, BSc(Hons) Real Estate

Postgraduate courses: MSc Building Surveying with Facilities Management, MSc Construction Project Management, MSc Environmental Surveying, MA Planning Built Environments, MSc/PGDip/PGCert Quantity Surveying, MSc Real Estate Management

School of Computing and Digital Technology; www.bcu.ac.uk/computing

BSc(Hons) Business Information Systems, BSc(Hons)/MSci Computer Forensics, BSc(Hons)/MSci Computer Games Technology, BSc(Hons)/MSci Computer Networks, BSc(Hons)/MSci Computer Networks and Security, BSc(Hons)/MSci Computer Science, BSc(Hons)/MSci Computing and Information Technology, BSc(Hons) Digital Media Computing

Postgraduate courses: MSc Advanced Computer Science, MSc/PGDip/PGCert Big Data Analytics, MSc Cyber Security, MSc Data Networks and Security, MSc Enterprise Systems Management

School of Engineering; www.bcu.ac.uk/engineering

BEng(Hons)/MEng Automotive Engineering, BEng(Hons)/MEng Electronic Engineering, BEng(Hons)/MEng Manufacturing Engineering, BEng(Hons)/MEng Mechanical Engineering

Postgraduate courses: MSc Automotive Engineering, MSc International Logistics and Supply Chain Management, MSc International Project Management (Distance Learning), MSc Logistics and Supply Chain Management, MSc Mechanical Engineering, MSc Project Management

BISHOP GROSSETESTE UNIVERSITY
www.bishopg.ac.uk

Undergraduate courses in archaeology, business (team entrepreneurship) counselling, drama, early childhood studies, education studies, history, mathematics, primary education, psychology, special educational needs, sport, theology & ethics, community health & social care, education, English, sociology, PGCE (primary/secondary), theology & ethics in society; MA in Education, EdD (doctor of education), MA English, PhD study

BLACKBURN COLLEGE
www.blackburn.ac.uk

Accounting Apprenticeship (Level 4 Higher), Accounting BA(Hons) Top Up, Accounting Foundation Degree FdA, Accounting with Financial Services BA(Hons) Top Up, Accounting with Financial Services Foundation Degree FdA, Applied Biology Higher National Diploma (HND), Applied Psychology (Counselling & Health) BSc(Hons), Applied Psychology (Counselling and Health) with Foundation Entry BSc(Hons), Apprenticeship in Care Leadership and Management (Higher Level 5), BA(Hons) Retail Management (Top Up), Business BA(Hons) Top up, Business Foundation Degree FdA, Business Studies BA(Hons) Top up (University of South Wales), Business with Human Resource Management BA(Hons), Business with Human Resource Management with Foundation Entry BA(Hons), Business with Human Resource Management with Industry Year BA(Hons), Business with Management BA(Hons), Business with Management with Foundation Entry BA(Hons), Business with Management with Industry Year BA(Hons), Certificate in Education and Training, Introductory, Certificate in Education and Training, Preparatory, Certificate of Higher Education in Legal Studies, Coaching & Mentoring Foundation Degree FdA, Coaching & Mentoring BA(Hons) Top Up, Community Coaching & Sports Development BSc(Hons) Top Up, Complementary and Integrative Health BSc(Hons) Top Up, Complementary Therapies FdSc, Computing BSc(Hons) Top Up, Computing Foundation Degree FdSc, Construction (Building Surveying) BSc(Hons), Construction (Building Surveying) with Foundation Entry BSc(Hons), Construction (Building Surveying) with Industry Year BSc(Hons), Construction (Project Management) BSc(Hons), Construction (Project Management) with Foundation Entry BSc(Hons), Construction (Project Management) with Industry Year BSc(Hons), Construction (Sustainable Design) BSc(Hons), Construction (Sustainable Design) with Foundation Entry BSc(Hons), Construction (Sustainable Design) with Industry Year BSc(Hons), Construction and the Built Environment HNC, Contemporary Design for Interiors BA(Hons) Top Up, Contemporary Fashion BA(Hons) (Top Up), Contemporary Fashion Foundation Degree FdA, Counselling BA(Hons) Top Up, Counselling Foundation Degree FdA, Criminology & Criminal Justice Foundation Degree FdA, Criminology BA(Hons) Top Up, Disability Studies (Inclusive Practice) BA(Hons) Top Up, Disability Studies (Inclusive Practice) Foundation Degree FdA, Early Childhood Studies BA(Hons) Top Up, Early Childhood Studies Foundation Degree FdA, Education Studies BA(Hons), Education Studies with Foundation Entry BA(Hons), Education Studies with Placement Year BA(Hons), Electrical and Electronic Engineering BEng(Hons), Electrical and Electronics Engineering (with Industry Year) BEng(Hons), Electrical and Electronics Engineering FdEng, Electrical and Electronics Engineering with Foundation Entry BEng(Hons), English Language and Literary Studies BA(Hons), English Language and Literary Studies with Foundation Entry BA(Hons), Fine Art BA(Hons), Fine Art with Foundation Entry BA(Hons), Fire & Rescue Service Management BA(Hons) Top Up, Fire & Rescue Service Management Foundation Degree FdA, General Engineering BEng(Hons), General Engineering FdEng, General Engineering with Foundation Entry BEng(Hons), General Engineering with Industry Year BEng(Hons), Graphic Communication BA(Hons), Graphic Communication with Foundation Entry BA(Hons), History and English Language BA(Hons), History and English Language with Foundation Entry BA(Hons), History and Literary Studies BA(Hons), History and Literary Studies with Foundation Entry BA(Hons), History and Politics BA(Hons), History and Politics with Foundation Entry BA(Hons), History and Sociology BA(Hons), History and Sociology with Foundation Entry BA(Hons), Hospitality Management BA(Hons) Top Up, Hospitality Management Foundation Degree FdA, Hospitality Management (with Events Management) Foundation Degree FdA, Human Resource Management (CIPD) Apprenticeship (Higher Level 5), Illustration and Animation BA(Hons), Illustration and Animation with Foundation Entry BA(Hons), Law LLB(Hons), Law LLB(Hons) Accelerated Route, Law Masters LLM, LLB(Hons) Law – Part-Time Only, Management Apprenticeship (ILM) (Higher Level 4), Management Apprenticeship (Level 5 Higher), Mechanical Engineering (with Industry Year) BEng(Hons), Mechanical Engineering BEng(Hons), Mechanical Engineering FdEng, Mechanical Engineering with Foundation Entry BEng(Hons), NVQ Diploma in Advice & Guidance Level 4, NVQ Diploma in Business & Administration Level 4,

PGCE (Education & Training) / CertEd (Education & Training), Photography BA(Hons) Top Up, Photography Foundation Degree FdA, Politics and English Language BA(Hons), Politics and English Language with Foundation Entry BA(Hons), Politics and Literary Studies BA(Hons), Politics and Literary Studies with Foundation Entry BA(Hons), Positive Practice with Children & Young People BA(Hons) Top Up, Positive Practice with Children & Young People Foundation Degree FdA, Public Health BSc(Hons) Top Up, Public Service Management BA(Hons) Top Up, Public Service Management Foundation Degree FdA, Public Service Management (Housing) BA(Hons) Top Up, Public Service Management (Housing) Foundation Degree FdA, Public Service Management (Uniformed Services) BA(Hons) Top Up, Public Service Management (Uniformed Services) Foundation Degree FdA, Retail Management Foundation Degree FdA, Social Science BA(Hons), Social Science with Foundation Entry BA(Hons), Sociology and English Language BA(Hons), Sociology and English Language with Foundation Entry BA(Hons), Sociology and Literary Studies BA(Hons), Sociology and Literary Studies with Foundation Entry BA(Hons), Sports Coaching & Performance BSc(Hons) Top Up, Sports Coaching & Performance Foundation Degree FdSc, Teaching & Learning Support (Primary) Foundation Degree FdA, Wellbeing and Social Care Practices BA(Hons) Top Up, Wellbeing and Social Care Practices Foundation Degree FdA

BOURNEMOUTH UNIVERSITY
www.bournemouth.ac.uk

Faculty of Science & Technology; www1.bournemouth.ac.uk/about/our-faculties/faculty-science-technology

Department of Archaeology, Anthropology & Forensic Science
BSc(Hons) Anthropology, BA(Hons) and BSc(Hons) Archaeology, BA(Hons) Archaeology & Anthropology, BSc(Hons) Archaeological & Forensic Sciences, BSc(Hons) Forensic Biology, BSc(Hons) Forensic Investigation, BSc(Hons) Forensic Science
Postgraduate courses: MSc Biological Anthropology, MSc Bioarchaeology, MSc Forensic Anthropology, MSc Forensic Archaeology, MSc Forensic Toxicology by Research, MSc Osteoarchaeology

Department of Computing & Informatics
BSc(Hons) Business Information Technology, BSc(Hons) Computing, BSc(Hons) Computer Networks, BSc(Hons) Cyber Security Management, BSc(Hons) Forensic Computing & Security, BSc(Hons) Information Technology Management, BSc(Hons) Software Engineering
Postgraduate courses: MSc Applied Data Analytics, MSc Cyber Security & Human Factors, MSc Information Technology, MSc Internet of Things, MSc Internet of Things with Cyber Security, MSc Internet of Things with Data Analytics, MRes (Master's by Research)

Department of Creative Technology
BSc(Hons) Games Software Engineering, BSc(Hons) Games Design, BA(Hons) Digital Creative Industries, BSc(Hons) Music & Audio Technology, BSc(Hons) Music & Sound Production Technology
Postgraduate courses: MSc Mobile App Development

Department of Design & Engineering
BSC(Hons) Design Engineering, BSc(Hons) Design Engineering (top-up), MEng Engineering (part-time), MEng(Hons) Mechanical Engineering, BA(Hons) Industrial Design, MDes(Hons) Product Design, BSc(Hons) Product Design, BA(Hons) Product Design
Postgraduate courses: MSc Engineering Project Management, MA Industrial Design, MSc Mechanical Engineering Design, MSc Product Design

Department of Life & Environmental Sciences
BSc(Hons) Biological Sciences, BSc(Hons) Ecology & Wildlife Conservation, BSc(Hons) Environmental Science, BSc(Hons) Geography, BSc(Hons) Marine Ecology & Conservation (top-up)
Postgraduate courses: MSc Biodiversity Conservation, MSc Green Economy

Department of Psychology
BSc(Hons) Psychology
Postgraduate courses: MSc Clinical and Developmental Neuropsychology, MSc Forensic and Neuropsychological Perspectives in Face-Processing, MSc

Foundations of Clinical Psychology, MSc Hypnosis in Research, Medicine and Clinical Practice, MSc Investigative Forensic Psychology

All departments conduct applied sciences by research

The Faculty of Management; www1.bournemouth.ac.uk/about/our-faculties/faculty-management

Bournemouth University School

Dept of Accounting, Finance & Economics

BA(Hons) Accounting & Business, BA(Hons) Accounting & Finance, MAccFin(Hons) Accounting & Finance, BA(Hons) Accounting & Law, BA(Hons) Accounting & Taxation, BA(Hons) Economics, BA(Hons) Finance & Business, BA(Hons) Finance & Economics, BA(Hons) Finance & Law – Top-up, BA(Hons) International Finance (Top-up)

Postgraduate courses: MSc Corporate Governance, MSc Finance, MSc International Accounting and Finance, MSc International Economics and Finance, MSc International Finance, MSc International Investment and Finance, MSc International Risk Management and Finance, MSc International Taxation and Finance

Dept of Leadership, Strategy & Organisation

BA(Hons) Business Studies, BA(Hons) Business Studies with Economics, BA(Hons) Business Studies with Enterprise, BA(Hons) Business Studies with Finance, BA(Hons) Business Studies with Human Resource Management, BA(Hons) Business Studies with Marketing, BA(Hons) Business Studies with Operations & Project Management, BA(Hons) International Business Studies, BA(Hons) Global Business Management (online, part-time), BA(Hons) Global Business Management (Top-up) (online, part-time), BA(Hons) Business & Management (Top-up), BA(Hons) International Management (Top-up)

Postgraduate courses: The Bournemouth MBA, MSc Professional Development (Loss Adjusting), MA Human Resource Management (part-time), MSc Innovation Management and Entrepreneurship, MSc International Management, MSc Management with Human Resources, MSc Management with Project Management

Dept of Events & Leisure

BA(Hons) Events Management, BA(Hons) Events & Leisure Marketing, MSc Events Management, MSc Events Marketing

Dept of Marketing

BSc(Hons) Marketing, BA(Hons) Retail Management, MSc Retail Management and Marketing, MSc Marketing Management

Dept of Sports & Physical Activity

BSc(Hons) Sport Development & Coaching Sciences, BSc(Hons) Sports Management, BSc(Hons) Sports Management (Golf), BSc(Hons) Sports Psychology & Coaching Sciences, MSc Sport Management

Dept of Tourism & Hospitality

BA(Hons) International Hospitality Management, BA(Hons) Tourism Management, BA(Hons) International Tourism and Hospitality Management, BA(Hons) International Hospitality & Tourism Management (Top-up), MSc Hotel and Food Services Management, MSc International Hospitality and Tourism Management, MSc Tourism Management, MSc Tourism Management & Marketing, PhD study

Faculty of Media & Communication; www1.bournemouth.ac.uk/about/our-faculties/faculty-media-communication

Department of Corporate & Marketing Communications

BA(Hons) Advertising, BSc(Hons) Marketing, BA(Hons) Marketing Communications, BA(Hons) Politics, BA(Hons) Public Relations, MA Advertising, MA Corporate Communication, MA International Political Communication, MA Political Psychology

Dept of Media Production

BA(Hons) Film, BA(Hons) Film Production & Cinematography, BA(Hons) History, BA(Hons) Media Production, BA(Hons) Photography, BA(Hons) Scriptwriting for Film and Television, BA(Hons) Television Production, MA Cinematography for Film and Television, MA Creative Media Arts: Data and Innovation, MA Directing Film and Television, MA Post Production Editing, MA Producing Film and Television, MA Radio Production, MA Scriptwriting, MA Sound Design for Film and Television

School of English, Communication and Journalism

BA(Hons) Communication & Media, BA(Hons) English, BA(Hons) Multimedia Journalism, MLit(Hons) English, MA Creative Writing and Publishing, MA Literary Media, MA Media and Communication, MA Multimedia Journalism

National Centre for Computer Animation
BA(Hons) Computer Animation Art and Design, BA(Hons) Computer Animation Technical Arts, MA 3D Computer Animation, MSc Computer Animation and Visual Effects, MA Digital Effects

Dept. of Law
LLB(Hons) Business Law, LLB(Hons) Entertainment Law, LLB(Hons) Law, LLB(Hons) Law with Economics, LLB(Hons) Law & Taxation, LLB(Hons) Law with Politics, BA(Hons) Law Top-Up, LLM Intellectual Property, LLM International Commercial Law, LLM International Tax Law, Graduate Diploma/CPE in Law, Postgraduate Certificate Intellectual Property, LLM Legal Practice, LPC Legal Practice, LLM Public International Law

Faculty of Health & Social Sciences; www1.bournemouth.ac.uk/about/our-faculties/faculty-health-social-sciences

Dept of Human Science & Public Health
BSc(Hons) Clinical Exercise Science, BSc(Hons) Midwifery, BSc(Hons) Nutrition and MNutr(Hons) Nutrition, BSc(Hons) Occupational Therapy, BSc(Hons) Physiotherapy, DipHE Operating Department Practice, BSc(Hons) Paramedic Science, BSc(Hons) Sports Therapy, PGDip Midwifery, MSc Nutrition & Behaviour, MSc Public Health, PGDip Public Health with Professional Registration as a Specialist Community Public Health Nurse (Health Visiting)

Department of Nursing & Clinical Sciences
BSc(Hons) Adult Nursing, BSc(Hons) Adult Nursing (Advanced Standing), BSc(Hons) Children & Young People's Nursing, BSc(Hons) Children & Young People's Nursing (Advanced Standing), BSc(Hons) Mental Health Nursing, BSc(Hons) Mental Health Nursing (Advanced Standing), PG Dip/MSc Advanced Clinical Practice, MA/PGDip/PGCert Care of Older People, PGDip Adult Nursing (with professional registration), PGDip Mental Health Nursing (with professional registration)

Dept of Social Work and Social Sciences
BA(Hons) Social Work, BA(Hons) Sociology, BA(Hons) Sociology & Anthropology, BA(Hons) Sociology & Criminology, MA Advanced Mental Health Practice, MA Advanced Practice (Child & Family Social Work), MA Advanced Practice (Vulnerable Adults), MA Leading & Developing Services, MA Social Care, MA Social Work, PGDip/MA Social Work (Children & Families)

UNIVERSITY OF BRADFORD
www.bradford.ac.uk

School of Engineering & Informatics
www.brad.ac.uk/ei

Faculty of Engineering & Informatics
School of Electrical Engineering and Computer Science
Computer Science; business computing, computer science, computer science for games, ICT with business; Postgraduate; advanced computer science, big data science and technology, computing, cyber security, mobile applications, software engineering
Electrical and Electronic Engineering; electrical and electronic engineering, medical electronics engineering, engineering and technology; Postgraduate; electrical and electronic engineering, personal, mobile and satellite communications, telecommunications engineering and entrepreneurship

School of Engineering
Chemical Engineering; chemical engineering; Postgraduate; chemical and petroleum engineering
Civil and Structural Engineering; civil and structural engineering; Postgraduate; civil and structural engineering
Mechanical and Automotive Engineering; mechanical engineering, mechanical and manufacturing engineering; Postgraduate; automotive engineering; mechanical engineering, information technology management, manufacturing management
Medical Engineering; Postgraduate; clinical technology, medical engineering, medical electronics engineering
Healthcare Technology; Postgraduate; medical engineering

School of Health Studies; www.brad.ac.uk/acad/health
clinical nursing practice, clinical practice, critical care, dementia studies, diagnostic radiography, health,

wellbeing and social care, midwifery studies, nursing (adult/child/mental health), occupational therapy, paramedic science, physiotherapy, sport rehabilitation; Postgraduate; adult cardiology, examination, assessment and intervention module, advanced care of the older person, advanced care of the older person, advanced practice (clinical practitioner),advanced practice (critical care), advanced practice (midwifery), advanced practice (minor injuries and minor illness),advancing transdisciplinary practice, applied physiotherapy, continence for physiotherapists, dementia studies, dementia studies (arts and activities/training in dementia care),diagnostic hysteroscopy and therapeutic diversity management, health and social care management, health wellbeing and social care, international health management, leadership, management and change in health and social care, leading service improvement, learning and talent development, managing health and social care, medical imaging, medical imaging (computed tomography/magnetic resonance imaging/medical image reporting/international), midwifery, musculoskeletal physiotherapy practice, nursing studies (international), patient safety, physiotherapy in women's health, professional healthcare practice, professional healthcare practice (cancer care), professional healthcare practice (children and young people/cognitive behavioural therapy/collaborative mental health care/diabetes care/end of life care/long term conditions/practice nursing/psychological therapies/public health/tissue viability), professional support, rehabilitation studies (continence for physiotherapists/musculoskeletal physiotherapy practice/physiotherapy in women's health/sports physiotherapy), sexual health, sports physiotherapy
AdvDip, BSc(Hons), CertHE, DipHE, FD, MSc, MPhil, PGDip/Cert, PhD, MPH

Faculty of Life Sciences; www.brad.ac.uk/acad/lifesci

Archaeological Sciences; archaeology, archaeological sciences, forensic archaeology and anthropology; Postgraduate; archaeological prospection, archaeological sciences, archaeology, forensic archaeology and crime scene investigation, human osteology & palaeopathology; Chemistry and Forensic sciences; chemistry, chemistry (analytical/materials/(medicinal), chemistry with industrial experience/research experience, integrated science; Postgraduate; analytical sciences, materials chemistry, science and entrepreneurship; Forensic and Medical sciences; forensic and medical sciences, forensic science, biomedical

science), healthcare science (life sciences); healthcare science (life sciences); clinical sciences; clinical sciences/medicine, clinical sciences; Postgraduate; biomedical science, cancer drug discovery, cancer pharmacology, cellular pathology laboratory practice, drug toxicology and safety pharmacology, science and entrepreneurship; Optometry and Vision Science; optometry, career progression programme; Pharmacy; pharmacy; Postgraduate; clinical pharmacy (community), clinical pharmacy (secondary care), pharmaceutical technology
BSc(Hons), MPhil, PhD, MChem, MPharm, CertHE, MSc, MSci(Hons), DPharm

Bradford School of Management; www.brad.ac.uk/management

Management; business and management studies, HRM, marketing, international business & management; Accounting and Finance; accounting and finance; Corporate management and business; Postgraduate; European and international business management, finance, accounting and management, international business and management, management, marketing and management, sustainable operations and management, applied management and entrepreneurship, innovation, enterprise and the circular economy: marketing and management, strategic marketing, media and entrepreneurship, science and entrepreneurship, telecommunications engineering and entrepreneurship
Executive MBA, MBA; BA(Hons), BSc(Hons), DBA, LlB, LlM, GradDip(Law), MBA, MRes, PhD, MSc, PGCert/Dip

School of Media, Design & Technology

Animation and Games; computer animation and visual effects, game design and development, graphics for games,
Film, TV and Media; film and TV production, film and media studies,
Web Design; web design and technology,
Postgraduate; digital filmmaking
BEng(Hons), BSc(Hons), BA(Hons), FD, MEng, MPhil, MSc, PhD

Faculty of Social Sciences; www.brad.ac.uk/acad/ssis

Economics; economics, business economics, financial economics
Peace Studies; development and peace studies, international relations and security studies, history and politics, politics, peace studies; PostGrad;African peace and conflict studies, applied dual-use

biosecurity education, conflict resolution, conflict, security and development, international politics and security studies, peace studies, peace, conflict and development, politics, violence & terrorism, Middle East violence & security studies
Psychology; psychology, psychology with counselling

Sociology & Criminology; applied criminal justice studies, sociology, sociology and psychology, psychology and crime
Social Work & Social Care; social work, working with children, young people and families; Postgraduate; social work
BA(Hons), BSc(Hons), MA, MPhil, PhD, PGDip, MPA

Degrees validated by University of Bradford offered at:

BRADFORD COLLEGE
www.bradfordcollege.ac.uk

accountancy, beauty therapy management, business management (HRM), business management (marketing), business management, childhood and youth studies, computer networks and systems support, computing and information systems, computing, construction management, counselling and psychology in community settings, education and training, early years, early years practice, education studies, fashion, film, games and digital media, graphic media design, health and social welfare, hospitality and travel management, interior design, internet applications, law (accountancy/marketing/social welfare), law and legal practice, law, lifelong learning, management and leadership, media make-up with special effects, photography, physical activity, health and well-being, primary education with QTS, public services management, secondary education (physics), social nutrition and health, sports coaching, supporting and managing learning in education, surface design and textile innovation, teaching and learning in the primary phase with QTS, visual arts, youth and community development; Postgraduate; applied business, PGCE (14-19), computing, education and training, education/leadership & management/inclusive education/early childhood/ICT, health and social care GCE (14-19), international business management, management, primary PGCE, youth and community development; BSc(Hons), CertHE, DipHE, BA(Hons), LlB(Hons), BEngTech, MA, MEd, PGDipCert, MSc, PGCE, FD, LawPGDip, LlM

UNIVERSITY OF BRIGHTON
www.brighton.ac.uk

School of Applied Social Science
Applied Psychology and Criminology BA(Hons), Applied Psychology and Sociology BA(Hons), Applied Psychology BSc(Hons), Criminology and Sociology BA(Hons), Criminology BA(Hons), Politics BA(Hons), Social Policy and Practice BSc(Hons), Social Science BA(Hons), Social Work BSc(Hons), Sociology BA(Hons)
Postgraduate courses: Advanced Social Work and Management MSc, Advanced Social Work MSc, Approved Mental Health Practice PGDip, Community Psychology MA, Humanistic Psychotherapeutic Counselling PGDip, Professional Social Work Practice PGCert, Professional Social Work Practice PGDip, Psychodynamic Psychotherapeutic Counselling PGDip, Psychotherapy MSc, Social Science MRes (PGCert), Social Work MSc

School of Architecture and Design
Architecture BA(Hons), Interior Architecture BA(Hons), Product Design Technology with Professional Experience BSc(Hons), Product Design with Professional Experience BSc(Hons), Sports Product Design with Professional Experience BSc(Hons)
Postgraduate courses: Architectural and Urban Design MA (PGCert PGDip), Architecture Post Part 2 Professional Experience, Architecture Professional Practice Pre-Diploma, Architecture RIBA Part 2 MArch, Interior Design MA (PGCert PGDip), Management, Practice and Law in Architecture PGDip, Sustainable Design MA, Town Planning MSc (PGCert PGDip)

School of Art

3D Design and Craft BA(Hons), 3D Design and Craft MDes, Fashion Communication with Business Studies BA(Hons), Fashion with Business Studies BA(Hons), Fine Art Painting BA(Hons), Fine Art Sculpture BA(Hons), Fine Art: Critical Practice BA(Hons), Fine Art: Printmaking BA(Hons), Graphic Design BA(Hons), Illustration BA(Hons), Textiles with Business Studies BA(Hons), Textiles with Business Studies MDes

Postgraduate courses: Arts and Cultural Research MRes (PGCert PGDip), Arts and Design by Independent Project MA, Craft MA (PGDip), Fine Art MA, Inclusive Arts Practice MA (PGCert PGDip), Sequential Design/Illustration MA, Textiles MA

Brighton Business School

Business and Management

Business BSc(Hons) top-up degree, Business Management BSc(Hons), Business Management with Economics and Placement Year BSc(Hons), Business Management with Economics BSc(Hons), Business Management with Finance and Placement Year BSc(Hons), Business Management with Finance BSc(Hons), Business Management with Human Resource Management and Placement Year BSc(Hons), Business Management with Human Resource Management BSc(Hons), Business Management with Marketing and Placement Year BSc(Hons), Business Management with Marketing BSc(Hons), Business Management with Placement Year BSc(Hons), International Business Management BSc(Hons)

Postgraduate courses: Human Resource Management MSc (PGCert PGDip), Human Resource Management PGDip, International Management MSc (PGCert PGDip), Management (Entrepreneurship) MSc (PGCert PGDip), Management (Human Resources) MSc (PGCert PGDip), Management (Innovation) MSc (PGCert PGDip), Management (Public Services) MSc (PGCert PGDip), Management MSc (PGCert PGDip), General Management (Full-time) MBA (PGCert PGDip), International Management MBA (PGCert PGDip)

Accounting, Finance and Economics

Accounting and Finance BSc(Hons), Economics BSc(Hons), Finance and Investment BSc(Hons)

Postgraduate courses: ACCA Professional Accountancy ACCA PROF, Accounting (ACCA) MSc (PGCert PGDip), Economics and Finance MSc (PGCert PGDIP), Finance and Accounting MSc, Finance and Banking MSc, Finance and Investment MSc (PGCert PGDip), Finance and Risk Management MSc

Law

Law LLB(Hons), Law with Business LLB(Hons), Law with Criminology LLB(Hons)

Marketing

Marketing Management BSc(Hons), Marketing Management with Placement Year BSc(Hons)

Postgraduate courses: Marketing (Branding and Communications) MSc (PGCert PGDip), Marketing (Digital Marketing) MSc (PGCert PGDip), Marketing (International Marketing) MSc (PGCert PGDip), Marketing (Social Marketing) MSc (PGCert PGDip), Marketing MSc (PGCert PGDip)

Brighton and Sussex Medical School; www.bsms.ac.uk/index.aspx

Bachelor of Medicine Bachelor of Surgery (BM BS)

Postgraduate courses: Anaesthesia and Perioperative Medicine, Cardiology, Clinical Radiology, Clinical Education, Dementia Studies, Diabetes in Primary Care, Global health, Global Pharmacy, Leadership and Commissioning, Medical Education, Medical Research, Paediatrics and Child Health, Physician Associate Studies, Psychiatry, Public Health

School of Computing, Engineering and Mathematics

Aeronautical Engineering BEng(Hons), Aeronautical Engineering BEng(Hons) (with integrated foundation year), Aeronautical Engineering BSc(Hons) top-up degree, Aeronautical Engineering MEng, Automotive Engineering BEng(Hons), Automotive Engineering BEng(Hons) (with integrated foundation year), Automotive Engineering BSc(Hons) top-up degree, Automotive Engineering MEng, Business Computer Systems BSc(Hons), Business Computer Systems MComp, Business Information Systems BA(Hons), Computer Science (Games) BSc(Hons), Computer Science BSc(Hons), Computer Science MComp, Digital Games Production BSc(Hons), Digital Media BSc(Hons), Digital Media Development BSc(Hons), Electrical and Electronic Engineering BEng(Hons), Electrical and Electronic Engineering BEng(Hons) (with integrated foundation year), Electrical and Electronic Engineering MEng, Electronic and Computer Engineering BEng(Hons), Electronic and Computer Engineering BEng(Hons) (with integrated foundation year), Electronic and Computer Engineering MEng, Electronic Engineering BSc(Hons) top-up degree, European Computing/DEST Informatique BSc(Hons), Mathematics BSc(Hons), Mathematics with Business BSc(Hons), Mathematics with

Economics BSc(Hons), Mathematics with Finance BSc(Hons), Mechanical and Manufacturing Engineering BSc(Hons) top-up degree, Mechanical Engineering BEng(Hons), Mechanical Engineering BEng(Hons) (with integrated foundation year), Mechanical Engineering MEng, Software Engineering BSc(Hons), Software Engineering MComp

Postgraduate courses: Automotive Electronic Engineering MSc (PGCert PGDip), By Learning Objectives MSc (PGCert PGDip), Computer Science MSc (PGCert PGDip), Computing MSc (PGCert PGDip), Data Analytics MSc (PGCert PGDip), Digital Media Production MSc, Information Security MSc (PGDip PGCert), Information Systems MSc (PGCert PGDip), User Experience Design MSc (PGCert PGDip)

School of Education

Primary Education (3-7 years) BA(Hons) with QTS, Primary Education (5-11 years) BA(Hons) with QTS, Primary English Education BA(Hons) with QTS, Primary Mathematics Education BA(Hons) with QTS, Secondary Mathematics Education BA(Hons) with QTS, Troops to Teachers non-graduate programme

Postgraduate courses: (Secondary) Art and Design PGCE, (Secondary) Biology PGCE, (Secondary) Chemistry PGCE, (Secondary) English PGCE, (Secondary) Geography PGCE, (Secondary) Mathematics PGCE, (Secondary) Modern Foreign Languages PGCE, (Secondary) Physics PGCE, (Secondary) Physics with Mathematics PGCE, (Secondary) Religious Studies PGCE, Early Years Initial Teacher Training, Further Education and Training PGCE, Primary Education (3-7 years) PGCE (PROFGCE), Primary Education PGCE (PROFGCE), School Direct Tuition and School Direct Salaried, Subject Knowledge Enhancement for teacher training, Autism PGCert, Primary Mathematics Specialist Teacher PGCert, Specific Learning Difficulties (Dyslexia) PGCert, MA Education

School of Environment and Education

Architectural Technology BSc(Hons), Building Surveying BSc(Hons), Civil Engineering (with integrated foundation year) BEng(Hons), Civil Engineering BEng(Hons), Civil Engineering MEng, Civil Engineering with Construction Management BEng(Hons), Civil Engineering with Construction Management MEng, Civil with Environmental Engineering BEng(Hons), Civil with Environmental Engineering MEng, Construction Management BSc(Hons), Earth and Ocean Science BSc(Hons), Environmental Sciences BSc(Hons), Geography BA(Hons), Geography BSc(Hons), Geography MGeog, Geography with Archaeology BSc(Hons), Geography with Geoinformatics BSc(Hons), Geology BSc(Hons), Geology MGeol, Physical Geography and Geology BSc(Hons), Project Management for Construction BSc(Hons)

Postgraduate courses: Civil Engineering MSc (PGCert PGDip), Construction Management MSc (PGCert PGDip), Environmental Assessment and Management MSc (PGCert PGDip), Geographical Information Systems and Environmental Management MSc (PGDip), Project Management for Construction MSc (PGCert PGDip), Water and Environmental Management MSc (PGDip)

School of Health Sciences

Acute Clinical Practice (Acute Care) GradCert, Acute Clinical Practice (Burn and Reconstructive Surgery) GradCert, Acute Clinical Practice (Cancer Care) GradCert, Acute Clinical Practice (Cardiac Care) GradCert, Acute Clinical Practice (Child Health) GradCert, Acute Clinical Practice (Emergency Care) GradCert, Acute Clinical Practice (Intensive Care) GradCert, Acute Clinical Practice (Neonatal Care) GradCert, Acute Clinical Practice (Ophthalmic Care) GradCert, Acute Clinical Practice (Renal Care) GradCert, Acute Clinical Practice BSc(Hons) top-up degree, Community Specialist Practice BSc(Hons), Health and Social Care Practice foundation degree, Health Studies BSc(Hons) top-up degree, Midwifery (3 years) BSc(Hons), Nurse Practitioner BSc(Hons) top-up degree, Nursing (Adult) BSc(Hons), Nursing (Child) BSc(Hons), Nursing (Mental Health) BSc(Hons), Occupational Therapy BSc(Hons), Paramedic Practice BSc(Hons), Physiotherapy BSc(Hons), Podiatry BSc(Hons), Professional Practice BSc(Hons) top-up degree, Public Health BSc(Hons), Specialist Community Public Health Nursing BSc(Hons)

Postgraduate courses: Advanced Practice (Health) MSc (PGDip), Clinical Research MRes (PGCert PGDip), Community Specialist Practice MSc PGDip, European MSc in Occupational Therapy, Health and Education MSc (PGCert PGDip), Health and Management MSc (PGCert PGDip), Health MSc (PGCert PGDip), Health Promotion MSc (PGCert PGDip), Musculoskeletal Physiotherapy MSc (PGCert PGDip), Occupational Therapy (Pre-Registration) MSc (PGCert PGDip), Physiotherapy and Education MSc (PGCert PGDip), Physiotherapy and Management MSc (PGCert PGDip), Physiotherapy MSc (PGCert PGDip), Podiatry (Pre-Registration) MSc, Podiatry MSc (PGCert PGDip), Podiatry with

Diabetes MSc (PGCert PGDip), Rehabilitation Science (Physiotherapy) MSc (PGCert PGDip), Specialist Community Public Health Nursing MSc (PGCert PGDip), Transforming Practice for Health Professionals through Education (PGCert)

School of Humanities
Advanced French Certificate, Advanced German Cert, Advanced Spanish Cert, Critical History BA(Hons), English Language and Creative Writing BA(Hons), English Language and English Literature BA(Hons), English Language and Linguistics BA(Hons), English Language and Media BA(Hons), English Language BA(Hons), English Literature and Creative Writing BA(Hons), English Literature and Linguistics BA(Hons), English Literature BA(Hons), Fashion and Dress History BA(Hons), Globalisation: History, Politics, Culture BA(Hons), History of Art and Design BA(Hons), History, Literature and Culture BA(Hons), Humanities BA(Hons), Humanities: War, Conflict and Modernity BA(Hons), Intermediate French Cert, Intermediate German Cert, Intermediate Spanish Cert, Linguistics BA(Hons), Media and English Literature BA(Hons), Philosophy, Politics and Ethics BA(Hons), Philosophy, Politics, Art BA(Hons), Visual Culture BA(Hons)
Postgraduate courses: Creative Writing MA (PGCert PGDip), Cultural and Critical Theory MA (PGCert PGDip), Cultural History, Memory and Identity MA (PGCert PGDip), English Language MA, Globalisation: Politics, Conflict and Human Rights MA (PGCert PGDip), History of Design and Material Culture MA, Linguistics MA MRes, Making of Histories PGCert, Making of Histories PGDip, Philosophy of Language MA (PGCert PGDip), TESOL Diploma, TESOL MA, TESOL with ICT MA, War: History and Politics MA (PGCert PGDip)

School of Media
Digital Film BA(Hons), Environment and Media Studies BA(Hons), Graphic Design for Digital Media BA(Hons), Illustration for Screen Arts BA(Hons), Media Studies BA(Hons), Media, Industry and Innovation BA(Hons), Multimedia Broadcast Journalism BA(Hons), Television and Digital Media Production BA(Hons), Digital Music and Sound Arts BA(Hons), Film and Screen Studies BA(Hons), Moving Image BA(Hons), Photography BA(Hons)
Postgraduate courses: Digital Media Arts MA, Digital Media, Culture and Society MA, Photography MA

School of Pharmacy and Biomolecular Sciences
Biological Sciences BSc(Hons), Biological Sciences BSc(Hons) (with integrated foundation year), Biological Sciences MSci, Biomedical Science BSc(Hons), Biomedical Science BSc(Hons) (with integrated foundation year), Biomedical Science MSci, Chemistry BSc(Hons), Chemistry BSc(Hons) (with integrated foundation year), Chemistry MChem, Ecology BSc(Hons), Ecology BSc(Hons) (with integrated foundation year), Ecology MSci, Pharmaceutical and Chemical Sciences BSc(Hons), Pharmaceutical and Chemical Sciences BSc(Hons) (with foundation year), Pharmacy MPharm, Pharmacy MPharm (with integrated foundation year)
Postgraduate courses: Biomedical Sciences MSc (PGCert PGDip), Bioscience MRes, Blood Sciences MSc (PGCert PGDip), Cellular Sciences MSc (PGCert PGDip), Chemistry MRes (PGCert PGDip), Clinical Pharmacy MSc, Ecology MRes (PGCert PGDip), General Pharmacy Practice PGDip (PGCert), Industrial Pharmaceutical Sciences MSc (PGCert PGDip), Infection Sciences MSc (PGCert PGDip), Non-Medical Prescribing for Pharmacists, Pharmaceutical and Biomedical Sciences MRes (PGCert PGDip), Pharmacology MSc (PGCert PGDip), Pharmacy (OSPAP) MSc (PGDip), Pharmacy (OSPAP) PGDip

School of Sport and Service Management
Euro BA in International Hospitality Management, International Event Management BA(Hons), International Event Management BA(Hons) top-up degree, International Hospitality Management BA(Hons), International Hospitality Management BA(Hons) top-up degree, International Tourism Management BA(Hons), International Tourism Management BA(Hons) top-up degree, Journalism BA(Hons), Physical Education BA(Hons), Physical Education BA(Hons) with QTS, Retail Management BA(Hons), Retail Management BA(Hons) top-up degree, Retail Marketing BA(Hons), Retail Marketing BA(Hons) top-up degree, Sport and Exercise Science BSc(Hons), Sport and Fitness BSc(Hons) top-up degree, Sport Business Management BSc(Hons), Sport Coaching and Development BA(Hons) top-up degree, Sport Coaching BSc(Hons), Sport Journalism BA(Hons), Sport Studies BA(Hons)
Postgraduate courses: (Secondary) Dance PGCE, (Secondary) Physical Education PGCE, Applied Exercise Physiology MSc (PGCert PGDip), Applied Sport Physiology MSc (PGCert PGDip), International Event Management MSc (PGCert PGDip),

International Hospitality Management MSc (PGCert PGDip), Sport and International Development MA, Sport Business Management MSc, Strength and

Conditioning MSc, Tourism and International Development MSc (PGCert PGDip)

MPhil/PhD study available in all departments

UNIVERSITY OF BRISTOL
www.bris.ac.uk

Faculty of Arts; www.bristol.ac.uk/arts

School of Arts; www.bristol.ac.uk/school-of-arts

Department of Anthropology and Archaeology
BA Anthropology, MArts Anthropology with Innovation, BA Archaeology and Anthropology

Department of Film and Television
BA Film and Television, BA Film and English, BA Film and French, BA Film and German, BA Film and Italian, BA Film and Portuguese, BA Film and Spanish, BA Theatre and Film, MArts Film and Television with Innovation
Postgraduate courses: MA in Film and Television, MA in Composition of Music for Film and Television

Department of Music
BA Music, BA Music and French, BA Music and German, BA Music and Italian, MArts Music with Innovation
Postgraduate courses: MA in Music, MA in Composition of Music for Film and Television

Department of Philosophy
BA Philosophy, BSc Philosophy and Economics, BA Philosophy and French, BA Philosophy and German, BA Philosophy and Italian, BSc Philosophy and Politics, BA Philosophy and Portuguese, BA Philosophy and Russian, BA Philosophy and Spanish, BA Philosophy and Theology

Department of Theatre
BA Theatre and Performance Studies, BA Theatre and English, BA Theatre and Film, BA Theatre and French, BA Theatre and German, BA Theatre and Italian, BA Theatre and Spanish, MArts Theatre with Innovation

School of Humanities; www.bristol.ac.uk/humanities

Department of Classics and Ancient History
BA Ancient History, BA Classical Studies, BA Classics

Department of English
BA English, BA English Literature and Community Engagement, BA English and Classical Studies, BA English and Philosophy, BA Film and English, BA Theatre and English
Postgraduate course: MA in English Literature

Department of History
BA History, MArts History with Innovation
Postgraduate course: MA in History

Department of History of Art
BA History of Art, BA History of Art and French, BA History of Art and German, BA History of Art and Italian, BA History of Art and Portuguese, BA History of Art and Russian, BA History of Art and Spanish
Postgraduate course: MA in History of Art

Department of Religion and Theology
BA Religion and Theology, MArts Religion and Theology with Study Abroad
Postgraduate course: MA in Religion

School of Modern Languages; www.bristol.ac.uk/sml

Department of French
BA French, BA Modern Languages, BA French and German, BA French and Italian, BA French and Portuguese, BA French and Russian, BA French and Spanish
Postgraduate courses: MA Comparative Literatures and Cultures, PG Dip/MA Translation

Department of German
BA German, BA Modern Languages, BA German and Italian, BA German and Portuguese, BA German and Russian, BA German and Spanish
Postgraduate courses: MA Comparative Literatures and Cultures, PG Dip/MA Translation

Department of Hispanic, Portuguese and Latin American Studies
BA Hispanic Studies, BA Modern Languages, BA Spanish, BA Spanish and Portuguese, BA Spanish and Russian
Postgraduate courses: MA Comparative Literatures and Cultures, PG Dip/MA Translation

Department of Italian
BA Italian, BA Modern Languages
Postgraduate courses: BA Italian and Portuguese, BA Italian and Russian, BA Italian and Spanish

Postgraduate courses: MA Comparative Literatures and Cultures, PG Dip/MA Translation

Department of Russian

BA Modern Languages, BA Russian, BA Czech and French, BA Czech and German, BA Czech and Italian, BA Czech and Portuguese, BA Czech and Russian, BA Czech and Spanish, BA Spanish and Russian

Postgraduate courses: MA Comparative Literatures and Cultures, PG Dip/MA Translation

Faculty of Biomedical Sciences; www.bristol.ac.uk/biomedical-sciences

School of Biochemistry; www.bristol.ac.uk/biochemistry

BSc Biochemistry, BSc Biochemistry with Medical Biochemistry, BSc Biochemistry with Molecular Biology and Biotechnology, MSci Biochemistry, MSci Biochemistry with Medical Biochemistry, MSci Biochemistry with Molecular Biology and Biotechnology

Postgraduate courses: MSc in Biomedical Sciences Research, MSc in Biophysics and Molecular Life Sciences

School of Cellular and Molecular Medicine; www.bristol.ac.uk/cellmolmed

BSc Cancer Biology and Immunology, BSc Cellular and Molecular Medicine, BSc Medical Microbiology, BSc Virology and immunology, Intercalated BSc in Pathology and Microbiology

Postgraduate courses: MSc in Transfusion and Transplantation Sciences, MSc in Biomedical Sciences Research

School of Physiology, Pharmacology and Neuroscience; www.bristol.ac.uk/phys-pharm-neuro

BSc Neuroscience, MSci Neuroscience with Study in Industry, BSc Pharmacology, MSci Pharmacology with Study in Industry, BSc Physiological Science, MSci Physiological Science with Study in Industry

Postgraduate courses: MSc in Biomedical Sciences Research, MRes Systems Neuroscience

Elizabeth Blackwell Institute for Health Research; www.bristol.ac.uk/blackwell

Faculty of Engineering; www.bristol.ac.uk/engineering

School of Computer Science, Electrical and Electronic Engineering, and Engineering Mathematics; www.bristol.ac.uk/engineering/about/school-sceem

Department of Computer Science

BSc Computer Science, MEng Computer Science, MEng Computer Science with Innovation, MEng Computer Science and Electronics, BSc Mathematics and Computer Science, MEng Mathematics and Computer Science

Postgraduate courses: MSc Advanced Computing, MSc Advanced Computing – Creative Technology, MSc Advanced Computing – Machine Learning, Data Mining and High-Performance Computing, MSc Computer Science

Department of Electrical and Electronic Engineering

BEng Electrical and Electronic Engineering, MEng Electrical and Electronic Engineering, MEng Electrical and Electronic Engineering with Innovation, BEng Mechanical and Electrical Engineering, MEng Mechanical and Electrical Engineering, MEng Computer Science and Electronics

Postgraduate courses: MSc in Communication Networks and Signal Processing, MSc in Image & Video Communications and Signal Processing, MSc in Optical Communications and Signal Processing, MSc in Wireless Communication Systems and Signal Processing, MSc in Advanced Microelectronics and Systems Engineering, MSc Biomedical Engineering

Department of Engineering Mathematics

BEng Engineering Mathematics, MEng Engineering Mathematics

Postgraduate courses: MSc in Engineering Mathematics, MSc in Robotics

School of Civil, Aerospace and Mechanical Engineering; www.bristol.ac.uk/engineering/about/school-came

Department of Aerospace Engineering

BEng Aerospace Engineering, MEng Aerospace Engineering

Postgraduate course: MSc Advanced Composites

Department of Civil Engineering

BEng Civil Engineering, MEng Civil Engineering

Postgraduate courses: MSc in Earthquake Engineering and Infrastructure Resilience, MSc Water and Environmental Management

Department of Mechanical Engineering
BEng in Mechanical Engineering, MEng in Mechanical Engineering, BEng Mechanical and Electrical Engineering, MEng Mechanical and Electrical Engineering
Postgraduate courses: MSc Nuclear Science and Engineering, MSc Advanced Composites, MSc Robotics

Faculty of Health Sciences; www.bristol.ac.uk/health-sciences

Bristol Dental School; www.bristol.ac.uk/dental
BDS Gateway to Dentistry, BDS Dentistry
Postgraduate courses: DDS Orthodontics Doctorate in Dental Surgery, MSc Dental Implantology, MSc Oral Medicine, Postgraduate Certificate Clinical Conscious Sedation and Anxiety Management, Postgraduate Certificate Clinical Oral Surgery, MSc/PGDip/PGCert Postgraduate Dental Studies

Bristol Medical School; www.bristol.ac.uk/medical-school
MB ChB Gateway to Medicine, MB ChB Medicine
Postgraduate courses: MRes Health Sciences Research, MSc Molecular Neuroscience, MSc Perfusion Science, MSc Reproduction and Development, MSc Stem Cells and Regeneration, MSc Translational Cardiovascular Medicine

Bristol Veterinary School; www.bristol.ac.uk/vetscience
BVSc Gateway to Veterinary Science, BVSc Veterinary Science, BSc Veterinary Nursing and Bioveterinary Science, BSc Veterinary Nursing and Companion Animal Behaviour
Postgraduate course: MSc Global Wildlife Health and Conservation

Centre for Health Sciences Education; www.bristol.ac.uk/health-sciences/chse
BSc Applied Anatomy
Postgraduate course: PGDip/PGCert/MSc Teaching and Learning for Health Professionals

Faculty of Science; www.bristol.ac.uk/science

School of Biological Sciences
BSc Biology, BSc Zoology, MSci Biology, MSci Zoology, MSci Palaeontology and Evolution
Postgraduate course: MSc Palaeobiology

School of Chemistry
BSc Chemistry, MSci Chemistry, BSc Chemical Physics, MSci Chemical Physics

School of Earth Sciences
BSc Environmental Geoscience, MSci Environmental Geoscience, BSc Geology, MSci Geology, BSc Geophysics, MSci Geophysics, BSc Palaeontology and Evolution, MSci Palaeontology and Evolution
Postgraduate courses: MSc Palaeobiology, MSc Volcanology

School of Experimental Psychology
BSc Psychology, MSci Psychology, MSci Psychology with Innovation
Postgraduate courses: MSc Experimental Psychology, MSc Clinical Neuropsychology, MSc in Applied Neuropsychology, Diploma in Applied Neuropsychology

School of Geographical Sciences
BSc Geography, MSci Geography with Innovation, BSc Geography with Quantitative Research Methods
Postgraduate courses: MSc in Climate Change Science and Policy, MSc in Environmental Policy and Management, MSc in Human Geography: Society and Space

School of Mathematics
Mathematics, BSc, Mathematics, MSci, Mathematics with Statistics, BSc, Mathematics with Statistics, MSci, Mathematics and Computer Science, BSc, Mathematics and Computer Science, MEng, Economics and Mathematics, BSc, Mathematics and Philosophy, BSc, Mathematics and Philosophy, MSci, Mathematics and Physics, BSc, Mathematics and Physics, MSci
Postgraduate course: MSc in Mathematical Sciences

School of Physics
MSci Physics, BSc Physics, MSci Physics with Astrophysics, BSc Physics with Astrophysics, MSci Physics with Innovation, MSci Physics and Philosophy, BSc Physics and Philosophy, MSci Theoretical Physics, MSci Chemical Physics, BSc Chemical Physics
Postgraduate courses: MSc Nanoscience and Functional Nanomaterials, MSc Nuclear Science and Engineering

Social Sciences and Law; *www.bristol.ac.uk/fssl*

School of Education; www.bristol.ac.uk/education

Education Studies, BSc, Psychology in Education, BSc

Postgraduate courses: MSc Education, MSc Educational Leadership, MSc Education Management, MSc Educational Research, MSc Psychology of Education, MSc Teaching English to Speakers of Other Languages

School for Policy Studies; www.bristol.ac.uk/sps

Childhood Studies

Childhood Studies, BSc, Childhood Studies with Management, BSc, Childhood Studies with Quantitative Research Methods, BSc, Childhood Studies with Quantitative Research Methods, MSci

Social Policy

Social Policy, BSc, Social Policy with Management, BSc, Social Policy and Politics Joint Honours, BSc, Social Policy and Sociology Joint Honours, BSc, Social Policy with Quantitative Research Methods, BSc, Social Policy with Criminology, BSc, Social Policy with Quantitative Research Methods, MSci

Criminology

Criminology, BSc

Postgraduate courses

MSc Disability Studies: Inclusive Theory and Research, MSc Nutrition, Physical Activity and Public Health, MSc Public Policy, MSc Policy Research, MSc Social Work Research, MRes Health and Wellbeing, MSc Social Work, MSc Advanced Social Work with Children and Families

School of Economics, Finance and Management; www.bristol.ac.uk/efm

BSc Accounting and Finance, BSc Accounting and Management, BSc Economics and Accounting, BSc Economics, BSc Economics and Econometrics, BSc Economics and Finance, BSc Economics and Mathematics, BSc Economics and Politics, BSc Management, BSc International Business Management

Postgraduate courses: MSc Accounting and Finance, MSc Economics, MSc Economics and Finance, MSc Finance and Investment, MSc Accounting, Finance and Management, MSc Economics, Accounting and Finance, MSc Economics, Finance and Management, MSc Management, MSc Management, MSc Management, MSc Management, MSc Social Science Research Methods, MSc Strategy, Change and Leadership, Graduate Diploma in Economics

School of Sociology, Politics and International Studies; www.bristol.ac.uk/spais

Politics and International Relations, BSc, Politics with Quantitative Research Methods, BSc, Politics with Quantitative Research Methods, MSci, Politics and Sociology, BSc, Economics and Politics, BSc, Philosophy and Politics, BSc, Social Policy and Politics, BSc, Politics and French, BA, Politics and German, BA, Politics and Italian, BA, Politics and Portuguese, BA, Politics and Russian, BA, Politics and Spanish, BA, Sociology, BSc, Sociology with Quantitative Research Methods, BSc, Sociology with Quantitative Research Methods, MSci, Social Policy and Sociology, BSc, Sociology and Philosophy, BSc, Theology and Sociology, BA

Postgraduate courses: MSc European and Global Governance, MSc Gender and International Relations, MSc International Relations, MSc International Security, LLM International Law and International Relations, MSc Social Science Research Methods, MSc Development and Security, MSc East Asian Development and the Global Economy, MSc International Development, MSc Contemporary Identities, MSc Ethnicity and Multiculturalism, MSc Social and Cultural Theory, MSc Social Science Research Methods, MSc Sociology

University of Bristol Law School

LLB Law, LLB Law and French, LLB Law and German, LLB Law and Spanish

LLM Commercial Law, LLM European Legal Studies, LLM General Legal Studies, LLM Health, Law and Society, LLM Human Rights Law, LLM International Commercial Law, LLM International Law, LLM International Law and International Relations, LLM Labour Law and Corporate Governance, LLM Law and Globalisation, LLM Public Law, MA Law, MSc Socio-Legal Studies, MRes Sustainable Futures

UNIVERSITY OF THE WEST OF ENGLAND, BRISTOL
www.uwe.ac.uk

Arts, Creative Industries and Education; www.uwe.ac.uk/cahe

Arts and Cultural Industries; www.uwe.ac.uk/cahe/artsandculturalindustries.aspx

BA(Hons) Creative and Professional Writing, BA(Hons) English, BA(Hons) English (with Foundation Year), BA(Hons) English and English Language, BA(Hons) English and History, BA(Hons) English Language and Linguistics, BA(Hons) English with Writing, BA(Hons) Film Studies, BA(Hons) Film Studies and Literature, BA(Hons) History, BA(Hons) History with Heritage, BA(Hons) Liberal Arts, BA(Hons) Media and Cultural Production, BA(Hons) Media Culture and Communication

Postgraduate courses: MA Contemporary Film Culture, MA Creative Producing, MRes Culture

Art and Design; www.uwe.ac.uk/cahe/artanddesign.aspx

BA(Hons) Creative Media Design, BA(Hons) Drawing and Print, BA(Hons) Fashion Communication, BA(Hons) Fashion Textiles, BA(Hons) Fine Art, BA(Hons) Graphic Design, BA(Hons) Illustration, BA(Hons) Interior Design

Postgraduate courses: MRes Culture, MA/MFA Curating, MA/PGDip/PGCert Design, MA/PGDip/PGCert Fine Art, MA/PGDip/PGCert Graphic Arts, MA/PGDip/PGCert Multi-Disciplinary Printmaking

Education and Childhood; www.uwe.ac.uk/cahe/edu.aspx

BA(Hons) Early Childhood, BA(Hons) Education in Professional Practice, BSc(Hons) Mathematics with Qualified Teacher Status, BA(Hons) Primary Education (ITE)

Postgraduate courses: MA Childhood and Culture, MA Education, ProfDoc Education, MA Education (Early Years), PGCE Primary Early Years Initial Teacher Education (3-7), PGCE Primary Initial Teacher Education (5-11), PGCE Secondary Initial Teacher Education Art and Design, PGCE Secondary Initial Teacher Education Biology with Science, PGCE Secondary Initial Teacher Education Business, PGCE Secondary Initial Teacher Education Chemistry with Science, PGCE Secondary Initial Teacher Education Computer Science, PGCE Secondary Initial Teacher Education English, PGCE Secondary Initial Teacher Education Geography, PGCE Secondary Initial Teacher Education History, PGCE Secondary Initial Teacher Education Mathematics, PGCE Secondary Initial Teacher Education Modern Languages, PGCE Secondary Initial Teacher Education Physics with Science

Film and Journalism; www.uwe.ac.uk/cahe/filmandjournalism.aspx

Filmmaking, Animation and Photography

BA(Hons) Animation, BA(Hons) Filmmaking, FdSc Games and Animation Production, BA(Hons) Photography

Postgraduate courses: MSc/PGDip/PGCert Animation, MA Cinematography, MA Contemporary Film Culture, MRes Culture, MA/PGDip/PGCert Documentary Production, MA/PGDip/PGCert Photography, MA/PGDip/PGCert Wildlife Filmmaking

Journalism, Media and Public Relations

BA(Hons) Journalism, BA(Hons) Journalism and Public Relations, BA(Hons) Media and Journalism

Postgraduate courses: MRes Culture, MA Documentary Production, MA Journalism, MA Radio Documentary

Drama and Acting

BA(Hons) Drama, BA(Hons) Drama and Acting

Business and Law; www.uwe.ac.uk/bl/

Bristol Business School; www.uwe.ac.uk/bl/bbs.aspx

Accounting, Economics and Finance

BA(Hons) Accounting and Finance, BA(Hons) Banking and Finance, BA(Hons) Business Management with Accounting and Finance, BA(Hons) Business Management and Economics, BA(Hons) Economics, BSc(Hons) Economics

Postgraduate courses: MSc/PGDip/PGCert Accounting and Financial Management, MSc Accounting and Financial Management (Fast Track route for qualified professionals), MSc/PGDip/PGCert Finance, MSc/PGDip/PGCert Global Political Economy

Business and Management

BA(Hons) Business (Team Entrepreneurship), BA(Hons) Business and Events Management, BA(Hons) Business and Human Resource Management, BA(Hons) Business and Law, BA(Hons) Business and Management, MBus Business Management, BA(Hons) Business Management and Economics,

BA(Hons) Business Management and Leadership, BA(Hons) Business Management Practice, BA(Hons) Business Management with Accounting and Finance, BA(Hons) Business Management with Law, BA(Hons) Business Management with Marketing, FdA Business with Management, BA(Hons) International Business, BA(Hons) International Business Management, BA(Hons)Marketing, BA(Hons) Marketing Communication Management, BA(Hons) Sports Business and Entrepreneurship

Postgraduate courses: MSc/PGDip/PGCert Business Management, PGCert Enterprise, MSc/PGDip/PGCert Events Management, MSc/PGDip/PGCert Human Resource Management, MSc/PGDip/PGCert Innovation and Applied Entrepreneurship, MSc/PGDip/PGCert International Management, PGCert Leadership and Management, PGCert Leadership and Management (Coaching and Mentoring), MSc/PGDip/PGCert Marketing, MSc/PGDip/PGCert Marketing Communications, MBA Master of Business Administration (MBA) (Full-time), PGCert Project Management (Professional Development)

Bristol Law School; www.uwe.ac.uk/bl/bls.aspx

BA(Hons) Business and Law, BA(Hons) Business Management with Law, LLB(Hons) Commercial Law, BA(Hons)Criminology and Law, LLB(Hons) European and International Law, LLB(Hons) Law, LLB(Hons) Law with Business

Postgraduate courses: LLM Advanced Legal Practice (LPC LLM), LLM Bar Professional Training Studies/PGDip BPTC, LLM/PGDip/PGCert Commercial Law, LLM/PGDip/PGCert Environmental Law and Sustainable Development, LLM/PGDip/PGCert International Banking and Finance Law, LLM/PGDip/PGCert International Law, LLM/PGDip/PGCert International Trade and Economic Law, GDL Law (full-time)

Environment and Technology; www.uwe.ac.uk/et/

Architecture and the Built Environment; www.uwe.ac.uk/et/abe.aspx

Architecture

BSc(Hons) Architectural Technology and Design, BSc(Hons) Architecture, BEng(Hons) Architecture and Environmental Engineering, BA(Hons) Architecture and Planning, BA(Hons) Interior Architecture

Postgraduate courses: MArch Architecture, MRes Architecture, Design and the Built Environment, MSc Facade Engineering, MA Place: Spaces, Environments, Design, PGCert Professional Practice and Management in Architecture

Built Environment

BEng(Hons) Building Services Engineering, BSc(Hons) Building Surveying, BSc(Hons) Construction Project Management, BA(Hons)Property Development and Planning, BSc(Hons) Quantity Surveying and Commercial Management, BSc(Hons) Real Estate

Postgraduate courses: MSc/PGDip/PGCert Building Information Modelling (BIM) in Design Construction and Operations, MSc Building Services Engineering, MSc/Graduate Diploma Building Surveying, MSc/PGDip/PGCert Construction Project Management, MSc Facade Engineering, MSc International Construction Law, PGDip International Construction Law, Graduate Diploma/MSc Quantity Surveying, MSc/PGDip/PGCert Real Estate Finance and Investment, MSc Real Estate Finance and Investment (Distance Learning), MSc/PGDip/PGCert Real Estate Management

Computer Science and Creative Technologies; www.uwe.ac.uk/et/csct.aspx

Computing

BSc(Hons) Applied Computing, FdSc Applied Computing, BSc(Hons) Computer Science, BEng(Hons) Computing for Embedded Systems, BSc(Hons) Computing, BSc(Hons) Forensic Computing and Security, BSc(Hons) Information Technology, BSc(Hons) Information Technology Management for Business (ITMB), BSc(Hons) Software Engineering for Business

Postgraduate courses: MRes Data Science, MSc/PGDip/PGCert Information Management, MSc/PGDip/PGCert Information Technology, MSc/PGDip/PGCert Software Engineering

Creative Technologies

BSc(Hons) Audio and Music Technology, BSc(Hons) Broadcast Audio and Music Technology, BSc(Hons) Creative Music Technology, BSc(Hons) Digital Media, BSc(Hons) Games Technology, BA(Hons) Product Design, BSc(Hons) Product Design Technology

Postgraduate courses: MSc Commercial Games Development, MSc Creative Technology, MSc Music Technology

Engineering Design and Mathematics; www.uwe.ac.uk/et/edm.aspx

Engineering

BEng(Hons)Aerospace Engineering, MEng Aerospace Engineering, FdSc Aerospace Engineering Manufacturing, BEng(Hons) Aerospace Engineering with Pilot Studies, MEng Aerospace Engineering with Pilot Studies, BEng(Hons) Automotive Engineering, MEng Automotive Engineering, BEng(Hons) Civil and Environmental Engineering, BEng(Hons) Electronic and Computer Engineering, FdSc Electronic and Computer Engineering, BEng(Hons) Electronic Engineering, MEng Electronic Engineering, BSc(Hons) Engineering, BEng(Hons) Mechanical Engineering, FdSc Mechanical Engineering, MEng Mechanical Engineering, FdSc Mechatronics, BEng(Hons) Robotics

Postgraduate courses: MSc/PGDip/PGCert Aerospace, MSc/PGDip/PGCert Automation and Computer Vision, MSc/PGDip/PGCert Embedded Systems and Wireless Networks, MRes Engineering, MSc Engineering Business Management, MSc/PGDip/PGCert Engineering Management, MSc/PGDip/PGCert Mechanical Engineering, MSc/PGDip/PGCert Professional Engineering, MSc/PGDip/PGCert Robotics, MSc Transport Engineering and Planning

Mathematics
BSc(Hons) Mathematics, MMath Mathematics, BSc(Hons) Mathematics and Statistics, BSc(Hons) Mathematics with Qualified Teacher Status

Geography and Environmental Management
BEng(Hons) Civil and Environmental Engineering, BSc(Hons) Environmental Resource Management, BA(Hons) Geography, BSc(Hons) Geography, BA(Hons) Geography and Planning, BA(Hons) Geography and Tourism, BSc(Hons) Geology, BA(Hons) Uniformed and Public Services, FdA Uniformed and Public Services, BSc(Hons) Urban Planning

Postgraduate courses: MRes Data Science, MSc/PGDip Environmental Consultancy, MSc/PGDip/PGCert Environmental Management, MRes Geography and Environmental Management, MSc Planning Major Projects, MSc/PGDip/PGCert Sustainable Development in Practice, MSc Transport Engineering and Planning, MSc/PGDip/PGCert Transport Planning, MSc/PGDip/PGCert Urban and Rural Planning, MSc/PGDip/PGCert Urban Planning

Health and Applied Sciences; www.uwe.ac.uk/hls/

Allied Health Professions; www.uwe.ac.uk/hls/ahp.aspx
BSc(Hons) Applied Paramedic Science, BSc(Hons) Diagnostic Imaging, BSc(Hons) Occupational Therapy, BSc(Hons) Paramedic Science, DipHE Paramedic Science, BSc(Hons) Physiotherapy, BSc(Hons) Radiotherapy and Oncology, BSc(Hons) Sport Rehabilitation

Postgraduate courses: MSc/PGDip/PGCert Medical Ultrasound, MSc/PGDip/PGCert Nuclear Medicine, MSc Physician Associate Studies, MSc Radiotherapy and Oncology, MSc Rehabilitation

Applied Sciences; www.uwe.ac.uk/hls/bbas.aspx
BSc(Hons) Biological Sciences, MSci Biological Sciences, BSc(Hons) Biomedical Science, MSci Biomedical Science, BSc(Hons) Environmental Science, MSci Environmental Science, BSc(Hons) Forensic Science, MSci Forensic Science, FdSc Healthcare Science, BSc(Hons) Healthcare Science (Clinical Engineering), BSc(Hons) Healthcare Science (Life Science), BSc(Hons) Healthcare Science (Physiological Sciences), FdSc Integrated Wildlife Conservation, CertHE Premedical Sciences, BSc(Hons) Wildlife Ecology and Conservation Science, MSci Wildlife Ecology and Conservation Science

Postgraduate courses: MSc/PGDip/PGCert Advanced Forensic Analysis, MSc/PGDip/PGCert Advanced Wildlife Conservation in Practice, MRes Applied Sciences, MSc/PGDip Biomedical Science, ProfDoc Biomedical Science, PGCert Practical Science Communication, MSc/PGDip Science Communication

Health and Social Sciences; www.uwe.ac.uk/hls/hss.aspx
Social Sciences
BA(Hons) Criminology, BA(Hons) Criminology and Law, BA(Hons) Criminology and Sociology, BSc(Hons) Criminology with Psychology, MSci Environmental Health and Practice, BA(Hons) Philosophy, BA(Hons) Politics and International Relations, BSc(Hons) Psychology, BSc(Hons) Psychology with Criminology, BSc(Hons) Psychology with Sociology, BSc(Hons) Public and Environmental Health, FdSc Public and Environmental Health, BSc(Hons) Public Health (Specialist Community Public Health Nursing), BA(Hons) Sociology, BSc(Hons) Sociology with Psychology, FdA Therapeutic Work with Children and Young People

Postgraduate courses: ProfDoc Counselling Psychology, MSc/PGDip Environmental Health, MSc/PGDip/PGCert Environmental Health (Distance Learning), MSc Environmental Health Professional Practice, MSc/PGDip/PGCert Health Psychology, ProfDoc Health Psychology, MA Music Therapy, MSc/PGDip/PGCert Occupational Psychology, MSc/PGDip/PGCert Public Health, MRes Social Sciences, MSc/PGDip/PGCert Sport and Exercise Psychology

Social Work

BSc(Hons) Social Work

Postgraduate courses: MSc/PGDip/PGCert Professional Development (Social Work), PGCert Approved Mental Health Practice

Nursing and Midwifery; www.uwe.ac.uk/hls/nm.aspx

FdSc Health and Social Care Practice, BSc(Hons) Midwifery, BSc(Hons)/BSc Nursing (Adult Nursing), BSc(Hons) Nursing (Children), BSc(Hons) Nursing (Learning Disabilities), BSc(Hons) Nursing (Mental Health), BSc(Hons) Public Health (Specialist Community Public Health Nursing), BSc(Hons) Specialist Practice

Postgraduate courses: MSc/PGDip/PGCert Advanced Practice, PGDip Public Health (Specialist Community Public Health Nursing), MSc/PGDip/PGCert Specialist Practice

BRUNEL UNIVERSITY
www.brunel.ac.uk

College of Engineering, Design and Physical Sciences; www.brunel.ac.uk/cedps

Computer Science; www.brunel.ac.uk/cedps/computer-science

Business Computing (eBusiness) BSc, Business Computing (Human Computer Interaction) BSc, Business Computing (Social Media) BSc, Business Computing BSc, Computer Science (Artificial Intelligence) BSc, Computer Science (Digital Media and Games) BSc, Computer Science (Network Computing) BSc, Computer Science (Software Engineering) BSc, Computer Science BSc

Postgraduate courses: Data Science and Analytics MSc, Digital Service Design MSc, Information Systems Management MSc

Design; www.brunel.ac.uk/design

Industrial Design and Technology BA, Product Design BSc, Product Design Engineering BSc

Postgraduate courses: Design and Branding Strategy MA, Design Strategy and Innovation MA, Integrated Product Design MSc

Electronic and Computer Engineering; www.brunel.ac.uk/cedps/electronic-computer-engineering

Electrical Engineering with Renewable Energy Systems MEng, Electronic and Communications Engineering BEng/MEng, Electronic and Computer Engineering BEng/MEng, Electronic and Electrical Engineering BEng/MEng, Computer Systems Engineering BEng/MEng

Postgraduate courses: Advanced Electronic and Electrical Engineering MSc, Distributed Computing Systems Engineering MSc, Wireless Communication Systems MSc, Sustainable Electrical Power MSc, Computer Communication Networks MSc

Mathematics; www.brunel.ac.uk/cedps/mathematics

Mathematics BSc, Financial Mathematics BSc, Mathematics and Statistics with Management BSc, Mathematics with Computer Science BSc, Mathematics MMath, Financial Mathematics MMath

Postgraduate courses: Financial Mathematics MSc, Statistics with Data Analytics MSc

Mechanical, Aerospace and Civil Engineering; www.brunel.ac.uk/cedps/mechanical-aerospace-civil-engineering

Aerospace Engineering BEng, Aerospace Engineering MEng, Automotive Engineering BEng, Automotive Engineering MEng, Aviation Engineering BEng, Aviation Engineering MEng, Aviation Engineering with Pilot Studies BEng, Aviation Engineering with Pilot Studies MEng, Civil Engineering BEng, Civil Engineering MEng, Civil Engineering with Sustainability BEng, Civil Engineering with Sustainability MEng, Mechanical and Energy Engineering BEng, Mechanical and Energy Engineering MEng, Mechanical Engineering BEng, Mechanical Engineering MEng, Mechanical Engineering with Aeronautics BEng, Mechanical Engineering with Aeronautics MEng, Mechanical Engineering with Automotive Design BEng, Mechanical Engineering with Automotive Design MEng, Mechanical Engineering with Building Services BEng, Mechanical Engineering with Building Services MEng, Motorsport Engineering BEng, Motorsport Engineering MEng

Postgraduate courses: Advanced Engineering Design MSc, Advanced Manufacturing Systems MSc, Advanced Mechanical Engineering MSc, Aerospace Engineering MSc, Automotive and Motorsport

Engineering MSc, Biomedical Genetics and Tissue Engineering MSc, Biomedical, Biomechanics and Bioelectronics Engineering MSc, Building Services Engineering Management MSc, Building Services Engineering MSc, Building Services Engineering with Sustainable Energy MSc, Engineering Management MSc, Oil and Gas Engineering PGCert/PGDipl/MSc, Project and Infrastructure Management MSc, Renewable Energy Engineering MSc, Structural Engineering MSc, Structural Integrity MSc, Sustainable Energy – Technologies and Management MSc, Water Engineering MSc

College of Business, Arts and Social Sciences; www.brunel.ac.uk/cbass

Brunel Business School

Business and Management (Accounting) BSc, Business and Management (Marketing) BSc, Business and Management BSc, International Business BSc
Postgraduate courses: MBA Business Administration, Accounting and Business Management MSc, Applied Corporate Brand Management MSc, Business Intelligence and Social Media MSc, Global Supply Chain Management MSc, Human Resource Management MSc, Human Resources and Employment Relations MSc, International Business MSc, Management MSc, Marketing MS

Arts and Humanities; www.brunel.ac.uk/cbass/arts-humanities

Anthropology BSc, Anthropology and Sociology BSc, English and Film and TV Studies BA, English BA, English with Creative Writing BA, Film and Television Studies BA, Journalism BA, Theatre and Creative Writing BA, Theatre and English BA, Theatre and Film and Television Studies BA, Theatre BA, Creative Writing BA, English with Creative Writing BA, Creative Writing and Games Design BA
Postgraduate courses: Anthropology of Childhood, Youth and Education MSc, Anthropology of International Development and Humanitarian Assistance MSc, Medical Anthropology MSc, Psychological and Psychiatric Anthropology MSc, Social Anthropology MRes, Children, Youth and International Development MA, International Journalism MA, MA Creative Writing: The Novel, MA Creative Writing

Economics and Finance; www.brunel.ac.uk/economics-and-finance

Economics and Accounting BSc, Economics and Business Finance BSc, Economics and Management BSc, Economics BSc, Finance and Accounting BSc

Postgraduate courses: Finance and Investment MSc, Finance and Accounting MSc, Business Finance MSc, Banking and Finance MSc

Education; www.brunel.ac.uk/cbass/education

Education BA
Postgraduate courses: Education MA, PGCE in Primary Education, PGCE in Secondary Education

Politics, History and the Brunel Law School; www.brunel.ac.uk/cbass/politics-history-law

History BA, International Politics BSc, Law LLB, Law with Criminal Justice LLB, Law with International Arbitration and Commercial Law LLB, Politics and Economics BSc, Politics and History BSc, Politics and Sociology BSc, Politics BSc
Postgraduate courses: CPE/Graduate Diploma in Law, Intellectual Property Law Postgraduate Certificate, Intelligence Analysis PG Cert (Distance Learning), Intelligence and Security Studies (Distance Learning) MA, Intelligence and Security Studies MA, International Commercial Law LLM, International Financial Regulation and Corporate Law LLM, International Human Rights Law LLM, International Intellectual Property Law LLM, International Relations MA, Master of Laws (LLM Law), Military History MA, Public Affairs and Lobbying MSc

Social Sciences, Media and Communications; www.brunel.ac.uk/subjects

Digital Design BSc, Visual Effects and Motion Graphics BSc, Sociology (Media) BSc, Sociology BSc
Postgraduate courses: Media and Communications MSc, Social Work MA, Digital Design and Branding MSc, Advanced Multimedia Design and 3D Technologies MSc

College of Health and Life Sciences; www.brunel.ac.uk/chls

Clinical Sciences; www.brunel.ac.uk/chls/clinical-sciences

Occupational Therapy BSc, Specialist Community Public Health Nursing BSc
Postgraduate courses: Occupational Therapy (Pre-Registration) MSc, Occupational Therapy (Post-Registration) MSc, Specialist Community Public Health Nursing PGDip and MSc, Physiotherapy BSc (full-time programme), Physiotherapy (Pre-Registration) MSc, Neurorehabilitation MSc, Physician

Associate MSc, Public Health and Health Promotion MSc

Life Sciences; www.brunel.ac.uk/chls/life-sciences

Biomedical Sciences (Biochemistry) BSc, Biomedical Sciences (Genetics) BSc, Biomedical Sciences (Human Health) BSc, Biomedical Sciences (Immunology) BSc, Biomedical Sciences BSc, Environmental Sciences BSc, Environmental Sciences MSci, Life Sciences BSc, Physical Education and Youth Sport BSc, Psychology BSc, Sport, Health and Exercise Sciences (Coaching) BSc, Sport, Health and Exercise Sciences (Human Performance) BSc, Sport, Health and Exercise Sciences (Sport Development) BSc, Sport, Health and Exercise Sciences BSc, Sport, Health and Exercise Sciences with Business Studies BSc

Postgraduate courses: Molecular Medicine and Cancer Research MSc, Psychological Sciences MSc, Sport and Exercise Psychology MSc, Sport, Health and Exercise Sciences MSc, Sustainability, Entrepreneurship and Design MSc

UNIVERSITY OF BUCKINGHAM
www.buckingham.ac.uk

Accounting

BSc Accounting and Finance, BSc Accounting with Communication Studies, BSc Accounting with French, BSc Accounting with Spanish, BSc Computing with Accounting and Finance

Postgraduate courses: MSc in Accounting and Finance, MSc in Finance and Investment, MSc in Financial Service Management, MSc in Money, Banking and Central Banking

Business

BSc (Econ) Business Economics, BSc Business and Management, BSc Business Enterprise, BSc Business and Management with Applied Computing, BSc Business and Management with French, BSc Business and Management with Spanish

Postgraduate courses: MBA, MSc in Entrepreneurial Consultancy and Practice, MSc in Lean Enterprise, MSc in Management in a Service Economy, MSc in Structured Innovation

Communication

BA English Studies, BA English Studies for Teaching, BA Communication (EFL) and Media Studies, BA English Studies with Media Communications, BA Journalism with Communication Studies, BSc Accounting with Communication Studies, BSc Business and Management with Communication Studies, BSc Marketing with Media Communications, BSc Psychology with Media Communications, BA English Language and Communication Studies, BA Communication, Media and Journalism

Computing

BSc Computing, BSc Computing and Software Entrepreneurship, BA Politics with Applied Computing, BSc Business and Management with Applied Computing, BSc Computing with Accounting and Finance, BSc Computing with Business and Management, BSc Computing with Economics, BSc Economics with Applied Computing, BSc Psychology with Applied Computing

Postgraduate courses: MSc in Applied Computing, MSc in Computing by Research, MSc in Innovative Computing

Diplomacy

Postgraduate course: MA in Security, Intelligence and Diplomacy

Economics

BSc (Econ) Business Economics, BSc (Econ) Economics, BSc Economics with Applied Computing, BSc Economics with English Language Studies, BSc Economics with French, BSc Economics with History, BSc Economics with Journalism, BSc Economics with Politics, BSc Economics with Spanish

Education

Postgraduate courses: Independent PGCE, International PGCE, MA in Education, MA in School-based Mentoring, MEd in Educational Leadership, Postgraduate Certificate in Middle Leadership, Primary PGCE with Qualified Teacher Status, Qualified Teacher Status (QTS) Conversion Course – Secondary, Qualified Teacher Status (QTS) Conversion Course – Primary, Secondary PGCE with Qualified Teacher Status, TA to Teacher

English Literature

BA English Literature, BA English Literature with English Language Studies, BA English Literature with French, BA English Literature with History, BA English Literature with History of Art, BA English Literature with Journalism, BA English Literature with Psychology, BA English Literature with Spanish

Postgraduate courses: MA in Biography, MA by research options

English Studies

BA English Studies, BA English Studies for Teaching, BA English Studies with Journalism, BA English Studies with Media Communications, BA English Language and Communication Studies

Entrepreneurship

BSc Business Enterprise

Postgraduate course: MSc in Entrepreneurial Consultancy and Practice

History and History of Art

BA History of Art, BA History of Art and Heritage Management, BA History of Art with English Literature, BA History of Art with French, BA History of Art with History, BA History of Art with Journalism, BA History of Art with Spanish, BA History with Economics, BA History with English Literature, BA History with Journalism, BA History with Politics, BA History and Economics, BA History and Politics

Postgraduate courses: MA in Decorative Arts and Historic Interiors, MA by research options

Intelligence

Postgraduate courses: MA in Law Enforcement, Security & Intelligence Studies, MA in Security and Intelligence Studies, MA in Security, Intelligence and Diplomacy, PGCert/PGDip in Law Enforcement, Security and Intelligence Studies

International Studies

BA International Studies, BA International Relations with Applied Computing, BA International Relations with Economics, BA International Relations with English Language Studies, BA International Relations with French, BA International Relations with Journalism, BA International Relations with Spanish, BA International Studies with English Language Studies, BA International Studies with French, BA International Studies with Journalism, BA International Studies with Spanish

Journalism

BA Journalism with Communication Studies, BA Journalism with English Literature, BA Journalism with French, BA Journalism with International Relations, BA Journalism with International Studies, BA Journalism with Politics, BA Journalism with Spanish, BA Communication, Media and Journalism

Law

LLB Law, LLB Law with Business and Management, LLB Law with Economics, LLB Law with English Language Studies, LLB Law with French, LLB Law with Politics, LLB Law with Spanish, LLB Law with Business Finance

Postgraduate courses: LLM International and Commercial Law, research options

Marketing

BSc Marketing with French, BSc Marketing with Media Communications, BSc Marketing with Spanish

Medicine

MB ChB Medicine

Philosophy

BA Philosophy, Politics and Economics

Politics

BA Politics with Applied Computing, BA Politics with Economics, BA Politics with English Language Studies, BA Politics with French, BA Politics with Journalism, BA Politics with Spanish, BA Politics and Economics, BA Politics and History, BA Philosophy, Politics and Economics, BA Politics, Economics and Law

Psychology

BSc Psychology, BSc Psychology with Applied Computing, BSc Psychology with Business and Management, BSc Psychology with English Literature, BSc Psychology with French, BSc Psychology with Marketing, BSc Psychology with Media Communications, BSc Psychology with Spanish

Postgraduate course: MSc in Health Psychology

BUCKINGHAMSHIRE NEW UNIVERSITY
www.bucks.ac.uk

School of Arts and Creative Industries; bucks.ac.uk/about-us/our-structure/ schools-and-departments/school-of-arts-and-creative-industries

Department of Art and Design; bucks.ac.uk/about-us/our-structure/ schools-and-departments/school-of-arts-and-creative-industries/art-and-design
BA(Hons) Creative Advertising, BA(Hons) Fashion Design, BA(Hons) Graphic Arts, BA(Hons) Graphic Design, BA(Hons) Illustration, BA(Hons) Interior and Spatial Design, BA(Hons) Product Design, BSc(Hons) Product Design, BA(Hons) Textiles and Surface Design

Department of Media Production; bucks.ac.uk/about-us/our-structure/ schools-and-departments/school-of-arts-and-creative-industries/media-production
BA(Hons) Animation and Visual Effects, BA(Hons) Audio and Music Production, BA(Hons) Creative Writing for Publication, BA(Hons) Film and Television Production

Department of Music and Events Management; bucks.ac.uk/about-us/our-structure/schools-and-departments/ school-of-arts-and-creative-industries/ music-and-events-management
BA(Hons) Music and Live Events Management, BA(Hons) Music Business, BA(Hons) Music Management and Studio Production, BA(Hons) Music Performance Management

School of Management and Professional Studies; bucks.ac.uk/about-us/our-structure/schools-and-departments/ school-of-management-and-professional-studies

Bucks Business School; bucks.ac.uk/about-us/our-structure/schools-and-departments/school-of-management-and-professional-studies/bucks-business-school
BSc(Hons) Accounting and Finance, BA(Hons) Advertising Management and Digital Communications, BA(Hons) Business and Finance, BA(Hons) Business and Human Resource Management, BA(Hons) Business Management, BA(Hons) Marketing, BA(Hons) Sport Business Management, BA(Hons) Sport Marketing, BA(Hons) Sports Business and Coaching, LLB(Hons) Business Law, LLB(Hons) Law

Department of Computing; bucks.ac.uk/ about-us/our-structure/schools-and-departments/school-of-management-and-professional-studies/computing
Foundation Degree (Science) Computing, BSc(Hons) Computing, BSc(Hons) Computing and Web Development, BSc(Hons) Games Development, BA(Hons) Independent Games Production, BSc(Hons) Software Engineering

Department of Security & Resilience, Policing and Law; bucks.ac.uk/about-us/ our-structure/schools-and-departments/ school-of-management-and-professional-studies/security-and-resilience
BA(Hons) Crowd Safety Management, BA(Hons) Security Consultancy, Business Continuity Management

Department of Aviation Events and Tourism; bucks.ac.uk/about-us/our-structure/ schools-and-departments/school-of-management-and-professional-studies/ aviation-events-tourism
BSc(Hons) Air Transport with Helicopter Pilot Training, BA(Hons) Airline and Airport Management, BA(Hons) International Tourism Management with Air Travel, BA(Hons) International Travel and Tourism Management, BSc(Hons) Air Transport with Commercial Pilot Training, BA(Hons) Event and Festivals Management, BA(Hons) International Hotel Management (Top-up), BA(Hons) International Hospitality Management (Top-Up)

School of Health and Social Sciences; bucks.ac.uk/about-us/our-structure/schools-and-departments/school-of-health-and-social-sciences

Department of Applied Health & Exercise Science; bucks.ac.uk/about-us/our-structure/schools-and-departments/school-of-health-and-social-sciences/applied-health-and-exercise-science

BA(Hons) Exercise, Health and Fitness Management, BA(Hons) Sport Development and Coaching, BSc(Hons) Sport and Exercise Science, BSc(Hons) Sports Therapy, BSc(Hons) Strength and Conditioning, Master of Science Advanced Practice, Master of Science Health Exercise and Wellbeing, Master of Science Professional Practice (Healthcare), BSc(Hons) Sports Psychology, BA(Hons) Sports Development and Coaching, BA(Hons) Sports Business and Sports Law, BA(Hons) Sport Business Management

Department of Community Health, Education & Social Sciences; bucks.ac.uk/about-us/our-structure/schools-and-departments/school-of-health-and-social-sciences/community-health,-education-and-social-sciences

BSc(Hons) Criminology, BSc(Hons) Police Studies and Criminal Justice, BSc(Hons) Police Studies with Criminal Investigation, BSc(Hons) Police Studies with Criminological Psychology, BSc(Hons) Health and Social Science, BSc(Hons) Community Health Care Nursing (District Nursing), BA(Hons) Professional Practice (Early Years), BA(Hons) Professional Practice (Primary Education and Education), BA(Hons) Professional Practice (Working with Children and Young People), Certificate in Knowledge of Policing, Foundation Degree (Arts) Early Years Practice, Foundation Degree (Arts) Policing, Foundation Degree (Arts) Working with Children and Young People, Master of Arts Education, Master of Science Criminology Communities and Disorder, Master of Science Specialist Community Public Health Nursing, Postgraduate Certificate Education

Department of Psychology; bucks.ac.uk/about-us/our-structure/schools-and-departments/school-of-health-and-social-sciences/psychology

BSc(Hons) Behavioural Sciences, BSc(Hons) Criminological Psychology, BSc(Hons) Psychology, BSc(Hons) Psychology and Criminology, BSc(Hons) Sports Psychology, Master of Science Cognitive Behavioural Therapy

Department of Social Work & Integrated Care; bucks.ac.uk/about-us/our-structure/schools-and-departments/school-of-health-and-social-sciences/social-work-and-integrated-care

BSc(Hons) Social Work, Foundation Degree (Arts) Health and Social Care

School of Pre-Qualifying Nursing and Vocational Health Care; bucks.ac.uk/about-us/our-structure/schools-and-departments/school-of-pre-qualifying-nursing-and-vocational-health-care

BSc(Hons) Nursing (Adult), BSc(Hons) Nursing (Children's), BSc(Hons) Nursing (Mental Health), DipHE Operating Department Practice, PGDip Nursing (Adult), PGDip Nursing (Mental Health)

UNIVERSITY OF CAMBRIDGE
www.cam.ac.uk

Flexible undergraduate programmes

BA(Hons) Anglo-Saxon, Norse, and Celtic, BA(Hons) Archaeology, BA(Hons) Architecture, BA(Hons) Asian and Middle Eastern Studies, BA(Hons)/MEng Chemical Engineering, BA(Hons) Classics, BA(Hons) Computer Science, BA(Hons) Economics, BA(Hons) Education, MEng Engineering, BA(Hons) English, BA(Hons) Geography, BA(Hons) History, BA(Hons) History and Modern Languages, BA(Hons) History and Politics, BA(Hons) History of Art, BA(Hons) Human, Social, and Political Sciences, BA(Hons) Land Economy, BA(Hons) Law, BA(Hons) Linguistics, Management Studies (Part II course), Manufacturing Engineering (Part II course), BA(Hons)/MMath Mathematics, MB/BChir Medicine, BA(Hons) Modern and Medieval Languages, BA(Hons) Music, BA(Hons)/MSci Natural Sciences, BA(Hons) Philosophy, BA(Hons) Psychological and Behavioural Sciences, BA(Hons) Theology, Religion, and Philosophy of Religion, VetMB Veterinary Medicine

Postgraduate courses

School of Arts and Humanities; www.csah.cam.ac.uk

MPhil in American Literature, MPhil in Anglo-Saxon, Norse and Celtic, MPhil in Architecture, MPhil in Architecture and Urban Design, MPhil in Architecture and Urban Studies, MPhil in Asian and Middle Eastern Studies (Arabic Studies), MPhil in Asian and Middle Eastern Studies (Chinese Studies), MPhil in Asian and Middle Eastern Studies (East Asian Studies), MPhil in Asian and Middle Eastern Studies (Hebrew Studies), MPhil in Asian and Middle Eastern Studies (Japanese Studies), MPhil in Asian and Middle Eastern Studies (Middle Eastern and Islamic Studies), MSt in Building History, MPhil in Classics, Dip in Conservation of Easel Paintings, MSt in Creative Writing, MLitt in English Literature, MPhil in English Studies: 18th Century and Romantic Studies, MPhil in English Studies: Criticism and Culture, MPhil in English Studies: Modern and Contemporary Literature, MPhil in European, Latin American and Comparative Literatures and Cultures, MPhil in Film and Screen Studies, MPhil in History of Art and Architecture, Master of Music, MPhil in Medieval and Renaissance Literature, MPhil in Music, MPhil in Philosophy, Postgraduate Certificate in Professional Practice in Architecture, CPGS in Theology and Religious Studies, MLitt in Theology and Religious Studies, MPhil in Theology, Religion and Philosophy of Religion, Advanced Diploma in Theology, Religion and Philosophy of Religion, MPhil in Theoretical and Applied Linguistics

School of Clinical Medicine; www.medschl.cam.ac.uk

MPhil in Biological Science (MRC Cognition and Brain Sciences Unit), PGCert in Clinical Medicine, MSt in Clinical Medicine (Intensive Care), MPhil in Clinical Science (Experimental Medicine), MPhil in Clinical Science (Rare Diseases), MPhil in Epidemiology, MPhil in Genomic Medicine, MSt in Genomic Medicine, PGDip in Genomic Medicine, PGCert in Genomic Medicine, MD (Doctor of Medicine), Postgraduate Certificate in Medical Education, MPhil in Medical Science (CIMR), MPhil in Medical Science (Clinical Biochemistry), MPhil in Medical Science (Clinical Neurosciences), MPhil in Medical Science (CRUKCI), MPhil in Medical Science (Medicine), MPhil in Medical Science (MRC Cancer Unit), MPhil in Medical Science (MRC Epidemiology Unit), MPhil in Medical Science (Obstetrics and Gynaecology), MPhil in Medical Science (Oncology), MPhil in Medical Science (Paediatrics), MPhil in Medical Science (Psychiatry), MPhil in Medical Science (Radiology), MPhil in Medical Science (Surgery), National Institutes of Health Oxford/Cambridge Programme, MPhil in Primary Care Research, MPhil in Public Health, MPhil in Translational Biomedical Research

School of Technology; www.tech.cam.ac.uk

MPhil in Advanced Chemical Engineering, MPhil in Advanced Computer Science, MPhil in Bioscience Enterprise, MPhil in Biotechnology, Master of Business Administration, Executive Master of Business Administration, MPhil in Chemical Engineering and Biotechnology, MSt in Construction Engineering, Doctor of Business, MPhil in Energy Technologies, MPhil in Engineering, MPhil in Engineering for Sustainable Development, Postgraduate Diploma in Entrepreneurship, Master of Finance, MPhil in Finance, MPhil in Industrial Systems, Manufacture, and Management, MPhil in Innovation, Strategy and Organisation, MSt in Interdisciplinary Design for the Built Environment, MPhil in Machine Learning and Machine Intelligence, MPhil in Management, Master of Accounting, MSt in Entrepreneurship, MPhil in Nuclear Energy, MSt in Social Innovation, MPhil in Strategy, Marketing and Operations, MSt in Sustainability Leadership, Postgraduate Certificate in Sustainable Business, Postgraduate Diploma in Sustainable Business, MPhil in Technology Policy, Postgraduate Certificate in Sustainable Value Chains

School of the Biological Sciences; www.bio.cam.ac.uk

MPhil in Basic and Translational Neuroscience, MPhil in Biological Science (Biochemistry), MPhil in Biological Science (Genetics), MPhil in Biological Science (MRC Laboratory of Molecular Biology), MPhil in Biological Science (MRC Mitochondrial Biology Unit), MPhil in Biological Science (Pathology), MPhil in Biological Science (Pharmacology), MPhil in Biological Science (Physiology, Development and Neuroscience), MPhil in Biological Science (Plant Sciences), MPhil in Biological Science (Psychology), MPhil in Biological Science (Sanger Institute), MPhil in Biological Science (Zoology), MPhil in Social and Developmental Psychology, Doctor of Veterinary Medicine, MPhil in Veterinary Science

School of the Humanities and Social Sciences; www.cshss.cam.ac.uk

MSt in Advanced Subject Teaching, MPhil in African Studies, MPhil in American History, MPhil in

Applied Biological Anthropology, MSt in Applied Criminology and Police Management, MSt in Applied Criminology, Penology and Management, MPhil in Archaeological Research, MPhil in Archaeology, MPhil in Assyriology, MPhil in Biological Anthropological Science, Master of Corporate Law (MCL), MPhil in Criminological Research, MPhil in Criminology, MPhil in Development Studies, MPhil in Early Modern History, MPhil in Economic and Social History, MPhil in Economic Research, MPhil in Economics, Advanced Diploma in Economics, Doctor of Education, MPhil in Education (Arts, Creativity & Education), MPhil in Education (Child and Adolescent Psychotherapeutic Counselling), MPhil in Education (Critical Approaches to Children's Literature), MPhil in Education (Educational Leadership and School Improvement), MPhil in Education (Educational Research), MPhil in Education (Globalisation and International Development), MPhil in Education (Mathematics Education), MPhil in Education (Perspectives on Inclusive and Special Education), MPhil in Education (Politics, Development and Democratic Education), MPhil in Education (Primary Education), MPhil in Education (Psychology and Education), MPhil in Education (Research in Second Language Education), Master of Education (Researching Practice), Master of Education (Science Teacher Researchers and Practitioners), Postgraduate Advanced Certificate in Educational Studies, Postgraduate Certificate in Educational Studies, Postgraduate Diploma in Educational Studies, Postgraduate Award in Educational Studies, Educational Studies: Child and Adolescent Psychotherapeutic Counselling, Postgraduate Award in Educational Studies: Contemporary Issues in Music Education, Postgraduate Award in Educational Studies: Dialogic Teaching, Postgraduate Award in Educational Studies: Introduction to Child and Adolescent Psychotherapeutic Counselling, Postgraduate Certificate in Educational Studies: Teaching Advanced Mathematics, Postgraduate Award in Educational Studies: Understanding Shakespeare through Performance, MPhil in Egyptology,

MPhil in Environmental Policy, MPhil in Finance and Economics, MPhil in Health, Medicine and Society, MPhil in Historical Studies, MSt in History, MPhil in History and Philosophy of Science and Medicine, MPhil in Human Evolutionary Studies, Postgraduate Diploma in International Law, MSt in International Relations, MPhil in International Relations and Politics, MPhil in Land Economy, MPhil in Land Economy Research, MPhil in Latin American Studies, Master of Law (LLM), MLitt in Law, Postgraduate Diploma in Legal Studies, MPhil in Medieval History, MPhil in Modern British History, MPhil in Modern European History, MPhil in Modern South Asian Studies, MPhil in Multi-disciplinary Gender Studies, MPhil in Planning, Growth and Regeneration, MPhil in Political Thought and Intellectual History, MPhil in Public Policy, MSt in Real Estate, MPhil in Real Estate Finance, MPhil in Social Anthropology, MRes in Social Anthropology, MPhil in Sociology (Political and Economic Sociology), MPhil in Sociology (The Sociology of Marginality and Exclusion), MPhil in Sociology (The Sociology of Media and Culture), MPhil in Sociology (The Sociology of Reproduction), MPhil in World History

School of the Physical Sciences; www.physsci.cam.ac.uk
MASt in Applied Mathematics, MPhil in Applied Mathematics and Theoretical Physics, MPhil in Astronomy, MASt in Astrophysics, MPhil in Chemistry, MPhil in Computational Biology, MPhil in Conservation Leadership, MPhil in Earth Sciences, MPhil in Geographical Research, MPhil in Geography, MASt in Materials Science, MPhil in Materials Science and Metallurgy, MASt in Mathematical Statistics, MPhil in Micro and Nanotechnology Enterprise, MASt in Physics, MPhil in Physics, MPhil in Polar Studies (Scott Polar Research Institute), MASt in Pure Mathematics, MPhil in Pure Mathematics and Mathematical Statistics, MPhil in Scientific Computing

CANTERBURY CHRIST CHURCH UNIVERSITY
www.canterbury.ac.uk

Faculty of Arts and Humanities; www.canterbury.ac.uk/arts-and-humanities

School of Humanities; www.canterbury.ac.uk/arts-and-humanities/school-of-humanities

American Studies, BA, Archaeology, BA, Creative and Professional Writing with Foundation Year, BA, Creative and Professional Writing, BA, English Literature with Foundation Year, BA, English Literature, BA, History with Foundation Year, BA, History, BA, Medieval and Early Modern Studies, BA, Religion, Philosophy and Ethics, BA, Theology, BA
Postgraduate courses: American Studies by Research, MA, Creative Writing: Prose Fiction, MA, English Literature by Research, MA, English Literature, MA, Theology and Religious Studies by Research, MA

School of Language Studies and Applied Linguistics; www.canterbury.ac.uk/arts-and-humanities/language-studies-and-applied-linguistics

English Language and Communication with Foundation Year, BA, English Language and Communication, BA, French, BA
Postgraduate courses: Teaching English to Speakers of Other Languages (TESOL), MA/PgDip

School of Music and Performing Arts; www.canterbury.ac.uk/arts-and-humanities/music-and-performing-arts

Creative Theatre Production, BA, Dance Education, BA, Dance, BA, Drama, BA, Music and Media Production, BA, Music Production, BA, Music, BA, Music, BMus, Music: Commercial Music, BA, Music: Creative Music Technology, BA, Performing Arts, BA
Postgraduate courses: Arts and Cultural Management, MA, Master of Music, MMus

School of Media, Art and Design; www.canterbury.ac.uk/arts-and-humanities/media-art-and-design

Animation Production, BA, Digital Media, BA, Film Production, BA, Film, Radio and Television Studies, BA, Games Design, BA, Graphic Design, BA, Illustration, BA, Journalism: Multimedia Journalism, BA, Media and Communications, BA, Photography, BA, Public Relations, Media and Marketing, BA, Television Production, BA, Web Design, BA

Postgraduate course: Media, Art and Design by Research, MA

Faculty of Education; www.canterbury.ac.uk/education

Childhood Studies, BA, Early Childhood Education and Care, BA Hons, Early Childhood Studies, BA, Early Years Initial Teacher Training (ITT), BA Pathway, Education and Professional Training, BA, Education Studies, BA, Mathematics with Secondary Education, BSc, Physical Education and Physical Activity, BA, Physical Education and Sport & Exercise Science, BA, Primary Education, BA, Spanish with Secondary Education, BA, Special Educational Needs and Inclusion Studies, BA, Special Educational Needs and Physical Activity, BA
Postgraduate courses: Career Management, MA, Early Childhood Education with Early Years Teacher Status, PGCE, Early Childhood Education, MA, Education (Academic Practice), MA, Education and Training, ProfGCE / Dip / Cert / Award, Education, Doctorate, Education, MA, Global and International Education, MA, INSPIRE, PGCE, Mathematics Specialist Teacher, PgCert, Myth, Cosmology and the Sacred, MA, National Award for SEN Co-ordination, Postgraduate Certificate, PGCE 7-14 Years, PGCE Applied Business Studies (14-19), PGCE Art and Design (Secondary), PGCE Citizenship (Secondary), PGCE Computing (Secondary), PGCE English (Secondary), PGCE Geography (Secondary), PGCE Health and Social Care (14-19), PGCE History (Secondary), PGCE Leisure and Tourism (14-19), PGCE Mathematics (Secondary), PGCE Modern Foreign Languages (Secondary), PGCE Music (Secondary), PGCE Physical Education (Secondary), PGCE Physics with Mathematics (Secondary), PGCE Post Compulsory Education, PGCE Primary – Full-time, PGCE Primary Modular, PGCE Primary with Mathematics Specialism, PGCE Psychology (14-19), PGCE Religious Education (Secondary), PGCE Sciences (Secondary), Physical Education and Physical Activity by Research, MA, Social and Emotional Learning, Postgraduate Certificate, Special Needs and Inclusion, MA, Transformational Leadership (Teach First), MA, Transformational Leadership, MA

Faculty of Health and Wellbeing; www.canterbury.ac.uk/health-and-wellbeing

School of Nursing; www.canterbury.ac.uk/health-and-wellbeing/nursing

BSc(Hons) Adult Nursing, BSc(Hons) Child Nursing, BSc(Hons) Mental Health Nursing, BSc(Hons) Nursing Studies for International Nurses

School of Allied Health Professions; www.canterbury.ac.uk/health-and-wellbeing/allied-health-professions

BSc(Hons) Diagnostic Radiography, BSc(Hons) Occupational Therapy, BSc(Hons) Operating Department Practice, BSc(Hons) Paramedic Science
Postgraduate courses: MSc Clinical Reporting, MSc Medical Imaging, MSc Health and Wellbeing

School of Public Health, Midwifery and Social Work; www.canterbury.ac.uk/health-and-wellbeing/public-health-midwifery-and-social-work

Foundation Degree in Social Care Studies, BSc(Hons) Health Studies/BSc(Hons) Public Health/BSc(Hons) Health Promotion, BSc(Hons) Midwifery, BA(Hons) Social Work, BSc(Hons) Specialist Community Public Health Nursing
Postgraduate courses: PgDip Specialist Community Public Health Nursing, MA Social Work, MSc Public Health, MSc Mental Health

Institute of Medical Sciences; www.canterbury.ac.uk/health-and-wellbeing/institute-of-medical-sciences

Postgraduate courses: MSc, Physician Associate Studies, MCh in Surgery – Otorhinolaryngology, MCh in Surgery – Orthopaedics and Regenerative Medicine, MCh in Surgery – Urology, MCh in Surgery – Ophthalmology

Faculty of Social and Applied Sciences; www.canterbury.ac.uk/social-and-applied-sciences

School of Psychology, Politics and Sociology; www.canterbury.ac.uk/social-and-applied-sciences/psychology-politics-and-sociology

European Politics, BSc, International Relations, BSc, Politics, BSc, Psychology (Sport and Exercise), BSc, Psychology, BSc, Sociology and Social Policy, BSc, Sociology, BA / BSc

Postgraduate courses: Clinical Psychology, DClinPsy, Cognitive Behavioural Therapy (High Intensity), Postgraduate Diploma, Cognitive Behavioural Therapy, MSc, European Politics (with Diplomacy Specialism), MSc, International Relations (with Security Studies Specialism), MSc, Politics (with Migration and Minorities Studies Specialism), MSc, Professional Practice: Psychological Perspectives, PhD, Psychology (Conversion Course), MSc

The Business School; www.canterbury.ac.uk/social-and-applied-sciences/christ-church-business-school

Accounting and Finance, BSc, Accounting and Management, BSc, Accounting, BSc, Advertising, BSc, Business Management, BSc, Business Studies, BSc, Digital Marketing Communications, BA, Finance, BSc, Human Resource Management, BSc, Logistics Management, BSc, Management (Sustainable and Ethical Business), BSc, Management, BSc, Marketing, BSc
Postgraduate courses: Collaborative Transformation, Postgraduate Certificate, Education Leadership and Management, MBA, Healthcare Leadership and Management, MBA, Human Resource Management, CIPD Advanced Diploma, Human Resource Management, MA, International Business, MSc, Management Studies, MA/PgDip/PgCert, Master of Business Administration (MBA), MBA

School of Law, Criminal Justice and Computing; www.canterbury.ac.uk/social-and-applied-sciences/law-criminal-justice-and-computing

Applied Criminology, BA / BSc, Business Information Systems, BSc, Computer Forensics and Security, BSc, Computer Science, BSc, Computing, BSc, Computing, Foundation Degree, Forensic Investigation, BSc, Information Technology, BSc, Law, LL.B., Policing (Crime Science), BSc, Policing (Criminal Investigation), BSc, Policing (Criminal Psychology), BSc, Policing (Critical Incidents), BSc, Policing (Cybersecurity), BSc, Policing (Global Perspectives), BSc, Policing (Terrorism and Political Violence), BSc, Policing (Youth Justice), BSc, Policing, BSc, Web Technology, BSc
Postgraduate courses: Applied Policing Practice, MSc, Policing, MSc

School of Human and Life Sciences; www.canterbury.ac.uk/social-and-applied-sciences/human-and-life-sciences

Animal Science with Foundation Year, BSc, Animal Science, BSc, Biology with Foundation Year, BSc, Biology, BSc, Biomolecular Science, BSc, Biosciences, BSc, Ecology, BSc, Environmental Science, BSc, Events Management, BSc, Geography, BA, Geography, BSc, Hospitality Management, BSc, Human Biology, BSc, Plant Science, BSc, Sport and Exercise Psychology, BSc, Sport and Exercise Science, BSc -2018/19, Sport Coaching Science, BSc, Tourism Management, BSc, Tourism Studies, BA/BSc

Postgraduate courses: Applied Ecology and Environmental Management, MSc, Applied Exercise and Health Science, MSc, Tourism and Event Management, MSc

CARDIFF UNIVERSITY
www.cardiff.ac.uk

College of Arts, Humanities and Social Sciences; www.cardiff.ac.uk/colleges/arts-humanities-social-sciences

Business School; www.cardiff.ac.uk/business-school

Accounting and Finance

Accounting (BSc), Accounting and Finance (BSc), Accounting with a European Language (French) (BSc), Accounting with a European Language (German) (BSc), Accounting with a European Language (Spanish) (BSc)

Postgraduate courses: MSc in Accounting and Finance, MSc in Finance

Business Management

Business Management (BSc), Business Management (Human Resources) (BSc), Business Management (International Management) (BSc), Business Management (Logistics and Operations) (BSc), Business Management (Marketing) (BSc), Business Management with a European Language (French) (BSc), Business Management with a European Language (German) (BSc), Business Management with a European Language (Spanish) (BSc), Business Studies and Japanese (BSc)

Postgraduate courses: MBA, MSc in Human Resource Management, MSc in International Human Resource Management, MSc in International Management, MSc in Business Strategy and Entrepreneurship, MSc in Strategic Marketing, MSc in Logistics and Operations Management, MSc in Maritime Policy and Shipping Management

Economics

Banking and Finance (BScEcon), Banking and Finance with French (BScEcon), Banking and Finance with German (BScEcon), Banking and Finance with Spanish (BScEcon), Banking and Finance with a Professional Placement Year (BScEcon), Business Economics (BScEcon), Business Economics with French (BScEcon), Business Economics with German (BScEcon), Business Economics with Spanish (BScEcon), Business Economics with a Professional Placement Year (BScEcon), Economics (BScEcon), Economics and Finance (BScEcon), Economics and Finance with a Professional Placement Year (BScEcon), Economics and Management Studies (BScEcon), Economics and Management Studies with a Professional Placement Year (BScEcon), Economics with French (BSc), Economics with German (BSc), Economics with Spanish (BSc)

Postgraduate courses: MSc in Financial Economics, MSc in International Economics, Banking and Finance

School of English, Communication and Philosophy; www.cardiff.ac.uk/english-communication-philosophy

English Language

BA English Language, BA English Language & Literature, BA English Language and Linguistics, BA English Language and French, BA English Language and German, BA English Language and Italian, BA English Language and Spanish, BA English Language and Welsh, BA English Language and Philosophy

English Literature

BA English Literature, BA English Literature and Creative Writing, BA English Literature and Ancient History, BA English Literature and Archaeology, BA English Literature and French, BA English Literature and German, BA English Literature and History, BA English Literature and Italian, BA English Literature, Journalism and Media, BA English Literature and Music, BA English Literature and Philosophy, BA English Literature and Religious Studies, BA English

Literature and Spanish, BA English Literature and Welsh

Philosophy

BA in Philosophy, BA in Philosophy and Ancient History, BA in Philosophy and Archaeology, BA in Philosophy and Economics, BA in Philosophy and French, BA in Philosophy and English Language, BA in Philosophy and English Literature, BA in Philosophy and History, BA in Philosophy and Italian, BA in Philosophy and Music, BA in Philosophy and Politics, BA in Philosophy and Religious Studies, BA in Philosophy and Spanish, BA in Philosophy and Welsh

Postgraduate courses

MA Applied Linguistics, MA Creative Writing, MA English Literature, MA Ethics and Social Philosophy, MA Forensic Linguistics, MA Language and Communication Research, MA Language and Linguistics

School of Geography and Planning; www.cardiff.ac.uk/geography-planning

Geography (Human) (BSc), Geography (Human) and Planning (BSc), Urban Planning and Development (BSc)

Postgraduate courses: City Futures (MSc), Eco-Cities (MSc), European Spatial Planning and Environmental Policy (MSc), Food, Space and Society (MSc), International Planning and Development (MSc), Planning Practice (PgCert), Social Science Research Methods (Environmental Planning) (MSc/PgDip), Spatial Planning and Development (MSc), Sustainability, Planning and Environmental Policy (MSc), Transport and Planning (MSc), Urban and Regional Development (MSc), Urban Design (MA)

School of History, Archaeology and Religion; www.cardiff.ac.uk/history-archaeology-religion

Ancient History

BA Ancient History, BA Archaeology and Ancient History, BA Ancient and Medieval History, BA Ancient History and History, BA Ancient History and French, BA Ancient History and German, BA Ancient History and Italian, BA Ancient History and Spanish, BA English Literature and Ancient History, BA Philosophy and Ancient History

Postgraduate courses: MA Ancient History, MA History and Archaeology of the Greek and Roman World, MA Ancient and Medieval Warfare, MA Late Antique and Byzantine Studies

Archaeology and Conservation

BA Archaeology, BA Archaeology and Ancient History, BA Archaeology and Medieval History, BA Archaeology and History, BA Archaeology and Religious Studies, BA Archaeology and French, BA Archaeology and German, BA Archaeology and Italian, BSc Archaeology

Postgraduate courses: MA Archaeology, MA Archaeology: Prehistoric Britain, MA Archaeology: Early Medieval Society and Culture, MA Archaeology: European Neolithic, MA Early Celtic Studies, MA History and Archaeology of the Greek and Roman World, MSc Archaeological Science, MSc Care of Collections, MSc Conservation Practice, MSc Professional Conservation

History

BA History, BA Ancient History and History, BA Archaeology and History, BA History and Economics, BA History and Italian, BA History and Music, BA History and Spanish, BA History and Welsh, BSc Econ Modern History and Politics, BA History with Welsh History, BA Ancient and Medieval History

Postgraduate courses: MA Medieval British Studies, MA Welsh History, MA History, MA Ancient and Medieval Warfare

Religious Studies and Theology

BA Religious Studies and Theology, BA Religious Studies and Ancient History, BA Religious Studies and Archaeology, BA Religious Studies and History, BA Religious Studies and English Literature, BA Religious Studies and German, BA Religious Studies and Music, BA Religious Studies and Philosophy, BA Religious Studies and Politics, BA Religious Studies and Italian, BA Religious Studies and Spanish

Postgraduate courses: MA/PgDip Islam in Contemporary Britain, MA in Religious Studies: Religion in Late Antiquity, MA in Religious Studies: Asian Religions, MA in Religious Studies, MA Late Antique and Byzantine Studies

Journalism, Media and Cultural Studies; www.cardiff.ac.uk/journalism-media-cultural-studies

Journalism and Communications (BA), Media and Communications (BA), Media, Journalism and Culture (BA), Journalism, Communications and Politics (BA), Journalism, Media and English Literature (BA), Journalism, Media and Sociology (BA)

Postgraduate courses: Broadcast Journalism (MA), Computational and Data Journalism (MSc), Digital Media and Society (MA), International Journalism (MA), International Public Relations and Global Communications Management (MA), Journalism, Media and Communications (MA), Magazine Journalism (MA), Media Management (MBA), News

Journalism (MA), Political Communication (MA), Science, Media and Communication (MSc)

School of Law and Politics; www.cardiff.ac.uk/law-politics
Law
LLB Law, LLB Law and Criminology, LLB Law and Politics, LLB Law and Sociology, LLB Law and French, LLB Law and German, LLB Law and Welsh
Postgraduate courses: LLM Canon Law, LLM European Legal Studies, LLM Governance and Devolution, LLM Human Rights Law, LLM Intellectual Property Law, LLM International Commercial Law, LLM Legal Aspects of Medical Practice, LLM Legal and Political Aspects of International Affairs, LLM Shipping Law, LLM Social Care Law, LLM Law

Politics and International Relations
Politics (BSc Econ), International Relations and Politics (BSc Econ), International Relations and Politics (with a Language) (BSc Econ), Politics and Sociology (BSc Econ), Politics and Spanish (BA), Politics and Welsh (BA)
Postgraduate courses: MSc Econ International Relations, MSc Econ Politics and Public Policy, MSc/PgDip Social Science Research Methods (International Relations), MSc/PgDip Social Science Research Methods (Politics), MSc Econ Welsh Government and Politics

School of Modern Languages; www.cardiff.ac.uk/modern-languages
Chinese
BA Modern Chinese, BA Modern Languages and Translation (Chinese)
French
French (BA), French and Economics (BA), French and English Literature (BA), French and German (BA), French and History (BA), French and Italian (BA), French and Japanese (BA), French and Music (BA), French and Philosophy (BA), French and Politics (BA), French and Portuguese (BA), French and Spanish (BA), French and Welsh (BA), Modern Languages and Translation (BA)
German
German (BA), German and Economics (BA), German and History (BA), German and Italian (BA), German and Japanese (BA), German and Music (BA), German and Politics (BA), German and Portuguese (BA), German and Spanish (BA), Modern Languages and Translation (BA)
Italian
Italian and Economics (BA), Italian and English Literature (BA), Italian and Japanese (BA), Italian and Music (BA), Italian and Philosophy (BA), Italian and Politics (BA), Italian and Spanish (BA), Modern Languages and Translation (BA)
Portuguese
Modern Languages and Translation (BA), Portuguese and Italian (BA), Portuguese and Japanese (BA), Portuguese and Spanish (BA)
Spanish
Spanish (BA), Spanish and Economics (BA), Spanish and English Literature (BA), Spanish and Japanese (BA), Spanish and Philosophy (BA)
Postgraduate course
Translation Studies (MA)

School of Music; www.cardiff.ac.uk/music
BMus Music, BA Music and Mathematics, BA Music and Philosophy, BA Music and Religious Studies, BA Music and Welsh
Postgraduate course: MA in Music

School of Social Sciences; www.cardiff.ac.uk/social-sciences
Criminology
Criminology (BSc), Criminology and Sociology (BSc), Criminology and Social Policy (BSc)
Education
Education (BSc), Education and Welsh (BA)
Sociology
Sociology (BSc), Sociology and Social Policy (BSc), Sociology and Education (BSc)
Social Science
Social Science (BSc)
Human and Social Sciences
Human and Social Sciences (BSc)
Social Analytics
Social Analytics (BSc)
Postgraduate courses
MSc in Childhood and Youth, MSc in Crime, Safety and Justice, MSc in Education, Policy and Society, MSc in Social Science, MSc in Social and Public Policy, MSc in Science, Media and Communication, MSc Social Science Research Methods (SSRM), MSc in Skills and Workforce Development (located in Singapore)

School of Welsh; www.cardiff.ac.uk/welsh
BA Welsh, Welsh and Italian (BA), Welsh and Journalism (BA), Welsh and Music (BA), Welsh and Religious Studies (BA), Welsh and Spanish (BA)
Postgraduate course: MA Welsh and Celtic Studies

College of Biomedical and Life Sciences; www.cardiff.ac.uk/colleges/biomedical-life-sciences

School of Biosciences; www.cardiff.ac.uk/biosciences

BSc Biological Sciences, BSc Biomedical Sciences, BSc Biochemistry, BSc Neuroscience, MBiol: Master's in Biological Sciences, MBiomed: Master's in Biomedical Sciences, MBiochem: Master's in Biochemistry, MNeuro; Master's in Neuroscience

Postgraduate course: Tissue Engineering (MSc/PgDip)

School of Dentistry; www.cardiff.ac.uk/dentistry

Dental Surgery (BDS), Dental Therapy and Hygiene (BSc), Dental Hygiene (Diploma)

Postgraduate courses: Clinical Dentistry (MClinDent), Implantology (MSc/PgDip), Orthodontics (MScD), Tissue Engineering (MSc), Oral Biology (MSc)

School of Healthcare Sciences; www.cardiff.ac.uk/healthcare-sciences

Adult Nursing (BN), Children's Nursing (BN), Diagnostic Radiography and Imaging (BSc), Mental Health Nursing (BN), Midwifery (BMid), Occupational Therapy (BSc), Operating Department Practice (BSc), Physiotherapy (BSc), Radiotherapy and Oncology (BSc)

Postgraduate courses: Advanced Clinical Practice MSc/PgCert, Advanced Practice MSc/PgCert, Community Health Studies (SPQ) MSc/PgDip, Clinical Photography PgCert, Image Appreciation PgDip/PgCert, Managing Care in Perioperative and Anaesthesia Practice MSc/PgDip/PgCert, Occupational Therapy (post-registration) MSc/PgDip, Physiotherapy MSc/PgDip, Radiographic Reporting PgDip/PgCert, Radiography MSc/PgDip, Specialist Community Public Health Nursing MSc/PgDip, Sport & Exercise Physiotherapy MSc/PgDip

School of Medicine; www.cardiff.ac.uk/medicine

Medical Pharmacology (Science route) (BSc), Medicine (MBBCh)

Postgraduate courses: Advanced Surgical Practice MSc, Ageing Health and Disease MSc, Bioinformatics MSc, Bioinformatics and Genetic Epidemiology MSc, Clinical Dermatology MSc, Critical Care MSc, Diabetes MSc/PgDip, Genetic and Genomic Counselling MSc, Medical Research and Innovation MSc/PgDip/PgCert, Medical Toxicology MSc/PgDip/PgCert,

Neonatal Medicine MSc/PgDip, Occupational Health (Policy and Practice) MSc, Pain Management MSc, Pain Management (Primary and Community Care) MSc/PgDip/PgCert, Palliative Medicine for Health Care Professionals MSc, Practical Dermatology MSc/PgDip, Psychiatry MSc, Public Health MPH, Therapeutics MSc/PgDip/PgCert, Wound Healing and Tissue Repair MSc

School of Optometry and Vision Sciences; www.cardiff.ac.uk/optometry-vision-sciences

BSc in Optometry

Postgraduate courses: MSc/Dip/PgCert Clinical Optometry, PGCert Glaucoma, PGCert Eye Care Governance

School of Pharmacy and Pharmaceutical Sciences; www.cardiff.ac.uk/pharmacy-pharmaceutical-sciences

Master of Pharmacy (MPharm)

Postgraduate courses: Cancer Biology and Therapeutics (MSc), Clinical Research MSc, Clinical Pharmacy (MSc/PgDip/PgCert)

School of Psychology; psych.cf.ac.uk

Psychology BSc

Postgraduate courses: MSc in Neuroimaging Methods and Applications, MSc in Social Science Research Methods

College of Physical Sciences and Engineering; www.cardiff.ac.uk/colleges/physical-sciences-engineering

Welsh School of Architecture; www.cardiff.ac.uk/architecture

BSc Architectural Studies

Postgraduate courses: PgDip in Architecture: Professional Practice (Part 3), MA Architectural Design, MSc in Building Diagnostics for Energy and Environmental Performance, Master of Design Administration (MDA), MA in Urban Design, MSc in Environmental Design of Buildings (local and distance learning), MSc in Sustainable Mega Buildings, MSc in Sustainable Building Conservation

School of Chemistry; www.cardiff.ac.uk/chemistry

Chemistry (BSc), Chemistry (MChem)

MSc Catalysis, MSc Biological Chemistry, MSc Medicinal Chemistry

School of Computer Science and Informatics; www.cardiff.ac.uk/computer-science

Applied Software Engineering (BSc), Computer Science (BSc)

Postgraduate courses: MSc Advanced Computer Science, MSc Information Security and Privacy, MSc Computational and Data Journalism, MSc Data Science and Analytics, MSc Computing, MSc Computing and IT Management

School of Earth and Ocean Sciences; www.cardiff.ac.uk/earth-ocean-sciences

Environmental Geography (BSc), Environmental Geography (MESci), Exploration and Resource Geology (BSc), Exploration and Resource Geology (MESci), Environmental Geoscience (BSc), Environmental Geoscience (MESci), Geology (BSc), Geology (MESci), Marine Geography (BSc), Marine Geography (MESci)

School of Engineering; www.cardiff.ac.uk/engineering

Architectural Engineering (BEng/MEng), Civil Engineering (BEng/MEng), Civil and Environmental Engineering (BEng/MEng), Electrical and Electronic Engineering (BEng/MEng), Integrated Engineering (BEng/MEng), Mechanical Engineering (BEng/MEng), Medical Engineering (BEng/MEng)

Postgraduate courses: MSc in Advanced Mechanical Engineering, MSc in Civil and Geoenvironmental Engineering, MSc in Civil and Water Engineering, MSc in Civil Engineering, MSc in Communication Technology and Entrepreneurship, MSc in Electrical Energy Systems, MSc in Manufacturing Engineering, Innovation and Management, MSc in Structural Engineering, MSc in Sustainable Energy and Environment, MSc in Wireless and Microwave Communication Engineering

School of Mathematics; www.cardiff.ac.uk/mathematics

Mathematics (BSc), Mathematics (MMath), Mathematics and its Applications (BSc), Mathematics, Operational Research and Statistics (BSc), Mathematics with Computer Science Options (BSc), Financial Mathematics (BSc), Mathematics and Music (BA)

Postgraduate courses: Operational Research and Applied Statistics (MSc), Operational Research, Applied Statistics and Financial Risk (MSc), Data Science and Analytics (MSc)

School of Physics and Astronomy; www.astro.cardiff.ac.uk

BSc Physics, MPhys Physics, BSc Theoretical and Computational Physics, BSc Physics with Medical Physics, BSc Physics with Astronomy, MPhys Physics with Astronomy, BSc Astrophysics, MPhys Astrophysics, BSc Maths and Physics

Postgraduate courses: MSc Astrophysics, MSc Physics

CARDIFF METROPOLITAN UNIVERSITY
www.cardiffmet.ac.uk

School of Art & Design; www.cardiffmet.ac.uk/artanddesign

Animation BA(Hons), Architectural Design & Technology BSc(Hons), Artist Designer: Maker BA(Hons), Ceramics BA(Hons), Fashion Design BA(Hons), Fine Art BA(Hons), Graphic Communication BA(Hons), Illustration BA(Hons), Interior Design BA(Hons), International Design BA/BSc(Hons), International Design (Architectural Design) BA/BSc(Hons), International Design (Digital Media Design) BA/BSc(Hons), International Design (Experience Design) BA/BSc(Hons), International Design (Graphic Design) BA/BSc(Hons), International Design (Interior Design) BA/BSc(Hons), International Design (Product Design) BA/BSc(Hons), International Design (Textiles Design) BA/BSc(Hons), International Foundation Course (Art & Design), Photographic Practice BA(Hons) (Delivered at Cardiff Arts Academy, Bridgend College), Product Design BA/Bsc(Hons), Textiles BA(Hons)

Postgraduate courses: Art & Design (Art History through Practice) MA/PgD/PgC, Art & Design (Art, Science & Technology) MA/PgD/PgC, Art & Design (Design Futures) MA/PgD/PgC, Art & Design (Ecologies) MA/PgD/PgC, Art & Design (Fashion Design Futures) MA/PgD/PgC, Art & Design (Illustration) MA/PgD/PgC, Art & Design (Philosophy) MA/PgD/PgC, Ceramics MA/PgD/PgC, Fine Art MFA, MRes: Master of Research in Art and Design MRes/PgC, Postgraduate Certificate in Professional and Research Skills: (Art & Design), Product Design MSc/PgD/PgC

School of Education;
www.cardiffmet.ac.uk/education

Creative Writing BA (Joint Hons), Creative Writing and Media BA(Hons), Drama BA (Joint Hons), Drama and Creative Writing BA(Hons), Drama and Media BA(Hons), Early Childhood Studies (Single Honours) BA(Hons), Education Studies & Drama BA(Hons), Education Studies & Early Childhood Studies BA(Hons), Education Studies & English BA(Hons), Education Studies & Sport & Physical Activity BA(Hons), Education, Psychology and Special Educational Needs BA(Hons), English BA (Joint Hons), English & Creative Writing BA(Hons), English & Drama BA(Hons), English & Media BA(Hons), English Language Teaching & Education Studies BA(Hons), English Language Teaching & English BA(Hons), English Language Teaching (ELT) BA (Joint Hons), Media BA (Joint Hons), Primary Education Studies BA(Hons), Primary Education Studies & English Language Teaching BA(Hons), Secondary Education: Music 11-16 (Leading to Qualified Teacher Status) BA(Hons), Secondary Education: Welsh 11-16 (Leading to Qualified Teacher Status) BA(Hons), Youth & Community Work BA(Hons), Youth & Community Work

Postgraduate courses: Creative Writing MA/PgD/PgC, Education (with pathways) MA/PgD/PgC, English Literature MA/PgD/PgC, English Literature & Creative Writing MA/PgD/PgC, Managing Community Practice MA, Post Compulsory Education & Training PGCE/PCE, Primary PGCE, Secondary PGCE, Specialist Journalism MA/PgD/PgC, TESOL MA, Youth & Community Work PgD

School of Health Sciences;
www.cardiffmet.ac.uk/health

iomedical Science BSc(Hons), Biomedical Sciences (Health Exercise & Nutrition) BSc(Hons), Complementary Healthcare (with Practitioner Status) BSc(Hons), Complementary Healthcare (with Practitioner Status) CertHE, Complementary Healthcare (with Practitioner Status) DipHE, Dental Technology BSc(Hons), Environmental Health BSc(Hons), Food Industry Management BSc(Hons), Food Science & Technology BSc(Hons), Foundation leading to BA/BSc Social Sciences, Foundation leading to BSc Health Sciences, Health & Social Care BSc(Hons), Health & Social Care HND, Healthcare Science BSc(Hons), Housing Studies BSc(Hons)/Diploma/HNC, Human Nutrition & Dietetics BSc(Hons), Nutrition BSc(Hons), Podiatry BSc(Hons), Psychology BSc(Hons), Public Health BSc(Hons), Social Work BSc(Hons), Speech and Language Therapy BSc(Hons)

Postgraduate courses: Advanced Practice (with specialist pathways) MSc/PgD/PgC, Applied Public Health MSc/PgD/PgC, Biomedical Science MSc/PgD/PgC, Dental Technology MSc/PgD/PgC, Dietetics MSc/PgD, Food Safety Management MSc/PgD, Food Science & Technology MSc/PgD/PgC, Food Technology for Industry MSc/PgD/PgC, Forensic Psychology Doctorate (D. Foren. Psy.), Forensic Psychology MSc/PgD/PgC, Forensic Psychology (Practitioner Programme) PgD, Health Psychology MSc/PgD/PgC, Master of Research (Biomedical Sciences) MRes/PgC, Master of Research (Health) MRes/PgC, Master of Research (Psychology) MRes/PgC, Occupational Safety, Health & Wellbeing MSc/PgD/PgC

School of Management;
www.cardiffmet.ac.uk/management

Accounting BA(Hons), Accounting & Finance BA(Hons), Business & Management Studies BA(Hons), Business & Management Studies with Finance BA(Hons), Business & Management Studies with Human Resource Management BA(Hons), Business & Management Studies with Information Systems Management BA(Hons), Business & Management Studies with International Business Management BA(Hons), Business & Management Studies with Law BA(Hons), Business & Management Studies with Marketing BA(Hons), Business Economics BA(Hons), Business Information Systems BSc(Hons), Banking & Finance BSc(Hons), Computer Science BSc(Hons), Computer Games Design & Development BSc(Hons), Digital Marketing Management BA(Hons), Economics BSc(Hons), Events Management BA(Hons), Foundation Programme: Cardiff School of Management, Fashion Marketing Management BA(Hons), International Hospitality & Tourism Management BA(Hons), International Hospitality Management BA(Hons), International Tourism & Events Management BA(Hons), International Tourism Management BA(Hons), International Business Management BA(Hons), International Economics & Finance BSc/BScEcon(Hons), International Hospitality & Events Management BA(Hons), International Business Administration (Top-Up) BA(Hons), Marketing Management BA(Hons), Software Engineering BSc(Hons)

Postgraduate courses: Accounting & Finance MSc, Banking & Finance MSc, Computing MSc/PgD/PgC, Data Science MSc/PgD/PgC, Digital Marketing Management MSc/PgD/PgC, Executive MBA, Events

Project Management MSc/PgD/PgC, Economics & Finance MSc, Financial Management MSc/PgD/PgC, Fashion Marketing Management MSc/PgD/PgC, Human Resource Management MSc/PgD/PgC, International Business Management MSc/PgD/PgC, Information Technology Management MSc/PgD/PgC, International Hospitality and Tourism Management MSc/PgD/PgC, International Supply Chain and Logistics Management MSc, LLM International Business Masters of Laws, Strategic Marketing MSc/PgD/PgC, MBA Advanced Entry, MBA Master of Business Administration (MBA), Masters of Research in Management (MRes Management), Doctor of Management (DMan) (Taught Doctorate Degree), Project Management MSc, Production Engineering Management MSc, Sustainable Leadership (PgC)/20Twenty Leadership Programme, Technology Project Management MSc/PgD/PgC

School of Sport; www.cardiffmet.ac.uk/schoolofsport

Dance & Physical Education BA(Hons), Astudiaethau Chwaraeon ac Addysg Gorfforol (dwyieithog)/Sport and Physical Education Studies (bilingual) BSc(Hons), Sport & Exercise Science (Intercalated) BSc(Hons), Sport Performance Analysis BSc(Hons), Sport Studies BSc(Hons), Sport & Exercise Science BSc(Hons), Sport & Physical Education BSc(Hons), Sport Coaching BSc(Hons), Sport Conditioning, Rehabilitation & Massage BSc(Hons), Sport Development BSc(Hons), Sport Management BSc(Hons)

Postgraduate courses: Taught Doctorate in Sport Coaching DSC, Strength & Conditioning MSc/PgD/PgC, Sport Psychology MSc/PgD/PgC, Sport Performance Analysis MSc/PgD/PgC, Sport Management & Leadership MSc/PgD/PgC, Sport Coaching and Pedagogy MSc/PgD/PgC, Sport Broadcast MSc/PgD/PgC, Sport & Exercise Science MSc/PgD/PgC, Sport & Exercise Medicine MSc/PgD/PgC, Sociology and Ethics of Sport MA/PgD/PgC, Professional Practice (Sport Performance Analysis) MSc/PgD

UNIVERSITY OF CENTRAL LANCASHIRE
www.uclan.ac.uk

Faculty of Business, Law and Applied Social Studies; www.uclan.ac.uk/faculties/business-law-applied-social-studies.php

Lancashire School of Business and Enterprise; www.uclan.ac.uk/schools/lancashire-school-business-enterprise/index.php

accounting and finance, accounting, advertising and marketing communications, business administration, accounting and financial studies, international financial management, retail management, business management by elearning, international tourism management, management in tourism, accounting and financial management, human resource management, global business management, international hospitality management, marketing management, international business and management, international business, business studies, management in events, business and management, economics, management in hospitality, business and marketing, marketing management (digital media), event management; Postgraduate courses in management coaching skills, management studies, finance and management, marketing management, international hospitality and event management, international festivals and event management, internship in international tourism, hospitality and event management, human resource management/development, international business and management, human resource management, leadership skills, business management, business administration, international festivals and tourism management, accounting and finance, international hospitality and tourism management, management (elearning); BA(Hons), BSc(Econ), MA, MSc, Cert, PGCert, PGDip, GradDip, MBA, DBA

Lancashire Law School; www.uclan.ac.uk/schools/lancashire-law-school/index.php

criminology and sociology, law, law with psychology, senior status, law with international studies, law with criminology, law with business, criminology and criminal justice; Postgraduate courses in financial and commercial law, law and international security, law, legal practice, international business law; BA(Hons), LLB(Hons), LLM, PGDip, PGCert, GDip

Centre for Excellence in Learning and Teaching; www.uclan.ac.uk/schools/celt/index.php

education and history, education studies, education and sociology, education and psychology; Postgraduate courses in education; BA(Hons), BSc(Hons), MEd, PGDip, EdD

Faculty of Clinical and Biomedical Sciences; www.uclan.ac.uk/faculties/clinical-biomedical-sciences.php

School of Dentistry; www.uclan.ac.uk/schools/dentistry/index.php

dental hygiene and dental therapy, dentistry, dental studies (dental care professionals); Postgraduate courses in prosthodontics, commissioning and dental advising, clinical periodontology, endodontology, mentoring in dental practice, dental implantology, oral surgery; BSc(Hons), BDS, MSc, PGCert, PGDip

School of Medicine; www.uclan.ac.uk/schools/medicine/index.php

physician associate studies, medicine (bachelor of medicine and bachelor of surgery), medical sciences; Postgraduate courses in sports medicine, physician associate studies, musculoskeletal management in primary care, general practice; BSc(Hons), MPAS, MBBS, MSc, PGDip

School of Pharmacy and Biomedical Sciences; www.uclan.ac.uk/schools/pharmacy-biomedical-sciences/index.php

pharmacy, physiology and pharmacology, biomedical science, healthcare science, biomedical science; Postgraduate courses in cancer biology and therapy, advanced pharmacy practice, industrial pharmaceutics; MPharm, BSc(Hons), MSc

Faculty of Culture and the Creative Industries; www.uclan.ac.uk/faculties/culture-creative-industries.php

School of Art, Design and Fashion; www.uclan.ac.uk/schools/art-design-fashion/index.php

fine art, architecture, architectural studies, illustration, textiles, fashion design (with sandwich), interior design, fashion promotion, product design, advertising, graphic design, architectural technology; Postgraduate courses in creative thinking (distance learning), ceramics, fashion and lifestyle promotion, building conservation and adaptation, design, architecture, surface pattern and textiles, graphic design,

product design, fashion design, fashion and lifestyle brand studies, fine art, arts – health, children€™s book illustration, interior design, antiques (distance learning); BA(Hons), BSc(Hons), MA, PGCert, PGDip, MSc

School of Journalism, Media and Performance; www.uclan.ac.uk/schools/journalism-media-performance/index.php

photography, acting, television production, games design, media production, publishing, journalism, animation, music production, sports journalism, film production, music theatre, music, theatre, screenwriting with film, television and radio, web design and development, international journalism, digital visual effects, dancer performance and teaching; Postgraduate courses in scriptwriting, film production, games design, music, photography, publishing, games design (distance learning), animation, journalism, music industry management and promotion, dance and somatic wellbeing; BA(Hons), BSc(Hons), MA, PGCert, PGDip

School of Humanities and the Social Sciences; www.uclan.ac.uk/schools/humanities-social-sciences/index.php

English language and linguistics, politics and philosophy, film and media studies, politics, liberal arts, sociology, English literature and creative writing, English and history, philosophy, English with a modern language, English language and creative writing, education and deaf studies, English language and literature, religion, culture and society, public services, British Sign Language and deaf studies, history, history and politics, English literature; Postgraduate courses in British Sign Language/English interpreting and translation, history, religion, culture and society; BA(Hons), MA, PGDip, MRes

School of Language and Global Studies; www.uclan.ac.uk/schools/language-global-studies/index.php

teaching English to speakers of other languages and modern languages, English for international corporate communication with a modern foreign language, modern languages (Arabic, French, German, Japanese or Spanish) for international business, Asia Pacific studies, English for international corporate communication, business management and Chinese, international business communication, modern languages (Arabic, Chinese, French, German, Japanese, Korean, Russian and Spanish); Postgraduate courses in interpreting and translation, intercultural business communication, teaching English to speakers of other languages (TESOL) with applied linguistics; BA(Hons), MA

Faculty of Health and Wellbeing; www.uclan.ac.uk/faculties/health-wellbeing.php

School of Community Health and Midwifery; www.uclan.ac.uk/schools/community-health-midwifery/index.php

neonatal practice, sexual health practice, health and social care, counselling and psychotherapy studies, midwifery (direct entry programme), specialist community public health nurse – health visiting or school nursing or sexual health adviser, health and social care, sexual health studies, health and social care, community specialist practitioner, midwifery for registered nurses; Postgraduate courses in specialist community public health nurse – health visiting or school nursing or sexual health adviser, supervision of counselling and psychotherapy, safeguarding in an international context, applied public health, health and social care education, community specialist practitioner, sexual health studies, sustainability, health and wellbeing, primary care mental health practice, applied public health, midwifery, psychosexual therapy, integrative psychotherapy; BSc(Hons), FCert, FDSC, FDA, PGDip, Cert, MSc, PGCert, MA

School of Health Sciences; www.uclan.ac.uk/schools/health-sciences/index.php

professional practice, nurse practitioner, paramedic practice, physiotherapy, enhanced paramedic practice, sports therapy, operating department practice; Postgraduate courses in advanced practice, clinical research, health informatics, enhanced clinical practice, health informatics, delivering quality cancer services, injection therapy, health informatics, health; BSc(Hons), DipHE, MSc, PGDip, PGCert, Cert, DProf

School of Nursing; www.uclan.ac.uk/schools/nursing/index.php

nursing, child and adolescent mental health, nursing (children), nursing (adult), nursing (mental health), psychosocial mental health care; Postgraduate courses in nursing, child and adolescent mental health, personality disorder, nursing (adult or mental health), personality disorder, personality disorder (research), conflict and violence minimisation, paediatric critical care, philosophy and mental health,

investigating serious incidents; BSc(Hons), MSc, PGCert, PGDip, MA

School of Social Work, Care and Community; www.uclan.ac.uk/schools/social-work-care-community/index.php

children, schools and families, community and social care: policy and practice, community and social care (integrated), community leadership, social policy and sociology, social work, children, schools and families, social pedagogy, advocacy and participation, community leadership; Postgraduate courses in professional development and practice, doctor of professional practice, community social care policy and practice, community leadership, advanced community justice, contemporary practice with children and young people, specialist practice with adults, specialist child care practice, leadership and management in social work and social care, mental health practice including approved mental health professional training, safeguarding children, social policy, equality and community leadership, social work; BA(Hons), FDA, MA, PGDip, PGCert, DProf

School of Sport and Wellbeing; www.uclan.ac.uk/schools/sport-wellbeing/index.php

sports coaching and development, sport and exercise physiology, outdoor adventure leadership, sport science, exercise and fitness management, sport (studies), sports (coaching and development), nutrition and exercise sciences, sport and physical education, sports coaching, sport business management, strength and conditioning, sports coaching (with optional sports coach UK endorsed pathway), sports (coaching), nutrition and exercise sciences (personal fitness training), sport business (management), nutrition and exercise sciences (human nutrition), strength and conditioning, outdoor leadership; Postgraduate courses in elite performance, nutrition and food sciences, elite coaching practice, hazard analysis critical control point (HACCP), sports leadership and professional development, sports marketing and business management, sports coaching, sport and exercise science, physical education and school sport, strength and conditioning, food safety management; BA(Hons), BSc(Hons), PGCert, PGDip, DProf, MRes, MA, MSc

Faculty of Science and Technology; www.uclan.ac.uk/faculties/science-technology.php

School of Engineering; www.uclan.ac.uk/schools/engineering/index.php

fire engineering, mechanical engineering, fire safety engineering, robotics engineering, electronic engineering, fire safety (management), robotics engineering, quantity surveying, construction project management, civil engineering, electronic engineering, motorsports engineering, facilities management, computer aided engineering, energy engineering, oil and gas safety engineering, aerospace engineering, building services and sustainable engineering, fire and leadership studies, fire engineering, mechanical maintenance engineering, aerospace engineering, fire safety (engineering), building surveying; Postgraduate courses in maintenance engineering, fire safety engineering, oil and gas engineering, nuclear security and safeguards, nuclear safety, renewable energy engineering, fire investigation, fire scene investigation, nuclear safety, security and safeguards, fire and rescue service management, mechanical engineering, project management, construction project management, building service, construction law and dispute resolution; MEng, BEng(Hons), BSc(Hons), MSc, PGDip, PGCert

School of Forensic and Applied Sciences; www.uclan.ac.uk/schools/forensic-applied-sciences/index.php

forensic science and molecular biology, archaeology, forensic science, environmental management, forensic science and criminal investigation, forensic science and anthropology, archaeology and anthropology, policing and criminal investigation, policing, archaeology, geography, biology, forensic science and chemical analysis; Postgraduate courses in forensic science, financial investigation, criminal investigation, professional practice (early action), forensic and conservation genetics, waste and resource management, document analysis, health safety and environmental management, forensic anthropology, criminal justice, counter terrorism, DNA profiling, energy and environmental management, cybercrime investigation; MSci, BSc(Hons), FDSC, BA(Hons), MSc, PGDip, PGCert

School of Physical Sciences and Computing; www.uclan.ac.uk/schools/physical-sciences-computing/index.php

computer games development, astrophysics, chemistry, physics with astrophysics, computing, computer network technology, physics, astronomy, forensic computing and security, computer networks and security, chemistry, mathematics, computer science, forensic computing, software engineering; Postgraduate courses in user experience design, IT security, interaction design, synthetic organic chemistry, child computer interaction, agile leadership, instrumental analysis, computing, forensic toxicology; MComp, MPhys, BSc(Hons), MChem, MMath, FDSc, MSc, MRes, PGDip

School of Psychology; www.uclan.ac.uk/schools/psychology/index.php

psychology of child development, forensic psychology, psychology with psychotherapy counselling, health psychology, psychology and criminology, social psychology, neuropsychology, neuroscience, psychology; Postgraduate courses in forensic psychology, psychology of child development, health psychology, psychology conversion, applied criminal psychology; BSc(Hons), MSc

UNIVERSITY OF CHESTER
www.chester.ac.uk

Dept of Acute Adult Care; www.chester.ac.uk/health/aac

advanced practice, critical care pathway, professional practice, professional nursing (international), return to practice nursing; BSc(Hons), MSc, GCert, PGCert, MSc

Dept of Archaeology; www.chester.ac.uk/departments/history-archaeology

history, combined history, archaeology, combined archaeology; Postgraduate courses in archaeology and heritage practice, archaeology of death and memory, history, past landscapes and environments, war, conflict and society, archaeology, history; BA(Hons, MA, MRes

Dept of Art and Design;
www.chester.ac.uk/art-design

animation, fashion design, fashion marketing and communication, fine art, graphic design, interior design, photography and product design; Postgraduate courses in fine art; BA(Hons), MRes, MA

Dept of Biological Sciences;
www.chester.ac.uk/departments/
biological-sciences

animal behaviour, animal behaviour & welfare, biology, biomedical science, bioveterinary science, conservation biology, forensic biology, wildlife conservation & ecology, top-up animal management, top-up healthcare science (anatomical pathology technology), top-up zoo management; Postgraduate courses in wildlife conservation, applied wildlife forensics, various research programmes; BSc(Hons), MSc, PGDip, PGCert

Dept of Business and Finance;
www.chester.ac.uk/bse

accounting and finance, banking and business finance, business finance, business management, international business management, international business management with a language, integrated master's in business, global entrepreneurship and business management; Postgraduate courses in management, international business, international finance, marketing management, business administration; BSc(Hons), MBus, BA(Hons), MSc, MBA

Dept of Chemical Engineering;
www.chester.ac.uk/chemical-engineering

chemical engineering; BSc

Chester Medical School;
www.chester.ac.uk/medicine

biochemistry, biotechnology, genetics and evolution, health and exercise science, immunology, medical biochemistry, medical genetics, medical science, microbiology, pharmacology; Postgraduate courses in biomedical science, cardiovascular disease, clinical bariatric practice, diabetes, gastroenterology, haematology, infection and immunity, medical genetics, medicine of ageing, medicolegal practice, oncology, orthopaedics, physician associate, psychiatric medicine, respiratory medicine, exercise medicine, stem cell and tissue regeneration, medical leadership and management; BSc(Hons), MSc, MBA

Dept of Clinical Sciences and Nutrition;
www.chester.ac.uk/csn

nutrition and exercise science, human nutrition, nutrition and dietetics, public health nutrition; Postgraduate courses in cardiovascular health and rehabilitation, exercise and nutrition science, exercise and nutrition science, human nutrition, nutrition and dietetics, obesity and weight management, public health nutrition; BSc, MSc, MPhil, PhD

Dept of Computer Science;
www.chester.ac.uk/csis

applied computing, computer science, computer science, cybersecurity, games development, software engineering; Postgraduate courses in advanced computer science, cybersecurity (conversion), project engineering, programme and project management; BSc, MComp, MSc, MRes, PhD

Faculty of Education and Children's Services; www.chester.ac.uk/education

childhood and youth professional studies, early childhood studies, education studies, teacher education: early years – primary education (3-7) with QTS, teacher education: primary education (5-11) with QTS; Postgraduate courses in primary (5-11 years), primary/early years (3-7 years), early years practice with EYTS, secondary, school direct initial teacher education, qualified teacher status (QTS) assessment only, creative practices in education, education, dyslexia research and practice, early childhood, education in society, educational leadership, educational practice, SENCO – national award for SEN coordination, special educational needs and disability; BA(Hons), PGCE, MA, EdD

Dept of Electronic and Electrical Engineering; www.chester.ac.uk/
electronic-engineering

electronic and electrical engineering; BEng, MEng

Dept of English; www.chester.ac.uk/english

English literature, English language, English language and literature, creative writing; Postgraduate courses in creative writing: writing and publishing fiction, English language and linguistics, modern and contemporary fiction, nineteenth-century literature and culture, gender studies, English, storytelling; BA(Hons), MA, MRes, MPhil, PhD

Dept of Geography and International Development; www.chester.ac.uk/geography

geography (single or combined), international development studies, natural hazard management; Postgraduate courses in regeneration for practitioners; BA(Hons), BSc(Hons), MA, MSc, PGCert, PGDip

Dept of Health and Social Care; www.chester.ac.uk/health

midwifery, pre-registration nursing (adult), pre-registration nursing (children), pre-registration nursing (learning disability), pre-registration nursing (mental health); health and social care, non-medical prescribing, professional practice, palliative and end of life care, return to practice (midwifery), return to practice (nursing), social work, specialist community practice health nursing, specialist practice community; Postgraduate courses in advanced practice, advancing community treatment options and responses, applied mental health practice, art therapy, cancer care, critical care, professional studies in health and social care, public health, endodontology, global health, maternal and women's reproductive health, non-medical prescribing, oncology for health and social care practitioners, professional education, professional education, professional nursing (international), professional studies, restorative dentistry, return to practice (midwifery), return to practice (nursing), social work, specialist community practice health nursing, specialist practice community; BSc, BN, BA, BSc(Hons), GDip, PGCert, PGDip, MSc, MEd, DProf, DrPH, MA

Dept of History & Archaeology; www.chester.ac.uk/departments/history-archaeology

history (single or combined), archaeology (single or combined); Postgraduate courses in archaeology and heritage practice, archaeology of death and memory, history, past landscapes and environments, war, conflict and society, archaeology; BA(Hons), MA, MRes

Institute of Food Science and Innovation; www.chester.ac.uk/isfi

advances in food and beverage packaging, food science & innovation, food manufacturing with operations management (top-up), dairy technology, bakery & patisserie technology, food manufacturing with business management; BSc(Hons), FdSc

Institute of Gender Studies; www.chester.ac.uk/igs

gender studies MRes

Dept of Law; www.chester.ac.uk/law

law, law with business, law with criminology, law with politics, contemporary legal studies; LLB, LLM

Dept of Marketing, Tourism & Events Management; www.chester.ac.uk/mtem

events management (single or combined), marketing management (single or combined), international tourism management (single, combined or with a language); BA(Hons)

Dept of Mathematics; www.chester.ac.uk/maths

mathematics; BSc(Hons), MSc, PGDip, PGCert, PhD, MPhil

Dept of Mechanical Engineering; www.chester.ac.uk/mechanical-engineering

manufacturing engineering, mechanical engineering; BEng, MEng

Dept of Media; www.chester.ac.uk/media

advertising, broadcast production and presenting, commercial music production, digital photography, film studies, journalism (single or combined), media, media studies, music journalism, music production and promotion, radio production, sports journalism, television production; Postgraduate courses in broadcast media, media, multiplatform production, radio production television production; BA(Hons), MA, PGDip, PGCert

Dept of Mental Health and Learning Disability; www.chester.ac.uk/health/mhld

art therapy, health and social care (assistant practitioner); MA, FdSc

Dept of Midwifery, Child and Reproductive Health; www.chester.ac.uk/health/mcrh

midwifery; maternal and women€™s reproductive health, return to practice (midwifery); BSc, MSc

Dept of Modern Languages

modern languages, Chinese studies, French (single or combined), German, Spanish (single or combined), Spanish, Portuguese and Latin American studies; Postgraduate courses in European languages and global cultures, modern languages; BA(Hons), MA, MRes

Dept of Natural Sciences; www.chester.ac.uk/natural-sciences

physics, chemistry; Postgraduate course in applied sciences; BSc, MRes

Dept of Performing Arts; www.chester.ac.uk/departments/performing-arts

dance, drama and theatre studies, music, music journalism, musical theatre, performing arts, popular music performance; Postgraduate courses in arts and media, dance, drama, popular music; BA(Hons), MA, PGDip, PGCert

Dept of Psychology; www.chester.ac.uk/psychology

psychology (single or combined), forensic psychology, applied psychology; Postgraduate courses in psychology, family and child psychology, cognitive & behavioural therapies: high intensity training, CBT clinical supervision: high intensity, CBT clinical supervision: low intensity; BSc(Hons), MSc, PGDip, PGCert, MRes, MPhil, PhD

Dept of Public Health and Wellbeing; www.chester.ac.uk/health/phw

advancing community treatment options and responses, public health, non-medical prescribing, palliative and end of life care, specialist community practice health nursing, specialist practice community; BSc(Hons), GDip, PGCert, PGDip, MSc

Dept of Social and Political Science; www.chester.ac.uk/sps

counselling skills, criminology (single or combined), economics, economics and business, international relations, politics (single or combined), sociology (single or combined); BA(Hons), BSc(Hons)

Dept of Social Work and Interprofessional Education; www.chester.ac.uk/health/swipe

advanced oral health sciences, applied mental health practice, cancer care, professional studies in health and social care, endodontology, health and social care, professional education, professional education, professional studies, restorative dentistry, social work; FdSc, BA(Hons), DProf, MSc, MA, PGCert, PGDip

Dept of Sport and Community Engagement; www.chester.ac.uk/space

sports coaching, sport development and coaching, sport development, physical activity and health, sport management; BSc(Hons), BA(Hons), FD

Dept of Theology and Religious Studies; www.chester.ac.uk/trs

religious studies, theology, theology and religious studies (single or combined); Postgraduate courses in theology, religions studies, practical theology; BA(Hons), MA, professional doctorate, MPhil, PhD

Warrington School of Management; www.chester.ac.uk/warrington-school-of-management

business, business management, marketing and advertising management, events management, hospitality management, events management and commercial music production, sports events management, sport marketing and management; Postgraduate courses in creative industries management, digital marketing, health services management, management, engineering management, sport management; BSc(Hons), BA(Hons), MSc, PGDip, PGCert

UNIVERSITY OF CHICHESTER
www.chiuni.ac.uk

Business School; www.chi.ac.uk/business-school

accounting and finance, business studies, charity development, data science, digital marketing, environmental management and sustainability in business, event and hospitality management, event management, human resource management, IT management for business, marketing, software development for business, sustainable tourism management, tourism management, tourism and hospitality management, international English studies, accounting & finance and IES, marketing and tourism management, event management and tourism management, marketing and tourism management, tourism management with international English studies; Postgraduate courses in leadership & management, digital marketing; BA(Hons), BSc(Hons), MA, MSc, PhD

Dept of Childhood, Social Work and Social Care; www.chi.ac.uk/department-childhood-social-work-social-care

social work, children & families, adult social care, foundation early years, early childhood studies; BA(Hons), PhD

Dept of Creative and Digital Technologies; www.chi.ac.uk/department-creative-digital-technologies

3D animation and visual effects, creative and digital media, digital film production and screenwriting, film and television studies, media and communications, screen acting and creative technologies, digital film technologies, screenwriting, sports media, creative writing and screenwriting; BA(Hons), BSc(Hons)

Dept of Dance; www.chi.ac.uk/department-dance

dance, dance performance, dance studies, dance science; Postgraduate courses in performance: dance (mapdance), somatic practices by independent research, dance research, choreography and professional practices, secondary dance; BA(Hons), MA, PGCE

Institute of Education; www.chi.ac.uk/institute-education

primary, secondary; Postgraduate courses in education, inclusive special education, growth mindsets, national award for SENCO, school business managers, workplace learning development, workplace learning development (send policy and practice); PGCE, PGCiPP, MA

Dept of Engineering and Design; www.chi.ac.uk/engineering-and-design

science and engineering – integrated foundation year, electronics & electrical engineering, mechanical engineering & materials, sports engineering, product design & innovation, biomedical materials engineering, creative science, product design, mechanical engineering; BEng(Hons), BSc(Hons), BA(Hons), MEng

Dept of English and Creative Writing; www.chi.ac.uk/department-english-and-creative-writing

English literature; creative writing and English, English literature and language, creative writing, English literature and drama studies, drama and theatre; BA(Hons), PhD

Dept of Fine Art; www.chi.ac.uk/fine-art

fine art, fine art with printmaking, fine art with sculpture, fine art with textiles, history of art and fine art, painting and drawing; Postgraduate course in fine art; BA(Hons), MA

Dept of History and Politics; www.chi.ac.uk/department-history-and-politics

history, medieval and early modern history, modern history, politics and contemporary history, politics; Postgraduate courses in cultural history, the history of Africa and the African diaspora; BA, BSc(Hons), MA, MRes, MPhil, PhD

Dept of Music; www.chi.ac.uk/department-music

acting for film, IES and music, music, music performance, music performance and acting for film, music and musical theatre, music with arts development, music with IES, music with jazz studies, music with musical theatre, music with teaching, music with workshop leadership, music, marketing and administration, musical theatre (triple threat), musical theatre performance, musical theatre and acting for film, musical theatre and arts development, choral directing, instrumental teaching, jazz performance, orchestral performance, performance, vocal performance, vocal teaching; Postgraduate courses in music performance, advanced performance; BA(Hons), BMus(Hons), MA

Dept of Psychology and Counselling; www.chi.ac.uk/department-psychology-and-counselling

psychology, humanistic counselling, counselling, advanced applied psychology; BSc(Hons), Dip, BA(Hons), Cert, MSci

Department of Sport Development and Management; www.chi.ac.uk/department-sport-development-management

community sport coaching, community sport coaching, football coaching and performance, sport business & management, sport development & coaching, sports media, sport studies, sport tourism; BA(Hons), BSc(Hons), FdSc

Department of Physical Education; www.chi.ac.uk/department-pe

PE and sports coaching, PE in the primary years, PE in the secondary years; BA(Hons)

Department of Adventure Education; www.chi.ac.uk/department-adventure-education

outdoor and adventure education, adventure facilitation and education; BA(Hons)

Department of Sport and Exercise Sciences; www.chi.ac.uk/department-sport-and-exercise-sciences

sport and exercise psychology, sport and exercise science (performance sailing), sport and exercise science (physical activity for health), sport and exercise science (sport performance), sport science and coaching, sports therapy, dance science; Postgraduate courses in sport and exercise biomechanics, sport and exercise physiology, sport and exercise psychology (BPS stage 1), sports coaching science, sports performance analysis, strength and conditioning, sport and exercise science, sports therapy; BSc(Hons), MSc, MSci

Department of Theatre; www.chi.ac.uk/department-theatre

acting, drama and theatre, theatre, performing arts (theatre performance and dance), theatre (performance and production); BA(Hons)

Department of Theology, Philosophy and Religious Studies; www.chi.ac.uk/department-theology-philosophy-and-religious-studies

philosophy and ethics, theology, religion, ethics and society; Postgraduate courses in Christian ministry, public theology, schools chaplaincy; BA(Hons), MA

CITY UNIVERSITY LONDON
www.city.ac.uk

Cass Business School; www.cass.city.ac.uk

accounting and finance, actuarial science, banking and international finance, business management, business management, digital innovation and entrepreneurship, business studies, business with finance, business with marketing, finance, international business, investment and financial risk management, management; Postgraduate courses in finance, corporate finance, investment management, banking & international finance, international accounting & finance, real estate investment, global finance (taught online), finance & investment (taught part-time), mathematical trading & finance, quantitative finance, financial mathematics, management, global supply chain management, marketing strategy & innovation, entrepreneurship, innovation, creativity and leadership, real estate, real estate investment, actuarial science, actuarial management, insurance & risk management, energy, trade & finance, shipping, trade & finance, actuarial management, finance & investment, insurance & risk management, global finance (taught online), voluntary sector management, charity accounting & financial management, charity marketing & fundraising, grantmaking, philanthropy & social investment, NGO management, business administration; BSc(Hons), MSc, PGCert, PGDip, MBA, EMBA

School of Arts & Social Sciences; www.city.ac.uk/arts-social-sciences

criminology, criminology and psychology, criminology and sociology, economics, economics with accounting, English, financial economics, history, international political economy, international politics, international politics and sociology, journalism, media, communication and sociology, music, music, sound and technology, politics, psychology, sociology, sociology with psychology; Postgraduate courses in audiovisual translation and popular culture, behavioural economics, broadcast journalism, business economics/international business economics, clinical, social and cognitive neuroscience, composition, creative writing (non-fiction/novels/playwriting and screenwriting), creative writing and publishing, criminology and criminal justice, culture, policy and management, development economics, diplomacy and foreign policy, economic evaluation in health care, economics, Erasmus Mundus masters: journalism, media and globalisation, ethnomusicology, financial economics, financial journalism, food policy, global political economy, counselling psychology, health economics, interactive journalism, international communications and development, international journalism, international politics, international politics and human rights, international publishing, investigative journalism, magazine journalism, media and communications, music, newspaper journalism, organisational psychology, counselling psychology, publishing, research methods, research methods with psychology, television journalism; BSc(Hons), BA, MA, MSc, GCert

School of Health Sciences; www.city.ac.uk/health

speech and language science, midwifery, nursing: adult, nursing: child, nursing: mental health, optometry, radiography (diagnostic imaging), radiography (radiotherapy and oncology), speech and language therapy, health and social care; postgraduate courses in adult and mental health nursing (pre-registration), speech and language therapy, midwifery, nursing (adult), nursing (child), nursing (mental health), public health (school nursing, health visiting and district nursing), adult and mental health nursing, speech and language therapy, nursing studies, return to practice nursing, primary care; BSc(Hons), MSc, PGDip

School of Mathematics, Computer Science & Engineering; www.city.ac.uk/mathematics-computer-science-engineering

aeronautical engineering, biomedical engineering, business computing systems, civil engineering, computer science, computer science with cyber security, computer science with games technology, data science, electrical and electronic engineering,

engineering, mathematics, mathematics and finance, mathematics with finance and economics, mechanical engineering, structural engineering; Postgraduate courses in air safety management, air transport management, aircraft maintenance management, airport management, biomedical engineering with healthcare technology management, business systems analysis and design, civil engineering structures, civil engineering structures (nuclear power plants) computer games technology, construction management, cyber security, data science, energy and environmental technology and economics, health informatics, human-computer interaction design, information science, information systems and technology, internet of things with entrepreneurship, library science, maritime operations and management, mechanical engineering, project management, finance and risk, renewable energy and power systems management, software engineering, temporary works and construction method engineering; BSc(Hons), BEng(Hons), MEng, MSci, MSc

City Law School; www.city.ac.uk/law

LLB, LLB in legal practice (online); Postgraduate courses in law, LLM, innovation, creativity and leadership; LLB, LLM, MSc, MA, MInnov, MPhil, PhD

GUILDHALL SCHOOL OF MUSIC & DRAMA
www.gsmd.ac.uk

Department of Music; www.gsmd.ac.uk/music/

BMus(Hons) with principal study in strings, harp & guitar, wind, brass & percussion, keyboard, vocal studies, composition, electronic music, jazz, early instruments, BA performance & creative enterprise; Postgraduate courses: Guildhall Artist Masters in performance, composition or leadership, orchestral artistry in association with London Symphony Orchestra, artist diploma (for strings, wind, brass, percussion, keyboard, vocal studies, opera studies), MA in music therapy, MA in opera making & writing in association with the Royal Opera House, PGCert performance teaching, MPhil/DMus, MPhil/PhD in music (including music therapy)

Department of Drama; www.gsmd.ac.uk/acting/

BA(Hons) acting; Postgraduate courses: MA acting, MA in training actors, PGCert performance teaching, BA performance & creative enterprise

Department of Technical Theatre; www.gsmd.ac.uk/technical.theatre

BA(Hons) technical theatre arts, with pathways in stage management, costume supervision, design realisation (scenic art, scenic construction & props), and theatre technology, BA(Hons) video design for live performance; Postgraduate courses: MA collaborative theatre production & design, PGCert performance teaching, MPhil/DMus, MPhil/PhD in music (including music therapy), and drama

Creative Learning

BA(Hons) performance & creative enterprise, MMus leadership

REGENTS UNIVERSITY LONDON
www.regents.ac.uk

Business & Management

global management – final year entry – BA(Hons), global management (enterprise & innovation) – BA(Hons), global management (enterprise & innovation) with integrated foundation – BA(Hons), global management (finance) – BA(Hons), global management (finance) with integrated foundation – BA(Hons), global management (leadership & management) – BA(Hons), global management (leadership & management) with integrated foundation – BA(Hons), global management (marketing) – BA(Hons), global management (marketing) with integrated foundation – BA(Hons), international business (French) – BA(Hons), international business (French) with integrated foundation – BA(Hons), international business (German) – BA(Hons), international business (German) with integrated foundation – BA(Hons), international business (Italian) – BA(Hons), international business (Italian) with integrated foundation – BA(Hons), international business (Japanese) – BA(Hons), international business (Japanese) with integrated foundation – BA(Hons), international business (mandarin Chinese) – BA(Hons), international business (mandarin Chinese) with integrated foundation – BA(Hons), international business (Russian) – BA(Hons), international business (Russian) with integrated foundation – BA(Hons), international business (Spanish) – BA(Hons), international business (Spanish) with integrated foundation – BA(Hons), international events management – BA(Hons), international events management with integrated foundation – BA(Hons)

Fashion & Design

fashion design – BA(Hons), fashion design – BA(Hons) with integrated foundation, fashion design with marketing – BA(Hons), fashion design with marketing – BA(Hons) with integrated foundation, fashion marketing – BA(Hons), fashion marketing – BA(Hons) with integrated foundation, interior design – BA(Hons), interior design – BA(Hons) with integrated foundation

Film, Media & Performance

acting & world theatre – BA(Hons), acting & world theatre – BA(Hons) with integrated foundation, film, tv & digital media production – BA(Hons), film, tv & digital media production – BA(Hons) with integrated foundation, screenwriting & producing – BA(Hons), screenwriting & producing – BA(Hons) with integrated foundation

Liberal Arts & Humanities

liberal studies (art history) – BA(Hons), liberal studies (art history) with integrated foundation – BA(Hons), liberal studies (business & management) – BA(Hons), liberal studies (business and management) with integrated foundation – BA(Hons), liberal studies (english) – BA(Hons), liberal studies (english) with integrated foundation – BA(Hons), liberal studies (history) – BA(Hons), liberal studies (history) with integrated foundation – BA(Hons), liberal studies (international relations) – BA(Hons), liberal studies (international relations) with integrated foundation – BA(Hons), liberal studies (journalism) – BA(Hons), liberal studies (journalism) with integrated foundation – BA(Hons), liberal studies (media & communications) – BA(Hons), liberal studies (media & communications) with integrated foundation – BA(Hons), liberal studies (political science) – BA(Hons), liberal studies (political science) with integrated foundation – BA(Hons), liberal studies (psychology) – BA(Hons), liberal studies (psychology) with integrated foundation – BA(Hons), liberal studies (public relations) – BA(Hons), liberal studies (public relations) with integrated foundation – BA(Hons)

Psychotherapy & Psychology

psychology – BSc(Hons), psychology with integrated foundation – BSc(Hons) with integrated foundation

THE NORDOFF-ROBBINS MUSIC THERAPY CENTRE
www.nordoff-robbins.org.uk

music therapy, music, health, society; MMusTherapy, PGDip, MPhil, PhD, DPsych

TRINITY LABAN CONSERVATOIRE OF MUSIC & DANCE
www.labantrinity.ac.uk

Music; www.trinitylaban.ac.uk/study/music

BMus(Hons) in music; Postgraduate courses: MA music education and performance, MA in music, master of music (MMus), MFA creative practice, postgraduate advanced diploma, postgraduate diploma; research degree programme: MPhil/PhD in dance/music/collaborative arts, the teaching musician – postgraduate certificate, diploma and MA

Musical Theatre; www.trinitylaban.ac.uk/study/musical-theatre

BA(Hons) musical theatre performance

Dance; www.trinitylaban.ac.uk/study/dance

BA(Hons) contemporary dance; Postgraduate courses: postgraduate diploma: community dance, MA dance performance (Transitions Dance Company), MA/MFA choreography, MA/MFA creative practice: transdisciplinary, MA/MFA creative practice: dance professional practice, MFA dance science, MSc dance science, MPhil/PhD in dance/music/collaborative arts

COVENTRY UNIVERSITY
www.coventry.ac.uk

Faculty of Arts and Humanities; www.coventry.ac.uk/study-at-coventry/faculties-and-schools/arts-and-humanities/

School of Art and Design; www.coventry.ac.uk/study-at-coventry/faculties-and-schools/arts-and-humanities/art-and-design/

Architecture BSc(Hons), Automotive and Transport Design MDes/BA(Hons), Fashion BA(Hons), Fine Art BA(Hons), Fine Art and Illustration BA(Hons), Foundation Diploma in Art and Design, Graphic Design BA(Hons), Illustration and Animation BA(Hons), Illustration and Graphic Design BA(Hons), Interior Design MDes/BA(Hons), Product Design MDes/BA(Hons); Postgraduate courses: Automotive Design MA, Contemporary Arts Practice MA, Design and Transport MSc, Graphic Design MA, Illustration and Animation MA, Industrial Product Design MSc, Interior Design MA, Painting MA

School of Humanities; www.coventry.ac.uk/study-at-coventry/faculties-and-schools/arts-and-humanities/humanities/

English BA(Hons), English and Creative Writing BA(Hons), English and Journalism BA(Hons), English and TEFL BA(Hons), French and International Relations BA(Hons), History BA(Hons), History and Politics BA(Hons), International Fashion Business BA(Hons), International Relations BA(Hons), Languages for International Business BA(Hons), Politics BA(Hons), Sociology BA(Hons), Sociology and Criminology BA(Hons), Spanish BA(Hons); Postgraduate courses: Diplomacy, Law and Global Change MA, English Language Teaching and Applied Linguistics MA, International Relations MA, Professional Creative Writing MA, Teaching English for Academic Purposes MA, Terrorism, International Crime and Global Security MA

School of Media and Performing Arts; www.coventry.ac.uk/study-at-coventry/faculties-and-schools/arts-and-humanities/media-and-performing-arts/

Dance BA(Hons), Digital Media BA(Hons), Journalism BA(Hons), Media and Communications BA(Hons), Media Production BA(Hons), Music BA(Hons), Music Technology BSc(Hons), Photography BA(Hons), Theatre and Professional Practice BA(Hons); Postgraduate courses: Automotive Journalism MA, Collaborative Theatre Making MA, Communication, Culture and Media MA, Film and TV MA (Online), Global Journalism MA, 21st Century Media Practice MA

Coventry Business School; www.coventry.ac.uk/study-at-coventry/faculties-and-schools/coventry-business-school/

Accountancy BA(Hons), Accounting and Finance BA(Hons), Advertising and Marketing BA(Hons),

Business Administration BA(Hons), Business and Finance BA(Hons), Business and Human Resource Management BA(Hons), Business and Marketing BA(Hons), Business Economics BA(Hons), Business Management BA(Hons), Digital Marketing BA(Hons), Economics BA(Hons), Enterprise and Entrepreneurship BA(Hons), European Business Management BA(Hons), Event Management BA(Hons), Finance BSc(Hons), Finance and Investment BA(Hons), Financial Economics BA(Hons), International Business Management BA(Hons), International Economics and Trade BA(Hons), Marketing BA(Hons), Sport Management BA(Hons), Sport Marketing BA(Hons); Postgraduate courses: Accounting and Financial Management MSc, Advertising and Marketing MA, Banking and Finance MSc, Brand Management MA, The MBA in Cyber Security, Digital Marketing MA, Finance MSc, Global Entrepreneurship MA, Human Resource Development PgDip, Human Resource Management PgDip, Human Resource Management MA, Human Resource Management MA Top Up, International Business MSc, International Business Economics MSc, International Business Management MSc, International Events Management MSc, International Human Resource Management MSc, International Marketing MSc, Investment Management MSc, Islamic Finance MSc, Leadership and Management MA, Marketing Management MA, Sport Management MSc, Sport Marketing MA, Strategic Marketing MSc

Faculty of Engineering, Environment and Computing; www.coventry.ac.uk/study-at-coventry/faculties-and-schools/engineering-environment-and-computing/

School of Computing, Electronics and Mathematics; www.coventry.ac.uk/study-at-coventry/faculties-and-schools/engineering-environment-and-computing/computing-electronics-and-mathematics/

Computer Hardware and Software Engineering BEng(Hons), Computer Science MSci/BSc(Hons), Computing BSc(Hons), Electrical and Electronic Engineering MEng/BEng(Hons), Electronic Engineering BEng(Hons), Ethical Hacking and Cybersecurity MSci/BSc(Hons), Games Technology BSc(Hons), Information Technology for Business BSc(Hons), Mathematics BSc(Hons), Mathematics and Data Analytics MSci/BSc(Hons), Mathematics and Physics BSc(Hons), Mathematics and Statistics BSc(Hons), Multimedia Computing BSc(Hons); Postgraduate courses: Computer Science MSc, Cyber Security MSc, Data Science and Computational Intelligence MSc, Digital Technology for Engineering MSc, Electrical and Electronic Engineering MSc, Electronic Engineering MSc, Embedded Microelectrics and Wireless Systems MSc, Forensic Computing Msc, Information Technology Management MBA, Information Technology MSc, Management Information Systems MSc, Management of Information Technology MSc, Network Computing MSc, Software Development MSc

School of Energy, Construction and Environment; www.coventry.ac.uk/study-at-coventry/faculties-and-schools/engineering-environment-and-computing/energy-construction-and-environment/

Architectural Technology BSc(Hons), Building Services Engineering BEng(Hons), Building Surveying BSc(Hons), Civil Engineering BEng(Hons), Civil Engineering BSc(Hons), Civil Engineering MEng, Construction Management BSc(Hons), Disaster Management and Emergency Planning BSc(Hons), Environmental Engineering MEng/BEng, Geography BA(Hons), Geography BSc(Hons), International Disaster Management BSc(Hons), Geography and Natural Hazards BSc(Hons), Oil, Gas and Energy Management BSc(Hons), Quantity Surveying and Commercial Management BSc(Hons); Postgraduate courses: Agroecology and Food Security MSc, Civil and Structural Engineering MSc, Civil Engineering MSc, Civil Engineering (Technical Route) MSc, Construction Management MSc, Construction Project and Cost Management MSc, Disaster Management MSc, Emergency Planning and Management MSc, Environmental Management MSc, Global Humanitarian Engineering MSc, Highways and Transportation Engineering MSc, Oil and Gas Engineering MSc, Oil and Gas Management MSc, Petroleum and Environmental Technology MSc

School of Mechanical, Aerospace and Automotive Engineering; www.coventry.ac.uk/study-at-coventry/faculties-and-schools/engineering-environment-and-computing/mechanical-aerospace-and-automotive-engineering/

Aerospace Systems Engineering BEng(Hons), Aerospace Technology BEng(Hons), Automotive Engineering MEng/BEng(Hons), Aviation Management

BSc(Hons), Engineering BSc (Part Time), Engineering Business Management BEng(Hons) Top Up, Global Logistics BSc, Manufacturing Engineering MEng/BEng(Hons), Mechanical Engineering MEng/BEng(Hons), Motorsport Engineering MEng/BEng(Hons); Postgraduate courses: Aerospace Engineering MSc, Air Transport Management MSc, Automotive Engineering MSc, Control Engineering MSc, Engineering and Management MSc, Engineering Business Management MSc, Engineering Project Management MSc, Global Logistics MSc, Global Logistics MBA, Human Factors in Aviation MSc, Mechanical Engineering MSc, Production Engineering and Operations Management MSc, Renewable Energy Engineering MSc, Supply Chain Management MBA, Supply Chain Management MSc, Systems and Control MSc

Faculty of Health and Life Sciences; www.coventry.ac.uk/study-at-coventry/faculties-and-schools/health-and-life-sciences/

School of Life Sciences; www.coventry.ac.uk/study-at-coventry/faculties-and-schools/health-and-life-sciences/life-sciences/

Analytical Chemistry and Forensic Science BSc(Hons), Biological and Forensic Sciences BSc(Hons), Biomedical Science/Applied Biomedical Science BSc(Hons), Food and Nutrition BSc(Hons), Food Safety, Inspection and Control BSc(Hons), Human Biosciences BSc(Hons), Medical and Pharmacological Sciences BSc(Hons), Nutrition and Health BSc(Hons), Sport and Exercise Science BSc(Hons), Sports Therapy BSc(Hons); Postgraduate courses: Applied Sport and Exercise Science MSc, Biomedical Science MSc, Biotechnology MSc, Molecular Biology MSc, Pharmacology and Drug Discovery MSc, Science of Youth Coaching and Development MSc, Sports and Exercise Nutrition MSc, Strength and Conditioning MSc

School of Psychological, Social and Behavioural Sciences; www.coventry.ac.uk/study-at-coventry/faculties-and-schools/health-and-life-sciences/psychological-social-and-behavioural-sciences/

Childhood and Youth Studies BA(Hons), Counselling, Coaching and Mentoring BA(Hons), Criminology BA(Hons), Criminology and Law BA(Hons), Criminal Psychology BSc(Hons), Criminology and Psychology BA(Hons), Forensic Investigations BSc(Hons), Psychology BSc(Hons), Social Sciences BSc, Social Work BA(Hons), Sport Psychology BSc(Hons); Postgraduate courses: Applied Psychology MSc, Business and Organisational Psychology MSc, Career Guidance (QCG) MA, Career Coaching MSc, Clinical Psychology Doctorate, Cognitive Behavioural Therapy PGDip/MSc, Forensic Psychology MSc, Forensic Psychology and Crime MSc, Fraud Investigation Management MSc, Health Care Management MBA, Health Psychology MSc, Mindfulness and Compassion MSc, Occupational Psychology MSc, Psychology MSc, Social and Health Care Leadership and Management MSc, Social Work MA

School of Nursing, Midwifery and Health; www.coventry.ac.uk/study-at-coventry/faculties-and-schools/health-and-life-sciences/nursing-midwifery-and-health/

Adult Nursing BSc(Hons), Children and Young People's Nursing BSc(Hons), Dietetics and Human Nutrition BSc(Hons), Learning Disabilities Nursing BSc(Hons), Mental Health Nursing BSc(Hons), Midwifery BSc(Hons), Midwifery (Shortened 88 Week Course) BSc(Hons), Occupational Therapy BSc(Hons), Operating Department Practice DipHE, Paramedic Science Foundation, Physiotherapy BSc(Hons); Postgraduate courses: Advanced Clinical Practice MSc, Advancing Physiotherapy Practice MSc, Global Healthcare Management MSc, Health Studies MSc, Manual Therapy MSc, Neurological Rehabilitation PGCert, Nursing Studies MSc, Public Health Nutrition MSc, Social and Therapeutic Horticulture MSc, Teenage and Young Adult Cancer Care PGCert

Coventry Law School; www.coventry.ac.uk/study-at-coventry/faculties-and-schools/coventry-law-school/

Business Law LLB(Hons), International Law LLB(Hons), Law LLB(Hons); Postgraduate courses: International Law LLM, Law LLM, International Business Law LLM

CRANFIELD UNIVERSITY
www.cranfield.ac.uk

Aerospace; www.cranfield.ac.uk/themes/aerospace/explore-aerospace-courses

Advanced Lightweight Structures and Impact MSc, Aircraft Design option in Aerospace Vehicle Design MSc, Avionic Systems Design option in Aerospace Vehicle Design MSc, Computer and Machine Vision MSc, Rotating Machinery, Engineering and Management option in Thermal Power MSc, Aerospace Propulsion option in Thermal Power MSc, Aerospace Computational Engineering MSc, Aircraft Engineering MSc, Computational and Software Techniques in Engineering MSc, Gas Turbine Technology option in Thermal Power MSc, Software Engineering for Technical Computing MSc, Aerospace Dynamics MSc, Astronautics and Space Engineering MSc, Computational Fluid Dynamics MSc, Power, Propulsion and the Environment option Msc in Thermal Power, Structural Design option in Aerospace Vehicle Design MSc, Aerospace Vehicle Design MSc, Autonomous Vehicle Dynamics and Control MSc, Computer Aided Engineering MSc, Pre-master's in Engineering, Thermal Power MSc/MSc by Research

Defence and Security; www.cranfield.ac.uk/themes/defence-and-security

Cyber Defence and Information Assurance MSc, Cyberspace Operations MSc, Defence Acquisition Management MSc, Defence Leadership MSc, Defence Simulation and Modelling MSc, Digital Forensics MSc, Explosives Ordnance Engineering MSc, Forensic Archaeology and Anthropology MSc, Forensic Ballistics MSc, Forensic Engineering and Science MSc, Forensic Explosive and Explosion Investigation MSc, Forensic Investigation MSc, Guided Weapon Systems MSc, Gun Systems Design MSc, Information Capability Management MSc, International Defence and Security MSc, Military Aerospace and Airworthiness MSc, Military Electronic Systems Engineering MSc, Military Operational Research MSc, Military Vehicle Technology MSc, Programme and Project Management (Defence) MSc, Security Sector Management MSc, Systems Engineering for Defence Capability MSc, Vehicle and Weapon Engineering (USA)

Energy and Power; www.cranfield.ac.uk/themes/energy-and-power

Advanced Chemical Engineering MSc, Advanced Mechanical Engineering MSc, Design of Rotating Machines MSc, Energy from Waste MSc, Energy Systems and Thermal Processes MSc, Flow Assurance for Oil and Gas Production MSc, Geothermal Engineering MSc, Offshore and Ocean Technology with Offshore Materials Engineering MSc, Offshore and Ocean Technology with Offshore Renewable Energy MSc, Offshore and Ocean Technology with Pipeline Engineering MSc, Offshore and Ocean Technology with Risk Management MSc, Offshore and Ocean Technology with Subsea Engineering MSc, Process Systems Engineering MSc, Renewable Energy Engineering MSc, Renewable Energy Technology MSc, MBA Energy

Environment and Agrifood; www.cranfield.ac.uk/themes/environment-and-agrifood

Applied Bioinformatics MSc, Food Chain Systems MSc, Future Food Sustainability MSc, Geographical Information Management MSc, Land Reclamation and Restoration MSc, Atmospheric Emission Technology MSc, Cleantech Entrepreneurship MSc, Environmental Management for Business MSc, Environmental Consultancy PGCert, Environmental Engineering MSc

Manufacturing; www.cranfield.ac.uk/themes/manufacturing

Advanced Materials MSc, Aerospace Manufacturing MSc, Aerospace Materials MSc, Applied Nanotechnology MSc, Cyber-Secure Manufacturing MSc, Engineering and Management of Manufacturing Systems MSc, Global Product Development and Management MSc, Knowledge Management for Innovation MSc, Management and Information Systems MSc, Manufacturing Consultancy MSc, Manufacturing Technology and Management MSc, Medical Technology Regulatory Affairs MSc, Operations Excellence MSc, Quality Management in Scientific Research and Development MSc, Through-life System Sustainment MSc, Welding Engineering MSc

Transport Systems; www.cranfield.ac.uk/themes/transport-systems

Advanced Motorsport Engineering MSc, Air Transport Management MSc, Air Transport Management MSc (Executive), Airport Planning and Management (Executive) MSc, Airport Planning and Management MSc, Airworthiness MSc, Automotive Engineering

MSc, Automotive Mechatronics MSc, Safety and Accident Investigation – Air Transport MSc, Safety and Accident Investigation – Marine Transport MSc, Safety and Accident Investigation – Rail Transport MSc, Safety and Human Factors in Aviation MSc

Water; www.cranfield.ac.uk/themes/water
Community Water and Sanitation MSc, Environmental Water Management MSc, Water and Wastewater Engineering MSc

School of Management; www.cranfield.ac.uk/som
Finance and Management MSc, Investment Management MSc, Strategic Marketing MSc, Logistics and Supply Chain Management MSc, Procurement and Supply Chain Management MSc, Logistics and Supply Chain Management MSc (Executive), Management MSc, Management and Entrepreneurship MSc, Management & Corporate Sustainability MSc; MBA Full-time, Executive MBA, MBA Energy, MBA Defence

UNIVERSITY FOR THE CREATIVE ARTS
www.uca.ac.uk (at Canterbury, Epsom, Farnham, Maidstone and Rochester)

BA(Hons) Acting & Performance, BA(Hons) Advertising, BA(Hons) Animation, BA(Hons) Architecture (ARB/RIBA Part 1), BA(Hons) Computer Animation Arts, BA(Hons) Computer Games Arts, BA(Hons) Computer Games Design, BSc(Hons) Computer Games Technology, BA(Hons) Contemporary Jewellery, BA(Hons) Creative Arts, BSc(Hons) Creative Coding & Technology, BA(Hons) Creative Writing, BA(Hons) Design for Theatre, Film & Performance, BA(Hons) Digital Film & Screen Arts, BA(Hons) Drawing, BA(Hons) Fashion, BA(Hons) Fashion Atelier, BA(Hons) Fashion Buying Retail Management, BA(Hons) Fashion Design, BA(Hons) Fashion Journalism, BA(Hons) Fashion Management & Marketing, BA(Hons) Fashion Media & Promotion, BA(Hons) Fashion Photography, BA(Hons) Fashion Promotion & Imaging, BA(Hons) Fashion Textiles: Print, BA(Hons) Film Production, BA(Hons) Fine Art, BA(Hons) Fine Art, BA(Hons) Fine Art, BA(Hons) Glass, Ceramics, Jewellery, Metalwork, BA(Hons) Graphic Communication, BA(Hons) Graphic Design, BA(Hons) Graphic Design: Visual Communications, BA(Hons) Graphic Design, BA(Hons) Hand Embroidery for Fashion, Interiors, Textile Art, BA(Hons) Illustration, BA(Hons) Illustration & Animation, BA(Hons) Illustration, BA(Hons) Interior Architecture & Design, BA(Hons) Interior Architecture & Design, BA(Hons) Interior Craft & Decorative Art, BA(Hons) Interior Styling & Design, BA(Hons) Journalism & Media Production, BA(Hons) Moving Image, BA(Hons) Music, BA/BSc(Hons) Music Composition & Technology, BA(Hons) Music Journalism, BA(Hons) Music Marketing & Promotion, BA(Hons) Music Performance, BA(Hons) Music Production, BA(Hons) Performance, BA(Hons) Painting, BA(Hons) Photography, BA(Hons) Product Design, BA(Hons) Silversmithing, Goldsmithing & Jewellery, BA(Hons) Sports Fashion & Branding, BA(Hons) Television Production, BA(Hons) Television & Media Production, BA(Hons) Textiles for Fashion & Interiors, BA(Hons) Textiles, BA(Hons) Visual Communications

Postgraduate courses: MA Animation, MA Architecture, MArch Master of Architecture (ARB/RIBA Part 2), MA Ceramics, MA Contemporary Jewellery, PGCert Creative Arts Education, MA Curatorial Practice, MA Design, Innovation & Brand Management, MA Documentary Practices, MBA Fashion Business, MA Fashion Business & Management, MA Fashion Marketing & Communication, MA Fashion Photography, MA Filmmaking, MA Fine Art, MA Graphic Design, MA Illustration, MA Interior Design, MA Jewellery, MA Photography, MFA Photography, MA Product Design, MA Printed Textiles for Fashion & Interiors, MA Textiles, MA Urban Design, MA Visual Communication

UNIVERSITY OF CUMBRIA
www.cumbria.ac.uk

Department of Business, Law, Policing and Social Sciences; www.cumbria.ac.uk/study/academic-departments/business-law-policing-and-social-sciences/

BA(Hons) Business Management, BA(Hons) Business Management with Human Resources Management, BA(Hons) Business Management with Marketing, BA(Hons) Business, Accounting and Finance, BSc(Hons) Computing and IT – Top Up (Full-time), BSc(Hons) Criminology, BSc(Hons) Criminology with Applied Psychology, BSc(Hons) Criminology with Forensic Investigation, BSc(Hons) Criminology with Law, BSc(Hons) Criminology with Policing and Investigation, BSc(Hons) Criminology with Social Science, BA(Hons) International Business Management, LLB(Hons) Law, FDSc Policing, FDSc Policing Studies (with pathways), BSc(Hons) Professional Policing

Postgraduate courses: MSc Applied Forensic Psychology, MSc Applied Social Science, PgD Business Administration, PgC Business Administration (Part-time), MSc Criminology and Criminal Justice, PgC Criminology and Criminal Justice, PgD Criminology and Criminal Justice, MSc Finance and Accounting & PgD target award, LLM Information Technology Law and International Communications, LLM International Commercial Law with International Dispute Resolution, LLM International Criminal Law, MSc International Management

Department of Health, Psychology and Social Studies; www.cumbria.ac.uk/study/academic-departments/health-psychology-and-social-studies/

BSc(Hons) Applied Psychology, BA(Hons) Contemporary Youth and Community Work, BSc(Hons) Occupational Therapy (pre-registration), BSc(Hons) Physiotherapy (pre-registration), BSc(Hons) Psychology, BA(Hons) Social Work, Certificate HE Working with Children and Families, BA(Hons) Working with Children and Families (Top-up), BA(Hons) Working with Children and Families, BA(Hons) Youth and Community Work

Postgraduate courses: MA Advanced Practice in Social Work, PgD Advanced Practice of Cognitive Behavioural Therapy, MA Counselling and Psychotherapy, PgD Counselling and Psychotherapy, PgC Management and Leadership in Health and Social Care, PgD Management and Leadership in Health and Social Care, MA Mental Health Practice, PgD Mental Health Practice, MSc Occupational Therapy (Pre-Registration), MSc Physiotherapy (Pre-registration), MA Social Work, PgC Working with Children, Adolescents and Families

Institute of the Arts; www.cumbria.ac.uk/study/academic-departments/institute-of-the-arts/

BA(Hons) Acting, Dip HE Creative Writing, BA(Hons) Creative Writing, BA(Hons) Dance, BA(Hons) Drama and Musical Theatre, Dip HE English Literature, BA(Hons) English Literature, BA(Hons) Film and Television, BA(Hons) Fine Art, BA(Hons) Games Design, BA(Hons) Graphic Design, BA(Hons) Illustration, BA(Hons) Musical Theatre, BA(Hons) Performing Arts, BA(Hons) Photography, BA(Hons) Wildlife Media

Postgraduate courses: MA Contemporary Fine Art, MA Creative Practice, MA Directing, MA Fashion Textiles, MA Photography

Institute of Education; www.cumbria.ac.uk/study/academic-departments/institute-of-education/

BA(Hons) Education Studies, Dip HE Education Studies, BA(Hons) Primary Education (3-11) with QTS, BA(Hons) Primary Education: Inclusion with SEND (with QTS), BA(Hons) Teaching and Learning

PGCE courses: PGCE General Primary with QTS (5 - 11 years), PGCE General Primary with QTS – Mathematics specialism (PGCE), PGCE General Primary with QTS – Modern Foreign Languages specialism, PGCE General Primary with QTS – Physical Education specialism, PGCE Lower Primary with QTS (3-7 year olds), PGCE Postgraduate Certificate in Education (non-QTS), PGCE Secondary Education with QTS: Art and Design, PGCE Secondary Education with QTS: Biology, PGCE Secondary Education with QTS: Chemistry, PGCE Secondary Education with QTS: Computer Science and ICT, PGCE Secondary Education with QTS: Design and Technology, PGCE Secondary Education with QTS: English, PGCE Secondary Education with QTS: Geography, PGCE Secondary Education with QTS: History, PGCE Secondary Education with QTS: Mathematics, PGCE Secondary Education with QTS: Modern Foreign Languages, PGCE Secondary

Education with QTS: Music, PGCE Secondary Education with QTS: Physical Education, PGCE Secondary Education with QTS: Physics, PGCE Secondary Education with QTS: Religious Education

Postgraduate courses: MA Education Professional Practice (with pathways), PgC Learning and Teaching for Higher Education, NPQ Middle Leadership (Now Recruiting for January 2017), PgC National Award for SEN Coordination, QTS Direct (Assessment Only), NPQ Senior Leadership, SKE Subject Knowledge Enhancement: Computing (8 weeks), SKE Subject Knowledge Enhancement: Mathematics (28 weeks)

Department of Medical and Sport Sciences; www.cumbria.ac.uk/study/academic-departments/medical-and-sport-sciences/

BSc(Hons) Sport Rehabilitation, BSc(Hons) Sport and Exercise Science, BA(Hons) Sport Coaching and Physical Education, BSc(Hons) Diagnostic Radiotherapy, BSc(Hons) Healthcare Science

Postgraduate courses: MSc Medical Imaging, PgC Medical Imaging, PgD Medical Imaging, MSc Medical Imaging (Ultrasound), MSc Medical Imaging: Magnetic Resonance Imaging

Department of Nursing, Health and Professional Practice; www.cumbria.ac.uk/study/academic-departments/nursing-health-and-professional-practice/

BSc(Hons) Nursing (Adult), BSc(Hons) Nursing (Child), BSc(Hons) Nursing (Learning Disabilty), BSc(Hons) Nursing (Mental Health), BSc(Hons) Midwifery, BSc(Hons) Practice Development: Developing Paramedic Practice, DipHE Paramedic Practice, ILM Level 5 certificate in Coaching and Mentoring, BSc(Hons) Management and Leadership in Health and Social Care programme, BSc Practice Management, DipHE Practice Management, ILM Executive Coaching and Mentoring Level 7 certificate, MSc Management and Leadership in Health and Social Care programme, BSc(Hons) Nursing Practice, BSc(Hons) Practice Development with pathways, UAD Practice Development with pathways, Grad Dip Practice Development, DipHE Practice Development, MSc Practice Development with pathways, PG Cert Practice Development with pathways, PG Dip Practice Development, BSc(Hons) Community Specialist Practice Top-up (District Nursing), BSc(Hons) Community Specialist Practice Top-up (General Practice Nursing), BSc(Hons) Practice Management, Dip HE Practice Management

Postgraduate courses: Graduate Diploma Practice Development: Developing Paramedic Practice, MSc Practice Development: Enhancing Paramedic Practice, MA Counselling and Psychotherapy, PgDip Counselling and Psychotherapy, MSc Advanced Practice (Clinical), PGc Advanced Practice (Clinical), Postgraduate Diploma Community Specialist Practice (District Nursing), Postgraduate Diploma Community Specialist Practice (General Practice Nursing), Graduate Diploma Community Specialist Practice (District Nursing), Graduate Diploma Community Specialist Practice (General Practice Nursing)

Department of Science, Natural Resources and Outdoor Studies; www.cumbria.ac.uk/study/academic-departments/science-natural-resources-and-outdoor-studies/

BSc(Hons) Animal Conservation Science, BSc(Hons) Applied Chemistry, Certificate HE Biology, BSc(Hons) Biology, BSc(Hons) Biomedical Sciences, BSc(Hons) Conservation Biology, BSc(Hons) Forensic and Investigative Science, BSc(Hons) Forest Management, FDSc Forestry, BSc(Hons) Geography, BSc(Hons) Marine and Freshwater Conservation, BSc(Hons) Outdoor Adventure and Environment, FDA Outdoor Education, BA(Hons) Outdoor Leadership, FDSc Radiation Protection, BSc(Hons) Woodland Ecology and Conservation, BSc(Hons) Zoology

Postgraduate courses: MSc Ecosystem Services Evaluation, PgD Outdoor and Experiential Learning, MA Outdoor and Experiential Learning, MA Transcultural European Outdoor Studies

DE MONTFORT UNIVERSITY
www.dmu.ac.uk

Leicester Castle Business School; www.lcbs.ac.uk

Global Finance BSc(Hons), Executive MBA (EMBA), Global MBA, Sustainable Business MBA, Intercultural Business Communication Intercultural Business Communication MSc, Business Management in Sport MSc, Business Management in the Creative Industries MSc, Creative Entrepreneurship

MSc Creative Enterprise MSc, Global Banking and Finance MSc, Global Finance and Investment MSc, Motorsport Business of Motorsport MA, Professional Coaching PGCert Professional Coaching PG Certificate

Leicester Media School; www.dmu.ac.uk/about-dmu/schools-and-departments/leicester-media-school/

Animation BA(Hons), Animation Visual Effects BA(Hons), Broadcast Journalism BA(Hons), Communication Arts BA(Hons), Film Studies BA(Hons), Film Studies BA(Hons) (Joint Honours), Film Studies with Languages BA(Hons), Media and Communication BA(Hons), Media and Communication with Languages BA(Hons), Media BA(Hons) (Joint Honours), Media Production BSc(Hons), Visual Effects BSc(Hons), Game Art BA(Hons) (Skillset accredited), Graphic Design BA(Hons), Graphic Design and Illustration BA(Hons), Graphic Design (Interactive) BA(Hons), Graphic Design and e-Media Foundation Degree (FdA), Journalism BA(Hons) (NCTJ-accredited), Journalism BA(Hons) BA(Hons) (Joint Honours), Audio and Recording Technology BSc(Hons), Creative Music Technology BA(Hons), Music Technology BSc(Hons), Music, Technology and Performance BA(Hons), Creative Sound Technology FdSc, Graphic Design and e-Media Foundation Degree FdA

Postgraduate courses: Independent Study MA, International Film Production MA, Investigative Journalism MA

School of Computer Science and Informatics; www.dmu.ac.uk/about-dmu/schools-and-departments/school-of-computer-science-and-informatics/

Computing BSc(Hons), Computing HND, Foundation Year in Computing, Computer Security BSc(Hons), Computer Science BSc(Hons), Forensic Computing BSc(Hons), Software Engineering BSc(Hons), Computer Games Programming BSc(Hons), Intelligent Systems BSc(Hons), Intelligent Systems MComp, Business Information Systems BSc(Hons), Computing for Business BSc(Hons), Information and Communication Technology BSc(Hons), Mathematics BSc(Hons)

Postgraduate courses: Cyber Security MSc, Cyber Technology MSc, Software Engineering MSc, Forensic Computing for Practitioners MSc/PG Dip/PG Cert, Professional Practice in Digital Forensics and Security MSc, Intelligent Systems MSc, Intelligent Systems and Robotics MSc, Business Intelligence Systems and Data Mining MSc, Computing MSc, Data Analytics MSc, Information Systems Management MSc

School of Engineering and Sustainable Development; www.dmu.ac.uk/about-dmu/schools-and-departments/school-of-engineering-and-sustainable-development/

Engineering Year Zero (Foundation year), Electrical and Electronic Engineering BEng/MEng(Hons), Mechanical Engineering BEng(Hons), Mechanical Engineering (Integrated Masters), Mechatronics BEng(Hons), Mechatronics (Integrated Masters), Physics BSc/MPhys(Hons)

Postgraduate courses: Electronic Engineering MSc, Engineering Management MSc, Mechanical Engineering MSc, Mechatronics MSc, Energy and Sustainable Building Design MSc, Energy and Sustainable Development MSc

Leicester Business School; http://www.dmu.ac.uk/about-dmu/schools-and-departments/leicester-business-school/

BA(Hons) Accounting and Business Management, BA(Hons) Accounting and Economics, BA(Hons) Accounting and Finance, BA(Hons) Advertising and Marketing Communications, BA(Hons) Business and Globalisation, BA(Hons) Business and Management, BA(Hons) Business and Marketing, BA(Hons) Business Entrepreneurship and Innovation, BA(Hons) Business Management and Economics, BA(Hons) Business Management and Finance, BA(Hons) Business Management and Human Resource Management, BA(Hons) Economics, BSc(Hons) Economics, BSc(Hons) Economics and Finance, BA(Hons) Economics and International Relations, BA(Hons) Economics and Politics, BSc(Hons) Global Finance, BSc(Hons) Global Leadership and Management, BA(Hons) Human Resource Management, BA(Hons) International Business, BA(Hons) International Relations and Politics, BA(Hons) International Marketing and Business, BA(Hons) International Relations, BA(Hons) Marketing, BA(Hons) Politics, BA(Hons) Public Administration and Management

Postgraduate courses: MSc Accounting and Finance, MSc Accounting and Finance – Fast track – Distance learning, MSc Advertising and Public Relations Management, MSc Business Economics and Business Analytics, MSc Business Economics and Business Finance, MSc Business Economics and International Relations, MSc Business Economics and Marketing, MSc Business Economics and Risk Management, MSc Business Management in the Creative Industries,

MSc Business Management in Sport, MA Business of Motorsport, MA Diplomacy and World Order, MSc Forensic Accounting, MSc Global Banking and Finance, MSc Global Investment and Risk, Housing Studies PG Cert, MSc Intercultural Business Communications, MSc International Business and Corporate Responsibility, MSc International Business and Entrepreneurship, MSc International Business and Finance, MSc International Business and Human Resource Management, MSc International Business and Management, MSc International Business and Marketing, MA International Relations, MA/ PG Dip Human Resource Management, MA/ PG Dip Human Resource Management ể' Part-time, MSc Marketing Management, MA Politics, MSc Project Management, MSc Risk Management, MSc Risk Management – Distance Learning, MSc Strategic and Digital Marketing, Executive MBA, MBA Master of Business Administration (Global), MBA Master of Business Administration (Lawyers) – Distance learning, MBA Master of Business Administration Sustainable Business

Leicester De Montfort Law School; www.dmu.ac.uk/about-dmu/schools-and-departments/leicester-de-montfort-law-school/

LLB Law(Hons), LLB Business Law(Hons), LLB Law and Criminal Justice(Hons), LLB Law, Human Rights & Social Justice(Hons), BA Business Management and Law (Joint Hons), BA Law and Economics (Joint Hons)

Postgraduate courses: LLM Business Law / LLM Law, LLM Business Law / LLM International Business Law – Distance Learning, LLM Employment Law & Practice – Distance Learning, LLM Environmental Law & Practice – Distance Learning, LLM Food Law – Distance Learning, LLM International Business Law, LLM International Human Rights – Distance Learning, LLM Legal Practice – Distance Learning, LLM Medical Law and Ethics – Distance Learning, LLM Sports Law & Practice – Distance Learning, Graduate Diploma in Law, Graduate Diploma in Law – Part-time, Legal Practice Course, Legal Practice Course – Part-time

Leicester School of Architecture; www.dmu.ac.uk/about-dmu/schools-and-departments/leicester-school-of-architecture/

Architecture BA(Hons), Architectural Technology BSc(Hons)

Postgraduate courses: Architecture March, Architectural Practice PG Dip, Architectural Design MA, Architecture and Sustainability MSc

School of Visual and Performance Arts, www.dmu.ac.uk/about-dmu/schools-and-departments/school-of-visual-and-performing-arts/

Dance BA(Hons), Dance BA (Joint Honours)(Hons), Drama Studies BA(Hons), Drama Studies (Joint Honours) BA(Hons), Performing Arts BA(Hons), Art and Design (Foundation Studies) BTEC Diploma, Fine Art BA(Hons), Photography and Video BA(Hons), Arts and Festivals Management BA(Hons), Arts and Festivals Management (Joint Honours) BA(Hons)

Postgraduate courses: Arts MA, Cultural Events Management MSc, Digital Arts MA, Fine Art MA, Performance Practices MA, Performance Practices MFA

School of Design; www.dmu.ac.uk/about-dmu/schools-and-departments/school-of-design/

Design Crafts BA(Hons), Design Products MDes(Hons), Digital Design BA(Hons), Interior Design BA(Hons), Interior Design MDes(Hons), Product Design BA(Hons), Product Design BSc(Hons), Product and Furniture Design BA(Hons), Contour Fashion BA(Hons), Contour Fashion Communication BA(Hons), Fashion Buying with Design BA(Hons), Fashion Buying with Garment Technology BA(Hons), Fashion Buying with Marketing BA(Hons), Fashion Buying with Merchandising BA(Hons), Fashion Design BA(Hons), Fashion Textile Design BA(Hons), Footwear Design BA(Hons), Textile Design BA(Hons)

Postgraduate courses: Design MA, Design Innovation MA, Design Management and Entrepreneurship MA, Digital Design MA, Fashion and Textiles MA, Fashion Management with Marketing MA, Interior Design MA, Product Design MA, Textile Design, Technology and Innovation MSc

School of Humanities; www.dmu.ac.uk/about-dmu/schools-and-departments/school-of-humanities/

Creative Writing (Joint Honours) BA(Hons), English BA(Hons), English (Joint Honours) BA(Hons), English with Languages BA(Hons), English Language (Joint Honours) BA(Hons), English Language with Languages BA(Hons), English Language with TESOL BA(Hons), History BA(Hons), History (Joint Honours) BA(Hons), History with Languages BA(Hons)

Postgraduate courses: English MA, English Language Teaching MA, History MA, Photographic History MA, Sports History and Culture MA, Management, Law and Humanities of Sport MA, Humanities research degree MPhil/PhD

Institute of Creative Technologies; www.ioct.dmu.ac.uk
IOCT Masters in Creative Technologies

Leicester De Montfort Law School; www.dmu.ac.uk/about-dmu/schools-and-departments/leicester-de-montfort-law-school/
LLB Law(Hons), LLB Business Law(Hons), LLB Law and Criminal Justice(Hons), LLB Law, Human Rights and Social Justice(Hons), BA Business Management and Law (Joint Hons), BA(Hons) Law and Economics
Postgraduate courses: LLM Business Law, LLM Employment Law and Practice, LLM Environmental Law and Practice, LLM Food Law, LLM International Business Law, LLM International Human Rights, LLM Medical Law and Ethics, LLM Sports Law and Practice

School of Allied Health Sciences; www.dmu.ac.uk/about-dmu/schools-and-departments/school-of-allied-health-sciences/
Biomedical Science BSc(Hons), Health and Wellbeing in Society BSc(Hons), Speech and Language Therapy BSc(Hons), Medical Science B Med Sci(Hons)
Postgraduate courses: Advanced Biomedical Science MSc/PG Dip/PG Cert, Master's by Research MA/MSc, Physician Associate Studies MSc

School of Applied Social Sciences; www.dmu.ac.uk/about-dmu/schools-and-departments/school-of-applied-social-sciences/
Criminology and Criminal Justice BA(Hons), Criminology and Criminal Justice with Psychology BA(Hons), Criminal Investigation with Policing BA(Hons), Education Studies BA(Hons), Education Studies with French BA(Hons), Education Studies with Mandarin BA(Hons), Education Studies with Psychology BA(Hons), Policing BA(Hons), Psychology BSc(Hons), Psychology with Criminology BSc(Hons), Psychology with Education Studies BSc(Hons), Psychology with Health Studies BSc(Hons), Social Work BA(Hons), Youth Work and Community Development BA(Hons)
Postgraduate courses: Education Practice MA, Health and Community Development Studies, Health Psychology MSc, Master's in Research (Applied Health Studies) MRes, Psychological Well-being MSc, Social Work MA, Youth and Community Development Studies MA, Youth Work and Community Development PQ, Youth Work, Health and Community Development PQ MA/PGDip

School of Nursing and Midwifery; www.dmu.ac.uk/about-dmu/schools-and-departments/the-leicester-school-of-nursing-and-midwifery/
Health and Professional Practice BSc(Hons), Learning Beyond Registration Professional, Midwifery (Pre-registration Midwifery) BSc(Hons), Non-medical Prescribing BSc, Nursing with Registration (Adult) BSc(Hons), Nursing with Registration (Child) BSc(Hons), Nursing with Registration (Mental Health) BSc(Hons), Nursing with Registration (Learning Disability) BSc(Hons)
Nursing MSc/PG Dip/PG Cert, Non-medical Prescribing PG Cert, Specialist Community Public Health Nursing MSc/PG Dip/PG Cert

Leicester School of Pharmacy; www.dmu.ac.uk/about-dmu/schools-and-departments/leicester-school-of-pharmacy/
Pharmaceutical and Cosmetic Science BSc(Hons), Forensic Science BSc(Hons), Pharmacy MPharm(Hons)
Postgraduate courses: Clinical Pharmacy MSc/PG Dip/PG Cert, Medical Leadership and Advanced Professional Skills MSc, Pharmaceutical Biotechnology MSc/PG Dip/PG Cert, Pharmaceutical Quality by Design MSc/PG Dip/PG Cert, Practice Certificate in Independent Prescribing for Pharmacists PG Cert, Quality by Design for the Pharmaceutical Industry MSc/PG Dip/PG Cert with professional qualification

UNIVERSITY OF DERBY
www.derby.ac.uk

College of Arts, Humanities and Education; www.derby.ac.uk/ahe

School of Arts; www.derby.ac.uk/arts

3D Animation BA(Hons), Animation BA(Hons), Animation MDes, Fine Art BA(Hons), Graphic Design BA(Hons), Graphic Design MDes, Illustration BA(Hons), Illustration MDes, Interior Design BA(Hons), Year Zero, Fashion BA(Hons), Fashion and Fashion Marketing BA(Hons), Textile Design BA(Hons), Year Zero, Film Production BA(Hons), Media Production BA(Hons), Photography and Film Production (BA(Hons), Radio Production BA(Hons), Television Production (Joint Honours), Visual Effects and Post Production BA(Hons), Year Zero, Music BA(Hons), Music Technology and Production BSc(Hons), Popular Music with Music Technology BA(Hons), Popular Music Production (Joint Honours), Year Zero, Contemporary Theatre and Performance BA(Hons), Costume and Set Design BA(Hons), Dance BA(Hons), Technical Theatre BA(Hons), Theatre Studies (Joint Honours), Year Zero, Commercial Photography BA(Hons), Photography BA(Hons), Photography and Film Production BA(Hons), Photography (Joint Honours), Year Zero, Product Design BA(Hons), Year Zero

Postgraduate courses: MA Fashion and Textiles, MA Film and Photography, MA Fine Art, MA Music Production, MA Visual Communication, MA Writing for Performance

Humanities; www.derby.ac.uk/departments/humanities

English, Creative Writing and Publishing
Creative & Professional Writing (Joint Honours), Creative & Professional Writing BA(Hons), Creative & Professional Writing BA(Hons) with Foundation Year, English (Joint Honours), English BA(Hons), English BA(Hons) with Foundation Year, English Integrated Masters (MLit), English Language (Joint Honours), English Literature and Language with Foundation Year with optional TESOL pathway BA(Hons), English Literature and Language with optional TESOL pathway BA(Hons), English for Academic Purposes Certificate of Credit, Foundation Certificate in Higher Education (Online), Publishing (Joint Honours), Technical English Certificate of Credit, Writing and Publishing BA(Hons)
Postgraduate courses: Public History and Heritage MA, Publishing MA

History
History (Joint Honours), History BA(Hons), History BA(Hons) with Foundation Year, History Integrated Masters (MHist); Postgraduate course: Public History and Heritage MA

Journalism
Football Journalism BA(Hons), Journalism (Joint Honours), Journalism BA(Hons), Journalism BA(Hons) with Foundation Year, Magazine Journalism BA(Hons), Magazine Journalism with Foundation Year BA(Hons), Specialist Sports Journalism BA(Hons), Specialist Sports Journalism with Foundation Year BA(Hons)

Media and Cultural Studies
American Studies (Joint Honours), Film and Television Studies (Joint Honours), Liberal Arts BA(Hons), Liberal Arts BA(Hons) with Foundation Year, Media Studies (Joint Honours), Media and Communication BA(Hons), Media and Communication BA(Hons) with Foundation Year, Popular Music in Society (Joint Honours), Writing and Publishing BA(Hons); Postgraduate courses: Public History and Heritage MA, Publishing MA

Institute of Education; www.derby.ac.uk/education

BEd(Hons) Primary Education with Qualified Teacher Status, Integrated Masters in Education (MEdu) (in curriculum enhancement) with Qualified Teacher Status, BA(Hons) Early Childhood Studies, BA(Hons) Early Childhood Studies with Foundation Year, BA(Hons) Early Childhood Studies with Early Years Teacher Status (0-5), Early Childhood Studies (Joint Honours), BA(Hons) Child and Youth Studies, BA(Hons) Child and Youth Studies with Foundation Year, BA(Hons) Education Studies with optional pathway in SEND, TESOL or Career Development, BA(Hons) Education Studies with Foundation Year, Education Studies (Joint Honours), BA(Hons) Special Educational Needs and Disability, BA(Hons) Special Educational Needs and Disability with Foundation Year, Delivered by Partner Colleges, FdA Special Educational Needs and Disabilities, FdA Children's and Young People's Services, FdA Post-14 Education and Training

Postgraduate courses: MA Careers Education and Coaching, MA Childhood, MA Inclusion and SEND, MA Educational Leadership, EdD Doctor of Education, MPhil or PhD Education, MA Education (full-time), MA Education (part time, on campus), MA Education (Workplace Contract), MA Education: Early Years, MA Education: Teaching English to Speakers of Other Languages (TESOL), MA Education: Leadership Coaching and Mentoring, MA Education: Leadership and Management, MA Education: Lifelong Learning, MA Education: Primary Mathematics, MA Education: Special Educational Needs and Disabilities, PG Cert Early Years with Early Years Teacher Status (0-5), PGCE Primary with Qualified Teacher Status, PGCE Primary (School Direct) with Qualified Teacher Status, PGCE Secondary (School Direct) with Qualified Teacher Status, PGCE Post-14 (Education and Training), PGDE Post-14 (Education and Training), Assessment Only Route to Qualified Teacher Status (QTS)

College of Business, Law and Social Sciences; www.derby.ac.uk/blss

Derby Business School; www.derby.ac.uk/departments/dbs

HND Business and Management (part-time), BA(Hons) Business Management (Top up), BSc(Hons) Logistics Management (Top up), MSc Human Resource Management (Top up), MSc Marketing Management, MSc Supply Chain Improvement, Master of Business Administration (MBA Global & MBA Global Finance), BA(Hons) Professional Culinary Arts (Top-up), BA(Hons) Professional Culinary Management (part-time), BA(Hons) International Tourism Management (part-time), BSc(Hons) International Spa Management (part-time), BA(Hons) International Hospitality Management (part-time), BA(Hons) Event Management (part-time)

Department of Hotel, Resort and Spa Management; www.derby.ac.uk/departments/hotel-resort-and-spa-management

Events Management

Event Management (part-time) BA(Hons), Event Management BA(Hons), Event Management FdA, Event Safety Management University Diploma, Sound, Light and Live Event Technology BSc(Hons); Postgraduate course: Events Management MSc

Hospitality and Culinary Management

International Hospitality Business Management (top up) BA(Hons), International Hospitality Management (part-time) BA(Hons), International Hospitality Management BA(Hons), International Hospitality Management FdA, Professional Culinary Arts (FdA), Professional Culinary Arts BA(Hons) (Top-Up), Professional Culinary Management (part-time) BA(Hons), Professional Culinary Management BA(Hons); Postgraduate course: International Hospitality Management MSc

Tourism Management

International Tourism Management (part-time) BA(Hons), International Tourism Management BA(Hons), International Tourism Management FdA; Postgraduate course: Tourism Management MSc

Spa and Wellness Management

International Spa Management (part-time) BSc(Hons), International Spa Management BSc(Hons), International Spa Management FdSc, Wellness Management BSc(Hons); Postgraduate course: International Spa Management MSc

Derby Law School; www.derby.ac.uk/departments/law/

International Relations and Diplomacy (Joint Honours), International Relations and Diplomacy (with optional year in Hague) BA(Hons), LLB(Hons), Law (Joint Honours), Law – LLB(Hons) with Criminology Postgraduate courses: LLM (including specialist pathways), LLM Legal Practice

Department of Criminology and Social Sciences; www.derby.ac.uk/departments/social-sciences/

Criminology and Policing

Criminal Psychology BSc(Hons), Criminal Psychology BSc(Hons) with Foundation Year, Criminology (Joint Honours), Criminology BSc(Hons), Criminology BSc(Hons) with Foundation Year, Law – LLB(Hons) with Criminology, Policing BA(Hons), Policing and Investigations BA(Hons)

Postgraduate courses: Criminal Investigation MSc, Criminal Justice and Criminology MSc, Financial Investigation and Digital Intelligence MSc, Intelligence, Security and Disaster Management MSc, Police Leadership, Strategy and Organisation MSc

Political Sciences

International Relations and Diplomacy (Joint Honours), International Relations and Diplomacy (with optional year in Hague) BA(Hons), Politics (Joint Honours); Postgraduate courses: MA Social Policy, Social and Political Studies MA

Social Sciences

Social Policy (Joint Honours), Sociology (Joint Honours), Sociology BA(Hons), Sociology BA(Hons) with Foundation Year; Postgraduate courses: Intelligence, Security and Disaster Management MSc, Understanding Radicalisation PG Cert

International Policing and Justice Institute; www.derby.ac.uk/departments/the-institute/

BA(Hons) Policing, LLB(Hons) with Criminology, BSc(Hons) Criminology, BSc(Hons) Criminal Psychology, BSc(Hons) Global Security, BSc(Hons) Intelligence, BSc(Hons) Policing, Global Security and Intelligence, Diploma in Policing, Certificate of Knowledge in Policing, FdSc Criminal Justice (Forensic Criminology), FdSc Criminal Justice (Security), FdA Criminal Justice (Human Rights), FdA Criminal Justice (Policing), BSc(Hons) Computer Forensic Investigation, BSc(Hons) Forensic Science, BSc(Hons) Forensic Science with Criminology, BSc(Hons) Forensic Science with Psychology

Postgraduate courses: MSc Police Leadership, Strategy and Organisation, Master of Business Administration (MBA Global & MBA Global Finance), MBA (Online), MSc Criminal Investigation, MSc Digital Forensics and Computer Security, MRes (Forensic Science), PG Cert Understanding Radicalisation

College of Engineering and Technology; www.derby.ac.uk/engineering-technology

Department of Electronics, Computing and Mathematics; www.derby.ac.uk/engineering-technology/elec-comp-maths/

Computer Games

Computer Games Modelling and Animation BA(Hons), Computer Games Programming, Engineering and Technology Year Zero; Postgraduate courses: Electronics, Computing or Mathematics MPhil or PhD, Mobile App Development MSc

Computer Science & IT

Analytics (Joint Honours), BSc(Hons) Computing and Information Technologies Top-Up (Online), Computer Forensic Investigation BSc(Hons), Computer Network Engineering BEng(Hons), Computer Networks and Security BSc(Hons), Computer Science BSc(Hons), Computing and Information Technologies University Advanced Diploma (Online), Cyber Security BSc(Hons), Data Science BSc(Hons),

Engineering and Technology Year Zero, Information Technology BSc(Hons)

Postgraduate courses:

Advanced Computer Networks MSc, Cyber Security MSc, Digital Forensics and Computer Security MSc, Electronics, Computing or Mathematics MPhil or PhD, Information Technology MSc, Information Technology MSc (Online), Mobile App Development MSc

Electrical and Electronic Engineering

Electrical and Electronic Engineering BSc(Hons), Electrical and Electronic Engineering FdEng, Electrical and Electronic Engineering with Industrial Year BEng(Hons), Engineering and Technology Year Zero

Postgraduate courses: Audio Engineering MSc, Control and Instrumentation MSc, Electronics, Computing or Mathematics MPhil or PhD, Innovative Engineering Solutions MSc, Professional Engineering (Online) MSc, Professional Engineering MSc

Entertainment Engineering

Broadcast Engineering and Live Event Technology BSc(Hons), Engineering and Technology Year Zero, Sound, Light and Live Event Technology BSc(Hons); Postgraduate course: Audio Engineering MSc

Mathematics

Engineering and Technology Year Zero, Foundation Certificate in Higher Education (Online), Introduction to Maths in Preparation for Higher Education Certificate of Credit, Mathematics (Joint Honours), Mathematics BSc(Hons), Mathematics and Computer Science BSc(Hons), Mathematics with Education BSc(Hons)

Postgraduate courses: Big Data Analytics MSc, Computational Mathematics MSc, Electronics, Computing or Mathematics MPhil or PhD, Innovative Engineering Solutions MSc

Department of Mechanical Engineering and the Built Environment; www.derby.ac.uk/engineering-technology/mech-built/

Architecture, Architectural Technologies and Interior Design

Architectural Design (Joint Honours), Architectural Studies FdSc, Architectural Technology and Practice BSc(Hons), Engineering and Technology Year Zero, Interior Architecture and Venue Design BA(Hons), Interior Design BA(Hons)

Postgraduate courses: Building Information Modelling (BIM) and Project Collaboration MSc, Innovative Engineering Solutions MSc, Mechanical Engineering and the Built Environment MPhil or PhD, Sustainable Architecture and Healthy Buildings MSc

Civil Engineering and Construction

Civil Engineering BSc(Hons), Civil Engineering FdEng, Civil Engineering MEng, Civil and Infrastructure Engineering BEng(Hons), Civil and Infrastructure Engineering with Industrial Year BEng(Hons), Construction FdSc, Construction Management and Property Development BSc(Hons), Engineering and Technology Year Zero, Property Development (Joint Honours), Quantity Surveying and Commercial Management BSc(Hons)

Postgraduate courses: Building Information Modelling (BIM) and Project Collaboration MSc, Civil Engineering and Construction Management MSc, Innovative Engineering Solutions MSc, Mechanical Engineering and the Built Environment MPhil or PhD, Professional Engineering MSc

Mechanical and Manufacturing Engineering

Engineering Management (Top Up) BEng(Hons), Engineering Planning and Control FdEng, Engineering and Technology Year Zero, Manufacturing and Production Engineering with Industrial Year BEng(Hons), Mechanical Engineering BEng/ Mechanical Engineering with Industrial Year BEng(Hons), Mechanical Engineering MEng, Mechanical and Manufacturing Engineering (HNC), Mechanical and Manufacturing Engineering BEng(Hons), Mechanical and Manufacturing Engineering FdSc

Postgraduate courses: Advanced Materials and Additive Manufacturing MSc, Advanced Materials and Additive Manufacturing MSc (Online), Innovative Engineering Solutions MSc, Mechanical Engineering and the Built Environment MPhil or PhD, Mechanical and Manufacturing Engineering MSc, Professional Engineering MSc, Strategic Engineering Management MSc,

Motorsport Engineering

Engineering and Technology Year Zero, Motorsport Engineering BEng(Hons), Motorsport Engineering FdEng, Motorsport Engineering MEng, Motorsport and Motorcycle Manufacturing Engineering BEng(Hons)

Innovative Engineering Solutions MSc, Mechanical Engineering and the Built Environment MPhil or PhD, Motorsport Engineering MSc, Professional Engineering MSc

Product Design

Engineering and Technology Year Zero, Product Design BA(Hons), Product Design Engineering BSc(Hons), Year Zero

Postgraduate courses: Art and Design MPhil or PhD, Mechanical Engineering and the Built Environment MPhil or PhD

College of Health and Social Care; www.derby.ac.uk/health-and-social-care/

Department of Healthcare Practice; www.derby.ac.uk/health-and-social-care/courses/health-care-practice/
Pre-Registration Courses

BSc(Hons) Nursing (Adult), BSc(Hons) Nursing (Mental Health), FdSc Professional Development (Health and Social Care)/Higher Apprenticeship Assistant Practitioner; Postgraduate courses: MSc Nursing (Adult) with NMC registration, MSc Nursing (Mental Health) with NMC registration

Post-Registration courses

BSc(Hons) Community Specialist Practice, BSc(Hons) Specialist Community Public Health Nursing

Postgraduate courses: PG Cert Interprofessional Practice Education, PG Cert Leadership for Healthcare Improvement, PG Cert Management of Long Term Conditions, MSc Advanced Practice, MSc Community Specialist Practice (District Nursing), MSc Health and Social Care Studies, MSc Specialist Community Public Health Nursing (Health Visiting or School Nursing), MSc Nursing (Adult) with NMC registration, MSc Nursing (Mental Health) with NMC registration, Return to Practice (Nursing), Doctor of Health and Social Care Practice

Diagnostic Imaging

BSc(Hons) Diagnostic Radiography, FdSc Professional Development (Health and Social Care)/Higher Apprenticeship Assistant Practitioner

Postgraduate courses: MSc Diagnostic Radiography (Pre-Registration), MSc Medical Ultrasound, PG Cert Osteoporosis and Falls Management, PG Cert Bone Densitometry Reporting

Department of Therapeutic Practice; www.derby.ac.uk/health-and-social-care/courses/therapeutic-practice/
Occupational Therapy

BSc(Hons) Occupational Therapy, MSc Hand Therapy (incorporating PG Cert/PG Dip), MSc Occupational Therapy (Pre-registration), MSc Advanced Occupational Therapy/Advanced Occupational Therapy Community (inc PG Cert/Dip), Return to Practice (Occupational Therapy), Doctor of Health and Social Care Practice, FdSc Professional Development (Health and Social Care)/Higher Apprenticeship Assistant Practitioner

Counselling and Psychotherapy

BSc(Hons) Counselling and Psychotherapy Principles and Practices, Counselling and Psychotherapy

Principles and Practices (Joint Honours), BSc(Hons) Nursing (Mental Health)

Postgraduate courses: PG Cert Systemic Thinking and Practice, PG Cert Compassion Focused Therapy, MSc Cognitive Behavioural Psychotherapy (BABCP accredited) (incorporating PG Cert/PG Dip), MSc Integrative Counselling and Psychotherapy (incorporating PG Cert/PG Dip) (BACP Accredited), MSc Systemic Psychotherapy, MSc Health and Social Care Studies, Doctor of Health and Social Care Practice

Therapeutic Arts
BA(Hons) Creative Expressive Therapies, Dance and Movement Studies (Joint Honours), MA Art Therapy, MA Dance Movement Psychotherapy, MA Dramatherapy, MA Music Therapy

Department of Social and Community Studies; www.derby.ac.uk/health-and-social-care/courses/social-community-studies/

BA(Hons) Applied Social Work, BA(Hons) Health and Social Care, BA(Hons) Working with Young People and Communities (Youth Work or Community Development), BSc(Hons) Child and Family Health and Wellbeing, Child and Family Health and Wellbeing (Joint Honours), MA Social Work

College of Life and Natural Sciences; *www.derby.ac.uk/science/*

Department of Life Sciences; www.derby.ac.uk/science/life/
Biomedical Health and Human Biology
BSc(Hons) Human Biology, BSc(Hons) Biomedical Health, MSci Biomedical Health

Psychology
BSc(Hons) Psychology, Psychology (Joint Honours); Postgraduate courses: MSc Behaviour Change (incorporating PG Dip/PG Cert), MSc Health Psychology,

MSc Applied Developmental Psychology, MRes Psychology

Sport and Exercise Science
BSc(Hons) Sport and Exercise Science, BSc(Hons) Strength, Conditioning and Rehabilitation, BSc(Hons) Performance Analysis and Coaching Science, BSc(Hons) Physical Activity, Nutrition and Health, BSc(Hons) Sport Therapy and Rehabilitation, BA(Hons) Sport Management, BA(Hons) Sport Coaching and Development, BA(Hons) Sport and Education, Sport and Exercise Studies (Joint Honours), FdA Sport Coaching; Postgraduate courses: MRes (Sport and Exercise), MSc Applied Sport and Exercise Science

Outdoor and Adventure Sport
BSc(Hons) Adventure Sport and Coaching Science, BA(Hons) Outdoor Leadership and Management, FdA Outdoor Activity Leadership

Department of Natural Sciences; www.derby.ac.uk/science/courses/science/natural/
BSc(Hons) Biology, Biology (Joint Honours), BSc(Hons) Zoology, Zoology (Joint Honours), BSc(Hons) Forensic Science, BSc(Hons) Forensic Science with Criminology, BSc(Hons) Forensic Science with Psychology, BSc(Hons) Geography, Geography (Joint Honours), Global Development (Joint Honours), BSc(Hons) Geology, Geology (Joint Honours), Environmental Hazards (Joint Honours)
Postgraduate courses: MSc Conservation Biology, MSc Environmental Assessment and Control, MSc Applied Petroleum Geoscience (incorporating PG Cert/PG Dip), MSc Applied Acoustics, MSc Environmental Assessment and Control, MSc Applied Petroleum Geoscience (incorporating PG Cert/PG Dip), MSc Applied Acoustics

UNIVERSITY CENTRE DONCASTER
www.don.ac.uk/university-centre-doncaster

Art, Design and Media
FdA Illustration and Concept Art, HND in Creative Media Production & Computer Games Design / Animation, BA(Hons) Fine Art and Crafts, BA(Hons) Games Design and Animation (Top Up), BA(Hons) Graphic Design, BA(Hons) Graphic Design (distance learning), BA(Hons) Illustration and Concept Art

Postgraduate courses: MA in Creative Industries: Practice, Business and Innovation, MA in Creative Pattern Cutting

Early Years
FdA Early Childhood Development and Learning in Practice, FdA Supporting Children with Special Educational Needs and Disability, BA(Hons) Early Childhood Studies, BA(Hons) Early Childhood

Studies (top up), BA(Hons) Early Childhood Studies (top up) BA(Hons) Early Childhood Studies (top up) Northern Ireland, BA(Hons) Early Childhood Studies (top up č distance learning)
Postgraduate courses: MA in Early Childhood Studies, MA in Early Childhood Studies (Distance Learning), MA in Education Studies (Primary / Secondary / SEND)

Education
BA(Hons) Education and Advancing Professional Practice

Counselling and Relationship Studies
BA(Hons) Counselling Solutions (Top Up)
Postgraduate courses: Postgraduate Diploma Psychosexual Therapy, MA in Contemporary Relationship Studies

Hospitality and Catering
Professional Culinary Arts Diploma Level 4

Humanities and Social Sciences
BA(Hons) Applied Social Science, BA(Hons) Criminal Justice, BA(Hons) English, BA(Hons) Psychology in the Community, FdSc Professional Practice in Health and Social Care; Postgraduate course: MA in Literature and Digital Culture

Leadership and Management
BA(Hons) Business Management, BA(Hons) International Football Business Management
Postgraduate courses: MBA Masters in Business Administration, Postgraduate Diploma in Human Resource Management, MSc in Human Resource Management

Music and Performing Arts
FdA Live Performance Technology, FdA Performing Arts in the Community (Dance, Drama, Music), BA(Hons) Creative Music Technology, BA(Hons) Performing Arts in the Community Top Up (Dance, Drama, Music)

Sports
BA(Hons) Physical Education and Sports Coaching, BSc(Hons) Sport Science and Coaching in Football (Distance Learning), BSc(Hons) Sports, Fitness and Exercise Science, BSc(Hons) Sports, Exercise and Health Science (Top Up)

Teacher Education and Professional Development:
Postgraduate courses: MEd in Advancing Professional Practice, Professional Graduate / Postgraduate Certificate in Education (PgCE / PGCE), Certificate in Education (Cert Ed)

UNIVERSITY OF DUNDEE
www.dundee.ac.uk

Duncan of Jordanstone College of Art & Design; www.dundee.ac.uk/djcad
Animation BDes, Art & Philosophy BA(Hons), Digital Interaction Design BSc(Hons), Fine Art BA(Hons), Art & Design (General Foundation) BA / BDes, Graphic Design BDes(Hons), Illustration BDes(Hons), Interior & Environmental Design BDes(Hons), Jewellery & Metal Design BDes(Hons), Product Design BSc(Hons), Textile Design BDes(Hons)
Postgraduate courses: Anatomy for Artists PGCert, Animation & VFX MSc, Art & Humanities MFA, Art, Society & Publics MFA, Design for Business MSc, Forensic Art MSc, Medical Art MSc, Product Design MSc, PhD/MPhil, Theatre Studies MLitt

School of Business; www.dundee.ac.uk/business/
Accountancy BAcc(Hons), Accountancy (without Honours) BAcc, Accountancy and Mathematics BSc(Hons), Accountancy with Business Finance BAcc(Hons), Accountancy with French BAcc(Hons), Accountancy with German BAcc(Hons), Accountancy with Spanish BAcc(Hons), Business Economics with Marketing BSc(Hons), Business Economics with Marketing MA(Hons), Business Economics with Marketing and European Studies MA(Hons), Business Economics with Marketing and Geography MA(Hons), Business Economics with Marketing and History MA(Hons), Business Economics with Marketing and Mathematics MA(Hons), Business Economics with Marketing and Politics MA(Hons), Business Economics with Marketing and Psychology MA(Hons), Business Economics with Marketing with French MA(Hons), Business Economics with Marketing with German MA(Hons), Business Economics with Marketing with Spanish MA(Hons), Business Management BSc(Hons), Business Management (Accounting & Finance) BSc(Hons), Economic Studies MA / BSc(Hons), Economics MA(Hons), Economics BSc(Hons), Economics and European Studies MA(Hons), Economics and History MA(Hons), Economics and International Relations MA(Hons), Economics and Politics MA(Hons), Economics with French MA(Hons),

Economics with German MA(Hons), Economics with Spanish MA(Hons), Finance BFin, Financial Economics BSc(Hons), Financial Economics MA(Hons), Financial Economics with French MA(Hons), Financial Economics with German MA(Hons), Financial Economics with Spanish MA(Hons), International Business BSc(Hons), International Business MA / BSc(Hons), International Business MA(Hons), International Business and Environmental Sustainability MA(Hons), International Business and Finance MA(Hons), International Business and International Relations MA(Hons), International Business with E-Commerce BSc(Hons), International Business with Financial Management BSc(Hons), International Business with French BSc(Hons), International Business with French MA(Hons), International Business with German BSc(Hons), International Business with German MA(Hons), International Business with Marketing BSc(Hons), International Business with Marketing MA(Hons), International Business with Spanish BSc(Hons), International Business with Spanish MA(Hons), International Finance BIFin
Postgraduate courses: Accountancy MSc, Accounting & Finance MRes, Accounting & Finance MSc, Accounting, Management and Strategy MSc, Banking and Finance MSc, Economics PGDip, Finance MSc, Financial Economics PGDip, International Accounting MSc, International Business MSc, International Business and Banking MSc, International Business and Finance MSc, International Business and Human Resource Management MSc, International Business and Management MSc, International Business and Marketing MSc, International Business, Accounting and Finance MSc, International Business, Banking and Finance MSc, International Business, Marketing and Human Resource Management MSc, Management MSc, Management and Accounting MSc

School of Dentistry; http://dentistry.dundee.ac.uk
Bachelor of Dental Surgery, BSc in Oral Health Sciences
Postgraduate courses: Dental Public Health MDPH, Endodontics MDSc, Forensic Dentistry MSc & MFOdont, Oral Biology MSc, Oral Cancer MRes, Orthodontics MSc (Egypt), Prosthodontics MDSc, Restorative Dental Care (Egypt)

School of Education & Social Work; www.dundee.ac.uk/esw
Childhood Practice/Childhood Studies BA, Community Learning and Development BA (Honours), Education (Primary) MA (Honours), Professional

Development BA, Professional Development (Leadership & Management) BA, Professional Development (Tertiary Education) BA, Professional Development (Community Engagement) BA, Professional Development (Volunteer Management) BA, Social Work BA (Honours), Teaching Qualification Further Education Cert
Postgraduate courses: Advanced Social Work Studies MSc, Community Learning and Development (Distance Learning) Masters, Education (including IB Certificate) Masters, Education (Leading Learning and Teaching) Masters, Education (Inclusion and Learner Support) Masters, Education (Nursery/Early Education) Masters, Education (Pupil Care and Support) Masters, Education (Adult Literacies) Masters, Education (International Education) Masters, Education (Developing Mathematical Thinking) Masters, Education (Primary) PGDE, Education, Secondary (Chemistry) PGDE, Education, Secondary (Mathematics) PGDE, Education, Secondary (Physics) PGDE, Education Secondary (Home Economics) PDGE, Educational Psychology MSc, Leadership and Innovation (Distance Learning) MSc, Social Work MSc, Teaching in Higher Education PGCert

School of Humanities; www.dundee.ac.uk/humanities
Arts and Social Sciences (3 year) MA, English MA(Hons), English and Creative Writing MA(Hons), English and European Studies MA(Hons), English and Film Studies MA(Hons), English and History MA(Hons), English and Mathematics MA(Hons), English and Philosophy MA(Hons), English and Politics MA(Hons), English and Psychology MA(Hons), English with French MA(Hons), English with German MA(Hons), English with Spanish MA(Hons), European Philosophy MA(Hons), European Philosophy with French MA(Hons), European Philosophy with German MA(Hons), European Philosophy with Spanish MA(Hons), European Studies MA(Hons), European Studies and European Languages & Culture MA(Hons), European Studies and Geography MA(Hons), European Studies and History MA(Hons), European Studies and International Relations MA(Hons), European Studies and Philosophy MA(Hons), European Studies and Psychology MA, European Studies with French MA(Hons), European Studies with German MA(Hons), European Studies with Spanish MA(Hons), History MA(Hons), History and International Relations MA(Hons), History and Philosophy MA(Hons), History and Politics MA(Hons), History

and Psychology MA(Hons), History with French MA(Hons), History with German MA(Hons), History with Spanish MA(Hons), Languages MA, BSc, LLB, Liberal Arts MA(Hons), Part-time Degree MA, Part-time Evening Certificate in Management CertHE, Part-time Evening Diploma in Management DipHE, Philosophy MA(Hons), Philosophy and Film MA(Hons), Philosophy and International Relations MA(Hons), Philosophy and Politics MA(Hons), Philosophy and Psychology MA(Hons), Philosophy with French MA(Hons), Philosophy with German MA(Hons), Philosophy with Spanish MA(Hons), Scottish Historical Studies MA(Hons), Scottish Historical Studies with French MA(Hons), Scottish Historical Studies with German MA(Hons), Scottish Historical Studies with Spanish MA(Hons)

Postgraduate courses: Archival Studies PGCert, Archives and Records Management MLitt / MSc, Comics & Graphic Novels MDes, Comics & Graphic Novels MLitt, Crime Writing and Forensic Investigation MLitt, Digital Recordkeeping PGCert, English Studies MLitt, English Studies part-time MLitt, Family and Local History MLitt, Film Studies MLitt, Graduate Diploma in French by Distance Learning GradDip, Graduate Diploma in German by Distance Learning GradDip, Graduate Diploma in Spanish by Distance Learning GradDip, History MRes, History MLitt, Humanities MLitt, Philosophy MLitt, Philosophy and Literature MLitt, Records Management PGCert, Records Management and Digital Preservation MSc, Records Management and Information Rights MSc, Science Fiction MLitt, Scottish History (by distance learning) MLitt, Theatre Studies MLitt, Writing Practice & Study MLitt

School of Life Sciences; www.lifesci.dundee.ac.uk

Biochemistry BSc(Hons), Biological Chemistry and Drug Discovery BSc(Hons), Biological Chemistry and Drug Discovery (with a year in industry) BSc, Biological Sciences BSc(Hons), Biological Sciences (with a year in industry) BSc(Hons), Biomedical Sciences BSc(Hons), Biomedical Sciences (with a year in industry) BSc(Hons), Life Sciences (with Dundee & Angus College) BSc(Hons), Microbiology BSc(Hons), Molecular Biology BSc(Hons), Molecular Genetics BSc(Hons), Neuroscience BSc(Hons), Pharmacology BSc(Hons), Physiological Sciences BSc(Hons)

School of Medicine; http://medicine.dundee.ac.uk

Anatomy (Intercalated) BMSc(Hons), Applied Orthopaedic Technology (Intercalated) BMSc(Hons), Cardiovascular and Diabetes Medicine (Intercalated) BMSc(Hons), Forensic Medicine (Intercalated) BMSc(Hons), Gateway to Medicine Year, Genetics, Cancer and Personalised Medicine (Intercalated) BMSc(Hons), Healthcare Improvement (Intercalated) BMSc(Hons), Human Reproduction, Assisted Conception and Embryonic Stem Cells (Intercalated) BMSc(Hons), International Health (Intercalated) BMSc(Hons), Medical Sciences BSc(Hons), Medicine MBChB, Neuropharmacology and Behaviour (Intercalated) BMSc(Hons), Scottish Graduate Entry Medicine Programme (ScotGEM) MBChB, Teaching in Medicine (Intercalated) BMSc(Hons)

Postgraduate courses: Cancer Biology MRes, Certificate in Urgent Care PGCert, Clinical Audit and Research for Healthcare Professionals PGCert, Cognitive Behavioural Psychotherapy PGCert / PGDip, Diabetes Care, Education & Management MSc, Diabetes Care, Education & Management PGDip, Diabetes Care, Education & Management PGCert, Human Clinical Embryology and Assisted Conception MSc, Medical Education MMEd, Medical Education (Part Time Distance Learning) MMEd, Motion Analysis MSc / PGDip / PGCert, Motion Analysis (Part Time by Distance Learning) MSc / PGDip / PGCert, Orthopaedic and Rehabilitation Technology MSc, Orthopaedic Science MSc, Orthopaedic Surgery MCh Orth, Palliative Care Research MPH, Psychological Therapy in Primary Care MSc, Public Health MPH, Quality Diabetes Care MSc/PGDip/PGCert, Sports Biomechanics and Rehabilitation MRes

School of Nursing and Health Sciences; http://nursing-health.dundee.ac.uk

Adult Nursing BSc, Adult Nursing (Fife campus) MSc, Adult Nursing (Fife Campus) BSc(Hons), Adult Nursing (Tayside campus) BSc, Adult Nursing (Tayside campus) MSc, Adult Nursing (Tayside Campus) BSc(Hons), Child Nursing BSc, Child Nursing MSc, Child Nursing BSc(Hons), Mental Health Nursing BSc, Mental Health Nursing MSc, Mental Health Nursing BSc(Hons), Nursing BSc

Postgraduate courses: Health Studies MSc, Infection: Prevention and Control MSc, Infection: Prevention and Control (Top Up) BSc, Infection: Prevention and Control (Top Up) Distance Learning BSc, Midwifery MSc / Maternal and Infant Health MSc, Nursing MSc,

Nursing & Health MSc, Post-Registration Nursing BSc, Quality Improvement MSc

School of Science and Engineering; www.dundee.ac.uk/scienceengineering

Anatomical Sciences BSc(Hons), Applied Computing BSc(Hons), Applied Computing: Games (with Dundee & Angus College) BSc(Hons), Applied Computing: Human Computer Interaction BSc, Applied Physics BSc(Hons), Biomedical Engineering BEng(Hons), Civil Engineering BEng / MEng(Hons), Civil Engineering MEng, Civil Engineering BEng, Computing Science BSc(Hons), Electronic Engineering BEng(Hons), Electronic Engineering & Physics BEng(Hons), Forensic Anthropology BSc(Hons), Mathematical Biology BSc(Hons), Mathematical Biology MSci, Mathematics MMath, Mathematics BSc(Hons), Mathematics and Astrophysics BSc(Hons), Mathematics and Economics BSc, Mathematics and Financial Economics BSc, Mathematics and Physics MSci, Mathematics and Physics BSc, Mathematics and Psychology BSc, Mechanical Engineering BEng(Hons), Mechanical Engineering with Renewables BEng, Physics MSci, Physics BSc(Hons), Physics BSc / MSci(Hons), Physics with Astrophysics BSc(Hons), Physics with Renewable Energy Science MSci, Physics with Renewable Energy Science BSc, Renewables MSci / BEng / BSc(Hons)

Postgraduate courses: Anatomy & Advanced Forensic Anthropology MSc, Anatomy for Artists PGCert, Applied Computing MSc, Applied Computing with Work Placement MSc, Applied Mathematics MSc, Biomedical Engineering MSc, Civil Engineering MSc, Computing MSc, Computing Research MSc, Computing with International Business MSc, Computing with International Business with Work Placement MSc, Computing with Vision and Imaging MSc, Computing with Work Placement MSc, Data Engineering MSc, Data Science PGCert, Data Science MSc, Data Science (part time) MSc, Design for Medical Technologies MSc, Forensic Anthropology MSc, Forensic Archaeology and Anthropology MSc, Forensic Art & Facial Identification MSc, Geotechnical Engineering MSc, Human Anatomy MSc, Industrial Engineering and International Finance MSc, Industrial Engineering and Management MSc, Information Technology & International Business MSc, Mathematical Biology MSc, Mathematics PGDip, Mathematics for the Financial Sector MSc, Medical Art MSc, Medical Imaging MSc, Renewable Energy and Environmental Modelling MSc, Structural Engineering and Concrete Materials MSc, User Experience Design MSc

School of Social Sciences; www.dundee.ac.uk/social-sciences

Architecture MArch(Hons), Architecture (RIBA Part II) MArch, Architecture (Wuhan) BA(Hons), Architecture Studies MArch, Architecture with Urban Planning MArch, English Law LLB, English Law with French LLB, English Law with German LLB, English Law with Spanish LLB, Environmental Science BSc(Hons), Environmental Science (with Dundee & Angus College) BSc(Hons), Environmental Science and Geography BSc(Hons), Environmental Science and Geography MA(Hons), Environmental Sustainability MA(Hons), Environmental Sustainability and Geography MA(Hons), European Politics MA(Hons), European Politics with French MA(Hons), European Politics with German MA(Hons), European Politics with Spanish MA(Hons), Geography BSc(Hons), Geography MA(Hons), Geography MA(Hons) / BSc(Hons), Geography and Economics MA(Hons), Geography and History MA(Hons), Geography and Planning MA(Hons), Geography and Politics MA(Hons), Geography and Psychology MA(Hons), Geography with French MA(Hons), Geography with German MA(Hons), Geography with Spanish MA(Hons), Geopolitics MA(Hons), Geopolitics MA(Hons), International Relations and Politics MA(Hons), Law (Dual Qualifying) with Oil and Gas Law LLB, Law (Eng/NI) − Accelerated LLB, Law (Eng/NI) with Oil and Gas Law LLB, Law (including Law with Languages) LLB, Law (Scots and English Dual Qualifying) LLB, Law (Scots) − Accelerated LLB, Law (Scots) with Oil and Gas Law LLB, Law − Accelerated LLB, Politics MA(Hons), Politics and Psychology MA(Hons), Politics with French MA(Hons), Politics with German MA(Hons), Politics with Spanish MA(Hons), Psychology MA(Hons) / BSc(Hons), Psychology BSc(Hons), Psychology with French BSc(Hons), Psychology with French MA(Hons), Psychology with German BSc(Hons), Psychology with German MA(Hons), Psychology with Spanish BSc(Hons), Psychology with Spanish MA(Hons), Scots Law LLB, Scots Law with French LLB, Scots Law with German LLB, Scots Law with Spanish LLB, Town and Regional Planning MA(Hons)

Postgraduate courses: Augmentative & Alternative Communication MSc, Comparative & European Private International Law LLM, Corporate & Commercial Law LLM, Developmental Psychology MSc,

Energy Law and Policy LLM, Energy Law and Policy (Distance Learning) LLM, Energy Studies with Specialisation in Energy and the Environment MSc, Energy Studies with Specialisation in Energy Economics MSc, Energy Studies with Specialisation in Energy Finance MSc, Energy Studies with Specialisation in Energy Policy MSc, Energy Studies with Specialisation in Oil and Gas Economics MSc, Energy Studies without specialisation (Distance Learning) MSc, Environmental Law LLM, Healthcare Law and Ethics LLM, International Commercial Law LLM, International Commercial Law (LLM) – Dual Qualifying Programme LLM, International Criminal Justice & Human Rights LLM, International Finance MFin, International Law & Security MSc, International Law & Security LLM, International Mineral Resources Management MSc, International Mineral Resources Management (Distance Learning) MBA, International Oil and Gas Management MSc, International Oil and Gas Management (Distance Learning) MBA, International Relations MSc, International Security MSc, International Security: Drugs and Organised Crime MSc, International Security: European Union MSc, International Security: Human Rights MSc, International Security: Russia MSc, International Security: Terrorism MSc, Law (General) LLM, Law, Banking and Finance LLM, Managing in the Energy Industries MSc, Mineral Law and Policy LLM, Mineral Law and Policy (Distance Learning) LLM, Natural Resources Law and Policy LLM, Natural Resources Law and Policy (Distance Learning) LLM, Oil and Gas Law and Policy LLM, Oil and Gas Law and Policy (Distance Learning) LLM, Petroleum Taxation and Finance LLM, Petroleum Taxation and Finance (Distance Learning) LLM, Professional Legal Practice PGDip, Psychological Research Methods MSc, Psychology of Language MSc, Psychology of Mental Health MSc, Social Research Methods MSc, Social Research Methods (Population and Welfare) MSc, Spatial Planning with Environmental Assessment MSc, Spatial Planning with Geographic Information Systems MSc, Spatial Planning with Marine Spatial Planning MSc, Spatial Planning with Sustainable Urban Design MSc, Spatial Planning with Urban Conservation MSc, Sustainability MSc, Sustainability and the Green Economy MSc, Sustainability and Water Security MSc, Sustainability: Climate Change and Low Carbon Futures MSc

DURHAM UNIVERSITY
www.dur.ac.uk

Department of Anthropology; www.dur.ac.uk/anthropology
Anthropology BA(Hons), Anthropology BSc(Hons), Health & Human Sciences BSc(Hons), BA(Hons) Anthropology and Archaeology, BA(Hons) Anthropology and Sociology
Postgraduate courses: Socio-Cultural Anthropology MA, MA Research Methods (Anthropology), Sustainability, Culture and Development MSc, Medical Anthropology MSc, Energy and Society MSc

School of Applied Social Sciences; www.dur.ac.uk/sass
BA Criminology, BA Single and Joint Honours in Sociology, BA Sport, Exercise and Physical Activity
Postgraduate courses: MSc Criminology and Criminal Justice, MA Social Research Methods (Criminology), MA Social Research Methods (Sociology), MA Social Research Methods (Social Policy), Master of Social Work, MA Social Research Methods (Social Work), MA Social Research Methods, MA International Social Work and Community Development

Department of Archaeology; www.dur.ac.uk/archaeology
BA Archaeology, BSc Archaeology, BA Archaeology and Ancient Civilisations, BA Combined Honours, Joint Honours with Anthropology, Joint Honours with Ancient History
Postgraduate courses: MA Archaeology, MA International Cultural Heritage Management, MSc in Archaeological Science, MSc Palaeopathology, MA Museum and Artefact Studies, MA in the Conservation of Archaeological and Museum Objects

Department of Biosciences; www.dur.ac.uk/biosciences
BSc Biological Sciences, MBiol Biosciences; Postgraduate opportunities on website

Business School; www.dur.ac.uk/business
BSc Accounting, BSc Accounting and Finance, BA Accounting and Management, BSc Finance, Business and Management (BA), Marketing and Management (BA), BA Economics, BA Economics with

Management, BA Economics with French, BA Economics and Politics, BA Philosophy, Politics and Economics

Postgraduate courses: Master of Business Administration, MSc Accounting, MSc Economics, MSc Environmental and Natural Resource Economics, MSc Experimental Economics, MSc Public Economics, MSc Finance, MSc Finance (Accounting and Finance), MSc Finance (Corporate and International Finance), MSc Finance (Economics and Finance), MSc Finance (Finance and Investment), MSc Finance (International Banking and Finance), MSc Finance (International Money, Finance and Investment), MSc Islamic Finance, MSc Islamic Finance and Management, MSc Management, MSc Management (Entrepreneurship), MSc Management (Finance), MSc Management (Human Resource Management), MSc Management (International Business), MSc Management (Supply Chain Logistics), Part-time MA Management, MSc Marketing

Department of Chemistry; www.dur.ac.uk/chemistry

BSc Chemistry, MChem Chemistry; Postgraduate courses: various research degrees

Department of Classics and Ancient History; www.dur.ac.uk/classics

BA in Ancient History, BA in Classical Civilisation, BA in Classics, Ancient History and Archaeology, BA in Ancient, Medieval and Modern History

Postgraduate courses: MA in Classics, MA in Ancient Philosophy, MA in Greece, Rome and the Near East

Department of Earth Sciences; www.dur.ac.uk/earth.sciences

BSc Geology, BSc Environmental Geoscience, BSc Geophysics with Geology, MSci Earth Sciences, BSc Geoscience; Postgraduate courses: various research degrees

School of Education; www.dur.ac.uk/education

BA(Hons) Education Studies, BA(Hons) Primary Education MA Education; Postgraduate courses: MSc in Educational Assessment, MA Intercultural Communication and Education, MA Research Methods, International Summer Postgraduate Institute (ISPI), Postgraduate Certificate in the Practice of Education

School of Engineering and Computing Sciences; www.dur.ac.uk/ecs

MEng Computer Science, BSc Computer Science, BSc Software Development for Business, MEng General Engineering, BEng General Engineering; Postgraduate courses: MSc Communications Engineering, MSc Internet Systems and eBusiness, MSc New and Renewable Energy

English Language Centre; www.dur.ac.uk/englishlanguage.centre

Postgraduate courses: MA TESOL, MA Applied Linguistics for TESOL

Department of English Studies; www.dur.ac.uk/english.studies

BA English Literature, BA English Literature and History, BA English Literature and Philosophy; Postgraduate courses: MA in English Literary Studies, MA in Medieval and Renaissance Literary Studies, MA in Romantic and Victorian Literary Studies, MA in Twentieth and Twenty-First Century Literary Studies, MA in Studies in Poetry, MA in Creative Writing

Department of Geography; www.dur.ac.uk/geography

BA Geography, BSc Geography, MArts Geography, MSci Geography; Postgraduate courses: Risk Masters MA/MSc, MA in Geography (Research Methods)

School of Government & International Affairs; www.dur.ac.uk/sgia

BA Politic, BA International Relations, BA Economics & Politics, BA Philosophy & Politics, BA Philosophy, Politics and Economics, BA Combined Honours in Social Sciences; Postgraduate courses: MSc Arab World Studies – Language Based (LBAS), MSc Conflict Prevention and Peacebuilding, MSc Defence, Development and Diplomacy, MSc Global Politics, MA Politics and International Relations (Political Theory), MA Research Methods (Politics, International Relations, Security), MA International Relations, MA International Relations (Europe), MA International Relations (East Asia), MA International Relations (Middle East)

Department of History; www.dur.ac.uk/history

BA History, BA Ancient, Medieval and Modern History, BA English Literature and History, BA Modern European Languages and History; Postgraduate courses: MA in Social & Economic History

(Research Methods), MA in History, MA in Medieval and Early Modern Studies

Durham Law School; www.dur.ac.uk/law

Law LLB; Postgraduate courses: LLM Master of Laws (General), LLM Corporate Law, LLM European Trade and Commercial Law, LLM International Trade and Commercial Law, LLM International Law and Governance

Department of Mathematical Sciences; www.dur.ac.uk/mathematical.sciences

Mathematics BSc, Mathematics MMath; Postgraduate courses: MSc in Mathematical Sciences, MSc in Particles, Strings and Cosmology, various research degrees

School of Modern Languages & Cultures; www.dur.ac.uk/mlac

BA Modern Languages and Cultures, BA in Modern Languages and History, BA in Chinese Studies, BA in Japanese Studies; Postgraduate courses: MA in Arabic-English Translation and Interpreting, MA in Translation Studies, MA in Visual Arts and Culture, MA in Medieval and Early Modern Studies

Department of Music; www.dur.ac.uk/music

Music BA; Postgraduate course: Music MA

Department of Natural Sciences; www.dur.ac.uk/natural.sciences

BSc Natural Sciences, MSci Natural Sciences

Department of Philosophy; www.dur.ac.uk/philosophy

BA Philosophy, BA Philosophy and Politics, BA Philosophy and Psychology, BA Philosophy and Theology, BA English Literature and Philosophy, BA Music and Philosophy, BA Philosophy, Politics and Economics (PPE), BA Education Studies & Philosophy; Postgraduate courses: Graduate Diploma in Philosophy, Philosophy (MA)

Department of Physics; www.dur.ac.uk/physics

BSc Physics, MPhys Physics, MPhys Physics and Astronomy, MPhys Theoretical Physics; Postgraduate courses: MSc Particles, Strings and Cosmology, MSc Biophysical Sciences

Department of Psychology; www.dur.ac.uk/psychology

BSc(Hons) in Psychology; Postgraduate courses: MSc Cognitive Neuroscience, MSc Developmental Psychopathology, MA Research Methods (Developmental Psychology)

Department of Theology and Religion

BA Theology and Religion, BA Philosophy and Theology; Postgraduate courses: MA in Biblical Studies, MA in Christian Theology, MA in Christian Theology (Anglican Studies), MA in Christian Theology (Catholic Studies), MA in Religion and Society, MA in Theology and Religion, MA in Spirituality, Theology & Health, Graduate Diploma

CRANMER HALL, ST JOHN'S COLLEGE
www.cranmerhall.com

Certificate in Theology, Ministry and Mission, Diploma in Theology, Ministry and Mission, BA in Theology, Ministry and Mission; Postgraduate courses: MA in Theology and Ministry, MA in Consultancy for Mission and Ministry, MA in Digital Theology

NEW COLLEGE DURHAM
www.newdur.ac.uk

Art & Design
FdA Visual Arts, FdA Graphic Design, FdA Graphic Design, BA(Hons) top-up Design, BA(Hons) top-up Visual Arts

Beauty
FdA Spa Management

Business & Management
BA(Hons) top-up Management, FdA Business & Management, FdA Business & Management, FdA Event Management

Computing
BSc(Hons) top-up Computing with Networking, BSc(Hons) top-up Business Computing, FdSc Computing with Networking, FdSc Cyber Security, FdSc Applied Business Computing, BSc(Hons) top-up Business Computing

Construction
HNC Civil Engineering, HND top-up Civil Engineering and the Built Environment, HND top-up

Construction & the Built Environment, HNC Construction & the Built Environment

Counselling
FdA Counselling, BA(Hons) top-up Counselling Studies

Early Years
FdA Supporting Learning & Teaching, FdA Childhood Studies & Professional Practice

Education
FdSc Cyber Security, FdSc Applied Health & Social Care (Adults), FdSc Applied Sport & Exercise Science, FdSc Computing with Networking, FdA Public & Community Services, FdA Roots and Popular Music, FdA Spa Management, FdA Supporting Learning & Teaching, FdA Tourism Management, FdA Visual Arts, FdSc Applied Business Computing, FdA Heritage & Cultural Tourism Management, FdA Hospitality Management, FdA Housing & Community Studies, FdA Film & Media Production, FdA Event Management, FdA Graphic Design, FdA Childhood Studies & Professional Practice, FdA Counselling, FdA Childhood Studies & Professional Practice, FdA Business & Management

Graphic Design & Media
FdA Film & Media Production, FdA Graphic Design, BA(Hons) top-up Visual Arts, BA(Hons) top-up Design

Health & Care
FdSc Applied Health & Social Care (Adults)

Housing
FdA Housing & Community Studies

Music
FdA Roots and Popular Music, BA(Hons) top-up Popular Music

Public Services
FdA Public & Community Services

Social Work
BA(Hons) Social Work

Sport
HND top-up Sport, HNC Sport, FdSc Applied Sport & Exercise Science, BA(Hons) top-up Sport & Exercise

Tourism, Hospitality & Events
FdA Event Management, FdA Hospitality Management, FdA Tourism Management

ROYAL ACADEMY OF DANCE
www.rad.org.uk

ballet education, ballet/dance teaching studies, Benesh, dance education, movement notation; BA(Hons), Dip/CertHE, MTeach(Dance), licenciate, PGCE

UNIVERSITY OF EAST ANGLIA
www.uea.ac.uk

School of Art, Media and American Studies; www.uea.ac.uk/web/ama
BA American and English Literature, BA American History, BA American Literature with Creative Writing, BA American Studies, BA American Studies (3 Years), BA Archaeology, Anthropology and Art History, BA Archaeology, BA Film and Television Studies, BA Film Studies and English Literature, BA History and Film Studies, BA History and History of Art, BA History of Art, BA History of Art and Literature, BA History of Art with Gallery and Museum Studies, BA Media Studies
Postgraduate courses: Graduate Diploma World Art Studies, MA American Studies, MA Cultural Heritage and Museum Studies, MA Film Studies, MA Film, Television and Creative Practice, MA History of Art, MA The Arts of Africa, Oceania and the Americas

School of Biological Sciences; www.uea.ac.uk/web/biological-sciences
BSc Biochemistry, BSc Biological Science (with Education), BSc Biological Sciences, BSc Biomedicine, BSc Ecology, BSc Molecular Biology and Genetics; Postgraduate courses in: Graduate Diploma Ecology, MSc Applied Ecology and Conservation, MSc Molecular Medicine, MSc Plant Genetics and Crop Improvement, MSci Biochemistry, MSci Biological Sciences

School of Chemistry; www.uea.ac.uk/web/chemistry

BSc Chemical Physics, BSc Chemistry, BSc Chemistry (with Education), BSc Physics, BSc Physics (with Education)

Postgraduate courses: Graduate Diploma Chemical Sciences, MChem Chemical Physics, MChem Chemistry, MChem Forensic and Investigative Chemistry, MPhys Physics, MSc Advanced Organic Chemistry

School of Computing Sciences; www.uea.ac.uk/web/computing

BEng Computer Systems Engineering, BSc Actuarial Sciences, BSc Applied Computing Science with a Foundation Year, BSc Business Information Systems, BSc Computer Graphics, Imaging and Multimedia, BSc Computing Science, BSc Computing Science (with Education)

Postgraduate courses: MComp Computing Science, MSc Advanced Computing Science, MSc Computing Science, MSc Information Systems, MSc Knowledge Discovery and Datamining,

School of Economics; www.uea.ac.uk/web/economics

BA Philosophy, Politics and Economics, BSc Business Economics, BSc Business Finance and Economics, BSc Economics, BSc Economics with Accountancy, BSc Politics and Economics

Postgraduate courses: Graduate Diploma Economics, MSc Behavioural and Experimental Economics, MSc Economics, MSc Economics and International Relations, MSc Economics of International Finance and Trade, MSc Economics of Money, Banking and Capital Markets, MSc Finance and Economics, MSc Industrial Economics, MSc International Business Economics, MSc International Business Finance and Economics, MSc Media Economics, MSc Quantitative Financial Economics

School of Education and Lifelong Learning; www.uea.ac.uk/web/education

BA Education, BA Physical Education

Postgraduate courses: MA Adult Literacy and Learning For Global Change, MA Education: Learning, Pedagogy and Assessment, MA Educational Practice and Research (Part Time), MA Mathematics Education, MA Second Language Education, PGCE Physics with Mathematics, PGCE Primary (General Class Teacher with Mathematics Specialism), PGCE Primary (Key Stage 2 with Primary Languages French/German/Spanish), PGCE Primary (Specialising in Foundation Stage and Key Stage 1/Key Stage 1 and Key Stage 2/Key Stage 2), PGCE Secondary English, PGCE Secondary Geography, PGCE Secondary History, PGCE Secondary Mathematics, PGCE Secondary Modern Foreign Languages, PGCE Secondary Physical Education, PGCE Secondary Science (Specialising in Biology/Chemistry/Physics)

School of Environmental Sciences; www.uea.ac.uk/web/environmental-sciences

BA / BSc Geography, BA Geography, BSc Climate Change, BSc Environmental Earth Sciences, BSc Environmental Geophysics, BSc Environmental Sciences, BSc Environmental Sciences (with Education), BSc Environmental Sciences and International Development, BSc Geography, BSc Geography (with Education), BSc Geology with Geography, BSc Geophysics

Postgraduate courses: BSc Meteorology and Oceanography, MSc Applied Ecology – International Programme, MSc Climate Change, MSc Environmental Assessment and Management, MSc Environmental Sciences, MSci Climate Change, MSci Environmental Earth Sciences, MSci Environmental Geophysics, MSci Environmental Sciences, MSci Geology with Geography, MSci Geophysics, MSci Meteorology and Oceanography

School of Health Sciences; www.uea.ac.uk/web/health-sciences

BSc Adult Nursing, BSc Children's Nursing, BSc Learning Disabilities Nursing, BSc Mental Health Nursing, BSc Midwifery, BSc Midwifery (Shortened), BSc Occupational Therapy, BSc Paramedic Science, BSc Physiotherapy, BSc Speech and Language Therapy

Postgraduate courses: Dip HE Operating Department Practice, MClinEd Clinical Education, MSc Adult Nursing – Preregistration, MSc Advanced Professional Practice, MSc Clinical Research NIHR, MSc Occupational Therapy, MSc Physiotherapy

School of History; www.uea.ac.uk/web/history

BA History, BA History and Politics, BA Modern History

Postgraduate courses: Graduate Diploma History, MA Early Modern History, MA Landscape History, MA Medieval History, MA Modern History

Interdisciplinary Institute for the Humanities; www.uea.ac.uk/web/humanities

BA American Studies (with a Foundation Year), BA English Literature (with a Foundation Year), BA Film and Television Studies (with a Foundation Year), BA History (with a Foundation Year), BA History of Art (with a Foundation Year), BA Intercultural Communication with Business Management (with a Foundation Year), BA Philosophy (with a Foundation Year), BA Politics (with a Foundation Year)

Postgraduate courses: MA Creative Entrepreneurship, MA Gender Studies

School of International Development; www.uea.ac.uk/web/international-development

BA Geography and International Development, BA International Development, BA International Development with Anthropology, BA International Development with Economics, BA International Development with Politics, BA Media and International Development, BSc International Development and the Environment

Postgraduate courses: MA Agriculture and Rural Development, MA Conflict, Governance and International Development, MA Education and Development, MA Gender Analysis in International Development, MA Globalisation, Business and Sustainable Development, MA International Development, MA International Social Development, MA Media and International Development, MSc Climate Change and International Development, MSc Development Economics, MSc Environment and International Development, MSc Impact Evaluation for International Development, MSc Water Security and International Development

School of Law; www.uea.ac.uk/web/law

LLB Law, LLB Law with American Law, LLB Law with European Legal Systems

Postgraduate courses: Graduate Diploma in Legal Studies, LLM Employment Law, LLM Information Technology and Intellectual Property Law, LLM International Commercial and Business Law, LLM International Commercial and Competition Law, LLM International Trade Law, LLM Master of Laws, LLM Media Law, Policy and Practice, PG Certificate Employment Law (Part Time)

School of Literature, Drama and Creative Writing; www.uea.ac.uk/web/literature

BA Drama, BA English and American Literature, BA English Literature, BA English Literature and Drama, BA English Literature with Creative Writing, BA Literature and History, BA Scriptwriting and Performance

Postgraduate courses: MA Biography and Creative Non-Fiction, MA Creative Writing Poetry, MA Creative Writing Prose Fiction, MA Creative Writing Scriptwriting, MA Literary Translation, MA Medieval and Early Modern Textual Cultures 1381 – 1688, MA Modern and Contemporary Writing, MA Theatre Directing: Text and Production, MFa Creative Writing

School of Mathematics; www.uea.ac.uk/web/mathematics

BEng Energy Engineering, BEng Energy Engineering with Environmental Management, BEng Engineering, BSc Mathematics, BSc Mathematics (with Education), BSc Mathematics with Business

Postgraduate courses: MEng Energy Engineering, MEng Engineering, MMath Master of Mathematics, MSc Energy Engineering with Environmental Management

School of Natural Sciences; www.uea.ac.uk/web/natural-sciences

BSc Natural Sciences; Postgraduate course: MNatSci Natural Sciences

Norwich Business School; www.uea.ac.uk/web/norwich-business-school

BSc Accounting and Finance, BSc Accounting and Management, BSc Business Finance and Management, BSc Business Management, BSc Marketing and Management

Postgraduate courses: MBA Master of Business Administration, MSc Accounting and Finance, MSc Banking and Finance, MSc Brand Leadership, MSc Business Management, MSc Enterprise and Business Creation, MSc Finance and Management, MSc Human Resource Management, MSc International Accounting and Financial Management, MSc Investment and Financial Management, MSc Management, MSc Marketing, MSc Marketing and Management, MSc Operations and Logistics Management

Norwich Medical School; www.uea.ac.uk/web/medicine

Postgraduate courses: CredPG Master of Surgery – Specialist Development Modules, MBBS Medicine, Mclined Clinical Education, MRes Clinical Science,

MS Oncoplastic Breast Surgery, MSc Clinical Research, MSc Health Economics, MSc Health Research, MSc Physician Associate Studies, MSc Regional Anaesthesia, PG Certificate Clinical Education (Part Time), PG Diploma Clinical Education, PG Diploma Clinical Research, PG Diploma Health Economics, PG Diploma Oncoplastic Breast Surgery, PG Diploma Regional Anaesthesia

School of Pharmacy; www.uea.ac.uk/web/pharmacy

BSc Pharmacology and Drug Discovery; Postgraduate courses: MPharm Pharmacy, PG Diploma Pharmacy Practice

School of Politics, Philosophy and Language and Communication Studies; www.uea.ac.uk/web/ppl

BA Culture, Literature and Politics, BA English Literature and Philosophy, BA Intercultural Communication with Business Management, BA International Relations, BA International Relations and Modern History, BA International Relations and Modern Languages, BA International Relations and Politics, BA Modern Language (3 Year Option with a Semester Abroad), BA Modern Language(s) with Management Studies, BA Modern Languages (Double Honours with a Year Abroad), BA Philosophy, BA Philosophy and History, BA Philosophy and Politics, BA Politics, BA Politics and Media Studies, BA Society, Culture and Media, BA Translation and Interpreting with Modern Languages (Double Honours with a Year Abroad), BA Translation, Media and Modern Language (3 Year Option with a Semester Abroad), BA Translation, Media and Modern Languages (Double Honours with a Year Abroad)
Postgraduate courses: MA Applied Translation Studies, MA Broadcast and Digital Journalism International, MA Broadcast and Digital Journalism UK, MA Global Intercultural Communication, MA International Relations, MA International Security, MA Media and Cultural Politics, MA Media, Culture and Society, MA Philosophy and Literature, MA Public Policy and Public Management, MRes Philosophy

School of Psychology; www.uea.ac.uk/web/psychology

BSc Cognitive Psychology, BSc Developmental Psychology, BSc Psychology, BSc Social Psychology
Postgraduate courses: MRes Social Science Research Methods, MSc Cognitive Neuroscience, MSc Developmental Science, MSc Social Psychology

School of Social Work; www.uea.ac.uk/web/socialwork

BA Social Work; Postgraduate course: MA Social Work

CITY COLLEGE NORWICH
www.ccn.ac.uk

BSc(Hons) Professional Aviation Engineering Practice, BSc(Hons) Applied Sport, Health and Exercise, BA(Hons) Tourism Management, BA(Hons) Psychology with Sociology, BA(Hons) Leadership in the Public Sector, BA(Hons) Leadership and Management, BA(Hons) Integrated Health and Social Care Top Up, BA(Hons) Hospitality and Event Management, BA(Hons) English and Social Sciences, BA(Hons) English, BA(Hons) Childhood Studies, BA(Hons) Business Management

EASTON & OTLEY COLLEGE
www.eastonotley.ac.uk

BA(Hons) Crime, Terrorism and Global Security, BSc(Hons) Agribiosciences, BSc(Hons) Agriculture, BSc(Hons) Animal Science and Welfare (Top-Up), BSc(Hons) Ecology and Conservation (Top-Up), BSc(Hons) Equine Science (Top-Up), BSc(Hons) Equitation & Coaching, BSc(Hons) Wildlife Management and Conservation (Top-Up), BSc(Hons) Zoology, BSc Sports Coaching Science (Top-Up), Certificate in Education (Lifelong Learning Sector), FdA Landscape and Garden Design, FdSc Agricultural Management Science, FdSc Animal Science & Welfare, FdSc Ecology & Conservation Management, FdSc Equine Science & Welfare, FdSc Fishery Management & Sustainable Aquaculture, FdSc Football Studies & Coaching (subject to approval), FdSc Health, Fitness, Strength & Conditioning (subject to approval), FdSc Sports Coaching Science, FdSc Wildlife Management & Conservation; Postgraduate course: Professional Graduate Certificate in Education (PGCE)

EDGE HILL UNIVERSITY
www.edgehill.ac.uk

Faculty of Arts and Sciences;
www.edgehill.ac.uk/fas

Department of Biology; www.edgehill.ac.uk/biology

BSc(Hons) Biology, BSc(Hons) Biotechnology, BSc(Hons) Ecology and Conservation, BSc(Hons) Food Science, BSc(Hons) Genetics, BSc(Hons) Human Biology, BSc(Hons) Plant Science
Postgraduate course: MSc Conservation Management

Business School; www.edgehill.ac.uk/business

BSc(Hons) Accountancy, BSc(Hons) Business and Economics, BSc(Hons) Business and Management, BSc(Hons) Business and Management with Accounting and Finance, BSc(Hons) Business and Management with Human Resource Management, BSc(Hons) Business and Management with Leisure and Tourism, BSc(Hons) Business and Management with Logistics and Supply Chain Management, BSc(Hons) Business and Management with Marketing, BSc(Hons) Business Innovation and Enterprise, BSc(Hons) International Business, BA(Hons) Advertising, BSc(Hons) Marketing, BSc(Hons) Marketing with Advertising, BSc(Hons) Marketing with Digital Communications, BSc(Hons) Marketing with Public Relations
Postgraduate courses: MSc Leadership and Management Development, Master of Business Administration, Master of Business Administration (Finance), Master of Business Administration (Human Resource Management), Master of Business Administration (Information Technology), Master of Business Administration (Marketing), Professional Doctorate Emergency Services Management, MA Marketing Communications and Branding, MBA Master of Business Administration (Marketing)

Department of Computer Science; www.edgehill.ac.uk/computerscience

BSc(Hons) Computer Science, BSc(Hons) Computer Science and Mathematics, BSc(Hons) Computing, BSc(Hons) Computing (Application Development), BSc(Hons) Computing (Games Programming), BSc(Hons) Computing (Networking, Security and Forensics), BSc(Hons) Data Science, BSc(Hons) Information Technology Management for Business, BSc(Hons) Software Engineering, BSc(Hons) Web Design and Development, MComp Business Information Systems, MComp Computer Security and Networks, MComp Computing, MComp Software Application Development, MComp Web Design and Development
Postgraduate courses: MSc Advanced Computer Networking, MSc Big Data Analytics, MSc Computing, MSc Cyber Security, MSc Games Programming and Visual Computing, MSc Information Security and IT Management

English, History and Creative Writing; www.edgehill.ac.uk/englishhistorycreativewriting

English

BA(Hons) English, BA(Hons) English Language, BA(Hons) English Literature, BA(Hons) Creative Writing and English Literature, BA(Hons) Drama and English Literature, BA(Hons) English and Film Studies, BA(Hons) English Literature and History, BA(Hons) English Literature with Creative Writing, BA(Hons) English with Creative Writing
Postgraduate courses: MA English, MA Popular Culture

History

BA(Hons) History, BA(Hons) History with Politics
Postgraduate courses: MA History and Culture, MA Popular Culture

Creative Writing

BA(Hons) Creative Writing, BA(Hons) Creative Writing and Drama, BA(Hons) Creative Writing and Film Studies
Postgraduate course: MA Creative Writing

Department of Geography; www.edgehill.ac.uk/geography

BSc(Hons) Environmental Science, BSc(Hons) Geoenvironmental Hazards, BA(Hons) Geography, BSc(Hons) Geography, BSc(Hons) Geology with Physical Geography, BA(Hons) Human Geography, BSc(Hons) Physical Geography, BSc(Hons) Physical Geography and Geology

Department of Law and Criminology; www.edgehill.ac.uk/law

LLB(Hons) Law, LLB(Hons) Law with Criminology, LLB(Hons) Law with Politics, BA(Hons) Childhood & Youth Studies and Criminology, [BA(Hons) Criminology, BA(Hons) Criminology and Law, BA(Hons)

Criminology and Psychology, BA(Hons) Criminology and Sociology, BSc(Hons) Psychology and Criminology

Department of Media; www.edgehill.ac.uk/media

BA(Hons) Animation, BA(Hons) Film Studies, BA(Hons) Film Studies with Film Production, BA(Hons) Film and Television Production, BA(Hons) Media, Film and Television, BA(Hons) Media, Music and Sound, BA(Hons) Public Relations, BA(Hons) Public Relations with Politics, BA(Hons) Television Production Management

Postgraduate courses: MA Critical Screen Practice, MA Film and Media, MSc Media Management

Department of Performing Arts; www.edgehill.ac.uk/performingarts

BA(Hons) Creative Performance, BA(Hons) Creative Writing and Drama, BA(Hons) Dance, BA(Hons) Dance and Drama, BA(Hons) Drama, BA(Hons) Drama and English Literature, BA(Hons) Drama & Film Studies, BA(Hons) Music, BA(Hons) Music Production, BA(Hons) Musical Theatre, BA(Hons) Popular Music

Postgraduate courses: PGCert Creative and Cultural Education, MA Making Performance

Department of Psychology; www.edgehill.ac.uk/psychology

BSc(Hons) Psychology, BSc(Hons) Educational Psychology, BSc(Hons) Sport and Exercise Psychology, BSc(Hons) Psychology and Criminology, BA(Hons) Criminology and Psychology

Postgraduate course: MSc Psychology (Conversion)

Department of Sport and Physical Activity; www.edgehill.ac.uk/sport

BA(Hons) Physical Education and School Sport, BSc(Hons) Sport and Exercise Psychology, BSc(Hons) Sport and Exercise Science, BA(Hons) Sports Coaching and Development, BA(Hons) Sports Development and Management, BA(Hons) Sports Management and Coaching, BSc(Hons) Sports Therapy, MSci Sports Coaching and Development

Postgraduate course: MSc Sport, Physical Activity and Mental Health

Faculty of Education; www.edgehill.ac.uk/education

Early Years Unit; www.edgehill.ac.uk/earlyyears

BA(Hons) Early Years Education with QTS, PGCE Early Years Education with QTS, Early Years Teacher Training (Routes to EYTS), FdA Early Years Leadership, FdA Early Years Practice, BA(Hons) Early Years Leadership, BA(Hons) Early Years Practice

Primary Education Unit; www.edgehill.ac.uk/children-education-and-communities

BA(Hons) Children and Young People's Learning and Development, BA(Hons) Teaching, Learning and Child Development, BA(Hons) Working with Children 5-11, BA(Hons) Primary Education with QTS, BA(Hons) Primary Education with QTS (School-Based Route)

Postgraduate courses: PGCE Primary Education with QTS, PGCE Primary Mathematics Specialist with QTS

Professional Learning Unit; www.edgehill.ac.uk/education/professional-learning

Postgraduate courses: PGCert/MA Specialist Primary Mathematics Practice, PGCert SpLD (Dyslexia) with AMBDA/ATS, Postgraduate Certificate Education (Dyscalculia), Postgraduate Certificate Education (Inclusion and SEN), MA Education, MA Educational Enquiry, MSc Education and Leadership

Secondary and Further Education Unit; www.edgehill.ac.uk/secondary-and-further-education

BA(Hons) Education, Secondary Undergraduate QTS Initial Teacher Training Degrees

Postgraduate course: PGCE

Further Education and Training Unit; www.edgehill.ac.uk/educationfe

University Higher Diploma Further Education and Training, FdA Teaching in the Lifelong Learning Sector, BA(Hons) Teaching in the Lifelong Learning Sector

Postgraduate course: PGCE Further Education and Training

Faculty of Health and Social Care; *www.edgehill.ac.uk/health*

Nursing; www.edgehill.ac.uk/health/nursing

BSc(Hons) Nursing (Adult), BSc(Hons) Nursing (Child), BSc(Hons) Nursing (Learning Disabilities), BSc (Hons Nursing (Mental Health), MNSW Adult Nursing and Social Work, MNSW Children's Nursing and Social Work, MNSW Learning Disabilities Nursing and Social Work, MNSW Mental Health Nursing and Social Work

Midwifery; www.edgehill.ac.uk/health/midwifery

BSc(Hons) Pre-Registration Midwifery

Operating Department Practice; www.edgehill.ac.uk/health/odp

BSc(Hons) Operating Department Practice

Paramedic Practice; www.edgehill.ac.uk/health/paramedic

BSc(Hons) Paramedic Practice, BSc Clinical and Professional Paramedic Practice

Applied Health and Social Care; www.edgehill.ac.uk/health/ahsc

BSc(Hons) Child and Adolescent Mental Health and Wellbeing, BSc(Hons) Child Health and Wellbeing, BA(Hons) Counselling and Psychotherapy, BSc(Hons) Family and Community Wellbeing, BSc(Hons) Global Public Health, BA(Hons) Health and Social Wellbeing, BSc(Hons) Nutrition and Health, MSci Nutrition, BSc(Hons) Psychosocial Analysis of Offending Behaviour

Postgraduate courses: PGCert Advanced Critical Care, PGCert Medical Leadership, PGCert Mental Health Law and Ethics, PGCert Simulation and Clinical Learning, PGCert Teaching and Learning in Clinical Practice, PGCert Workplace-based Postgraduate Medical Education, MSc Advanced Fertility Practice, MSc Advanced Practice, MSc Applied Clinical Nutrition, MSc Child and Adolescent Mental Health and Wellbeing, MA Clinical Education, MSc Clinical Reproductive Medicine, MClin Res Master of Clinical Research, MSc Dental Implantology, MHealth Res Master of Health Research, MSc Leadership Development, MSc Midwifery, MSc Professional Clinical Practice, MSc Public Health Nutrition, MA Social Work, MSc Surgical Care Practice

Social Work; www.edgehill.ac.uk/health/socialwork

BA(Hons) Social Work, MNSW Adult Nursing and Social Work, MNSW Children's Nursing and Social Work, MNSW Learning Disabilities Nursing and Social Work, MNSW Mental Health Nursing and Social Work

Postgraduate course: MA Social Work

THE UNIVERSITY OF EDINBURGH
www.ed.ac.uk

School of Biological Sciences; www.ed.ac.uk/biology

Biological Sciences (BSc), Biological Sciences (Biochemistry) (BSc), Biological Sciences (Biotechnology) (BSc), Biological Sciences (Cell Biology) (BSc), Biological Sciences (Development, Regeneration and Stem Cells) (BSc), Biological Sciences (Ecology) (BSc), Biological Sciences (Evolutionary Biology) (BSc), Biological Sciences (Genetics) (BSc), Biological Sciences (Immunology) (BSc), Biological Sciences (Molecular Biology) (BSc), Biological Sciences (Molecular Genetics) (BSc), Biological Sciences (Plant Science) (BSc), Biological Sciences (Zoology) (BSc), Biological Sciences with Management (BSc)

Postgraduate courses: Animal Breeding & Genetics MSc/PgDip, Biochemistry MSc/PgDip, Biodiversity & Taxonomy of Plants MSc/PgDip, Bioinformatics MSc, PgDip, Biotechnology MSc/PgDip, Drug Discovery & Protein Biotechnology (Online Distance Learning) MSc/PgDip/PgCert/PgProfDev, Drug Discovery & Translational Biology MSc/PgDip, Evolutionary Genetics MSc/PgDip, Human Complex Trait Genetics MSc/PgDip, Next Generation Drug Discovery (Online Distance Learning) MSc/PgDip/PgCert/PgProfDev, Quantitative Genetics & Genome Analysis MSc/PgDip, Synthetic Biology & Biotechnology MSc/PgDip, Systems & Synthetic Biology MSc/PgDip

Business School; www.business-school.ed.ac.uk

MA Accounting and Finance, MA Business and Accounting, MA Business and Finance, MA Business Management, MA Business with Decision Sciences, MA Business with Enterprise and Innovation, MA Business with Human Resource Management, MA

Business with Marketing, MA Business with Strategic Economics, MA International Business, MA International Business with Arabic, MA International Business with Chinese, MA International Business with French, MA International Business with German, MA International Business with Italian, MA International Business with Japanese, MA International Business with Russian, MA International Business with Spanish, MA Business and Law, MA Business and Geography, MA Business and Economics, BSc Computer Science and Management Science, BSc Mathematics and Business, LLB Law and Business, LLB Law and Accountancy, MA Arabic and Business, MA Economics and Accounting, MA French and Business, MA German and Business, MA Italian and Business, MA Portuguese and Business, MA Psychology and Business, MA Russian Studies and Business, MA Spanish and Business

Postgraduate courses: MSc Accounting and Finance, MSc Banking and Risk, MSc Business Analytics, MSc Carbon Finance, MSc Entrepreneurship and Innovation, MSc Finance, MSc Human Resource Management, MSc International Business and Emerging Markets, MSc International Human Resource Management, MSc Management, MSc Marketing, MSc Marketing and Business Analysis, Master of Business Administration

School of Chemistry; www.chem.ed.ac.uk

Chemical Physics (BSc), Chemical Physics (MChemPhys), Chemistry (BSc), Chemistry (MChem), Medicinal and Biological Chemistry (BSc), Medicinal and Biological Chemistry (MChem)

Postgraduate courses: Materials Chemistry MSc, Medicinal & Biological Chemistry MSc

School of Divinity; www.ed.ac.uk/divinity

Divinity (BD), Divinity – Graduate Entry (MDiv), Divinity and Classics (MA), Philosophy and Theology (MA), Religious Studies (MA), Religious Studies and English Literature (MA), Religious Studies and Scottish Literature (MA), Theology (MA)

Biblical Studies MTh/MSc, Religious Studies MSc, Science & Religion MSc, Theology in History MTh/MSc, World Christianity MTh/MSc

School of Economics; www.ed.ac.uk/economics

Economics (MA), Economics and Accounting (MA), Economics and Economic History (MA), Economics and Mathematics (MA), Economics and Politics (MA), Economics and Sociology (MA), Economics and Statistics (MA), Economics with Environmental Studies (MA), Economics with Finance (MA), Economics with Management Science (MA)

Postgraduate courses: Economics MSc, Economics (Econometrics) MSc, Economics (Finance) MSc

Edinburgh College of Art; www.eca.ed.ac.uk

Animation (BA), Architectural History and Archaeology (MA), Architectural History and Heritage (MA), Architecture (BA/MA), Art (BA), Fashion (BA), Film and Television (BA), Fine Art (5-year programme) (MA), Graphic Design (BA), History of Art (MA), History of Art and Architectural History (MA), History of Art and Chinese Studies (MA), History of Art and English Literature (MA), History of Art and History of Music (MA), History of Art and Scottish Literature (MA), Illustration (BA), Interior Design (BA), Intermedia Art (BA), Jewellery and Silversmithing (BA), Landscape Architecture (MA), Music (BMus), Music (MA), Painting (BA), Performance Costume (BA), Photography (BA), Product Design (BA), Sculpture (BA), Textiles (BA)

Postgraduate courses: Acoustics & Music Technology MSc, Advanced Sustainable Design MSc, Animation Master of Fine Art, Architectural & Urban Design MSc, Architectural Conservation MSc, Architectural History & Theory MSc, Architectural Project Management (Online Distance Learning) MSc, Architecture, Master of (ARB/RIBA Part 2) MArch ARB Pt 2, Art in the Global Middle Ages MSc, Art, Space & Nature Master of Fine Art, MA, Composition (TBC), Composition for Screen MSc, Contemporary Art Practice Master of Fine Art, MA, Contemporary Art Theory MFA, Cultural Landscapes MSc, Cultural Studies MSc, Design & Digital Media MSc, Design Informatics Master of Fine Art, MA, Digital Composition & Performance MSc, Digital Media Design (Online Distance Learning) MSc, European Masters in Landscape Architecture European Masters, Fashion Master of Fine Art, Film Directing Master of Fine Art, MA, Glass Master of Fine Art, MA, Graphic Design Master of Fine Art, MA, History of Art, Theory & Display MSc, Illustration Master of Fine Art, MA, Interior Design MA, Jewellery Master of Fine Art, Landscape & Wellbeing MSc, Landscape Architecture MLA, Material Practice MSc, Modern & Contemporary Art: History, Curating & Criticism MSc, Musical Instrument Research MMus, Musicology MMus, Performance Costume Master of Fine Art, Product Design MA, Renaissance & Early Modern Studies (TBC), Scottish Art & Visual Culture MSc, Sound

Design MSc, Textiles Master of Fine Art, Urban Strategies & Design MSc

Edinburgh Medical School; www.ed.ac.uk/medicine-vet-medicine/edinburgh-medical-school

Medicine (MBChB), BSc(Hons) in Medical Sciences, BSc in Oral Health Sciences, BSc Biomedical Sciences, BSc Infectious Diseases, BSc Neuroscience, BSc Pharmacology, BSc Physiology, BSc Reproductive Biology

Postgraduate courses: Anatomical Sciences (Online Distance Learning) PgDip/PgCert/PgProfDev, Biodiversity, Wildlife & Ecosystem Health (Online Distance Learning) MSc/PgCert/PgDip/PgProfDev, Clinical Microbiology & Infectious Diseases (Online Distance Learning) MSc, Global Health & Infectious Diseases (Online Distance Learning) MSc/PgDip/PgCert/PgProfDev, Global Health Studies (Online Distance Learning) PgCert, Human Anatomy MSc, International Animal Health (Online Distance Learning) MSc/PgDip/PgCert/PgProfDev, Science Communication & Public Engagement MSc, Science Communication & Public Engagement (Online Distance Learning) MSc/PgCert/PgDip, Clinical Management of Pain (Online Distance Learning) MSc/PgDip/PgCert/PgProfDev, Clinical Ophthalmology (Online Distance Learning) ChM (Clinical Ophthalmology), General Surgery (Online Distance Learning) ChM (General Surgery), Imaging (Online Distance Learning) MSc/PgDip/PgCert/PgProfDev, Internal Medicine (Online Distance Learning) MSc/PgCert/PgDip, Neuroimaging for Research (Online Distance Learning) MSc/PgDip/PgCert/PgProfDev, Oral Surgery MClinDent, Oral Surgery/Orthodontics/Paediatric Dentistry or Prosthodontics DClinDent, Orthodontics MClinDent, Paediatric Dentistry MClinDent, Paediatric Emergency Medicine (Online Distance Learning) MSc/PgCert/PgDip, Primary Care Ophthalmology (Online Distance Learning) MSc, Primary Dental Care (Online Distance Learning) MSc/PgCert/PgDip, Prosthodontics MClinDent, Regenerative Medicine: Clinical & Industrial Delivery MSc, Stem Cells and Translational Neurology (Online Distance Learning) MSc/PgDip/PgCert/PgProfDev, Surgical Sciences (Online Distance Learning) MSc, Transfusion, Transplantation & Tissue Banking MSc, Trauma & Orthopaedics (Online Distance Learning) ChM (Trauma & Orthopaedics), Urology (Online Distance Learning) ChM (Urology), Vascular & Endovascular Surgery (Online Distance Learning) ChM (Vascular and Endovascular Surgery), Clinical Education (Online Distance Learning) MSc/PgCert/PgDip, Clinical Trials (Online Distance Learning) MSc/PgCert/PgDip, Data Science, Technology & Innovation (Online Distance Learning) MSc/PgDip/PgCert/PgProfDev, Family Medicine (Online Distance Learning) MFM, Global eHealth (Online Distance Learning) MSc/PgCert/PgDip/PgProfDev, Global Health Challenges (Online Distance Learning) PgCert/PgProfDev, Public Health MPH, Public Health (Online Distance Learning) MPH/PgCert/PgDip

The Moray House School of Education; www.ed.ac.uk/education

Applied Sport Science (BSc), Childhood Practice (BA), Community Education (BA), Physical Education (MA), Primary Education with Gaelic (Fluent Speakers/Learners) (MA), Sport and Recreation Management (BSc)

Postgraduate courses: Dance Science & Education MSc/PgDip, Digital Education (Online Distance Learning) MSc/PgDip/PgCert, Education MSc, Inclusive Education MSc/PgDip/PgCert, Language Teaching MSc/PgDip, Learning for Sustainability MSc/PgDip/PgCert, Outdoor Education MSc/PgDip/PgCert, Outdoor Environmental & Sustainability Education MSc/PgDip/PgCert, Performance Psychology MSc/PgDip, Physical Activity for Health MSc/PgDip/PgCert, Professional Graduate Diploma in Education (Primary) PGDE, Professional Graduate Diploma in Education (Secondary) PGDE, Social Justice & Community Action (Online Distance Learning) MSc/PgDip/PgCert, Sport Policy/Management & International Development MSc, Strength & Conditioning MSc/PgDip, Teaching English to Speakers of Other Languages (TESOL) MSc/PgDip, Transformative Learning and Teaching MSc

School of Engineering; www.eng.ed.ac.uk

Chemical Engineering (BEng/MEng), Civil Engineering (BEng/MEng), Electrical and Mechanical Engineering (BEng/MEng), Electronics and Computer Science (BEng/MEng), Electronics and Electrical Engineering (BEng/MEng), Engineering (BEng/MEng), Mechanical Engineering (BEng/MEng), Structural and Fire Safety Engineering (BEng/MEng), Structural Engineering with Architecture (BEng/MEng)

Postgraduate courses: Advanced Chemical Engineering MSc, Electrical Power Engineering MSc, Electronics MSc, International Master of Science in Fire Safety Engineering MSc, Sensor & Imaging Systems MSc, Signal Processing & Communications MSc,

Structural & Fire Safety Engineering MSc, Sustainable Energy Systems MS/PgDip

School of Geosciences; www.ed.ac.uk/geosciences

Ecological and Environmental Sciences (BSc), Ecological and Environmental Sciences with Management (BSc), Environmental Geoscience (BSc), Geography (MA), Geography (BSc), Geography and Archaeology (MA), Geography and Economics (MA), Geography and Politics (MA), Geography and Social Anthropology (MA), Geography and Social Policy (MA), Geography and Sociology (MA), Geography with Environmental Studies (MA), Geology (BSc), Geology (MEarthSci), Geology and Physical Geography (BSc), Geology and Physical Geography (MEarthSci), Geophysics (MEarthPhys), Geophysics (BSc), Geophysics and Geology (BSc), Geophysics and Geology (MEarthPhys), Geophysics and Meteorology (BSc), Geophysics and Meteorology (MEarthPhys)

Postgraduate courses: Applied Geoscience (Geoenergy) MSc, Carbon Capture & Storage MSc, Carbon Innovation (Online Distance Learning) PgCert, Carbon Management MSc, Carbon Management (Online Distance Learning) MSc, Climate Change Management (Online Distance Learning) PgCert, Earth Observation & Geoinformation Management MSc, Ecological Economics MSc, Ecosystem Services MSc, Energy, Society and Sustainability MSc, Environment & Development MSc, Environment, Culture & Society MSc, Environmental Protection & Management MSc, Environmental Sustainability MSc, Food Security MSc, Geographical Information Science MSc, Geographical Information Science & Archaeology MSc, Global Environment Challenges (Online Distance Learning) PgCert, Marine Systems & Policies MSc, Soils & Sustainability MSc, Sustainable Plant Health MSc

School of Health in Social Science; www.ed.ac.uk/health

Health, Science and Society (MA), Nursing Studies (BN)

Postgraduate courses: Advancing Nursing Practice MSc/PgCert/PgDip, Applied Psychology (Healthcare) For Children & Young People MSc, Children & Young People's Mental Health & Psychological Practice MSc, Children & Young People's Mental Health & Psychological Practice (Online Distance Learning) MSc/PgDip/PgCert, Clinical Psychology DClinPsychol, Counselling MCouns/PgCert/PgDip, Counselling (Interpersonal Dialogue) MCouns, Counselling Studies MSc, Psychological Therapies MSc, Psychology of Mental Health (Conversion) MSc, Psychotherapy and Counselling DPsychotherapy

School of History, Classics and Archaeology; www.ed.ac.uk/history-classics-archaeology

Ancient and Medieval History (MA), Ancient History (MA), Ancient History and Classical Archaeology (MA), Ancient History and Greek (MA), Ancient History and Latin (MA), Ancient Mediterranean Civilisations (MA), Archaeology (MA), Archaeology and Ancient History (MA), Archaeology and Social Anthropology (MA), Classical and Middle East Studies (MA), Classical Archaeology and Greek (MA), Classical Archaeology and Latin (MA), Classical Studies (MA), Classics (MA), Classics and English Language (MA), Classics and Linguistics (MA), Economic History (MA), Greek Studies (MA), History (MA), History and Archaeology (MA), History and Classics (MA), History and History of Art (MA), History and Politics (MA), History and Scottish History (MA), Latin Studies (MA)

Postgraduate courses: American History MSc, Ancient History MSc, Archaeology MSc, Classical Art & Archaeology MSc, Classics MSc, Contemporary History MSc, European Archaeology MSc, History MSc, History (Online Distance Learning) (TBC), Human Osteoarchaeology MSc, Intellectual History MSc, Late Antique, Islamic & Byzantine Studies MSc, Medieval History MSc, Mediterranean Archaeology MSc, Scottish History MSc

School of Informatics; www.ed.ac.uk/informatics

Artificial Intelligence (BSc), Artificial Intelligence and Computer Science (BSc), Artificial Intelligence and Mathematics (BSc), Artificial Intelligence and Software Engineering (BEng), Artificial Intelligence with Management (BEng), Cognitive Science (BSc), Computer Science (BSc), Computer Science (BEng), Computer Science and Management Science (BSc), Computer Science and Mathematics (BSc), Computer Science and Physics (BSc), Computer Science with Management (BEng), Informatics (5-year undergraduate Masters Programme) (MInf), Software Engineering (BEng), Software Engineering with Management (BEng)

Postgraduate programmes: Advanced Design Informatics MSc, Artificial Intelligence MSc, Cognitive Science MSc, Computer Science MSc, Data Science MSc, Design Informatics MSc, Informatics MSc

School of Law; www.law.ed.ac.uk

Law (Graduate Entry) (LLB), Law (Ordinary and Honours) (LLB), Law and Accountancy (LLB), Law and Business (LLB), Law and Celtic (LLB), Law and Economics (LLB), Law and French (LLB), Law and German (LLB), Law and History (LLB), Law and International Relations (LLB), Law and Politics (LLB), Law and Social Anthropology (LLB), Law and Social Policy (LLB), Law and Sociology (LLB), Law and Spanish (LLB)

Postgraduate courses: Commercial Law LLM, Comparative & European Private Law LLM, Corporate Law LLM, Criminal Law & Criminal Justice LLM, Criminology & Criminal Justice MSc, European Law LLM, Global Crime, Justice & Security MSc, Global Environment & Climate Change Law LLM, Human Rights LLM, Information Technology Law (Online Distance Learning) LLM, Innovation, Technology & the Law LLM, Innovation, Technology & the Law (Online Distance Learning) LLM, Intellectual Property Law LLM, Intellectual Property Law (Online Distance Learning) LLM, International Banking Law & Finance LLM, International Commercial Law & Practice (Online Distance Learning) LLM, International Economic Law LLM, International Law LLM, Law LLM, Law (Online Distance Learning) LLM, Law (Online Distance Learning) PgCert, Law & Chinese LLM, Medical Law & Ethics LLM, Medical Law & Ethics (Online Distance Learning) LLM, Professional Legal Practice Diploma

School of Literatures, Languages and Culture; www.ed.ac.uk/literatures-languages-cultures

Arabic (MA), Arabic and Ancient Greek/Business/Economics/French/History/History of Art/Persian/Politics/ Religious Studies/Social Anthropology/Spanish (MA), Celtic (MA), Celtic and Archaeology/English Language/English Literature/French/German/Linguistics/Scandinavian Studies/Scottish History/Scottish Literature (MA), Chinese (MA), Chinese and Economics/French/German/History/Italian/Linguistics/Russian Studies/Spanish (MA), English and Scottish Literature (MA), English Literature (MA), English Literature and Classics/History (MA), French (MA), French and Business/Classics/English Language/English Literature/German/History/History of Art/Italian/Linguistics/Philosophy/Politics/Portuguese/Russian Studies/Scandinavian Studies/Scottish Literature/Social Policy/Spanish (MA),, German (MA), German and Business/Classics/English Language/English Literature/History/History of Art/

Italian/Linguistics/Philosophy/Politics/Portuguese/Russian Studies/Scandinavian Studies/Scottish Literature/Social Policy/Spanish (MA), Islamic Studies (MA), Italian (MA), Italian and Business/Classics/English Language/English Literature/History/History of Art/Linguistics/Philosophy/Politics/Portuguese/Russian Studies/Scandinavian Studies/Scottish Literature /Social Policy /Spanish (MA), Japanese (MA), Japanese and Linguistics (MA), Middle Eastern Studies (MA), Persian and English Literature/Middle Eastern Studies/Politics/Social Anthropology (MA), Persian Studies (MA), Portuguese and Business/English Language/English Literature/History/History of Art/Linguistics/Philosophy/Politics/Russian Studies/Scandinavian Studies/Scottish Literature/Social Policy (MA), Russian Studies (MA, Russian Studies and Business/Classics/English Language/English Literature/History/History of Art/Linguistics/Philosophy/Politics/Scandinavian Studies/Scottish Literature/Social Policy/Spanish (MA), Scandinavian Studies (Danish, Norwegian, Swedish) (MA), Scandinavian Studies and Classics/English Language/English Literature/History/Linguistics/Philosophy/Politics/Scottish Literature/Social Policy/Spanish (MA), Scottish Ethnology (MA), Scottish Ethnology and Archaeology/Celtic/English Language/English Literature/Scandinavian Studies/Scottish History/Scottish Literature, Scottish Literature (MA), Scottish Literature and Classics/History/Scottish History (MA), Scottish Studies (MA), Spanish (MA), Spanish and Business/Classics/English Language/English Literature/History/History of Art/Linguistics/Philosophy/Politics/Portuguese/Scottish Literature/Social Policy (MA)

Postgraduate courses: Advanced Arabic MSc, Book History & Material Culture MSc, Celtic & Scottish Studies MSc, Chinese Society & Culture MSc, Chinese Studies MSc, Comparative Literature MSc, Creative Writing MSc, East Asian Relations MSc, English Literature: Literature & Modernity: 1900 to the Present MSc, English Literature: Literature & Society: Enlightenment, Romantic & Victorian MSc, English Literature: US Literature – Cultural Values from Revolution to Empire MSc, Film Studies MSc, Film, Exhibition & Curation MSc, Islamic & Middle Eastern Studies MSc, Japanese Society & Culture MSc, Medieval Literatures & Cultures MSc, Middle Eastern Studies with Advanced Arabic MSc, Middle Eastern Studies with Arabic MSc, Persian Civilisation MSc, Diploma, Playwriting MSc, Scottish Culture & Heritage (Online Distance Learning) PgCert, Theatre & Performance Studies MSc, Translation Studies MSc

School of Mathematics; www.maths.ed.ac.uk

Applied Mathematics (BSc), Mathematics (MA), Mathematics (BSc), Mathematics and Biology/Business/Music/Physics/Statistics (BSc), Mathematics with Management (BSc), MMath (MMath)

Postgraduate courses: Computational Applied Mathematics MSc, Computational Mathematical Finance MSc/PgDip, Financial Mathematics MSc, Financial Modelling & Optimization MSc/PgDip, Operational Research MSc/PgDip, Operational Research with Computational Optimization MSc/PgDip, Operational Research with Data Science MSc, Operational Research with Risk MSc/PgDip, Statistics & Operational Research MSc, Statistics with Data Science MSc

School of Philosophy, Psychology and Language Sciences; www.ed.ac.uk/ppls

Cognitive Science (Humanities) (MA), English Language (MA), English Language and Literature (MA), Linguistics (MA), Linguistics and English Language/Social Anthropology (MA), Philosophy (MA), Philosophy and Economics/English Language/English Literature/Greek/Linguistics/Mathematics/Politics/Psychology/Scottish Literature (MA), Psychology (BSc), Psychology (MA), Psychology and Business/Economics/Linguistics (MA)

School of Physics and Astronomy; www.ph.ed.ac.uk

Astrophysics (MPhys), Astrophysics (BSc), Computational Physics (MPhys), Computational Physics (BSc), Mathematical Physics (MPhys), Mathematical Physics (BSc), Physics (BSc), Physics (MPhys), Physics and Music (BSc), Physics with a Year Abroad (MPhys), Physics with Meteorology (BSc), Physics with Meteorology (MPhys), Theoretical Physics (BSc), Theoretical Physics (MPhys)

Postgraduate courses: High Performance Computing MSc/PgDip, High Performance Computing with Data Science MSc, Mathematical Physics MSc, Theoretical Physics MSc

School of Social and Political Science; www.sps.ed.ac.uk

Government, Policy and Society (MA), Government, Policy and Society with Quantitative Methods (MA), International Relations (MA), International Relations and International Law (MA), International Relations with Quantitative Methods (MA), Politics (MA), Politics and Economic and Social History (MA), Politics with Quantitative Methods (MA), Social Anthropology (MA), Social Anthropology and Politics/Social Policy/Development (MA), Social Anthropology with Social History (MA), Social Policy and Economics/Law/Politics/Social and Economic History/Sociology (MA), Social Policy with Quantitative Methods (MA), Social Work (BSc), Sociology (MA), Sociology and Politics/Psychology/Social Anthropology (MA), Sociology with Quantitative Methods (MA), Sustainable Development (MA)

Postgraduate courses: Advanced Professional Studies (Adult Protection) PgCert, Advanced Social Work Studies (Mental Health Officer Award) PgCert, Africa & International Development MSc, Africa & International Development (Online Distance Learning) PgCert, African Studies MSc, Childhood Studies MSc, Comparative Public Policy MSc, Digital Society MSc, Global Challenges (Online Distance Learning) MSc/PgCert, Global Development Challenges (Online Distance Learning) PgCert, Global Environment, Politics & Society MSc, Global Health Policy MSc, Global Health Policy (Online Distance Learning) PgCert, Health Policy MSc, International & European Politics MSc, International Development MSc, International Development (Online Distance Learning) MSc/PgCert/PgDip, International Political Theory MSc, International Relations MSc, International Relations of the Middle East MSc, International Relations of the Middle East with Arabic/Advanced Arabic MSc, Making Use of Digital Research (Online Distance Learning) PgCert, Management of Bioeconomy, Innovation & Governance MSc, Medical Anthropology MSc, Nationalism Studies MSc, Policy Studies MSc, Public Policy MPP/PgDip/PgCert, Science & Technology in Society MSc, Social Anthropology MSc, Social Research MSc/PgCert, Social Work, Master of MSW, Sociology & Global Change MSc

Royal (Dick) School of Veterinary Studies; www.ed.ac.uk/vet

Veterinary Medicine (5-year programme) (BVM&S); Veterinary Medicine (Graduate Entry Programme – 4-year programme) (BVM&S)

Postgraduate courses: Advanced Clinical Practice (Online Distance Learning) MVetSci/PgDip/PgCert/PgProfDev, Animal Biosciences MSc, Applied Animal Behaviour & Animal Welfare MSc, Clinical Animal Behaviour (Online Distance Learning) MSc/PgDip/PgCert, Conservation Medicine (Online Distance Learning) MVetSci/PgDip/PgCert/PgProfDev, Equine Science (Online Distance Learning) MSc/PgDip/PgCert/PgProfDev, International Animal Welfare,

Ethics & Law (Online Distance Learning) PgProfDev, One Health (Online Distance Learning) MSc/PgDip/PgCert/PgProfDev, RCVS Certificate in Advanced Veterinary Practice (Online Distance Learning)

PgProfDev, Veterinary Anaesthesia & Analgesia (Online Distance Learning) MSc/PgDip/PgCert, Veterinary Epidemiology (Online Distance Learning) MSc/PgCert/PgDip/PgProfDev

EDINBURGH NAPIER UNIVERSITY
www.napier.ac.uk

Arts and Media; www.napier.ac.uk/ courses/browse-interests/arts-and-media

Acting & English BA/BA(Hons), Acting for Stage and Screen (Advance entry) BA/BA(Hons), Communication, Advertising and Public Relations BA/BA(Hons), English BA/BA(Hons), English & Film BA(Hons), Film BA/BA(Hons), Journalism BA/BA(Hons), Music BMus/BMus(Hons), Music (Popular) BA/BA(Hons), Photography BA/BA(Hons), Interactive Media Design BSc/BSc(Hons), Television BA/BA(Hons)
Postgraduate courses: Advanced Film Practice MFA, Directing MFA, International Journalism for Media Professionals MA, Playwriting MFA, Publishing MSc, Journalism MA, Screenwriting MA, Screenwriting PGCert, Creative Advertising MSc, Creative Writing MA, Film MA

Business and Languages; www.napier.ac.uk/courses/browse-interests/business-and-languages

Accounting BA/BA(Hons) & Joint Honours, Financial Services BA/BA(Hons), LLB/LLB(Hons) & Joint Honours, Business Management BA/BA(Hons) & Joint Honours, Business Management BA Advanced entry (various specialisms), Business & Enterprise BA Advanced Entry, Business & Enterprise in Sport BA/BA(Hons), Business Studies (Sandwich) BA/BA(Hons) & Joint Honours, International Business Management BA/BA(Hons), International Business Management & Language (French/German/Spanish) BA/BA(Hons), Languages & Intercultural Communication BA/BA(Hons), Communication, Advertising & Public Relations BA/BA(Hons) Advanced Entry, Business Information Systems BSc/BSc(Hons), Information Technology Management BSc/BSc(Hons), Marketing Management BA/BA(Hons), Marketing with Digital Media BA/BA(Hons), International Festival & Event Management BA(Hons) & Joint Honours, International Hospitality Management BA(Hons) & Joint Honours, International Tourism Management BA(Hons) & Joint Honours, International Tourism & Airline Management BA(Hons), Sales Management BA

Postgraduate courses: International Banking & Finance MSc, International Finance MSc, MBA (Leadership Practice), The Edinburgh Napier MBA, Executive MBA, MBA (various specialisms), Learning, Teaching and Assessment Practice in HE, Business Management MSc (various specialisms), International Business Management MSc, Business Management MSc (various specialisms), Intercultural Business Communication MSc, Intercultural Business Communication with TESOL MSc, Real Estate Management & Investment MSc, Facilities Management MSc, Human Resource Management MSc, International Human Resource Management MSc, Human Resource Management MSc, Creative Advertising MSc, Marketing MSc (various specialisms), International Marketing MSc, Business Information Technology MSc

Computing; www.napier.ac.uk/courses/browse-interests/computing

Business Information Systems BSc/BSc(Hons), Computer Systems and Networks BEng(Hons), Computing BEng/BEng(Hons), Computing BSc/BSc(Hons), Computer Security and Forensics BEng/BEng(Hons), Computing Science BSc/BSc(Hons), Creative Computing BSc/BSc(Hons), Digital Media BSc/BSc(Hons), Games Development BSc(Hons), Information Technology Management BSc(Hons), Interactive Media Design BSc/BSc(Hons), Software Engineering BEng/BEng(Hons), Software Engineering MEng, Sound Design BSc(Hons), Web Design and Development BSc(Hons)
Postgraduate courses: Advanced Networking MSc/PGDip/PGCert, Advanced Security and Digital Forensics MSc, Business Information Technology MSc, Computing MSc, Sound Design MSc, Advanced Security and Cybercrime MSc, Data Science MSc, Project and Programme Management MSc, Strategic ICT Leadership MSc

Criminology, Psychology and Law; www.napier.ac.uk/courses/browse-interests/criminology-psychology-and-law

Criminology BA/BA(Hons), Psychology BA(Hons)/BSc(Hons), Psychology with Sociology BA/BA(Hons), Social Science BA/BA(Hons), Law LLB/LLB(Hons), Law joint honours LLB/LLB(Hons), Law LLB (Graduate Entry)

Postgraduate courses: Applied Criminology and Forensic Psychology MSc, Career Guidance & Development PGDip

Design; www.napier.ac.uk/courses/browse-interests/design

Graphic Design BDes/BDes(Hons), Interior & Spatial Design BDes/BDes(Hons), Product Design BDes/BDes(Hons), Web Design and Development BSc(Hons), Photography BA/BA(Hons), Interactive Media Design BSc/BSc(Hons), Marketing with Digital Media BA/BA(Hons)

Postgraduate courses: Environmental Graphics MA/MDes, Exhibition Design MA/MDes, Interaction Design MA/MDes, Interior Architecture MA/MDes, Lighting Design MA/MDes, Motion Graphics MA/MDes, Product Design Prototyping MA/MDes, Sound Design MSc, Creative Advertising MSc

Engineering and the Built Environment; www.napier.ac.uk/courses/browse-interests/engineering

Architectural Technology BSc/BSc(Hons), Building Surveying BSc/BSc(Hons), Civil Engineering BEng/BEng(Hons), Civil Engineering MEng, Civil & Transportation Engineering MEng, Construction & Project Management BSc/BSc(Hons), Electrical Engineering BEng/BEng(Hons), Electronic Engineering BEng/BEng(Hons), Electronic & Electrical Engineering BEng/BEng(Hons), Electronic & Electrical Engineering MEng, Energy & Environmental Engineering BEng/BEng(Hons), Engineering with Management BEng/BEng(Hons), Mechatronics BEng/BEng(Hons), Mechanical Engineering BEng/BEng(Hons), Mechanical Engineering MEng, Quantity Surveying BSc/BSc(Hons), Real Estate Surveying BSc/BSc(Hons)

Postgraduate courses: Advanced Materials Engineering MSc, Advanced Structural Engineering MSc, Architectural Technology & Building Performance MSc, Automation & Control MSc, Construction Project Management MSc, Energy & Environmental Engineering MSc, Environmental Sustainability MSc, Facilities Management MSc, MBA (Logistics & Supply Chain Management), Renewable Energy MSc, Real Estate Management & Investment MSc, Safety & Environmental Management MSc, Transport Planning and Engineering MSc

Health and Social Care; www.napier.ac.uk/courses/browse-interests/health-and-social-care

Nursing (Adult) BN, Nursing (Child) BN, Nursing (Learning Disabilities) BN, Nursing (Mental Health) BN, Nursing Studies (Option Rich Programme) BSc, Midwifery BM, Care of People with Epilepsy Graduate Certificate, Psychology BA(Hons)/BSc(Hons), Psychology with Sociology BA(Hons)/BSc(Hons), Veterinary Nursing BSc/BSc(Hons), Biological Sciences BSc/BSc(Hons), Biomedical Sciences BSc/BSc(Hons), Sport & Exercise Science BSc/BSc(Hons), Physical Activity & Health BSc/BSc(Hons), Sports Coaching BSc/BSc(Hons)

Postgraduate courses: Advanced Practice MSc (and flexible managed programmes), Healthcare Management MSc, MBA (Health Management) MBA, Sport & Exercise Science MSc by research, Sport Performance Enhancement MSc, Drug Design & Biomedical Science MSc, Medical Biotechnology MSc, Clinical Exercise Science PgCert/PgDip/MSc, Pharmaceutical Science MSc, Masters in Midwifery MM, Masters in Nursing (Adult) MN, Masters in Nursing (Child) MN, Masters in Nursing (Learning Disability) MN, Masters in Nursing (Mental Health) MN

Life Sciences; www.napier.ac.uk/courses/browse-interests/life-sciences

Animal & Conservation Biology BSc/BSc(Hons), Biological Sciences BSc/BSc(Hons), Biomedical Sciences BSc/BSc(Hons), Marine & Freshwater Biology BSc/BSc(Hons), Applied Microbiology BSc/BSc(Hons), Veterinary Nursing BSc/BSc(Hons)

Postgraduate courses: Biomedical Science MSc, Clinical Exercise Science PGCert/PGDip/MSc, Biotechnology for Environmental Sustainability MSc, Drug Design & Biomedical Science MSc, Medical Biotechnology MSc, Pharmaceutical Science MSc, Wildlife Biology & Conservation MSc, Ecotourism MSc

Sports and Exercise Sciences; www.napier.ac.uk/courses/browse-interests/sport-and-exercise-sciences

Physical Activity and Health BSc/BSc(Hons), Sport & Exercise Science BSc/BSc(Hons) (Including advanced entry), Sports Coaching BSc/BSc(Hons), Business & Enterprise in Sport BA/BA(Hons)

Postgraduate courses: Clinical Exercise Science PGCert/PgDip/MSc, Sport & Exercise Science MSc by research, Sport Performance Enhancement MSc

Tourism; www.napier.ac.uk/courses/browse-interests/tourism

International Hospitality Management BA(Hons) & Joint Honours, International Tourism Management BA(Hons) & Joint Honours, International Tourism & Airline Management BA(Hons), International Festival & Event Management BA(Hons) & Joint Honours

Postgraduate courses: Business Event Management MSc, International Tourism Management MSc, International Event & Festival Management MSc, Heritage & Cultural Tourism Management MSc, Tourism Marketing MSc, Tourism & Hospitality Management MSc, Ecotourism MSc

UNIVERSITY OF ESSEX
www.essex.ac.uk

School of Biological Sciences; www.essex.ac.uk/bs

BSc Biological Sciences, BSc Microbiology (subject to approval), BSc Biochemistry, BSc Biomedical Science, BSc Genetics, BSc Genetics and Genomics, BSc Marine Biology, MMarBiol Marine Biology (Integrated Masters)

Postgraduate courses: MSc Biotechnology, MSc Cancer Biology, MSc Tropical Marine Biology, MSc Molecular Medicine

School of Computer Science and Electronic Engineering; www.essex.ac.uk/csee

BSc Computer Science, BSc Computer Games, BEng Computer Networks, BSc Information and Communication Technology, MSci Computer Science (integrated Masters), BSc Data Science and Analytics, BEng Robotic Engineering, BEng Computer Systems Engineering, BEng Computers with Electronics, BEng Electronic Engineering, BEng Communications Engineering, MEng Electronic Engineering (integrated Masters), MEng Communications Engineering (integrated Masters)

Postgraduate courses: MSc Advanced Computer Science, MSc Advanced Web Engineering, MSc Artificial Intelligence, MSc Big Data and Text Analytics, MSc Data Science, MSc Cloud Computing, MSc Computer Engineering, MSc Computer Games, MSc Computer Science, MSc Internet of Things, MSc Intelligent Systems and Robotics, MSc Computer Networks and Security, MSc Electronic Engineering, MSc Advanced Communication Systems, MSc Computational Finance, MSc Algorithmic Trading

East 15 Acting School; www.east15.ac.uk

BA Acting, BA Acting (International), BA Acting and Contemporary Theatre, BA Stage and Production Management, BA Acting and Community Theatre, BA Acting and Stage Combat, BA Physical Theatre, BA World Performance, Certificate of Higher Education in Theatre Arts

Postgraduate courses: MA Acting, MA/MFA Acting (International), MA/MFA Theatre Directing

Department of Economics; www.essex.ac.uk/economics

BA/BSc Economics, BA/BSc Management Economics, BA/BSc International Economics, BA/BSc Financial Economics, BA Financial Economics and Accounting, BSc Economics with Mathematics, BSc Economics and Mathematics, BA History and Economics, BSc Accounting with Economics, BA Philosophy, Politics and Economics, BA Economics and Politics, BA Political Economics, BA Economics with a Modern Language

Postgraduate courses: MRes Economics, MA Economics, MSc Economics, MSc Behavioural Economics, MSc Applied Economics and Data Analysis, MSc Computational Economics, Financial Markets and Policy, MSc Economics and Econometrics, MSc International Economics, MSc Management Economics, MSc Money and Banking, MSc Accounting and Financial Economics, MSc Financial and Business Economics, MSc Financial Economics, MSc Financial Econometrics, MSc Financial Economics and Econometrics, PG Diploma Statistics and Finance, Graduate Diploma Economics

Essex Business School; www.essex.ac.uk/ebs

BSc Accounting, BSc Accounting and Finance, BSc Accounting and Management, BSc Accounting with Economics, BSc Finance, BSc Financial Management, BSc Finance with Mandarin, BSc Banking and Finance, BSc Marketing, BSc Management and Marketing, BSc Business Management, BBA Business Administration, BSc Tourism Management, BA Business Management and Modern Languages, BA Business Management with a Modern Language,

BSc Management with Mandarin, BSc Management and Marketing, BSc International Business and Entrepreneurship

Postgraduate courses: MSc Accounting, MSc Accounting and Finance, MSc Accounting and Financial Management, MSc International Accounting and Banking, MRes Accounting, MSc Finance, MSc Banking and Finance, MSc Finance and Investment, MSc Finance and Management, MSc Financial Engineering and Risk Management, MSc International Finance, MSc Finance and Data Analytics, MSc Finance and Global Trading, MSc Management, Master of Business Management (MBM), MSc International Management, The Essex MBA, MRes Management and Organisation, MSc Business Analytics, MSc Human Resource Management, MSc Global Project Management, MSc International Logistics and Supply Chain Management, MSc Entrepreneurship and Innovation, MSc International Business and Entrepreneurship, MSc International Marketing and Entrepreneurship, MSc Marketing and Brand Management, MSc Marketing Management

Department of Government; www.essex.ac.uk/government

BA Politics, BA International Relations, BA Politics and International Relations, BA Political Economics, BA Political Theory and Public Policy, BA Philosophy, Politics and Economics, BA Economics and Politics, BA Politics with Human Rights, BA International Relations and Modern Languages, BA Sociology and Politics, BA Modern History and International Relations, BA Modern History and Politics, BA Philosophy and Politics, LLB Law with Politics

Postgraduate courses: Graduate Diploma Politics, MA/MSc Political Science, MA Politics, MA/MSc Conflict Resolution, MA United States Politics, MA/MSc Global and Comparative Politics, MA Ideology and Discourse Analysis, MA/MSc International Relations, MA/MSc Political Economy, MA Political Theory, MA/MSc Public Opinion and Political Behaviour, MRes International Relations, MRes Political Economy, MRes Political Science

School of Health and Social Care; www.essex.ac.uk/hhs

FdSc Health Science, Graduate Certificate Psychological Well-Being Practitioner, BSc Nursing (Mental Health), BSc Nursing (Adult), FdSc Oral Health Science (Hygiene), BSc Oral Health Science (Therapy), BSc Occupational Therapy, BA Social Work, BSc Speech and Language Therapy (TBC)

Postgraduate courses: Postgraduate Certificate Psychological Well-Being Practitioner, MSc Nursing (Adult) (pre-registration), MSc Nursing (Mental Health) (pre-registration), MSc Periodontology and MSc Advanced Periodontal Practice, MSc Occupational Therapy (Pre-Registration), MSc Speech and Language Therapy (Pre-Registration)

Department of History; www.essex.ac.uk/history

BA History, BA Modern History, BA History and Literature, BA History with Film Studies, BA Philosophy and History, BA Art History and History, BA Modern History and Politics, BA Modern History and International Relations, BA History with Human Rights, BA History and Sociology, BA History and Criminology, BA History and Economics, BA English Language and History

Postgraduate course: MA History

Department of Language and Linguistics; www.essex.ac.uk/langling

BA English Language and Language Development, BA English Language and Linguistics, BA Linguistics, BA English Language and History, BA English Language and Literature, BA English Language and Sociology, BA Teaching English as a Foreign Language (TEFL), BA Language Studies (no year abroad), BA French/German/Italian/Portuguese/Spanish and Modern Languages, MLang Modern Languages (Translation), BA Modern Languages and English Language, BA Modern Languages and Linguistics, BA Modern Languages and Teaching English as a Foreign Language, BA Modern Languages with Latin American Studies, BA Spanish, Portuguese and Brazilian Studies, BA International Relations and Modern Languages, BA European Studies and Modern Languages, BA Business Management with a Modern Language, BA Business Management and Modern Languages, LLB English and French Law, BA Art History and Modern Languages, BA Art History with Modern Languages

Postgraduate courses: MA Applied Linguistics, MA English Language and Linguistics, MA Linguistics, MA Linguistic Studies, MA Psycholinguistics, MA Language in Society, MA Teaching English to Speakers of Other Languages (TESOL), Postgraduate Diploma Chinese-English Translation and Interpreting, MA Business Translation and Interpreting (Chinese-English), MA Conference Interpreting and Translation (Chinese-English), MA Translation, Interpreting and Subtitling, MA Translation and Literature, MA Translation and Professional Practice

School of Law; www.essex.ac.uk/law

LLB Law with Business, LLB Law with Human Rights, LLB Law with Politics, LLB Law with Philosophy, BA Philosophy and Law, BA Latin American Studies with Human Rights, BA Philosophy with Human Rights, BA Politics with Human Rights, BA Sociology with Human Rights

LLM International Human Rights Law, LLM International Human Rights and Humanitarian Law, LLM International Humanitarian Law, LLM Economic, Social and Cultural Rights, LLM International Commercial and Business Law, LLM International Trade Law, LLM International Trade and Maritime Law, LLM European Union Commercial Law, MA Theory and Practice of Human Rights, MA Human Rights and Cultural Diversity, LLB Law (Senior Status)

Department of Literature, Film, and Theatre Studies; www.essex.ac.uk/lifts

BA Creative Writing, BA Literature and Creative Writing, BA Film and Creative Writing, BA Drama, BA Drama and Literature, BA English Literature, BA English and United States Literature, BA Literature and Creative Writing, BA Drama and Literature, BA Film Studies and Literature, BA English Language and Literature, BA History and Literature, BA Philosophy and Literature, BA Literature and Sociology, BA Literature and Art History, BA Film Studies, BA Film and Creative Writing, BA Film Studies and Literature, BA American (United States) Studies with Film, BA Film Studies and Art History, BA History and Film Studies, BA History with Film Studies, BA Multimedia Journalism, BA Journalism and Criminology/Economics/English Language/Liberal Arts/Literature/Modern Languages/Philosophy/Politics/Sociology, BA Journalism with Business Management/Human Rights

Postgraduate courses: MA Creative Writing, MA Playwriting, MA Avant-Gardes, MA Literature, MA American Literatures, MA Film and Literature, MA Wild Writing: Literature, Landscape and the Environment, MA Translation and Literature, MA Film Studies

Department of Mathematical Sciences; www.essex.ac.uk/maths

BSc Mathematics, BSc Mathematics and Statistics, BSc Actuarial Science, BSc Economics and/with Mathematics, BSc Finance and Mathematics, BSc Mathematics with Computing, BSc Data Science and Analytics, BSc Mathematics with Physics

Postgraduate courses: MSc Actuarial Science, PG Diploma Actuarial Science, MSc Data Science, MSc Mathematics, Graduate Diploma Mathematics, MSc Mathematics and Finance, PG Diploma Mathematics and Finance, MSc Statistics, MSc Statistics and Finance, PG Diploma Statistics and Finance, MSc Statistics and Operational Research, PG Diploma Statistics and Operational Research

School of Philosophy and Art History; www.essex.ac.uk/depts/spah.aspx

BA Art History, BA Curatorial Studies, BA Philosophy and Art History, BA Art History and History, BA Art History with Modern Languages, BA Art History and Modern Languages, BA Film Studies and Art History, BA Literature and Art History, BA Philosophy, BA Philosophy, Religion and Ethics, BA Philosophy and Art History/History/Human Rights/Law/Literature/Politics/Sociology/Philosophy, Politics and Economics, LLB Law and Philosophy

Postgraduate courses: MA Art History and Theory, MA Curating, MA Philosophy and Art History, Graduate Diploma Art History and Theory, Graduate Diploma Art History with English for Academic Purposes, MA Philosophy

Department of Psychology; www.essex.ac.uk/psychology

BA Psychology, BSc Psychology, BSc Psychology with Cognitive Neuroscience

Postgraduate courses: MSc Psychology, MSc Advanced Psychology, MSc Cognitive Neuropsychology, MSc Cognitive Neuroscience, MSc Research Methods in Psychology, MSc Language and the Brain

Department of Psychosocial and Psychoanalytic Studies; www.essex.ac.uk/cps

FdA/BA Therapeutic Communication and Therapeutic Organisations, BA Childhood Studies, BA Psychoanalytic Studies, BA Therapeutic Care, BA Sociology with Psychosocial Studies

Postgraduate courses: MA Psychoanalytic Studies, MA Jungian and Post-Jungian Studies, MA Psychodynamic Counselling, MA Refugee Care, PG Diploma/MA Management and Organisational Dynamics

Department of Sociology; www.essex.ac.uk/sociology

BA Sociology, BSc Sociology with Applied Quantitative Research Methods, BA Communications and Digital Culture, BA Sociology and Politics, BA Sociology with Human Rights, BA Sociology with Social Psychology, BA History and Sociology, BA Philosophy and Sociology, BA English Language and

Sociology, BA Literature and Sociology, BA Criminology, BA Sociology and Criminology, BA Criminology with Social Psychology, BA Criminology and American Studies, BA Social Anthropology, BA Social Anthropology with Human Rights, BA Sociology with Psychosocial studies

Postgraduate courses: MA Sociology, MA Advertising, Marketing and the Media, MA Criminology, MSc Criminology and Socio-Legal Research, MSc Organised Crime, Terrorism and Security, MA Sociological

Research Methods, MSc Survey Methods for Social Research, MA Sociology and Management

School of Sport, Rehabilitation and Exercise Sciences; www.essex.ac.uk/sres
BSc Physiotherapy, BSc Sports and Exercise Science, BSc Sports Performance and Coaching, BSc Sports Therapy

Postgraduate courses: MSc Physiotherapy (Pre-registration), MSc Sport and Exercise Science

WRITTLE COLLEGE
www.writtle.ac.uk

Agriculture
BSc(Hons) Agriculture, BSc(Hons) Agriculture (Arable Crop Management), BSc(Hons) Agriculture (Farm Livestock Production), BSc(Hons) Agriculture (Sustainable Environments), Diploma of Higher Education in Agriculture, Diploma of Higher Education in Agriculture (Arable Crop Management), Diploma of Higher Education in Agriculture (Farm Livestock Production), Diploma of Higher Education in Agriculture (Sustainable Environments), Certificate of Higher Education in Agriculture

Postgraduate courses: MSc Sustainable Land Management under Global Change, MSc Crop Production (Agriculture)

Animal Science and Animal Management
BSc(Hons) Animal Science, BSc(Hons) Animal Management, Diploma of Higher Education in Animal Science, Diploma of Higher Education in Animal Management, Certificate of Higher Education in Animal Studies

Postgraduate course: MSc Animal Welfare and Conservation

Art and Design
BA(Hons) Contemporary Art and Design
Postgraduate course: MA by Dissertation in Art and Design

Bioveterinary Science
MSci Bioveterinary Science, BSc(Hons) Bioveterinary Science

Equine
BSc(Hons) Equine Behavioural Science, BSc(Hons) Equine Performance and Business Management, BSc(Hons) Equine Sports Therapy and Rehabilitation, Diploma of Higher Education Equine Behavioural Science, Diploma of Higher Education Equine Performance and Business Management, Diploma of

Higher Education Equine Sports Therapy and Rehabilitation

Floristry
BA(Hons) Professional Floristry and Floral Design, BA(Hons) Professional Floristry (Top-up Year), Certificate of Higher Education in Floristry

Global Ecosystem Management
BSc(Hons) Global Ecosystem Management, Diploma of Higher Education in Global Ecosystem Management, Certificate of Higher Education in Natural Ecosystems

Horticulture
BSc(Hons) Horticulture, BSc(Hons) Horticulture and International Business, Diploma of Higher Education Horticulture, Certificate of Higher Education in Horticulture

Postgraduate courses: MSc Horticulture, MSc Sustainable Land Management under Global Change, MSc Crop Production (Horticulture), MSc Postharvest Technology, Postgraduate Certificate in Postharvest Technology

Landscape Architecture and Garden Design
BSc(Hons) Landscape Architecture, BSc(Hons) Landscape and Garden Design, Diploma of Higher Education in Garden Design, Diploma of Higher Education in Landscape Design

Postgraduate courses: MA Landscape Architecture, MA Garden Design, Postgraduate Diploma in Landscape Architecture

Sports, Cycling and Aerial Performance
BSc(Hons) Sports and Exercise Performance, Foundation Degree (FdSc) Sports Science with Aerial Performance, Foundation Degree (FdSc) Cycling Performance, Diploma of Higher Education Sports and Exercise Performance

Sustainable Land Management
Postgraduate course: MSc Sustainable Land Management under Global Change

Veterinary Physiotherapy
MVetPhys Veterinary Physiotherapy, BSc(Hons) Animal Therapy, BSc(Hons) Equine Sports Therapy and Rehabilitation
Postgraduate course: MSc Veterinary Physiotherapy

UNIVERSITY OF EXETER
www.exeter.ac.uk

Accounting and Finance; www.exeter.ac.uk/undergraduate/degrees/accounting

Accounting and Finance BSc, Accounting and Finance with European Study BSc, Accounting and Finance with Industrial Experience BSc, Accounting and Finance with International Study BSc, Business and Accounting BSc, Business and Accounting with European Study BSc, Business and Accounting with Industrial Experience BSc, Business and Accounting with International Study BSc, Professional exemptions
Postgraduate courses: Accounting and Finance MSc, Accounting and Taxation MSc

Anthropology; www.exeter.ac.uk/undergraduate/degrees/anthropology

Anthropology BA, Anthropology with Study Abroad BA, Anthropology BSc, Anthropology with Study Abroad BSc
Postgraduate course: Anthrozoology MA

Arab and Islamic Studies; www.exeter.ac.uk/undergraduate/degrees/arabislamic

Arabic and Islamic Studies MArabic, Middle East Studies BA
Postgraduate courses: Islamic Studies MA, Middle East and Islamic Studies MA, Middle East Studies MRes
Read more at http:// www.exeter.ac.uk/postgraduate/courses-by-subject/#eYlgpHZo10vT3dTT.99

Archaeology; www.exeter.ac.uk/undergraduate/degrees/archaeology

Archaeology BA, Archaeology with Employment Experience / Employment Experience Abroad BA, Archaeology with Study Abroad BA, Archaeology and Anthropology BA, Archaeology and Anthropology with Employment Experience / Employment Experience Abroad BA, Archaeology and Anthropology with Study Abroad BA, Archaeology with Forensic Science BSc, Archaeology with Forensic Science with Employment Experience / Employment Experience Abroad BSc, Archaeology with Forensic Science with Study Abroad BSc
Postgraduate courses: Archaeology MA, Bioarchaeology MSc, Experimental Archaeology MA, Roman Archaeology MA

Art History & Visual Culture; www.exeter.ac.uk/undergraduate/degrees/art

Art History & Visual Culture BA, Art History & Visual Culture with Employment Experience / Employment Experience Abroad BA, Art History & Visual Culture with Study Abroad BA, Art History & Visual Culture and Classical Studies BA, Art History & Visual Culture with Classical Studies with Employment Experience / Employment Experience Abroad BA, Art History & Visual Culture and Classical Studies with Study Abroad BA, Art History & Visual Culture with Drama with Employment Experience / Employment Experience Abroad BA, Art History & Visual Culture and English BA, Art History & Visual Culture with English with Employment Experience / Employment Experience Abroad BA, Art History & Visual Culture and English with Study Abroad BA, Art History & Visual Culture and History BA, Art History & Visual Culture with History with Employment Experience / Employment Experience Abroad BA, Art History & Visual Culture and History with Study Abroad BA, Art History & Visual Culture and Modern Languages BA

Biosciences; www.exeter.ac.uk/undergraduate/degrees/biosciences

Animal Behaviour BSc, Animal Behaviour MSci, Animal Behaviour with Professional Placement BSc, Animal Behaviour with Study Abroad BSc, Biochemistry BSc, Biochemistry with Industrial Experience BSc, Biochemistry with Study Abroad BSc, Biological and Medicinal Chemistry BSc, Biological and Medicinal Chemistry with Industrial Experience BSc, Biological and Medicinal Chemistry with Study

Abroad BSc, Biological Sciences BSc, Biological Sciences with Professional Placement BSc, Biological Sciences with Study Abroad BSc, Conservation Biology and Ecology BSc, Conservation Biology and Ecology MSci, Conservation Biology and Ecology with Professional Placement BSc, Conservation Biology and Ecology with Study Abroad BSc, Evolutionary Biology BSc, Evolutionary Biology MSci, Evolutionary Biology with Professional Placement BSc, Evolutionary Biology with Study Abroad BSc, Marine Biology BSc, Marine Biology MSci, Marine Biology with Professional Placement BSc, Marine Biology with Study Abroad BSc, Zoology BSc, Zoology MSci, Zoology with Professional Placement BSc, Zoology with Study Abroad BSc

Postgraduate courses: Conservation and Biodiversity MSc, Evolutionary and Behavioural Ecology MSc, Food Security and Sustainable Agriculture MSc

Business and Management; www.exeter.ac.uk/undergraduate/degrees/business

Business and Management BA, Business and Management with European Study BA, Business and Management with Industrial Experience BA, Business and Management with International Study BA, Management with Marketing BA, Management with Marketing with European Study BA, Management with Marketing with Industrial Experience BA, Management with Marketing with International Study BA, Business BSc, Business with European Study BSc, Business with Industrial Experience BSc, Business with International Study BSc

Postgraduate courses: International Management MSc, Marketing MSc, Human Resource Management MSc/PgDip, International Tourism Management MSc, International Hospitality Management MSc, Management MRes, MBA – The Exeter MBA, Global Political Economy MRes, Finance and Investment MSc, Finance and Management MSc, Financial Analysis and Fund Management MSc, Finance and Marketing MSc

Classics and Ancient History; www.exeter.ac.uk/undergraduate/degrees/classics

Ancient History BA, Ancient History with Employment Experience / Employment Experience Abroad BA, Ancient History with Study Abroad BA, Classical Studies BA, Classical Studies with Employment Experience / Employment Experience Abroad BA, Classical Studies with Study Abroad BA, Classics BA, Classics with Employment Experience / Employment Experience Abroad BA, Classics with Study Abroad BA, Ancient History and Archaeology BA, Ancient History and Archaeology with Employment Experience / Employment Experience Abroad BA, Ancient History and Archaeology with Study Abroad BA, Classical Studies and English BA, Classical Studies and English with Employment Experience / Employment Experience Abroad BA, Classical Studies and English with Study Abroad BA, Classical Studies and Modern Languages BA, Classical Studies and Philosophy BA, Classical Studies and Philosophy with Employment Experience / Employment Experience Abroad BA, Classical Studies and Philosophy with Study Abroad BA, Classical Studies and Theology BA, Classical Studies and Theology with Employment Experience / Employment Experience Abroad BA, Classical Studies and Theology with Study Abroad BA

Postgraduate courses: Classics and Ancient History MA, Ancient Philosophy, Science & Medicine, Ancient Politics & Society, Classical Receptions, Cultural Histories & Material Exchanges, Literary Interactions

Computer Science and IT; www.exeter.ac.uk/undergraduate/degrees/computerscience

Computer Science BSc, Computer Science MSci, Computer Science with Industrial Placement BSc, Computer Science and Mathematics BSc, Computer Science and Mathematics MSci, Computer Science and Mathematics with Industrial Placement BSc, Digital and Technology Solutions degree apprenticeship

Postgraduate courses: Computer Science MSc, Computer Science with Business MSc, Data Science (Professional) MSc, Data Science MSc

Drama; www.exeter.ac.uk/undergraduate/degrees/drama

Drama BA, Drama with Employment Experience / Employment Experience Abroad BA, Drama with Study Abroad BA, Art History & Visual Culture and Drama BA, Art History & Visual Culture and Drama with Study Abroad BA

Postgraduate courses: Theatre Practice MA

Economics; www.exeter.ac.uk/undergraduate/degrees/economics

Economics BSc, Economics with European Study BSc, Economics with Industrial Experience BSc, Economics with International Study BSc, Business Economics BSc, Business Economics with European Study BSc,

Business Economics with Industrial Experience BSc, Business Economics with International Study BSc, Economics with Econometrics BSc, Economics with Econometrics with European Study BSc, Economics with Econometrics with Industrial Experience BSc, Economics with Econometrics with International Study BSc, Economics and Finance BSc, Economics and Finance with European Study BSc, Economics and Finance with Industrial Experience BSc, Economics and Finance with International Study BSc, Economics and Politics BSc, Economics and Politics with European Study BSc, Economics and Politics with Industrial Experience BSc, Economics and Politics with International Study BSc
Postgraduate courses: Economics MSc, Economics and Econometrics MSc, Behavioural Economics and Finance MSc, Economics MRes, Financial Economics MSc, Money and Banking MSc

Education; www.exeter.ac.uk/postgraduate/taught/education
Postgraduate courses: MA Education, Professional Development in Education, MEd/PgDip/PgCert Teaching English to Speakers of Other Languages, MEd Teaching English to Speakers of Other Languages (Part time Intensive Summer Programme), MSc Educational Research, EdD Education

Engineering; www.exeter.ac.uk/undergraduate/degrees/engineering
Civil Engineering BEng, Civil Engineering MEng, Civil Engineering with Industrial Experience MEng, Civil Engineering with International Study MEng, Civil and Environmental Engineering MEng, Civil and Environmental Engineering with Industrial Experience MEng, Civil and Environmental Engineering with International Study MEng, Electronic Engineering BEng, Electronic Engineering MEng, Electronic Engineering with Industrial Experience MEng, Electronic Engineering with International Study MEng, Electronic Engineering and Computer Science BEng, Electronic Engineering and Computer Science MEng, Electronic Engineering and Computer Science with Industrial Experience MEng, Electronic Engineering and Computer Science with International Study MEng, Engineering BEng, Engineering MEng, Engineering and Management BEng, Engineering and Management MEng, Engineering and Management with Industrial Experience MEng, Civil Engineering Site Management, Engineering and Entrepreneurship MEng, Engineering and Management with International Study MEng, Materials Engineering BEng, Materials Engineering MEng, Materials Engineering with Industrial Experience MEng, Materials Engineering with International Study MEng, Mechanical Engineering BEng, Mechanical Engineering MEng, Mechanical Engineering with Industrial Experience MEng, Mechanical Engineering with International Study MEng, Mining Engineering BEng, Mining Engineering MEng, Renewable Energy Engineering BEng, Renewable Energy Engineering MEng
Postgraduate courses: Civil Engineering MSc, Civil Engineering with Management MSc, Engineering Business Management MSc, Engineering conversion, International Supply Chain Management MSc, Materials Engineering MSc, Materials Engineering with Management MSc, Mechanical Engineering MSc, Mechanical Engineering with Management MSc, Renewable Energy Engineering MSc, Structural Engineering MSc, Structural Engineering with Management MSc, Water Engineering MSc, Water Engineering with Management MSc

English; www.exeter.ac.uk/undergraduate/degrees/english
English BA (Exeter), English with Employment Experience / Employment Experience Abroad BA (Exeter), English with Study Abroad BA (Exeter), English with Study in North America BA, English and Drama BA, English and Drama with Employment Experience / Employment Experience Abroad BA, English and Drama with Study Abroad BA, English and Film Studies BA, English and Film Studies with Employment Experience / Employment Experience Abroad BA, English and Film Studies with Study Abroad BA, English and Modern Languages BA, English BA (Penryn), English with Study Abroad BA (Penryn), English and History BA, English and History with Study Abroad BA
Postgraduate courses: Creative Writing MA, English Literary Studies MA

Environmental Science; www.exeter.ac.uk/undergraduate/degrees/envsci
Environmental Science BSc, Environmental Science with Professional Placement BSc, Environmental Science with Study Abroad BSc, Environmental Science MSci
Postgraduate courses: Conservation Science and Policy MSc, Sustainable Development MSc, Sustainable Development (Climate Change and Risk Management) MSc

Film Studies; www.exeter.ac.uk/ undergraduate/degrees/film

Film Studies BA, Film Studies with Employment Experience / Employment Experience Abroad BA, Film Studies with Study Abroad BA, Film Studies and Modern Languages BA

Postgraduate course: International Film Business MA

Geography; www.exeter.ac.uk/ undergraduate/degrees/geography

Geography BA/BSc (Penryn), Geography with Professional Placement BA/BSc (Penryn), Geography with Study Abroad BA/BSc (Penryn), Geography BA (Exeter), Geography with European Study BA (Exeter), Geography with Study Abroad BA (Exeter), Geography BSc (Exeter), Geography with European Study BSc (Exeter), Geography with Study Abroad BSc (Exeter)

Postgraduate courses: Sustainable Development MSc, Critical Human Geographies MRes, Sustainable Development (Climate Change and Risk Management) MSc, Sustainable Futures MRes, Conservation Science and Policy MSc

Geology; www.exeter.ac.uk/ undergraduate/degrees/geology

Applied Geology BSc, Applied Geology MGeol, Engineering Geology and Geotechnics BSc, Engineering Geology and Geotechnics MGeol, Geology BSc, Geology MGeol

Postgraduate courses: Applied Geotechnics MSc, Mining Geology MSc, Exploration Geology MSc, Geotechnical Engineering MSc

History; www.exeter.ac.uk/undergraduate/ degrees/history

History BA (Exeter), History with Employment Experience / Employment Experience Abroad BA (Exeter), History with Study Abroad BA (Exeter), History and Ancient History BA, History and Ancient History with Employment Experience / Employment Experience Abroad BA, History and Ancient History with Study Abroad BA, History and Archaeology BA, History and Archaeology with Employment Experience / Employment Experience Abroad BA, History and Archaeology with Study Abroad BA, History and International Relations BA, History and International Relations with Employment Experience / Employment Experience Abroad BA, History and International Relations with Study Abroad BA, History and Modern Languages BA, History BA (Penryn), History with Study Abroad BA (Penryn), History and Politics BA (Penryn), History

and Politics with Study Abroad BA (Penryn), History and International Relations BA (Penryn), History and International Relations with Study Abroad BA (Penryn)

Postgraduate courses: Economic and Social History MRes, History MA, Medieval Studies MA, International Heritage Management and Consultancy MA/ MRes/PGDip/PGCert

Human Sciences; www.exeter.ac.uk/ undergraduate/degrees/humansciences

Human Sciences BA/BSc, Human Sciences with Professional Placement BA/BSc, Human Sciences with Study Abroad BA/BSc

Law; www.exeter.ac.uk/undergraduate/ degrees/law

Graduate Law LLB, Law LLB, Law with European Study LLB, LLB (English Law and French Law) Master 1 (Maitrise en Droit)

Postgraduate courses: LLM Master of Laws, Socio-Legal Research MRes

Liberal Arts; www.exeter.ac.uk/ undergraduate/degrees/libarts

Liberal Arts BA, Liberal Arts with Employment Experience / Employment Experience Abroad BA (Exeter), Liberal Arts with Study Abroad BA

Mathematics; www.exeter.ac.uk/ undergraduate/degrees/mathematics

Mathematical Sciences BSc, Mathematical Sciences (Ecology and Evolution) MSci, Mathematical Sciences (Energy Systems and Control) MSci, Mathematical Sciences (Environmental Science) MSci, Mathematics BSc, Mathematics MMath, Mathematics with International Study MMath, Mathematics with Professional Experience MMath, Mathematics (Climate Science) MSci, Mathematics (Geophysical and Astrophysical Fluid Dynamics) MSci, Mathematics (Mathematical Biology) MSci, Mathematics with Accounting BSc, Mathematics with Economics BSc, Mathematics with Finance BSc, Mathematics with Management BSc, Mathematics and Physics BSc, Mathematics with Accounting MSci, Mathematics with Economics MSci, Mathematics with Finance MSci, Mathematics with Management MSci

Postgraduate courses: Advanced Mathematics MSc, Financial Mathematics MSc

Medical Imaging (Radiography); www.exeter.ac.uk/undergraduate/degrees/ medical-imaging

Medical Imaging (Diagnostic Radiography) BSc

Medical Sciences; www.exeter.ac.uk/undergraduate/degrees/medicine

Medical Sciences BSc, Medical Sciences with Professional Training Year BSc, Sport and Exercise Medical Sciences BSc, Sport and Exercise Medical Sciences with Professional Training Year BSc

Medicine; www.exeter.ac.uk/undergraduate/degrees/medicine

Medicine BMBS

Postgraduate courses: Clinical Education MSc, Environment and Human Health MSc, Healthcare Leadership and Management PgCert

Mining Engineering; www.exeter.ac.uk/undergraduate/degrees/mining

Mining Engineering BEng, Mining Engineering MEng

Postgraduate courses: Mining Engineering MSc/PgDip, Surveying and Land/Environmental Management MSc/PgDip, Mining Lifecycle (Professional) PgCert, Mining Engineering (Professional) MSc, Tunnel Engineering MSc

Modern Languages; www.exeter.ac.uk/undergraduate/degrees/languages

Modern Languages BA, Chinese, French, German, Italian, Portuguese, Russian, Spanish, Modern Languages and Arabic BA, Modern Languages and Latin BA

Postgraduate courses: Translation Studies MA, Global Literatures and Cultures MA

Natural Sciences; www.exeter.ac.uk/undergraduate/degrees/natural-sciences

Natural Sciences BSc, Natural Sciences MSci

Philosophy; www.exeter.ac.uk/undergraduate/degrees/philosophy

Philosophy BA, Philosophy with Study Abroad BA, Philosophy and History BA, Philosophy and History with Study Abroad BA, Philosophy and Modern Languages BA, Philosophy and Politics BA, Philosophy and Politics with Study Abroad BA, Philosophy and Sociology BA, Philosophy and Sociology with Study Abroad BA, Philosophy and Theology BA, Philosophy and Theology with Study Abroad BA, Philosophy Combined Honours

Postgraduate courses: Philosophy MA, Philosophy and Sociology of Science MA

Physics and Astronomy; www.exeter.ac.uk/undergraduate/degrees/physics

Physics BSc, Physics MPhys, Physics with Astrophysics BSc, Physics with Astrophysics MPhys, Physics with North American Study MPhys, Physics with Professional Experience MPhys, Physics with Study in Australia MPhys, Physics with Study in New Zealand MPhys

Politics and International Relations; www.exeter.ac.uk/undergraduate/degrees/politics

International Relations BA, International Relations with Study Abroad BA, Politics BA, Politics with Study Abroad BA, Politics, Philosophy and Economics BA, Politics, Philosophy and Economics with Study Abroad BA, Politics and International Relations BSc (Exeter), Politics and International Relations with Study Abroad BSc (Exeter), Politics Combined Honours, International Relations and Modern Languages BA, Politics and Modern Languages BA, Politics and Sociology BA, Politics and Sociology with Study Abroad BA, Politics and International Relations BA (Penryn), Politics and International Relations with Study Abroad BA (Penryn), International Relations BA (Penryn), International Relations with Study Abroad BA (Penryn)

Postgraduate courses: Applied Security Strategy MA, Conflict, Security and Development MA, European Politics MA, International Relations MA, MPA – see Public Administration Masters, Public Administration Masters (MPA), Political Thought MA, Politics and International Relations of the Middle East MA, Policy Analytics MSc, Politics MRes, Security – see MA Applied Security Strategy, Security Conflict and Human Rights MRes, Advanced Quantitative Methods (AQM) In Social Sciences MRes

Psychology; www.exeter.ac.uk/undergraduate/degrees/psychology

Applied Psychology (Clinical) MSci, Psychology BSc, Psychology with Sport and Exercise Science BSc

Postgraduate courses: Animal Behaviour MSc, Psychological Research Methods MSc, Social and Organisational Psychology MSc

Renewable Energy Engineering; www.exeter.ac.uk/undergraduate/degrees/energy

Renewable Energy Engineering BEng, Renewable Energy Engineering MEng, Renewable Energy BSc, Renewable Energy Engineering with Industrial Experience MEng

Sociology (and Criminology); www.exeter.ac.uk/undergraduate/degrees/sociology

Criminology BSc, Criminology with Study Abroad BSc, Sociology BA, Sociology with Study Abroad BA, Sociology BSc, Sociology with Study Abroad BSc, Sociology and Anthropology BA, Sociology and Anthropology with Study Abroad BA, Sociology and Criminology BSc, Sociology and Criminology with Study Abroad BSc, Sociology Combined Honours, Sociology and Modern Languages BA
Postgraduate courses: Science and Technology Studies MRes, Sociology MA, Cultural Sociology MA

Sport and Health Sciences; www.exeter.ac.uk/undergraduate/degrees/sport

Exercise and Sport Sciences BSc, Exercise and Sport Sciences with Study Abroad BSc, Exercise and Sport Sciences MSci, Human Biosciences BSc
Postgraduate courses: Health and Wellbeing MRes, Paediatric Exercise and Health MSc, Sport and Health Sciences MSc

Theology and Religion; www.exeter.ac.uk/undergraduate/degrees/theology

Theology and Religion BA, Theology and Religion with Study Abroad BA, Theology and Religion with Employment Experience / Employment Experience Abroad BA (Exeter)
Postgraduate courses: Theology MA

UNIVERSITY OF ST MARK & ST JOHN
www.marjon.ac.uk

Faculty of Education, Enterprise & Culture; www.marjon.ac.uk/courses/our-faculties/faculty-of-education–social-sciences

BA(Hons) Childhood Practice, BA(Hons) Criminology, BA(Hons) Early Childhood Studies – Progression, FdA Early Years, BA(Hons) Education Studies, BSc(Hons) Forensic Criminology, BSc(Hons) Global Education, FdA Learning and Teaching, BA(Hons) Outdoor Adventure Education, BA(Hons) Performing Arts Education, BEd(Hons) Physical Education – Secondary Ed (with QTS), BEd(Hons) Primary Education (with QTS), BA(Hons) Primary Education, BEd(Hons) Primary Education – Early Years (with QTS), BEd Primary Education – Physical Education (with QTS), BSc(Hons) Psychology, BSc(Hons) Psychotherapy & Counselling, BA(Hons) Social Sciences, BA(Hons) Sociology, BA(Hons) Special Educational Needs & Disability Studies, BA(Hons) Theology, BA(Hons) Youth and Community Work
Postgraduate courses: MA Literature for Children and Young Adults, MA Education, MRes Outdoor Education or Outdoor Learning, Postgraduate Diploma in Early Years with Initial Teacher Training, PGCE in Secondary Education with Art and Design, PGCE Primary, PGCE Secondary Education with Drama, PGCE Secondary Education with English, PGCE Secondary Education with Geography, PGCE Secondary Education with Media Studies, PGCE Secondary Education with Modern Foreign Languages, PGCE Secondary Education with Physical Education, PGCE Secondary Education with Psychology, PGCE Secondary Education with Religious Education (RE), Postgraduate Certificate in Coaching & Mentoring, MSc Psychology, School Direct, MA Social Policy, MRes Social Science, MSc Sport & Exercise Psychology, PG Dip/MA Youth and Community Work

Faculty of Sport, Health and Wellbeing; www.marjon.ac.uk/courses/our-faculties/faculty-of-sport–health-sciences/

BSc(Hons) Exercise Physiology, BA(Hons) Football Development & Coaching, BSc(Hons) Human Biosciences, MOst Master of Osteopathic Medicine (Undergraduate Pre-registration Master), BSc(Hons) Nutrition, BA(Hons) Outdoor Adventure Education, BA(Hons) Physical Education (non QTS), BEd(Hons) Physical Education – Secondary Ed (with QTS), BSc(Hons) Rehabilitation in Sport and Exercise – Progression, BSc(Hons) Rehabilitation in Sport and Exercise, BSc(Hons) Sport & Exercise Psychology, BSc(Hons) Sport and Exercise Science, BA(Hons) Sport Coaching, BA(Hons) Sport Development – Coaching and School Sport, BA(Hons) Sport Development – Progression, BA(Hons) Sport Development – Sport Management, BA(Hons) Sport Development, FdA Sport Development and Coaching, BSc(Hons) Sport, Physical Activity and Health, BSc(Hons) Sports Therapy – Progression, BSc(Hons) Sports Therapy, BSc(Hons) Strength and Conditioning – Progression, BSc(Hons) Strength and Conditioning

Postgraduate courses: MRes Outdoor Education or Outdoor Learning, MRes Sport and Exercise Medicine, MRes Sport and Exercise Science, MRes Sport and Health Sciences, MRes Sport Development, MRes Sport Management, PGCE Secondary Education with Physical Education, Master of Public Health (MPH), MSc Sport & Exercise Psychology, MSc Sport Rehabilitation (Pre-Registration)

FALMOUTH UNIVERSITY
www.falmouth.ac.uk

Academy of Music and Theatre Arts; www.falmouth.ac.uk/academy-of-music-theatre-arts

Acting BA(Hons), Creative Events Management BA(Hons), Creative Music Technology BA(Hons), Dance & Choreography BA(Hons), Music BA(Hons), Music, Theatre & Entertainment Management BA(Hons), Popular Music BA(Hons), Technical Theatre Arts BA(Hons), Theatre & Performance BA(Hons)
Postgraduate course: Creative Events Management MA

Falmouth Business School; www.falmouth.ac.uk/falmouth-business-school

Business Entrepreneurship BA(Hons)
Postgraduate courses: Creative Education MA, Launchpad (with MA Entrepreneurship), Leasing & Asset Finance MA

Falmouth School of Art; www.falmouth.ac.uk/falmouth-school-of-art

Drawing BA(Hons), Fine Art BA(Hons), Illustration BA(Hons)
Postgraduate course: Illustration: Authorial Practice MA

Fashion & Textiles Institute; www.falmouth.ac.uk/fashion-textiles-institute

Fashion Design BA(Hons), Fashion Marketing BA(Hons), Fashion Photography BA(Hons), Sportswear Design BA(Hons), Textile Design BA(Hons)
Postgraduate course:
Postgraduate course: Postgraduate Certificate in Higher Education (PGCHE)

Games Academy; www.falmouth.ac.uk/games-academy

Computing for Games BSc(Hons), Game Art BA(Hons), Game Development BA(Hons)

Postgraduate course: Creative App Development MA

Institute of Photography; www.falmouth.ac.uk/institute-of-photography

Postgraduate course: Photography MA
Marine & Natural History Photography BA(Hons), Photography BA(Hons), Press & Editorial Photography BA(Hons)

School of Architecture, Design & Interiors; www.falmouth.ac.uk/school-of-architecture-design-interiors

Architecture BA(Hons), Interior Design BA(Hons), Sustainable Product Design BA(Hons)

School of Communication Design; www.falmouth.ac.uk/school-of-communication-design

Creative Advertising BA(Hons), Graphic Design BA(Hons)
Postgraduate courses: Advertising Strategy & Planning MA, Communication Design MA, Creative Advertising MA

School of Film & Television; www.falmouth.ac.uk/school-of-film-television

Animation & Visual Effects BA(Hons), Film BA(Hons), Television BA(Hons)
Postgraduate course: Film & Television MA

School of Writing & Journalism; www.falmouth.ac.uk/school-of-writing-journalism

Creative Writing BA(Hons), English BA(Hons), English with Creative Writing BA(Hons), Journalism and Communications BA(Hons), Journalism and Creative Writing BA(Hons), Journalism BA(Hons), Sports Journalism BA(Hons)
Postgraduate courses: Professional Writing MA, Writing for Script & Screen MA

UNIVERSITY OF GLASGOW
www.gla.ac.uk

Accounting and Finance; www.gla.ac.uk/ subjects/accountingfinance

Accountancy & Finance [BAcc], Accounting & Mathematics [BSc], Accounting & Statistics [BSc], Finance & Mathematics [BSc], Finance & Statistics [BSc]

Postgraduate courses: Accounting Professional Pathway 1 (ICAEW) [MAcc], Corporate Governance & Accountability [MSc], Financial Modelling [MSc], International Accounting & Financial Management [MAcc], International Corporate Finance & Banking [MSc], International Finance [MFin], International Financial Analysis [MSc]

Archaeology; www.gla.ac.uk/subjects/ archaeology

Archaeology (MA/BSc/MA(SocSci))

Postgraduate courses: Ancestral Studies [MSc/PgDip], Ancient Cultures [MLitt], Celtic & Viking Archaeology [MLitt/PgDip], Conflict Archaeology & Heritage [MLitt], Material Culture & Artefact Studies [MLitt/PgDip], Museum Studies [MSc]

Biodiversity, Animal Health and Comparative Medicine; www.gla.ac.uk/ subjects/bahcm

Marine & Freshwater Biology [BSc], Zoology [BSc]

Postgraduate courses: Animal Welfare Science, Ethics & Law [MSc], Conservation Management of African Ecosystems [MSc], Ecology & Environmental Biology [MRes], Quantitative Methods in Biodiversity, Conservation and Epidemiology [MSc], Wildlife & Livestock Management [MSc/PgDip/PgCert: online distance learning]

Business; www.gla.ac.uk/subjects/ business

Accountancy & Finance [BAcc], Accounting & Mathematics [BSc], Accounting & Statistics [BSc], Business & Management [MA(SocSci)/MA/LLB/BSc], Business Economics [MA(SocSci)/LLB], Economics [MA(SocSci)/BSc/BAcc/MA/LLB], Finance & Mathematics [BSc], Finance & Statistics [BSc]

Postgraduate courses: Accounting Professional Pathway 1 (ICAEW) [MAcc], Aerospace Engineering & Management [MSc], Asset Pricing & Investment [MSc], Banking & Financial Services [MSc], Biotechnology and Management [MSc/PgDip], Civil Engineering & Management [MSc], Corporate

Governance & Accountability [MSc], Creative Industries and Cultural Policy [MSc], Development Studies [MSc], Economic Development [MSc], Economics [MRes], Economics, Banking & Finance [MSc], Electronics & Electrical Engineering & Management [MSc], Environment & Sustainable Development [MSc], Finance & Economic Development [MSc], Finance & Management [MSc], Financial Economics [MSc], Financial Forecasting & Investment [MSc], Financial Modelling [MSc], Financial Risk Management [MSc], Geomatics & Management [MSc], Global Markets, Local Creativities (Erasmus Mundus International Master) [IntM], Intellectual Property, Innovation & the Creative Economy [MSc/PgDip/PgCert: online distance learning], International Accounting & Financial Management [MAcc], International Banking & Finance [MSc], International Business & Entrepreneurship [MSc], International Corporate Finance & Banking [MSc], International Finance [MFin], International Financial Analysis [MSc], International Human Resource Management & Development [MSc], International Management & Design Innovation [MSc], International Real Estate & Management [MSc], International Strategic Marketing [MSc], International Trade & Finance [MSc], Investment Banking & Finance [MSc], Investment Fund Management [MSc], Management [MSc], Management [MRes], Management & Sustainable Tourism [MSc], Management with Enterprise & Business Growth [MSc], Management with Human Resources [MSc], Management with International Finance [MSc], MBA (Master of Business Administration) [MBA], Mechanical Engineering & Management [MSc], Media Management [MSc], Public Policy & Management [MSc], Quantitative Finance [MSc]

Cancer Sciences; www.gla.ac.uk/subjects/ cancersciences

Postgraduate courses: Advanced Lymphoedema Management [PgCert], Cancer Sciences [MSc], Molecular Pathology [MSc/PgDip/PgCert]

Cardiovascular and Medical Sciences; www.gla.ac.uk/subjects/cms

Biomedical Engineering [BEng/MEng]

Postgraduate courses: Applied Neuropsychology [MSc(MedSci)], Cardiovascular Sciences [MSc(MedSci)], Clinical Pharmacology [MSc(MedSci)], Clinical Trials & Stratified Medicine

[MSc], Diabetes [MSc(MedSci)], Sport and Exercise Science & Medicine [MSc], Stratified Medicine and Pharmacological Innovation [MSc], Translational Medicine [MRes]

Celtic and Gaelic; www.gla.ac.uk/subjects/celticgaelic
Celtic Civilisation [MA/MA(SocSci)], Celtic Studies [MA], Gaelic [LLB/MA]
Postgraduate courses: Ancestral Studies [MSc/PgDip], Ancient Cultures [MLitt], Celtic Studies [MLitt]

Central and East European Studies; www.gla.ac.uk/subjects/cees
Central & East European Studies [MA/MA(SocSci)], Russian [MA]
Postgraduate courses: Central and East European, Russian and Eurasian Studies (Erasmus Mundus International Master) [IntM], Global Security [MRes], Global Security [MSc], Russian for Social Scientists [PgDip], Russian for Social Scientists [PgCert], Russian Language [PgCert], Russian Language [PgDip], Russian, East European & Eurasian Studies [MSc], Russian, East European & Eurasian Studies [MRes]

Chemistry; www.gla.ac.uk/subjects/chemistry
Chemical Physics [MSci/BSc], Chemistry [BSc/MSci], Chemistry with Medicinal Chemistry [BSc/MSci]
Postgraduate courses: Chemistry [MSc], Chemistry with Medicinal Chemistry [MSc]

Classics; www.gla.ac.uk/subjects/classics
Classics (Classical Civilisation) [MA/MA(SocSci)], Greek [MA], Latin [MA]
Postgraduate courses: Ancestral Studies [MSc/PgDip], Ancient Cultures [MLitt], Classics [MLitt]

Comparative Literature; www.gla.ac.uk/subjects/comparativeliterature
Comparative Literature [MA]
Postgraduate courses: Comparative Literature [MLitt], Translation Studies: Translation & Professional Practice [MSc/PgDip/PgCert]

Computing Science; www.gla.ac.uk/subjects/computing
Computing Science [BSc/MSci/MA(SocSci)/MA], Digital Media & Information Studies [MA], Electronic & Software Engineering [BSc/BEng/MEng], Software Engineering [BSc/MSci]
Postgraduate courses: Bioinformatics [MSc/PgDip/PgCert], Computer Systems Engineering [MSc],

Computing Science [MSc], Data Analytics [MSc: online distance learning], Data Analytics [MSc], Data Science [MSc], Information Security [MSc], Information Technology [MSc], IT Cyber Security [MSc], Security, Intelligence and Strategic Studies (Erasmus Mundus International Master) [IntM], Software Development [MSc], Software Engineering [MSc]

Creative Writing; www.gla.ac.uk/subjects/creativewriting
Postgraduate courses: Creative Writing [MLitt: online distance learning], Creative Writing [MLitt]

Dentistry; www.gla.ac.uk/schools/dental/
Dentistry [BDS]
Postgraduate courses: Endodontics [MSc(DentSci)], Oral & Maxillofacial Surgery [MSc(DentSci)], Oral Sciences [MSc], Orthodontics [DClinDent]

Economic and Social History; www.gla.ac.uk/subjects/economicsocialhistory
Economic & Social History [MA(SocSci)/LLB/MA]
Postgraduate courses: Chinese Studies [MSc], Global Economy [MSc], Global Markets, Local Creativities (Erasmus Mundus International Master) [IntM], History [MLitt/MSc/PgDip], History (with an emphasis on the History of Medicine) [MLitt/MSc]

Economics; www.gla.ac.uk/subjects/economics
Business Economics [MA(SocSci)/LLB], Economics [MA(SocSci)/BSc/BAcc/MA/LLB]
Postgraduate courses: Asset Pricing & Investment [MSc], Banking & Financial Services [MSc], Development Studies [MSc], Economic Development [MSc], Economics [MRes], Economics, Banking & Finance [MSc], Environment & Sustainable Development [MSc], Finance & Economic Development [MSc], Finance & Management [MSc], Financial Economics [MSc], Financial Forecasting & Investment [MSc], Financial Risk Management [MSc], Global Markets, Local Creativities (Erasmus Mundus International Master) [IntM], International Banking & Finance [MSc], International Trade & Finance [MSc], Investment Banking & Finance [MSc], Investment Fund Management [MSc], Quantitative Finance [MSc]

Education; www.gla.ac.uk/subjects/education
Childhood Practice, Community Development [BA], Education with Teaching Qualification (Primary) [MEduc], Primary Education with Teaching

Qualification (Dumfries Campus) [MA(D)], Religious & Philosophical Education [MA(Ed)], Technological Education [BTechEd]

Postgraduate courses: Academic Practice [PgCert], Adult Education for Social Change (Erasmus Mundus International Master) [IntM], Adult Education, Community Development & Youth Work [MEd/PgDip], Advanced Educational Leadership [PgCert: online distance learning], Assessment in Education [MSc: online distance learning], Childhood Practice [MEd/PgDip], Children's Literature & Literacies [MEd], Children's Literature, Media & Culture [IntM], Doctorate in Education (Research) [EdD: online distance learning available], Education [MSc: online distance learning], Education (Primary) [PGDE], Education (Secondary) [PGDE], Education, Public Policy & Equity [MSc], Educational Studies [MSc], Educational Studies [MEd], Educational Studies (Adult Education, Community Development & Youth Studies) [MSc], Enhanced Practice in Education (Dumfries Campus) [MSc], Health-Professions Education / Health Professions Education (with Research) [MSc/MSc(with Research)/PgDip/PgCert: online distance learning], Inclusive Education: Research, Policy & Practice [PgDip/PgCert: online distance learning available], Inclusive Education: Research, Policy & Practice [MEd], Learning & Teaching in Higher Education [MEd: online distance learning], Learning and Teaching of Modern Languages in the Primary School [PgCert], Middle Leadership and Management in Schools [PgCert], Museum Education [MSc: online distance learning], Museum Education [MSc], Professional Learning & Enquiry [MEd], Professional Practice with PGDE [MEd], Psychological Studies (conversion) [MSc], Religious Education by Distance Learning (CREDL) [PgCert: online distance learning], Teacher Leadership and Learning [PgCert], Teaching Adults [MSc], TESOL: Teaching of English to Speakers of Other Languages [MSc], TESOL: Teaching of English to Speakers of Other Languages [MEd]

Engineering; www.gla.ac.uk/subjects/engineering

Aeronautical Engineering [MEng/BEng], Aeronautical Engineering (in partnership with SIT), Aerospace Systems [MEng/BEng], Aerospace Systems (in partnership with SIT), Biomedical Engineering [BEng/MEng], Civil Engineering [MEng/BEng], Civil Engineering (jointly offered with SIT), Civil Engineering with Architecture [MEng/BEng], Electronic & Software Engineering [BSc/BEng/MEng], Electronics & Electrical Engineering [BEng/MEng], Electronics & Electrical Engineering (in partnership with UESTC), Electronics with Music [BEng/MEng], Mechanical Design Engineering [BEng/MEng], Mechanical Design Engineering (in partnership with SIT), Mechanical Engineering [BEng/MEng], Mechanical Engineering with Aeronautics [BEng/MEng], Mechatronics [BEng/MEng], Mechatronics (in partnership with SIT), Product Design Engineering [BEng/MEng]

Postgraduate courses: Aerospace Engineering [MSc], Aerospace Engineering & Management [MSc], Biomedical Engineering [MSc], Civil Engineering [MSc], Civil Engineering & Management [MSc], Computer Systems Engineering [MSc], Electronics & Electrical Engineering [MSc], Electronics & Electrical Engineering & Management [MSc], Mechanical Engineering [MSc], Mechanical Engineering & Management [MSc], Mechatronics [MSc], Nanoscience and Nanotechnology [MSc], Product Design Engineering [MSc], Sensor and Imaging Systems [MSc], Software Engineering [MSc], Structural Engineering [MSc], Sustainable Energy [MSc], Urban Transport [MSc]

English Language and Linguistics; www.gla.ac.uk/subjects/englishlanguage

English Language [MA]

Postgraduate courses: English Language & English Linguistics [MSc], TESOL: Teaching of English to Speakers of Other Languages [MSc], TESOL: Teaching of English to Speakers of Other Languages [MEd]

English Literature; www.gla.ac.uk/subjects/englishliterature

English Literature [MA/LLB]

Postgraduate courses: American Studies [MLitt], Creative Writing [MLitt], Creative Writing [MLitt: online distance learning], English Literature [MLitt], English Literature: Early Modern Literature and Culture [MLitt], English Literature: Fantasy [MLitt], English Literature: Modernities – Literature, Culture, Theory [MLitt], English Literature: Victorian Literature [MLitt], Environment, Culture & Communication (Dumfries Campus) [MLitt]

Film and Television Studies; www.gla.ac.uk/subjects/filmtelevision

Film & Television Studies [MA]

Postgraduate courses: Creative Industries and Cultural Policy [MSc], Film & Television Studies [MLitt], Film Curation [MSc], Filmmaking and Media Arts [MSc], Media Management [MSc]

Geographical and Earth Sciences; www.gla.ac.uk/subjects/ges

Earth Science [BSc], Geography [BSc/MA/MA(SocSci)]

Postgraduate courses: Geoinformation Technology and Cartography [MSc/PgDip/PgCert], Geomatics & Management [MSc], Geospatial and Mapping Sciences [MSc/PgDip/PgCert], Human Geography: Spaces, Politics, Ecologies [MRes]

Health and Wellbeing; www.gla.ac.uk/subjects/healthwellbeing

Applied Neuropsychology [MSc(MedSci)], Clinical Neuropsychology [MSc(MedSci)], Clinical Psychology [DClinPsy], Global Health [MSc], Global Mental Health [MSc/PgDip/PgCert: online distance learning], Global Mental Health [MSc], Health Technology Assessment [MSc/PgDip/PgCert: online distance learning], Molecular Pathology [MSc/PgDip/PgCert], One Health [MSc/PgDip/PgCert: online distance learning], Primary Care [MSc: online distance learning], Public Health [MPH], Public Health [MPH/PgDip/PgCert: online distance learning]

History; www.gla.ac.uk/subjects/history

History [MA/MA(SocSci)/LLB], Scottish History [MA/MA(SocSci)]

Postgraduate courses: American Studies [MLitt], Ancestral Studies [MSc/PgDip], Early Modern History [MLitt], Gender History [MSc/PgDip], Global Security [MRes], Global Security [MSc], History [MLitt/MSc/PgDip], History (with an emphasis on the History of Medicine) [MLitt/MSc], Medieval History [MLitt], Modern History [MLitt], Scottish History [MLitt], Security, Intelligence and Strategic Studies (Erasmus Mundus International Master) [IntM], War Studies [MLitt]

History of Art; www.gla.ac.uk/subjects/historyofart

History of Art [MA]

Postgraduate courses: Antiquities Trafficking & Art Crime [PgCert: online distance learning], Art History: Art: Politics: Transgression: 20th Century Avant-Gardes [MLitt], Art History: Collecting and Provenance in an International Context [MSc], Art History: Dress and Textile Histories [MLitt], Art History: Inventing Modern Art, 1768-1918 [MLitt], Art History: Technical Art History, Making & Meaning [MLitt], Art History: The Renaissance in Northern Europe and Italy [MLitt], Curatorial Practice (Contemporary Art) [MLitt], Museum Studies [MSc], Textile Conservation [MPhil]

Infection, Immunity and Inflammation; www.gla.ac.uk/subjects/iii

Immunology [BSc], Medicine [MBChB], Microbiology [BSc], Parasitology [BSc], Veterinary Biosciences [BSc], Veterinary Medicine & Surgery [BVMS], Virology [BSc]

Postgraduate courses: Immunology & Inflammatory Disease [MSc], Infection Biology (with specialisms) [MSc]

Information Studies; www.gla.ac.uk/subjects/informationstudies

Digital Media & Information Studies [MA]

Postgraduate courses: Information Management & Preservation (Digital)/(Archives & Records Management) [MSc/PgDip/PgCert], Museum Studies [MSc]

Law; www.gla.ac.uk/subjects/law

Common Law [LLB], Common Law (graduate entry) [LLB], Scots Law [LLB], Scots Law (graduate entry) [LLB]

Postgraduate courses: Common Law (graduate entry) [LLB], Corporate & Financial Law [LLM], Diploma in Professional Legal Practice [PgDip], Global Security [MRes], Global Security [MSc], Intellectual Property & the Digital Economy [LLM], Intellectual Property, Innovation & the Creative Economy [LLM/PgDip/PgCert: online distance learning], Intellectual Property, Innovation & the Creative Economy [MSc/PgDip/PgCert: online distance learning], International Commercial Law [LLM], International Competition Law & Policy [LLM], International Economic Law [LLM], International Law [LLM], International Law & Security [LLM], Law [LLM], Law [MRes], Scots Law (graduate entry) [LLB], Socio-Legal Studies [MRes]

Life Sciences; www.gla.ac.uk/subjects/lifesciences

Anatomy [BSc], Biochemistry [BSc], Biomedical Engineering [BEng/MEng], Genetics [BSc], Human Biology [BSc], Human Biology & Nutrition [BSc], Immunology [BSc], Marine & Freshwater Biology [BSc], Microbiology [BSc], Molecular & Cellular Biology [BSc], Molecular & Cellular Biology (with Biotechnology) [BSc], Molecular & Cellular Biology (with Plant Science) [BSc], Neuroscience [BSc], Parasitology [BSc], Pharmacology [BSc], Physiology [BSc], Physiology & Sports Science [BSc], Physiology, Sports Science & Nutrition [BSc], Virology [BSc], Zoology [BSc]

Postgraduate courses: Bioinformatics [MSc/PgDip/PgCert], Biomedical Sciences [MSc], Biomedical

Sciences [MRes], Human Anatomy [PgCert], Medical Visualisation & Human Anatomy [MSc]

Management; www.gla.ac.uk/subjects/ management

Accounting & Statistics [BSc], Business & Management [MA(SocSci)/MA/LLB/BSc], Business Economics [MA(SocSci)/LLB]

Postgraduate courses: Aerospace Engineering & Management [MSc], Biotechnology and Management [MSc/PgDip], Civil Engineering & Management [MSc], Creative Industries and Cultural Policy [MSc], Electronics & Electrical Engineering & Management [MSc], Finance & Management [MSc], Geomatics & Management [MSc], Intellectual Property, Innovation & the Creative Economy [MSc/PgDip/PgCert: online distance learning], International Business & Entrepreneurship [MSc], International Human Resource Management & Development [MSc], International Management & Design Innovation [MSc], International Real Estate & Management [MSc], International Strategic Marketing [MSc], Management [MSc], Management [MRes], Management & Sustainable Tourism [MSc], Management with Enterprise & Business Growth [MSc], Management with Human Resources [MSc], Management with International Finance [MSc], MBA (Master of Business Administration) [MBA], Mechanical Engineering & Management [MSc], Media Management [MSc], Public Policy & Management [MSc]

Mathematics; www.gla.ac.uk/subjects/ mathematics

Accounting & Mathematics [BSc], Finance & Mathematics [BSc], Mathematics [BSc/MSci/MA/ MA(SocSci)]

Postgraduate courses: Data Analytics [MSc], Data Analytics [MSc: online distance learning], Financial Modelling [MSc], Mathematics / Applied Mathematics [MSc]

Medicine; www.gla.ac.uk/subjects/ medicine

Biomedical Engineering [BEng/MEng], Immunology [BSc], Medicine [MBChB], Physiology, Sports Science & Nutrition [BSc], Virology [BSc]

Postgraduate courses: Advanced Lymphoedema Management [PgCert], Advanced Practice in Health Care [MSc(MedSci)], Child Health [PgCert], Clinical Genetics [MSc(MedSci)], Clinical Nutrition [MSc(MedSci)], Critical Care [MSc], Endodontics [MSc(DentSci)], Forensic Toxicology [MSc(MedSci)], Genetic and Genomic Counselling (with Work Placement) [MSc(MedSci)], Health-Professions Education / Health Professions Education (with Research) [MSc/MSc(with Research)/PgDip/PgCert: online distance learning], Healthcare Chaplaincy [PgCert], Human Nutrition [MSc(MedSci)], Leadership in Health & Social Care [PgCert: online distance learning], Medical Genetics and Genomics [MSc(MedSci)], Medical Physics [MSc], Molecular Pathology [MSc/PgDip/PgCert], Nursing: see Advanced Practice in Health Care [MSc(MedSci)], Oral & Maxillofacial Surgery [MSc(DentSci)], Sports Nutrition: see Human Nutrition [MSc(MedSci)], Sports Nutrition [PgCert]

Modern Languages and Cultures; www.gla.ac.uk/subjects/modernlanguages

Comparative Literature [MA], French [MA], German [MA], Italian [MA], Portuguese [MA], Russian [MA], Spanish [MA]

Postgraduate courses: Comparative Literature [MLitt], Translation Studies: Translation & Professional Practice [MSc/PgDip/PgCert], Russian for Social Scientists [PgCert], Russian for Social Scientists [PgDip], Russian Language [PgDip], Russian Language [PgCert]

Molecular, Cell and Systems Biology; www.gla.ac.uk/subjects/mcsb

Biotechnology [MSc], Biotechnology and Management [MSc/PgDip], Food Security [MSc]

Music; www.gla.ac.uk/subjects/music

Electronics with Music [BEng/MEng], Music BMus [BMus], Music MA [MA]

Postgraduate courses: Composition and Creative Practice [MMus], Historically Informed Performance Practice (in conjunction with RCS) [MMus], Musicology [MMus], Sound Design & Audiovisual Practice [MSc]

Neuroscience and Psychology; www.gla.ac.uk/subjects/ neurosciencepsychology

Neuroscience [BSc], Psychology [BSc/MA/ MA(SocSci)]

Postgraduate courses: Applied Neuropsychology [MSc(MedSci)], Brain Sciences [MSc], Clinical Neuropsychology [MSc(MedSci)], Psychological Science (conversion) [MSc], Psychological Science, Research Methods of [MSc], Psychological Studies (conversion) [MSc]

Nursing and Health Care; www.gla.ac.uk/subjects/nursing
Nursing [BN(Hons)]
Postgraduate courses: Advanced Nursing Science [MSc], Advanced Practice in Health Care [MSc(MedSci)], Leadership in Health & Social Care [PgCert: online distance learning]

Philosophy; www.gla.ac.uk/subjects/philosophy
Philosophy [MA/BSc/MA(SocSci)/LLB]
Postgraduate courses: Philosophy [MLitt], Philosophy [MSc]

Physics and Astronomy; www.gla.ac.uk/subjects/physics
Astronomy [BSc/MSci], Chemical Physics [MSci/BSc], Physics / Theoretical Physics [BSc/MSci], Physics with Astrophysics [BSc/MSci]
Postgraduate courses: Astrophysics [MSc], Physics: Advanced Materials [MSc], Physics: Energy and the Environment [MSc], Physics: Global Security [MSc], Physics: Nuclear Technology [MSc], Sensor and Imaging Systems [MSc], Sustainable Energy [MSc], Theoretical Physics [MSc]

Politics; www.gla.ac.uk/subjects/politics
Politics [MA(SocSci)/MA/LLB]
Postgraduate courses: Chinese Studies [MSc], Global Security [MRes], Global Security [MSc], Human Rights & International Politics [MRes], Human Rights & International Politics [MSc], International Relations [MRes], International Relations [MSc], Political Communication [MSc/PgDip], Political Communication [MRes], Security, Intelligence and Strategic Studies (Erasmus Mundus International Master) [IntM], Transnational Crime, Justice & Security [MSc]

Psychology; www.gla.ac.uk/subjects/psychology
Psychology [BSc/MA/MA(SocSci)]
Postgraduate courses: Brain Sciences [MSc], Clinical Neuropsychology [MSc(MedSci)], Psychological Science (conversion) [MSc], Psychological Science, Research Methods of [MSc], Psychological Studies (conversion) [MSc], Psychology (conversion) [MSc: online distance learning]

Scottish Literature; www.gla.ac.uk/subjects/scottishliterature
Scottish Literature [MA]

Sociology; www.gla.ac.uk/subjects/sociology
Sociology [MA/MA(SocSci)]

Postgraduate courses: Antiquities Trafficking & Art Crime [PgCert: online distance learning], Criminology [MRes], Criminology & Criminal Justice [MSc], Equality & Human Rights [MRes], Equality & Human Rights [MSc], Global Migrations & Social Justice [MRes], Global Migrations & Social Justice [MSc], Global Security [MRes], Global Security [MSc], Media, Communications & International Journalism [MSc], Sociology [MSc], Sociology & Research Methods [MRes], Transnational Crime, Justice & Security [MSc]

Statistics; www.gla.ac.uk/subjects/statistics
Accounting & Statistics [BSc], Finance & Statistics [BSc], Statistics [BSc/MSci]
Postgraduate courses: Advanced Statistics [MRes], Banking & Financial Services [MSc], Biostatistics [MSc], Data Analytics [MSc: online distance learning], Data Analytics [MSc], Environmental Statistics [MSc], Financial Modelling [MSc], Statistics [MSc]

Teaching
Education with Teaching Qualification (Primary) [MEduc], Primary Education with Teaching Qualification (Dumfries Campus) [MA(D)], Religious & Philosophical Education [MA(Ed)], Technological Education [BTechEd]

Theatre Studies; www.gla.ac.uk/subjects/theatre
Theatre Studies [MA]
Postgraduate courses: Playwriting & Dramaturgy [MLitt], Theatre Practices [MLitt], Theatre Studies [MLitt]

Theology and Religious Studies; www.gla.ac.uk/subjects/theology
Theology & Religious Studies [MA/BD/BD(Min)]
Postgraduate courses: Ancient Cultures [MLitt], Political Islam [MSc], Religion, Literature & Culture [MLitt/MTh], Religious Education by Distance Learning (CREDL) [PgCert: online distance learning]

Translation Studies; www.gla.ac.uk/subjects/translationstudies
Postgraduate courses: Translation Studies: Translation & Professional Practice [MSc/PgDip/PgCert]

Urban Studies; www.gla.ac.uk/subjects/urbanstudies
Social & Public Policy [MA/MA(SocSci)/LLB]
Postgraduate courses: City & Regional Planning [MSc], City Planning & Real Estate Development [MSc], City Planning & Regeneration [MSc], City

Planning & Transport [MSc], Housing Studies [MSc/PgDip], International Planning Studies [MSc], International Real Estate [MSc], International Real Estate & Management [MSc], Public and Urban Policy [MSc/PgDip], Public Policy & Management [MSc], Public Policy Research [MRes], Real Estate [PgCert], Real Estate [MSc], Real Estate & Regeneration [MSc], Spatial Planning [PgCert], Urban Research [MRes], Urban Transport [MSc]

Veterinary Medicine; www.gla.ac.uk/subjects/veterinary

Veterinary Biosciences [BSc], Veterinary Medicine & Surgery [BVMS]

Postgraduate courses: Advanced Practice in Veterinary Nursing [MSc/PgDip/PgCert: online distance learning], Veterinary Public Health [MVPH], Wildlife & Livestock Management [MSc/PgDip/PgCert: online distance learning]

GLASGOW CALEDONIAN UNIVERSITY
www.gcu.ac.uk

School of Engineering and Built Environment; www.gcu.ac.uk/ebe

3D Animation and Visualisation BSc(Hons), Audio Technology BSc(Hons), Building Services Engineering BEng(Hons), Building Surveying BSc(Hons), Building Surveying Pathway BSc(Hons), Computer Games (Art and Animation) BSc(Hons), Computer Games (Design) BSc(Hons), Computer Games (Indie Development) BSc(Hons), Computer Games (Software Development) BSc(Hons), Computer Networking BEng(Hons), Computer-Aided Mechanical Engineering BEng(Hons), Computer-Aided Mechanical Engineering MEng, Computing BSc(Hons), Construction Management BSc(Hons), Construction Management Pathway BSc(Hons), Cyber Security and Networks BSc(Hons), Cyber Security and Networks Pathway BSc(Hons), Digital Design (Graphics) BSc(Hons), Digital Security and Forensics BSc(Hons), Electrical Power Engineering MEng, Electrical Power Engineering BEng(Hons), Electrical Power Engineering Pathway MEng, Electrical and Electronic Engineering BEng(Hons), Electrical and Electronic Engineering MEng, Electrical and Electronic Engineering Pathway MEng, Electrical, Electronic and Energy Engineering MEng, Electrical, Electronic and Energy Engineering BEng(Hons), Environmental Civil Engineering BSc(Hons), Environmental Management BSc(Hons), Fire Risk Engineering BEng(Hons), Forensic Investigation BSc(Hons), Health and Safety Management BSc, Health, Safety and Environmental Management BSc(Hons), IT Management for Business BSc(Hons), Mechanical Electronic Systems Engineering MEng, Mechanical Electronic Systems Engineering BEng(Hons), Mechanical and Power Plant Systems BEng(Hons), Networked Systems Engineering BEng(Hons), Quantity Surveying BSc(Hons), Quantity Surveying Pathway BSc(Hons), Real Estate BSc(Hons), Software Development for Business BSc(Hons)

Postgraduate courses: 3D Design for Virtual Environments MSc, Advanced Internetwork Engineering MSc, Applied Instrumentation and Control MSc, Applied Instrumentation and Control (Oil and Gas) MSc, Big Data Technologies MSc, Building Services Engineering MSc, Climate Justice MSc, Electrical and Electronic Engineering MSc, Environmental Management (Waste, Energy, Water, Oil and Gas) MSc, International Project Management (Energy, Construction Management, Oil and Gas) MSc, Mechanical Engineering MSc, Quantity Surveying MSc

Glasgow School for Business and Society; www.gcu.ac.uk/gsbs

Accountancy BA(Hons), Accountancy Pathway BA/BA(Hons), Bachelor of Laws LLB, Bachelor of Laws with Risk LLB, Business Management BA(Hons), Finance, Investment and Risk BA(Hons), Finance, Investment and Risk Pathway BA(Hons), International Business BA(Hons), International Business and Human Resource Management BA(Hons), International Business and Tourism Management BA(Hons), International Business with Language BA(Hons), International Events Management BA(Hons), International Events Management Pathway BA(Hons), International Fashion Branding BA(Hons), International Fashion Business BA(Hons), International Marketing BA(Hons), International Sports Management BA(Hons), International Supply Chain Management BA(Hons), Media and Communication BA(Hons), Multimedia Journalism BA(Hons), Risk Management BA(Hons), Social Sciences BA(Hons)

Postgraduate courses: Accounting and Finance MSc, Captive Insurance Management Certificate, Digital Brand Marketing MSc, Health History MSc, Human Resource Management MSc, International Banking,

Finance and Risk Management MSc, International Business Management MSc, International Events Management MSc, International Fashion Marketing MSc, International Human Resource Management MSc, International Marketing MSc, International Operations and Supply Chain Management MSc, International Tourism Management MSc, Multimedia Journalism MA, Risk Management MSc, Social Business and Microfinance MSc, Social Sciences BA(Hons), Strategic Human Resource Management for Business Executives PgC, Television Fiction Writing MA

School of Health and Life Sciences; www.gcu.ac.uk/hls

Postgraduate courses: Applied Biomedical Science/ Biomedical Science BSc(Hons), Applied Psychology BSc(Hons), Biomolecular and Biomedical Sciences MSc, Cell and Molecular Biology BSc(Hons), Diagnostic Imaging BSc(Hons), Food Bioscience BSc(Hons), Human Nutrition and Dietetics BSc(Hons), Microbiology BSc(Hons), Nursing Studies (Adult) BSc, Nursing Studies (Adult) BSc(Hons), Nursing Studies (Child) BSc, Nursing Studies (Child) BSc(Hons), Nursing Studies (Dual Registration Learning Disability/Child) BSc(Hons), Nursing Studies (Learning Disability) BSc, Nursing Studies (Learning Disability) BSc(Hons), Nursing Studies (Mental Health) BSc, Nursing Studies (Mental Health) BSc(Hons), Occupational Therapy BSc(Hons), Ophthalmic Dispensing BSc, Optometry BSc(Hons), Oral Health Science BSc, Orthoptics BSc, Paramedic Science BSc, Pharmacology BSc(Hons), Physiotherapy BSc(Hons), Podiatry BSc(Hons), Professional Studies in Nursing BSc(Hons), Radiotherapy and Oncology BSc(Hons), Social Work BSc(Hons)

GCU London; www.gculondon.ac.uk

Postgraduate courses: Fashion Business Creation MSc, Fire Risk Engineering BEng(Hons), Global Marketing MSc, International Banking, Finance and Risk Management MSc, International Fashion Marketing MSc, International Management and Business Development MSc, International Project Management (Energy, Construction Management, Oil and Gas) MSc, Luxury Brand Management MBA, Luxury Brand Marketing MSc, Masters of Business Administration MBA, Public Health MSc, Quantity Surveying MSc, Risk Management MSc

THE GLASGOW SCHOOL OF ART
www.gsa.ac.uk

BSc(Hons) Immersive Systems Design, BArch/ DipArch Architecture, BA(Hons) Communication Design, BEng/MEng Engineering with Architecture, BA(Hons) Fashion Design, BA(Hons) Fine Art Photography, BA(Hons) Interaction Design, BA(Hons) Interior Design, BDes/MEDes Product Design, BEng/MEng Product Design Engineering, BA(Hons) Sculpture & Environmental Art, BA(Hons) Silversmithing and Jewellery Design, BDes(Hons) Sound for the Moving Image, BA(Hons) Textile Design

Postgraduate courses: MArch in Architectural Studies, MDes Communication Design, MLitt Curatorial Practice (Contemporary Art), MDes in Design Innovation and Citizenship, MDes in Design Innovation and Collaborative Creativity, MDes in Design Innovation and Environmental Design, MDes in Design Innovation and Interaction Design, MDes in Design Innovation and Service Design, MDes in Design Innovation and Transformation Design, MSc in Environmental Architecture, MDes Fashion + Textiles, MDes in Graphics/Illustration/Photography, MDes in Interior Design, MSc International Heritage Visualisation, MSc International Management and Design Innovation, MFA Master of Fine Art, MLitt Fine Art Practice, MRes in Creative Practices, Master of Research, MSc Medical Visualisation and Human Anatomy, PG Certificate in Learning and Teaching, PG Cert in Supervision, MSc Product Design Engineering, MSc Serious Games and Virtual Reality, MDes Sound for the Moving Image

UNIVERSITY OF GLOUCESTERSHIRE
www.glos.ac.uk

School of Art and Design; www.glos.ac.uk/academic-schools/art-and-design

Advertising BA(Hons), Fashion Design BA(Hons), Fine Art BA(Hons), Graphic Design BA(Hons), Illustration BA(Hons), Interior Design BA(Hons), Landscape Architecture BA(Hons), Photography BA(Hons), Photography: Editorial and Advertising BA(Hons), Photojournalism and Documentary Photography BA(Hons), Visual Communication (Level 6) BA(Hons)

Postgraduate courses: Fine Art PGCert/PGDip/MA, Illustration MA, Landscape Architecture PGDip/MA, MA/MDes Graphic Design Full-Time/Part-Time, Photography PGCert/PGDip/MA, Visual Communication PGCert/PGDip/MA

Business School; www.glos.ac.uk/academic-schools/business

Accounting and Business Management BA(Hons), Accounting and Finance BA(Hons), Accounting and Financial Management Studies BA(Hons), Business and Management Studies BA(Hons), Business and Marketing Management BA(Hons), Business Computing BSc(Hons), Business Management BA(Hons), Business Management and Strategy BA(Hons), Computer and Cyber Forensics BSc(Hons), Computer Games Design BSc(Hons), Computer Games Programming BSc(Hons), Computing BSc(Hons), Computing (Level 6) BSc(Hons), Cyber and Computer Security BSc(Hons), Digital Marketing BA(Hons), Digital Media and Web Technologies BSc(Hons), Events Management BA(Hons), Hotel Resort and Tourism Management BA(Hons), Hotel, Resort and Events Management BA(Hons), International Business Management BA(Hons), International Business Studies BA(Hons), Logistics Management BA(Hons), Marketing, Advertising and Branding BA(Hons), Product Design (BSc/BA Hons), Sports Management BA(Hons), Top-up degree BA(Hons) Level 6 International Business

Postgraduate courses: Accounting and Finance MSc, Accounting and Finance (Masters Stage) MSc, Computing (Masters Stage) MSC Masters Stage, Cyber Security (MSc) MSc, Marketing PGCert/PGDip/MSc, MBA Business Administration PGCert/PGDip/MBA, MBA Business Administration (Masters stage) MBA, MSc Finance PGCert/PGDip/MSc, MSc Human Resource Management PGDip/MSc, MSc Human Resource Management (Masters Stage) MSc

School of Education; www.glos.ac.uk/academic-schools/education

Early Childhood Studies BA(Hons), Education BA(Hons), Post-Compulsory Education and Training (PCET), Primary – general (FS/KS1, ages 3-7) BEd(Hons), Primary – general (KS1/KS2, ages 5-11) BEd(Hons), Primary – general (maths) (KS1/KS2, ages 5-11) BEd(Hons)

Postgraduate courses: Academic Practice PGCert, Early Years with EYTS PGCert, Education MA, Educational Leadership PGCert/PGDip/MA/MEd, Inclusive Education PGCert/PGDip/MA/MEd, Mentoring and Coaching PGCert, National Award for Special Educational Needs Co-ordination PGCert, Specific Learning Difficulties PGCert, Teacher Training PGCE (Primary) PGCE Primary, Teacher Training PGCE (Secondary) PGCE

School of Health and Social Care; www.glos.ac.uk/academic-schools/health-and-social-care

Community and Health Management (Level 6) BSc(Hons), Nursing (Adult) BSc(Hons), Social Care (Adult/Mental Health) BSc(Hons), Social Work BSc(Hons)

Postgraduate courses: Advancing Practice (Health) PGCert/PGDip/MSc, Community and District Nursing Specialist Practice PGDip, Community and Primary Care Practice PGCert/PGDip/MSc, Social Work PGCert/PGDip/MA

School of Law; www.glos.ac.uk/academic-schools/law

Law LLB

School of Liberal and Performing Arts; www.glos.ac.uk/academic-schools/liberal-and-performing-arts

Creative Writing BA(Hons), Dance BA(Hons), Drama BA(Hons), English BA(Hons), English Language and Creative Writing BA(Hons), English Literature and Creative Writing BA(Hons), Film Studies BA(Hons), History BA(Hons), Performing Arts BA(Hons), Religion, Philosophy and Ethics BA(Hons)

Postgraduate courses: Creative and Critical Writing PGCert/PGDip/MA

School of Media; www.glos.ac.uk/academic-schools/media

Animation BA(Hons), Creative Music Technology BA(Hons), Film and Television Production (Level 6) BA(Hons), Film Production BA(Hons), Journalism BA(Hons), Magazine Journalism and Production, Media Production BA(Hons), Music Business BA(Hons), Popular Music BA(Hons), Sports Journalism BA(Hons), Television Production BA(Hons)
Postgraduate course: Film Production MA

School of Natural and Social Sciences; www.glos.ac.uk/academic-schools/natural-and-social-sciences

Animal Biology BSc(Hons), Applied Social Sciences (Level 6) BSc(Hons), Biology BSc(Hons), Criminology BSc(Hons), Criminology and Psychology BSc(Hons), Criminology and Sociology BSc(Hons), Ecology and Environmental Science BSc(Hons), Geography BSc(Hons), Geography BA(Hons), Policing BSc(Hons), Psychology BSc(Hons), Sociology BA(Hons)

Postgraduate courses: Applied Ecology PGCert/PGDip/MSc, Criminology PGCert/PGDip/MSc, Forensic Psychology PGCert/PGDip/MSc, Occupational Psychology PGCert/PGDip/MSc, Psychology PGCert/PGDip/MSc, Public Protection PGCert

School of Sport and Exercise; www.glos.ac.uk/academic-schools/sport-and-exercise/

Applied Sport and Exercise Studies (Level 6) BSc(Hons), Exercise, Fitness and Health Foundation Degree, Physical Education BSc(Hons), Physical Education and Coaching BSc(Hons), Sport and Exercise Sciences BSc(Hons), Sports Coaching BSc(Hons), Sports Coaching and Development Foundation Degree, Sports Development and Coaching BSc(Hons), Sports Strength and Conditioning BSc(Hons), Sports Therapy BSc(Hons)
Professional Doctorate in Sport and Exercise (Postgraduate Research), Professional Practice in Sports Coaching PGDip/MSc, Professional Practice in Sports Therapy PGDip/MSc, Sports Strength and Conditioning PGCert/PGDip/MSc, Sports Therapy MSc

GLYNDWR UNIVERSITY
www.glyndwr.ac.uk

School of Creative Arts; www.glyndwr.ac.uk/en/AcademicSchools/CreativeArts

Applied Art
MDes Animation, BA(Hons) Animation, MDes Applied Arts, BA(Hons) Applied Arts
Postgraduate courses: MA Art Practice, MA Design Practice

Design Communication & Digital Art
MDes Game Art, BA (Hons Game Art, MDes Graphic Design, BA(Hons) Graphic Design, MDes Illustration, Graphic Novels & Children€™s Publishing, BA(Hons) Illustration, Graphic Novels and Children€™s Publishing, MDes Photography & Film, BA(Hons) Photography & Film

Fine Art
MFA Fine Art
BA(Hons) Fine Art

Creative Media Technology
BSc(Hons) Music Technology, BSc(Hons) Professional Sound and Video, BA(Hons) Radio Production, BSc(Hons) Sound Technology, BSc(Hons) Television Production and Technology

Broadcasting & Journalism
BA(Hons) Broadcasting, Journalism and Media Communications, BA(Hons) Journalism, Certificate of Higher Education in Journalism

Creative Writing
BA(Hons) History and Creative Writing, BA(Hons) English and Creative Writing

English
BA(Hons) English, BA(Hons) English and Creative Writing, BA(Hons) English and History

History
BA(Hons) History, BA(Hons) History and Creative Writing, BA(Hons) English and History

Theatre
BA(Hons) Theatre, Television and Performance

School of Social and Life Sciences; www.glyndwr.ac.uk/en/AcademicSchools/SocialandLifeSciences

Animal Studies and Equine Science
FdSc Animal Studies, FdSc Animal Studies (three years including foundation year), BSc(Hons) Animal Studies (top up), BSc(Hons) Animal Science,

BSc(Hons) Equine Science and Welfare Management, BSc(Hons) Wildlife and Plant Biology

Complementary Medicine

BSc(Hons) Acupuncture, BSc(Hons) Complementary Therapies for Healthcare, BSc(Hons) Complementary Therapies for Healthcare (four years including foundation year), BSc(Hons) Rehabilitation and Injury Management

Childhood Studies

BA(Hons) Childhood, Education and Welfare, BA(Hons) Education and Childhood Studies, BA(Hons) Families and Childhood Studies, BA(Hons) Childhood Studies (top-up year), FdA Early Childhood Practice, FdA Early Childhood Practice (Early Years Practitioner)

Education

BA(Hons) Education (ALN/SEN), BA(Hons) Education (Counselling Skills and Psychology), BA(Hons) Education Studies (top-up)

Postgraduate courses: MA Education, Professional Graduate Certificate in Education, MSc Learning and Technology, Graduate Diploma in Professional Development (Education), Continuing Professional Development (CPD) Rethinking Child Development, Professional Graduate Certificate in Education, Graduate Certificate in Professional Development (Education), Graduate Diploma in Professional Development (Education)

Counselling

Diploma of Higher Education in Counselling, Counselling Adults (top up), BSc(Hons) Counselling Children and Young People (top up)

Health Care Studies

Dip HE Contemporary Health Studies, BSc(Hons) Health and Wellbeing, BSc(Hons) Mental Health and Wellbeing

Postgraduate courses: MSc Advanced Clinical Practice, MSc Health Sciences, MSc Specialist Community Public Health Nursing, Emotions, Interpreting and Healthcare Settings, Introduction to Counselling

Nursing pre-registration

BN(Hons) Nursing (Adult)

Nursing post-registration

BSc(Hons) Community Specialist Practice (District Nursing), BSc(Hons) Healthcare Leadership and Management (Level 6 top-up), BSc(Hons) Specialist Community Public Health Nursing (Health Visiting), BSc(Hons) Specialist Community Public Health Nursing (School Nursing)

Postgraduate courses: Postgraduate Diploma Specialist Community Public Health Nursing (School Nursing), Postgraduate Diploma Specialist Community Public Health Nursing (Health Visiting), District Nursing, Return to Practice in Nursing

Occupational Therapy

BSc(Hons) Occupational Therapy

Psychology

BSc(Hons) Psychology

Postgraduate course: MSc Psychology of Religion

Criminal Justice

BA(Hons) Criminology and Criminal Justice, BA(Hons) Policing

Postgraduate course: MA Criminology and Criminal Justice

Social Care

BA(Hons) Social Work, FdA Therapeutic Child Care, BA(Hons) Therapeutic Child Care (top-up year)

Postgraduate courses: MA Education (Youth and Community Work), MA Education (Counselling Children and Young People), MA Education (counselling skills for Education)

Youth and Community

BA(Hons) Youth and Community Work (JNC)

Sport

BSc(Hons) Football Coaching and the Performance Specialist, BSc(Hons) Sport and Exercise Sciences, BSc(Hons) Sports Coaching for Participation and Performance Development, BSc(Hons) Sports Management

School of Applied Science, Computing and Engineering; www.glyndwr.ac.uk/en/AcademicSchools/AppliedScienceComputingEngineering

Aeronautical Engineering

BEng(Hons) Aeronautical and Mechanical Engineering, BEng(Hons) Aircraft Maintenance (Level 6 top-up)

Postgraduate courses: MSc Aeronautical Engineering, MSc Aircraft Structure, MSc Unmanned Aircraft System Technology

Automotive

BEng(Hons) Automotive Engineering, Building and Civil Engineering, BSc(Hons) Architectural Design Technology, BSc Civil Engineering Studies, BSc(Hons) Construction Management , BSc(Hons) Real Estate Management

Postgraduate course: MSc Automotive Engineering

Computing

BSc(Hons) Computing, BSc(Hons) Computer Science, BSc(Hons) Computer Game Design and Enterprise, MComp Computer Game Development, BSc(Hons) Computer Game Development, BSc(Hons) Computer Network and Security, BSc(Hons) Creative

Computing, BSc(Hons) Cyber Security, HNC Cyber Security, HND Cyber Security, BSc(Hons) Library and Information Management (Level 6 top-up), FdSc Library and Information Practice

Postgraduate courses: MSc Affective Computing, MSc Computer Game Development, MSc Computer Networking, MSc Learning and Technology, MSc Computer Science, MSc Computing, Postgraduate Certificate in Computing (PGCert), CCNA Cisco Networking Academy, MSc Robotics, MSc Mechatronics

Design

BEng(Hons) Composite Design (Level 6 top-up)

Electrical and Electronic Engineering

BEng(Hons) Electrical and Electronic Engineering

Housing

FdSc Housing and Sustainable Communities, BSc(Hons) Housing Studies (top-up)

Industrial Engineering

BEng(Hons) Automation Engineering, FdEng Industrial Engineering, BEng(Hons) Industrial Engineering (Level 6 top-up)

Postgraduate courses: MSc Mechanical Manufacturing, MSc Composite Material Engineering, MSc Electrical Power Engineering, MSc Electronic

Engineering, MSc Renewable Engineering and Sustainable Energy

Science and Environment

BSc(Hons) Chemistry with Green Nanotechnology, BSc(Hons) Forensic Science, BEng(Hons) Renewable and Sustainable Engineering

North Wales Business School; www.glyndwr.ac.uk/en/AcademicSchools/ NorthWalesBusinessSchool

Business

BA(Hons) Applied Business, BA(Hons) Business

Postgraduate courses: MA Human Resource Management, MBA Master of Business, Executive MBA

Entrepreneurship

BSc(Hons) Digital Enterprise and Innovation

Finance

BA(Hons) Accounting and Finance, BSc(Hons) Financial Technology Management

Hospitality, Leisure and Retail

BA(Hons) Hospitality Tourism and Event Management, BSc(Hons) Sports Management

Marketing

BA(Hons) Business, Marketing and Consumer Behaviour

UNIVERSITY OF GREENWICH
www.gre.ac.uk

Faculty of Architecture, Computing and Humanities; www.gre.ac.uk/ach

Animation, BA Hons, Architecture, BA Hons, Building Studies, HNC (LSEC Bexley Campus), Business Computing, BSc Hons, Business Information Technology (Extended), BSc Hons, Business Information Technology, BSc Hons, Computer Science, BSc Hons, Computer Security and Forensics, BSc Hons, Computer Systems and Networking, BSc Hons, Computing (Extended), BSc Hons, Computing with Games Development, BSc Hons, Computing, BSc Hons, Construction Management, BSc Hons, Creative Digital Media (Extended), BSc Hons, Creative Digital Media, BSc Hons, Creative Writing and English Literature, BA Hons, Creative Writing, BA Hons, Criminology (Extended), BA Hons, Criminology and Criminal Psychology (Extended), BSc Hons, Criminology and Criminal Psychology, BSc Hons, Criminology, BA Hons, Digital Arts Practice, BA Hons, Digital Film Production, BSc Hons, Drama and English Literature, BA Hons, Drama, BA Hons,

English Language and English Language Teaching (ELT), BA Hons, English Language and Literature, BA Hons, English Literature with Creative Writing, BA Hons, English Literature, BA Hons, Film and Television Production, BA Hons, Film Studies, BA Hons, Financial Mathematics, BSc Hons, Games Design and Development, BSc Hons, Garden Design, BA(Hons), Graphic and Digital Design, BA Hons, Graphic and Digital Design, HND, History and English, BA Hons, History and Politics, BA Hons, History and Sociology, BA Hons, History, BA Hons, Landscape Architecture, BA Hons, Languages and International Relations, BA Hons, Law (Extended), LLB Hons, Law Senior Status, LLB Hons, Law, LLB Hons, Mathematics and Computing, BSc Hons, Mathematics with Business, BSc Hons, Mathematics with Economics, BSc Hons, Mathematics, BSc Hons, Mathematics, BSc Hons (Extended), Media and Communications, BA Hons, Occupational Safety, Health and Environment, BSc Hons (Top-up), Photography (Top-up), BA(Hons) (North Kent College),

Politics and International Relations, BA Hons, Property Development and Management, BA Hons, Quantity Surveying, BSc Hons, Sociology (Extended), BA Hons, Sociology and Criminology, BSc Hons, Sociology and Psychology, BSc Hons, Sociology, BA Hons, Software Engineering, BEng Hons, Sound Design, BA Hons, Statistics and Operational Research, BSc Hons

Postgraduate courses: Architectural Practice, PGDip (ARB/RIBA Part 3 Exemption), Architecture Part 2, MArch, Architecture, Landscape and Urbanism, MSc, Big Data and Business Intelligence, MSc, Computer Forensics and Cyber Security, MSc, Computer Science, MSc, Computer Systems and Network Engineering, MSc, Computing and Information Systems, MSc, Construction Management and Economics, MSc, Criminology and Criminal Psychology, MSc, English: Literary London, MA, Enterprise Systems and Database Administration, MSc, Facilities Management (Distance Learning), MSc, Film Production MA/MSc, Information Systems Management, MSc, International and Commercial Law, LLM, International Criminology, MA, International Maritime Policy, MA, Landscape Architecture, MA, Landscape Architecture, MLA, Management of Business Information Technology, MSc, Mathematics, MMath, Occupational Hygiene, MSc/PGDip, Project Management – International (Distance Learning), MSc, Project Management – International, MSc, Real Estate (Distance Learning), MSc, Real Estate Development and Investment, MSc, Safety, Health and Environment, PGDip/MSc, Second Language Learning and Teaching, MA, Software Engineering, MSc, Spatial Data Science, MSc, Sustainable Building Design and Engineering, MSc, Web Design and Content Planning, MA

Faculty of Education and Health; www.gre.ac.uk/eduhea

Adult Nursing, BSc Hons, Assistant Health and Social Care Practitioner, FdS, Childhood and Youth Studies (Extended), BA Hons, Childhood and Youth Studies, BA Hons, Children's Nursing, BSc Hons, Early Years, BA Hons, Early Years, BA Hons (Top-up), Education Studies, BA Hons, FdA Community Sport, Health and Social Care, BA Hons (Top-up), Health and Wellbeing (Extended), BSc Hons, Health and Wellbeing, BSc Hons, Language and Literacy Education (2-Year Accelerated Degree), BA Hons, Learning Disabilities Nursing, BSc Hons, Mathematics Education (2-Year Accelerated Degree), BA Hons, Mental Health Nursing, BSc Hons, Mental Health Work, BSc Hons (Top-up), Midwifery, BSc Hons, Paramedic Science, BSc Hons, Physical Education and Sport (Extended), BA Hons, Physical Education and Sport, BA Hons, Primary Education (2-Year Accelerated Degree), BA Hons, Primary Education with Qualified Teacher Status (QTS), BA Hons, Psychology with Counselling, BSc Hons, Psychology, BSc Hons, Public Health (Extended), BSc Hons, Public Health, BSc Hons, School Direct Training Programmes (Early Years), School Direct Training Programmes (Primary), Sexual Health, BSc Hons (Top up), Social Work, BA Hons, Specialist Community Public Health (Health Visiting and School Nursing), BSc Hons (Top-up), Specialist Practitioner (District Nursing), BSc Hons (Top up)

Postgraduate courses: Advanced Practice, MSc, Child and Adolescent Psychology, MSc, Doctorate in Education, EdD, Early Years Teacher Status (Professional), PGCE, Early Years Teacher Status, PGCE, Education and Training, MPhil/PhD, Education, MA, Education, MPhil/PhD, Health and Social Care Research, MPhil/PhD, Healthcare Practice, MA, Higher Education, PGCert, Lifelong Learning Sector (ESOL and Literacy), PCE, Lifelong Learning Sector (ESOL and Literacy), PGCE, Lifelong Learning Sector (ESOL), PCE, Lifelong Learning Sector (ESOL), PGCE, Lifelong Learning Sector (Literacy), PCE, Lifelong Learning Sector (Literacy), PGCE Nursing (Adult Nursing), MSc, Lifelong Learning Sector (Numeracy), PCE, Lifelong Learning Sector (Numeracy), PGCE, Lifelong Learning Sector, PCE, Lifelong Learning Sector, PGCE, Nursing (Children€™s Nursing), MSc, Nursing (Mental Health Nursing), MSc, Nursing, PGDip (Adult Nursing), Nursing, PGDip (Mental Health Nursing), Primary Education, PGCE, Primary Mathematics (Subject Specialist), PGCE, Primary Professional Development, PGCert, Professional Certificate in Education/ProfGCE (Bromley), Psychology, MPhil/PhD, Psychology, MSc (Conversion Degree), Psychology, MSc by Research, School Direct Training Programme (Secondary), PGCE, Secondary Education Mathematics, PGCE, Secondary Education Modern Languages (French), PGCE, Secondary Education Physical Education, PGCE, Secondary Education Science with Biology, PGCE, Secondary Education Science with Chemistry, PGCE, Secondary Education Science with Physics, PGCE, Secondary Musicians in Education, PGCE, Social Work, MA, Specialist Practitioner (District Nursing), PGDip, Sport and Exercise Psychology, MSc, Therapeutic Counselling, MSc

Faculty of Engineering and Science; www.gre.ac.uk/engsci

Applied Biomedical Science, BSc Hons, Applied Bioscience Technology, Foundation Degree, Biology (Extended), BSc Hons, Biology, BSc Hons, Biomedical Science (Extended), BSc Hons, Biomedical Science, BSc Hons, Building Services Engineering, FdE (RSME), Business Administration (Extended), BA Hons, Business Administration with Accounting and Finance, BA Hons, Business Administration with Marketing, BA Hons, Business Administration, BA Hons, Business Administration, FdA, Chemical Engineering (Extended), BEng Hons, Chemical Engineering, BEng Hons, Chemistry (Extended), BSc Hons, Chemistry BSc(Hons), (Degree Apprenticeship), Chemistry FdSc, (Higher Apprenticeship), Chemistry HNC, (Higher Apprenticeship), Chemistry, BSc Hons, Chemistry, HNC, Civil Engineering (Extended), BEng Hons, Civil Engineering, BEng Hons, Civil Engineering, FdSc (RSME), Computer Engineering (Extended), BEng Hons, Computer Engineering, BEng Hons, Construction Management, FdSc (RSME), Cybernetics (Extended), BEng Hons, Cybernetics, BEng Hons, Design, Innovation and Entrepreneurship (Extended), BEng Hons, Design, Innovation and Entrepreneurship, BEng Hons, Digital and Technology Solutions BSc(Hons), (Degree Apprenticeship), Electrical and Electronic Engineering (Extended), BEng Hons, Electrical and Electronic Engineering, BEng Hons, Electrical and Electronic Engineering, Foundation Degree, Electrical Engineering, FdE (RSME), Engineering Management (Extended), BEng Hons, Engineering Management, BEng Hons, Engineering Technology, BEng Hons, Environmental Science, BSc Hons, Forensic Science (Extended), BSc Hons, Forensic Science with Criminology (Extended), BSc Hons, Forensic Science with Criminology, BSc Hons, Forensic Science, BSc Hons, Geography, BSc Hons, Human Nutrition (Extended), BSc Hons, Human Nutrition, BSc Hons, Industrial Engineering (Extended), BEng Hons, Industrial Engineering, BEng Hons, Information Technology Management for Business, BSc Hons, Mechanical Engineering (Extended), BEng Hons, Mechanical Engineering, BEng Hons, Mechanical Engineering, Foundation Degree, Natural Sciences (Extended) BSc, Natural Sciences, BSc Hons, Pharmaceutical Sciences (Extended), BSc Hons, Pharmaceutical Sciences BSc(Hons), (Degree Apprenticeship), Pharmaceutical Sciences FdSc, (Higher Apprenticeship), Pharmaceutical Sciences, BSc Hons, Pharmacology and Physiology (with Integrated Foundation Year), BSc Hons, Pharmacology and Physiology, BSc Hons, Sports Science (Extended), BSc Hons, Sports Science with Coaching (Extended), BSc Hons, Sports Science with Coaching, BSc Hons, Sports Science with Professional Football Coaching (Extended), BSc Hons, Sports Science with Professional Football Coaching, BSc Hons, Sports Science, BSc Hons

Postgraduate courses: Agricultural and Food Sciences – Research, MPhil/PhD, Agriculture for Sustainable Development, MSc, Applied Plant Science, MSc, Biology, MBiol, Biomedical Sciences (Online), MSc/ PGDip/PGCert, Biotechnology, MSc, Chemical Engineering, MEng, Chemistry, MChem, Civil Engineering, MEng, Civil Engineering, MSc, Computer Engineering, MEng, Cybernetics, MEng, Design, Innovation and Entrepreneurship, MEng, Development Studies – Research, MPhil/PhD, Electrical and Electronic Engineering, MEng, Electrical and Electronic Engineering, MSc, Electrical Power Engineering, MSc, Engineering – Research, MPhil/PhD, Engineering Management, MEng, Engineering Management, MSc, Engineering, MSc by Research, Environmental Conservation, PGDip/MSc, Food Innovation, MSc, Food Safety and Quality Management e-learning, MSc/PGDip/PGCert, Food Safety and Quality Management, PGDip/MSc, Formulation Science, MSc, Future Intelligent Technologies, MSc, General Pharmacy Practice, PGCert/PGDip/MSc, Global Oil and Gas Management, MSc, Global Shipping Management, MSc, Independent/Supplementary Prescribing, PGCert, Industrial Engineering, MEng, Mechanical and Manufacturing Engineering, MSc, Mechanical Engineering, MEng, Medicines Management, PGCert/PGDip/MSc, Natural Resources, MSc by Research, Pharmaceutical Biotechnology, MSc, Pharmaceutical Sciences, MSc/PGDip, Pharmacy, MPharm, Science – Research, MPhil/PhD, Science, MSc by Research, Strength and Conditioning, MSc, Sustainable Environmental Management, MSc, Water, Waste and Environmental Engineering, MSc

GRIMSBY INSTITUTE/UNIVERSITY CENTRE
www.grimsby.ac.uk

Animal Care
HNC Animal Management

Business
BA Business Management, BA Business Management with Accounting, BA Business Management with Marketing, Level 7 Award, Certificate, Diploma in Strategic Management and Leadership

Computing
BSc(Hons) Computing Technologies, FdSc Computing Technologies

Community Studies
BA Criminological Studies with Social Science, FdA Children, Young People and Families

Creative Arts, Performance & Music
BA(Hons) Design, BA(Hons) Music Production, BA(Hons) Popular Music Performance, BA(Hons) Special Effects Make-up Design and Prosthetics, FdA Performing Arts

Early Years
BA Early Childhood Studies Top up, FdEd Early Childhood Studies

Education
FdEd Primary Education Studies, HEA Leadership and Teacher Excellence CPD Programme, In-Service Certificate in Education, Professional Graduate Certificate in Education and Postgraduate Certificate in Education (Teaching in the Lifelong Learning Sector), Level3 Award in Education and Training (C&G 6502), Pre-Service Certificate in Education, Professional Graduate Certificate in Education and Postgraduate

Certificate in Education (Teaching in the Lifelong Learning Sector)

Engineering & Construction
HNC Mechanical Engineering, HNC Construction, HND Construction, HND Mechanical Engineering, HND Construction Top Up, HND Electrical and Electronic Engineering

Health & Social Care
BSc Applied Psychology, BSc Health and Social Care Top Up, FdA Counselling Studies, FdSc Mental Health Studies (Nursing pathway), FdSc Community Mental Health, FdSc Hospital and Health Care (Adult), FdSc Health and Social Care, FdSc Gerontology and Dementia Studies

Leisure
BA Tourism and Business Management Top up, FdA Tourism Management, FdA Events Management, FdA Sport and Recreation Management

Postgraduate
Level 7 Award, Certificate, Diploma in Strategic Management and Leadership

Media & Writing
BA(Hons) Independent Game Design (Game Art), BA(Hons) Independent Game Design (Game Development), BA(Hons) Professional and Creative Writing, FdA TV Production, FdA Photography

Sport
HNC Sport and Exercise Sciences, HND Sport and Exercise Sciences

HARPER ADAMS UNIVERSITY
www.harper-adams.ac.uk

Agriculture
BSc(Hons) Agriculture, FdSc Agriculture, BSc(Hons) Agriculture with Animal Science, BSc(Hons) Agriculture with Crop Management, BSc(Hons) Agriculture with Farm Business Management, FdSc Agriculture with Mechanisation, BSc(Hons) Agriculture with Mechanisation

Animal Sciences
BSc(Hons)/BSc Animal Behaviour and Welfare (Clinical), BSc(Hons)/BSc Animal Behaviour and Welfare (Non-clinical), BSc(Hons) Animal Health and Welfare, FdSc Animal Management and Welfare,

BSc(Hons) Animal Production Science, MSci Animal Production Science, BSc(Hons) Bioveterinary Science, MSci Bioveterinary Science

Business and Agri-food
BSc(Hons) Agri-business, FdSc Agri-business, BSc(Hons) Agri-food Marketing with Business, FdSc Agri-food Marketing with Business, BSc(Hons) Business Management with Marketing, FdSc Business Management with Marketing

Countryside, Environment and Wildlife
BSc(Hons) Countryside and Environmental Management, BSc(Hons) Countryside Management, FdSc

Countryside Management, BSc(Hons) Wildlife Conservation and Environmental Management

Engineering

BEng(Hons) Agricultural Engineering, MEng Agricultural Engineering, MEng Automotive Engineering (Off-Highway), BEng(Hons) Automotive Engineering (Off-Highway), BEng(Hons) Mechanical Engineering, MEng Mechanical Engineering, BSc(Hons) Product Support Engineering

Food Science, Technology and Innovation

BSc(Hons) Food and Public Health Nutrition, BSc(Hons) Food Business Innovation and Entrepreneurship, BSc(Hons) Food Manufacture with Marketing, BSc(Hons) Food Sustainability Management, BSc(Hons) Food Technology and Product Development, BSc(Hons) Food Technology with Nutrition

Geography

BSc(Hons) Geography and Environmental Management

Land and Property Management

BSc(Hons) Real Estate, BSc(Hons) Rural Enterprise and Land Management (REALM), BSc(Hons) Rural Property Management

Veterinary Nursing

Dip AVN Advanced Veterinary Nursing, BSc/BSc(Hons) Veterinary Nursing, BSc(Hons) Veterinary Nursing (with Advanced Standing), BSc/BSc(Hons) Veterinary Nursing with Companion Animal Behaviour, BSc(Hons) Veterinary Nursing with Small Animal Rehabilitation

Zoology

BSc(Hons) Applied Zoology, BSc(Hons) Applied Zoology with Entomology, BSc(Hons) Applied Zoology with Environmental Management

Postgraduate courses

PgD/MSc Advanced Veterinary Practice Sciences, PgC/PgD/MSc Agricultural Engineering (Mobile Machinery), PgC Agricultural Law, PgC/PgD/MSc Agricultural Sciences and Production Systems, PgC/PgD/MSc/MRes Agroecology, MRes Applied Ecology, PgC/PgD/MSc/MREs Applied Mechatronic Engineering, PgC/PgD/MSc/MRes Aquaculture, PgC/PgD/MSc Automotive Engineering (Off-Highway), PgC/PgD/MSc/MRes Conservation and Forest Protection, PgD/MSc Ecological Applications, PgC/PgD/MSc /MRes Entomology, PgC Equine Medicine, PgC Exotic Animal Studies, PgC Feline Veterinary Studies, PgC/PgD/MSc/MRes Food Industry Management, PgC/PgD/MSc/MRes Forestry Management, PgC/PgD/MSc/MRes Integrated Pest Management, PgC/PgD/MSc International Agri-Business and Food Chain Management, MRes Land and Property Management, MRes Master of Research, PgC/PgD Meat Business Management, PgC/PgD/MSc Negotiated Studies, PgC/PgD/MSc/MRes Plant Pathology, PgC Poultry Business Management, PgC/PgD/MSc/MRes Poultry Production, PgC/PgD/MSc/MRes Ruminant Nutrition, MProf/MSc Rural Estate and Land Management, PgC Small Animal Cardiology Studies, PgC Small Animal Diagnostic Imaging, PgC Small Animal Emergency Medicine and Surgery, PgC Small Animal Medicine, PgC Small Animal Ophthalmology, PgC Small Animal Surgery, PgC Veterinary Nurse Practitioner, PgD/MSc Veterinary Nursing, PgC Veterinary Oncology Nursing, UDip/PgC/PgD/MSc Veterinary Pharmacy, PgD/MSc Veterinary Physiotherapy, PgC Veterinary Rehabilitation Nursing, PgC Western Veterinary Acupuncture and Chronic Pain Management

ASKHAM BRYAN COLLEGE
www.askham-bryan.ac.uk

Agriculture

BSc/BSc(Hons) Agricultural Management, BSc/BSc(Hons) Agriculture, BSc/BSc(Hons) Applied Agriculture, Extended Foundation Degree Countryside Management, Foundation Degree (FdSc) Agriculture, Foundation Degree Enterprise (Land-Based)

Animal Management

BSc/BSc(Hons) Animal Conservation, BSc/BSc(Hons) Animal Management, BSc/BSc(Hons) Animal Management and Science, BSc/BSc(Hons) Canine and Feline Behaviour and Welfare, BSc/BSc(Hons) Zoo Management, Extended Foundation Degree Animal Management, Foundation Degree (FdSc) Animal Management, Foundation Degree (FdSc) Canine and Feline Training and Behaviour, Foundation Degree (FdSc) Management of Animal Collections with Conservation, Foundation Degree Animal Management, Foundation Degree Canine and Feline Training and Behaviour, Foundation Degree Management of Animal Collections with Conservation

Countryside and the Environment

BSc/BSc(Hons) Countryside Management, Extended Foundation Degree Agriculture, Extended Foundation Degree Countryside Management, Foundation

Degree (FdSc) Countryside Management, Foundation Degree Enterprise (Land-Based)

Equine

BSc/BSc(Hons) Equine Business Management, BSc/BSc(Hons) Equine Science, BSc/BSc(Hons) Equine Science and Management, Foundation Degree (FdSc) Equine Business Management, Foundation Degree (FdSc) Equine Science and Management, Extended Foundation Degree Equine Management

Floristry

Foundation Degree (FdSc) Sports Surface Management, City and Guilds Higher Diploma (ICSF) Level 4 Floristry

Horticulture

BSc/BSc(Hons) Applied Horticulture, BSc/BSc(Hons) Horticulture with Landscape Garden Management, Foundation Degree (FdSc) Horticulture, Foundation Degree (FdSc) Sports Surface Management, Extended Foundation Degree Horticulture, Foundation Degree (FdSc) Arboriculture and Urban Forestry, Foundation Degree Enterprise (Land-Based, Foundation Degree Sports Surface Management

Outdoor Adventure Sport

Foundation Degree (FdSc) Sport (Coaching and Fitness), Foundation Degree (FdSc) Sport (Adventure and Outdoor Education)

Professional Tree Surgery and Management

BSc/BSc(Hons) Applied Horticulture, Foundation Degree (FdSc) Sports Surface Management, Foundation Degree (FdSc) Arboriculture and Urban Forestry

Sport

Foundation Degree (FdSc) Sport (Coaching and Fitness), Foundation Degree (FdSc) Sport (Adventure and Outdoor Education), Foundation Degree (FdSc) Sports Surface Management, Foundation Degree Sport (Coaching and Fitness)

Uniformed Public Services

HNC/HND Public Services

Veterinary Nursing

BSc(Hons) Veterinary Health Studies, BSc(Hons) Veterinary Nursing (Top Up), Foundation Degree (FdSc) Veterinary Health Studies

HERIOT-WATT UNIVERSITY
www.hw.ac.uk

School of Energy, Geoscience, Infrastructure and Society; www.hw.ac.uk/schools/energy-geoscience-infrastructure-society.htm

Architectural Engineering

Architectural Engineering BEng(Hons), Architectural Engineering MEng, Architectural Engineering with International Studies MEng

Biology

Marine Biology BSc(Hons), Biological Sciences BSc(Hons), Biological Sciences (Cell and Molecular Biology) BSc(Hons), Biological Sciences (Human Health) BSc(Hons), Biological Sciences (Microbiology) BSc(Hons), Brewing and Distilling BSc(Hons)

Civil Engineering and Structural Engineering

Civil Engineering BEng(Hons), Civil Engineering MEng, Civil Engineering with International Studies MEng, Structural Engineering BEng(Hons), Structural Engineering MEng, Structural Engineering with Architectural Design BEng(Hons), Structural Engineering with Architectural Design MEng, Structural Engineering with International Studies MEng

Postgraduate courses: Civil Engineering MSc/Diploma, Civil Engineering and Construction Management MSc/Diploma, Safety and Risk Management (distance learning only) MSc/Diploma, Safety, Risk and Reliability Engineering (distance learning only) MSc/Diploma, Structural and Foundation Engineering MSc/Diploma, Water and Environmental Management MSc/Diploma, Water Technology and Desalination MSc/Diploma

Construction Management and Surveying

Construction Project Management BSc(Hons), Quantity Surveying BSc(Hons)

Postgraduate courses: Commercial Management and Quantity Surveying MSc/Diploma, Construction Project Management MSc/Diploma

Energy and Renewables

Postgraduate courses: Energy MSc/Diploma, Oil and Gas Technology MSc, Renewable Energy and Distributed Generation MSc, Renewable Energy Development (RED) MSc/Diploma, Renewable Energy Engineering MSc/Diploma/Certificate, Smart Grid Demand Management MSc/Diploma

Food Science, Health and Nutrition

Biotechnology MSc/Diploma, Food and Beverage Science MSc/Diploma/Certificate, Food Science and Nutrition MSc/Diploma/Certificate, Food Science,

Safety and Health MSc/Diploma/Certificate, Human Health and Disease MSc/Diploma

Geoscience

Postgraduate courses: Applied Petroleum Geoscience MSc, Reservoir Evaluation and Management MSc

Marine, Environment and Climate Change

Postgraduate courses: Climate Change: Impacts and Mitigation MSc/Diploma/Certificate, Climate Change: Managing the Marine Environment MSc/Diploma/Certificate, Integrative Marine Data Skills MSc/Diploma, Marine Biodiversity and Biotechnology MSc/Diploma/Certificate, Marine Planning for Sustainable Development MSc/Diploma, Marine Renewable Energy MSc/Diploma, Marine Resource Development and Protection MSc/Diploma/Certificate, Marine Resource Management (MRM) MSc/Diploma, Marine Science MSc/Diploma

Petroleum Engineering

Postgraduate course: Petroleum Engineering MSc

Real Estate

Postgraduate courses: Real Estate and Planning MSc/Diploma, Real Estate Investment and Finance MSc/Diploma, Real Estate Management and Development MSc/Diploma

Urban Studies

Urban Planning and Property Development BSc(Hons), Geography, Society and Environment MA(Hons)

Postgraduate courses: Architectural Project Management MSc/Diploma, Building Conservation (Technology and Management) MSc/Diploma, Building Services Engineering MSc/Diploma, Sustainable Building Design MSc, Sustainable Urban Management MSc/Diploma, Urban and Regional Planning MSc/Diploma, Urban Strategies and Design MSc/Diploma

School of Engineering and Physical Sciences; www.hw.ac.uk/schools/engineering-physical-sciences/

Chemistry

BSc Chemistry, MChem Chemistry, BSc(Hons) Chemistry and Professional Education, MChem Chemistry with a European Language, MChem Chemistry with a year in Australia, BSc(Hons) Chemistry with a year in Australia, MChem Chemistry with a Year in Europe, MChem Chemistry with a Year in North America, MChem Chemistry with Biochemistry, BSc(Hons) Chemistry with Biochemistry, MChem Chemistry with Computational Chemistry, BSc(Hons) Chemistry with Computational Chemistry, MChem Chemistry with Industrial Experience, MChem Chemistry with Materials, BSc(Hons) Chemistry with Materials, MChem Chemistry with Materials and Nanoscience, MChem Chemistry with Nanotechnology, MChem Chemistry with Pharmaceutical Chemistry, BSc(Hons) Chemistry with Pharmaceutical Chemistry

Chemical Engineering

MEng Chemical Engineering, BEng(Hons) Chemical Engineering, MEng Chemical Engineering and Diploma in Industrial Training, BEng(Hons) Chemical Engineering and Diploma in Industrial Training, MEng Chemical Engineering with Energy Engineering, MEng Chemical Engineering with Oil and Gas Technology, MEng Chemical Engineering with Pharmaceutical Chemistry

Postgraduate course: Sustainability Engineering, MSc/Diploma/Certificate

Electrical, Electronic and Computer Engineering

Electrical and Electronic Engineering BEng(Hons), Electrical and Electronic Engineering MEng, Computing and Electronics BEng(Hons), Computing and Electronics MEng, Electrical Power and Energy BEng(Hons), Electrical Power and Energy MEng, Robotics, Autonomous and Interactive Systems BEng(Hons), Robotics, Autonomous and Interactive Systems MEng

Postgraduate courses: Embedded Systems, MSc/Diploma, Mobile Communications, MSc/Diploma/Certificate, Robotics, Autonomous and Interactive Systems, MSc/Diploma, Renewable Energy and Distributed Generation, MSc, Smart Systems Integration (Erasmus Mundus), MSc, Vision Image & Robotics (VIBOT) (Erasmus Mundus), MSc

Mechanical Engineering

MEng/BEng Mechanical Engineering, MEng/BEng Mechanical Engineering and Energy Engineering

Postgraduate courses: Advanced Mechanical Engineering, MSc/Diploma, Energy, MSc/Diploma, Renewable Energy and Distributed Generation, MSc, Renewable Energy Engineering, MSc/Diploma/Certificate, Smart Grid Demand Management, MSc/Diploma

Physics

Physics BSc(Hons)/MPhys, Chemical Physics BSc(Hons)/MPhys, Engineering Physics BSc(Hons)/MPhys, Mathematical Physics BSc(Hons)/MPhys, Physics and Professional Education BSc(Hons)

Postgraduate courses: Photonics and Optoelectronic Devices, MSc

School of Mathematical and Computer Sciences; www.hw.ac.uk/schools/mathematical-computer-sciences.htm

Actuarial Mathematics and Statistics

Actuarial Science BSc(Hons), Actuarial Science and Diploma in Industrial Training BSc(Hons), Financial Mathematics BSc(Hons), Statistical Modelling BSc(Hons)

Postgraduate courses: Actuarial Management MSc/Diploma/Certificate, Actuarial Science MSc/Diploma/Certificate, Actuarial Science and Management MSc/Diploma, Financial Mathematics MSc, Quantitative Financial Engineering MSc, Quantitative Financial Risk Management MSc/Diploma

Computer Science

Computer Science BSc(Hons), Computer Science (Artificial Intelligence) BSc(Hons), Computer Science (Games Programming) BSc(Hons), Computer Science (Software Engineering) BSc(Hons), Computer Science and Diploma in Industrial Training BSc(Hons), Computer Systems BSc(Hons), Computer Systems (Games Programming) BSc(Hons), Computer Systems and Diploma in Industrial Training BSc(Hons), Information Systems BSc(Hons), Information Systems (Interaction Design) BSc(Hons), Information Systems (Internet Systems) BSc(Hons), Information Systems (Management) BSc(Hons), Information Systems and Diploma in Industrial Training BSc(Hons), Software Engineering MEng

Postgraduate courses: Artificial Intelligence MSc/Diploma, Artificial Intelligence with Speech and Multimodal Interaction MSc/Diploma, Business Information Management MSc/Diploma, Computer Systems Management MSc/Diploma, Data Science MSc/Diploma, Information Technology (Business) MSc/Diploma, Information Technology (Graduate Diploma) Diploma, Information Technology (Software Systems) MSc/Diploma, Network Security MSc/Diploma, Software Engineering MSc/Diploma

Mathematics

Mathematics BSc, Mathematics MMath, Mathematical, Statistical and Actuarial Sciences BSc(Hons), Mathematical, Statistical and Actuarial Sciences and Diploma in Industrial Training BSc(Hons), Mathematics with Computer Science BSc(Hons), Mathematics and Computer Science BSc(Hons), Mathematics with Finance BSc, Mathematics with Finance and Diploma in Industrial Training BSc, Mathematics with French BSc(Hons), Mathematics with German BSc(Hons), Mathematics with Spanish BSc(Hons), Mathematics with Physics BSc, Mathematics with Statistics BSc

Postgraduate courses: Applied Mathematical Sciences MSc/Diploma, Applied Mathematical Sciences Climate Change Modelling MSc/Diploma, Applied Mathematical Sciences with Biological and Ecological Modelling MSc/Diploma MSc/Diploma, Computational Mathematics MSc/Diploma, Graduate Certificate in the Mathematical Sciences Diploma/Certificate, Mathematical Biology, Ecology and Medicine MSc/Diploma, Mathematics MSc/Diploma, Quantitative Finance and Mathematics MSc/Diploma

School of Social Sciences; www.hw.ac.uk/schools/social-sciences

Accountancy and Finance

Accountancy and Business Law MA(Hons), Accountancy and Finance MA(Hons), Business and Finance MA(Hons), Finance MA(Hons), Finance and Business Law MA(Hons)

Postgraduate courses: MSc International Accounting and Finance, MSc International Accounting and Management, MSc International Accounting and Environmental Economics, MSc Strategy and International Management Accounting, MSc Finance, MSc Finance and Management, MSc International Banking and Finance, MSc International Finance and Corporate Accountability, MSc International Finance and Environmental Economics, MSc Investment Management

Business Management

International Business Management MA(Hons), International Business Management with Business Law MA(Hons), International Business Management with Enterprise MA(Hons), International Business Management with Human Resource Management MA(Hons), International Business Management with Marketing MA(Hons), International Business Management with Year Abroad MA(Hons), Bachelor of Business Administration BBA

Postgraduate courses: Business Psychology MSc/Diploma, International Business Management with Finance MSc, International Business Management with HRM MSc, International Business Management with Logistics MSc, International Business Management with Marketing MSc, International Business Management with Performance Management MSc, International Business Management with Project Management MSc, International Business Management with Sustainability Management MSc, International Business Management with Tourism MSc,

International Fashion Marketing MSc, International Marketing Management MSc, International Marketing Management with Consumer Psychology MSc, International Marketing Management with Digital Marketing MSc, International Marketing Management with Sustainability MSc, International Marketing Management with Tourism MSc,, Business Strategy, Leadership and Change MSc, Lean Six Sigma for Operational Excellence MSc, Managing Business Performance MSc, Operations Management MSc, Strategic Project Management MSc, Logistics and Supply Chain Management MSc, Logistics and Supply Chain Management with Business Performance MSc, Logistics and Supply Chain Management with Lean Six Sigma MSc, Logistics and Supply Chain Management with Marketing MSc, Logistics and Supply Chain Management with Shipping and Port Operations MSc, Logistics with Green and Sustainable Supply Chain Management MSc

Economics

Economics MA(Hons), Economics and Accountancy MA(Hons), Economics and Business Law MA(Hons), Economics and Business Management MA(Hons), Economics and Finance MA(Hons), Economics and Marketing MA(Hons)

Postgraduate courses: MSc Economics, Banking and Finance, MSc Energy and Economics, MSc International Finance and Economic Development

Languages and Intercultural Studies

Applied Languages and Translating (French/German) MA(Hons), Applied Languages and Translating (French/Spanish) MA(Hons), Applied Languages and Translating (German/ Spanish) MA(Hons), British Sign Language (Interpreting, Translating and Applied Language Studies) MA(Hons), Languages (Interpreting and Translating) (French/German) MA(Hons), Languages (Interpreting and Translating) (French/Spanish) MA(Hons), Languages

(Interpreting and Translating) (German/Spanish) MA(Hons), Languages (Interpreting and Translating) (French/British Sign Language) MA(Hons), Languages (Interpreting and Translating) (German/British Sign Language) MA(Hons), Languages (Interpreting and Translating) (Spanish/British Sign Language) MA(Hons), French and Applied Language Studies MA(Hons), German and Applied Language Studies MA(Hons), Spanish and Applied Language Studies MA(Hons), International Business Management and Languages: Chinese as Main Language MA(Hons), International Business Management and Languages: French as Main Language MA(Hons), International Business Management and Languages: German as Main Language MA(Hons), International Business Management and Languages: Spanish as Main Language MA(Hons)

Psychology

Psychology (Applied) BSc(Hons), Psychology BSc(Hons), Psychology with Management BSc(Hons)

School of Textiles and Design; www.hw.ac.uk/schools/textiles-design.htm

Postgraduate courses: BSc Fashion Technology, BA Fashion, BA Interior Design, BA Fashion Communication, BA Fashion Marketing and Retailing, BA Design for Textiles

Postgraduate courses: MA Fashion and Textiles Design, MA Interior Architecture and Design, MA Knitwear (Design, Heritage and Production), MSc Ethics in Fashion, MSc Fashion Textiles Management

Edinburgh Business School; www.ebsglobal.net

Postgraduate courses: MBA, DBA, MSc Masters Strategic Planning, MSc Masters Marketing, MSc Masters Financial Management, MSc Masters Human Resource Management

UNIVERSITY OF HERTFORDSHIRE
www.herts.ac.uk

Hertfordshire Business School; www.herts.ac.uk/apply/schools-of-study/business

BA(Hons) Accounting, BA(Hons) Accounting & Finance, BA(Hons) Business Administration, BA(Hons) Business Economics, BA(Hons) Business Studies, BA(Hons) Economics, BA(Hons) Event Management, BA(Hons) Finance, BA(Hons) Human

Resource Management, BA(Hons) IT Management for Business (ITMB), BA(Hons) International Business, BA(Hons) International Management (Dual Award), BA(Hons) International Tourism Management, BA(Hons) Management, BA(Hons) Marketing, BA(Hons) Tourism Management, BA(Hons) Business and Accounting, BA(Hons) Business and Economics, BA(Hons) Business and Finance, BA(Hons) Business and Information Systems, BA(Hons) Business and Event Management, BA(Hons) Business and Marketing, BA(Hons) Business and Human Resources, BA(Hons) Business and Tourism, BA(Hons) Accounting and Economics, BA(Hons) Event Management and Marketing, BA(Hons) Event Management and Tourism, BA(Hons) Finance and Economics, BA(Hons) Marketing and Advertising, BA(Hons) Marketing with Digital Communications, BA(Hons) Marketing with Fashion

Postgraduate courses: MSc Accounting & Financial Management, MSc Business Analysis and Consultancy, MSc Business and Organisational Strategy, MSc Finance and Investment Management, MSc Global Business (Dual Award), MA Human Resource Management, MSc International Business, MSc International Tourism and Hospitality Management, MSc Leadership and Management in Public Services, MSc Management, MSc Marketing, MBA Master of Business Administration, MSc Project Management

School of Computer Science; www.herts.ac.uk/apply/schools-of-study/computer-science

MEng Computer Science, BSc(Hons) Computer Science, BSc(Hons) Computer Science (Artificial Intelligence), BSc(Hons) Computer Science (Networks), BSc(Hons) Computer Science (Software Engineering), BSc(Hons) Information Technology, BSc(Hons) Computer Science with a year abroad

Postgraduate courses: MSc Artificial Intelligence with Robotics, MSc Computer Networking Principles and Practice, MSc Software Engineering, MSc Cyber Security

School of Creative Arts; www.herts.ac.uk/apply/schools-of-study/creative-arts

Design

Architecture BA(Hons), Design Crafts: Textiles BA(Hons), Design Crafts: Ceramics and Glass BA(Hons), Design Crafts: Jewellery BA(Hons), Fashion Design BA(Hons), Fashion and Fashion Business BA(Hons), Graphic Design BA(Hons), Illustration BA(Hons), Interior Architecture and Design BA(Hons), Product and Industrial Design BA(Hons), Model Design (Model Effects BA(Hons), Model Design (Character and Creative Effects) BA(Hons), Model Design (Special Effects) BA(Hons)

Postgraduate courses: MA Graphic Design, MA Illustration, MA Graphic Design (online), MA Illustration (online), MA Product Design, MA Fashion, MA Interior Architecture and Design, MA Experience Design

Film and Media

Film and Television Production BA Hons, Digital Media Design BA(Hons), Photography BA(Hons), Model Design (Model Effects) BA(Hons), Model Design (Special Effects) BA(Hons), Model Design (Character and Creative Effects) BA(Hons), 2D Animation and Character for Digital Media BA(Hons), 3D Computer Animation and Modelling BA(Hons), 3D Games Art and Design BA(Hons), Visual Effects for Film and Television BA(Hons)

Postgraduate courses: MA Film & TV Production, MA Games Art and Design, MA Photography, MA Digital Media Arts, MA Experience Design, MA Animation

Music

Music Composition and Technology BSc Hons, Music Composition and Technology for Film and Games BSc Hons, Songwriting and Music Production BSc Hons, Audio Recording and Production BSc Hons, Music Technology BSc Hons, Sound Design Technology BSc Hons, Music Industry Management BA/BSc Hons

Postgraduate courses: Music Composition for Film and Media MSc, Music and Sound Technology (Audio Engineering/Programming) MSc

Therapies

Postgraduate course: Art Therapy MA

Visual Arts

BA(Hons) Fine Art, BA(Hons) Photography

Postgraduate courses: MA Fine Art, MA Contemporary Textiles

School of Education; www.herts.ac.uk/apply/schools-of-study/education

Bachelor of Education (BEd), BA(Hons) Early Childhood Education, Foundation degree in Early Years, BA(Hons) Education Studies, BA(Hons) Education Studies with Learning and Teaching, BA(Hons) Education Studies with Special Educational Needs & Disability

Postgraduate courses: Postgraduate Certificate in Education (PGCE), MA Education Framework, Doctorate in Education

School of Engineering and Technology; www.herts.ac.uk/apply/schools-of-study/engineering-and-technology

Aerospace

Aerospace Engineering (BEng), Aerospace Engineering (MEng), Aerospace Engineering with Space Technology (BEng Hons), Aerospace Engineering with Space Technology (MEng), Aerospace Systems Engineering (BEng), Aerospace Systems Engineering

(MEng), Aerospace Systems Engineering with Pilot Studies (BEng), Aerospace Systems Engineering with Pilot Studies (MEng), Aerospace Technology with Management (BSc), Aerospace Technology with Pilot Studies (BSc)

Postgraduate course: Aerospace Engineering (MSc)

Automotive

Automotive Engineering (BEng), Automotive Engineering (MEng), Automotive Engineering with Motorsport (BEng), Automotive Engineering with Motorsport (MEng), Automotive Technology with Management (BSc), Motorsport Technology (BSc)

Postgraduate course: Automotive Engineering MSc

Biomedical Engineering

BEng(Hons) Biomedical Engineering, MEng Biomedical Engineering

Digital Technologies

Computer Technology and Networks BSc(Hons), Multimedia and Internet Technology BSc(Hons)

Electrical, Electronic and Communications Engineering

Electronics and Computer Engineering (BEng), Electronics and Computer Engineering (MEng), Electronics and Communication Engineering (BEng), Electronics and Communication Engineering (MEng), Electrical and Electronic Engineering (BEng), Electrical and Electronic Engineering (MEng), Electronic Engineering and Mechatronics (BEng), Electronic Engineering and Mechatronics (MEng)

Postgraduate courses: MSc in Embedded Intelligent Systems, MSc in Radio and Mobile Communication System, MSc in Microelectronics and Computer Engineering, MSc in Power Electronics and Control, MSc in Mechatronics, MSc in Communications and Information Engineering

Manufacturing and Operations Management

Manufacturing Management (MSc), Operations and Supply Chain Management (MSc)

Mechanical Engineering

Mechanical Engineering (BEng), Mechanical Engineering (MEng), Mechanical Engineering and Mechatronics (BEng), Mechanical Engineering and Mechatronics (MEng)

Postgraduate course: Mechanical Engineering MSc

Civil Engineering

BEng(Hons) Civil Engineering, MEng(Hons) Civil Engineering

School of Health and Social Work; www.herts.ac.uk/apply/schools-of-study/ health-and-social-work

Diagnostic radiography

Diagnostic Radiography and Imaging BSc(Hons), Radiotherapy and Oncology BSc(Hons)

Postgraduate courses: Medical Imaging and Radiation Sciences Diagnostic Imaging MSc, Medical Imaging and Radiation Sciences Image Interpretation MSc, Medical Imaging and Radiation Sciences Oncological Sciences MSc, Medical Imaging and Radiation Sciences Ultrasound MSc

Dietetics and nutrition

Nutrition (BSc Hons), Dietetics (BSc Hons)

Postgraduate course: MSc Dietetics (Advanced Practice)

Health visiting

BSc(Hons) Specialist Community Nursing (Community Children's Nursing), BSc(Hons) Specialist Community Nursing (Community District Nursing), BSc(Hons) Specialist Community Nursing (General Practice Nursing), BSc(Hons) Specialist Community Public Health Nursing (Health Visiting), BSc(Hons) Specialist Community Public Health Nursing (School Nursing)

Postgraduate courses: MSc/PgDip Specialist Community Nursing (Community Children's Nursing), MSc/PgDip Specialist Community Nursing (Community District Nursing), MSc/PgDip Specialist Community Nursing (General Practice Nursing), MSc/PgDip Specialist Community Public Health Nursing (Health Visiting), MSc/PgDip Specialist Community Public Health Nursing (School Nursing)

Midwifery

Midwifery with RM BSc(Hons), Midwifery with RM Shortened (BSc Hons), Midwifery and Women's Health (BSc)

Postgraduate courses: Master of Midwifery (Masters), Midwifery and Women's Health (MSc)

Nursing

Adult Nursing Bsc(Hons), Children's Nursing BSc(Hons), Learning Disability Nursing BSc(Hons), Mental Health Nursing BSc(Hons), Contemporary Nursing BSc(Hons)

Postgraduate courses: MSc Adult Nursing, Mental health recovery and social inclusion MSc/PgDip/ PgCert (Online), Contemporary Nursing (MSc)

Radiotherapy

Radiotherapy and Oncology BSc(Hons)

Postgraduate courses: Medical Imaging and Radiation Sciences Diagnostic Imaging (MSc/PgD/PgC), Medical Imaging and Radiation Sciences Image

Interpretation (MSc/PgD/PgC), Medical Imaging and Radiation Sciences Oncological Sciences (MSc/PgD/PgC), Medical Imaging and Radiation Sciences Ultrasound (MSc/PgD/PgC)

Paramedic sciences
Paramedic Science BSc(Hons)
Postgraduate course: Paramedic Science (MSc)

Physiotherapy
Physiotherapy BSc(Hons)
Postgraduate courses: Advanced Physiotherapy (Neuromusculoskeletal) (MSc/PgD), Advanced Physiotherapy (MSc/PgD/PgC)

Social work
Social Work BSc/BSc(Hons)
Postgraduate course: Social Work MSc

School of Humanities; www.herts.ac.uk/apply/schools-of-study/humanities

American Studies
BA(Hons) English Language & Communication with American Studies, BA(Hons) English Literature with American Studies, BA(Hons) History with American Studies, BA(Hons) Philosophy with American Studies

Creative Writing
BA(Hons) Creative Writing and English Literature & Communication, BA(Hons) Creative Writing and Literature, BA(Hons) Creative Writing and History, BA(Hons) Creative Writing and Philosophy, BA(Hons) Journalism and Creative Writing, BA(Hons) Media and Creative Writing
Postgraduate course: MA in Creative Writing

English Language and Communication
English Language & Communication BA, English Language & Communication BA (with various joint options)

English Literature
English Literature BA(Hons), English Literature BA(Hons) (with various joint options)

Film
BA(Hons) English Language & Communication with Film, BA(Hons) History with Film, BA(Hons) Philosophy with Film, BA(Hons) Mass Communications

History
History BA(Hons), History BA(Hons) (with various joint options), BA(Hons) English Language & Communication with Public History, BA(Hons) English Literature with Public History, BA(Hons) History with Public History, BA(Hons) Philosophy with Public History

Journalism
BA(Hons) Mass Communications, BA(Hons) Journalism and Creative Writing, BA(Hons) Journalism and Media, BA(Hons) English Language & Communication and Journalism, BA(Hons) English Literature and Journalism, BA(Hons) History and Journalism, BA(Hons) Journalism and Philosophy

Media Cultures

Philosophy
Philosophy BA(Hons), Philosophy BA(Hons) (with various joint options)

Religious Studies
BA(Hons) English Language & Communication with Religious Studies, BA(Hons) English Literature with Religious Studies, BA(Hons) History with Religious Studies, BA(Hons) Philosophy with Religious Studies

School of Law, Criminology and Political Science

Accelerated (Two-Year) LLB(Hons), LLB(Hons) Law, LLB(Hons) Commercial Law, LLB(Hons) Government and Politics, LLB(Hons) Criminal Justice, BA(Hons) Criminal Justice and Criminology, BA(Hons) Politics and International Relations
Postgraduate course: LLM Master̕sU̕es in Law

School of Life and Medical Sciences; www.herts.ac.uk/apply/schools-of-study/life-and-medical-sciences

Biosciences
Biochemistry (BSc Honours), Biological Sciences (BSc Honours), Biomedical Science (BSc Honours), Healthcare Science (Life Sciences) (BSc Hons), Molecular Biology (BSc Hons), Pharmacology (BSc Hons)
Postgraduate courses: Biotechnology (MSc/PgD/PgC), Molecular Biology (MSc/PgD/PgC), Pharmacology (MSc/PgD/PgC), Pharmacovigilance (MSc/PgD/PgC)

Dietetics and Nutrition
Nutrition (BSc Hons), Dietetics (BSc Hons)
Postgraduate course: MSc Dietetics (Advanced Practice)

Geography, Environment and Agriculture
Geography (BSc Honours), Human Geography (BSc Honours), Human Geography with Environmental Studies (BSc Honours), Physical Geography (BSc Honours), Environmental Management and Ecology (BSc Honours), Environmental Management with Agriculture (BSc Honours)
Postgraduate courses: Environmental Management (MSc/PgD/PgC/AIEMA), Environmental Management for Agriculture (MSc), Sustainable Planning

(MSc), Sustainable Planning and Environmental Management (MSc), Sustainable Planning and Transport (MSc), Water and Environmental Management (MSc/PgD/PgC/AIEMA)

Optometry
Postgraduate course: Optometry (Masters in Optometry MOptom)

Pharmacy
Pharmacy courses MPharm
Postgraduate courses: MSc/PgD/PgC Pharmacy Practice, MSc Advancing Clinical Pharmacy Practice, MSc Advancing Clinical Pharmacy Practice with extended placement, PgDip Pharmacy (Overseas Pharmacists Assessment Programme), MSc in Regulatory Affairs with TOPRA

Pharmacology
Pharmacology (BSc Hons)
Postgraduate course: MSc Pharmacology

Pharmaceutical Science
Pharmaceutical Science BSc(Hons)

Postgraduate medicine
Postgraduate courses: MSc Cardiology and Stroke, MSc Clinical Dermatology, MSc Public Health (online), MSc Health and Medical Simulation, MSc Health and Medical Education, MSc Clinical Skin Integrity and Wound Management, MSc Physician Associate Studies

Psychology
BSc Psychology

Postgraduate courses: Business Psychology (MSc), Occupational Psychology (MSc), Psychology Conversion Course (MSc), Research Methods in Psychology (MSc), Research in Clinical Psychology (MSc), Doctorate in Clinical Psychology (DClinPsy)

Public Health
Postgraduate course: Master of Public Health (Online)

Sports, health and exercise
Sport and Exercise Science (BSc Hons), Sports Studies (BSc/BSc Hons), Sports Therapy (BSc/BSc Hons)

School of Physics, Astronomy and Mathematics; www.herts.ac.uk/apply/schools-of-study/physics-astronomy-and-mathematics

Physics
BSc(Hons) in Physics, BSc(Hons) Physics with Science Education
Postgraduate course: MPhys Physics

Astrophysics
BSc(Hons) in Astrophysics, BSc(Hons) Astrophysics with Science Education
Postgraduate course: MPhys in Astrophysics

Mathematics
Mathematics BSc Honours, Financial Mathematics BSc Honours

HERTFORDSHIRE REGIONAL COLLEGE
www.hrc.ac.uk

Access to higher education courses in the following areas: 3D dimensional design, art & design, business with HRM/accounting/information systems/ marketing computing technologies, fine art practice, graphic design, visual merchandising

NORTH HERTFORDSHIRE COLLEGE
www.nhc.ac.uk

Foundation and extended degrees and other courses covering the following subjects: accounting/information systems/ computing technology, business/with HRM, creative enterprises-fashion & textile, early years, marketing, sports studies, business with HRM/accounting/information systems/marketing

OAKLANDS COLLEGE
www.oaklands.ac.uk

HNC/HND Courses
HNC Civil Engineering Studies (Part-time), HNC in Construction Management, HND Electrical and Electronic Engineering, Extended Degree in Engineering and Technology (Initial Year), HNC Engineering (Mechanical), HNC/HND Music, HNC/HND in Performing Arts, HNC/HND Art and

Design, HNC Electrical and Electronic Engineering, HND Engineering (Mechanical)

Foundation Degrees

Foundation Degree in Animal Management, Foundation Degree in Business Management, Foundation Degree in Business Management with Accounting, Foundation Degree in Business Management with Law, Foundation Degree in Business Management with Marketing, Foundation Degree in Business Management with Event Management, Foundation Degree in Early Years (part-time), Foundation Degree in Media Production, Foundation Degree in Sports Studies

Other Courses

Initial Degree for Extended Degree Programme in Engineering & Technology, BA(Hons) Agriculture

WEST HERTS COLLEGE
www.westherts.ac.uk

Foundation degrees covering the following subjects: Accounting, HRM, Information systems, Law, Marketing, Media systems, Networks, Software development, Early Years, Fashion, Media Production, Photography, Sports Studies

HND courses covering the following subjects: Health and Social Care, Hospitality & Event, Management, Music, Performing Arts, Public Services, Travel and Tourism

THE UNIVERSITY OF HUDDERSFIELD
www.hud.ac.uk

A to D

Accountancy and Finance BA(Hons), Accountancy BA(Hons), Accountancy with Financial Services BA(Hons), Advertising and Marketing Communications BA(Hons), Air Transport and Logistics Management BSc(Hons), Animation BA(Hons), Applied Computing (Top-up) BSc(Hons), Architectural Technology BSc(Hons), Architecture/Architecture (International) (RIBA Part 1) BA(Hons), Automotive and Motorsport Engineering BEng(Hons), Automotive and Motorsport Engineering MEng, Behavioural Sciences BSc(Hons), Biochemistry BSc(Hons), Biochemistry with Research Placement BSc(Hons), Biological Sciences BSc(Hons), Biology (Molecular and Cellular) BSc(Hons), Biomedicine BSc(Hons), Broadcast Journalism BA(Hons), Business Accounting (Top-up) BA(Hons), Business Administration and Management (Top-up) BA(Hons), Business and Human Resource Management BA(Hons), Business and Marketing BA(Hons), Business Economics BSc(Hons), Business Law LLB(Hons), Business Management and Leadership BA(Hons), Business Management BA(Hons), Business Management with Finance BA(Hons), Business Strategy BA(Hons), Business Studies BA(Hons), Business with Financial Services BA(Hons), Business with Supply Chain Management BA(Hons), Business with Sustainability BA(Hons), Certificate in Management Studies (CMS), Cervical Screening (H), Chemical Engineering and Chemistry BSc(Hons), Chemical Engineering BEng(Hons), Chemical Engineering MEng, Chemistry BSc(Hons), Chemistry MChem, Chemistry with Chemical Engineering BSc(Hons), Chemistry with Forensic Science BSc(Hons), Chemistry with Industrial Experience MChem, Childhood Studies BA(Hons), Computer Games Design BA(Hons), Computer Systems Engineering BEng(Hons), Computing BSc(Hons), Computing in Business BA(Hons), Computing MComp, Computing Science BSc(Hons), Computing Science MSci, Computing Science with Games Programming BSc(Hons), Construction Project Management BSc(Hons), Contemporary Art and Illustration BA(Hons), Contemporary Art BA(Hons), Continuing Professional Development for Pharmacy Technicians, Costume with Textiles BA(Hons), Counselling Studies with Mentoring BSc(Hons), Creative Music Technology BMus(Hons), Criminology BSc(Hons), Criminology with Law BSc(Hons), Digital and Social Media Marketing BA(Hons), Drama and English Language BA(Hons), Drama and English Literature BA(Hons), Drama BA(Hons), Drama with Creative Writing BA(Hons)

Postgraduate courses: Accounting MSc, Advanced Architectural Design MA, Advanced Computer Science MSc, Advanced Project Management in Construction MSc, Analytical Bioscience MSc, Analytical Chemistry MSc, Master of Architecture/Architecture (International) (RIBA Part 2), Automotive

Engineering MSc, Banking and Finance MSc, Business Economics MSc, Business English and Intercultural Communication MA, Business MSc, Business with Finance MSc, Business with Human Resource Management MSc, Commercial Law LLM, Creative Pattern Cutting MA, Design Integration and Building Information Modelling (BIM) MSc, Digital Media MA, Drug Discovery and Business Strategy MSc

E to I

Early Years BA(Hons), Economics and Politics BSc(Hons), Economics BSc(Hons), Economics with Financial Services BSc(Hons), Education and Professional Development BA/BA(Hons), Education Human Resource Development and Training BA(Hons), Electronic and Communication Engineering BEng(Hons), Electronic and Electrical Engineering MEng/BEng(Hons), Electronic Engineering and Computer Systems BEng(Hons), Electronic Engineering BEng(Hons), Electronic Engineering MEng, Energy Engineering BEng(Hons), Energy Engineering MEng, English Language and Literature BA(Hons), English Language BA(Hons), English Language with a Modern Language BA(Hons), English Language with Creative Writing BA(Hons), English Literature and History BA(Hons), English Literature BA(Hons), English with a Modern Language BA(Hons), English Literature with Creative Writing BA(Hons), Entrepreneurship BA(Hons), Events Management BA(Hons), Exercise Science BSc(Hons), Fashion Brand Marketing BA(Hons), Fashion Creative Direction BA(Hons), Fashion Design (Fashion Design with Marketing and Production) BA(Hons), Fashion Design (Fashion Design with Textiles) BA(Hons), Film Studies and Drama BA(Hons), Film Studies and English Literature BA(Hons), Film Studies and History BA(Hons), Forensic and Analytical Science BSc(Hons), Forensic and Analytical Science MSci, Geography BSc(Hons), Global Business Administration and Management (Top-up) BA(Hons), Global Business and Logistics Management (Top-up) BA(Hons), Global Marketing (Top-up) BA(Hons), Graphic Design and Animation BA(Hons), Graphic Design BA(Hons), Health and Social Care MSci, History and English Language BA(Hons), History and Politics BA(Hons), History BA(Hons), Hospitality Business Management BA(Hons), Hospitality Business Management with a Modern Language BA(Hons), Human Geography BSc(Hons), Human Resource Management BA(Hons), Illustration BA(Hons), Information and Communication Technology BSc(Hons), Interior Design BA(Hons), International Accountancy (Top-up) BA(Hons), International Business BA(Hons), International Fashion Buying Management BA(Hons), International Politics BSc(Hons), International Trade and Investment (Top-up) BA(Hons)

Postgraduate courses: Early Childhood Studies MA, Early Years Initial Teacher Training (EYTS) – Graduate Entry Mainstream, Economics MSc, Education and Youth Work Studies MA, Education MA, Electronic and Communication Engineering MSc, Electronic and Embedded Systems Engineering MSc, Engineering Control Systems and Instrumentation MSc, Engineering Management MSc, English Language and Applied Linguistics MA, Fashion Textile Practices MA, Finance MSc, Financial Economics MSc, Forensic and Analytical Science MSc, Forensic Science (Forensic Anthropology) MSc, Forensic Science (Forensic Biology) MSc, Forensic Science (Forensic Entomology) MSc, Forensic Science (Forensic Toxicology) MSc, Graphic Design MA, Guidance Professional Studies PgDip, Health Service Research MSc, Hospitality Management Master of Business Administration (MBA), Information Systems Management MSc, Intercultural Communication MA, International Business Law LLM, International Business Management MSc, International Business with Financial Services MSc, International Business with Hospitality MSc, International Business with Tourism MSc, International Education MA, International Fashion Design Management MA, International Finance with Law MSc, International Hospitality and Tourism Management MSc, International Hospitality Management MSc, International Human Resource Management (HRM) MA, International Law LLM, International Marketing MSc, Investigative Psychology MSc

J to N

Journalism BA(Hons), Law (Exempting) Master of Law and Practice (MLP) incorporating LLB(Hons), Law LLB(Hons), Law with Criminology LLB(Hons), Learning Support BA(Hons), Lifelong Learning Cert Ed pre-service/in-service, Logistics and Supply Chain Management BSc(Hons), Marketing BA(Hons), Marketing with Public Relations BA(Hons), Mechanical Engineering (Top-up) BEng(Hons), Mechanical Engineering BEng(Hons), Mechanical Engineering MEng, Media and Popular Culture BA(Hons), Medical Biochemistry BSc(Hons), Medical Biology BSc(Hons), Medical Genetics BSc(Hons), Midwifery Studies BSc(Hons), Music and Sound for Image BA(Hons), Music BMus(Hons), Music Journalism BA(Hons), Music Performance BMus(Hons), Music Technology and Audio Systems BSc(Hons), Music Technology and Popular Music BA(Hons), Music Technology BA(Hons), Nursing (Adult) BSc(Hons), Nursing (Child) BSc(Hons), Nursing (Learning Disability) BSc(Hons), Nursing (Mental Health) BSc(Hons), Nursing Studies (Top-up) (Distance Learning) BSc(Hons)

Postgraduate courses: Law with Finance LLM, Learning and Development Management MA, Lifelong Learning PGCE pre-service, Logistics and Supply Chain Management MSc, Management MSc, Management with Entrepreneurship MSc, Management with Hospitality MSc, Management with International Business MSc, Management with Leadership MSc, Management with Marketing MSc, Marketing Communications MSc, Marketing MSc, Master of Business Administration (MBA), Master of Law LLM, Mechanical Engineering Design MSc, Mechanical Engineering MSc, Music Performance Postgraduate Diploma

O to S

Occupational Therapy BSc(Hons), Operating Department Practice BSc(Hons), Perioperative Studies (Top-up) (Distance Learning) BSc(Hons), Pharmaceutical Chemistry BSc(Hons), Pharmaceutical Chemistry MSci, Pharmacology BSc(Hons), Pharmacy MPharm, Photography BA(Hons), Physical Geography BSc(Hons), Physiotherapy BSc(Hons), Podiatry BSc(Hons), Policing and Investigation BSc(Hons), Politics and Criminology BSc(Hons), Politics BSc(Hons), Politics with Sociology BSc(Hons), Popular Music BMus(Hons), Popular Music Production BA(Hons), Popular Music Production BSc(Hons), Primary Education (Early Years and Key Stage 1) BA(Hons) with QTS, Product Design BA/BSc(Hons), Psychology BSc(Hons), Psychology with Counselling BSc(Hons), Psychology with Criminology BSc(Hons), Religion and Education BA(Hons), Science Extended Degree leading to a BSc(Hons) Degree, Secondary Music Education BA(Hons) with QTS, Secondary Religious Education BA(Hons) with QTS, Social Work MSc, Social Work MSci, Sociology and Criminology BSc(Hons), Sociology and Psychology BSc(Hons), Sociology BSc(Hons), Software Engineering BSc(Hons), Software Engineering MEng, Sport and Exercise Nutrition MSci, Sport Exercise and Nutrition BSc(Hons), Sport Science BSc(Hons), Sport, Exercise and Nutrition BSc(Hons), Sports Journalism BA(Hons), Supply Chain Management BSc(Hons), Supply Chain Management with Logistics (Top-up) BSc(Hons), Supporting Learning and Assessment in Practice (Distance Learning), Surveying (Building Surveying) BSc(Hons), Surveying (Quantity Surveying) BSc(Hons)

Postgraduate courses: Oil and Gas Engineering with Management MSc, Operations and Supply Chain Management MSc, Pharmaceutical and Analytical Science MSc, Pharmaceutical Formulation and Business Strategy MSc, Podiatry MSc, Primary Education (Early Years and Key Stage 1) PGCE with QTS, Primary Education PGCE with QTS, Project Management MSc, Psychology MSc, Risk Disaster and Environmental Management MSc, School Direct (Primary/Secondary) PGCE with QTS, Secondary Business Education PGCE with QTS, Secondary Computer Science PGCE with QTS, Secondary English PGCE with QTS, Secondary Mathematics PGCE with QTS, Secondary Music PGCE with QTS, Secondary Science with Biology PGCE with QTS, Secondary Science with Chemistry PGCE with QTS, Secondary Science with Physics PGCE with QTS, Social Research and Evaluation MSc (Distance Learning), Strategic Human Resource Management MSc, Stylistics MA, Sustainable Architecture MSc

T to Y

TESOL (Top-up) BA(Hons), TESOL and Education BA(Hons), TESOL and Younger Learners (Top-up) BA(Hons), Textile Practice (Surface Design) BA/BSc(Hons), Textile Practice (Textile Crafts and Art) BA/BSc(Hons), Textile Practice (Textile Design) BA/BSc(Hons), Transport and Logistics Management BSc(Hons), Travel and Tourism Management BA(Hons), Web Design BSc(Hons), Web Technologies BSc(Hons), Youth and Community Studies (Top up) BA(Hons), Youth and Community Work BA(Hons), Youth and Community Work In-Service BA(Hons)

Postgraduate courses: Teaching English to Speakers of Other Languages MA, Technology Enhanced Learning and Innovation MA, Theory of Podiatric Surgery MSc, Urban Design MA, Youth and Community Work Professional Studies PgDip

UNIVERSITY OF HULL
www.hull.ac.uk

Faculty of Arts, Cultures and Education;
www.hull.ac.uk/Faculties/face.aspx

School of Arts; www.hull.ac.uk/Faculties/face/arts.aspx

Drama

BA(Hons) Drama, BA(Hons) Drama and English, BA(Hons) Drama and Film Studies, BA(Hons) Drama with a Modern Language, BA(Hons) Music and Théatre

Postgraduate course: MA in Theatre Making

English

BA(Hons) Creative Writing and English, BA(Hons) Creative Writing and Film Studies, BA(Hons) Drama and English, BA(Hons) English, BA(Hons) English and American Literature and Culture, BA(Hons) English and Film Studies, BA(Hons) English and Music, BA(Hons) English and Philosophy, BA(Hons) English Language, Linguistics and Cultures, BA(Hons) English with a Modern Language, BA(Hons) History and English

Postgraduate course: MA/MRes in English (Creative Writing and English Literature)

Film and Digital Media

BA(Hons) Creative Writing and Film Studies, BA(Hons) Digital Design, BA(Hons) Digital Design with a Modern Language, BA(Hons) Drama and Film Studies, BA(Hons) English and Film Studies, BA(Hons) Film Studies, BA(Hons) Film Studies with a Modern Language, BA(Hons) Game and Entertainment Design, BA(Hons) Game and Entertainment Design with a Modern Language, BA(Hons) Media Studies, BA(Hons) Music and Film Studies

Postgraduate course: MA in Digital Media

Music

BA(Hons) Creative Music Technology, BA(Hons) English and Music, BA(Hons) Music (Jazz), BA(Hons) Music (Popular), BA(Hons) Music and Film Studies, BA(Hons) Music and Theatre, BA Music, BMus Music, BA(Hons) Music with a Modern Language

Postgraduate course: MMus in Music (Musicology, Composition, Performance, Technology)

School of Education and Social Sciences; www.hull.ac.uk/Faculties/face/ess.aspx

Criminology

BA(Hons) Criminology, BA(Hons) Criminology and Sociology, BA(Hons) Criminology with Forensic Science, BA(Hons) Criminology with Law, BA(Hons) Criminology with Psychology, LLB Law with Criminology, BSc(Hons) Psychology with Criminology

Postgraduate course: MA in Criminal Justice and Crime Control

Education, Teaching and Childhood Studies

BA(Hons) Early Childhood Studies, BA(Hons) Education Studies, BA(Hons) Education Studies with TESOL, BA(Hons) Education Studies, Social Inclusion and Special Needs, FdA Early Childhood Studies, BA(Hons) Learning and Teaching (Primary QTS) (top-up), FdEd Learning Support (part-time), BA(Hons) Primary Teaching, BA(Hons) Working with Children, Young People and Families, BA(Hons) Youth Work and Community Development

Postgraduate courses: MA in Education, MA in Education and Digital Technologies, MA in Education and Early Childhood, MA in Education and Leadership, MA in Education, Inclusion and Special Needs, MA in Pedagogy and Practice

Sociology and Social Sciences

BA(Hons) Criminology and Sociology, BA(Hons) Philosophy and Religion, BA(Hons) Sociology, BA(Hons) Sociology (Social Anthropology)

Postgraduate courses: MA in Women's and Gender Studies (GEMMA), MSc/MA in Social Research

Social Work, Youth and Community Development

BA(Hons) Education Studies, Social Inclusion and Special Needs, BA(Hons) Social Work, BA(Hons) Working with Children, Young People and Families, BA(Hons) Youth Work and Community Development

Postgraduate course: MA in Social Work

School of Histories, Languages and Cultures; www.hull.ac.uk/Faculties/face/hlc.aspx

American Studies

BA(Hons) American Studies, BA(Hons) American Studies with a Modern Language, BA(Hons) English and American Literature and Culture, BA(Hons) History and American Studies

History

BA(Hons) Heritage and History, BA(Hons) History, BA(Hons) History and American Studies, BA(Hons) History and Archaeology, BA(Hons) History and English, BA(Hons) History and Politics, BA(Hons) History with a Modern Language
Postgraduate courses: MA in History

Languages

BA(Hons) American Studies with a Modern Language, BA(Hons) Chinese and French (Dual Languages), BA(Hons) Chinese and German (Dual Languages), BA(Hons) Chinese and Italian (Dual Languages), BA(Hons) Chinese and Spanish (Dual Languages), BA(Hons) Chinese Studies, BA(Hons) Combined Three Languages, BA(Hons) Digital Design with a Modern Language, BA(Hons) Drama with a Modern Language, BA(Hons) Dual Languages, BA(Hons) English Language, Linguistics and Cultures, BA(Hons) English with a Modern Language, BA(Hons) Film Studies with a Modern Language, BA(Hons) French and German (Dual Languages), BA(Hons) French and Italian (Dual Languages), BA(Hons) French and Spanish (Dual Languages), BA(Hons) French Studies, BA(Hons) Game and Entertainment Design with a Modern Language, BA(Hons) German and Italian (Dual Languages), BA(Hons) German and Spanish (Dual Languages), BA(Hons) German Studies, BA(Hons) History with a Modern Language, BA(Hons) Italian and Spanish (Dual Languages), BA(Hons) Italian Studies, LLB Law with a Modern Language, BA(Hons) Music with a Modern Language, BA(Hons) Spanish and Latin American Studies
Postgraduate courses: MA in TESOL, MA in TESOL with Translation Studies, MA in Translation Studies, MA in Translation Studies with TESOL

Philosophy

BA(Hons) English and Philosophy, BA(Hons) Philosophy, BA(Hons) Philosophy and Politics, BA(Hons) Philosophy and Religion, BA(Hons) Philosophy, Politics and Economics

Faculty of Business, Law and Politics; www.hull.ac.uk/Faculties/fblp.aspx

Hull University Business School; www.hull.ac.uk/Faculties/fblp/hubs.aspx

Accounting and Finance

BSc(Hons) Accounting, BSc(Hons) Accounting and Financial Management, BA(Hons) Business Management and Accounting, BA(Hons) Business Management and Financial Management, BSc(Hons) Economics and Accounting, BSc(Hons) Economics and Financial Management, BSc(Hons) Financial Management
Postgraduate courses: MSc in Accounting and Finance, MSc in Finance and Investment, MSc in Financial Management, MSc in Professional Accounting

Business and Management

BA(Hons) Business Economics, BA(Hons) Business Management, BA(Hons) Business Management (part-time), BA(Hons) Business Management and Accounting, BA(Hons) Business Management and Economics, BA(Hons) Business Management and Financial Management, BA(Hons) Business Management and Marketing, BA(Hons) Business Management and Supply Chain, BA(Hons) Business Management with Entrepreneurship, BA(Hons) Business Management with Human Resource Management, BA(Hons) Business Management with ICT, BA(Hons) Business Management with Sustainability, BA(Hons) International Business, BA(Hons) International Business Management (1 year top up), LLB Law with Business Management, MBus Management
Postgraduate courses: Hull Executive MBA (EMBA), MSc in Business Management, MSc in Business Management (with Internship), MSc in Economics and Business, MSc in Human Resource Management, MSc in International Business

Economics and Business Economics

BA(Hons) Business Economics, BA(Hons) Business Economics and Marketing, BA(Hons) Business Management and Economics, BSc(Hons) Economics, BSc(Hons) Economics and Accounting, BSc(Hons) Economics and Financial Management, BA(Hons) Philosophy, Politics and Economics
Postgraduate course: MSc in Economics and Business

Marketing

BA(Hons) Business Economics and Marketing, BA(Hons) Business Management and Marketing, BA(Hons) Marketing
Postgraduate courses: MSc in Advertising and Marketing, MSc in Marketing Management

Logistics and Supply Chain Management

BA(Hons) Business Management and Supply Chain, BSc(Hons) Logistics and Supply Chain Management
Postgraduate course: MSc in Logistics and Supply Chain Management

School of Law and Politics

Law

BA(Hons) Criminology with Law, LLB International Law, LLB Law, LLB Law (Senior Status), LLB Law

with a Modern Language, LLB Law with Business Management, LLB Law with Criminology, LLB Law with Legislative Studies, LLB Law with Politics
Postgraduate course: LLM in International Law

Politics and International Relations

BA(Hons) British Politics and Legislative Studies, BA(Hons) History and Politics, LLB Law with Legislative Studies, LLB Law with Politics, BA(Hons) Philosophy and Politics, BA(Hons) Philosophy, Politics and Economics, BA(Hons) Politics, BA(Hons) Politics and International Relations, BA(Hons) War and Security Studies
Postgraduate courses: MA in Applied Global Ethics, MA in International Politics, MA in Strategy and International Security

Faculty of Health Sciences; www.hull.ac.uk/Faculties/fhs.aspx

Hull York Medical School; www.hyms.ac.uk

Hull MBBS, BSc Biomedical Sciences
Postgraduate courses: Certificate in Health Professions Education, Diploma in Health Professions Education, MSc in Health Professions Education, MSc in Physician Associate Studies, MSc Clinical Anatomy, MSc Clinical Anatomy and Education, MSc in Human Anatomy & Evolution, Masters in Public Health

School of Health and Social Work; www.hull.ac.uk/Faculties/fhs/shsw.aspx

Health, Nursing and Midwifery

BSc(Hons) Midwifery, BSc(Hons) Midwifery (Short Programme), BSc(Hons) Nursing (Adult), BSc(Hons) Nursing (Child), BSc(Hons) Nursing (Learning Disability), BSc(Hons) Nursing (Mental Health), BSc(Hons) Nursing Studies, BSc(Hons) Operating Department Practice, BSc(Hons) Paramedic Science
Postgraduate courses: MRes in Health Studies, MSc in Advanced Practice, MSc in Colonoscopy, MSc in Gastroenterology Care, MSc in Health Studies, MSc in Healthcare Improvement Leadership, MSc in Leadership in Health and Social Care, PGCert Educator in Practice, PGCert Practice Teacher, PGCert/PGDip Cognitive Behavioural Therapy (Secondary Care), Postgraduate Diploma in Midwifery (Short Programme)

Social Work, Youth and Community Development

BA(Hons) Education Studies, Social Inclusion and Special Needs, BA(Hons) Social Work, BA(Hons) Working with Children, Young People and Families, BA(Hons) Youth Work and Community Development

Postgraduate course: MA in Social Work

School of Life Sciences; www.hull.ac.uk/Faculties/fhs/sls.aspx

Biomedical Sciences

BSc(Hons) Biomedical Science, BSc(Hons) Human Biology
Postgraduate courses: MSc in Biomedical Science, MSc in Cancer Imaging, MSc in Translational Oncology

Psychology

BSc(Hons) Criminology with Psychology, BSc(Hons) Psychology, BSc(Hons) Psychology with Criminology
Postgraduate courses: MSc in Clinical Applications of Psychology, MSc in Health Psychology

Sport, Health and Exercise Sciences

BSc(Hons) Applied Exercise Science for Health, BSc(Hons) Applied Sport Science for Performance, BSc(Hons) Sport and Exercise Nutrition, BSc(Hons) Sport Rehabilitation, BSc(Hons) Sports Coaching and Performance Science
MSc in Cancer Rehabilitation, MSc in Cardiovascular Rehabilitation, MSc in Clinical Exercise Physiology

Faculty of Science and Engineering

School of Engineering and Computer Science

Chemical Engineering

MEng Chemical and Energy Engineering, BEng Chemical Engineering
Postgraduate courses: MSc in Chemical Engineering, MSc in Energy Engineering, MSc in Public Engagement and Science Communication

Electrical and Electronic Engineering

BEng Control and Instrumentation Engineering, BEng Electrical and Electronic Engineering, MEng Electrical, Electronic and Energy Engineering, BEng Electronic Engineering
Postgraduate courses: MSc in Electrical and Electronic Engineering, MSc in Energy Engineering, MSc in Public Engagement and Science Communication

Computer Science

BSc(Hons) Computer Science, BSc(Hons) Computer Science (Software Engineering), BSc(Hons) Computer Science (with Teacher Training), BSc(Hons) Computer Science for Games Development, BSc(Hons) Computing
Postgraduate courses: MSc in Advanced Computer Science, MSc in Computer Science (Security and Distributed Computing), MSc in Computer Science (Software Engineering), MSc in Computer Science for

Games Development, MSc in Public Engagement and Science Communication

Mechanical Engineering

MEng Mechanical and Energy Engineering, BEng Mechanical and Medical Engineering, BEng Mechanical Engineering, BEng Mechanical Engineering and Manufacturing

Postgraduate courses: MSc in Energy Engineering, MSc in Mechanical Engineering, MSc in Public Engagement and Science Communication

Medical and Biomedical Engineering

BEng Biomedical Engineering, BEng Mechanical and Medical Engineering

Postgraduate courses: MSc in Biomedical Engineering, MSc in Public Engagement and Science Communication

School of Environmental Sciences
www.hull.ac.uk/Faculties/fse/es.aspx

Biological and Environmental Science

BSc(Hons) Biology, BSc(Hons) Biology with Ecology, BSc(Hons) Ecology and Environment, BSc(Hons) Human Biology, BSc(Hons) Marine Biology, BSc(Hons) Zoology

Postgraduate courses: MSc in Environmental Change, Management and Monitoring, MSc in Public Engagement and Science Communication

Geography and Geology

BA(Hons) Geography, BSc(Hons) Geography, BSc(Hons) Geology, BSc(Hons) Geology with

Physical Geography, BA(Hons) Human Geography, BSc(Hons) Physical Geography

Postgraduate courses: MSc in Public Engagement and Science Communication, MSc in Renewable Energy

School of Mathematics and Physical Sciences; www.hull.ac.uk/Faculties/fse/mp.aspx

Chemistry

BSc(Hons) Biochemistry, BSc(Hons) Chemistry (top-up) (part-time), BSc(Hons) Chemistry, BSc(Hons) Chemistry (Forensic and Analytical Science), FdSc Chemical Sciences (part-time), NEBOSH National Diploma in Environmental Management (part-time), NEBOSH National Diploma in Occupational Health and Safety (part-time), BSc(Hons) Safety and Environmental Management (with NEBOSH) (part-time)

Postgraduate courses: MSc in Analytical and Forensic Chemistry, MSc in Public Engagement and Science Communication, MSc/MRes Environmental Management (in partnership with NEBOSH), MSc/MRes in Occupational Health and Safety Management (in partnership with NEBOSH), MSc/MRes in Occupational Health, Safety and Environmental Management (in partnership with NEBOSH)

Mathematics

BSc(Hons) Mathematics

Physics and Astrophysics

BSc(Hons) Physics, MPhys Physics (with Teacher Training), BSc(Hons) Physics with Astrophysics, BSc(Hons) Theoretical Physics

---

BISHOP BURTON COLLEGE
www.bishopburton.ac.uk

FdSc Sport, Exercise Science and Health, FdSc Animal Management and Behaviour, FdSc Applied Canine Behaviour and Training, FdA Design, FdA Fashion and Clothing Design, FdA Professional Practice for Early Years, FdSc Agriculture, FdSc Agriculture (Farm Business Administration), FdSc Agriculture (Precision Crop Technology), FdSc Ecology and Environmental Management, FdSc Equine Therapy and Rehabilitation, FdSc Equine Sports Science and Coaching, FdSc Business Management for the Equine Industry, FdA Floristry Design, FdA Policing and Criminology, HNC in Precision Technology (leading to a BTEC HNC/Diploma in General Engineering), BSc(Hons) Agricultural Resource Management (Top Up), BSc Applied Animal Behaviour and Training, BSc Bioveterinary Science, BSc Animal Behaviour and Welfare (Top Up), BSc Canine

Behaviour Management (Top Up), MSc Applied Animal Behaviour and Training, BA Design (Top Up), BA Fashion, Design and Manufacture (Top Up), HNC/HND in Business, HNC/HND in Travel and Tourism Management, BSc Ecology and Environmental Management (Top Up), BSc Sport, Exercise Science and Health, FdSc Wildlife and Conservation Management, BSc Wildlife and Conservation Management (Top Up), BSc(Hons) Equine Therapy and Rehabilitation, BSc(Hons) Equine Sports Science and Coaching, BSc(Hons) Equine Science, BSc(Hons) Business Management for the Equine Industry, BA Floristry Design (Top Up), HND Horticulture (Garden Design), HNC Horticulture (Garden Design), BA Policing and Criminology (Top Up), City and Guilds Level 3 Award in Education and Training, Professional Graduate Certificate in Education (Lifelong

Learning) and Certificate in Education, City and Guilds Level 5 Diploma in Education and Training, BA(Hons) Education and Professional Development

DONCASTER COLLEGE
www.don.ac.uk

Art, Design and Media
FdA Illustration and Concept Art, HND in Creative Media Production – Computer Games Design/Animation, BA(Hons) Fine Art and Crafts, BA(Hons) Games Design and Animation (Top Up), BA(Hons) Graphic Design, BA(Hons) Graphic Design (distance learning), BA(Hons) Illustration and Concept Art
Postgraduate courses: MA in Creative Industries: Practice, Business and Innovation, MA in Creative Pattern Cutting

Computing
HNC Computing & Systems Development, HND Computing & Systems Development

Early Years
FdA Early Childhood Development and Learning in Practice, FdA Supporting Children with Special Educational Needs and Disability, BA(Hons) Early Childhood Studies, BA(Hons) Early Childhood Studies (top up), BA(Hons) Early Childhood Studies (top up) Northern Ireland, BA(Hons) Early Childhood Studies (top up – distance learning)
Postgraduate courses: MA in Early Childhood Studies, MA in Early Childhood Studies (Distance Learning), MA in Education Studies (Primary/Secondary/SEND)

Education
BA(Hons) Education and Advancing Professional Practice

Foundation for Counselling and Relationship Studies
BA(Hons) Counselling Solutions (Top Up)
Postgraduate courses: Postgraduate Diploma Psychosexual Therapy, MA in Contemporary Relationship Studies

Hospitality and Catering
Professional Culinary Arts Diploma Level 4

Humanities and Social Sciences
BA(Hons) Applied Social Science, BA(Hons) Criminal Justice, BA(Hons) English, BA(Hons) Psychology

in the Community, HNC in Health and Social Care, HND in Health and Social Care, FdSc Professional Practice in Health and Social Care
Postgraduate courses: MA in Literature and Digital Culture

Leadership and Management
BA(Hons) Business Management, BA(Hons) International Football Business Management
Postgraduate courses: MBA Masters in Business Administration, Postgraduate Diploma in Human Resource Management, MSc in Human Resource Management

Music and Performing Arts
FdA Live Performance Technology, FdA Performing Arts in the Community (Dance, Drama, Music), BA(Hons) Creative Music Technology, BA(Hons) Performing Arts in the Community Top Up (Dance, Drama, Music)

Sports
BA(Hons) Physical Education and Sports Coaching, BSc(Hons) Sport Science and Coaching in Football (Distance Learning), BSc(Hons) Sports, Fitness and Exercise Science, BSc(Hons) Sports, Exercise and Health Science (Top Up)

Advanced Technologies
HNC Construction, HND Construction, HND Construction (one year conversion), HNC Electrical/Electronic Engineering, HND Electrical/Electronic Engineering (top-up), HNC Mechanical Engineering, HND Mechanical Engineering (one year conversion)

Teacher Education and Professional Development
Postgraduate courses: MEd in Advancing Professional Practice, Professional Graduate/Postgraduate Certificate in Education (PgCE/PGCE), Certificate in Education (Cert Ed)

IMPERIAL COLLEGE, LONDON
www.imperial.ac.uk

Department of Aeronautics;
www.imperial.ac.uk/engineering/
departments/aeronautics

MEng Aeronautical Engineering, MEng Aeronautics with Spacecraft Engineering

Postgraduate courses: MSc Advanced Aeronautical Engineering, MSc Advanced Computational Methods for Aeronautics, Flow Management and Fluid-Structure Interaction, MSc Composites: the Science, Technology and Engineering Application of Advanced Composites, MRes Fluid Dynamics Across Scales

Department of Bioengineering;
www.imperial.ac.uk/engineering/
departments/bioengineering

MEng Biomedical Engineering, MEng Molecular Bioengineering, Biomedical Science, BSc Medical Biosciences, BSc Medical Biosciences with Management

Postgraduate courses: MRes Bioengineering, MSc Biomedical Engineering, MSc Human and Biological Robotics, MRes Medical Device Design and Entrepreneurship, MRes Neurotechnology

Imperial College Business School;
www.imperial.ac.uk/business-school

Postgraduate courses: MSc Business Analytics, MSc Climate Change, Management and Finance (delivered in partnership with the Grantham Institute), MSc Economics and Strategy for Business, MSc Finance, MSc Finance and Accounting, MBA, MSc Innovation, Entrepreneurship and Management, MSc International Health Management, MSc Investment and Wealth Management, MSc Management, MBA (Executive), MBA (Global Online), MBA (Weekend), MSc Risk Management and Financial Engineering, MSc Strategic Marketing

Department of Chemical Engineering;
www.imperial.ac.uk/engineering/
departments/chemical-engineering

BSc Chemical Engineering, BSc Chemical with Nuclear Engineering

Postgraduate courses: MSc Advanced Chemical Engineering, MSc Advanced Chemical Engineering with Biotechnology, MSc Advanced Chemical Engineering with Process Systems Engineering, MSc Advanced Chemical Engineering with Structured

Product Engineering, MRes Molecular Science and Engineering (delivered by the Institute for Molecular Science and Engineering), MSc/PGDip/PGCert Process Automation, Instrumentation and Control

Department of Chemistry;
www.imperial.ac.uk/natural-sciences/
departments/chemistry

BSc Chemistry, MSCi Chemistry, MSCi Chemistry with French for Science, MSCi Chemistry with German for Science, BSc Chemistry with Management, MSCi Chemistry with Medicinal Chemistry, MSCi Chemistry with Molecular Physics, MSCi Chemistry with Spanish for Science

Postgraduate courses: MRes Bioimaging Sciences, MRes Catalysis: Chemistry and Engineering, MRes Chemical Biology: Multidisciplinary Physical Scientists for Next Generation Biological, Biomedical and Pharmaceutical Research and Development, MRes Drug Discovery and Development: Multidisciplinary Science for Next Generation Therapeutics, MRes Green Chemistry, Energy and the Environment, MRes Nanomaterials, MRes Plant Chemical Biology: Multidisciplinary Research for Next Generation Agri-Sciences

Department of Civil and Environmental Engineering; www.imperial.ac.uk/
engineering/departments/civil-engineering

MEng Civil Engineering

Postgraduate courses: MSc Concrete Structures, MSc Concrete Structures and Business Management, MSc Earthquake Engineering, MSc Engineering Fluid Mechanics for the Offshore, Coastal and Built Environments, MSc Environmental Engineering, MSc Environmental Engineering and Business Management, MSc Environmental Engineering and Sustainable Development, MSc General Structural Engineering, MSc Hydrology and Business Management, MSc Hydrology and Sustainable Development, MSc Hydrology and Water Resources Management, MSc Soil Mechanics, MSc Soil Mechanics and Business Management, MSc Soil Mechanics and Engineering Seismology, MSc Soil Mechanics and Environmental Geotechnics, MSc Soil Mechanics and Sustainable Development, MSc Structural Steel Design, MSc Structural Steel Design and Business Management,

MSc Transport, MSc Transport and Business Management, MSc Transport and Sustainable Development

Department of Computing;
www.imperial.ac.uk/engineering/departments/computing

MEng Computing (Artificial Intelligence), BEng Computing, MEng Computing (Computation in Biology and Medicine), MEng Computing (Computational Management), MEng Computing (Games, Vision, Interaction), MEng Computing (International Programme of Study), MEng Computing, MEng Computing (Software Engineering), BEng Mathematics and Computer Science, MEng Mathematics and Computer Science (Computational Statistics), MEng Mathematics and Computer Science, MEng Mathematics and Computer Science (Pure Maths and Computational Logic)

Postgraduate courses: MSc Advanced Computing, MRes Advanced Computing, MSc Computing (Artificial Intelligence), MSc Computing (Computational Management), MSc Computing (Machine Learning), MSc Computing (Security and Reliability), MSc Computing (Software Engineering), MSc Computing (Visual Computing and Robotics), MSc Computing Science

Dyson School of Design Engineering;
www.imperial.ac.uk/engineering/departments/design-engineering

MEng Design Engineering

Postgraduate courses: MA/MSc Global Innovation Design, MA/MSc Innovation Design Engineering

Department of Earth Science and Engineering; www.imperial.ac.uk/engineering/departments/earth-science

BSc Geology, MSci Geology, MSci Geology and Geophysics, BSc Geophysics, MSci Geophysics, MSci Petroleum Geoscience

Postgraduate courses: MSc Metals and Energy Finance, MSc Petroleum Engineering, MSc Petroleum Geoscience

Department of Electrical and Electronic Engineering; www.imperial.ac.uk/engineering/departments/electrical-engineering

BEng Electrical and Electronic Engineering, MEng Electrical and Electronic Engineering, MEng Electrical and Electronic Engineering with Management, BEng Electronic and Information Engineering, MEng Electronic and Information Engineering

Postgraduate courses: MSc Analogue and Digital Integrated Circuit Design, MSc Communications and Signal Processing, MSc Control Systems, MSc Future Power Networks

Centre for Environment Policy;
www.imperial.ac.uk/natural-sciences/departments/environmental-policy

Postgraduate courses: MSc Environmental Technology; MSc Sustainable Retirement Investment and Management

Department of Life Sciences;
www.imperial.ac.uk/natural-sciences/departments/life-sciences

BSc Biochemistry, BSc Biochemistry with French for Science, BSc Biochemistry with German for Science, BSc Biochemistry with Management, BSc Biochemistry with Spanish for Science, BSc Biological Sciences, BSc Biological Sciences with French for Science, BSc Biological Sciences with German for Science, BSc Biological Sciences with Management, BSc Biological Sciences with Spanish for Science, BSc Biotechnology, BSc Biotechnology with French for Science, BSc Biotechnology with German for Science, BSc Biotechnology with Management, BSc Biotechnology with Spanish for Science, BSc Ecology and Environmental Biology, BSc Microbiology

Postgraduate courses: MSc Applied Biosciences and Biotechnology, MSc Bioinformatics and Theoretical Systems Biology, MRes Biosystematics, MSc Computational Methods in Ecology and Evolution, MRes Computational Methods in Ecology and Evolution, MSc Conservation Science, MSc Ecological Applications, MSc Ecology, Evolution and Conservation, MRes Ecology, Evolution and Conservation Research, MRes Ecosystem and Environmental Change, MRes Molecular and Cellular Biosciences, MRes Molecular Plant and Microbial Sciences, MRes Structural Molecular Biology, MRes Systems and Synthetic Biology, MSc Taxonomy and Biodiversity, MRes Tropical Forest Ecology

Department of Materials;
www.imperial.ac.uk/engineering/departments/materials

MEng Biomaterials and Tissue Engineering, BEng Materials Science and Engineering, MEng Materials Science and Engineering, BEng Materials with Management, MEng Materials with Nuclear Engineering

Postgraduate courses: MSc Advanced Materials Science and Engineering, MSc Advanced Nuclear Engineering

Department of Mathematics; www.imperial.ac.uk/natural-sciences/ departments/mathematics

BSc Mathematics, MSci Mathematics, BSc Mathematics (Pure Mathematics), BSc Mathematics with Applied Mathematics/Mathematical Physics, BSc Mathematics with Education, BSc Mathematics with Mathematical Computation, BSc Mathematics with Statistics, BSc Mathematics with Statistics for Finance, BSc Mathematics, Optimisation and Statistics

Postgraduate courses: MSc Applied Mathematics, MSc Mathematics and Finance, MSc Pure Mathematics, MSc Statistics, MRes Stochastic Analysis and Mathematical Finance

Department of Mechanical Engineering; www.imperial.ac.uk/engineering/ departments/mechanical-engineering

MEng Mechanical Engineering, MEng Mechanical with Nuclear Engineering

Postgraduate courses: MSc Advanced Mechanical Engineering, MSc Sustainable Energy Futures (delivered by Energy Futures Lab)

Department of Medicine; www.imperial.ac.uk/medicine/ departments/department-of-medicine

MBBS Medicine (Lee Kong Chian School of Medicine, Singapore), MBBS/BSc Medicine

Postgraduate courses: MBBS Medicine (Graduate entry), MSc/PGCert Allergy, MRes Bacterial Pathogenesis and Infection, MRes Clinical Research (Diabetes and Obesity), MRes Clinical Research (Human Nutrition), MRes Clinical Research (Human Vaccinology), MRes Clinical Research (Translational Medicine), MRes Experimental Neuroscience, MSc Functional Omics, MSc Human Molecular Genetics, MSc Immunology, MRes Molecular and Cellular Basis of Infection, MRes Molecular Basis of Human Disease, MSc Molecular Biology and Pathology of Viruses, MSc Molecular Medicine, PGCert Paediatrics and Child Health, PGDip Paediatrics and Child Health, MSc Paediatrics and Child Health, MSc Translational Neuroscience

National Heart and Lung Institute; www.imperial.ac.uk/medicine/ departments/nhli

Postgraduate courses: MSc Cardiorespiratory Nursing, PGCert/PGDip/MSc Cardiovascular and Respiratory Healthcare, PGCert/MSc Genes, Drugs and Stem Cells – Novel Therapies, PGCert/PGDip/Msc Genomic Medicine, Msc Medical Ultrasound, PGCert/Msc Innovations in Cardiological Science, PGCert/PGDip/MSc Preventive Cardiology, MRes Respiratory and Cardiovascular Science

Department of Physics; www.imperial.ac.uk/natural-sciences/ departments/physics

BSc Physics, MSci Physics, BSc Physics and Music Performance, BSc Physics with Science Education, MSci Physics with Science Education, BSc Physics with Theoretical Physics, MSci Physics with Theoretical Physics

Postgraduate courses: MRes Controlled Quantum Dynamics, MSc Optics and Photonics, MRes Photonics, MSc Physics, MSc Physics with Extended Research, MSc Physics with Nanophotonics, MSc Physics with Shock Physics, MRes Plastic Electronic Materials, MSc Quantum Engineering, MSc Quantum Fields and Fundamental Forces, MSc Theory and Simulation of Materials

School of Public Health; www.imperial.ac.uk/medicine/ departments/school-public-health

Postgraduate courses: MSc Epidemiology, MRes Epidemiology, Evolution and Control of Infectious Diseases, MPH Public Health

Science Communication Unit

Postgraduate courses: MSc Science Communication; MSc Science Media Production

Student Recruitment and Outreach

PGCE INSPIRE teacher training programme

Department of Surgery and Cancer; www.imperial.ac.uk/medicine/ departments/department-surgery-cancer

Postgraduate courses: MRes Anaesthetics, Pain Medicine and Intensive Care, MRes Biomedical Research, MRes Cancer Biology, MRes Cancer Informatics, MRes Data Science, PGCert/PGDip/MSc Health Policy (delivered by the Institute of Global Health Innovation), MSc Healthcare and Design (delivered by the Institute of Global Health Innovation), MRes Medical Robotics and Image-Guided Intervention (delivered by the Institute of Global Health, MRes Microbiome in Health and Disease (delivered by the Institute of Global Health Innovation), PGCert/PGDip/MSc Patient Safety (delivered by the Institute of Global Health Innovation), PGCert/PGDip Patient Safety (delivered by the Institute of Global Health Innovation), PGCert/MSc Reproductive and Developmental Biology, PGDip/MEd Surgical Education, PGCert/PGDip/MSc Surgical Innovation

KEELE UNIVERSITY
www.keele.ac.uk

A to D

BSc(Hons) Accounting and Astrophysics, BA(Hons) Accounting and Business Management, BA(Hons) Accounting and Finance, BA(Hons) Accounting and Marketing, BSc(Hons) Accounting and Mathematics, BSc(Hons) Accounting and Physics, BA(Hons) Accounting, Finance and International Business, BSc(Hons) Adult Nursing, BA(Hons) American Studies, BA(Hons) American Studies and English Literature, BA(Hons) American Studies and Film Studies, BA(Hons) American Studies and History, BA(Hons) American Studies and International Business, BA(Hons) American Studies and Politics, BSc(Hons) Astrophysics and Chemistry, BSc(Hons) Astrophysics and Computer Science, BSc(Hons) Astrophysics and Education, BSc(Hons) Astrophysics and Environmental Science, BSc(Hons) Astrophysics and Forensic Science, BSc(Hons) Astrophysics and Geography, BSc(Hons) Astrophysics and Geology, BSc(Hons) Astrophysics and Human Geography, BSc(Hons) Astrophysics and Mathematics, BSc(Hons) Astrophysics and Medicinal Chemistry, BSc(Hons) Astrophysics and Music Technology, BSc(Hons) Astrophysics and Physical Geography, BSc(Hons) Biochemistry, BSc(Hons) Biochemistry and Biology, BSc(Hons) Biochemistry and Chemistry, BSc(Hons) Biochemistry and Human Biology, BSc(Hons) Biochemistry and Medicinal Chemistry, BSc(Hons) Biochemistry and Neuroscience, BSc(Hons) Biology, BSc(Hons) Biology and Chemistry, BSc(Hons) Biology and Computer Science, BSc(Hons) Biology and Criminology, BSc(Hons) Biology and Education, BSc(Hons) Biology and Forensic Science, BSc(Hons) Biology and Geography, BSc(Hons) Biology and Geology, BSc(Hons) Biology and Human Geography, BSc(Hons) Biology and Mathematics, BSc(Hons) Biology and Physical Geography, BSc(Hons) Biology and Psychology, BSc(Hons) Biomedical Science, BA(Hons) Business and Human Resource Management, BA(Hons) Business Management and Computer Science, BA(Hons) Business Management and Criminology, BA(Hons) Business Management and Economics, BA(Hons) Business Management and Finance, BA(Hons) Business Management and Geography, BA(Hons) Business Management and Human Geography, BA(Hons) Business Management and International Relations, BSc(Hons) Business Management and Mathematics, BA(Hons) Business Management and Media, BA(Hons) Business Management and Politics, BA(Hons) Business Management and Psychology, BSc(Hons) Chemistry, MChem Chemistry: Integrated Masters, BSc(Hons) Chemistry and Environmental Science, BSc(Hons) Chemistry and Forensic Science, BSc(Hons) Chemistry and Geology, BSc(Hons) Chemistry and Human Biology, BSc(Hons) Chemistry and Mathematics, BSc(Hons) Chemistry and Neuroscience, BSc(Hons) Chemistry and Physics, BSc(Hons) Children's Nursing, BSc(Hons) Computer Science, MComp Computer Science: Integrated Masters, BSc(Hons) Computer Science and Film Studies, BSc(Hons) Computer Science and Forensic Science, BSc(Hons) Computer Science and Geology, BSc(Hons) Computer Science and Mathematics, BSc(Hons) Computer Science and Music, BSc(Hons) Computer Science and Music Technology, BSc(Hons) Computer Science and Neuroscience, BSc(Hons) Computer Science and Physics, BA(Hons) Criminology, BA(Hons) Criminology and History, BSc(Hons) Criminology and Human Biology, BA(Hons) Criminology and Law, BSc(Hons) Criminology and Neuroscience, BA(Hons) Criminology and Philosophy, BSc(Hons) Criminology and Psychology, BA(Hons) Criminology and Sociology

Postgraduate courses: Adult Nursing (MSc), Advanced Clinical Practice (MSc), Advanced Computer Science, Advanced Critical Care Practitioner (PgCert), Advanced Practice in Computed Tomographic Colongraphy (PgCert), Advanced Professional Practice (Pharmacy), Advancing Professional Practice (MSc), Advancing Professional Practice (Nursing), Analytical Science for Industry, Applied Clinical Anatomy PG Cert, Biomedical Blood Science,

Biomedical Engineering, Biomedical Science (Graduate Diploma), Cell and Tissue Engineering, Certificate in Counselling / Part-Time MSc in Counselling and Psychotherapy, Certificate in Research and Evaluation, Child Care Law and Practice, Child Development, Clinical Pharmacy (Hospital Pharmacists only), Clinical Practice (BSc), Cognitive Psychology, Contemporary Literature and Film, Continuing Professional Development, Creative Music Technology, Creative Writing, Criminology and Criminal Justice, Critical Care Practice (PgCert), Diplomatic Studies, Doctorate in Pharmacy

E to I

BA(Hons) Economics, BA(Hons) Economics and Finance, BA(Hons) Economics and History, BA(Hons) Economics and International Business, BA(Hons) Economics and Marketing, BA(Hons) Economics and Mathematics, BA(Hons) Economics and Philosophy, BA(Hons) Economics and Politics, BA(Hons) Economics and Sociology, BA(Hons) Education, BA(Hons) Education and English Literature, BA(Hons) Education and History, BSc(Hons) Education and Human Biology, BSc(Hons) Education and Mathematics, BA(Hons) Education and Music, BA(Hons) Education and Philosophy, BSc(Hons) Education and Physics, BA(Hons) Education and Sociology, BA(Hons) English and American Literature, BA(Hons) English Literature, BA(Hons) English Literature and Creative Writing, BA(Hons) English Literature and Film Studies, BA(Hons) English Literature and History, BA(Hons) English Literature and International Relations, BA(Hons) English Literature and Law, BA(Hons) English Literature and Media, BA(Hons) English Literature and Music, BA(Hons) English Literature and Philosophy, BA(Hons) English Literature and Psychology, BA(Hons) English Literature and Sociology, BSc(Hons) Environment and Sustainability, BSc(Hons) Environmental Science, BSc(Hons) Environmental Science and Geography, BSc(Hons) Environmental Science and Human Biology, BSc(Hons) Environmental Science and Human Geography, BSc(Hons) Environmental Science and Medicinal Chemistry, BSc(Hons) Environmental Science and Physical Geography, BSc(Hons) Environmental Science and Physics, BA(Hons) Film Studies, BA(Hons) Film Studies and Creative Writing, BA(Hons) Film Studies and Media, BA(Hons) Film Studies and Music Technology, BA(Hons) Finance and Marketing, MSci Forensic and Analytical Investigation, BSc(Hons) Forensic Science, BSc(Hons) Forensic Science and Criminology, BSc(Hons) Forensic Science and Human Biology, BSc(Hons) Forensic Science and Law, BSc(Hons) Forensic Science and Neuroscience, BSc(Hons) Forensic Science and Physics, BSc(Hons) Forensic Science and Psychology, BA(Hons) or BSc(Hons) Geography, BSc(Hons) Geography and Geology, BA(Hons) Geography and History, BSc(Hons) Geography and Human Biology, BSc(Hons) Geography and Mathematics, BSc(Hons) Geography and Physics, BA(Hons) Geography and Politics, BA(Hons) Geography and Sociology, BSc(Hons) Geology and Human Biology, BSc(Hons) Geology and Human Geography, BSc(Hons) Geology and Physical Geography, BSc(Hons) Geology and Physics, BSc(Hons) Geoscience, MGeoscience Geoscience: Integrated Masters, BA(Hons) History, BA(Hons) History and Human Geography, BA(Hons) History and International Relations, BA(Hons) History and Law, BSc(Hons) History and Physical Geography, BA(Hons) History and Politics, BSc(Hons) History and Psychology, BSc(Hons) Combined Human Biology, BSc(Hons) Human Biology and Human Geography, BSc(Hons) Human Biology and Mathematics, BSc(Hons) Human Biology and Medicinal Chemistry, BSc(Hons) Human Biology and Physical Geography, BSc(Hons) Human Biology and Psychology, BA(Hons) Human Geography, BSc(Hons) Human Geography and Mathematics, BSc(Hons) Human Geography and Physics, BA(Hons) Human Geography and Politics, BA(Hons) Human Geography and Sociology, BA(Hons) Human Resource Management and International Business, BA(Hons) Human Resource Management and Marketing, BSc(Hons) Human Resource Management and Psychology, University Certificate Industrial Relations (University Certificate), BA(Hons) International Business and International Relations, BA(Hons) International Business and Marketing, BA(Hons) International Business and Media, BA(Hons) International Business Management, BA(Hons) International Relations, BA(Hons) International Relations and Philosophy, BA(Hons) International Relations and Politics, BA(Hons) International Relations and Sociology

Postgraduate courses: English Literatures, Environmental Politics and Climate Change, Environmental Sustainability and Green Technology, Foundation Medical Practice, Foundation Medical Practice / GP Induction and Refresher Scheme, Geoscience Research, Global Media and Culture, Global Media and Management, Global Media and Management (subject to validation), Global Security, GP Induction and Refresher Scheme, Health Professions Education: Accreditation and Assessment (FAIMER-Keele), Health Sciences, History, Human Rights, Globalisation and Justice, Humanities MRes, Independent Prescribing, Individual Health Modules, Industrial Relations and Employment Law, International Law, International Relations

J to N

LLB(Hons) Law, BA(Hons) Law and Music, BA(Hons) Law and Philosophy, BA(Hons) Law and Politics, LLB(Hons) Law with Business, LLB(Hons) Law with Criminology, LLB(Hons) Law with Politics, BSc(Hons) Learning Disability Nursing, BA(Hons) Liberal Arts, MLibArts Liberal Arts: Integrated Masters, BA(Hons) Management, BA(Hons) Marketing and Management, BA(Hons) Marketing and Media, BSc(Hons) Marketing and Psychology, BSc(Hons) Mathematics, MMath Mathematics: Integrated Masters, BSc(Hons) Mathematics and Music, BSc(Hons) Mathematics and Philosophy, BSc(Hons) Mathematics and Physical Geography, BSc (Hon) Mathematics and Physics, BSc(Hons) Mathematics and Psychology, BA(Hons) Media and Music Technology, BA(Hons) Media and Sociology, BA(Hons) Media, Culture and Creative Practice, BSc(Hons) Medicinal Chemistry and Biology, BSc(Hons) Medicinal Chemistry and Forensic Science, BSc(Hons) Medicinal Chemistry and Geology, BSc(Hons) Medicinal Chemistry and Mathematics, BSc(Hons) Medicinal Chemistry and Neuroscience, BSc(Hons) Medicinal Chemistry and Physics, MB ChB Medicine, BSc(Hons) Mental Health Nursing, BSc(Hons) Midwifery, BA(Hons) Music, BA(Hons) Music and Music Technology, BSc(Hons) Music and Psychology, BA(Hons) Music Technology, BSc(Hons) Music Technology and Neuroscience, BSc(Hons) Music Technology and Physics, BSc(Hons) Music Technology and Psychology, BSc(Hons) or MSci Integrated Master€™s Natural Sciences, BSc(Hons) Neuroscience, BSc(Hons) Neuroscience and Psychology, BSc(Hons) Nursing Studies

Postgraduate courses: Law and Society, Learning and Teaching in Higher Education, MA Education, MA Education (Developing Educational Practice), MA Education (International Education), MA Education (Leadership and Management), MA European Industrial Relations and Human Resource Management (or PG Diploma), MA Human Resource Management (or PG Diploma), MA Industrial Relations (or PG Diploma), MA Industrial Relations and Employment Law (or PG Diploma), MA Industrial Relations and

Human Resource Management (or PG Diploma), MA International Business, MA Management, Medical Education, Medical Education (Intercalated), Medical Engineering Design, Medical Engineering Design, Medical Ethics and Law, Medical Ethics and Palliative Care, Medical Science, Medical Science (Anatomical Sciences), Medical Science (Clinical Audit) PG Cert, Medical Science (Frailty and Integrated Care), Medical Science (Leadership and Management), Medical Science (Oncology), Medical Science (Oncology) – (not recruiting in 2017/18), Medical Science (Paediatric Respiratory Medicine), Medical Science (Stroke), Molecular Parasitology and Vector Biology, MSc Accounting and Financial Management, MSc Biosciences, MSc Finance, MSc Finance and Management, MSc in Counselling and Psychotherapy (formerly MSc in Counselling Psychology), MSc in Counselling and Psychotherapy 3 year Part-Time, MSc Neuroscience, Music, Neurological Rehabilitation, Neuromusculoskeletal Health Care

O to U

BSc(Hons) Pharmaceutical Science, Technology and Business, MPharm(Hons) Pharmacy, MPharm (only available to international students) Pharmacy with Integrated Training Year, BA(Hons) Philosophy, BA(Hons) Philosophy and Politics, BSc(Hons) Philosophy and Psychology, BSc(Hons) Physical Geography, BSc(Hons) Physical Geography and Physics, BSc(Hons) Physical Geography and Politics, BSc(Hons) Physical Geography and Sociology, BSc(Hons) Physics, BSc(Hons) Physics with Astrophysics, BSc(Hons) Physiotherapy, BA(Hons) Politics, BA(Hons) Politics and Sociology, BSc(Hons) Psychology, BSc(Hons) Psychology (Single Honours) with Placement Year, BSc(Hons) Psychology and Sociology, BSc(Hons) Psychology with Counselling, BSc(Hons) Radiography (Diagnostic Imaging), BSc(Hons) Rehabilitation Science, BA(Hons) Social Work, BA(Hons) Sociology

Postgraduate courses: Pain Science and Management, PGCE (Academic Award), PGCE International, Physiotherapy (Cardio-respiratory), Physiotherapy (Full-Time), Physiotherapy (Neurology), Physiotherapy (Part-Time), Politics, Practice Education (Social Work), Primary Teacher Teaching, Professional Doctorate (Criminology & Criminal Justice), Professional Doctorate (Education), Professional Doctorate (Social Work), Professional MSc, Psychology of Health and Wellbeing, Rheumatology Practice (entry alternate years), Rheumatology Practice (MSc), Safeguarding Adults – Law, Policy and Practice, Scientific Research

Training (with International Placement): MSc Biosciences or MSc Neuroscience, Secondary Teacher Training, Social and Community Psychology, Social Science Research Methods MRes, Social Work, Specialist Community Nursing – District Nursing Pathway, Specialist Community Nursing – District Nursing Pathway (BSc), Specialist Community Nursing – District Nursing Pathway (PgDip), Specialist Community Public Health Nursing – Health Visiting Pathway, Specialist Community Public Health Nursing – Health Visiting Pathway (BSc), Specialist Community Public Health Nursing – Health Visiting Pathway (PgDip), Specialist Community Public Health Nursing & School Nursing Pathway, Specialist Community Public Health Nursing – School Nursing Pathway (BSc), Specialist Community Public Health Nursing & School Nursing Pathway (PgDip), University Certificate Industrial Relations, US Politics

UNIVERSITY OF KENT
www.kent.ac.uk

American Studies
American Studies BA(Hons), American Studies (History) BA(Hons), American Studies (Latin America) BA(Hons), American Studies (Literature) BA(Hons)
Postgraduate course: American Studies MA

Anthropology and Conservation
Anthropology BSc(Hons), Biological Anthropology BSc(Hons), Cultural Studies and Social Anthropology BA(Hons), Environmental Social Sciences BA(Hons), History and Social Anthropology BA(Hons), Human Ecology BSc(Hons), Law and Social Anthropology BA(Hons), Philosophy and Social Anthropology BA(Hons), Psychology and Social Anthropology BSc(Hons), Social Anthropology BA(Hons), Social Anthropology and Politics BA(Hons), Social Anthropology and Social Policy BA(Hons), Social Anthropology with French BA(Hons), Social Anthropology with German BA(Hons), Social Anthropology with Italian BA(Hons), Social Anthropology with Spanish BA(Hons), Sociology and Social Anthropology BA(Hons), Wildlife Conservation BSc(Hons), Wildlife Conservation with a Year in Professional Practice BSc(Hons)
Postgraduate courses: Conservation and International Wildlife Trade MSc, Conservation and Rural Development MSc, Conservation and Tourism MSc, Conservation Biology MSc, Environmental Anthropology MA, MSc, Ethnobotany MSc, Evolution and Human Behaviour MSc, Forensic Osteology and Field Recovery Methods MSc, Social Anthropology MA, Social Anthropology and Conflict MA, Social Anthropology of Europe MA, Social Anthropology with Visual Ethnography MA

Archaeology, Ancient History and Classics
Ancient History BA(Hons), Ancient, Medieval and Modern History BA(Hons), Asian Studies and Classical & Archaeological Studies BA(Hons), Classical and Archaeological Studies BA(Hons), Classical & Archaeological Studies and Comparative Literature BA(Hons), Classical & Archaeological Studies and Drama BA(Hons), Classical and Archaeological Studies and English and American Literature BA(Hons), Classical and Archaeological Studies and Film BA(Hons), Classical and Archaeological Studies and French BA(Hons), Classical and Archaeological Studies and German BA(Hons), Classical and Archaeological Studies and Hispanic Studies BA(Hons), Classical and Archaeological Studies and Italian BA(Hons), Classical and Archaeological Studies and Philosophy BA(Hons), Classical and Archaeological Studies and Religious Studies BA(Hons), Classical Studies BA(Hons), History and Archaeological Studies BA(Hons)

Architecture
Architecture MArch, Architecture BA(Hons)
Postgraduate courses: Architectural Conservation MSc, Architectural Visualisation MA, Architecture and the Sustainable Environment MSc, Architecture and Urban Design MA, Master of Architecture MArch

Arts
Art History BA(Hons), Art History and Classical & Archaeological Studies BA(Hons), Art History and English and American Literature BA(Hons), Art History and Film BA(Hons), Art History and French BA(Hons), Art History and German BA(Hons), Art History and Hispanic Studies BA(Hons), Art History and History BA(Hons), Art History and Italian BA(Hons), Cultural Studies and Art History BA(Hons), Digital Arts MArt, Digital Arts BA(Hons), Drama and Theatre and Art History BA(Hons), Event and Experience Design BA(Hons), Event and Experience Management BA(Hons), Fine Art BA(Hons), Liberal Arts BA(Hons), Media Studies BA(Hons),

Multimedia Technology and Design BSc(Hons), Philosophy and Art History BA(Hons)

Postgraduate courses: Advanced Communications Engineering (RF Technology and Telecommunications) MSc, Advanced Communications Engineering (Wireless Systems and Networks) MSc, Advanced Digital Systems Engineering MSc, Advanced Digital Systems Engineering (Communications) MSc, Advanced Digital Systems Engineering (Integrated Circuit Design) MSc, Advanced Electronic Systems Engineering MSc, Architectural Visualisation MA, Computer Animation MSc, Creative Producing MA, Curating MA, Digital Visual Effects MSc, European Theatre MA, Film MA, Film with Practice MA, Fine Art MA, History and Philosophy of Art MA, Information Security and Biometrics MSc, Mobile Application Development MSc, Music (Research, Composition or Performance) MA, Music Technology MA, Physical Acting MA, Popular Music (Research, Production or Performance) MA, Stand-Up Comedy MA, Theatre Making MA

Biosciences

Biochemistry BSc(Hons), Biology BSc(Hons), Biomedical Engineering BEng(Hons), Biomedical Science BSc(Hons)

Postgraduate courses: Biotechnology and Bioengineering MSc, Cancer Biology MSc, Conservation Biology MSc, Drug Design MSc, Infectious Diseases MSc, Reproductive Medicine: Science and Ethics MSc, Advanced and Specialist Healthcare MSc, Analysis and Intervention in Intellectual and Developmental Disabilities PDip, MSc, Autism Studies PCert, PDip, MA, Biotechnology and Bioengineering MSc, Cancer Biology MSc, Drug Design MSc, Infectious Diseases MSc, Intellectual and Developmental Disabilities PCert, PDip, MA, Intellectual and Developmental Disabilities and Forensic Issues MSc, Intellectual and Developmental Disabilities (Distance Learning) PCert, PDip, MA, Reproductive Medicine: Science and Ethics MSc, Strategic Leadership and Multi-professional Education in Healthcare MSc, PDip

Business, Accounting, Finance and Marketing

Accounting and Finance BA(Hons), Accounting and Finance and Economics BA(Hons), Business Administration with Business Analytics BBA(Hons), Business and Management with a Year in Industry BA(Hons), Business (top-up) BA(Hons), Economics and Management BA(Hons), English Language and Linguistics and Management BA(Hons), French and Management BA(Hons), German and Management BA(Hons), Hispanic Studies and Management BA(Hons), International Business BSc(Hons), International Business with a Year Abroad BSc(Hons), International Business with a Year in Industry BSc(Hons), Italian and Management BA(Hons), Law and Accounting and Finance BA(Hons), Law and Management BA(Hons), Management BSc(Hons), Management with a Year in Industry BSc(Hons), Marketing BSc(Hons), Mathematics and Accounting and Finance BA(Hons), Philosophy and Management BA(Hons)

Postgraduate courses: Business Analytics MSc, Computing and Entrepreneurship MSc, Digital Marketing and Analytics MSc, Human Resource Management MSc, Logistics and Supply Chain Management MSc, Management MSc, Management (International Business) MSc, Marketing MSc, Organisational Psychology MSc/PDip/PCert, The Kent MBA, Finance (Finance and Management) MSc, Finance (Finance, Investment and Risk) MSc, Finance (Financial Markets) MSc, Finance (International Banking and Finance) MSc, International Accounting and Finance MSc

Computing

Business Information Technology BSc(Hons), Computer Science BSc(Hons), Computer Science (Artificial Intelligence) BSc(Hons), Computer Science (Consultancy) BSc(Hons), Computer Science for Health BSc(Hons), Computer Science (Networks) BSc(Hons), Computing BSc(Hons), Computing (Consultancy) BSc(Hons)

Postgraduate courses: Advanced Computer Science MSc, Advanced Computer Science (Cloud Computing and Big Data) MSc, Advanced Computer Science (Computational Intelligence) MSc, Advanced Software Development MSc, Computer Animation MSc, Computer Science MSc, Computer Security MSc, Computing and Entrepreneurship MSc, Cyber Security MSc, Networks and Security MSc

Criminology

Criminal Justice and Criminology BA(Hons), Criminology BA(Hons), Criminology and Cultural Studies BA(Hons), Criminology and Social Policy BA(Hons), Criminology and Sociology BA(Hons), Criminology with Quantitative Research BA(Hons), Law and Criminology BA(Hons)

Postgraduate course: Criminology MA

Cultural Studies

Criminology and Cultural Studies BA(Hons), Cultural Studies and Art History BA(Hons), Cultural Studies and Comparative Literature BA(Hons), Cultural Studies and Film BA(Hons), Cultural Studies and Media BA(Hons), Cultural Studies and Media and Journalism BA(Hons), Cultural Studies and Social Anthropology BA(Hons), Philosophy and Cultural Studies BA(Hons)

Digital Arts

BA(Hons), Digital Arts MArt, Multimedia Technology and Design BSc(Hons)

Drama and Theatre

Classical & Archaeological Studies and Drama BA(Hons), Comparative Literature and Drama BA(Hons), Drama and English and American Literature BA(Hons), Drama and English Language and Linguistics BA(Hons), Drama and Theatre BA(Hons), Drama and Theatre and Art History BA(Hons), Film and Drama BA(Hons), French and Drama BA(Hons), German and Drama BA(Hons), Hispanic Studies and Drama BA(Hons), History and Drama BA(Hons), Italian and Drama BA(Hons), Philosophy and Drama BA(Hons), Religious Studies and Drama BA(Hons)

Economics

Accounting and Finance and Economics BA(Hons), Economics BSc(Hons), Economics and Management BA(Hons), Economics and Politics BA(Hons), Economics with a Language (Spanish) BSc(Hons), Economics with Computing BSc(Hons), Economics with Econometrics BSc(Hons), European Economics BSc(Hons), European Economics (French) BSc(Hons), European Economics (German) BSc(Hons), European Economics (Spanish) BSc(Hons), Financial Economics BSc(Hons), Financial Economics with Econometrics BSc(Hons), Law and Economics BA(Hons), Sociology and Economics BA(Hons), Sociology with Quantitative Research BA(Hons)

Postgraduate courses: Agri-Environmental Economics and Policy MSc, Applied Economics and International Development MSc, Economics MSc, Economics and Econometrics MSc, Economics and Finance MSc, Economics Conversion Programme/Diploma in Economic Analysis MSc, PDip, Finance and Econometrics MSc, International Business and Economic Development MSc, International Finance and Economic Development MSc

Education

Postgraduate courses: Higher Education PGCert/PGDip/MA

Engineering and Electronics

Biomedical Engineering BEng(Hons), Computer Systems Engineering BEng(Hons), Computer Systems Engineering MEng, Electronic and Communications Engineering BEng(Hons), Electronic and Communications Engineering MEng, Electronic and Computer Systems (top-up) BEng(Hons)

Postgraduate courses: Advanced Communications Engineering (RF Technology and Telecommunications) MSc, Advanced Communications Engineering (Wireless Systems and Networks) MSc, Advanced Digital Systems Engineering MSc, Advanced Digital Systems Engineering (Communications) MSc, Advanced Digital Systems Engineering (Integrated Circuit Design) MSc, Advanced Electronic Systems Engineering MSc, Architectural Visualisation MA, Computer Animation MSc, Digital Visual Effects MSc, Information Security and Biometrics MSc, Mobile Application Development MSc

English Literature and Comparative Literature

Asian Studies and Comparative Literature BA(Hons), Asian Studies and English and American Literature BA(Hons), Classical & Archaeological Studies and Comparative Literature BA(Hons), Classical and Archaeological Studies and English and American Literature BA(Hons), Comparative Literature BA(Hons), Comparative Literature and Drama BA(Hons), Comparative Literature and English, American and Postcolonial Literature BA(Hons), Comparative Literature and English and American Literature BA(Hons), Comparative Literature and English Language and Linguistics BA(Hons), Comparative Literature and Film BA(Hons), Comparative Literature and French with a Year Abroad BA(Hons), Comparative Literature and German with a Year Abroad BA(Hons), Comparative Literature and Hispanic Studies with a Year Abroad BA(Hons), Comparative Literature and History BA(Hons), Comparative Literature and Italian with a Year Abroad BA(Hons), Comparative Literature and Philosophy BA(Hons), Comparative Literature and Religious Studies BA(Hons), Contemporary Literature BA(Hons), Cultural Studies and Comparative Literature BA(Hons), Drama and English and American Literature BA(Hons), English, American and Postcolonial Literature and Film BA(Hons), English, American and Postcolonial Literatures BA(Hons), English and American Literature BA(Hons), English and American Literature and Creative Writing BA(Hons), English and American Literature and Film BA(Hons), English and American Literature and Hispanic Studies BA(Hons), English and American Literature and Journalism BA(Hons), English and American Literature and Sociology BA(Hons), English and American Literature with an Approved Year Abroad BA(Hons), English Language and Linguistics and English and American Literature BA(Hons), French and English and American Literature BA(Hons), German and English and American

Literature BA(Hons), History and English, American and Postcolonial Literatures BA(Hons), History and English and American Literature BA(Hons), Italian and English and American Literature BA(Hons), Law and English Literature BA(Hons), Philosophy and English and American Literature BA(Hons), Religious Studies and English and American Literature BA(Hons), World Literature BA(Hons)

Postgraduate courses: Comparative Literature MA, Critical Theory MA, European Culture MA, French and Comparative Literature MA, Applied Linguistics for Teaching English to Speakers of Other Languages (TESOL) MA, Creative Writing MA, Critical Theory MA, Dickens and Victorian Culture MA, Eighteenth-Century Studies MA, English and American Literature MA, Language and Literature MA, Linguistics MA, Medieval and Early Modern Studies MA, Postcolonial Studies MA, The Contemporary MA

Film

Classical and Archaeological Studies and Film BA(Hons), Comparative Literature and Film BA(Hons), Cultural Studies and Film BA(Hons), English, American and Postcolonial Literature and Film BA(Hons), English and American Literature and Film BA(Hons), Film BA(Hons), Film and Drama BA(Hons), Film and Religious Studies BA(Hons), French and Film BA(Hons), German and Film BA(Hons), Hispanic Studies and Film BA(Hons), History and Film BA(Hons), Italian and Film BA(Hons), Philosophy and Film BA(Hons)

Health and Social Care

Applied Behaviour Analysis GCert, Autism Studies Cert, Autism Studies Foundation FdSc, Health and Social Care BA(Hons), Positive Behaviour Support Diploma, Professional Practice (Top-Up) BSc(Hons), Social Work BA(Hons)

Postgraduate courses: Advanced Child Protection PCert, PDip, MA

History

Ancient History BA(Hons), Ancient, Medieval and Modern History BA(Hons), Asian Studies and Classical & Archaeological Studies BA(Hons), Classical and Archaeological Studies BA(Hons), Classical & Archaeological Studies and Comparative Literature BA(Hons), Classical & Archaeological Studies and Drama BA(Hons), Classical and Archaeological Studies and English and American Literature BA(Hons), Classical and Archaeological Studies and Film BA(Hons), Classical and Archaeological Studies and French BA(Hons), Classical and Archaeological Studies and German BA(Hons), Classical and Archaeological Studies and Hispanic Studies

BA(Hons), Classical and Archaeological Studies and Italian BA(Hons), Classical and Archaeological Studies and Philosophy BA(Hons), Classical and Archaeological Studies and Religious Studies BA(Hons), Classical Studies BA(Hons), Comparative Literature and History BA(Hons), European History with a Year Abroad BA(Hons), French and History BA(Hons), German and History BA(Hons), Hispanic Studies and History BA(Hons), History BA(Hons), History and Archaeological Studies BA(Hons), History and Drama BA(Hons), History and English, American and Postcolonial Literatures BA(Hons), History and English and American Literature BA(Hons), History and English Language and Linguistics BA(Hons), History and Film BA(Hons), History and Philosophy BA(Hons), History and Politics BA(Hons), History and Religious Studies BA(Hons), History and Social Anthropology BA(Hons), Italian and History BA(Hons), Law and History BA(Hons), Military History BA(Hons)

Postgraduate courses: Ancient History MA, Archaeology MA, Heritage Management MA, History and Philosophy of Art MA, History of Medicine and Health MA, Medieval and Early Modern Studies MA, Modern History MA, Roman History and Archaeology MA, Rome Ancient and Modern MA, War, Media and Society MA

Journalism

Cultural Studies and Media and Journalism BA(Hons), Cultural Studies and Media with Journalism BA(Hons), English and American Literature and Journalism BA(Hons), Journalism BA(Hons)

Postgraduate courses: International Multimedia Journalism MA, Multimedia Journalism MA

Languages and Linguistics

Art History and French BA(Hons), Art History and Italian BA(Hons), Asian Studies and Classical & Archaeological Studies BA(Hons), Asian Studies and Comparative Literature BA(Hons), Asian Studies and English and American Literature BA(Hons), Asian Studies and English Language and Linguistics BA(Hons), Asian Studies and French BA(Hons), Asian Studies and German BA(Hons), Asian Studies and Hispanic Studies BA(Hons), Asian Studies and Italian BA(Hons), Asian Studies and Philosophy BA(Hons), Asian Studies and Religious Studies BA(Hons), Classical and Archaeological Studies and French BA(Hons), Classical and Archaeological Studies and German BA(Hons), Classical and Archaeological Studies and Italian BA(Hons), Comparative Literature and English Language and Linguistics BA(Hons), Comparative Literature and French with a

Year Abroad BA(Hons), Comparative Literature and German with a Year Abroad BA(Hons), Comparative Literature and Hispanic Studies with a Year Abroad BA(Hons), Comparative Literature and Italian with a Year Abroad BA(Hons), Drama and English Language and Linguistics BA(Hons), English and American Literature and Hispanic Studies BA(Hons), English Language and Linguistics BA(Hons), English Language and Linguistics and English and American Literature BA(Hons), English Language and Linguistics and Management BA(Hons), European Studies (Combined Languages) BA(Hons), European Studies (French) BA(Hons), European Studies (German) BA(Hons), European Studies (Italian) BA(Hons), European Studies (Spanish) BA(Hons), French BA(Hons), French and Drama BA(Hons), French and English and American Literature BA(Hons), French and English Language and Linguistics BA(Hons), French and Film BA(Hons), French and Hispanic Studies BA(Hons), French and History BA(Hons), French and Management BA(Hons), French and Philosophy BA(Hons), French and Religious Studies BA(Hons), German BA(Hons), German and Drama BA(Hons), German and English and American Literature BA(Hons), German and English Language and Linguistics BA(Hons), German and Film BA(Hons), German and French BA(Hons), German and History BA(Hons), German and Management BA(Hons), German and Philosophy BA(Hons), German and Religious Studies BA(Hons), Hispanic Studies BA(Hons), Hispanic Studies and Drama BA(Hons), Hispanic Studies and English Language and Linguistics BA(Hons), Hispanic Studies and Film BA(Hons), Hispanic Studies and German BA(Hons), Hispanic Studies and History BA(Hons), Hispanic Studies and Italian BA(Hons), Hispanic Studies and Management BA(Hons), Hispanic Studies and Religious Studies BA(Hons), History and English Language and Linguistics BA(Hons), Italian BA(Hons), Italian and Drama BA(Hons), Italian and English and American Literature BA(Hons), Italian and English Language and Linguistics BA(Hons), Italian and Film BA(Hons), Italian and French BA(Hons), Italian and German BA(Hons), Italian and History BA(Hons), Italian and Management BA(Hons), Italian and Philosophy BA(Hons), Italian and Religious Studies BA(Hons), Philosophy and English Language and Linguistics BA(Hons), Philosophy and Hispanic Studies BA(Hons), Politics and English Language and Linguistics BA(Hons)

Law

Certificate in Law Cert, English and French Law LLB(Hons), European Legal Studies LLB(Hons), International Legal Studies with a Year Abroad LLB(Hons), Law LLB(Hons), Law and Accounting and Finance BA(Hons), Law and Criminology BA(Hons), Law and Economics BA(Hons), Law and English Literature BA(Hons), Law and History BA(Hons), Law and Management BA(Hons), Law and Philosophy BA(Hons), Law and Social Anthropology BA(Hons), Law and Sociology BA(Hons), Law and Welfare BA(Hons), Law (Senior Status) LLB(Hons), Law with a Language (French) LLB(Hons), Law with a Language (German) LLB(Hons), Law with a Language (Spanish) LLB(Hons), Law with Quantitative Research LLB(Hons), Politics and Law BA(Hons)

Human Rights Law LLM, International Law LLM, Law LLM, PDip, PCert, Law (Erasmus-Europe) LLM

Liberal Arts

Liberal Arts BA(Hons)

Mathematics, Statistics and Actuarial Sciences

Actuarial Science BSc(Hons), Financial Mathematics BSc(Hons), Mathematics BSc(Hons), Mathematics MMath, Mathematics and Accounting and Finance BA(Hons), Mathematics and Statistics BSc(Hons), Mathematics and Statistics MMathStat, Mathematics with Secondary Education (QTS) BSc(Hons)

Postgraduate courses: Actuarial Science Pdip, Applied Actuarial Science MSc, International Master's in Applied Actuarial Science MSc, International Master's in Mathematics and its Applications MSc, International Master's in Statistics MSc, International Master's in Statistics with Finance MSc, Mathematics and its Applications MSc, Statistics MSc, Statistics with an Industrial Placement MSc, Statistics with Finance MSc

Music

Music Business and Production BA(Hons), Music, Performance and Production BA(Hons), Music Technology and Audio Production BSc(Hons)

Pharmacy

Pharmacology and Physiology BSc(Hons), Pharmacy MPharm

Postgraduate courses: General Pharmacy Practice PCert/ PDip/MSc, General Pharmacy Practice PCert/ PDip/MS, Independent/Supplementary Prescribing PCert, Medicines Management MSc/PDip/PCert

Philosophy

Asian Studies and Philosophy BA(Hons), Classical and Archaeological Studies and Philosophy BA(Hons), Comparative Literature and Philosophy

BA(Hons), French and Philosophy BA(Hons), German and Philosophy BA(Hons), History and Philosophy BA(Hons), Italian and Philosophy BA(Hons), Law and Philosophy BA(Hons), Philosophy BA(Hons), Philosophy and Art History BA(Hons), Philosophy and Cultural Studies BA(Hons), Philosophy and Drama BA(Hons), Philosophy and English and American Literature BA(Hons), Philosophy and English Language and Linguistics BA(Hons), Philosophy and Film BA(Hons), Philosophy and Hispanic Studies BA(Hons), Philosophy and Management BA(Hons), Philosophy and Politics BA(Hons), Philosophy and Social Anthropology BA(Hons), Philosophy and Sociology BA(Hons), Religious Studies and Philosophy BA(Hons)

Postgraduate courses: Medical Humanities MA, Philosophy MA, Reasoning MA

Physical Sciences

Astronomy, Space Science and Astrophysics MPhys, Astronomy, Space Science and Astrophysics BSc(Hons), Astronomy, Space Science and Astrophysics with a Year Abroad MPhys, Chemistry BSc(Hons), Chemistry MChem, Forensic Science MSci, Forensic Science BSc(Hons), Physics BSc(Hons), Physics MPhys, Physics with Astrophysics MPhys, Physics with Astrophysics BSc(Hons)

Postgraduate courses: Forensic Science MSc, Physics (Euromasters) MSc

Politics and International Relations

Economics and Politics BA(Hons), History and Politics BA(Hons), Philosophy and Politics BA(Hons), Politics BA(Hons), Politics and English Language and Linguistics BA(Hons), Politics and International Relations BA(Hons), Politics and International Relations (Bi-diplme) BA(Hons), Politics and International Relations with a Language BA(Hons), Politics and International Relations with Quantitative Research BA(Hons), Politics and Law BA(Hons), Social Anthropology and Politics BA(Hons), Social Policy and Politics BA(Hons), Sociology and Politics BA(Hons), War and Conflict BA(Hons)

EU External Relations MA, International Conflict Analysis PDip, MA, International Conflict and Security MA, International Development MA, International Migration MA, International Political Economy MA, International Relations MA, PDip, International Relations MA, International Relations with International Law MA, PDip, Peace and Conflict Studies (International Joint Award) MA, Political Strategy and Communication MA, Terrorism and Society PDip, MA

Psychology

Applied Psychology BSc(Hons), Applied Psychology with Clinical Psychology BSc(Hons), Psychology BSc(Hons), Psychology and Social Anthropology BSc(Hons), Psychology with Clinical Psychology BSc(Hons), Psychology with Forensic Psychology BSc(Hons), Psychology with Studies in Europe BSc(Hons), Social Psychology BSc(Hons)

Postgraduate courses: Cognitive Psychology / Neuropsychology MSc, Developmental Psychology MSc, Forensic Psychology MSc, Group Processes and Intergroup Relations MSc, Organisational Psychology MSc, PDip, PCert, Political Psychology MSc, Research Methods in Psychology MSc, Social and Applied Psychology MSc

Religious Studies

Asian Studies and Religious Studies BA(Hons), Classical and Archaeological Studies and Religious Studies BA(Hons), Comparative Literature and Religious Studies BA(Hons), Film and Religious Studies BA(Hons), French and Religious Studies BA(Hons), German and Religious Studies BA(Hons), Hispanic Studies and Religious Studies BA(Hons), History and Religious Studies BA(Hons), Italian and Religious Studies BA(Hons), Religious Studies BA(Hons), Religious Studies and Drama BA(Hons), Religious Studies and English and American Literature BA(Hons), Religious Studies and Philosophy BA(Hons)

Postgraduate course: Religion MA

Sociology and Social Policy

Criminology and Social Policy BA(Hons), English and American Literature and Sociology BA(Hons), Law and Sociology BA(Hons), Law and Welfare BA(Hons), Philosophy and Sociology BA(Hons), Social Anthropology and Social Policy BA(Hons), Social Policy BA(Hons), Social Policy and Politics BA(Hons), Social Policy and Sociology BA(Hons), Social Policy with Quantitative Research BA(Hons), Social Sciences BSc(Hons), Sociology BA(Hons), Sociology and Economics BA(Hons), Sociology and Politics BA(Hons), Sociology and Social Anthropology BA(Hons), Sociology with Quantitative Research BA(Hons)

Postgraduate courses: Analysis and Intervention in Intellectual and Developmental Disabilities PDip, MSc, Applied Behaviour Analysis PCert, PDip, MSc, Autism Studies PCert, PDip, MA, Intellectual and Developmental Disabilities PCert, PDip, MA, Intellectual and Developmental Disabilities and Forensic Issues MSc, Positive Behaviour Support PDip, MSc, Social Work MA, Sociology MA

Sports and Exercise Sciences

Sport and Exercise for Health BSc(Hons), Sport and Exercise Management BA(Hons), Sport and Exercise Science BSc(Hons), Sport Management BA(Hons), Sport Management MSport, Sports Therapy BSc(Hons)

Postgraduate course: Sports Science for Optimal Performance MSc

---

KINGSTON UNIVERSITY
www.kingston.ac.uk

Kingston School of Art; http://fada.kingston.ac.uk

Architecture BA(Hons), Art & Design History and Practice BA(Hons), Creative and Cultural Industries: Art Direction BA(Hons), Creative and Cultural Industries: Curation, Exhibition and Events BA(Hons), Creative and Cultural Industries: Design Marketing BA(Hons), Fashion BA(Hons), Filmmaking BA(Hons), Fine Art BA(Hons), Fine Art & Art History BA(Hons), Graphic Design BA(Hons), Historic Building Conservation FdSc and BSc(Hons), Illustration Animation BA(Hons), Interior Design BA(Hons), Photography BA(Hons), Product & Furniture Design BA(Hons)

Postgraduate courses: Architecture (ARB/RIBA Part 2) MArch, Art and Design History MA, Art Market and Appraisal (Professional Practice) MA, Art & Space MA, Communication Design: Graphic Design MA, Communication Design: Illustration MA, Curating Contemporary Design MA, Experimental Film MA, Fashion MA, Fashion MA: Knit pathway, Fine Art MFA, Film making MA, Graduate Diploma Creative Practice, Historic Building Conservation MSc, Landscape Architecture MLA (LI accredited), Landscape Architecture PgDip (LI accredited), Landscape and Urbanism MA, Museum and Gallery Studies MA, Photography MA, Product & Furniture Design MA, Professional Practice Architecture (ARB/RIBA Part 3 exemption) PgDip, Project Management for Creative Practitioners MSc, Sustainable Design MA

Faculty of Arts and Social Sciences; http://fass.kingston.ac.uk

Business BA/BSc(Hons), Business Economics BSc(Hons), Creative Writing BA(Hons), Criminology BSc(Hons), Dance BA(Hons), Drama BA(Hons), Economics BSc(Hons), English Language & Linguistics BA(Hons), English Literature BA(Hons), Film BA(Hons), Financial Economics BSc(Hons), Forensic Psychology BSc(Hons), History BA(Hons), Human Rights BA(Hons), International Law LLB(Hons), International Relations BSc(Hons), Journalism BA(Hons), Law LLB(Hons), Media Skills BA(Hons), Media & Communication BA(Hons), Music Technology BA(Hons), Politics & International Relations BA(Hons), Popular Music BA(Hons), Psychology BSc(Hons), Publishing BA(Hons), Sociology BSc(Hons)

Postgraduate courses: Aesthetics and Art Theory MA, Applied Linguistics for Language Teaching MA, Behavioural Decision Science MSc, Child Psychology MSc, Clinical Applications of Psychology MSc, Composing for Film and Television MMus, Contemporary European Philosophy MA, Creative Writing and Publishing MA, Creative Writing Distance Learning MA, Creative Writing MA, Creative Writing MFA, Criminology MA, Criminology with Forensic Psychology MA, Development and International Economics MA, English Literature MA, Film Studies MA, Financial Economics MA, Forensic Psychology MSc, Gender Without Borders MA, General Law LLM, History MA, Human Rights MA, International Conflict MSc, International Politics and Economics MA, International Relations MSc, Journalism PgDip/MA, Literature and Philosophy MA, Magazine Journalism MA, Media and Communication MA, Modern European Philosophy MA, Music Education MA, Music MA, Music Performance MMus, Philosophy and Contemporary Critical Theory MA, Philosophy MPhilStud, Political Economy MA, Production of Popular Music MMus, Psychology MSc, Publishing MA, Terrorism and Political Violence MSc

Kingston Business School; http://business.kingston.ac.uk

Accounting & Finance BSc(Hons), Business Finance BA(Hons), Business Management BA(Hons), Human Resource Management BA(Hons), International Business BSc(Hons), Marketing Management BA(Hons), Marketing & Advertising BSc(Hons), Real Estate Management with Business Experience BSc(Hons)

Postgraduate courses: Accounting and Finance MSc, Banking and Finance MSc, Business and Management MRes, Creative Industries & the Creative Economy MA, Finance MSc, Financial and Business

Management MSc, Human Resource Management MSc, Innovation Management & Entrepreneurship MSc, International Business Management MSc, International Business Management with Entrepreneurship MSc, International Business Management with Marketing MSc, International Business Management with Project Management MSc, International Human Resource Management MSc, International Human Resource Management MSc, Investment and Financial Risk Management MSc, Leadership and Management in Health PgCert/PgDip/MSc top-up/MSc, Logistics and Supply Chain Management MSc, Marketing and Strategy MSc, Marketing Communications and Advertising MSc, Marketing & Brand Management MSc, Master of Business Administration MBA, Occupational and Business Psychology MSc, Public Relations and Corporate Communications MA, Real Estate MSc

Faculty of Health, Social Care and Education www.healthcare.ac.uk

Adult Nursing BSc(Hons), Child Centred Interprofessional Practice BA(Hons) top-up/FdA, Children's Nursing BSc(Hons), Early Years FdA, Early Years: Education & Leadership in Practice BA(Hons) top-up, Early Years: Leadership & Management FdA, Early Years: Teaching & Learning BA(Hons) top-up, Healthcare Practice DipHE and BSc(Hons), Healthcare Practice FdSc, Learning Disability Nursing BSc(Hons), Mental Health Nursing BSc(Hons), Midwifery / Registered Midwife BSc(Hons), Occupational Therapy BSc(Hons), Paramedic Practice BSc(Hons), Paramedic Science BSc(Hons), Physical Education, Sport and Activity (PESA) FdA, Physiotherapy BSc(Hons), Primary Teaching leading to Qualified Teacher Status BA(Hons), Radiography, Diagnostic BSc(Hons), Radiography, Therapeutic BSc(Hons), Social Work BA(Hons), Special Educational Needs & Inclusive Practice BA(Hons) top-up, Special Educational Needs & Inclusive Practice FdA, Working with Children & Young People BA(Hons)

Postgraduate courses: Adult Nursing PgDip, Advanced Social Work MA, Applied Exercise for Health MSc, Children's Nursing PgDip, Clinical Leadership MSc, Clinical Research MClinRes, Early Years Teacher Initial Teacher Training (ITT), Education MRes, Healthcare Practice MSc, Leadership and Management in Social Care PgCert, Mental Health Nursing PgDip, Midwifery/Registered Midwife for registered nurses PgDip, Midwifery/Registered Midwife PgDip, Physiotherapy MSc, Practice Education PgCert, Primary Teaching leading to Qualified Teacher Status (QTS) PGCE, Professional Education and Training PgCert/PgDip/MA, Radiography: Breast Evaluation PgCert/PgDip/MSc, Radiography: Medical Imaging PgCert/PgDip/MSc, Radiography: Medical Imaging (Mammography) PgCert/PgDip/ MSc, Radiography: Oncology Practice PgCert/ PgDip/MSc, Rehabilitation PgCert/PgDip/MSc, Secondary Teaching leading to Qualified Teacher Status (QTS) PGCE, Social Work MSW

Faculty of Science, Engineering and Computing; http://sec.kingston.ac.uk

Actuarial Mathematics & Statistics BSc(Hons), Actuarial Science BSc(Hons), Aerospace Engineering, Astronautics & Space Technology MEng/BEng(Hons), Aerospace Engineering BSc(Hons), Aerospace Engineering MEng/BEng(Hons), Aerospace Engineering (Maintenance, Repair & Overhaul) Foundation Degree (FdEng), Aircraft Engineering BSc(Hons), Aircraft Engineering BSc(Hons) top-up, Aircraft Engineering Foundation Course, Automotive Engineering BSc(Hons), Automotive Engineering MEng/BEng(Hons), Automotive Engineering (Motorsport) MEng/BEng(Hons), Aviation Operations with Commercial Pilot Training BSc(Hons), Aviation Operations & Technology BSc(Hons), Aviation Studies for Commercial Pilot Training BSc(Hons) top-up, Biochemistry BSc(Hons), Biological Sciences BSc(Hons), Biological Sciences (Environmental Biology) BSc(Hons), Biological Sciences (Genetics and Molecular Biology) BSc(Hons), Biological Sciences (Human Biology) BSc(Hons), Biological Sciences (Medical Biology) BSc(Hons), Biomedical Science BSc(Hons), Building Surveying BSc(Hons), Chemistry BSc(Hons), Chemistry MChem(Hons), Civil Engineering BEng(Hons), Civil Engineering BSc(Hons), Computer Graphics Technology BSc(Hons), Computer Science BSc(Hons), Computer Science (Games Programming) BSc(Hons), Computer Science (Network Communications) BSc(Hons), Computing and Mathematics foundation year, Computing with Business BSc(Hons), Construction Management BSc(Hons), Creative Technology BSc(Hons), Cyber Security & Computer Forensics with Business BSc(Hons), Engineering Foundation with pathways in Aerospace, Civil, Mechanical Engineering, Environmental Hazards & Disaster Management BSc(Hons), Environmental Management BSc(Hons), Environmental Management with Business BSc(Hons) only, Environmental Science BSc(Hons), Financial Mathematics with Business BSc(Hons), Forensic Science BSc(Hons), Games Technology

BSc(Hons), Geography BA/BSc(Hons), Geology BSc(Hons), Human Geography BA(Hons), Information Systems BSc(Hons), Information Systems (Internet Business) BSc(Hons), International Foundation Year (delivered by Study Group), Mathematics BSc(Hons), Mathematics with Business BSc(Hons), Mathematics & Statistics BSc(Hons), Mechanical Engineering BSc(Hons), Mechanical Engineering MEng/BEng(Hons), Motorsport Engineering/Motorsport Engineering (Motorcycle) BSc(Hons), Nutrition (Exercise and Health) BSc(Hons), Nutrition (Human Nutrition) BSc(Hons), Pharmaceutical Science BSc(Hons), Pharmaceutical Science MPharmSci(Hons), Pharmaceutical & Chemical Sciences FdSc, Pharmacology BSc(Hons), Pharmacy MPharm(Hons), Quantity Surveying Consultancy BSc(Hons), Science foundation year, Software Engineering BSc(Hons), Sport Coaching FdSc, Sport Science BSc(Hons), Sport Science (Coaching) BSc(Hons)

Postgraduate courses: Advanced Industrial & Manufacturing Systems MSc, Advanced Product Design Engineering MSc, Aerospace Engineering MSc, Analytical Chemistry MSc, Analytical Chemistry with Management Studies, Biomedical Science with Management Studies MSc, Biomedical Science (Haematology/Medical Microbiology) MSc, Building Surveying MSc, Cancer Biology MSc, Computer Animation MA, Embedded Systems MSc, Embedded Systems with Management Studies MSc, Embedded Systems (Computer Vision) MSc, Embedded Systems (Computer Vision) with Management Studies MSc, Engineering Projects & Systems Management MSc, Environmental Management MSc, Environmental Management (Energy) MSc, Environmental Management (Water Resources) MSc, Forensic Analysis MSc, Game Development (Design) MA, Game Development (Programming) MSc, Geographical Information Systems & Science MSc, Hazards & Disaster Management MSc, Information Systems MSc, Information Systems (Health Information Management) MSc, International Enterprise Information Management MSc, IT & Strategic Innovation MSc, Management in Construction MSc, Management in Construction with Law MSc, Management in Construction (Civil Engineering) MSc, Mechanical Engineering MSc, Mechatronic Systems MSc, Network & Information Security MSc, Network & Information Security with Management Studies MSc, Networking & Data Communications MSc, Networking & Data Communications with Management Studies MSc, Pharmaceutical Analysis MSc, Pharmaceutical Analysis with Management Studies MSc, Pharmaceutical Science MSc, Pharmaceutical Science with Management Studies MSc, Pharmaceutical Technology MSc, Pharmacy Practice (Overseas Pharmacists Assessment Programme) PgDip/MSc top-up, Professional Engineering MSc, Quantity Surveying MSc, Renewable Energy Engineering MSc, Software Engineering MSc, Software Engineering with Management Studies MSc, Sport and Exercise Science MSc, Structural Design & Construction Management MSc, Structural Design & Construction Management with Sustainability MSc, User Experience Design MSc

LANCASTER UNIVERSITY
www.lancs.ac.uk

Faculty of Arts and Social Sciences; www.lancaster.ac.uk/arts-and-social-sciences

Department of English Literature and Creative Writing; www.lancaster.ac.uk/english-literature-and-creative-writing

English Literature BA(Hons), English Literature and History BA(Hons), English Literature and Linguistics BA(Hons), English Literature and Philosophy BA(Hons), English Literature and Religious Studies BA(Hons), English Literature with Creative Writing BA(Hons), English Literature, Creative Writing and Practice BA(Hons)

Postgraduate courses: MA in Creative Writing, MA in English Literary Research, MA in English Literary Studies, MA in English Literary Studies with Creative Writing

Department of History; www.lancaster.ac.uk/history

History BA(Hons), History and International Relations BA(Hons), History and Philosophy BA(Hons), History and Politics BA(Hons), History and Religious Studies BA(Hons), History, Philosophy and Politics BA(Hons), Medieval and Renaissance Studies BA(Hons)

Postgraduate course: MA in History

Lancashire Institute for the Contemporary Arts; www.lancaster.ac.uk/lica

Design BA(Hons), Drama, Theatre and Performance BA(Hons), Film Studies BA(Hons), Film and Creative Writing BA(Hons), Film and English Literature BA(Hons), Film and Philosophy BA(Hons), Film and Sociology BA(Hons), Film and Theatre BA(Hons), Film, Media and Cultural Studies BA(Hons), Fine Art BA(Hons), Fine Art and Creative Writing BA(Hons), Fine Art and Film BA(Hons), Fine Art and Theatre BA(Hons), Marketing and Design BSc(Hons), Theatre and Creative Writing BA(Hons), Theatre and English Literature BA(Hons)

Postgraduate courses: Arts Management MA, Design Management MA

Department of Languages and Cultures; www.lancaster.ac.uk/languages-and-cultures

Environmental Sustainability in Contemporary China BA(Hons) L270, French Studies BA(Hons), French Studies and Computing BSc(Hons), French Studies and English Literature BA(Hons), French Studies and Film BA(Hons), French Studies and Geography BA(Hons), French Studies and German Studies BA(Hons), French Studies and History BA(Hons), French Studies and Linguistics BA(Hons), French Studies and Mathematics BA(Hons), French Studies and Philosophy BA(Hons), French Studies and Politics BA(Hons), French Studies and Psychology BA(Hons), French Studies and Spanish Studies BA(Hons), French Studies and Theatre BA(Hons), French Studies with Chinese BA(Hons), French Studies with Italian BA(Hons), German Studies BA(Hons), German Studies and Computing BSc(Hons), German Studies and English Literature BA(Hons), German Studies and Film BA(Hons), German Studies and Geography BA(Hons), German Studies and History BA(Hons), German Studies and Linguistics BA(Hons), German Studies and Mathematics BA(Hons), German Studies and Philosophy BA(Hons), German Studies and Politics BA(Hons), German Studies and Psychology BA(Hons), German Studies and Spanish Studies BA(Hons), German Studies and Theatre BA(Hons), German Studies with Chinese BA(Hons), German Studies with Italian BA(Hons), International Relations in Contemporary China BA(Hons), Linguistics with Chinese BA(Hons), Management Studies and European Languages BA(Hons), Modern Languages BA(Hons), Modern Languages and Cultures MLang(Hons), Spanish Studies BA(Hons), Spanish Studies and Computing BSc(Hons), Spanish Studies and English Literature BA(Hons), Spanish Studies and Film BA(Hons), Spanish Studies and Geography BA(Hons), Spanish Studies and History BA(Hons), Spanish Studies and Linguistics BA(Hons), Spanish Studies and Mathematics BA(Hons), Spanish Studies and Philosophy BA(Hons), Spanish Studies and Politics BA(Hons), Spanish Studies and Psychology BA(Hons), Spanish Studies and Theatre BA(Hons), Spanish Studies with Chinese BA(Hons), Spanish Studies with Italian BA(Hons)

Postgraduate courses: MA in Translation, MA in Languages and Cultures, European Languages and Cultures MPhil/PhD, MSc in International Innovation

Law School; www.lancaster.ac.uk/law

Law LLB(Hons), Law with Criminology LLB(Hons), Law with Politics LLB(Hons), BA(Hons) Criminology, BA Joint(Hons) Criminology and Psychology, BA Joint(Hons) Criminology and French Studies, BA Joint(Hons) Criminology and Sociology

Postgraduate courses: LLM Law, PGDip Law, LLM International Business and Corporate Law, LLM International Human Rights Law, LLM International Human Rights and Terrorism Law, LLM International Law, LLM Criminology and Criminal Justice, MA Criminology and Criminal Justice, MSc Criminal Justice and Social Research Methods, MSc Criminology and Social Research Methods

Department of Linguistics and English Language; www.lancaster.ac.uk/linguistics

English Language BA(Hons), English Language (Study Abroad) BA(Hons), English Language and Creative Writing BA(Hons), English Language and French Studies BA(Hons), English Language and German Studies BA(Hons), English Language and Linguistics BA(Hons), English Language and Literature BA(Hons), English Language and Spanish Studies BA(Hons), English Language in the Media BA(Hons), English Language in the Media (Study Abroad) BA(Hons), English Language with Chinese BA(Hons), English Literature and Linguistics BA(Hons), Linguistics BA(Hons), Linguistics and Philosophy BA(Hons), Linguistics and Psychology BA(Hons), Linguistics with Chinese

Postgraduate courses: Applied Linguistics and TESOL MA, Discourse Studies MA, English Language (Distance) MA, English Language and Literary Studies MA, Language Testing (Distance) MA, Language and Linguistics MA, Teaching English to Speakers of Other Languages (by Distance) MA

Department of Politics, Philosophy and Religion; www.lancaster.ac.uk/ppr

Ethics, Philosophy and Religion BA(Hons), International Relations BA(Hons), International Relations and Religious Diversity BA(Hons), Peace Studies and International Relations BA(Hons), Philosophy BA(Hons), Philosophy and Politics BA(Hons), Philosophy and Religious Studies BA(Hons), Philosophy with Chinese BA(Hons), Philosophy, Politics and Economics BA(Hons), Politics BA(Hons), Politics and International Relations BA(Hons), Politics and Religious Studies BA(Hons), Politics and Sociology BA(Hons), Politics with Chinese BA(Hons), Politics, International Relations and Management BSc(Hons), Religious Studies BA(Hons), Religious Studies and Sociology BA(Hons), Religious Studies with Chinese BA(Hons), Social Work, Ethics and Religion MSocial Work(Hons)

Postgraduate courses: MA Conflict, Development and Security, MA Conflict Resolution and Peace Studies, MA Diplomacy and Foreign Policy, MA/LLM Diplomacy and International Law, MA Diplomacy and International Law (Distance Learning), LLM Diplomacy and International Law (Distance Learning), MA Diplomacy and International Relations (Distance Learning), MA Diplomacy and Religion, MA/LLM International Law and International Relations, MA International Relations, MA Politics, MA Politics, Philosophy and Religion, MA Politics and Philosophy, MA Religion and Conflict, MRes International Relations, MSc Politics, Philosophy and Management, MA Philosophy, MA Philosophy and Religion, MA Politics, Philosophy and Religion, MA Politics and Philosophy, PGCert Philosophy, MA Diplomacy and Religion, MA Philosophy and Religion, MA Politics, Philosophy and Religion, MA Quakerism in the Modern World (Distance Learning), MA Religion and Conflict, MA Religious Studies, PGCert Religious Studies, PGCert Religious Studies (Distance Learning), Postgraduate Certificate in Quaker Studies (Distance Learning)

Department of Sociology; www.lancaster.ac.uk/sociology

Social Work BA(Hons), Social Work, Ethics and Religion MSocial Work, Sociology BA(Hons)

Postgraduate courses: Child Welfare MRes, Environment, Culture and Society MA, Gender and Women's Studies MA, Gender and Women's Studies and English MA, Gender and Women's Studies and Sociology MA, Media and Cultural Studies MA, Social Research MA, Social Work MA, Sociology MA

Faculty of Health and Medicine; www.lancaster.ac.uk/fhm

Biochemistry BSc(Hons), Biochemistry MSci(Hons), Biochemistry with Biomedicine BSc(Hons), Biochemistry with Genetics BSc(Hons), Biological Sciences BSc(Hons), Biological Sciences MSci(Hons), Biological Sciences with Biomedicine BSc(Hons), Biology BSc(Hons), Biology MSci(Hons), Biology with Psychology BSc(Hons), Biomedical Science BSc(Hons), Biomedicine BSc(Hons), Biomedicine MSci(Hons), Bioscience with Entrepreneurship BSc(Hons), Medicine and Surgery MBChB, Sports and Exercise Science BSc(Hons)

Postgraduate courses: MSc in Ageing, MSc in Biomedicine, MSc in Clinical Research, MRes in Global Health: translational research and quantitative skills, MSc in Health Economics and Policy, MSc in Innovation and Improvement Science, MSc in Medical Education, MSc in Medical Leadership, MA in Professional Practice

Management School; www.lancaster.ac.uk/lums

Accounting and Economics BSc(Hons), Accounting and Finance BSc(Hons), Accounting and Management BSc(Hons), Accounting, Finance and Mathematics BSc(Hons), Advertising and Marketing BA(Hons), Bioscience with Entrepreneurship BSc(Hons), Business Administration BBA(Hons), Business Analytics and Consultancy BSc(Hons), Business Economics (Industry) BSc(Hons), Business Management BSc(Hons), Economics BSc(Hons), Economics and Geography BA(Hons), Economics and International Relations BA(Hons), Economics and Mathematics BSc(Hons), Economics and Politics BA(Hons), Entrepreneurship and Management BSc(Hons), Finance BSc(Hons), Finance and Economics BSc(Hons), Financial Mathematics BSc(Hons), Financial Mathematics MSci(Hons), International Business Management (America/France/Germany/Italy/Mexico/Spain) BBA(Hons), International Management BSc(Hons), International Management in Contemporary China BA(Hons), Management Studies and European Languages BA(Hons), Management and Human Resources BSc(Hons), Management and Information Technology (4 years including placement) BSc(Hons), Management and Organisational Behaviour BSc(Hons), Management and Psychology BA(Hons), Management and Sociology BA(Hons), Marketing BSc(Hons), Marketing Management BSc(Hons), Marketing and Design BSc(Hons), Marketing with Psychology BSc(Hons),

Mathematics, Operational Research, Statistics and Economics (MORSE) BSc(Hons), Philosophy, Politics and Economics BA(Hons), Politics, International Relations and Management BSc(Hons)

Postgraduate courses: MSc Accounting & Financial Management, MSc Advanced Financial Analysis (including CFA training), MSc/MRes Advanced Marketing Management, MSc Business Analytics, MSc/PGDip E-Business & Innovation, MSc Economics, GradDip Economics (9 months), MSc Entrepreneurship, Innovation & Practice, MSc Finance, MBA Full-time MBA, MSc Human Resource Management, MA Human Resources & Consulting, MSc/MRes Information Technology, Management & Organisational Change (ITMOC), MSc International Business & Strategy, MSc Logistics & Supply Chain Management, MSc Management, MRes Management Science, MSc Management Science & Marketing Analytics, MSc Marketing, MSc Money, Banking & Finance, MSc Politics, Philosophy & Management, MSc Project Management, MSc Quantitative Finance

Faculty of Science and Technology; www.lancaster.ac.uk/sci-tech
Biology and Biological Sciences
Biology BSc(Hons), Biology MSci(Hons), Biological Sciences BSc(Hons), Biological Sciences MSci(Hons), Biochemistry BSc(Hons), Biochemistry with Biomedicine BSc(Hons), Biological Sciences with Biomedicine BSc(Hons), Biology with Psychology BSc(Hons), Biochemistry with Genetics BSc(Hons), Biomedical Science BSc(Hons), Biomedicine BSc(Hons), Biomedicine: MSci(Hons), Bioscience with Entrepreneurship BSc(Hons)
Chemistry
Chemistry BSc(Hons), Chemistry MChem(Hons), Chemistry (Study Abroad) MChem(Hons)
Computing and Communications
Computer Science BSc(Hons), Computer Science and Mathematics BSc(Hons), Computer Science and Mathematics MSci(Hons), Management and Information Technology BSc(Hons), Software Engineering BSc(Hons)
Ecology and Conservation
Ecology and Conservation BSc(Hons)
Engineering
Engineering BEng(Hons), Mechanical Engineering BEng(Hons), Mechanical Engineering MEng(Hons), Chemical Engineering BEng(Hons), Chemical Engineering MEng(Hons), Electronic and Electrical Engineering BEng(Hons), Electronic and Electrical Engineering MEng(Hons), Mechatronics BEng(Hons), Mechatronics MEng(Hons), Nuclear Engineering BEng(Hons), Nuclear Engineering MEng(Hons)
Environmental and Earth Sciences
Earth and Environmental Science BSc(Hons), Earth and Environmental Science MSci(Hons), Environmental Science BSc(Hons), Environmental Science MSci(Hons)
Geography
Geography BA(Hons), Geography BSc(Hons), Geography MArts(Hons), Geography MSci(Hons), Physical Geography BSc(Hons), Physical Geography MSci(Hons), Human Geography BA(Hons)
Mathematics and Statistics
Mathematics BSc(Hons), Mathematics MSci(Hons), Mathematics and Philosophy BA(Hons), Mathematics with Statistics BSc(Hons), Mathematics with Statistics MSci(Hons), Mathematics, Operational Research, Statistics and Economics (MORSE) BSc(Hons), Statistics BSc(Hons), Statistics MSci(Hons), Theoretical Physics with Mathematics BSc(Hons), Theoretical Physics with Mathematics MSci(Hons), Financial Mathematics BSc(Hons), Financial Mathematics MSci(Hons)
Natural Sciences
Natural Sciences BSc(Hons), Natural Sciences MSci(Hons)
Physics
Physics BSc(Hons), Physics MPhys(Hons), Physics with Particle Physics and Cosmology BSc(Hons), Physics with Particle Physics and Cosmology MPhys(Hons), Physics, Astrophysics and Cosmology BSc(Hons), Physics, Astrophysics and Cosmology MPhys(Hons), Theoretical Physics BSc(Hons), Theoretical Physics MPhys(Hons), Theoretical Physics with Mathematics BSc(Hons), Theoretical Physics with Mathematics MSci(Hons)
Psychology
Psychology BA(Hons), Psychology BSc(Hons), Psychology MPsych(Hons)
Postgraduate courses
Computer Science MSc, Conservation and Biodiversity MSc, Cyber Security MSc, Data Science MSc, Developmental Disorders MSc, Developmental Psychology MSc, Electronic Engineering MSc, Engineering Project Management MSc, Environment and Development MSc, Environment and Development MA, Environment and Law LLM, Environment, Culture and Society MA, Environmental Management MSc, Flood and Coastal Risk Management PgCert, Food Challenges for the 21st Century PgCert, Human Rights and the Environment LLM, Mechanical Engineering MSc, Mechanical Engineering with

Project Management MSc, Psychological Research Methods MSc, Psychology of Advertising MSc, Quantitative Finance MSc, Statistics MSc, Statistics PGDip, Statistics and Operational Research (STOR-i)

MRes, Sustainable Water Management MSc, Volcanology and Geological Hazards MSc, Wireless Communication Systems MSc

BLACKPOOL AND THE FYLDE COLLEGE
www.blackpool.ac.uk

Accounting and Finance
Accounting Level 4 Higher Apprenticeship (AAT)

Administration
Business Administration Level 4 Higher Apprenticeship (OCR), Human Resource Management Level 5 Diploma (CIPD)

Architecture and Advanced Construction
Construction and the Built Environment HNC (Edexcel)

Automotive and Motorsport
Automotive Engineering and Technology (Automotive) BEng(Hons), Automotive Engineering and Technology (Automotive) FdA, Automotive Engineering and Technology (Motorsport) BEng(Hons), Automotive Engineering and Technology (Motorsport) FdA, Automotive Engineering and Technology with Foundation Year (Automotive) FdA, Automotive Engineering and Technology with Foundation Year (Motorsport) FdA

Building and Construction
Civil Engineering HNC (Edexcel)

Business and Project Management
Business and Financial Management BA(Hons), Business and Financial Management FdA, Human Resource Management Level 5 Intermediate Diploma (CIPD), Management FdA, Management and Leadership Level 5 Higher Apprenticeship (OCR), Management in the Workplace BA(Hons), Project Management BSc(Hons), Project Management FdA, Project Management Level 4 Higher Apprenticeship (EAL)

Child Development and Wellbeing
Early Childhood Studies BA(Hons), Early Childhood Studies Level 5 FdA, Family Support and Wellbeing BA(Hons), Family Support and Wellbeing FdA, Working with Young People FdA

Computing – Digital Media and ICT
Digital and Technology Solutions (Cyber Security Analyst) Apprenticeship, Digital and Technology Solutions (Network Engineer) Apprenticeship, Digital and Technology Solutions (Software Engineering) Apprenticeship, Interactive Media Development BSc(Hons), Interactive Media Development FdA, Network Engineering (Cyber Security) BSc(Hons), Network Engineering (Cyber Security) FdA, Network Engineering (Systems Administration) BSc(Hons), Network Engineering (Systems Administration) FdA, Network Engineering Security and Systems Administration BSc(Hons), Software Engineering (App Development) FdA, Software Engineering (Game Development) FdA, Software Engineering and Game Development BSc(Hons)

Creative Arts, Design and Crafts
Fashion Design (Contemporary Costume) BA(Hons), Fashion Design BA(Hons), Fine Art Professional Practice BA(Hons), Graphic Design and Visual Communication BA(Hons), Photography BA(Hons)

Criminology and Criminal Justice
Criminology and Criminal Justice BA(Hons), Criminology and Criminal Justice FdA

Engineering
Aerospace Engineering BEng(Hons), Aerospace Engineering FdA, Electrical and Electronic Engineering HNC (Edexcel), Engineering (Mechanical Engineering) BEng(Hons), Engineering (Mechanical Engineering) BEng(Hons), Engineering (Mechatronics Engineering) BEng(Hons), Engineering (Mechatronics Engineering) BENg(Hons), General Engineering HNC (Edexcel), Mechanical Engineering HNC (Edexcel)

English and ESOL
English: Language, Literature and Writing BA(Hons)

Health and Social Care
Health and Social Care (Adult) BA(Hons), Health and Social Care (Child) BA(Hons), Leadership for Health and Social Care and Children and Young People's Services Level 5 Higher Apprenticeship (NCFE Cache), Professional Practice Health and Social Care (Children and Families) FdA, Professional Practice Health and Social Care (Combined) FdA, Professional Practice Health and Social Care (Mental Health) FdA

Hospitality and Catering
Hospitality and Events Management BA(Hons), Hospitality and Events Management FdA

Learning Support
Teaching and Learning Support BA(Hons), Teaching and Learning Support FdA

Media Production, Film and Television
Scriptwriting for Stage, Screen and Gaming BA(Hons)

Performing Arts and Music
Acting BA(Hons), Musical Theatre BA(Hons)

Public Services
Public Services FdA, Public Services and The Community BSc(Hons)

Science
Human Biosciences BSc(Hons), Human Biosciences FdA, Marine Biology and Coastal Zone Management BSc(Hons), Marine Biology and Coastal Zone Management FdA

Sport, Leisure and Recreation
Physical Activity, Nutrition and Health FdA, Sports Coaching and Exercise Instruction BSc(Hons), Sports Coaching and Exercise Science FdA, Sports Studies and Development BA(Hons)

Teaching and Lecturing
Professional Certificate in Education PCE, Professional Graduate Certificate in Education PGCE

Travel and Tourism
Tourism Management BA(Hons), Tourism Management FdA

UNIVERSITY OF LEEDS
www.leeds.ac.uk

Faculty of Arts, Humanities and Cultures; www.leeds.ac.uk/info/130500/faculties

Faculty of Arts; www.leeds.ac.uk/arts

BA Arabic and Islamic Studies, BA Arabic and Middle Eastern Studies UG, BA Asia Pacific Studies, BA Asia Pacific Studies (International), BA Biomedical and Health Care Ethics, BA Chinese (Modern), BA Classical Civilisation, BA East Asian Religions and Cultures, BA English Language and Literature, BA English Literature, BA English Literature and Theatre Studies, BA French, BA German, BA History, BA International History and Politics, BA Islamic Studies, BA Italian, BA Japanese, BA Linguistics and Phonetics, BA Middle Eastern Studies, BA Philosophy, BA Philosophy, Ethics and Religion, BA Russian, BA Spanish, BA Thai Studies, BA Theatre and Performance with Enterprise, BA Theology and Religious Studies, various joint honours options

Postgraduate courses: MA American Literature and Culture PGT, MA Applied and Professional Ethics (Online), MA Applied Translation Studies, MA Arabic/English Translation, MA Audiovisual Translation Studies, MA Biomedical and Health Care Ethics, MA Biomedical and Health Care Ethics (Online), MA Biomedical and Health Care Ethics, MA Business and Public Service Interpreting and Translation Studies, MA Chinese and Management, MA Conference Interpreting and Translation Studies, MA East Asian Cultures and Societies, MA East Asian Cultures and Societies (Language Pathway), MA English Literature, MA English Literature (Modern and Contemporary pathway), MA English Literature (Renaissance pathway), MA English Literature (Romantic pathway), MA English Literature (Victorian pathway), MA History of Health, Medicine and Society, MA History of Science, Technology and Medicine, MA in Social and Cultural History, MA Linguistics, MA Linguistics and English Language Teaching, MA Medieval History, MA Medieval Studies, MA Middle Eastern and Islamic Studies, MA Modern History, MA Philosophy, MA Philosophy of Religion and Ethics, MA Postcolonial Literary and Cultural Studies, MA Professional Language and Intercultural Studies, MA Race and Resistance, MA Religion and Public Life, MA Religious Studies and Global Development, MA Theology and Religious Studies, MA War and Strategy, MA Writing Identities: Critical and Creative Practices, MRes Biomedical and Healthcare Ethics, MRes Classics, MRes East Asian Studies, ND Language for Engineering, ND Language for Science, ND Language for Science: Engineering, ND Language for Science: General Science, PGCert Philosophy of Religion and Ethics, PGCert Theology and Religious Studies, PGDip Applied and Professional Ethics (Online), PGDip Applied Translation Studies, PGDip Biomedical and Health Care Ethics, PGDip Biomedical and Health Care Ethics (Online), PGDip Business and Public Service Interpreting, PGDip Conference Interpreting, PGDip Philosophy of Religion and Ethics, PGDip Theology and Religious Studies

School of Media and Communication; www.media.leeds.ac.uk

BA Hons Journalism, BA Hons Film, Photography and Media, BA Hons Communication and Media, BA Hons Digital Media

Postgraduate courses: MA Film, Photography and Media, MA Communication and Media, MA International Communication, MA International Journalism, MA Media Industries, MA New Media, MA Political Communication, MA Public Relations and Society

School of Design; www.design.leeds.ac.uk

BA Art and Design, BA Fashion Design, BA Fashion Marketing, BA Fashion Technology, BA Graphic and Communication Design, BA Textile Design

Postgraduate courses: MA Advertising and Design, MA Design, MA Design Future Society, MA Fashion, Enterprise and Society, MSc Textiles

School of Fine Art, History of Art and Cultural Studies; www.fine-art.leeds.ac.uk

BA Art Gallery and Museum Studies, BA Cultural and Media Studies, BA Fine Art, BA Fine Art with Contemporary Cultural Theory, BA Fine Art with History of Art, BA Fine Art with Museum and Gallery Studies, BA History of Art, BA History of Art with Cultural Studies

Postgraduate courses: MA in Art Gallery and Museum Studies, MA in Arts Management and Heritage Studies, MA in Critical and Cultural Theory, MA in Fine Art (MAFA), MA in History of Art

School of Music; www.music.leeds.ac.uk

Music BA, Music (Performance) BMus, Music with Enterprise BA, Music, Multimedia and Electronics BSc, Music and Music Psychology MArts BA

Postgraduate courses: Applied Psychology of Music MA, Critical and Applied Musicology MA, Critical and Experimental Composition MMus, Electronic and Computer Music MA, Music and Management MA, Performance MMus or Postgraduate Diploma, Graduate Diploma in Music

School of Performance and Cultural Industries; www.pci.leeds.ac.uk

BA Theatre and Performance, BA Theatre and Performance with Enterprise

Postgraduate courses: MA Applied Theatre and Intervention, MA Culture, Creativity and Entrepreneurship, MA Performance Design, MA Writing for Performance and Publication

Faculty of Biological Sciences; www.fbs.leeds.ac.uk

BSc Biochemistry, MBiol Biochemistry, BSc Biological Sciences, MBiol Biological Sciences, BSc Biology, MBiol Biology, BSc Biology and Mathematics, BSc Biology with Enterprise, MBiol Biology with Enterprise, BSc Biotechnology with Enterprise, MBiol Biotechnology with Enterprise, BSc Ecology and Conservation Biology, MBiol Ecology and Conservation Biology, BSc Genetics, MBiol Genetics, BSc Human Physiology, MBiol Human Physiology, BSc Medical Biochemistry, MBiol Medical Biochemistry, BSc Medical Microbiology, BSc Medical Sciences, MBiol Medical Sciences, BSc Microbiology, MBiol Microbiology, BSc Natural Sciences, BSc Neuroscience, MBiol Neuroscience, BSc Pharmacology, MBiol Pharmacology, BSc Sport and Exercise Sciences, MSci Sport and Exercise Sciences, BSc Sports Science and Physiology, MSci Sports Science and Physiology, BSc Zoology

Postgraduate courses: MSc Biodiversity and Conservation, MSc Biodiversity and Conservation with African Field Course, MRes Biodiversity and Conservation, MRes Biodiversity and Conservation with African Field Course, MSc Biopharmaceutical Development, MSc Bioscience, MSc Infection, Immunity & Human Disease, MSc Plant Science and Biotechnology, MSc Sport and Exercise Medicine

Faculty of Business; www.business.leeds.ac.uk

BSc Accounting and Finance, BSc Banking and Finance, BSc Business Analytics, BSc Business Economics, BSc Economics, BSc Economics and Finance, BSc Economics and Management, BA Human Resource Management, BSc International Business, BSc International Business and Finance, BSc International Business and Marketing, BA Management, BA Management and the Human Resource, BA Management with Marketing, various joint honours options

Postgraduate courses: Master of Business Administration, MSc Accounting and Finance, MSc Actuarial Finance, MSc Banking and International Finance, MSc Finance and Investment, MSc Financial Mathematics, MSc Financial Risk Management, MSc Economics, MSc Economics and Finance, MSc Business Analytics and Decision Sciences, MSc Business Psychology (also available part-time), MSc Enterprise and Enterpreneurship (also available part-time), MSc Global Strategy and Innovation Management, MSc Global Supply Chain Management, MSc Information Systems and Information Management, MSc

Management, MSc Management Consulting, MSc Organizational Psychology, MA Human Resource Management (also available part-time), MSc International Business, MA Advertising and Marketing, MSc Consumer Analytics and Marketing Strategy, MA Corporate Communications, Marketing and Public Relations, MSc International Marketing Management, MSc Business Management

Faculty of Education, Social Sciences and Law; www.essl.leeds.ac.uk

School of Education; www.education.leeds.ac.uk

BA Childhood Studies, BA Education, BA Teaching English to Speakers of Other Languages (TESOL), BSc Psychology with Education, BA English, Language and Education, BA Social Science
Postgraduate courses: MA Childhood Studies, MA Education, MA Technology, Education and Learning, MA English Language Teaching and Digital Technologies, MA International Education Leadership and Policy, MA Education and Professional Enquiry, MA Special Educational Needs, PGCert Provision for Children with Developmental Disorders, MA Deaf Education (Teacher of the Deaf Qualification) (Distance learning), MA Teaching English to Speakers of Other Languages (TESOL), MEd Teaching English to Speakers of Other Languages (TESOL), MA TESOL Studies, MA Teaching English to Speakers of Other Languages (China), MA Teaching English to Speakers of Other Languages and Information and Communications Technology, MA Teaching English to Speakers of Other Languages for Young Learners, MA Teaching English to Speakers of Other Languages (Teacher Education)

School of Sociology and Social Policy; www.sociology.leeds.ac.uk

BA(Hons) Sociology, BA(Hons) Social Policy, BA(Hons) Social Policy and Crime, BA(Hons) Social Policy with Enterprise, BA(Hons) Social Policy and Sociology, various joint honours options
Postgraduate courses: MA Social and Public Policy, MA Social Research, MA Society, Culture and Media, MPA Public Administration, MSc Inequalities and Social Science, MA Social and Political Thought, MA Disability Studies, MA Gender Studies

School of Politics and International Studies; www.polis.leeds.ac.uk

BA International Development, BA International Relations, BA Politics, BA Economics and Politics

Postgraduate courses: MA Global Development, MA International Relations, MA International Relations and Politics of the Middle East, MA Conflict, Development and Security, MA Security, Terrorism and Insurgency, MA Politics, MA Public Administration

School of Law; www.law.leeds.ac.uk

LLB Law, LLB Law with European Legal Studies, LLB Law with International Legal Studies, LLB Law with French Law, LLB Law with German Law, LLB Law with Hispanic Law, BA Criminal Justice and Criminology
Postgraduate courses: LLM Criminal Justice and Criminal Law, MSc Criminal Justice and Criminology, LLM Intellectual Property Law, LLM International Banking and Finance Law, LLM International Business Law, LLM International Corporate Law, LLM International Human Rights Law, LLM International Law, LLM International Trade Law, LLB Law (graduate programme), MSc Law and Finance, MSc Security, Conflict and Justice

Faculty of Engineering; www.engineering.leeds.ac.uk

School of Chemical and Process Engineering; www.engineering.leeds.ac.uk/info/20135/school_of_chemical_and_process_engineering

Aviation Technology and Management BSc, Aviation Technology with Pilot Studies BSc, Chemical Engineering MEng/BEng, Chemical and Energy Engineering MEng/BEng, Chemical and Materials Engineering MEng/BEng, Chemical and Nuclear Engineering MEng/BEng, Petroleum Engineering MEng/BEng
Postgraduate courses: Advanced Chemical Engineering MSc, Chemical Process Engineering MSc, Energy and Environment MSc, Materials Science and Engineering MSc, Petroleum Production Engineering MSc

School of Civil Engineering; www.engineering.leeds.ac.uk/info/20131/school_of_civil_engineering

Architectural Engineering MEng/BEng, Architecture MEng/BEng, Civil and Environmental Engineering MEng/BEng, Civil and Structural Engineering MEng/BEng, Civil Engineering with Project Management MEng/BEng, Civil Engineering with Transport MEng/BEng
Postgraduate courses: Advanced Concrete Technology MSc (Eng), Advanced Concrete Technology

PGDip, Engineering Project Management MSc (Eng), Environmental Engineering and Project Management MSc (Eng), International Construction Management and Engineering MSc (Eng), Structural Engineering MSc (Eng), Water, Sanitation and Health Engineering MSc (Eng)

School of Computing;
www.engineering.leeds.ac.uk/info/20132/
school_of_computing

Applied Computer Science MEng, BSc, Computer Science MEng/BSc, Computer Science (Digital & Technology Solutions) BSc, Computer Science with Artificial Intelligence MEng/BSc, Computer Science with High Performance Graphics and Games Engineering MEng/BSc, Computer Science with Mathematics MSci/BSc, Electronics and Computer Engineering MEng/BEng

Postgraduate courses: Advanced Computer Science MSc, Advanced Computer Science (Cloud Computing) MSc, Advanced Computer Science (Data Analytics) MSc, Advanced Computer Science (Intelligent Systems) MSc, High-Performance Graphics and Games Engineering MSc, Mathematics and Computer Science MSc

School of Electronic and Electrical Engineering;
www.engineering.leeds.ac.uk/info/20133/
school_of_electronic_and_
electrical_engineering

Electronic and Communications Engineering MEng/BEng, Electronics and Computer Engineering MEng/BEng, Electronic and Electrical Engineering MEng/BEng, Electronic Engineering MEng/BEng, Electronics and Renewable Energy Systems MEng/BEng, Mechatronics and Robotics MEng/BEng, Music Multimedia and Electronics BSc

Postgraduate courses: Communications and Signal Processing MSc (Eng), Digital Communications Networks MSc (Eng), Electrical Engineering and Renewable Energy Systems MSc (Eng), Electronic and Electrical Engineering MSc (Eng), Embedded Systems Engineering MSc (Eng), Engineering, Technology and Business Management MSc (Eng), Mechatronics and Robotics MSc (Eng)

School of Mechanical Engineering;
www.engineering.leeds.ac.uk/info/20134/
school_of_mechanical_engineering

Aeronautical and Aerospace Engineering MEng/BEng, Automotive Engineering MEng/BEng, Mechanical Engineering MEng/BEng, Mechatronics

and Robotics MEng/BEng, Medical Engineering MEng/BEng, Product Design MDes/BSc

Postgraduate courses: Advanced Mechanical Engineering MSc (Eng), Aerospace Engineering MSc, Automotive Engineering MSc (Eng), Mechatronics and Robotics MSc (Eng), Medical Engineering MSc (Eng), Joint European Master in Tribology of Surface and Interfaces

Faculty of Environment;
www.environment.leeds.ac.uk

BSc Geography-Geology, BSc Geological Sciences, MGeol Geological Sciences, BSc Geophysical Sciences, MGeophys Geophysical Sciences, BSc Environmental Science, MEnv Environmental Science, BSc Geography, BSc Meteorology and Climate Science, MEnv Meteorology and Climate Science, BSc Geography and Environmental Mathematics, BA Geography, BA Geography with Transport Studies, BA Geography Joint Honours Courses, BA Environment and Business, MEnv Environment and Business, BSc Sustainability and Environmental Management, MEnv Sustainability and Environmental Management

Postgraduate courses: MSc Engineering Geology, MSc Exploration Geophysics, MSc Structural Geology with Geophysics, MRes Climate and Atmospheric Science, MSc Environmental Water Consultancy, MSc Geographical Information Systems (GIS), MSc Geographical Information Systems (GIS) (Online distance learning), MSc River Basin Dynamics and Management with GIS, MSc Climate Change and Environmental Policy, MSc Ecological Economics, MSc Environment and Development, MSc Environment and Development with Integrated International Fieldwork, MSc Sustainability and Business, MSc Sustainability and Consultancy, MSc Sustainability in Transport, MSc Sustainable Cities, MSc Mathematical Modelling for Transport, MSc Transport Economics, MSc Transport Planning, MSc (Eng) Transport Planning and Engineering, MSc Transport Planning and the Environment, MSc Sustainability in Transport

Faculty of Mathematics and Physical Sciences; www.maps.leeds.ac.uk

BSc Actuarial Mathematics, BSc Chemistry, BSc/MChem Chemistry, BSc Food Science and Nutrition, BSc Food Science, BSc Mathematical Studies, BSc Mathematics and Statistics, BSc/MMath Mathematics and Statistics, BSc Mathematics with Finance, BSc Mathematics, BSc/MMath Mathematics, BSc Medicinal Chemistry, BSc/MChem Medicinal Chemistry,

BSc Nutrition, BSc Physics with Astrophysics, MPhys Physics with Astrophysics, BSc Physics, MPhys Physics, BSc Theoretical Physics, MPhys Theoretical Physics

Postgraduate courses: MSc Chemical Biology and Drug Design, MSc Polymers, Colorants and Fine Chemicals, MSc Food Quality and Innovation, MSc Food Science, MSc Food Science (Food Biotechnology), MSc Food Science and Nutrition, MSc Nutrition, MSc Atmosphere-Ocean Dynamics, MSc Data Science and Analytics, MSc Mathematics, MSc Mathematics and Computer Science, MSc Medical Statistics, MSc Statistics, MSc Statistics with Applications to Finance, MSc Financial Mathematics, MSc Actuarial Finance, MSc Physics, MSc Physics and Business Management

Faculty of Medicine and Health; *www.medhealth.leeds.ac.uk*

BA Social Work, BSc Midwifery, BSc Nursing (Adult), BSc Nursing (Child), BSc Nursing (Mental Health), BSc Psychology

Postgraduate courses: MA Psychotherapy and Counselling, MA Social Work, MPH Public Health (International), MPH Public Health – Health Management, Planning and Policy (International), MPH Public Health – Health Management, Planning and Policy (International), MSc Advanced Practice, MSc Clinical Care, MSc Clinical Research Methods, MSc Health Informatics, MSc International Health, MSc Pharmacy Practice, MSc Pharmacy Practice with Prescribing, ND Systemic Practice (Foundation), ND Systemic Practice (Intermediate), PGCert Clinical Assessment, PGCert Health Informatics (Part Time – 12 months), PGCert Public Health (International), PGCert Public Health – Health Management, Planning and Policy (International), PGCert Systemic Practice, PGDip Clinical Embryology (Distance Learning), PGDip Health Informatics, PGDip Pharmacy Practice, PGDip Pharmacy Practice with Prescribing, PGDip Public Health (International), PGDip Public Health – Health Management, Planning and Policy (International)

COLLEGE OF THE RESURRECTION
college.mirfield.org.uk

BA(Hons) in Theological Studies

Postgraduate courses: MA/PGDip in Ministry & Theology, MA in Liturgy

---

LEEDS ARTS UNIVERSITY
www.leeds-art.ac.uk

BA(Hons) Animation, BA(Hons) Fashion, BA(Hons) Fashion Photography, BA(Hons) Graphic Design, BMus(Hons) Popular Music Performance, BA(Hons) Comic & Concept Art, BA(Hons) Fashion Branding With Communication, BA(Hons) Filmmaking, BA(Hons) Illustration, BA(Hons) Printed Textiles & Surface Pattern Design, BA(Hons) Creative Advertising, BA(Hons) Fashion Design, BA(Hons) Fine Art, BA(Hons) Photography, BA(Hons) Visual Communication

Postgraduate courses: MA Creative Practice, MA Curation Practices

---

LEEDS COLLEGE OF MUSIC
www.lcm.ac.uk

BA(Hons) Music (Business), BA(Hons) Music (Classical With Jazz), BA(Hons) Music (Classical With Popular), BA(Hons) Music (Classical With Production), BA(Hons) Music (Classical)

Postgraduate course: MMus/PGDip Creative Musician

LEEDS TRINITY UNIVERSITY
www.leedstrinity.ac.uk

Undergraduate degrees in the following subjects

Business
Accounting and Business, Business and Economics, Business and Management, Business and Marketing, Economics, International Business

Childhood and Education
Early Childhood Studies, Education and Religious Studies, Education Studies, Working with Children, Young People and Families

Criminology and Sociology
Criminology, Criminology and Sociology, Criminology with Police Studies, Psychology and Criminology, Psychology and Sociology, Sociology, Sociology with Police Studies

English
Creative and Professional Writing, English and Creative Writing, English and Film, English and History, English and Media, English Language and Linguistics, English Literature

Health and Nutrition
Exercise, Health and Fitness, Exercise, Health and Nutrition, Public Health and Individual Wellbeing

Humanities
History, History and Philosophy, History and Politics, Philosophy, Ethics and Religion, Politics and Economics, Politics and International Relations, Theology and Religious Studies

Journalism
Broadcast Journalism, Journalism, Journalism and Politics, Sports Journalism

Law
Law

Media and Film
Film, Media, Media and Marketing, Photography, Television Production

Primary Education
Primary Education – Early Years (QTS), Primary Education – Later Years (QTS)

Psychology
Counselling, Psychology, Forensic Psychology, Media and Psychology, Psychology, Psychology and Business, Psychology and Child Development, Sport Psychology

Sport and Physical Education
Physical Education, Secondary Education, Physical Education and Sport (2 years), Sport and Exercise Sciences, Sport and Exercise Sciences (Sports Nutrition), Sport Management, Sport Therapy and Rehabilitation, Sports Coaching, Strength and Conditioning

Postgraduate degrees in the following subjects:International Business, Marketing, MBA, MBA in Finance, Family Support, MA in Education, Creative Writing, History, Victorian Studies, Journalism, Primary Education, PGCE Primary (3-7), PGCE Primary (5-11), Psychology, PGCE Business, PGCE Computer Science with ICT, PGCE English, PGCE Geography, PGCE History, PGCE Mathematics, PGCE Modern Foreign Languages (MFL), PGCE Religious Education, PGCE Science with Biology, PGCE Science with Chemistry, PGCE Science with Physics, Health and Wellbeing Sport Management

NORTHERN SCHOOL OF CONTEMPORARY DANCE
www.nscd.ac.uk

BA(Hons) Dance (Contemporary)

Postgraduate courses: MA Dance & Creative Enterprise, MA Contemporary Dance Performance (Verve)

YORK ST JOHN UNIVERSITY
www.yorksj.ac.uk

Art and Design
Animation BA(Hons), Fine Art BA(Hons), Furniture Design BA(Hons), Games Design BA(Hons), Graphic Design BA(Hons), Illustration BA(Hons), Interior Design BA(Hons), Photography BA(Hons), Product Design BA(Hons)

Postgraduate course: Fine Arts MA/PgDip/PgCert

Business
Accounting & Business Management BA(Hons), Accounting & Finance BA(Hons), Business and Economics BA(Hons), Business Information Technology BA(Hons), Business Studies BA(Hons), Business

Management BA(Hons), Business Management & Finance BA(Hons), Business Management & HR Management BA(Hons), Business Management and BSL BA(Hons), Business Information Management BA(Hons), Business Management & French BA(Hons), Business Management & German BA(Hons), Business Management & Japanese BA(Hons), Business Management & Spanish BA(Hons), Economics & Finance BSc(Hons), Events and International Hospitality Management BA(Hons), Events Management BA(Hons), International Business Management BA(Hons), International Hospitality Management BA(Hons), International Tourism and Hospitality Management BA(Hons), Marketing and Events Management BA(Hons), Marketing and International Hospitality Management BA(Hons), Marketing Management BA(Hons), Sports Management BA(Hons), Sports Marketing Management BA(Hons), Tourism Management BA(Hons), Tourism Management & Marketing BA(Hons), Tourism Management & Spanish BA(Hons), Tourism and Events Management BA(Hons)

Postgraduate courses: Coaching & Mentoring PgCert, Creative & Cultural Marketing MSc, Digital Marketing MSc, International Business Management MSc, International Marketing MSc, Leadership & Management MSc, Masters of Business Administration MBA, MBA: Finance MBA, MBA: Human Resource Management MBA, Masters of Business Conversion MBA

Computing

Computer Science BSc(Hons), Games Development BSc(Hons), Software Engineering BSc(Hons)

Health Sciences

Biomedical Science BSc(Hons), Occupational Therapy BHSc(Hons), Physiotherapy BHSc(Hons)

Humanities

American Studies BA(Hons), Creative Writing BA(Hons), English Literature BA(Hons), Environmental Geography BSc(Hons), Geography BSc(Hons), Human Geography BA(Hons), Human Geography with American Studies BA(Hons), Human Geography with History BA(Hons), Human Geography with Media Studies BA(Hons), History BA(Hons), War Studies BA(Hons), History & American Studies BA(Hons), American Studies & Film Studies BA(Hons), Creative Writing & English Language BA(Hons), Creative Writing & Media BA(Hons), English Language & English Literature BA(Hons), English Language & Education Studies BA(Hons), English Literature & BSL BA(Hons), English Literature & French BA(Hons), English Literature & German BA(Hons), English Literature & Japanese BA(Hons), English Literature & Spanish BA(Hons), English Literature & History BA(Hons), English Literature & Film Studies BA(Hons), English Literature & Education Studies BA(Hons), Media & English Literature BA(Hons)

Postgraduate courses: American Studies MA, Contemporary Literature MA, Creative Writing MA, International History MA

Languages and Linguistics

English Language & Linguistics BA(Hons), Linguistics & TESOL BA(Hons), TESOL & French BA(Hons), TESOL & German BA(Hons), TESOL & Japanese BA(Hons), TESOL & Spanish BA(Hons), French & German BA(Hons), French & Spanish BA(Hons), German & Spanish BA(Hons), Spanish with British Sign Language BA(Hons), Spanish with Japanese BA(Hons), French with British Sign Language BA(Hons), French with Japanese BA(Hons), French with Spanish BA(Hons), English Language & BSL BA(Hons), German with British Sign Language BA(Hons), German with Japanese BA(Hons), English Language & French BA(Hons), English Language & German BA(Hons), German with Spanish BA(Hons), English Language & Japanese BA(Hons), English Language & Spanish BA(Hons)

Postgraduate courses: Applied Linguistics: TESOL MA, Applied Linguistics: Translation MA, Clinical Linguistics MSc/PgDip/PgCert, Language and Linguistics MA/PgDip/PgCert, Japanese Language Teaching MA

Media and Production

Film Studies BA(Hons), Media BA(Hons), Media Production BA(Hons), Media Production: Journalism BA(Hons), Media Production: Film and Television BA(Hons), Media & Film Studies BA(Hons)

Performance

Drama & Dance BA(Hons), Drama: Education & Community BA(Hons), Drama & Theatre BA(Hons), Music BA(Hons), Music Composition BA(Hons), Music: Education & Community BA(Hons), Music: Performance BA(Hons), Music Production BA(Hons)

Postgraduate courses: Applied Theatre MA/PgDip/PgCert, Music Composition MA/PgDip/PgCert, Music Production MA, Theatre & Performance MA/PgDip/PgCert

Psychology and Counselling

Counselling, Coaching & Mentoring BA(Hons), Psychology BSc(Hons), Psychology with Counselling BSc(Hons)

Postgraduate courses: Counselling MA/PGDip, Psychology of Child & Adolescent Development MSc

Religion and Philosophy

Christian Theology BA(Hons), Religion, Philosophy & Ethics BA(Hons), Religious Studies BA(Hons), Theology & Religious Studies BA(Hons)

Postgraduate course: Contemporary Religion MA

Social Sciences

Sociology BA(Hons), Criminology BA(Hons), Sociology with Criminology BA(Hons), Police Studies BA(Hons), Criminology with Police Studies BA(Hons), Sociology with Police Studies BA(Hons)

Postgraduate courses: Occupational Therapy (pre-registration) MSc, Physiotherapy (Pre-registration) MSc, Leadership in Health & Social Care MSc, Professional Health & Social Care MSc, Promoting Health in Long Term Conditions MSc

Sport

Sport & Exercise Science BSc(Hons), Sport & Exercise Therapy BSc(Hons), Physical Education & Sports Coaching BA(Hons), Sport Development & Business Management BA(Hons)

Postgraduate course: Strength & Conditioning MSc

Education

Children, Young People & Families BA(Hons), Children, Young People & Families with British Sign Language (BA Hons), Children, Young People & Families with Special Educational Needs & Inclusion BA(Hons), Children, Young People & Families and Education Studies BA(Hons), Early Childhood Studies BA(Hons), Education Studies BA(Hons), Education Studies with French BA(Hons), Education Studies with German BA(Hons), Primary Education 3 – 7 years BA(Hons), Primary Education 5 – 11 years BA(Hons), Education Studies with Japanese BA(Hons), Education Studies with Spanish BA(Hons), Education Studies with Special Educational Needs & Inclusion BA(Hons), Education Studies & Sociology BA(Hons)

Postgraduate courses: Primary Education PGCE, Secondary Education RE PGCE, Secondary Education (School Direct) PGCE, Education MA, Education: Early Childhood MA, Education: Mentoring MA, Education: Post-compulsory Education MA, Education: Research-engaged Setting MA

LEEDS BECKETT UNIVERSITY
www.leedsbeckett.ac.uk

Faculty of Arts, Environment & Technology; www.leedsbeckett.ac.uk/ aet

The Leeds School of Art, Architecture & Design; www.leedsbeckett.ac.uk/aet/#art-architecture-design

architecture, architectural professional practice, art & design, artist teacher in art & design, design practice, fashion, fine art, interior architecture & design, urban design, graphic art & design, professional studies, landscape architecture & design, urban design

School of Built Environment & Engineering; www.leedsbeckett.ac.uk/aet/#built-environment-engineering

adv engineering management, building/engineering studies/services engineering, civil engineering/& construction, construction/commercial/management, strategic/project management, facilities management, architectural technology, building/quantity surveying, environmental engineering & construction, health & neighbourhood planning, housing/strategy, housing, regeneration & urban management, planning law & practice, strategic project management, project management/construction, town & regional planning, UK planning law & dispute practice, sustainable urban planning

School of Computing, Creative Technology & Engineering; www.leedsbeckett.ac.uk/ aet/#computing-creative-technology

advanced engineering management, business information technology/intelligence, computer forensics/& security, computer science computing/systems engineering, computer sustainable engineering, creative media/technology, digital forensics & security/journalism/photography, electrical & electronic engineering, engineering robotics & automation, food engineering, games design, information management/systems, web applications development, mathematics & computer science, mobile device applications, information & technology/management, broadcast media technologies, computer animation/& special effects & visual effects, sustainable computing/technology, creative technology, 3D visualisation & interactive environments, networking systems engineering

School of Cultural Studies & Humanities; www.leedsbeckett.ac.uk/as/cs

English/& history/media/creative writinf, English literature, history, media, communication & cultures, English contemporary literature, social history; BA(Hons), BSc(Hons), DipHE, FdAA, GradCert, MPhil, MRes, MSc, PGDip

School of Film, Music & Performing Arts; www.leedsbeckett.ac.uk/aet/#film-music-performingarts

music performance/production/technology, dance, audio engineering, performance, music for moving image, sound & music for interactive games, sound design, pop music & culture, documentary film making

Northern Film School

animation, film making, film & TV

Faculty of Business and Law; www.leedsbeckett.ac.uk/fbl

Leeds Business School; www.leedsbeckett.ac.uk/fbl/ leeds_business_school

business analytics/finance/marketing, business management development, business studies/administration/economics, business & management/HRM/management studies, action by facilitation, corporate governance/communications, executive leadership/business coaching, entrepreneurship & business, HRM, international HRM, international business/communications/business law/trade & finance/banking & investment/leadership/marketing, journalism, leadership & change, management, marketing, marketing & advertising management, PR & communication/journalism/strategic communication, retail marketing management, strategic & digital marketing, supply chain management & logistics, MBA (Executive/Graduate)

Leeds Law School; www.leedsbeckett.ac.uk/lbs/law

law, legal practice, international business law, law & finance/international business/management; BA(Hons), HND, LlB(Hons), LlM, MA, MSc, PGDip/Cert, MBA, DBA

Faculty of Health & Social Sciences; www.leedsbeckett.ac.uk/hss

Social Sciences & Psychology

playwork, youth work & community development, young people, communities and society, criminology, criminology & psychology, psychology, psychology & society, social psychology, social work, sociology, therapeutic counselling, young people, communities and society, youth work & community development,- Postgraduate; advanced social work practice, art psychotherapy practice, criminology, interdisciplinary psychology, interpersonal & counselling skills, mental health practice, psychological therapies, psychology, psychotherapy, youth work & community development, community & youth studies

Health

environmental health, toxicological sciences, nutrition adult nursing, biomedical sciences (human biology/microbiology/molecular biology), dietetics, environmental health, health and community care, mental health nursing, nutrition, nutritional health, physiotherapy, safety, health & environmental management, speech & language therapy, sports and exercise therapy, support work; Postgraduate; acoustics, advanced practice, advanced social work practice, applied biomedical sciences research, chaplaincy in health & social care, community & youth studies, community specialist practitioner – district nursing, dietetics, eating disorders, environmental health, health and community care, health and safety, mental health practice, microbiology and biotechnology, nutrition in practice, occupational therapy, physiotherapy, play therapy, practice based play therapy, public health, health promotion, social work, specialist community public health nursing – health visiting/occupational health nursing/school nursing, therapeutic play skills, toxicological sciences
Short Courses and CP; BA(Hons), BSc(Hons), CertHE, MA, MSc, PGDip/Cert, Prof Dip, DipHE, FdAA, GradCert, MPhil, MRes, PGDip, MBioms

Carnegie Faculty; www.leedsbeckett.ac.uk/carnegie

childhood and early years, higher and further education, childhood studies, education studies, internationalisation inclusion training in intellectual disability for educators in Europe, partnerships with schools playwork researchers, childhood outdoor & adventurous activities, psychology, strength & coordination, PE, leisure, sport & culture, PE with outdoor education, sport & exercise science, sport & business management/development/management/coaching/studies, sport physical activity & health, sport & exercise medication, psychology of sport & exercise, international/event management, sport event management, sport & exercise/biomedicine/

nutrition/physiology/health/psychology/science/therapy, sport, law & society, conference & exhibition management, entertainment management, managing cultural & major events, event sponsorship and fundraising; BA(Hons), BSc(Hons), FdSc, PGCE, PGCert/Dip, MA, PhD, Prof DocEd

UNIVERSITY OF LEICESTER
www.le.ac.uk

Department of American Studies; www2.le.ac.uk/departments/americanstudies
BA American Studies

School of Archaeology and Ancient History; www2.le.ac.uk/departments/archaeology
BA Archaeology, BA Ancient History and Archaeology, BA Ancient History
Postgraduate courses: MA Archaeology, MA Classical Mediterranean

School of Arts; www2.le.ac.uk/departments/arts
English
BA English, BA English and American Studies, BA English and History, BA French and English, BA Italian and English, BA Spanish and English, BA Film Studies and English, BA History of Art and English
Postgraduate courses: MA in Applied Linguistics and TESOL, MA in Creative Writing, MA in English Language and Linguistics, MA in English Studies, MA in Modern Literature/Modern Literature and Creative Writing, MA in TESOL, MA in Victorian Studies

History of Art and Film
BA History of Art, BA History of Art and English, BA Film Studies and Visual Arts, BA Film Studies and English, BA Film and Media Studies
Postgraduate courses: MA/PGDip/PGCert Country House (Art, History and Literature), MA in Film and Film Cultures

Modern Languages
French and Italian BA, French and Spanish BA, Italian and Spanish BA, French and English BA, Italian and English BA, Spanish and English BA, European Studies BA, Modern Language Studies BA, Modern Languages with Management BA, Modern Languages with Film Studies BA, Modern Languages with Translation BA, Modern Languages and Translation BA, Translation and Interpreting BA
Postgraduate course: Translation Studies MA

School of Biological Sciences; www2.le.ac.uk/departments/biologicalsciences
Molecular and Cell Biology
BSc Biological Sciences (Biochemistry), BSc Biological Sciences (Physiology with Pharmacology), BSc Biological Sciences (Neuroscience), BSc Medical Biochemistry, BSc Medical Physiology
Postgraduate courses: MSc Bioinformatics, MSc Cancer Cell and Molecular Biology

Genetics
BSc Biological Sciences (Genetics), BSc in Medical Genetics
Postgraduate courses: MSc Molecular Genetics, MSc in Bioinformatics

Infection, Immunity & Inflammation
BSc Biological Sciences, BSc Biological Sciences (Microbiology), BSc Medical Microbiology
Postgraduate courses: MSc Infection and Immunity, MSc Chronic Disease and Immunity

Neuroscience, Psychology and Behaviour
BSc Psychology, BSc Applied Psychology, BSc Psychology with Cognitive Neuroscience, BSc Psychology with Sociology
Postgraduate courses: MSc Psychological Research Methods, MSc Occupational Psychology (DL), MSc Psychology of Work (DL)

School of Business; www2.le.ac.uk/departments/business
Accounting and Finance
BSc Accounting and Finance, Major in Accounting and Finance, Minor in Accounting and Finance
Postgraduate courses: MSc Accounting and Finance, MSc Management, Finance and Accounting, MSc Banking and International Finance, MSc Business Analysis and Finance, MSc Finance, MSc Financial Risk Management

Economics
BA Banking and Finance and BSc Banking and Finance, BA Business Economics and BSc Business Economics, BA Economics and BSc Economics, BA Economics and Accounting and BSc Economics and

Accounting, BA Financial Economics and BSc Financial Economics
Postgraduate courses: MSc Economics, MSc Financial Economics

Management and Marketing
BA Management Studies, BA Management Studies (Finance), BA Management Studies (Marketing), BA Management Studies (Organisation Studies), BA Management Studies and Economics, Major in Human Resource Management, Major in Management Studies, Minor in Entrepreneurship, Minor in Human Resource Management, Minor in Management Studies, Minor in Marketing
Postgraduate courses: MSc Human Resource Management and Training, MSc International Management, MSc Management, MSc International Marketing, MSc Marketing, MSc Marketing for the Creative Industries, MSc Marketing for Places and Tourism

Department of Chemistry; www2.le.ac.uk/departments/chemistry
Chemistry BSc, Pharmaceutical Chemistry BSc, Chemistry with Forensic Science BSc, Chemistry MChem, Pharmaceutical Chemistry MChem, Chemistry with Forensic Science MChem
Postgraduate courses: MSc Chemical Research – Biological Chemistry, MSc Chemical Research – Green Chemistry, MSc Chemical Research – Physical Chemistry, MSc Forensic Science and Criminal Justice

Department of Criminology; www2.le.ac.uk/departments/criminology
Criminology BSc, Major in Criminology, Minor in Criminal Justice, Minor in Criminal Behaviour
Postgraduate courses: Criminology MSc, Criminology in Practice MSc, Terrorism, Security and Policing MSc, Crime, Justice and Psychology MSc

School of Education; www2.le.ac.uk/departments/education
Postgraduate courses: PGCE Primary (University-led), PGCE Primary (School Direct), PGCE Secondary (University-led), PGCE Secondary (School Direct), International Education MA

Department of Engineering; www2.le.ac.uk/departments/engineering
MEng/BEng General Engineering, MEng/BEng Aerospace Engineering, MEng/BEng Electrical and Electronic Engineering, MEng/BEng Communications and Electronic Engineering, MEng/BEng Software and Electronic Engineering, MEng/BEng Mechanical Engineering

Postgraduate courses: MSc Advanced Control and Dynamics, MSc Advanced Electrical and Electronic Engineering, MSc Advanced Engineering, MSc Advanced Materials Engineering, MSc Advanced Mechanical Engineering, MSc Embedded Systems and Control Engineering, MSc Information and Communication Engineering, MSc in Reliable Embedded Systems

Centre for English Local History; www2.le.ac.uk/centres/elh?uol_r=948a87cd
Postgraduate course: MA in English Local and Family History

School of Geography, Geology and the Environment; www2.le.ac.uk/departments/geoggeolenv
Geography
BA Geography, BA Human Geography, BA Major in Human Geography, BSc Geography, BSc Physical Geography
Postgraduate courses: MRes in Geography, MSc Environmental Informatics, MSc in GIS, MSc Sustainable Management of Natural Resources

Geology
BSc/MGeol Geology, BSc/MGeol Applied and Environmental Geology, BSc/MGeol Geology with Geophysics, BSc/MGeol Geology with Palaeobiology

Department of Health Sciences; www2.le.ac.uk/departments/health-sciences
Postgraduate courses: Medical Statistics (MSc/PgDip), Diabetes (MSc/PG Dip/PG Cert), Quality and Safety in Healthcare (MSc/PG Dip/PG Cert), MRes in Applied Health Research

Department of History; www2.le.ac.uk/departments/history
BA History, BA Contemporary History, BA History and Politics, BA International Relations and History, BA History and American Studies, BA English and History, BA History and Archaeology, BA Ancient History and History
Postgraduate courses: MA History, MRes History, MA English Local and Family History, MA Urban History, MA Urban Conservation

Leicester Law School; www2.le.ac.uk/departments/law
LLB Law, LLB Law (Senior Status), LLB with a Year Abroad, LLB/Maîtrise Double degree, LLB Law with

Criminology, LLB Law with a Modern Language, LLB Law with Politics

Postgraduate courses: LLM International Commercial Law, LLM International Human Rights Law, LLM International Law, LLM Public International Law, LLM General Law

Department of Mathematics; www2.le.ac.uk/departments/mathematics

BSc Mathematics, MMath Mathematics, BSc Mathematics and Actuarial Science, Major in Mathematics

Postgraduate courses: MSc in Actuarial Science, MSc in Applied Computation and Numerical Modelling, MSc in Financial Mathematics and Computation, MSc in Data Analysis in Business Intelligence programme

Department of Media and Communication; www2.le.ac.uk/departments/media

BA Media and Communication, BA Media and Society, BA Film and Media

Postgraduate courses: MA Global Media and Communication, MA Mass Communications, MA Media and Public Relations, MA Media and Advertising, MA Media, Culture and Society, MA New Media and Society

Department of Medical and Social Care Education; www2.le.ac.uk/departments/msce

MBChB Medicine, BSc(Hons) Operating Department Practice

Department of Museum Studies; www2.le.ac.uk/departments/museumstudies

MA/MSc/PGDip Museum Studies, MA/PGDip Art Museum and Gallery Studies

Department of Physics and Astronomy; www2.le.ac.uk/departments/physics

Physics BSc, Physics MPhys, Physics with Astrophysics BSc, Physics with Astrophysics MPhys, Physics with Space Science BSc, Physics with Space Science MPhys

Postgraduate courses: Applied Computation and Numerical Modelling MSc, Space Exploration Systems MSc/PGDip

Department of Politics and International Relations; www2.le.ac.uk/departments/politics

BA Politics, BA International Relations, BA International Relations and History, BA Politics and Economics, BA Politics and Sociology, BA History and Politics, BA Politics and International Relations

Postgraduate courses: MA Diplomatic Studies, MA Human Rights and Global Ethics, MA International Relations and World Order, MA Intelligence and Security, MA International Security, MA Politics in the EU, MA Politics of Conflict and Violence

School of Psychology; www2.le.ac.uk/departments/psychology

BSc Psychology, BSc Psychology with Cognitive Neuroscience, BSc Applied Psychology

Postgraduate courses: MSc in Psychological Research Methods, MSc Occupational Psychology, MSc/PGDip Psychology of Work

Department of Sociology; www2.le.ac.uk/departments/sociology

BA Sociology

Postgraduate courses: MA Contemporary Sociology, MSc Social Research, MA Media, Culture and Society

NEWMAN UNIVERSITY
www.newman.ac.uk

Accounting and Finance BA(Hons), Applied Social Science BA(Hons), Education Studies BA(Hons), Sport and Exercise Science full-time top up BSc(Hons), Business Management BA(Hons), Mathematics with opt-in route to QTS BSc(Hons), Counselling Studies and Working with Children, Young People and Families BA(Hons), Creative Writing BA(Hons), Criminology BA(Hons), BA(Hons) Drama, Theatre and Applied Performance, Drama and Education BA(Hons), Drama and English BA(Hons), Business Economics BA(Hons), Education and Counselling Studies BA(Hons), Early Childhood Education and Care BA(Hons), English BA(Hons), English and Creative Writing BA(Hons), English and Education BA(Hons), English Literature BA(Hons), English and Theology BA(Hons), Health and Social Care BSc(Hons), Applied Health and Social Care BA/BSc(Hons) Top-Up Award, History BA(Hons), History and Education BA(Hons), History and Theology BA(Hons), Counselling Studies top-up award BA(Hons), Mathematics BSc(Hons), Philosophy, Religion & Education BA(Hons), Primary Education (with recommendation for QTS) Top-up BA(Hons), Psychology BSc(Hons), Psychology and Counselling

Studies BSc(Hons), Sport and Education BA(Hons), Sport and Exercise Psychology BSc(Hons), Sport Coaching Science BSc(Hons), Sport Coaching Science (Tournament Golf) BSc(Hons), Sport and Exercise Science BSc(Hons), Sport and Exercise Studies BA(Hons), Studies in Primary Education BA(Hons), Theology and Education BA(Hons), Theology BA(Hons), Working with Children, Young People and Families BA(Hons), Working with Children, Young People & Families and Education BA(Hons), Working with Children, Young People and Families part-time top-up award BA(Hons), Youth and Community Work BA(Hons), Professional Practice Top-up award BA Hons, Psychology and Childhood Studies BSc(Hons), Working with Children Young People and Families / International Social Work (dual award) BA(Hons), Business and Marketing BA(Hons)

Postgraduate courses: Business: Master of Business Administration (MBA), Doctor of Education EdD, Education MA, Catholic School Leadership PGCert, Early Childhood Education and Care PGCert, Higher Education Practice PGCert, Safeguarding PGCert, Heritage and Public History PGCert, Victorian Studies MA, Human Sciences MRes, Humanities MRes, Applications of Psychology MSc, Clinical Applications of Psychology MSc, Integrative Psychotherapy MSc, Primary Initial Teacher Education PGCE, Secondary Initial Teacher Education PGCE, Contemporary Christian Theology MA, Catholic Social Teaching Grad Cert/PGCert, Chaplaincy with Young People Prof Cert/PGCert, Work-Based Learning MA/MSc, Youth and Community Work MA/PGDip

UNIVERSITY OF LINCOLN
www.lincoln.ac.uk

College of Arts; www.lincoln.ac.uk/home/collegeofarts

Lincoln School of Architecture and the Built Environment; www.lincoln.ac.uk/home/abe
Architecture BA(Hons), Bachelor of Architecture with Honours BArch(Hons)
Postgraduate courses: Architecture MArch Global Practice, Master of Architecture MArch

Lincoln School of Design; www.lincoln.ac.uk/home/lsd
Creative Advertising BA(Hons), Design for Exhibition and Museums BA(Hons), Graphic Design BA(Hons), Illustration BA(Hons), Interactive Design BA(Hons), Interior Architecture and Design BA(Hons), Product Design BA(Hons)
Postgraduate courses: Design MA, Design for Exhibition and Museums MA, Graphic Design MA, Interior Architecture and Design MA, Professional Practice and Management in Architecture PG Dip

Lincoln School of Film & Media; www.lincoln.ac.uk/home/fm
Animation BA(Hons), Audio Production BA(Hons), Film and Television BA(Hons), Media Production BA(Hons), Media Studies BA(Hons), Photography BA(Hons)
Digital Media MA, Media & Cultural Studies MA by Research, Media (including by practice) MPhil/PhD, Media, Film and TV Production MA, Photography MA, Studies in Media and Culture MA

Lincoln School of English and Journalism; www.lincoln.ac.uk/home/ej
English BA(Hons), English and Creative Writing BA(Hons), English and History BA(Hons), English and Journalism BA(Hons), Journalism BA(Hons), Journalism and Public Relations BA(Hons), Journalism Studies BA(Hons), Public Relations BA(Hons)
Postgraduate courses: 21st Century Literature MA, Creative Writing MA, English Studies MA, Journalism MA, Journalism (Arts) MA, Journalism (Digital) MA, Journalism (Science and Environment) MA, Journalism (Sports) MA, Journalism (War and International Human Rights) MA, Nineteenth Century Studies MA, Public Relations MA

School of Fine & Performing Arts; www.lincoln.ac.uk/home/fpa
Dance BA(Hons), Drama and English BA(Hons), Drama and Theatre BA(Hons), Fashion BA(Hons), Fine Art BA(Hons), Music BA(Hons)
Postgraduate courses: Choreography MA, Drama MA, Fine Art MA

School of History and Heritage; www.lincoln.ac.uk/home/hh
Art History and History BA(Hons), Conservation of Cultural Heritage BA(Hons), English and History BA(Hons), History BA(Hons), Philosophy BA(Hons)

Postgraduate courses: Conservation of Cultural Heritage MA, Conservation Studies Graduate Diploma, Historical Studies MA, Medieval Studies MA

College of Science; www.lincoln.ac.uk/home/collegeofscience

School of Chemistry; www.lincoln.ac.uk/home/chemistry
Chemistry BSc(Hons), Chemistry MChem, Chemistry for Drug Discovery and Development BSc(Hons), Chemistry for Drug Discovery and Development MChem, Chemistry with Education BSc(Hons), Chemistry with Education MChem, Chemistry with Mathematics BSc(Hons), Chemistry with Mathematics MChem, Forensic Chemistry BSc(Hons), Forensic Chemistry MChem, Forensic Science BSc(Hons)
Postgraduate courses: Analytical Sciences MSc, Forensic Science MSc

School of Computer Science; www.lincoln.ac.uk/home/socs
Computer Science BSc(Hons), Computer Science MComp, Games Computing BSc(Hons), Games Computing Mcomp
Postgraduate courses: Computer Science MSc, Intelligence Systems MSc

School of Engineering; www.lincoln.ac.uk/home/engineering
Automation Engineering BEng(Hons), Electrical Engineering (Control Systems) BEng/MEng(Hons), Electrical Engineering (Electronics) BEng/MEng(Hons), Electrical Engineering (Power and Energy) BEng/MEng(Hons), Mechanical Engineering BEng/MEng(Hons), Mechanical Engineering (Control Systems) BEng/MEng(Hons), Mechanical Engineering (Power and Energy) BEng/MEng(Hons)
Postgraduate courses: Engineering Management MSc, Mechanical Engineering MSc

School of Geography; www.lincoln.ac.uk/home/geography
Geography BA/BSc(Hons)

School of Life Sciences; www.lincoln.ac.uk/home/lifesciences
Animal Behaviour and Welfare BSc(Hons), Animal Behaviour and Welfare MBio, Biochemistry BSc(Hons), Biochemistry MBio, Biology BSc(Hons), Biology MBio, Biomedical Science BSc(Hons), Biomedical Science MBio, Bioveterinary Science BSc(Hons),

Bioveterinary Science MBio, Zoology BSc(Hons), Zoology MBio
Postgraduate courses: Biotechnology MSc, Clinical Animal Behaviour MSc, Microbial Biotechnology MSc, Microbiology MSc

School of Mathematics and Physics; www.lincoln.ac.uk/home/smp
Mathematics BSc(Hons), Mathematics MMath, Mathematics and Computer Science BSc(Hons), Mathematics and Physics BSc(Hons), Mathematics and Physics MMath, Physics BSc(Hons), Physics MPhys

School of Pharmacy; www.lincoln.ac.uk/home/lsp
Pharmaceutical Science BSc(Hons), Pharmacy MPharm

National Centre for Food Manufacturing; www.lincoln.ac.uk/home/holbeach/degreefoundation
Food and Drink Operations and Manufacturing Management BSc(Hons), Food and Drink Operations and Manufacturing Management FdSc, Food Science and Technology BSc(Hons), Food Science and Technology FdSc
Postgraduate course: MSc Agri-food Technology

College of Social Science; www.lincoln.ac.uk/home/collegeofsocialscience

School of Education; www.lincoln.ac.uk/home/education
Education BA(Hons), Education and Psychology BSc(Hons)
Postgraduate courses: Education MA, Postgraduate Certificate in Education (Primary) PGCE, Postgraduate Certificate in Education (Secondary) PGCE

School of Health and Social Care; www.lincoln.ac.uk/home/shsc
Health and Social Care BSc(Hons), Nursing with Registered Nurse (Adult) BSc(Hons), Nursing with Registered Nurse (Mental Health) BSc(Hons), Paramedic Science BSc(Hons), Professional Practice BSc(Hons)
Postgraduate courses: Advanced Clinical Practice MSc, Advanced Clinical Practice (Primary Care) MSc, Advanced Clinical Practice (Urgent Care) MSc, Erasmus Mundus Master Advanced Development in Social Work EMMA, Health and Social Care Integration and Innovation MSc, Healthcare in Secure

Environments MSc, Interprofessional Practice (Approved Mental Health Professional) PG Dip, Physiotherapy (pre-registration) MSc, Postgraduate Certificate in Non-Medical Prescribing/Practice Certificate in Independent Prescribing (Level 7, Level M) PG Cert, Social Work MSc, Social Work Advanced Professional Practice MSc, Specialist Practice Frail Older Adults for Health and Social Care MSc

Lincoln Law School; www.lincoln.ac.uk/home/law

Law LLB(Hons), Law and Criminology LLB(Hons)
Postgraduate courses: International Business Law LLM, International Law LLM

School of Psychology; www.lincoln.ac.uk/home/psychology

Psychology BSc(Hons), Psychology with Clinical Psychology BSc(Hons), Psychology with Forensic Psychology BSc(Hons)
Postgraduate courses: Developmental Psychology MSc, Forensic Psychology MSc, Psychological Research Methods MSc, Psychology DclinPsy

School of Social & Political Sciences; www.lincoln.ac.uk/home/socialsciences

Criminology BA(Hons), Criminology and Social Policy BA(Hons), Criminology and Sociology BA(Hons), International Relations BA(Hons), International Relations and Politics BA(Hons), International Relations and Social Policy BA(Hons), Politics BA(Hons), Politics and Social Policy BA(Hons), Politics and Sociology BA(Hons), Social Policy BA(Hons), Social Policy and Sociology BA(Hons), Sociology BA(Hons)
Postgraduate courses: Gender Studies MA, International Relations MA, Politics MA

School of Sport and Exercise Science; www.lincoln.ac.uk/home/sport

Health and Exercise Science BSc(Hons), Physical Education and Sport BSc(Hons), Sport and Exercise Science BSc(Hons), Sport Development and Coaching BSc(Hons), Strength and Conditioning in Sport BSc(Hons)
Postgraduate courses: Sport Science MSc, Sports Therapy MSc

Lincoln International Business School; www.lincoln.ac.uk/home/lbs

Accountancy and Finance BA(Hons), Advertising and Marketing BA(Hons), Banking and Finance (MFin), Banking and Finance BSc(Hons), Business and Enterprise Development BA(Hons), Business and Finance BA(Hons), Business and Management (with Professional Practice) BA(Hons), Business and Marketing (with Professional Practice) BA(Hons), Business Economics BA(Hons), Business Psychology BSc(Hons), Business Studies (with Professional Practice) BA(Hons), Economics BSc(Hons), Economics and Finance (MEcon), Economics and Finance BSc(Hons), Events Management BSc(Hons), International Business Management BA(Hons), International Tourism Management BA(Hons), Marketing Management BA(Hons), Sports Business Management BA(Hons)
Postgraduate courses: Accounting MSc, Accounting and Finance MSc, Crisis and Disaster Management MSc, Culture and Heritage Management MA, Events Management MSc, Fashion Management MSc, Finance MSc, Human Resource Management Full Time MSc, Human Resource Management Part Time MSc, International Business MSc, International Business Economics MSc, International Investment Banking MSc, Logistics and Global Operations MSc, Management MSc, Management and International Relations MSc, Marketing MSc, Marketing with Luxury Brands MSc, Master of Business Administration (Full-time) MBA, Master of Business Administration (Part-time) MBA, Project Management MSc, Tourism and Marketing MSc

EAST RIDING COLLEGE
www.eastridingcollege.ac.uk

BA(Hons) Contemporary Media, Design and Production, BA(Hons) Education and Professional Development, BA(Hons) in Early Childhood Policy and Practice (Top-up), BA(Hons) Social Science, BSc(Hons) Sports, Coaching and Health Sciences (Top-up), Foundation Degree in Computing, Foundation Degree in Early Childhood Policy and Practice, Foundation Degree in Learning Support, Foundation Degree in Leisure Management, Foundation Degree in Public Services Management, Foundation Degree in Sport, Exercise and Health Sciences, ILM Level Seven NVQ Diploma in Strategic Management and Leadership, In-Service Certificate in Education (Lifelong Learning) and Professional Graduate Certificate in Education (Lifelong Learning), Masters in Education, Pre-Service Certificate in Education (Lifelong

Learning), Pre-Service Professional Graduate Certificate in Education (PGCE)

HULL COLLEGE
www.hull-college.ac.uk

BA(Hons) Architecture, BA(Hons) Dance, BA(Hons) Fashion, BA(Hons) Film-Making and Creative Media Production, BA(Hons) Fine Art, BA(Hons) Games Design, BA(Hons) Graphic Design, BA(Hons) Illustration, BA(Hons) Journalism and Digital Media, BA(Hons) Music Performance, BA(Hons) Music Production, BA(Hons) Musical Theatre, BA(Hons) Photography, BA(Hons) Technical and Theatre Production, BA(Hons) Textiles, Foundation Degree Digital Design and Development, BA(Hons) Digital Design and Development, Foundation Degree Sound Design for Games and Media, Foundation Degree Sound Design for Games and Media, Foundation Degree Performing Arts, FdA Performing Arts, MA Creative Practice, MArch Architecture, BA(Hons) Applied Social Science, BA(Hons) Business and Management, BA(Hons) Business and Management (Top Up), BA(Hons) Criminology (Top Up), BA(Hons) Health and Social Care, BA(Hons) Young Children's Learning and Development, BEng(Hons) Engineering Technology, BSc(Hons) Computing, BSc(Hons) Construction Management (Top-Up), BEng(Hons) Engineering Technology, BSc(Hons) Sport and Health Sciences, Foundation Degree Business and Management, Foundation Degree Young Children's Learning and Development, Foundation Degree Criminology, Foundation Degree Travel and Tourism Management, Professional Graduate Certificate in Education (In-Service), Professional Graduate Certificate in Education (Pre-Service)

NORTH LINDSEY COLLEGE
www.northlindsey.ac.uk

Business, Education and Professional Development
BA(Hons) English and History Studies, BA(Hons) Business Studies, FdA Leadership and Management, FdA Business and Human Resource Management, Professional Graduate Certificate in Education (PGCE), Certificate in Education, FdA Children Learning and Development (Early Childhood), FdA Children Learning and Development (Learning Support), BA(Hons) Children, Learning and Development

Engineering and Technology
FdEng Materials Engineering, FdEng Integrated Engineering (Electrical), FdEng Integrated Engineering (Mechanical)
Health, Life and Social Sciences
BA(Hons) Social Science, BSc(Hons) Sport and Exercise, FdSc Bioscience, FdSc Sport & Exercise (Personal Training) (Coaching), FdA Counselling, FdSc Biochemistry, FdSc Professional Practice in Health and Social Care

UNIVERSITY OF LIVERPOOL
www.liv.ac.uk

Department of Archaeology, Classics and Egyptology; www.liverpool.ac.uk/archaeology-classics-and-egyptology
Ancient History BA(Hons), Archaeology BA(Hons), Archaeology BSc(Hons), Archaeology of Ancient Civilisations BA(Hons), Classical Studies BA(Hons), Classics BA(Hons), Egyptology BA(Hons), Evolutionary Anthropology BSc(Hons), Heritage Studies (Honours Select)
Postgraduate courses: Advanced Transdisciplinary Design MSc (Based in London campus), Architecture MA, Arts: Architecture MRes, Building Information Modelling (BIM) MSc, Digital Integrated Design MSc, Master of Architecture MArch, Sustainable Environmental Design in Architecture (SEDA) MSc

Department of Architecture; www.liverpool.ac.uk/architecture
Architecture BA(Hons), Master of Architecture MArch
Postgraduate courses:

Department of Chemistry; www.liverpool.ac.uk/chemistry

Chemical Sciences BSc(Hons), Chemistry BSc(Hons), Chemistry for Sustainable Energy (MChem), Chemistry MChem, Chemistry with a Year in Industry BSc(Hons), Chemistry with Research in Industry MChem, Medicinal Chemistry BSc(Hons), Medicinal Chemistry with Pharmacology MChem, Heritage Studies (Honours Select)

Postgraduate course: Advanced Chemical Sciences MSc

Department of Communication and Media; www.liverpool.ac.uk/communication-and-media

Communication and Media; Film Studies (Honours Select)

Postgraduate courses: Arts: Communication and Media MRes, Media and Communication: Digital Culture and Communication pathway MA, Media and Communication: Media and Politics pathway MA, Strategic Communication MSc (Based in London campus)

Department of Computer Science; www.liverpool.ac.uk/computer-science

Computer Science BSc(Hons), Computer Science MEng(Hons), Financial Computing BSc(Hons), Mathematics and Computer Science BSc (Joint Honours), Software Development BSc(Hons)

Postgraduate courses: Advanced Computer Science MSc, Advanced Computer Science with Internet Economics MSc, Big Data and High Performance Computing MSc, Computer Science MSc

Department of Dental Sciences; www.liverpool.ac.uk/study/ undergraduate/courses/departments/ index.php?department=dental-sciences

Dental Surgery BDS

Postgraduate courses: Endodontics DDSc, Orthodontics DDSc, Special Care Dentistry DDSc

Department of Earth Sciences; www.liverpool.ac.uk/earth-ocean-and-ecological-sciences

Earth Sciences entry route leading to BSc(Hons), Geology (North America) MESci(Hons), Geology and Geophysics MESci(Hons), Geology and Physical Geography BSc(Hons), Geology and Physical Geography MESci(Hons), Geology BSc(Hons), Geology MESci(Hons), Geophysics (Geology) BSc(Hons), Geophysics (North America) MESci(Hons), Geophysics (Physics) BSc(Hons)

Postgraduate course: Petroleum Reservoir Geoscience MSc

Department of Ecology and Marine Biology; www.liverpool.ac.uk/ecolog

Conservation and Biodiversity BSc(Hons), Conservation and Biodiversity MEcol(Hons), Marine Biology BSc(Hons), Marine Biology MMarBiol(Hons)

Postgraduate courses: Conservation and Resource Management MRes, Conservation and Resource Management MSc

Department of Electrical Engineering and Electronics; www.liverpool.ac.uk/ electrical-engineering-and-electronics

Avionic Systems BEng(Hons), Avionic Systems MEng(Hons), Computer Science and Electronic Engineering BEng(Hons), Computer Science and Electronic Engineering MEng(Hons), Electrical and Electronic Engineering BEng(Hons), Electrical and Electronic Engineering MEng(Hons), Mechatronics and Robotic Systems BEng(Hons), Mechatronics and Robotic Systems MEng(Hons)

Postgraduate courses: Energy and Power Systems MSc (Eng), Microelectronic Systems MSc (Eng), Sensor Technologies and Enterprise MSc, Telecommunications and Wireless Systems MSc (Eng)

Department of Engineering; www.liv.ac.uk/ engineering

Aerospace Engineering BEng(Hons), Aerospace Engineering MEng(Hons), Aerospace Engineering with Pilot Studies BEng(Hons), Aerospace Engineering with Pilot Studies MEng(Hons), Architectural Engineering BEng(Hons), Architectural Engineering MEng(Hons), Civil and Structural Engineering MEng(Hons), Civil Engineering BEng(Hons), Civil Engineering MEng(Hons), Engineering BEng(Hons), Engineering Foundation BEng(Hons), Engineering MEng(Hons), Industrial Design BEng, Industrial Design MEng, Mechanical Engineering BEng(Hons), Mechanical Engineering MEng(Hons)

Postgraduate courses: Advanced Aerospace Engineering MSc (Eng), Advanced Manufacturing Systems and Technology MSc (Eng), Advanced Mechanical Engineering MSc (Eng), Biomedical Engineering MSc (Eng), Product Design and Management MSc(Eng), Risk and Uncertainty MSc (Eng), Sustainable Civil and Structural Engineering MSc (Eng)

Department of English; www.liverpool.ac.uk/english

Applied English BA(Hons), English BA(Hons), English Language BA(Hons), English Literature BA(Hons)

Postgraduate courses: Applied Linguistics MA, Arts: English MRes, English MA, English: Modern and Contemporary Literature MA, English: Renaissance and Eighteenth-Century Literature MA, English: Victorian Literature MA, Teaching English to Speakers of Other Languages (TESOL) MA

Department of Geography; www.liverpool.ac.uk/geography

Environmental Science BSc(Hons), Geography BA(Hons), Geography BSc(Hons)

Postgraduate courses: Contemporary Human Geography (Research Methods) MA, Environment and Climate Change MSc, Environmental Sciences MSc, Geographic Data Science MSc, Population and Health MSc

Department of Health Sciences; www.liv.ac.uk/healthsciences

Diagnostic Radiography BSc(Hons), Nursing BN(Hons), Occupational Therapy BSc(Hons), Orthoptics BSc(Hons), Physiotherapy BSc(Hons), Radiotherapy BSc(Hons)

Postgraduate courses: Advanced Practice in Healthcare MSc/PGDip/PGCert, Nursing MSc/PGDip/PGCert, Radiotherapy MSc, Radiotherapy PGDip

Department of History; www.liverpool.ac.uk/history

History BA(Hons)

Postgraduate courses: Archives MRes, Archives and Records Management MARM, Archives and Records Management (International Pathway) MARMI, History MRes, History: Cultural History MA, History: Eighteenth-Century Worlds MA, History: Medieval and Renaissance Studies MA, History: Twentieth-Century History MA, International Slavery Studies MA

Department of Irish Studies; www.liverpool.ac.uk/irish-studies

Irish Studies BA(Hons)

Postgraduate courses: Irish Studies MRes, Irish Studies MA/PGDip

Department of Law; www.liverpool.ac.uk/law

Law LLB(Hons), Law with Accounting and Finance LLB(Hons), Law with French LLB(Hons), Law with Spanish LLB(Hons)

Postgraduate courses: LLB Law for Graduates, International Human Rights Law LLM/PGDip/PGCert, Law, Medicine and Healthcare LLM/PGDip/PGCert, LLM (General) LLM/PGDip/PGCert

Department of Life Sciences; www.liverpool.ac.uk/life-sciences

Anatomy and Human Biology BSc(Hons), Biochemistry MBiolSci, Biochemistry BSc(Hons), Biological and Medical Sciences MBiolSci, Biological and Medical Sciences BSc(Hons), Biological Sciences MBiolSci, Biological Sciences BSc(Hons), Biological Sciences MBiolSci, Bioveterinary Science MBiolSci, Bioveterinary Science BSc(Hons), Genetics MBiolSci, Genetics BSc Hons, Human Physiology MBiolSci, Human Physiology BSc(Hons), Microbiology MBiolSci, Microbiology BSc(Hons), Molecular Biology and Biotechnology MBiolSci, Molecular Biology and Biotechnology BSc(Hons), Pharmacology MBiolSci, Pharmacology BSc(Hons), Tropical Disease Biology MBiolSci, Tropical Disease Biology BSc(Hons), Zoology MBiolSci, Zoology BSc(Hons)

Postgraduate courses: Advanced Biological Sciences MSc, Advanced Biological Sciences MRes, Biomedical Sciences and Translational Medicine MRes, Clinical Sciences MRes, Musculoskeletal Ageing MRes

Management School; www.liverpool.ac.uk/management

Accounting and Finance BA(Hons), Business Economics BA(Hons), Business Management BA(Hons), Economics BSc(Hons), International Business BA(Hons), Marketing BA(Hons)

Postgraduate courses: Financial and Actuarial Mathematics MSc (Based in London campus), Accounting MSc (Based in London campus), Accounting and Finance MSc, Banking and Finance MSc (based in London campus), Business Administration (Football Industries) PG Cert, Business Analytics and Big Data MSc, Business Law and Economics MSc (Based in London campus), Digital Business Enterprise Management MSc, Economics MSc, Entrepreneurship and Innovation Management MSc, Finance and Investment Management MSc (Based in London campus), Finance MSc, Financial Risk Management MSc MSc, Football Industries MBA, Human Resource Management (CIPD Accredited) MSc, International Business MSc, Management MRes, Marketing MSc, Master in

Management MIM, MBA (The Liverpool MBA) on campus MBA, Operations and Supply Chain Management MSc, Programme and Project Management MSc, Sports Business MSc, Thoroughbred Horseracing Industries MBA

Department of Mathematical Sciences; www.liverpool.ac.uk/mathematical-sciences

Actuarial Mathematics BSc(Hons), French and Mathematics BA (Joint Hons), Mathematical Physics MMath, Mathematical Sciences entry route leading to BSc(Hons), Mathematical Sciences with a European Language BSc(Hons), Mathematics and Business Studies BSc (Joint Hons), Mathematics and Economics BSc(Hons), Mathematics and Statistics BSc(Hons), Mathematics BSc(Hons), Mathematics MMath, Mathematics with Finance BSc(Hons), Physics and Mathematics BSc (Joint Hons), Theoretical Physics MPhys

Postgraduate courses: Financial Mathematics MSc/PGDip/PGCert, Mathematical Sciences MSc/PGDip/PGCert

Department of Medicine; www.liverpool.ac.uk/medicine

Foundation to Health and Veterinary Studies, Medicine – Foundation to Health and Veterinary Studies, Medicine and Surgery MBChB

Postgraduate courses: Medicine and Surgery MBChB (Graduate Entry), Master of Public Health MPH, Medical Education PGCert/PGDip/MSc, Physician Associate Studies PGDip, Master of Public Health MPH (Based in London campus)

Department of Modern Languages and Cultures; www.liverpool.ac.uk/modern-languages-and-cultures

Basque (Honours Select), Chinese (Honours Select), French BA(Hons), German BA(Hons), Hispanic Studies BA(Hons), Italian (Honours Select), Italian BA(Hons), Modern European Languages BA(Hons), Modern Language Studies BA (Joint Hons), Portuguese (Honours Select), Spanish (Honours Select)

Postgraduate courses: Basque Studies – Modern Languages and Cultures MRes, Catalan Studies – Modern Languages and Cultures MRes, Chinese Studies – Modern Languages and Cultures MRes, Film Studies – Modern Languages and Cultures MRes, French Studies – Modern Languages and Cultures MRes, German Studies – Modern Languages and Cultures MRes, Hispanic Studies – Modern Languages and Cultures MRes, Italian

Studies – Modern Languages and Cultures MRes, Latin American Studies MRes, Modern Languages and Cultures MRes, Portuguese Studies – Modern Languages and Cultures MRes, Spanish Studies – Modern Languages and Cultures MRes

Department of Music; www.liverpool.ac.uk/music

Music and Popular Music BA(Hons), Music and Technology BA(Hons), Music BA(Hons), Popular Music BA(Hons)

Postgraduate courses: Arts: Music MRes, Music MMus, Music Industry Studies MA, The Business of Classical Music MA

Department of Ocean Sciences; www.liverpool.ac.uk/earth-ocean-and-ecological-sciences

Earth Sciences entry route leading to BSc(Hons), Geography and Oceanography BSc(Hons), Marine Biology with Oceanography BSc(Hons), Mathematics with Ocean and Climate Sciences BSc(Hons), Ocean Sciences BSc(Hons), Ocean Sciences MOSci(Hons)

Postgraduate course: Sea Level: From Coast to Global Ocean MSc

Department of Philosophy; www.liverpool.ac.uk/philosophy

Mathematics and Philosophy BA (Joint Hons), Philosophy BA(Hons), Philosophy, Politics and Economics BA

Postgraduate courses: Art, Aesthetics and Cultural Institutions MA, Arts: Philosophy MRes, Philosophy MA

Department of Physics; www.liverpool.ac.uk/physics

Astrophysics MPhys, Physical Sciences entry route leading to BSc(Hons), Physics BSc(Hons), Physics for New Technology BSc(Hons), Physics MPhys, Physics with Astronomy BSc(Hons), Physics with Medical Applications BSc(Hons), Physics with Nuclear Science BSc(Hons), Physics with Radiation Protection BSc(Hons)

Postgraduate courses: Nuclear Science and Technology MSc, Radiometrics: Instrumentation and Modelling MSc

Department of Planning; www.liverpool.ac.uk/geography-and-planning

Environment and Planning BA(Hons), Geography and Planning BA(Hons), Town and Regional

Planning MPlan, Urban Regeneration and Planning BA(Hons)

Postgraduate courses: Environmental Assessment and Management MSc, Marine Planning and Management MSc, Town and Regional Planning M/CD, Town and Regional Planning MA, Urban Design and Property Development MSc (Based in London campus), Urban Planning MSc (Based in London campus), Urban Regeneration and Management MSc

Department of Politics; www.liverpool.ac.uk/politics

International Politics and Policy BA(Hons), Politics and International Business BA (Joint Hons), Politics BA(Hons)

Postgraduate courses: International Relations and Security MA, International Relations and Security MRes

Department of Psychology; www.liverpool.ac.uk/psychology

Psychology BSc(Hons), Psychology BSc(Hons) (2+2 programme with Foundation Element), Psychology MPsycholSci(Hons)

Postgraduate courses: Doctor of Clinical Psychology DClinPsychol, Investigative and Forensic Psychology MSc/PGDip/PGCert, Reading for Life MSc, Research Methods in Psychology MSc/PGDip/PGCert

Department of Sociology, Social Policy and Criminology; www.liverpool.ac.uk/ sociology-social-policy-and-criminology

Criminology and Security BA(Hons), Criminology BA(Hons), Social Policy (Honours Select), Sociology BA(Hons)

Postgraduate courses: Criminological Research MRes, Social Research MRes, Social Research Methods MA

Department of Veterinary Science; www.liverpool.ac.uk/veterinary-science

Veterinary Conservation Medicine Intercalated Honours BSc, Veterinary Science – Foundation to Health and Veterinary Studies, Veterinary Science BVSc

Postgraduate courses: Bovine Reproduction DBR, Veterinary Business Management PGCert, Veterinary Physiotherapy MSc/PGDip, Veterinary Professional Studies MSc, Veterinary Postgraduate Unit, Veterinary Science MSc

LIVERPOOL HOPE UNIVERSITY
www.hope.ac.uk

Business School; www.hope.ac.uk/businessschool

BA Accounting & Finance, BA Business Management, BA Marketing

Postgraduate courses: MA Business and Management, MA Human Resource Management and Development, International MBA

Disability and Education; www.hope.ac.uk/disabilityandeducation

BA Disability Studies in Education, BA Special Educational Needs

Postgraduate courses: MA Disability Studies, MA Special Educational Needs

Drama, Dance and Performance Studies; www.hope.ac.uk/dramadanceandperformance

BA Creative and Performing Arts, BA Dance, BA Drama and Theatre Studies/Drama

Postgraduate course: MA Contemporary Popular Theatres

Early Childhood; www.hope.ac.uk/earlychildhood

BA Early Childhood

Postgraduate course: MA Developmental Psychology and Early Childhood

Education Studies; www.hope.ac.uk/educationstudies

BA Education

Postgraduate courses: MA Education, MA International Education, MA Interdisciplinary Studies in Education

English; www.hope.ac.uk/english

BA English Language, BA English Literature

Postgraduate courses: MA English Language, MA English Literature

Fine and Applied Art; www.hope.ac.uk/fineandappliedart

BA Art and Design History, BA Design, BA Fine Art, BA Graphic Design

Postgraduate courses: MA/PG Cert Art History and Curating, MA Creative Practice, MA Museum and Heritage Studies

Geography and Environmental Science; www.hope.ac.uk/geography

BSc Environmental Science, BSc Geography, BSc Tourism, BA Tourism Management
Postgraduate course: MSc Ecology and Environmental Management

Health Sciences; www.hope.ac.uk/healthsciences

BSc Biological Sciences, BSc Biology, BSc Human Biology, BSc Nutrition, BSc Sport and Exercise Science, BSc Sport and Physical Education, BSc Sport Psychology
Postgraduate courses: MSc Diabetes, Sport and Exercise Science (MRes)

History and Politics; www.hope.ac.uk/historyandpolitics

BA History, BA International Relations, BA Politics, BA Politics and International Relations
Postgraduate courses: MA History, MA International Relations, MA Peace Studies

Law; www.hope.ac.uk/law

LLB Law (Qualifying Law Degree), BA Law

Mathematics and Computer Science; www.hope.ac.uk/mathematicsandcomputerscience

BSc Computer Science, BEng Electronic and Computer Engineering, MEng Electronic and Computer Engineering
Postgraduate courses: MSc Computer Science, MSc Mathematical Informatics (Dual International Masters)

Media and Communication; www.hope.ac.uk/mediaandcommunication

BA Media and Communication, BA Creative Writing, BA Film and Visual Culture
Postgraduate courses: MA Film, Media and Society

Music; www.hope.ac.uk/music

BA Music, BA Popular Music
Postgraduate courses: MA Creative Practice, MA Music, MA The Beatles, Popular Music and Society

Psychology; www.hope.ac.uk/psychology

BSc Psychology, BSc Sport Psychology
Postgraduate courses: MSc Cognitive Neuroscience and Neuroimaging, MSc Psychology

Social Science; www.hope.ac.uk/socialscience

BA Criminology, BA Sociology
Postgraduate courses: MA Criminology, MA Sociology

Social Work, Care and Justice; www.hope.ac.uk/socialworkcareandjustice

BA Childhood and Youth, BA Health and Wellbeing, BA Health and Social Care, BA Social Policy, BA Social Work
Postgraduate courses: MA Social Policy, MA Social Work, MA Youth and Community Work

School of Teacher Education; www.hope.ac.uk/teachereducation

BA Primary Education (QTS)
Postgraduate courses: PGCE Primary (QTS), PGCE Early Years (QTS), PGCE Secondary (QTS), PGDE, MA/MEd Professional Practice, Education Doctorate EdD, School Direct

Theology, Philosophy and Religion; www.hope.ac.uk/theology

BA Christian Theology, BA Philosophy and Ethics, BA Philosophy, Ethics and Religion, BA Religious Studies, BA Theology, BA Theology and Religious Studies
Postgraduate courses: MA Biblical and Pastoral Theology, PG Cert Biblical Studies

LIVERPOOL JOHN MOORES UNIVERSITY
www.ljmu.ac.uk

Faculty of Arts, Professional and Social Studies; www.ljmu.ac.uk/about-us/faculties/faculty-of-arts-professional-and-social-studies

Liverpool School of Art and Design; www.ljmu.ac.uk/about-us/faculties/faculty-of-arts-professional-and-social-studies/liverpool-school-of-art-and-design

Architecture BA(Hons), Fashion: Design and Communication BA(Hons), Fine Art BA(Hons), Graphic Design and Illustration BA(Hons), History of Art and Museum Studies BA(Hons)

Postgraduate courses: Architecture MArch, Art and Design MRes, Art in Science MA, Contemporary Art MPhil, Exhibition Studies MA, Fashion Innovation and Realisation MA, Fine Art MA, Graphic Design and Illustration MA, Urban Design MA

Liverpool Screen School; www.ljmu.ac.uk/about-us/faculties/faculty-of-arts-professional-and-social-studies/liverpool-screen-school

Creative Writing BA(Hons), Creative Writing and Film Studies BA(Hons), Drama BA(Hons), Drama and Creative Writing BA(Hons), Drama and English BA(Hons), English and Creative Writing BA(Hons), Film Studies BA(Hons), International Journalism BA(Hons), Journalism BA(Hons), Media Production BA(Hons), Sports Journalism BA(Hons)

Cities, Culture and Creativity MA, Documentary MA, International Journalism MA, International News Journalism MA, Musical Theatre MA, Screenwriting MA, Writing MA

Liverpool Centre for Advanced Policing; www.ljmu.ac.uk/about-us/faculties/faculty-of-arts-professional-and-social-studies/liverpool-centre-advanced-policing-studies

Policing Studies BA(Hons), Policing Studies FDA, Policing Studies and Computer Forensics BSc(Hons), Policing Studies and Cybercrime BSc(Hons), Policing Studies and Evidence-based Practice BSc(Hons), Policing Studies and Forensic Psychology BSc(Hons), Policing Studies and Forensics BSc(Hons)

Postgraduate courses: Advanced Policing MSc, Doctor of Policing, Security and Criminal Justice, Evidence-Informed Practice (Criminal Justice and Policing) PGDip, International and Transnational Policing MSc, Policing and Criminal Investigation MSc, Policing and Cybercrime MSc, Policing, Port and Maritime Security MSc

School of Humanities and Social Science; www.ljmu.ac.uk/about-us/faculties/faculty-of-arts-professional-and-social-studies/school-of-humanities-and-social-science

Criminology BA(Hons), Criminology and Psychology BSc(Hons), Criminology and Sociology BA(Hons), English BA(Hons), English, Media and Cultural Studies BA(Hons), History BA(Hons), History and English BA(Hons), Media, Culture, Communication BA(Hons), Policing Studies BA(Hons), Sociology BA(Hons)

Postgraduate courses: Critical Social Science MRes, English MRes, International Relations MA, Mass Communications MA, Modern History MRes

School of Law; www.ljmu.ac.uk/about-us/faculties/faculty-of-arts-professional-and-social-studies/school-of-law

Criminal Justice BA(Hons), Forensic Psychology and Criminal Justice BSc(Hons), Law LLB(Hons), Law and Business BA(Hons), Law and Criminal Justice LLB(Hons)

Postgraduate courses: Criminal Justice MA, Global Crime, Justice and Security Master of Laws (LLM)/MSc, International Business Corporate and Finance Law LLM (Master of Laws), Legal Practice Course LPC, Legal Practice LLM (LPC BPTC Conversion), LLM (Master of Laws), Qualifying Law LLM

Faculty of Education, Health and Community; www.ljmu.ac.uk/about-us/faculties/faculty-of-education-health-and-community

School of Education; www.ljmu.ac.uk/about-us/faculties/faculty-of-education-health-and-community/school-of-education

Early Childhood Studies BA(Hons), Education Studies and Early Years BA(Hons), Education Studies and Inclusion BA(Hons), Learning, Development and Support BA(Hons), Primary Education with recommendation for Qualified Teacher Status (QTS) BA(Hons)

Postgraduate courses: Advanced Educational Practice: Autism PgDip/PgCert/MA, Advanced Educational Practice: Dyslexia PgDip/PgCert/MA, Advanced Educational Practice: Leadership and Management PgDip/PgCert/MA, Advanced Educational Practice: Mentoring and Coaching PgDip/PgCert/MA, Advanced Educational Practice: Religious Education PgDip/PgCert/MA, Advanced Educational Practice: Special Educational Needs PgDip/PgCert/MA, Advanced Educational Practice: Teaching and Learning PgDip/PgCert/MA, Art and Design: Secondary with Qualified Teacher Status (QTS) PGDE, Biology: Secondary with Qualified Teacher Status (QTS) PGDE, Chemistry: Secondary with Qualified Teacher Status (QTS) PGDE, Computer Science: Secondary with Qualified Teacher Status (QTS) PGDE, Design and Technology: Secondary PGDE with QTS, Digital Literacies and Learning MA, Education, Globalisation and Social Change MA, Education Practice MA, English: Secondary with Qualified Teacher Status (QTS) PGDE, Geography: Secondary with Qualified Teacher Status (QTS) PGDE, History: Secondary with Qualified Teacher Status (QTS) PGDE, International Approaches to Early Childhood Education MA, Mathematics: Secondary with Qualified Teacher Status (QTS) PGDE, Media Studies: Secondary with Qualified Teacher Status (QTS) PGDE, Modern Foreign Languages: Secondary with Qualified Teacher Status (QTS) PGDE, Performing Arts (Dance): Secondary with Qualified Teacher Status (QTS) PGDE, Performing Arts (Drama): Secondary with Qualified Teacher Status (QTS) PGDE, PGDE Primary Key Stage 1/2 (5-11 years) with Qualified Teacher Status (QTS), Physical Education: Secondary with Qualified Teacher Status (QTS) PGDE, Physics: Secondary with Qualified Teacher Status (QTS) PGDE, Physics with Mathematics: Secondary with Qualified Teacher Status (QTS) PGDE, Primary Foundation Stage/Key Stage 1 (3-7 years) with QTS PGDE, Primary with Mathematics Specialism (5-11 years) with QTS PGDE, Primary with Physical Education Specialism (5-11 years) and QTS PGDE, Religious Education: Secondary with Qualified Teacher Status (QTS) PGDE, School Direct Initial Teacher Training (salaried) with QTS PGCert, School Direct Primary Initial Teacher Training with QTS, School Direct Secondary Initial Teacher Training with QTS, Special Educational Needs Co-ordinator (SENCO) PGCert

School of Nursing and Allied Health; www.ljmu.ac.uk/about-us/faculties/faculty-of-education-health-and-community/school-of-nursing-and-allied-health

Adult Nursing BSc(Hons), Child Nursing BSc(Hons), Health and Social Care for Individuals, Families and Communities BA(Hons), Mental Health Nursing BSc(Hons) with Registered Nurse Status, Midwifery BA(Hons) with Registered Midwife Status, Nursing (International) BSc(Hons), Paramedic Science BSc(Hons), Paramedic Science (International) Top up degree BSc(Hons)

Postgraduate courses: Advanced Healthcare Practice (Clinical) MSc, Advanced Practice Paediatrics MSc, Counselling and Psychotherapy Practice MA, Improving Access to Psychological Therapies in Primary Care PGCert, Social Work MA, Specialist Community Practitioner Children's Nursing PGDip/BSc(Hons), Specialist Community Practitioner/ District Nursing BSc(Hons)/PGDip, Specialist Community Public Health Nurse (Health Visiting / School Nursing) BSc(Hons)/PGDip

School of Sport Studies, Leisure and Nutrition; www.ljmu.ac.uk/about-us/faculties/faculty-of-education-health-and-community/school-of-sport-studies-leisure-and-nutrition

Dance Practices BA(Hons), Disability Sport Coaching and Development Foundation Degree, Events Management BA(Hons), Food Development and Nutrition BSc(Hons), International Tourism Management BA(Hons), Nutrition BSc(Hons), Outdoor Education BSc(Hons), Physical Education BA(Hons), Sport and Nutrition for Health BSc(Hons), Sport Business BA(Hons), Sport Coaching BSc(Hons), Sport Development BA(Hons)

Postgraduate courses: International Events Management MSc, International Tourism Management MSc, MA Dance Practices, Public Health Nutrition MSc/PgDip/PgCert, Sport Coaching MSc

Faculty of Science; www.ljmu.ac.uk/about-us/faculties/faculty-of-science

School of Natural Sciences and Psychology; www.ljmu.ac.uk/about-us/faculties/faculty-of-science/school-of-natural-sciences-and-psychology

Animal Behaviour BSc(Hons), Biology BSc(Hons), Forensic Anthropology BSc(Hons), Geography

BSc(Hons), Psychology BSc(Hons), Wildlife Conservation BSc(Hons), Zoology BSc(Hons)

Postgraduate courses: Bioarchaeology MSc, Forensic Anthropology MSc, Health Psychology MSc, Primate Behaviour and Conservation MSc, Professional Doctorate in Health Psychology DHealthPsych, Wildlife Conservation and UAV Technology MSc

School of Pharmacy and Biomolecular Sciences; www.ljmu.ac.uk/about-us/faculties/faculty-of-science/school-of-pharmacy-and-biomolecular-sciences

Biochemistry BSc(Hons), Biomedical Science BSc(Hons), Chemistry BSc(Hons), Forensic Science BSc(Hons), Pharmaceutical Science BSc(Hons), Pharmacy MPharm

Postgraduate courses: Clinical Pharmacy for Primary and Interface Care PGCert/PGDip/MSc, Clinical Pharmacy for Secondary and Tertiary Care PGCert/PGDip/MSc, Cosmetic Science MSc, Drug Discovery and Design PGCert/PGDip/MSc, Forensic Bioscience MSc, Industrial Biotechnology MSc, Pharmaceutical Manufacture and Quality Control PGCert/PGDip/MSc, Virology MSc

School of Sport and Exercise Sciences; www.ljmu.ac.uk/about-us/faculties/faculty-of-science/school-of-sport-and-exercise-sciences

Applied Sport Psychology BSc, Science and Football BSc, Sport and Exercise Science BSc

Postgraduate courses: Clinical Exercise Physiology MSc, Exercise Physiology PGCert/PGDip/MSc, Professional Doctorate in Applied Sport and Exercise Science, Professional Doctorate in Sport and Exercise Psychology, Sport and Clinical Biomechanics MSc, Sport Nutrition MSc, Sport Psychology MSc, Strength and Conditioning MSc

Faculty of Engineering and Technology; www.ljmu.ac.uk/about-us/faculties/faculty-of-engineering-and-technology

Department of Applied Mathematics; www.ljmu.ac.uk/about-us/faculties/faculty-of-engineering-and-technology/department-of-applied-mathematics

Applied Mathematics with Engineering BSc(Hons), Mathematics BSc(Hons), Mathematics and Data Science BSc(Hons), Mathematics with Finance BSc(Hons)

Department of the Built Environment; www.ljmu.ac.uk/about-us/faculties/faculty-of-engineering-and-technology/department-of-the-built-environment

Architectural Engineering BEng(Hons), Architectural Engineering MEng(Hons), Architectural Technology BSc(Hons), Building Services Engineering BEng/MEng(Hons), Building Services Engineering Project Management BSc(Hons), Building Surveying BSc(Hons), Civil Engineering HNC, Construction and Property HNC, Construction Management BSc(Hons), Facilities Management BSc(Hons), Quantity Surveying BSc(Hons), Real Estate BSc(Hons)

Postgraduate courses: Applied Facilities Management MSc/PGDip/PGCert/CPD, Architectural Engineering MSc, Commercial Building Surveying MSc, Construction Project Management MSc, Integrated Building Information Management (BIM) MSc, Project Management MSc, Quantity Surveying and Commercial Management MSc, Real Estate MSc, Water, Energy and the Environment MSc/PGDip/PGCert

Department of Civil Engineering; www.ljmu.ac.uk/about-us/faculties/faculty-of-engineering-and-technology/department-of-civil-engineering

Civil and Environmental Engineering MEng, Civil and Offshore Engineering MEng(Hons), Civil and Structural Engineering MEng(Hons), Civil and Transportation Engineering MEng(Hons), Civil Engineering MEng/BEng, Civil Engineering and Architecture MEng(Hons), Civil Engineering and Construction Management MEng(Hons)

Postgraduate course: Civil Engineering MSc

Department of Computer Science; www.ljmu.ac.uk/about-us/faculties/faculty-of-engineering-and-technology/department-of-computer-science

Computer Forensics MComp/BSc(Hons), Computer Games Development MComp/BSc(Hons), Computer Networks MComp/BSc(Hons), Computer Science MComp/BSc(Hons), Computer Security MComp/BSc(Hons), Computer Studies MComp/BSc(Hons), Data Science MComp/BSc(Hons), Multimedia Computing MComp/BSc(Hons), Software Engineering MComp/BSc(Hons)

Postgraduate courses: Advanced Computer Studies MSc, Computer Forensics MSc, Computer Network Security MSc, Computer Science MSc, Computing and Information Systems MSc, Software Engineering MSc

Department of Electronics and Electrical Engineering

Audio and Music Production BSc(Hons), Computer Technology BEng/MEng(Hons), Control and Automation Engineering BEng/MEng(Hons), Electrical and Electronic Engineering BEng(Hons), Electrical Power Engineering BEng(Hons), Electronic Engineering BEng(Hons), Product Design Engineering BSc(Hons), Video Production and Streaming BSc(Hons)

Postgraduate courses: Electrical Power and Control Engineering MSc, Sensor Technologies and Enterprise MSc

Department of Maritime and Mechanical Engineering; www.ljmu.ac.uk/about-us/faculties/faculty-of-engineering-and-technology/department-of-maritime-and-mechanical-engineering

Management, Transport and Logistics BSc(Hons), Manufacturing Systems Engineering BEng(Hons) Part time, Marine and Offshore Engineering BEng/MEng(Hons), Marine Operations Foundation (FdSc), Maritime Business and Management BSc(Hons), Mechanical and Manufacturing Engineering BEng/MEng(Hons), Mechanical and Marine Engineering BEng/MEng(Hons), Mechanical Engineering BEng/MEng(Hons), Mechanical Engineering with Management BEng/MEng(Hons), Nautical Science BSc(Hons)

Postgraduate courses: Drone Technology and Applications MSc, International Transport, Trade and Logistics MSc, Logistics and Supply Chain Management MSc, Manufacturing Engineering MSc, Marine and Offshore Engineering MSc, Mechanical Engineering MSc, Port Management MSc

Liverpool Business School; www.ljmu.ac.uk/about-us/faculties/liverpool-business-school

Accounting and Finance BSc(Hons), Business and Human Resource Management BA(Hons), Business and Public Relations BA(Hons), Business Management BA(Hons), Business Studies BA(Hons), Business with Finance BA(Hons), Business with International Business Management BA(Hons), Business with Marketing BA(Hons), Human Resource Management BA(Hons), Marketing BA(Hons)

Postgraduate courses: Digital Marketing MSc, Doctor of Business Administration DBA, Doctor of Business Administration, Engineering and Technology DBA, Entrepreneurship MSc, Financial Management MSc, Human Resource Management MA, International Business and Management MSc, International Human Resource Management MSc, International Public Relations MSc, Management and Digital Business MSc, Management MSc, MBA, Public Relations MSc

UNIVERSITY OF THE ARTS LONDON
www.arts.ac.uk

Camberwell College of Arts; www.arts.ac.uk/camberwell

FdA Graphic Design, FdA Illustration, BA(Hons) Drawing, BA(Hons) Graphic Design, BA(Hons) Illustration, BA(Hons) Painting, BA(Hons) Photography, BA(Hons) Sculpture, BA(Hons) 3D Design

Postgraduate courses: MA Conservation, MA Visual Arts: Book Arts, MA Visual Arts: Designer Maker, MA Visual Arts: Fine Art Digital, MA Visual Arts: Illustration, MA Visual Arts: Printmaking

Central Saint Martins; www.arts.ac.uk/csm

BA(Hons) Acting – Drama Centre London, BA(Hons) Architecture, BA(Hons) Ceramic Design, BA(Hons) Culture, Criticism and Curation, BA(Hons) Fashion, BA(Hons) Fashion: Fashion Design with Knitwear, BA(Hons) Fashion: Fashion Design with Marketing, BA(Hons) Fashion: Fashion Design Menswear,

BA(Hons) Fashion: Fashion Design Womenswear, BA(Hons) Fashion: Fashion Print, BA(Hons) Fashion Communication, BA(Hons) Fashion Communication: Fashion History and Theory, BA(Hons) Fashion Communication: Fashion Journalism, BA(Hons) Fashion Communication: Fashion Communication and Promotion, BA(Hons) Fine Art, BA(Hons) Graphic Communication Design, BA(Hons) Jewellery Design, BA(Hons) Performance: Design and Practice, BA(Hons) Product Design, BA(Hons) Textile Design

Postgraduate courses: Central Saint Martins Birkbeck MBA, Graduate Diploma in Fashion, MA Acting – Drama Centre London, MA Applied Imagination in the Creative Industries, MA Architecture: Cities and Innovation, M Arch Architecture, MA Arts and Cultural Enterprise, MA Art and Science, MA Character Animation, MA Culture, Criticism and Curation, MA Design (Ceramics/Furniture/

Jewellery), MA Dramatic Writing, MA Fashion, MA Fashion Communication, MA Fine Art, MA Graphic Communication Design, MA Industrial Design, MA Innovation Management, MA Material Futures, MA Narrative Environments, MA Performance Design and Practice, MA Photography, MA Screen: Acting – Drama Centre London, MA Screen: Directing – Drama Centre London, MRes Art: Exhibition Studies, MRes Art: Moving Image, MRes Art: Theory and Philosophy

Chelsea College of Arts; www.arts.ac.uk/chelsea

FdA Interior Design, BA(Hons) Fine Art, BA(Hons) Graphic Design Communication, BA(Hons) Interior & Spatial Design, BA(Hons) Textile Design

Postgraduate courses: MA Curating & Collections, MA Fine Art, MA Graphic Design Communication, MA Interior & Spatial Design, MA Textile Design

London College of Communication; www.arts.ac.uk/lcc

BA(Hons) Advertising, BA(Hons) Animation, BA(Hons) Contemporary Media Cultures, BA(Hons) Design for Art Direction, BA(Hons) Design for Branded Spaces, BA(Hons) Design Management and Cultures, BA(Hons) Film Practice, BA(Hons) Film and Television, BA(Hons) Games Design, BA(Hons) Graphic and Media Design, BA(Hons) Graphic Branding and Identity, BA(Hons) Illustration and Visual Media, BA(Hons) Information and Interface Design, BA(Hons) Interaction Design Arts, BA(Hons) Journalism, BA(Hons) Live Events and Television, BA(Hons) Magazine Journalism and Publishing, BA(Hons) Media Communications, BA(Hons) Photography, BA(Hons) Photojournalism and Documentary Photography, BA(Hons) Public Relations, BA(Hons) Sound Arts and Design, BA(Hons) Sports Journalism

Postgraduate courses: Graduate Diploma Photography

MA Advertising, MA Animation, MA Arts and Lifestyle Journalism, MA Design Management and Cultures, MA Documentary Film, MA Film, MA Games Design, MA Graphic Branding and Identity, MA Graphic Media Design, MA Illustration and Visual Media, MA Interaction Design Communication, MA Media, Communications and Critical Practice, MA Photography, MA Photojournalism and Documentary Photography, MA Photojournalism and Documentary Photography (Part Time/Online Mode), MA Public Relations, MA Publishing, MA Screenwriting, MA Service Experience Design

and Innovation, MA Sound Arts, MA Television, Postgraduate Certificate Design for Visual Communication, Postgraduate Diploma Design for Visual Communication

London College of Fashion; www.arts.ac.uk/fashion

International Preparation for Fashion (Certificate in Higher Education), BA(Hons) 3D Effects for Performance and Fashion, BA(Hons) Bespoke Tailoring, BA(Hons) Cordwainers Fashion Bags and Accessories: Product Design and Innovation, BA(Hons) Cordwainers Footwear: Product Design and Innovation, BA(Hons) Costume for Performance, BA(Hons) Creative Direction for Fashion, BA(Hons) Fashion Buying and Merchandising, BA(Hons) Fashion Contour, BA(Hons) Fashion Design and Development, BA(Hons) Fashion Design Technology: Menswear, BA(Hons) Fashion Design Technology: Womenswear, BA(Hons) Fashion Illustration, BA(Hons) Fashion Jewellery, BA(Hons) Fashion Journalism, BSc(Hons) Fashion Management, BA(Hons) Fashion Marketing, BA(Hons) Fashion Pattern Cutting, BA(Hons) Fashion Photography, BA(Hons) Fashion Public Relations and Communication, BA(Hons) Fashion Sportswear, BA(Hons) Fashion Styling and Production, BA(Hons) Fashion Textiles: Embroidery, BA(Hons) Fashion Textiles: Knit, BA(Hons) Fashion Textiles: Print, BA(Hons) Fashion Visual Merchandising and Branding, BA(Hons) Hair and Make-up for Fashion, BA(Hons) Hair, Make-up and Prosthetics for Performance, BSc(Hons) Psychology of Fashion

Postgraduate courses: Executive MBA (Fashion), Graduate Diploma Fashion Management, MA Fashion Design Management, MA Fashion Entrepreneurship and Innovation, MA Fashion Retail Management, MA Strategic Fashion Marketing, Postgraduate Certificate Fashion: Buying and Merchandising, MA Psychology for Fashion Professionals, MSc Applied Psychology in Fashion, Graduate Diploma Fashion Media Styling, MA Costume Design for Performance, MA Fashion Cultures, MA Fashion Curation, MA Fashion Journalism, MA Fashion Media Production, Postgraduate Certificate Fashion: Fashion and Lifestyle Journalism, MA Fashion Photography, Graduate Diploma Fashion Design Technology, MA Fashion Artefact, MA Footwear, MA Fashion Futures, MA Fashion Design Technology Menswear, MA Fashion Design Technology Womenswear, MA Pattern and Garment Technology, Postgraduate Certificate Fashion: Fashion Visual Merchandising

Wimbledon College of Arts; www.arts.ac.uk/wimbledon

BA(Hons) Fine Art: Painting, BA(Hons) Fine Art: Print & Time-Based Media, BA(Hons) Fine Art: Sculpture, BA(Hons) Costume for Theatre & Screen, BA(Hons) Production Arts for Screen, BA(Hons) Theatre Design

MA Drawing, MA Painting, MA Theatre Design, MFA Fine Art

LONDON CONTEMPORARY DANCE SCHOOL
www.theplace.org.uk

BA(Hons) in Contemporary Dance

Postgraduate courses: PGDip/MA in Contemporary Dance, PGDip/MA in Developing Artistic Practice

---

LONDON METROPOLITAN UNIVERSITY
www.londonmet.ac.uk

Guildhall School of Business and Law; www.londonmet.ac.uk/schools/business-and-law

Accounting and Finance BA(Hons), Accounting and Finance (Extended Degree) BA(Hons), Advertising, Marketing Communications and Public Relations BA(Hons), Airline, Airport and Aviation Management BSc(Hons), Banking and Finance BSc(Hons), Banking and Finance (with Integrated Professional Training) BSc(Hons), Business Economics BA(Hons), Business Law LLB(Hons), Business Management BA(Hons), Business Management (Extended Degree) BA(Hons), Business Management and Marketing BA(Hons), Business Studies BA(Hons), CICM Diploma in Credit Management Level 3 Diploma, CICM Diploma in Credit Management Level 5 Diploma, CIM Certificate in Professional Marketing Certificate, CIM Diploma in Professional Marketing Diploma, Economics BSc(Hons), Economics and Finance BSc(Hons), Events Management BA(Hons), Fashion Marketing and Business Management BA(Hons), Human Resource Management Int Dip PD, International Business Management BSc(Hons), International Business Management (Top-Up) BSc(Hons), Law BA(Hons), Law (with International Relations) LLB(Hons), LLB (Criminal Law)(Hons), LLB Law(Hons), Music Business and Live Entertainment BA(Hons), Tourism and Travel Management BA(Hons), Translation BA(Hons)

Postgraduate courses: Common Professional Exam GDL, Conference Interpreting MA, Corporate Social Responsibility and Sustainability Adv Dip Pro Dev, Corporate Social Responsibility and Sustainability MSc, Employment Law and Practice Adv Dip Pro Dev, Financial Services Law, Regulation and Compliance LLM, Financial Services Law, Regulation and Compliance PG Dip, Global Transport and Logistics MSc, Global Transport and Logistics PG Dip, Human Resource Management MA, Human Resource Management PG Dip, International Oil, Gas and Energy Law LLM, International Oil, Gas and Energy Law PG Dip, International Trade and Finance MSc, Interpreting MA, Legal Practice LLM, Legal Practice Course PG Dip, LLM Legal Practice LLM, Management and Strategic Leadership (Top-Up) MA, Maritime Law (Top-Up) (Distance Learning) LLM, Marketing MA, Master of Business Administration MBA, Master of Business Administration (Architecture) MBA, Master of Business Administration (Arts Management) #MBA, Master of Business Administration (Business Psychology) MBA, Master of Business Administration (Cyber Security) MBA, Master of Business Administration (Data Analytics) MBA, Master of Business Administration (Islamic Finance) MBA, MBA (Top Up) MBA, Media and Entertainment Law LLM, Media and Entertainment Law PG Dip, Public-Private Partnerships Adv Dip Pro Dev, Teaching Languages (Arabic) MA, Teaching Languages (English) MA, Translation MA

School of Computing and Digital Media; www.londonmet.ac.uk/schools/computing-and-digital-media

Beauty Marketing and Journalism BA(Hons), Business Computer Systems (Top Up) BSc(Hons), Business Information Technology BSc(Hons), Computer Games Programming BSc(Hons), Computer Network Engineering Extended Degree BSc(Hons), Computer

Networking BEng(Hons), Computer Networking and Cyber Security BSc(Hons), Computer Science BSc(Hons), Computer Systems Engineering BEng(Hons), Computing BSc(Hons), Computing Extended Degree BSc(Hons), Computing, Technology and Mathematics Extended Degree BSc(Hons), Creative Music Technologies BA(Hons), Cyber Security Extended Degree BSc(Hons), Digital Forensics and Cyber Security BSc(Hons), Digital Media BA(Hons), Electronic and Communications Engineering BEng(Hons), Fashion Marketing and Journalism BA(Hons), Film and Broadcast Production BA(Hons), Film and Television Studies BA(Hons), Games Modelling, Animation and Effects BSc(Hons), Journalism BA(Hons), Journalism FdA, Journalism, Film and Television Studies BA(Hons), Mathematical Sciences BSc(Hons), Mathematics BSc(Hons), Mathematics Extended Degree BSc(Hons), Media and Communications BSc(Hons), Media and Communications Extended Degree (including Foundation Year) BSc(Hons), Media and Marketing BA(Hons), Media and Public Relations BA(Hons), Media with Arabic BA(Hons), Media with French BA(Hons), Media with Languages BA(Hons), Media with Spanish BA(Hons), Media, Communications and Journalism BSc(Hons), Multimedia Journalism BA(Hons), Photojournalism BA(Hons), Software Engineering (Top-up) BEng(Hons)

Postgraduate courses: Computer Networking and Cyber Security MSc, Computing and Information Systems MSc, Data Analytics MSc, Digital Media MA, Information Technology (Distance Learning) MSc

School of Human Sciences; www.londonmet.ac.uk/schools/human-sciences

Biochemistry BSc(Hons), Biochemistry Extended Degree BSc(Hons), Biological Science BSc(Hons), Biological Sciences Extended Degree BSc(Hons), Biology of Infectious Disease BSc(Hons), Biomedical Science BSc(Hons), Biomedical Science Extended Degree BSc(Hons), Biomedical Science leading to MD BSc(Hons), Biotechnology BSc(Hons), Biotechnology Extended Degree BSc(Hons), Chemistry BSc(Hons), Chemistry Extended Degree BSc(Hons), Crime Scene and Forensic Investigation (Top-Up) BSc(Hons), Dietetics and Nutrition BSc(Hons), Forensic Science BSc(Hons), Forensic Science Extended Degree BSc(Hons), Herbal Medicinal Science (Top-Up) BSc(Hons), Human Nutrition BSc(Hons), Human Nutrition Extended Degree BSc(Hons), Medical

Bioscience BSc(Hons), Medical Bioscience Extended Degree BSc(Hons), Personal Training with Strength and Conditioning (Top-up) BSc(Hons), Pharmaceutical Science BSc(Hons), Pharmaceutical Science Extended Degree BSc(Hons), Pharmacology BSc(Hons), Pharmacology Extended Degree BSc(Hons), Physical Education and Coaching (Top-up) BSc(Hons), Physical Education and Football Coaching with Arsenal in the Community FdSc, Sciences Extended Degree (Biology, Chemistry, Health, Psychology) BSc(Hons), Sport and Exercise Science BSc(Hons), Sport Psychology, Coaching and Physical Education BSc(Hons), Sports and Dance Therapy BSc(Hons), Sports Science Extended Degree BSc(Hons), Sports Therapy BSc(Hons), Sports Therapy Extended Degree BSc(Hons)

Postgraduate courses: Biomedical Science MSc, Biomedical Studies (Distance Learning) MSc, Blood Science MSc, Blood Science (Distance Learning) MSc, Cancer Immunotherapy MSc, Cancer Pharmacology MSc, Dietetics and Nutrition MSc, Dietetics and Nutrition PG Dip, Food Science MSc, Human Nutrition (Public Health / Sports) MSc, Medical Genomics MSc, Pharmaceutical Science and Drug Delivery Systems MSc, Sports Therapy MSc

School of Social Professions; www.londonmet.ac.uk/schools/social-professions

Community Development and Leadership BSc(Hons), Community Development and Youth Extended Degree BSc(Hons), Creative Writing and English Literature Extended Degree BA(Hons), Criminology, Policing and Law Extended Degree BSc(Hons), Early Childhood Studies BA(Hons), Early Childhood Studies FdA, Early Childhood Studies Extended Degree (including Foundation Year) BA(Hons), Education and Social Policy BA(Hons), Education Studies BA(Hons), Education Studies and English Literature BA(Hons), Education Studies Extended Degree (including Foundation Year) BA(Hons), Health and Community Development BSc(Hons), Health and Social Care BSc(Hons), Health and Social Policy BSc(Hons), Health and Wellbeing in Early Childhood BA(Hons), International Foundation Programme Architecture and Interior Design Prep Diploma, International Foundation Programme Art Media and Design Prep Diploma, International Foundation Programme Business Management Prep Diploma, International Foundation Programme Computing, Technology and Mathematics Prep Diploma, International

Foundation Programme Law Prep Diploma, International Foundation Programme Sciences Prep Diploma, International Foundation Programme Social Sciences and Humanities Prep Diploma, Montessori Early Childhood Practice FdA, Public Health and Health Promotion (Top-up) BSc(Hons), Social Work BSc(Hons), Wellbeing in Later Life (Top-Up) BA(Hons), Working with Older People FdA, Youth Studies BSc(Hons)

Postgraduate courses: Early Childhood Studies MA, Education MA, Health and Social Care Management and Policy MSc, Learning and Teaching in Higher Education MA, Master of Public Administration (MPA) MA, PGCE Early Childhood (Employment-based), PGCE Early Years (3 7), PGCE Early Years (3 7) (Aylward Academy), PGCE Early Years (3 7) (Cardinal Pole), PGCE Early Years (3 7) (Princess May), PGCE Primary (5 11) (Aylward Academy), PGCE Primary (5 11) (Cardinal Pole), PGCE Primary (5 11) (Princess May), PGCE Primary (5-11), PGCE Primary (Viridis), PGCE Secondary English with Media (Cardinal Pole), PGCE Secondary Mathematics, PGCE Secondary Mathematics (Aylward Academy), PGCE Secondary Mathematics (Cardinal Pole), PGCE Secondary Modern Languages, PGCE Secondary Modern Languages (Aylward Academy), PGCE Secondary Modern Languages (Cardinal Pole), PGCE Secondary Science with Biology, PGCE Secondary Science with Biology (Aylward Academy), PGCE Secondary Science with Biology (Cardinal Pole), PGCE Secondary Science with Chemistry, PGCE Secondary Science with Chemistry (Aylward Academy), PGCE Secondary Science with Chemistry (Cardinal Pole), PGCE Secondary Science with Physics, PGCE Secondary Science with Physics (Aylward Academy), PGCE Secondary Science with Physics (Cardinal Pole), Public Health MSc, QTS Only School Direct (Salaried) Early Years (3 7) (Cardinal Pole) PGCE, QTS Only School Direct (Salaried) Primary (5 11) (Cardinal Pole) PGCE, QTS Only School Direct (Salaried) Secondary Mathematics QTS, QTS Only School Direct (Salaried) Secondary Modern Languages QTS, Social Work MSc, Teaching Adult Dyslexic Learners in Higher and Further Education PG Cert

School of Social Sciences; www.londonmet.ac.uk/schools/social-sciences

Criminology BSc(Hons), Criminology and International Security BA(Hons), Criminology and Law BA(Hons), Criminology and Policing BSc(Hons), Criminology and Psychology BSc(Hons), Criminology and Sociology BSc(Hons), Criminology and Youth Studies BSc(Hons), Diplomacy and International Relations BA(Hons), Diplomacy and Law BA(Hons), International Relations BA(Hons), International Relations and Law BA(Hons), International Relations and Politics BA(Hons), International Relations and Politics Extended Degree BA(Hons), International Relations with Arabic BA(Hons), International Relations with French BA(Hons), International Relations with Languages BA(Hons), International Relations with Spanish BA(Hons), International Relations, Peace and Conflict Studies BA(Hons), Police Studies, Procedure and Investigation BSc(Hons), Politics BA(Hons), Psychology BSc(Hons), Psychology and Sociology BSc(Hons), Psychology Extended Degree BSc(Hons), Social Sciences and Humanities Extended Degree BA(Hons), Sociology BSc(Hons), Sociology and Social Policy BA(Hons)

Postgraduate courses: Applied Psychology MSc, Applied Psychology PG Dip, Counselling Psychology Prof Doc, Counter-Terrorism Studies (Distance Learning) MSc, Counter-Terrorism Studies (Distance Learning) PG Cert, Counter-Terrorism Studies (Distance Learning) PG Dip, Crime, Violence and Prevention MSc, Criminology MSc, Diplomacy and Security Studies (Distance Learning) MSc, Diplomacy and Security Studies (Distance Learning) PG Cert, Diplomacy and Security Studies (Distance Learning) PG Dip, Health Psychology Prof Doc, Human Rights and International Conflict MA, Intelligence and Security Studies MSc, Intelligence and Security Studies PG Cert, Intelligence and Security Studies PG Dip, International Relations MA, Occupational and Business Psychology MSc, Occupational Psychology Prof Doc, Policing, Security and Community Safety Prof Doc, Psychological Therapy MSc, Psychology for Graduates (by Distance Learning) Uni Cert, Psychology of Mental Health MSc, Security and Terrorism Law (distance learning) MA, Security and Terrorism Law (Distance Learning) PG Cert, Security and Terrorism Law (distance learning) PG Dip, Security Management (Distance Learning) MSc, Security Management (Distance Learning) PG Cert, Security Management (Distance Learning) PG Dip, Security Studies MSc, Security Studies PG Cert, Security Studies PG Dip, Terrorism, Policing and Security (Distance Learning) MSc, Terrorism, Policing and Security (Distance Learning) PG Cert, Terrorism, Policing and Security (Distance Learning) PG Dip, Woman and Child Abuse MA

The Sir John Cass School of Art, Architecture and Design; www.londonmet.ac.uk/schools/the-cass

Architecture BA(Hons), Creative Writing and English Literature BA(Hons), Dance FdA, Design for Publishing BA(Hons), Design Studio Practice BA(Hons), English Literature BA(Hons), Fashion BA(Hons), Fashion Accessories and Jewellery BA(Hons), Fashion Photography BA(Hons), Fine Art BA(Hons), Furniture FdA, Furniture and Product Design BA(Hons), Graphic Design BA(Hons), Illustration BA(Hons), Illustration and Animation BA(Hons), Interior Architecture and Design BA(Hons), Interior Design BA(Hons), Interior Design and Decoration BA(Hons), Material and Visual Culture BA(Hons), Painting BA(Hons), Photography BA(Hons), Publishing BA(Hons), Textile Design BA(Hons), Theatre and Film BA(Hons), Theatre and Film Production Design BA(Hons), Theatre and Performance Practice BA(Hons)

Postgraduate courses: Architecture MA, Creative, Digital and Professional Writing MA, Examination in Professional Practice in Architecture RIBA3, Master of Fine Arts MFA, Professional Diploma in Architecture RIBA2, Spatial Planning and Urban Design MA

THE LONDON SCHOOL OF OSTEOPATHY
www.lso.ac.uk

MOst Osteopathy; BOst Osteopathy

LONDON SOUTH BANK UNIVERSITY
www.lsbu.ac.uk

School of Applied Sciences; www.lsbu.ac.uk/schools/applied-sciences
Food Sciences
BSc(Hons) Baking Science and Technology, BSc(Hons) Baking Science and Technology (New Product Development), BSc(Hons) Baking Science and Technology (Nutrition), BSc(Hons) Food and Nutrition, BSc(Hons) Food Science, BSc(Hons) Food Science (Food Safety), BSc(Hons) Food Science (New Product Development), BSc(Hons) Human Nutrition, BSc(Hons) Human Nutrition (Exercise Science), BSc(Hons) Human Nutrition (Psychology), FdSc Baking Science and Technology, FdSc Baking Science and Technology (New Product Development), FdSc Baking Science and Technology (Nutrition), FdSc Foundation Degree Baking Science and Technology (Management), FdSc Foundation Degree Culinary Arts

Postgraduate course: MSc/Top-up to MSc Food Safety and Control
Human Sciences
BSc(Hons) Bioscience, BSc(Hons) Forensic Science, BSc(Hons) Sport and Exercise Science, BSc(Hons) Sports Coaching and Analysis, Extended Degree Programme Science, HND Applied Biology

Psychology
BSc(Hons) Psychological Counselling, BSc(Hons) Psychology, BSc(Hons) Psychology (Addiction Psychology), BSc(Hons) Psychology (Child Development), BSc(Hons) Psychology (Clinical Psychology), BSc(Hons) Psychology (Forensic Psychology), BSc(Hons) Psychology (Health and Nutrition), BSc(Hons) Psychology (Sport Psychology), Extended Degree Programme Science

Postgraduate courses: MRes Psychology, MSc Addiction Psychology and Counselling, MSc Psychology, MSc/PgDip/PgCert Mental Health and Clinical Psychology

School of Arts and Creative Industries; www.lsbu.ac.uk/schools/arts-and-creative-industries
BA(Hons) Creative Advertising with Marketing, BA(Hons) Digital Design, BA(Hons) Drama and Performance, BA(Hons) English with Creative Writing, BA(Hons) Fashion Promotion with Marketing, BA(Hons) Film Practice, BA(Hons) Film Studies, BA(Hons) Journalism, BA(Hons) Liberal Arts, BA(Hons) Photography, BA(Hons) Theatre Technologies, BA(Hons) Visual Effects (VFX), BA (hons) Music Industry Management with Marketing, BA/

BSc(Hons) Game Design and Development, BA/BSc(Hons) Sound Design

Postgraduate courses: MA Creative Performance Practice, MA Editing and Post Production (EPP), MA Journalism with Development Studies, MRes Arts and Creative Industries

School of the Built Environment and Architecture; www.lsbu.ac.uk/schools/the-built-environment-and-architecture

Architecture

BA(Hons) Architecture, MArch Architecture

Postgraduate courses: MSc Architecture, MSc Digital Architecture and Robotic Construction, Professional Practice Part 3 RIBA

Civil and Building Services Engineering

BEng(Hons) Building Services Engineering, BEng(Hons) Civil Engineering, BSc(Hons) Civil Engineering, BTEC HNC Civil Engineering, BTEC HND Building Services Engineering, Diploma IOA Acoustics and Noise Control

Postgraduate courses: MSc Building Services Engineering, MSc Civil Engineering, MSc Environmental and Architectural Acoustics, MSc Structural Engineering, MSc Sustainable Energy Systems, MSc Transport Engineering and Planning

Construction, Property and Surveying

BSc(Hons) Architectural Engineering, BSc(Hons) Architectural Technology, BSc(Hons) Building Surveying, BSc(Hons) Commercial Management (Quantity Surveying), BSc(Hons) Construction Management, BSc(Hons) Property Management (Building Surveying), BSc(Hons) Quantity Surveying, BSc(Hons) Real Estate, BTEC HNC Construction, Extended Degree Programme Built Environment

Postgraduate courses: MBA Construction and Infrastructure Management, MSc Construction Project Management, MSc International Real Estate, MSc/Top-up to MSc Property Development and Planning, PgDip/MSc Quantity Surveying, PgDip/MSc/Top-up to MSc Building Surveying, PgDip/MSc/Top-up to MSc Real Estate

School of Business; www.lsbu.ac.uk/schools/business

Accounting and Finance

BA(Hons) Accounting and Finance, BSc(Hons) Economics, BSc(Hons) Economics with Accounting, BSc(Hons) Economics with Business Management, BSc(Hons) Economics with E-Business, BSc(Hons) Economics with Enterprise and Entrepreneurship, BSc(Hons) Economics with Finance, BSc(Hons) Economics with Human Resources, BSc(Hons) Economics with Law, BSc(Hons) Economics with Marketing, BSc(Hons) Economics with Project Management, BSc(Hons) Economics with Retail Management, Foundation Course Business

Postgraduate courses: MSc Applied Accounting, MSc Corporate Governance with Graduate ICSA, MSc International Accounting and Finance, MSc International Finance

Business and Enterprise

International Diploma Programme, BA(Hons) Business Management, BA(Hons) Business Management with Accounting, BA(Hons) Business Management with E-Business, BA(Hons) Business Management with Economics, BA(Hons) Business Management with Enterprise and Entrepreneurship, BA(Hons) Business Management with Finance, BA(Hons) Business Management with Human Resources, BA(Hons) Business Management with Law, BA(Hons) Business Management with Marketing, BA(Hons) Business Management with Project Management, BA(Hons) Business Management with Retail, BA(Hons) International Business Management Top-up, BTEC HND Business Studies, FdA Foundation Degree Business, Foundation Course Business

Postgraduate courses: MSc Business Project Management, MSc International Business Management, MSc International Business Management with Finance, MSc International Business Management with HRM, MSc International Business Management with Marketing, MSc International Business Management with Project Management

Management, Marketing and People

BA(Hons) Marketing, BA(Hons) Marketing with Accounting, BA(Hons) Marketing with Advertising and Digital Communications, BA(Hons) Marketing with Economics, BA(Hons) Marketing with Enterprise and Entrepreneurship, BA(Hons) Marketing with Finance, BA(Hons) Marketing with Human Resources, BA(Hons) Marketing with Law, BA(Hons) Marketing with Luxury Brand Management, BA(Hons) Marketing with Project Management, BA(Hons) Marketing with Public Relations, BA(Hons) Marketing with Retail, BA(Hons) Marketing with Supply Chain and Procurement, CIPD Certificate Human Resource Practice, CM Certificate in Management, DMS Diploma in Management Studies, Foundation Course Business

Postgraduate courses: MBA Construction and Infrastructure Management, MBA Master of Business Administration, MPA Executive Master in Public Administration, MSc International Health Services and Hospital Management, MSc International

Human Resources, MSc International Human Resources Management (IGS), MSc International Marketing (with internship), MSc Marketing, MSc Marketing (with internship), MSc Marketing Communications, MSc Marketing Communications (with internship), MSc Marketing Management (CIM and IDM Top Up), MSc/PgDip/PgCert International Marketing, PgCert Leadership and Management: Homelessness and Housing, PgDip/MSc Human Resource Development, PgDip/MSc Human Resource Management

School of Engineering; www.lsbu.ac.uk/schools/engineering

Chemical and Petroleum Engineering

BEng(Hons) Chemical and Process Engineering, BEng(Hons) Petroleum Engineering, BTEC HND Chemical Engineering, MEng(Hons) Chemical and Process Engineering, MEng(Hons) Petroleum Engineering

Postgraduate courses: MSc Chemical Engineering and Process Management, MSc Engineering Project Management, MSc Petroleum Engineering

Computer Science and Informatics

BSc(Hons) Applied Computing, BSc(Hons) Business Information Technology, BSc(Hons) Computer Science, BSc(Hons) Computer Systems Management, BSc(Hons) Data Science, BSc(Hons) Information Technology, BSc(Hons) Web Development (IT), Foundation Year Computing

Postgraduate courses: MSc Data Science, MSc Internet, Mobile Systems and Applications, MSc Systems and Cyber Security

Electrical and Electronic Engineering

BEng(Hons) Computer Engineering, BEng(Hons) Computer Systems and Networks Engineering, BEng(Hons) Electrical and Electronic Engineering, BEng(Hons) Electrical Engineering and Power Electronics, BEng(Hons) Telecommunications Engineering, BTEC HND Electrical and Electronic Engineering, MEng(Hons) Computer Engineering, MEng(Hons) Computer Systems and Networks Engineering, MEng(Hons) Electrical and Electronic Engineering, MEng(Hons) Electrical Engineering and Power Electronics, MEng(Hons) Telecommunications Engineering

Postgraduate courses: MEM Master of Engineering Management, MRes General Engineering, MRes Master of Research in Electrical and Electronic Engineering, MSc Advanced Telecommunication and Wireless Engineering, MSc Electrical and Electronic Engineering

Mechanical Engineering and Design

BEng(Hons) Advanced Vehicle Engineering, BEng(Hons) Mechanical Engineering, BSc(Hons) Engineering Product Design, BSc(Hons) Product Design, BSc(Hons) Special Effects Design, Extended Degree Programme Engineering, MEng(Hons) Advanced Vehicle Engineering, MEng(Hons) Mechanical Engineering

Postgraduate courses: MSc Mechanical Engineering, MSc Mechatronics, Robotics and Embedded Systems

School of Health and Social Care; www.lsbu.ac.uk/schools/health-and-social-care

Adult Nursing and Midwifery

BSc(Hons) Adult Nursing, BSc(Hons) Midwifery (3 year), BSc(Hons) Midwifery (Shortened Course)

Postgraduate courses: PgDip/MSc Mental Health Advanced Nurse Practitioner, MSc Midwifery and Excellence in Practice, PgCert/PgDip/MSc Palliative and End of Life Care, PgCert/PgDip/MSc Perinatal Mental Health, PgDip/MSc (Top-up) Adult Nursing, PgCert/PgDip/MSc Palliative and End of Life Care, PgCert/PgDip/MSc Perinatal Mental Health, PgDip/MSc (Top-up) Adult Nursing, PgDip/MSc Mental Health Advanced Nurse Practitioner, PgCert/PgDip/MSc Palliative and End of Life Care, PgCert/PgDip/MSc Perinatal Mental Health, PgDip/Top up to MSc Advanced Clinical Practice

Allied Health Sciences

BSc(Hons) Chinese Medicine: Acupuncture, BSc(Hons) Diagnostic Radiography, BSc(Hons) Occupational Therapy, BSc(Hons) Operating Department Practice, BSc(Hons) Physiotherapy, BSc(Hons) Radiographic Studies, BSc(Hons) Sport Rehabilitation, BSc(Hons) Therapeutic Radiography, DipHE Diagnostic Imaging, DipHE Radiotherapy Practice, Integrated Masters Physiotherapy, Integrated Masters Sport Rehabilitation

Postgraduate courses: GradCert/PgCert Non-Medical Prescribing, Professional Doctorate in Health and Social Care, M.CMAc Chinese Medicine: Acupuncture, PgCert/PgDip/MSc Diagnostic Imaging, Masters Chiropractic, PgCert Breast Imaging, PgCert/PgDip/MSc Diagnostic Imaging, PgCert/PgDip/MSc Professional Development in Occupational Therapy, PgCert/PgDip/MSc Radiographic Reporting, PgCert/PgDip/MSc Diagnostic Imaging, PgDip/MSc Occupational Therapy (pre-registration mode), PgDip/MSc (Top-up)/MSc Therapeutic Radiography, PgDip/Top up to MSc Advanced Clinical Practice

Children's Nursing

BSc(Hons) Children's Nursing, BSc(Hons)/PgDip Children's Nursing – Second registration programme Postgraduate courses: MSc Children's Nursing, PgDip Children's Nursing, PgDip/MSc Advanced Neonatal Nurse Practitioner, PgDip/MSc Children's Advanced Nurse Practitioner, PgDip/MSc Professional Practice: Children's Nursing, PgDip/Top up to MSc Advanced Clinical Practice

Mental Health and Learning Disabilities Nursing

BSc(Hons) Learning Disability Nursing, BSc(Hons) Mental Health Nursing
Postgraduate courses: MSc Advanced CBT Practice (Resilience and Positive Development), PgDip/MSc Learning Disability Nursing, PgCert/PgDip/MSc Perinatal Mental Health, PgDip/MSc (Top-up) Mental Health Nursing, PgCert Advanced CBT Practice for the Treatment of Anxiety and Depression, PgCert/ PgDip/MSc Perinatal Mental Health, PgDip Advanced CBT Practice (Resilience and Positive Development), PgDip/MSc Learning Disability Nursing, PgDip/MSc (Top-up) Mental Health Nursing, PgCert/PgDip/MSc Perinatal Mental Health, PgDip/ Top up to MSc Advanced Clinical Practice

Primary and Social Care

BA(Hons) Social Work
BSc(Hons) District Nursing
BSc(Hons) Health and Social Care: Administration and Management
BSc(Hons) Health Visiting (Specialist Community Public Health Nursing)
BSc(Hons) Occupational Health Nursing (Specialist Community Public Health Nursing)
BSc(Hons) School Nursing (Specialist Community Public Health Nursing)
Grad Cert / BSc(Hons) Workplace Health Management
Postgraduate courses: MA Social Work, MSc (top-up) Advanced Nurse Practitioner, MSc/PgDip Public Health and Health Promotion, PgCert/PgDip/Msc Leadership and Service Improvement, PgCert/Community/Specialist Practice Teacher Award/Practice Educator Award (Social Work)/PgDip/MA Practice Education/Associate Fellow/Fellow of the HEA, PgDip Health Visiting (Specialist Community Public Health Nursing), PgDip Occupational Health Nursing (Specialist Community Public Health Nursing), PgDip Primary Care District Nursing, PgDip School Nursing (Specialist Community Public Health Nursing), PgDip/Top up to MSc Advanced Clinical Practice, PgCert/Community/Specialist Practice Teacher Award/Practice Educator Award (Social Work)/

PgDip/MA Practice Education/Associate Fellow/Fellow of the HEA

School of Law and Social Sciences; www.lsbu.ac.uk/schools/law-and-social-sciences

Centre for Education and School Partnerships

BA(Hons) Education – Top Up, BA(Hons) Education Studies
Postgraduate courses: MA Education – Autism, MA Education – Special Educational Needs and Disability (SEND), MA Programme in Education, PGCE Primary (5-11), PGCE School Direct, PgCert Autism, PgCert Mentoring, PgCert National Award for Special Educational Needs Coordinator

Law

LLB(Hons) Business Law, LLB(Hons) Criminal Law, LLB(Hons) Entertainment and Media Law, LLB(Hons) Family Law, LLB(Hons) Human Rights, LLB(Hons) Law, LLB(Hons) Law with Criminology
Postgraduate courses: LLM Civil Litigation and Dispute Resolution, LLM Crime and Litigation, LLM International Commercial Law, LLM International Criminal Law and Procedure, LLM International Human Rights and Development

Social Sciences

BA(Hons) History, BA(Hons) History with Criminology, BA(Hons) History with Politics, BA(Hons) History with Sociology, BA(Hons) International Relations, BA(Hons) International Relations with Criminology, BA(Hons) International Relations with Politics, BA(Hons) International Relations with Sociology, BA(Hons) Liberal Arts, BA(Hons) Politics, BSc(Hons) Criminology, BSc(Hons) Criminology with Law, BSc(Hons) Criminology with Politics, BSc(Hons) Criminology with Psychology, BSc(Hons) Sociology, BSc(Hons) Sociology with Criminology, BSc(Hons) Sociology with Politics
Postgraduate courses: MSc Criminology and Social Research Methods, MSc Development and Urbanisation, MSc Development Studies, MSc Refugee Studies, MSc/PgDip Education for Sustainability

Urban, Environment and Leisure Studies

BA(Hons) Events and Entertainment Management, BA(Hons) Housing Studies, BA(Hons) Human Geography, BA(Hons) Human Geography with Housing, BA(Hons) Human Geography with Planning, BA(Hons) Human Geography with Tourism Development, BA(Hons) Tourism and Hospitality Management, BA(Hons) Urban and Environmental Planning, BTEC HNC Housing Studies

Postgraduate courses: MA Housing and Society, MA London and Global Cities, MA Planning, Policy and Practice, MA Urban Design and Planning, MSc/Top-up International Tourism and Hospitality Management, PgCert/PgDip/MA Housing Studies, PgDip/MA Town Planning

UNIVERSITY OF EAST LONDON
www.uel.ac.uk

School of Architecture, Computing and Engineering; www.uel.ac.uk/schools/ace

Architecture and Design

BSc(Hons) Architectural Design Technology (Accredited by CIAT), BSc(Hons) Architecture (ARB/RIBA Part 1), BA(Hons) Interior Design, BSc(Hons) Product Design

Postgraduate courses: MArch Architecture (ARB/RIBA Part 2), MRes Architecture (Reading the Neoliberal City), MA Architecture and Urbanism, PGDip Landscape Architecture, MA Professional Landscape Architecture, MA Interior Design

Computer Science and Informatics

BSc(Hons) Computer Science, BSc(Hons) Computing for Business

Postgraduate courses: MSc Computer Science, MSc Data Science, MSc Information Security and Digital Forensics, Prof Doc Data Science, Prof Doc Information Security

Civil and Structural Engineering

BEng(Hons) Civil Engineering, MEng Civil Engineering (Integrated Master's), FdSc Civil Engineering and Construction Management, BSc(Hons) Construction Management

Postgraduate courses: MSc Civil Engineering, MSc Structural Engineering, PGDip Civil Engineering, PGDip Structural Engineering, MSc Construction Engineering Management

Mechanical Engineering

BEng(Hons) Design Engineering, BEng(Hons) Engineering Management, BEng(Hons) General Engineering, BEng(Hons) Mechanical Engineering, MEng Mechanical Engineering (Integrated Master's)

Surveying and Construction

BSc(Hons) Construction Management, BSc(Hons) Surveying and Mapping Sciences

Postgraduate courses: MSc Construction Engineering Management, MSc Civil Engineering, MSc Structural Engineering, PGDip Civil Engineering, PGDip Structural Engineering

School of Arts and Digital Industries; www.uel.ac.uk/schools/adi

Art and Design

BA Animation, BA Illustration, BA Graphic Design, BA Fine Art, BA Photography

Fashion & Textiles

BA Fashion Design, BA Fashion Textiles, BA Fashion Marketing

Humanities and Creative Industries

BA Advertising, BA Creative and Professional Writing, BA English Literature, BA History, BA Journalism, BA Sports Journalism

Media and Screen subjects

BSc Computer Game Development, BA Computer Games Design: Story Development, BA Film, BA Media and Communication

Performing Arts

BA Dance Urban Practice, BA Drama Applied Theatre and Performance, BA Music Technology and Production, BA Music Performance and Production, BA Hons Performing Arts

Postgraduate courses

MA Acting, MA Contemporary Performance Practices, MA Digital Advertising, MA Filmmaking, MA Fine Art, MA International Fashion Business, MA Media Communication and Global Development, MA Theatre Directing

Cass School of Education and Communities; www.uel.ac.uk/schools/cass

Early Childhood

BA(Hons) Social and Community Work, BA(Hons) Early Childhood and Special Education, BA(Hons) Early Childhood with Education and QTS, BA(Hons) Early Childhood Studies

Postgraduate course: MA Early Childhood Studies

Education

BA Hons (Education Studies)

Postgraduate courses: MA Education, MA Leadership in Education

English Language Teaching

Postgraduate course: MA English Language Teaching

Social Work

BA(Hons) Social Work

Postgraduate courses: MA Post Qualifying Professional Practice, MA Social Work

Special Educational Needs

BA(Hons) Special Education

Postgraduate courses: MA/PgDip/PgCert Special and Additional Learning Needs, MA Special Educational Needs, PGCert Autism Spectrum Conditions and Learning, PGCert Special Educational Needs Coordination, PGCert Understanding and Supporting Behaviour

Teacher Training

Postgraduate courses: PGCE iPGCE, PGCE Non-Qualified Teacher Status (QTS), PGCE Primary (5-11), PGCE Primary with Early Years (3-7), PGCE Primary with English, PGCE Primary with English as an Additional Language, PGCE Primary with Humanities and Religious Education, PGCE Primary with ICT and Computing, PGCE Secondary Biology, PGCE Secondary Chemistry, PGCE Secondary Community Languages, PGCE Secondary Computing, PGCE Secondary Design and Technology, PGCE Secondary Drama, PGCE Secondary English, PGCE Secondary French, PGCE Secondary French with German, PGCE Secondary French with Italian, PGCE Secondary French with Spanish, PGCE Secondary Geography, PGCE Secondary German with French, PGCE Secondary Mathematics, PGCE Secondary Music, PGCE Secondary Physical Education, PGCE Secondary Physics, PGCE Secondary Physics with Mathematics, PGCE Secondary Religious Education, PGCE Secondary Spanish with French

Youth and Community

Postgraduate course: MA Youth and Community

School of Health, Sport and Bioscience; www.uel.ac.uk/schools/health-sport-and-bioscience

Applied Sport and Exercise Sciences

Football Coaching West Ham FdSc, BSc(Hons) Sport and Exercise Science, BSc(Hons) Sport and Exercise Science (with Foundation year), BSc(Hons) Sport Physical Education and Development, BSc(Hons) Sport, Physical Education and Development (with Foundation year), BSc(Hons) Sports Coaching, BA(Hons) Sports Journalism, BSc(Hons) Sports Therapy

Postgraduate courses: MSc Applied Sport and Exercise Sciences (with specialism), MSc Sports Management, MRes Sports Science

Bioscience

BSc(Hons) Biochemistry, BSc(Hons) Biomedical Science, BSc(Hons) Chemistry, BSc(Hons) Medical

Physiology, DipHE Medical Sciences, BSc(Hons) Pharmaceutical Science, BSc(Hons) Pharmacology

Postgraduate courses: MSc Biomedical Science (with specialism), MRes Bioscience, MSc Pharmaceutical Science (with specialism)

Health

BSc(Hons) Nursing (Adult), BSc(Hons) Public Health, BSc(Hons) Public Health and Health Promotion, BSc(Hons) Public Health and Health Services Management

Postgraduate courses: MRes Health Science, MSc Public Health

Physiotherapy and Podiatry

BSc(Hons) BSc(Hons) Physiotherapy, BSc(Hons) Podiatry

Postgraduate course: PGCert Musculoskeletal Ultrasonography

School of Psychology; www.uel.ac.uk/schools/psychology

BSc(Hons) Business Psychology, BSc(Hons) Child Psychology, BSc(Hons) Clinical and Community Psychology, BSc(Hons) Counselling, BSc(Hons) Forensic Psychology, BSc(Hons) Psychology

Postgraduate courses: MSc Applied Positive Psychology and Coaching Psychology, MSc Business Psychology, PGDip Career Coaching, MSc Career Coaching, MSc Clinical and Community Psychology, PGDip Counselling and Psychotherapy, MA Counselling & Psychotherapy, PGDip in Integrative Counselling and Coaching, MSc Integrative Counselling and Coaching, MSc Occupational and Organisational Psychology, MSc Psychology

Royal Docks School of Business and Law; www.uel.ac.uk/schools/royal-docks

Accounting, Finance and Economics

BA(Hons) Accounting and Finance, MAccFin Accounting and Finance, BSc(Hons) Economics

Postgraduate courses: MSc International Accounting and Finance, MSc Professional Accounting, MSc Finance and Risk

Business

BA(Hons) Business Management, BA(Hons) Business Management (Human Resource Management), BA(Hons) Business Management (Marketing)

Postgraduate courses: MBA Master of Business Administration, MSc International Business Management, MSc Oil and Gas Management, MSc Sports Management

Criminology

BA(Hons) Criminology and Criminal Justice, BA(Hons) Criminology and Law, BA(Hons)

Criminology and Psychology, BA(Hons) Policing, BA(Hons) Sociology with Criminology
Postgraduate course: MSc Terrorism and Counter-terrorism Studies

Law
LLB(Hons) Business Law, LLB(Hons) Law, FdA Law (Paralegal Studies), LLB(Hons) Law with Criminology, LLB(Hons) Law with International Relations
Postgraduate courses: LLM (Business and Financial Law), LLM (General), LLM (Human Rights Advocacy), LLM (International Law and Legal Practice), LLM (Transitional Justice and Conflict), LLM Energy and Natural Resources Law

Tourism, Hospitality and Events
BA(Hons) Events Management, BA(Hons) Tourism Management, BA(Hons) Hospitality Management

School of Social Sciences; www.uel.ac.uk/schools/social-sciences
Global Studies
BA(Hons) International Relations, BA(Hons) International Development, BA(Hons) International Development with NGO Management

Postgraduate courses: MSc International and Comparative Public Policy, MSc/PGCert NGO and Development Management, MA Media, Communication and Global Development, MSc International Relations, MA Refugee Studies, MA Conflict, Displacement and Human Security

Sociology
BA(Hons) Sociology, BA(Hons) Sociology with Criminology
Postgraduate courses: MA Media, Communication and Global Development, PGCert Narrative Research via Distance Learning

Psychosocial
BA(Hons) Psychosocial Theory and Practice
Postgraduate courses: MA Psychosocial Studies via Distance Learning

---

UNIVERSITY OF WEST LONDON
www.uwl.ac.uk

London School of Film, Media and Design; www.uwl.ac.uk/academic-schools/film-media-design
BA(Hons) Advertising and Public Relations, BA(Hons) Broadcast and Digital Journalism, BA(Hons) Journalism, BA(Hons) English and Media and Communications, BA(Hons) English and Film, BA(Hons) English and Creative Writing, BA(Hons) Fashion Branding and Marketing, BA(Hons) Fashion Buying and Management, BA(Hons) Fashion Promotion and Imaging, BA(Hons) Fashion and Textiles, BA(Hons) Film Production, BA(Hons) Graphic Design (Visual Communication and Illustration), BA(Hons) Media and Communications, BA(Hons) Photography, BA(Hons) Commercial Photography, FdA Photography, BA(Hons) Radio and Digital Media, BA(Hons) Visual Effects, BA(Hons) Games, Design and Animation
Postgraduate courses: MA Advertising, Branding & Communication, MA Film Production, MA Luxury Design, Innovation & Brand management, MPhil in Creative Writing, MA Creative Media Start Up

The Claude Littner Business School; www.uwl.ac.uk/academic-schools/business
BA(Hons) Accounting and Finance, BSc(Hons) Business Economics, BA(Hons) Business Studies, BA(Hons) Business Studies with Finance, BA(Hons) Business Studies with Human Resource Management, BA(Hons) Business Studies with Marketing, BSc(Hons) Human Resource Management, BA(Hons) International Business Management, BSc(Hons) Social Media Marketing
Postgraduate courses: MSc Digital Marketing, MSc Finance and Accounting, MSc Finance and Risk Management, MA/PGDip Human Resource Management, MSc International Business Management, MSc International Marketing, MBA Masters in Business Administration

School of Computing and Engineering; www.uwl.ac.uk/academic-schools/computing
BEng(Hons) Civil and Environmental Engineering, BEng(Hons) Electrical and Electronic Engineering, BSc(Hons) Applied Sound Engineering, BSc(Hons)

Architectural Design and Technology, BSc(Hons) Building Surveying, BSc(Hons) Computer Games Technology, BSc(Hons) Computer Science, BSc(Hons) Computing and Information Systems (part-time only), BSc(Hons) Construction Project Management, BSc(Hons) Creative Computing, BSc(Hons) Cyber Security, BSc(Hons) Information Technology, BSc(Hons) Information Technology Management for Business (ITMB), BSc(Hons) Mathematics and Statistics, BSc(Hons) Mobile Computing, FdEng Civil and Environmental Engineering (part-time only), FdSc Architectural Design and Technology (part-time only), FdSc Building Surveying, FdSc Computing and Information Systems (part-time only), FdSc Construction Project Management (part-time only)
Postgraduate courses: MSc Applied Project Management, MSc Civil and Environmental Engineering, MSc Cyber Security, MSc Digital Audio Engineering, MSc Health Informatics, MSc Information Systems, MSc Software Engineering

London Geller College of Hospitality and Tourism; www.uwl.ac.uk/academic-schools/hospitality-tourism

BA(Hons) Airline and Airport Management, BA(Hons) Event Management, BA(Hons) Event Management with Hospitality, BA(Hons) Event Management with Tourism, BA(Hons) Food and Professional Cookery (top-up), BA(Hons) Hospitality Management, BA(Hons) Hospitality Management and Food Studies, BA(Hons) International Hotel Management, BA(Hons) Leisure Management, BA(Hons) Strategic Transport Management, BA(Hons) Travel and Tourism Management, BSc(Hons) Culinary Arts Management, FdA Airline and Airport Management, FdA Event Management, FdA Event Management with Hospitality, FdA Event Management with Tourism, FdA Hospitality Management, FdA Hospitality Management and Food Studies, FdA International Hotel Management, FdA Travel and Tourism Management
Postgraduate courses: MA International Tourism and Aviation Management, MA Food Business Management, MA Luxury Hospitality Management, MA Luxury Hospitality Management with Internship, MPhil Hospitality

School of Law and Criminology; www.uwl.ac.uk/academic-schools/law

BA(Hons) Criminology, BA(Hons) Criminology with Law, BA(Hons) Criminology with Psychology, BA(Hons) Criminology, Policing and Forensics, BA(Hons) Criminology with Sociology, BA(Hons) Criminology with Criminal Justice, BA(Hons) Sociology, BA(Hons) Sociology with Criminology, LLB(Hons) Law
Postgraduate courses: MA Criminology, MA Criminology and Global Security, MA Criminology and Global Crime, MA/LLM International Criminal Justice, PGCert Legal Practice (LPC Stage 1), LLM Legal Practice, LLM International Business and Commercial Law, LLM International Banking and Finance Law, LLM International Studies in Intellectual Property Law

London College of Music; www.uwl.ac.uk/academic-schools/music

BA(Hons) Acting, BA(Hons) Actor Musicianship, BA(Hons) Electronic Music Production, BA(Hons) Live Sound Production, BA(Hons) Music Management, BA(Hons) Music Mixing and Mastering, BA(Hons) Music Recording and Production, BA(Hons) Music Technology – Audio Post Production, BA(Hons) Music Technology (Top-up), BA(Hons) Music Technology and Radio Broadcasting, BA(Hons) Music Technology and Video Production, BA(Hons) Music Technology Specialist, BA(Hons) Music Technology with Composition, BA(Hons) Music Technology with Performance, BA(Hons) Music Technology with Popular Music Performance, BA(Hons) Musical Theatre, BA(Hons) Text and Performance, BA(Hons) Theatre Production (Design and Management), BA(Hons) Voice in Performance, BMus(Hons) Composition, BMus(Hons) Composition and Recording, BMus(Hons) Film Composition, BMus(Hons) Music Performance and Recording, BMus(Hons) Music Performance with Music Management, BMus(Hons) Music Performance with Technology, BSc(Hons) Applied Sound Engineering, DipHE Music Technology
Postgraduate courses: DMus Composition, DMus Electronic/Electro-acoustic Composition, DMus Performance, MA Advanced Music Technology, MA Music Industry Management and Artist Development, MMus Composition (Electronic Music, Concert Music or Film and Television), MMus Performance, MMus Popular Music Performance, PGDip Performance

College of Nursing, Midwifery and Healthcare; www.uwl.ac.uk/academic-schools/nursing-midwifery

BSc(Hons) Adult Nursing, BSc(Hons) Nursing (Children's Nursing), BSc(Hons) Health Promotion and Public Health, BSc(Hons) Midwifery (pre-/post-registration), BSc(Hons) Nursing (Learning Disabilities),

BSc(Hons) Nursing (Mental Health), BSc(Hons) Operating Department Practice, BSc(Hons) Professional Practice (Top-up)

Postgraduate courses: MPhil Nursing, MSc Advanced Practice, MSc Bioinformatics, MSc Improvement Science, MSc Nursing (top-up), MSc Nursing and Healthcare/MSc Nursing and Healthcare – Integrated, MSc Public Health and Wellbeing, PGCert Strategic Workforce Planning, PGCert/PGDip/MSc Professional Practice, PGCert/PGDip/MSc Psychosocial Interventions for Psychosis, PGDip Nursing (Adult), PGDip Nursing (Mental Health), PGDip/MSc Management Studies (Health and Social Care)

School of Human and Social Sciences; www.uwl.ac.uk/academic-schools/psychology

BA(Hons) Early Years, BA(Hons) Education Studies, BA(Hons) Politics and International Relations, BSc(Hons) Forensic Science, BSc(Hons) Psychology with Applied Forensic Investigation, BSc(Hons) Psychology with Counselling Theory, BSc(Hons) Psychology with Criminology, BSc(Hons) Psychology with Substance Use and Misuse Studies, BSc(Hons) Social Work, BSc(Hons) Substance Use and Misuse Studies (Top-up), BSc Nutritional Therapy, DipHE Nutritional Therapeutics, FdSc Nutritional Therapeutics

Postgraduate courses: PGCert/PGDip Clinical Hypnotherapy, MSc Dementia Care, MSc Health Psychology, MSc Psychology Conversion, MPhil Psychology

---

UNIVERSITY OF LONDON; BIRKBECK
www.bbk.ac.uk

School of Arts; www.bbk.ac.uk/arts

Department of English and Humanities; www.bbk.ac.uk/english

Creative Writing (BA), Theatre and Drama Studies (BA), Theatre Studies and English (BA), Arts and Humanities (BA), English (BA)

Postgraduate courses: Contemporary Literature and Culture (MA), Creative Producing (MA), Creative Writing (MA), Cultural and Critical Studies (MA), Humanities and Cultural Studies (MRes), Medical Humanities (MA/PGDip/PGCert), Medical Leadership (MSc/PGDip/PGCert), Medieval Literature and Culture (MA), Modern and Contemporary Literature (MA), Renaissance Studies (MA), Romantic Studies (MA/PGDip/PGCert), Screenwriting (MA/PGCert), Shakespeare and Contemporary Performance (MA), Text and Performance (MA), Text and Performance (with RADA) (MA), Theatre Directing (MFA), Victorian Studies (MA)

Department of Cultures and Languages; www.bbk.ac.uk/languages

BA French Studies, BA German Studies, BA Iberian and Latin American Studies (Spanish or Portuguese pathways), BA Modern Languages (with two of French, German, Japanese, Portuguese or Spanish), BA Linguistics and Languages (with one of French/German/Japanese/Portugues/Spanish), BA Language and Management/Management and Language (with one of French/German/Japanese/Portuguese/Spanish), BA Language and History/History and Language (with one of French/German/Japanese/Portuguese/Spanish), BA Language and Film/Media

Postgraduate courses: Comparative Literature, Cultures and Thought (MA), French Studies (GradDip), German Studies (GradDip), Iberian and Latin American Studies (GradCert), International Foundation Programme for Postgraduate Study (GradDip), Japanese Cultural Studies (MA), Language Teaching (MA), Politics with [Language] (Intensive) (MRes), Spanish, Portuguese and Latin American Cultural Studies (MA), Teaching English to Speakers of Other Languages (TESOL) (MA), World Cinema (MA)

Department of History of Art; www.bbk.ac.uk/art-history

History of Art (CertHE), BA History of Art, BA History of Art with Curating, BA History of Art with Film, BA History of Art with History, History of Art and Architecture (GradCert)

Postgraduate courses: MA History of Art, MA History of Art with History and Theory of Photography

Department of Film, Media and Cultural Studies; www.bbk.ac.uk/culture

Arts and Media Management (Foundation Degree), BA Film and Media, BA Journalism and Media, BA

Media and Culture, BA Global Cinemas and Screen Arts

Postgraduate courses: Arts Policy and Management (MA/PGDip/PGCert), Digital Media Culture (MA), Digital Media Design (MA), Digital Media Management (MA), Film, Television and Screen Media (MA), Film Programming and Curating (MA), Journalism (MA/PGCert), Investigative Reporting (MA), Screenwriting (MA/PGCert), Digital Media Management (PGCert), Web Design and Development (PGCert)

School of Business, Economics and Informatics; www.bbk.ac.uk/business

Department of Economics, Mathematics and Statistics; www.bbk.ac.uk/ems

BSc Economic and Social Policy, BSc Economics, BSc Economics and Business, BSc Financial Economics, BSc Financial Economics with Accounting, BSc Mathematics, BSc Mathematics and Accounting, BSc Mathematics and Economics, BSc Mathematics and Management, BSc Mathematics and Statistics, BSc Statistics and Economics

Postgraduate courses: MSc Applied Statistics, MSc Applied Statistics and Financial Modelling, MSc Economics, MSc Finance, MSc Finance (with advanced pathways), MSc Financial Economics, MSc Financial Risk Management, MSc Mathematical Finance, MSc Mathematics, MSc Mathematics and Financial Modelling, PGCert in Econometrics

Department of Computer Science and Information Systems; www.dcs.bbk.ac.uk

BSc in Computing, BSc in Digital and Technology Solutions Degree Apprenticeship (Software Engineering), BSc in Information Systems and Management, FdSc in Computing/Information Technology/Web Development, CertHE in Information Technology, CertHE in Web Design Technologies

Postgraduate courses: MSc in Computer Science, MSc in Data Science, MSc in Information Technology, PGCert in Cloud and Data Technologies, MSc in Advanced Computing Technologies, MSc in Computing for the Financial Services, MSc in Data Analytics, MSc in Information and Web Technologies, MSc in Information Systems and Management

Department of Management; www.bbk.ac.uk/management

Accounting (BSc), Accounting and Management (BA), Accounting with Finance (BSc), Applied Accounting and Business (BSc), Business (BSc), Funeral Management (CertHE), Management (BA),

Management (CertHE), Management (Foundation Degree), Management and Accounting (Foundation Degree), Management for Personal Assistants (CertHE), Marketing (BSc), Professional Studies (BSc Top-Up)

Postgraduate courses: Accounting and Financial Management (MSc), Business Innovation (PGCert), Business Innovation with E-Business (MSc), Business Innovation with Entrepreneurship and Innovation Management (MSc), Business Innovation with International Technology Management (MSc), Corporate Governance and Business Ethics (MSc), Corporate Responsibility & Sustainability (MSc), Creative Industries (Management) (MSc), Creative Industries (PGCert), International Business (MSc), International Business and Development (MSc), International Management (MSc), International Marketing (MSc), Investment Management (MSc), Management (MRes/MSc/PGCert/PGDip), Management with Business Innovation (MSc), Management with Business Strategy and the Environment (MSc), Management with Corporate Governance and Business Ethics (MSc), Management with Creative Industries (MSc), Management with Human Resource Management (MSc), Management with International Business (MSc), Management with International Business and Development (MSc), Management with Marketing (MSc), Management with Sport Management (MSc), Marketing (MSc), Marketing Communications (MSc), Sport Governance (PGCert), Sport Management (MSc/PGCert), Sport Management and Marketing (MSc), Sport Management and the Business of Football (MSc), Sport Management, Governance and Policy (MSc), Sport Marketing (MSc)

Department of Organisational Psychology; www.bbk.ac.uk/orgpsych

Business Psychology (BSc)

Postgraduate courses: Career Management and Coaching (MSc), Coaching (PGCert), Human Resource Development and Consultancy (MSc), Human Resource Management (MSc), Management Consultancy and Organisational Change (MSc), Occupational Psychology (MSc), Organizational Behaviour (MSc)

School of Law; www.bbk.ac.uk/law

Department of Criminology; www.bbk.ac.uk/law/departments/department-of-criminology

Criminology (CertHE), Criminology and Criminal Justice (BSc)

Postgraduate courses: Criminal Law and Criminal Justice (MA/LLM), Global Criminology (MSc)

Department of Law; www.bbk.ac.uk/law/departments/department-of-law
Legal Method (CertHE)
Law (LLB)
Language and/with International Law (French, German, Japanese, Portuguese, Spanish) (BA)
Postgraduate courses: Constitutional Politics, Law and Theory (LLM), Criminal Law and Criminal Justice (MA/LLM), Human Rights (LLM/MA), International Economic Law (Finance or Justice and Development Pathway) (Intensive) (LLM), International Economic Law, Justice and Development (Evening) (LLM), Law General (LLM), Law, Democracy, and Human Welfare: Global Perspectives (Intensive) (LLM), Qualifying Law Degree (LLM)

School of Science; www.bbk.ac.uk/science

Department of Biological Sciences
Biomedicine (BSc), Structural Molecular Biology (BSc), Laboratory Science (Foundation Degree/Higher Apprenticeship), Life Sciences for Subjects Allied to Medicine (CertHE), Physics and Mathematics (CertHE)
Postgraduate courses: Analytical Bioscience (MSc/PGDip), Analytical Chemistry (MSc/PGDip), Biobusiness (MSc), Bioinformatics with Systems Biology (MRes/MSc), Chemical Research (MRes), Microbiology (MRes/MSc), Principles of Protein Structure (PGCert), Protein Crystallography (PGCert), Structural Biology (MRes), Structural Molecular Biology (MSc), Techniques in Structural Molecular Biology (PGCert)

Department of Earth and Planetary Sciences; www.bbk.ac.uk/geology
Earth History and Palaeontology (CertHE), Earth Sciences (BSc), Environmental Geology (BSc), Environmental Geology (GradCert), Geology (BSc), Geology (CertHE/GradCert), Mineralogy and Volcanology (CertHE), Planetary Science with Astronomy (BSc/CertHE)
Postgraduate courses: Environmental Geology (GradCert), Geology (GradCert), Planetary Sciences (GradCert)

Department of Psychological Sciences; www.bbk.ac.uk/psychology
Business Psychology (BSc), Psychodynamic Counselling and Organisational Dynamics (CertHE),

Psychology (BSc), Psychology for Education (BA), Psychology for Education Professionals (Foundation Degree), Applied Psychology (CertHE), Counselling and Counselling Skills (CertHE), Psychology (CertHE)
Postgraduate courses: Cognition and Computation (MA), Cognition and Computation (MSc), Cognitive Neuroscience and Neuropsychology (MSc/MA), Developmental Sciences (MA/MSc), Educational Neuroscience (MA/MSc), Functional Neuroimaging (MRes), Psychoanalytic Studies (MA), Psychodynamic Counselling & Psychotherapy with Children and Adolescents (MSc), Psychodynamic Counselling and Psychotherapy (MSc), Psychodynamics of Human Development (MSc/PGDip), Psychological Research Methods (MSc), Psychology (MRes/MSc/PGDip), Psychosocial Studies (MA/GradCert)

School of Social Sciences, History and Philosophy; www.bbk.ac.uk/sshp

Department of Applied Linguistics and Communication; www.bbk.ac.uk/linguistics
CertHE Higher Education Introductory Studies, CertHE Introduction to History, CertHE Introduction to Geography, CertHE Introduction to Politics, CertHE Introduction to Social Sciences, CertHE Linguistics and Language, BA Linguistics and Language
Postgraduate courses: GradCert Linguistic Studies, IPGCert Intercultural Communication, PGDip Intercultural Communication, MA Applied Linguistics and Communication, MA Intercultural Communication for Business and Professions, MA Language Teaching, MA TESOL (Teaching English to Speakers of Other Languages)

Department of Geography; www.bbk.ac.uk/geography
Community Development and Public Policy (BSc), Community Leadership (CertHE), Development and Globalisation (BSc), Development Studies (CertHE), Environmental Management (BSc), Geography (BSc), Human Geography (BA), Introduction to Social Sciences (CertHE), Social Anthropology (CertHE), Social Sciences (BSc)
Postgraduate courses: Children, Youth and International Development (MSc), Climate Change (MSc/PGDip/PGCert), Environment and Sustainability (MSc/PGDip), Geographic Information Science (MSc/PGDip/PGCert), Geography (MSc/PGDip/PGCert), Global Environmental Politics and Policy

(MSc), International Development (MSc/PGDip/PGCert), International Development and Social Anthropology (MSc/PGDip), Social and Cultural Geography (MA), War and Humanitarianism (MSc)

Department of History, Classics and Archaeology; www.bbk.ac.uk/history

BA Archaeology, BA Classics/BA Classical Studies, BA Contemporary History and Politics, BA History, BA History and Archaeology, BA History and International Relations

Postgraduate courses: MA Archaeological Practice, MA Classical Archaeology, MA Classical Civilisation/MA Classics, MA Contemporary History and Politics, MA Early Modern History, MA European History, MA Gender, Sexuality and Culture, MSc Gender, Sexuality and Society, MA Global History: Empires, States and Cultures, MA Historical Research, MA History of Ideas, MA History of Science and Medicine, MA History of the British Isles, MA Medieval History, MA Public Histories, MRes History, MSc War and Humanitarianism, GradCert in History

Department of Philosophy; www.bbk.ac.uk/philosophy

CertHE Philosophy, BA Philosophy

Postgraduate course: PGCert/PGDip/MA/MRes Philosophy

Department of Politics; www.bbk.ac.uk/politics

International Studies (CertHE), Politics (CertHE), Global Politics and International Relations (BA), Politics (BA), Politics, Philosophy and History (BA)

Postgraduate courses: European Politics and Policy (MSc), Global Governance and Emerging Powers (MSc), Global Politics (MRes/MSc), Government, Policy and Politics (MSc), International Security and Global Governance (MSc), Middle East in Global Politics: Islam, Conflict and Development (MSc), Nationalism and Ethnic Conflict (MSc), Politics (MRes), Politics of Population, Migration and Ecology (MSc), Public Policy and Management (MRes/MSc), Social and Political Theory (MSc), Social Research (MSc/PGCert/PGDip)

Department of Psychosocial Studies; www.bbk.ac.uk/psychosocial

Counselling and Counselling Skills (CertHE), Psychodynamic Counselling and Organisational Dynamics (CertHE), Psychosocial Studies (BA), Psychosocial Studies and Principles of Psychodynamic Counselling (BA)

Postgraduate courses: Culture, Diaspora, Ethnicity (PGDip), Culture, Diaspora, Ethnicity (PGCert/MA), Education, Power and Social Change (MSc/PGCert/PGDip), Psychoanalytic Studies (MA), Psychodynamic Counselling & Psychotherapy with Children and Adolescents (MSc), Psychodynamic Counselling and Psychotherapy (MSc), Psychodynamics of Human Development (PGDip/MSc), Psychosocial Studies (GradCert), Psychosocial Studies (MA), Social Research and Psychosocial Studies (MRes)

UNIVERSITY OF LONDON; COURTAULD INSTITUTE OF ART
www.courtauld.ac.uk

BA History of Art

Postgraduate courses: GradDip in the History of Art, MA History of Art, MA Curating the Art Museum, MA Buddhist Art: History and Conservation, PGDip in the Conservation of Easel Paintings, MA Conservation of Wall Painting

UNIVERSITY OF LONDON; GOLDSMITHS
www.goldsmiths.ac.uk

Department of Anthropology; www.gold.ac.uk/anthropology

BA(Hons) Anthropology, BA(Hons) Anthropology & Media, BA(Hons) Anthropology & Sociology, BA(Hons) Anthropology & Visual Practice, BA(Hons) History & Anthropology, BA(Hons) Politics, Philosophy & Economics, BA Religion

Postgraduate courses: MA in Anthropology & Cultural Politics, MA in Anthropology & Museum Practice, MA in Applied Anthropology & Community & Youth Work, MA in Applied Anthropology & Community Arts, MA in Applied Anthropology & Community Development, MA in Development & Rights, MA in Migration & Mobility, MA in Social Anthropology, MA in Visual Anthropology, MRes in Anthropology, MRes in Visual Anthropology

Department of Art; www.gold.ac.uk/art

BA(Hons) Fine Art, BA(Hons) Fine Art & History of Art, BSc(Hons) Digital Arts Computing
Postgraduate courses: MA in Artists' Film & Moving Image, MFA in Curating, MFA in Fine Art

Department of Computing; www.gold.ac.uk/computing

BA(Hons) Journalism, BMus/BSc(Hons) Music Computing, BSc(Hons) Business Computing & Entrepreneurship, BSc(Hons) Computer Science, BSc(Hons) Computing & Chinese, BSc(Hons) Creative Computing, BSc(Hons) Digital Arts Computing, BSc(Hons) Games Programming, BSc Data Science, BSc Maths and Computer Science, BSc Maths and Economics
Postgraduate courses: MA in Computational Arts, MA in Computer Games Art & Design, MA in Creative & Cultural Entrepreneurship: Computing Pathway, MA Independent Games and Playable Experience Design

Confucius Institute for Dance and Performacne; www.gold.ac.uk/confucius-institute

BA(Hons) International Relations & Chinese, BA(Hons) Sociology & Chinese, BSc(Hons) Computing & Chinese

Department of Design; www.gold.ac.uk/design

BA(Hons) Design
Postgraduate courses: MA in Design: Expanded Practice, PGCE (Secondary): Design and Technology, Graduate Diploma in Design

Department of Educational Studies; www.gold.ac.uk/educational-studies

BA(Hons) Education, Culture & Society
Postgraduate courses: MA in Artist Teachers & Contemporary Practices, MA in Children's Literature, MA in Children's Literature: Children's Illustration, MA in Creative Writing and Education, MA in Education: Culture, Language & Identity, MA in Multilingualism, Linguistics & Education, PGCE

(Primary with Modern Languages), PGCE (Primary), PGCE (Secondary) Art & Design, PGCE (Secondary) Standard Programme, PGCE (Secondary): Design and Technology, PGCE (Secondary): Drama, PGCE (Secondary): English

Department of English and Comparative Literature; www.gold.ac.uk/ecl

BA(Hons) English, BA(Hons) English & American Literature, BA(Hons) English & Comparative Literature, BA(Hons) English & Drama/Drama & English, BA(Hons) English & History, BA(Hons) English Language & Literature, BA(Hons) English with Creative Writing, BA(Hons) Media & English
Postgraduate courses: MA in Black British Writing, MA in Children's Literature, MA in Creative & Life Writing, MA in Creative Writing and Education, MA in Literary Studies, MA in Literary Studies: Pathway in American Literature & Culture, MA in Literary Studies: Pathway in Comparative Literature & Criticism

English Language Centre; www.gold.ac.uk/english-language-centre

Postgraduate courses: Graduate Diploma in Creative & Cultural Industries, Graduate Diploma in Design, Graduate Diploma in Media, Culture & Social Sciences, Graduate Diploma in Music

Department of History; www.gold.ac.uk/history

BA(Hons) English & History, BA(Hons) History, BA(Hons) History & Anthropology, BA(Hons) History & History of Ideas, BA(Hons) History & Politics, BA History & Journalism
Postgraduate courses: MA in History, MA in Queer History, MPhil & PhD in History, MRes in History

Institute for Creative and Cultural Entrepreneurship (ICCE); www.gold.ac.uk/icce

BA(Hons) Arts Management
Postgraduate courses: MA in Events and Experience Management, MA in Arts Administration & Cultural Policy, MA in Arts Administration & Cultural Policy: Music Pathway, MA in Creative & Cultural Entrepreneurship, MA in Creative & Cultural Entrepreneurship: Computing Pathway, MA in Creative & Cultural Entrepreneurship: Design Pathway, MA in Creative & Cultural Entrepreneurship: Fashion Pathway, MA in Creative & Cultural Entrepreneurship: Leadership Pathway, MA in Creative & Cultural Entrepreneurship: Media & Communications Pathway, MA in Creative & Cultural Entrepreneurship:

Music Pathway, MA in Creative & Cultural Entrepreneurship: Theatre & Performance Pathway, MA in Cultural Policy, Relations & Diplomacy, MA in Luxury Brand Management, MA in Social Entrepreneurship, MA in Tourism & Cultural Policy, MA in Translation, PGCert in Museums & Galleries Entrepreneurship, Graduate Diploma in Creative & Cultural Industries

Institute of Management Studies; www.gold.ac.uk/institute-management-studies

BA(Hons) Economics, BSc(Hons) Economics with Econometrics, BSc(Hons) Management with Economics, BSc(Hons) Management with Entrepreneurship, BSc(Hons) Management with Marketing, BSc(Hons) Marketing, BSc(Hons) Psychology with Management, BSc Maths and Economics

Postgraduate courses: MSc in Consumer Behaviour, MSc in Management of Innovation, MSc in Occupational Psychology, MSc Marketing & Technology

Department of Media and Communications; www.gold.ac.uk/media-communications

BA(Hons) Media & Communications, BA(Hons) Media & English, BA(Hons) Media & Sociology

Postgraduate courses: MA in Brands, Communication & Culture, MA in Children's Literature: Children's Illustration, MA in Creative & Cultural Entrepreneurship: Media & Communications Pathway, MA in Cultural Studies, MA in Culture Industry, MA in Digital Media: Technology & Cultural Form, MA in Film & Screen Studies, MA in Filmmaking, MA in Filmmaking (Cinematography), MA in Filmmaking (Directing Fiction), MA in Filmmaking (Editing), MA in Filmmaking (Producing), MA in Filmmaking (Screen Documentary), MA in Filmmaking (Sound Recording, Post-Production & Design), MA in Gender, Media & Culture, MA in Global Media & Transnational Communications, MA in Journalism, MA in Media & Communications, MA in Photography: The Image & Electronic Arts, MA in Political Communications, MA in Postcolonial Culture & Global Policy, MA in Promotional Media: Public Relations, Advertising & Marketing, MA in Race, Media & Social Justice, MA in Radio, MA in Script Writing, MA in Television Journalism, MA/MSc in Digital Journalism, MRes in Filmmaking, Photography & Electronic Arts, MRes in Media & Communications

Department of Music; www.gold.ac.uk/music

BMus(Hons) Music, BMus(Hons) Popular Music, BMus/BSc(Hons) Music Computing

Postgraduate courses: MA in Arts Administration & Cultural Policy: Music Pathway, MA in Creative & Cultural Entrepreneurship: Music Pathway, MA in Music, MA in Music (Contemporary Music Studies), MA in Music (Ethnomusicology), MA in Music (General), MA in Music (Historical Musicology), MA in Music (Popular Music Research), MMus in Composition, MMus in Creative Practice, MMus in Performance, MMus in Popular Music, MMus in Sonic Arts, Graduate Diploma in Music

Department of Politics and International Relations; www.gold.ac.uk/politics-and-international-relations

BA(Hons) Economics, Politics & Public Policy, BA(Hons) History & Politics, BA(Hons) International Relations, BA(Hons) International Relations & Chinese, BA(Hons) Politics, BA(Hons) Politics & International Relations, BA(Hons) Politics, Philosophy & Economics, BA(Hons) Sociology & Politics, BA Religion

Postgraduate courses: MA in Art & Politics, MA in International Relations, MA in Politics, Development and the Global South

Department of Psychology; www.gold.ac.uk/psychology

BSc(Hons) Psychology, BSc(Hons) Psychology with Clinical Psychology, BSc(Hons) Psychology with Cognitive Neuroscience, BSc(Hons) Psychology with Forensic Psychology, BSc(Hons) Psychology with Management

Postgraduate courses: MRes in Research Methods in Psychology, MSc Computational Cognitive Neuroscience, MSc in Cognitive & Clinical Neuroscience, MSc in Forensic Psychology, MSc in Foundations in Clinical Psychology & Health Services, MSc in Music, Mind & Brain, MSc in the Psychology of Social Relations, MSc Psychology of the Arts, Neuroaesthetics & Creativity

Department of Social, Therapeutic and Community Studies (STACS); www.gold.ac.uk/stacs

BA(Hons) Applied Social Science, Community Development & Youth Work, BA(Hons) Psychosocial Studies, BA(Hons) Social Work

Postgraduate courses: Graduate Certificate in Humanistic & Psychodynamic Counselling, MA in

Advanced Social Work: Practice Education (qualified Social Workers), MA in Applied Anthropology & Community & Youth Work, MA in Applied Anthropology & Community Arts, MA in Applied Anthropology & Community Development, MA in Art Psychotherapy, MA in Counselling, MA in Dance Movement Psychotherapy, MA in Practice Education (non-Social Work qualified staff working in Social Welfare roles), MA in Social Work, MA in Understanding Domestic Violence & Sexual Abuse, MSc/PGDip in Cognitive Behavioural Therapy

Department of Sociology; www.gold.ac.uk/ sociology

BA(Hons) Anthropology & Sociology, BA(Hons) Criminology, BA(Hons) Media & Sociology, BA(Hons) Politics, Philosophy & Economics, BA(Hons) Sociology, BA(Hons) Sociology & Chinese, BA(Hons) Sociology & Politics, BA(Hons) Sociology with Criminology, BA Religion

Postgraduate courses: MA in Brands, Communication & Culture, MA in Cities & Society, MA in Critical & Creative Analysis, MA in Gender, Media & Culture, MA in Human Rights, Culture & Social Justice, MA in Photography & Urban Cultures, MA in Race, Media & Social Justice, MA in Social Research, MA in Visual Sociology

Department of Theatre and Performance; www.gold.ac.uk/theatre-performance

BA(Hons) Drama & Theatre Arts, BA(Hons) Drama: Comedy and Satire, BA(Hons) Drama: Performance, Politics and Society, BA(Hons) English & Drama/ Drama & English, BA Drama: Musical Theatre

Postgraduate courses: MA in Applied Theatre: Drama in Educational, Community & Social Contexts, MA in Black British Writing, MA in Creative & Cultural Entrepreneurship: Theatre & Performance Pathway, MA in Dramaturgy and Writing for Performance, MA in Musical Theatre, MA in Performance & Culture: Interdisciplinary Perspectives, MA in Performance Making, MA in World Theatres

Department of Visual Cultures; www.gold.ac.uk/visual-cultures

BA(Hons) Curating, BA(Hons) Fine Art & History of Art, BA(Hons) History of Art

Postgraduate courses: MA in Contemporary Art Theory, MA in Research Architecture, MRes in Curatorial/Knowledge, MRes in Visual Cultures, Graduate Diploma in Contemporary Art History

UNIVERSITY OF LONDON; INSTITUTE IN PARIS
www.ulip.lon.ac.uk

BA in French Studies, BA in French Studies with Business, BA in French Studies with History, BA in French Studies with International Relations, BA in International Politics, BA in International Politics with French Studies

Postgraduate courses: LLM (Master of Laws) in Paris – QMUL, MA in International Relations (Paris) – QMUL, MA in Urban History and Culture, Sorbonne Law School–Queen Mary University of London Double LLM

UNIVERSITY OF LONDON; INSTITUTE OF EDUCATION
www.ioe.ac.uk

Undergraduate courses

Psychology with Education BA/BSc, Social Sciences BSc, Social Sciences with Quantitative Methods BSc, Working with Children: Education and Wellbeing (Top-Up) BA/BEd, Education Studies BA

Postgraduate courses

Culture, Communication and Media

Applied Linguistics MA, Art and Design in Education MA, Digital Media, Culture and Education MA, Education and Technology MA, English Education MA, Museums and Galleries in Education MA, Music Education MA, Teaching of English to Speakers of Other Languages (TESOL) MA, Teaching of English to Speakers of Other Languages (TESOL) Pre-Service MA

Curriculum, Pedagogy and Assessment

Advanced Educational Practice Grad Dip, Advanced Educational Practice MA, Citizenship, History or Religious Education (Humanities) MA, Curriculum, Pedagogy and Assessment MA, Development Education and Global Learning MA, Education MA,

Educational Assessment MA, Effective Learning and Teaching MA, Mathematics Education MA, Science Education MA, Teaching MTeach

Education Practice and Society

Comparative Education MA, Education and International Development MA, Education, Gender and International Development MA, Education, Health Promotion and International Development MA, Educational Planning, Economics and International Development MA, Higher and Professional Education MA, Higher Education Management MBA, Lifelong Learning and Leadership (Singapore) MA, Philosophy of Education MA, Policy Studies in Education MA, Professional Education and Training MA, Social Justice and Education MA, Sociology of Education MA

Learning and Leadership

Applied Educational Leadership and Management MA, Early Years Education MA, Educational Leadership (International) MBA, Leadership MA, Literacy Learning and Literacy Difficulties MA, Primary Education (Policy and Practice) MA, Reading Recovery and Literacy Leadership MA, Social Science Research Methods PG Dip

Psychology and Human Development

Child Development MSc, Developmental and Educational Psychology MSc, Education (Psychology) MA, Educational Neuroscience MA/MSc, Habilitation and Disabilities of Sight (Children and Young People) Grad Dip, International Leadership in Inclusive Education MA, National Award for Special Educational Needs Co-ordination PG Cert, Psychology Grad Cert, Psychology of Education MSc, Special and Inclusive Education MA, Specific Learning Difficulties (Dyslexia) MA, Speech, Language and Communication Needs in Schools: Advanced Practice MSc

Social Science

Social Policy and Social Research MSc, Social Research Methods MSc, Sociology of Childhood and Children's Rights MA, Systematic Reviews for Social Policy and Practice MSc

Teacher training

University-led

PGCE Early years: Initial Teacher Training (Employment/Mainstream Pathway), PGCE Primary (including EYFS/KS1 or Specialist Mathematics), PGCE Secondary (Art and Design/Biology/Business Education/Chemistry/Citizenship/Computing and ICT/Economics/English/English with Drama/Geography/History/Languages/Mathematics/Music/Physics/Physics with Mathematics/Psychology/Religious Education/Social Science), PGCE Post-Compulsory (Education)

School Direct (Salaried or Tuition Fee)

PGCE Primary, PGCE Primary Mathematics Specialist, PGCE Secondary (Art and Design/Biology/Business Education/Chemistry/Citizenship/Computing and ICT/Economics/English/English with Drama/Geography/History/Languages/Mathematics/Music/Physics/Physics with Mathematics/Psychology/Religious Education/Social Science)

UNIVERSITY OF LONDON; KING'S COLLEGE LONDON
www.kcl.ac.uk

Arts, Culture and Media

Comparative Literature with Film Studies BA, Digital Culture BA, Film Studies BA, French with Film Studies with a year abroad BA, German & Music with a year abroad BA, German with Film Studies with a year abroad BA, Liberal Arts BA, Music BMus, Spanish with Film Studies with a year abroad BA

Postgraduate courses: Advanced Musical Studies PG Cert, Arts & Cultural Management MA, Big Data in Culture & Society MA, Christianity & the Arts MA, Classical Art & Archaeology MA, Cultural & Creative Industries MA, Digital Asset & Media Management MA, Digital Culture & Society MA, Digital Curation MA, Digital Humanities MA, Film Studies MA (Film & Philosophy pathway available), Music MMus (Composition or Musicology and Ethnomusicology), Shakespeare Studies MA, Theatre & Performance Studies MA

Biomedical and Life Sciences

Anatomy, Developmental & Human Biology BSc, Biochemistry BSc, Biochemistry MSci, Biomedical Science BSc, Global Health & Social Medicine BSc, Medical Physiology BSc, Molecular Genetics BSc, Molecular Genetics MSci, Neuroscience BSc, Neuroscience MSci, Nutrition BSc, Pharmacology MSci, Pharmacology BSc, Pharmacology & Molecular Genetics BSc

Postgraduate courses: Aerospace Medicine MSc / PG Dip, Biomedical and Molecular Sciences Research MSc/ MRes, Cardiovascular Research MSc, Cellular

Therapy from Bench to Market MSc, Chemistry MPhil / PhD, Global Air Quality: Management and Science MSc, Genomic Medicine MSc/ PG Dip / PG Cert, Human and Applied Physiology MSc, Immunology MSc, Medical Engineering and Physics MSc, Medical Humanities MSc, Medical Imaging Sciences MRes, Molecular Biophysics for Medical Sciences MRes, Nutrition MSc / PG Dip, PGCE Biology, Regenerative Dentistry MSc, Space Physiology and Health MSc, Translational Cancer Medicine MRes

Chemistry

Chemistry BSc, Chemistry MSci, Chemistry with Biomedicine BSc, Chemistry with Biomedicine MSci

Computer Science

Computer Science BSc, Computer Science MSci, Computer Science with Intelligent Systems BSc, Computer Science with Management BSc, Computer Science with Robotics BSc

Postgraduate courses: Advanced Computing MSc, Advanced Computing with Management MSc, Advanced Software Engineering MSc, Advanced Software Engineering with Management MSc, Big Data in Culture & Society MA, Computational Finance MSc, Computer Systems Engineering with Management MSc, Computing & Internet Systems MSc, Computing & Security MSc, Data Science MSc, Postgraduate Certificate in Education (Computer Science) PGCE, Robotics MSc, Web Intelligence MSc

Conflict and Security

History & International Relations BA, International Relations BA, War Studies BA, War Studies & History BA, War Studies & Philosophy BA

Postgraduate courses: Air Power in the Modern World MA/PGDip, Arms Control & International Security MA / PG Dip / PG Cert, Conflict Resolution in Divided Societies MA, Conflict, Security & Development MA, Geopolitics, Territory & Security MA, History of War MA, Intelligence & International Security MA, International Conflict Studies MA, International Peace & Security MA, International Relations & Contemporary War MA/PGDip, International Relations MA, National Security Studies MA, Non-Proliferation & International Security MA, Science & Security MA, South Asia & Global Security MA, Terrorism, Security & Society MA, War in the Modern World MA/PGDip, War Studies MA

Dental Training and Science

Postgraduate courses: Advanced Minimum Intervention Dentistry MSc, Aesthetic Dentistry MSc, Conscious Sedation for Dentistry PG Dip, Dental Cone

Beam CT Radiological Interpretation PG Cert, Dental Public Health MSc, Endodontics MSc, Endodontics PG Dip, Endodontology MClinDent, Fixed & Removable Prosthodontics MClinDent, Maxillofacial & Craniofacial Technology MSc, Maxillofacial Prosthetic Rehabilitation MSc, Operative Dentistry PG Dip, Orthodontics MSc, Paediatric Dentistry MSc, Periodontology MClinDent, Prosthodontics MClinDent, Regenerative Dentistry MSc, Special Care Dentistry MSc

Dentistry

Dentistry BDS, Dentistry Entry Programme for Medical Graduates BDS, Dentistry Graduate/Professional Entry Programme BDS, Enhanced Support Dentistry Programme BDS

Education Management and Policy

Postgraduate courses: Applied Linguistics and English Language Teaching MA, Child Studies MA, Computing in Education MA, Education & Professional Studies MA, Education in Arts & Cultural Settings MA, Education Management MA, Education, Policy & Society MA, English in Education MA, International Child Studies MA, Mathematics Education MA, Modern Foreign Languages Education MA, Science Education MA

Engineering

Biomedical Engineering BEng, Biomedical Engineering MEng, Computer Science with Intelligent Systems BSc, Computer Science with Robotics BSc, Electronic & Information Engineering BEng/MEng, Electronic Engineering BEng/MEng, Electronic Engineering with Management BEng/MEng

Postgraduate courses: Computer Systems Engineering with Management MSc, Electronic Engineering with Management MSc, Engineering with Management MSc, Intelligent Systems MSc, Mobile & Personal Communications MSc, Robotics MSc, Telecommunications & Internet Technology MSc

Finance

Accounting, Accountability & Financial Management MSc, Banking & Finance MSc, Computational Finance MSc, Finance (Asset Pricing) MSc, Finance (Corporate Finance) MSc, Financial Mathematics MSc

Geography and the Environment

Geography BA/BSc

Postgraduate courses: Climate Change: Environment, Science & Policy MSc, Climate Change: History, Culture & Society MA, Disasters, Adaptation & Development MA/MSc, Environment &

Development MA/MSc, Environment, Politics & Globalisation MA/MSc, Environmental Monitoring, Modelling & Management MSc, Geography MA/MSc, Geopolitics, Territory & Security MA, Global Air Quality: Management and Science MSc, Risk Analysis MA/MSc, Sustainable Cities MA/MSc, Tourism, Environment & Development MA / MSc, Water: Science & Governance MSc

History and Classics

Ancient History BA, Classical and Modern Greek Studies BA, Classical Archaeology BA, Classical Studies and Comparative Literature BA, Classical Studies and French with a year abroad BA, Classical Studies BA, Classical Studies with English BA, Classics (Greek & Latin) BA, French & History with a year abroad BA, German & History with a year abroad BA, Greek with English BA, History and International Relations BA, History BA, War Studies and History BA

Postgraduate courses: Ancient History MA, Classical Art & Archaeology MA, Classical Studies Grad Dip, Classics MA, Contemporary British History MA, Early Modern History MA, Eighteenth-Century Studies MA, History MRes (with Ancient History, Medieval History, Early Modern History or Modern History pathways), History of War MA, Late Antique & Byzantine Studies Grad Dip, Late Antique & Byzantine Studies MA, Medieval History MA, Medieval Studies MA, Modern History MA, Politics & Contemporary History MA, Postgraduate Certificate in Education (Latin with Classics), Science, Technology & Medicine in History MA, The Classical World & Its Reception MA, World History & Cultures MA

Imaging Sciences

Biomedical Engineering BEng/MEng
Postgraduate courses: Medical Engineering & Physics MSc/PG Dip, Medical Imaging Sciences MRes, Medical Ultrasound MSc/PG Dip/PG Cert, Nuclear Medicine: Science & Practice MSc/PG Dip/PG Cert, Radiopharmaceutics and PET Radiochemistry MSc/PG Dip/PG Cert, Specialist Ultrasound Practice PG Cert, Vascular Ultrasound MSc/PG Dip/PG Cert

International Affairs and Development

Geography BA/BSc, Global Health & Social Medicine BA/BSc, International Development BA
Postgraduate courses: Brazil in Global Perspective MSc, China & Globalisation MSc, Conflict Resolution in Divided Societies MA, Conflict, Security & Development MA, Contemporary India (Research) MRes, Contemporary India MA, Disasters, Adaptation & Development MA/MSc, Emerging Economies & Inclusive Development MSc, Emerging Economies & International Development MSc, Environment & Development MA/MSc, Eurasian Political Economy & Energy MSc, European Political Economy MA, Geography MA/MSc, Geopolitics, Territory & Security MA, Global Ethics & Human Values MA, Global Health & Social Justice MSc/PG Dip/PG Cert, Global Health MSc/PG Dip/PG Cert, Global Mental Health MSc, History of War MA, Intelligence & International Security MA, International Conflict Studies MA, International Peace & Security MA, International Political Economy MA, International Relations & Contemporary War MA, International Relations MA, Latin American Development MSc, Leadership & Development MSc/PG Dip, Middle Eastern Studies MA, Political Economy of Emerging Markets MSc, Political Economy of the Middle East MA, Russia in Global Systems MSc, Russian Politics & Society MSc, Security, Leadership & Society MSc / PG Dip, South Asia & Global Security MA, Sustainable Cities MA/MSc, Tourism, Environment & Development MA/MSc, War Studies MA, Water: Science & Governance MSc

Languages and Literature

Classical Studies & Comparative Literature BA, Classical Studies & French with a year abroad BA, Classical Studies with English BA, Comparative Literature BA, Comparative Literature with Film Studies BA, English BA, English Language & Linguistics BA, English with Film Studies BA, European Studies (French/German/Spanish pathways) with a year abroad BA, French & German with a year abroad BA, French & History with a year abroad BA, French & Management with a year abroad BA, French & Philosophy with a year abroad BA, French & Spanish with a year abroad BA, French (four year) with a year abroad BA, French (three year) BA, French with English with a year abroad BA, French with Film Studies with a year abroad BA, German & History with a year abroad BA, German & Management with a year abroad BA, German & Philosophy with a year abroad BA, German & Portuguese with a year abroad BA, German & Spanish with a year abroad BA, German BA, German with English with a year abroad BA, German with Film Studies with a year abroad BA, Greek with English BA, Portuguese & French with a year abroad BA, Spanish & Latin American Studies with a year abroad BA, Spanish & Management with a year abroad BA, Spanish & Portuguese with a year abroad BA, Spanish with English with a year abroad BA, Spanish with Film Studies with a year abroad BA

Postgraduate courses: Ancient History MA, Classical Art & Archaeology MA, Classical Studies Grad Dip, Classics MA, Comparative Literature MA, Contemporary Literature, Culture & Theory MA, Critical Methodologies MA, Early Modern English Literature: Text & Transmission MA, Eighteenth Century Studies MA, English 1850 & Present MA, French Literature & Culture MA, Language & Cultural Diversity MA, Late Antique & Byzantine Studies Grad Dip, Late Antique & Byzantine Studies MA, Medieval Studies MA, PGCE (English), PGCE (Latin with Classics), PGCE (Modern Foreign Languages), Shakespeare Studies MA, Spanish, Portuguese & Latin American Studies MA, Teaching English to Speakers of Other Languages (TESOL) MA, The Classical World & Its Reception MA, Theatre & Performance Studies MA

Law

Law LLB, English Law & German Law LLB and MLLP or Certificate in Rechtswissenschaften (with Humboldt University of Berlin), English Law & French Law LLB and Maitrise en droit (with Universit Paris 2, Panthon-Assas), Politics, Philosophy & Law LLB

Postgraduate courses: Competition Law LLM, European Law LLM, Intellectual Property & Information Law LLM, International Business Law LLM, International Corporate & Commercial Law LLM, International Dispute Resolution LLM, International Financial Law LLM, International Tax LLM, Master of Laws LLM, Transnational Law LLM

Management

Business Management BSc, International Management BSc

Postgraduate courses: Accounting, Accountability & Financial Management MSc, International Marketing MSc, Human Resource Management & Organisational Analysis MSc, Organisational Psychiatry & Psychology MSc, International Management MSc, Public Policy & Management MSc

Mathematics

Mathematics & Philosophy BA, Mathematics with Management & Finance BSc, Mathematics BSc/MSci, Mathematics with Statistics BSc

Postgraduate courses: Complex Systems Modelling – From Biomedical and Natural to Economic and Social Sciences MSc, Financial Mathematics MSc, Mathematics Grad Dip, Mathematics MSc, Non-

Equilibrium Systems: Theoretical Modelling, Simulation and Data-Driven Analysis MSc, Postgraduate Certificate in Education (Mathematics), Postgraduate Certificate in Education (Physics with Mathematics), Theoretical Physics MSc

Medicine

Extended Medical Degree Programme MBBS, Medicine Maxfax Entry Programme MBBS, Medicine Graduate/Professional Entry Programme MBBS, Medicine MBBS

Nursing and Midwifery

Clinical Practice BSc, Midwifery with Registration as a Midwife BSc, Nursing Studies (for qualified healthcare professionals) BSc, Nursing with Registration as a Children's Nurse BSc, Nursing with Registration as a Mental Health Nurse BSc, Nursing with Registration as an Adult Nurse BSc, Specialist Community Public Health Nursing (Health Visiting/School Nursing) BSc

Postgraduate courses: Advanced Practice (District Nursing) MSc/PG Dip/PG Cert, Advanced Practice (Leadership) MSc/PG Dip/PG Cert, Advanced Practice (Midwifery) MSc/PG Dip/PG Cert, Advanced Practice (Specialist Community Public Health Nursing/ Health Visiting/School Nursing) PG Dip, Advanced Practice MSc/PG Dip/PG Cert, Clinical Research MRes, Implementation and Improvement Science MSc, Midwifery Practice with Registration as a Midwife PG Dip, Nursing with registration (graduate entry) PG Dip

Pharmacy, pharmacology and forensic science

Pharmacology & Molecular Genetics BSc, Pharmacology BSc, Pharmacology iBSc, Pharmacology MSci, Pharmacy MPharm

Biopharmaceuticals MSc, Clinical Pharmacology MSc/PG Dip/PG Cert, Drug Development Science MSc/PG Dip/PG Cert, Drug Discovery Skills MSc, Forensic Science MSc/MRes/PG Dip/PG Cert, Independent Prescribing PG Cert, Pharmaceutical Analysis & Quality Control MSc, Pharmaceutical Technology MSc, Pharmacology MSc/MRes, Pharmacy Practice Prescribing MSc/PG Dip/PG Cert, Postgraduate courses: Analytical Toxicology MSc, Radiopharmaceutics & PET Radiochemistry MSc, Translational Medicine MRes

Philosophy and religion

Philosophy & Spanish with a year abroad BA, Philosophy BA, Philosophy, Politics & Economics

(PPE) BA, Religion, Philosophy & Ethics BA, Religion, Politics & Society BA, Theology BA
Postgraduate courses: Biblical Studies (with Language & Literature or Theology pathways) MA, Christianity & the Arts MA, History of Philosophy MA, Jewish Studies MA, Philosophy MA, Philosophy of Medicine and Psychiatry MA, Philosophy of Psychology MA, Systematic Theology MA, Theology & Religious Studies Grad Dip

Physics

Physics BSc/MSci, Physics & Philosophy BSc/MSci, Physics with Medical Applications BSc, Physics with Theoretical Physics BSc/MSci
Postgraduate courses: Non-Equilibrium Systems: Theoretical Modelling, Simulation and Data-Driven Analysis MSc, Physics MSc, Physics Grad Dip, Theoretical Physics MSc

Policy and society

Global Health & Social Medicine BA/BSc
Postgraduate courses: Ageing & Society MA/MSc/PG Dip/PG Cert, Bioethics & Society MA/PG Dip/PG Cert, Brazil in Global Perspective MSc, Child & Adolescent Mental Health MSc, Child Studies MA, China & Globalisation MSc, Climate Change: Environment, Science & Policy MSc, Climate Change: History, Culture, Society MA, Conflict Resolution in Divided Societies MA, Conflict, Security & Development MA, Contemporary India MA, Emerging Economies & Inclusive Development MSc, Emerging Economies & International Development MSc, Environment, Politics & Globalisation MA/MSc, Gerontology MSc/PG Dip/PG Cert, Global Mental Health MSc, International Child Studies MA, Medical Humanities MSc, Medicine, Health and Public Policy MSc/PG Dip/PG Cert, Mental Health, Ethics and Law MSc, Public Policy & Ageing MA/PG Dip/ PG Cert, Public Policy & Management MSc, Public Policy MA, Research Methods for Social Science & Health MSc/ PG Dip/PG Cert

Politics and economics

Economics & Management BA, Economics BSc, European Politics BA, European Studies with a year abroad (French, German or Spanish pathway) BA, Political Economy BA/BSc, Politics BA/BSc, Religion, Politics and Society BA
Postgraduate courses: Double Master's in Asian and European Affairs MA, Emerging Economies & Inclusive Development MSc, Emerging Economies & International Development MSc, Eurasian Political Economy & Energy MSc, European Political

Economy MA, European Studies MA, International Political Economy MA, Political Economy MA, Political Economy of Emerging Markets MSc, Political Economy of the Middle East MA, Politics & Contemporary History MA, Public Policy MA, Russian Politics & Society MSc

Psychiatry, psychology and neuroscience

Neuroscience BSc/iBSc/MSci, Psychology BSc/iBSc
Postgraduate courses: Addiction Studies MSc/PG Cert, Affective Disorders MSc, Applied Neuroscience MSc, Child & Adolescent Mental Health MSc, Clinical Neurodevelopmental Sciences MSc, Clinical Neuropsychiatry MSc, Clinical Neuroscience MSc, Cognitive Behavioural Therapies PG Dip, Early Intervention in Psychosis MSc, Family Therapy MSc/Grad Cert, Forensic Mental Health MSc/PG Dip, Genes, Environment & Development in Psychology & Psychiatry MSc, Global Mental Health MSc, Health Psychology MSc, International Programme in Addiction Studies MSc Distance Learning, Medical Humanities MSc, Mental Health Studies MSc, Mental Health, Ethics & Law MSc, Neuroimaging MSc, Neuroscience MSc, Organisational Psychiatry & Psychology MSc, Philosophy of Medicine & Psychiatry MA, Philosophy of Psychology MA, Psychiatric Research MSc/PG Cert, Psychology & Neuroscience of Mental Health MSc/PG Dip/PG Cert Distance Learning, War & Psychiatry MSc

Public health

Postgraduate courses: Dental Public Health MSc, Global Air Quality: Management & Science MSc, Global Health and Social Justice MSc/PG Dip/PG Cert, Palliative Care MSc/PG Dip/PG Cert, Public Health MPH (with Environmental Health, Primary Care or Allied Health pathways)

Specialist training for medical professionals

Postgraduate courses: Advanced (Neuromusculoskeletal) Physiotherapy MSc, Advanced Paediatrics MSc, Aerospace Medicine MSc/PG Dip, Cardiovascular Research MSc, Clinical Dermatology MSc, Dental Public Health MSc, Dentistry BDS (Entry programme for Medical Graduates), Dietetics MSc/PG Dip, Genomic Medicine MSc/PG Dip/PG Cert, Global Health MSc/PG Dip/PG Cert, Maxillofacial & Craniofacial Technology MSc, Maxillofacial Prosthetic Rehabilitation MSc, Medical Immunology MSc/PG Dip/PG Cert, Medical Ultrasound MSc/PG Dip/PG Cert, Nuclear Medicine: Science & Practice MSc/PG Dip/PG Cert, Nutrition MSc/PG Dip, Orofacial Pain MSc, Palliative Care MSc/PG Dip/PG Cert,

Physiotherapy (pre-registration) MSc, Radiopharmaceutics & PET Radiochemistry MSc, Rheumatology MSc/PG Dip, Specialist Ultrasound Practice PG Cert, Translational Cancer Medicine MRes, Vascular Ultrasound MSc/PG Dip/PG Cert

Teaching

Postgraduate courses: Biology PGCE, Chemistry PGCE, Computer Science PGCE, English PGCE, Latin with Classics PGCE, Mathematics PGCE,

Modern Foreign Languages PGCE, Physics PGCE, Physics with Mathematics PGCE, Postgraduate Certificate in Education (PGCE), Religious Education PGCE, Science Education MA, Teaching English to Speakers of Other Languages (TESOL) MA

Therapeutic health

Nutrition & Dietetics BSc, Nutrition BSc, Physiology iBSc, Physiotherapy BSc

UNIVERSITY OF LONDON; LONDON SCHOOL OF ECONOMICS & POLITICAL SCIENCE
www.lse.ac.uk

Department of Accounting; www.lse.ac.uk/accounting

BSc/Dip Accounting and Finance

Postgraduate courses: MSc Accounting, Organisations and Institutions, MSc Accounting and Finance, MSc Law and Accounting

Department of Anthropology; www.lse.ac.uk/anthropology

BA/BSc Social Anthropology, BA Anthropology and Law

Postgraduate courses: MSc Social Anthropology, MSc Social Anthropology (Learning and Cognition), MSc Social Anthropology (Religion in the Contemporary World), MSc Anthropology and Development, MSc Anthropology and Development Management, MSc China in Comparative Perspective

Department of Economics; www.lse.ac.uk/economics

BSc Economics, BSc Econometrics and Mathematical Economics, BSc Economics with Economic History

Postgraduate courses: MSc Economics, MSc Econometrics and Mathematical Economics, MSc Economics and Management, MSc Economics and Philosophy, MSc Finance and Economics

Department of Economic History; www.lse.ac.uk/economicHistory

BSc Economic History, BSc Economic History with Economics

Postgraduate courses: MSc Economic History, MSc Economic History (Research), Erasmus Mundus MA Global Studies, MSc Political Economy of Late Development, MSc Quantitative Economic History

Department of Finance; www.lse.ac.uk/finance

BSc Finance

Postgraduate courses: MSc Finance and Economics, MSc Risk and Finance, MSc Finance, MSc Finance and Private Equity

Department of Gender Studies; www.lse.ac.uk/Gender

Postgraduate courses: MSc Gender, MSc Gender (Research), MSc Gender (Sexuality), MSc Gender, Development and Globalisation, MSc Gender, Media and Culture, MSc Gender, Policy and Inequalities, MSc Women, Peace and Security

Department of Geography and Environment; www.lse.ac.uk/geographyAndEnvironment

BA Geography, BSc Geography with Economics, BSc Environment and Development, BSc Environmental Policy with Economics

Postgraduate courses: MSc Environment and Development, MSc Environmental Economics and Climate Change, MSc Environmental Policy and Regulation, MSc Human Geography and Urban Studies (Research), MSc Local Economic Development, MSc Real Estate Economics and Finance, MSc Regional and Urban Planning Studies, MSc Urbanisation and Development, Double Master's Degree in Urban Policy

Department of Government; www.lse.ac.uk/government

BSc Government, BSc Government and Economics, BSc Government and History, BSc Politics and International Relations, BSc Politics and Philosophy, BSc Philosophy, Politics and Economics

Postgraduate courses: MSc Comparative Politics, MSc Conflict Studies, MSc Global Politics, MSc Public Policy and Administration, MSc Political Science and Political Economy, MSc Political Theory, MSc Regulation

Department of Health Policy; www.lse.ac.uk/health-policy

Postgraduate courses: MSc Global Health, MSc Health Policy, Planning, and Financing (HPPF), MSc International Health Policy (IHP-HP), MSc International Health Policy (Health Economics) (IHP-HE), eMSc Health Economics, Policy, and Management

Department of International Development; www.lse.ac.uk/internationalDevelopment

Postgraduate courses: MSc African Development, MSc Development Management, MSc Development Studies, MSc International Development and Humanitarian Emergencies, MSc Health and International Development

Department of International History; www.lse.ac.uk/internationalHistory

BA History

Postgraduate courses: MSc Empires, Colonialism and Globalisation, MSc History of International Relations, MSc Theory and History of International Relations, LSE-Columbia University Double MSc in International and World History, LSE-Peking University Double MSc in International Affairs

Department of International Relations; www.lse.ac.uk/internationalRelations

BSc International Relations, BSc International Relations and History

Postgraduate courses: MSc in International Relations, MSc in International Political Economy, Sciences Po-LSE Double Degree in Affaires Internationales and IR/IPE, MSc International Relations Theory

Department of Law; www.lse.ac.uk/collections/law

LLB Bachelor of Laws

Postgraduate courses: LLM Master of Laws, Executive LLM, MSc Law and Accounting

Department of Management; www.lse.ac.uk/management

Postgraduate courses: Global Master's in Management, Master's in Management, MSc Economics and Management, MSc Human Resources and Organisations, MSc Management and Strategy, MSc Management of Information Systems and Digital Innovation, MSc Marketing, MSc Social Innovation and Entrepreneurship

Department of Mathematics; www.lse.ac.uk/maths

BSc Financial Mathematics and Statistics, BSc Mathematics and/with Economics

Postgraduate courses: MSc Operations Research & Analytics, MSc Applicable Mathematics, MSc Financial Mathematics

Department of Media and Communications; www.lse.ac.uk/media@lse

Postgraduate courses: MSc Global Media and Communications (with Year 2 in either University of Southern California, Fudan University or University of Cape Town), MSc Media and Communications, MSc Media and Communications (Research track), MSc Media and Communications (Data and Society), MSc Media and Communications (Governance), MSc Media, Communication and Development, MSc Politics and Communication, MSc in Strategic Communications

Department of Methodology; www.lse.ac.uk/methodology

Postgraduate course: MSc in Applied Social Data Science

Department of Philosophy, Logic and Scientific Method; www.lse.ac.uk/philosophy

BSc Philosophy & Economics, BSc Philosophy, Logic & Scientific Method, BSc Philosophy, Politics & Economics, BSc Politics & Philosophy

Postgraduate courses: MSc Economics & Philosophy, MSc Philosophy & Public Policy, MSc Philosophy of Science, MSc Philosophy of the Social Sciences

Department of Psychological and Behavioural Science; www.lse.ac.uk/DPBS

Postgraduate courses: MSc in Organisational and Social Psychology, MSc in the Psychology of Economic Life, MSc in Social and Cultural Psychology, MSc in Social and Public Communication, Executive MSc in Behavioural Science

Department of Social Policy; www.lse.ac.uk/socialPolicy

BSc Social Policy, BSc Social Policy and Economics, BSc Social Policy and Sociology, BSc Social Policy with Government

Postgraduate courses: Masters of Public Administration (MPA), MSc Criminal Justice Policy, MSc Global

Population Health, MSc Social Policy (European and Comparative), MSc Social Policy (Research), MSc Social Policy (Social Policy and Planning), MSc Social Policy and Development, MSc Social Policy and Development (Non-Governmental Organisations)

Department of Sociology; www.lse.ac.uk/sociology

BSc Sociology

Postgraduate courses: MSc Sociology, MSc Sociology (Research), MSc Sociology (Contemporary Social Thought), MSc Political Sociology, MSc City Design

and Social Science, MSc Culture and Society, MSc Economy, Risk and Society, MSc Human Rights, MSc Inequalities and Social Science, MSc International Migration and Public Policy

Department of Statistics; www.lse.ac.uk/statistics

BSc Actuarial Science, BSc Business Mathematics and Statistics, BSc Financial Mathematics and Statistics

Postgraduate courses: MSc Statistics, MSc Quantitative Methods for Risk Management, MSc Data Science

UNIVERSITY OF LONDON; LONDON SCHOOL OF JEWISH STUDIES
www.lsjs.ac.uk

BA(Hons) Jewish Education

Postgraduate courses: MA Jewish Education, MA Jewish Studies

UNIVERSITY OF LONDON; QUEEN MARY
www.qmul.ac.uk

Faculty of Humanities and Social Sciences; www.qmul.ac.uk/about/hss

School of Business and Management; www.busman.qmul.ac.uk

BSc Business Management, BSc Marketing and Management, BSc Accounting and Management

Postgraduate courses: Accounting and Management MSc, Business Analytics MSc, Business and Management MRes, Development and International Business MSc, Innovation and Enterprise MRes, International Business and Politics MRes/MSc, International Business MRes/MSc, International Financial Management MRes/MSc, International Human Resource Management MRes, International Human Resource Management MSc Management and Organisational Innovation MSc Management MSc Marketing MSc, Public Administration MPA, Public Services MRes, Work and Organisation MRes

School of Economics and Finance; www.econ.qmul.ac.uk

Economics BSc(Hons), Economics and Finance BSc(Hons), Economics and International Finance BSc(Hons), Economics, Finance and Management BSc(Hons), Economics and Politics BSc(Hons), Economics, Statistics and Mathematics BSc(Hons)

Postgraduate courses: Accounting and Finance MSc, Banking and Finance MSc, Behavioural Finance MSc, Business Finance MSc, Economics MSc, Finance MSc, Finance and Econometrics MSc, Investment Banking MSc, Investment and Finance MSc, Law and Economics LLM, Law and Finance MSc, Mathematical Finance MSc, Wealth Management MSc

School of English and Drama; www.sed.qmul.ac.uk

BA(Hons) Drama, BA(Hons) English, BA(Hons) English and Drama, BA(Hons) English with Creative Writing, BA(Hons) English and History, BA(Hons) English and Film Studies, BA(Hons) English and French, BA(Hons) English and German, BA(Hons) English and Hispanic Studies, BA(Hons) English and Russian, BA(Hons) English Literature and Linguistics

Postgraduate courses: MA Theatre and Performance, MSc Creative Arts and Mental Health, MA in English Studies, MA in Poetry

School of Languages, Linguistics and Film; www.sllf.qmul.ac.uk

Comparative Literature and Film BA, Comparative Literature and Linguistics BA, Comparative Literature BA, English Language and Linguistics BA, English Literature and Linguistics BA, Film Studies and Drama BA, Film Studies and French BA, Film

Studies and German BA, Film Studies and Hispanic Studies BA, Film Studies and History BA, Film Studies and Russian BA, Film Studies BA, French and Comparative Literature BA, French and German BA, French and Hispanic Studies BA, French and Linguistics BA, French and Portuguese BA, French and Russian BA, French BA, French with Business Management BA, German and Comparative Literature BA, German and Hispanic Studies BA, German and Linguistics BA, German and Russian BA, German BA, German with Business Management BA, Hispanic Studies and Catalan BA, Hispanic Studies and Comparative Literature BA, Hispanic Studies and Linguistics BA, Hispanic Studies and Portuguese BA, Hispanic Studies and Russian BA, Hispanic Studies BA, Hispanic Studies with Business Management BA, Russian and Comparative Literature BA, Russian and Linguistics BA, Russian BA, Russian with Business Management BA

Postgraduate courses: Anglo-German Cultural Relations MA, Applied Linguistics for English Language Teaching MA/PGCert/PGDip, Comparative Literature MA, Documentary Practice MA, Film Studies MA, Linguistics MA, MRes in Linguistics (1 year full time)

School of Geography; www.geog.qmul.ac.uk

Geography BA/BSc, Human Geography BA, Geography with Business Management BSc, Environmental Science BSc, Environmental Science with Business Management BSc

Postgraduate courses: Cities and Cultures MA/MRes, Development and Global Health MA, Development and International Business MSc, Environmental Science by Research MSc, Geography MA/MSc/MRes, Global Development Futures MA/MRes, Global Health Geographies MA/MRes, Integrated Management of Freshwater Environments MSc/PGCert/PGDip, London Studies MA/PGCert

School of History; www.history.qmul.ac.uk

BA History, BA Medieval History, BA Modern and Contemporary History, BA History and Film Studies, BA History and Comparative Literature

Postgraduate courses: MA History, MA History of Political Thought and Intellectual History, MA Global and Imperial History, MA Modern and British Contemporary History, MA Urban History and Culture

School of Law; www.law.qmul.ac.uk

LLB Law, LLB Law Senior Status, LLB Global Law, LLB English and European Law, LLB Law with History, LLB Law and Politics

Postgraduate courses: LLM in Art, Business and Law, LLM in Banking and Finance Law, LLM in Commercial and Corporate Law, LLM in Comparative and International Dispute Resolution, LLM in Competition Law, LLM in Computer and Communications Law, LLM in Criminal Justice, LLM in Energy and Natural Resources Law, LLM in Environmental Law, LLM in European Law, LLM in Human Rights Law, LLM in Immigration Law, LLM in Insurance Law, LLM in Intellectual Property Law, LLM in International Business Law, LLM in International Economic Law, LLM in International Shipping Law, LLM in Legal Theory, LLM in Media Law, LLM in Medical Law, LLM in Public International Law, LLM in Tax Law, Master of Laws

School of Politics and International Relations; www.politics.qmul.ac.uk

BA(Hons) International Relations, BA(Hons) Politics and International Relations, BA(Hons) Politics with Business Management, BA(Hons) Politics

Postgraduate courses: MSc European Public Policy, MSc International Business and Politics, MSc International Public Policy, MA/MRes/PGCert/PGDip International Relations, MRes/MSc Public Policy

Faculty of Medicine and Dentistry; www.smd.qmul.ac.uk

Barts and the London School of Medicine and Dentistry; www.smd.qmul.ac.uk

Undergraduate degrees

Medicine MBBS, Dentistry BDS, Global Health BSc

Medicine postgraduate degrees

Aesthetic Medicine MSc/PGCert/PGDip, Biomedical Science (Medical Microbiology) MSc, Burn Care MSc, Burn Care PGCert, Cancer and Clinical Oncology MSc/PGDip, Cancer and Molecular and Cellular Biology MSc/PGDip, Cancer and Molecular Pathology and Genomics MSc/PGDip, Cancer and Therapeutics MSc/PGDip, Clinical Dermatology PgDip, Clinical Drug Development MSc/PGDip, Clinical Endocrinology MSc/PgDip, Clinical Microbiology MSc/PGDip, Creative Arts and Mental Health MSc/PGDip, Critical Care MSc, Cultural and Global Perspectives in Mental Health Care MSc/PGDip, Education for Clinical Contexts MA, Endocrinology and Diabetes MSc/PgDip, Forensic Medical Sciences MSc, Gastroenterology MSc/PGDip, Genomic

Medicine MSc, Global Health, Law and Governance MSc, Global Public Health and Policy MSc, Health Systems and Global Policy MSc, Healthcare Research Methods MSc, Healthcare Research Methods PGDip, Inflammation: Cellular and Vascular Aspects MRes, International Primary Healthcare MSc, Mental Health and Law MSc/PGDip, Mental Health: Psychological Therapies MSc/PGDip, Migration, Culture and Global Health MSc, Orthopaedic Trauma Science MSc, Physician Associate Studies MSc, Podiatric Sports Medicine PGCert, Professional Doctorate Intercultural Psychoanalytical Psychotherapy, Reconstructive Microsurgery MSc, Regenerative Medicine MSc, Sports and Exercise Medicine MSc/PGDip (Medics), Sports and Exercise Medicine MSc/PGDip (Physio), Surgical Skills and Sciences MSc, Trauma Sciences (Military and Humanitarian) MScg, Trauma Sciences MSc

Dentistry postgraduate degrees

Advanced Oral Biology MSc, Craniofacial Trauma Reconstruction MSc, Dental Materials MSc, Dental Public Health MSc, Dental Science for Clinical Practice MSc, Dental Technology MSc, Endodontic Practice MSc, Experimental Oral Pathology (Oral Sciences) MSc, Oral Biology MSc, Oral Medicine MClinDent, Oral Surgery MClinDent, Orthodontics DClinDent, Paediatric Dentistry DClinDent, Periodontology DClinDent, Prosthodontics DClinDent

Faculty of Science and Engineering; www.qmul.ac.uk/about/se

School of Biological and Chemical Sciences; www.sbcs.qmul.ac.uk

BSc(Hons) Biochemistry with a Year in Industry/Research, BSc/MSci(Hons) Biochemistry, BSc(Hons) Biology, BSc(Hons) Biomedical Sciences, BSc(Hons) Chemistry with a Year in Industry/Research, BSc/MSci(Hons) Chemistry, BSc(Hons) Genetics, BSc(Hons) Medical Genetics, BSc(Hons) Neuroscience, BSc/MSci(Hons) Pharmaceutical Chemistry, BSc(Hons) Pharmacology and Innovative Therapeutics, BSc(Hons) Psychology, BSc(Hons) Zoology Postgraduate courses: MSc Aquatic Ecology by Research, MSc Bioinformatics, MSc Chemical Research, MSc Ecological and Evolutionary Genomics, MSc/PGCert Ecology and Evolutionary Biology, MSc/PGCert Freshwater and Marine Ecology, MSc Plant and Fungal Taxonomy Diversity and Conservation

School of Electronic Engineering and Computer Science; www.eecs.qmul.ac.uk

BEng Electrical and Electronic Engineering, BEng Electronic Engineering, BSc (Eng) Creative Computing, BSc (Eng) IT Management for Business (ITMB), BSc Computer Science, BSc Computer Science with Accounting, BSc Computer Science with Business Management, BSc Computer Science with Mathematics, BSc Computer Science with Multimedia, BSc Software Engineering for Business, MEng/BEng Computer Systems Engineering, MEng/BEng Electronic Engineering and Telecommunications

Postgraduate courses in the following subjects: Big Data Science, Computer Science, Computer Science by Research, Computer Vision, Computing and Information Systems, Electronic and Electrical Engineering, Electronic Engineering by Research, Financial Computing, Media and Arts Technology by Research, Network Science, Software Engineering, Telecommunication and Wireless Systems, Telecommunication and Wireless Systems Management

School of Engineering and Materials Science; www.sems.qmul.ac.uk

MEng/BEng Aerospace Engineering, MEng/BEng Biomaterials for Biomedical Sciences, BSc/MSci Biomedical Engineering, MEng/BEng Chemical Engineering, MEng/BEng Dental Materials, MEng/BEng Design, Innovation and Creative Engineering, MEng/BEng Materials and Design, MEng/BEng Materials Science and Engineering, MEng/BEng Mechanical Engineering, MEng/BEng Robotics Engineering, MEng/BEng Sustainable Energy Engineering

Postgraduate courses: MSc Advanced Mechanical Engineering, MSc Aerospace Engineering, MSc Biomaterials, MSc Biomedical Engineering, MSc Biomedical Engineering (conversion programme), MSc Biomedical Engineering with Biomaterials and Tissue Engineering, MSc Biomedical Engineering with Imaging and Instrumentation, MSc Computer Aided Engineering, MSc Dental Materials, MSc/MRes Materials Research, MSc Mechanical Engineering (conversion programme), MSc Polymer Science and Nanotechnology, MSc Regenerative Medicine, MSc Sustainable Energy Engineering (conversion programme), MSc Sustainable Energy Systems

School of Mathematical Sciences; www.maths.qmul.ac.uk

BSc/MSci Mathematics, BSc Pure Mathematics, BSc/MSci Mathematics and Statistics, BSc Mathematics, Statistics and Financial Economics, BSc Mathematics with Business Management, BSc Mathematics,

Business Management and Finance, BSc Mathematics with Management, BSc Mathematics with Actuarial Science, BSc Mathematics with Finance and Accounting, MSci Financial Mathematics
Postgraduate courses: MSc Mathematics, MSc Mathematical Finance, MSc Financial Computing, MSc Network Science

School of Physics and Astronomy; www.ph.qmul.ac.uk
BSc/MSci Physics, BSc/MSci Astrophysics, BSc/MSci Physics with Astrophysics, BSc/MSci Theoretical Physics, BSc/MSci Physics with Particle Physics, BSc Physics with Management
Postgraduate courses: MSc Condensed Matter Physics, MSc Particle Physics, MSc Theoretical Physics, MSc (EuroMasters), PGCert Astronomy and Astrophysics

UNIVERSITY OF LONDON; ROYAL HOLLOWAY
www.rhul.ac.uk

School of Biological Sciences; www.royalholloway.ac.uk/ biologicalsciences
Biochemistry BSc, Biology BSc, Biomedical Sciences BSc, Ecology and Conservation BSc, Medical Biochemistry BSc, Molecular Biology BSc, Zoology BSc

Department of Classics; www.royalholloway.ac.uk/classics
Ancient History BA, Ancient History and Philosophy BA, Classical Archaeology and Ancient History BA, Classical Studies BA, Classical Studies and Comparative Literature and Culture BA, Classical Studies and Drama BA, Classical Studies and Philosophy BA, Classical Studies with Philosophy BA, Classics BA, Classics and Philosophy BA, Classics with Philosophy BA, Greek BA, Latin BA
Postgraduate courses: Ancient History MA, Classical Art and Archaeology MA, Classical Reception by Research MRes, Classics MA

Department of Computer Science; www.royalholloway.ac.uk/ computerscience
Computer Science BSc/MSci, Computer Science (Artificial Intelligence) BSc/MSci, Computer Science (Distributed & Networked Systems) BSc/MSci, Computer Science (Information Security) BSc/MSci, Computer Science (Software Engineering) BSc/MSci, Computer Science and Mathematics BSc, Computer Science with a year in industry BSc, Digital Media Culture & Technology BA/BSc
Postgraduate courses: Computational Finance MSc, Data Science and Analytics MSc, Distributed and Networked Systems MSc, Information Security MSc, Machine Learning MSc, The Internet of Things MSc

Department of Drama, Theatre and Dance; www.royalholloway.ac.uk/ dramaandtheatre
Dance BA, Drama and Creative Writing BA, Drama and Dance BA, Drama and Music BA, Drama and Philosophy BA, Drama and Theatre Studies BA, Drama with Film BA, Drama with Philosophy BA
Postgraduate courses: Contemporary Performance Practices MA, Playwriting MA, Theatre Directing MA

Department of Earth Sciences; www.royalholloway.ac.uk/earthsciences
Digital Geosciences BSc, Environmental Geology BSc/MSci, Geology BSc, Geoscience MSci, Petroleum Geology BSc
Postgraduate courses: Environmental Diagnosis and Management MSc, Petroleum Geoscience MSc, Petroleum Geoscience (By Distance Learning) MSc

Department of Economics; www.royalholloway.ac.uk/economics
Economics BSc (Econ), Economics and Management BSc, Economics and Mathematics BSc, Economics with French BSc (Econ), Economics with German BSc (Econ), Economics with Italian BSc (Econ), Economics with Music BSc (Econ), Economics with Political Studies BSc (Econ), Economics with Spanish BSc (Econ), Economics, Politics and International Relations BSc, Finance and Mathematics BSc, Financial and Business Economics BSc (Econ), Politics, Philosophy and Economics BA
Postgraduate courses: Computational Finance MSc, Economics MSc, Finance MSc

Department of Electronic Engineering; www.royalholloway.ac.uk/ electronicengineering

Electronic Engineering BEng/MEng
Postgraduate course: Engineering Management MSc

Department of English; www.royalholloway.ac.uk/english

American Literature and Creative Writing BA, Comparative Literature and Culture and English BA, English BA, English and American Literature BA, English and Classical Studies BA, English and Creative Writing BA, English and Drama BA, English and Film Studies BA, English and History BA, English and Latin BA, English and Philosophy BA, English with Philosophy BA
Postgraduate courses: Creative Writing MA, English Literature MA, Medieval Studies MA, Shakespeare MA, Victorian Literature, Art and Culture MA

Department of Geography; www.royalholloway.ac.uk/geography

Geography BA/BSc, Human Geography BA, Physical Geography BSc
Postgraduate courses: Cultural Geography (Research) MA by Research, Geopolitics and Security MSc, Practising Sustainable Development MSc, Quaternary Science MSc, Sustainability and Management MSc

Department of History; www.royalholloway.ac.uk/history

Ancient and Medieval History BA, History BA, History and Music BA, History and Philosophy BA, History, Politics and International Relations BA, Modern and Contemporary History BA
Postgraduate courses: Crusader Studies MA, History MA, Holocaust Studies MA, Late Antique and Byzantine Studies MA, Medieval Studies MA, Public History MA

School of Law; www.royalholloway.ac.uk/ criminologyandsociology

Criminology and Psychology BSc, Criminology and Sociology BSc, Law LLB, Law (Senior Status) LLB, Law with Criminology LLB, Law with Sociology LLB
Postgraduate courses: Consumption, Culture and Marketing MA, Forensic Psychology MSc

School of Management; www.royalholloway.ac.uk/management

Accounting and Finance BSc, Business and Management BSc, Management with Accounting BSc, Management with Digital Innovation BSc, Management with Entrepreneurship BSc, Management with Human Resources BSc, Management with International Business BSc, Management with Marketing BSc, Management with Mathematics BSc, Management with Sustainability BSc
Postgraduate courses: Business Information Systems MSc, Consumption, Culture and Marketing MA, Entrepreneurship MSc, International Accounting MSc, International Human Resource Management MSc, International Management MBA/MSc, International Management (Marketing) MSc, Managing Digital Innovation MSc, Marketing MA, MBA (Year in Business) MBA

Department of Mathematics; www.royalholloway.ac.uk/mathematics

Mathematical Studies BSc, Mathematics BSc/MSci, Mathematics and Management BSc, Mathematics and Music BA, Mathematics and Physics BSc, Mathematics and Physics MSci, Mathematics with French BSc, Mathematics with German BSc, Mathematics with Italian BSc, Mathematics with Management BSc, Mathematics with Philosophy BSc, Mathematics with Spanish BSc, Mathematics with Statistics BSc
Postgraduate courses: Mathematics for Applications MSc, Mathematics of Cryptography and Communications MSc

Department of Media Arts; www.royalholloway.ac.uk/mediaarts

Digital Media Culture & Technology BA/BSc, Drama with Film BA, Film Studies BA, Film Studies with Philosophy BA, Film, Television and Digital Production BA
Postgraduate courses: Documentary by Practice MA, International Television Industries MA, Media Management MA, Producing Film and Television MA, Screenwriting for Television and Film (in Retreat) MA

School of Modern Languages, Literatures and Cultures; www.royalholloway.ac.uk/ mllc

Comparative Literature and Culture BA, Comparative Literature and Culture and Drama BA, Comparative Literature and Culture and English BA, Comparative Literature and Culture and Philosophy BA, Comparative Literature and Culture with History of Art and Visual Culture BA, Comparative Literature and Culture with International Film BA, Comparative Literature and Culture with Philosophy BA, European and International Studies (French) BA,

European and International Studies (German) BA, European and International Studies (Italian) BA, European and International Studies (Spanish) BA, History of Art and Visual Culture & Comparative Literature and Culture BA, Modern Languages BA, Modern Languages and Classical Studies BA, Modern Languages and Comparative Literature and Culture BA, Modern Languages and Drama BA, Modern Languages and English BA, Modern Languages and Greek BA, Modern Languages and History BA, Modern Languages and History of Art and Visual Culture BA, Modern Languages and Latin BA, Modern Languages and Management BA, Modern Languages and Music BA, Modern Languages and Philosophy BA, Modern Languages and Translation Studies BA, Modern Languages with History of Art and Visual Culture BA, Modern Languages with International Film BA, Modern Languages with International Relations BA, Modern Languages with Mathematics BA, Modern Languages with Music BA, Modern Languages with Philosophy BA, Modern Languages with Translation Studies BA, Translation Studies BA, Translation Studies and Comparative Literature and Culture BA, Translation Studies and History of Art and Visual Culture BA, Translation Studies with History of Art and Visual Culture BA, Translation Studies with International Film BA

Department of Music; www.royalholloway.ac.uk/music

Music BMus, Music and English BA, Music and Philosophy BA, Music with French BA, Music with German BA, Music with Italian BA, Music with Philosophy BA, Music with Political Studies BA, Music with Spanish BA
Postgraduate courses: Advanced Musical Studies MMus, Music Performance PG Dip

Department of Philosophy; www.royalholloway.ac.uk/philosophy

Philosophy BA

Department of Phsyics; www.royalholloway.ac.uk/physics

Astrophysics BSc/MSci, Experimental Physics BSc/MSci, Physics BSc/MSci, Physics with Music BSc, Physics with Particle Physics BSc/MSci, Physics with Philosophy BSc, Theoretical Physics BSc/MSci
Postgraduate courses: Physics (Euromasters) MSc, Physics by Research MSc

Department of Politics and International Relations; www.royalholloway.ac.uk/politicsandir

International Relations BA, Politics BA, Politics and International Relations BA, Politics and International Relations and Philosophy BA, Politics with Philosophy BA, Politics, Philosophy and Economics BA
Postgraduate courses: Elections, Campaigns and Democracy MSc, International Public Policy MSc, International Relations MSc, International Security MSc, Media, Power and Public Affairs MSc, Politics of Development MA

Department of Psychology; www.royalholloway.ac.uk/psychology

Applied Psychology BSc, Psychology BSc/MSci, Psychology, Clinical and Cognitive Neuroscience BSc, Psychology, Clinical Psychology and Mental Health BSc, Psychology, Development and Developmental Disorders BSc
Postgraduate courses: Applied Social Psychology MSc, Clinical Psychology MSc, Forensic Psychology MSc

Department of Social Work; www.royalholloway.ac.uk/socialwork

Postgraduate courses: Advanced Practice MSc, Social Work MSc, Social Work (Step up to Social Work) PG Dip

UNIVERSITY OF LONDON; ROYAL VETERINARY COLLEGE
www.rvc.ac.uk

BSc Agriculture, BSc Biological Sciences, BSc Biological Sciences (Animal Behaviour, Welfare and Ethics), BSc Biological Sciences or BSc Bioveterinary Sciences with a Certificate in Work-Based Learning and Research, BSc Bioveterinary Sciences, BSc Veterinary Nursing, BVetMed Bachelor of Veterinary Medicine, FdSc Veterinary Nursing, Graduate Diploma in Equine Locomotor Research, Graduate Diploma Veterinary Nursing, Intercalated BSc Bioveterinary Science, Intercalated BSc Bioveterinary Science, Intercalated BSc Comparative Pathology, Intercalated BSc Comparative Pathology, MSci

Applied Biological Research, MSci Applied Bioveterinary Research, MSci Biological Sciences, MSci Bioveterinary Sciences, MSci Wild Animal Biology Postgraduate courses: GradDip in Equine Locomotor Research, GradDip in Veterinary Nursing, MSc Wild Animal Biology, MSc Wild Animal Health, MSc/Cert

Intensive Livestock Health and Production, MSc/Dip/Cert Livestock Health and Production, MSc/Dip/Cert Veterinary Education, MSc/Dip/Cert Veterinary Epidemiology and Public Health, MSc/PGDip One Health (Infectious Diseases), MSc/PGDip Veterinary Epidemiology, PGCert in Veterinary Clinical Studies

UNIVERSITY OF LONDON; SCHOOL OF ORIENTAL AND AFRICAN STUDIES
www.soas.ac.uk

Department of Anthropology and Sociology; www.soas.ac.uk/anthropology
BA Social Anthropology, various joint options
Postgraduate courses: MA Anthropological Research Methods, MA Anthropological Research Methods and Intensive Language, MA Anthropological Research Methods and Nepali, MA Anthropology of Food, MA Anthropology of Media, MA Anthropology of Media with Intensive Language, MA Anthropology of Travel and Tourism, MA Medical Anthropology, MA Medical Anthropology and Intensive Language, MA Migration and Diaspora Studies and Intensive Language, MA Museums, Heritage and Material Culture Studies, MA Social Anthropology, MA Social Anthropology Programme with Intensive Language, MA Social Anthropology of Development, MA in Migration and Diaspora Studies

Centre for English Studies; www.soas.ac.uk/english-studies
BA English, various joint options

Department of History of Art and Archaeology; www.soas.ac.uk/art
BA History of Art, BA History of Art (Asia, Africa and Europe), BA History of Art and Archaeology, various joint options
Postgraduate courses: MA Arts of Asia and Africa, MA Contemporary Art and Art Theory of Asia and Africa, MA Critical Media and Cultural Studies, MA Global Creative and Cultural Industries, MA History of Art and Archaeology of East Asia, MA History of Art and Archaeology of East Asia and Intensive Language, MA History of Art and Architecture of the Islamic Middle East, MA History of Art and/or Archaeology, MA Museums, Heritage and Material Culture Studies, MA Religious Arts of Asia

Department of Music; www.soas.ac.uk/music
BA Music, BA in Global Popular Music, various joint options
Postgraduate courses: MA Global Creative and Cultural Industries, MA Music in Development, MMus Ethnomusicology, MMus Performance

Department of Development Studies; www.soas.ac.uk/development
BA Development Studies, various joint options
Postgraduate courses: MSc Development Studies, MSc Development Studies (Central Asia Pathway), MSc Development Studies (Contemporary India Pathway), MSc Development Studies (Palestine Pathway), MSc Environment, Politics and Development, MSc Globalisation and Development, MSc Labour, Social Movements and Development, MSc Migration Mobility and Development, MSc Research for International Development, MSc Violence, Conflict & Development, MSc Violence, Conflict & Development (Palestine Pathway)

Department of East Asian Languages and Cultures; www.soas.ac.uk/east-asia
BA Chinese (Modern and Classical), BA Chinese Studies, BA Japanese, BA Japanese Studies, BA Korean, BA Korean Studies, various joint options
Postgraduate courses: MA ... and Intensive Language (Japanese), MA ... and Intensive Language (Korean), MA Applied Japanese Linguistics, MA Chinese Studies, MA Japanese Studies, MA Japanese Studies (Dual Degree Programme), MA Japanese Studies (Literature Pathway), MA Korean Studies, MA Korean Studies (Literature Pathway), MA Sinology, MA Sinology (Chinese Literature Exit Award)

Department of Economics; www.soas.ac.uk/economics
BSc Development Economics, BSc Economics, various joint options

Postgraduate courses: MSc Development Economics, MSc Economics, MSc Economics with reference to Africa, MSc Economics with reference to Environment and Development, MSc Economics with reference to South Asia, MSc Economics with reference to the Asia Pacific Region, MSc Economics with reference to the Middle East, MSc Global Economic Governance and Policy, MSc International Finance and Development, MSc Political Economy of Development, MSc Research for International Development

School of Finance and Management; www.soas.ac.uk/finance-and-management

BA International Management and South East Asian Studies, BSc International Management (China), BSc International Management (Japan and Korea), BSc International Management (Middle East and North Africa), BSc Management, various joint options

Postgraduate courses: MRes in Finance and Management, MSc Finance and Financial Law, MSc International Management (China), MSc International Management (Japan), MSc International Management (Middle East and North Africa), MSc Public Financial Management, MSc Public Policy and Management, MSc in Finance

Department of History; www.soas.ac.uk/history

BA Ancient Near Eastern Studies, BA Global Liberal Arts, BA History, various joint options

Postgraduate courses: MA Ancient Near Eastern Languages, MA Historical Research Methods and Intensive Language, MA History, MA History and Intensive Language, MA in Historical Research Methods

Department of Religions and Philosophies; www.soas.ac.uk/religions-and-philosophies

BA Study of Religions, BA World Philosophies, various joint options

Postgraduate courses: MA Buddhist Studies, MA Islamic Societies and Cultures, MA Religion in Global Politics, MA Religions of Asia and Africa, MA Religions of Asia and Africa and Intensive Language, MA Traditions of Yoga and Meditation

Centre for Development, Environment and Policy; www.soas.ac.uk/cedep

Postgraduate courses: PGCert/PGDip/MSc Agricultural Economics, PGCert/PGDip/MSc Climate Change and Development, PGCert/PGDip/MSc Environmental Economics, PGCert/PGDip/MSc Environmental Management, PGCert/PGDip/MSc Poverty Reduction: Policy and Practice, PGCert/PGDip/MSc Sustainable Development

Centre for Gender Studies; www.soas.ac.uk/genderstudies

Postgraduate courses: MA Gender Studies, MA Gender Studies and Law, MA Gender and Sexuality, MA in Gender Studies with special reference to the Middle East

Centre for Global Media and Communications; www.soas.ac.uk/global-media-and-communications

Postgraduate courses: MA Global Digital Cultures, MA International Journalisms, MA Media and the Middle East, MA Media in Development, MA in Global Media and Postnational Communication

Centre for International Studies and Diplomacy; www.soas.ac.uk/cisd

Postgraduate courses: MA Globalisation and Multinational Corporations, MA/PGDip International Studies and Diplomacy, MSc Global Energy and Climate Policy, MA Global Diplomacy (Online), MA Global Diplomacy: MENA (Online), MA Global Diplomacy: South Asia (Online), MSc Global Corporations and Policy (Online), MSc Global Energy and Climate Policy (Online)

School of Languages, Cultures and Linguistics; www.soas.ac.uk/languages-cultures-linguistics

BA African Language and Culture, BA African Studies, BA Arabic, BA Arabic and .... (a language), BA Arabic and Islamic Studies, BA Hebrew and Israeli Studies, BA International Management and South East Asian Studies (3 years), BA Islamic Studies, BA Linguistics, BA Middle Eastern Studies, BA Persian, BA South Asian Studies, BA South Asian Studies (Bengali/Hindi/Nepali/Sanskrit/Urdu pathways), BA South East Asian Studies, BA Turkish, various joint options

Postgraduate courses: MA ... and Intensive Language (Arabic), MA African Studies, MA African Studies (Literature Pathway), MA Applied Linguistics and Language Pedagogy, MA Arabic Language Learning and Teaching, MA Arabic Literature, MA Chinese Language Learning and Teaching, MA Islamic Studies, MA Israeli Studies, MA Japanese Language Learning and Teaching, MA Korean Language Learning and Teaching, MA Language Documentation and Description, MA Linguistics, MA Linguistics and Intensive Language, MA Near and Middle Eastern Studies, MA Pacific Asian Studies, MA Palestine Studies, MA South Asian Area Studies, MA South East Asian Studies, MA Translation, MA Turkish Studies, MA in Iranian Studies, MA in the Study of Contemporary Pakistan

School of Law; www.soas.ac.uk/law

LLB Single Honours, Senior Status LLB, various joint options
Postgraduate courses: LLM (Master of Laws), LLM in Chinese Law, LLM in Dispute and Conflict Resolution, LLM in Environmental Law, LLM in Human Rights, Conflict and Justice, LLM in International Economic Law, LLM in International Law, LLM in International and Comparative Commercial Law, LLM in Islamic Law, LLM in Law and Gender, LLM in Law in the Middle East and North Africa, LLM in Law, Development and Globalisation, MA Legal Studies (General Programme), MA in Chinese Law, MA in Dispute and Conflict Resolution, MA in Environmental Law and Sustainable Development, MA in Human Rights Law, MA in International Law, MA in International and Comparative Commercial Law, MA in Islamic Law, MA in Law, Development and Globalisation

Department of Politics and International Studies; www.soas.ac.uk/politics

BA International Relations, BA Politics, BA Politics and International Relations, various joint options
Postgraduate courses: MRes Politics with (Language), MSc African Politics, MSc Asian Politics, MSc Comparative Political Thought, MSc International Politics, MSc Middle East Politics, MSc Politics of China, MSc Politics of Conflict, Rights & Justice, MSc State, Society and Development

UNIVERSITY OF LONDON; THE SCHOOL OF PHARMACY
www.pharmacy.ac.uk

Master of Pharmacy (MPharm)
Postgraduate courses: MSc in Pharmaceutics, MSc Drug Discovery and Development, MSc Drug Discovery and Pharma Management, MSc in Medicinal Natural Products and Phytochemistry, MSc in Pharmaceutical Formulation and Entrepreneurship, MSc Experimental Pharmacology and Therapeutics, MSc Clinical Pharmacy, International Practice and Policy

UNIVERSITY OF LONDON; UNIVERSITY COLLEGE LONDON (UCL)
www.ucl.ac.uk

Anthropology
BSc Anthropology
Postgraduate courses: MRes Anthropology, MSc Anthropology, Environment and Development, MA Creative and Collaborative Enterprise, MSc Digital Anthropology, MA Ethnographic and Documentary Film (Practical), MSc Human Evolution and Behaviour, MA Material and Visual Culture, MA Materials, Anthropology and Design, MSc Medical Anthropology, MSc Social and Cultural Anthropology

Applied Medical Sciences
BSc/MSci Applied Medical Sciences

Archaeology
BA/BSc Archaeology, BA Archaeology and Anthropology, BA Classical Archaeology and Classical Civilisation, BA Egyptian Archaeology
Postgraduate courses: MSc Archaeological Science: Technology and Materials, MA Archaeology, Grad Dip Archaeology, MA Archaeology and Heritage of Asia, MA Archaeology of Egypt and the Near East, MA Artefact Studies, MSc Bioarchaeological and Forensic Anthropology, MA Comparative Art and Archaeology, MSc Computational Archaeology: GIS, Data Science and Complexity, MSc Conservation for Archaeology and Museums, MA Cultural Heritage Studies, MSc Environmental Archaeology, MA Managing Archaeological Sites, MA Mediterranean Archaeology, MA Museum Studies, MSc Palaeoanthropology and Palaeolithic Archaeology, MA Principles of Conservation, MA Public Archaeology, MA Research Methods for Archaeology, MSc Built Environment: Sustainable Heritage, MRes Science and Engineering in Arts, Heritage and Archaeology

Architecture

BSc Architecture, MEng Engineering and Architectural Design, BSc Architectural and Interdisciplinary Studies

Postgraduate courses: PGCert Advanced Architectural Research, MRes Architectural Computation, MSc Architectural Computation, MArch Architectural Design, MA Architectural History, MArch (ARB/RIBA Part 2) Architecture, MRes Architecture and Digital Theory, MA Architecture and Historic Urban Environments, MArch Design for Manufacture, MArch Design for Performance and Interaction, MA Situated Practice, MRes Space Syntax: Architecture and Cities, MSc Space Syntax: Architecture and Cities, MArch Urban Design

Arts and Sciences

BASc Arts and Sciences

Biochemical Engineering and Bioprocessing

BSc Bioprocessing of New Medicines (Business and Management), BSc Bioprocessing of New Medicines (Science and Engineering), BEng/MEng Engineering (Biochemical)

Biochemistry and Biotechnology

BSc/MSci Biochemistry, BSc Biotechnology

Postgraduate courses: MSc Biochemical Engineering, MRes Synthetic Biology

Biological/Biomedical Sciences

BSc/MSci Biological Sciences, BSc Biomedical Sciences

Postgraduate courses: MRes Biodiversity, Evolution and Conservation, MSc Biomedical Sciences, MRes Biosciences, MRes Brain Sciences, MSc Experimental Pharmacology and Therapeutics, MSc Genetics of Human Disease, MSc Neuroscience, MRes Modelling Biological Complexity

Cancer

BSc Cancer Biomedicine

Postgraduate course: MSc Cancer

Chemical Engineering

BEng/MEng Engineering (Chemical)

Postgraduate courses: MSc Chemical Process Engineering, MSc Global Management of Natural Resources

Chemistry

BSc/MSci Chemistry, BSc/MSci Chemical Physics, BSc/MSci Chemistry with Management Studies, BSc/MSci Chemistry with Mathematics, BSc/MSci Chemistry with a European Language, BSc/MSci Medicinal Chemistry

Postgraduate courses: MSc Advanced Materials Science, MSc Applied Analytical Chemistry, MSc Chemical Research, MSc Materials for Energy and Environment, MSc Molecular Modelling, MRes Molecular Modelling and Materials Science, MRes Organic Chemistry: Drug Discovery

Child Health

Postgraduate courses: MSc Advanced Physiotherapy: Cardiorespiratory, MSc Advanced Physiotherapy: Neurophysiotherapy, MSc Advanced Physiotherapy: Paediatrics, MSc Applied Paediatric Neuropsychology, MRes Biomedicine, MSc Cell and Gene Therapy, MRes Child Health, MSc Child and Adolescent Mental Health, MSc Clinical Paediatric Neuropsychology, MSc Infancy and Early Childhood Development, MSc Paediatrics and Child Health with Clinical Practice, MSc Paediatrics and Child Health: Advanced Paediatrics, MSc Paediatrics and Child Health: Community Child Health, MSc Paediatrics and Child Health: Global Child Health, MSc Paediatrics and Child Health: Intensive Care, MSc Paediatrics and Child Health: Molecular and Genomic Paediatrics, MSc Physiotherapy Studies: Cardiorespiratory, MSc Physiotherapy Studies: Neurophysiotherapy, MSc Physiotherapy Studies: Paediatrics

Civil and Environmental Engineering

BEng/MEng Engineering (Civil)

Postgraduate courses: MSc Civil Engineering, Grad Dip Civil Engineering, MSc Civil Engineering (with Environmental Systems), MSc Civil Engineering (with Geographic Information Science), MSc Civil Engineering (with Infrastructure Planning), MSc Civil Engineering (with Integrated Design), MSc Civil Engineering (with Seismic Design), MSc Civil Engineering (with Surveying), MSc Earthquake Engineering with Disaster Management, MSc Engineering for International Development, MSc Environmental Systems Engineering, MSc GIS (Geographic Information Science), MSc Geoinformatics for Building Information Modelling, MSc Spatio-temporal Analytics and Big Data Mining, MSc Transport, MSc Transport with Business Management, MRes Urban Sustainability and Resilience, MSc Built Environment: Environmental Design and Engineering, MSc Health, Wellbeing and Sustainable Buildings, MSc Light and Lighting

Classical World

BA Ancient World, BA Classics, BA Greek and English, BA Greek with Latin, BA Latin and English, BA Latin with Greek

Postgraduate courses: MA Classics, MA Reception of the Classical World

Computer Science

BSc/MEng Computer Science, MEng Mathematical Computation

Postgraduate courses: MSc Business Analytics (with specialisation in Computer Science), MSc Computational Finance, MSc Computational Statistics and Machine Learning, MRes Computational Statistics and Machine Learning, MSc Computer Graphics, Vision and Imaging, MSc Computer Science, MSc Data Science (with specialisation in Computer Science), MSc Financial Risk Management, MSc Financial Systems Engineering, MSc Information Security, MSc Machine Learning, MRes Robotics, MSc Robotics and Computation, MSc Software Systems Engineering, MRes Virtual Reality, MRes Web Science and Big Data Analytics, MSc Web Science and Big Data Analytics

Dentistry

Postgraduate courses: PGCert Advanced Aesthetic Dentistry, MSc Conservative Dentistry, PGCert Dental Sedation and Pain Management, PGDip Endodontic Practice, MSc Endodontics, MClinDent Endodontology, MClinDent Endodontology (Advanced Training), PGDip Implant Dentistry, MSc Oral Medicine, MClinDent Oral Surgery, MClinDent Oral Surgery (Advanced Training), MSc Oral and Maxillofacial Surgery, MClinDent Orthodontics, MClinDent Orthodontics (Advanced Training), MSc Paediatric Dentistry, MClinDent Periodontology, MClinDent Prosthodontics, MClinDent Prosthodontics (Advanced Training), MSc Restorative Dental Practice, MSc Special Care Dentistry, PGCert Special Care Dentistry

Development Planning

Postgraduate courses: MSc Building and Urban Design in Development, MSc Development Administration and Planning, MSc Environment and Sustainable Development, MSc Social Development Practice, MSc Urban Development Planning, MSc Urban Economic Development, MSc Digital Innovation in Built Asset Management

Ear Institute

Postgraduate courses: MSc Advanced Audiology, MSc Audiological Science, MSc Audiological Science with Clinical Practice, MSc Otology and Audiology, MRes Sensory Systems, Technologies and Therapies

Earth Sciences

MSci Earth Sciences, MSci Earth Sciences (International Programme), BSc/MSci Environmental Geoscience, BSc/MSci Geology, BSc/MSci Geophysics Postgraduate courses: MSc Geophysical Hazards, MSc Geoscience, PGCert Natural Hazards, PGCert Natural Hazards for Insurers, MRes Risk and Disaster Reduction, PGCert Risk and Disaster Reduction, MSc Risk and Disaster Science, MSc Risk, Disaster and Resilience, MSc Sustainable Resources

Economics and Business

BSc (Econ) Economics, BA Economics and Business with East European Studies
Postgraduate courses: MSc Economic Policy, MSc Economics

Education

BA Education Studies
Postgraduate courses: Grad Dip Advanced Educational Practice, MA Advanced Educational Practice, MA Applied Educational Leadership and Management, MA Art and Design in Education, MA Citizenship, History or Religious Education (Humanities), MA Comparative Education, MA Curriculum, Pedagogy and Assessment, MA Digital Media, Culture and Education, MA Early Years Education, MA Education, MA Education and Technology, MA Educational Assessment, MA Effective Learning and Teaching, MA English Education, MA Higher and Professional Education, MA Leadership, MA Lifelong Learning and Leadership (Singapore), MA Mathematics Education, MA Museums and Galleries in Education, MA Music Education, MA Philosophy of Education, MA Primary Education (Policy and Practice), MA Professional Education and Training, MA Science Education, MBA Educational Leadership (International), MBA Higher Education Management, MTeach Teaching, PGDip Social Science Research Methods

Electronic and Electrical Engineering

BEng/MEng Engineering (Electronic and Electrical)
Postgraduate courses: MRes Integrated Photonic and Electronic Systems, MSc Internet Engineering, MSc Nanotechnology, MSc Telecommunications, MRes Telecommunications, MSc Telecommunications with Business, MSc Wireless and Optical Communications

Energy

Postgraduate courses: MSc Economics and Policy of Energy and the Environment, MRes Energy Demand Studies

English

BA English
Postgraduate courses: MA English Linguistics, MA English: Issues in Modern Culture

European Languages, Culture and Society

BA Comparative Literature, BA Dutch, BA French, BA French and an Asian or African Language, BA German, BA German and History, BA Icelandic, BA Italian, BA Italian Studies and History of Art: UCL–Venice Double Degree, BA Italian Studies:

UCL–Venice Double Degree, BA Language and Culture, BA Modern Language Plus, BA Modern Languages, BA Scandinavian Studies, BA Scandinavian Studies and History, BA Spanish and Latin American Studies, BA Viking and Old Norse Studies
Postgraduate courses: MA Dutch Studies: Language, Culture and History, MA French and Francophone Studies: Language, Culture and History, MA German History: Language, Culture and History, MA German Studies: Language, Culture and History, MA Hispanic Studies: Language, Culture and History, MA Italian Studies: Language, Culture and History, MA Language, Culture and History, MA Scandinavian Studies: Language, Culture and History

European Social and Political Studies
BA European Social and Political Studies

Fine Art
BA/BFA Fine Art
Postgraduate courses: MA/MFA Fine Art

Geography
BSc (Econ) Economics and Geography, BSc Environmental Geography, BA/BSc Geography
Postgraduate courses: MSc Aquatic Science, MSc Climate Change, MSc Conservation, MSc Environment, Politics and Society, MSc Environmental Mapping, MSc Environmental Modelling, MSc Geospatial Analysis, MSc Global Migration, MSc Remote Sensing, MSc Urban Studies

Hebrew and Jewish Studies
BA Ancient Languages, BA Hebrew and Jewish Studies, BA History (Central and East European) and Jewish Studies
Postgraduate course: MA Jewish Studies

History
BA Ancient History, BA History, BA History with a European Language
Postgraduate courses: MA Ancient History, MA Chinese Health and Humanity, MA European History, MA History, MA Late Antique and Byzantine Studies, MA Medieval and Renaissance Studies, MA Transnational Studies

History of Art
BA History of Art, BA History of Art with Material Studies
Postgraduate course: MA History of Art

History, Politics and Economics
BA History, Politics and Economics

Human Sciences
BSc Human Sciences, MSci Human Sciences and Evolution

Infection and Immunity
BSc Infection and Immunity

Postgraduate course: MSc Infection and Immunity

Information Studies and Information Management for Business
BSc/MSci Information Management for Business
Postgraduate courses: MA Archives and Records Management, MA/MSc Digital Humanities, MSc Information Science, MRes Information Studies, MA Library and Information Studies, MA Publishing

International Development and Education
Postgraduate courses: MA Development Education and Global Learning, MA Education and International Development, MA Education, Gender and International Development, MA Education, Health Promotion and International Development, MA Educational Planning, Economics and International Development, MA International Leadership in Inclusive Education

Law
LLB Bachelor of Law (UCL) and Bachelor of Law (HKU), LLB English and German Law Dual Degree, LLB Law, LLB Law with French Law, LLB Law with German Law, LLB Law with Hispanic Law
Postgraduate course: LLM Law

Linguistics
BA Linguistics
Postgraduate courses: MA Applied Linguistics, MA Teaching of English to Speakers of Other Languages (TESOL), MA Linguistics, MA Linguistics with a specialisation in Phonology/Pragmatics/Semantics/Syntax

Management
BSc/MSci Management Sciences,
Postgraduate courses: MBA Business Administration, MSc Business Analytics (with specialisation in Management Science), MSc Entrepreneurship, MSc Finance, MSc Management

Mathematics
BSc/MSci Mathematics, BSc/MSci Mathematics and Physics, BSc/MSci Mathematics and Statistical Science, BSc/MSci Mathematics with Economics, BSc/MSci Mathematics with Management Studies, BSc/MSci Mathematics with Mathematical Physics, BSc/MSci Mathematics with Modern Languages
Postgraduate courses: MSc Financial Mathematics, MSc Mathematical Modelling

Mechanical Engineering
BEng/MEng Engineering (Mechanical with Business Finance), BEng/MEng Engineering (Mechanical)
Postgraduate courses: MSc Biomaterials and Tissue Engineering, MSc Engineering with Finance, MSc Engineering with Innovation and Entrepreneurship, MSc Marine Engineering (Mechanical and Electrical

Options), MSc Mechanical Engineering, MSc Naval Architecture, MSc Power Systems Engineering

Medical Physics and Biomedical Engineering

BEng/MEng Engineering (Biomedical), MSci Medical Physics, BSc Physics with Medical Physics

Postgraduate courses: BSc Cardiovascular Science, MRes Medical Physics and Biomedical Engineering, MRes Medical Technology Entrepreneurship, MSc Physics and Engineering in Medicine by Distance Learning, MSc Physics and Engineering in Medicine: Biomedical Engineering and Medical Imaging, MSc Physics and Engineering in Medicine: Radiation Physics

Medicine

MBBS BSc Medicine

Postgraduate courses: MSc Clinical Trials, MA Clinical Education, MSc Clinical and Professional Education, MSc Medical Education, MSc Advanced Biomedical Imaging, MRes Clinical Drug Development, MSc Clinical Drug Development, MSc Clinical and Public Health Nutrition, MSc Drug Design, MRes Drug Design, MSc Eating Disorders and Clinical Nutrition, MSc/MRes Human Tissue Repair, MRes Human Tissue Repair, MSc Prenatal Genetics and Fetal Medicine, MSc Reproductive Science and Women's Health, MRes Reproductive Science and Women's Health

Centre for Multidisciplinary and Intercultural Inquiry

Postgraduate courses: MA African Studies with Education, MSc African Studies with Environment, MSc African Studies with Health, MA African Studies with Heritage, MA Comparative Literature, MA Early Modern Studies, MA European Culture and Thought: Culture, MA European Culture and Thought: Thought, MA European Studies: European Society, MA European Studies: Modern European Studies, MA Film Studies, MA Gender, Society and Representation, MA Health Humanities, MA Philosophy, Politics and Economics of Health, MSc Specialised Translation (Audiovisual), MSc Specialised Translation (Scientific, Technical and Medical), MSc Specialised Translation (with Interpreting), MA Translation: Research, MA Translation: Translation Studies, MA Translation: Translation and Culture

Natural Sciences

BSc/MSci Natural Sciences

Neuroscience

BSc/MSci Neuroscience

Postgraduate courses: MSc Advanced Neuroimaging, MSc Brain and Mind Sciences, MSc Clinical Neurology, MSc Clinical Neurology (by Distance Learning), MSc Clinical Neuroscience, MSc Dementia: Causes, Treatments and Research (Neuroscience), MRes Neuromuscular Disease, MSc Neuromuscular Disease, MRes Stroke Medicine, MSc Stroke Medicine, MRes Translational Neurology

Nutrition

BSc Nutrition and Medical Sciences

Ophthalmology

Postgraduate courses: MSc Biology of Vision, PGCert Clinical Ophthalmic Practice, MSc Clinical Ophthalmology, MSc Ophthalmology with Clinical Practice, MRes Vision Research

Pharmacology

BSc/MSci Pharmacology

Pharmacy

MPharm Pharmacy

Postgraduate courses: MSc Clinical Pharmacy, International Practice and Policy, MSc Drug Discovery and Development, MSc Drug Discovery and Pharma Management, MRes Drug Sciences, MSc Medicinal Natural Products and Phytochemistry, MSc Pharmaceutical Formulation and Entrepreneurship, MSc Pharmaceutics

Philosophy

BA Philosophy, BA Philosophy and Economics, BA Philosophy and Greek, BA Philosophy and History of Art

Postgraduate course: MA Philosophy

Physics and Astrophysics

BSc/MSci Astrophysics, BSc/MSci Physics, BSc/MSci Theoretical Physics

Postgraduate courses: MSc Astrophysics, MSc Biological Physics, MSc Physics, MSc Planetary Science, MSc Quantum Technologies, MSc Scientific Computing

Political Science and Politics

BSc Philosophy, Politics and Economics, BA Politics, Sociology and East European Studies

Postgraduate courses: MSc Democracy and Comparative Politics, MSc European Public Policy, MSc Global Governance and Ethics, EMPA Global Public Policy and Management, MA Human Rights, MSc International Public Policy, MA Legal and Political Theory, MPA Public Administration and Management, MSc Public Policy, MSc Security Studies

Population Health

BSc Population Health

Postgraduate courses: MSc Dental Public Health, MSc Health Psychology, MSc Health and Society: Social Epidemiology, MSc Population Health, MSc Global Health and Development, MSc Global Health and Development: tropEd programme, MSc Health Economics and Decision Science, MSc Global Prosperity,

MSc Data Science for Research in Health and Biomedicine, MSc Health Informatics

Project Management for Construction

BSc Project Management for Construction

Postgraduate courses: MSc Construction Economics and Management, MSc Infrastructure Investment and Finance, MSc Project and Enterprise Management, MSc Strategic Management of Projects

Psychology, Psychiatry, Language Sciences and Special Educational Needs

BSc/MSci Psychology, BA/BSc Psychology with Education, BSc/MSci Psychology and Language Sciences

Postgraduate courses: GradCert Psychology, Grad Dip Habilitation and Disabilities of Sight (Children and Young People), Language and Cognition, Language and Communication Needs in Schools: Advanced Practice, MA Education (Psychology), MA Literacy Learning and Literacy Difficulties, MA Reading Recovery and Literacy Leadership, MA Special and Inclusive Education, MA Special and Inclusive Education (Cairo), MA Specific Learning Difficulties (Dyslexia), MA/MSc Educational Neuroscience, MRes Applied Research in Human Communication Disorders, MRes Cognitive Neuroscience, MRes Developmental Neuroscience and Psychopathology, MRes Speech, MSc Behaviour Change, MSc Child Development, MSc Clinical Mental Health Sciences, MSc Cognitive and Decision Sciences, MSc Cognitive Behavioural Therapy for Children and Young People, MSc Cognitive Neuroscience, MSc Dementia: Causes, MSc Developmental and Educational Psychology, MSc Developmental Psychology and Clinical Practice, MSc Human-Computer Interaction, MSc Industrial/Organisational and Business Psychology, MSc Language Sciences (with specialisation in Language Development/Linguistics with Neuroscience/Neuroscience and Communication/Sign Language and Deaf Studies/Speech and Hearing Sciences), MSc Mental Health Sciences Research, MSc Psychoanalytic Developmental Psychology, MSc Psychological Sciences, MSc Psychology of Education, MSc Social Cognition: Research and Applications, MSc Speech, MSc Speech and Language Sciences, MSc Theoretical Psychoanalytic Studies (Non-Clinical), PGCert Child and Young Persons Psychological Wellbeing Practice, PGCert Low Intensity Cognitive Behavioural Interventions, PGCert National Award for Special Educational Needs Co-ordination, PGDip Child and Young Person IAPT Therapy, PGDip Cognitive Behaviour Therapy with Counselling for Depression, Treatments and Research (Mental Health)

Russian and East European Languages and Culture

BA Bulgarian and East European Studies, BA Czech (with Slovak) and East European Studies, BA Finnish and East European Studies, BA Hungarian and East European Studies, BA Polish and East European Studies, BA Romanian and East European Studies, BA Russian Studies, BA Russian and History, BA Russian with an East European Language, BA Serbian/Croatian and East European Studies, BA Slovak (with Czech) and East European Studies, BA Ukrainian and East European Studies

Postgraduate courses: MA Central and South-East European Studies, MA Comparative Business Economics, MA Comparative Economics and Policy, MRes East European Studies, MA (International) Economy, State and Society: Economics and Business, MA (International) Economy, State and Society: History and Society, MA (International) Economy, State and Society: Politics and Security, MA (International) Economy, State and Society: Politics and the International Economy, MA History (SSEES), MA Political Analysis (Russia and Eastern Europe), MA Political Sociology (Russia and Eastern Europe), MRes Politics and Economics of Eastern Europe, MA Russian Studies, MA Russian and East European Literature and Culture, MA Russian and Post-Soviet Politics

Science and Technology Studies

BSc History and Philosophy of Science, BSc Science and Society

Postgraduate courses: MSc History and Philosophy of Science, MSc Science, Technology and Society, MPA Development, Technology and Innovation Policy, MPA Energy, Technology and Climate Policy, MPA Science, Engineering and Public Policy, MPA Urban Innovation and Policy

Security and Crime Science

BSc Security and Crime Science

Postgraduate courses: MSc Countering Organised Crime and Terrorism, MSc Crime Science, MSc Crime and Forensic Science, MSc Policing, PGCert Security and Crime Science

Social Sciences

BSc Social Sciences, BSc Social Sciences with Quantitative Methods

Postgraduate courses: MA Policy Studies in Education, MA Social Justice and Education, MSc Social Policy and Social Research, MSc Social Research Methods, MA Sociology of Childhood and Children's Rights, MA Sociology of Education, MSc Systematic Reviews for Social Policy and Practice

Space and Climate Physics

Postgraduate courses: PGCert Defence Systems Engineering, MSc Management of Complex Projects, PGCert Rail Systems Engineering, MSc Space Risk and Disaster Reduction, MSc Space Science and Engineering: Space Science, MSc Space Science and Engineering: Space Technology, PGCert Space Systems Engineering, MSc Systems Engineering Management, MSc Technology Management

Statistical Science

BSc (Econ) Economics and Statistics, MSci Statistical Science (International Programme), BSc Statistics, BSc Statistics and Management for Business, BSc Statistics, Economics and Finance, BSc Statistics, Economics and a Language

Postgraduate courses: MSc Data Science (with specialisation in Statistics), MSc Statistics, MSc Statistics (Medical Statistics)

Surgery and Interventional Science

BSc/MSci Medical Sciences and Engineering

Postgraduate courses: MS Advanced Minimally-Invasive Surgery, MSc Burns, Plastic and Reconstructive Surgery, MSc Evidence-Based Healthcare, MSc Musculoskeletal Science, MSc Musculoskeletal Science (by Distance Learning), MSc Nanotechnology and Regenerative Medicine, MSc Performing Arts Medicine, MSc Perioperative Medicine, MSc Physical Therapy in Musculoskeletal Healthcare and Rehabilitation, MSc Rehabilitation Engineering and Assistive Technologies, MSc Sports Medicine, Exercise and Health, MSc Surgical and Interventional Sciences

The Americas

BA History and Politics of the Americas

Postgraduate courses: MA Caribbean and Latin American Studies, MSc Globalisation and Latin American Development, MSc International Relations of the Americas, MSc Latin American Politics, MA Latin American Studies, MA United States Studies: History and Politics

Urban Planning, Design and Real Estate

BSc Planning and Real Estate, BSc Urban Planning, Design and Management, BSc Urban Studies

Postgraduate courses: MPlan City Planning, MSc Housing and City Planning, MSc Infrastructure Planning, Appraisal and Development, MRes Interdisciplinary Urban Design, MSc International Planning, MSc International Real Estate and Planning, MSc Mega Infrastructure Planning, Appraisal and Delivery, MSc Spatial Planning, MSc Sustainable Urbanism, MSc Transport and City Planning, MSc Urban Design and City Planning, MSc Urban Regeneration, MSc Smart Cities and Urban Analytics, MSc Smart Cities and Urban Analytics (RTPI Pathway), MRes Spatial Data Science and Visualisation, MSc Spatial Data Science and Visualisation

UNIVERSITY OF LOUGHBOROUGH
www.lboro.ac.uk

Department of Aeronautical and Automotive Engineering; www.lboro.ac.uk/departments/aae

BEng/MEng(Hons) Aeronautical Engineering, BEng/MEng(Hons) Automotive Engineering

Postgraduate courses: MSc Automotive Systems Engineering, PGCert Powertrain Simulation and Test, PGCert Intelligent Vehicle Systems, PGCert Body and Chassis Simulation and Test

School of Architecture, Building and Civil Engineering; www.lboro.ac.uk/departments/abce

BSc(Hons) Architectural Engineering and Design Management, BArch(Hons) Architecture

Postgraduate courses: MSc Air Transport Management, MRes Built Environment: Energy Demand Studies, MSc Construction Management, MSc Construction Project Management, MSc Infrastructure in Emergencies (Distance or Blended Learning), MSc Low Carbon Building Design and Modelling, MSc Low Energy Building Services Engineering, MSc Water and Environmental Management, MSc Water and Waste Engineering

School of the Arts, English and Drama; www.lboro.ac.uk/departments/aed

BA(Hons) Drama, BA(Hons) Drama with English, BA(Hons) Drama with Business Studies, BA(Hons) English, BA(Hons) English and Drama, BA(Hons) English and Sport Science, BA(Hons) English Literature, BA(Hons) English with Business Studies, BA(Hons) English with Creative Writing, BA(Hons) Fine art, BA(Hons) Graphic Communication and Illustration, BA(Hons) Publishing and English, BA(Hons) Textiles: Innovation and Design

Postgraduate courses: MA Graphic Design and Visualisation, MA Art and Design (Studio Practice),

MA Creative Writing, MA English, MA Animation for Health and Wellbeing

School of Business and Economics; www.lboro.ac.uk/departments/sbe

BSc(Hons) Accounting and Financial Management, BSc(Hons) Banking, Finance and Management, BSc(Hons) Business Economics and Finance, BSc(Hons) Economics, BSc(Hons) Economics and Management, BSc(Hons) Economics with Accounting, BSc(Hons) Economics with Geography, BSc(Hons) Economics with Politics, BSc(Hons) Information Management and Business, BSc(Hons) International Business, BSc(Hons) International Economics, BSc(Hons) Management Sciences, BSc(Hons) Retailing, Marketing and Management

Postgraduate courses: Master of Business Administration, MSc Banking and Finance, MSc Business Analytics Consulting, MSc Business Psychology, MSc Corporate Finance, MSc Economics and Business Strategy, MSc Economics and Finance, MSc Economics and International Business, MSc Employment Relations and HRM, MSc Finance and Investment, MSc Finance and Management, MSc Finance, MSc Human Resource Management, MSc Information Management and Business Technology, MSc International Management, MSc Management, MSc Marketing, MSc Work Psychology

Department of Chemical Engineering; www.lboro.ac.uk/departments/chemical

BEng/MEng(Hons) Bioengineering, BEng/MEng(Hons) Biomaterials Engineering, BEng/MEng Chemical Engineering

Postgraduate courses: MSc Advanced Process Engineering, MSc Advanced Chemical Engineering with IT and Management

Department of Chemistry; www.lboro.ac.uk/departments/chemistry

BSc/MChem(Hons) Chemistry, BSc/MChem(Hons) Medicinal and Pharmaceutical Chemistry, BSc/MSci(-Hons) Natural Sciences

Postgraduate courses: MSc/PGDip/PGCert Analytical Chemistry, MSc/PGDip/PGCert Analytical and Pharmaceutical Science, MSc/PGDip/PGCert Pharmaceutical Science and Medicinal Chemistry

Department of Computer Science; www.lboro.ac.uk/departments/compsci

BSc/MSci Computer Science, BSc/MSci Computer Science, BSc/MSci Computer Science and Artificial Intelligence, BSc/MSci Computing and Management, BSc/MSci Computer Science and Mathematics, BSc/

MSci Information Technology Management for Business

Postgraduate courses: MSc Advanced Computer Science, MSc Internet Computing and Network Security

Design School; www.lboro.ac.uk/departments/design-school

BA(Hons) Industrial Design & Technology, BSc(Hons) Product Design & Technology, BSc(Hons) User Centred Design

Postgraduate courses: MSc/PGDip/PGCert Ergonomics & Human Factors, MSc/PGDip/PGCert Human Factors in Transport, MSc/PGDip/PGCert Human Factors for Inclusive Design, MSc/PGDip/PGCert Ergonomics in Health & Community Care, MSc/PGDip/PGCert Human Factors & Ergonomics for Patient Safety, MA User Experience Design, MA Industrial Design & Technology

Department of Geography; www.lboro.ac.uk/departments/geography

BA/BSc(Hons) Geography, MSci(Hons) Geography, BSc(Hons) Geography and Management, BSc(Hons) Geography and Sport Management, BSc(Hons) Geography and Sport Science, BSc(Hons) Geography with Economics

Postgraduate courses: MSc Environmental Monitoring for Management, MSc International Financial and Political Relations, MSc Globalization and Cities

Department of Materials; www.lboro.ac.uk/departments/materials

BEng/MEng(Hons) Materials Science and Engineering, BEng/MEng(Hons) Automotive Materials, BEng/MEng(Hons) Biomaterials Engineering, BEng/MEng(Hons) Bioengineering

Postgraduate courses: MSc/PGDip/PGCert Materials Science and Technology, MSc/PGDip/PGCert Polymer Science and Technology

Department of Mathematical Sciences; www.lboro.ac.uk/departments/maths

BSc/MMath(Hons) Mathematics, BSc(Hons) Mathematics and Accounting and Financial Management, BSc(Hons) Mathematics with Economics, BSc(Hons) Mathematics with Management, BSc(Hons) Mathematics with Mathematics Education, BSc(Hons) Mathematics and Sport Science, BSc(Hons) Mathematics with Statistics, BSc(Hons) Financial Mathematics, BSc/MSci(Hons) Natural Sciences

Postgraduate courses: MSc Industrial Mathematical Modelling, MSc Mathematical Finance

Department of Mechanical, Electrical and Manufacturing Engineering; www.lboro.ac.uk/departments/meme

BEng/MEng(Hons) Electronic and Computer Systems Engineering, BEng/MEng(Hons) Electronic and Electrical Engineering, BSc(Hons) Engineering Management, BEng/MEng(Hons) Manufacturing Engineering, BEng/MEng(Hons) Mechanical Engineering, BEng/MEng(Hons) Product Design Engineering, BEng/MEng(Hons) Robotics, Mechatronics and Control Engineering, BSc(Hons) Sports Technology, BEng/MEng(Hons) Systems Engineering

Postgraduate courses: MSc Advanced Manufacturing Engineering and Management, MSc Digital Communication Systems, MSc Electronic and Electrical Engineering, MSc Engineering Design, MSc European Masters in Renewable Energy, MSc Mechanical Engineering, MSc Mobile Communications, MSc Networked Communications, MSc Renewable Energy Systems Technology (Distance Learning), MSc Renewable Energy Systems Technology, MSc Systems Engineering

Department of Physics; www.lboro.ac.uk/departments/physics

BSc/MPhys(Hons) Physics, BSc/MPhys(Hons) Engineering Physics, BSc(Hons) Physics with Astrophysics and Cosmology, BSc/MPhys(Hons) Physics and Mathematics, BSc/MSci(Hons) Natural Sciences

Postgraduate courses: MSc Advanced Physics, MSc Physics of Materials

Department of Politics, History and International Relations; www.lboro.ac.uk/departments/phir

BA(Hons) History, BA(Hons) History and International Relations, BA(Hons) History and Politics, BA(Hons) International Relations, BA(Hons) Politics, BA(Hons) Politics and International Relations, BA(Hons) Politics with Economics, BA(Hons) Politics with History, BA(Hons) Politics with International Relations, BA(Hons) Politics, History and International Relations

Department of Social Sciences; www.lboro.ac.uk/departments/socialsciences

BSc(Hons) Communication and Media Studies, BSc(Hons) Criminology and Social Policy, BSc(Hons) Psychology with Criminology, BSc(Hons) Sociology, BSc(Hons) Sociology with Criminology, BSc(Hons) Social Psychology

MA Global Media and Cultural Industries, MA Media and Cultural Analysis, MA Digital Media and Society, MA Global Political Communication

School of Sport, Exercise and Health Sciences; www.lboro.ac.uk/departments/ssehs

BSc(Hons) Human Biology, BSc(Hons) Psychology, BSc(Hons) Sport and Exercise Psychology, BSc(Hons) Sport and Exercise Science, BSc(Hons) Sport Management, BSc/MSci(Hons) Biochemistry, BSc/MSci(Hons) Biological Sciences

Department of Teacher Education; www.lboro.ac.uk/departments/teacher-education

Postgraduate courses: Mathematics PGCE/MSc with QTS, Physical Education PGCE/MSc with QTS

Loughborough University in London; www.lborolondon.ac.uk

Postgraduate courses: Cyber Security and Big Data MSc, Design and Culture MA, Design Innovation MA/MSc/MRes, Design Innovation Management MSc, Digital Creative Media MSc, Digital Technologies MRes, Diplomacy and International Governance MRes, Diplomacy, Business and Trade MSc, Diplomacy, Statecraft and Foreign Policy MSc, Entrepreneurial Design Management MSc, Entrepreneurship and Innovation Management MSc, Entrepreneurship and Innovation MRes, Entrepreneurship, Finance and Innovation MSc, Internet Technologies with Business Management MSc, Managing Innovation in Creative Organisations MSc, Media and Creative Industries MA/MRes, Mobile Communication Systems MSc, Security, Peace-Building and Diplomacy MSc, Sport Business and Innovation MSc, Sport Business and Leadership MSc, Sport Business MRes, Sport Digital and Media Technologies MSc

UNIVERSITY OF MANCHESTER
www.manchester.ac.uk

Faculty of Biology, Medicine and Health; www.bmh.manchester.ac.uk

BNurs Adult Nursing, BSc Anatomical Sciences, BSc Biochemistry, BSc Biology, BSc Biology with Science & Society, BSc Biomedical Sciences, BSc Biotechnology, BSc Cell Biology, BNurs Children's Nursing, BSc Cognitive Neuroscience and Psychology, BDS Dentistry (first-year entry), BSc Developmental Biology, BSc Genetics, BSc Healthcare Science (Audiology), BSc Immunology, BSc Life Sciences, BSc Management and Innovation in Healthcare, BSc Medical Biochemistry, MBChB Medicine, BNurs Mental Health Nursing, BSc Microbiology, BMidwif Midwifery, BSc Molecular Biology, BSc Neuroscience, BSc/MSci Optometry, BSc Oral Health Science, BSc Pharmacology and Physiology, BSc Pharmacology, MPharm Pharmacy, BSc Physiology, BSc Plant Science, BSc Psychology, BSc Speech and Language Therapy, MSpchLangTher Speech and Language Therapy, BSc Zoology

Postgraduate courses: MSc/PGDip/PGCert Advanced Audiology Studies, MSc/PGDip/PGCert Advanced Clinical Practice – Paediatric Anaesthesia, MSc Advanced General Dental Practice, MSc/PGDip Advanced Practice in Forensic Mental Health, MSc Advanced Practice and Leadership, MSc Advanced Professional Practice and Leadsership, MSc Advanced Nursing Practice and Leadership, MSc Advanced Midwifery Practice and Leadership, MSc Advanced Social Work Practice and Leadership, PGCert Advanced Specialist Training in Emergency Medicine, PGCert Approved Mental Health Professional Practice, MSc Audiology, MSc Biochemistry, MSc Bioinformatics and Systems Biology, MRes Biological Sciences, MSc Biotechnology and Enterprise, MSc/PGDip/PGCert Cancer Biology and Radiotherapy Physics, MSc Cancer Research and Molecular Biomedicine, MRes Cardiovascular Health and Disease, MSc Cell Biology, MSc/PGDip/PGCert Chemical Food Safety and Integrity, MSc Clinical and Health Psychology, MSc Clinical Biochemistry, MSc/PGDip Clinical Pharmacy, MClin Res/PGDip Clin Res/PGCert Clin Res Clinical Research, MSc Clinical Rheumatology & Musculoskeletal Medicine, MSc/PGDip/PGCert Clinical Trials (Pharmaceutical Industrial Advanced Training), MSc/PGDip Deaf Education, MSc/PGDip Dementia Care (APIMH), MSc/PGDip/PGCert Dental Implantology, MDPH/PGDip/ PGCertDental Public Health, MResDental Public Health, MSc Developmental Biology, MSc Endodontics, MSc Evidence-Based Health Care, MRes Experimental Cancer Medicine, MSc Fixed and Removable Prosthodontics, MSc/PGDip Forensic Psychology and Mental Health, MSc Genetic Counselling, MSc Genomic Medicine, MRes HSC/PGDip Res HSC/ PGCert Res HSC Health and Social Care, MSc/PGDip/PGCert Health Data Science, MSc Health Psychology, MSc History of Science, Technology and Medicine, MSc/PGDip/PGCert Industrial Pharmacy (Pharmaceutical Industrial Advanced Training), MSc Investigative Ophthalmology and Vision Sciences, MSc/PGDip/PGCert Medical Education, MSc/PGDip Medical Imaging Science, MSc/PGDip Medical Microbiology, MRes Medical Sciences, MSc/PGDip Medical Virology, MSc Model-Based Drug Development, MSc Molecular Pathology, MSc Neuroscience, MSc Neuroimaging for Clinical and Cognitive Neuroscience, MSc/PGDip/PGCert Occupational Hygiene, MSc/Advanced Diploma/PGCert Occupational Medicine, MSc Occupational Medicine (Dubai), MRes Oncology, MSc/PGDip Oral and Maxillofacial Surgery, MSc Clin Oral and Maxillofacial Surgery, MSc Clin Orthodontics, MSc Paediatric Dentistry, MSc Clin Periodontology, MSc/PGDip/ PGCert Pharmaceutical Business Development and Licensing (Pharmaceutical Industrial Advanced Training), MSc/PGDip/PGCert Pharmaceutical Microbiology (Pharmaceutical Industrial Advanced Training), MSc/PGDip/PGCert Pharmaceutical Technology and Quality Assurance, PGDip Physician Associate Studies, MSc/PGDip Primary Mental Health Care (APIMH), MRes Psychology, MSc/ PGDip Psychosocial Interventions for Psychosis (APIMH), MPH/MRes Public Health and Primary Care, MPH Master of Public Health, MRes Primary Care, MRes Public Health, MRes Reproduction and Pregnancy, PGDip Restorative and Aesthetic Dentistry, MSc Science Communication, MSc/PGDip Skin Ageing and Aesthetic Medicine, MA Social Work, MSc/PGDip/PGCert/CPD units Specialist Practice (Cancer), PGCert Teaching and Learning in Biology, Medicine and Health Sciences, MRes Tissue Engineering for Regenerative Medicine, MRes Translational Medicine (Interdisciplinary Molecular Medicine), PGCert Translational Medicine (Interdisciplinary Molecular Medicine)

Faculty of Science and Engineering; *www.se.manchester.ac.uk*

School of Chemical Engineering and Analytical Science; www.ceas.manchester.ac.uk

BEng/MEng Chemical Engineering, MEng Chemical Engineering (Energy and Environment)
Postgraduate courses: MSc Advanced Chemical Engineering, MSc Advanced Process Integration and Design

School of Chemistry; www.chemistry.manchester.ac.uk

BSc/MChem Chemistry, BSc/MChem Chemistry with Medicinal Chemistry
MSc Chemistry, MSc Polymer Materials Science and Engineering

School of Computer Science; www.cs.manchester.ac.uk

BSc/MEng Artificial Intelligence, BSc/MEng Computer Science, BEng/MEng Computer Systems Engineering, BSc/MEng Software Engineering, BSc Computer Science with Business and Management, BSc Computer Science and Mathematics, BSc/MEng Computer Science (Human Computer Interaction)
Postgraduate courses: MSc Advanced Computer Science, MSc Advanced Computer Science and IT Management, MRes Advanced Computer Science Master of Research

School of Earth and Environmental Sciences; www.sees.manchester.ac.uk

BEng/MEng Petroleum Engineering, BSc Environmental and Resource Geology, BSc Environmental Science, BSc Geochemistry, BSc Geography and Geology, BSc Geology, BSc/MEarthSci Geology with Planetary Science, MEarthSci Earth Sciences
MSc Applications in Environmental Sciences, MSc Environmental Sciences, Policy and Management (MESPOM), MSc Petroleum Geoscience, MSc Pollution and Environmental Control

School of Electrical and Electronic Engineering; www.eee.manchester.ac.uk

BEng/MEng Electrical and Electronic Engineering, BEng/MEng Electronic Engineering, BEng/MEng Mechatronic Engineering
Postgraduate courses: MSc Advanced Control and Systems Engineering, MSc Communication Engineering, MSc Digital Signal Processing, MSc Electrical Power Systems Engineering, MSc Advanced Electrical Power Systems Engineering, MSc Power Electronics, Machines and Drives, MSc Renewable Energy and Clean Technology

School of Materials; www.materials.manchester.ac.uk

BSc/MEng Materials Science and Engineering, MEng Materials Science and Engineering with Biomaterials, MEng Materials Science and Engineering with Polymers, MEng Materials Science and Engineering with Metallurgy, MEng Materials Science and Engineering with Corrosion, MEng Materials Science and Engineering with Textile Technology, BSc Fashion Buying and Merchandising, BSc Fashion Management, BSc Fashion Marketing
Postgraduate courses: MSc Advanced Engineering Materials, MSc Biomaterials, MSc Corrosion Control Engineering, MSc International Fashion Marketing, MSc International Fashion Retailing, MSc Polymer Materials Science and Engineering, MSc Textile Technology (Technical Textiles)

School of Mathematics; www.maths.manchester.ac.uk

BSc/MMath Mathematics, BSc/MMath Mathematics with Financial Mathematics, BSc/MMath Mathematics and Statistics, BSc Actuarial Science and Mathematics, BSc Mathematics with Finance, BSc Mathematics and Philosophy, BSc Mathematics with a Modern Language
MSc Actuarial Science, MSc Applied Mathematics, MSc Mathematical Finance, MSc Pure Mathematics and Mathematical Logic, MSc Statistics

School of Mechanical, Aerospace and Civil Engineering; www.mace.manchester.ac.uk

BEng/MEng Aerospace Engineering, MEng Aerospace Engineering with Management, BEng/MEng Civil Engineering, MEng Civil Engineering (Enterprise), MEng Civil and Structural Engineering, BEng/MEng Mechanical Engineering, MEng Mechanical Engineering, BEng/MEng Mechanical Engineering with Management
Postgraduate courses: MSc Adv. Manufacturing Tech. and Systems Management, MSc Aerospace Engineering, MSc Commercial Project Management, MSc Construction Project Management, MSc Engineering Project Management, MSc Management of Projects, MSc Mechanical Engineering Design, MSc Project Management Professional Development Programme, MSc Reliability Engineering and Asset Management, MSc Renewable Energy and Clean Technology, MSc Structural Engineering, MSc Thermal Power and Fluid Engineering

School of Physics and Astronomy;
www.physics.manchester.ac.uk

BSc/MMath & Phys Mathematics and Physics, BSc/MPhys Physics, BSc/MPhys Physics with Astrophysics, BSc/MPhys Physics with Philosophy, BSc/MPhys Physics with Theoretical Physics

Faculty of Humanities;
www.humanities.manchester.ac.uk

Alliance Manchester Business School;
www.mbs.ac.uk

BSc(Hons) Accounting, BSc(Hons) IT Management for Business, BSc(Hons) IT Management for Business (Accounting), BSc(Hons) IT Management for Business (Marketing), BSc(Hons) IT Management for Business (Strategy and Economics), BSc(Hons) International Business, Finance and Economics, BSc(Hons) International Management, BSc(Hons) International Management with American Business Studies, BSc(Hons) Management, BSc(Hons) Management (Accounting and Finance), BSc(Hons) Management (Human Resources), BSc(Hons) Management (Innovation, Strategy and Entrepreneurship), BSc(Hons) Management (International Business Economics), BSc(Hons) Management (Marketing), BSc(Hons) Management (Sustainable and Ethical Business), BSc(Hons) Management Singapore

Postgraduate courses: MBA Master of Business Administration, MEnt Master of Enterprise, MSc Accounting, MSc Accounting and Finance, MSc Business Analysis and Strategic Management, MSc Business Analytics: Operational Research and Risk Analysis, MSc Business Psychology, MSc Corporate Communications and Reputation Management, MSc Finance, MSc Human Resource Management and Industrial Relations, MSc Innovation Management and Entrepreneurship, MSc International Business and Management (Management), MSc International Healthcare Leadership, MSc International Human Resource Management and Comparative Industrial Relations, MSc Management, MSc Marketing, MSc Operations, Project and Supply Chain Management, MSc Organisational Psychology, MSc Quantitative Finance

School of Arts, Languages and Cultures;
www.alc.manchester.ac.uk

BA American Studies, BA Ancient History and Archaeology/History, BA Ancient History, BA Arabic and a Modern European Language, BA Arabic Studies, BA Archaeology and Anthropology/History, BA Archaeology, BA Art History and History, BA Chinese and Japanese/Linguistics, BA Chinese Studies, BA Classical Studies, BA Classics, BA Drama and English Literature/Screen Studies, BA Drama, BA East Asian Studies, BA English Language and Arabic/Chinese/English Literature/French/German/Italian/Japanese/Portuguese/Russian/Spanish, BA English Language, BA English Literature and a Modern Language (French/German/Italian/Spanish), BA English Literature and American Studies/History, BA English Literature, BA English Literature with Creative Writing, BA Film Studies and Arabic/Archaeology/Chinese/East Asian Studies/English Language/English Literature/French/German/History/History of Art/Italian/Japanese/Linguistics/Middle Eastern Studies/Portuguese/Russian/Spanish, BA French and Chinese/German/Italian/Japanese/Linguistics/Portuguese/Russian/Spanish, BA French Studies, BA German and Chinese/Italian/Japanese/Linguistics/Portuguese/Russian/Spanish, BA German Studies, BA History and American Studies/Arabic/French/German/Italian/Portuguese/Russian/Sociology/Spanish, BA History, BA History of Art, BSc International Disaster Management & Humanitarian Response, BA Italian and Chinese, BA Italian and Japanese/Linguistics/Portuguese/Russian/Spanish, BA Italian Studies, BA Japanese Studies, BA Latin and English Literature/Italian/Linguistics/Spanish, BA Latin with French, BA Linguistics and Arabic/Japanese/Portuguese/Russian/Social Anthropology/Sociology/Spanish), BA Linguistics, BA Middle Eastern Studies, BA Modern History with Economics, BA Modern Language and Business & Management (Arabic/Chinese/French/German/Italian/Japanese/Portuguese/Russian/Spanish), BA Music and Drama, MusB Music, BA Politics and Arabic/Chinese/French/German/Italian/Japanese/Modern History/Portuguese/Russian/Spanish, BA Portuguese and Chinese/Japanese, BA Religion and Anthropology, BA Religions and Theology, BA Russian and Chinese/Japanese/Portuguese/Spanish, BA Russian Studies, BA Spanish and Chinese/Japanese/Portuguese, BA Spanish, Portuguese and Latin American Studies, BA Theological Studies in Philosophy and Ethics

MA Archaeology, MA Art Gallery and Museum Studies, MA Arts Management, Policy and Practice, MA Classics and Ancient History, MusM Composition (Electroacoustic Music and Interactive Media), MusM Composition (Instrumental and Vocal music), Conference Interpreting, MA Creative Writing, MA English Literature and American Studies, MA Film Studies, MA Gender, Sexuality and Culture, PGCert Global Health, MA History, MSc History of Science,

Technology and Medicine (including Medical Humanities award route), Humanitarianism and Conflict Response, MA Intercultural Communication, MSc International Disaster Management, MA Linguistics, MA Medieval and Early Modern Studies, MA Modern and Contemporary Literature, MusM Music (Ethnomusicology), MusM Music (Musicology), MA Religions and Theology, MA Screenwriting

School of Environment, Education and Development; www.seed.manchester.ac.uk

BA Architecture, BA English Language for Education, BA Environmental Management, BSc Geography and Geology, BA/BSc Geography, BSc International Disaster Management & Humanitarian Response, BA Management, Leadership and Leisure, MPlan Master of Planning, MPRE Master of Planning with Real Estate, BA Urban and Regional Planning
Postgraduate courses: MA Architecture and Urbanism, MArch Architecture, MSc Development Economics and Policy, MSc Development Finance, MA Digital Technologies, Communication and Education, MA Education (International), MA Educational Leadership, MSc Environmental Governance, MSc Environmental Impact Assessment & Management, MSc Environmental Monitoring, Modelling and Reconstruction, MSc Geographical Information Science, MSc Global Urban Development and Planning, MSc Human Resource Development (International Development), MSc ICTs for Development, MSc International Development: Development Management, MSc International Development: Environment Climate Change and Development, MSc International Development: Globalisation, Trade and Industry, MSc International Development, MSc International Development: Politics, Governance and Development Policy, MSc International Development: Poverty Conflict and Reconstruction, MSc International Development: Poverty, Inequality and Development, MSc International Development: Public Policy and Management, MSc Management and Implementation of Development Projects, MSc Management and Information Systems: Change and Development, MSc Organisational Change and Development, PGCE Primary, PGCE Primary School Direct 5-11, PGCE Sec Sch Dir: Geography (Cheadle & Marple College), PGCE Sec Sch Dir: History (Cheadle & Marple College), PGCE Secondary Business Education, PGCE Secondary Chemistry, PGCE Secondary Economics and Business Education, PGCE Secondary English, PGCE Secondary French, PGCE Secondary (Geography), PGCE Secondary German, PGCE

Secondary (History), PGCE Secondary Mathematics, PGCE Secondary Physics, PGCE Secondary Physics with Maths, PGCE Secondary School Direct (English), PGCE Secondary School Direct (Mathematics), PGCE Secondary School Direct Science: Biology (11-16 or 11-18), PGCE Secondary School Direct Science: Chemistry (11-16 or 11-18), PGCE Secondary School Direct Science: Physics (11-16 or 11-18), PGCE Secondary Science Biology, PGCE Secondary Spanish, Planning MSc, PGCE Secondary School Direct (French), PGCE Secondary School Direct (German), PGCE Secondary School Direct (Physics with Maths), PGCE Secondary School Direct (Spanish), MEd Psychology of Education, MSc Real Estate Asset Management, MSc Real Estate Development, MA TESOL, MSc Urban Design and International Planning, MSc Urban Regeneration and Development

School of Law; www.law.manchester.ac.uk

BASS Criminology & Quantitative Methods, BA Criminology, LLB Law, LLB Law with Criminology, LLB Law with Politics, BASS Philosophy & Criminology, BASS Politics & Criminology, BASS Social Anthropology & Criminology, BASS Sociology & Criminology
Postgraduate courses: LLM Corporate Governance, MA/MRes/PGDip Criminology, MRes Criminology (Social Statistics), LLM/MA/PGDip Healthcare Ethics and Law, PGCert Healthcare Ethics, PGCert Healthcare Law, LLM Intellectual Property Law, LLM International Business and Commercial Law, LLM International Financial Law, LLM International Trade Transactions, LLM Law, LLM Public International Law, LLM/MA Security and International Law, LLM Transnational Dispute Resolution

School of Social Sciences; www.socialsciences.manchester.ac.uk

BAEcon Accounting and Finance, BAEcon Business Studies and Economics/Politics/Sociology, BAEcon Business Studies, BASS Criminology & Quantitative Methods, BAEcon Development Studies, BAEcon Economics and Finance/Philosophy/Politics/Sociology, BAEcon/BSc Economics, BAEcon Finance, BASS Philosophy and Criminology/Politics/Quantitative Methods, BA Philosophy, BASS Politics and Criminology/International Relations/Quantitative Methods, BSocSc Politics and International Relations, BASS Politics and Quantitative Methods/Social Anthropology/Sociology, BA Politics, Philosophy and Economics, BASS Social Anthropology and Criminology/Philosophy/Sociology, BSocSc Social Anthropology, BASS Social Sciences (Social

Anthropology & Quantitative Methods), BASS Sociology and Criminology/Philosophy/Quantitative Methods, BSocSc Sociology

MA Anthropological Research, MSc Econometrics, MSc Economics and Econometrics, MSc Economics (Economics of Health), MSc Economics (Environmental Economics), MA/MSc Economics, MSc Financial Economics, MA Human Rights – Law/Political Science Pathway, MA International Political Economy, MA International Relations, MA Peace and Conflict Studies, MA Philosophy, MA Political Economy, MA Political Science – Democracy and Elections, MA Political Science – European Politics & Policy Pathway, MA Political Science – Governance and Public Policy Pathway, MA Political Science – Philosophy and Political Theory, MA Political Science – Political Theory Pathway, MA Politics, MA Social Anthropology – Culture, Ethnography and Development Pathway, MA Social Anthropology, MA Social Anthropology – Visual and Sensory Media Pathway, MSc Social Research Methods and Statistics, MSc Sociological Research, MSc Sociology, MA Visual Anthropology

MANCHESTER METROPOLITAN UNIVERSITY
www.mmu.ac.uk

Faculty of Arts and Humanities; www.mmu.ac.uk/artshumanities

Manchester School of Art; www.art.mmu.ac.uk

Foundation Diploma in Art and Design, BA Acting, BA Animation, BA Architecture, BA Art History, BA Art History and Curating, BA Fashion, BA Fashion Art Direction, BA Filmmaking, BA Fine Art, BA Fine Art and Art History, BA Fine Art and Curating, BA Graphic Design, BA Illustration with Animation, BA Interactive Arts, BA Interior Design, BA Photography, BA Textiles in Practice, BA Three Dimensional Design

Postgraduate courses: MA/MFA Animation, MA/MFA Architecture MArch, MA Architecture & Urbanism MA, MA/MFA Collaborative Practice, MA/MFA Contemporary Curating, MA/MFA Design: Ceramics, MA/MFA Design: Embroidery, MA/MFA Design: Fashion, MA/MFA Design: Fashion Art Direction, MA/MFA Design: Furniture, MA/MFA Design: Glass, MA/MFA Design: Graphic Design & Art Direction, MA/MFA Design: Illustration, MA/MFA Design: Interior Design, MA/MFA Design: Jewellery, MA/MFA Design: Lab, MA/MFA Design: Textile Practice, MA/MFA Design: Textiles for Fashion, MA/MFA Filmmaking, MA/MFA Fine Art, MA/MFA Landscape Architecture MLA, MA/MFA Photography, MA/MFA Product Design MA/MSc/MFA, MA/MFA Visual Culture

Humanities, Languages and Social Science; www.mmu.ac.uk/hlss

English

BA(Hons) English, BA(Hons) English and American Literature, BA(Hons) English and Creative Writing, BA(Hons) English and Film, BA(Hons) English and Multimedia Journalism, BA(Hons) English and History, BA(Hons) English and Philosophy, BA(Hons) English and Politics, BA(Hons) English and Linguistics, BA(Hons) English and French, BA(Hons) English and Spanish, BA(Hons) English with a minor route language

Postgraduate courses: MA English Studies, MA/MFA Creative Writing

History, Politics and Philosophy

BA(Hons) American History, BA(Hons) Ancient and Medieval History, BA(Hons) Ancient History, BA(Hons) Ethics, Religion & Philosophy, BA(Hons) History, BA(Hons) History and International Politics, BA(Hons) History and International Politics, BA(Hons) History and Philosophy, BA(Hons) History and Politics, BA(Hons) History and Sociology, BA(Hons) International Politics, BA(Hons) International Politics and French, BA(Hons) International Politics and Philosophy, BA(Hons) International Politics and Philosophy, BA(Hons) International Politics and Philosophy, BA(Hons) International Politics and Spanish, BA(Hons) International Politics with a minor route language, BA(Hons) Modern History, BA(Hons) Philosophy, BA(Hons) Philosophy and Politics, BA(Hons) Philosophy and Politics, BA(Hons) Philosophy and Psychology, BA(Hons) Philosophy and Sociology, BA(Hons) Politics, BA(Hons) Public Services, BA(Hons) Public Services

(Governance), BA(Hons) Public Services (Social Policy), BA(Hons) Public Services (Uniformed Services), BA(Hons) War and Society, BSc(Hons) Medieval and Early Modern History

Postgraduate courses: MA Creative Writing, MFA Creative Writing, MA English Studies, MA History, MA International Relations and Global Communications, MA European Philosophy, Master of Public Administration, MA Library and Information Management, MSc Information and Data Management, MA Multimedia Journalism, MA Journalism, MSc Communication, Behaviour and Credibility Analysis, MA Teaching English to Speakers of Other Languages (TESOL) and Applied Linguistics, MA Linguistics and English Studies, MA Linguistics and English Language, MA Sociology and Global Change, MA Criminology, MSc Applied Quantitative Methods, MSc Science Communication

Sociology

BA(Hons) Sociology, BSc(Hons) Sociology with Quantitative Methods, BA(Hons) Criminology, BSc(Hons) Criminology and Sociology with Quantitative Methods, BSc(Hons) Criminology with Quantitative Methods, BA(Hons) Criminology and Politics, BA/BSc(Hons) Criminology and Psychology

Postgraduate courses: MA Sociology and Global Change, MA Criminology, MSc Applied Quantitative Methods

Languages, Linguistics and TESOL

BA(Hons) English and Teaching English to Speakers of Other Languages, BA(Hons) French and Spanish, BA(Hons) French Studies, BA(Hons) French with German, BA(Hons) French with Italian, BA(Hons) French with Japanese, BA(Hons) French with Mandarin Chinese, BA(Hons) French with Modern Standard Arabic, BA(Hons) French with Urdu, BA(Hons) Linguistics and French, BA(Hons) Linguistics and Spanish, BA(Hons) Linguistics with German, BA(Hons) Linguistics with Italian, BA(Hons) Linguistics with Japanese, BA(Hons) Linguistics with Mandarin Chinese, BA(Hons) Linguistics with Modern Standard Arabic, BA(Hons) Linguistics with Urdu, BA(Hons) Spanish Studies, BA(Hons) Spanish with German, BA(Hons) Spanish with Italian, BA(Hons) Spanish with Japanese, BA(Hons) Spanish with Mandarin Chinese, BA(Hons) Spanish with Modern Standard Arabic, BA(Hons) Spanish with Urdu, BA(Hons) Teaching English to Speakers of other Languages and French, BA(Hons) Teaching English to Speakers of Other Languages and Linguistics, BA(Hons) Teaching English to Speakers of other Languages and Spanish, BA(Hons) Teaching English

to Speakers of other Languages with German, BA(Hons) Teaching English to Speakers of other Languages with Italian, BA(Hons) Teaching English to Speakers of other Languages with Japanese, BA(Hons) Teaching English to Speakers of other Languages with Mandarin Chinese, BA(Hons) Teaching English to Speakers of other Languages with Modern Standard Arabic, BA(Hons) Teaching English to Speakers of other Languages with Urdu

Postgraduate courses: MA Teaching English to Speakers of Other Languages (TESOL) and Applied Linguistics, MA Linguistics and English Studies, MA Linguistics and English Language

Journalism, Information and Communications

BA(Hons) Multimedia Journalism, BSc(Hons) Digital Media and Communications, BA(Hons) Multimedia Journalism with a minor route language

Postgraduate courses: MA Library and Information Management, MSc Information and Data Management, MA Multimedia Journalism, MA Journalism, MSc Communication, Behaviour and Credibility Analysis

Manchester Fashion Institute; http://fashioninstitute.mmu.ac.uk

Fashion Design and Technology: BA(Hons) Womenswear, BA(Hons) Fashion Design and Technology: Menswear, BA(Hons) Fashion Design and Technology: Sportswear, BA(Hons) Fashion Promotion, BA(Hons) Fashion Buying and Merchandising, BA(Hons) Fashion Business and Management, BA(Hons) Fashion, BA(Hons) Fashion Art Direction

Postgraduate courses: MA International Fashion Business: Marketing Management, MA International Fashion Business: Buying and Merchandising Management, MA Responsible Fashion, MA Fashion Innovation, MA/MFA Design: Fashion Art Direction, MA/MFA Design: Fashion

Faculty of Business and Law; www.mmu.ac.uk/business-and-law

Business School; www.mmu.ac.uk/business-school

BA(Hons) Accounting and Finance, BA(Hons) Advertising and Brand Management, BA(Hons) Banking and Finance, BA(Hons) Business and Economics, BA(Hons) Business and Human Resource Management, BA(Hons) Business and Marketing, BA(Hons) Business Enterprise and Human Resource Management, BA(Hons) Business Enterprise and Marketing, BA(Hons) Business Management, BA(Hons) Business Management Professional

(Degree Apprenticeship), BA(Hons) Business Management Professional in Hospitality (Degree Apprenticeship), BA(Hons) Business Management Professional in Retail (Degree Apprenticeship), BA(Hons) Business Management with Law, BA(Hons) Digital Media and Marketing, BA(Hons) Economics and International Business, BA(Hons) Economics and Politics, BA(Hons) Economics and Banking, BA(Hons) Economics and Finance, BA(Hons) Events Management, BA(Hons) Hospitality Business Management, BA(Hons) Human Resource Management, BA(Hons) International Business and Marketing, BA(Hons) International Business Management, BA(Hons) Marketing Management, BA(Hons) Public Relations and Marketing, BA(Hons) Retail Management and Marketing, BA(Hons) Sports Management, BA(Hons) Sports Marketing Management, BA(Hons) Sustainable Performance Management (CIMA), BA(Hons) Tourism Management, BA/BSc(Hons) Economics, BSc(Hons) Business Technology, BSc(Hons) Digital & Technology Solutions (Degree Apprenticeship), MBus(Hons) Business, M.HRM(Hons) Human Resource Management

Postgraduate courses: Certificate in Professional Studies: Management and Leadership, MA International Events Management, MA International Tourism and Hospitality Management, MA Master of Sports Directorship, MBA Master of Business Administration (MBA), MBA Master of Business Administration (MBA) in Digital Management, MBA Master of Business Administration (MBA) in Financial Services, MBA Strategic Health and Social Care Pathway (MBA), MSc Accounting and Finance, MSc Banking and Finance, MSc Business Analytics, MSc Crowd Safety and Risk Analysis, MSc Digital Marketing, MSc Digital Marketing Communications, MSc Economic and Finance Analysis, MSc Human Resource Management with CIPD, MSc International Business Management, MSc International Finance and Management, MSc International Finance and Management, MSc International Human Resource Management, MSc International Human Resource Management with CIPD, MSc Logistics and Supply Chain Management, MSc Management, MSc Marketing, MSc Marketing (Communications), MSc Marketing (Creative Advertising), MSc Place Management and Leadership, MSc Project Management, MSc Public Relations, MSc Public Relations and Media Management, MSc Strategic Business Management, PgCert Public Relations and Digital Communications

Law School; www.mmu.ac.uk/law

LLB(Hons) Law, LLB(Hons) in Legal Practice

Postgraduate courses: Bar Professional Training Course, Legal Practice Course, LLM Legal Practice, Graduate Diploma in Law, LLM (Master of Laws)

Faculty of Education; www.mmu.ac.uk/education

BA(Hons) Early Years and Childhood Studies, BA(Hons) Education Studies, BSc(Hons) Educational Psychology, BA(Hons) Primary Education with Mathematics with QTS, BA(Hons) Primary Education with QTS, BSc(Hons) Secondary Mathematics Education with QTS

Postgraduate courses: MA Autism Spectrum Conditions, MA Bilingualism, Education and Society, MA Childhood and Youth Studies, MA Coaching and Mentoring, MA/PgDip Community Development and Youth Work: Leadership and Practice, PgCert Dyscalculia, MA Early Childhood Studies, MA Education, MRes Education and Society, MA Education Studies, MA Educational Leadership, MA Educational Leadership and Management, MA Inclusive Education and Disability, MA Inclusive Education and Special Educational Needs and Disability (SEND), MA Language Education, MA Leadership in Early Years, PgCert National Award for Special Educational Needs Coordination, PGCE Primary Education with QTS, PGCE Primary Education with QTS (Early Years), MA Professional Development and Enquiry, MSc Science, Technology, Engineering and Mathematics (STEM), PGCE Secondary Art and Design with QTS, PGCE Secondary Biology with QTS, PGCE Secondary Business with QTS, PGCE Secondary Chemistry with QTS, PGCE Secondary Computing and ICT with QTS, PGCE Secondary Design and Technology with QTS, PGCE Secondary Drama with QTS, PGCE Secondary English with QTS, PGCE Secondary Geography with QTS, PGCE Secondary History with QTS, PGCE Secondary Mathematics with QTS, PGCE Secondary Modern Foreign Languages with QTS, PGCE Secondary Music with QTS, PGCE Secondary Music with Specialist Instrument Teaching with QTS, PGCE Secondary Physical Education with QTS, PGCE Secondary Physics with Mathematics with QTS, PGCE Secondary Physics with QTS, PGCE Secondary Psychology with QTS, PGCE Secondary Religious Education with QTS, PGCE Secondary Social Science with QTS, MA Social Research, PgCert/PgDip/MA Specific Learning Difficulties, MA Teaching and Learning

Faculty of Health, Psychology and Social Care; www.mmu.ac.uk/hpsc

Department of Health Professions; www.mmu.ac.uk/health-professions

BSc Nutritional Sciences, BSc Physiotherapy, BSc Speech and Language Therapy, BSc Sport and Exercise Nutrition

Postgraduate courses: MSc/PgDip/PgCert Advanced Physiotherapy, MSc Nutrition and Health, MSc Food Safety, MSc Food Innovation, MSc/PgDip/PgCert Emergency Medicine, MSc Sport and Exercise Medicine

Department of Nursing; www.mmu.ac.uk/nursing

Postgraduate course: PgDip Adult Nursing
BSc Adult Nursing, BSc Community Health, BSc Mental Health Nursing

Department of Psychology; www.mmu.ac.uk/psychology

BSc Forensic Psychology, BSc Psychology, BSc Psychology Foundation, BSc Psychology with Counselling and Psychotherapy, BSc Psychology with Foundation Year, BSc Philosophy and Psychology, BSc Psychology and Sociology

Postgraduate courses: MSc Clinical Skills in Integrative Psychotherapy, MSc Psychological Wellbeing in Clinical Practice, PgCert Integrative Therapies, MSc Psychology

Department of Social Care; www.mmu.ac.uk/social-care-and-social-work

BSc Integrated Health and Social Care, BSc Social Care with a foundation year, BSc Social Work
Postgraduate courses: PgCert Augmentative and Alternative Communication, MSc Occupational Safety, Health and Environment, MA Social Work, MSc Advanced Practice in Health and Social Care, Professional Doctorate in Health and Social Care

Faculty of Science and Engineering; www.mmu.ac.uk/science-engineering

Biology

MBiol/BSc(Hons) Biology, BSc(Hons) Biology, BSc(Hons) Animal Behaviour, BSc(Hons) Microbiology and Molecular Biology, BSc(Hons) Wildlife Biology

Postgraduate courses: MSc Animal Behaviour, MSc Biological Recording, MSc Bird Conservation, MSc Conservation Biology, MSc Conservation Genetics, MSc Zoo Conservation Biology

Chemistry

MChem/BSc(Hons) Pharmaceutical Chemistry, BSc(Hons) Medicinal and Biological Chemistry, BSc(Hons) Chemistry

Computing and Digital Technology

MComp Computer Science, BSc(Hons) Computer Science, BSc(Hons) Computing, BSc(Hons) Software Engineering, BSc(Hons) Computer Forensics and Security, BSc(Hons) Computer Games Technology, BSc(Hons) Web Technologies, BSc(Hons) Computer Animation and Visual Effects

Postgraduate courses: MSc Computing, MSc Information Systems, MSc Data Science, MSc Data Analytics, MSc Advanced Computer Science, MSc Cyber Security

Engineering

BEng/MEng(Hons) Mechanical Engineering, BEng/MEng(Hons) Electrical and Electronic Engineering, BSc(Hons) Product Design and Technology, BSc(Hons) Computer and Network Technology, BSc(Hons) Design Engineering

Postgraduate courses: MSc Automotive Engineering, MSc Control and Instrumentation for Nuclear Engineering, MSc Electronic Engineering, MSc Engineering Management, MSc Industrial Communication and Automation, MSc Mechanical Engineering, MSc Rail Engineering

Environmental Science

BSc Environmental Science

Geography

MGeog(Hons) Geography, BSc(Hons) Geography, BSc(Hons) Human Geography, BSc(Hons) Physical Geography

Healthcare Science

MBioMedSci(Hons) Biomedical Science, BSc(Hons) Biomedical Science, BSc(Hons) Human Biosciences, BSc(Hons) Human Physiology, BSc(Hons) Sport Science and Physiology, BSc(Hons) Healthcare Science (Life Sciences), BSc(Hons) Healthcare Science (Physiological Sciences)

Postgraduate courses: MSc Biomedical Science, MSc Cellular Pathology, MSc Clinical Biochemistry, MSc Haematology and Transfusion Science, MSc Medical Microbiology

Mathematics

MMath(Hons) Mathematics, BSc(Hons) Mathematics

Science communication

Postgraduate course: MSc Science Communication

MIDDLESEX UNIVERSITY
www.mdx.ac.uk

Art and Design
Animation
Foundation Year in Visual Arts, Animation BA Honours, 3D Animation & Games BA Honours
Fashion
Fashion Textiles BA Honours, Fashion Design BA Honours, Design Crafts BA Honours, Fashion Communication and Styling BA Honours
Postgraduate courses: Fashion MA, Jewellery Futures MA
Fine art
Fine Art BA Honours, Intensive Foundation in Art and Design (iFAD)
Postgraduate courses: Fine Art MA, Printmaking MA, Art and Social Practice MA
Graphic design
Graphic Design BA Honours
Postgraduate course: Graphic Design MA
Illustration
Illustration BA Honours
Postgraduate course: Children's Book Illustration and Graphic Novels MA
Interiors
Architectural Technology BSc Honours, Interior Design BA Honours, Interior Architecture BA Honours
Postgraduate course: Interiors (Architecture and Design) MA
Photography
Photography BA Honours
Postgraduate course: Photography MA
Design crafts
Design Crafts BA Honours
Postgraduate course: Jewellery Futures MA
Product design
Product Design BA, Design Crafts BA Honours, Product Design Engineering BEng/MEng

Business
Accounting and finance
Accounting and Finance BA Honours, Banking and Finance BSc Honours, Business Accounting BA Honours, Business Management (Finance) BA Honours
Postgraduate courses: Accounting Practice MProf, Banking and Finance MSc/PG Cert/PG Dip, Finance Practice MProf, Financial Management MSc/PG Cert/PG Dip, Investment and Finance MSc/PGDip/PGCert

Business and management
Business Management (Finance) BA Honours, Business Management (Human Resources) BA Honours, Business Management (Innovation) BA Honours, Business Management (Mandarin) BA Honours, Business Management (Marketing) BA Honours, Business Management (Project Management) BA Honours, Business Management (Spanish) BA Honours, Business Management (Supply Chain) BA Honours, Business Management BA Honours, International Business Admin BA Honours, International Business and Trade BA, International Business BA Honours
Postgraduate courses: Arts Management MA, Global Supply Chain Management MSc/PG Dip/PG Cert, Innovation Management and Entrepreneurship MSc/PG Dip/PG Cert, International Business Management MA/PG Dip/PG Cert, Management MSc/PGDip/PGCert, Marine Surveying (Top up) MSc, Master of Business Administration in Oil and Gas MBA, Master of Business Administration MBA, Media Management MSc, Shipping and Logistics MBA
Economics
Economics BA/BSc Honours, Business Economics BSc Honours
Postgraduate courses: Behavioural Economics in Action MSc/PGDip/PGCert
Human resource management
Business Management (Human Resources) BA Honours, Human Resource Management BA Honours
Postgraduate courses: Organisational Change MA/PGDip/PGCert, Work and Organisations MSc/PGDip/PGCert, People Management and Development MA/PGDip/PGCert (CIPD Accredited), Diversity Management MA/PGDip/PGCert, Human Resource Practice MProf, Leadership in Organisations MA, International Human Resource Management MA/PGDip/PGCert (CIPD Accredited), Diversity and Organisational Change MA
Marketing
Marketing BA Honours
Postgraduate courses: Strategic Marketing MSc/PGDip/PGCert, Digital Marketing MSc/PGDip/PGCert, Corporate and Marketing Communications MSc/PGDip/PGCert, Strategic Branding and Stakeholder Communication MA/PGDip/PGCert

Tourism and hospitality management

International Tourism Management BA Honours, International Tourism Management (Mandarin) BA Honours, International Tourism Management (Spanish) BA Honours, International Hospitality and Tourism Management Top Up BA Honours

Postgraduate course: International Tourism Management MSc

Computer Sciences, Engineering and Maths

Computer and communications engineering

Computer Forensics BSc Honours, Computer Networks BSc Honours, Robotics BEng(Hons)/MEng, Computer Systems Engineering BEng(Hons)/MEng, Computer Communication and Networks BEng(Hons)/MEng

Postgraduate courses: Computer Networks and Network Design MSc, Telecommunications Engineering MSc, Network Security and Pen Testing MS/PGDip/PGCert, Network Management and Cloud Computing MSc, Building Information Modelling Management MSc/PGDip/PGCert

Computer science and informatics

Information Technology BSc Honours, Computer Science BSc Honours, Business Information Systems BSc Honours, Mathematics with Computing BSc/MSci

Postgraduate courses: Creative Technology MA/MSc, Robotics MSc/PGDip/PGCert, Electronic Security and Digital Forensics MSc, Computer Science MSc, Cybercrime and Digital Investigation MSc, Business Information Systems Management MSc

Design engineering

Product Design BA, Design Engineering BEng(Hons)/MEng, Robotics BEng(Hons)/MEng, Mechatronics BEng(Hons)/MEng, Product Design Engineering BEng/MEng, Electronic Engineering BEng(Hons)/MEng

Postgraduate courses: Creative Technology MA/MSc, Engineering Management MSc, Robotics MSc/PGDip/PGCert, Mechatronic Systems Engineering MSc, Building Information Modelling Management MSc/PGDip/PGCert

Engineering project management

Engineering Management MSc, Building Information Modelling Management MSc/PGDip/PGCert

Mathematics

Mathematics BSc(Hons)/MMath, Mathematics with Computing BSc/MSci

Postgraduate courses: Applied Statistics MSc/PGDip, Operational Research MSc/PGDip, Financial Mathematics MSc/PGDip

Construction and Architecture

Architecture and Construction

Architectural Technology BSc Honours, Interior Architecture BA Honours

Postgraduate courses: Engineering Management MSc, Building Information Modelling Management MSc/PGDip/PGCert

Construction professional practice

Professional Practice in Engineering Management BSc Honours, Foundation degree Professional Practice in Construction Operations Management, Professional Practice in Construction Site Management BA Honours, Professional Practice in Quantity Surveying and Commercial Management BA Honours

Education Studies

Early childhood studies

Early Childhood Studies BA Honours

Postgraduate course: Early Years Initial Teacher Training

Education studies

Education Studies BA Honours, Early Childhood Studies BA Honours, Learning and Teaching BA Honours, Learning and Teaching Foundation FdA

Postgraduate courses: Leading Inclusive Education MA, Higher Education MA, Education MA, Higher Education PGCert

Teacher training

Postgraduate courses: PGCE Secondary Education Mathematics, PGCE Primary Education with QTS, PGCE Secondary Education Science with Physics, PGCE Secondary Education Music, PGCE Secondary Education English, PGCE Secondary Education Business Studies, PGCE Secondary Education Drama with English, PGCE Secondary Education Science with Biology, PGCE Secondary Education Science with Chemistry, PGCE Secondary Education Computer Science with ICT

Film, Media and English

Creative writing

Creative Writing and Journalism BA Honours

Postgraduate courses: Novel Writing (Online Distance Learning) MA, Writing for Creative and Professional Practice MA/PGDip

English

English BA Honours

Film and television

Visual Effects BA Honours, Film BA Honours, Television Production BA Honours, Professional Practice in Visual Effects BA Honours

Postgraduate courses: Professional Practice in Visual Effects MA, Film MA

Interpreting and translation

Legal Interpreting Diploma, Medical Interpreting Diploma, Interpreting and Translation BA Honours

Postgraduate courses: Translation (Business and Legal) MA/PGDip, Translation (Audiovisual and Literary) MA/PGDip

Journalism

Journalism BA Honours, Journalism and Media BA Honours, Creative Writing and Journalism BA Honours

Postgraduate courses:

Media

Popular Music BA Honours, Digital Media BA Honours, Film BA Honours, Television Production BA Honours, Games Design BA/BSc Honours, Journalism and Media BA Honours, Publishing and Digital Culture BA Honours, Media and Cultural Studies BA Honours, Advertising, Public Relations and Media BA Honours

Postgraduate courses: Creative Technology MA/MSc, Media Management MSc

Games

Visual Effects BA Honours, Games Design BA/BSc Honours, Professional Practice in Visual Effects BA Honours, 3D Animation & Games BA Honours

Postgraduate courses: Creative Technology MA/MSc, Professional Practice in Visual Effects MA

Healthcare and Social Work

Healthcare science

Public Health BSc, Healthcare Science (Audiology) BSc Honours, Healthcare Science (Neurophysiology) BSc Honours, Healthcare Science (Cardiac Physiology) BSc Honours

Postgraduate courses: Cardiac Ultrasound MSc/PGDip/PGCert, Cardiac Rhythm Management and Electrophysiology MSc/PGDip/PGCert, Cardiopulmonary Exercise Testing MSc/PGDip/PGCert

Mental health

Nursing (Mental Health) BSc Honours, Higher Apprenticeship/Higher Diploma Care Leadership and Management, Professional Practice in Mental Health Nursing BSc Honours

Postgraduate courses: Mental Health Studies MSc, Dementia Care and Practice GradCert/PGCert, Nursing (Mental Health) (Pre-registration programme) PGDip, Mental Health and Substance Use (Dual Diagnosis) MSc, Professional Practice (Health, Social Care, Public and Community Sectors) MA/MSc

Midwifery

Midwifery Top Up BSc Honours, Midwifery BSc Honours, Midwifery with Professional Registration (Shortened Programme for Registered Adult Nurses) BSc(Hons)

Postgraduate courses: Neonatal Care GradCert/PGCert, Midwifery Studies MSc

Nursing

Nursing Studies BSc Honours, Professional Practice in Nursing BSc Honours, Nursing (Adult) BSc Honours, Nursing Degree (Child) BSc Honours, Veterinary Nursing BSc Honours, Nursing (Mental Health) BSc Honours, European Nursing Degree (Adult) BSc Honours, Professional Practice in Mental Health Nursing BSc Honours, Higher Apprenticeship/Higher Diploma Care Leadership and Management

Postgraduate courses: Nursing (Adult) (Pre-registration programme) PGDip, Nursing (Mental Health) (Pre-registration programme) PGDip, Nursing Studies MSc / Nursing Studies (Advanced Nursing Practice) MSc, Professional Practice (Health, Social Care, Public and Community Sectors) MA/MSc

Social work

Social Work BA Honours

Postgraduate courses: Dementia Care and Practice GradCert/PGCert, Evidence Based Parenting Programmes Supervision & Leadership PGDip, Evidence Based Parenting Programmes Supervision Theory PGCert, Professional Practice (Health, Social Care, Public and Community Sectors) MA/MSc, Social Work MA

Veterinary nursing

Veterinary Nursing BSc Honours

Natural Sciences

Biosciences

Biochemistry BSc Honours, Neuroscience BSc(Hons) BSc Honours, Biology BSc Honours, Foundation Year in Science, Biology (Biotechnology) BSc Honours, Biology (Molecular Biology) BSc Honours, Biology (Environmental Biology) BSc Honours, Psychology with Neuroscience BSc Honours, Medical Biochemistry/Clinical Biochemistry BSc(Hons)/MSci

Postgraduate course: Biodiversity, Evolution and Conservation in Action MSc/PGDip

Environmental, occupational and public health

Public Health BSc, Environmental Health CertHE, Environmental Health BSc Honours, Environmental and Public Health BSc Honours, Occupational Safety, Health and Environment (Top Up) BSc Honours

Postgraduate courses: Applied Public Health MSc/PgDip/PgCert, Global Governance and Sustainable Development MA, Environmental Health MSc, Biodiversity, Evolution and Conservation in Action MSc/

PGDip, Sustainability and Environmental Management MSc, Occupational Safety, Health and Environmental Management MSc/PGDip

Medical science and technology

Biochemistry BSc Honours, Biomedical Engineering BEng(Hons)/MEng, Biomedical Science BSc Honours, Foundation Year in Science, Healthcare Science (Audiology) BSc Honours, Healthcare Science (Cardiac Physiology) BSc Honours, Healthcare Science (Neurophysiology) BSc Honours, Medical Biochemistry/Clinical Biochemistry BSc(Hons)/MSci, Medical Physiology (Cardiovascular Science) BSc Honours, Medical Physiology (Neuroscience) BSc Honours, Neuroscience BSc(Hons) BSc Honours, Nutrition BSc, Pharmaceutical Chemistry BSc/MSci

Postgraduate courses: Biomedical Science (Cellular Pathology) MSc/PGDip/PGCert, Biomedical Science (Clinical Biochemistry) MSc/PGDip/PGCert, Biomedical Science (Haematology and Transfusion Science) MSc/PGDip/PGCert, Biomedical Science (Medical Immunology) MSc/PGDip/PGCert, Biomedical Science (Medical Microbiology) MSc/PGDip/PGCert, Cardiac Rhythm Management and Electrophysiology MSc/PGDip/PGCert, Cardiac Ultrasound MSc/PGDip/PGCert, Cardiopulmonary Exercise Testing MSc/PGDip/PGCert, Clinical Physiology (Cardiology) MSc/PGDip, Clinical Physiology (Neurophysiology) MSc/PGDip

Law

Foundation Year in Law and Social Sciences, International Politics and Law BA Honours, International Politics BA Honours, International Politics, Economics and Law BA Honours, Law BA Honours, LLB Commercial Law, LLB European Law and Politics, LLB Law, LLB Law with Criminology, LLB Law with Human Rights, LLB Law with International Relations

Postgraduate courses: Cybercrime and Digital Investigation MSc, Environmental Law and Justice MA, Global Governance and Sustainable Development MA, International Business Law LLM/PGDip/PGCert, International Relations MA, LLM/PGDip/PGCert Commercial Law, LLM/PGDip/PGCert Employment Law, LLM/PGDip/PGCert European Law, LLM/PGDip/PGCert Human Rights Law, LLM/PGDip/PGCert International Law, LLM/PGDip/PGCert International Minority Rights Law, LLM/PGDip/PGCert Law (General), Migration, Society and Policy MA

Performing Arts

Dance

Dance Studies BA Honours, Foundation Year in Performing Arts, Dance Performance BA Honours

Postgraduate courses: Arts Management MA, Professional Practice, Dance (specialisation) MA, Professional Practice (Somatic Studies) MA, Professional Practice (Dance Technique Pedagogy) MA, Professional Practice in Arts MA

Music

Jazz BA Honours, Music BA Honours, Foundation Year in Performing Arts, Music Business and Arts Management BA Honours

Postgraduate courses: Arts Management MA, Creative Entrepreneurship (Media/Music) MA

Theatre

Theatre Arts BA Honours

Postgraduate courses: Arts Management MA, Theatre Arts MA, Professional Practice in Arts MA

Psychology

Sociology with Psychology BA Honours, Psychology Foundation Year, Psychology BSc Honours, Psychology with Neuroscience BSc Honours, Psychology with Education Degree BSc Honours, Psychology with Counselling Skills BSc Honours, Psychology with Criminology Degree BSc Honours

Postgraduate courses: Health Psychology MSc, Applied Clinical Health Psychology MSc, Criminology with Forensic Psychology MSc, Applied Psychology MSc, Forensic Psychology MSc, Psychology Conversion MSc

Social Sciences

Criminology and policing

Criminology (Policing) BA Honours, Criminology BA Honours, LLB Law with Criminology, Criminology (Youth Justice) BA Honours, Criminology (Criminal Justice) BA Honours, Criminology with Psychology BA Honours, Psychology with Criminology Degree BSc Honours

Postgraduate courses: Criminology with Forensic Psychology MSc, Comparative Drug and Alcohol Studies MA, Criminology MA, Cybercrime and Digital Investigation MSc, Youth Justice, Community Safety and Applied Criminology MA

Politics and international relations

International Politics and Law BA Honours, International Politics BA Honours, International Politics, Economics and Law BA Honours

Postgraduate courses: Environmental Law and Justice MA, Global Governance and Sustainable

Development MA, International Relations MA, Migration, Society and Policy MA

Sociology

Sociology BA Honours, Sociology with Psychology BA Honours, Sociology with Criminology BA Honours, Sociology and Social Policy BA Honours

Postgraduate courses: Comparative Drug and Alcohol Studies MA, Global Governance and Sustainable Development MA, Migration, Society and Policy MA

Sport and Exercise Science and Rehabilitation Courses

Nutrition BSc, Football Science (top-up) BSc Honours, Sport and Exercise Science BSc Honours, Sport and Exercise Rehabilitation BSc Honours, Sport and Community Development (top-up) BA Honours, Sport and Exercise Science (Performance Analysis) BSc Honours, Sport and Exercise Science (Strength and Conditioning) BSc Honours, Sport and Exercise Science (Teaching and Coaching Sport) BSc Honours

Postgraduate courses: Sport Performance Analysis MSc, Sport Rehabilitation MSc/PGDip, Strength and Conditioning MSc, Master of Philosophy MPhil and Doctor of Philosophy PhD, Sport and Exercise Science MSc, Sport and Exercise Nutrition MSc, Sport, Exercise and Physical Activity for Special Populations MSc

---

UNIVERSITY OF NEWCASTLE UPON TYNE
www.ncl.ac.uk

Accounting and Finance

Accounting and Finance BA/BSc Honours, Mathematics and Accounting BSc Honours, Business Accounting and Finance BA Honours

Agri-Business Management

Agri-Business Management BSc Honours, Food Business Management and Marketing BSc Honours

Agriculture

Agri-Business Management BSc Honours, Agriculture BSc Honours, Agriculture with Agronomy BSc Honours, Agriculture with Animal Production Science BSc Honours, Agriculture with Farm Business Management BSc Honours, Applied Plant Science BSc Honours

Postgraduate courses: Agricultural and Environmental Science MSc, Biodiversity Conservation and Ecosystem Management MSc, Environmental Resource Assessment MSc, Food and Rural Development Research MSc, Organic Farming and Food Production Systems MSc, Sustainable Agriculture and Food Security MRes/MSc

Ancient History

Ancient History BA Honours, Ancient History and Archaeology BA Honours

Animal Science

Animal Science BSc Honours

Postgraduate courses: Agricultural and Environmental Science MSc, Animal Behaviour MRes, Applied Animal Behaviour and Welfare MSc, PGDip, Organic Farming and Food Production Systems MSc

Archaeology

Ancient History and Archaeology BA Honours, Archaeology BA Honours, History and Archaeology BA Honours

Postgraduate courses: Archaeology MA, Roman Frontier Studies MA

Architecture, Planning and Landscape

Architecture BA Honours, Architecture and Urban Planning BA Honours, Urban Planning BA Honours

Postgraduate courses: Architectural Design Research MA, Architectural Practice and Management PGDip, Architecture Graduate Diploma, Architecture, Master of (MArch), Architecture, Planning and Landscape MA, Business and Humanities Graduate Diploma, Experimental Architecture MSc, International Spatial Planning MSc, Landscape Architecture Studies MA, Planning and Environment Research MA, Planning for Sustainability and Climate Change MSc, Regional Development and Spatial Planning MA/PGDip, Spatial Planning PGDip, Sustainable Buildings and Environments MSc, Town Planning Diploma/MSc, Urban Design MA/PGDip, Urban Energy Technology and Policy MRes/MSc

Biochemistry

Biochemistry BSc Honours, Biochemistry (Integrated Master's) MSci Honours

Biology and Zoology

Applied Plant Science BSc Honours, Biology BSc Honours, Biology MBiol Honours, Biology (Cellular and Molecular Biology) BSc Honours, Biology (Cellular and Molecular Biology) MBiol Honours, Biology

287

(Ecology and Conservation) BSc Honours, Biology (Ecology and Conservation) MBiol Honours, Biology and Psychology BSc Joint Honours, Zoology BSc Honours, Zoology MBiol Honours

Postgraduate courses: Ecological Consultancy MSc, Industrial and Commercial Biotechnology MSc, Wildlife Management MSc

Biomedical and Biomolecular Sciences

Biochemistry BSc Honours, Biochemistry (Integrated Master's) MSci Honours, Biomedical Genetics BSc Honours, Biomedical Genetics (Integrated Master's) MSci Honours, Biomedical Sciences BSc Honours, Biomedical Sciences (Integrated Master's) MSci Honours, Medical Science (Deferred Choice) BSc Honours, Pharmacology BSc Honours, Physiological Sciences BSc Honours

Postgraduate courses: Ageing and Health MRes, Clinical and Health Sciences with Ageing MSc/PGDip/PGCert, Clinical Research/Clinical Research (Ageing) MClinRes, PGDip/PGCert, Medical Sciences MSc, Musculoskeletal Ageing (CIMA) MRes, Systems Biology MRes, Cardiovascular Science in Health and Disease MRes, Cell Signalling in Health and Disease MRes, Clinical and Health Sciences with Clinical Research MSc/PGDip/PGCert, Clinical and Health Sciences with Molecular Pathology MSc/PGDip/PGCert, Clinical and Health Sciences MSc/PGDip/PGCert, Clinical and Health Sciences with Allergy PGCert, Clinical and Health Sciences with Therapeutics MSc/PGDip/PGCert, Clinical and Health Sciences with Ageing MSc/PGDip/PGCert, Clinical Research/Clinical Research (Ageing) MClinRes/PGDip/PGCert (E-learning), Clinical Research/Clinical Research (Leadership) MClinRes/PGDip/PGCert, Clinical Science (pathways in Medical Physics and Physiological Sciences) MSc, Diabetes MRes, Immunobiology MRes, Medical Sciences MRes/MSc, Medical Technology Innovation MRes, Mitochondrial Biology and Medicine MRes, Musculoskeletal Ageing (CIMA) MRes, Stem Cells and Regenerative Medicine MRes, Systems Biology MRes, Toxicology MRes, Translational Medicine and Therapeutics MRes, Transplantation MRes/PGCert, Biosciences MRes, Medical and Molecular Biosciences MRes, Medical Sciences MRes/MSc, Molecular Microbiology MRes, Systems Biology MRes, Biotechnology and Business Enterprise MRes, Industrial and Commercial Biotechnology MSc, Medical Technology Innovation MRes, Cancer MRes, Cancer Studies PGCert, Medical Sciences MSc, Oncology MSc/PGDip, Oncology for the Pharmaceutical Industry MSc/PGDip, Palliative Care MSc/PGDip, Stem Cells and Regenerative Medicine MRes, Medical Education MMedEd/PGDip/PGCert, Physician Associate Studies PGDip

Business Management

Agri-Business Management BSc Honours, Business Management BA Honours, Food Business Management and Marketing BSc Honours, International Business Management BSc Honours, International Business Management BSc Honours, International Marketing and Management BSc Honours, Marketing and Management BSc Honours

Postgraduate courses: Accounting, Finance and Strategic Investment MSc, Advanced International Business Management and Marketing (Dual Award) MSc/MSc, Advanced International Business Management (Dual Award) MSc/MSc, Arts, Business and Creativity MA, Business and Humanities Graduate Diploma, Business and Humanities Graduate Diploma with Pre-Sessional English, Cross-Cultural Communication and International Management MA, E-Business (E-Marketing) MSc, E-Business (Information Systems) MSc, E-Business MSc, Employee Relations MA/PGDip/PGCert, Global Human Resource Management MSc, Human Resource Management MA, Innovation, Creativity and Entrepreneurship MSc, International Business Management MSc, International Human Resource Management MA, International Marketing MSc, Management and Business Studies (Research) MA/PGDip, Master of Business Administration MBA, Operations Management (Dual Award) MSc/MSc, Operations Management, Logistics and Accounting MSc, Operations, Logistics and Supply Chain Management MSc, Banking and Finance MSc, Finance MSc, Finance, Accounting and Business Graduate Diploma, International Economics and Finance MSc, International Financial Analysis MSc, Operations Management, Logistics and Accounting MSc, Quantitative Finance and Risk Management MSc

Chemical Engineering

Chemical Engineering BEng Honours, Chemical Engineering MEng Honours, Chemical Engineering with Bioprocess Engineering MEng Honours, Chemical Engineering with Process Control MEng Honours, Chemical Engineering with Sustainable Engineering MEng Honours

Postgraduate courses: Applied Process Control MSc/PGDip, Chemical Engineering MSc, Clean Technology MSc/PGDip, Sustainable Chemical Engineering MSc/PGDip

Chemistry

Chemistry BSc/MChem Honours, Chemistry with Medicinal Chemistry BSc/MChem Honours
Postgraduate courses: Chemistry MSc, Drug Chemistry MSc

Civil Engineering

Civil Engineering BEng/MEng Honours, Civil and Structural Engineering BEng/MEng Honours, Civil and Surveying Engineering BEng/MEng Honours
Postgraduate courses: Environmental Engineering MSc, Engineering Geology MSc, Geotechnical Engineering MSc, Structural Engineering MSc, Business and Humanities Graduate Diploma, Transport PGDip, Transport Planning and Business Management MSc, Transport Planning and Engineering MSc, Transport Planning and Intelligent Transport Systems (ITS) MSc, Transport Planning and Modelling MSc, Transport Planning and the Environment MSc, Flood Risk Management MSc, Hydrogeology and Water Management MSc, Hydroinformatics MSc, Hydroinformatics and Water Management (Euro Aquae) MSc, Hydrology and Climate Change MSc

Classics and Ancient History

Ancient History BA Honours, Ancient History and Archaeology BA Honours, Classical Studies BA Honours, Classical Studies and English BA Honours, Classics BA Honours
Postgraduate course: Classics and Ancient History MA, Classics MLitt

Computing Science

Computer Science BSc/MComp Honours, Computer Science (Bio-Computing) BSc/MComp Honours, Computer Science (Game Engineering) BSc/MComp Honours, Computer Science (Human-Computer Interaction) BSc/MComp Honours, Computer Science (Mobile and Distributed Systems) BSc/MComp Honours, Computer Science (Security and Resilience) BSc/MComp Honours, Computer Science (Software Engineering) BSc/MComp Honours
Postgraduate course: Advanced Computer Science MSc, Bioinformatics MSc, Cloud Computing for Big Data MRes/PGDip, Cloud Computing MSc, Computational Neuroscience and Neuroinformatics MSc, Computational Systems Biology MSc, Computer Game Engineering MSc, Computer Science MSc, Computer Security and Resilience MSc, Digital Civics MRes, E-Business MSc, Synthetic Biology MSc, Animal Behaviour MRes, Computational Neuroscience and Neuroinformatics MSc, Evolution and Human Behaviour MRes, Neuroscience MRes

Dentistry

Dental Surgery BDS Honours, Oral and Dental Health Sciences BSc Honours
Postgraduate courses: Clinical Implant Dentistry PGDip, Conscious Sedation in Dentistry PGDip, Orthodontics MSc, Restorative Dentistry MClinDent

Earth Science

Earth Science BSc/MEarthSci Honours

Economics

Economics BSc Honours, Economics and Business Management BA Honours, Economics and Finance BSc Honours
Postgraduate course: International Economics and Finance MSc

Education

Education BA Honours
Postgraduate courses: Business and Humanities Graduate Diploma, Coaching and Mentoring for Teacher Development PGCert, Cross-Cultural Communication and Education MA, Education Research MA, Education: International Perspectives (Development and Education) MA, Education: International Perspectives (Leadership and Management) MA, Education: International Perspectives (Teaching and Learning) MA, Education: International Perspectives (Technology in Education) MA, Educational Leadership PGCert, Educational Research and Innovation PGCert, Innovative Pedagogy and Curriculum PGCert, International Development and Education with Cross Cultural Communication MA, International Development and Education MA, Medical Education MMedEd/PGDip/PGCert, Physician Associate Studies PGDip, Postgraduate Certificate in Education (PGCE) – School Direct, Postgraduate Certificate in Education (PGCE) Primary (with Qualified Teacher Status QTS), Postgraduate Certificate in Education (PGCE) Secondary (with Qualified Teacher Status QTS)

Electrical and Electronic Engineering

Automation and Control BEng/MEng Honours, Digital Electronics BEng/MEng Honours, Electrical and Electronic Engineering BEng/Meng Honours, Electrical Power Engineering BEng/MEng Honours, Electronic Communications BEng/MEng Honours, Electronics and Computer Engineering BEng/MEng Honours, Microelectronic Engineering BEng/MEng Honours
Postgraduate courses: Advanced Electrical Power Engineering MSc, Automation and Control MSc, Communications and Signal Processing MSc,

Electrical Power MSc, Materials Design and Engineering MSc, Microelectronics MSc, Power Distribution Engineering MSc/PGDip/PGCert, Wireless Embedded Systems MSc

English Literature, Language and Linguistics

English Literature and History BA Honours, English Language BA Honours, English Language and Literature BA Honours, English Literature BA Honours, English Literature with Creative Writing BA Honours, Linguistics BA Honours, Linguistics with Chinese or Japanese BA Honours, Linguistics with French BA Honours, Linguistics with German BA Honours, Linguistics with Spanish BA Honours
Postgraduate courses: Creative Writing MA/PGCert, Writing Poetry MA, English Language and/or Linguistics MLitt, English Literature MA/MLitt, Modern and Contemporary Literature MA, Applied Linguistics and TESOL MA, Applied Linguistics Research MA, Clinical Linguistics and Evidence Based Practice (Research) MSc/PGDip, Cross-Cultural Communication and Applied Linguistics MA, English Language and/or Linguistics MLitt, Linguistics (with specialist pathways in English Language, Language Acquisition, and European Languages) MA, Sociolinguistics (Research) MA/PGDip

Environmental and Rural Studies

Countryside Management BSc Honours, Environmental Science BSc Honours, Environmental Sciences (Agricultural and Environmental Science) MEnvSci, Environmental Sciences (Clean Technology) MEnvSci Honours, Environmental Sciences (Ecosystem Management) MEnvSci Honours, Environmental Sciences (Environmental Geochemistry) MEnvSci Honours, Rural Studies BSc Honours
Postgraduate courses: Biodiversity Conservation and Ecosystem Management MSc, Ecological Consultancy MSc, Environmental Resource Assessment MSc, Food and Rural Development Research MSc, Sustainable Agriculture and Food Security MRes/MSc

Exercise

Sport and Exercise Science BSc Honours

Film Studies

Film and Media BA Honours, Film Practices BA Honours
Postgraduate courses: Film Studies MLitt, Film: Theory and Practice MA

Fine Art

Fine Art BA Honours

Postgraduate course: Fine Art MFA,, Art Museum and Gallery Practice MPrac/MA/PGDip, Business and Humanities Graduate Diploma, Heritage Practice MPrac, Heritage Studies MA/PGDip, Heritage, Gallery and Museum Studies PGCert, Heritage, Museums and Galleries MLitt, Museum Practice MPrac/MA/PGDip

Genetics

Biomedical Genetics BSc Honours, Biomedical Genetics (Integrated Master's) MSci Honours
Postgraduate courses: Genomic Medicine MSc/PGDip/PGCert, Medical Genetics MRes, Mitochondrial Biology and Medicine MRes, Neuromuscular Diseases MRes, Stem Cells and Regenerative Medicine MRes

Geography

Geographic Information Science BSc Honours, Geographic Information Science BSc Honours, Geography BSc/BA Honours, Geography and Planning BA Honours, Physical Geography BSc Honours, Surveying and Mapping Science BSc Honours
Postgraduate courses: Environmental and Petroleum Geochemistry MSc, Environmental Consultancy MSc, Petroleum Geochemistry MSc, Business and Humanities Graduate Diploma, Human Geography Research MA, Local and Regional Development (Research) MA, Regional Development and Spatial Planning MA/PGDip

History

History BA Honours, History and Archaeology BA Honours
Postgraduate courses: British History MA, Classics and Ancient History MA, Classics MLitt, European History MA, History MA/MLitt, History MLitt, History of Medicine MA

Journalism

Journalism, Media and Culture BA Honours
Postgraduate course: International Multimedia Journalism MA

Law

Law LLB Honours
Postgraduate courses: Business and Humanities Graduate Diploma, Environmental Law and Policy (Research) LLM, Environmental Regulation and Sustainable Development LLM, International Business Law LLM, International Law LLM, Law and Society (Legal Research) LLM, Law LLM

Marine Sciences

Marine Biology BSc Honours, Marine Biology and Oceanography BSc Honours, Marine Zoology BSc Honours

Marine Technology

Marine Technology with Marine Engineering BEng/MEng Honours, Marine Technology with Naval Architecture BEng/MEng Honours, Marine Technology with Offshore Engineering BEng/MEng Honours, Marine Technology with Small Craft Technology BEng/MEng Honours

Postgraduate courses: Marine Engineering MSc, Marine Technology Education Consortium (MTEC) MSc/PGDip/PGCert, Marine Technology (International) – Singapore MSc, Marine Transport Management MSc, Naval Architecture MSc, Offshore Engineering MSc, Pipeline Engineering MSc/PGDip/PGCert, Subsea Engineering and Management MSc, Technology in the Marine Environment MRes

Marketing

Marketing BSc Honours, Marketing and Management BSc Honours

Postgraduate courses: Advanced International Business Management and Marketing (Dual Award) MSc/MSc, Cross-Cultural Communication and International Marketing MA, E-Business (E-Marketing) MSc, International Marketing MSc, International Marketing MSc (London campus)

Mathematics and Statistics

Mathematics and Accounting BSc Honours, Mathematics and Economics BSc Honours, Mathematics BSc/MMath Honours, Mathematics and Psychology BSc Joint Honours, Mathematics and Statistics BSc/MMath Honours, Mathematics with Finance BSc Honours, Mathematics with Management BSc Honours, Statistics BSc Honours

Mechanical and Systems Engineering

Mechanical and Low Carbon Transport Engineering MEng Honours, Mechanical Design and Manufacturing Engineering BEng/MEng Honours, Mechanical Engineering BEng/MEng Honours, Mechanical Engineering with Biomedical Engineering MEng Honours, Mechanical Engineering with Mechatronics MEng Honours, Mechanical Engineering with Energy MEng Honours

Postgraduate courses: Renewable Energy, Enterprise and Management (REEM) MSc/PGDip/PGCert, Renewable Energy Flexible Training Programme (REFLEX) MSc/PGDip/PGCert, Urban Energy Technology and Policy MRes, Urban Energy Technology and Policy (with specialist pathways in Planning, Architecture) MSc, Biomedical Engineering MSc, Design and Manufacturing Engineering MSc, Mechanical Engineering MSc, Mechatronics MSc, Rail and Logistics MSc/PGDip/PGCert, Sustainable Transport Engineering MSc

Media, Communication and Cultural Studies

Film and Media BA Honours, Film Practices BA Honours, Journalism, Media and Culture BA Honours, Media, Communication and Cultural Studies BA Honours

Postgraduate courses: Creative Arts Practice MA, Cross-Cultural Communication and Media Studies MA, Media and Cultural Studies MPhil, PhD, Media and Journalism MA, Media and Public Relations MA, Media and Society (Research) MA

Medicine

Medicine and Surgery MB BS Honours

Postgraduate courses: Cardiovascular Science in Health and Disease MRes, Clinical and Health Sciences with Clinical Research MSc/PGDip/PGCert, Clinical and Health Sciences with Molecular Pathology MSc/PGDip/PGCert, Clinical and Health Sciences MSc/PGDip/PGCert, Clinical and Health Sciences with Allergy PGCert, Clinical and Health Sciences with Surgery PGCert, Clinical and Health Sciences with Therapeutics MSc/PGDip/PGCert, Clinical and Health Sciences with Ageing MSc/PGDip/PGCert, Clinical Leadership PGCert, Clinical Research/Clinical Research (Ageing) MClinRes/PGDip/PGCert (E-learning), Clinical Research/Clinical Research (Leadership) MClinRes/PGDip/PGCert, Neuromuscular Diseases MRes, Physician Associate Studies PGDip, Translational Medicine and Therapeutics MRes, Transplantation MRes, Epidemiology MRes, Health Services Research MSc/PGDip, Public Health MPH/PGDip, Public Health and Health Services Research MSc/PGDip/PGCert, Social Science and Health Research MSc

Modern Languages

Chinese Studies OR Japanese Studies BA Honours, Modern Languages BA Honours, Modern Languages and Business Studies BA Honours, Modern Languages and Linguistics BA Honours, Modern Languages, Translation and Interpreting, Spanish, Portuguese and Latin American Studies BA Honours

Postgraduate courses: Chinese Studies MLitt, French MLitt, German MLitt, Japanese Studies MLitt, Latin American Interdisciplinary Studies MA, Latin

American Studies MLitt, Portuguese MLitt, Professional Translation for European Languages MA, Spanish MLitt

Music

Contemporary and Popular Music BA Honours, Folk and Traditional Music BA Honours, Music BA/BMus Honours
Postgraduate courses: Music Graduate Diploma, Music MLitt

Nutrition and Food

Food and Human Nutrition BSc Honours, Food Business Management and Marketing BSc Honours, Nutrition and Psychology BSc Joint Honours, Nutrition with Food Marketing BSc Honours
Postgraduate courses: Security MRes/MSc

Pharmacology

Pharmacology BSc Honours

Pharmacy

Pharmacy MPharm Honours

Philosophy

Philosophy BA Honours
Postgraduate course: Philosophy MLitt

Physics

Physics BSc/MPhys Honours, Theoretical Physics BSc/MPhys Honours

Physiological Sciences

Physiological Sciences BSc Honours

Politics

Government and European Union Studies BA Honours, Politics BA Honours, Politics and Economics BA Honours, Politics and History BA Honours, Politics and Sociology BA Honours
Postgraduate courses: Cross-Cultural Communication and International Relations MA, European Union Studies MA, International Politics (Global Justice and Ethics) MA, International Politics (Globalisation, Poverty and Development) MA, International Development and Education MA, International Political Economy MA, International Politics (Critical Geopolitics) MA, International Relations MA, Politics (Research) MA, World Politics and Popular Culture MA

Psychology

Psychology BSc Honours, Psychology and Biology BSc Joint Honours, Psychology and Mathematics BSc Joint Honours, Psychology and Nutrition BSc Joint Honours, Psychology and Sport and Exercise Science BSc Joint Honours
Postgraduate courses: Animal Behaviour MRes, Cognitive Behavioural Therapy for Anxiety Disorders PGCert, Cognitive Behavioural Therapy PGDip, Evolution and Human Behaviour MRes, Forensic Psychology MSc, Foundations in Clinical Psychology MSc, Low Intensity Psychological Therapies PGCert, Neuroscience MRes, Praxis Cognitive Behavioural Therapy Studies PGCert, Psychology (Foundations in Clinical and Forensic Psychology) MSc

Sociology

Sociology BA Honours
Postgraduate courses: Sociology and Social Research MA, Sociology MA

Speech and Language Sciences

Speech and Language Sciences BSc Honours, Speech and Language Therapy BSc Honours
Postgraduate course: Master of Speech and Language Sciences MSc Honours, Clinical Linguistics and Evidence Based Practice (Research) MSc/PGDip, Language Pathology MSc

Sport and Exercise Science

Sport and Exercise Science BSc Honours

Surveying and Mapping Science

Postgraduate course: Master of Planning MPlan Honours

TESOL, Cross-Cultural Communication, Translating and Intrepreting

Postgraduate courses: Applied Linguistics and TESOL MA, Cross-Cultural Communication and Applied Linguistics MA, Cross-Cultural Communication and Education MA, Cross-Cultural Communication and Media Studies MA, Cross-Cultural Communication and International Marketing MA, Cross-Cultural Communication and International Relations MA, Cross-Cultural Communication and International Management MA, Cross-Cultural Communication MA, Educational and Applied Linguistics Integrated PhD, International Development and Education with Cross Cultural Communication MA, Interpreting MA, Professional Translation for European Languages MA, Translating and Interpreting MA, Translating MA, Translation Studies MA, Translation Studies MLitt

Zoology

Marine Zoology BSc Honours, Zoology BSc/MBiol Honours

UNIVERSITY OF NORTHAMPTON
www.northampton.ac.uk

Faculty of Health and Society; www.northampton.ac.uk/about-us/ academic-faculties

Adult Nursing BSc(Hons), Applied Criminal Justice Studies (Top-Up) BA(Hons), Child Nursing BSc(Hons), Criminology BA(Hons), Criminology (Joint Honours) BA/BSc(Hons), Dental Nursing FdSc, Health and Social Care FdSc, Health and Social Care (Top-up) BSc(Hons), Health Studies (Joint Honours) BA/BSc(Hons), Human Bioscience BSc(Hons), Investigative Practice BA(Hons), Learning Disability Nursing BSc(Hons), Mental Health Nursing BSc(Hons), Midwifery BSc(Hons), Occupational Therapy BSc(Hons), Paramedic Science FdSc, Paramedic Science BSc(Hons), Podiatry BSc(Hons), Policing BA(Hons), Professional Practice (Top-Up) BSc(Hons), Psychology BSc(Hons), Psychology – Developmental and Educational BSc(Hons), Psychology (Joint Honours) BA/BSc(Hons), Psychology and Counselling BSc(Hons), Psychology and Criminology (Joint Honours) BA/BSc(Hons), Social and Community Development BA(Hons), Social Care (Joint Honours) BSc(Hons), Social Care and Health Studies (Joint Honours) BA/BSc(Hons), Social Work BA(Hons), Sociology BA(Hons), Sociology (Joint Honours) BA/BSc(Hons), Sociology and Psychology (Joint Honours) BA/BSc(Hons), Sport and Exercise Science BSc(Hons), Sport Development and Physical Education BA(Hons), Sports Studies (Joint Honours) BA/BSc(Hons), Sports Studies and Psychology (Joint Honours) BA/BSc(Hons), Sports Therapy BSc(Hons), Sports Therapy FdSc

Postgraduate courses: Advanced Occupational Therapy PGCert, Advanced Professional Practice MSc, Advanced Professional Practice (Occupational Therapy) MSc, Child and Adolescent Mental Health Services (CAMHs) MSc, Counselling MSc, Counselling Children and Young People MSc, Leadership for Health & Social Care MSc, Public Health MSc, Social Work MA, Specialist Community Public Health Nursing PGDip, Strength and Conditioning MSc

Faculty of Education and Humanities; www.northampton.ac.uk/about-us/ academic-faculties

Childhood and Youth BA(Hons), Creative Writing BA(Hons), Creative Writing (Joint Honours) BA(Hons), Early Childhood Studies BA(Hons), Early Years Foundation Degree FdA, Education Studies BA(Hons), Education Studies (Joint Honours) BA/BSc(Hons), English BA(Hons), English (Joint Honours) BA(Hons), English and Education Studies Joint Honours BA/BSc(Hons), Higher Level Teaching Assistant (HLTA), History BA(Hons), History (Heritage) BA, History (Joint Honours) BA/BSc(Hons), History and Education Studies Joint Honours BA(Hons), History and English (Joint Honours) BA/BSc(Hons), International Business Communications (Top-Up) BA(Hons), Learning and Teaching (FDLT), Learning and Teaching (top-up) BA(Hons), OCR Level 5 and Level 7 Diploma Specific Learning Difficulties/Dyslexia University Diploma, Primary Education 5-11 (QTS) BA(Hons), Special Educational Needs and Inclusion BA(Hons)

Postgraduate courses: Early Years Teacher Status (0-5), Education MA, Education (Early Years Pathway) MA, Education (English Language Teaching) MA, Education (Mathematics Pathway) MA, Education Management and Leadership MA, English – Contemporary Literature MA, History MA, PGCE QTS Primary Education School Direct Route PGCE, PGCE Top-up Primary/Early Years/Secondary, Postgraduate Certificate in Primary English PGCert, Postgraduate Certificate Primary Computing PGCert, Postgraduate Certificate Primary Maths PGCert, Primary Education (3-7) (QTS) PGCE, Primary Education (5-11) (QTS) PGCE, Special Educational Needs and Inclusion MA, Special Educational Needs and Inclusion (Autism Pathway) MA, The National Award for SEN Co-ordination PGCert

Faculty of Business and Law; www.northampton.ac.uk/about-us/ academic-faculties

Accounting (fast track NHS) FdA, Accounting (Joint Honours) BA/BSc(Hons), Accounting and Finance BSc(Hons), Advertising (Joint Honours) BA/BSc(Hons), Advertising & Digital Marketing BA(Hons), Banking and Financial Planning BSc(Hons), Business HND, Business (Joint Honours) BA/BSc(Hons), Business and Accounting (Joint Honours) BA/BSc(Hons), Business and Business Entrepreneurship (Joint Honours) BA/BSc(Hons), Business and Management (Top-Up) BA(Hons), Business Entrepreneurship FdA, Business Entrepreneurship BA(Hons), Business Entrepreneurship (Joint

Honours) BA/BSc(Hons), Business Studies BA(Hons), Economics BSc(Hons), Economics (Joint Honours) BA/BSc(Hons), Economics and Accounting (Joint Honours) BA/BSc(Hons), Economics and Business (Joint Honours) BA/BSc(Hons), Events Management BA(Hons), Events Management (Joint Honours) BA/BSc(Hons), Events Management (Top-up) BA(Hons), Fashion Marketing BA(Hons), Human Resource Management BA(Hons), Human Resource Management PGDip, Human Resource Management (Joint Honours) BA/BSc(Hons), Human Resource Management (Top-Up) BA(Hons), Human Resource Management and Business (Joint Honours) BA/BSc(Hons), International Accounting BSc(Hons), International Business BA(Hons), International Development BA(Hons), International Development (Joint Honours) BA/BSc(Hons), International Development and Economics (Joint Honours) BA/BSc(Hons), International Hospitality Management Top-up BA, International Logistics and Trade Finance (Top-Up) BA(Hons), International Relations and Politics BA(Hons), International Tourism Management BA(Hons), International Tourism Management (Joint Honours) BA/BSc(Hons), International Tourism Management (Top-Up) BA(Hons), International Tourism Management and Events Management (Joint Honours) BA/BSc(Hons), Law LLB(Hons), Law (Joint Honours) BA/BSc(Hons), Law and Business (Joint Honours) BA/BSc(Hons), Management BA(Hons), Management (Joint Honours) BA(Hons), Management and Business Entrepreneurship (Joint Honours) BA/BSc(Hons), Management and International Tourism Management (Joint Honours) BA/BSc(Hons), Marketing (Joint Honours) BA/BSc(Hons), Marketing and Advertising (Joint Honours) BA/BSc(Hons), Marketing and Business (Joint Honours) BA/BSc(Hons), Marketing and Events Management (Joint Honours) BA/BSc(Hons), Marketing and Management (Joint Honours) BA/BSc(Hons), Marketing Management BSc(Hons), Marketing Management (Top-Up) BA(Hons), Psychology and Marketing (Joint Honours) BA/BSc(Hons), Supply Chain Leadership FdA, Travel and Tourism Management HND

Postgraduate courses: Accounting and Finance MSc, Accounting and Finance (Top-up) MSc, Corporate Governance and Leadership MSc, Economics MSc, Human Resource Management (Top-Up) MA, International Banking and Finance MSc, International Commercial Law LLM, International Criminal Law and Security (LLM ICLAS) LLM, International Hotel Management MA, International Logistics MSc, International Marketing Strategy MSc, International Relations MA, International Special Events Management MSc, International Tourism Development MA, IT Service Management (Distance Learning) MSc, Legal Practice LLM, Management MSc, Marketing Top-Up MA, Master of Business Administration MBA, Master of Business Administration (Executive) MBA, Project Management MSc, Social Innovation MA

Faculty of Arts, Science and Technology; www.northampton.ac.uk/about-us/academic-faculties

Acting BA(Hons), Acting (Creative Theatre) BA(Hons), Architectural Technology BSc(Hons), Biology BSc(Hons), Business Computing (Systems) BSc(Hons), Business Computing (Systems) HND, Business Computing (Web Design) HND, Business Computing (Web Design) BSc(Hons), Civil Engineering (top-up) BSc(Hons), Computer Games Development BSc(Hons), Computer Networks Engineering BEng(Hons)/MEng, Computing BSc(Hons), Computing HND, Computing (Computer Networks Engineering) HND, Computing (Computer Networks Engineering) BEng(Hons), Computing (Computer Systems Engineering) BEng(Hons), Computing (Computer Systems Engineering) HND, Computing (Graphics and Visualisation) HND, Computing (Graphics and Visualisation) BSc(Hons), Computing (Mobile Computing) BSc(Hons), Computing (Software Engineering) HND, Computing (Software Engineering) BSc(Hons), Computing (Web Technology and Security) HND, Computing (Web Technology and Security) BSc(Hons), Countryside and Wildlife Management FdSc, Drama BA(Hons), Drama (Joint Honours) BA/BSc(Hons), Engineering HND, Engineering BSc(Hons), Environmental Science BSc(Hons), Fashion Promotion and Communication BA(Hons), Film and Screen Studies (Joint Honours) BA/BSc(Hons), Fine Art BA(Hons), Fine Art Painting and Drawing BA(Hons), Footwear and Accessories BA(Hons), Geography BSc(Hons), Geography (Human Geography) BSc(Hons), Geography (Physical Geography) BSc(Hons), Graphic Communication BA(Hons), Human Geography (Joint Honours) BA/BSc(Hons), Illustration BA(Hons), Interior Design BA(Hons), Leather for Fashion BA(Hons), Leather Technology top-up BSc(Hons), Leatherseller's Certificate/Diploma, Lift Engineering FdSc/HNC, Mechanical Engineering BEng(Hons)/MEng, Media Production & Moving Image (Joint Honours) BA/BSc(Hons), Media Production and Moving Image

BA(Hons), Media Production and Multimedia Journalism Joint Honours BA(Hons), Multimedia Journalism BA(Hons), Multimedia Journalism (Joint Honours) BA/BSc(Hons), Multimedia Sports Journalism BA(Hons), Non-Destructive Testing FdSc, Photography BA(Hons), Popular Music BA(Hons), Popular Music (Joint Honours) BA/BSc, Product Design BSc, Product Design HND, Wastes Management (distance learning) HNC

Postgraduate courses: Computing MSc, Computing (Computer Networks Engineering) MSc, Computing (Internet Technology and Security) MSc, Computing (Serious Games) MSc, Computing (Software Engineering) MSc, Engineering MSc, Fine Art MA, International Environmental Management (distance learning), Leather Technology (Professional) MSc, Lift Engineering MSc, Wastes Management (Distance Learning) MSc

UNIVERSITY OF NORTHUMBRIA AT NEWCASTLE
www.northumbria.ac.uk

Department of Applied Sciences; www.northumbria.ac.uk/about-us/academic-departments/applied-sciences

Biology BSc(Hons), Biomedical Science BSc(Hons), Chemistry BSc(Hons), Chemistry MChem, Criminology and Forensic Science BSc(Hons), Food Science and Nutrition BSc(Hons), Forensic Science BSc(Hons), Medical Sciences Diploma (followed by study on the Doctor of Medicine degree at St. George's University in Grenada)

Postgraduate courses: Biotechnology MSc, Forensic Science MSc, Microbiology MSc, Nutritional Science MSc

Department of Architecture and Built Environment; www.northumbria.ac.uk/about-us/academic-departments/architecture-and-built-environment

Architecture BA(Hons), Building Surveying BSc(Hons), Interior Architecture BA(Hons), Quantity Surveying Bsc, Real Estate BSc(Hons)

Postgraduate courses: Architecture MArch, Interior Architecture Postgraduate Certificate, Real Estate (International) MSc, Real Estate MSc, Surveying (Building Surveying) MSc, Surveying (Housing) MSc, Surveying (Quantity Surveying) MSc, Surveying (Real Estate) MSc

Department of Arts; www.northumbria.ac.uk/about-us/academic-departments/arts

Animation BA(Hons), Art and Design History BA(Hons), Drama BA(Hons), Film and Television Studies BA(Hons), Film and TV Production BA(Hons), Fine Art BA(Hons)

Postgraduate courses: Animation MA, Arts MRes, Conservation of Fine Art MA, Creative and Cultural Industries Management MA, Master of Fine Art (MFA), Preventive Conservation MA, Theatre and Performance MA

Department of Computer and Information Sciences; www.northumbria.ac.uk/about-us/academic-departments/computer-and-information-sciences

Applied Computing (top-up award) BSc(Hons), Computer and Digital Forensics BSc(Hons)/MComp, Computer Networks and Cyber Security BSc(Hons)/MComp, Computer Science BSc(Hons)/MComp, Computer Science with Animation, Graphics and Vision BSc(Hons)/MComp, Computer Science with Artificial Intelligence BSc(Hons)/MComp, Computer Science with Games Development BSc(Hons)/MComp, Computer Science with Web Development BSc(Hons)/MComp, Information Technology and Data Science BSc(Hons), Information Technology Management for Business BSc(Hons)

Postgraduate courses: Computer Network Technology MSc, Computer Science MSc, Computing and Information Technology MSc, Computing and Information Technology MSc (London Campus), Computing and Information Technology with Advanced Practice (London Campus)) MSc, Cyber Security MSc (London Campus), Cyber Security MSc Part-time (London Campus), Cyber Security with Advanced Practice MSc (London Campus), Information Science (Data Analytics) MSc, Information Science MSc – Library Management, Web and Mobile Development Technologies (Part-time) MSc, Multidisciplinary Innovation MA MSc

Department of Geography and Environmental Sciences; www.northumbria.ac.uk/about-us/ academic-departments/geography

Environmental Geography BSc(Hons), Environmental Science BSc(Hons), Geography BA/BSc(Hons), Human Geography (MGeog), Physical Geography MGeog/BSc(Hons)

Postgraduate courses: Disaster Management and Sustainable Development MSc, Environmental Health MSc, Safety, Health and Environmental Management MSc

Department of Humanities; www.northumbria.ac.uk/about-us/ academic-departments/humanities

American Studies BA(Hons), English Language and Literature BA(Hons), English Language Studies BA(Hons), English Literature and Creative Writing BA(Hons), English Literature and History BA(Hons), English Literature BA(Hons), History and Politics BA(Hons), History BA(Hons)

Postgraduate courses: Applied Linguistics for TESOL MA, Creative Writing MA, English Literature MA, English Literature MRes, History MA, History MRes, TESOL MA

Department of Mathematics, Physics and Electrical Engineering; www.northumbria.ac.uk/about-us/ academic-departments/mathematics- physics-and-electrical-engineering

Electrical and Electronic Engineering BEng/MEng(Hons), Electronic Design Engineering Top Up BEng, Mathematics BSc/MMath(Hons), Mobile Communications Engineering (top-up award) BEng(Hons), Physics BSc(Hons), Physics MPhys(Hons), Physics with Astrophysics BSc/MPhys(Hons)

Postgraduate courses: Electrical Power Engineering MSc, Microelectronic and Communications Engineering MSc

Department of Mechanical and Construction Engineering; www.northumbria.ac.uk/about-us/ academic-departments/mechanical-and- construction-engineering

Automotive Engineering BEng/MEng(Hons), Building Services Engineering BEng/MEng(Hons), Civil Engineering BEng/MEng(Hons), Construction Engineering Management BSc(Hons), Mechanical and Architectural Engineering BEng/MEng(Hons), Mechanical and Automotive Engineering BEng/ MEng(Hons), Mechanical Engineering BEng/ MEng(Hons)

Postgraduate courses: Construction Project Management with BIM MSc, Engineering Management MSc, Mechanical Engineering MSc, Pipeline Integrity Management MSc/PGDip, Professional Practice in Project Management MSc Part-time (London Campus), Project Management MSc, Renewable and Sustainable Energy Technologies MSc

Newcastle Business School; www.northumbria.ac.uk/about-us/ academic-departments/newcastle- business-school

Accounting and Finance BA(Hons), Accounting BA(Hons), Business (top up award) BA(Hons), Business (with Law) BA(Hons), Business and Finance (top up award) BA(Hons), Business and International Management (top up award) BA(Hons), Business and Marketing (top up award) BA(Hons), Business Enterprise, Creation and Management BA(Hons) (London Campus), Business Leadership and Management Practice BA(Hons) Degree Apprenticeship, Business Management BA(Hons), Business Top-up BA(Hons) (London Campus), Business with Accounting BA(Hons), Business with Economics BA(Hons), Business with Entrepreneurship BA(Hons), Business with Financial Management BA(Hons), Business with Human Resource Management BA(Hons), Business with International Management BA(Hons), Business with Logistics and Supply Chain Management BA(Hons), Business with Management BA(Hons), Business with Marketing Management BA(Hons), Business with Tourism Management BA(Hons), Entrepreneurial Business Management BA(Hons), Finance and Investment Management BA(Hons), Human Resource Management BA(Hons), International Banking and Finance (Completion award) BA(Hons), International Business Management BA(Hons), International Business Management with French BA(Hons), International Business Management with Spanish BA(Hons), International Hospitality and Tourism Management (Top-Up) BA(Hons), Leadership and Management BA(Hons), Logistics and Supply Management BA(Hons), Marketing Management BA(Hons), Tourism and Events Management BA(Hons)

Postgraduate courses: Business Graduate Diploma, Business with Business Analytics MSc, Business with Entrepreneurship MSc, Business with Entrepreneurship with Advanced Practice (London) MSc, Business with Financial Management MSc, Business with

Hospitality and Tourism Management MSc, Business with Human Resource Management MSc, Business with International Management and Finance MSc, Business with International Management MSc, Business with Logistics and Supply Chain Management MSc, Business with Management and Marketing MSc, Business with Management MSc, Business with Marketing Management MSc, Coaching MA/PGCert/PGDip, Digital Marketing MSc, Forensic Accounting MSc/PGCert, Global Logistics, Operations and Supply Chain Management MSc, Human Resource Management and Development MA, International Business Management MSc, International Finance and Investment MSc, International Financial Management MSc, Leadership and Management MSc, MBA, MSc Business with Management and Finance, MSc Digital Marketing with Advanced Practice (London Campus), Multidisciplinary Innovation MA MSc

Northumbria Law School; www.northumbria.ac.uk/about-us/academic-departments/northumbria-law-school

Law LLB(Hons), Law with Business LLB(Hons), Law with International Business LLB(Hons), M Law
Postgraduate courses: Advanced Legal Practice LLM, Commercial Law LLM, Data Protection Law and Information Governance Postgraduate Certificate, Employment Law in Practice Postgraduate Certificate/Diploma/LLM, Information Rights Law and Practice Postgraduate Certificate, International Commercial Law LLM, Legal Practice Postgraduate Diploma, LLM in Bar Professional Training, LLM in Legal Practice, Medical Law Postgraduate Certificate, Mental Health Law Postgraduate Certificate/Diploma/LLM, Professional Practice in Mental Health Law Postgraduate Certificate

Northumbria School of Design; www.northumbria.ac.uk/about-us/academic-departments/northumbria-school-of-design

3D Design BA(Hons), Design for Industry BA(Hons), Fashion BA(Hons), Fashion Communication BA(Hons), Fashion Design and Marketing BA(Hons), Graphic Design BA(Hons), Interaction Design BA(Hons), Interactive Media Design BA(Hons), Interior Design BA(Hons)
Postgraduate courses: Design MA, Design Management MA, Design Management MA (London Campus), Design MRes, Multidisciplinary Innovation MA MSc

Department of Nursing, Midwifery & Health; www.northumbria.ac.uk/about-us/academic-departments/nursing-midwifery-health

Midwifery Studies BSc(Hons), Nursing Science BSc(Hons), Nursing Studies/Registered Nurse Adult BSc(Hons), Nursing Studies/Registered Nurse Child BSc(Hons), Nursing Studies/Registered Nurse Learning Disabilities BSc(Hons), Nursing Studies/Registered Nurse Mental Health BSc(Hons), Operating Department Practice Diploma of Higher Education
Postgraduate courses: Master of Clinical Practice (Advanced Critical Care Practice), Midwifery Studies PGDip, Nursing (Adult) MNurs, Nursing (Child) MNurs, Nursing (Mental Health) MNurs, Nursing Leadership MSc, Nursing MSc, Professional Non-Surgical Aesthetic Practice MSc/PGCert, Teaching and Learning in Professional Practice PGCert

Department of Psychology; www.northumbria.ac.uk/about-us/academic-departments/psychology

Psychology BSc(Hons), Psychology with Criminology BSc(Hons)
Postgraduate courses: Health Psychology MSc, Occupational and Organisational Psychology MSc, Psychology MRes, Psychology MSc, Sport and Exercise Psychology MSc

Department of Social Sciences; www.northumbria.ac.uk/about-us/academic-departments/social-sciences-languages

Criminology and Sociology BSc(Hons), Criminology BSc(Hons), International Relations and Politics BA(Hons), Journalism and English Literature BA(Hons), Journalism BA(Hons), Mass Communication (Completion Award) BA(Hons), Mass Communication BA(Hons), Mass Communication with Advertising BA(Hons), Mass Communication with Business BA(Hons), Mass Communication with Public Relations BA(Hons), Media and Journalism BA(Hons), Sociology BSc(Hons)
Postgraduate courses: Criminology and Criminal Justice MA, International Development MSc, Mass Communication Management MSc, Social Sciences MRes

Department of Social Work, Education & Community Wellbeing; www.northumbria.ac.uk/about-us/ academic-departments/social-work-education-community-wellbeing

Childhood and Early Years Studies BA(Hons), Guidance and Counselling BA(Hons), Integrated Health and Social Care BSc(Hons), Occupational Therapy BSc(Hons), Primary Education BA(Hons), Social Work BSc(Hons)

Postgraduate courses: Autism MA, Early Years and Primary (Flexible) PGCE, Early Years Education (Early Years Teacher Status) PGCert, Education MA, Master of Education, Master of Public Health, Occupational Therapy (Pre-Registration) MSc, Primary Education PGCE, Secondary Art, Craft and Design PGCE, Social Work MA, Teaching Pupils with Dyslexia within an Education and Training Setting PGCert

Department of Sport, Exercise and Rehabilitation; www.northumbria.ac.uk/ about-us/academic-departments/sport-exercise-and-rehabilitation

Applied Sport and Exercise Science BSc(Hons), Applied Sport Science with Coaching BSc(Hons), Physiotherapy BSc(Hons), Sport Coaching BSc(Hons), Sport Development BA(Hons), Sport Management BSc(Hons), Sport, Exercise and Nutrition BSc(Hons)

Clinical Exercise Physiology MSc, Exercise Science MRes, International Sport Management MSc, Physiotherapy (Pre-registration) MSc, Strength and Conditioning MSc

UNIVERSITY OF NOTTINGHAM
www.nottingham.ac.uk

Faculty of Arts; www.nottingham.ac.uk/ arts

American and Canadian Studies

American and Canadian Literature, History and Culture BA, American and Canadian Literature, History and Culture (International Study) BA, Film and Television Studies and American Studies BA, American Studies and English BA, American Studies and History BA, American Studies and Latin American Studies BA, Politics and American Studies BA

Postgraduate courses: American Studies MA, American and Canadian Studies MRes, Comparative Literature MA, Languages and Intercultural Studies MA

Archaeology

Archaeology BA, Archaeology BSc, Historical Archaeology BA, Ancient History and Archaeology BA, Archaeology and Classical Civilisation BA, Archaeology and Geography BA, Archaeology and History of Art BA

Postgraduate courses: Archaeological Science MSc (by Research), Archaeology MA (by Research)

Classics

Classics BA, Classics and English BA, Classical Civilisation BA, Latin BA

Postgraduate courses: Ancient History MA, Classical Literature MA, The Visual Culture of Classical Antiquity MA, Classical Civilisation and Philosophy BA

Culture, Film and Media

Film and Television Studies BA, International Media and Communications Studies BA, Film and Television Studies and American Studies BA

Postgraduate courses: Critical Theory and Cultural Studies MA, Critical Theory and Politics MA, Cultural Industries and Entrepreneurship MSc, International Media and Communication Studies MA, Film, Television and Screen Industries MA

English

English BA, English Language and Literature BA, English with Creative Writing BA, English and French BA, English and German BA, English and Hispanic Studies BA, English and History BA, English and Philosophy BA

Postgraduate courses: Applied Linguistics MA, Applied Linguistics and English Language Teaching MA, Applied Linguistics and English Language Teaching by Web-based Distance Learning MA, Applied Linguistics by Web-based Distance Learning MA, Communication and Entrepreneurship MSc, Creative Writing MA, English Literature MA, English Studies MA, English Studies by Web-based Distance Learning MA, Health Communication by Web-based Distance Learning MA, Literary Linguistics MA, Literary Linguistics by Web-based Distance Learning MA, Modern English Language by Web-based Distance Learning MA, Viking and Anglo-Saxon Studies MA

French and Francophone Studies

French Studies BA, Modern European Studies BA, French and Contemporary Chinese Studies BA, French and History BA, French and Politics BA, French and Philosophy BA, French and International Media and Communications Studies BA

Postgraduate courses: Languages and Intercultural Studies MA, Digital Technologies for Language Teaching (Distance Learning) MA, French MA (by research), Translation Studies MA

German Studies

German BA, German and Contemporary Chinese Studies BA, German and History BA, Modern European Studies BA, German and Politics BA, German and International Media and Communications Studies BA

Postgraduate courses: German MA (by research), Digital Technologies for Language Teaching (Distance Learning) MA, Translation Studies MA

History

History BA, Ancient History and History BA, History and History of Art BA, History and Politics BA, History with Contemporary Chinese Studies BA, History and East European Cultural Studies BA

Postgraduate course: History MA

History of Art

History of Art and English BA, History of Art BA

Postgraduate courses: Art History MA, Visual Culture MA

Modern Languages

Modern Languages BA, Modern European Studies BA, Modern Language Studies BA, Modern Languages with Business BA, Modern Languages with Translation BA

Postgraduate courses: Chinese/English Translation & Interpreting MA, Comparative Literature MA, Languages and Intercultural Studies MA, Digital Technologies for Language Teaching (Distance Learning) MA, Southeast European Studies MA (by research), Translation Studies MA

Music

Music BA, Music and Music Technology BA, Music and Philosophy BA

Postgraduate courses: Music MA

Philosophy

Philosophy and Theology BA, Philosophy BA, Philosophy, Politics and Economics BA

Postgraduate courses: Philosophy MA

Russian and Slavonic Studies

Russian Studies BA, Russian and Contemporary Chinese Studies BA, Russian and History BA, History and East European Cultural Studies BA

Postgraduate courses: Russian Studies MA (by research), Slavonic Studies MA (by research), Southeast European Studies MA (by research), Translation Studies MA

Spanish, Portuguese and Latin American Studies

Portuguese and International Media and Communications Studies BA, Economics with Hispanic Studies BA, Hispanic Studies and History BA, Hispanic Studies BA, Spanish and Contemporary Chinese Studies BA, Spanish and International Media and Communications Studies BA

Postgraduate courses: Modern Languages MA (by research), Digital Technologies for Language Teaching (Distance Learning) MA, Comparative Literature MA, Languages and Intercultural Studies MA, Translation Studies MA

Theology and Religious Studies

Theology and Religious Studies BA, Biblical Studies and Theology BA, Religion, Culture and Ethics BA, Religion, Philosophy and Ethics BA

Postgraduate courses: Church History (distance learning) MA, Systematic and Philosophical Theology (distance learning) MA

Faculty of Engineering; www.nottingham.ac.uk/engineering

Aerospace

Aerospace Engineering BEng/MEng

Postgraduate course: Aerospace Technologies MSc

Architecture and Built Environment

BArch/MArch Architecture, Architectural Environment Engineering BEng, Architecture and Environmental Design MEng

Postgraduate courses: Design MArch, Digital Architecture and Tectonics MArch, Energy Conversion and Management MSc, Environmental Design MArch, Professional Practice in Architecture PGCert ARB RIBA Part 3, Renewable Energy and Architecture MSc, Sustainable Building Technology MSc, Sustainable Building Technology Collaborative MSc, Sustainable Energy and Entrepreneurship MSc, Sustainable Urban Design MArch

Chemical and Environmental Engineering

Chemical Engineering BEng/MEng, Chemical Engineering with Environmental Engineering BEng/MEng, Environmental Engineering BEng/MEng

Postgraduate courses: Chemical Engineering MSc, Environmental Engineering MSc, Efficient Fossil Energy Technologies MSc, Bioengineering MSc, Bioengineering: Biomaterials and Biomechanics MSc, Sustainable Energy Engineering MSc

Civil Engineering

Civil Engineering BEng/MEng

Postgraduate courses: Civil Engineering MSc, Civil Engineering: Structural Engineering MSc, Environmental Management and Earth Observation MSc

Electrical and Electronic Engineering

Electrical and Electronic Engineering BEng/MEng, Electrical Engineering BEng/MEng, Electronic Engineering BEng/MEng, Electronic and Computer Engineering BEng/MEng

Postgraduate courses: Electrical Engineering MSc, Electrical and Electronic Engineering MSc, Electrical and Electronic Engineering and Entrepreneurship MSc, Electrical Engineering for Sustainable and Renewable Energy MSc, Electronic Communications and Computer Engineering MSc, Modern Telecommunications MSc, Power Electronics and Drives MSc, Sustainable Transportation and Electrical Power Systems Erasmus Mundus MSc, Sustainable Energy Engineering MSc

Mechanical, Materials and Manufacturing Engineering

Manufacturing Engineering BEng/MEng, Mechanical Engineering BEng/MEng, Product Design and Manufacture BEng/MEng

Postgraduate courses: Advanced Materials MSc, Applied Ergonomics and Human Factors (Distance Learning) MSc/PGCert, Human Factors and Ergonomics MSc, Manufacturing Engineering and Management MSc, Bioengineering MSc, Mechanical Engineering MSc, Human Computer Interaction MSc, Bioengineering: Biomaterials and Biomechanics MSc

Medicine and Health Sciences; www.nottingham.ac.uk/mhs

Applied Psychology

Postgraduate courses: Clinical Psychology DClinPsy, Forensic Psychology – Full Programme DForenPsy, Forensic Psychology – top-up programme DForenPsy, Health Psychology MSc, Management Psychology MSc, Management Psychology PGDip, Mental Health Research MSc, Occupational Psychology MSc, Rehabilitation Psychology MSc, Work and Organisational Psychology MSc, Work and Organisational Psychology PGDip, Workplace Health and Wellbeing MSc (Distance eLearning)

Medical Physiology and Therapeutics

Medical Physiology and Therapeutics BSc

Postgraduate courses:

Medicine

Medicine BMBS

Postgraduate courses: Assisted Reproduction Technology MMedSci, Oncology MSc, Applied Sport and Exercise Medicine MSc, Cancer Immunology and Biotechnology MSc, Drug Discovery and Pharmaceutical Sciences MSc, Health Psychology MSc, Management Psychology MSc, Master of Public Health MPH, Medical Education MMedSci, Mental Health Research MSc, Occupational Psychology MSc, Oncology PGCert, Public Health (International Health) MPH, Rehabilitation Psychology MSc, Sports and Exercise Medicine MSc, Stem Cell Technology MSc, Work and Organisational Psychology MSc, Work and Organisational Psychology PGDip, Workplace Health and Wellbeing MSc (Distance eLearning), Immunology and Allergy MSc, Microbiology and Immunology MSc, Molecular Genetics and Diagnostics MSc, Clinical Microbiology MSc (Distance Learning), Clinical and Molecular Microbiology MSc, Cancer Immunology and Biotechnology MSc

Nursing, Midwifery, Physiotherapy and Rehabilitation Sciences

Midwifery BSc(Hons), Nursing (Adult) BSc, Nursing (Child) BSc, Nursing (Mental Health) BSc, Nursing (Graduate Entry) Adult MSc, Nursing (Graduate Entry) Child MSc, Nursing (Graduate Entry) Mental Health MSc, Physiotherapy BSc, Sport Rehabilitation BSc

Postgraduate courses: Advanced Clinical Practice MSc, Advanced Clinical Skills PGCert, Advanced Nursing MSc, Cognitive Behavioural Therapy MSc, Cognitive Behavioural Therapy PGDip, Graduate Entry Nursing – Adult MSc, Graduate Entry Nursing – Child Branch MSc, Graduate Entry Nursing – Mental Health MSc, Quality and Patient Safety Improvement MSc, Quality and Patient Safety Improvement PGCert, Quality and Patient Safety Improvement PGDip, Maternal and Newborn Health MSc, Midwifery MSc, Midwifery PGDip, Physiotherapy MSc, Physiotherapy PGDip, Physiotherapy PGCert, Practice Teacher in Health and Social Care PGCert, Research Methods (Health) MA

Sport and Exercise Science

Sport and Exercise Science BSc

Veterinary Medicine and Science

Veterinary Medicine and Surgery – BVM BVS with BVMed Sci

Postgraduate courses: Veterinary Education PGCert, Veterinary Medicine and Surgery PGCert

Faculty of Science; www.nottingham.ac.uk/science

Biochemistry

Biochemistry BSc, Biochemistry MSci, Biochemistry and Biological Chemistry BSc, Biochemistry and

Biological Chemistry MSci, Biochemistry and Genetics BSc, Biochemistry and Genetics MSci, Biochemistry and Molecular Medicine BSc, Biochemistry and Molecular Medicine MSci

Postgraduate course: Biological Photography and Imaging MSc

Biology, Genetics, Tropical Biology and Zoology

Biology BSc, Biology MSci, Zoology BSc, Zoology MSci, Tropical Biology BSc, Genetics MSci, Genetics BSc

Postgraduate courses: Biological Photography and Imaging MSc

Biosciences

Agriculture BSc, Integrated Agricultural Business Management BSc, Integrated Agricultural Business Management with Industrial Placement Award BSc, Agricultural and Crop Science BSc, Agricultural and Livestock Science BSc, International Agricultural Science BSc, Animal Science BSc, Biotechnology BSc, Environmental Science BSc, Environmental Science MSci, International Environmental Science BSc, International Environmental Science MSci, Environmental Biology BSc, Microbiology BSc, Nutrition BSc, Nutrition and Dietetics MNutr, Plant Science BSc, Food Science and Nutrition MSci, Pre-Veterinary Science Certificate, Food Science BSc, Food Science and Nutrition BSc, Food Science MSci

Postgraduate courses: Advanced Dietetic Practice MSc, Advanced Dietetic Practice PGDip, Advanced Dietetic Practice PGCert, Agrifood MSc, Agrifood PGDip, Agrifood PGCert, Animal Nutrition MSc, Animal Nutrition PGDip, Applied Biomolecular Technology for the Biopharmaceutical, Food and Biotechnology Industries MSc, Applied Biopharmaceutical Biotechnology and Entrepreneurship (ABBE) MSc, Brewing Science MSc, Brewing Science and Practice MSc, Brewing Science PGDip, Brewing Science MRes, Brewing: Principles and Practice (E Learning) PGCert, Clinical Nutrition MSc, Clinical Nutrition PGDip, Crop Improvement MSc, Crop Improvement PGDip, Food Production Management MSc, Food Production Management PGDip, Food Science and Engineering MRes, Industrial Physical Biochemistry MRes, Nutritional Sciences MSc, Sensory Science MRes, Sensory Science PGCert

Chemistry

Chemistry BSc, Chemistry with a Year in Industry MSci, Chemistry MSci, Medicinal and Biological Chemistry BSc, Chemistry with an International Study Year MSci, Medicinal and Biological Chemistry MSci, Medicinal and Biological Chemistry with an Assessed Year in Industry MSci, Chemistry and Molecular Physics BSc, Chemistry and Molecular Physics MSci

Postgraduate courses: Green and Sustainable Chemistry MSc, Chemistry MSc (by Research)

Computer Science

Computer Science BSc, Computer Science MSci, Computer Science including International Year MSci, Computer Science With Year in Industry BSc, Computer Science with Artificial Intelligence BSc, Computer Science with Artificial Intelligence MSci, Computer Science with Artificial Intelligence including International Year MSci, Computer Science and Artificial Intelligence with Year in Industry BSc, Data Science BSc

Postgraduate courses: Computer Science MSc, Human Computer Interaction MSc

Mathematical Sciences

Statistics BSc, Mathematics (International Study) BSc, Mathematics MMath, Mathematics and Economics BSc, Mathematics BSc, Financial Mathematics BSc

Postgraduate courses: Financial and Computational Mathematics MSc, Gravity, Particles and Fields MSc, Mathematical Medicine and Biology MSc, Pure Mathematics MSc, Scientific Computation MSc, Statistics MSc, Statistics and Applied Probability MSc

Natural Sciences

Natural Sciences BSc, Natural Sciences MSci

Neuroscience

Neuroscience BSc, Neuroscience MSci

Pharmacy

Pharmaceutical Sciences (with a Year in Industry) MSci, Pharmacy MPharm

Postgraduate course: Drug Discovery and Pharmaceutical Sciences MSc

Physics and Astronomy

Physics BSc, Physics MSci, Mathematical Physics BSc, Mathematical Physics MSci, Physics with Astronomy BSc, Physics with Astronomy MSci, Physics with European Language BSc, Physics with European Language MSci, Physics with Medical Physics BSc, Physics with Medical Physics MSci, Physics with Nanoscience BSc, Physics with Nanoscience MSci, Physics with Theoretical Astrophysics BSc, Physics with Theoretical Astrophysics MSci, Physics with Theoretical Physics BSc, Physics with Theoretical Physics MSci, Physics and Philosophy BSc

Postgraduate courses: Physics MSc (by Research), Gravity, Particles and Fields MSc

Psychology

Psychology BSc, Psychology MSci, Psychology and Cognitive Neuroscience BSc

Postgraduate courses: Applied Educational Psychology Doctorate DAppEdPsy, Brain Imaging MSc, Psychology (Conversion Course) PGDip, Psychology (Conversion) MSc, Psychology Research Methods MSc

Faculty of Social Sciences;
www.nottingham.ac.uk/social-sciences
Business
Accountancy BSc, Finance, Accounting and Management BSc, International Management BSc, Industrial Economics BSc, Industrial Economics with Insurance BSc, Management BSc, Management with Chinese Studies BA

Postgraduate courses: Accounting and Finance MSc, Banking and Finance MSc, Business Analytics MSc, Business and Management MSc, Social Science Research (Management and Business Studies) MSc, Communication and Entrepreneurship MSc, Entrepreneurship, Innovation and Management MSc, Finance and Investment MSc, Human Resource Management and Organisation MSc, Industrial Engineering and Operations Management MSc, Information Systems and Operations Management MSc, International Business MSc, Logistics and Supply Chain Management MSc, Management MSc, Marketing MSc, Master of Business Administration – General MBA, Master of Business Administration (Executive) MBA, Master of Business Administration (Executive) – Healthcare MBA, Master of Business Administration – Singapore MBA, Risk Management MSc, Supply Chain and Operations Management MSc, Sustainable Business MSc, Sustainable Energy and Entrepreneurship MSc

Economics
Economics BA/BSc, Economics and Econometrics BSc, Economics and International Economics BA/BSc, Economics with Chinese Studies BA, Economics with French BA, Economics with German BA, Economics with Hispanic Studies BA, Economics with Russian BA, Economics and Philosophy BA, Philosophy, Politics and Economics BA, Mathematics and Economics BSc, Politics and Economics BA

Postgraduate courses: Economics MSc, Economics of Monetary and Financial Policy MSc, Economic Development and Policy Analysis MSc, Behavioural Economics MSc, Economics and Development Economics MSc, Economics and Econometrics MSc, Economics and Financial Economics MSc, Economics and International Economics MSc, Economics (Conversion) GDip

Education
Education BA, Education MArts, Humanistic Counselling Practice BA

Postgraduate courses: Creativity, Arts, Literacies and Learning MA, Education MA, Education (Flexible) MA, Educational Leadership and Management MA, Educational Leadership and Management (by distance learning) MA, International Student Advice and Support PGCert, Learning, Technology and Education MA, Learning, Technology and Education (online) MA, Mentoring and Coaching Beginning Teachers PGCert, Person-Centred Experiential Counselling and Psychotherapy Practice MA, Special and Inclusive Education MA, Special and Inclusive Education (online) MA, Teaching Chinese to Speakers of Other Languages (TCSOL) MA, Teaching English to Speakers of Other Languages (TESOL) MA, Teaching English for Academic Purposes (TEAP) by distance learning MA, Teaching English to Speakers of Other Languages (TESOL) by Web-based Distance Learning MA, PGCE Postgraduate Certificate in Primary Education, Trauma Studies MA, PGCE Postgraduate Certificate in Secondary Education, PGCE (International) Postgraduate Certificate in Education PGCEi

Geography
Geography BA, Geography BSc, Environmental Geoscience BSc, Geography with Business BA

Postgraduate courses: Environmental Management MA, Environmental Management MSc, Geography (Sc) MRes, Geography MSc (by research), Geography MA (by research), Geography MRes, Human Geography MSc, Landscape and Culture MA

Law
Law BA, Law LLB, Law with French and French Law BA, Law with German and German Law BA, Law with Spanish and Spanish Law BA

Postgraduate courses: Master of Laws LLM, Criminal Justice LLM, Environmental Law LLM, European Law LLM, Human Rights Law LLM, International Commercial Law LLM, International Criminal Justice and Armed Conflict LLM, International Law and Development LLM, International Law LLM, Maritime Law LLM, Public International Law LLM, International Law, Security and Terrorism MA, Social Science Research (Socio-Legal Studies) MA, Law and Environmental Science MSc, Public Procurement Law and Policy LLM/PGDip/PGCert

Politics and International Relations
Politics and International Relations BA, International Relations and Global Issues MSci, Politics and American Studies BA, Politics and Economics BA,

French and Politics BA, German and Politics BA, French and Contemporary Chinese Studies BA, History and Politics BA, German and Contemporary Chinese Studies BA, Philosophy, Politics and Economics BA, Russian and Contemporary Chinese Studies BA, Spanish and Contemporary Chinese Studies BA, History with Contemporary Chinese Studies BA

Postgraduate courses: Asian and International Studies MA, Slavery and Liberation MA/PGDip/PGCert, Diplomacy MA, International Relations MA, Governance and Political Development MA, Politics and Contemporary History MA, International Security and Terrorism MA, Social Science Research (Political Science and International Relations) MA

Sociology and Social Policy

Criminology BA, Criminology and Social Policy BA, Criminology and Sociology BA, Social Work BA, Sociology BA, Sociology and Social Policy BA

Postgraduate courses: Criminology MA, Criminology PGDip, Global Citizenship, Identities and Human Rights MA, Global Citizenship, Identities and Human Rights PGDip, International Social Policy MA, Master of Public Administration MPA, Public Administration PGDip, Public Policy MA, Public Policy PGDip, Social Work MA, Social Science Research (Social Policy and Social Work) MA, Social Science Research (Sociology) MA

NOTTINGHAM TRENT UNIVERSITY
www.ntu.ac.uk

School of Animal, Rural and Environmental Sciences; www.ntu.ac.uk/ares

Animal Biology BSc(Hons), Ecology BSc(Hons), Ecology and Conservation BSc(Hons), Environmental Science BSc(Hons), Equestrian Psychology and Sports Science BSc(Hons), Equine Sports Science BSc(Hons), Food Science and Technology BSc(Hons), Geography MGeog, Geography BSc(Hons), Geography (Physical) BSc(Hons), Horticulture (final year top-up) BSc(Hons), Wildlife Conservation BSc(Hons), Wildlife Conservation and Management (final year top-up) BSc(Hons), Zoo Biology BSc(Hons)

Postgraduate courses: MSc/MRes Animal Health and Welfare, MRes Applied Anthrozoology, MSc/MRes Biodiversity Conservation, MSc/MRes Endangered Species Recovery and Conservation, MRes Equine Health and Welfare, MRes Equine Performance, MSc Equine Performance, Health and Welfare, MSc/MRes Global Food Security and Development

School of Architecture, Design and the Built Environment; www.ntu.ac.uk/adbe

Architectural Design

BArch(Hons) Architecture (ARB/RIBA Part 1), BA(Hons) Interior Architecture and Design, BSc(Hons) Architectural Technology

Postgraduate courses: MArch Architecture, MA Interior Architecture and Design, Professional Certificate in Architecture

Civil Engineering

BEng(Hons) Civil Engineering, BSc(Hons) Civil Engineering, MEng(Hons) Civil Engineering Design and Construction

Postgraduate courses: MSc Civil Engineering, MSc Structural Engineering with Management, MSc Structural Engineering with Materials

Construction Management and Quantity Surveying

BSc(Hons) Construction Management, BSc(Hons) Quantity Surveying and Commercial Management, Level 6 Chartered Surveyor (Degree Apprenticeship), Studying BSc(Hons) Quantity Surveying and Commercial Management

Postgraduate courses: MSc Construction Management, MSc Project Management (Construction), Online MSc in Construction Project Management (Distance Learning), MSc Quantity Surveying

Property Management and Development

BSc(Hons) Building Surveying, BSc(Hons) Property Development and Planning, BSc(Hons) Property Finance and Investment, BSc(Hons) Real Estate

Postgraduate courses: MSc Building Surveying, MSc Planning and Development, MSc Real Estate, MSc International Real Estate Investment and Finance

Product Design

BA(Hons) Product Design, BSc(Hons) Product Design, BA(Hons) Furniture and Product Design

Postgraduate courses: MA Design: Products and Furniture, MSc Design: Products and Technology

School of Art & Design; www.ntu.ac.uk/art

BArch(Hons) Architecture, BA(Hons) Animation, BA(Hons) Art & Design Media Practice (one year top-up), BA(Hons) Costume Design and Making, BA(Hons) Decorative Arts, BA(Hons) Design for Film and Television, BA(Hons) Fashion Accessory Design, BA(Hons) Fashion Communication and Promotion, BA(Hons) Fashion Design, BA(Hons) Fashion Knitwear Design and Knitted Textiles, BA(Hons) Fashion Management, BA(Hons) Fashion Marketing and Branding, BA(Hons) Filmmaking, BA(Hons) Fine Art, BA(Hons) Furniture and Product Design, BA(Hons) Graphic Design, BA(Hons) Interior Architecture and Design, BA(Hons) International Fashion Business (one year top-up), BA(Hons) Photography, BA(Hons) Product Design, BA(Hons) Textile Design, BA(Hons) Theatre Design, BSc(Hons) Product Design
Postgraduate courses: MA Fashion Knitwear Design, MA Branding and Identity, MA Commercial Photography, MA Culture, Style and Fashion, MA Culture, Style and Fashion, MA Fashion and Textile Design, MA Fashion Marketing, MA Fashion Marketing, MA Fashion Communications, MA Fashion Communications, MA Fashion Design, MA Graphic Design, MA Graphic Design Theory and Practice, MA Illustration, MA International Fashion Management, MA International Fashion Management, MA Luxury Fashion Brand Management, MA Luxury Fashion Brand Management, MA Photography, MA Photography, MA Textile Design Innovation, MFA Fine Art, MFA Fine Art, PG Cert Creative Pattern Cutting

School of Arts and Humanities; www.ntu.ac.uk/hum

BA(Hons) Broadcast Journalism, BA(Hons) Journalism, BA(Hons) Media, BA(Hons) English, BA(Hons) History, various joint options
Postgraduate courses: MA/PGDip Broadcast Journalism, MA/PGDip Digital and Newspaper Journalism, MA/PGDip Documentary Journalism, MA/PGDip Magazine Journalism, MA Creative Writing, MA English Language Teaching, MA History, MA Holocaust and Genocide (by research), MA Linguistics (by research), MA Media and Globalisation, MA Philosophy (by research), MA TESOL (Teaching English to Speakers of Other Languages), MA/ PGDip/ PGCert Museum and Heritage Development, MRes English Literary Research

Nottingham Business School; www.ntu.ac.uk/nbs

BA(Hons) Accounting and Finance, BA(Hons) Business, BA(Hons) Business Management and Accounting and Finance, BA(Hons) Business Management and Economics, BA(Hons) Business Management and Entrepreneurship, BA(Hons) Business Management and Human Resources, BA(Hons) Business Management and Marketing, BA(Hons) Economics, BA(Hons) Economics with Business, BA(Hons) Economics with International Finance and Banking, BA(Hons) Economics with International Trade and Development, BA(Hons) International Business, BA(Hons) International Business (with French), BA(Hons) International Business (with German), BA(Hons) International Business (with Spanish), BA(Hons) Marketing
Postgraduate courses: MSc Branding and Advertising, MSc Digital Marketing, MSc Economics, MSc Economics and Investment Banking, MSc Entrepreneurship, MSc Finance, MSc Finance and Accounting, MSc Finance and Investment Banking, MSc Human resource Management (full-time), MSc International Business, MSc Management, MSc Management and Finance, MSc Management and Global Supply Chain Management, MSc Management and Innovation and Enterprise, MSc Management and International Business, MSc Management and Marketing, MSc Marketing, MSc Project Management

Nottingham Institute of Education; www.ntu.ac.uk/edu

BA(Hons) Primary Education, BA(Hons) Childhood Studies, BA(Hons) Education Studies, BA(Hons) Early Years and Psychology, BA(Hons) Early Years and Special and Inclusive Education, BA(Hons) Education Studies and Early Years, BA(Hons) Education Studies and Psychology, BA(Hons) Education Studies and Special and Inclusive Education, BA(Hons) Education
Postgraduate course: MA Education, various teacher training options

Nottingham Law School; www.ntu.ac.uk/nls

LLB(Hons) Law (Full-time), LLB(Hons) Law (Sandwich), LLB(Hons) Business Law, LLB(Hons) / LLM European Law, LLB(Hons) International Law, LLB(Hons) Law with Business, LLB(Hons) Law with Criminology, LLB(Hons) Law with Psychology, LLB(Hons) Law (Distance Learning), LLB(Hons) Law (Flexible Learning), LLB(Hons) Law Senior Status
Postgraduate courses: Master of Law (LLM) courses in the following areas: Corporate and Insolvency Law, Dual LLM in Corporate and Insolvency Law/ European and Insolvency Law, General Law, Health Law and Ethics, Human Rights and Justice,

Intellectual Property Law, International Financial Law, International Trade and Commercial Law, Oil, Gas and Mining Law, Sports Law, Legal Practice

School of Science and Technology; www.ntu.ac.uk/sat

Engineering

MEng(Hons) Biomedical Engineering, BEng(Hons) Biomedical Engineering, MEng(Hons) Electronic Engineering, BEng(Hons) Electronic Engineering, MEng(Hons) Sport Engineering, BEng(Hons) Sport Engineering, MEng(Hons) Mechanical Engineering, BEng(Hons) Mechanical Engineering

Biosciences

BSc(Hons) Biological Sciences, BSc(Hons) Biological Sciences (Part-time), BSc(Hons) Biomedical Science, BSc(Hons) Biochemistry, MBiol Biochemistry, BSc(Hons) Microbiology, MBiol Microbiology, BSc(Hons) Pharmacology, MBiol Pharmacology

Postgraduate courses: MSc Biomedical Science, MSc Biotechnology, MSc Molecular Cell Biology, MSc Pharmacology, MSc Neuropharmacology, MSc Molecular Microbiology, MRes Biotechnology, MRes Cancer Biology, MRes Cell Biology, MRes Molecular Biology, MRes Molecular Microbiology, MRes Neuropharmacology, MRes Pharmacology

Chemistry

BSc(Hons) Chemistry, BSc(Hons) Pharmaceutical and Medicinal Chemistry, MChem Chemistry

Postgraduate courses: MSc Chemistry/Chemistry (Professional Practice), MRes Chemistry, MRes Advanced Materials Engineering, MRes Analytical Chemistry, MRes Pharmaceutical Analysis, MRes Pharmaceutical and Medicinal Science

Computing and Technology

BSc(Hons) Computer Science, BSc(Hons) Computer Science (Games Technology), BSc(Hons) Software Engineering, BSc(Hons) Computer Systems Engineering, BSc(Hons) Computer Systems (Networks), BSc(Hons) Computer Systems (Forensic and Security), BSc(Hons) Computing, BSc(Hons) Digital Media Technology, BSc(Hons) Information Systems, BSc(Hons) Information and Communications Technology, MComp(Hons) Computer Science, MComp(Hons) Computer Systems Engineering

Postgraduate courses: MSc Computer Science, MSc Computing Systems, MSc Computer Games Systems, MSc IT Security, MSc Cloud and Enterprise Computing, MSc Interactive Media Engineering, MSc Engineering (Cybernetics and Communications), MSc Engineering (Electronics), MSc Engineering

Management, MSc Data Analytics for Business, MRes Computer Science, MRes Electronic Systems

Forensics

BSc(Hons) Forensic Science

Mathematics

BSc(Hons) Mathematics, BSc(Hons) Financial Mathematics, BSc(Hons) Computer Science and Mathematics, BSc(Hons) Sport Science and Mathematics, BSc(Hons) Physics and Mathematics, BSc(Hons) Data Science, MMath(Hons) Mathematics

Postgraduate courses: MRes Mathematical Sciences, MSc Data Analytics for Business

Physics

BSc(Hons) Physics, BSc(Hons) Physic with Nuclear Technology, BSc(Hons) Physics with Astrophysics, MSci Physics

Postgraduate course: MRes Medical and Materials Imaging

Sport Science

BSc(Hons) Sport Science and Management, BSc(Hons) Sport and Exercise Science, BSc(Hons) Coaching and Sport Science, BSc(Hons) Exercise, Nutrition and Health

Postgraduate courses: MRes Sport Science, MRes Exercise Physiology, MRes Performance Nutrition, MRes Performance Analysis, MRes Biomechanics, MRes Sport and Exercise Psychology

School of Social Sciences; www.ntu.ac.uk/soc

BA(Hons) Criminology, BA(Hons) Policing, BA(Hons) Health and Social Care, BA(Hons) International Relations, BA(Hons) Politics, BA(Hons) Politics and International Relations, BSc(Hons) Psychology (British Psychological Society accredited), BSc(Hons) Psychology with Criminology (British Psychological Society accredited), BSc(Hons) Psychology with Sociology (British Psychological Society accredited), BA(Hons) Sociology, BA(Hons) Social Work, BA(Hons) Youth Justice, BA(Hons) Youth Studies

Postgraduate courses: MSc/ PGDip Psychology, MSc Applied Child Psychology, MRes/ MSc Psychological Research Methods, MSc Forensic Mental Health, MSc Forensic Psychology, MSc Cyberpsychology, MSc Psychology in Clinical Practice, MSc Psychological Wellbeing and Mental Health, MA Criminology, MA Sociology, MA Politics, MA International Relations, Online MA International Relations (Distance learning), MA Public Health, PG Cert/ MA Career Development

SOUTHAMPTON SOLENT UNIVERSITY
www.solent.ac.uk

www.solent.ac.uk/courses

Art, Design & Fashion

Fashion

beauty management, fashion, fashion buying & merchandising, fashion graphics,/journalism/film fashion marketing with management, fashion photography, fashion promotion & communication, fashion styling, visual merchandising & retail design

Photography

photography, fashion photography, photojournalism

Visual Arts & Design

animation, computer & video games, computer generated images, digital animation, fine art, graphic design/web & mobile devices, illustration, interior design/decoration, product design, special effects, visual arts, fashion, web design & development, digital graphics for web; BA(Hons), BSc(Hons), FdA, MA

Built Environment

architectural technology, construction management, interior design/decoration, civil engineering, quantity surveying, international construction, design & managemenr; BA(Hons), BSc(Hons)

Business, Management and Economics

accounting & finance, business economics, business enterprise & entrepreneurship, creative enterprise, advertising/& PR, international/business management, business (professional development), business administration, international management, business, business & management/marketing, law, promotional media, business information technology, information technology management, information technology for business, festival/& events management, fashion buying & merchandising, fashion promotion & communication, fashion with PR, international tourism management, international air travel & tourism management, maritime business,, ship & port management, marketing/with advertising/management, PR & communication, advertising & PR, media communication & culture, music management/promotion, creative advertising, sports marketing, visual marketing & retail distribution,, marketing, advertising & outdoor marketing, fitness management & personal training, football studies & business, PR; BA(Hons), BSc(Hons), LlB, LlM, FdA, MBA, PGD, MSc

Computing, Games and Networking

animation, digital animation, computing & video games, computer games, software development, computer generation imagery, computer networks & web design, computer systems & networks, network security management, web design & management/development, computing, software engineering, information technology for business; BA(Hons), BSc(Hons)

Engineering and Yacht Design

electronic engineering, engineering design & manufacture, production design, manufacturing & mechanical engineering, applied acoustics, yacht & power craft design, yacht design, & production, BEng(Hons), BA(Hons), BSc(Hons), MSc

Maritime & Geography

geography with environmental studies/marine studies, maritime, business, shipping & port management, marine engineering & management, marine electrical & electronic engineering, marine engineering; BEng(Hons), BSc(Hons), FdEng, MSc

Media and Media Technology

audio & acoustics, audio engineering, broadcasting systems, computer generated imagery, digital music pop journalism/performance/production, performance & promotion, songwriting, film, film & TV studies, film production, live sound, technology, music systems, outside broadcasting (production operations), screenwriting, sound engineering, sound for film, TV special effects/production, TV & video production, TV postproduction/studio production, marketing with advertising management, music management/promotion, media culture & production, media production/writing, audio engineering/technology, digital music, live sound technology, media technology, music studio technology, outside broadcast/production operations, social media, sound engineering, sound for film, TV & games, TV production technology; BSc(Hons), BA(Hons)

Music and Performance

pop music journalism/production, TV & games, music management & promotion; BSc(Hons), BA(Hons)

Health and Social Sciences

criminal investigation with psychology, criminology/psychology, psychology (criminal behaviour/counselling), fitness/management & personal training, health, exercise & physical activity, psychology (counselling/criminal behaviour/education/health), criminology & counselling, social work, criminology & criminal justice; BA(Hons), BSc(Hons), MSc

Sport and Fitness

applied sport science, fitness & personal training, training, fitness management & sport training, health, exercise & physical activity, sports coaching & development, adventure & extreme sport management; BA(Hons), BSc(Hons), MA, MSc

Writing and Communication

advertising & PR, creative enterprise, English & creative writing/film/magazine journalism/PR/advertising/media, fashion & events management,, fashion journalism, journalism, magazine journalism, multimedia journalism, photojournalism, pop music/sports journalism, advertising/& PR, event management, fashion buying & merchandising, fashion promotion & communication, fashion with PR, PR & communications, promotional media, marketing with advertising management, media communication & culture, promotional media, music/production/promotion/management, sports marketing; BA(Hons)

Postgraduate; international accounting and finance, HRM, personnel and development, Master of Business Administration, international business management, management, project management, applied computing, computer engineering, cyber security engineering, data analytics engineering, digital design, applied acoustics, biography and life writing, creative direction for fashion and beauty, fashion merchandise management, film production, athletic development and peak performance, sports broadcast journalism, international trade regulation, criminology and criminal justice, creative advertising, creative enterprise, marketing, management, PR and multimedia communications, visual communication, MBA international maritime management, international maritime business, international shipping and logistics, shipping operations; MA, MSc, MBA, LlM

THE OPEN UNIVERSITY
www.open.ac.uk

Arts & Humanities

BA (Honours) Arts and Humanities, BA (Honours) Arts and Humanities (Philosophy), BA (Honours) Arts and Humanities (Religious Studies), BA (Honours) Criminology and Law, Bachelor of Laws (Honours) (LLB), Bachelor of Laws (Honours) (graduate entry), BA (Honours) Philosophy and Psychological Studies, BA (Honours) Politics, Philosophy and Economics, BSc (Honours) Psychology and Law, BA (Honours) Youth Justice Studies (England and Wales), BA (Honours) Arts and Humanities (Music), BA (Honours) Classical Studies, BA (Honours) Arts and Humanities (Classical Studies), BA (Honours) Arts and Humanities (Creative Writing), BA (Honours) Arts and Humanities (English Language), BA (Honours) Arts and Humanities (English Literature), BA (Honours) Arts and Humanities (History), BSc (Honours) Computing & IT and Design, BSc (Honours) Computing & IT and a second subject, BA/BSc (Honours) Design and Innovation, BA (Honours) Economics and History, BA (Honours) English Language and Literature, BA (Honours) English Literature, BA (Honours) English Literature and Creative Writing, BA (Honours) History, BA (Honours) History and Politics, BA (Honours) Arts and Humanities (Art History), BSc (Honours) Combined STEM, BA (Honours) Language Studies, BA (Honours) Arts and Humanities (French), BA (Honours) Arts and Humanities (German), BA (Honours) Arts and Humanities (Spanish), BA (Honours) Language Studies with English and French, BA (Honours) Language Studies with English and German, BA (Honours) Language Studies with English and Spanish, BA (Honours) Language Studies with French and German, BA (Honours) Language Studies with French and Spanish, BA (Honours) Language Studies with German and Spanish

Business & Management

BA (Honours) Business Management, BA (Honours) Business Management (Economics), BA (Honours) Business Management (Leadership Practice), BA (Honours) Business Management (Sport and Football), BSc (Honours) Computing & IT and Business, BSc (Honours) Computing & IT and a second subject, BA (Honours) Business Management (Innovation and Enterprise), BA (Honours) Business Management (Accounting), BA (Honours) Business Management (Marketing)

Computing & IT
BSc (Honours) Computing and IT, Top-up BSc (Honours) Computing and IT Practice, BSc (Honours) Combined STEM, BSc (Honours) Computing & IT and Psychology, BSc (Honours) Computing & IT and a second subject

Design
BSc (Honours) Computing & IT and Design, BA/BSc (Honours) Design and Innovation, BSc (Honours) Computing & IT and a second subject, BSc (Honours) Combined STEM

Education, Childhood & Youth
BA (Honours) Childhood and Youth Studies, BA (Honours) Early Childhood, Top-up BA (Honours) Early Childhood, BA (Honours) Health and Social Care, BSc (Honours) Sport, Fitness and Coaching, BA (Honours) Youth Justice Studies (England and Wales), BA (Honours) Education Studies (Primary), BSc (Honours) Mathematics and its Learning

Engineering
Bachelor of Engineering (Honours), Top-up Bachelor of Engineering (Honours), BSc (Honours) Combined STEM, BA/BSc (Honours) Design and Innovation, BSc (Honours) Environmental Management and Technology

Environment & Development
BSc (Honours) Combined STEM, BSc (Honours) Environmental Management and Technology, BSc (Honours) Environmental Science, BA (Honours) Environmental Studies, BSc (Honours) Geography and Environmental Science, BA (Honours) International Studies, BA/BSc (Honours) Design and Innovation

Health & Social Care
BA (Honours) Health and Social Care, BSc (Honours) Health Sciences, BSc (Honours) Healthcare and Health Science, BSc (Honours) Nursing Practice, BSc (Honours) Adult Nursing, BSc (Honours) Psychology with Counselling, BA (Honours) Childhood and Youth Studies, BSc (Honours) Mental Health Nursing, BA (Honours) Social Work (England), BA (Honours) Social Work (Scotland), BA (Honours) Social Work (Scotland) (graduate entry), BA (Honours) Social Work (Wales), BA (Honours) Youth Justice Studies (England and Wales)

Health & Wellbeing
BSc (Honours) Sport, Fitness and Coaching, BSc (Honours) Health Sciences, BA (Honours) Health and Social Care, BSc (Honours) Healthcare and Health Science, BSc (Honours) Mental Health Nursing

Languages
BA (Honours) Arts and Humanities, BA (Honours) Language Studies, BA (Honours) Arts and Humanities (English Language), BA (Honours) Arts and Humanities (English Literature), BA (Honours) English Language and Literature, BA (Honours) Language Studies with English and French, BA (Honours) Language Studies with English and German, BA (Honours) Language Studies with English and Spanish, BA (Honours) Language Studies with French and German, BA (Honours) Language Studies with French and Spanish, BA (Honours) Language Studies with German and Spanish, BA (Honours) Arts and Humanities (French), BA (Honours) Arts and Humanities (German), BA (Honours) Arts and Humanities (Spanish), BA (Honours) English Literature, BA (Honours) English Literature and Creative Writing, BA (Honours) Classical Studies

Law
Bachelor of Laws (Honours) (LLB), Bachelor of Laws (Honours) (graduate entry), BA (Honours) Criminology and Law, BSc (Honours) Psychology and Law, BA (Honours) Youth Justice Studies (England and Wales)

Mathematics & Statistics
BSc (Honours) Mathematics and Statistics, BSc (Honours) Computing & IT and Mathematics, BSc (Honours) Computing & IT and a second subject, BSc (Honours) Economics and Mathematical Sciences, BSc (Honours) Mathematics, BSc (Honours) Mathematics and Physics, BSc (Honours) Mathematics and its Learning, BSc (Honours) Combined STEM, BSc (Honours) Computing & IT and Statistics

Medical Sciences
BSc (Honours) Health Sciences

Nursing & Healthcare Practice
BSc (Honours) Nursing Practice, BSc (Honours) Health Sciences, BA (Honours) Health and Social Care, BSc (Honours) Healthcare and Health Science, BSc (Honours) Adult Nursing, BSc (Honours) Mental Health Nursing

Psychology & Counselling
BSc (Honours) Combined STEM, BSc (Honours) Computing & IT and Psychology, BSc (Honours) Computing & IT and a second subject, BA (Honours) Criminology and Psychology, BA (Honours) Philosophy and Psychological Studies, BSc (Honours)

Psychology, BSc (Honours) Psychology and Law, BSc (Honours) Psychology with Counselling, BA (Honours) Social Sciences (Psychology), BSc (Honours) Forensic Psychology, BSc (Honours) Social Psychology, BA (Honours) Childhood and Youth Studies

Science

BSc (Honours) Geography and Environmental Science, BSc (Honours) Health Sciences, BSc (Honours) Healthcare and Health Science, BSc (Honours) Combined STEM, BSc (Honours) Natural Sciences, BSc (Honours) Natural Sciences (Chemistry), BSc (Honours) Natural Sciences (Environmental Science), BSc (Honours) Natural Sciences (Physics), BSc (Honours) Mathematics and Physics, BSc (Honours) Environmental Science, BSc (Honours) Natural Sciences (Astronomy and Planetary Science), BSc (Honours) Natural Sciences (Biology), BSc (Honours) Natural Sciences (Earth Sciences), BA (Honours) Environmental Studies, BSc (Honours) Environmental Management and Technology, BSc (Honours) Sport, Fitness and Coaching

Social Sciences

BA (Honours) Social Sciences, BA (Honours) Social Sciences (Criminology), BA (Honours) Social Sciences (Economics), BA (Honours) Social Sciences (Geography), BA (Honours) Social Sciences (Politics), BA (Honours) Social Sciences (Psychology), BA (Honours) Social Sciences (Sociology), BA (Honours) Business Management (Economics), BA (Honours) Economics and History, BSc (Honours) Economics and Mathematical Sciences, BA (Honours) Politics, Philosophy and Economics, BSc (Honours)

Combined STEM, BSc (Honours) Computing & IT and Psychology, BSc (Honours) Computing & IT and a second subject, BA (Honours) Criminology and Psychology, BA (Honours) Environmental Studies, BSc (Honours) Forensic Psychology, BSc (Honours) Geography and Environmental Science, BA (Honours) History and Politics, BA (Honours) Philosophy and Psychological Studies, BSc (Honours) Psychology, BSc (Honours) Psychology and Law, BSc (Honours) Psychology with Counselling, BA (Honours) Criminology and Law, BA (Honours) International Studies, BSc (Honours) Social Psychology, BA (Honours) Youth Justice Studies (England and Wales), BA (Honours) Childhood and Youth Studies

Technology

BSc (Honours) Combined STEM, BSc (Honours) Environmental Management and Technology

Postgraduate courses

Master's degrees in the following subjects: Advanced Networking, Advancing Healthcare Practice, Art History, Childhood and Youth, Classical Studies, Computing, Creative Writing, Crime and Justice, Development Management, Education, Engineering, English, Environmental Management, Finance, Forensic Psychological Studies, History, Human Resource Management, Laws, Mathematics, MBA (Master of Business Administration), MBA (Technology Management), Medicinal Chemistry, Mental Health Science, Music, Online and Distance Education, Philosophy, Psychology, Science, Social Work, Space Science and Technology, Systems Thinking in Practice, Technology Management, Translation

---

UNIVERSITY OF OXFORD
www.ox.ac.uk

Division of Humanities; www.ox.ac.uk/divisions/humanities

Rothermere American Institute; www.rai.ox.ac.uk

American studies/history/politics/literature; MSt

Faculty of Classics; www.classics.ox.ac.uk

BA(Hons), MPhil, MSt and DPhil degrees in the following areas: classics, classics and English/ modern languages/ oriental studies, classical archaeology and ancient history, ancient and modern history, Greek and/or Roman history, Greek and/or Latin languages and literature, ancient history, classical

languages and literature, classical archaeology, late antique & Byzantine

Ruskin School of Drawing and Fine Art; www.ruskin-sc.ox.ac.uk

BFA, MLitt, DPhil in the following areas: art history & theory, contemporary art, drawing, fine art, theoretical & practice-led research, history of art & visual culture

Faculty of English, Language & Literature; www.english.ox.ac.uk

BA(Hons), DPhil, MLitt, MPhil, MSt degrees in the following areas: English language and literature (650-

1550; 1550-1700; 1600-1830; 1800-1914; 1900-present day), English & modern languages/classics/history, literature in English, English language, English & American studies, English studies/medieval studies, history & English, Shakespeare, women's studies: film aesthetics, studio world literatures in English

History of Art Department; www.hoa.ox.ac.uk

BA(Hons), DPhil, MLitt and MSt degrees in the following areas: history of art, topics include art and culture in Renaissance Florence and Venice, The Dutch Golden Age: 1618-72, painting and culture in Ming China, English architecture, art and its public in France, 1815-67, authenticity and replication in art and visual culture, French painting, 1880-1912, gothic: artistic originality and the transmission of style in medieval art, image and thought, media and modernity: art and mass culture, 1880&'2000, portraiture as genre, the apparatus of art history, theories of vision: the eye and the gaze, women, art and culture in early modern Europe

Faculty of History; www.history.ox.ac.uk

BA(Hons), DPhil, MPhil, MSc, MSt and MLetters degrees in the following areas: history of the British Isles, general history,,historical methods, British history, general history, ancient and modern history, history and economics, history and English, history and modern languages, history and politics; Postgraduate studies include; British and European history, from 1500 to the present, economic and social history, global and imperial history, history of art and visual culture, history of science, medicine and technology, late antique and Byzantine studies, medieval history, medieval studies, modern south Asian studies, US history

Faculty of Linguistics, Philology and Phonetics; www.ling-phil.ox.ac.uk

BA, MPhil, PhD and MSt degrees in the following areas: modern languages and linguistics, psychology, philosophy and linguistics, Graduate Courses; general linguistics and comparative philology, general linguistics and comparative philology, comparative philology and general linguistics

Faculty of Medieval & Modern Languages; www.mod-langs.ox.ac.uk

BA(Hons), DPhil, MPhil and MSt degrees in the following areas: Arabic, Czech (with Slovak, modern Greek, classics, French, German, Hebrew, history, Italian, linguistics, Persian, philosophy, Polish, Portuguese, Russian, Spanish, Turkish; Graduate Taught Courses; modern languages, Celtic studies, Slavonic studies, Yiddish studies, women's studies, film aesthetics, medieval studies

Faculty of Music; www.music.ox.ac.uk

BMus, DPhil, MA(Hons), MPhil, MSt and MLitt degrees in the following areas: chamber music, choral studies/conducting performance, composition & analysis, dance music, musicology, ethnomusicology, historical musicology, jazz, musical history/theory, the motet in the 14/15th centuries, orchestration, music analysis & criticism, performance & interpretation, psychology of music, theory & analysis, source studies, technology of composition, south Western music theory; Masters;composition, ethnomusicology, musicology, performance, psychology of music

Faculty of Oriental Studies; www.orinst.ox.ac.uk

BA(Hons), DPhil, MPhil and MSt degrees in the following areas: Arabic, Aramaic with Syriac, Armenian, Asia & Near Asian studies, bible interpretation, Buddhist studies, Chinese studies, classic & oriental studies, Classical Armenian studies, Classical Hebrew studies, Classical Indian religion, Coptic, Cuneiform studies, Eastern Christian studies, eastern Christianity, Egyptology, Egyptology & ancient Near East, European & Middle East languages, Hebrew & Jewish studies, Hindi & Urdu, Hindi and Urdu, Islamic art and archaeology, Islamic studies and history, Islamic world, Japanese studies, Jewish studies, Jewish studies in the Graeco-Roman period, Judaism and Christianity in the Graeco-Roman World, Korean, Korean studies, Medieval Arabic thought, Modern Chinese studies, Modern Jewish studies, Modern Middle Eastern studies, Modern South Asian studies, Old Iranian, Oriental studies, Ottoman Turkish studies, Pali, Pali and Prakrit, Persian, Sanskrit, Syriac studies, theology & oriental studies, Tibetan and Himalayan studies, Traditional East Asia, Turkish

Faculty of Philosophy; www.philosophy.ox.ac.uk

BA(Hons), BPhil, MPhil and PhD degrees in the following areas: philosophy and modern languages; philosophy and theology; physics and philosophy; mathematics and philosophy; psychology, philosophy and linguistics; computer science and philosophy

early modern philosophy, knowledge and reality, ethics: philosophy of mind, philosophy of science and social science, philosophy of religion, the philosophy of logic and language, aesthetics, medieval philosophy: Aquinas/Duns Scotus and Ockham, the philosophy of Kant, post-Kantian philosophy, theory of politics, Plato, Republic, Aristotle, Frege, Russell and Wittgenstein, formal logic, philosophy of physics, philosophy of mathematics, philosophy of science, philosophy of cognitive science, the philosophy and economics of the environment, philosophical logic, Plato, Latin philosophy, jurisprudence

Faculty of Theology; www.theology.ox.ac.uk

BA(Hons), BTh, MTh, MSt, MLitt, MPhil, DPhil, PGDip/Cert degrees in the following areas: theology & religion/oriental studies, philosophy & theology, applied theology, theology in applied theology, sociology of religion, pastoral psychology, science and faith in the modern world, the use of the bible, Christian spirituality, liturgy and worship, Christian ethics, mission in the modern world, inter-faith dialogue, ecclesiology in an ecumenical context, Old Testament, New Testament, biblical interpretation, Christian ethics, philosophical theology, science & religion, modern/Reformation/scholastic/patristic theology, ecclesiastical history, the study of religions, issues in theology, Judaism and Christianity in the Graeco-Roman world

Division of Mathematical, Physical and Life Sciences; www.ox.ac.uk/divisions/mpls

Dept of Chemistry; www.chem.ox.ac.uk

DPhil, MChem, MSc degrees in the following areas: chemical biology, inorganic chemistry, organic chemistry, physical chemistry, mathematical techniques, molecular biochemistry/& chemical biology, organic chemistry/reactions/synthesis, organometallic chemistry, physical & theoretical chemistry, quantum mechanics, reaction mechanisms, solid state chemistry, spectroscopy, theoretical chemistry, thermodynamics

Dept of Computer Science; www.cs.ox.ac.uk

BA(Hons), MSc, DPhil, PhD degrees in the following areas: computer science, mathematics/ & computer science, modelling & scientific computing, mathematics & foundations of computer science & philosophy, software engineering, software & systems security

Dept of Engineering Science; www.eng.ox.ac.uk

DPhil, MEng, MSc, EngD degrees in the following areas: engineering science, autonomous intelligent machines and systems, gas turbines aerodynamics, synthetic biology, renewable energy marine structures; research in engineering science, automotive engineering, aerothermal engineering, micromechanics and materials modelling, mechanical performance and integrity, advanced structures, biotechnics, hydraulics, sustainable energy, environmental engineering, bioprocesses, process systems, chemical engineering, production engineering, optoelectronics, microelectronics, communications, power electronics, machine vision and robotics, machine learning, multivariable control, nonlinear and predictive control, medical imaging and informatics, cellular engineering and therapy, dynamic systems, chaos, optimization and mathematical models, autonomous intelligent machines and systems CDT, gas turbines aerodynamics CDT

Life Science Interface; Doctoral Training Centre; www.lsi.ox.ac.uk

DPhil degrees in the following areas; biological systems, biological experimental techniques, biological physics, organic chemistry, molecular genetics & cell biology, mathematical biology, medicinal chemistry, programming, bioinformatics, statistical data systems, structural biology

Division of Materials; www.materials.ox.ac.uk

DPhil, MEng, MSc, MS, MEm degrees in the following areas: materials science, materials structures & mechanical properties of metals, electrical/mechanical properties, nanoelectronics, materials economics, non-metallic materials, composites, polymers, packaging/superconducting/semiconducting materials, structural & nuclear materials, device materials, nanomaterials, process & manufacturing, characterisation, computational nuclear modelling

Mathematical Institute; www.maths.ox.ac.uk

BA(Hons), DPhil, MCF, MFoCS, MS, MSc, MMath degrees in the following areas: mathematics, mathematics and statistics/philosophy/computer science/theoretical physics; Research Areas; algebra, combinatorics, functional analysis, geometry, history of mathematics, logic, mathematical and computational finance, mathematical physics, number theory, numerical analysis, industrial and applied mathematics, nonlinear partial differential equations, stochastic analysis, topology, mathematical biology

Dept of Physics; www.physics.ox.ac.uk

BA(Hons), DPhil, MPhys, MPhysPhil degrees in the following areas: physics, atmospheric oceanic & planetary physics, astrophysics, condensed matter physics, cosmology, general relativity, quantum theory, sub-atomic physics, particle physics, physics, atomic & laser/theoretical physics, physics & philosophy

Dept of Plant Science; www.plants.ox.ac.uk/plants

DPhil, MRes, MSc degrees in the following areas: biochemistry & systems biology, biological science, cell biology/physiology, cell & development biology, comparative developmental genetics, ecology, evolution & systematics, plant science

Dept of Statistics; www.stats.ox.ac.uk

BA(Hons), DPhil, MMath, MSc, PGDip degrees in the following areas: applied statistics, mathematics & statistics, applied probability & research in statistics

Dept of Zoology; www.zoo.ox.ac.uk

DPhil, MRes, MSc degrees in the following areas: animal behaviour/welfare, ageing biology, biological science, infectious disease, ecology & conservation, evolution & development, food science, molecular biology & bioinformatics, indigenous biology, ornithology, integrative bioscience, wildlife conservation

Biological Science; www.biologyy.ox.ac.uk

organisms, cells & genes, ecology, qualitative methods, evolution, adaptation to the environment, cell & developmental biology, animal behaviour, disease, plants

Division of Medical Sciences; www.ox.ac.uk/divisions/ medical_science

Dept of Biochemistry; www.bioch.ox.ac.uk

DPhil, MBiochem, MSc, PhD degrees in the following areas: biochemistry, molecular & cellular biology, structural chromosome and developmental biology, infection, immunity and translational medicine, neuroscience, integrative systems biology, life sciences interface systems approaches to biomedical science e biochemistry, biomedical imaging, synthetic biology, iological chemistry and biophysical chemistry, organic chemistry and maths & statistics, macromolecular structure and function, bioenergetics and metabolism, genetics and molecular biology, cell biology, molecular immunology, plant molecular biology, neuropharmacology, membrane transport, glycobiology, human disease, bionanotechnology, systems biology and signalling to the nucleus, biochemistry, medical sciences, chromosome & developmental biology, structural biology, infection, immunity and translational medicine

Nuffield Dept of Clinical Medicine; www.ndm.ox.ac.uk

PhD, MSc degrees in the following areas: cancer biology, genetic medicine, immunology & infectious diseases, protein science & structural biology, physiology, cellular & molecular biology, tropical medicine & global health

Dept of Clinical Neurosciences; www.ndcn.ox.ac.uk

DPhil, MSc degrees in the following areas: medicine, medical sciences, sleep medicine, MRT physics/analysis, biomedical sciences, experimental psychology, clinical neurology, functional MRI of the brain, anaesthesia

Dept of Experimental Psychology; www.psy.ox.ac.uk

BA(Hons), DPhil, MSc degrees: experimental psychology, psychology, philosophy & linguistics, psychological research;

Radcliffe Department of Medicine

Division of Cardiovascular Medicine, Oxford Centre for Diabetes, Endocrinology and Metabolism, MRC Weatherall Institute of Molecular Medicine, Nuffield Division of Clinical Laboratory Sciences, The Oxford Acute Vascular Imaging Centre, Centre for the Advancement of Sustainable Medical Innovation Investigative Medicine Division

Nuffield Dept of Obstetrics & Gynaecology; www.obs-gyn.ox.ac.uk

obstetrics & gynaecology, clinical embryology; MSc, DPhil

Dept of Oncology; www.oncology.ox.ac.uk

oncology, radiation biology, experimental therapeutics, medical oncology, radiation oncology & radiobiology; DPhil, MRes, MSc

Department of Orthopaedics, Rheumatology and Musculoskeletal Sciences; www.ndorms.ox.ac.uk

orthopaedics, rheumatology, musculoskeletal sciences, translational medicine & medical technology, immunology; MSc, DPhil

Dept of Paediatrics;
www.paediatrics.ox.ac.uk
medicine, paediatric infection and immunity, paediatric infectious diseases, international child health, paediatric endocrinology and diabetes, paediatric haematology, neonatology, paediatric gastroenterology and nutrition, HIV infection and immune control, molecular infectious diseases, developmental immunology, paediatric neuroimaging and pain, vaccinology; PhD, MSc, DPhil

Sir William Dunn School of Pathology;
www.path.ox.ac.uk
bacteriology and virology, cell biology, infection,immunology & molecular medicine, microbiology and molecular biology; DPhil

Dept of Pharmacology;
www.pharm.ox.ac.uk
pharmacology, cardiovascular/autonomic in vivo/ systems neuroscience, drug discovery/medicinal chemistry, cell signalling, molecular neuroscience and disease, cellular neuroscience, experimental therapeutics, practical drug therapy, medical chemistry for cancer; MSc, DPhil

Dept of Physiology, Anatomy and Genetics;
www.dpag.ox.ac.uk
functional genomics, cell physiology, development cell biology,neuroscience, cardiac science; BA, MPhil, MSc, DPhil

Nuffield Department of Population Health;
www.ndph.ox.ac.uk
global health science, population technology, population health, ethics & law, medical sociology, population pathology, integrated population health, global health, preventive medicine; DPhil, MSc

Nuffield Dept of Primary Health Sciences;
www.phc.ox.ac.uk
evidence-based health care, health research, primary healthcare, behavioural medicine, evidence-based medicine, health service economics and organisation, chronic kidney disease, clinical trials, tobacco addiction, diabetes and long-term conditions, health, heart failure research, hypertension, infectious diseases research; DPhil, MSc

Dept of Psychiatry;
www.psychiatry.ox.ac.uk
experimental psychology, eating disorders, suicide, child & adolescent psychiatry, clinical psychopharmacology, bipolar research, experimental psychopathology & cognitive therapies, forensic psychiatry,

neural correlates of gene function, neurobiology and experimental therapeutics, neurobiology of ageing, autism, eating disorders, human brain activity, cognitive approaches to psychosis, cognitive health and neuroscience clinical trials, mindfulness, perinatal psychopathology and offspring development, psychological medicine, psychopharmacology and emotion, social psychiatry, translational neurobiology of psychosis, translational neuroimaging, translational neuroscience & dementia MSc, DPhil, MRCPsych

Nuffield Dept of Surgical Science;
www.surgery.ox.ac.uk
surgical science, endovascular neurosurgery, integrated immunology, surgical science and practice; DPhil, MCh, MS, MSc

Division of Social Sciences;
www.socsci.ox.ac.uk

School of Anthropology and Museum Ethnography; www.anthro.ox.ac.uk
anthropology, archaeology & anthropology, human science, medical anthropology, cognitive & evolutionary anthropology, visual material & museum anthropology, migration studies; BA, BSc, DPhil, MPhil, MSc

Pitt Rivers Museum; www.prm.ox.ac.uk
visual, material & museum anthropology, material culture, visual anthropology, art and aesthetics, sensory anthropology, ethnographic photography and film, and museum anthropology; DPhil, MPhil, MSc

School of Archaeology; www.arch.ox.ac.uk
archaeology & anthropology, bioarchaeology, Eurasian prehistory, classical archaeology & ancient history, historical & classical chronology, materials & technology, chronology, Eurasian prehistory, Palaeolithic archaeological science; BA(Hons), DPhil, MLitt, MSc, MSt

SAID Business School; www.sbs.ox.ac.uk
law and finance, major programme management, MBA economics and management, management studies, executive MBA, financial economics, strategic management, financial strategy, global business, organisational leadership, strategy and innovation, cyber risk for managers, finance, high performance leadership, performing leaders, private equity, real estate, women transforming leadership; BA, Dip, MBA, Exec MBA, MSc

Dept of Economics;
www.economics.ox.ac.uk

economics, macroeconomics, microeconomics, quantitative economics, British economic history since 1870, command & transitional economies, comparative demographic systems, econometrics, economics of developing countries, economics of industry, finance, game theory, international economics, labour economics & industrial relations, mathematical methods, microeconomic theory, money & banking, philosophy & economics of the environment, public economics, advanced econometrics, advanced macroeconomics, advanced microeconomics, behavioural economics, development economics, economic history, financial economics, industrial organisation, international trade, labour economics, public economics,
theory based empirical analysis; BA(Hons), DPhil, MEng, MSc, MPhil

Dept of Education;
www.education.ox.ac.uk

applied linguistics, education (comparative & international education/higher education/learning & technology/children & education/research), learning and teaching/in HE, PGCE (numerous secondary subjects, Schools Direct), teaching English in university setting; DPhil, MSc, PGCE, PGDip

School of Geography & the Environment;
www.geog.ox.ac.uk

geographical research, space, place and society, earth system dynamics, biogeography, biodiversity and conservation, climate change and variability, climate change impacts and adaptation, complexity, contemporary urban life, island life, cultural spaces: geographies of affective experience, desert landscapes and dynamics, environmental change & management, environmental geography, European integration, forensic geography, geographies of finance, geographies of nature, geopolitics in the margin, heritage science & conservation, post-Soviet Russia in transition, quaternary period: natural & human systems, transport & mobilities, geography & the environment, conservation/environmental change & management, nature, society & environmental governance, water science, policy & management; BA(Hons), BCL, Dip, DPhil, MJur, MLitt, MPhil, MSc, MSt, PGDip

School of Interdisciplinary Area Studies;
www.area-studies.ox.ac.uk

African studies, Latin American studies, contemporary Chinese studies, contemporary India, modern Japanese studies, Middle East studies, Russian and East European studies, MBA, MSc, MPhil, DPhil

Dept of International Development;
www.qeh.ox.ac.

international development, development studies, economics for development, global governance and diplomacy, migration studies;MPhil, MSc, DPhil

Oxford Internet Institute; www.oii.ox.ac.uk

social science of the internet, information, communication & the social sciences; DPhil, MSc

Faculty of Law; www.law.ox.ac.uk

law, jurisprudence, jurisprudence with senior status, law with law studies in Europe, legal studies, Postgraduate; civil law, magister juris, criminology and criminal justice, law and finance, taxation, international human rights law, intellectual property law and practice
BA(Hons), BCL, Dip. DPhil, MJur, MLitt, MPhil, MSc, MSt, PGDip, MJur

Oxford Martin School;
www.oxfordmartin.ox.ac.uk

research in health & medicine, energy & environment, technology & society, ethics & governance

Oxford-Man Institute of Quantitative Finance; www.oxford-man.ox.ac.uk

data analysis and patterns in data, decision making under uncertainty and asset allocation, efficient markets, risk premia and market anomalies, electronic trading, numerical methods and high performance computing in finance, pensions, investments and hedge fund industry, stability of financial systems

Dept of Politics & International Relations;
www.politics.ox.ac.uk

history and politics, international relations, politics (political theory/European politics & society), political/political theory research, philosophy, politics and economics; BA(Hons), DPhil, MLitt, MPhil, MSc

Dept of Social Policy & Intervention;
www.spi.ox.ac.uk

comparative social policy, evidence-based social intervention and policy evaluation, social policy or social intervention, social policy, social intervention
BA, MPhil, MSc

Dept of Sociology; www.sociology.ox.ac.uk
sociology, history & politics, human sciences, philosophy, politics & economics, sociology and demography; BA(Hons), DPhil, MPhil, MSc

OXFORD BROOKES UNIVERSITY
www.brookes.ac.uk

Business School; www.brookes.ac.uk/OBBS
Undergraduate degrees in the following subjects: Accounting and Economics (BSc), Accounting and Finance, Business and Enterprise (FdA), Business and Management, Business and Management (BA top-up), Business and Marketing Management, Business Management, Business Management, International, Business, Enterprise and Entrepreneurship, Business, Management and Communications (BA top-up), Business, Management and Communications (FdA), Economics, Economics, Finance and International Business, Economics, Politics and International Relations, Events Management, Events Management (FdA), Finance, Accounting and, Finance, International Business, and Economics, Human Resource Management, International Business Management, International Business, Finance, and Economics, International Relations, Economics and Politics, Management, Business, Management, Business and, Management, Business and Marketing, Management, International Business, Management, Marketing, Marketing (and Business) Management, Marketing Management, Politics, Economics and International Relations
Postgraduate courses in the following subjects: Accounting, Accounting and Finance, Applied Accounting MSc, Brand Management, Marketing and, Business Management, Business Management (Corporate Social Responsibility), Business Management (Economics), Business Management (Entrepreneurship), Business Management (Human Resource Management), Business Management (Marketing), Coaching and Mentoring Practice, Digital Marketing, Doctor of Coaching and Mentoring, Economics, International Business, Events Management, International, Finance, Finance, Accounting and, Human Resource Management (MSc), Human Resource Management (part-time MA), Human Resource Management MA, International Business Economics, International Events Management, International Events Marketing, International Luxury Marketing,

International Management, International Management and International Relations, International Relations, International Management and, International Trade and Logistics, Management, Business, Management, Business (Corporate Social Responsibility), Management, Business (Economics), Management, Business (Entrepreneurship), Management, Business (Human Resources Management), Management, Business (Marketing), Management, Human Resource (part-time MA), Management, Human Resources (MSc), Management, International, Marketing, Marketing and Brand Management, Marketing, Digital, Marketing, International Events, Marketing, International Luxury, MBA, Oxford Brookes, Mentoring and Coaching, Doctor of, Oxford Brookes MBA, Trade and Logistics, International

Department of Biological and Medical Sciences; www.brookes.ac.uk/bms
Undergraduate degrees in the following subjects: Animal Behaviour and Welfare (BSc top-up), Animal Behaviour and Welfare (FdSc), Animal Biology and Conservation, Animal Conservation (BSc top-up), Animal Conservation (FdSc), Applied Animal Management (BSc top-up), Applied Animal Management (FdSc), Applied Biosciences (Health Informatics) (BSc top-up), Applied Biosciences (Health Informatics) (FdSc), Biological Sciences, Biology, Biology, MBiol, Biomedical Science, Conservation, Animal Biology and, Environmental Sciences, Equine Science (BSc Hons), Equine Science and Thoroughbred Management (BSc Hons), Human Biology, Life Sciences Foundation, MBiol Biology, Medical Science
Postgraduate courses in the following subjects: Conservation Ecology, Genetics and Genomics, Medical, Medical Genetics and Genomics

Department of English and Modern Languages; www.brookes.ac.uk/english-languages
Undergraduate degrees in the following subjects: Applied Languages, Creative Writing, English Literature with, Drama, English Literature, English

Literature with Creative Writing, BA(Hons), Japanese Studies, Languages Applied, Literature, English, Studies, Japanese

Postgraduate courses in the following subjects: Business, Culture and Languages, International, Creative Writing MA, English Literature, International Business, Culture and Languages, Literature, English, Writing, Creative

Department of Midwifery, Community and Public Health; www.brookes.ac.uk/mcph

Midwifery BSc(Hons)

Postgraduate courses in the following subjects: Health, Public, Midwifery – Pre-Registration, Pre-Registration, Midwifery, Public Health, Specialist Community Public Health Nursing (Health Visiting or School Nursing)

Department of Nursing; www.brookes.ac.uk/nursing

Undergraduate degrees in the following subjects: Adult and Mental Health Nursing, MSci, Adult Nursing, Children's Nursing, Health and Social Care (FdSc), Mental Health and Child Nursing, MSci, Mental Health Nursing, MSci Nursing (Adult and Mental Health), MSci Nursing (Mental Health and Child), Nursing (Adult), Nursing (Children's), Nursing (Mental Health)

Postgraduate courses in the following subjects: Acute Care of the Older Person with Frailty, Postgraduate Certificate, Adult Intensive Care Practice, Postgraduate Certificate, Adult Nursing – Pre-Registration MSc, Advanced Nursing Practice, Advanced Practice (Clinical), Cancer Studies, Cardio Respiratory Practice, Postgraduate Certificate, Children's High Dependency Practice, Postgraduate Certificate, Children's Nursing Pre-Registration MSc, Children's Nursing, Community, Community Children's Nursing, District Nursing, Emergency Nursing Practice, Postgraduate Certificate, Mental Health Nursing – Pre-Registration, Neonatal Practice, Postgraduate Certificate, Nursing (Adult) – Pre-Registration, Nursing (Children's) Pre-Registration, Nursing (Mental Health) – Pre-Registration, Nursing Practice, Advanced, Nursing Studies Leadership in Clinical Practice, Nursing, District, Orthopaedic Practice, Postgraduate Certificate, Postgraduate Certificate in Acute Care of the Older Person with Frailty, Postgraduate Certificate in Adult Intensive Care Practice, Postgraduate Certificate in Cardio Respiratory Practice, Postgraduate Certificate in Children's High Dependency Practice, Postgraduate Certificate in Emergency Nursing Practice, Postgraduate Certificate in Neonatal Practice,

Postgraduate Certificate in Orthopaedic Practice, Postgraduate Certificate in Renal and Urology Practice, Renal and Urology Practice, Postgraduate Certificate, Studies, Nursing

Department of Psychology, Health and Professional Development; www.brookes.ac.uk/phpd

Undergraduate degrees in the following subjects: Health Sciences Open Award, Operating Department Practice BSc, Paramedic Science, Psychology

Postgraduate courses in the following subjects: Adult High Dependency Care Practice, Postgraduate Certificate, Health and Social Care, Management in, Health Sciences Open Award, Higher Professional Education, Management in Health and Social Care, Minor Injury and Illness Management, Postgraduate Certificate, Postgraduate Certificate in Adult High Dependency Care Practice, Postgraduate Certificate in Minor Injury and Illness Management, Professional Education, Higher, Psychology (MSc), Psychology (Qualifying Certificate), Qualifying Certificate Psychology

Department of Social Sciences; www.brookes.ac.uk/social-sciences

Undergraduate degrees in the following subjects: Anthropology, Anthropology, Biological, Anthropology, Social, Biological Anthropology BSc(Hons), Geography, International Relations, International Relations and Politics, Policing (FdA), Politics, Politics, International Relations and, Social Anthropology BA(Hons), Sociology

Postgraduate courses in the following subjects: Anthropology, Conservation, Primate – Apes in the Anthropocene (MSc), Conservation, Primate – Apes in the Anthropocene (PGCert), Conservation, Primate – Apes in the Anthropocene (PGDip), Conservation, Primate – Human-Primate Interface (MSc), Conservation, Primate – Human-Primate Interface (PGCert), Conservation, Primate – Human-Primate Interface (PGDip), Conservation, Primate – Lemurs and Nocturnal Primates (MSc), Conservation, Primate – Lemurs and Nocturnal Primates (PGCert), Conservation, Primate – Lemurs and Nocturnal Primates (PGDip), Conservation, Primate (MSc), Conservation, Primate (PGCert), Conservation, Primate (PGDip), Conservation, Primatology and (MRes), International Relations, International Security, PGCert Primate Conservation – Lemurs and Nocturnal Primates, Primate Conservation – Apes in the Anthropocene (MSc), Primate Conservation – Apes in the Anthropocene (PGCert), Primate Conservation – Apes in the

Anthropocene (PGDip), Primate Conservation – Human-Primate Interface (MSc), Primate Conservation – Human-Primate Interface (PGCert), Primate Conservation – Human-Primate Interface (PGDip), Primate Conservation – Lemurs and Nocturnal Primates (MSc), Primate Conservation – Lemurs and Nocturnal Primates (PGDip), Primate Conservation (MSc), Primate Conservation (PGCert), Primate Conservation (PGDip), Primatology and Conservation (MRes), Relations, International, Security, International

Department of Sport, Health Sciences and Social Work; www.brookes.ac.uk/shssw

Undergraduate degrees in the following subjects: Applied Sports Science (BSc top-up), Coaching Science (FdSc), Coaching, Sport and Physical Education, Nutrition, Occupational Therapy, Physical Education, Sport and Coaching, Physiotherapy, Social Work, Sport and Exercise Science, Sport, Coaching and Physical Education, Sports Coaching, Fitness and Rehabilitation (FdSc), Sports Science with Sports Coaching Education (FdSc)

Postgraduate courses in the following subjects: Applied Human Nutrition, Applied Sport and Exercise Nutrition, Child Protection Practice, Child Welfare and Wellbeing, Nutrition, Applied Human, Occupational Therapy (Pre-Registration), Physiotherapy (Pre-Registration), Pre-Registration, Physiotherapy, Rehabilitation, Social Work, Sport and Exercise Nutrition, Applied, Therapy, Occupational

School of Architecture; www.architecture.brookes.ac.uk

Undergraduate degrees in the following subjects: Architecture, Architecture, Interior, Interior Architecture

Postgraduate courses in the following subjects: Architectural Regeneration and Development, International, Architecture, Applied Design in, MArchD (ARB and RIBA part 2), Architecture, MArch, Development and Emergency Practice, Disaster, Shelter, Emergency Practice, and Development, Humanitarian Action and Peacebuilding, International Architectural Regeneration and Development, MArch Architecture, MArchD Applied Design in Architecture (ARB and RIBA part 2), Shelter after Disaster, Sustainable Building – Performance and Design

School of Arts; www.brookes.ac.uk/school-of-arts

Undergraduate degrees in the following subjects:]Art and Design Foundation, Art, Fine, Creative Arts and Design Practice (BA top-up), Creative Arts and Design Practice (FdA), Creative Music Production, Digital Media Production, Film Studies, Fine Art, Furniture Design and Make (BA top-up), Furniture Design and Make (FdA), Graphic Design (BA Hons), Illustration (BA Hons), Media Production, Digital, Music, Publishing Media

Postgraduate courses in the following subjects: Art, Fine (MFA), Connective Practice, MA Social Structure, Digital Media Production, Digital Publishing, Film Studies: Popular Cinema, Fine Art (MFA), Media Production, Digital, Music, Popular Cinema: Film Studies, Publishing Media (MA), Publishing Studies (distance learning), Publishing, Digital, Sculpture, Social, Social Sculpture and Connective Practice, Sound Arts (MA)

School of Education; www.brookes.ac.uk/education

Undergraduate degrees in the following subjects: Childhood Studies, Early, Communication, and English Language, Early Childhood Studies, Early Childhood Studies (BA top-up), Early Years (FdA), Education and Lifelong Learning (BA top-up), Education Studies, Education Studies: SEN, Disabilities and Inclusion, Education, Primary Teacher (Campus-Based), Educational Practice (FdA), English Language and Communication, Primary Teacher Education (Campus-Based)

Postgraduate courses in the following subjects: Advanced Study in SEMH Difficulties, PGCert Education, Challenging Behaviour, PGCert Education, Childhood and Youth Studies, MA Education, Children's Literature, PGCert Education, Doctor of Education, Early Childhood, PGCert Education, Education (MA), Education, Doctor of, Further Education, PGCert Education, Higher Education, MA in Education, Leadership and Management, MA Education, Leadership and Management, PGCert Education, Literacy Difficulties, Working with Children With, MA Education – Leadership and Management, MA Education – TESOL, MA Education: Childhood and Youth Studies, MA in Education – Higher Education, National Award for SEN Coordination, PGCert Education, PGCE Education – Post-compulsory, PGCE Primary (campus based) 3-7, PGCE Primary (campus based) 5-11, PGCE without QTS, PGCert Education: Advanced

Study in SEMH Difficulties, PGCert Education: Challenging Behaviour, PGCert Education: Children's Literature, PGCert Education: Early Childhood, PGCert Education: Further Education, PGCert Education: Leadership and Management, PGCert Education: National Award for SEN Coordination, PGCert Education: Teaching English as an Additional Language (EAL), PGCert Education: Understanding and Managing SEMH Difficulties, Post-compulsory Education (PGCE), Postgraduate Certificate: Working with Children with Literacy Difficulties, Teaching English as an Additional Language (EAL), PGCert Education, TESOL, MA Education, Understanding and Managing SEMH Difficulties, PGCert Education

School of Engineering, Computing and Mathematics; www.brookes.ac.uk/ecm

Undergraduate degrees in the following subjects: Automotive Engineering (BEng / MEng), Business Management, Information Technology, Business, Software Development, Computer Science, Computer Science for Cyber Security, Computing (FdSc), Computing for Robotic Systems, Computing Foundation, Computing, Network, Cyber Security, Computer Science for, Electrical and Electronic Engineering (FdEng, Abingdon and Witney College), Electrical and Electronic Engineering (FdEng, Solihull College), Electronic Engineering (BSc top-up course), Electronic Engineering (BSc top-up), Engineering Foundation, Engineering, Automotive (BEng / MEng), Engineering, Mechanical, Engineering, Mechanical (BEng / MEng), Engineering, Motorsport (BEng / MEng), Foundation, Engineering, Information Technology Management for Business, Mathematical Sciences, Mathematics, Mathematics, MMath, Mechanical Engineering, Mechanical Engineering (BEng / MEng), Mechanical Engineering (BSc top-up), Mechanical Engineering (FdEng, Abingdon and Witney College), Mechanical Engineering (FdEng, Solihull College), MMath Mathematics, Motorsport Engineering (BEng / MEng), Motorsport Engineering (FdEng, Bridgwater and Taunton College), Motorsport Engineering (FdEng, Brooklands College), Motorsport Technology (BSc top-up), Motorsport Technology (BSc), Motorsports – Performance and Automotive Technology (FdEng), Network Computing, Robotics System Engineering, Software Development for Business, Technology, Motorsport

Postgraduate courses in the following subjects: Automotive Engineering (MSc), Computer Science, Computer Science for Cyber Security, Computing, Cyber Security, Computer Science for, Data Analytics for Government, eBusiness, Engine Design, Racing, Engineering, Automotive, Engineering, Mechanical MSc, Engineering, Motorsport, Engineering, Software, Government, Data Analytics for, IT Systems Administration and Management, Mechanical Engineering MSc, Mobile and High Speed Telecommunication Networks, Motorsport Engineering, Racing Engine Design, Software Engineering, Systems Administration and Management, IT, Telecommunication Networks, Mobile and High Speed

School of History, Philosophy and Culture; www.brookes.ac.uk/hpc

Undergraduate degrees in the following subjects: Art, History of, Communication, Media and Culture, Criminology, History, History of Art, Philosophy

Postgraduate courses in the following subjects: History, History of Medicine, MA History, MA History (History of Medicine)

School of Law; www.brookes.ac.uk/school-of-law

LLB Law

Postgraduate courses in the following subjects: Graduate Diploma in Law, Human Rights, International law, International Economic Law, LLM, International Human Rights, Law, International Law, Globalisation and Development, International Law, LLM, Law (GDL), Law, International, Law, International Economic, Law, International Human Rights, Law, International Trade and Commercial, LLM in International Economic Law, LLM in International Human Rights Law, LLM in International Law, LLM in International Law, Globalisation and Development, LLM in International Trade and Commercial Law

School of the Built Environment; be.brookes.ac.uk

Undergraduate degrees in the following subjects: Built Environment Foundation, Commercial Management, Quantity Surveying and, Construction Project Management, Estate Management, Real, Foundation in Built Environment, Management (Commercial), Quantity Surveying and, Management, Construction, Management, Real Estate, Planning and Property Development, Planning, Development and Urban Design, Project Management (Construction), Property Development and Planning, Quantity Surveying and Commercial Management, Real Estate Management, Surveying (Planning and Property Development course), Urban Design, Planning and Development

Postgraduate courses in the following subjects: Building Information Modelling and Management, Certificate in Spatial Planning Studies, Commercial and Residential, Real Estate, Commercial Management, Quantity Surveying and, Conservation, Historic, Construction Project Management, Design, Urban (MA), Diploma in Planning, EAM, Environmental Assessment and Management, Historic Conservation, Investment Finance, Real Estate, Management, Environmental Assessment, Planning, Diploma in, Planning, Spatial, Planning, Urban, Developing and Transitional Regions, Project Management in the Built Environment, Project Management, Construction, Quantity Surveying and Commercial Management MSc, Real Estate, Real Estate Investment Finance, Spatial Planning, Spatial Planning Studies, Certificate in, Urban Design (MA),

Urban Planning, Developing and Transitional Regions

The Oxford School of Hospitality Management; www.brookes.ac.uk/hospitality

Undergraduate degrees in the following subjects: Hospitality Management, International, International Hospitality Management, Management, International Hospitality

Postgraduate courses in the following subjects: Hospitality, Events and Tourism Management, International, Hotel and Tourism Management, International, International Hospitality, Events and Tourism Management, International Hotel and Tourism Management, International Tourism Management, Tourism Management, International

UNIVERSITY OF PLYMOUTH
www.plymouth.ac.uk

Plymouth Business School; www.plymouth.ac.uk/schools/plymouth-business-school

BSc(Hons) Business Enterprise and Entrepreneurship (2 year Fast Track), BSc(Hons) Business Management (2 Year Fast Track), BSc(Hons) Business Management, BSc(Hons) Cruise Management, BSc(Hons) Economics, BSc(Hons) Economics with International Relations, BSc(Hons) Economics with Law, BSc(Hons) Economics with Politics, BSc(Hons) Events Management, BSc(Hons) Financial Economics, BSc(Hons) Financial Management, BSc(Hons) Hospitality Management, BSc(Hons) International Business Economics, BSc(Hons) International Hospitality Management, BSc(Hons) International Supply Chain and Shipping Management, BSc(Hons) International Tourism Management, BSc(Hons) Management Practice, BSc(Hons) Maritime Business and Logistics, BSc(Hons) Maritime Business and Maritime Law, BSc(Hons) Maritime Transport and Logistics, BSc(Hons) Marketing, BSc(Hons) Professional Management Practice, BSc(Hons) Tourism and Hospitality Management, BSc(Hons) Tourism Management

Postgraduate courses: DBA Business Administration, DPA Public Administration, MA Human Resource Management, MA Human Resource Management, MA Human Resource Management (top-up), Management, Government and Law (Foundation Route for Specified Qualification), MBA Master of Business

Administration (top-up), MSc Accounting and Finance, MSc Brand and Design Management, MSc Business and Management, MSc Digital and Social Media Marketing, MSc Entrepreneurship, MSc Entrepreneurship and International Development, MSc Finance, MSc Finance and Investment, MSc International Business, MSc International Hospitality Management, MSc International Logistics and Supply Chain Management, MSc International Procurement and Supply Chain Management, MSc International Shipping, MSc Management, MSc Operations and Supply Chain Management, MSc Tourism and Hospitality Management

Plymouth Institute of Education; www.plymouth.ac.uk/schools/education

BA(Hons) Early Childhood Studies, BA(Hons) Education Studies, BEd(Hons) Primary (Art and Design), BEd(Hons) Primary (Early Childhood Studies), BEd(Hons) Primary (English), BEd(Hons) Primary (Humanities), BEd(Hons) Primary (Mathematics), BEd(Hons) Primary (Music), BEd(Hons) Primary (Physical Education), BEd(Hons) Primary (Science), BEd(Hons) Primary (Special Educational Needs), CertEd Certificate in Education (incorporating the Diploma in Education and Training), CertEd Certificate in Education (incorporating the Diploma in Education and Training)

Postgraduate courses: EdD Education, MA Education, PGCE (incorporating the Diploma in Education and Training), PGCE (incorporating the Diploma in Education and Training), PGCE Primary (Early Years), PGCE Primary, PGCE Secondary (Art & Design), PGCE Secondary (Computer Science), PGCE Secondary (Design and Technology), PGCE Secondary (Drama), PGCE Secondary (English), PGCE Secondary (Geography), PGCE Secondary (Mathematics), PGCE Secondary (Music), PGCE Secondary (Science with Biology), PGCE Secondary (Science with Chemistry), PGCE Secondary (Science with Physics), PgCert Education: Autism, PgCert Post-16 Mathematics Education, PgCert The National Award for Special Educational Needs Coordination, PhD Education

Plymouth University Peninsula School of Dentistry; www.plymouth.ac.uk/schools/peninsula-school-of-dentistry

BDS Dental Surgery, BSc(Hons) Dental Therapy and Hygiene
Postgraduate courses: MSc Minor Oral Surgery, MSc Periodontology, MSc Restorative Dentistry

Plymouth University Peninsula School of Medicine; www.plymouth.ac.uk/schools/peninsula-school-of-medicine

BMBS Bachelor of Medicine, Bachelor of Surgery
Postgraduate courses: MClinEd Clinical Education, MClinEd Clinical Education, MSc Global and Remote Healthcare, MSc Global and Remote Healthcare, MSc Healthcare Management, Leadership and Innovation, MSc Healthcare Management, Leadership and Innovation, MSc Simulation and Patient Safety, MSc Simulation and Patient Safety, PgCert Clinical Education, PgCert Healthcare Management, Leadership and Innovation, PgCert Simulation and Patient Safety, PgDip Clinical Education, PgDip Healthcare Management, Leadership and Innovation, PgDip Physician Associate Studies, PgDip Simulation and Patient Safety

School of Art, Design and Architecture; www.plymouth.ac.uk/schools/school-of-art-design-and-architecture

BA(Hons) 3D Design, BA(Hons) Architectural Technology and the Environment, BA(Hons) Architecture, BA(Hons) Digital Media Design, BA(Hons) Documentary Photography, BA(Hons) Film & Television Production, BA(Hons) Fine Art, BA(Hons) Game Arts and Design, BA(Hons) Graphic Communication with Typography, BA(Hons) Illustration, BA(Hons) Internet Design, BA(Hons) Media Arts, BA(Hons) Photography, BA(Hons) Publishing, BSc(Hons) Architectural Engineering, BSc(Hons) Building Surveying and the Environment, BSc(Hons) Construction Management and the Environment, BSc(Hons) Digital Media Design, BSc(Hons) Internet Design
Postgraduate courses: MA Architecture, MA Contemporary Art Practice, MA Design, MA Photography, MA Publishing, MA Publishing, MArch Architecture, MFA Photographic Arts, MRes Digital Art and Technology, MSc High Performance Buildings, ResM Art, Design and Architecture

School of Biological and Marine Sciences; www.plymouth.ac.uk/schools/school-of-biological-and-marine-sciences

BSc(Hons) Animal Behaviour and Welfare, BSc(Hons) Animal Conservation Science, BSc(Hons) Biological Sciences, BSc(Hons) Biosciences, BSc(Hons) Conservation Biology, BSc(Hons) Marine Biology, BSc(Hons) Marine Biology and Coastal Ecology, BSc(Hons) Marine Biology and Oceanography, BSc(Hons) Ocean Exploration and Surveying, BSc(Hons) Ocean Science and Marine Conservation, BSc(Hons) Oceanography and Coastal Processes
Postgraduate courses: MRes Applied Marine Science, MRes Marine Biology, MRes Marine Renewable Energy, MSc Applied Marine Science, MSc Hydrography, MSc Marine Renewable Energy, MSc Sustainable Aquaculture Systems, MSc Zoo Conservation Biology, MSci(Hons) Ocean Science, ResM Biological Sciences

School of Biomedical and Healthcare Sciences

BSc(Hons) Biomedical Science, BSc(Hons) Health and Fitness, BSc(Hons) Healthcare Science (Life Sciences), BSc(Hons) Healthcare Science (Physiological Sciences), BSc(Hons) Human Biosciences, BSc(Hons) Nutrition, Exercise and Health
Postgraduate courses: MSc Biomedical Science, MSc Biomedical Science, PgDip Biomedical Science

School of Computing, Electronics and Mathematics; www.plymouth.ac.uk/schools/school-of-computing-electronics-and-mathematics

BEng(Hons) Civil Engineering with Foundation Year, BEng(Hons) Electrical and Electronic Engineering, BEng(Hons) Electrical and Electronic Engineering with Foundation Year, BEng(Hons) Mechanical Engineering with Foundation Year, BEng(Hons) Robotic Engineering with Foundation Year, BEng(Hons) Robotics, BSc(Hons) Computer and Information Security, BSc(Hons) Computer Science, BSc(Hons)

Computer Systems and Networks, BSc(Hons) Computing & Games Development, BSc(Hons) Computing, BSc(Hons) Computing with Foundation Year, BSc(Hons) Data Modelling and Analytics, BSc(Hons) Electrical and Electronic Engineering, BSc(Hons) Mathematics, BSc(Hons) Mathematics and Statistics, BSc(Hons) Mathematics with Education, BSc(Hons) Mathematics with Finance, BSc(Hons) Mathematics with Foundation Year, BSc(Hons) Mathematics with High Performance Computing, BSc(Hons) Mathematics with Theoretical Physics, BSc(Hons) Robotics
Postgraduate courses: MEng(Hons) Electrical and Electronic Engineering, MEng(Hons) Robotics, MRes Robotics, MSc Computer and Information Security, MSc Computer Science (Conversion), MSc Data Science and Business Analytics, MSc Electrical and Electronic Engineering, MSc Robotics, MSci(-Hons) Computer Science

School of Engineering; www.plymouth.ac.uk/schools/school-of-engineering
BEng(Hons) Civil and Coastal Engineering, BEng(Hons) Civil Engineering, BEng(Hons) Marine Technology, BEng(Hons) Mechanical Engineering, BEng(Hons) Mechanical Engineering with Composites, BSc(Hons) Marine and Composites Technology, BSc(Hons) Mechanical Design and Manufacture, BSc(Hons) Navigation and Maritime Science, FdSc Navigation and Maritime Science
MEng(Hons) Civil and Coastal Engineering, MEng(Hons) Civil Engineering, MEng(Hons) Marine Technology, MEng(Hons) Mechanical Engineering, MEng(Hons) Mechanical Engineering with Composites, MSc Advanced Engineering Design, MSc Civil Engineering, MSc Coastal Engineering

School of Geography, Earth and Environmental Sciences; www.plymouth.ac.uk/schools/school-of-geography-earth-and-environmental-sciences
BA(Hons) Geography, BA(Hons) Geography with International Relations, BSc(Hons) Applied Geology, BSc(Hons) Biology with Foundation Year, BSc(Hons) Chemistry, BSc(Hons) Chemistry with Foundation Year, BSc(Hons) Earth Sciences with Foundation Year, BSc(Hons) Environmental Management and Sustainability, BSc(Hons) Environmental Science, BSc(Hons) Environmental Science with Foundation Year, BSc(Hons) Extended Science, BSc(Hons) Geography, BSc(Hons) Geography with Ocean Science, BSc(Hons) Geology, BSc(Hons) Geology with Ocean Science, BSc(Hons) Human Biology with Foundation Year, BSc(Hons) Marine Biology with Foundation Year, BSc(Hons) Marine Sciences with Foundation Year, BSc(Hons) Physical Geography and Geology MChem Analytical Chemistry, MGeol Geology, MRes Sustainable Environmental Management, MSc Analytical Chemistry, MSc Environmental Consultancy, MSc Planning, MSc Sustainable Environmental Management, MSc Sustainable Geoscience

School of Health Professions; www.plymouth.ac.uk/schools/school-of-health-professions
BA(Hons) Social Work, BSc(Hons) Dietetics, BSc(Hons) Occupational Therapy, BSc(Hons) Optometry, BSc(Hons) Paramedic Practitioner, BSc(Hons) Physiotherapy, BSc(Hons) Podiatry
Postgraduate courses: MA Social Work, MClinRes Clinical Research, MSc Advanced Professional Practice (Health and Social Care Professions), MSc Advanced Professional Practice in Dietetics, MSc Advanced Professional Practice in Neurological Rehabilitation, MSc Advanced Professional Practice in Occupational Therapy, MSc Advanced Professional Practice in Paediatric Dietetics, MSc Advanced Professional Practice in Physiotherapy, MSc Advanced Professional Practice in Safeguarding Adults, MSc Human Nutrition, MSc Occupational Therapy (Pre-Registration), MSc Pre-Hospital Critical Care/Retrieval and Transfer

School of Humanities and Performing Arts; www.plymouth.ac.uk/schools/hpa
BA(Hons) Acting, BA(Hons) Anthropology, BA(Hons) Art History, BA(Hons) Dance, BA(Hons) English, BA(Hons) English and Creative Writing, BA(Hons) English with French, BA(Hons) English with History, BA(Hons) English with Publishing, BA(Hons) English with Spanish, BA(Hons) Fine Art and Art History, BA(Hons) History, BA(Hons) History with English, BA(Hons) History with International Relations, BA(Hons) History with Politics, BA(Hons) Music, BA(Hons) Theatre and Performance
Postgraduate courses: MA Archival Practice, MA Creative Writing, MA English Literature, MA English Literature, MA History, MA Performance Training, MFA Performance Training, MRes English, ResM Art History, ResM Computer Music, ResM Dance, ResM History, ResM Theatre and Performance

School of Law, Criminology and Government; www.plymouth.ac.uk/schools/law-criminology-government

BSc(Hons) Criminology and Criminal Justice Studies, BSc(Hons) Criminology and Criminal Justice Studies with International Relations, BSc(Hons) Criminology and Criminal Justice Studies with Law, BSc(Hons) Criminology and Criminal Justice Studies with Psychology, BSc(Hons) Criminology and Criminal Justice Studies with Sociology, BSc(Hons) International Relations, BSc(Hons) International Relations with Law, BSc(Hons) International Relations with Politics, BSc(Hons) International Relations with Psychology, BSc(Hons) International Relations with Spanish, BSc(Hons) Law with Business, BSc(Hons) Law with Criminology and Criminal Justice Studies, BSc(Hons) Police and Criminal Justice Studies, BSc(Hons) Politics with History, BSc(Hons) Politics with International Relations, BSc(Hons) Politics with Law, BSc(Hons) Public Services (Policing), BSc(Hons) Sociology, GradDip Law, LLB(Hons) Law, LLB(Hons) Law with Business, LLB(Hons) Law with Criminology and Criminal Justice Studies
Postgraduate courses: MA International Relations: Global Security and Development, MSc Criminology

School of Nursing and Midwifery; www.plymouth.ac.uk/schools/school-of-nursing-and-midwifery

BSc(Hons) Critical Care (Intercalated), BSc(Hons) Critical Care, BSc(Hons) Nursing (Adult), BSc(Hons) Nursing (Child Health), BSc(Hons) Nursing (Mental Health), BSc(Hons) Pre-Registration Midwifery, BSc(Hons) Professional Development in Advancing Practice, BSc(Hons) Professional Development in Community and Primary Care, BSc(Hons) Professional Development in Critical Care, BSc(Hons) Professional Development in End of Life Care, BSc(Hons) Professional Development in Health and Social Care, BSc(Hons) Professional Development in Long Term Conditions, BSc(Hons) Professional Development in Mental Health, BSc(Hons) Professional Development in Neonatal Care, BSc(Hons) Professional Development in Nursing, BSc(Hons) Urgent and Emergency Care (Intercalated), BSc(Hons) Urgent and Emergency Care
Postgraduate courses: MSc Advanced Critical Care Practitioner, MSc Advanced Neonatal Nurse Practitioner, MSc Advanced Professional Practice (Clinical Practitioner), MSc Advanced Professional Practice (Community and Primary Care Practitioner), MSc Advanced Professional Practice (Mental Health Practitioner), MSc Advanced Professional Practice (Nursing and Midwifery Professions), MSc Contemporary Healthcare (Education), MSc Surgical Care Practitioner (Abdominal, Pelvic and General Surgery), MSc Surgical Care Practitioner (Cardiothoracic Surgery), MSc Surgical Care Practitioner (Trauma and Orthopaedic Surgery), PgDip Advanced Critical Care Practitioner, PgDip Surgical Care Practitioner (Abdominal, Pelvic and General Surgery), PgDip Surgical Care Practitioner (Cardiothoracic Surgery), PgDip Surgical Care Practitioner (Trauma and Orthopaedic Surgery)

School of Psychology; www.plymouth.ac.uk/schools/psychology

BSc(Hons) Psychological Studies, BSc(Hons) Psychology, BSc(Hons) Psychology with Criminology and Criminal Justice Studies, BSc(Hons) Psychology with Human Biology, BSc(Hons) Psychology with Sociology
Postgraduate courses: DClinPsy Clinical Psychology, MPsych Advanced Psychology, MSc Psychological Research Methods, MSc Psychology

SOUTH DEVON COLLEGE
www.southdevon.ac.uk

FdSc Adventure Leadership, FdSc Animal Science, BSc(Hons) Applied Animal Science, FdSc Biosciences, FdA Business & Management, BA(Hons) Child Development and Education, FdSc/HNC Civil and Coastal Engineering, BSc(Hons) Civil Engineering, BSc(Hons) Coaching (Outdoor Leadership), BSc(Hons) Coaching (Sports Performance and Development), FdSc Computing, FdSc Criminology and Psychology, BSc(Hons) Digital and Technology Solutions, FdA Digital Marketing, FdA Drama, Performance and Arts Management, FdA Early Years Care and Education, FdSc/HNC Electronics and Robotic Control Engineering, BSc Extended Science (Year 0), FdA Fashion with Textiles, FdA Film and Photography, FdA Games and Interactive Design, FdSc Healthcare Practice, BSc(Hons) Healthcare Practice, FdA History with English, FdA Illustration Arts, FdSc Law, BA(Hons) Leadership and Management, FdSc/HNC Manufacturing and Mechatronic Engineering, FdSc Marine Technologies,

PGCE (incorporating the Diploma in Education and Training), FdA Professional Practice in Construction Operations Management, FdSc Psychology with Sociology, FdSc Sport and Exercise Science, FdSc Sustainable Construction and the Built Environment, FdA Teaching and Learning, FdA Tourism, Hospitality and Events Management, FdSc Yacht Operations

---

TRURO & PENWITH COLLEGE
www.trurocollege.ac.uk

BA(Hons) Applied Media, BA(Hons) Business, Enterprise and Leadership, BA(Hons) Education and Training, BA(Hons) Human Behavioural Studies, BA(Hons) Silversmithing and Jewellery, BSc(Hons) Applied Computing Technologies, BSc(Hons) Applied Social Science, BSc(Hons) Applied Sport and Health Science, BSc(Hons) Archaeology, FDA Business, FDA Childhood Education, FDA Childhood Education, FDA Children and Young Peoples Workforce, FDA Commercial Music Performance and Production, FDA Computer Games Design and Production, FDA Counselling Studies, FDA English Studies, FDA Health and Social Care, FDA History, Heritage and Archaeology, FDA Illustration (Digital), FDA Interior Design Practice, FDA Photography and Digital Imaging, FDA Silversmithing and Jewellery, FDSc Archaeology, FDSc Biomedical Studies, FDSc Community Studies (Development and Youth Work), FDSc Computer Technology, FDSc Exercise, Health and Fitness, FDSc Health and Nutrition, FDSc Law, FDSc Outdoor Education, FDSc Public Services, FDSc Public Services, FDSc Sports Coaching, FDSc Sports Coaching, FDSc Sports Rehabilitation, FDSc Web Technology, HNC Applied Psychology, HNC Applied Psychology, HNC Art and Design, HNC Business, HNC Children and Young Peoples Workforce, HNC Children and Young Peoples Workforce, HNC Computer Games Design and Production, HNC Hospitality Management, HND Applied Psychology, HND Applied Psychology, HND Art and Design, HND Fine Art: Methods and Materials, HND Hospitality Management, HND Media Moving Image, Postgraduate Certificate in Education

---

UNIVERSITY OF PORTSMOUTH
www.port.ac.uk

Faculty of Creative and Cultural Industries; www.port.ac.uk/faculty-of-creative-and-cultural-industries

Portsmouth School of Architecture; www.port.ac.uk/portsmouth-school-of-architecture

Architecture BA(Hons), Interior Architecture and Design BA(Hons)

Postgraduate courses: Final Examination in Professional Practice (Part 3) Architecture, Historic Building Conservation MSc, Interior Design MA, International Professional Practice (Part 3) Architecture, Architecture MArch, Professional Design Practice MA, Sustainable Cities MA

School of Art and Design; www.port.ac.uk/school-of-art-and-design

Fashion and Textile Design BA(Hons), Graphic Design BA(Hons), Illustration BA(Hons), Photography BA(Hons)

Postgraduate courses: Data Visualisation Design MA, Fashion and Textiles MA, Graphic Design MA, Illustration MA, Photography MA

School of Creative Technologies; www.port.ac.uk/school-of-creative-technologies

Animation BA(Hons), Broadcast Journalism BSc(Hons), Computer Animation and Visual Effects BSc(Hons), Computer Games Enterprise BSc(Hons), Computer Games Technology BSc(Hons), Creative Media Technologies BSc(Hons), Digital Media BSc(Hons), Film Production BA(Hons), Film Production with Business Communication BA(Hons), Music and Sound Technology BSc(Hons), Music Computing BSc(Hons), Television and Broadcasting BSc(Hons)

Postgraduate courses: Creative Technologies MSc, Digital Media MSc, Creative Industries MRes

School of Media and Performing Arts; www.port.ac.uk/school-of-media-and-performing-arts

Creative Writing BA(Hons), Drama and Performance BA(Hons), English and Creative Writing BA(Hons), Film Industries BA(Hons), Film Industries and Creative Writing BA(Hons), Media and Digital Practice BA(Hons), Media Studies BA(Hons), Musical Theatre BA(Hons)

Postgraduate courses: Creative Writing MA, Media and Communication MA, Creative Industries MRes

Faculty of Humanities and Social Sciences; www.port.ac.uk/faculty-of-humanities-and-social-sciences

School of Education and Childhood Studies; www.port.ac.uk/school-of-education-and-childhood-studies

Further Education and Training CertEd, Childhood and Youth Studies BA(Hons), Childhood and Youth Studies with Psychology BA(Hons), Early Childhood Studies BA(Hons), Early Childhood Studies with Psychology BA(Hons), Early Years Care and Education FdA, Education Studies (Top-Up) BA(Hons), Early Years Initial Teacher Training GradCert, Learning Support FdA

Postgraduate courses: Education Studies MA, Educational Leadership and Management PgDip, Educational Leadership and Management PgCert, Educational Leadership and Management MSc, Early Years Initial Teacher Training GradCert, MRes Humanities and Social Sciences MRes, PGCE Computer Science, PGCE English, Further Education and Training PGCE, PGCE Geography, PGCE Mathematics, PGCE Modern Foreign Languages, PGCE Science, Professional Doctorate in Education EdD

School of Languages and Area Studies; www.port.ac.uk/school-of-languages-and-area-studies

American Studies BA(Hons), American Studies and History BA(Hons), Applied Languages BA(Hons), Applied Languages MLang, Combined Modern Languages BA(Hons), Communication and English Studies BA(Hons), English and American Studies BA(Hons), English Language and Linguistics BA(Hons), French Studies BA(Hons), German Studies BA(Hons), International Business Communication BA(Hons), International Development Studies BA(Hons), International Development Studies and Languages BA(Hons), International Relations and Languages BA(Hons), International Trade and Business Communication BA(Hons), Languages, Cultures and Communication BA(Hons), Spanish and Latin American Studies BA(Hons), Spanish Studies BA(Hons)

Postgraduate courses: Applied Linguistics and TESOL MA, Communication and Applied Linguistics MA, International Development Studies MSc, International Development Studies PgCert, International Development Studies PgDip, MRes Humanities and Social Sciences MRes, TESOL, Leadership and Management (Distance Learning) MA, Translation Studies MA

School of Social, Historical and Literary Studies; www.port.ac.uk/school-of-social-historical-and-literary-studies

English and History BA(Hons), English and Media Studies BA(Hons), English Language and Literature BA(Hons), English Literature BA(Hons), History BA(Hons), History and Politics BA(Hons), International Relations BA(Hons), International Relations and History BA(Hons), International Relations and Politics BA(Hons), Journalism BA(Hons), Journalism with English Language BA(Hons), Journalism with English Literature BA(Hons), Journalism with Media Studies BA(Hons), Politics BA(Hons), Sociology BSc(Hons), Sociology and Criminology BSc(Hons), Sociology and Media Studies BA(Hons), Sociology with Psychology BSc(Hons)

Postgraduate courses: European Politics MA, International Relations MA, Public Administration MPA, MRes Humanities and Social Sciences MRes, Naval History MA

Portsmouth Business School; www.port.ac.uk/portsmouth-business-school

Accounting and Financial Management; www.port.ac.uk/accounting-and-financial-management

Accountancy and Financial Management (Top-up) BA(Hons), Accounting with Finance BA(Hons), Finance with Business Communication (Top-up) BA(Hons), Financial Management for Business BA(Hons)

Postgraduate courses: Accounting and Finance MSc, Financial Decision Analysis MSc, Forensic Accounting MSc

Economics and Finance; www.port.ac.uk/economics-and-finance

Business Economics BSc (Econ)(Hons), Economics BSc (Econ)(Hons), Economics and Management BA(Hons), Economics, Finance and Banking BSc (Econ)(Hons)

Postgraduate courses: Corporate Finance MSc, Economics, Finance and Banking MSc, Finance MSc, International Finance and Banking MSc

Marketing and Sales; www.port.ac.uk/marketing-and-sales

Digital Marketing BA(Hons), Marketing BA(Hons), Marketing with Psychology BA(Hons)

Postgraduate courses: Digital Marketing MA, Marketing MA, Sales Management MA

Organisation Studies and Human Resource Management; www.port.ac.uk/organisation-studies-and-human-resource-management

Business and Human Resource Management BA(Hons), Human Resource Management with Psychology BA(Hons)

Postgraduate courses: Coaching and Development MSc, Coaching and Development PgCert, Coaching and Development PgDip, Human Resource Development (Top-up) MSc, Human Resource Development and Training Management PgDip, Human Resource Management PgDip, Human Resource Management MSc, International Human Resource Management MSc, Leadership and Management (Top-up) MSc

Operations and Systems Management; www.port.ac.uk/operations-and-systems-management

Business and Supply Chain Management BSc(Hons), Business and Systems Management BSc(Hons)

Postgraduate courses: Project Management MSc, Strategic Quality Management MSc/PGDip/PGCert

Strategy, Enterprise and Innovation; www.port.ac.uk/strategy-enterprise-and-innovation

Business Management and Entrepreneurship BA(Hons)

Postgraduate courses: Innovation Management and Entrepreneurship MSc, Risk, Crisis and Resilience Management MSc

School of Law; www.port.ac.uk/school-of-law

Law LLB(Hons), Law with Business LLB(Hons), Law with Criminology LLB(Hons), Law with International Relations LLB(Hons)

Postgraduate courses: Corporate Governance and Law/Grad ICSA LLM, Law LLM, Alternative Dispute Resolution LLM, Alternative Dispute Resolution PgCert

Faculty of Science; www.port.ac.uk/faculty-of-science

School of Biological Sciences; www.port.ac.uk/school-of-biological-sciences

Biochemistry BSc(Hons), Biochemistry MBiol, Biology MBiol, Biology BSc(Hons), Marine Biology BSc(Hons), Marine Biology MBiol

Postgraduate courses: Applied Aquatic Biology MSc, Biotechnology MSc, Science MRes

School of Earth and Environmental Sciences; www.port.ac.uk/school-of-earth-and-environmental-sciences

Engineering Geology and Geotechnics BEng(Hons), Environmental Science MEnvSci, Environmental Science BSc(Hons), Geological Hazards MGeol, Geological Hazards BSc(Hons), Geology MGeol, Geology BSc(Hons), Marine Environmental Science BSc(Hons), Marine Environmental Science MEnvSci, Palaeontology MGeol, Palaeontology BSc(Hons), Physics BSc(Hons), Applied Physics MPhys(Hons), Physics, Astrophysics and Cosmology BSc(Hons), Physics, Astrophysics and Cosmology MPhys(Hons)

Postgraduate courses: Crisis and Disaster Management MSc, MSc Engineering Geology MSc, Environmental Geology and Contamination MSc, Geological and Environmental Hazards MSc, Science MRes

Department of Geography; www.port.ac.uk/department-of-geography

Geography BSc(Hons), Geography BA(Hons), Sustainable Environmental Management BSc(Hons)

Postgraduate courses: Coastal and Marine Resource Management MSc, Geographical Information Systems MSc, Science MRes

School of Health Sciences and Social Work; www.port.ac.uk/school-of-health-sciences-and-social-work

Diagnostic Radiography and Medical Imaging BSc(Hons) Approved, Human Communication Science (Top-up) BSc(Hons), Nursing (Adult)

BN(Hons), Operating Department Practice BSc(Hons), Optometry MOptom, Paramedic Science BSc(Hons), Radiotherapy and Oncology BSc(Hons) Approved, Social Work BSc(Hons) Approved

Postgraduate courses: Science MRes, Optometry MOptom, Professional Doctorate in Health and Social Care ProfDoc, Social Work MSc Approved, Systematic Reviews in Health PgCert

School of Pharmacy and Biomedical Sciences; www.port.ac.uk/school-of-pharmacy-and-biomedical-sciences

Biomedical Science BSc(Hons), Pharmaceutical Science (Top-up) BSc(Hons), Pharmacology BSc(Hons), Pharmacy MPharm(Hons)

Postgraduate courses: Medical Biotechnology MSc, Science MRes, Prescribing and Therapeutics PgCert

Dental Academy; www.port.ac.uk/dental-academy

Dental Hygiene and Dental Therapy BSc(Hons), Dental Nursing CertHE

Department of Psychology; www.port.ac.uk/department-of-psychology

Forensic Psychology BSc(Hons), Psychology BSc(Hons)

Postgraduate courses: Child Forensic Studies: Psychology and Law MSc, Forensic Psychology MSc, Forensic Psychology Practice PgDip, Health Psychology MSc Subject to approval, Science MRes, Professional Doctorate in Forensic Psychology DForenPsy, Psychology and Learning Disability MSc

Department of Sport and Exercise Science; www.port.ac.uk/department-of-sport-and-exercise-science

Exercise and Fitness Management BSc(Hons), Sport and Exercise Psychology BSc(Hons), Sport and Exercise Science BSc(Hons), Sports Management and Development BSc(Hons), Sports Science and Management (Top-up) BSc(Hons)

Postgraduate courses: Clinical Exercise Science MSc, Human and Applied Physiology MSc, Science MRes, Clinical Exercise Science PgCert, Clinical Exercise Science PgDip, Physical Activity, Exercise and Health MSc, Sport and Exercise Psychology ProfDoc, Sport and Exercise Psychology (BPS) MSc, Sport, Exercise and Health Science ProfDoc, Sports Management MSc, Sports Performance MSc

Faculty of Technology; www.port.ac.uk/faculty-of-technology

School of Civil Engineering and Surveying; www.port.ac.uk/school-of-civil-engineering-and-surveying

Building Surveying BSc(Hons), Civil Engineering MEng, Civil Engineering BEng(Hons), Construction Engineering Management BEng(Hons), Property Development BSc(Hons), Quantity Surveying BSc(Hons)

Postgraduate courses: Building Information Management (BIM) MSc, Civil Engineering MSc, Civil Engineering with Environmental Engineering MSc, Civil Engineering with Geotechnical Engineering MSc, Civil Engineering with Structural Engineering MSc, Construction Project Management MSc, Quantity Surveying MSc, Real Estate Management MSc

School of Computing; www.port.ac.uk/school-of-computing

Business Information Systems BSc(Hons), Computer Science BSc(Hons), Computer Science MEng, Computing BSc(Hons), Data Science and Analytics BSc(Hons) Subject to approval, Forensic Computing BSc(Hons), Software Engineering BSc(Hons)

Postgraduate courses: Data Analytics MSc, Forensic Information Technology MSc, Information Systems MSc

School of Engineering; www.port.ac.uk/school-of-engineering

Computer Networks BSc(Hons), Electronic Engineering BEng(Hons), Electronic Engineering MEng, Engineering and Technology BEng(Hons), Industrial Design BSc(Hons), Innovation Engineering BEng(Hons), Innovation Engineering MEng, Mechanical and Manufacturing Engineering BEng(Hons), Mechanical Engineering BEng(Hons), Mechanical Engineering MEng, Petroleum Engineering BEng(Hons), Petroleum Engineering MEng, Product Design and Innovation BSc(Hons)

Postgraduate courses: Advanced Manufacturing Technology MSc, Computer Network Administration and Management MSc, Electronic Engineering MSc, Energy and Power Systems Management MSc, Mechanical Engineering MSc, Petroleum and Gas Engineering MSc

Department of Mathematics; www.port.ac.uk/department-of-mathematics

Mathematics BSc(Hons), Mathematics MMath, Mathematics for Finance and Management BSc(Hons), Mathematics with Statistics BSc(Hons)

Postgraduate course: Logistics and Supply Chain Management MSc

QUEEN MARGARET UNIVERSITY COLLEGE
www.qmu.ac.uk

BA(Hons) Acting for Stage and Screen, BSc Applied Nursing, BSc(Hons) Applied Pharmacology, BA(Hons) Business Management, BA(Hons) Business Management (Fast-Track), BA(Hons) Costume Design and Construction, BSc(Hons) Diagnostic Radiography, BSc(Hons) Dietetics, BA/BA(Hons) Drama and Performance, BA(Hons) Events Management, BA(Hons) Film and Media, Diploma in Higher Education Hearing Aid Audiology, BSc(Hons) Human Biology, BA(Hons) International Hospitality and Tourism Management, BA/BA(Hons) Media – No longer running for 2018 entry, BSc(Hons) Nursing, BSc(Hons) Nutrition, BSc(Hons) Nutrition and Food Science, BSc(Hons) Occupational Therapy, BSc(Hons) Physical Activity, Health and Wellbeing, BSc(Hons) Physiotherapy, BSc(Hons) Podiatry, BSc Professional Practice Framework, BSc(Hons) Psychology, BSc(Hons) Psychology and Sociology, BA(Hons) Public Relations and Media, BA(Hons) Public Relations, Marketing and Events, BSc(Hons) Public Sociology, BSc(Hons) Speech and Language Therapy, BA(Hons) Theatre and Film, BSc(Hons) Therapeutic Radiography

Postgraduate courses: PgCert Applied Social Development, MSc Art Psychotherapy (International), MA Arts, Festival and Cultural Management, Audiology (PgDip/MSc Rehabilitative Audiology (Post-Registration)), PgDip/MSc Audiology (Pre-Registration), MSc Cognitive Behavioural Therapy, PgCert Collaborative Working: Education and Therapy, MSc Diabetes, PgDip/MSc Dietetics, MSc PgDip/PgCert Dispute Resolution, MSc Gastronomy, MSc Global Health, PgCert Health in Fragile and Conflict-Affected States, MSc International Management and Leadership, MSc International Management and Leadership with Events, MSc International Management and Leadership with Family and Smaller Enterprises, MSc International Management and Leadership with Hospitality, MSc International Management and Leadership with Tourism, MSc Mammography, Master of Clinical Research, Master of Research, MBA, MBA Family and Smaller Enterprises, MBA Hospitality, MBA Tourism, MSc Medical Imaging, MSc Music Therapy, PgDip/MSc Occupational Therapy (Post-Registration), MSc Occupational Therapy (Pre-Registration), PgCert Palliative Care, MSc/PgDip/PgCert Person-Centred Practice, PgDip Person-Centred Practice (District Nursing), PgDip Person-Centred Practice (Health Visiting), MSc/PgDip Person-Centred Practice (Palliative Care), MSc/PgDip Person-Centred Practice (Public Health and Wellbeing), PgDip Person-Centred Practice (School Nursing), PhD, Physiotherapy (MSc Advancing Physiotherapy Practice), PgDip/MSc Physiotherapy (Pre-Registration), MSc Play Therapy, Podiatry (MSc Theory of Podiatric Surgery, MSc Podiatry/Podiatry by Distance e-Learning, MSc/PgDip/e-PgCert Professional and Higher Education, Professional Doctorate, Master of Public Administration (MPA), PgCert Public Health and Wellbeing, MSc Public Health Nutrition, Public Relations (MSc Strategic Communication and Public Relations), Public Relations (CIPR Diploma in Internal Communications Practice), Public Relations (CIPR Diploma in Public Affairs Practice), Public Relations (CIPR Professional Diploma in Public Relations), Radiography (MSc Diagnostic Radiography (Pre-Registration)), MSc Radiotherapy (Post-Registration), PgDip/MSc Radiotherapy and Oncology (Pre-Registration), MSc Sexual and Reproductive Health, MSc Social Development and Health, PgDip/MSc Speech and Language Therapy (Pre-Registration), MA Stage Management

UNIVERSITY OF READING
www.reading.ac.uk

School of Agriculture, Policy and Development; www.reading.ac.uk/apd

BSc Agricultural Business Management, BSc Agriculture, BSc Animal Science, BSc Consumer Behaviour and Marketing, BSc Environmental Management, BSc Food Marketing and Business Economics, BSc International Development

Postgraduate courses in the following subjects: Agriculture and Development, Applied International Development, Climate Change and Development, Communication for Development, Development Finance, Environment and Development, Food Security and Development, Agricultural Economics, Food Economics and Marketing, Research Agricultural and Food Economics, Research Agriculture, Ecology and Environment, Postgraduate Certificate in Sustainable Livestock Production

Department of Archaeology; www.reading.ac.uk/archaeology

BA Archaeology, BA Archaeological Science, BA Archaeology and Ancient History, BA Archaeology and Classical Studies, BA Archaeology and History, BA Museum Studies and Archaeology

Postgraduate courses: MA Archaeology, MA Archaeology (Bioarchaeology), MA Archaeology (Medieval Europe), MA Archaeology (Middle East), MA by Research Archaeology, MSc Environmental Archaeology

School of Architecture; www.reading.ac.uk/architecture

BSc Architecture

School of Art; www.reading.ac.uk/fineart

BA Art, BA Fine Art, BA Art and English Literature, BA Art and Film, BA Art and Film and Theatre, BA Art and History of Art, BA Art and Philosophy, BA Art and Psychology, BA Art and Theatre

Postgraduate courses: MFA Fine Art, MA Creative Enterprise: Art pathway, MA Creative Enterprise (Film Pathway), MA Book Design, MA Creative Enterprise (Communication Design Pathway), MA Information Design, MA Typeface Design

School of Biological Sciences; www.reading.ac.uk/biologicalsciences

BSc Biochemistry, BSc Biological Sciences, BSc Biomedical Sciences, BME Undergraduate courses, BEng/MEng Biomedical Engineering, BSc Ecology and Wildlife Conservation, BSc Microbiology, BSc Zoology

Postgraduate courses: MSc by Research Entomology, MSc by Research Biomedicine, MSc Molecular Medicine, MSc Plant Diversity, MSc Wildlife Management & Conservation, MSc Species Identification and Survey Skills

School of the Built Environment; www.reading.ac.uk/built-environment

BSc Building Surveying, BSc Construction Management, BSc Construction Management and Surveying, BSc Quantity Surveying

Postgraduate courses: MSc Construction Cost Management, MSc Construction in Emerging Economies, MSc Construction Management, MSc Design and Management of Sustainable Built Environments, MSc Information Management for Design, Construction and Operation, MSc Project Management Project Management, MSc Renewable Energy: Technology and Sustainability

Department of Chemistry; www.reading.ac.uk/chemistry

MChem Chemistry, BSc Chemistry

Postgraduate course: MSc in Chemical Research

Department of Classics; www.reading.ac.uk/classics

BA Ancient History, BA Classical Studies, BA Classics, BA Ancient History and Archaeology, BA Ancient History and History, BA Archaeology and Classical Studies, BA Classical Studies and English Literature, BA Classical Studies and Medieval Studies, BA Italian and Classical Studies, BA Museum and Classical Studies, BA Philosophy and Classical Studies

Postgraduate courses: MA Classics and Ancient History, MA Classical Tradition, MA City of Rome

Department of Computer Science; www.reading.ac.uk/dcs-computer-science.aspx

BSc Computer Science

Postgraduate course: MSc Advanced Computer Science

Department of Economics; www.reading.ac.uk/economics

BSc Economics, BA Economics, BSc Business Economics, BSc Economics and Econometrics, BSc Economics and Finance

Postgraduate courses: MSc Economics, MSc Business Economics, MSc Economics and Finance, MA Public Policy

Institute of Education; www.reading.ac.uk/education

BA Children's Development and Learning, BA Education Studies, BA Primary Education with Art Specialism (QTS), BA Primary Education with English Specialism (QTS), BA Primary Education with Mathematics Specialism (QTS), BA Primary Education with Music Specialism (QTS)

Postgraduate courses: MA Education, MA Education (Early Years), MA Education (English Language Teaching), MA Education (Inclusive Education), MA Education (Leadership and Management), MA Education (Music Education), PGCert Special Education Needs Coordinator (SENCO), various PGCE options

Department of English Language and Applied Linguistics; www.reading.ac.uk/english-language-and-applied-linguistics

BA English Language, BA English Language and Literature

Postgraduate courses: MA in Applied Linguistics, MA in TESOL

English Literature; www.reading.ac.uk/english-literature

BA English Literature, BA English Literature and Italian, BA English Literature and Politics, BA English Literature and German, BA English Literature with French, BA English Literature and International Relations, BA English Literature and Film and Theatre, BA English Literature and Film, BA English Literature and Theatre, BA English Language and Literature

Postgraduate course: MA in English

Department of Film, Theatre & Television; www.reading.ac.uk/ftt

BA Film, BA Theatre, BA Film and Theatre

Postgraduate courses: MA Creative Enterprise

Food and Nutritional Sciences; www.reading.ac.uk/food

BSc Food Science, BSc Food Technology with Bioprocessing, BSc Nutrition and Food Science, BSc Nutrition with Food Consumer Sciences, BSc Food Science with Business

Postgraduate courses: MSc Food Science, MSc Nutrition and Food Science, MSc Food Technology – Quality Assurance, MSc Sustainable Food Quality for Health

Department of Geography and Environmental Science; www.reading.ac.uk/geographyandenvironmentalscience

BSc Environmental Science, MEnvSci Environmental Science, BSc Geography and Economics, BSc Human and Physical Geography, BSc Human Geography, BSc Physical Geography

Postgraduate courses: MSc Environmental Management, MSc Environmental Pollution

Henley Business School; www.henley.reading.ac.uk

BA Accounting and Business, BSc Accounting and Finance, BA Accounting and Management, BA Accounting (Beijing Institute of Technology), BA Business and Management, BA Entrepreneurship, BA Entrepreneurship and Management, BA International Business and Management, BA International Management and Business Administration with French, BA International Management and Business Administration with German, BA International Management and Business Administration with Italian, BA International Management and Business Administration with Spanish, BSc International Business and Finance, BSc Management with Information Technology, BSc Finance and Investment Banking, BSc Finance and Management with the University of Venice, BSc Economics and Finance, BSc Mathematics with Finance and Investment Banking, BSc Real Estate, BSc Investment and Finance in Property, BSc Real Estate with MSc/Dip Urban Planning & Development

Postgraduate courses: Doctor of Business Administration (DBA), Executive MBA (EMBA), Flexible Executive MBA, MA Leadership, MBA, MRes Informatics, MSc Accounting and Finance, MSc Accounting and Financial Management, MSc Accounting and International Management, MSc Behavioural Finance, MSc Business Technology Consulting, MSc Capital Markets, Regulation and Compliance, MSc Conservation of the Historic Environment, MSc Corporate Finance, MSc Economics and Finance, MSc Entrepreneurship (Creative Industries), MSc Entrepreneurship (Financing), MSc Entrepreneurship (Leadership), MSc Financial Engineering, MSc

Financial Risk Management, MSc in Coaching and Behavioural Change, MSc Informatics (Beijing), MSc Information Management & Big Data in Business, MSc Information Management & Business Analysis and Service Design, MSc Information Management & Systems Analysis and Design, MSc International Business, MSc International Business and Finance, MSc International Human Resource Management, MSc International Securities, Investment and Banking, MSc International Shipping and Finance, MSc Investment Management, MSc Management, MSc Management Information Systems (Ghana), MSc Marketing (Digital Marketing), MSc Marketing (International Marketing), MSc Real Estate, MSc Real Estate Finance, MSc Real Estate Investment and Finance, MSc Rural Land and Business Management, MSc Spatial Planning and Development, IPF Certificate, IPF Diploma & MSc Real Estate Investment and Finance (IPF Entry Route)

Department of History; www.reading.ac.uk/history

BA History, BA Ancient History and History, BA Archaeology and History, BA History and Economics, BA History and English Literature, BA History and International Relations, BA History and Philosophy, BA History and Politics, BA Classical Studies and Medieval Studies

Postgraduate courses: MA History, MRes Medieval Studies

School of Law; www.reading.ac.uk/law

LLB Law, LLB Law with Legal Studies in Europe
Postgraduate courses: LLM/PGDiploma/PGCertificate/Certificate of Completion in Global Crisis, Conflict and Disaster Management, LLM Advanced Legal Studies, LLM International Law, LLM Human Rights, MSc Oil and Gas Law, MRes (Law), MRes (Law and Society), MA (Res) Legal History

Department of Mathematics and Statistics; www.reading.ac.uk/maths-and-stats

BSc Mathematics, MMath Mathematics, BSc Computational Mathematics, BSc Mathematics and Economics, BSc Mathematics with Finance and Investment Banking, BSc Mathematics and Meteorology, MMath Mathematics and Meteorology, BSc Mathematics and Psychology, BSc Mathematics and Statistics
Postgraduate course: MSc in Financial Engineering

Department of Meteorology; www.met.reading.ac.uk

BSc/MMet Meteorology and Climate, BSc Environmental Physics

Postgraduate courses: MSc Atmosphere, Oceans and Climate (MSc AOC), MSc Applied Meteorology (MSc AM), MSc AM with Management (MSc AMCM)

Department of Modern Languages and European Studies; www.reading.ac.uk/modern-languages-and-european-studies

French and Economics BA, French and English Literature BA, French and German BA, French and History BA, French and International Relations BA, French and Italian BA, French and Management BA, French Studies and English Language BA, International Management and Business Administration with French BA, German BA, German and Economics BA, German and English Literature BA, German Studies and English Language BA, German and History BA, German and International Relations BA, German and Italian BA, German and Management BA, International Management and Business Administration with German BA, Italian BA, Italian and Classical Studies BA, Italian and Economics BA, Italian and English Literature BA, Italian Studies and English Language BA, Italian and History BA, Italian and International Relations BA, Italian and Management BA, International Management and Business Administration with Italian BA, Spanish BA, Spanish and French BA, Spanish and German BA, Spanish and Italian BA, Spanish and Economics BA, Spanish and English Literature BA, Spanish and History BA, Spanish and Management Studies BA, Spanish and International Relations BA, Spanish Studies and English Language BA, International Management and Business Administration with Spanish BA

School of Pharmacy; www.reading.ac.uk/pharmacy

MPharm Pharmacy

Department of Philosophy; www.reading.ac.uk/Phil

BA Ethics, Value and Philosophy, BA Philosophy, BA Philosophy and Classical Studies, BA Philosophy and English Literature, BA Philosophy and International Relations, BA Philosophy and Politics, BA Philosophy, Politics and Economics, BA Psychology and Philosophy, BA Art and Philosophy, BA History and Philosophy
Postgraduate course: MRes Philosophy

Department of Politics and International Relations; www.reading.ac.uk/spirs

BA Politics and International Relations, BA War, Peace and International Relations, BA Politics and

Economics, BA International Relations and Economics, BA Philosophy, Politics and Economics
Postgraduate courses: MA International Relations, MA Diplomacy, MA International Security Studies, MA Strategic Studies, MA Public Policy, MRes Politics and International Relations

School of Psychology and Clinical Language Sciences; www.reading.ac.uk/psychology/

BSc Psychology, BSc Language Sciences & Psychology, BSc Speech & Language Therapy, BSc Psychology with Neuroscience, MSci Applied Psychology (Clinical)

Postgraduate courses: MSc Clinical Aspects of Psychology, MSc Cognitive Neuroscience, MSc Development and Psychopathology, MSc Language Sciences, MSc Research Methods in Psychology, MSc Speech and Language Therapy, Postgraduate Certificate in Evidence-based Psychological Treatments, Postgraduate Diploma in Evidence-based Psychological Treatment, Postgraduate Professional Development Certificate/Diploma in Evidence-based Psychological Treatment

ROBERT GORDON UNIVERSITY
www.rgu.ac.uk

Aberdeen Business School; http://www.rgu.ac.uk/about/schools-and-departments/aberdeen-business-school

BA(Hons) Accounting and Finance, BSc Accounting with CIMA – Distance Learning, BA(Hons) Business Management, BA(Hons) International Business Management, BA(Hons) Management Degree, BA(Hons) Management with Human Resource Management, BA(Hons) Management with Marketing
Postgraduate courses: MSc Accounting and Finance, MSc Energy Management, MSc Financial Management, MSc Health Safety and Risk Management, MSc Human Resource Management, MSc International Business, MSc Management, Master of Business Administration, MBA Oil and Gas Management, MSc Oil and Gas Accounting, MSc Oil and Gas Finance, MSc Project Management, MSc Purchasing and Supply Chain Management, MSc Quality Management, MSc Strategic Accounting – Online Top Up, MBA Oil and Gas Management

School of Applied Social Studies; http://www.rgu.ac.uk/about/schools-and-departments/school-of-applied-social-studies

BA(Hons) Applied Social Sciences, BA(Hons) Social Work, BA(Hons) Social Work – Distance Learning, BA Residential Child Care
Postgraduate courses: MSc Applied Psychology, MSc Corporate Social Responsibility, MSc Social Work

School of Computing Science and Digital Media; http://www.rgu.ac.uk/about/schools-and-departments/school-of-computing-science-and-digital-media

BSc(Hons) Computing (Application Software Development), BSc(Hons) Computer Network Management and Design, BSc(Hons) Computer Science, BSc(Hons) Cyber Security, BSc(Hons) Digital Media – Design, Production and Development, BSc(Hons) IT Management for Business, BSc(Hons) Software Development for Business
Postgraduate courses: MSc Computer Science, MSc Cyber Security, MSc Data Science, MSc Information Technology, MSc Information Technology with Business Intelligence, MSc Information Technology with Cyber Security, MSc Information Technology with Network Management, MSc IT for the Oil and Gas Industry

School of Creative and Cultural Business; http://www.rgu.ac.uk/about/schools-and-departments/school-of-creative-and-cultural-business

BA(Hons) Events Management, BA(Hons) Fashion Management, BA(Hons) Journalism, BA(Hons) Media, BA(Hons) Public Relations, BA(Hons) International Tourism Management, BA(Hons) International Hospitality Management
Postgraduate courses: MSc Corporate Communications and Public Affairs, MSc Digital Marketing, MSc Information and Library Studies, MSc Journalism, MSc International Marketing Management, MSc Information Management, MSc Fashion

Management, MSc International Tourism and Hospitality Management

School of Engineering; http://www.rgu.ac.uk/about/schools-and-departments/school-of-engineering

BEng(Hons) Electronic and Electrical Engineering, BEng(Hons) Mechanical and Electrical Engineering, BEng(Hons) Mechanical and Offshore Engineering, BEng(Hons) Mechanical Engineering Degree, MEng Electronic and Electrical Engineering, MEng Mechanical and Electrical Engineering, MEng Mechanical and Offshore Engineering, MEng Mechanical Engineering Degree

Postgraduate courses: MSc Asset Integrity Management, MSc Drilling and Well Engineering, MSc Engineering, MSc Offshore Oil and Gas Engineering, MSc Oil and Gas Engineering, MSc Oil and Gas Innovation, MSc Petroleum Production Engineering, MSc Subsea Engineering

Gray's School of Art; http://www.rgu.ac.uk/about/schools-and-departments/gray-s-school-of-art

BA(Hons) Communication Design – Graphics, Illustration, Photography, BA(Hons) Contemporary Art Practice – Moving Image, Photography, Printmaking, Sculpture, BA(Hons) Fashion and Textile Design, BA(Hons) Painting, BA(Hons) Three Dimensional Design, BA Commercial Photography

Postgraduate courses: MA Communication Design, MA Curatorial Studies, MA Fashion & Textiles, MA Fine Art, MA Jewellery, MA Product Design

School of Health Sciences; http://www.rgu.ac.uk/about/schools-and-departments/school-of-health-sciences

BSc(Hons) Applied Sport and Exercise Science, BSc(Hons) Occupational Therapy, BSc(Hons) Physiotherapy, BSc(Hons) Diagnostic Radiography

Postgraduate courses: MSc Applied Sports Performance Analysis, MSc Public Health and Health Promotion, MSc Physiotherapy (Pre-registration)

The Law School; http://www.rgu.ac.uk/about/schools-and-departments/the-law-school

BA(Hons) Law and Management Degree, LLB(Hons) Law

Postgraduate courses: LLM Employment Law and Practice, LLM Law, LLM MSc Construction Law and Arbitration, LLM Oil and Gas Law

School of Nursing and Midwifery; http://www.rgu.ac.uk/about/schools-and-departments/school-of-nursing-and-midwifery

Bachelor of Nursing – Children and Young People BNursing, Bachelor of Nursing – Mental Health BNursing, Bachelor of Nursing – Adult BNursing, Bachelor of Nursing(Hons) – Adult Nursing BNursing(Hons), Bachelor of Midwifery

Postgraduate course: MSc Advancing Nursing Practice

School of Pharmacy and Life Sciences; http://www.rgu.ac.uk

BSc(Hons) Biomedical Science, BSc(Hons) Applied Biomedical Science, BSc(Hons) Bioscience with Biomedical Sciences, BSc(Hons) Forensic and Analytical Science, MPharm Pharmacy, BSc(Hons) Nutrition, BSc(Hons) Nutrition and Dietetics

Postgraduate courses: MSc Clinical Pharmacy Practice, MSc Instrumental Analytical Science – Environmental Analysis, MSc Instrumental Analytical Science – Drug Analysis and Toxicology, MSc Instrumental Analytical Science – Oilfield Chemicals, MSc Instrumental Analytical Science – DNA Analysis, Proteomics & Metabolomics, MSc Clinical Pharmacy Service Development

The Scott Sutherland School of Architecture and Built Environment; http://www.rgu.ac.uk/about/schools-and-departments/the-scott-sutherland-school-of-architecture-and-built-environment

BSc(Hons) Architectural Technology, BSc(Hons) Construction Management, BSc(Hons) Surveying, BSc MArch Architecture

Postgraduate courses: MArch Architecture Part 2, MSc Commercial Practice for the Energy Sectors, MSc Construction Project Management Degree

ROEHAMPTON UNIVERSITY
www.roehampton.ac.uk

Business School; www.roehampton.ac.uk/business

Undergraduate degrees in the following subjects: Accounting, Business Management, Business Management and Economics, Business Management and Entrepreneurship, Human Resource Management, International Business, Marketing, Retail Marketing and Management

Postgraduate degrees in the following subjects: International Management, International Management with Finance, International Management with HRM, International Management with Marketing, MBA

Dance; www.roehampton.ac.uk/dance

Undergraduate degrees in the following subject: Dance Studies

Postgraduate degrees in the following subjects: Choreography, Choreography and Performance (MRes), Choreomundus: International Master in Dance Knowledge, Practice and Heritage, Dance Anthropology, Dance Philosophy and History, Dance Politics and Sociology

Drama, Theatre and Performance; www.roehampton.ac.uk/drama-theatre-and-performance

Undergraduate degrees in the following subjects: Drama Studies, Drama, Theatre and Performance Studies

Postgraduate degrees in the following subject: London's Theatre and Performance: Viewing, Making, Writing

Education; www.roehampton.ac.uk/education

Undergraduate degrees in the following subjects: Early Childhood Studies, Education Studies, Primary Education (QTS), Sport Coaching, Sports Coaching Practice

Postgraduate degrees in the following subjects: Early Childhood Studies, Education Leadership and Management, Education Policy, Educational Practice, National Award for SEN Coordinators, PGCE Primary, PGCE Primary – general (with Mathematics), PGCE Secondary, School Direct – Primary and Secondary, Social Research Methods, Sounds of Intent, Special Educational Needs (Inclusive or Psychological Perspectives)

English and Creative Writing; www.roehampton.ac.uk/english-and-creative-writing

Undergraduate degrees in the following subjects: Creative Writing, English Literature

Postgraduate degrees in the following subjects: Children's Literature, Children's Literature (Distance Learning), Creative Writing, Creative Writing (specialist pathway)

Humanities; www.roehampton.ac.uk/humanities

Undergraduate degrees in the following subjects: Classical Civilisation, History, Ministerial Theology (FdA/BTh), Ministerial Theology (Graduate Diploma), Philosophy, Theology and Religious Studies

Postgraduate degrees in the following subjects: Christian Ministry, Classical Research, Historical Research, History, Practical Theology (DTh), Theology and Religious Studies

Life Sciences; www.roehampton.ac.uk/life-sciences

Undergraduate degrees in the following subjects: Anthropology, Biological Sciences, Biomedical Science, Nutrition and Health, Social Anthropology, Sport and Exercise Sciences, Sport Psychology, Zoology

Postgraduate degrees in the following subjects: Anthropology of Health, Biomechanics, Cell Biomedicine (MRes), Clinical Neuroscience, Clinical Nutrition, Health Sciences, Nutrition and Metabolic Disorders (MRes), Primate Biology, Behaviour and Conservation, Psychology of Sport and Exercise (BPS Accredited), Sport and Exercise Physiology, Sport and Exercise Science, Stress and Health

Media, Culture and Language; www.roehampton.ac.uk/media-culture-and-language

Undergraduate degrees in the following subjects: Digital Media, English Language and Linguistics, Film, Journalism, Languages and Global Communication, Mass Communications, Media, Culture and Identity, Photography

Postgraduate degrees in the following subjects: Applied Linguistics and TESOL, Audiovisual Translation, Film and Screen Cultures, Intercultural

Communication in the Creative Industries, Journalism, Media Communication and Culture, Specialised Translation

Psychology; www.roehampton.ac.uk/ psychology

Undergraduate degrees in the following subjects: Psychology, Psychology and Counselling, Therapeutic Psychology

Postgraduate degrees in the following subjects: Art Psychotherapy, Attachment Studies, Counselling Psychology (HCPC approved and BPS accredited), Dance Movement Psychotherapy, Dramatherapy, Integrative Counselling and Psychotherapy, Music Therapy, Play Therapy

Social Sciences; www.roehampton.ac.uk/ social-sciences

Undergraduate degrees in the following subjects: Criminology, LLB(Hons) Law, LLB(Hons) Law and Criminology, Sociology

Postgraduate degrees in the following subjects: Erasmus Mundus Human Rights Policy and Practice, Global Criminology, Graduate Diploma in Law, Human Rights, Human Rights and International Relations

THE ROYAL ACADEMY OF DANCE
www.rad.org.uk

BA(Hons) Ballet Education, BA(Hons) Dance Education, Certificate in Ballet Teaching Studies, Certificate of Higher Education: Dance Education, Diploma in Dance Teaching Studies, Diploma of Higher Education: Dance Education, Licentiate of the Royal Academy of Dance, MA in Education (Dance Teaching), PGCE: Dance Teaching, Professional Dancers' Postgraduate Teaching Certificate, Professional Dancers' Teaching Diploma

ROYAL ACADEMY OF DRAMATIC ART
www.rada.ac.uk

BA(Hons) in Acting, Foundation Course in Acting, MA in Text and Performance, MA Theatre Lab, Foundation Degree (FdA) in Technical Theatre and Stage Management, BA(Hons) in Technical Theatre & Stage Management (Progression Year), Postgraduate Diploma in Theatre Costume

ROYAL AGRICULTURAL UNIVERSITY
www.rau.ac.uk

BSc(Hons) Agricultural Management (Top-up), BSc(Hons) Agriculture, FdSc Agriculture and Farm Management, BSc(Hons) Applied Equine Science and Business, BSc(Hons) Applied Farm Management, BSc(Hons) Bloodstock and Performance Horse Management, FdSc British Wildlife Conservation, FdSc Business and Enterprise, BSc(Hons) Countryside Management (Top-up), FdSc Environmental Conservation and Heritage Management, BSc(Hons) Equine Studies (Top-up), BSc(Hons) Food Production and Supply Management, BSc(Hons) International Business Management, BSc(Hons) International Business Management (Food and Agribusiness), BSc(Hons) International Equine and Agricultural Business Management, BSc(Hons) Real Estate, Diploma in Real Estate Valuation, BSc(Hons) Rural Land Management, BSc(Hons) Wildlife and Countryside Management (Top Up)

Postgraduate courses: MBA Advanced Farm Management, MSc Agricultural Technology and Innovation, MSc Business Management, MSc Food Safety and Quality Management, Graduate Certificate in Agriculture, Graduate Diploma in Agriculture, MBA International Food and Agribusiness, MSc by Research Programme, MSc Real Estate, MSc Rural Estate Management, MSc Sustainable Agriculture and Food Security

ASKHAM BRYAN COLLEGE
www.askham-bryan.ac.uk

(See Harper Adams University)

ROYAL BALLET SCHOOL
www.royalballetschool.org.uk

Diploma of Dance Teaching, various training programmes for young dancers

ROYAL COLLEGE OF ART
www.rca.ac.uk

School of Architecture; www.rca.ac.uk/schools/school-of-architecture

Degrees in the following subjects: Architecture, City Design, Environmental Architecture, Interior Design, MRes RCA: Architecture Pathway, Current Research

School of Arts & Humanities; www.rca.ac.uk/schools/school-of-arts-humanities

Degrees in the following subjects: Ceramics & Glass, Contemporary Art Practice, Critical Writing in Art & Design, Curating Contemporary Art, Jewellery & Metal, Painting, Photography, Print, Sculpture, V&A/RCA History of Design, MRes RCA: Fine Art Pathway, MRes RCA: Humanities Pathway, Current Research: Applied Arts, Current Research: Fine Art, Current Research: Humanities, Fine Art Research Gallery, Facilities, Visual Cultures Lecture Series, StudioRCA, Dyson Gallery: Orientations & Locate & Reshape Exhibition Series, The Peter Dormer Lecture

School of Communication; www.rca.ac.uk/schools/school-of-communication

Degrees in the following subjects: Animation, Digital Direction, Information Experience Design, Visual Communication, MRes RCA: Communication Design Pathway, Communication Research, Communication Research Gallery, Facilities

School of Design; www.rca.ac.uk/schools/school-of-design

Degrees in the following subjects: Design Products, Global Innovation Design, Innovation Design Engineering, Intelligent Mobility, MRes Healthcare & Design, Service Design, MRes RCA: Design Pathway, Current Research, Design Research Gallery, Funded Research, Facilities, Fashion Menswear, Fashion Womenswear, Textiles

ROYAL COLLEGE OF MUSIC
www.rcm.ac.uk

BMus(Hons) Bachelor of Music

Postgraduate courses: MPerf Master of Performance, MMus Master of Music, ArtDip Artist Diploma in Performance

THE ROYAL COLLEGE OF ORGANISTS
www.rco.org.uk

Courses in playing, teaching and choral directing leading to the following qualifications: CertRCO, ARCO, FRCO, LTRCO, DipCHD

ROYAL CONSERVATOIRE OF SCOTLAND
www.rcs.ac.uk

BA(Hons) Ballet Education, BA(Hons) Dance Education, Certificate in Ballet Teaching Studies, Certificate of Higher Education: Dance Education, Diploma in Dance Teaching Studies, Diploma of Higher Education: Dance Education, Licentiate of the Royal Academy of Dance, MA in Education (Dance Teaching), PGCE: Dance Teaching, Professional Dancers' Postgraduate Teaching Certificate, Professional Dancers' Teaching Diploma

Postgraduate courses: MA Classical and Contemporary Text (Acting) or (Directing), MA Musical Theatre (Performance) or (Musical Directing) or (Choreography), MMus/MA Music (Brass, Chamber Music, Composition, Conducting, Guitar and Harp, Historically Informed Performance Practice, Jazz, Keyboard, Opera, Piano Accompaniment, Piano for Dance, Repetiteurship, Scottish Music, Strings, Timpani and Percussion, Vocal Studies, Woodwind), MEd Learning and Teaching in the Performing Arts, MA Learning and Teaching (Gaelic Arts), PG Cert Learning Support and Administration in Higher Arts Education, PG Cert Learning and Teaching in Arts Education, PG Cert Learning and Teaching in Higher Arts Education

ROYAL NORTHERN COLLEGE OF MUSIC
www.rncm.ac.uk

BA(Hons) Music, Bachelor of Music(Hons) Popular Music, Graduate Diploma of the Royal Northern College of Music; Postgraduate courses: Master of Music, Master of Performance, PG Dip Advanced Studies, Master of Philosophy and Doctor of Philosophy, Conducting, Postgraduate Diploma (International Artist), Hall/RNCM Strings Leadership Course, Northern Ballet / RNCM Postgraduate Diploma: Pianist for Ballet, PGCE in Music with Specialist Instrumental Teaching

UNIVERSITY OF ST ANDREWS
www.st-andrews.ac.uk

Ancient History
Ancient History MA(Hons), Ancient History & Archaeology MA(Hons), Classical Studies (Ancient History & Archaeology pathway),BA (International Hons)
Postgraduate courses: Classics MLitt, Classics MPhil
Arabic
Postgraduate courses:
Middle Estern Literary and Cultural Studies MLitt, Comparative Literature MLitt, Cultural Identity Studies MLitt

Archaeology
Ancient History & Archaeology MA(Hons), Ancient History & Archaeology and Social Anthropology MA(Hons), Mediaeval History & Archaeology MA(Hons), Classical Studies – Ancient History and Archaeology pathway BA (International Hons)
Postgraduate courses:
Art History MLitt, Museum and Gallery Studies MLitt, Classics MLitt, Classics MPhil, Anthropology, Art and Perception MRes, Mediaeval History MLitt,

Mediaeval Studies MLitt, Scottish Historical Studies MLitt

Art History

Art History MA(Hons)

Postgraduate courses:

Art History MLitt, History of Photography MLitt, Museum and Gallery Studies MLitt

Biology

Biology BSc(Hons), Biology MBiol(Hons), Behavioural Biology BSc(Hons), Biochemistry BSc(Hons), Biochemistry MBiochem(Hons), Biomolecular Science BSc(Hons), Cell Biology BSc(Hons), Ecology and Conservation BSc(Hons), Evolutionary Biology BSc(Hons), Marine Biology BSc(Hons), Marine Biology MMarBiol(Hons), Molecular Biology BSc(Hons), Neuroscience BSc(Hons), Sustainable Development BSc(Hons), Sustainable Development MA(Hons), Zoology BSc(Hons),

Postgraduate courses: Marine Mammal Science MSc, Sustainable Aquaculture – Distance Learning PGDip/MSc, Sustainable Aquaculture – Distance Learning PG Certificate

Chemistry

Chemistry BSc(Hons), Chemistry MChem(Hons), Biomolecular Science BSc(Hons), Chemical Sciences BSc(Hons), Chemistry with Medicinal Chemistry BSc(Hons), Chemistry with Medicinal Chemistry MChem(Hons), Materials Chemistry BSc(Hons), Materials Chemistry MChem(Hons), Sustainable Development BSc(Hons), Sustainable Development MA(Hons)

Postgraduate courses:

Catalysis MSc, Chemical Science MSc

Classics and Classical Studies

Classics MA(Hons), Classical Studies MA(Hons), Classical Studies BA (International Hons), Greek MA(Hons), Latin MA(Hons)

Postgraduate courses:

Classics MLitt, Classics MPhil

Comparative Literature

Postgraduate courses:

Comparative Literature MLitt, Crossways in Cultural Narratives International MLitt, German and Comparative Literature MLitt

Computer Science

Computer Science BSc(Hons), Computer Science, MSci(Hons), Computer Science (Gateway) BSc(Hons), Computer Science (Gateway), MSci(Hons)

Postgraduate courses:

Advanced Computer Science MSc, Artificial Intelligence MSc, Computer Communication Systems MSc,

Computing and Information Technology MSc, Data-Intensive Analysis MSc, Dependable Software Systems MSc European Masters, Human Computer Interaction MSc, Information Technology MSc, Management and Information Technology MSc, Software Engineering MSc

Divinity

Biblical Studies MA(Hons), Divinity BD(Hons), Hebrew MA (joint Hons), New Testament MA (joint Hons), Theological Studies MA(Hons), Theology MTheol(Hons)

Postgraduate courses:

Analytic and Exegetical Theology MLitt, Bible and the Contemporary World MLitt, Bible and the Contemporary World – Distance Learning PGDip/MLitt, Biblical Languages and Literature MLitt, Systematic and Historical Theology MLitt, Theology, Imagination and the Arts MLitt

Earth and Environmental Sciences

Earth Sciences MGeol(Hons), Environmental Earth Sciences BSc(Hons), Geology BSc(Hons)

Postgraduate courses:

Geochemistry MSc, Mineral Resources MSc, Oil and Gas Innovation MSc

Economics and Finance

Economics BSc(Hons), Economics MA(Hons), Economics BA (International Hons), Financial Economics BSc(Hons), Financial Economics MA(Hons)

Postgraduate courses:

Economics MSc, Finance and Economics MSc, Finance MSc, Money, Banking and Finance MSc, Banking and Finance MSc

English

English MA(Hons), English BA (International Hons)

Postgraduate courses:

Creative Writing MLitt, Medieval English MLitt, Modern and Contemporary Literature and Culture MLitt, Playwriting and Screenwriting MLitt, Postcolonial and World Literatures MLitt, Romantic and Victorian Studies MLitt, Shakespeare and Renaissance Literary Culture MLitt, Women, Writing and Gender MLitt

Film Studies

Film Studies MA(Hons), Film Studies BA (International Hons)

Postgraduate courses: Film Studies MLitt

French

French MA(Hons)

Postgraduate courses: French Studies MLitt, Comparative Literature MLitt, Crossways in Cultural Narratives International MLitt, Cultural Identity Studies MLitt

Geography
Geography BSc(Hons), Geography MA(Hons)
Postgraduate courses:
Sustainable Development MSc, Sustainable Development and Energy MSc, Sustainable Development and Environmental Economics MSc, Human Geography/ Sustainable Development MRes,

German
German MA(Hons)
Postgraduate courses:
German Studies MLitt, German and Comparative Literature MLitt, Comparative Literature MLitt, Crossways in Cultural Narratives International MLitt, Cultural Identity Studies MLitt

Greek
Greek MA(Hons), Classical Studies (Greek and Latin pathway) BA (International Hons), Classics MA(Hons)
Postgraduate courses:
Classics MLitt, Classics MPhil

History
History MA(Hons), History BA (International Hons), Ancient History MA(Hons), Mediaeval History MA(Hons), Middle East Studies MA (joint Hons), Modern History MA(Hons), Scottish History MA(Hons)
Postgraduate courses:
Central and Eastern European Studies MLitt, Early Modern History MLitt, Environmental History MLitt, History of Philosophy MLitt, Intellectual History MLitt, Iranian Studies MLitt, Legal and Constitutional Studies MLitt/PGDip, Mediaeval History MLitt, Mediaeval Studies MLitt, Middle Eastern History MLitt, Modern History MLitt, Reformation Studies MLitt, Scottish Historical Studies MLitt, The Book. History and Techniques of Analysis MLitt, Transnational, Global and Spatial History MLitt

International relations
International Relations MA(Hons), International Relations BA (International Hons)
International Political Theory MLitt, International Security Studies MLitt, Legal and Constitutional Studies MLitt, Middle East, Caucasus and Central Asian Security Studies MLitt, Peace and Conflict Studies MLitt, Strategic Studies MLitt, Terrorism and Political Violence MLitt, Terrorism and Political Violence ể' Distance Learning MLitt

Italian
Italian MA(Hons)
Postgraduate courses:
Italian Studies MLitt, Comparative Literature MLitt, Crossways in Cultural Narratives International MLitt, Cultural Identity Studies MLitt

Management
Management BSc(Hons), Management MA(Hons), Management Science BSc(Hons)
Postgraduate courses:
Banking and Finance MSc, Finance and Management MSc, Human Resource Management MLitt, International Business MLitt, Management MLitt, Management and Information Technology MSc, Marketing MLitt

Marine Biology
Marine Biology BSc(Hons), Marine Biology MMarBiol(Hons)
Postgraduate courses:
Marine Mammal Science MSc, Sustainable Aquaculture – Distance Learning PGDip/MSc, Sustainable Aquaculture – Distance Learning PG Certificate

Mathematics
Mathematics BSc(Hons), Mathematics MA(Hons), Mathematics MMath(Hons), Applied Mathematics MMath(Hons), Pure Mathematics MMath(Hons), Statistics BSc(Hons), Statistics MA(Hons), Statistics MMath(Hons)
Postgraduate courses:
Mathematics MSc, Applied Statistics and Datamining PGDip/MSc, Data-Intensive Analysis MSc, Statistics MSc

Mediaeval Studies
Postgraduate courses: Mediaeval Studies MLitt, Mediaeval History MLitt, Medieval Englis MLitt

Medicine
Medicine A100 (Scotland, England and No Preference routes) BSc(Hons), Medicine A990 (Canada route) BSc(Hons), Medicine (Gateway) BSc(Hons), ScotGEM (2018 graduate entry programme) MBChB
Postgraduate courses:
Global Health Implementation MSc, Health Psychology MSc, MD

Middle East Studies
Postgraduate courses:
Cultural Identity Studies MLitt
Iranian Studies MLitt, Middle East, Caucasus and Central Asian Security Studies MLitt, Middle Eastern Literary and Cultural Studies MLitt, Middle Eastern History MLitt

Neuroscience
Neuroscience BSc(Hons)
Postgraduate courses:
Neuroscience MRes

Persian

Postgraduate courses:

Middle Eastern Literary and Cultural Studies MLitt, Comparative Literature MLitt, Cultural Identity Studies MLitt

Philosophy

Philosophy MA(Hons)

Postgraduate courses:

Conversion to Philosophy GradDip, Epistemology, Mind and Language MLitt, History of Philosophy MLitt, Logic and Metaphysics MLitt, Moral, Political and Legal Philosophy MLitt, Philosophy MLitt

Physics and astronomy

Physics BSc(Hons), Physics MPhys(Hons), Astrophysics BSc(Hons), Astrophysics MPhys(Hons), Theoretical Physics MPhys(Hons), Physics and Astronomy (Gateway) BSc(Hons), Physics and Astronomy (Gateway) MPhys(Hons), International Physics and Astronomy (Gateway) BSc(Hons), International Physics and Astronomy (Gateway) MPhys(Hons)

Postgraduate courses:

Astrophysics MSc, Photonics and Optoelectronic Devices MSc

Psychology

Psychology BSc(Hons), Psychology MA(Hons)

Postgraduate courses:

Adults with Learning Disabilities who have Significant and Complex Needs PGDip, Evolutionary and Comparative Psychology: The Origins of the Mind MSc, Health Psychology MSc, Neuroscience MRes, Psychology (Conversion) MSc, Research Methods in Psychology MSc, The Psychology of Dementia Care PGCert

Russian

Russian MA(Hons)

Postgraduate courses:

Russian Studies MLitt, Comparative Literature MLitt, Cultural Identity Studies MLitt

Social Anthropology

Social Anthropology MA(Hons)

Postgraduate courses:

Anthropology, Art and Perception MRes, Social Anthropology MRes, Social Anthropology and Amerindian Studies MRes, Social Anthropology with Pacific Studies MRes

Spanish

Spanish MA(Hons)

Postgraduate courses:

Spanish and Latin American Studies MLitt, Comparative Literature MLitt, Crossways in Cultural Narratives International MLitt, Cultural Identity Studies MLitt

Statistics

Statistics BSc(Hons), Statistics MA(Hons), Statistics MMath(Hons), Mathematics BSc(Hons), Mathematics MA(Hons), Mathematics MMath(Hons), Applied Mathematics MMath(Hons), Pure Mathematics MMath(Hons)

Postgraduate courses:

Statistics MSc, Applied Statistics and Datamining PGDip/MSc, Data-Intensive Analysis MSc, Mathematics MSc

Sustainable development

Sustainable Development BSc(Hons), Sustainable Development MA(Hons)

Postgraduate courses:

Sustainable Development MSc, Sustainable Development and Energy MSc, Sustainable Development and Environmental Economics MSc, Human Geography/Sustainable Development MRes

UNIVERSITY OF SALFORD
www.salford.ac.uk

School of Arts and Media; http://www.salford.ac.uk/arts-media/courses

Art and Design: Foundation Year Art and Design Foundation Year, BA(Hons) Fashion Design, BA(Hons) Fashion Image Making and Styling, BA(Hons) Film and TV Set Design, FdA Games Design (Taught at Salford City College), BA(Hons) Graphic Design, BA(Hons) Graphic Design (First year taught at Carmel College), FdA Graphic Design (Taught at Salford City College), BA(Hons) Interior Design, FdA Media Make-up For Fashion (Taught at Salford City College), BA(Hons) Photography, BA(Hons) Photography with Industry Placement, BA(Hons) Visual Arts

Postgraduate courses: MA Contemporary Arts Practice with Industry Experience, MA Design for Communication with Industry Experience, MA Socially Engaged Arts Practice with Community Experience

English and Creative Writing: BA(Hons) Drama and Creative Writing, BA(Hons) English and Creative Writing, BA(Hons) English and Drama, BA(Hons)

English Language, BA(Hons) English Language and Creative Writing, BA(Hons) English Literature, BA(Hons) English Literature with English Language Postgraduate courses: MA/PgDip Creative Writing: Innovation and Experiment, MA/PgDip Literature, Culture and Modernity
Postgraduate courses: MA International Journalism for Digital Media, MA/PgDip Journalism: News/Broadcast/Sport, MA Public Relations and Digital Communications
Journalism: BA(Hons) Journalism (Broadcast), BA(Hons) Journalism (Multimedia)
Media: BA(Hons) Animation, BA(Hons) Animation with Industry Placement, BSc(Hons) Computer and Video Games, BSc(Hons) Computer and Video Games with Industry Placement, BA(Hons) Digital Media, BA(Hons) English and Film, BA Hons Film Production, BA(Hons) Film Studies, FdA Media Production (Taught at Salford City College), BSc(Hons) Media Technology, BSc(Hons) Professional Broadcast Techniques (One year top-up), BA(Hons) Television and Radio
Postgraduate courses: MA/PgDip Media Production: Animation, MA/PgDip Media Production: Children's TV Production, MA/PgDip Media Production: Post-Production for TV, MA/PgDip Media Production: TV Documentary Production, MA/PgDip Media Production: TV Drama Production, MA Wildlife Documentary Production
Music: BA(Hons) Music: Creative Music Technology, BA(Hons) Music: Musical Arts, BA(Hons) Music: Popular Music and Recording
Postgraduate courses: MA Music
Performing Arts: BA(Hons) Comedy Writing & Performance, BA(Hons) Dance, BA(Hons) Media and Performance, BA(Hons) Technical Theatre (Production and Design), BA(Hons) Theatre and Performance Practice
Postgraduate courses: MA Contemporary Performance Practice
Politics and History: BA(Hons) Contemporary History and Politics, BA(Hons) Contemporary Military and International History, BA(Hons) International Politics and Security, BA(Hons) International Relations and Politics, BA(Hons) Politics
Postgraduate courses: MA/PgDip Intelligence and Security Studies, MA/PgDip Terrorism and Security

School of the Built Environment; http://www.salford.ac.uk/built-environment
BSc(Hons) Architectural Design and Technology, BSc(Hons) Architecture, MArch Architecture,

BSc(Hons) Architectural Engineering, BSc(Hons) Building Surveying, MSci(Hons) Building Surveying, BSc(Hons) Construction Project Management, BSc(Hons) Property and Real Estate, BSc(Hons) Quantity Surveying
Postgraduate courses: MSc BIM and Digital Built Environments, MSc/LLM Construction Law and Practice, MSc Building Surveying, MSc Construction Management, MSc Project Management in Construction, MSc Quantity Surveying, MSc Quantity Surveying (M&E), MSc Real Estate and Property Management, March

School of Computing, Science and Engineering; http://www.salford.ac.uk/computing-science-engineering
Acoustics, Audio and Video: BEng(Hons) Audio Acoustics, BEng(Hons) Audio Acoustics with Foundation Year, BSc(Hons) Professional Sound and Video Technology
Postgraduate courses: MSc/PgDip Audio Acoustics, MSc/PgDip Environmental Acoustics, MSc/PgDip Audio Production
Aeronautical Engineering: BEng(Hons) Aeronautical Engineering, MEng(Hons) Aeronautical Engineering, BEng(Hons) Aeronautical Engineering with Foundation Year, BEng(Hons) Aircraft Engineering with Pilot Studies, MEng(Hons) Aircraft Engineering with Pilot Studies, BSc(Hons) Aviation Technology with Pilot Studies
Postgraduate courses: MSc/PgDip/PgCert Aerospace Engineering
Civil and Structural Engineering: BEng(Hons) Civil Engineering, BSc(Hons) Civil Engineering, MEng(Hons) Civil Engineering, BEng(Hons) Civil Engineering with Foundation Year, BEng(Hons) Civil and Architectural Engineering, MEng(Hons) Civil and Architectural Engineering
Postgraduate courses: MSc/PgDip/PgCert Structural Engineering, MSc Transport Engineering and Planning
Computer Networking and Telecommunications: BSc(Hons) Computer Networks
Postgraduate courses: MSc/PgDip Data Telecommunication Networks
Computer Science: BSc(Hons) Computer Science, BSc(Hons) Computer Science with Professional Experience, BSc(Hons) Computer Science with Foundation Year, BSc(Hons) Computer Science with Web Development, BSc(Hons) Computer Science with Web Development and Professional Experience, BSc(Hons) Computer Science with Cyber Security,

BSc(Hons) Computer Science with Cyber Security and Professional Experience, BSc(Hons) Computer Science with Data Analytics, BSc(Hons) Computer Science with Data Analytics and Professional Experience, BSc(Hons) Software Engineering, BSc(Hons) Software Engineering with Professional Experience
Postgraduate courses: MSc/PgDip Databases and Web-based Systems, MSc/PgDip Cyber Security, Threat Intelligence and Forensics, MSc/PgDip Data Science
Mathematics: BSc(Hons) Mathematics, BSc(Hons) Financial Mathematics
Mechanical Engineering: BEng(Hons) Mechanical Engineering, MEng(Hons) Mechanical Engineering, BEng(Hons) Mechanical Engineering with Foundation Year
Petroleum and Gas Engineering: BEng(Hons) Petroleum and Mechanical Engineering
Postgraduate courses: MSc/PgDip Gas Engineering and Management, MSc/PgDip/PgCert Industrial and Commercial Combustion Engineering, MSc/PgDip Petroleum and Gas Engineering
Physics: BSc(Hons) Physics, MPhys(Hons) Physics, BSc(Hons) Physics with Acoustics, MPhys(Hons) Physics with Acoustics, MPhys(Hons) Physics with Studies in North America, BSc(Hons) Pure and Applied Physics, BSc(Hons) Physics with Foundation Year
Postgraduate courses: MSc Renewable Energy Materials
Electronic Engineering: BEng(Hons) Electronic Engineering, BEng(Hons) Electronic Engineering with Foundation Year
Robotics and System Engineering: MSc/PgDip Advanced Control System, MSc/PgDip Robotics and Automation

School of Environment and Life Sciences; http:// www.salford.ac.uk/environment-life-sciences/courses

BA(Hons) Archaeology and Geography with Professional Practice, BSc(Hons) Biochemistry, BSc(Hons) Biochemistry with Studies in the USA, BSc(Hons) Biology, Foundation Year Biology Foundation Year, BSc(Hons) Biology with Studies in the USA, BSc(Hons) Biomedical Science, BSc(Hons) Chemistry, BSc(Hons) Environmental Management, Foundation Year Environmental Management Foundation Year, BSc(Hons) Geography, BA(Hons) Geography, BSc(Hons) Human Biology and Infectious Diseases, BSc(Hons) Medicinal Chemistry, BSc(Hons) Pharmaceutical Science, BSc(Hons) Wildlife and Practical Conservation, BSc(Hons) Wildlife Conservation with Zoo Biology, BSc(Hons) Zoology
Postgraduate courses: MSc Biomedical Science, MSc Biotechnology, MSc Drug Design and Discovery, MSc Environmental and Public Health, MSc Environmental Assessment and Management, MSc/PgDip/PgCert Environmental Modelling, MSc/PgDip/PgCert Geographical Information Systems, Msc/PgDip Molecular Parasitology and Vector Biology, MSc/PgDip Occupational Safety, Health and Wellbeing, MSc Safety, Health and Environment, MSc Science Communication and Future Media, MSc/PgDip Sustainability, MSc/PgDip/PgCert Wildlife Conservation

School of Health Sciences; http:// www.salford.ac.uk/health-sciences

BSc(Hons) Diagnostic Radiography, BSc(Hons) Exercise, Nutrition and Health, BSc(Hons) Occupational Therapy, BSc(Hons) Physiotherapy, BSc(Hons) Podiatry, BSc(Hons) Prosthetics and Orthotics, BSc(Hons) Psychology, BSc(Hons) Psychology (First year taught at Salford City College), BSc(Hons) Psychology and Counselling, BSc(Hons) Psychology and Criminology, BSc(Hons) Psychology and Criminology (First year taught at Salford City College), BSc(Hons) Psychology of Sport, BSc(Hons) Public Health, BSc(Hons) Public Health with Placement, BSc(Hons) Sport Rehabilitation, FdSc Sports Coaching (Taught at Hopwood Hall College), BSc(Hons) Sports Science (Human Performance, Performance Analysis or Strength and Conditioning pathways)
Postgraduate courses: MSc/PgDip/PgCert Advanced Medical Imaging, MSc/PgDip/PgCert Advanced Occupational Therapy, MSc/PgDip/PgCert Advanced Physiotherapy, MSc/PgDip/PgCert Applied Psychology (Addictions), MSc/PgDip/PgCert Applied Psychology (Therapies), MSc/PgDip/PgCert Geriatric Medicine, MSc/PgDip/PgCert Media Psychology, MSc/PgDip Nuclear Medicine Imaging, MSc/PgDip/PgCert Occupational and Vocational Rehabilitation, MSc/PgDip/PgCert Performance Analysis in Sport, MSc Pre-registration Masters Podiatry Programme, MSc/PgDip/PgCert Psychology of Coercive Control, MSc/PgDip/PgCert Public Health, PgCert Public Health (Block and Blend), MSc/PgDip/PgCert Sports Injury Rehabilitation, MSc/PgDip/PgCert Strength and Conditioning, MSc/PgDip/PgCert Trauma and Orthopaedics, MSc/PgDip/PgCert Trauma and Orthopaedics: Lower Limb, MSc/PgDip/PgCert Trauma and Orthopaedics: Spinal, MSc/PgDip/PgCert Ultrasound Imaging

School of Health and Society; http://www.salford.ac.uk/about-us/corporate-information/leadership-and-management/schools-and-colleges

Counselling and Psychotherapy: BSc(Hons) Counselling and Psychotherapy: Professional Practice, BSc(Hons) Criminology with Counselling,
Postgraduate courses: MSc/PgDip/PgCert Advanced Counselling and Psychotherapy Studies, PgCert Cognitive Behaviour Therapy, MSc/PgDip/PgCert Cognitive Behavioural Psychotherapy, MSc/PgDip Counselling and Psychotherapy Studies (Professional Training)
Midwifery:
BSc(Hons) Midwifery (156 weeks), BSc(Hons) Midwifery (Post RN)
Postgraduate courses: MSc/PgDip/PgCert Advanced Practice (Neonates), MSc/PgDip/PgCert Midwifery
Nursing: BSc(Hons) Integrated Practice in Learning Disabilities Nursing and Social Work, BSc(Hons) Nursing /RN Adult, BSc(Hons) Nursing /RN Children and Young People's, BSc(Hons) Nursing /RN Mental Health, BSc(Hons) Nursing Studies
Postgraduate courses: MSc/PgDip/PgCert Advanced Practice (Health and Social Care), MSc/PgDip/PgCert Dementia: Care and the Enabling Environment, MSc/PgDip/PgCert Diabetes Care, PgCert Gastrointestinal Disorders, MSc/PgDip/PgCert Leadership and Management for Healthcare Practice, MSc Leading Education for Health and Social Care Reform, PgCert Leading Education in Practice: NMC Practice Teacher Award, MSc/PgDip/PgCert Military Veterans' Health and Wellbeing, Multi-professional Support of Learning and Assessment in Practice – Non-Credited, MSc/PgDip/PgCert Nursing (Block and Blend), MA/RN Nursing/RN (Adult, Mental Health or Children & Young People), MSc/PgDip/PgCert Nursing: Research, Practice, Practice (Neuroscience), Education, International, Prof Doc Professional Doctorate (Health and Social Care), PgCert Simulation in Health and Social Care, PgCert Work Based Learning: Using and Disseminating Evidence into Practice
Social Work and Social Policy: BSc(Hons) Social Policy, Foundation Year Social Sciences Foundation Year, BA(Hons) Social Work, BSc(Hons) Integrated Practice in Learning Disabilities Nursing and Social Work
Postgraduate courses: MSc/PgDip/PgCert Applied Social Work Practice, MA Social Pedagogy, MSc/PgDip/PgCert Social Policy, MA Social Work

Sociology and Criminology: BSc(Hons) Criminology, BSc(Hons) Criminology and Sociology, BSc(Hons) Criminology with Counselling, BSc(Hons) Sociology
Postgraduate courses: MSc/PgCert/PgDip The Criminal Justice Process

Salford Business School; http://www.salford.ac.uk/business-school

BSc(Hons) Accounting and Finance, BSc(Hons) Business and Economics, FdSc Business and Events Management (Taught at Salford City College), BSc(Hons) Business and Financial Management, BSc Business and Financial Management (First Year taught at Salford City College), FdSc Business and Financial Management (Taught at Salford City College), FdSc Business and Hospitality Management (Taught at Salford City College), BSc(Hons) Business and Management, BSc(Hons) Business and Management (First year taught at Salford City College), FdSc Business and Management (Taught at Salford City College), FdSc Business and Marketing (Taught at Salford City College), Foundation Year Business Foundation Year, BSc(Hons) Business Information Technology, BSc(Hons) Business Management with Law, BSc(Hons) Business Management with Sport, LLB(Hons) Corporate Law, BSc(Hons) Human Resource Management, BSc(Hons) Human Resource Management (First year taught at Salford City College), Graduate Certificate Human Resource Management (HRM) with CIPD Intermediate Level Diploma, BSc(Hons) International Business, BSc(Hons) International Events Management, LLB(Hons) Law, LLB(Hons) Law (Media and Digital Industries), LLB(Hons) Law with Criminology, LLB(Hons) Law with Management, BSc(Hons) Marketing, BSc(Hons) Marketing (First year taught at Salford City College)
Postgraduate courses: MSc/PgDip/PgCert Accounting and Finance, MSc/PgDip/PgCert Digital Marketing, MSc/PgDip/PgCert Financial Services Management, MSc/PgDip/PgCert Global Management, MSc/PgDip/PgCert Human Resource Management and Development, MSc/PgDip/PgCert Human Resource Management and Development – part time evening attendance, MSc/PgDip/PgCert Information Systems Management, MSc/PgDip/PgCert International Banking and Finance, MSc/PgDip/PgCert International Business, LLM/PgDip/PgCert International Business Law, MSc/PgDip/PgCert International Business with Law, LLM/PgDip/PgCert International Commercial Law, MSc/PgDip/PgCert International Corporate Finance, MSc/PgDip/PgCert International Events

Management, Graduate Certificate International Management, MSc/PgDip/PgCert Islamic Banking and Finance, MSc/PgDip/PgCert Management, PgCert Management and Personal Development, MSc/PgDip/PgCert Marketing, MSc/PgDip/PgCert

Procurement, Logistics and Supply Chain Management, MSc/PgDip/PgCert Project Management, MSc Risk and Crisis Management (Food Safety Assurance), MSc Sports Directorship, MBA The Salford MBA, MBA The Salford MBA Part-time Executive

---

RIVERSIDE COLLEGE, HALTON
www.riversidecollege.ac.uk

sport coaching and sport development, sport coaching, counselling, education, health & social care; Dip, FD, FdSc, BSc(Hons), PCET

SCARBOROUGH TEC
www.scarboroughtec.ac.uk/about-scarborough-tec/

Certificate in Education, Professional Graduate Certificate in Education, Postgraduate Certificate in Education (Teaching in the Lifelong Learning Sector)

UNIVERSITY OF SHEFFIELD
www.sheffield.ac.uk

Faculty of Arts and Humanities; www.sheffield.ac.uk/faculty/arts-and-humanities

Department of Archaeology
BA Archaeology, BSc Archaeology, BA Archaeology and History, BA Classical and Historical Archaeology, BA Prehistoric Archaeology
Postgraduate courses: MA Aegean Archaeology, MA Archaeology, MA Archaeology of the Classical Mediterranean, MA Medieval Archaeology, MA Landscape Archaeology, MA Cultural Heritage Management, MA Cultural Materials, MSc Environmental Archaeology & Palaeoeconomy, MSc Osteoarchaeology, MSc Human Osteology & Funerary Archaeology, MSc Palaeoanthropology

School of English
BA (honours) in English Language & Linguistics, BA (honours) in English Language & Literature, BA (honours) in English Literature, BA (honours) in English & Theatre
Postgraduate courses: MA Applied Linguistics with TESOL, MA Creative Writing, MA Eighteenth Century Studies, MA English Language and Linguistics, MA English Literature, MA Nineteenth Century Studies, MA Theatre and Performance Studies

Department of History
BA History
Postgraduate courses: MA in Historical Research, MA in Medieval History, MA in Early Modern History, MA in Modern History, MA in American History, MA in Global History

School of Languages and Cultures
Single honours, programmes with two languages, programmes with three languages in French, Germanic Studies, Hispanic Studies, Russian and Slavonic Studies
Postgraduate MA courses: MA Crossways in Cultural Narratives (Mundus), MA in Intercultural Communication, MA in Intercultural Communication and International Development, MA in Multilingual Information Management, MA in Screen Translation, MA in Translation Studies, MA in Hispanic Studies, MA in Latin American Studies, MA in Catalan Studies, MA in French Studies

Department of Music
BMus
Postgraduate courses: MA Composition, MA Ethnomusicology, MA Music Management, MA Musicology, MA Music Performance Studies, MA Music Psychology in Education, MA Psychology of Music,

MA Sonic Arts, MA Traditional Music of the British Isles, MA World Music Studies

Department of Philosophy
Philosophy (Single Honours)

Faculty of Engineering; www.sheffield.ac.uk/faculties/ engineering

Dept of Aerospace Engineering; www.sheffield.ac.uk/aerospace
adv aerospace materials, aerospace engineering/with private pilot instruction, aerostructures & aerodynamics, adv manufacturing technologies, adv control systems & systems engineering; BEng, MEng, MPhil, MSc, PhD, PGDip, MSc(Res), MSc, MSc(Eng)

Dept of Automatic Control & Systems Engineering; www.sheffield.ac.uk/acse
adv control & systems, computer systems engineering, computational intelligence & robotics, mechatronic & robotic engineering, systems & control engineering, engineering management; BEng, MEng, MPhil, MSc, PhD

Dept of Bioengineering; www.sheffield.ac.uk/bioengineering
bioengineering, biomedical engineering, biomanufacture, biomaterials with tissue engineering, biomaterials & regenerative medicine, dental materials science, medical devices & systems; BEng, MEng, MSc

Dept of Chemical & Biological Engineering; www.sheffield.ac.uk/cbe
biological and bioprocessing engineering, biochemical engineering & industrial management, chemical engineering, chemical engineering with energy/chemistry/biotechnology/nuclear technology/modern language, environmental & energy engineering, energy engineering with industrial management, process safety & loss prevention; BEng, MEng, MPhil, MSc, MSc(Eng), PhD

Dept of Civil & Structural Engineering; www.sheffield.ac.uk/civil
civil engineering, civil and structural engineering, structural engineering and architecture, architectural engineering design, civil engineering with a modern language, architectural engineering design, earthquake and civil engineering dynamics, steel construction, structural engineering, structural and concrete engineering, water engineering; BEng, MEng, MPhil, MSc, PGDip/Cert, PhD

Dept of Computer Science; www.sheffield.ac.uk/dcs
computer science, computer science and mathematics, artificial intelligence and computer science, software engineering, information technology management for business, software development for business, physics with computer science, advanced software engineering, advanced computer science, advanced computer science (enterprise computing/verification and testing), computer science & management/with speech and language processing, data science, IT management for business, software systems and internet technology, software engineering, data communications, information systems; BEng, BSc, MComp, MEng, MPhil, MSc, MSc(Eng), PhD

Dept of Electronic & Electrical Engineering; www.sheffield.ac.uk/eee
electrical engineering, electronic engineering, electrical and electronic engineering, electronic and communications engineering, digital electronics, microelectronics, electronic & electrical engineering, advanced electrical machines, power electronics and drives, data communications, electronic and electrical engineering, semiconductor photonics and electronics, wireless communication systems; BEng, MEng, MPhil, MSc, PhD

Dept of Materials Science & Engineering; www.sheffield.ac.uk/materials
aerospace materials, nuclear materials manufacturing, adv metallurgy, materials science & engineering (biomaterials), polymers & polymer composites science & engineering, nanomaterials & materials science,, nuclear materials/engineering & science, biomaterials & regenerative medicine, material science & nanomaterials; BEng, EngD, MEng, MPhil, MSc, MRes, PhD, MMet

Dept of Mechanical Engineering; www.sheffield.ac.uk/mecheng
advanced/mechanical engineering, advanced manufacturing technologies, aerodynamics & aerostructures, mechanical engineering with Spanish/French/Italian/German/industrial management/biomechanics, nuclear technology; BEng, MEng, MPhil, MSc, MSc(Res), PhD

Faculty of Medicine, Dentistry & Health; *www.sheffield.ac.uk/faculties/ medicine-dentistry-health*

The Medical School; www.sheffield.ac.uk/ medicine

human metabolism/nutrition, infection & immunity, medicine, medical education, molecular/& genetic medicine, musculoskeletal ageing, reproductive & developmental medicine, translational oncology, orthoptics, surgery, vision & strabismus; medical education, physician's associate, medical science, clinical neurology, genomic medicine, translational neuroscience, translational pathology (neuroscience); BMedSci, MBChB, MD, PhD, PGCert/Dip

School of Clinical Dentistry; www.sheffield.ac.uk/dentalschool

clinical dentistry, dental hygiene and therapy, dental implantology, dental materials science, dental public health, dental surgery, dentistry, endodontics, diagnostic oral pathology, orthodontics, paediatric dentistry, periodontics, prosthodontics, dental public health, dental technology, restorative dentistry; BDS, ClinDent, Diploma, MSc, MClinD, MDPH, MMedSci, MPhil, PhD

Health & Related Research; www.sheffield.ac.uk/scharr

adv emergency care, clinical research, health services, public health (management & leadership), health economics & decision making, European public health (health service research/management & leadership), international health technical assessment/ management & leadership; MSc, PGDip/Cert, MPH, MEuro PubHealth

Dept of Human Communication Sciences; www.sheffield.ac.uk/hcs

acquired communication disorders, cleft & speech, cleft palate studies, clinical communication studies, language & communication impairment in children, language & literacy, speech difficulties, speech & language sciences;

Dept of Infection & Immunity & cardiovascular disease; www.sheffield.ac.uk/ infectionandimmunity

molecular medicine (cancer, cardiovascular, experimental medicine, genetic mechanisms,microbes & infection, translational neuroscience; BMedSci, MSc, MRCPsych

Dept of Neuroscience; www.sheffield.ac.uk/neuroscience

translational pathology (neuroscience) genomic medicine; BMedSci, MSc, MRCPsych

School of Nursing & Midwifery; www.sheffield.ac.uk/snm

acute care, cancer care, adult nursing studies, advanced practice, adv neonatal nurse practitioner, dementia care, health & social care studies/human sciences, high dependency & critical care, infection control, long term conditions, maternity care, midwifery, neonatal intensive care, nursing studies, nurse practitioner, occupational health nursing, palliative care, public health, primary/critical/cancer/neonatal intensive care, advanced paediatric nurse practitioner, dementia studies, specialist practice, advanced nursing studies, primary care and community nursing, general practice advanced nurse practitioner; BMedSci, MMedSci, MMid, MPhil, PGCert, PhD

Dept of Oncology; www.sheffield.ac.uk/ oncology

clinical oncology, molecular oncology, human nutrition, ophthalmology and orthoptics, supportive care, surgical oncology,urology, inflammation and tumour targeting; MSc, MSD, PhD

The Faculty of Science; *www.sheffield.ac.uk/faculties/science*

Dept of Animal & Plant Sciences; www.sheffield.ac.uk/aps

biology, ecology & conservation biology, plant sciences, ecology & environment, evolution & behaviour, environmental science, plant & microbial biology, zoology; MBiolSci, PhD, MPhil, MEnvSci

Dept of Biomedical Science; www.sheffield.ac.uk/bms

biomedical science, genomic approaches to drug discovery, integrative physiology and pharmacology, sensory neuroscience, stem cell and regenerative medicine; BSc(Hons), MSc, PhD

Dept of Chemistry; www.sheffield.ac.uk/ chemistry

chemistry, polymers for advanced technologies, science communication, chemical physics, chemistry with biological & medicinal chemistry; BSc, MChem, MPhil, MPhys, PhD

School of Mathematics & Statistics; www.sheffield.ac.uk/maths

mathematics, statistics, financial maths, statistics with medical applications, maths with language, science communication studies; BSc, MSc, PhD, MMath, MComp

Dept of Molecular Biology & Biotechnology; www.sheffield.ac.uk/mbb

biochemistry, biochemistry & genetics/microbiology, chemistry with biological & medical chemistry, molecular cell biology, genetics/& molecular cell biology, human & molecular biosciences, medical genetics/biochemistry, microbiology/molecular cell biology, biochemistry, microbiology, molecular biology/& biotechnology, biology, medical microbiology, science communication; BSc(Hons), MBiolSci, PhD

Dept of Physics & Astronomy; www.sheffield.ac.uk/physics

astronomy & astrophysics, physics with astrophysics/computer science/philosophy, biophysics, chemical physics, inorganic semiconductors, medical physics, particle physics & particle astrophysics, soft matter, physics, theoretical physics; BSc(Hons), MPhys, MSc, PhD

Dept of Psychology; www.sheffield.ac.uk/psychology

cognitive studies, cognitive & computational neuroscience, cognitive neuroscience & human neuroimaging, science communication, psychology, psychological research methods; BA(Hons), BSc(Hons), DClinPsych, MA, MPhil, MSc, PhD

Faculty of Social Science; www.sheffield.ac.uk/faculty/social-science

School of Architecture; www.sheffield.ac.uk/architecture

architecture, architecture and landscape, engineering and architecture, architectural and interdisciplinary studies, architecture and TRP, architecture and landscape architecture, architecture: collaborative practice; Postgraduate; digital design and interactive built environments, sustainable architecture studies, urban design, architectural design; BA(Hons), MArch, MPhil, MSc, PhD, MEng

School of East Asian Studies; www.sheffield.ac.uk/seas

Chinese studies, East Asian studies, Japanese studies, /Korean studies, jt honours degrees; Postgraduate; contemporary China, Teaching Chinese as a foreign language, contemporary Japan, East Asian business, media in East Asia; BA(Hons), MA, PhD

Dept of Economics; www.sheffield.ac.uk/economics

economics, accounting & financial management & economics, business management & economics, economics & mathematics/politics/philosophy/finance, economics & public policy, business finance & economics, finance, financial economics, economics & health economics, international finance and economics, money, banking & finance, French/German/Hispanic studies/Russian & economics; Adv Cert, BA(Hons), BSc(Hons), MSc, PhD

Sheffield School of Law; www.sheffield.ac.uk/law

law, corporate & commercial law, European law, law with French/German/Spanish law, criminology, law & criminology, international law & global justice, international criminology, international/& European law, legal practice; LlB, LlM, MAPhil, PhD, GradDip

Sheffield Management School; www.sheffield.ac.uk/management

accounting and financial management, business management, international business management, business management with Japanese studies/Chinese studies/French/German/Hispanic studies/Korean studies/Russian, accounting and financial management and economics/mathematics, business management & economics/mathematics, business management and economics/mathematics/social policy/sociology; Postgrad; accounting, governance, & financial management, creative and cultural industries management, entrepreneurship and management, finance and accounting, global marketing management, HRM, information systems management, international management, international management and marketing, leadership and management, logistics and supply chain management, management, management (international business), marketing, marketing management practice, occupational psychology, work psychology; MSc, MPhil, PhD, Sheffield MBA, Exec MBA, adv manufacturing management, MBA with engineering

Dept of Politics; www.sheffield.ac.uk/politics

politics, European law/& governance & politics, European & global affairs, international relations/political economy, global politics and law/security/justice, globalisation & development, global justice/

security, governance & public policy, international relations & politics, international politics & security studies/public policy, political theory, politics with research methods, sociology with public policy, politics/& history/sociology/economics/philosophy/French/German/Russian/Hispanic studies; BA, MA, MPhil, PhD

Dept of Sociological Studies; www.sheffield.ac.uk/socstudies

business management & social policy/sociology, dementia studies, sociology/& English language/history/politics/criminology, digital media & society, integrated practice with children & families, international social change & policy, social policy/politics & sociology, sociology with public policy, social research, sociology, social work; BA(Hons), MA, MPhil, PhD

Dept of Urban Studies & Planning; www.sheffield.ac.uk/usp

cities & global development, commercial real estate, geography & planning, commercial real estate planning/& development, town & regional planning, urban studies/design & planning & planning, planning research, applied GIS, TR; BA(Hons), MA, MPlan, PhD

The School of Education; www.sheffield.ac.uk/education

applied professional studies in education, children, schools & families, education, culture & childhood, education, policy & practice, education: early childhood, globalising education: policy and practice, psychology and education, educational research, education: language and education, applied professional studies in education, teaching and learning in higher education, higher education learning, applied professional studies in education, education: early childhood education/early childhood/language &

education, educational child psychology, globalising education, higher education, language, learning & teaching, literacy & learning, policy & practice, PGDE (11-18 age range in English, geography, history, mathematics, modern languages & science), school direct, psychology & education, educational research; EdD, MA, MEd, MPhil, MSc, PGDE, PGCE, PhD, PCHE, DEdPsy

Dept of Geography; www.sheffield.ac.uk/geography

geography, applied GIS, environmental change & international development, environmental science, food security & food justice, geography & planning, international development, polar & alpine change; BA(Hons), BSc(Hons), MEnvSci, PhD, MPH, MGeogSci

School of Information; www.sheffield.ac.uk/is

data science, digital library management, health informatics, information management, information systems/management, librarianship, library & information service management, multilingual information management; MA, MChem, MSc, MSc(Res), PhD/MPhil

Dept of Journalism Studies; www.sheffield.ac.uk/journalism

global/magazine journalism, journalism studies, international political communication, broadcast journalism, print journalism, science communication; BA, MPhil, PhD

Dept of Landscape; www.sheffield.ac.uk/landscape

landscape architecture, landscape management, architecture & landscape, landscape studies, landscape research; BA(Hons), BSc(Hons), MA, PGDip, PhD, MLA, BA/BSc

SHEFFIELD HALLAM UNIVERSITY
www.shu.ac.uk

Faculty of Arts, Computing, Engineering & Science; www.shu.ac.uk/about-us/academic-departments/faculty-of-arts-computing-engineering-and-sciences

Sheffield Institute of Arts

BA (Honours) Animation, BSc (Honours) Architectural Technology, BSc (Honours) Architectural Technology (Part & Time), BSc (Honours) Architecture, BA (Honours) Fine Art, BA (Honours) Fine Art (part-time), BA (Honours) Creative Writing, BA (Honours) Fashion Design, BA (Honours) Fashion Management and Communication, BA (Honours) Digital Media Production, BA (Honours) Film and Media Production, BA (Honours) Games Design, BA (Honours) Graphic Design, BA (Honours)

Illustration, BA (Honours) Interior Design, BA (Honours) Jewellery and Metalwork, BA(Hons)Journalism, BA (Honours) Media, BA(Hons) Public Relations, BA(Hons) Public Relations and Media, BA (Honours) Performance and Professional Practice (top up), BA (Honours) Performance for Stage and Screen, BA (Honours) Photography, BA (Honours) Product Design, BA (Honours) Product Design: Furniture

Postgraduate courses: MA/MFA Fine Art, MA Animation and Digital Effects, MArt Animation, MA Arts and Cultural Management, MA Digital Media Managemnet, MArt Digital Media Production, MA Journalism, MA International Journalism, MA Sports Journalism, MA Filmmaking, MA Public Relations, MSc Games Software Development, MArch Architecture, MSc Technical Architecture, MA Creative Writing

Department of Computing

BSc (Honours) Computing Management (top-up), PGCE Secondary Computing, BSc (Honours) Business and ICT, BSc (Honours) Computer Security with Forensics, BSc (Honours) Information Technology with Business Studies, BSc (Honours) Information Technology with Business Technologies (top up), BSc (Honours) Information Technology with Digital Media (top up), MEng Software Engineering, BSc (Honours) Information Technology with Networks (top up), BA (Honours) Animation, BSc (Honours) Computing, BEng (Honours) Software Engineering, BSc (Honours) Computer Networks, BSc (Honours) Computer and Information Security, BSc (Honours) Computer Science for Games, BA (Honours) Digital Media Production, BEng (Honours) Computer Systems Engineering, BA (Honours) Games Design, BSc (Honours) Computer Science

Postgraduate courses: MPhil/PhD Research Degrees Ě' Materials and Engineering Research Institute, MPhil/PhD Research Degrees Ě' Cultural, Communication and Computing Research Institute, MComp Computer Science for Games, MSc Big Data Analytics, MSc Games Software Development, MSc Advanced Computer Networks, MSc Computing, MRes Computing (Enterprise Systems, Transformation and Innovation), MSc Information Systems Security, MA Animation and Digital Effects, MSc Computer and Network Engineering, MSc Information Technology Management

Department of Engineering

Engineering

PGCE Engineering, BEng (Honours) Mechanical Engineering top up, BEng (Honours) Food Engineering, BEng (Honours) Aerospace Engineering, BEng (Honours) Aerospace Manufacturing Engineering (top up), BEng (Honours) Automotive Engineering, BEng (Honours) Chemical Engineering, BEng (Honours) Electrical and Electronic Engineering, BEng (Honours) Computer Systems Engineering, BEng (Honours) Food Engineering, BEng (Honours) Electrical Power Engineering, BEng (Honours) Electrical Power Engineering, BEng (Honours) Electronic Engineering, BEng (Honours) Mechanical Engineering, BSc (Honours) Physics, BEng (Honours) Railway Engineering

Postgraduate courses: MEng Food Engineering, MEng Aerospace Engineering, MSc Telecommunication and Electronic Engineering, MSc Mechanical Engineering, MSc Electrical and Electronic Engineering, MSc Food Processing Engineering, MEng Automotive Engineering, MEng Electrical and Electronic Engineering, MEng Chemical Engineering, MSc Automation, Control and Robotics, MSc Advanced Mechanical Engineering, MSc Computer and Network Engineering, MSc Logistics and Supply Chain Management, MSc Advanced Engineering and Management, MBA Industrial Management, MSc Advanced Materials Engineering, MSc Sports Engineering, BEng (Honours) Materials Engineering, MEng Mechanical Engineering, MEng Materials Engineering, MSc Advanced Engineering

Mathematics

PGCE Secondary Mathematics, BSc (Honours) Mathematics with Education and Qualified Teacher Status, BSc (Honours) Mathematics, BSc (Honours) Physics

Department of Media Arts and Communication

Media Arts

BA (Honours) Public Relations (Part-Time), BA (Honours) Public Relations and Media, BA (Honours) Public Relations, BA (Honours) Film and Media Production, BA (Honours) Animation, BA (Honours) Fine Art, BA (Honours) Photography, BA (Honours) Journalism, BSc (Honours) Computer Science for Games, BA (Honours) Media, BA (Honours) Digital Media Production, BA (Honours) Games Design

Postgraduate courses: MArt Animation, MArt Digital Media Production, MComp Computer Science for Games, MA Filmmaking, MSc Games Software

Development, MA Games Design, MA Digital Media Management, MA Animation and Digital Effects, MA/MFA Fine Art

Media, PR and Journalism

BA (Honours) Public Relations (Part-Time), BA (Honours) Media, BA (Honours) Journalism (Part-Time), BA (Honours) Public Relations and Media (Part-Time), BA (Honours) Public Relations and Media, BA (Honours) Public Relations, BA (Honours) Marketing Communications and Advertising, BA (Honours) Film and Media Production, BA (Honours) Photography, BA (Honours) Journalism, BA (Honours) Media, BA (Honours) Digital Media Production, BA (Honours) Games Design

Postgraduate courses: MA International Journalism, MA Journalism, MA Arts and Cultural Management, MA Digital Media Management, MA Sports Journalism, MA Public Relations

Faculty of Development and Society; www.shu.ac.uk/about-us/academic-departments/development-and-society

Humanities
English

BA (Honours) Creative Writing, BA (Honours) English Literature, BA (Honours) English Language, BA (Honours) English, MA English by Research, MA Teaching English to Speakers of Other Languages (TESOL), MA Teaching English to Speakers of Other Languages (TESOL), MA Creative Writing

History

BA (Honours) History, MA History by Research

Stage and Screen

BA (Honours) Performance and Professional Practice (top up), BA (Honours) Film Studies and Screenwriting, BA (Honours) Film and Media Production, BA (Honours) Performance for Stage and Screen, BA (Honours) Film Studies, MPhil/PhD Stage and Screen

Law and Criminology

LLM International Sports Law in Practice, MPhil/PhD Law and Criminology, LLM Masters in Law by Research, BA (Honours) Forensic Accounting, LLB (Honours) Law with Criminology, LLB (Honours) Law, MSc Forensic Accounting, MA Applied Human Rights, MSc Forensic Psychology, LLM/PgDip/PgCert International Commercial Law, LLM Applied Human Rights

Department of the Natural and Built Environment

Undergraduate and postgraduate courses in Architecture, Construction, Building and Surveying, Environment, Geography, Planning, Housing and Regeneration, Real estate

Department of Psychology, Sociology and Politics
Psychology

BSc (Honours) Criminology and Psychology, BA (Honours) Education with Psychology and Counselling, BSc (Honours) Psychology, MSc Health Psychology, MSc Forensic Psychology, MSc Sport and Exercise Psychology, MSc Clinical Cognitive Neuroscience, MSc Psychology, MSc Developmental Psychology

Sociology

BA (Honours) Sociology, BA (Honours) Applied Social Science

Politics

BA (Honours) Politics

Faculty of Development & Society; www.shu.ac.uk/faculties/ds/nbe

Natural & Built Environment

architectural technology, architecture, building/quantity surveying, construction, project management, built environment, environmental science/management, human/geography, GIS, planning & geography, urban regeneration planning, real estate, project management in the built environment, transport planning, urban planning/regeneration; BSc(Hons), MPhil, MSc, PGDip/Cert, PhD, MBA

Criminology & Community Justice; www.shu.ac.uk/prospectus/subject/law

law, law & criminology, applied human rights, forensic criminology/science/law/psychology/accounting, international commercial law; BEng, BSc(Hons), FdSc, MA/PGDip/PGCert, MSc

Education; www.shu.ac.uk/prospectus/subject/education-studies

Asperger syndrome, autism spectrum, design 7 technology education & QTS, early/childhood studies, early years/education with QTS/teaching, design & technology, education, educational studies with psychology & counselling, education & learning support, education: early years teaching for academic purposes, English & educational studies, knowledge enhancement in mathematics, languages & TESOL (French/Spanish/German), learning & teaching in

HE/in primary education with QTS, mathematics/ science with education & QTS, mathematics with education & QTS, PE & school sport, post-16 education & training, teaching & learning in early years & the primary sector/with QTS/early years/HE, special needs coordination, education studies, primary ed with QTS, science with education & QTS, PGCE (early years education, learning & skills, mathematics education, primary, secondary,broad range of taught subjects, secondary citizenship), youth work

Teacher Education: post-16 education & FE, teach first, school direct, special educational needs coordination, teaching English for academic purposes; BA(Hons), CertE, EdD, FdA, MA, MPhil, MSc, PGCert/Dip, PhD, PGCE

English; www.shu.ac.uk/prospectus/subject/english

creative writing, writing, English & history, English/ language/literature, TESOL, English language teaching, ESOL, secondary English, English by research; BA(Hons), PGCE, MA, PGDip, MPhil, PhD

Environment; www.shu.ac.uk/prospectus/subject/environment

environmental management/science; BSc(Hons), MPlan, MSc/PGDip/PGCert

Geography; www.shu.ac.uk/prospectus/subject/geography

geography/and planning, GIS, human geography; BA(Hons), BSc(Hons), MSc, PGDip/Cert, PGCE

History; www.shu.ac.uk/prospectus/subject/history

history, English & history, criminology, politics, local & global history, imperialism & culture, history by research; PGCE, BA(Hons), MA, PGDip, MPhil, PhD

Law; www.shu.ac.uk/prospectus/subject/law

law applied human rights, international sport law in practice, global communication law, law with criminology; LlB, LLM, MSc, PGCert/Dip

Planning, Regeneration & Housing; www.shu.ac.uk/planning

geography & planning, built environment, business property management, urban planning, urban regeneration; BA(Hons), BSc(Hons), MPlanning and Transport, MSc/PGDip, DipHE, MBA

Psychology; www.shu.ac.uk/psychology

psychology, applied cognitive neuroscience, cognitive analytic therapy, criminology & psychology, developmental/health psychology, clinical cognitive neuroscience, education with psychology & counselling, psychology & sociology, sport & exercise psychology; BSc(Hons), MRes/PGDip/PGCert, MSc, ExecMBA

Sociology & Politics; www.shu.ac.uk/prospectus/subject/sociology-politics

applied social science, applied human rights, criminology/& sociology,, politics, psychology/& sociology, public health, social sciences, sociology, planning and policy; BA(Hons), GradDip, MA, MPhil/PhD, MRes/PGDip/PGCert

Stage & Screen; www.shu.ac.uk/prospectus/subject/stage-screen

animation & visual effects, film studies, film and media/production, international documentary production, performance & professional practice/for stage & screen, film studies & screenwriting; BA(Hons), FdA, MA, MArt, MA/PGDip/PGCert

Faculty of Health & Wellbeing; www.shu.ac.uk/faculties/hwb

Sport and Active Lifestyles; www.shu.ac.uk/prospectus/subject/sport-active-lifestyles

adv sport coaching practice, PE & school sport, sports development/with coaching, sport engineering/studies/coaching, sport & physical activity, physical activity, sport & health, sports studies, app/sport & exercise science, sport & exercise technology, sport business management; BA(Hons), BSc(Hons), MA, MSc, PGDip/Cert, ProfDoc, PGCE

Biosciences & Chemistry; www.shu.ac.uk/bio

analytical chemistry, biochemistry, biology, biomedical/laboratory sciences, biosciences, biotechnology, chemistry, forensic science, human biology, molecular & cell biology, pharmaceutical analysis, pharmacology and biotechnology, professional studies, secondary science; BSc(Hons), MSc/PGDip/PGCert, ProfDocBiomedSc, PGCE

Centre for Medical & Dental Education; www.shu.ac.uk/faculties/hwb/medical
MSc, PGCert/Dip

Diagnostic Radiography; www.shu.ac.uk/prospectus/subject/diagnostic-radiography

advanced diagnostic imaging practice, advancing professional practice, diagnostic radiography, medical ultrasound, radiological studies; DocProf Studies (Health and Social Care), BA(Hons), BSc(Hons), MSc/PGDip/PGCert

Nursing & Midwifery; www.shu.ac.uk/faculties/lwb/departments/nursing-midwifery

applied nursing (learning disability) and generic social work, perinatal and maternal mental health, specialist practice district nursing, specialist community public health nursing, health visiting/school nursing, acute and critical care of the child, child, adolescent and family mental health, nursing, nursing (adult/child/mental health), specialist practice district nursing, midwifery, advancing professional practice (paediatrics), approved mental health professional nursing, public health/primary & community care, health and social care leadership & management, healthcare education, maternal health care, midwifery, medical ultrasound, supportive and palliative care, primary care nursing/district nursing, professional practice (nursing/midwifery), prostate cancer care, health visiting and school nursing; AdvDip, AdvProfDev, BA(Hons), BSc(Hons), DocProfStud, FD, MSc/PGDip/PGCert

Occupational Therapy; www.shu.ac.uk/occupational

applying/occupational therapy, advancing (paediatric) practice, vocational rehabilitation; BSc(Hons), DocProf, MSc/PGDip/PGCert

Operating Department Practice; www.shu.ac.uk/odp

operating dept practice, advancing professional practice; DipHE, DocProfStud, MSc/PGDip/Cert

Paramedic Studies; www.shu.ac.uk/paramedic

paramedic practice; DipHE, MSc, PGDip/Cert, ProfDoc

Physiotherapy; www.shu.ac.uk/physio

advancing/applying physiotherapy practice, physiotherapy (practice based), adv professional practice (paediatrics), vocational rehabilitation, medical ultrasound therapy, manual therapy; BA(Hons), BSc(Hons), MSc, PGCert, PGDip, ProfDoc

Radiotherapy and Oncology; www.shu.ac.uk/radiotherapy

adv practice radiotherapy & oncology, prostrate cancer care, radiotherapy planning, radiotherapy & oncology in practice, supportive and palliative care,,

radiological studies; BA(Hons), BSc(Hons), DipHE, MSc/PGDip/PGCert, ProfDoc

Social Work; www.shu.ac.uk/socialwork

applied nursing (learning disabilities) & generic social work, social work, specialist mental health practice/practitioner, working with children, young people & families, youth & community work, youth work, health and social care leadership & management; BA(Hons), GradDip, MSc, PGDip, MSW, PGCert, DocSocWork, FD

Sheffield Business School; www.shu.ac.uk/sbs

Accounting, Banking & Finance; www.shu.ac.uk/prospectus/subject/accounting-banking-finance

accounting & finance/economics, banking & finance, economics, financial management, forensic accounting, risk management, wealth management; BA(Hons), MA, MSc, PGDip/Cert

Business & Management; www.shu.ac.uk/prospectus/subject/business-management

business and management/finance/HRM/English, business administration, business administration (facilities management), business analytics/ economics/ management/finance/financial management/ HRM/marketing/ studies, business and enterprise, coaching and mentoring, economics, executive MBA (psychology/facilities management/built environment), international business with Spanish/French/German, international HRM, international business management, international business, international marketing, logistics and supply chain management, oil and gas management, managing global business, total/ quality management and organisational excellence, marketing, communications and advertising, business information systems, charity research management, coaching & mentoring, facilities management, financial management, food marketing management, global supply chain management, HRM/D, IT with business studies, HRM/HR development, leadership & management, logistics & supply chain management, organisational development & consultancy, industrial management,languages with business/tourism, sales leadership, total, strategic operations management, Exec MBAs (psychology/facility management/built environment); BSc(Hons), DBA, FD, GradDip, Exec MBA, PGCE, MBA, MPhil, MSc, PGCert, PGDip, PhD, MRes, MBusiness

Sheffield Hallam University

Languages; www.shu.ac.uk/prospectus/subject/languages/

business & English, English language teaching, languages with TESOL/international business/tourism/marketing, international business studies & languages (French/German/Spanish), teaching English for academic purposes; GradDip/Cert, MPhil, PGCert, PhD

Tourism, Hospitality & Events Management; www.shu.ac.uk/prospectus/subject/tourism-hospitality-events

tourism management, international tourism management, event management, tourism management or event management with accounting, business, economics, European studies, finance, human resources, information systems, marketing or a language; either French, German, Spanish, Italian or mandarin Chinese; Postgraduate; international tourism and hospitality management

BSc(Hons), FdSc, MA, MPhil, MSc, PGCert, PGDip, PhD

UNIVERSITY OF SOUTH WALES
www.southwales.ac.uk

Faculty of Life Sciences and Education; www.southwales.ac.uk/courses/faculty/FLSE/?faculty_title=Faculty+of+Life+Sciences+and+Education

BA(Hons) Early Years Education and Practice (with Early Years Practitioner status), BA (Anrh) Astudiaethau Cynradd gyda SAC, BA(Hons) Counselling and Therapeutic Practice, BA(Hons) Creative and Therapeutic Arts, BA(Hons) Primary Studies with QTS, BA(Hons) Sports Leadership and Development, BA(Hons) Working with Children and Families, BSc(Hons) Acute and Critical Care, BSc(Hons) Childhood Development, BSc(Hons) Childhood Studies (Top Up), BSc(Hons) Community Health & Wellbeing (Top-Up), BSc(Hons) Community Health Studies (Specialist Practitioner Community Children's Nursing), BSc(Hons) Community Health Studies (Specialist Practitioner District Nursing) with integrated V100, BSc(Hons) Community Health Studies (Specialist Practitioner General Practice Nursing), BSc(Hons) Football Coaching and Performance, BSc(Hons) Football Coaching, Development and Administration, BSc(Hons) Health and Social Care Management, BSc(Hons) Police Sciences, BSc(Hons) Professional Practice (Health Care Studies), BSc(Hons) Professional Practice (Violence Reduction), BSc(Hons) Psychology, BSc(Hons) Psychology with Behaviour Analysis, BSc(Hons) Psychology with Cognitive Behavioural Therapy, BSc(Hons) Psychology with Counselling, BSc(Hons) Psychology with Criminology & Criminal Justice, BSc(Hons) Psychology with Developmental Disorders, BSc(Hons) Public Health, BSc(Hons) Rugby Coaching and Performance, BSc(Hons) Secondary Design and Technology with QTS, BSc(Hons) Secondary Mathematics with ICT with QTS, BSc(Hons) Secondary Mathematics with Science with QTS, BSc(Hons) Secondary Science with ICT with QTS, BSc(Hons) Secondary Science with Mathematics with QTS, BSc(Hons) Social Work, BSc(Hons) Specialist Community Public Health Nursing (Health Visiting), BSc(Hons) Specialist Community Public Health Nursing (Occupational Health Nursing), BSc(Hons) Specialist Community Public Health Nursing (School Nursing), BSc(Hons) Sport Psychology, BSc(Hons) Sport and Exercise Science, BSc(Hons) Sports Coaching, BSc(Hons) Sports Coaching and Development, BSc(Hons) Sports Studies, BSc(Hons) Strength and Conditioning, BSc(Hons) Systemic Counselling, Bachelor of Midwifery(Hons) Registered Midwife, Bachelor of Nursing(Hons)(Adult), Bachelor of Nursing(Hons)(Child Health), Bachelor of Nursing(Hons)(Learning Disabilities), Bachelor of Nursing(Hons)(Mental Health) Postgraduate courses: MA Art Psychotherapy, MA CAMH (Child and Adolescent Mental Health), MA Consultative Supervision, MA Counselling Children and Young People, MA Education (Innovation in Learning and Teaching), MA Integrative Counselling and Psychotherapy, MA Leadership & Management (Education), MA Leadership in Sport, MA Music Therapy, MA SEN/ALN (Additional Learning Needs), MA SEN/ALN (Autism), MA TESOL (Teaching English to Speakers of Other Languages), MSc Advanced Clinical Practitioner, MSc Advanced Performance Football Coaching, MSc Advanced Practice, MSc Applied Health Economics, MSc Behaviour

352

Analysis and Therapy, MSc Clinical Endodontics, MSc Clinical and Abnormal Psychology, MSc Cognitive Behavioural Psychotherapy, MSc Community Health Studies (Children's Community Nursing), MSc Community Health Studies (District Nursing), MSc Community Health Studies (Practice Nursing), MSc Dermatology in Clinical Practice, MSc Diabetes (Online Delivery), MSc Disaster Healthcare (Online Delivery), MSc Endocrinology (Online Delivery), MSc International Security and Risk Management (Online delivery), MSc Medical Education, MSc Obesity and Weight Management (Online Delivery), MSc Pain Management, MSc Play Therapy, MSc Preventative Cardiovascular Medicine (Online delivery), MSc Professional Practice, MSc Psychology by Research, MSc Public Health, MSc Respiratory Medicine (Online Delivery), MSc Rheumatology (Online Delivery), MSc Sexual and Reproductive Medicine, MSc Specialist Community Public Health Nursing (Health Visiting), MSc Specialist Community Public Health Nursing (School Nursing), MSc Sport, Health and Exercise Science, MSc Sports Coaching and Performance, MSc Systemic Psychotherapy

Faculty of Creative Industries; www.southwales.ac.uk/courses/faculty/ FCI/?faculty_title=Faculty+ of+Creative+Industries

BA (Anrh) Theatr a Drama, BA(Hons) Advertising Design, BA(Hons) Animation (2D and Stop Motion), BA(Hons) Computer Animation, BA(Hons) Computer Games Design, BA(Hons) Creative Industries (Photography) (Top Up), BA(Hons) Creative Music Technologies, BA(Hons) Dance, BA(Hons) Documentary Photography, BA(Hons) Fashion Design, BA(Hons) Fashion Marketing and Retail Design, BA(Hons) Fashion Promotion, BA(Hons) Film, BA(Hons) Film Studies, BA(Hons) Game Art, BA(Hons) Graphic Communication, BA(Hons) Illustration, BA(Hons) Interior Design, BA(Hons) Journalism, BA(Hons) Media Production, BA(Hons) Media, Culture and Journalism, BA(Hons) Music Business, BA(Hons) Performance and Media, BA(Hons) Performing Arts, BA(Hons) Photography, BA(Hons) Photojournalism, BA(Hons) Popular and Commercial Music, BA(Hons) Sports Journalism, BA(Hons) TV and Film Set Design, BA(Hons) Theatre and Drama, BA(Hons) Visual Effects and Motion Graphics, BMus(Hons) Contemporary Music Performance, BSc(Hons) Creative Industries (Popular Music Technology) (Top-Up), BSc(Hons) Sound Engineering

Postgraduate courses: MA Animation, MA Arts Practice (Art, Health and Wellbeing), MA Arts Practice (Fine Art), MA Documentary Photography, MA Drama, MA Games Enterprise, MA Graphic Communication, MA Songwriting and Production, MSc Music Engineering and Production

Faculty of Computing, Engineering and Science

BEng(Hons) Aeronautical Engineering, BEng(Hons) Aeronautical Engineering (Including Foundation Year), BEng(Hons) Civil Engineering, BEng(Hons) Electrical and Electronic Engineering, BEng(Hons) Electrical and Electronic Engineering (Including Foundation Year), BEng(Hons) Mechanical Engineering, BSc(Hons) Aircraft Maintenance Engineering, BSc(Hons) Analytical and Forensic Science (Top Up), BSc(Hons) Applied Cyber Security, BSc(Hons) Biology, BSc(Hons) Chemistry, BSc(Hons) Civil Engineering, BSc(Hons) Computer Applications Development, BSc(Hons) Computer Forensics, BSc(Hons) Computer Games Development, BSc(Hons) Computer Science, BSc(Hons) Computer Security, BSc(Hons) Computing Mathematics, BSc(Hons) Construction Project Management, BSc(Hons) Electrical and Electronic Engineering (Top Up), BSc(Hons) Forensic Biology, BSc(Hons) Forensic Investigation, BSc(Hons) Forensic Science, BSc(Hons) Forensic Science with Criminology, BSc(Hons) Geography, BSc(Hons) Geology, BSc(Hons) Geology and Physical Geography, BSc(Hons) Human Biology, BSc(Hons) Information Communication Technology, BSc(Hons) International Wildlife Biology, BSc(Hons) Lighting Design and Technology, BSc(Hons) Live Event Technology, BSc(Hons) Mathematics, BSc(Hons) Mechanical Engineering, BSc(Hons) Medical Sciences, BSc(Hons) Medicinal and Biological Chemistry, BSc(Hons) Natural History, BSc(Hons) Pharmaceutical Science, BSc(Hons) Project Management (Surveying), BSc(Hons) Quantity Surveying and Commercial Management, MBiol Biology, MComp Computer Applications Development, MComp Computer Forensics, MComp Computer Games Development, MComp Computer Science, MComp Computer Security, MComp Information Communication Technology, MEng Aeronautical Engineering, MEng Civil Engineering, MEng Electrical and Electronic Engineering, MEng Mechanical Engineering, MGeog Geography, MMath Computing Mathematics, MMath Mathematics, MSci Chemistry, MSci Forensic Biology, MSci Forensic Investigation, MSci Forensic

Science, MSci Forensic Science with Criminology, MSci Pharmaceutical Science

Postgraduate courses: MSc Aeronautical Engineering, MSc Analytical and Forensic Science, MSc Aviation Engineering and Management, MSc Civil Engineering and Environmental Management, MSc Civil and Structural Engineering, MSc Computer Forensics, MSc Computer Systems Security, MSc Computing and Information Systems, MSc Construction Project Management, MSc Cyber Security, MSc Electronics and Information Technology, MSc Embedded Systems Design (with Internship), MSc Hazard and Disaster Management, MSc Mechanical Engineering, MSc Mobile and Satellite Communications (with internship), MSc Optoelectronics (with internship), MSc Pharmaceutical Chemistry, MSc Professional Engineering, MSc Renewable Energy and Resource Management, MSc Safety, Health and Environmental Management, MSc Wildlife and Conservation Management

Faculty of Business and Society; www.southwales.ac.uk/courses/faculty/FBS/?faculty_title=Faculty+of+Business+and+Society

BA(Hons) Accounting and Finance, BA(Hons) Business, BA(Hons) Business Management, BA(Hons) Business Studies (Top Up), BA(Hons) Business and Accounting (Top Up), BA(Hons) Business and Finance (Top Up), BA(Hons) Business and Human Resource Management (Top Up), BA(Hons) Business and Marketing (Top Up), BA(Hons) Business and Supply Chain Management (Top Up), BA(Hons) English, BA(Hons) English and Creative Writing, BA(Hons) Event Management, BA(Hons) Forensic Accounting, BA(Hons) History, BA(Hons) Hotel and Hospitality Management, BA(Hons) Human Resource Management, BA(Hons) International Business (Top Up), BA(Hons) Logistics and Supply Chain Management, BA(Hons) Marketing, BA(Hons) Public Services, BA(Hons) Youth and Community Work, BA(Hons) Youth and Community Work (Youth Justice), BSc(Hons) Banking, Finance and Investment (Top Up), BSc(Hons) Criminology & Criminal Justice and Youth Justice, BSc(Hons) Criminology and Criminal Justice, BSc(Hons) Criminology and Criminal Justice and Sociology, BSc(Hons) Criminology and Criminal Justice with Psychology, BSc(Hons) Sociology, Chartered Institute of Management Accountants (CIMA) Certificate in Business Accounting, Chartered Institute of Procurement and Supply (CIPS) Diploma in Procurement and Supply, Chartered Institute of Procurement and Supply (CIPS) Professional Diploma in Procurement and Supply, Institute of Chartered Accountants in England and Wales (ICAEW), LLB(Hons) Law, LLB(Hons) Law Accelerated Route, LLB(Hons) Law with Criminology and Criminal Justice, LLB(Hons) Legal Practice (Exempting)

Postgraduate courses: Association of Chartered Certified Accountants (ACCA), Chartered Institute of Management Accountants (CIMA) Professional Scheme, LLM Laws, MA Buddhist Studies, MA English by Research, MA History by Research, MA Working for Children and Young People (Youth Work Initial Qualifying), MBA (Master of Business Administration), MSc Accounting, MSc Crime and Justice, MSc Engineering Management, MSc Finance and Investment, MSc Forensic Audit and Accounting, MSc Global Governance, MSc Health and Public Service Management, MSc Human Resource Management, MSc International Banking and Finance, MSc International Business and Enterprise, MSc International Logistics and Supply Chain Management, MSc Leadership and Management, MSc Management, MSc Marketing, MSc Project Management, MSc Public Relations, MSc Public Service Management, MSc Strategic Digital Marketing, MSc Strategic Leadership (Health and Social Care), MSc Strategic Procurement Management, MSc Working with Adult and Young Offenders

UNIVERSITY OF SOUTHAMPTON
www.soton.ac.uk

Accounting and Finance
BSc Accounting and Economics, BSc Accounting and Finance, BSc Accounting and Finance with placement year, BSc Economics and Actuarial Science, BSc Economics and Finance, BSc Mathematics with Actuarial Science, BSc Mathematics with Finance

Postgraduate courses: MSc Accounting and Finance, MSc Accounting and Management, MSc Finance, MSc Finance and Econometrics, MSc Finance and

Economics, MSc in Operational Research and Finance, MSc International Banking and Financial Studies, MSc International Financial Markets, MSc/PG Dip in Actuarial Science

Acoustical Engineering
BEng/MEng(Hons) Acoustical Engineering, BSc(Hons) Acoustics with Music, MEng Mechanical Engineering and Acoustical Engineering
Postgraduate course: MSc Acoustical Engineering

Aeronautics and Astronautics
MEng Aeronautics & Astronautics, MEng Aeronautics & Astronautics and Aerodynamics, MEng Aeronautics & Astronautics and Airvehicle Systems Design, MEng Aeronautics & Astronautics and Computational Engineering and Design, MEng Aeronautics & Astronautics and Engineering Management, MEng Aeronautics & Astronautics and Materials and Structures, MEng Aeronautics & Astronautics and Semester Abroad, MEng Aeronautics & Astronautics and Semester in Industry, MEng Aeronautics & Astronautics and Spacecraft Engineering
Postgraduate courses: MSc Aerodynamics and Computation, MSc Race Car Aerodynamics, MSc Space Systems Engineering, MSc Unmanned Aircraft Systems Design

Ageing and Gerontology
Postgraduate courses: MSc Gerontology, MSc Gerontology (Distance Learning), MSc Gerontology (Research), MSc Global Ageing and Policy (Distance Learning), PG Cert Gerontology, PG Cert Gerontology (Distance Learning), PG Cert Global Ageing and Policy (Distance Learning), PG Dip Gerontology (Distance Learning), PG Dip Global Ageing and Policy (Distance Learning)

Anthropology
BA Archaeology and Anthropology, BA Archaeology and Anthropology (with a Year Abroad), BSc Sociology with Anthropology

Archaeology
BA Ancient History and Archaeology, BA Ancient History and Archaeology with Year Abroad, BA Archaeology, BA Archaeology (with a Year Abroad), BA Archaeology and Anthropology, BA Archaeology and Anthropology (with a Year Abroad), BA Archaeology and Geography, BA Archaeology and Geography (with Year Abroad), BA Archaeology and History, BA Archaeology and History (with a Year Abroad), BSc Archaeology, BSc Archaeology (with a Year Abroad), MArc Archaeology Integrated Master, MSci Archaeology

Postgraduate courses: MA Osteoarchaeology, MA/MSc Maritime Archaeology, MSc Archaeology, MSc Archaeology (Bioarchaeology), MSc Archaeology (Higher Archaeological Practice), MSc Archaeology (Palaeoanthropology), MSc Business and Heritage Management

Astronomy
MPhys with Astronomy, MPhys with Astronomy (with a year abroad)

Audiology
BSc/BSc/MSci Healthcare Science (Audiology), MSci Hearing Science
Postgraduate courses: MSc Audiology and MSc Audiology (with Clinical Placement)

Biochemistry
BSc Biochemistry, MBiochem Master of Biochemistry, MSci Chemistry and Biochemistry
Postgraduate course: MRes in Advanced Biological Sciences degree

Biology
BSc Biology, BSc Mathematics with Biology, MSci Biology, MSci Biology and Marine Biology
Postgraduate courses: MRes in Advanced Biological Sciences degree, MRes Wildlife Conservation

Biomedical Sciences
BEng Biomedical Electronic Engineering, BSc Biomedical Sciences, MBioSci Master of Biomedical Sciences, MEng Biomedical Electronic Engineering
Postgraduate course: MSc Biomedical Engineering, MRes in Advanced Biological Sciences degree

Business
BSc Business Analytics, BSc Business Analytics with placement year, BSc Business Entrepreneurship, BSc Business Entrepreneurship with placement year, BSc Business Management, BSc Business Management and Spanish, BSc Business Management with placement year
Postgraduate courses: Master of Business Administration (full-time), MSc Business Analytics and Finance, MSc Business Risk and Security Management, MSc Business Strategy and Innovation Management, MSc Cyber Security Risk Management, MSc Digital Business and Entrepreneurship, MSc Entrepreneurship and Management, MSc Human Resource Management, MSc International Management, MSc Knowledge and Information Systems Management, MSc Marketing Management, MSc Project Management, MSc Risk and Finance, MSc Risk Management, MSc Supply Chain Management and Logistics

Chemistry
BSc Chemistry, MChem Chemistry, MChem Chemistry with a six month placement, MChem Chemistry with Maths, MChem Chemistry with Medicinal Sciences, MChem Chemistry with one year placement, MSci Chemistry and Biochemistry
Postgraduate courses: MSc Chemistry, MSc Chemistry by Research, MSc Electrochemistry, MSc Instrumental Analytical Chemistry

Civil Engineering
BEng Civil Engineering, MEng Civil and Environmental Engineering, MEng Civil Engineering, MEng Civil Engineering and Architecture
Postgraduate courses: MSc Civil Engineering, MSc Coastal and Marine Engineering and Management (2 years), MSc Engineering in the Coastal Environment, MSc Transportation Planning & Engineering, MSc Transportation Planning and Engineering (Infrastructure), MSc Transportation Planning and Engineering (Operations), MSc Transportation Planning and Engineering (Behaviour)

Computer Science and Software Engineering
BEng Software Engineering, BSc Computer Science, BSc Mathematics with Computer Science, MEng Computer Science, MEng Computer Science with Artificial Intelligence, MEng Computer Science with Cyber Security, MEng Computer Science with Distributed Systems and Networks, MEng Computer Science with Image and Multimedia Systems, MEng Computer Science with Mobile and Secure Systems, MEng Software Engineering
Postgraduate courses: MSc Artificial Intelligence, MSc Computer Science, MSc Cyber Security, MSc Data Science, MSc Embedded Systems, MSc Software Engineering, MSc Web Technology

Criminology
BSc Criminology, BSc Criminology and Psychology, BSc Social Policy and Criminology, BSc Sociology and Criminology
Postgraduate course: MSc Criminology

Demography
BSc Quantitative Social Science
Postgraduate courses: MA Transnational Studies, MSc Demography, MSc Global Health, MSc Social Statistics (Research Methods pathway), MSc Social Statistics (Statistics pathway), PG Cert/PG Dip/MSc Official Statistics

Design
Postgraduate courses: MA Communication Design, MA Cultural Politics, MA Design Management, MA Global Advertising and Branding, MA Global Media Management, MA Luxury Brand Management

Ecology
BSc Ecology & Conservation, MSci Ecology and Conservation
Postgraduate courses: MRes in Advanced Biological Sciences, MRes Wildlife Conservation

Economics International Foundation Year
BA Economics and Philosophy, BA Economics and Philosophy (with Year Abroad), BSc Accounting and Economics, BSc Economics, BSc Economics and Actuarial Science, BSc Economics and Finance, BSc Economics and Management Sciences, BSc MORSE (Mathematics, Operational Research, Statistics and Economics), BSc Politics and Economics, MEcon Master in Economics, MMORSE (Mathematics, Operational Research, Statistics and Economics)

Education Studies International Foundation Year
BSc(Hons) Education, BSc(Hons) Education and Psychology

Electrical and Electronic Engineering
BEng Electrical and Electronic Engineering, MEng Electrical and Electronic Engineering
Postgraduate courses: SKE Computer Sciences Subject Knowledge Enhancement, SKE Mathematics Subject Knowledge Enhancement, SKE Physics Subject Knowledge Enhancement, MA Applied Linguistics for Language Teaching, MA ELT/TESOL Studies, MA English Language Teaching, MSc Education, MSc Education Management and Leadership, MSc Education Practice and Innovation, PGCE English, PGCE FE Learning and Skills Sector, PGCE Geography, PGCE History, PGCE Information Technology and Computer Science (IT&CS), PGCE Mathematics, PGCE Modern Languages, PGCE Physical Education, PGCE Physics with Mathematics, PGCE Primary, PGCE Sciences, PGCE Secondary, PhD (Integrated) in Education (4 years), PhD Education (3 years), School Direct PGCE

Electrical Engineering
BEng Electrical and Electronic Engineering, BEng Electrical Engineering, MEng Electrical and Electronic Engineering, MEng Electrical Engineering
Postgraduate courses: EMECS European Masters in Embedded Computing Systems (2 years), MSc Biodevices, MSc Energy and Sustainability With Electrical Power Engineering, MSc Microelectromechanical Systems (Mems), MSc Microelectronics Systems Design, MSc Micro and Nanotechnology (1 year full-time), MSc Nanoelectronics and Nanotechnology, MSc System On Chip, MSc Systems, Control and Signal Processing, MSc Wireless Communications

Electronic Engineering

BEng Aerospace Electronic Engineering, BEng Biomedical Electronic Engineering, BEng Electronic Engineering, MEng Aerospace Electronic Engineering, MEng Biomedical Electronic Engineering, MEng Electronic Engineering, MEng Electronic Engineering with Artificial Intelligence, MEng Electronic Engineering with Computer Systems, MEng Electronic Engineering with Mobile and Secure Systems, MEng Electronic Engineering with Nanotechnology, MEng Electronic Engineering with Photonics, MEng Electronic Engineering with Wireless Communications

Postgraduate courses: EMECS European Masters in Embedded Computing Systems (2 years), MSc Biodevices, MSc Electronic Engineering, MSc Microelectromechanical Systems (Mems), MSc Microelectronics Systems Design, MSc Micro and Nanotechnology (1 year full-time), MSc Nanoelectronics and Nanotechnology, MSc System On Chip, MSc Systems, Control and Signal Processing MSc Wireless Communications

English

BA English, BA English and French, BA English and French, BA English and German, BA English and History, BA English and History with a year abroad, BA English and Music, BA English and Spanish, BA English Literature, Language and Linguistics, BA Film and English, BA Philosophy and English, MLang Languages and Contemporary European Studies (Integrated Masters in Languages)

Postgraduate courses: MA 20th and 21st Century Literature, MA Creative Writing, MA Eighteenth-Century Studies, MA English Literary Studies, MA English Literary Studies, MA English Literary Studies (Eighteenth Century), MA English Literary Studies (Nineteenth Century), MA English Literary Studies (Postcolonial and World Literatures), MA English Literary Studies (Twentieth Century and Contemporary), MA Global Englishes, MA Medieval and Renaissance Culture

Entrepreneurship

BSc Business Entrepreneurship, BSc Business Entrepreneurship with placement year

Postgraduate courses: MSc Digital Business and Entrepreneurship

Environmental Engineering

MEng Civil and Environmental Engineering

Postgraduate courses: MSc Coastal and Marine Engineering and Management (2 years), MSc Energy and Sustainability (Energy, Environment and Buildings), MSc Energy and Sustainability (Energy, Resources and Climate Change), MSc Engineering in the Coastal Environment, MSc Marine Technology, MSc Maritime Engineering Science / Advanced Materials, MSc Maritime Engineering Science / Marine Engineering, MSc Maritime Engineering Science / Maritime Computational Fluid Dynamics, MSc Maritime Engineering Science / Naval Architecture, MSc Maritime Engineering Science / Offshore Engineering, MSc Maritime Engineering Science / Yacht and Small Craft, MSc Sustainable Energy Technologies

Environmental Science

BSc Environmental Management with Business, BSc Environmental Monitoring and Modelling, BSc(Hons) Environmental Science, MEnvSci(Hons) Environmental Science

Postgraduate courses: MRes in Advanced Biological Sciences, MSc Biodiversity and Conservation, MSc Environmental Monitoring and Assessment, MSc Environmental Pollution Control, MSc Integrated Environmental Studies, MSc Water Resources Management

Fashion

BA(Hons) Fashion and Textile Design, BA(Hons) Fashion Marketing/Management

Postgraduate courses: MA Fashion Design, MA Fashion Management, MA Fashion Marketing and Branding, MA Textile Design

Film

BA Film and English, BA Film and French, BA Film and German, BA Film and History, BA Film and Philosophy, BA Film and Spanish, BA Film Studies, BA(Hons) Film and Philosophy

Postgraduate courses: MA Film and Cultural Management, MA Film Studies

Fine Art

BA(Hons) Fine Art

Postgraduate courses: MA Contemporary Curation, MA Fine Art

French

BA Ancient History and French, BA English and French, BA English and French, BA Film and French, BA French, BA French (Linguistic Studies, BA French and German, BA French and German (Linguistic Studies), BA French and Music, BA French and Philosophy, BA French and Portuguese, BA French and Spanish, BA French and Spanish (Linguistic Studies), BA Politics and French, BA French and History, BSc Business Management and French, BSc Management Sciences and French, BSc Mathematics with French, MLang French (Integrated Masters in Languages), MLang French (Linguistic Studies) (Integrated Masters in Languages), MLang French and German (Integrated Masters in Languages), MLang French and German Linguistic Studies (Integrated Masters in Languages), MLang French and Portuguese (Integrated Masters in Languages), MLang French and Spanish (Integrated Masters in Languages), MLang French and Spanish Linguistic Studies (Integrated Masters in Languages), MLang Languages and Contemporary European Studies (Integrated Masters in Languages), MSci Oceanography with French

Games Design and Art
BA(Hons) Games Design and Art
Postgraduate courses: MA Games Design

Geography
BA Archaeology and Geography, BA Archaeology and Geography (with Year Abroad), BA Geography, BSc Geography, BSc Geology with Physical Geography, BSc Oceanography with Physical Geography, BSc Population and Geography,
Postgraduate courses: MSc Applied Geographical Information Systems and Remote Sensing MSc Engineering in the Coastal Environment, MSc Geographical Information Systems (Online) (3 years), MSc Sustainability

Geology Science
BSc Geology, BSc Geology with Physical Geography, MSci Geology, MSci Geology with study abroad
Postgraduate courses: MRes Marine Geology and Geophysics

Geophysics
BSc Geophysical Sciences, BSc Geophysics with Foundation Year, MSci Geophysics, MSci Geophysics with study abroad
Postgraduate courses: MRes Marine Geology and Geophysics

German
BA Ancient History and German, BA English and German, BA Film and German, BA French and German, BA French and German (Linguistic Studies), BA German, BA German (Linguistic Studies), BA German and Music, BA German and Philosophy, BA German and Spanish, BA German and Spanish (Linguistic Studies), BA Politics and German, BA German and History, BSc Management Sciences and German, BSc Mathematics with German, BSc Business Management and German, MLang French and German (Integrated Masters in Languages), MLang French and German Linguistic Studies (Integrated Masters in Languages), MLang German (Integrated Masters in Languages), MLang German (Linguistic Studies) (Integrated Masters in Languages), MLang German and Spanish, MLang German and Spanish

Linguistic Studies, MLang Languages and Contemporary European Studies (Integrated Masters in Languages)

Graphic Arts
BA(Hons) Graphic Arts

Healthcare
BSc/MSci Healthcare Science (Audiology), BSc(Hons) Clinical Practice, BSc(Hons) Healthcare: Management, Policy and Research, BSc(Hons) Healthcare Science (Cardiovascular & Respiratory and Sleep Science)
Postgraduate courses: MRes Clinical and Health Research, MSc Advanced Clinical Practice (Advanced Critical Care Practitioner), MSc Advanced Clinical Practice (Critical Care), MSc Advanced Clinical Practice (Standard pathway), MSc Clinical Leadership in Cancer, Palliative and End of Life Care, MSc Complex Care in Older People, MSc Health Sciences, MSc Health Sciences – Amputation & Prosthetic Rehabilitation, MSc Health Sciences – Neonatal, MSc Leadership and Management in Health and Social Care, MSc Public Health, MSc Trauma Sciences, MSc Psychological Therapies and Mental Health, Postgraduate Certificate Low Intensity Cognitive Behavioural Therapy with IAPT PWP status

History
BA Ancient History, BA Ancient History and Archaeology, BA Ancient History and Archaeology with Year Abroad, BA Ancient History and French, BA Ancient History and German, BA Ancient History and History, BA Ancient History and History with Year Abroad, BA Ancient History and Philosophy, BA Ancient History and Philosophy with Year Abroad, BA Ancient History and Spanish, BA Ancient History with Year Abroad, BA Archaeology and History, BA Archaeology and History (with a Year Abroad), BA English and History, BA English and History with a year abroad, BA Film and History, BA Film and History (with a Year Abroad), BA History, BA History (with a Year Abroad), BA Modern History and Politics (with a Year Abroad), BA Philosophy and History, BA Philosophy and History (with Year Abroad), BA French and History, BA German and History, BA Modern History and Politics, BA Spanish and History
Postgraduate courses: MA Eighteenth-Century Studies, MA History, MA Jewish History and Culture, MA Medieval and Renaissance Culture, MA Transnational Studies

Information Technology
BSc Information Technology in Organisations, MComp Information Technology in Organisations

Language

BA Applied English Language Studies (Non-native English speakers only), BA English Literature, Language & Linguistics (with Year Abroad), BA English Literature, Language and Linguistics, BA Language and Society, BA Language Learning, BA Languages and Contemporary European Studies, BA Languages and Contemporary European Studies (English) (Non-native English speakers only), BA Modern Languages, MLang Language and Society (Integrated Masters in Languages), MLang Language Learning (Integrated Masters in Languages)

Postgraduate courses: MA Applied Linguistics (Research Methodology), MA Applied Linguistics for Language Teaching, MA English Language Teaching, MA English Language Teaching: Online (part time – 2.5 years), MA Language Acquisition Research

Law

BSc(Hons) Psychology with Law, LLB Accelerated Graduate Programme (2 years), LLB JD Accelerated Pathway Graduate Programme (2 years), LLB(Hons) Bachelor of Laws, LLB(Hons) European Legal Studies, LLB(Hons) International Legal Studies, LLB(Hons) Law with Psychology, LLB(Hons) Maritime Law

Postgraduate courses: LLM Commercial and Corporate Law, LLM General, LLM Information Technology and Commerce, LLM Insurance Law, LLM International Business Law, LLM International Law, LLM Maritime Law, PhD in Law

Management and Management Sciences

BA Music and Business Management, BA Music and Business Management (with a Year Abroad), BA Music and Management Sciences, BA(Hons) Fashion Marketing/Management, BSc Business Management and French, BSc Economics and Management Sciences, BSc Management Sciences and French, BSc Management Sciences and German, BSc Management Sciences and Spanish, BSc Business Management and German

Postgraduate courses: MSc Business Analytics and Management Sciences, MSc Education Management and Leadership, MSc Leadership and Management in Health and Social Care

Marine Biology

BSc Marine Biology with Oceanography, MSci Biology and Marine Biology, MSci Marine Biology, MSci Marine Biology with study abroad

Postgraduate courses: MSc Coastal and Marine Engineering and Management (2 years), MSc Marine Technology, MSc Maritime Engineering Science / Advanced Materials, MSc Maritime Engineering Science / Marine Engineering, MSc Maritime Engineering Science / Maritime Computational Fluid Dynamics, MSc Maritime Engineering Science / Naval Architecture, MSc Maritime Engineering Science / Offshore Engineering, MSc Maritime Engineering Science / Yacht and Small Craft

Marketing International Foundation Year

BA(Hons) Fashion Marketing/Management, BSc Marketing, BSc Marketing with Placement Year, BSc Marketing with Study Abroad

Postgraduate courses: MA Fashion Marketing and Branding, MSc Digital Marketing, MSc Marketing Analytics, MSc Marketing Management

Mathematical Sciences

BA Philosophy and Mathematics, BA Philosophy and Mathematics (with Year Abroad), BSc Mathematical Studies, BSc Mathematics, BSc Mathematics with Actuarial Science, BSc Mathematics with Biology, BSc Mathematics with Computer Science, BSc Mathematics with Finance, BSc Mathematics with French, BSc Mathematics with German, BSc Mathematics with Music, BSc Mathematics with Spanish, BSc Mathematics with Statistics, BSc MORSE (Mathematics, Operational Research, Statistics and Economics), MChem Chemistry with Maths, MMath Mathematical Physics, MMath Mathematics, MMORSE (Mathematics, Operational Research, Statistics and Economics)

Postgraduate courses: MSc in Operational Research, MSc in Operational Research and Finance, MSc in Statistics with Applications in Medicine, MSc Operational Research and Statistics, MSc Statistics, MSc/PG Dip in Actuarial Science PhD (Integrated) in Mathematical Sciences (4 years)

Mechanical Engineering

BEng(Hons) Mechanical Engineering, MEng Mechanical Engineering, MEng Mechanical Engineering and Acoustical Engineering, MEng Mechanical Engineering and Advanced Materials, MEng Mechanical Engineering and Aerospace, MEng Mechanical Engineering and Automotive, MEng Mechanical Engineering and Biomedical Engineering, MEng Mechanical Engineering and Computational Engineering and Design, MEng Mechanical Engineering and Engineering Management, MEng Mechanical Engineering and Mechatronics, MEng Mechanical Engineering and Naval Engineering, MEng Mechanical Engineering and Sustainable Energy Systems, MEng Mechanical Engineering

Postgraduate courses: MSc Biomedical Engineering, MSc Computational Engineering Design (Advanced

Mechanical Engineering Science), MSc Engineering Materials (Advanced Mechanical Engineering Science), MSc Mechatronics (Advanced Mechanical Engineering Science), MSc Propulsion and Engine Systems Engineering (Advanced Mechanical Engineering Sciences), MSc Surface Engineering and Coatings (Advanced Mechanical Engineering Sciences)

Mechatronic Engineering

BEng Mechatronic Engineering, MEng Mechatronic Engineering

Medicine

BMBS Medicine (BM4, graduate entry), BMBS Medicine and BMedSc (BM5), BMBS Medicine and, BMedSc (BM6, widening access), MChem Chemistry with Medicinal Sciences

Postgraduate courses: Masters of Research in Stem Cells, Development and Regenerative Medicine, MSc Allergy, MSc Diabetes Best Practice, MSc Genomic Medicine, MSc in Statistics with Applications in Medicine, MSc Public Health

Midwifery

BSc(Hons) Midwifery

Postgraduate course: MSc Midwifery (pre-registration)

Music

BA English and Music, BA English and Music (with Year Abroad), BA French and Music, BA German and Music, BA Music, BA Music (with a Year Abroad), BA Music and Business Management, BA Music and Business Management (with a Year Abroad), BA Philosophy and Music, BA Philosophy and Music (with Year Abroad), BSc Mathematics with Music, BSc(Hons) Acoustics with Music

Postgraduate course: MMus Music (Performance, Composition, Musicology)

Natural Sciences

MSci Natural Sciences

Neurosciences

MRes in Advanced Biological Sciences, Postgraduate Certificate Low Intensity Cognitive Behavioural Therapy with IAPT PWP status

Nursing

BN(Hons) Bachelor of Nursing (Adult), BN(Hons) Bachelor of Nursing (Adult and Child), BN(Hons) Bachelor of Nursing (Adult and Mental Health), BN(Hons) Bachelor of Nursing (Child), BN(Hons) Bachelor of Nursing (Child and Mental Health), BN(Hons) Bachelor of Nursing (Mental Health), BN(Hons) Bachelor of Nursing Top Up Degree for Advanced Diplomates, BSc(Hons) Public Health

Practice: Specialist Community Public Health Nursing (SCPHN)

Postgraduate courses: MSc Advanced Clinical Practice (Advanced [Nurse] Practitioner), MSc Advanced Clinical Practice (Advanced Neonatal Nurse Practitioner; Advanced Neonatal Practitioner), MSc Advanced Clinical Practice (District Nursing/Children's Community Nursing), MSc Nursing Studies (Top-up for Postgraduate Diploma in Nursing or SCPHN), Postgraduate Diploma in Nursing – Adult (pre-registration), Postgraduate Diploma in Nursing – Child (pre-registration), Postgraduate Diploma in Nursing – Mental Health (pre-registration), Postgraduate Diploma in Public Health Practice: Specialist Community Public Health Nursing [SCPHN]

Occupational Therapy

BSc(Hons) Occupational Therapy

Oceanography

BSc Marine Biology with Oceanography, BSc Oceanography (single honours), BSc Oceanography with Physical Geography, MSci Oceanography, MSci Oceanography with French, MSci Oceanography with study abroad

Postgraduate courses: MRes Marine Geology and Geophysics, MRes Ocean Science, MSc Engineering in the Coastal Environment, MSc Marine Environment and Resources (2 years), MSc Oceanography

Optoelectronics

Postgraduate courses: MSc Optical Fibre Technologies, MSc Photonics Technologies

Pharmacology

BSc Pharmacology

Philosophy

BA Ancient History and Philosophy, BA Ancient History and Philosophy with Year Abroad, BA Economics and Philosophy, BA Economics and Philosophy (with Year Abroad), BA Film and Philosophy, BA French and Philosophy, BA German and Philosophy, BA Philosophy, BA Philosophy, Ethics and Religion, BA Philosophy, Ethics and Religion with Year Abroad, BA Philosophy, Politics and Economics with Year Abroad, BA Philosophy (with Year Abroad), BA Philosophy and English, BA Philosophy and English (with Year Abroad), BA Philosophy and History, BA Philosophy and History (with Year Abroad), BA Philosophy and Mathematics, BA Philosophy and Mathematics (with Year Abroad), BA Philosophy and Music, BA Philosophy and Music (with Year Abroad), BA Philosophy and Politics, BA Philosophy and Politics (with Year Abroad), BA Philosophy and Sociology, BA

Philosophy and Sociology (with Year Abroad), BA(Hons) Film and Philosophy with Year Abroad
Postgraduate course: MA Philosophy

Physics

BSc Physics MMath Mathematical Physics, MPhys Physics, MPhys Physics with a Year of Experimental Research, MPhys Physics with Industrial Placement, MPhys Physics with Mathematics, MPhys Physics with Nanotechnology, MPhys Physics with Particle Physics, MPhys Physics with Photonics, MPhys Physics with Space Science

Physiotherapy

BSc(Hons) Physiotherapy; MSc Physiotherapy (pre-registration)

Podiatry

BSc(Hons) Podiatry

Politics

BA Modern History and Politics (with a Year Abroad), BA Philosophy and Politics, BA Philosophy and Politics (with Year Abroad), BA Politics and French, BA Politics and German, BA Politics and Spanish and Latin American Studies, BA Modern History and Politics, BSc International Relations, BSc Politics, BSc Politics and Economics, BSc Politics and International Relations
Postgraduate courses: LLM International Business Law, MA Transnational Studies, MSc Governance and Policy (Research) MSc International Politics (Research), MSc International Security and Risk, PG Dip/MSc Governance and Policy, PG Dip/MSc International Politics

Psychology

BSc Criminology and Psychology, BSc(Hons) Education and Psychology, BSc(Hons) Psychology, BSc(Hons) Psychology with Law LLB(Hons) Law with Psychology
Postgraduate courses: MSc Foundations of Clinical Psychology, MSc Health Psychology, MSc Research Methods in Psychology, Postgraduate Certificate Low Intensity Cognitive Behavioural Therapy with IAPT PWP status, Postgraduate Diploma in CBT (Advanced level practice), Postgraduate Certificate in CBT (Advanced level practice), Postgraduate Certificate in CBT (Introductory level practice), Postgraduate Certificate in CBT Theory, Postgraduate Diploma CBT for Anxiety and Depression (IAPT)

Ship Science

BEng(Hons) Ship Science, MEng Ship Science, MEng Ship Science and Advanced Materials, MEng Ship Science and Engineering Management, MEng Ship Science and Naval Architecture, MEng Ship Science and Naval Engineering, MEng Ship Science and Offshore Engineering, MEng Ship Science and Yacht and Small Craft

Sociology and Social Policy

BA Philosophy and Sociology, BA Philosophy and Sociology (with Year Abroad), BSc Population and Geography, BSc Social Policy and Criminology, BSc Sociology, BSc Sociology and Criminology, BSc Sociology and Social Policy, BSc Sociology with Anthropology
Postgraduate courses: MA Transnational Studies, MSc International Social Policy, MSc Public Health, MSc Sociology and Social Policy, MSc Sociology and Social Research

Spanish, Portuguese and Latin American Studies

BA Ancient History and Spanish, BA English and Spanish, BA Film and Spanish, BA French and Portuguese, BA French and Spanish, BA French and Spanish (Linguistic Studies), BA German and Spanish, BA German and Spanish (Linguistic Studies), BA Politics and Spanish and Latin American Studies, BA Spanish, BA Spanish (Latin American Studies), BA Spanish (Linguistic Studies), BA Spanish (The Spanish Speaking World), BA Spanish and Portuguese Studies, BA Spanish and History, BSc Business Management and Spanish, BSc Management Sciences and Spanish, BSc Mathematics with Spanish, MLang French and Portuguese (Integrated Masters in Languages), MLang French and Spanish (Integrated Masters in Languages), MLang French and Spanish Linguistic Studies (Integrated Masters in Languages), MLang German and Spanish, MLang German and Spanish Linguistic Studies, MLang Languages and Contemporary European Studies (Integrated Masters in Languages), MLang Spanish (Integrated Masters in Languages), MLang Spanish and Latin American Studies (Integrated Masters in Languages), MLang Spanish and Portuguese (Integrated Masters in Languages), MLang Spanish Linguistic Studies (Integrated Masters in Languages), MLang The Spanish Speaking World (Integrated Masters in Languages)

Zoology Science

BSc Zoology, MSci Zoology
Postgraduate courses: MRes in Advanced Biological Sciences, MRes Wildlife Conservation

STAFFORDSHIRE UNIVERSITY
www.staffs.ac.uk

School of Business, Leadership and Economics; www.staffs.ac.uk/about/departments/

Accounting And Business BA(Hons), Accounting And Finance BA(Hons), Business HND, Business And Marketing Management BA(Hons), Business Management BA(Hons), Certificate In Professional Marketing The Chartered Institute of Marketing (CIM), Diploma In Professional Marketing The Chartered Institute of Marketing (CIM), Events Management BA(Hons), International Business Management BA(Hons), Leadership And Management FdA, Level 5 Intermediate Certificate In Human Resource Management CIPD, Tourism Management BA(Hons), Visitor Attraction And Resort Management FdA

Postgraduate courses: Accounting And Finance MSc, Digital Marketing Management MSc, Economics For Business Analysis MSc, Economics Of Globalisation And European Integration MA, Human Resource Management PG Dip, Human Resource Management PG Cert, Human Resource Management MA, International Accounting And Financial Management MSc, International Business Management MSc, Islamic Finance And Accounting MSc, Master Of Business Administration MBA, Strategic Human Resource Management MA

Computing and Digital Technologies; www.staffs.ac.uk/about/departments/

Advertising, Film And Music Video Production BA(Hons), Animation BA(Hons), Applied Computing HND, Broadcast Journalism BA(Hons), Business Information Technology BSc(Hons), CGI And Visual Effects BSc(Hons), Cloud Computing BSc(Hons), Computer Gameplay Design And Production BEng(Hons), Computer Gameplay Design And Production BEng(Hons), Computer Games Animation BA(Hons), Computer Games Design BSc(Hons), Computer Games Design And Programming MEng, Computer Games Design With Foundation Year BSc(Hons), Computer Games Development BSc(Hons), Computer Games Programming BSc(Hons), Computer Games Programming (Virtual Reality) BSc(Hons), Computer Networks BSc(Hons), Computer Networks & Security MSci, Computer Networks And Security BSc(Hons), Computer Science BSc(Hons), Computer Science MSci, Computer Science BSc(Hons), Computing Science HND, Concept Art For Games And Film BA(Hons), Cyber Security BSc(Hons), Data Science BSc(Hons), Digital Film And Post Production Technology BSc(Hons), Digital Film And TV Production BA(Hons), Digital Media Production FdA, Electronic Music (Composition And Performance) BA(Hons), Experimental Film Production BA(Hons), Film And Television Production Technology FdSc, Film And Television Production Technology BSc(Hons), Film, Television And Radio Studies BA(Hons), Forensic Computing BSc(Hons), Games Art BA(Hons), Games Art And Animation BA(Hons), Games Journalism And PR BA(Hons), Games Studies BA(Hons), Indie Games Development BSc(Hons), Information Systems BSc(Hons), Internet Of Things BSc(Hons), Journalism BA(Hons), Media (Film) Production BA(Hons), Music And Audio Production FdA, Music And Audio Production FdSc, Music Business And Production BA(Hons), Music Production BA(Hons), Music Technology BSc(Hons), Network Computing BSc(Hons), Photojournalism BA(Hons), Professional Sports Writing And Broadcasting BA(Hons), Software App Development BSc(Hons), Software Engineering MSci, Software Engineering BSc(Hons), Sound Design BSc(Hons), Sports Journalism BA(Hons), Sports PR And Journalism BA(Hons), Stop-Motion Animation And Puppet-Making BA(Hons), Web Design BSc(Hons), Web Development BSc(Hons)

Postgraduate courses:

3D Computer Games Design MSc, Big Data MSc, Broadcast Journalism MA, Cloud Computing MSc, Computer Games Programming MSc, Computer Networks And Security MSc, Computer Science MSc, Computing MSc, Cyber Security MSc, Digital Forensics And Cybercrime Analysis MSc, Digital Forensics And Cybercrime Analysis MSc, Feature Film Production MA, Film By Negotiated Learning MA, Information Systems MSc, Internet Of Things MSc, Journalism MA, Mobile Device Application Development MSc, Music Production MA, Music Technology MSc, Professional Computing MSc, Software Engineering MSc, Sports Broadcast Journalism MA, Web Development MSc

Creative Arts and Engineering;
www.staffs.ac.uk/about/departments/
3D Design: Ceramics BA(Hons), 3D Design: Contemporary Jewellery And Fashion Accessories BA(Hons), 3D Design: Crafts BA(Hons), Acting BA(Hons), Acting And Screen Performance BA(Hons), Acting And Theatre Arts BA(Hons), Aeronautical Technology BSc(Hons), Automotive Engineering MEng, Automotive Engineering BEng(Hons), Cartoon And Comic Arts BA(Hons), Contemporary Art Practice FdA, Contemporary Creative Practice: Design Craft (Top-Up) BA(Hons), Contemporary Creative Practice: Fashion (Top-Up) BA(Hons), Contemporary Creative Practice: Fine Art (Top-Up) BA(Hons), Contemporary Creative Practice: Graphic Design (Top-Up) BA(Hons), Contemporary Creative Practice: Illustration (Top-Up) BA(Hons), Contemporary Creative Practice: Photography (Top-Up) BA(Hons), Contemporary Creative Practice: Textiles And Surface Pattern (Top-Up) BA(Hons), Dance And Theatre Arts FdA, Electrical And Electronic Engineering MEng, Electrical And Electronic Engineering BEng(Hons), Electrical And Electronic Technology BSc(Hons), Electrical And Electronic Technology FdSc, Electrical Engineering MEng, Electrical Engineering BEng(Hons), Electronic Engineering BEng(Hons), Electronic Engineering MEng, English BA(Hons), English And Creative Writing BA(Hons), Fashion BA(Hons), Fashion Studies FdA, Fine Art BA(Hons), Geography BSc(Hons), Geography With Mountain Leadership BSc(Hons), Graphic Design BA(Hons), Graphics And Digital Design FdA, History, Modern BA(Hons), History, Modern And International BA(Hons), Human Geography BA(Hons), Illustration BA(Hons), Manufacturing Technology BSc(Hons), Manufacturing Technology BSc(Hons), Manufacturing Technology FdSc, Mechanical Engineering MEng, Mechanical Engineering BEng(Hons), Mechanical Technology BSc(Hons), Mechanical Technology FdSc, Mechatronics MEng, Mechatronics BEng(Hons), Motorsport Technology BSc(Hons), Motorsport Technology Top Up BSc(Hons), Music Performance And Industry BA(Hons), Musical Theatre BA(Hons), Performing Arts (Musical Theatre) FdA, Photography BA(Hons), Physical Geography BSc(Hons), Product Design BA(Hons), Professional Musical Theatre BA(Hons), Surface Pattern Design BA(Hons), Telecommunication Engineering BEng(Hons), Telecommunication Engineering MEng, Textile Surfaces BA(Hons), Transport Design BA(Hons)

Postgraduate courses: Aeronautical Engineering MSc, Automotive Engineering MSc, Autosport Engineering MSc, Ceramic Design MA, Creative Futures: 3D Design MA, Creative Futures: Advertising And Brand Management MA, Creative Futures: Animation MA, Creative Futures: Applied Theatre MA, Creative Futures: Contemporary Art Practice MA, Creative Futures: Design MA, Creative Futures: Graphic Design MA, Creative Futures: Illustration MA, Creative Futures: Photography MA, Creative Futures: Product Design MA, Creative Futures: Surface Pattern Design MA, Creative Futures: Textile Design MA, Creative Futures: VFX MA, Creative Futures: Writing MA

Health and Social Care;
www.staffs.ac.uk/about/departments/
Health And Social Care BSc(Hons), Health Studies BSc(Hons), Midwifery Practice BSc(Hons), Nursing Practice (Adult) BSc(Hons), Nursing Practice (Children) BSc(Hons), Nursing Practice (Mental Health) BSc(Hons), Paramedic Science FdSc, Social Welfare Law, Policy And Advice Practice BA(Hons), Social Work BA(Hons), Specialist Practice – District Nursing BSc(Hons)

Postgraduate courses: Advanced Clinical Practice MSc, Advanced Forensic Practice (Custody Health Professional) PG Cert, Advanced Forensic Practice (Custody Health Professional) PG Dip, Advanced Forensic Practice (Custody Health Professional) MSc, Advanced Forensic Practice (Sexual Assault And Custody Health) PG Dip, Advanced Forensic Practice (Sexual Assault Health Professional) PG Cert, Advanced Forensic Practice (Sexual Assault Health Professional) MSc, Advanced Forensic Practice (Sexual Assault Health Professional) PG Dip, Advanced Health Assessment And Clinical Decision Making PG Cert, Health And Social Care By Negotiated Learning MSc, Health And Social Care By Negotiated Learning PG Dip, In Medical Education MSc, Master of Public Health MPH, Medical Education PG Cert, Medical Education PG Dip

Law, Policing and Forensics;
www.staffs.ac.uk/about/departments/
Business Law LLB(Hons), Criminology LLB(Hons), Forensic Investigation MSci, Forensic Investigation BSc(Hons), Forensic Science MSci, Forensic Science BSc(Hons), Law LLB(Hons), Law Studies (Progression) Full-Time BA(Hons), Policing And Criminal Investigation MSci, Policing And Criminal Investigation BSc(Hons), Sociology BA(Hons), Sociology,

raffordantuniv

Criminology And Deviance BA(Hons), Terrorism And Criminology BA(Hons)

Postgraduate courses: Crime Scene Investigation MSc, Family Law And Society MA, Fire Investigation MSc, Firearm Examination MSc, Forensic Science MSc, Human Resource Management And Employment Law Masters, International Relations And Russian Studies MA, Legal Practice LLM, Legal Practice PG Dip, Social And Cultural Theory MA, Sociology MA, Terrorism, Crime And Global Security MA, Transnational Organised Crime MA

Life Sciences and Education;
www.staffs.ac.uk/about/departments/

Animal Biology And Conservation MSci, Animal Biology And Conservation BSc(Hons), Animal Science With Animal Behaviour BSc(Hons), Animal Science With Animal Behaviour FdSc, Animal Science With Animal Health Management FdSc, Biological Science MSci, Biology BSc(Hons), Biomedical Science BSc(Hons), Biomedical Science MSci, Biomedical Science BSc(Hons), Early Childhood Studies BA(Hons), Early Childhood Studies With Early Years Teacher Status BA(Hons), Education BA(Hons), Education Studies BA(Hons), Football Coaching And Development FdA, Football Coaching And Performance BSc(Hons), Forensic Biology MSci, Forensic Biology BSc(Hons), Forensic Psychology BSc(Hons), Human Biology MSci, Human Biology BSc(Hons), Pharmaceutical Science MSci, Pharmaceutical Science BSc(Hons), Physical Education And Youth Sport Coaching BSc(Hons), Psychology BSc(Hons), Psychology And Child Development BSc(Hons), Psychology And Counselling BSc(Hons), Psychology And Criminology BSc(Hons), Sport And Exercise Sciences BSc(Hons), Sport Coaching And Sport Development BA(Hons), Sport Coaching And Sport Development BA(Hons), Sports Coaching And Physical Education FdSc, Sports Development And Coaching FdA, Sports Development And Coaching BA(Hons), Sports Strength And Conditioning BSc(Hons), Sports Therapy BSc(Hons)

Postgraduate courses: Applied Research MSc, Applied Research MA, Applied Sport And Exercise Psychology MSc, Art & Design PGCE, Clinical Psychology Professional Doctorate, Cognitive Behavioural Therapy PG Dip, Computer Science PGCE, Economics And Business Education PGCE, Education MA, English PGCE, Geography PGCE, Health Psychology MSc, Health Psychology Professional Doctorate, Mathematics PGCE, Molecular Basis Of Disease PG Cert, Molecular Biology MSc, Postgraduate Certificate In Education (Pcet) PGCE, Primary (General) PGCE, Psychology (Conversion) MSc

UNIVERSITY OF STIRLING
www.stir.ac.uk

School of Arts and Humanities;
www.stir.ac.uk/arts-humanities/courses/

Digital Media BA(Hons), English Studies BA(Hons), Film and Media BA(Hons), French BA(Hons), Heritage and Tourism BA; BA(Hons), History BA(Hons), International Management Studies and Intercultural Studies Double Degree BA(Hons), Journalism Studies BA(Hons), Law BA, Law LLB, Modern Languages BA(Hons), Philosophy BA(Hons), Politics BA(Hons), Politics (International Politics) BA(Hons), Politics, Philosophy and Economics: PPE BA(Hons), Religion BA(Hons), Scottish History BA(Hons), Spanish and Latin American Studies BA(Hons)

Postgraduate courses: Creative Writing (MLitt), Doctor of Diplomacy (DDipl), English Language and Linguistics (MLitt), Environment, Heritage and Policy (MSc), Environmental Policy and Governance (LLM/MSc), Gender Studies (Applied) (MSc/MLitt), Historical Research MRes, Postgraduate Certificate, International Conflict and Cooperation (MSc), International Energy Law and Policy (LLM), Law: Accelerated Graduate LLB, Media Management MSc, Postgraduate Diploma, Media Research MRes, Postgraduate Diploma, Philosophy Postgraduate Diploma, MLitt, Public Policy (MPP), Publishing Studies (MLitt), Publishing Studies (MRes), Renaissance Studies Postgraduate Diploma, Postgraduate Certificate, MRes, Scottish Literature (MLitt), Strategic Communication & Public Relations (Joint Degree), Strategic Public Relations & Communication Management Postgraduate Certificate, Postgraduate Diploma, MSc, Strategic Public Relations Postgraduate Certificate, Postgraduate Diploma, MSc, The Gothic Imagination (MLitt), Translation Studies (MSc), Translation Studies with TESOL (MSc)

Faculty of Natural Sciences;
www.stir.ac.uk/natural-sciences/

Undergraduate degrees in Applied Biological Sciences, Applied Computing, Aquaculture, Biology, Business Computing, Cell Biology, Computing Science, Conservation Biology and Management, Ecology, Environmental Geography, Environmental Geography and Outdoor Education, Environmental Science, Environmental Science (Integrated Masters), Environmental Science and Outdoor Education, Marine Biology, Mathematics, Applied Mathematics, Psychology, Software Engineering

Postgraduate courses: Aquaculture: Sustainable Aquaculture Postgraduate Certificate, Postgraduate Diploma, MSc, Aquaculture: Sustainable Aquaculture Postgraduate Certificate, Postgraduate Diploma, MSc, Aquatic Food Security MSc, Aquatic Pathobiology MSc, Aquatic Veterinary Studies MSc, Big Data MSc, Computing for Business MSc, Computing for Financial Markets MSc, Environmental Management Postgraduate Certificate, Postgraduate Diploma, MSc, Environmental Management (Conservation) Postgraduate Certificate, Postgraduate Diploma, MSc, Environmental Management (Energy) MSc, Postgraduate Diploma, Postgraduate Certificate, Health Psychology MSc, Postgraduate Certificate, Postgraduate Diploma, Human Animal Interaction MA, MSc, Postgraduate Certificate, Postgraduate Diploma, Information Technology Postgraduate Diploma, MSc, Marine Biotechnology MSc, Postgraduate Diploma, Psychological Research Methods (Autism Research) MSc, Postgraduate Certificate, Postgraduate Diploma, Psychological Research Methods (Bilingualism Research) MSc, Postgraduate Certificate, Postgraduate Diploma, Psychological Research Methods (Child Development) MSc, Postgraduate Certificate, Postgraduate Diploma, Psychological Research Methods (Cognition and Neuropsychology) MSc, Postgraduate Diploma, Postgraduate Certificate, Psychological Research Methods (Evolutionary Psychology) MSc, Postgraduate Certificate, Postgraduate Diploma, Psychological Research Methods (Perception and Action) MSc, Postgraduate Certificate, Postgraduate Diploma, Psychological Research Methods (Psychology of Faces) MSc, Postgraduate Certificate, Postgraduate Diploma, Psychological Therapy in Primary Care MSc, Software Engineering MSc, Postgraduate Diploma

The Faculty of Social Sciences;
www.stir.ac.uk/social-sciences/

Criminology and Social Policy BA(Hons), Criminology and Sociology BA(Hons), Education (Primary) BA(Hons), BSc(Hons), Education (Secondary) BA(Hons), BSc(Hons), Social Work BA(Hons), Sociology and Social Policy BA(Hons)

Postgraduate courses: Applied Social Research (Criminology) MSc, Postgraduate Diploma, Applied Social Research (MRes), Applied Social Research (MSc), Applied Social Research (Social Statistics and Social Research) (MSc), Applied Social Research Doctorate, Criminological Research (MRes), Dementia Studies Postgraduate Certificate, Postgraduate Diploma, MSc, Doctorate in Education (EdD), Education Studies and TESOL Postgraduate Certificate, Postgraduate Diploma, MSc, Educational Leadership (leading to Specialist Qualification for Headship) MSc, Postgraduate Diploma, Postgraduate Certificate, Educational Research Postgraduate Certificate, Postgraduate Diploma, MRes, Housing Studies MSc, Postgraduate Diploma, Postgraduate Certificate, Management and English Language Teaching MSc, Postgraduate Diploma, Postgraduate Certificate, PhD TESOL Research, Professional Education and Leadership MSc, Postgraduate Certificate, Postgraduate Diploma, Social Enterprise MSc, Postgraduate Diploma, Postgraduate Certificate, Social Work Studies Postgraduate Diploma, MSc, Teaching English to Speakers of Other Languages (TESOL) (Online) MSc, Postgraduate Certificate, Postgraduate Diploma, Teaching Qualification in Further Education (TQFE) – In-service Postgraduate Certificate, Teaching Qualification in Further Education (TQFE) – Pre-service Postgraduate Diploma, TESOL – Teaching English to Speakers of Other Languages Postgraduate Certificate, Postgraduate Diploma, MSc

Stirling Management School;
www.stir.ac.uk/management/

Accountancy BAcc(Hons), Accountancy and Finance BAcc(Hons), Business Studies BA(Hons), Economics BA(Hons), Finance BA(Hons), Human Resource Management BA(Hons), International Management Studies and Intercultural Studies Double Degree BA(Hons), International Management Studies with European Languages and Society BA(Hons), Management BSc, BSc(Hons), Marketing BA, BA(Hons), Retail Marketing BA, BA(Hons), Sport Business Management BA(Hons), Sustainable Events Management BA(Hons)

Postgraduate courses: Banking and Finance MSc, Postgraduate Diploma, Postgraduate Certificate, Behavioural Science for Management MSc, Postgraduate Diploma, Business and Management MSc, Business and Management Research Methods Postgraduate Diploma, Postgraduate Certificate, MRes, Data Science for Business MSc, Postgraduate Diploma, Postgraduate Certificate, DBA Doctor of Business Administration, Economics for Business and Policy MSc, Finance MSc, Postgraduate Certificate, Postgraduate Diploma, International Accounting and Finance MSc, Postgraduate Diploma, Postgraduate Certificate, International Business MSc, Postgraduate Diploma, International Human Resource Management MSc, Postgraduate Diploma, Postgraduate Certificate, Investment Analysis Postgraduate Certificate, Postgraduate Diploma, MSc, Management and English Language Teaching MSc, Postgraduate Diploma, Postgraduate Certificate, MSc Marketing, MBA Master of Business Administration, Strategic Sustainable Business MSc

Faculty of Health Sciences and Sport; www.stir.ac.uk/health-sciences-sport/

Nursing & Adult BSc, Nursing – Adult (Honours) BSc(Hons), Nursing – Mental Health BSc, Nursing – Mental Health (Honours) BSc(Hons), Sport and Exercise Science BSc(Hons), Sports Studies BA(Hons)
Postgraduate courses: Advancing Practice MSc, Postgraduate Diploma, Postgraduate Certificate, Clinical Doctorates Doctorate, MSc, Postgraduate Diploma, Early Years Practice Health Visiting MSc, Postgraduate Diploma, Global Issues in Gerontology and Ageing MSc, Postgraduate Diploma, Postgraduate Certificate, Health Research (Online) MRes, Postgraduate Diploma, Postgraduate Certificate, Performance Coaching MSc, Postgraduate Diploma, Postgraduate Certificate, Psychology of Sport (Accredited) MSc, Postgraduate Diploma, Postgraduate Certificate, Public Health MPH, Postgraduate Certificate, Postgraduate Diploma, Sport Nutrition MSc

---

STOCKPORT COLLEGE
www.stockport.ac.uk

BA(Hons) Contemporary Photography, BA(Hons) Illustration, BA(Hons) Childhood Studies, HNC/D-Computing and Systems Development, HNC/D-Computing and Systems Development, HNC Sport (Coaching and Development)

UNIVERSITY OF STRATHCLYDE
www.strath.ac.uk

Faculty of Engineering; https:// www.strath.ac.uk/engineering/ studywithus/undergraduate/

Department of Architecture
BSc Architectural Studies
Postgraduate courses: MArch/PgDip Advanced Architectural Design, MSc/PgDip/PgCert Advanced Construction Technologies & BIM, March Architectural Design (International), MSc/PgDip/PgCert Architectural Design for the Conservation of Built Heritage, MSc/ PgDip/ PgCert Sustainable Engineering: Architecture & Ecology, MSc/PgDip/PgCert Urban Design

Biomedical Engineering
BEng Biomedical Engineering, MEng Biomedical Engineering, BSc Prosthetics & Orthotics

Postgraduate courses: MSc/PgDip/PgCert Biofluid Mechanics, MSc Biomedical Engineering, MSc Medical Devices, MSc Prosthetics & Orthotics, MSc/PgDip/PgCert Prosthetics &/or Orthotics Rehabilitation Studies

Chemical & Process Engineering
BEng Chemical Engineering, MEng Chemical Engineering
Postgraduate courses: MSc Oil & Gas Innovation, MSc Process Technology and Management

Design, Manufacture & Engineering Management
BSc Product Design & Innovation, BEng Product Design Engineering, MEng Product Design Engineering, BEng Production Engineering & Management,

MEng Production Engineering & Management, BEng Sports Engineering, MEng Sports Engineering

Postgraduate courses: MSc/PgDip/PgCert Advanced Manufacture: Technology & Systems, MSc/PgDip/ PgCert Design Engineering, MSc/PgDip Digital Manufacturing, MSc Engineering Management for Process Excellence, MSc Global Innovation Management, MSc/PgDip/PgCert Mechatronics & Automation, MSc/PgDip/PgCert Product Design, MSc/PgDip/ PgCert Supply Chain & Logistics Management, MSc/PgDip Supply Chain & Sustainability Management, EngD/MSc/PgDip/PgCert Systems Engineering Management

Electronic & Electrical Engineering

BEng Computer & Electronic Systems, MEng Computer & Electronic Systems, BEng Electrical & Mechanical Engineering, MEng Electrical & Mechanical Engineering, MEng Electrical Energy Systems, MEng Electronic & Digital Systems, MEng Electronic & Electrical Engineering, MEng Electronic & Electrical Engineering with Business Studies

Postgraduate courses: MSc 5G Advanced Communications, MSc Advanced Electrical Power Engineering, MSc Autonomous Robotic Intelligent Systems, MSc Communications, Control & Digital Signal Processing, MSc Electrical Power Engineering with Business, MSc Electronic & Electrical Engineering, MSc Wind Energy Systems

Mechanical & Aerospace Engineering

BEng in Aero-Mechanical Engineering, BEng in Mechanical Engineering, BEng Mechanical Engineering with International Study, MEng Aero-Mechanical Engineering, MEng Mechanical Engineering, MEng Mechanical Engineering with Aeronautics, MEng Mechanical Engineering with Financial Management, MEng Mechanical Engineering with International Study, MEng Mechanical Engineering with Materials Engineering

Postgraduate courses: MSc/PgDip/PgCert Advanced Mechanical Engineering, MSc Advanced Mechanical Engineering with Aerospace, MSc Advanced Mechanical Engineering with Energy Systems, MSc Advanced Mechanical Engineering with Materials, MSc Advanced Mechanical Engineering with Power Plant Technologies, MSc/PgDip/PgCert Sustainable Engineering: Renewable Energy Systems & the Environment

Naval Architecture, Ocean & Marine Engineering

BEng Naval Architecture & Marine Engineering, MEng Naval Architecture & Marine Engineering, BEng Naval Architecture with High Performance Marine Vehicles, MEng Naval Architecture with High Performance Marine Vehicles, BEng Naval Architecture with Ocean Engineering, MEng Naval Architecture with Ocean Engineering

Faculty of Humanities & Social Sciences; www.strath.ac.uk/humanities/

School of Education

Childhood Practice BA, Education & Economics BA, Education & Human Resource Management BA, Education & Social Policy BA, Education & Social Services BA, Education & Sport BA, English & Education BA, French & Education, History & Education, Journalism & Creative Writing & Education BA, Law & Education BA, Mathematics with Teaching BSc, Physics with Teaching BSc, Politics & International Relations & Education BA, Primary Education BA, Psychology & Education BA, Spanish & Education

Postgraduate courses: Applied Educational & Social research MSc, Autism MEd, Autism MSc, Children & Young People€™s Literacy, Language and Literature MEd, Early Years Pedagogue, Education EdD, Education Studies MSc, Educational Leadership MEd, Educational Psychology MSc, Gaelic Immersion for Teachers PgDip, MSc/PgDip/PgCert Genealogical, Palaeographic & Heraldic Studies, Inclusive Education MEd, Philosophy with Children PgCert, Primary Education PGDE, Professional Practice Med, Safety and Risk Management MSc/Pg, Secondary Education PGDE, Dip/PgCert, PgCert Supporting Bilingual Learners in the Mainstream Classroom, PgCert Supporting Teacher Learning

School of Government & Public Policy

Philosophy, Politics & Economics BA, Politics & International Relations BA, Politics & International Relations & Social Policy BA

Postgraduate courses: European Politics MSc, International Relations MSc, International Relations, Law & Security MSc/LLM, Political Research MSc, Politics MSc, Public Policy MSc

School of Humanities

English (BA), History (BA), BA in Journalism & Creative Writing, BA French, BA Italian, BA Spanish

Postgraduate courses: Digital Journalism (MLitt/ PgDip), Literature, Culture & Place (MLitt/PgDip/ PgCert), Media & Communication (MLitt), Historical Studies (MSc), Health History (MSc), MLitt Digital Journalism, MRes/MPhil in Modern Languages

Law School

LLB Scots Law, LLB Law (Scots & English), LLB English Law, Clinical LLB, LLB Scots & English Law (Clinical), Graduate Entry LLB Scots Law, Graduate Entry LLB (Scots & English Law)

Postgraduate courses: LLM/PgDip/PgCert Climate Change Law & Policy, LLM/PgDip/PgCert Construction Law, LLM/MSc Criminal Justice & Penal Change, LLM/PgDip/PgCert Global Environmental Law & Governance, LLM/PgDip/PgCert Human Rights Law, LLM/PgDip/PgCert International Commercial Law, LLM/PgDip/PgCert International Law & Sustainable Development, MSc International Management & Law, MSC/LLM International Relations, Law & Security, LLM/PgDip/PgCert Internet Law & Policy/ IT Telecommunications Law, LLM/PgDip/PgCert Law, LLM Law & Finance LLM/PgDip/PgCert Law of the Sea, Sustainable Development and International Law, LLM/MSc/PgDip/PgCert Mediation & Conflict Resolution, Diploma Professional Legal Practice

Psychology Sciences & Health

BA Psychology, BSc Psychology & Counselling

Postgraduate courses: Clinical Health Psychology MSc, Educational Psychology MSc, Psychology MPhil/PhD/DEdPsy, Psychology with Business MSc, Research Methods in Psychology MSc

School of Social Work & Social Policy

BA(Hons) Social Work, BA Social Policy

Postgraduate courses: Postgraduate Diploma/Master in Social Work (MSW), MSc Advanced Residential Childcare, MSc Child & Youth Care Studies by Distance Learning, MSc Social Policy & MSc Social Policy (Research Methods)

Faculty of Science; www.strath.ac.uk/ science/

Computer & Information Science

BEng/MEng Computer & Electronic Systems, BSc/ MEng Computer Science, BSc(Hons) Data Analytics, BSc Software Engineering

Postgraduate courses: MSc Advanced Computer Science, MSc Advanced Computer Science with Big Data, MSc Advanced Software Engineering, MSc/ PgDip Data Analytics, MSc Digital Health Systems, MSc Enterprise Information Systems, MSc Information & Library Studies, MSc Information Management

Mathematics & Statistics

BSc(Hons) Data Analytics, BSc/MMAth Mathematics, BSc Mathematics, Statistics & Accounting

Postgraduate courses: MSc Quantitative Finance, MSc Applied Statistics in Health Sciences, MSc Applied Mathematical Sciences, MSc Data Analytics

Physics

BSc/MPhys Physics, MPhys Physics with Advanced Research

Postgraduate courses: MSc Advanced Physics, MSc Applied Physics, MSc Industrial Photonics, MSc Nanoscience, MSc Optical Technologies

Strathclyde Institute of Pharmacy & Biomedical Sciences,

Biochemistry MSci, BSc Biochemistry & Immunology, BSc Biochemistry & Microbiology, BSc Biochemistry & Pharmacology, BSc Biomedical Science, BSc Biomolecular Sciences, MSci Immunology, BSc Immunology & Microbiology, BSc Immunology & Pharmacology, MSci Microbiology, MSci Pharmacology, BSc Pharmacology & Microbiology, MPharm Pharmacy

Postgraduate courses: MPharm Pharmacy, MSc Advanced Biochemistry, MSc Advanced Immunology, MSc Advanced Pharmacology, MSc Advanced Clinical Pharmacy Practice, MSc Advanced Pharmaceutical Manufacturing, MSc Biomedical Sciences, MSc Industrial Biotechnology, MSc Pharmaceutical Analysis, MSc Pharmaceutical Quality & Good Manufacturing Practice, MSc Pharmacy Practice, Practice Certificate Pharmacist Independent Prescribing – Conversion Course, Practice Certificate Pharmacist Independent Prescribing – Full Course

[B] Strathclyde Business School; www.strath.ac.uk/ business/

BA degrees in Accounting, Business Analysis & Technology, Business Enterprise, Economics, Finance, Hospitality & Tourism Management, Human Resource Management, Management, Marketing

Postgraduate courses: Accounting & Finance, Economics, Human Resource Management, Entrepreneurship, Innovation & Technology, Entrepreneurial Management & Leadership, Management Science, Marketing, Strategy & Organisation, Strathclyde MBA

UNIVERSITY OF SUFFOLK
www.uos.ac.uk

Faculty of Arts, Business and Applied Social Science; www.ucs.ac.uk/ Faculties-and-Centres/Faculty-of-Arts,- Business-and-Applied-Social-Science/ Faculty-of-Arts,-Business-and-Applied- Social-Science.aspx

Department of Arts and Humanities

BA(Hons) Digital Film Production, BA(Hons) English, BA(Hons) Fine Art, BA(Hons) Graphic Design, BA(Hons) Graphic Design (Graphic Illustration), BA(Hons) History, BA(Hons) Interior Architecture and Design, BA(Hons) Photography, BA(Hons) Screenwriting, BA(Hons) Screenwriting and Film Studies; MA Fine Art

Department of Children, Young People and Education

BSc(Hons) Child Development and Developmental Therapies, MA/PG Dip/PG Cert Childhood Studies, BA(Hons) Early and Primary Education Studies, BA(Hons) Early Childhood Studies, BA(Hons) Early Learning, FdA Early Years Practice, MA Education Studies, Suffolk and Norfolk Primary SCITT, Suffolk and Norfolk Secondary SCITT, North East Essex Secondary SCITT, BA(Hons) Special Educational Needs and Disability Studies, Subject Knowledge Enhancement Secondary Mathematics

Department of Psychology, Sociology and Social Work

MSc Crime and Community Safety: Evidence Based Practice, BSc(Hons) Criminology, BSc(Hons) Criminology and Youth Studies, BSc(Hons) Criminology and Sociology, LLB(Hons) Law with Criminology, LLB(Hons) Law with Sociology, BSc(Hons) Psychology, BSc(Hons) Psychology and Criminology, BSc(Hons) Psychology and Sociology, BSc(Hons) Psychology and Youth Studies, BA(Hons) Sociology and Youth Studies, BSc(Hons) Sociology, BA(Hons) Social Work, FdA Counselling, BA(Hons) Counselling (Progression Route)

Faculty of Health and Science; www.ucs.ac.uk/faculty-of-health-and- science

Department of Health Sciences

BSc(Hons) Acute Health Care Practice, BSc(Hons) Adult Nursing, BSc(Hons) Adult Nursing: Work-Based Learning Pathway, MSc Advanced Health Care Practice, BSc(Hons) Child Health Nursing, BSc(Hons) Diagnostic Radiography, MA Healthcare Education, FdA HealthCare Practice (Acute Care), FdA Health Care Practice (Dementia Care), FdA Health Care Practice (End of Life), FdA Health Care Practice (Long Term Care), FdA Health Care Practice (Mental Health), BSc(Hons) Mental Health Nursing, BSc(Hons) Mental Health Nursing: Work-Based Learning Pathway, BSc(Hons) Midwifery, BSc(Hons) Nurse Practitioner, BSc(Hons) Operating Department Practice, BSc(Hons) Paramedic Science, Preparation for Mentorship, FdSc Public Health, BSc(Hons) Public Health, BSc(Hons) Radiotherapy and Oncology, BSc(Hons) Specialist Community Public Health Nursing (School Nurse or Health Visiting)

Department of Science and Technology

BSc(Hons) Bioscience, BSc(Hons) Bioscience with Foundation Year, BSc(Hons) Business Management and Information Technology, FdSc Network Engineering, BSc(Hons) Network Engineering (Progression Route), FdSc Software Engineering, BSc(Hons) Software Engineering (Progression Route), BA(Hons) Computer Games Design, BSc(Hons) Computer Games Programming, MSci Football Coaching, BSc(Hons) Mobile and Web Engineering, BSc(Hons) Nutrition and Human Health, BSc(Hons) Nutrition and Human Health with Foundation Year, MSci Performance Analysis for Football, BSc(Hons) Sport and Exercise Science, BSc(Hons) Sports Coaching, BSc Sports Performance Analysis, MSci Sports Psychology, MSci Strength and Conditioning

UNIVERSITY OF SUNDERLAND
www.sunderland.ac.uk

Faculty of Applied Sciences;
www.sunderland.ac.uk/faculties/apsc

Dept of Computing, Engineering & Technology; www.sunderland.ac.uk/faculties/apsc/ourdepartments/cet

mechanical engineering, engineering management, power engineering, engineering management, automotive engineering, information computing, extended computing, manufacturing engineering, computer systems engineering, engineering, network systems, electronic and electrical engineering, computer forensics, telecommunications engineering, project management, network computing, health information management, games software development, computing, information technology management, applied business computing, computer science, network systems; BA, BEng, BSc, FdSc, MSc

Dept of Pharmacy, Health & Wellbeing; www.sunderland.ac.uk/faculties/apsc/ourdepartments/phw

nursing, medicines management, biopharmaceutical science, pharmacy, clinical pharmacy, pharmaceutical science, drug discovery and development, independent prescribing for pharmacists, biomedical science, biopharmaceutical science, pharmaceutical and biopharmaceutical formulations, healthcare science: physiological/life sciences, healthcare science: physiological/life sciences, environmental management and assessment, sports coaching, practice development in chronic heart failure, cosmetic science
BA, BSc, FdA, MPharm, MSc, PGCE, Univ Dip, PGDip, Adv Dip

Dept of Psychology; www.sunderland.ac.uk/faculties/apsc/ourfaculty/ourdepartments/psychology

counselling, psychology, psychology with counselling, psychological research, extended psychology; BA, FdA, MA, MSc

Dept of Sport & Exercise Sciences; www.sunderland.ac.uk/faculties/apsc/ourdepartments/sport/

sport & exercise sciences, sports coaching/development, exercise, health & fitness, sport, exercise & fitness; BA, BSc, FdA, MSc

Faculty of Arts, Design & Media;
www.sunderland.ac.uk/faculties/adm/

Dept of Arts & Design; www.sunderland.ac.uk/faculties/adm/ourfaculty/ourdepartments/departmentofartsdesign

Numerous qualifications grouped under following subject headings;
animation, broadcast & digital media, dance, drama music, fashion, film, media and cultural studies, fine art, foundation art and design, glass and ceramics, graphics & advertising, illustration, PR, photography, Postgraduate; art and design, media; BA, BSc, FdA, MA

Faculty of Business & Law;
www.sunderland.ac.uk/faculties/bl

Sunderland Business School; www.sunderland.ac.uk/faculties/bl/departments/business

accounting & finance/financial management, accountancy & management, applied management/investment, banking & finance, business administration, business & financial management, business management/enterprise management/HRM/marketing, finance & management, marketing management, HRM, innovation & enterprise, investigative management, international management, marketing/management, MBA (HRM/hospitality management/innovation & enterprise/supply chain management/transformation/global business/finance/general management/marketing/finance); BA(Hons), FD, CertHE, MBM, MBA, MA, MSc, PGDip

Dept of Law; www.sunderland.ac.uk/faculties/bl/departments/law

law, criminal law & procedure, international, international law, legal practice, human rights, business law; LlB, LlM, LPC, BA(Hons)

Dept of Tourism, Hospitality & Events; www.sunderland.ac.uk/faculties/bl/departments/tourism

international hospitality & tourism management, tourism management, events management, travel & tourism, tourism & events/hospitality (jt degrees); BA(Hons), BA/BSc, FD, BSc(Hons)

Faculty of Education & Society

Dept of Education; www.sunderland.ac.uk/faculties/es/ourfaculty/ourdepartments/departmentofeducation

childhood studies, community and youth work studies, early years teaching, history, English education with QTS, education and care, education and training, education studies – combined subjects, social sciences, criminology, health and social care, social work, English and creative writing, combined subjects, education and curriculum studies secondary, English education, mathematics education ostgrad; post compulsory education, education, PGCE; business/design and technology/English/geography/computer science education/mathematics/primary education/science with biology/science with chemistry/science with physics education, School Direct, international education, special educational needs coordination, social work, teaching and learning in HE,

TESOL, education overseas; BA, BSc, MA, PGCE, FD, PGDip/Cert, MSc

Dept of Culture; www.sunderland.ac.uk/faculties/es/ourfaculty/ourdepartments/departmentofculture

English, creative writing, history, modern foreign languages, politics, TESOL; BA, BSc, MA, PGCE

Dept of Social Sciences; www.sunderland.ac.uk/faculties/es/ourfaculty/ourdepartments/departmentofsocialsciences

childhood studies, community & youth studies, community engagement, criminology, education & care, health & social care, practice development, social work, sociology, supporting career learning & development, working with young people, social sciences; BA, FdA, MA, BA(Hons), BEng(Hons), BSc(Hons), EdEng, FdSc, LLM, MBA, MSc, PGCE, PGCert

Degrees validated by University of Sunderland offered at:

SUNDERLAND COLLEGE
www.sunderlandcollege.ac.uk

applied music practice, biomedical science, biopharmaceutical science,, psychology, counselling, health & social care, practice dance, drama, exercise health & fitness, health & safety management, leadership & management, post compulsory education & training; FdA, FdSc, BSc

UNIVERSITY OF SURREY
www.surrey.ac.uk

Faculty of Arts and Science; www.surrey.ac.uk/faculty-arts-social-sciences

School of Economics

Business Economics BSc(Hons), Economics BSc(Hons), Economics and Finance BSc(Hons), Economics and Mathematics BSc(Hons), Politics and Economics BSc(Hons)

Postgraduate courses: MSc Business Economics and Finance, MSc Economics, MSc Economics and Finance, MSc Energy Economics and Policy, MSc International Economics, Finance and Development

Guildford School of Acting

BA(Hons) Acting, BA(Hons) Actor Musician, BA(Hons) Dance, BA(Hons) Musical Theatre, BA(Hons) Theatre (Conversion course by distance learning), BA(Hons) Theatre and Performance, BA(Hons) Theatre Production

Postgraduate courses: MA Acting, MA Creative Practices and Direction, MA Musical Theatre, MFA Acting, MFA Musical Theatre

School of Hospitality and Tourism Management

International Event Management BSc(Hons), International Hospitality and Tourism Management BSc(Hons), International Hospitality Management BSc(Hons) / MBus(Hons), International Tourism Management, BSc(Hons) / MBus(Hons)

Postgraduate courses:

MSc Air Transport Management, MSc International Event Management (Euromasters), MSc International Events Management, MSc International Hospitality

371

Management (Euromasters), MSc International Hotel Management, MSc International Tourism Development, MSc International Tourism Management, MSc International Tourism Management (Euromasters), MSc International Tourism Marketing, MSc Strategic Hotel Management

School of Law
Law LLB(Hons), Law (JD Pathway) LLB(Hons), Law with Criminology LLB(Hons), Law with International Relations LLB(Hons)
postgraduate courses: LLM International Commercial Law, PhD Law

School of Literature and Languages
BA French, BA German, BA English literature, BA Modern Langauges
Postgraduate courses: MA Communication and International Marketing, MA Intercultural Communication with International Business, MA Interpreting, MA Interpreting (Chinese Pathway), MA TESOL (Teaching English to Speakers of Other Languages), MA Translation, MA Translation and Interpreting, MRes Translation and Interpreting Studies, MA Creative Writing, MFA Creative Writing, MA English Literature

Department of Music and Media
Music BMus(Hons), Creative Music Technology BMus(Hons), Music and Sound Recording (Tonmeister) BMus(Hons) or BSc(Hons), Film and Video Production Technology BA(Hons) /BSc(Hons), Digital Media Arts BA(Hons)
Postgraduate courses: MMus Music (Composition), MMus Music (Conducting), MMus Music (Creative Practice), MMus Music (Musicology), MMus Music (Performance)

Department of Politics
International Politics BSc(Hons), Politics BSc(Hons), Politics and Economics BSc(Hons), Politics and Sociology BSc(Hons)

Surrey Business School
Business and Retail Management BSc(Hons) / MBus(Hons), Business Management BSc(Hons) / MBus(Hons), Business Management (Entrepreneurship) BSc(Hons) / MBus(Hons), Business Management (Human Resource Management) BSc(Hons) / MBus(Hons), Business Management (Marketing) BSc(Hons) / MBus(Hons), Business Management and French BSc(Hons), Business Management and German BSc(Hons), Business Management and Spanish BSc(Hons), International Business Management BSc(Hons) / MBus(Hons), Accounting and Finance BSc(Hons), Economics and Finance BSc(Hons)
Postgraduate courses: MSc Accounting and Finance, MSc Business Analytics, MSc Business Economics and Finance, MSc Corporate Finance, MSc Entrepreneurship, MSc Human Resource Management, MA Intercultural Communication with International Business, MSc International Business Management, MSc International Financial Management, MSc International Marketing Management, MSc International Retail Marketing, MSc Investment Management, PGCert Management Learning, MSc Marketing Management, MBA Master of Business Administration, MSc Occupational and Organizational Psychology, MSc Operations and Logistics Management, MSc Accounting and Finance, MSc Corporate Finance, MSc Economics and Finance, MSc International Financial Management, MSc Investment Management
Postgraduate courses: MSc International Relations

Department of Sociology
BSc Sociology, BSc Criminology and Sociology, BSc Criminology, BSc Media, Culture and Society, BA Media Studies
Postgraduate courses: MSc in Social Research Methods, MSc Criminology, Criminal Justice and Social Research, MSc Social Science and Complexity

Faculty of Engineering and Physical Sciences; www.surrey.ac.uk/faculty-engineering-physical-sciences

Department of Chemistry
BCs/MChem Chemistry, Chemistry with Forensic Investigation BSc(Hons) or MChem(Hons), Medicinal Chemistry BSc(Hons) or MChem(Hons)
Postgraduate courses: MRes Chemistry, PhD Chemistry

Department of Physics
Mathematics and Physics BSc(Hons) / MMath(Hons) / MPhys(Hons), Physics BSc(Hons) / MPhys(Hons), Physics with Astronomy BSc(Hons) / MPhys(Hons), Physics with Nuclear Astrophysics BSc(Hons) / MPhys(Hons), Physics with Quantum Technologies, BSc(Hons) / MPhys(Hons)
Postgraduate courses: MSc Medical Physics, MSc Nuclear Science and Applications, MSc Physics, MSc Radiation and Environmental Protection, PhD Physics

Department of Computer Science

Computer Science BSc, Computing and Information Technology BSc, Software Development for Business BSc, Data Science for Health BSc

Postgraduate courses: MSc in Information Systems, MSc in Information Security, PhD study

Department of Chemical and Process Engineering

Chemical and Petroleum Engineering BEng(Hons) / MEng(Hons), Chemical Engineering BEng(Hons) / MEng(Hons)

Postgraduate courses: MSc Information and Process Systems Engineering, MSc Petroleum Refining Systems Engineering, MSc Process and Environmental Systems Engineering, MSc Process Systems Engineering, MSc Renewable Energy Systems Engineering, PhD Chemical and Process Engineering

Department of Mechanical Engineering Sciences

Postgraduate courses: MSc in Advanced Materials, MSc in Biomedical Engineering, MPhil/PhD study

Department of Civil and Environmental Engineering

BEng/MEng Civil Engineering

Postgraduate courses: Bridge Engineering MSc, Civil Engineering MSc, Structural Engineering MSc, Water and Environmental Engineering MSc, Infrastructure Engineering and Management MSc, Advanced Geotechnical Engineering MSc

Department of Mathematics

BSc/MMath Mathematics

Postgraduate courses: MSc Mathematics, PhD study

Department of Electrical and Electronic Engineering

Biomedicine with Electronic Engineering BSc(Hons), Communication Systems BEng(Hons) / MEng(Hons), Computer and Internet Engineering BEng(Hons) / MEng(Hons), Electrical and Electronic Engineering BEng(Hons) / MEng(Hons), Electronic Engineering BEng(Hons) / MEng(Hons), Electronic Engineering for Medicine and Healthcare BEng(Hons) / MEng(Hons), Electronic Engineering with Computer Systems BEng(Hons) / MEng(Hons), Electronic Engineering with Nanotechnology BEng(Hons) / MEng(Hons), Electronic Engineering with Space Systems BEng(Hons) / MEng(Hons)

Postgraduate courses: MSc Communications, Networks and Software, MSc Computer Vision, Robotics and Machine Learning, MSc Electronic Engineering, MSc Electronic Engineering (Euromasters), MSc Medical Imaging, MSc Mobile and Satellite Communications, MSc Mobile Communications Systems, MSc Mobile Media Communications, MSc Nanotechnology and Renewable Energy, MSc RF and Microwave Engineering, MSc Satellite Communications Engineering, MSc Space Engineering, PhD Electronic Engineering

Faculty of Health and Medical Sciences; www.surrey.ac.uk/faculty-health-medical-sciences

School of Biosciences and Medicine

Biochemistry BSc(Hons), Biological Sciences BSc(Hons), Biomedical Science BSc(Hons). Biomedicine with Data Science BSc(Hons), Biomedicine with Electronic Engineering BSc(Hons), Biotechnology BSc(Hons), Food Science and Microbiology BSc(Hons), Microbiology BSc(Hons), Microbiology (Medical) BSc(Hons), Nutrition BSc(Hons), Nutrition and Food Science BSc(Hons), Nutrition/Dietetics BSc(Hons), Sport and Exercise Science BSc(Hons), Veterinary Biosciences BSc(Hons)

Postgraduate courses: MSc Medical Microbiology, MSc Medical Microbiology (Euromasters), PGDip Physician Associate, PhD and MD study

Food, Nutrition and Dietetics

Food Science and Microbiology BSc(Hons), Nutrition BSc(Hons), Nutrition and Food Science BSc(Hons), Nutrition/Dietetics BSc(Hons)

Postgraduate courses: MSc Human Nutrition, MSc Nutritional Medicine, PhD Nutritional Sciences, MD Nutritional Sciences

Sport and Exercises Sciences

Nutrition/Dietetics BSc(Hons), Sport and Exercise Science BSc(Hons)

School of Health Sciences

Health Sciences, Nursing and Midwifery

Electronic Engineering for Medicine and Healthcare BEng(Hons) / MEng(Hons), Midwifery: Registered Midwife BSc(Hons), Nursing Studies (Registered Nurse Adult Nursing) BSc(Hons), Nursing Studies (Registered Nurse Children's Nursing) BSc(Hons), Nursing Studies (Registered Nurse Mental Health Nursing) BSc(Hons), Operating Department Practice DipHE, Paramedic Science BSc(Hons)

Postgraduate courses: MSc Delivering Quality Healthcare, PGCert Education for Professional Practice, PGDip Nursing Studies (Adult Nursing), PGDip Nursing Studies (Mental Health Nursing), PGDip Physician Associate, MSc Primary and Community

Care (Community Children's Nursing), MSc Primary and Community Care (District Nursing), MSc Primary and Community Care (General Practice Nursing), MSc Public Health Practice with SCPHN (Health Visiting), MSc Public Health Practice with SCPHN (School Nursing), PhD study

School of Psychology
Psychology BSc(Hons)
Postgraduate courses: MSc Environmental Psychology, MSc Health Psychology, MSc Psychology (conversion), MSc Research Methods in Psychology, MSc Social Psychology, MSc Supervision and Consultation: Psychotherapeutic and Organisational Approaches, Psychological Intervention (CBT)

School of Veterinary Medicine
Veterinary Medicine and Science BVMSci, Veterinary Biosciences BSc(Hons)
Postgraduate courses: MSc Veterinary Microbiology, PhD Veterinary Medicine and Science

---

FARNBOROUGH COLLEGE OF TECHNOLOGY
www.farn-ct.ac.uk

business management/& computing, early childhood studies/early years practice/learning, criminology & sociology, documentary film/radio/TV, early years education and practice, early years care and education, electronic engineering, English literature & criminology/sociology, graphic design, health care practice, hospitality management, HR management, photography, media production, psychology & criminology, sports science/human performance, sports coaching,, software engineering; BA(Hons), BSc(Hons), FdA, FdSc, FdEng, PGEd

---

NESCOT (NORTH EAST SURREY COLLEGE OF TECHNOLOGY)
www.nescot.ac.uk

applied biological and healthcare science, computing, business accounting & technology management, osteopathic medicine, perfusion science, sports therapy, education and training, educational support, PGCE education & training, education studies; Additional Nongraduate Courses;acoustics, biomedical science, business management, health & social care, computing/& IT, early years, educational support, music technology, orthopaedic medicine, osteopathic medicine, photography, photo-imaging, perfusion science, psychodynamic counselling, sports therapy, teacher training, teaching & learning in lifelong learning sector, travel & tourism management; BA(Hons), BSc(Hons), DipHE, FdA, FdSc,MSc, PGDip, Masters, MOst, BOst

---

ST MARYS UNIVERSITY
www.smuc.ac.uk

acting, business law/management, business & finance/management & entrepreneurship, creative writing/first novel, criminology & society, drama, drama and applied/physical theatre/theatre arts, education and social science/drama, English/ & drama, film & screen media, geography, health & exercise science, history, international business management, law/with criminology, media arts, nutrition, philosophy, psychology, sociology, sport rehabilitation, science sport science, sports coaching science, tourism/management; Postgraduate; applied linguistics and ELT, applied sport and exercise, physiology, applied sport psychology, applied sports nutrition, bioethics and medical law, catholic school leadership, charity management, creative writing: first novel, education, culture and society,education: leading innovation and change, education: pedagogical leadership in physical education and sport, education: pedagogy, education: pedagogy, Gothic: culture, subculture, counterculture, human nutrition, Irish studies, international business practice, international tourism development,PGCE primary/secondary, physical theatre, public history, sport, health and applied science, sport rehabilitation, sports journalism, strength and conditioning,theatre directing, theology; BA, BSc, FdA, LlB, LLM, MA, MPhil, MSc, MRes, PGCE, PGCert, PGDip, PhD

UNIVERSITY OF SUSSEX
www.sussex.ac.uk

School of Business, Management and Economics; www.sussex.ac.uk/bmec/

Department of Business and Management

Accounting and finance

Accounting and Finance BSc, Accounting and Finance (with a professional placement year) BSc, Finance BSc, Finance (with a professional placement year) BSc, Finance with a Language BSc

Business and Management

Business and Management Studies BSc, Business and Management Studies (with a professional placement year) BSc, Business and Management Studies with a Language BSc, International Business BSc, International Business (with a professional placement year) BSc, International Business with a Language BSc, Marketing and Management BSc, Marketing and Management (with a professional placement year) BSc, Marketing and Management with Psychology BSc, Marketing and Management with Psychology (with a professional placement year) BSc

Postgraduate courses: Master of Business Administration – the Sussex MBA, Banking and Finance MSc, Entrepreneurship and Innovation MSc, Financial Risk and Investment Analysis MSc, Global Supply Chain and Logistics Management MSc, Human Resource Management MSc, International Accounting and Corporate Governance MSc, International Management MSc, International Marketing MSc, Management MSc, Management and Finance MSc, Marketing and Consumer Psychology MSc

Department of Economics

Economics BA, Economics (with a professional placement year) BA, Economics BSc, Economics (with a professional placement year) BSc, Economics and Finance BSc, Economics and International Development BA, Economics and International Relations BA, Economics and Management Studies BSc, Economics and Politics BA

Postgraduate courses: Economics MSc, Development Economics MSc, International Business Economics MSc, International Finance and Economics MSc

Science Policy Research Unit

Energy Policy MSc, Project Management MSc, Science and Technology Policy MSc, Strategic Innovation Management MSc, Sustainable Development MSc

School of Education and Social Work; www.sussex.ac.uk/esw/

Department of Education

Childhood and Youth: Theory and Practice BA, Primary and Early Years Education BA, Primary and Early Years Education (with Qualified Teacher Status) BA, Psychology with Education BSc

Postgraduate courses: Childhood and Youth Studies MA, Early Years in Education MA, Education MA, International Education and Development MA, International Teacher Education PGDip, Social Research Methods MSc, Media Studies PGCE, Primary PGCE, Secondary Classics PGCE, Secondary Drama PGCE, Secondary English PGCE, Secondary Geography PGCE, Secondary History PGCE, Secondary Mathematics PGCE, Secondary Modern Foreign Languages PGCE, Secondary Music PGCE, Secondary Psychology PGCE, Secondary Science PGCE, Education PhD

Department of Work and Social Care

Social Work BA, Health, Wellbeing and Social Care BA

Postgraduate courses: Social Work MA, Childhood and Youth Studies MA, Wellbeing MRes, Social Work & Social Care PhD

School of Engineering and Informatics; www.sussex.ac.uk/ei/

Department of Engineering and Design

Engineering

Automotive Engineering BEng, Automotive Engineering MEng, Automotive Engineering (with an industrial placement year) BEng, Automotive Engineering (with an industrial placement year) MEng, Electrical and Electronic Engineering BEng, Electrical and Electronic Engineering MEng, Electrical and Electronic Engineering (with an industrial placement year) BEng, Electrical and Electronic Engineering (with an industrial placement year) MEng, Mechanical Engineering BEng, Mechanical Engineering MEng, Mechanical Engineering (with an industrial placement year) BEng, Mechanical Engineering (with an industrial placement year) MEng

Postgraduate courses: Advanced Mechanical Engineering MSc, Digital Communication Systems MSc, Embedded Digital Systems MSc, Engineering Business Management MSc, Robotics and Autonomous

Systems MSc, Robotics and Autonomous Systems (with a Masters industrial placement) MSc, Robotics and Autonomous Systems (with an industrial placement year) MSc, PhD study

Product Design

Product Design BSc, Product Design (with an industrial placement year) BSc

Informatics

Computer Science BSc, Computer Science MComp, Computer Science (with an industrial placement year) BSc, Computer Science (with an industrial placement year) MComp, Computer Science and Artificial Intelligence BSc, Computer Science and Artificial Intelligence (with an industrial placement year) BSc, Computing for Business and Management BSc, Computing for Business and Management (with an industrial placement year) BSc, Computing for Digital Media BSc, Computing for Digital Media (with an industrial placement year) BSc, Games and Multimedia Environments (GAME) BSc, Games and Multimedia Environments (GAME) (with an industrial placement year) BSc

Postgraduate courses: Advanced Computer Science MSc, Computing with Digital Media MSc, Human-Computer Interaction MSc, Information Technology with Business and Management MSc, Intelligent and Adaptive Systems MSc, Management of Information Technology MSc, Web Development PGCert

School of English; www.sussex.ac.uk/ english/

American Studies and English (with a study abroad year) BA, BA, Drama and English BA, Drama and Film Studies BA, Drama with a Language BA, Drama, Theatre and Performance BA, English and Art History BA, English and Film Studies BA, English and History BA, English and Media Studies BA, English BA, English Language and Linguistics BA, English Language and Literature BA, Philosophy and English BA

Postgraduate courses: Masters in Literature, Theory and Culture, Modern and Contemporary Literature, Applied Linguistics, Creative and Critical Writing, Sexual Dissidence, PhD study

School of Global Studies; www.sussex.ac.uk/global/

Department of Anthropology

Anthropology BA, Anthropology and Cultural Studies BA, Anthropology and History BA, Anthropology and International Development BA, Anthropology with a Language BA, Geography and Anthropology BA, Geography and Anthropology MArts, International Relations and Anthropology BA

Postgraduate courses: Anthropology MA, Anthropology of Development and Social Transformation MA, Social Anthropology of the Global Economy MA, Social Research Methods MSc, PhD studies

Department of Geography

Geography BA, Geography BSc, Geography MArts, Geography MSci, Geography (research placement) MSci, Geography and Anthropology BA, Geography and Anthropology MArts, Geography and International Development BA, Geography and International Development BSc & 2018 entry only, Geography and International Development MArts, Geography and International Development MSci & 2018 entry only, Geography and International Relations BA, Geography and International Relations MArts, Geography with a Language BA

Postgraduate courses: Climate Change, Development and Policy MSc, Migration and Global Development MA, Social Research Methods MSc, African Studies PhD, Geography PhD, Migration Studies PhD

Department of International Development

Anthropology and International Development BA, Economics and International Development BA, Geography and International Development BA, Geography and International Development MArts, International Development BA, International Development with a Language BA, International Relations and Development BA, Sociology and International Development BA

Postgraduate courses: Anthropology of Development and Social Transformation MA, Conflict, Security and Development MA, Development Studies MA, Environment, Development and Policy MA, Gender and Development MA, Gender, Violence and Conflict MA, Globalisation, Business and Development MA, Governance and Development MA, Human Rights MA, International Education and Development MA, Media Practice for Development and Social Change MA, Migration Studies MA, Participation, Power and Social Change MA, Poverty and Development MA, Sexual Dissidence MA, Social Anthropology of the Global Economy MA, Social Development MA, Climate Change, Development and Policy MSc, Social Research Methods MSc, Development Studies (Global Studies) PhD, Development Studies (IDS) PhD, Human Rights PhD

Department of International Relations

Economics and International Relations BA, Geography and International Relations BA, Geography and International Relations MArts, International Relations BA, International Relations and a Language (with a study abroad year) BA, International Relations and Anthropology BA, International Relations and Development BA, International Relations and Sociology BA, International Relations with a Language BA, Law with International Relations LLB, Politics and International Relations BA

Postgraduate courses: Conflict, Security and Development MA, Geopolitics and Grand Strategy MA, Global Political Economy MA, International Relations MA, International Security MA, Social Research Methods MSc, International Relations PhD

School of History, Art History and Philosophy; www.sussex.ac.uk/hahp/

Department of History

American Studies and History (with a study abroad year) BA, Anthropology and History BA, English and History BA, English and History (with a study abroad year) BA, History BA, History and Film Studies BA, History and Philosophy BA, History and Politics BA, History and Sociology BA

Postgraduate courses: Contemporary History MA, Intellectual History MA, Contemporary History PhD, History PhD, Intellectual History PhD

Department of Art History

Art History BA, Art History (with a professional placement year) BA, Art History and Film Studies BA, English and Art History BA, English and Art History (with a study abroad year) BA

Postgraduate courses: Art History MA, Art History and Museum Curating MA, Art History and Museum Curating with Photography MA, Photography Studies MA, Art History PhD

Department of Philosophy

History and Philosophy BA, Philosophy BA, Philosophy and English BA, Philosophy and Sociology BA, Politics and Philosophy BA, Philosophy, Politics and Economics (PPE) BA

Postgraduate courses: Literature and Philosophy MA, Philosophy MA, Social and Political Thought MA, Philosophy PhD, Social and Political Thought PhD

Sussex Centre for American Studies

American Studies (with a study abroad year) BA, American Studies and English (with a study abroad year) BA, American Studies and Film Studies (with a study abroad year) BA, American Studies and History (with a study abroad year) BA, American Studies and Politics (with a study abroad year) BA, Law with American Studies (with a study abroad year) LLB

Postgraduate courses: American History PhD, American Literature PhD

School of Law, Politics and Sociology; www.sussex.ac.uk/lps/

Department of Law

Law LLB, Law (Graduate Entry) LLB, Law with a Language LLB, Law with a Language (with a study abroad year) LLB, Law with American Studies (with a study abroad year) LLB, Law with Business and Management LLB, Law with Criminology LLB, Law with International Relations LLB, Law with Media LLB, Law with Politics LLB

Postgraduate courses: Corruption, Law and Governance (delivered in Qatar) LLM, Criminal Law and Criminology LLM, Environmental Law LLM, Information Technology and Intellectual Property Law LLM, International Commercial and Trade Law LLM, International Criminal Law LLM, International Financial Law LLM, International Human Rights Law LLM, International Law LLM, Law LLM, Graduate Diploma in Law (GDL)/Common Professional Examination (CPE), Social Research Methods MSc, Law Studies PhD

Department of Politics

American Studies and Politics (with a study abroad year) BA, Economics and Politics BA, History and Politics BA, Law with Politics LLB, Philosophy, Politics and Economics (PPE) BA, Politics BA, Politics and International Relations BA, Politics and Philosophy BA, Politics and Sociology BA

Postgraduate courses: Corruption and Governance MA, European Governance and Policy MA, International Politics MA, Social Research Methods MSc, Contemporary European Studies PhD, Politics PhD

Department of Sociology

Sociology

History and Sociology BA, International Relations and Sociology BA, Philosophy and Sociology BA, Politics and Sociology BA, Sociology BA, Sociology and Cultural Studies BA, Sociology and International Development BA, Sociology and Media Studies BA, Sociology with a Language BA

Postgraduate courses: Criminology and Criminal Justice MA, Gender Studies MA, Social Research Methods MSc, Sociology PhD, Gender Studies (Social Sciences) PhD

Criminology

Criminology BA, Law with Criminology LLB, Criminology and Sociology BA, Psychology with Criminology BSc

School of Life Sciences; www.sussex.ac.uk/lifesci/

Biochemistry and Biomedicine

Biochemistry BSc, Biochemistry MSci, Biochemistry (research placement) MSci, Biochemistry (with an industrial placement year) BSc, Biomedical Science BSc, Biomedical Science MSci, Biomedical Science (research placement) MSci

Postgraduate courses: Genetic Manipulation and Molecular Cell Biology MSc, Biochemistry PhD

Chemistry

BSc/MChem Chemistry

Postgraduate courses: Chemistry PhD

Evolution, Behaviour and Environment

Biology BSc, Biology MSci, Biology (research placement) MSci, Ecology, Conservation and Environment BSc, Ecology, Conservation and Environment MSci, Ecology, Conservation and Environment (research placement) MSci, Genetics BSc, Genetics MSci, Genetics (research placement) MSci, Zoology BSc, Zoology MSci, Zoology (research placement) MSci

Postgraduate courses: Animal Behaviour MRes, Conservation Biology MRes, Evolutionary Biology MRes, Global Biodiversity Conservation MSc, Biology PhD, Environmental Science PhD

Neuroscience

Medical Neuroscience BSc, Medical Neuroscience MSci, Medical Neuroscience (research placement) MSci, Neuroscience BSc, Neuroscience MSci, Neuroscience (research placement) MSci, Neuroscience with Cognitive Science BSc, Neuroscience with Cognitive Science MSci, Neuroscience with Cognitive Science (research placement) MSci, Psychology with Neuroscience BSc

Postgraduate courses: Neuroscience MRes, Neuroscience MSc, Neuroscience PhD, Sussex Neuroscience 4-Year PhD Programme

School of Mathematical and Physical Sciences; www.sussex.ac.uk/mps/

Department of Mathematics

Mathematics BSc, Mathematics MMath, Mathematics (research placement) MMath, Mathematics with Economics BSc, Mathematics with Economics MMath, Mathematics with Finance BSc, Mathematics with Finance MMath

Postgraduate courses: Corporate and Financial Risk Management MSc, Data Science MSc, Financial Mathematics MSc, Mathematics MSc, Mathematics PhD

Department of Physics and Astronomy

Astrophysics MPhys, Physics BSc, Physics MPhys, Physics (research placement) MPhys, Physics (with an industrial placement year) BSc, Physics (with an industrial placement year) MPhys, Physics with Astrophysics BSc, Physics with Astrophysics MPhys, Theoretical Physics BSc, Theoretical Physics MPhys

Postgraduate courses: Astronomy MSc, Cosmology MSc, Frontiers of Quantum Technology MSc, Particle Physics MSc, Physics MSc, Astronomy PhD, Physics PhD

School of Media, Film and Music

Cultural Studies

Anthropology and Cultural Studies BA, Media and Cultural Studies BA, Sociology and Cultural Studies BA

Postgraduate courses: Digital Media MA, Gender and Media MA, Media and Cultural Studies MA, Gender Studies PhD, Cultural Studies PhD

Film Studies

American Studies and Film Studies (with a study abroad year) BA, Art History and Film Studies BA, Drama and Film Studies BA, English and Film Studies BA, Film Studies BA, Filmmaking BA, History and Film Studies BA, Media Production BA

Postgraduate courses: Film Studies MA Digital Documentary MA, Filmmaking MA, Media Practice for Development and Social Change MA, Film Studies PhD, Media, Film and Music by Published Works PhD, Creative and Critical Practice PhD

Journalism

Journalism BA

Postgraduate courses: International Journalism MA, Journalism MA, Journalism and Documentary Practice MA, Journalism and Media Studies MA,

Journalism Studies PhD, Media, Film and Music by Published Works PhD, Creative and Critical Practice PhD

Media and Communications

English and Media Studies BA, English and Media Studies (with a study abroad year) BA, Global Media and Communications (with a study abroad year) BA, Law with Media LLB, Media and Communications BA, Media and Cultural Studies BA, Sociology and Media Studies BA

Postgraduate courses: Digital Media MA, Gender and Media MA, Media and Cultural Studies MA, Digital Media PhD, Media and Communications PhD

Media Practice

Filmmaking BA, Media Production BA

Postgraduate courses: Digital Documentary MA, Filmmaking MA, Media Practice for Development and Social Change MA, Media, Film and Music by Published Works PhD, Creative and Critical Practice PhD

Music

Music BA, Music Technology BA

Postgraduate courses: Music and Sonic Media MA, Music PhD, Musical Composition PhD, Music Theatre PhD

School of Psychology;
www.sussex.ac.uk/psychology/

Marketing and Management with Psychology BSc, Marketing and Management with Psychology (with a professional placement year) BSc, Psychology BSc, Psychology (with a professional placement year) BSc, Psychology with Business and Management BSc, Psychology with Clinical Approaches BSc, Psychology with Cognitive Science BSc, Psychology with Criminology BSc, Psychology with Economics BSc, Psychology with Education BSc, Psychology with Neuroscience BSc

Postgraduate courses: Applied Social Psychology MSc, Cognitive Neuroscience MSc, Experimental Psychology MSc, Foundations of Clinical Psychology and Mental Health MSc, Low-Intensity Psychological Interventions for Children and Young People PGCert, Mental Health Practice PGCert, Psychological Methods MRes, Psychological Therapy PGDip, Psychology PhD

Brighton and Sussex Medical School;
www.bsms.ac.uk/index.aspx

Bachelor of Medicine Bachelor of Surgery (BM BS)

Postgraduate courses: Anaesthesia and Perioperative Medicine, Cardiology, Clinical Radiology, Clinical Education, Dementia Studies, Diabetes in Primary Care, Global health, Global Pharmacy, Leadership and Commissioning, Medical Education, Medical Research, Paediatrics and Child Health, Physician Associate Studies, Psychiatry, Public Health

---

SWANSEA UNIVERSITY
www.swansea.ac.uk

College of Arts & Humanities;
www.swansea.ac.uk/artandhumanities

English Language/TEFL and Literature

BA degrees in English Language, TESOL, English Literature, English Literature with Creative Writing

Languages, Translation and Communication

BA degrees in French, German, Italian, Spanish, English-Chinese Translation & Interpreting, Modern Languages, Translation and Interpreting, Media and Public Relations, Media and Public Relations (Welsh-medium);

History

BA degrees in Classics, Ancient History and Egyptology, Ancient and Medieval History, History, Medieval Studies

Political and Cultural Studies

BA degrees in American Studies, Philosophy, Politics and Economics (PPE), Politics and International Relations, War and Society,

Cymraeg / Welsh

BA degrees in Cymraeg (1st language), Cymraeg/ Welsh (2nd language), BA Cymraeg a'r Cyfryngau,

College of Engineering

Aerospace

BEng Aerospace Engineering, MEng Aerospace Engineering, BEng Aerospace Engineering (with a Year in Industry), MEng Aerospace Engineering (with a Year in Industry)

Chemical

BEng Chemical Engineering, MEng Chemical Engineering, BEng Chemical Engineering (with a Year in Industry), MEng Chemical Engineering (with a Year in Industry)

Civil

BEng Civil Engineering, MEng Civil Engineering, BEng Civil Engineering (with a Year in Industry), MEng Civil Engineering (with a Year in Industry)

Electronic and Electrical

BEng Electronic and Electrical Engineering, MEng Electronic and Electrical Engineering, BEng Electronic and Electrical Engineering (with a year in Europe, N. America, Australia or industry), MEng Electronic and Electrical Engineering (with a year in Europe, N. America, Australia or industry)

Foundation Year

Engineering Foundation Year, Aerospace Engineering Foundation Year, Chemical Engineering Foundation Year, Civil Engineering Foundation Year, Electrical and Electronic Engineering Foundation Year, Materials Science and Engineering Foundation Year, Mechanical Engineering Foundation Year, Medical Engineering Foundation Year

Materials

BEng Materials Science and Engineering, MEng Materials Science and Engineering, BEng Materials Science and Engineering (with a Year in Industry), MEng Materials Science and Engineering (with a Year in Industry), BEng Materials Science and Engineering (with a Year Abroad)

Mechanical

BEng Mechanical Engineering, MEng Mechanical Engineering, BEng Mechanical Engineering (with a Year in Industry), MEng Mechanical Engineering (with a Year in Industry), BEng Mechanical Engineering (with a year in Europe), BEng Mechanical Engineering (with a year in North America)

Medical

BEng Medical Engineering, MEng Medical Engineering, BEng Medical Engineering (with a Year in Industry), MEng Medical Engineering (with a Year in Industry)

Sports Science

BSc Sport and Exercise Science

College of Human and Health Sciences

Education

Education, BA(Hons), Education and Computing, BSc(Hons), Education and Mathematics, BSc(Hons), Education and Psychology, BSc(Hons), Education and Welsh, BA(Hons)

Healthcare Science

Healthcare Science (Audiology), BSc(Hons), Healthcare Science (Cardiac Physiology), BSc(Hons), Healthcare Science (Nuclear Medicine), BSc(Hons), Healthcare Science (Neurophysiology), BSc(Hons), Healthcare Science (Radiotherapy Physics), BSc(Hons), Healthcare Science (Radiation Physics), BSc(Hons), Healthcare Science (Respiratory and Sleep Physiology), BSc(Hons)

Nursing and Midwifery

Adult Nursing, Swansea BSc(Hons), Adult Nursing (Carmarthen campus) BSc(Hons), Child Nursing BSc(Hons), Mental Health Nursing, Swansea BSc(Hons), Maternity Care CertHE, Maternity Care (part-time) CertHE, Midwifery BMid

Osteopathy

Osteopathy, M.Ost,

Paramedic Science

Paramedic Science, DipHE

Psychology

Criminology & Psychology BSc(Hons), Psychology, BSc(Hons)

Society and Wellbeing

Health and Social Care, BSc(Hons), Criminology & Social Policy, BSc, Geography & Social Policy, BSc, Politics & Social Policy, BA, Social Policy, BSc(Hons), Social Sciences, BSc(Hons), Social Work, BSc(Hons); Postgraduate courses: MSc/PGCert/PGDip Gerontology and Ageing Studies, MSc International Gerontology and Ageing Studies, MA/PGDip/PGCert Childhood Studies, MA/PGDip/PGCert Developmental and Therapeutic Play, PGCert Enhanced Neonatal Care, MSc/PGDip/PGCert Child Public Health, MA/PGDip/PGCert Education for Health Professions, MSc/PGDip Advanced Critical Care Practice, MSc/PGDip Advanced Practice in Health Care, MSc/PGDip/PGCert Advanced Specialist Blood Transfusion Practice, PGCert Approved Mental Health Professional, PGCert Blood Component Transfusion, MSc/PgD/PgC Community and Primary Health Care Practice, MSc/PGDip/PGCert Enhanced Professional Practice, MSc/PGDip Enhanced Professional Midwifery Practice, MSc Long Term and Chronic Conditions Management, MA Medical Law and Ethics, PGCert Non-Medical Prescribing for Nurses and Midwives, PGCert Non-Medical Prescribing for Allied Health Professionals, PGCert Non-Medical Prescribing for Pharmacists, MSc Nursing Pre-Registration (Adult), MSc Nursing Pre-Registration (Child), MSc Nursing Pre-Registration (Mental Health), MSc/PgD Public Health & Health Promotion, MSc Social Work, MSc Health Care Management, MSc Leadership, Management and Innovation in Health Care, MSc Abnormal and Clinical Psychology, MSc Research Methods in Psychology and Cognitive Neuroscience, MSc Research Methods in Psychology, MSc Social Research Methods, MPhil and PhDss

College of Law and Criminology; *www.swansea.ac.uk/law*

BSc Criminology & Criminal Justice, BSc Criminology & Psychology, BSc Criminology & Social Policy, LLB Law and Criminology, LLB Single Honours Law, LLB Law (Crime and Criminal Justice), LLB Business Law, MLaw Human Rights; Postgraduate courses: MA Applied Criminal Justice & Criminology, LLM in Human Rights, LLM Intellectual Property & Commercial Practice, LLM in International Commercial Law, LLM in International Commercial and Maritime Law, LLM in International Maritime Law, LLM in International Trade Law, LLM in Legal Practice and Advanced Drafting, LLM in Oil and Gas Law, Law PhD/MPhil

College of Science http:// *www.swansea.ac.uk/science*

Department of biosciences

BSc Biology, BSc Biological Sciences (with deferred specialisation), BSc Marine Biology, BSc Zoology, BSc Biology (with Integrated Foundation), BSc Biology with a Year in Industry, BSc Marine Biology with a Year in Industry, BSc Zoology with a Year in Industry; Postgraduate courses: MSc Environmental Biology: Conservation and Resource Management, MSc High Performance and Scientific Computing, MRes Biosciences
PhD/MPhil Biological Sciences

Department of Computer Science

BSc Computer Science, MSci Computer Science, BSc Software Engineering, MEng Computing, BSc Computer Science (including Foundation Year), BSc Computer Science with a Year in Industry, BSc Software Engineering with a Year in Industry, MEng Computing with a Year in Industry, MSci Computer Science with a Year in Industry, BSc Education and Computing; Postgraduate courses: MSc Computer Science, MSc Advanced Computer Science, MSc Advanced Software Technology, MSc High Performance and Scientific Computing, MSc Data Science, MSc Computer Science: Informatique (Swansea route), MSc Computer Science: Informatique (Grenoble route), MSc by Research in Human Computer Interaction, MSc by Research in Theoretical Computer Science, MSc by Research in Visual

and Interactive Computing, MRes Computing and Future Interaction Technologies, MRes Visual Computing, MRes Logic and Computation, PhD/MPhil/MSc by Research in Computer Science

Department of Chemistry

BSc Chemistry, BSc Chemistry with a Year in Industry, MChem Chemistry, MChem Chemistry with a Year in Industry; Postgraduate research degrees also available

Department of Geography

BA Geography, BSc Geography, BA Human Geography, BSc Physical Geography, BSc Geography (with Integrated Foundation), BSc Physical Earth Science, BSc Geography and Geo-Informatics, BSc Geography with a Year Abroad, BSc Geography with a Year in Industry, BA Geography with a Year in Industry, BA Human Geography with a Year in Industry, BSc Physical Earth Science with a Year in Industry, BSc Physical Geography with a Year in Industry; Postgraduate courses: MSc Environmental Dynamics and Climate Change, MSc Geographic Information and Climate Change, MSc High Performance and Scientific Computing, MSc by Research in Earth Observation, MSc by Research in Environmental Dynamics, MSc by Research in Glaciology, MSc by Research in Global Environmental Modelling, MSc by Research in Global Migration, MSc by Research in Media Geographies, MSc by Research in Social Theory and Space, MSc by Research in Urban Studies, PhD/MPhil Human Geography, PhD/MPhil Physical Geography

Department of Mathematics

MMath Mathematics, BSc Mathematics, BSc Pure Mathematics, BSc Applied Mathematics, BSc Mathematics for Finance, BSc Mathematics (with Integrated Foundation), BSc Mathematics with a Year in Industry, BSc Mathematics for Finance with a Year in Industry; Postgraduate courses: MSc Maths & Computing for Finance, MSc High Performance and Scientific Computing, MSc Mathematics, MRes Stochastic Processes: Theory and Application, MSc by Research in Mathematics, PhD/MPhil/MSc by Research in Mathematics

Department of Physics

BSc Physics, BSc Physics (with Integrated Foundation), BSc with a Year Abroad, BSc Theoretical Physics, BSc Physics with Nanotechnology, BSc Physics with Particle Physics and Cosmology, BSc Physics with a Year in Industry, BSc Theoretical Physics with a Year in Industry, MPhys Physics, MPhys with a Year Abroad, MPhys Theoretical

Physics, MPhys Theoretical Physics with a Year in Industry, MPhys Physics with a Year in Industry ; Postgraduate courses: MSc High Performance and Scientific Computing, MSc by Research in Antimatter Physics, Cold Atoms and Quantum Optics, Laser Physics, Lattice Gauge Theory, Nanotechnology, Quantum Fields & Strings, Theoretical Particle Physics, PhDs and MPhils available

Swansea University Medical School

BSc Applied Medical Sciences, BSc Applied Medical Sciences (with a Foundation Year), Biochemistry BSc, Genetics BSc, MSci Biochemistry, MSci Genetics, BSc Medical Biochemistry, BSc Medical Genetics, BSc Biochemistry and Genetics, MSci Medical Biochemistry, MSci Medical Genetics, MSci Biochemistry and Genetics; Postgraduate courses: PG Dip Physician Associate Studies, MSc Nanomedicine, MSc Clinical Science (Medical Physics), MSc Medical Radiation Physics, MSc Health Informatics, MSc Autism and Related Conditions, MSc Applied Analytical Science (LCMS), MSc Health Data Science, MSc Leadership for the Health Professions, MRes Applied Analytical Science (LCMS), MRes Health Informatics, MRes Life Science and Healthcare Enterprise, MRes Medicine and Life Sciences, DProf/MRes Research in Health Professions Education; Postgraduate research degrees available

School of Management; www.swansea.ac.uk/som

Accounting and Finance

BSc Accounting & Finance, BSc Accounting, BSc Finance; Postgraduate courses: MSc Accounting & Finance, MSc Financial Management, MSc Finance and Business Analytics, MSc Finance, MSc International Banking & Finance, MSc Investment Management, MSc Strategic Accounting

Business

BSc Business Management, BSc Business Management (Entrepreneurship), BSc Business Management (Operations & Supply Management), BSc Business Management (Finance), BSc Business Management (e-Business), BSc Business Management (Management Consulting), BSc Business Management (Business Analytics), BSc Business Management (Human Resource Management), BSc Business Management (Marketing); Postgraduate courses: MSc Management, MSc Management (Marketing), MSc Management (Finance), MSc Management (Human Resource Management), MSc Management (Entrepreneurship), MSc Management (Operations and Supply Management), MSc Management (International Management), MSc Management (International Standards), MSc Management (e-Business); PhD

Economics

BSc Economics, BSc Economics and Business, BSc Economics and Finance; Postgraduate degrees: MSc Economics, MSc Economics & Finance

Marketing

BSc Business Management (Marketing), BSc Marketing; Postgraduate courses: MSc Management (Marketing), PhD

UNIVERSITY OF TEESSIDE
www.tees.ac.uk

School of Computing, Media and the Arts; www.tees.ac.uk/schools/sam

Art: digital arts & design, fine art

BA(Hons) Design: Comics, Graphic Novels and Sequential Design, Contemporary Fashion, FdA Design For the Creative Industries, BA(Hons) Fashion Design, BA(Hons) Fashion Enterprise, BA(Hons) Fine Arts, BA(Hons) Graphic Design,, BA(Hons) Interior Design, BA(Hons) Textile Design, BA(Hons) Product Design and Innovation; Postgraduate courses in MA Fine Art, MA Digital Arts And Design, MA Future Design

Computer Animation and Visual Effects

2D Animation BA(Hons), Computer Animation BA(Hons), Computer Animation and Visual Effects BA(Hons), Computer Character Animation BA(Hons), Technical Direction for Visual Effects BSc(Hons), Visual Effects BA(Hons), Visual Effects MComp(Hons); Postgraduate courses: Computer Animation and Visual Effects MA

Computer Games

Computer Games Animation BA(Hons), Computer Games Art BA(Hons), Computer Games Design BA(Hons), Computer Games Design MComp(Hons), Computer Games Programming BSc(Hons), Computer Games Programming MComp(Hons), Concept Art BA(Hons), Indie Games Development BA(Hons) ,

Technical Game Development BSc(Hons); Postgraduate courses: Concept Art for Games and Animation MA, Games Development MA
Computing and the Web
Computer Science BSc(Hons), Computer Science MComp(Hons), Computing BSc(Hons), Computing FdSc, Computing (Networking) FdSc, Cybersecurity and Networks BSc(Hons), Health Informatics BSc(Hons), Information Technology (IT) BSc(Hons), Web Production BSc(Hons); Postgraduate courses: Computer Security and Networks MSc, Computing MSc, IT Project Management MSc
Media and Journalism
Broadcast Media Production BA(Hons), Film and Television Production BA(Hons), Film, Media and Culture BA(Hons), Journalism BA(Hons), Sport Journalism BA(Hons); Postgraduate courses: Digital Media and Communications MA , Journalism MA , Multimedia Journalism MA , Multimedia Public Relations MA , Producing for Film and Television MA
Performing Arts and Music
Music Technology BSc(Hons), Performing Arts BA(Hons)

School of Health and Social care; www.tees.ac.uk/Undergraduate_courses/ Health_Social_Care/

Health, Care and Wellbeing BSc(Hons), Health, Wellbeing and Social Support FdSc, Social Care Cert HE, Dental Hygiene and Dental Therapy BSc(Hons), Dental Nurse Practice Cert HE, Diagnostic Radiography BSc(Hons), Midwifery BSc(Hons), Nursing Studies (Adult) BSc(Hons), Nursing Studies (Child) BSc(Hons), Nursing Studies (Learning Disabilities) BSc(Hons), Nursing Studies (Mental Health) BSc(Hons), Occupational Therapy BSc(Hons), Operating Department Practice Studies BSc(Hons), Paramedic Practice BSc(Hons), Physiotherapy BSc(Hons), Social Work BA(Hons), Integrated Care Studies BSc(Hons), Operating Department Practice BSc(Hons), Paramedic Science (Top-up) BSc(Hons), Specialist Community Public Health Nursing (Health Visiting) BSc(Hons), Specialist Community Public Health Nursing (Occupational Health) BSc(Hons), Specialist Community Public Health Nursing (School Nursing) BSc(Hons), Specialist Practice in District Nursing BSc(Hons); Postgraduate courses: Advanced Clinical Practice MSc, Advanced Clinical Practice (Management of Long-term Health Conditions) MSc, Advanced Clinical Practice (Neuromusculoskeletal Therapy) MSc, Advanced Practitioner MSc,

Advancing Human Factors in Health and Social Care PgCert, Advancing Quality Improvement in Health and Social Care PgCert, Advancing Quality, Safety and Governance in Health and Social Care MA, Autism Practice PgDip/MSc Clinical Psychology (DClinPsy), Clinical Research MRes, Clinical Research and Evidence-based Medicine PgCert, Cognitive Behavioural Therapy MSc, Cognitive Behavioural Therapy PgDip, Diagnostic Imaging Reporting PgCert/PgDip/MSc, Diagnostic Radiography (Pre-registration) PgDip/MSc, Evidence-based Medicine PgDip/MSc, Evidence-based Medicine (Anaesthesia, Perioperative Medicine and Pain) PgDip/MSc, Evidence-based Orthopaedics PgDip, Evidence-based Practice MSc, Forensic Radiography PgCert/MSc, General and Oncoplastic Breast Surgery MCh, Health and Social Care Professional Practice Doctorate, Health and Social Care Sciences (Generic pathway) MSc, Low Intensity Assessment and Intervention Skills for Psychological Wellbeing Practice PgCert, Master of Public Health MPH, Medical Ultrasound MSc, Medical Ultrasound PgCert, Medical Ultrasound PgDip, Midwifery Studies (Pre-registration) PgDip, Neuromusculoskeletal Therapy PgCert, Occupational Therapy (Pre-registration) PgDip/MSc, Orthopaedics, Physiotherapy (Pre-registration) MSc, Public Health (DrPH), Social Work MA, Specialist Community Public Health Nursing (Health Visiting) MSc, Specialist Community Public Health Nursing (Health Visiting) PgDip, Specialist Community Public Health Nursing (Occupational Health Nursing) PgDip, Specialist Community Public Health Nursing (School Nursing) MSc, Specialist Community Public Health Nursing (School Nursing) PgDip, Specialist Practice in District Nursing PgDip/MSc, Specialist Practice in District Nursing Professional Graduate Certificate, Surgical Gastroenterology and Minimally Invasive Surgery MCh, The Management of Long-term Health Conditions PgCert, Transformational Leadership in Health and Social Care MSc

Science & Engineering; www.tees.ac.uk/ schools/sse

Crime scene & Forensic science
Computer and Digital Forensics BSc(Hons), Computer and Digital Forensics with Professional Experience BSc(Hons), Crime Scene Science BSc(Hons), Crime Scene Science with Professional Experience BSc(Hons), Forensic and Investigative Sciences MSci(Hons), Forensic and Investigative Sciences with Professional Experience MSci(Hons), Forensic Biology BSc(Hons), Forensic Biology with

Professional Experience BSc(Hons) , Forensic Science BSc(Hons), Forensic Science with Professional Experience BSc(Hons); Postgraduate courses: Crime Intelligence and Data Analytics PgDip/MSc, Crime Intelligence and Data Analytics with Advanced Practice MSc, Forensic Science PgDip/MSc, Forensic Science with Advanced Practice MSc

Engineering

Aerospace Engineering BEng(Hons), Aerospace Engineering MEng(Hons), Aerospace Engineering with Industry BEng(Hons), Aerospace Engineering with Industry MEng(Hons), Chemical Engineering BEng(Hons), Chemical Engineering MEng(Hons), Chemical Engineering with Industry BEng(Hons), Chemical Engineering with Industry MEng(Hons), Civil Engineering BEng(Hons), Civil Engineering MEng(Hons), Civil Engineering with Disaster Management BEng(Hons), Civil Engineering with Disaster Management with Industry BEng(Hons), Civil Engineering with Industry BEng(Hons), Civil Engineering with Industry MEng(Hons), Control/Technical Support Engineer Degree Apprenticeship, Electrical and Electronic Engineering BEng(Hons), Electrical and Electronic Engineering MEng(Hons), Electrical and Electronic Engineering with Industry BEng(Hons), Electrical and Electronic Engineering with Industry MEng(Hons), Electrical/Electronic Technical Support Engineer Degree Apprenticeship, Embedded Electronic Systems Design and Development Engineer Degree Apprenticeship, Instrumentation and Control Engineering BEng(Hons), Instrumentation and Control Engineering MEng(Hons), Instrumentation and Control Engineering with Industry BEng(Hons), Instrumentation and Control Engineering with Industry MEng(Hons), Manufacturing Engineer Degree Apprenticeship, Mechanical Engineering BEng(Hons), Mechanical Engineering MEng(Hons), Mechanical Engineering with Industry BEng(Hons) , Mechanical Engineering with Industry MEng(Hons), Product Design and Development Engineer Degree Apprenticeship; Postgraduate courses: Advanced Home Futures MSc, Civil and Structural Engineering PgDip/MSc , Civil and Structural Engineering with Advanced Practice MSc, Electrical Power and Energy Systems PgDip/MS, Electrical Power and Energy Systems with Advanced Practice MSc, Food Processing Engineering PgDip/MSc, Food Processing Engineering with Advanced Practice MSc, Instrumentation and Control Engineering PgDip/MSc, Instrumentation and Control Engineering with Advanced Practice MSc, Mechanical Engineering PgDip/MSc, Mechanical Engineering with Advanced

Practice MSc, Oil and Gas Management PgDip/MSc, Oil and Gas Management with Advanced Practice MSc, Petroleum Engineering PgDip/MSc, Petroleum Engineering with Advanced Practice MSc, Project Management PgDip/MSca, Project Management with Advanced Practice MSc

Mathematics

Financial Mathematics BSc(Hons), Mathematics BSc(Hons)

Science and Environment

Biochemistry BSc(Hons), Biological Sciences BSc(Hons), Biological Sciences with Professional Experience BSc(Hons), Biomedical Science BSc(Hons), Chemistry BSc(Hons), Chemistry with Professional Experience BSc(Hons), Environmental Science BSc(Hons), Environmental Science with Professional Experience BSc(Hons), Food and Nutrition BSc(Hons), Food and Nutrition with Professional Experience BSc(Hons), Food Science and Engineering BSc(Hons), Food Science and Engineering with Professional Experience BSc(Hons), Health Sciences BSc(Hons), Human Biology BSc(Hons), Human Biology with Professional Experience BSc(Hons), Laboratory Scientist Degree Apprenticeship, Pharmaceutical Science BSc(Hons), Pre-Medical Science Cert HE, Pre-Veterinary Science Cert HE; Postgraduate courses: Energy and Environmental Management PgDip/MSc, Energy and Environmental Management with Advanced Practice MSc, Food Science and Biotechnology PgDip/MSc, Food Science and Biotechnology with Advanced Practice MSc

School of Social Sciences, Business & Law; www.tees.ac.uk/schools/sssbl

Criminology and Sociology

Criminology BSc(Hons), Criminology and Sociology BSc(Hons), Criminology with Law BSc(Hons), Criminology with Psychology BSc(Hons), Criminology with Youth Studies BSc(Hons), International Foundation Year (Social Sciences and Law), Social and Public Sector Evolution FdA, Sociology BSc(Hons),; Postgraduate courses: Criminology MSc, Social Research Methods MSc

Education, Early Childhood and Youth

Childhood and Youth Studies BA(Hons), Early Childhood Studies BA(Hons), Early Years Sector Endorsed FdA, Education and Training BA(Hons), Education and Training Certificate in Education, Education and Training (Supporting Teaching and Learning) BA(Hons), Education Studies BA(Hons), Supporting Teaching and Learning FdA, Teaching English to Speakers of Other Languages (CELTA),

Working With Children and Young People FdA, Working with Children and Young People (Top-up) BA(Hons), Young Children and Early Childhood (Top-up) BA(Hons); Postgraduate courses: Applied Education Leadership PgCert, Education Doctorate, Education MA, Education (Early Childhood Studies) MA, Education (Educational Leadership) MA, Education and Training Professional Graduate Certificate in Education

English

English Studies BA(Hons), English Studies with Creative Writing BA(Hons); Postgraduate courses: Creative Writing MA, Creative Writing (Distance Learning) MA, English MA

History

History BA(Hons), History MA

Law, Policing and Investigation

Crime and Investigation BSc(Hons), International Foundation Year (Social Sciences and Law), Law LLB(Hons), Law with Business Management LLB(Hons), Police Studies (Top-up) BSc(Hons), Policing BSc(Hons); Postgraduate courses: CILEx Graduate Fast-track Diploma, Criminal Investigation MSc, LLM Master of Laws, LLM (Criminal Law) Master of Laws, LLM (International Law) Master of Laws, LLM (Medical Law)

Psychology

Counselling FdA, Forensic Psychology BSc(Hons), Psychology BSc(Hons), Psychology and Counselling BSc(Hons), Psychology and Criminology BSc(Hons), Psychology with Business BSc(Hons), Therapeutic Counselling (Top-up) BA(Hons); Postgraduate courses: Counselling Psychology Doctorate, Forensic Psychology MSc, Health Psychology and Clinical Skills MSc, Psychology (Graduate Conversion) Diploma, Psychology (Top-up) Doctorate

Sport and Exercise

Applied Sport and Exercise (Top-up) BSc(Hons), Physical Activity, Exercise and Health BSc(Hons) , Sport and Exercise (Applied Sport Science) BSc(Hons), Sport and Exercise (Coaching Science) BSc(Hons), Sport and Exercise (Sport Studies) BSc(Hons), Sports Development BA(Hons), Sports Therapy and Rehabilitation BSc(Hons); Postgraduate courses: Applied Sports Rehabilitation MSc, Sport and Exercise MSc, Sports Rehabilitation MSc

Teesside University Business School

Accounting and Finance BA(Hons), Business Management BA(Hons), Business with Accountancy BA(Hons), Business with Enterprise and Innovation BA(Hons), Business with Human Resource Management BA(Hons), Business with International Management BA(Hons), Business with Marketing BA(Hons), Business with Tourism BA(Hons), Chartered Manager Degree Apprenticeship, Digital Marketing BSc(Hons), Economics BA(Hons), International Foundation Year (Business and Computing), Management Practice BA(Hons), Marketing BA(Hons), Sports Management and Marketing BA(Hons); Postgraduate courses: Accounting and Finance MSc, Business Administration (DBA) Doctorate, Human Resource Management MA, Human Resource Management (Applied) MA, International Management MSc, International Management PgDip, International Management (Accountancy) MSc, International Management (Applied) MSc, International Management (Digital Business) MSc, International Management (Human Resource Management) MSc, International Management (Marketing Management) MSc, International Management (Operations) MSc, Master of Business Administration MBA, Master of Business Administration (Applied) MBA,

ASKHAM BRYAN COLLEGE
www.askham-bryan.ac.uk

Agriculture

BSc/BSc(Hons) Agriculture,

UNIVERSITY CENTRE GRIMSBY
www.grimsby.ac.uk

computing technologies; commercial photography; design; games design and development; music; professional writing; special effects make-up design for TV, film and theatre; BA(Hons), BSc(Hons), FdSc

TRINITY COLLEGE LONDON
www.trinitycollege.co.uk

dance, drama & speech, music, performing & teaching, rock & pop, DaDa, English language, teaching English; PGDip, Music Diplomas, Teaching Diplomas

UNIVERSITY OF ULSTER
www.ulster.ac.uk

Faculty of Arts, Design & the Built Environment; www.ulster.ac.uk/faculties/art-design-and-built-environment

Belfast School of Art

BDes(Hons) Animation, BA(Hons) Art & Design, BA(Hons) Ceramics, Jewellery and Silversmithing, BA(Hons) Fine Art, BDes(Hons) Graphic Design and Illustration, BDes (Interaction Design), BA(Hons) Photography with Video, BDes(Hons) Product and Furniture Design, BA(Hons) Textile Art, Design and Fashion; Postgraduate courses: MSc Arts Therapies: Art Therapy; Music Therapy, MFA Design, MFA Photography

Belfast School of Architecture and the Built Environment

Architectural Engineering – BEng(Hons), Architectural Technology and Management – BSc(Hons), Architecture – BA(Hons), Building Surveying – BSc(Hons), Civil Engineering – BEng(Hons)/MEng(Hons), Civil Engineering (Geoinformatics) – BSc(Hons), Construction Engineering and Management – BSc(Hons), Energy – BSc(Hons), Environmental Health – BSc(Hons), Planning, Regeneration and Development – MSci(Hons), Quantity Surveying and Commercial Management – BSc(Hons), Real Estate – BSc(Hons), Safety Engineering and Disaster Management – MEng(Hons); Postgraduate courses: Community Planning and Governance – PgDip/MSc, Construction Business and Leadership (with management specialisms) – PgCert/PgDip/MSc, Fire Safety Engineering – PgDip/MSc, Infrastructure Engineering – PgDip/MSc, Real Estate – PgCert/PgDip/MSc, Renewable Energy and Energy Management – PgDip/MSc

Faculty of Arts; www.ulster.ac.uk/faculties/arts

School of Creative Arts and Technologies, School of English and History, School of Irish Language and Literature

Cinematic Arts – BSc(Hons), Creative Technologies – BSc(Hons), Drama – BA Hons (Modular), English – BA Hons (Modular), History – BA Hons (Modular), Irish Language & Diploma, Irish Language and Literature – BA Hons (Modular), Irish Studies & CertHE, Music – BMus(Hons), plus a range of joint honours degrees available; Postgraduate courses: Creative Musicianship & Mmus, Cultural Heritage and Museum Studies & MA, English Literature & MA, History – PgDip/MA, Irish History and Politics – PgDip/MA, Irish Language Translation, Interpreting and Professional Language Skills & MA, Museum Practice and Management – PgDip/MA

School of Media Film and Journalism

Journalism with Education & BA(Hons), Journalism with English & BA(Hons), Journalism with History & BA(Hons)

Faculty of Computing and Engineering; www.ulster.ac.uk/faculties/computing-and-engineering

School of Computing and Engineering; School of Computing and Intelligent Systems

Computer Engineering – BEng(Hons), Computer Games Development – BEng(Hons), Computer Science – BSc Hons (Modular), Computer Science (Software Systems Development) – BSc(Hons), Electrical and Electronic Engineering – BEng(Hons), Information Technologies – BSc(Hons), Mechanical and Manufacturing Engineering – BEng(Hons), Renewable Energy Engineering – BEng(Hons); Postgraduate courses: Data Science & MSc, Professional Software Development – MSc, MPhil and PhD

School of Computing & Mathematics

Computing Science – BSc(Hons), Computing Systems – BSc(Hons), Computing Technologies – BSc(Hons), Interactive Multimedia Design – BSc(Hons), Software Engineering – BEng(Hons),

School of Engineering

Biomedical Engineering – BSc(Hons), Electronic Engineering – BEng(Hons), Electronic Engineering + German Masters Degree – MEng(Hons), Engineering Management – BEng(Hons), Mechanical Engineering – MEng(Hons), Mechatronic Engineering – BEng(Hons), Mechatronic Engineering + German Masters Degree – MEng(Hons), Technology with Design – BSc(Hons); Postgraduate courses: Advanced Composites and Polymers & PgDip, Advanced Composites and Polymers & MSc, Biomedical Engineering & PgDip, Biomedical Engineering & MSc, Manufacturing Management – PgDip

Faculty of Life & Health Sciences; www.ulster.ac.uk/faculties/life-and-health-sciences

School of Biomedical Sciences

Biology – BSc(Hons), Biomedical Science – BSc(Hons), Biomedical Science with DPP (Pathology) – BSc(Hons), Biomedical Science with DPP/DIAS – BSc(Hons), Biotechnology – BSc(Hons), Dietetics – BSc(Hons), Food and Nutrition – BSc(Hons), Human Nutrition – BSc(Hons), Optometry – BSc Hons/ MOptom Hons, Stratified Medicine – BSc(Hons); Postgraduate courses: Biotechnology Research & MSc, Dietetics & MSc, Food Regulatory Affairs – PgCert/PgDip/MSc, Food and Nutrition – PgCert/ PgDip/MSc, Human Nutrition & MSc, Physician Associate Studies – PgDip/MSc, Stratified Medicine & MSc, Stem Cell Biology & PgCert, Theory of Independent Prescribing for Optometrists & PgCert, Veterinary Public Health & PgCert; PhDs

School of Geography and Environmental Sciences

Environmental Science – BSc Hons (Modular), Environmental Science with Education – BSc(Hons), Environmental Science with Psychology – BSc(Hons), Environmental Science with Psychology – BSc(Hons), Geography – BSc(Hons) (Modular), Geography with Education – BSc(Hons), Geography with Psychology – BSc(Hons); Postgraduate courses: Coastal Zone Management – PgDip/MSc, Environmental Management – PgDip/MSc, Environmental Management and Geographic Information Systems – PgDip/MSc,

Environmental Toxicology and Pollution Monitoring – PgDip/MSc, Geographic Information Systems – PgDip/MSc, Marine Spatial Planning – PgDip/MSc; PhDs

School of Health Sciences

Diagnostic Radiography & Imaging – BSc(Hons), Health Physiology / Healthcare Science – BSc(Hons), Occupational Therapy – BSc(Hons), Physiotherapy – BSc(Hons), Podiatry – BSc(Hons), Radiotherapy and Oncology – BSc(Hons), Speech and Language Therapy – BSc(Hons); Postgraduate courses: Professional Development in Occupational Therapy & MSc, Advancing Practice – PgCert/PgDip/MSc, Lower Limb Preservation in Diabetes – PgCert/PgDip/MSc, Medicines Management & PgCert, Professional Development in Occupational Therapy & MSc, Professional Development in Physiotherapy & MSc, Sensory Integration – PgCert/PgDip/MSc

School of Nursing

Applied Health Studies – BSc(Hons), Developing Practice in Healthcare – BSc(Hons), Health and Wellbeing – BSc(Hons), Nursing (Adult) – BSc(Hons), Nursing (Mental Health) – BSc(Hons), Specialist Community Public Health Nursing – BSc(Hons), Health Promotion and Public Health – PgCert/PgDip/MSc, Health and Wellbeing – PgDip/ MSc, Nursing – PgCert/PgDip/MSc, Specialist Community Public Health Nursing & PgDip, Palliative Care – PgDip/MSc; PhDs

School of Pharmacy and Pharmaceutical Sciences

Pharmaceutical Bioscience – MSci(Hons), Pharmacy – MPharm(Hons); Postgraduate courses in Pharmaceutical Sciences – PgDip/MSc, Pharmacy Management – PgDip

School of Psychology

Psychology – BSc Hons (Modular), Social Psychology – BSc(Hons); Postgraduate courses in Applied Behaviour Analysis & MSc, Applied Psychology (Mental Health and Psychological Therapies) & MSc, Family Therapy and Systemic Practice & PgCert, Health Psychology & MSc; PhD

School of Sports

Football Coaching and Business Management – BSc(Hons), Performance Analysis and Coaching Practice & AdvCert, Sports Coaching – BSc(Hons), Sport Studies – BSc(Hons), Sport and Exercise Sciences – BSc(Hons), Sport, Physical Activity and Health – BSc(Hons), Sports Coaching – BSc(Hons);

Postgraduate courses in Physical Activity and Public Health č' MSc, Sport and Exercise Medicine – PgDip/ MSc, Sport and Exercise Nutrition – PgDip/MSc, Sport and Exercise Psychology č' MSc, Sports Coaching č' MSc, Sport and Exercise Medicine – PgDip/MSc, Sport and Exercise Nutrition – PgDip/ MSc

Faculty of Social Sciences; www.ulster.ac.uk/socialsciences

School of Communication

Communication Management and Public Relations – BSc(Hons), Communication, Advertising and Marketing – BSc(Hons), Counselling – Professional Development – BSc(Hons), Interactiv e Media – BA(Hons), Journalism with Education – BA(Hons), Language and Linguistics – BSc(Hons), Media Studies and Production – BA(Hons), Media Studies with English – BA(Hons), Media Studies with History – BA(Hons), Therapeutic Communication and Counselling Studies – BSc(Hons); Postgraduate courses in Communication Management in Healthcare č' PgCert, Communication and Public Relations – PgDip/MSc, Counselling Studies and Therapeutic Communication – PgDip/MSc, Digital Media Communication – PgDip/MSc, English Language and Linguistics – PgDip/MSc, Journalism č' MA; PhDs

School of Criminology, Politics & Social Policy

Community Development – BSc(Hons), Community Youth Work – BSc(Hons), Criminology and Criminal Justice – BSc Hons (Modular), Health and Social Care Policy – BSc(Hons), Politics – BSc Hons (Modular), Politics with Criminology – BSc(Hons), Social Policy – BSc Hons (Modular), Social Policy with Criminology – BSc(Hons), Social Work BSc(Hons), Sociology – BSc Hons (Modular), Sociology with Criminology – BSc(Hons), Sociology with Politics – BSc(Hons); Postgraduate courses in Applied Peace and Conflict Studies – PgDip/MSc, Public Administration č' MPA, Restorative Practices č' MSc; PhDs

School of Education

Education with Specialisms – PgDip/MEd, Headship č' PgDip, Library and Information Management – PgDip/MSc, Middle, Leadership č' PgCert, PGCE Art and Design, PGCE Further Education, PGCE English with Drama and Media Studies, PGCE Geography, PGCE History, PGCE Home Economics, PGCE Home Economics, PGCE Physical Education, PGCE Primary Education, PGCE Technology and Design,

Teaching of English to Speakers of Other Languages č' MA

School of Law

Law – LLB Hons (Modular), Law with Accounting – LLB(Hons), Law with Criminology – LLB(Hons), Law with Human Resource Management – LLB(Hons), Law with Irish – LLB(Hons), Law with Marketing – LLB(Hons), Law with Politics – LLB(Hons); Postgraduate courses in Clinical Legal Education č' LLM, Commercial Law č' LLM, Employment Law and Practice č' PgCert, Gend, er, Conflict and Human Rights č' LLM, Human Rights Law and Transitional Justice č' LLM

School of Sociology and Applied Social Studies

Community Development – BSc(Hons), Community Youth Work – BSc(Hons), Criminology and Criminal Justice – BSc Hons, Health and Social Care Policy – BSc(Hons), Politics – BSc Hons, Politics with Criminology – BSc(Hons), Social Policy – BSc Hons (Modular), Social Policy with Criminology – BSc(Hons), Social Work (3 year full-time course) – BSc(Hons), Sociology – BSc Hons; Postgraduate courses in Applied Peace and Conflict Studies – PgDip/MSc, Public Administration č' MPA, Restorative Practices č' MSc; PhDs

Ulster Business School; www.ulster.ac.uk/faculties/ulster-university-business-school

Department of Accounting Finance and Economics

Accounting (Pathways) – BSc(Hons), Accounting and Law – BSc(Hons), Accounting and Management – BSc(Hons), Business Technology – BSc(Hons), Business Economics – BSc Hons, Business Economics with Accountancy Studies – BSc(Hons), Business Economics with Marketing – BSc(Hons), Economics – BSc Hons, Economics with Finance – BSc(Hons), Finance and Investment Management – BSc(Hons); Postgraduate courses in Accounting č' GradDip, Advanced Accounting č' MSc, Applied Finance č' MSc; PhDs

Department of Hospitality and Tourism Management

Consumer Management and Food Innovation – BSc Hons, Culinary Arts Management – BSc(Hons), International Hospitality Management – BSc(Hons), International Travel and Tourism Management – BSc Hons, Leisure and Events Management – BSc(Hons);

Postgraduate courses in International Event Management &' MSc, International Hospitality Management &' MSc, International Tourism Management – MSc

Department of International Business
International Business &' MSc; PhDs

Department of Management and Leadership
Business Studies – BSc(Hons), Human Resource Management – BSc(Hons), Management and Leadership Development – BSc(Hons), Marketing – BSc Hons; Postgraduate courses in Business Development and Innovation &' MSc, Business Improvement &' MSc, MBA (Master of Business Administration) &' MBA, Management &' MSc, Management and Corporate Governance &' MSc, Marketing &' MSc, Sport Management – MSc

Department of Marketing, Entrepreneurship and Strategy
Business Studies – BSc(Hons), Human Resource Management – BSc(Hons), Management and Leadership Development – BSc(Hons), Marketing – BSc Hons; PhDs

Business Institute,
Civic Leadership and Community Planning (Advanced Diploma), Customer Contact (Bachelor of Science Hons), Executive Leadership (MSc), Management Practice (Advanced Diploma), Management Practice (Bachelor of Science Hons), Social Enterprise (Advanced Diploma)

UNIVERSITY OF WALES TRINITY SAINT DAVID
www.uwtsd.ac.uk

Faculty of Architecture, Computing & Engineering; www.uwtsd.ac.uk/face

School of Applied Computing
BCs/HND/HNC and Four-year courses in Applied Computing, Business Information Technology, Computer Games Development, Computer Networks, Computing and Information Systems, Software Engineering, Web Development, BEng Computer Systems and Electronics, BEng Electrical and Electronic Engineering, HND/HNC Electronics Engineering, Foundation Year in STEM (1 year)

School of Architecture, Built & Natural Environment
BSc Architecture, BSc/HND Architectural Technology, Building Surveying, Civil Engineering and Environmental Management, Project & Construction Management, Quantity Surveying: Postgraduate courses: MSc Sustainable Construction, MSc Property and Facilities Management

School of Automotive Engineering
BSc/HND Automotive Engineering, Motorsport Engineering, BEng and Meng Automotive Engineering, Motorsport Engineering

Logistics and Transport
BSc/HND Logistics and Supply Chain Management, Logistics and Transport, Motorsport Management; Postgraduate courses: MSc Logistics, MSc Lean and Agile Manufacturing

Mechanical and Manufacturing Engineering
BEng/MEng Mechanical and Manufacturing Engineering, Mechanical and Manufacturing Engineering Four-Year Foundation Entry, Mechanical Engineering, Mechanical Engineering Four-Year Foundation Entry, Energy and Environmental Engineering, Energy and Environmental Engineering Four-Year Foundation Entry, Extreme Sports Engineering, Extreme Sports Engineering Four-Year Foundation Entry; Postgraduate courses: MSc Engineering Project Management, MSc Lean and Agile Manufacturing, MSc Logistics, MSc Non-destructive Testing and Evaluation, MSc Engineering Product Design, MSc Mechanical Engineering

Natural Environments
BSc/HND Environmental Conservation; Postgraduate course: MSc Environmental Conservation and Management

Swansea College of Art; www.uwtsd.ac.uk/art-design

Advertising Graphic Design Illustration
BA Graphic Design, BA Illustration, BA Advertising and Brand Design, MDes Graphic Design, MDes Illustration, MDes Advertising and Brand Design; Postgraduate courses: MA Visual Communication, MPhil/PhD

Automotive, Transport and Product Design

BA(Hons) Product Design, MDes(Hons) Product Design, BSc(Hons) Product Design & Technology, MDes(Hons)Product Design & Technology, BA(Hons) Automotive Design, MDes(Hons) Automotive Design, BA(Hons) Transport Design, MDes(Hons) Transport Design; Postgraduate courses: MA Product Design, MSc Industrial Design, MA Transportation Design, MPhil/PhD

Film & Digital Media

MMus Tech Music Technology, BA Music Technology, MArts Creative Computer Games Design, BA Creative Computer Games Design, MArts 3D Computer Animation, BA 3D Computer Animation, MArts Digital Film & Television Production, BA Digital Film & Television Production, MA 3D Computer Animation, MA Creative Sound Production, BA Set Design, MDes Set Design, BA Film and Visual Culture, BA New Media Production; Postgraduate courses: MPhil and PhD

Fine Art & Photography

Certificate of Higher Education Art and Design Foundation, BA Fine Art: Studio, Site & Context, BA(Hons) Photography in the Arts, BA(Hons) Photojournalism & Documentary Photography, MArts Fine Art: Studio Site and Context, MArts Photography in the Arts, MArts Photojournalism & Documentary Photography; Postgraduate courses: MRes Art & Design, MA Fine Art, MA Photography, MPhil/PhD

Glass

BA(Hons) Glass Contemporary Practice, BA(Hons) Glass Architectural Arts, MDes Glass Contemporary Practice, MDes Glass Architectural Art; Postgraduate courses: MA Glass, MPhil/PhD

Surface Pattern Design and Glass

BA Surface Pattern Design (Maker), BA(Hons) Surface Pattern Design (Textiles for Fashion), BA(Hons) Surface Pattern Design (Textiles for Interiors), BA(Hons) Surface Pattern Design (Fashion Object), MDes Surface Pattern Design (Maker), MDes Surface Pattern Design (Textiles for Fashion), MDes Surface Pattern Design (Textiles for Interiors), MDes Surface Pattern Design (Fashion Object); Postgraduate courses: MA textiles (Contemporary Dialogues), MA Surface Pattern Design

Faculty of Business and Management; www.uwtsd.ac.uk/business-management/

Swansea Business School

BA(Hons) Accounting, BA(Hons) Business and Finance, BA(Hons) Business Management, BA(Hons) Human Resource Management, BA(Hons) International Business, BA(Hons) Marketing Management, BA(Hons) Law and Business, HND Business Management, HND Business and Finance, Fda Business and Finance; Postgraduate courses: MBA, E-MBA, MSc Financial Management, MA Human Resource Management, MSc Trading and Financial Markets, CIPD Postgraduate Diploma in Human Resource Management, CIPD Intermediate Certificate in Human Resource Management, CIM Postgraduate Diploma in Marketing

Carmarthen Business School

BA Business and Management, BA Rural Enterprise Management, BA Cultural Industries Management; Postgraduate courses: MBA General Management,, MA Technology Enhanced Learning

Sport, Health and Outdoor Education: Carmethen

BSc Sport and Exercise Science, BSc Sport and Exercise Science (Sports Nutrition), BSc Sport and Exercise Science (Personal Training), BSc Sport and Exercise Science (Outdoor Fitness), BSc Sport and Exercise Science (Clinical Exercise Physiology), BSc Sport Therapy, BSc Public Health, BSc Health, Nutrition and Lifestyle, BA Outdoor Adventure Education, BA Physical Education, Dip HE Nursing Studies and Health; MA Outdoor Education, MA Physical Education

Sport, Health and Public Services: Swansea

BA Public Services I HND Public Services, BSc Policing, BSc Policing & Criminology, BA Law & Business, BA Law & Public Services, BA Law & Criminology, BA Law & Policing, BSc Health and Social Care, HND Health and Social Care, BSc Health Management, HND Health Management, BSc Health and Care of Children and Young People, FdSc Health and Care of Children and Young People, DipHE Nursing Studies & Health, BA International Sports Management, BA Sports Management, FDA Sports Management, HND Sports Management, BA Stadium and Sports Facility Management, BA Watersports Management

Swansea School of Tourism & Hospitality

BA and HNDs in Events Management, International Travel and Tourism Management, Leisure Management, Tourism Management, International Hotel Management; Postgraduate courses in MA International Tourism Management

Faculty of Education and Communities; www.uwtsd.ac.uk/education-and-communities/

School of Early Years

Foundation Degree Early Childhood, BA Early Years Education & Care, BA Early Years Education & Care – 2 Years, BA Early Years Education & Care (Early Years Practitioner), BA Early Years Education & Care (Early Years Practitioner) – 2 Years, Integrated Masters Early Years Education & Care, Integrated Masters Early Years Education & Care (Early Years Practitioner); Postgraduate courses: MA/Postgraduate Diploma Early Years Education & Care

School of Psychology

BSc Applied Psychology, BSc Psychology (BPS accredited), BA Counselling Studies and Psychology (BPS accredited), BA Education Studies and Psychology (BPS accredited), BSc Mental Health, MSc Applied Social and Health Psychology

School of Social Justice and Inclusion

Carmarthen: Certificate of Higher Education in Advocacy, Certificate of Higher Education in Playwork, Certificate of Higher Education Young Peoples Health and Wellbeing, Certificate of Higher Education Health and Wellbeing for Carers, Certificate of Higher Education Workplace Health and Wellbeing, Foundation Degree Inclusive Education, BA Social Studies: Additional Needs, BA Social Studies: Advocacy, BA Social Studies: Communities, Families and Individuals, BA Social Studies: Health and Social Care, BA Youth and Community Work, BA Gwaith Ieuenctid a Chymuned, BA Education Studies: Primary, BA Astudiaethau Addysg Gynradd; Postgraduate courses: Integrated Masters in Social Studies: Additional Needs, Integrated Masters in Social Studies: Advocacy, Integrated Masters in Social Studies: Communities, Families and Individuals, Integrated Masters in Social Studies: Health and Social Care, MA Youth Work, MA Equality and Diversity in Society, Graduate Certificate in Additional Learning Needs; Swansea: BA Counselling Skill and Interdisciplinary Studies, BA Counselling Studies and Psychology, BA Humanistic Counselling,

Integrated Masters in Humanistic Counselling, Graduate Certificate in Counselling Skills, MA Psychotherapeutic Practice: Emotion-Focused Therapy, Foundation Degree in Inclusive Education, BA Education Studies, BA Education Studies: Additional Learning Needs & Inclusion, BA Education Studies: Contemporary Learners & Learning, BA Education Studies: International Perspectives, BA Humanities with Education Studies

SWW Centre of Teacher Education

BA Primary Education with QTS, BA Addysg Gynradd gyda SAC, PGCE Primary with QTS, PGCE Secondary Art & Design with QTS, PGCE Secondary Computing and ICT with QTS, PGCE Secondary Business Studies with QTS, PGCE Secondary Maths 11-18 with QTS, PGCE Secondary Maths 11-16 with ICT and QTS, PGCE Secondary Biology with QTS, PGCE Secondary Design and Technology with QTS, PGCE Secondary Geography with QTS, PGCE Secondary Physics with QTS, PGCE Secondary Science 11-16 with QTS, PGCE Secondary English with QTS, PGCE Secondary History with QTS, PGCE Secondary Modern Foreign Languages with QTS, PGCE Secondary Religious Education with QTS, PGCE Secondary Welsh with QTS, PGCE Secondary Chemistry with QTS

Faculty of Humanities & Performing Arts; www.uwtsd.ac.uk/faculty-of-humanities-performingarts

Anthropology

BA Anthropology, BA Applied Anthropology, BA Archaeology and Anthropology

School of Archaeology

History and Anthropology BA Anthropology with Applied Psychology, BA Anthropology with Education Studies, BA Anthropology with Heritage Management; Postgraduate courses: MA Cultural Astronomy and Astrology, MA Ecology and Spirituality, MA Engaged Anthropology, MRes Anthropology, MRes Cultural Astronomy and Astrology

Ancient World

BA Ancient and Medieval History, BA Ancient Civilisations, BA Ancient History, BA Ancient History and Archaeology, BA Ancient History with Ancient Egyptian Culture, BA Ancient History with Ancient Egyptian Culture, BA Ancient History with Ancient Egyptian Culture, BA Ancient History with Education Studies, BA Ancient History with Heritage Management, BA Ancient History with Latin, BA

Ancient History, Anthropology, Education Studies, BA Ancient History, Archaeology, Education Studies, BA Ancient History, Classical Studies, Education Studies, BA Ancient History, History, Education Studies, BA Ancient History, Religious Studies, Education Studies, BA Classical Civilisation, BA Classical Civilisation, BA Classical Studies, BA Classical Studies with Ancient Egyptian Culture, BA Classical Studies with Ancient Egyptian Culture, BA Classical Studies with Ancient Egyptian Culture, BA Classical Studies with Greek, BA Classical Studies with Heritage Management, BA Classical Studies with Latin, BA Classical Studies, Ancient History, Education Studies, BA Classical Studies, Anthropology, Education Studies, BA Classical Studies, Archaeology, Education Studies, BA Classical Studies, English, Education Studies, BA Classical Studies, History, Education Studies, BA Classical Studies, Religious Studies, Education Studies, BA Classics, BA Conflict and War; Postgraduate courses: MA Ancient History, MA Ancient Religions, MA Classical Studies, MA Classics, MRes Ancient History, MRes Classical Studies

Performing Arts

BA(Hons) Acting, BA(Hons) Dance, BA(Hons) Theatre Design and Production, BA(Hons) Applied Drama, BA(Hons) Performing Arts (Contemporary Performance), BA Perfformio

Archaeology

BA Archaeology, BA Archaeology and Anthropology, BA Archaeology of Egypt and the Near East, BA Archaeology Professional Practice, BA Nautical Archaeology, BA Environmental Archaeology, MArts Archaeology, BA Archaeology with Ancient Egyptian Culture, BA Archaeology with Education Studies, BA Archaeology with Forensic Studies, BA Archaeology with Heritage Management; Postgraduate courses: MA Landscape Management and Environmental Archaeology, MRes Landscape and Environmental Archaeology

Chinese Studies

BA Chinese Studies, BA Chinese Civilisation and Anthropology, BA Chinese Civilisation and English, BA Chinese Civilisation and Medieval Studies, BA Chinese Civilisation and Philosophy, BA Chinese Civilisation and Religious Studies

English & Creative Writing

BA English, BA Creative Writing; Postgraduate courses: MA Creative and Script Writing, MA Creative Writing, MA Modern Literature, MA Medieval and Early Modern Literature, MRes Contemporary Literature, MRes Early Modern Literature, MRes Medieval Literature

Environment & Ecology

BA Philosophy, Politics and Economics, BA Political Ecology, BA Political Ecology with Humanitarianism and Law

Heritage

BA Heritage Studies, BA Heritage Studies with Museums & Archives, BA Heritage Studies with Nautical Archaeology; Postgraduate courses: MA Heritage Practice, MA Heritage Tourism

International Development, Humanitarianism & Law

BA International Development, Humanitarianism and Law

Modern History & Medieval Studies

BA Ancient and Medieval History, BA Celtic Studies, BA Chinese Civilisation and Medieval Studies, BA Chinese Studies and Medieval Studies, BA History, BA History and Ancient History, BA History and Anthropology, BA History and Archaeology, BA History and English, BA History and Theology, BA History with Education Studies, BA Medieval Studies, BA Medieval Studies and Anthropology, BA Medieval Studies and Archaeology, BA Medieval Studies and Classical Studies, BA Medieval Studies and English, BA Medieval Studies and History, BA Medieval Studies and History, BA Medieval Studies and Modern Historical Studies, BA Medieval Studies and Modern Historical Studies, BA Medieval Studies with Latin, BA Modern Historical Studies, BA Philosophy and History, BA Philosophy and Medieval Studies, MArts History; Postgraduate courses: MA Heritage Practice, MA Local History, MA Medieval Studies, MRes Heritage Practice, MRes Medieval Studies

Philosophy

BA Philosophy, BA Ethical and Political Studies, MArts Philosophical Studies; Postgraduate courses: MA Ecology and Spirituality, MA Philosophy, MA Philosophy and Religion: Eastern and Western Thought, Master of Philosophy (MPhil), MRes Philosophy

Politics & Economics

BA Philosophy, Politics and Economics

Religion

Carmarthen: BA Religious Studies, BA Astudiaethau Crefyddol, BA Religious Studies and Islamic Studies;

Lampeter: BA Religious Studies, MArts Religious Studies, MArts Theology

The School of Performing Arts, BA Theology and Classical Studies, BA Theology and History, BA Theology and Philosophy, BA Theology and Heritage Studies, BA Theology with Heritage Management, BA Theology with Education Studies; Postgraduate courses: MA Biblical Interpretation, MA Islamic Studies, MA Study of Religions, MTh Christian Theology, MTh Church History, MRes Biblical Interpretation, MRes Islamic Studies, MRes Religious Experience, MRes Study of Religions; MPhil/PhD

Welsh International Academy of Voice
MA in Advanced Vocal Studies, Post Graduate Diploma in Advanced Pianoforte Studies

UNIVERSITY OF WARWICK
www.warwick.ac.uk

Centre for Applied Linguistics
Undergraduate degrees in English Language and Linguistics, Language, Culture and Communication with Year Abroad, Linguistics with Arabic, Linguistics with Chinese, Linguistics with French, Linguistics with German, Linguistics with Italian, Linguistics with Japanese, Linguistics with Portuguese, Linguistics with Russian, Linguistics with Spanish ; Postgraduate courses: MRes Applied Linguistics, MPhil/PhD in Discourse Studies, MPhil/PhD in Intercultural Communication, MPhil/PhD in English Language Teaching, MPhil/PhD in English Language teaching and Applied Linguistics

Warwick Business School
Undergraduate degrees in Accounting and Finance, Accounting and Finance (with foundation year), Digital Innovation and Entrepreneurship, International Business with French, International Business with German, International Business with Italian, International Business with Spanish, International Management, Management, Management (with foundation year); Postgraduate courses: DBA, MPhil/PhD in Business and Management, Finance and Econometrics

Department of Chemistry
Undergraduate degrees in Chemistry, Chemistry (MChem), Chemistry with Medicinal Chemistry, Chemistry with Medicinal Chemistry (MChem)/ (MBio), Chemistry with Industrial Placement (MChem), Chemistry with International Placement (MChem); Postgraduate courses: MSc in Chemistry, PhD in Chemistry, PhD in Chemistry with Industrial Collaboration

Department of Classics and Ancient History
Undergraduate degrees in Ancient History and Classical Archaeology, Ancient History and Classical Archaeology with Study in Europe, Classical Civilisation, Classical Civilisation with Philosophy, Classical Civilisation with Study in Europe, Classics, Classics (Ancient Greek) with Study in Europe, Classics (Latin) with Study in Europe, Classics and English; Postgraduate courses: MRes in Classics and Ancient history, MPhil in Classics and Ancient History, PhD in Classics and Ancient History

Department of Computer Science
Undergraduate degrees in Computer Science, Computer Science (MEng), Computer and Management Sciences, Computer Systems Engineering, Computer Systems Engineering (MEng), Discrete Mathematics, Discrete Mathematics (MEng); Postgraduate courses: MSc Computer Science, PhD Computer Science, PhD Urban Science

Department of Economics
Undergraduate degrees in Economics, Economics and Industrial Organization, Economics, Politics and International Studies; Postgraduate courses: MRes/PhD Economics

Centre for Education Studies
Undergraduate course in Education Studies

School of Engineering
Undergraduate degrees Automotive Engineering (BEng), Automotive Engineering (MEng), Civil Engineering (BEng), Civil Engineering (MEng), Electrical and Electronic Engineering (BEng), Electrical and Electronic Engineering (MEng), Electronic Engineering (BEng), Electronic Engineering (MEng),

Engineering (BEng), Engineering (MEng), Engineering and Business Studies (BSc), Engineering Business Management (BEng), Manufacturing and Mechanical Engineering (BEng), Manufacturing and Mechanical Engineering (MEng), Mechanical Engineering (BEng), Mechanical Engineering (MEng); Postgraduate courses: MPhil/PhD in Engineering, EngD/EngD(Int) Engineering

Department of English and Comparative Literary Studies

Undergraduate degrees in English Literature, English Literature and Creative Writing, English and Theatre Studies (QW34), English and History; Postgraduate courses: MPhil/PhD in English and Comparative Literary Studies, MPhil/PhD in Translation Studies, MPhil/PhD Writing

Department of Film and Television Studies

Undergraduate degrees in Film Studies, Film and Literature; Postgraduate courses: MPhil/PhD in Film and/or Television Studies

Department of Global Sustainable Development

Undergraduate degrees in Global Sustainable Development, Economic Studies and Global Sustainable Development, Global Sustainable Development and Business Studies, History and Global Sustainable Development, Life Sciences and Global Sustainable Development, Philosophy and Global Sustainable Development, Politics, International Studies and Global Sustainable Development, Psychology and Global Sustainable Development, Sociology and Global Sustainable Development, Theatre and Performance Studies and Global Sustainable Development

Department of History

Undergraduate degrees in History, History and Philosophy, History and Politics, History and Sociology; Postgraduate courses: MPhil/PhD History

Department of History of Art

Undergraduate degrees in History of Art, History of Art with Italian; Postgraduate courses: MA History of Art, MPhil History of Art, PhD History of Art

School of Law

Undergraduate degrees in Law (3 years), Law (4 years), Law (4 years – Study Abroad in English), Law and Business Studies, Law and Sociology (4 years), Law with French Law (4 years), Law with German Law (4 years), Law with Humanities, Law with Social Sciences; Postgraduate courses: MPhil/PhD Law, LLM

Department of Liberal Arts

Undergraduate degree in Liberal Arts

School of Life Sciences

Undergraduate degrees in Biochemistry, Biochemistry (MBio), Biological Sciences, Biological Sciences (MBio), Biomedical Science, Biomedical Science (MBio); Postgraduate courses: MSc Biological Sciences, PhD Biological Sciences, PhD Synthetic Biology

Warwick Mathematics Institute

Mathematics (BSc), Mathematics (MMath); Postgraduate courses: PhD/MPhils in Mathematics, Statistics

Warwick Medical School

MD Doctor of Medicine, PhDs in Health Science, Medical Sciences, Clinical Education, medicine, Interdisciplinary Biomedical Research, Nursing, PhD by published work

School of Modern Languages and Cultures

Undergraduate degrees in Modern Languages (BA), Modern Languages and Economics, Modern Languages and Linguistics, Modern Languages with Linguistics, French Studies, German Studies, Italian Studies, Spanish Studies; Postgraduate courses: MA/MPhil/PhD in French, German, Hispanic and Italian studies

MORSE

Undergraduate degrees in MMORSE (Mathematics, Operational Research, Statistics and Economics), MORSE (Mathematics, Operational Research, Statistics and Economics)

Department of Philosophy

Undergraduate degrees in Philosophy (V500), Philosophy and Literature, Philosophy with Classical Civilisation, Philosophy with Psychology,

Mathematics and Philosophy; Postgraduate courses: MA/MPhil/PhD in Philosophy

Department of Philosophy, Politics and Economics

Undergraduate degree in Philosophy, Politics and Economics

Department of Physics

Undergraduate degrees in Physics, Physics (MPhys), Physics and Business Studies, Mathematics and Physics, Mathematics and Physics (MPhys); Postgraduate courses: MPhil/PhD in Physics

Department of Politics and International Studies

Undergraduate degrees in Politics, Politics and International Studies, Politics, International Studies and French, Politics, International Studies and German, Politic, International Studies and Hispanic Studies, Politics, International Studies and Italian, Politics, International Studies and Quantitative Methods, Politics and Sociology, Politics and International Studies with Chinese: Postgraduate courses: PhD in Politics and International Studies

Department of Psychology

Undergraduate degrees in Psychology, Psychology with Linguistics; Postgraduate courses: MSc/MPhil/PhD in Psychology

Department of Sociology

Undergraduate degrees in Sociology, Sociology and Quantitative Methods; Postgraduate courses: PhD in Sociology, Women€™s and Gender Studies

Department of Statistics

Undergraduate degrees in Data Science, Mathematics and Statistics, Mathematics and Statistics (MMathStat); Postgraduate courses: PhD/MPhil in Statistics, Mathematics and Statistics

School of Theatre and performance Studies

Undergraduate degree in Theatre and Performance Studies; Postgraduate courses: MA/MPhil/PhD in Theatre and Performance Studies

The Yesu Persaud Centre for Caribbean Studies

MRes in Caribbean Studies, MPhil/PhD in Caribbean Studies

UNIVERSITY OF WEST OF SCOTLAND
www.uws.ac.uk

School of Business and Enterprise; www.uws.ac.uk/schools/business-school/

BAcc & BAcc(Hons) Accounting, BA & BA(Hons) Business, BA Business & English Language (3rd Year Entry), BA & BA(Hons) Business & Finance, BA & BA(Hons) Business & Human Resource Management, BA & BA(Hons) Business & Marketing, CertHE Business with English, CertHE Business with English Language (London), BA & BA(Hons) Events Management, BA & BA(Hons) Human Resource Management, BA & BA(Hons) International Business (Accelerated), BA & BA(Hons) Law, BA & BA(Hons) Law & Business, BA & BA(Hons) Legal Studies, BA & BA(Hons) Marketing, BA & BA(Hons) Tourism Management (3rd Year Entry); Postgraduate courses: MSc Accounting, MSc Digital Marketing, Doctor of Business Administration, MSc Finance and Accounting with CIMA MSc Financial Accounting, MSc Human Resource Management, MSc International Events Management, MSc International Management, MSc International Marketing Management, MSc Logistics and Supply Chain, MSc Management Accounting, Master of Business Administration

School of Education; www.uws.ac.uk/schools/school-of-education/courses/

BA Childhood Practice (PT), BA & BA(Hons) Childhood Studies (2nd year entry), BA & BA(Hons) Community Education, BA & BA(Hons) Education, BA & BA(Hons) English as a Second Language (3rd or 4th year entry); Postgraduate courses: MEd Artist Teacher, Postgraduate Cert. Child Protection, Graduate Dip. Childhood Practice, Postgraduate Cert. Coaching and Mentoring, MSc Critical Youth and Community Studies, MEd Early years, MEd Enhanced Educational Practice, MEd Higher Education Practice, MSc Inclusive Education, MEd Leadership for Learning, MSc Mental Health and Education, Postgraduate Cert. Primary Physical Education, Professional Graduate Dup. in education (Secondary), MEd Teaching of English to Speakers of other Languages (TESOL)

School of Engineering and Computing; www.uws.ac.uk/schools/school-of-engineering-and-computing/

BEng & BEng(Hons) Aircraft Engineering, BSc & BSc(Hons) Business Technology, BEng & BEng(Hons) Chemical Engineering, BEng & BEng(Hons) Civil Engineering, BSc & BSc(Hons) Computer Animation Arts, BSc & BSc(Hons) Computer Games Development, BSc & BSc(Hons) Computer Games Technology, BSc & BSc(Hons) Computer Networking, BSc & BSc(Hons) Computer-Aided Design (3rd Year entry), BSc & BSc(Hons) Computing Science, BEng & BEng(Hons) Engineering Management (2nd Year and 3rd Year Entry), BEng & BEng(Hons) Mechanical Engineering, BSc & BSc(Hons) Music Technology, BSc & BSc(Hons) Physics, BSc & BSc(Hons) Physics with Nuclear Technology, BEng & BEng(Hons) Product Design & Development, BSc & BSc(Hons) Web and Mobile Development; Postgraduate courses: MSc Advanced Computer Systems Development, MSc Advanced Computing, MSc Advanced Film Technologies, MSc Big Data, MSc Chemical Engineering, MSc Civil Engineering, MSc Construction Management and Digital Engineering, MSc e-Health, MSc Engineering Management, MSc Information and Network Security, MSc Information Technology, MSc Internet of Things, MSc mechanical Engineering, MSc Mobile Web Development, MSc Smart Networks

School of Health, Nursing & Midwifery; www.uws.ac.uk/schools/school-of-health-nursing-and-midwifery/

BSc Adult Nursing, Certificate of Higher Education in Health and Social Care, BA & BA(Hons) Integrated Health and Social Care (2nd Year Entry), BA & BA(Hons) Integrated Health and Social Care with Administration (2nd Year Entry), BSc Mental Health Nursing, BSc Midwifery, BSc(Hons) Nursing Studies (3rd Year Entry), BSc Professional Health Studies (3rd Year Entry), BSc(Hons)Professional Health Studies (Part-Time); Postgraduate courses: MSc Advancing Practice, Postgraduate Cert. Child Protection, MSc Cognitive Behavioural Therapy, Graduate Dip. District Nurse, MSc Forensic Mental Health, MSc Gerontology, MSc Health Studies, MSc Health Studies (Family health), Graduate Cert. Health Visiting, Graduate Cert. Manging Respiratory Disorders, MSc Mental Health Nursing, MSc Mental Health Practice, MSc Midwifery, Graduate Cert. Neonatal Nursing, Graduate Dip. Occupational Health, Graduate Cert. Palliative Care, Graduate Cert. Personality Disorder, Graduate Dip. School Nursing, Graduate Cert. Sexual and Reproductive Health, Graduate Cert. Unscheduled Care, MSc Vulnerability

School of Media, Culture and Society; www.uws.ac.uk/schools/school-of-media-culture-and-society

BA & BA(Hons) Broadcast Production TV and Radio, BA & BA(Hons) Commercial Music, BA Commercial Sound Production (3rd year entry), BA & BA(Hons) Criminal Justice, BA & BA(Hons) Digital Art and Design (3rd Year Entry), BA & BA(Hons) Filmmaking and Screen Writing, BA & BA(Hons) Journalism (with option in Sport), BA & BA(Hons) Performance (3rd Year Entry), BSc & BSc(Hons) Psychology, BA & BA(Hons) Social Science, BA(Hons) Social Work, BA & BA(Hons) Society, Politics and Policy, BA & BA(Hons) Technical Theatre & Production (3rd year entry); Postgraduate courses: MA Broadcast Journalism, MA Creative Media Practice, MA Cultural Diplomacy, MA Cultural Diplomacy and International Events, MA Cultural Diplomacy and International Music and International Sport, MA Filmmaking, MA Music, Maters in Public Administration (MPA), MSc Applied Social Science, MSc Career Guidance and Development, MSc Contemporary Drug and Alcohol Studies, MSc Policy Analysis and Global Governance, MSc Psychology, MSc Social Work, Postgraduate Cert. Child Protection

School of Science and Sport; www.uws.ac.uk/schools/school-of-science/

BSc & BSc(Hons) Applied Bioscience, BSc & BSc(Hons) Applied Bioscience and Zoology, BSc & BSc(Hons) Applied Bioscience with Forensic Investigation (3rd year entry), BSc & BSc(Hons) Biomedical Science – Applied Biomedical Science, BSc & BSc(Hons) Chemistry, BSc & BSc(Hons) Environmental Health, BSc & BSc(Hons) Forensic Science, BSc & BSc(Hons) Occupational Safety and Health, BSc & BSc(Hons) Pharmacy Science and Health, BSc & BSc(Hons) Physics with Education, BSc & BSc(Hons) Sport and Exercise Science, BSc & BSc(Hons) Sport Coaching, BSc & BSc(Hons) Sport Development; Postgraduate courses: MSc Advanced Biomedical Science, MSc Biotechnology, MSc Formulation Science, MSc Project Management, MSc Project Management (International), MSc Quality Management, MSc Quality Management (International), MSc Waste and Resource Management

THE UNIVERSITY OF WESTMINSTER
www.wmin.ac.uk

Faculty of Architecture and the Built Environment; www.westminster.ac.uk/about-us/faculties/architecture-and-the-built-environment

Architecture and Interiors
Architectural Technology BSc Honours, Architecture and Environmental Design BSc Honours, Architecture BA Honours, Designing Cities: Planning and Architecture BA Honours, Interior Architecture BA Honours; Postgraduate courses: Architecture and Environmental Design MSc, Architecture MA, Interior Design MA, Master of Architecture (MArch) (RIBA pt II), Urban Design MA, Urban Design Postgraduate Diploma,

Planning, Housing and Urban Design

Planning, Housing and Urban Design
Designing Cities: Planning and Architecture BA Honours, Property and Planning BSc Honours; Postgraduate courses; Energy and Environmental Change MA, Energy and Environmental Change MA (January), International Planning and Sustainable Development MA, Urban and Regional Planning MA, Urban Design MA, Urban Design Postgraduate Diploma

Property and Construction
Architectural Technology BSc Honours, Building Engineering BSc Honours, Building Surveying BSc Honours, Construction Management BSc Honours, Property and Planning BSc Honours, Quantity Surveying and Commercial Management BSc Honours, Real Estate BSc Honours; Postgraduate courses: Building Information Management MSc, Building Information Management Postgraduate Diploma, Construction Commercial Management MSc, Construction Project Management MSc, Facilities and Property Management MSc, Property Finance MSc, Property Finance Postgraduate Diploma, Real Estate Development MSc

Tourism and Events
Tourism and Events Management BA Honours, Tourism Planning and Management BA Honours, Tourism with Business BA Honours; Postgraduate courses: Events and Conference Management MA, Tourism Management MA; PhD and MPhil study

Transport and Logistics
Air Transport Planning and Management MSc, Air Transport Planning and Management MSc (January), Logistics and Supply Chain Management MSc, Transport Planning and Management MSc

Westminster School of Media Arts and Design; www.westminster.ac.uk/about-us/faculties/westminster-school-of-media-arts-and-design

Art and Design
Animation BA Honours, Animation BA Honours, Fine Art Mixed Media BA Honours, Fine Art Mixed Media BA Honours, Graphic Communication Design BA Honours, Graphic Communication Design BA Honours, Illustration and Visual Communication BA Honours, Illustration and Visual Communication BA Honours; Postgraduate courses: Creative Practice MRes, Design for Communication MA, Interactive Media Practice MA,

Fashion
Fashion Buying Management BA Honours, Fashion Buying Management BA Honours, Fashion Design BA Honours, Fashion Design BA Honours, Fashion Marketing and Promotion BA Honours, Fashion Marketing and Promotion BA Honours, Fashion Merchandise Management BA Honours, Fashion Merchandise Management BA Honours; Postgraduate courses: Fashion Business Management MA, Menswear MA

Journalism and Mass Communication
Digital Media and Communication BA Honours, Digital Media and Communication BA Honours; Postgraduate courses: Communication MA, Communication Policy MA, Digital and Interactive Storytelling LAB MA, Diversity and the Media MA, Global Media Business MA, Global Media MA, International Media Business MA, Media and Development MA, Media Management MA, Media, Campaigning and Social Change MA, Media, Campaigning and Social Change PG Diploma, Multimedia Journalism (Broadcast) MA, Multimedia Journalism (Broadcast) PG Diploma, Multimedia Journalism (Print & Online) MA, Multimedia Journalism (Print & Online) PG Diploma, Public Relations MA, Social Media, Culture and Society MA

Commercial Music

Commercial Music BA Honours, Commercial Music BA Honours, Commercial Music Performance BMus Honours, Commercial Music Performance BMus Honours; Postgraduate courses: Audio Production MA, Music Business Management MA

Photography

Contemporary Media Practice BA Honours, Contemporary Media Practice BA Honours, Photography BA Honours, Photography BA Honours, Photography BA Honours, Photography BA Honours; Postgraduate courses: Documentary Photography and Photojournalism MA, Photography Arts MA

Television, Film and Moving Image

Contemporary Media Practice BA Honours, Contemporary Media Practice BA Honours, Film BA Honours, Film BA Honours, Television Production BA Honours, Television Production BA Honours

Faculty of Science and Technology; www.westminster.ac.uk/about-us/ faculties/science-and-technology

Biomedical Sciences

Biomedical Sciences BSc Honours, Biomedical Sciences with Foundation BSc Honours; Postgraduate courses: Biomedical Sciences (Cancer Biology) MSc, Biomedical Sciences (Cellular Pathology) MSc, Biomedical Sciences (Clinical Biochemistry) MSc, Biomedical Sciences (Haematology) MSc, Biomedical Sciences (Immunology) MSc, Biomedical Sciences (Medical Microbiology) MSc, Biomedical Sciences (Medical Molecular Biology) MSc, Biomedical Sciences MSc; PhD, MPhil, DProf and MRes study

Biosciences

Biochemistry BSc Honours, Biochemistry with Foundation BSc Honours, Biological Sciences BSc Honours, Biological Sciences with Foundation BSc Honours, Pharmacology & Physiology BSc Honours, Pharmacology and Physiology with Foundation BSc Honours; Postgraduate courses: Applied Biotechnology MSc; PhD, MPhil, DProf and MRes study

Business Information Systems

Business Information Systems BSc Honours, Business Information Systems with Foundation BSc Honours, Digital Media Development BSc Honours; Postgraduate courses: Business Intelligence and Analytics MSc, Business Systems Design and Integration MSc, Big Data Technologies MSc; PhD, MPhil, DProf and MRes study

Complementary Medicine

Chinese Medicine Acupuncture BSc Honours, Chinese Medicine Acupuncture with Foundation BSc Honours, Herbal Medicine BSc Honours, Herbal Medicine with Foundation BSc Honours; Postgraduate courses: Chinese Herbal Medicine MSc; PhD, MPhil, DProf and MRes study

Computer and Network Engineering

computer network security/with foundation; computer networks and communications/with foundation; computer systems and robotics/with foundation; computer systems engineering/with foundation; Postgrad: computer networks and communications; computer networks with cloud technologies/with security; BSc(Hons), DProf, MSc, MPhil, MRes, PhD

Computer Science and Software Engineering

Computer Network Security BSc Honours, Computer Network Security with Foundation BSc Honours, Computer Networks and Communications BSc Honours, Computer Systems and Robotics BEng Honours, Computer Systems Engineering BSc Honours, Computer Systems Engineering with Foundation BSc Honours; Postgraduate courses: Computer Networks with Cloud Technologies MSc, Computer Networks with Communications MSc, Computer Networks with Security MSc; PhD, MPhil, DProf and MRes study

Electronic Engineering

Biomedical Electronic and Instrumentation Engineering BSc Honours, Electronic & Electrical Engineering BEng Honours, Electronic Engineering BEng Honours, Electronic Engineering BSc Honours; Postgraduate courses: Electrical Engineering for Modern Sustainable Transport Systems MSc, Electronics with Embedded Systems MSc, Electronics with Medical Instrumentation MSc, Electronics with Robotic and Control Systems MSc, Electronics with System-on-Chip Technologies MSc, Telecommunications with Digital Signal Processing MSc, Telecommunications with Satellite and Broadband Technologies MSc, Telecommunications with Wireless Technologies MSc; PhD, MPhil, DProf and MRes study

Multimedia and Games Computing

Computer Games Development BSc Honours, Computer Games Development with Foundation BSc Honours, Digital Media Development BSc Honours, Digital Media Development with Foundation BSc Honours; Postgraduate courses: Interaction Design and Computing MSc, Interactive Media Practice MA; PhD, MPhil, DProf and MRes study

Nutrition
Human Nutrition BSc Honours, Human Nutrition with Foundation BSc Honours; Postgraduate courses: Global Public Health Nutrition MSc, Sport and Exercise Nutrition MSc; PhD, MPhil, DProf and MRes study

Psychology
Cognitive and Clinical Neuroscience BSc Honours, Psychology and Counselling BSc Honours, Psychology BSc Honours; Postgraduate courses: Business Psychology MSc, Health Psychology MSc, Psychology MSc; PhD, MPhil, DProf and MRes study

Faculty of Social Sciences and Humanities; www.westminster.ac.uk/ about-us/faculties/social-sciences-and-humanities

Criminology
Criminology BA Honours, Sociology and Criminology BA Honours; Postgraduate courses: PhD, MPhil, DProf and MRes study

English
Arabic and English Language BA Honours, Arabic and English Literature BA Honours, Chinese and English Language BA Honours, Chinese and English Literature BA Honours, Creative Writing and English Language BA Honours, Creative Writing and English Literature BA Honours, English Language and Linguistics BA Honours, English Literature and History BA Honours, English Literature and Language BA Honours, English Literature BA Honours, French and English Language BA Honours, French and English Literature BA Honours, Spanish and English Language BA Honours, Spanish and English Literature BA Honours; Postgraduate courses: Creative Writing: Writing the City MA, Creative Writing: Writing the City MA (January), Cultural and Critical Studies MA, Cultural and Critical Studies MA (January), English Language and Linguistics MA, English Language and Linguistics MA (January), English Language and Literature MA (January), English Language and Literature MA, English Literature: Modern and Contemporary Fictions MA, English Literature: Modern and Contemporary Fictions MA (January), Teaching English to Speakers of Other Languages MA (January), Teaching English to Speakers of Other Languages MA; PhD, MPhil, DProf and MRes study

History
English Literature and History BA Honours, History and Politics BA Honours, History BA Honours; PhD, MPhil, DProf and MRes study

Languages
Arabic and English Language BA Honours, Arabic and English Literature BA Honours, Arabic and International Relations BA Honours, Arabic and Linguistics BA Honours, Chinese and English Language BA Honours, Chinese and English Literature BA Honours, Chinese and International Relations BA Honours, Chinese and Linguistics BA Honours, French and English Language BA Honours, French and English Literature BA Honours, French and International Relations BA Honours, French and Linguistics BA Honours, French and Spanish BA Honours, Modern Languages: Arabic and Global Communication BA Honours, Modern Languages: Chinese and Global Communication BA Honours, Modern Languages: French and Global Communication BA Honours, Modern Languages: Spanish and Global Communication BA Honours, Spanish and English Language BA Honours, Spanish and English Literature BA Honours, Spanish and International Relations BA Honours, Spanish and Linguistics BA Honours, Translation Studies (French) BA Honours, Translation Studies (Spanish) BA Honours; Postgraduate courses: International Liaison and Communication MA, International Liaison and Communication MA (January), Specialised Translation MA, Translating Cultures MRes, Translation and Interpreting MA (January), Translation and Interpreting MA; PhD, MPhil, DProf and MRes study

Law
European Legal Studies LLB Honours, Law LLB Honours, Law with French Law LLB Honours, M-Law (Integrated Masters of Law); Postgraduate courses: Conflict Prevention, Dispute Resolution MA, Conflict Prevention, Dispute Resolution MA (January), Corporate Finance Law LLM, Corporate Finance Law LLM (January), Energy and Environmental Change MA, Energy and Environmental Change MA (January), Entertainment Law LLM (January), Entertainment Law LLM, Graduate Diploma in Law, International and Commercial Dispute Resolution Law LLM, International and Commercial Dispute Resolution Law LLM (January), International Commercial Law LLM (January), International Commercial Law LLM, International Law LLM, International Law LLM (January), Legal Practice LLM, Religion, Law and Society MA/LLM

Linguistics

Arabic and Linguistics BA Honours, Chinese and Linguistics BA Honours, English Language and Linguistics BA Honours, French and Linguistics BA Honours, Spanish and Linguistics BA Honours; Postgraduate courses: Teaching English to Speakers of Other Languages MA, Teaching English to Speakers of Other Languages MA (January); PhD, MPhil, DProf and MRes study

Politics and International Relations

Arabic and International Relations BA Honours, Chinese and International Relations BA Honours, French and International Relations BA Honours, History and Politics BA Honours, International Relations and Development BA Honours, International Relations BA Honours, Politics and International Relations BA Honours, Politics BA Honours, Spanish and International Relations BA Honours; Postgraduate courses: Energy and Environmental Change MA (January), Energy and Environmental Change MA, International Relations and Democratic Politics MA (January), International Relations and Democratic Politics MA, International Relations and Security MA (January), International Relations and Security MA, International Relations MA (January), International Relations MA; PhD, MPhil, DProf and MRes study

Sociology

Sociology and Criminology BA Honours, Sociology BA Honours; PhD, MPhil, DProf and MRes study

Visual Culture

Art and Visual Culture MA, Art and Visual Culture MA (January), Cultural and Critical Studies MA, Cultural and Critical Studies MA (January), Museums, Galleries and Contemporary Culture MA, Museums, Galleries and Contemporary Culture MA (January); PhD, MPhil, DProf and MRes study

Westminster Business School;
www.westminster.ac.uk/about-us/
faculties/westminster-business-school

Accounting, Finance and Economics

Accounting BSc Honours, Business Economics BSc Honours, Business Management (Accounting) BA Honours, Business Management (Economics) BA Honours, Business Management (Finance) BA Honours, Finance BSc Honours; Postgraduate courses: Finance and Accounting MSc, Finance and Accounting MSc (January), Finance, Banking and Insurance MSc, Global Finance MSc, International Economic

Policy & Analysis MSc, Investment and Risk Finance MSc (January), Investment and Risk Finance MSc; PhD, MPhil, DProf and MRes study

Business and Management

Business Management (Accounting) BA Honours, Business Management (Economics) BA Honours, Business Management (Entrepreneurship) BA Honours, Business Management (Finance) BA Honours, Business Management (Human Resource Management) BA Honours, Business Management (Marketing) BA Honours, Business Management BA Honours, Entrepreneurship BA Honours, Human Resource Management BA Honours, International Business (Arabic) BA Honours, International Business (Chinese) BA Honours, International Business (French) BA Honours, International Business (Spanish) BA Honours, International Business BA Honours, International Marketing BA Honours, Marketing Communications BA Honours, Marketing Management BA Honours; Postgraduate courses: Entrepreneurship, Innovation and Enterprise Development MSc, Human Resource Management MA, Human Resource Management MA (January), International Business and Management MA/MSc, International Business and Management MA/MSc (January), International Development Management MSc, International Human Resource Management MA, Management MA (January), Management MA, Marketing Communications MA, Marketing Communications MA (January), Marketing Management MA/MSc, Marketing Management MA/MSc (January), Master of Business Administration (MBA), Project Management MSc, Purchasing and Supply Chain Management MSc, Purchasing and Supply Chain Management MSc (January); PhD, MPhil, DProf and MRes study

Human Resource Management

Business Management (Human Resource Management) BA Honours, Human Resource Management BA Honours; Postgraduate courses: Human Resource Management MA, Human Resource Management MA (January), International Human Resource Management MA; PhD, MPhil, DProf and MRes study

Marketing

Business Management (Marketing) BA Honours, International Marketing BA Honours, Marketing Communications BA Honours, Marketing Management BA Honours; Postgraduate courses: Marketing Communications MA, Marketing Communications MA (January), Marketing Management MA/MSc,

Marketing Management MA/MSc; PhD, MPhil, DProf and MRes study

Education

Higher Education Postgraduate Certificate, Higher Education Postgraduate Certificate (January), Special Study in Supporting Learning University Certificate (January), Special Study in Supporting Learning University Certificate

Westminster Law School; www.westminster.ac.uk/about-us/ faculties/law

Law

See entry for Faculty of Social Sciences and Humanities.

THE UNIVERSITY OF WINCHESTER
www.winchester.ac.uk

Faculty of Arts; www.winchester.ac.uk/ aboutus/Universitystructure/arts/Pages/ faculty_of_arts.aspx

English, Creative Writing and American Studies

BA(Hons) American Studies, BA(Hons) American Studies & Politics, BA(Hons) American Studies & History BA(Hons) Creative Writing, BA(Hons) English Literature, BA(Hons) English Language Studies, BA(Hons) English with American Literature, BSc(Hons) English Linguistics with Forensic Linguistics (with optional sandwich year) (subject to validation), Postgraduate courses: MA Creative and Critical Writing,, MA Writing for Children, MA English Literature

Performing Arts

BA(Hons) Choreography and Dance, BA(Hons) Comedy Performance and Production, BA(Hons) Drama, BA(Hons) Musical Theatre, BA(Hons) Performing Arts, BA(Hons) Theatre for Children and Young People, BA(Hons) Theatre Production (Arts and Stage Management), Postgraduate courses: MA Cultural and Arts Management, Doctor of Creative Arts (Performing Arts)

School of Media and Film

BA Broadcast Television and Media Production, BA Creative Screen Production, BA Film and American Studies, BA Film Production, BA Film Studies, BA Film Studies and Production, BA Film Studies and Screenwriting, BA Journalism, BA Media and Audio Communication, BA Media and Communication, BA Media, Communication and Advertising, BA Media, Communication and Journalism, BA Media, Communication and Social Media, BA Music and Sound Production

Faculty of Business, Law and Sport; www.winchester.ac.uk/aboutus/ Universitystructure/BLS/Pages/ FacultyofBusiness/LawandSport.aspx

Winchester Business School

FdA Business Management for Information Technology, BA(Hons) Fashion: Media and Marketing, BA(Hons) Accounting and Finance, BA(Hons) Accounting and Management, BA(Hons) Business Management (top up), BA(Hons) Business Management for Information Technology, BA(Hons) Business Management with Enterprise and Innovation, BA(Hons) Business Management, BA(Hons) Event Management, BA(Hons) Marketing, BSc(Hons) Information Systems Management, FdSc Information Systems Management, MAcc(Hons) Accounting and Finance, MAcc(Hons) Accounting and Management; Postgraduate courses: MSc Project Management, (DBA) Doctor of Business Administration, Executive MBA, MA Applied Global Practice (Management), MSc Accounting and Finance, MSc Applied Global Practice (Management), MSc Insight Management, MSc International Business, MSc Marketing Innovation

Law

LLB(Hons) Law, BA(Hons) Law, LLM Medical Law and Ethics

Sport and Exercise

BSc Sport and Exercise Science, MSci Sport and Exercise Science, BSc Sport Psychology and Coaching, BSc Sports Coaching, BA Sports Business and Marketing, BA Sports Studies, BSc Strength, Conditioning and Fitness; Postgraduate courses: MSc Applied Sport & Exercise Science, MSc Sport and Exercise Psychology, MRes Sport and Exercise

Faculty of Education, Health and Social Care; *www.winchester.ac.uk/aboutus/ Universitystructure /BLS/Pages/ FacultyofEducation/ HealthandSocialCare.aspx*

Education Studies and Liberal Arts

BA(Hons) Education Studies, BA(Hons) Education Studies (Early Childhood), BA(Hons) Education Studies (Special and Inclusive Education), BA(Hons) Modern Liberal Arts; Postgraduate courses: MA Philosophy of Education, MA Modern Liberal Arts, MEd Stud(Hons) Education Studies, MEd Stud(-Hons) Education Studies (Early Childhood), MEd Stud(Hons) Education Studies (Special and Inclusive Education)

Teacher Development

BEd(Hons) Primary Education with Recommendation of Qualified Teacher Status 3 Years, BEd(Hons) Primary Education with Recommendation of Qualified Teacher Status 4 Years, MEd(Hons) Primary Education with Recommendation of Qualified Teacher Status 4 Years; Postgraduate courses: Doctor of Education, MA Education, Masters in Research, PGCE in Primary Education (3-7 full time and 5-11 full and part time), PGCE Secondary Religious Education, Postgraduate Early Years ITT, School Direct Route

Interprofessional Studies

BA Childhood, Youth and Community Studies, BSc Health, Community and Social Care Studies, BA Childhood Studies (top-up), BSc(Hons) Social Work; Postgraduate courses: Mid-Wessex GP Education, PGCert and MSc Delivery of Primary Health Care, MA Medical Education, MSc Social Work,

Faculty of Humanities and Social Sciences; *www.winchester.ac.uk/ aboutus/Universitystructure/HSS/ Pages/FacultyofHumanitiesand SocialSciences.aspx*

Applied Social Sciences

BA(Hons) Criminology, BA(Hons) Criminology and Sociology, BA(Hons) Forensic Studies, BSc(Hons) Geography; Postgraduate courses: MSc in Applied Criminology

Archaeology and Anthropology

BA(Hons) Anthropology, BSc(Hons) Archaeology, BA(Hons) Archaeology, BSc(Hons) Archaeological Practice, BSc(Hons) Archaeological Practice with Professional Placement, BA(Hons) History and Archaeology, BA(Hons) Ancient, Classical and Medieval Studies, BA(Hons) Classical Studies; Postgraduate courses: MA Cultural Heritage and Resource Management, MSc Human Osteology and Funerary Studies, MRes Archaeology, MRes Human Bioarchaeology

History

BA(Hons) History, BA(Hons) History and the Medieval World, BA(Hons) History and the Modern World; Postgraduate courses: MA History

Politics and Society

BA(Hons) Animal Welfare and Society, BA(Hons) Politics and Global Studies, BA(Hons) Philosophy, Politics and Economics, BA(Hons) Global History and Politics, BA(Hons) Sociology: Postgraduate course: MSc Animal Welfare Science, Ethics and Law

Psychology

BSc(Hons) Psychology (single/combined honours), BSc(Hons) Psychology and Cognition (single honours),, BSc(Hons) Psychology and Child Development (single honours), BSc(Hons) Psychological Science (single honours), BSc(Hons) Social Psychology; Postgraduate courses: MSc Forensic Psychology (BPS-accredited); MPhil and PhD study in a range of subjects

Theology, Religion and Philosophy

BA(Hons) Philosophy, Religion and Ethics, BA(Hons) Theology, Religion and Ethics, BA(Hons) Philosophy, Politics and Economics; Postgraduate courses: MA Reconciliation, MA Reconciliation and Peacebuilding

Faculty of Arts; www.wlv.ac.uk/about-us/our-schools-and-institutions/faculty of arts

Wolverhampton School of Art

applied arts; fashion and textiles; fine art; interior design; photography; product design; visual communication; visual communication (graphic design/illustration); Postgrad: design and applied arts; fine art; digital and visual communications; BA(Hons), BDes(Hons), MA, PhD

School of Humanities

English; English & deaf studies/education studies/film studies/history/philosophy; Postgrad: English; BA(Hons), MA

Creative and Professional Writing; creative and professional writing and English/film studies/media and communication studies/philosophy; BA(Hons)

English Language; English language and creative and professional writing/ linguistics/media and communication studies/media and cultural studies; BA(Hons)

Linguistics; linguistics and English language/deaf studies, linguistics and TESOL; Postgrad: language and information processing; BA(Hons), MA

Philosophy; philosophy and creative professional writing/English/film studies/law/politics/religious studies/sociology/war studies; Postgrad: human sciences; BA(Hons), MRes

Religious Studies; religious studies and education studies/history/philosophy/sociology; BA(Hons)

Cultural Heritage; cultural heritage; Postgrad: popular culture; BA(Hons), MA

School of Media

Animation, Games & Film Production; animation, computer games design, video and film production, art and design, commercial video production; BA(Hons), FdA

Broadcasting, Film & Media Studies; broadcasting and journalism, film studies, media and communication studies, media and cultural studies, film studies and philosophy, film, media and cultural studies, English and film studies, creative and professional writing and film studies, media and cultural studies and English language, media and cultural studies and sociology, film, media and communication studies, broadcast journalism, public relations;

Postgrad: contemporary media; film studies; PR & corporate communication; BA(Hons), FdA, MA

School of Performing Arts

dance; dance and drama; drama; drama and musical theatre; music; music technology, musical theatre, music technology and popular music, popular music, sound production; Postgrad: dance; dance science; music; audio technology; BA(Hons), BMus(Hons), MA, MMus, MSc

Faculty of Education, Health and Wellbeing; www.wlv.ac.uk/about-us/our-schools-and-institutes/faculty-of-education-health-and-wellbeing

Institute of Education

chemistry or computer science or mathematics with education; childhood studies; family and community studies; childhood and family studies and education studies/social policy/sociology/special educational needs, disability, inclusion; childhood studies with early years teacher status; education; education (learning education with progression); education studies; education studies and English; early years primary; early years services; primary education; special educational needs, disability, inclusion studies; special educational needs, disability, inclusion studies and education studies; supporting children in primary education; Postgrad: education; higher education and professional practice; PGCE; professional graduate certificate post-compulsory education; professional practice and lifelong education; BA(Hons), BA (PCE), BEd(Hons), BSc(Hons), CertED, PGCert, DEd, EDD, PGCE, PhD, FdA

Institute of Health Professions

developing palliative and end of life care practice; emergency practitioner (top-up); nursing (adult/children's/mental health/community health/learning disabilities); health and social care practice/top-up/restraint reduction; health and wellbeing (learning, education and progression); health studies (top-up); lymphoedema care; nursing studies fast track/top-up/subject-specific pathways (acute care/care of the older person/critical care/mental health and psychological interventions/orthopaedic care/renal care); midwifery; palliative and end-of-life care/for adults with life-limiting illness/for adults with progressive life-limiting illness; paramedic science; podiatry; special educational needs, inclusion and childhood and family studies; Postgrad: adult nursing; advanced clinical practice; advanced practice for allied health professionals (diabetology/musculoskeletal disorders); commissioning for health and social care; education for health social care and allied professionals; emergency planning, resilience and response; health and social care; health and wellbeing; health and wellbeing top-up; healthcare leadership; medical education; mental health; mental health nursing; midwifery studies; nursing; physician associate studies; return to nursing; service improvement; specialist clinical nursing; specialist community public health nursing (health visiting); BA(Hons), BNurs(Hons), BSc, BSc(Hons), MNurs, MAN, MMHN, MSc, PGCert, PGDip, ProfDoc

Institute of Psychology

psychology; psychology (counselling psychology/criminal behaviour); Postgrad: counselling psychology; forensic and investigative psychology; psychology; psychology (forensic/occupational); BSc(Hons), PGCert, MSci(Hons), PhD, ProfDoc

Institute of Public Health, Social Work & Care

health studies; health studies (top-up); health and social care; public health; social care; social care and criminology and criminal justice/deaf studies/health studies/sociology/social policy; social care (learning, education and progression); social work; social work studies; specialist social work studies; Postgrad: health and social care; health and wellbeing; master of public health; mental health practice for approved mental health professions; BSc(Hons), FD, MA/MSc, MPH, PGCert, PGDip

Institute of Sport

exercise and health; physical education; sport and exercise science; sport, culture, media and development; sport and exercise; sports coaching practice; sports coaching practice (football/martial arts); strength and conditioning; youth sport; Postgrad: sport and exercise science; BA(Hons); BSc(Hons); MRes; MSci(Hons); PhD

Faculty of Science & Engineering; www.wlv.ac.uk/about-us/our-schools-and-institutes/faculty-of-science-and-engineering

School of Architecture & Built Environment

architecture; architectural design technology; building surveying; civil engineering; civil and environmental engineering; constructional management; environmental health; geography, urban environments and climate change; infrastructure engineering management; interior architecture and property development; quantity surveying; Postgrad: building information modelling; civil engineering; civil engineering management; computer aided design for construction; construction law dispute and resolution; climate change management; construction project management; environmental management; environmental technology; BSc(Hons), BEng(Hons), MSc, PGCert

School of Biology, Chemistry & Forensic Science

Biology: animal behaviour and wildlife conservation; biochemistry; biological sciences; biotechnology; genetics and molecular biology; microbiology; molecular bioscience

Chemistry: chemistry, chemistry with secondary education (QTS)

Forensic Science: forensic science; forensic science and criminology

Postgrad: animal behaviour and wildlife conservation; molecular biology with bioinformatics, computational bioinformatics, forensic genetics and human identification, forensic mark comparison, fire scene investigation, medical biotechnology, applied microbiology and biotechnology; wildlife conservation; BSc(Hons), MSc, MSci

School of Biomedical Science & Physiology

biomedical science; healthcare science (biomedical science/physiological sciences); human biology; medical physiology and diagnostics; medical science; Postgrad: biomedical science; biomedical science (cellular pathology/clinical biochemistry/haematology)/medical microbiology); BSc(Hons), BMedSci(Hons), MSc, DMedSci

School of Engineering

aerospace engineering; automotive engineering; chemical engineering; electronic and telecommunications engineering; mechanical engineering; mechatronics engineering; motorsport engineering; Postgrad: advanced technology management;

advanced technology management – engineering analysis/manufacturing/sustainability; manufacturing engineering; BEng(Hons), MEng(Hons), MSc, PGCert

School of Mathematics & Computer Science

business intelligence; cloud computing; computer networks (top-up); computer science; computer science (games development/software engineering); computer science with secondary education (QTS); computer science (smart technologies); computer security (top-up); computing; computing games development (top-up); computing software development (top-up); cyber security; data science; industrial mathematics; mathematics; mathematics with secondary education (QTS); mathematical sciences; Postgrad: computer science; information technology; information technology management; mathematics; web and mobile application development; BSc(Hons), MSc, PGCert

School of Pharmacy

pharmaceutical science; pharmacology; pharmacy; Postgrad: pharmaceutical science (drug discovery & design/pharmacological sciences), independent prescribing; BSc(Hons), MPharm, MSc

Faculty of Social Sciences; www.wlv.ac.uk/about-us/our-schools-and-institutions/faculty-of-social-sciences

The Wolverhampton Business School

accounting & finance; business and accounting/economics/finance/HR management/marketing management; business management; business management with foundation year; event and venue management; economics; economics and politics/social policy/sociology; human resource management; international business management; international hospitality management; marketing management; tourism management; Postgrad: coaching and mentoring, finance and accounting, healthcare leadership, HR development and organisational change, HR management, innovation and entrepreneurship, international banking and finance, international business management, management, marketing, event and venue management, international hospitality management/managing PR for events and venues; Postgrad Certs, Dips: coaching and mentoring; event and venue management; healthcare leadership; HRD and organisational change; HRM; international hospitality management; leadership; management studies; marketing (CIM); medical education; MBA, BA(Hons), BSc(Hons), FdA, MA, MBA, PGCert/Dip, MSc

Wolverhampton Law School; law, accounting and law, business and law

accounting and law; business and law; HR management and law; law; law and philosophy, law and social sciences with foundation year; social policy and law; Postgrad: Chartered Institute of Legal Executives certification; common professional examination; international commercial and financial law; international corporate and financial law; law; professional practice top-up; legal practice; BA(Hons), LLB(Hons), PGDip/Cert, LLM

School of Sociology, History & Political Studies

criminal justice and sociology/social policy; criminology; criminology and criminal justice; criminology and criminal justice and law/social care/social policy/sociology; deaf studies and English/linguistics/social policy/special educational needs, disability and inclusion studies; English and history; history; history and religious/war studies; politics and history/media and communication studies/philosophy/social policy/war studies; childhood and family studies/media cultural studies/philosophy/religious studies/social care and sociology; childhood and family studies/social care and social policy; social policy and law; interpreting; interpreting with foundation year; sociology; sociology and history/politics/social policy; war studies; war studies and philosophy; Postgrad: conflict studies; military history by distance learning; history of the first world war; second world war studies, conflict, society, holocaust; BA(Hons), MA

UNIVERSITY COLLEGE WORCESTER
www.worc.ac.uk

Institute of Education; www.worc.ac.uk/discover/institute-of-education

Collaborative Working with Children, Young People & Families FdA, Diploma in Education and Training, Doctor of Education EdD, Early Childhood (Professional Practice) BA(Hons), Early Years Foundation Degree (Flexible and Distributed Learning Pathway), Early Years Foundation Degree, Early Years Initial Teacher Training, Education MA/PGDip/PGCert, Education MPhil/PhD, Education MRes, Education Studies BA(Hons), Education Studies degrees, Higher Education Practice MA/PGDip/PGCert, Integrated Working with Children & Families BA(Hons) Top-up Degree, Leading Early Years Practice PGCert, Learning Support FdA, Learning and Development from Early Years to Adolescence (0-19) FdA, Learning and Teaching in Higher Education PG Cert, MA / PG Dip / PG Cert Education (Church School Leadership), MA / PG Dip / PG Cert Education (Early Childhood), MA / PG Dip / PG Cert Education (Leadership and Management), MA / PG Dip / PG Cert Education (Leading Learning and Teaching), MA / PG Dip / PG Cert Education (Mentoring and Coaching), MA / PG Dip / PG Cert Education (Religions and Values Education), MA / PG Dip / PG Cert Education (Special and Inclusive Education), Mentoring in Early Childhood PGCert, Music Education MMusEd, National Award SENCo (NASENCO) PG Cert Education (Special Educational Needs Coordination), PGCE – Primary (QTS), PGCE – Primary Mathematics, PGCE – Primary Physical Education, PGCE – School Direct Primary, PGCE – School Direct Secondary, PGCE – Secondary, Primary Initial Teacher Education (with QTS) BA(Hons), Primary and Outdoor Education BA(Hons), Professional Practice BA(Hons) Top-up Degree, Religion, Philosophy & Values in Education BA(Hons), Special Educational Needs, Disabilities and Inclusion BA(Hons), Subject Knowledge Enhancement, Teaching and Learning FdA, University Diploma in Private Tutoring

Institute of Health & Society; www.worc.ac.uk/discover/institute-of-health-and-society.html

Advancing Practice MSc, Advocacy for Victims of Sexual Violence PGCert, Allied Health Studies MPhil/PhD, Applied Criminology BA(Hons), Applied Health & Social Science BA(Hons) Top-up Degree, Birth and Beyond BA(Hons), Birth and Beyond FdA, Business Psychology BSc(Hons), Child & Adolescent Mental Health FdSc, Child and Adolescent Mental Health BSc Hons Top-up Degree, Clinical Education MRes, Clinical Psychology BSc(Hons), Counselling FdSc, Counselling MSc, Counselling Psychology BSc(Hons), Criminology BA(Hons), Criminology MPhil/PhD, Dementia Studies Foundation Degree, Dementia Studies MPhil/PhD, Developmental Psychology BSc(Hons), Diet, Nutrition and Health MSc/PGDip/PGCert, EMDR Therapy MSc, Forensic Psychology BSc(Hons), Health Sciences BSc(Hons) Top-up Degree, Health and Social Care FdSc, Integrative Counselling BA(Hons), Integrative Counselling FdA, Mental Health FdSc, Midwifery BSc(Hons), Midwifery MPhil/PhD, Nursing BSc(Hons), Nursing MPhil/PhD, Nursing Studies BSc(Hons), Nutrition and Health Access module, Nutritional Therapy PGDip / MSc, Occupational Therapy BSc(Hons), Occupational Therapy MPhil/PhD, Occupational/Business Psychology MSc, PG Cert in Supervision, Paramedic Science BSc, Paramedic Science FdSc, Physician Associate MSc, Physiotherapy BSc(Hons), Psychology BSc(Hons), Psychology MPhil/PhD, Psychology MSc, Psychology degrees, Public Health MSc, Social Work & Social Policy MPhil/PhD, Social Work BA(Hons), Social Work MA (Subject to approval), Sport & Exercise Psychology BSc(Hons), Understanding Domestic and Sexual Violence MA

Institute of Humanities & Creative Arts; www.worc.ac.uk/discover/institute-of-humanities-and-creative-arts.html

Animation BA(Hons), Animation and Computing BA/BSc(Hons), Animation degrees, Art & Design BA(Hons), Art & Design degrees, Art and Design MPhil/PhD, Creative & Professional Writing (Joint Honours), Creative & Professional Writing degrees, Creative Digital Media BA(Hons), Creative Digital Media MPhil/PhD, Creative Digital Media degrees, Creative Media MA, Dance HND, Design MRes, Drama & Performance degrees, Drama MA, Drama and Performance BA(Hons), Drama and Performance MPhil/PhD, English Language (Joint Honours), English Language degrees, English Literature BA(Hons), English Literature and Language MPhil/PhD, English Literature degrees, Film Production BA(Hons), Film

Production degrees, Film Studies BA(Hons), Film Studies MPhil/PhD, Film Studies degrees, Fine Art BA(Hons), Fine Art degrees, Game Art BA(Hons), Game Art and Graphic Design, Graphic Design BA(Hons), Graphic Design degrees, History BA(Hons), History MPhil/PhD, Illustration BA(Hons), Illustration degrees, Journalism BA(Hons), Law LLB(Hons), Law with Criminology LLB(Hons), Law with Forensic Psychology LLB(Hons), Media & Culture BA(Hons), Media & Culture degrees, Media and Cultural Studies MPhil/PhD, Politics (Joint Honours), Screenwriting (Joint Honours), Screenwriting degrees, Sociology BA(Hons), Sociology MPhil/PhD, Sociology degrees, Touring Theatre MTheatre, Urban & Electronic Music Production HND

Institute of Science & the Environment; www.worc.ac.uk/discover/institute-of-science-and-the-environment

Animal Biology BSc(Hons), Animal Biology MBiol (Integrated Masters), Animal Biology MPhil/PhD, Animal Biology degrees, Archaeological Landscapes MA, Archaeology & Heritage Studies degrees, Archaeology MPhil/PhD, Archaeology MRes, Archaeology and Heritage Studies BA(Hons), Atmospheric Sciences MPhil/PhD, Biochemistry BSc(Hons), Biochemistry MBiol (Integrated Masters) Biochemistry MPhil/PhD, Biological Sciences degrees, Biology BSc(Hons), Biology MBiol (Integrated Masters), Biology MRes, Biology and Mathematics BSc(Hons), Biomedical Science BSc(Hons), Computing and Mathematics BSc(Hons), Ecology BSc(Hons), Ecology MPhil/PhD, Ecology and Environmental Management MRes, Ecology degrees, Education Studies and Mathematics BSc(Hons), Environmental Science BSc(Hons), Environmental Science degrees, Environmental Studies/Science MPhil/PhD, Forensic and Applied Biology BSc(Hons), Geography BSc(Hons), Geography and Mathematics BSc(Hons), Geography degrees, Human Biology BSc(Hons), Human Biology MBiol (Integrated Masters), Human Biology MPhil/PhD, Human Biology degrees, Human Geography BA(Hons), Human Geography MPhil/PhD, Human Geography degrees, Human Nutrition BSc(Hons), Human Nutrition degrees, Mathematics BSc(Hons), Mathematics MPhil/PhD, Mathematics and Physical Education BSc(Hons), Mathematics and Psychology BSc(Hons), Mathematics degrees, Physical Geography BSc(Hons), Physical Geography MPhil/PhD, Physical Geography degrees, Plant Biology MPhil/PhD, Plant Science BSc(Hons), Plant Science MBiol (Integrated Masters), Postgraduate Certificate in Evaluation for a Sustainable Future, River Science MRes

Institute of Sport & Exercise Science; www.worc.ac.uk/discover/institute-of-sport-and-exercise-science

Applied Sport Science MSc, Applied Sports Performance Analysis MSc, Cricket Coaching & Management BSc(Hons), Dance and Community Practice BA(Hons), Football Business Management and Coaching FdSc, International Sport Management MSc, Outdoor Adventure Leadership & Management BSc(Hons), Outdoor Education MA, Physical Education BSc(Hons), Physical Education and Dance BA(Hons), Physical Education and Outdoor Education BSc(Hons), Physical Education degrees, Socio-Cultural Studies of Sport and Exercise MRes, Sport & Exercise Science BSc(Hons), Sport & Exercise Science MPhil/PhD, Sport Business Management BA(Hons), Sport Development & Coaching BA(Hons), Sport, Coaching & Physical Education HND, Sports Coaching HND, Sports Coaching MSc, Sports Coaching Science BSc(Hons), Sports Coaching Science degrees, Sports Coaching Science with Disability Sport BSc(Hons), Sports Performance & Coaching HND, Sports Studies BSc(Hons), Sports Studies degrees, Sports Therapy BSc(Hons)

Worcester Business School; www.worc.ac.uk/discover/worcester-busines-school

Accounting and Finance BA(Hons), Business & Accountancy BA(Hons), Business & Digital Communications BA(Hons), Business & Enterprise BA(Hons), Business & Finance BA(Hons), Business & Human Resource Management BA(Hons), Business & Marketing BA(Hons), Business Administration BA(Hons) – Online with NCC Education, Business Information Technology BSc(Hons), Business MPhil/PhD, Business Management BA(Hons) Top-Up, Business Management BA(Hons), Business Management HND, Business Management degrees, Business Studies BA(Hons), Business, Accountancy & Marketing BA(Hons), Business, Economics & Finance BA(Hons), Computer Games Design & Development BSc(Hons), Computing BSc(Hons), Computing HND, Computing MPhil/PhD, Computing degrees, Doctor of Business Administration DBA, Entrepreneurship BA(Hons), Finance MSc, Human Resource Management MA, Human Resource Management MSc International Business Management BA(Hons),

International Finance BA(Hons) top-up, International Management MSc, Leadership and Management FdA/BA(Hons), MBA – Master of Business Administration, MBA in Executive Leadership & Management (Part-Time), Marketing BA(Hons), Marketing MSc, Marketing, Advertising and Public Relations BA(Hons), University Diploma in Leadership and Management (UDLM), Web Development BSc(Hons)

UNIVERSITY OF YORK
www.york.ac.uk

Dept of Archaeology; www.york.ac.uk/archaeology

BA and BSc archaeology; BA archaeology and heritage; BA historical archaeology; BSc bioarchaeology; Postgrad: MSc archaeological information systems; MSc bioarchaeology; MA Conservation Studies; MA in Cultural Heritage Management, MSc digital heritage; MA/MSc early prehistory; MA/MSc funerary archaeology; MA historical archaeology; zooarchaeology; the archaeology of buildings; conservation studies; cultural heritage management; field archaeology; historical archaeology; medieval archaeology; landscape archaeology; mesolithic studies

Dept of Biology; www.york.ac.uk/biology

biology; biochemistry; biomedical sciences; biotechnology & microbiology; ecology; genetics; molecular cell biology; industrial biotechnology (MSc only); BSc, MPhil, MRes, MSc, PhD, MBiol

Dept of Chemistry; www.york.ac.uk/chemistry

chemistry; chemistry, management & industry; chemistry, resources & the environment; chemistry, biological and medicinal chemistry; green chemistry and sustainable industrial technology; BSc, MChem, MPhil, MSc, PhD

Dept of Computer Science; www.cs.york.ac.uk

advanced computer science; computer science; computer science with artificial intelligence; computer science with embedded systems; computer science and mathematics; computing; cyber security; doctorate in intelligent games and game intelligence; human-centred interactive technologies; information technology; safety critical systems engineering; safety critical systems engineering with automotive applications; social media & interactive technology; software engineering; systems safety engineering; BEng, BSc, MEng, MMath, MPhil, MSc, PGCert, PGDip

Dept of Economics & Related Studies; www.york.ac.uk/economics

economics; economics and finance; economics and econometrics; economics, econometrics and finance; economics and mathematics; economics and philosophy; economics and politics; history and economics; mathematics and finance; philosophy, politics and economics; Postgrad: development economics and emerging markets; econometrics and economics; economics; economics and finance; economics and public policy; finance and econometrics; financial engineering; health economics; project analysis, finance and investment; BA, BSc, MPhil, MSc, PGCert, PGDip, PhD

Dept of Education; www.york.ac.uk/education

education; English in education; sociology and education; psychology in education, PGCE (English, history, maths, economics, geography, foreign languages, sciences, teaching & learning, teacher training); Postgrad: applied linguistics; applied linguistics for ELT; applied linguistics for language teaching; global & international citizenship education; science education; social justice and education; teaching English to speakers of other languages; teaching English to young learners; BA, MA, MPhil, PhD, PGCE

Dept of Electronics; www.york.ac.uk/electronics

electronic engineering; electronic and communication engineering; electronic and computer engineering; electronic engineering with nanotechnology; electronic engineering with business management; music technology systems; Postgrad: audio and music technology; communications engineering; digital systems engineering; electronic engineering; embedded wireless systems; engineering management; intelligent robotics; music technology; nanoscale VLSI design; BEng, MEng, MSc, MPhil, PhD

Centre for Eighteenth Century Studies; www.york.ac.uk/eighteenth-century-studies

MA in eighteenth century studies; MA

Dept of English & Related Literature; www.york.ac.uk/english

English; English/history; English/history of art; English/linguistics; English/philosophy; English/politics; Postgrad: culture & thought after 1945, eighteenth century studies; English literary studies; film and literature; global literature and cultures; literature of the Romantic period, 1775-1832; medical history and humanities; medieval literatures & languages, modern and contemporary literature and culture; poetry and poetics, Renaissance literature, 1500-1700; Victorian literature and culture; BA, MA, MPhil, PhD

Dept of Environment; www.york.ac.uk/environment

environment, economics and ecology; environmental geography; environmental science; human geography and environment; Natural Sciences specialising in Environment; Postgrad: environmental economics & environmental management; environmental science and management; marine environmental management; corporate social responsibility and environmental management; BSc, MPhil, MSc, MEnv, PhD

Centre for Health Economics; www.york.ac.uk/che

economic evaluation of health technologies; economic evaluation for health technology assessment, health econometrics & data; health economics; health economics for healthcare professionals; health policy, mental health policy; MSc, PhD

Dept of Health Sciences; www.york.ac.uk/healthsciences

biomedical sciences; nursing (adult); nursing (child); nursing (learning disability); nursing (mental health); midwifery practice; applied health research, health research and statistics; health sciences; health & social care; international humanitarian affairs; public health; BA, BSc, DipHE, MPhil, MSc, PGCert, PGDip, PhD, MPH, FD, MNursing, Dip

Dept of History; www.york.ac.uk/history

history; English history; French history; history/economics; history/philosophy; history/politics; history of art; Postgrad: contemporary history and international politics; culture and thought after 1945; early modern history; eighteenth century studies; heritage, history and the parish church; medical history and humanities; medieval history; medieval studies; modern history; public history; Renaissance and early modern studies, women's studies; BA, MA, MPhil, PhD, PGDip

Dept of History of Art; www.york.ac.uk/history-of-art

history of art, English/history of Art; history/history of Art; Postgrad: history of art; history of art (architectural history and theory); history of art (British art); history of art (medieval art and medievalisms); history of art (modern and contemporary art); history of art (sculpture studies); stained glass conservation & heritage management; BA, MA, MPhil, PhD

Hull York Medical School; www.hyms.ac.uk

undergraduate qualifying medical courses; biomedical sciences; clinical anatomy; clinical anatomy and education; human sciences, medical sciences; medicine; public health; health professions education; human anatomy and evolution; physicians associate studies; MBBS, MSc, PGCert, MD, PhD, MPhil, BSc

Centre for Applied Human Rights; www.york.ac.uk/cahr

applied human rights, international human rights law & practice; LLM, MA, PhD, PGCert

Dept of Language & Linguistic Science; www.york.ac.uk/language

studying two languages: French and German/Italian/Spanish; German and Italian/Spanish; Italian and Spanish; studying one language and linguistics: French/German/Italian/Spanish; linguistics with French/German/Italian/Spanish; history/French; French/philosophy; German/philosophy; studying English, English language & linguistics; English/linguistics; studying linguistics: linguistics; linguistics/mathematics; philosophy/linguistics; Postgrad: linguistics; comparative syntax and semantics; forensic speech science; language and communication; language variation and change; linguistics by research; phonetics and phonology; phonological development, psycholinguistics; sociolinguistics; BA, MA, MPhil, MSc, PhD

York Law School; www.york.ac.uk/law

law, international corporate governance & commercial law, international human rights law & practice; legal & political theory; LLB, LLM, MPhil, PhD

York Management School; www.york.ac.uk/management

business and management; accounting, business finance and management; actuarial science; marketing; Postgrad: accounting and financial management; global marketing; human resource management; international business and strategic management; management; management with business finance; BA, BSc, MA, MPhil, MRes, MSc, PhD

Dept of Mathematics; maths.york.ac.uk/www/Home

mathematics; actuarial science; mathematics with computer science/economics/physics/statistics/finance/philosophy; Postgrad: advanced mathematical biology; financial engineering, mathematical finance (distance learning also available); statistics & computational finance; BA, BSc, MMath, MPhil, MRes, MSc, PGCert, PGDip, PhD

Centre for Modern Studies; www.york.ac.uk/modernstudies

culture & thought after 1945; MA

Dept of Music; www.york.ac.uk/music

music; music and sound recording; Postgrad: music; community music; music education; music production, music technology; BA, MA, MPhil, PhD, PGDip/Cert

Dept of Philosophy; www.york.ac.uk/philosophy

philosophy, philosophy with economics/politics/politics & economics/mathematics & physics/neuroscience/social & political sciences/English/French/German/ History/ mathematics/linguistics/sociology/physics; BA, BSc, GradDip, MA, MPhil, MPhys, PhD

Dept of Physics; www.york.ac.uk/physics

physics; physics with astrophysics/mathematics/philosophy; theoretical physics, fusion energy; BA, BSc, MMath, MPhil, MPhys, MSc, PhD

Dept of Politics; www.york.ac.uk/politics

politics; politics with international relations/English/history/economics/philosophy (including PPE); social and political sciences; Postgrad: conflict, governance & development; environment and politics; international political economy; international relations; political research, political theory; political philosophy, public administration; public administration & public policy/international development; postwar recovery studies; BA, MA, MSc, PhD

Dept of Psychology; www.york.ac.uk/psychology

psychology; Postgrad: applied forensic psychology; cognitive neuroscience; forensic psychology studies; development, disorders and clinical practice; developmental cognitive neuroscience; research in psychology; BSc, MPsych, MPhil, MRes, MSc, PhD

Dept of Social Policy & Social Work; www.york.ac.uk/spsw

applied social science (children & young people/crime & criminal justice); applied social science & social policy; criminology; social and political sciences; social policy; social work; Postgrad: comparative and international social policy; comparative applied social and public policy; global crime and justice; global social policy; master of public administration; master of public administration, international development; public policy and management; public policy and management (online); social and public policy (online); social policy; BA, MA, MPA, MPhil, MRes, PhD

Dept of Sociology; www.york.ac.uk/sociology

sociology, sociology with criminology/ social psychology, sociology/education, philosophy/sociology, social and political sciences/ with philosophy; Postgrad; criminology/ and social research, culture, society and globalization, social media and social research, social media and management, social media and interactive technologies; BA, MA, MPhil, MSc, PhD

Dept of Theatre, Film & Television; www.york.ac.uk/tft

interactive media; theatre writing, directing & performance; film & TV production; Postgrad: digital film & TV production; post-production with visual effects/sound design; theatre – writing direction and performance; theatre, film, TV and interactive media by research; BA, BSc, MA, MPhil, MSc, PhD

Part 5

Qualifications Awarded by Professional and Trade Associations

THE FUNCTIONS OF PROFESSIONAL ASSOCIATIONS

Qualifications

Some associations qualify individuals to act in a certain professional capacity. They also try to safeguard high standards of professional conduct. Few associations have complete control over the profession with which they are concerned. Some professions are regulated by the law, and their associations act as the central registration authority. Entry to others is directly controlled by associations that alone award the requisite qualifications. If a profession is required to be registered by the law and is controlled by the representative council, a practitioner found guilty by his or her council of misconduct may be suspended from practice or completely debarred by the removal of his or her name from the register of qualified practitioners. In other professions the consequence of misdemeanour may not be so serious, because the profession does not exercise the same degree of control.

The professions registered by statute, and therefore subject to restrictions on entry and loss of either privileges or the right to practise on erasure, are listed in Table 5.1. Certain other professions are closed.

Table 5.1 Professions registered by statute

Profession	Statutory committee controlling professional conduct
Architects	Architects Registration Board
Dentists	General Dental Council
Doctors	General Medical Council
Professions supplementary to medicine: arts therapists, biomedical scientists, chiropodists/podiatrists, clinical scientists, dieticians, hearing aid dispensers, occupational therapists, operating department practitioners, orthoptists, paramedics, physiotherapists, practitioner psychologists, prosthetists/orthotists, radiographers, speech and language therapists and social workers	Health and Care Professions Council (HCPC)
Nurses and midwives	Nursing and Midwifery Council
Opticians and optometrists	General Optical Council
Osteopaths	General Osteopathic Council
Patent attorneys	Chartered Institute of Patent Attorneys
Pharmacists, pharmacy technicians	General Pharmaceutical Council
Teachers	The National College for Teaching and Leadership

Study

Some associations give their members an opportunity to keep abreast of a particular discipline or to undertake further study in it. Such associations are especially numerous in medicine, science and applied science. Many qualifying associations also provide an information and study service for their members. Some of the more famous learned societies confer added status upon distinguished practitioners by electing them to membership or honorary membership.

Protection of Members' Interests

Some associations exist mainly to look after the interests of individual practitioners and the group. A small number are directly concerned with negotiations over salary and working conditions.

MEMBERSHIP OF PROFESSIONAL ASSOCIATIONS

Qualifying associations

The principal function of qualifying associations is to examine and qualify people who wish to become practitioners in the field with which they are concerned. As already indicated, some regulate professional conduct and many offer opportunities for further study. Membership is divided into grades, usually classified as corporate and non-corporate. Non-corporate members are those not yet admitted to full membership, mainly students; they are divided from corporate membership by barriers of age and levels of responsibility and experience. The principal requirement for admission to membership is the knowledge and ability to pass the association's exams; candidates may be exempted from the association's exams if they have acceptable alternative qualifications.

Non-corporate or affiliated members

Non-corporate members are those who are as yet unqualified or only partly qualified. They are accorded limited rights and privileges, but may not vote at meetings of the corporate body. Most associations have a student membership grade. Students are those who are preparing for the exams that qualify them for admission to corporate membership. Some associations have licentiate and graduate membership grades, which are senior to the student grade. Graduates are those who have passed the qualifying exams but lack other requirements, such as age and experience, for admission to corporate membership.

Corporate or full members

Corporate members are the fully qualified constituent members of incorporated associations. They are accorded full rights and privileges and may vote at meetings of the corporate body. Corporate membership is often divided into two grades: a senior grade of members or fellows and a general grade of associate members or associates.

Honorary members

Some associations have a special class of honorary members or fellows for distinguished members or individuals who have made an outstanding contribution to the profession in question.

Examinations and requirements

Professionals normally become corporate members by exam or exemption, with or without additional requirements. Many final professional exams are of degree standard, and a number of professional qualifications are accepted by employers as evidence of competence at operational level. Ongoing professional development is encouraged by most associations to ensure members' skills and knowledge are up to date and relevant.

The transition from the general grade of membership to the senior can be automatic in some associations (for instance, on reaching a prescribed age), but in others the higher grade is reached only after the submission of evidence of research or progress in the profession.

Qualifying exams are usually conducted in two or more stages. The first stage leads to an Intermediate or Part I qualification, the second leads to a Final or Part II or Part III qualification, which is about the standard of a degree.

Gaining professional qualifications

Prospective students can study by any of the following means:

- correspondence courses (distance learning and/or online support);

- personal attendance at the schools maintained by some associations (eg the Architectural Association School of Architecture);

- further and higher education institutions.

ACCOUNTANCY
Membership of Professional Institutions and Associations

ASSOCIATION OF ACCOUNTING TECHNICIANS

140 Aldersgate Street
London EC1A 4HY
Tel: +44 (0)20 3735 2434
Fax: 020 7397 3009
E-mail: aat@aat.org.uk
Website: www.aat.org.uk

AAT is the UK's leading qualification and membership body for accounting professionals. We have over 125,000 members including students, people working in accountancy and self-employed business owners, in more than 90 countries worldwide. Established in 1980 to ensure consistent training and regulation for accounting staff, our qualifications provide a progression route to CIMA, CIPFA, ICAS, ICAEW and ACCA.

MEMBERSHIP
Student Member
Affiliate Member
Full Member (MAAT)
Fellow Member (FMAAT)

QUALIFICATION/EXAMINATIONS
AAT Accounting Qualifications
Entry Award in Accounting (AAT Access)
Entry Certificate in Accounting
Introductory Certificate in Accounting
Introductory Diploma in Accounting and Business

(16–19-year-olds)
Intermediate Diploma in Accounting
Advanced Diploma in Accounting
Advanced Certificate in Taxation and Ethics
AAT Bookkeeping
Introductory Award in Bookkeeping
Intermediate Certificate in Bookkeeping
Advanced Certificate in Bookkeeping and Ethics
AAT Computerised Accounting
Introductory Award in Computerised Accounting
Intermediate Award in Computerised Accounting
Advanced Certificate in Computerised Accounting and Ethics
AAT Small Business Courses
Introductory Award in Accounting Skills to Run Your Business
AAT Essentials (One day courses)

DESIGNATORY LETTERS
MAAT and FMAAT

ASSOCIATION OF CHARITY INDEPENDENT EXAMINERS

The Gatehouse
White Cross
South Road
Lancaster
Lancashire LA1 4XQ
Tel: 01524 34892
E-mail: info@acie.org.uk
Website: www.acie.org.uk

ACIE provides support, training, conferences, resources and qualifications for independent examiners of charity accounts throughout the UK (*subscriptions apply*). Further information at the website: **www.acie.org.uk**

Registered charity in E&W 1139609 & SC039066. Registered company limited by guarantee 7461134; registered in England at The Gatehouse, White Cross, Lancaster LA1 4XQ.

MEMBERSHIP
Affiliate
Full Member (*with category of either Associate or Fellow*)

QUALIFICATION/EXAMINATIONS
Associate (*limited re: size and type of charity by one of several authorisation bands – see website*): ACIE
Fellow (*all UK charities eligible for IE*): FCIE

DESIGNATORY LETTERS
ACIE, FCIE

CHARTERED INSTITUTE OF INTERNAL AUDITORS

13 Abbeville Mews
88 Clapham Park Road
London SW4 7BX
Tel: 020 7498 0101
Fax: 020 7978 2492
E-mail: membership@iia.org.uk
Website: www.iia.org.uk

The Chartered Institute of Internal Auditors (IIA) is the only professional body in the UK and Ireland focused exclusively on internal auditing and we are passionate about supporting, promoting and training the professionals who work in it. Every year we help internal auditors at every stage of their career with training, qualifications and technical resources.

MEMBERSHIP
Student Member
Affiliate Member
Voting Member (PIIA, CMIIA)
Head of Internal Audit Service Member
Fellow (FIIA, CFIIA)

QUALIFICATION/EXAMINATIONS
IIA Certificate in Internal Audit and Business Risk (IA Cert)
IIA Diploma (PIIA)
IIA Advanced Diploma (CMIIA)
IT Auditing Certificate

DESIGNATORY LETTERS
IA Cert, PIIA, CMIIA, FIIA, CFIIA

CIMA – THE CHARTERED INSTITUTE OF MANAGEMENT ACCOUNTANTS

26 Chapter Street
London SW1P 4NP
Tel: 020 8849 2251
E-mail: cima.contact@cimaglobal.com
Website: www.cimaglobal.com

CIMA is the employers' choice when recruiting financially qualified business leaders.

The Chartered Institute of Management Accountants, founded in 1919, is the world's leading and largest professional body of Management Accountants, with 183,000 members and students operating at the heart of business in 168 countries. CIMA works closely with employers and sponsors leading-edge research, constantly updating its qualification, professional experience requirements and continuing professional development to ensure it remains the most relevant international accountancy qualification for business.

MEMBERSHIP
Member
Associate (ACMA)
Fellow (FCMA)

QUALIFICATION/EXAMINATIONS
Certificate in Business Accounting
CIMA Professional
Certificate in Islamic Finance
Diploma in Islamic Finance

DESIGNATORY LETTERS
ACMA, FCMA

ICAEW (THE INSTITUTE OF CHARTERED ACCOUNTANTS IN ENGLAND AND WALES)

Metropolitan House
321 Avebury Boulevard
Milton Keynes MK9 2FZ
Tel: 01908 248 250
E-mail: careers@icaew.com
Website: icaew.com/careers

ICAEW is a world leading professional membership organisation that promotes, develops and supports over 140,000 chartered accountants worldwide. We provide qualifications and professional development, share our knowledge, insight and technical expertise, and protect the quality and integrity of the accountancy and finance profession.

MEMBERSHIP
ACA (Associate of the Institute of Chartered Accountants in England and Wales)
FCA (Fellow Chartered Accountant)

QUALIFICATION/EXAMINATIONS
The ICAEW chartered accountancy qualification, the ACA, is one of the most advanced learning and professional development programmes available. It has integrated components which give an in-depth understanding across accountancy, finance and business. Combined they help build the technical knowledge, professional skills and practical experience needed to become an ICAEW Chartered Accountant. There is more than one way to start the ACA, find out more at icaew.com/careers

The ICAEW Certificate in Finance, Accounting and Business (ICAEW CFAB) provides fundamental knowledge and skills in finance, accounting and business. ICAEW CFAB consists of the same six exam modules as the first level of the ACA qualification. It can be studied as a stand-alone qualification or as an entry route to the ACA. There are no entry requirements and it is achievable in as little as 12 months through online learning, self-study or classroom tuition. Find out more at icaew.com/cfab

DESIGNATORY LETTERS
ACA, FCA

ICAS (INSTITUTE OF CHARTERED ACCOUNTANTS OF SCOTLAND)

CA House
21 Haymarket Yards
Edinburgh EH12 5BH
Tel: 0131 347 0100
E-mail: caeducation@icas.com
Website: icas.com

ICAS is a professional body for around 19,000 world class business professionals who work in the UK and in more than 100 countries around the world. Our members have all achieved the internationally recognised and respected CA qualification. We are an educator, examiner, regulator, and thought leader. ICAS is the first professional body for accountants and was created by Royal Charter in 1854.

MEMBERSHIP

To qualify as a CA, trainees must enter and complete a training contract with an ICAS authorised employer for a prescribed period, normally three years. They must achieve relevant work experience requirements and key competencies, study for and pass three stages of examinations and complete a course and assignment in Business Ethics. For further information please see the ICAS website.

QUALIFICATION/EXAMINATIONS

The CA qualification syllabus contains ten subjects leading to three stages of exams.

Test of Competence (TC) contains five subjects: Financial Accounting, Principles of Auditing and Reporting, Finance, Business Management, Business Law.

Test of Professional Skills (TPS): Taxation, Advanced Finance, Financial Reporting, Assurance and Business Systems.

Test of Professional Expertise (TPE) contains a multidisciplinary case study designed to apply theoretical knowledge and practical skills to a real-life situation.

In addition to including ethics within the three levels, Business Ethics forms a standalone subject and assessment.

DESIGNATORY LETTERS
CA

INSTITUTE OF FINANCIAL ACCOUNTANTS

Burford House
44 London Road
Sevenoaks
Kent TN13 1AS
Tel: 01732 458080
Fax: 01732 455848
E-mail: mail@ifa.org.uk
Website: www.ifa.org.uk

The IFA was established in 1916 and is the oldest body of non-Chartered Accountants in the world. We represent members and students in more than 80 countries, providing qualifications for those wishing to work in financial management and accountancy, and CPD for qualified Financial Accountants, particularly in SMEs.

MEMBERSHIP
Financial Accounting Executive
Associate (AFA)

Fellow (FFA)

QUALIFICATION/EXAMINATIONS
IFE Level 4 Award for SME Tax Advisers (QCF)
IFA Level 4 Award for SME Financial Accounting (International Standards) (QCF)
IFA Level 4 Diploma for SME Financial Accountants (QCF)
IFA Level 5 Diploma for SME Financial Managers (QCF)

IFA Level 5 Diploma for SME Finance and Business Managers (QCF)
The Diploma in IFRS for Accounting Professionals and the Diploma in IFRS for Business

DESIGNATORY LETTERS
QCF

INTERNATIONAL ASSOCIATION OF BOOKKEEPERS

Suite 5
20 Churchill Square
Kings Hill
West Malling
Kent ME19 4YU
Tel: 0844 3303527
Fax: 0844 3303514
E-mail: mail@iab.org.uk
Website: www.iab.org.uk

The IAB specializes in providing high-quality, accredited and regulated financial and business qualifications. We continue to be the leading international membership body for professional bookkeepers. Established in 1973, we now have many thousands of students and members worldwide.

MEMBERSHIP
Associate (AIAB)
Member (MIAB)
Fellow (FIAB)

QUALIFICATION/EXAMINATIONS
Award in Bookkeeping (Level 1)
Award in Manual Bookkeeping (Level 1)
Award in Computerized Bookkeeping (Level 1)
Certificate in Bookkeeping (Level 2)
Award in Manual Bookkeeping (Level 2)
Award in Computerized Bookkeeping (Level 2)
Certificate in Bookkeeping (Level 1)
Certificate in Bookkeeping (Level 3)
Diploma in Bookkeeping (Level 3)
Certificate in Manual Bookkeeping (Level 3)
Award in Computerized Bookkeeping (Level 3)
Diploma in Accounting to International Standards (Level 4)
Certificate in Payroll (Level 1)
Certificate in Payroll (Level 2)
Award in Computerized Payroll (Level 2)

Diploma in Payroll (Level 2)
Diploma in Payroll (Level 3)
Award in Computerized Payroll (Level 1)
Award in Computerized Payroll for Business (Level 1)
Certificate in Computerized Payroll for Business (Level 2)
Certificate in Computerized Payroll for Business (Level 3)
Award in Computerized Payroll (Level 3)
Award in Computerized Accounting for Business (Level 1)
Certificate in Computerized Accounting for Business (Level 2)
Certificate in Computerized Accounting for Business (Level 3)
Diploma in Accounting and Advanced Bookkeeping (Level 3)
Diploma in Small Business Financial Management (Level 3)
Diploma in Cost and Management Accounting (Level 3)
Diploma in Financial Information for Managers (Level 4)
Diploma in Personal and Business Tax (Level 4)

DESIGNATORY LETTERS
NCF, QCF

THE ASSOCIATION OF CHARTERED CERTIFIED ACCOUNTANTS

London WC2A 3EE
Tel: 020 7059 5000
Fax: 020 7059 5050
E-mail: info@accaglobal.com
Website: www.accaglobal.com

ACCA is the largest and fastest-growing international accountancy body, with over 424,000 students and 147,000 members in 170 countries. The ACCA Qualification is an established route to professional status, and we offer continued support to our members throughout their careers.

MEMBERSHIP
Associate (ACCA)
Fellow (FCCA)

QUALIFICATION/EXAMINATIONS
Foundations in Accountancy

Certificate in International Finance Reporting
Certificate in International Finance Reporting Standard for SMEs
Diploma in International Finance Reporting
The ACCA Qualification
MBA (awarded by Oxford Brookes University; accredited by the Association of MBAs)

DESIGNATORY LETTERS
ACCA, FCCA

THE ASSOCIATION OF CORPORATE TREASURERS

68 King William Street
London EC4N 7DZ
Tel: 020 7847 2540
E-mail: act@treasurers.org
Website: www.treasurers.org

The ACT is the professional chartered body for treasury and sets the benchmark for international treasury excellence. The ACT leads the profession through its globally recognised treasury qualifications by defining standards and championing continuing professional development.

MEMBERSHIP
eAffiliate Member
Student Member
Affiliate Member
Associate Member
Fellow
Business Member

QUALIFICATION/EXAMINATIONS
Treasury qualifications pathway
Certificate in Treasury Fundamentals
Certificate in Treasury
Diploma in Treasury Management
MCT Advanced Diploma
Cash management qualifications
Award in Cash Management Fundamentals
Certificate in International Cash Management

DESIGNATORY LETTERS
CertTF, CertT, AMCT, MCT, AwardCMF, CertICM,

THE ASSOCIATION OF INTERNATIONAL ACCOUNTANTS

Staithes 3
The Watermark
Metro Riverside
Newcastle upon Tyne
Tyne & Wear NE11 9SN
Tel: 0191 493 0277
Fax: 0191 493 0278
E-mail: aia@aiaworldwide.com
Website: www.aiaworldwide.com

AIA was founded in 1928 as a global accountancy body and has recognition as a Recognised Qualifying Body for statutory auditors, supervisory status for its members in the Money Laundering Regulations 2007 and an Awarding Body in the UK. AIA is a Prescribed Body in ROI and is recognised worldwide.

MEMBERSHIP
Student Member
Graduate Member
Academic Member
Associate (AAIA)
Fellow (FAIA)
Honorary Member
Retired Member

QUALIFICATION/EXAMINATIONS
Professional Accountancy Qualification
Recognised Professional Qualification (Statutory Audit)
QCF Level 5 Certificate in Accountancy
QCF Level 6 Diploma in Accountancy
QCF Level 7 Diploma in Professional Accountancy
Auditing Diploma
IFRS Diploma
Management Accounting & Costing Diploma
IFRS for SMEs Certificate

DESIGNATORY LETTERS
AAIA, FAIA

THE CHARTERED INSTITUTE OF PUBLIC FINANCE AND ACCOUNTANCY (CIPFA)

77 Mansell Street
London E1 8AN
Tel: 020 7543 5600
Fax: 020 7543 5700
E-mail: students@cipfa.org.uk
Website: www.cipfa.org.uk

The Chartered Institute of Public Finance and Accountancy (CIPFA) is *the* professional body for people in public finance. Our 14,000 members work throughout the public services and as the only UK professional accountancy body to specialise in public services, CIPFA's qualifications are the foundation for a career in public finance.

MEMBERSHIP
Affiliate
Associate
Full Member

QUALIFICATION/EXAMINATIONS
CIPFA Professional Qualification
Professional Qualification in Public & Corporate Accounting
Integrated Qualification for Auditors
Certificate in International Public Sector Financial Reporting
Certificate in International Public Sector Accounting Standards
Certificate in Financial Reporting for Academies

DESIGNATORY LETTERS
CPFA

THE INSTITUTE OF CERTIFIED BOOKKEEPERS

London Underwriting Centre
3 Minster Court
Mincing Lane
City of London EC3R 7DD
Tel: 0845 060 2345
Fax: 01635 298960
E-mail: info@bookkeepers.org.uk
Website: www.bookkeepers.org.uk

The ICB is the largest bookkeeping institute in the world. Our aims are to promote bookkeeping as a profession, to improve training in the principles of bookkeeping, and to establish qualifications and the award of grades of membership that recognize academic attainment, work experience and professional competence, and thereby enable qualified bookkeepers to gain recognition as an integral part of the financial world.

MEMBERSHIP
Registered Student
Affiliate
Associate Member (AICB)
Member (MICB)
Fellow (FICB)

QUALIFICATION/EXAMINATIONS
Level 1: Certificate in Basic Bookkeeping

Level 2: (Intermediate): Certificate in Computerized Bookkeeping
Level 2: (Intermediate): Certificate in Manual Bookkeeping
Level 3: (Advanced): Diploma in Computerized Bookkeeping
Level 3: (Advanced): Diploma in Manual Bookkeeping
Level 3: (Advanced): Diploma in Payroll Management
Level 3: (Advanced): Diploma in Self-Assessment Tax Returns
Level 4: (Advanced): Diploma in Financial Management (Drafting Financial Statements, Management Accounting, Personal Taxation and Business Taxation)

DESIGNATORY LETTERS
AICB, MICB, FICB

ACOUSTICS
Membership of Professional Institutions and Associations

INSTITUTE OF ACOUSTICS

St Peter's House
45–49 Victoria Street
St Albans
Hertfordshire AL1 3WZ
Tel: 01727 848195
Fax: 01727 850553
E-mail: ioa@ioa.org.uk
Website: www.ioa.org.uk

The IOA is the UK's professional body for those working in acoustics, noise and vibration, and has more than 3,000 members in research, educational, environmental, government and industrial organizations. It offers professionally recognized courses and is licensed by the Engineering Research Council to offer registration at Chartered and Incorporated Engineer levels.

MEMBERSHIP
Student

Affiliate
Technician Member (TechIOA)
Associate Member (AMIOA)
Member (MIOA)
Fellow (FIOA)
Honorary Fellow (HonFIOA)
Incorporated Engineer (IEng)
Chartered Engineer (CEng)
Sponsor

QUALIFICATION/EXAMINATIONS
Certificate of Competence in Environmental Noise
Measurement

Certificate of Competence in Workplace Noise Risk
Assessment
Certificate Course in the Management of Occupational Exposure to Hand–Arm Vibration
Certificate Course in Building Acoustics
Measurements
Diploma in Acoustics and Noise Control

DESIGNATORY LETTERS
TechIOA, AMIOA, MIOA, FIOA, HonFIOA, IEng,
CEng

ADVERTISING AND PUBLIC RELATIONS
Membership of Professional Institutions and Associations

CHARTERED INSTITUTE OF PUBLIC RELATIONS

52–53 Russell Square
London WC1B 4HP
Tel: 020 7631 6900
Fax: 020 7631 6944
E-mail: info@cipr.co.uk
Website: www.cipr.co.uk

The CIPR, founded in 1948, is the professional body for PR practitioners and has more than 9,000 members, to whom it offers information, advice, support and training. Our aim is to raise standards within the profession through the promotion of best practice and our members abide by our strict code of professional conduct.

MEMBERSHIP
Student
Affiliate
Associate (ACIPR)

Member (MCIPR)
Fellow (FCIPR)
Global Affiliate

QUALIFICATION/EXAMINATIONS
Foundation Award in Public Relations
Advanced Certificate
Diploma

DESIGNATORY LETTERS
ACIPR, MCIPR, FCIPR

INSTITUTE OF PRACTITIONERS IN ADVERTISING

44 Belgrave Square
London SW1X 8QS
Tel: 020 7235 7020
Fax: 020 7245 9904
E-mail: web@ipa.co.uk
Website: www.ipa.co.uk

The IPA is the UK's leading professional body for advertising, media and marketing communications agencies. We promote the services of our member agencies, which have access to a range of services and benefits, including a Legal Department, Information Centre and training courses provided by our Professional Development Department.

MEMBERSHIP
Personal Member (MIPA)
Fellow/Honorary Fellow (FIPA)
Member Agency

QUALIFICATION/EXAMINATIONS
Foundation Certificate

Advanced Certificate
LegRgs Certificate
Commercial Certificate
Search Certificate
Excellence Diploma
Eff Test

DESIGNATORY LETTERS
MIPA, FIPA

INSTITUTE OF PROMOTIONAL MARKETING

193-197 High Holborn
London WC1V 7BD
Tel: 020 3848 0444
E-mail: training@theipm.org.uk
Website: www.theipm.org.uk

The Institute of Promotional Marketing represents promoters, agencies and service partners engaged in promotional marketing in the UK by protecting, promoting and progressing effective sales promotion across all media channels through its education, legal advice, awards, and other products and services.

MEMBERSHIP
Corporate Member

QUALIFICATION/EXAMINATIONS
IPM Foundation Certificate
IPM Incentive & Motivation Diploma
IPM Diploma
Legal Code Certification (LCC)

DESIGNATORY LETTERS
MISP

LONDON SCHOOL OF PUBLIC RELATIONS

118A Kensington Church Street
London W8 4BH
Tel: 020 7221 3399
Fax: 020 7243 1730
E-mail: info@lspr-education.com
Website: www.lspr-education.com

Established in 1992, the London School of Public Relations (LSPR) provides up-to-date pracitical, hands-on training courses for those wishing to enter public relations as a career or for those already in a PR or communications role. They are suitable for anyone who needs up-to-date practical training awarded with a professional development qualification.

LSPR provides the following courses:
  DIPLOMA:
• PR & Reputation Management – 5 day course
  ADVANCED CERTIFICATES:

• Business Strategy for PR – 2 day course
• Branding -2 day course
• Corporate Social Responsibility & Sustainability – 2 day course
• Risk & Crisis Management – 2 day course
  CERTIFICATES:
• Business Writing – 1 day workshop
• Copy Editing – 1 day course
• Impression Management (Personal Branding) – 1 day course
• On Camera – Media Handeling – 1 day
• Press Release Writing – 1 day course

- Presentation Skills – 1 day course

Our Diploma, *PR & Reputation Management*, is awarded to delegates upon successful completion of a 5 day full-time intensive course: Monday–Friday.

The Advanced Certificate courses run for 2 days.

Certificate courses are intensive short workshops run for 1 day on Thursday or Friday (Presentation Skills and Press Release Writing)

All the courses are also offered in-house for clients.

LSPR training programmes are approved and recognised by Continuous Professional Development (CPD).

LSPR operates globally with headquarters in London and international partners, in association with PR bodies and agencies.

MEMBERSHIP
Continuous Professional Development (CPD)

QUALIFICATION/EXAMINATIONS
- Diploma: In class assessment and a Final project
- Advanced Certificates: In class critical thinking exercises
- Certificates: Attendance based and in class presentations and group work

AGRICULTURE AND HORTICULTURE
Membership of Professional Institutions and Associations

INSTITUTE OF HORTICULTURE

Capel Manor College
Bullsmoor Lane
Enfield
Middlesex EN1 4RQ
Tel: 01992 707025
E-mail: ioh@horticulture.org.uk
Website: www.horticulture.org.uk

The IoH represents all those professionally engaged in horticulture in the UK and the Republic of Ireland. Our main aim is to promote the profession and its importance in food and ornamental plant production, improving the environment, providing employment and as the leisure pursuit of gardening. We are also developing CPD and mentoring schemes for our members and liaise with government and other bodies on matters of interest or concern.

MEMBERSHIP
Student Member, Affiliate, e-Affiliate, Associate (AI Hort), Member (MI Hort), Fellow (FI Hort), Group Membership

DESIGNATORY LETTERS
AI Hort, MI Hort, FI Hort

ROYAL HORTICULTURAL SOCIETY

RHS Garden Wisley
Woking
Surrey GU23 6QB
Tel: 01483 226500
E-mail: qualifications@rhs.org.uk
Website: www.rhs.org.uk

The Royal Horticultural Society is a recognized awarding body offering a range of qualifications in horticultural knowledge and skills. Part-time courses leading to RHS qualifications are offered by approved centres throughout the UK and Ireland, and by distance-learning providers. The RHS School of Horticulture provides courses in practical horticultural skills.

QUALIFICATION/EXAMINATIONS
RHS Level 1 Introductory Award in Practical Horticulture
RHS Level 1 Award in Practical Horticulture
RHS Level 2 Certificate in the Principles of Plant Growth, Propagation and Development
RHS Level 2 Certificate in the Principles of Garden Planning, Establishment and Maintenance
RHS Level 2 Certificate in the Principles of Horticulture
RHS Level 2 Certificate in Practical Horticulture
RHS Level 2 Diploma in the Principles and Practices of Horticulture
RHS Level 3 Certificate in the Principles of Plant Growth, Health and Applied Propagation
RHS Level 3 Certificate in the Principles of Garden Planning, Construction and Planting
RHS Level 3 Certificate in Practical Horticulture
RHS Level 3 Diploma in the Principles and Practices of Horticulture
Master of Horticulture (RHS)
RHS Level 3 Diploma in Horticultural Practice

THE ROYAL BOTANIC GARDEN EDINBURGH

20A Inverleith Row
Edinburgh EH3 5LR
Tel: 0131 552 7171
Fax: 01312 482901
E-mail: education@rbge.org.uk
Website: www.rbge.org.uk

The RBGE was founded in the 17th century as a physic garden, growing medicinal plants. Now it extends over four gardens boasting a rich living collection of plants, and is a world-renowned centre for plant science and education.

QUALIFICATION/EXAMINATIONS
Certificate in Botanic Illustration
Certificate in Herbology
Certificate in the Principles of Horticulture (RHS Level 2)
Certificate in Practical Field Botany
Certificate in Practical Horticulture
Diploma in Botanical Illustration
Diploma in Garden Design
Diploma in Garden History
Diploma in Herbology
HND/BSc in Horticulture with Plantsmanship
MSc in The Biodiversity and Taxonomy of Plants

AMBULANCE SERVICE
Membership of Professional Institutions and Associations

AMBULANCE SERVICE INSTITUTE

Suite 183
Maddison House
226 High Street
Croydon CR9 1DF
E-mail: enquiries@asi-international.com
Website: www.asi-international.com

The ASI is a non-union, non-political, independent institute whose membership is dedicated to raising the standards and quality of ambulance provision and thereby improving the professionalism and quality of care available to patients. Membership is open to non-NHS personnel as well as to employees of NHS Ambulance Services.

MEMBERSHIP
Student
Member (MASI)
Licentiate (LASI)
Associate (AASI)
Graduate (GASI)
Fellow (FASI)

QUALIFICATION/EXAMINATIONS
The Institute offers professional examinations and qualifications in the areas of Pre-Hospital Care, Control and Communications, and Management, for those who desire a career in the ambulance service.

DESIGNATORY LETTERS
MASI, LASI, AASI, GASI, FASI

ARBITRATION
Membership of Professional Institutions and Associations

THE CHARTERED INSTITUTE OF ARBITRATORS

12 Bloomsbury Square
London WC1A 2LP
Tel: 020 7421 7444
Fax: 020 7404 4023
E-mail: info@ciarb.org
Website: www.ciarb.org

The CIArb is a not-for-profit, UK-registered charity with 12,000 members worldwide that exists to promote and facilitate the settlement of private disputes by arbitration and alternative dispute resolution. We provide training for arbitrators, mediators and adjudicators and act as an international centre for practitioners, policy-makers, academics and those in business concerned with the cost-effective and early settlement of disputes.

MEMBERSHIP
Associate (ACIArb)

Member (MCIArb)
Fellow (FCIArb)

QUALIFICATION/EXAMINATIONS
Introductory Certificate
Advanced Certificate
Diploma

DESIGNATORY LETTERS
ACIArb, MCIArb, FCIArb

ARCHAEOLOGY
Membership of Professional Institutions and Associations

CHARTERED INSTITUTE FOR ARCHAEOLOGISTS

Miller Building
University of Reading
Reading
Berkshire RG6 6AB
Tel: 0118 378 6446
E-mail: admin@archaeologists.net
Website: www.archaeologists.net

CIfA is the leading professional body representing archaeologists working in the UK and overseas. We promote high professional standards and strong ethics in archaeological practice, to maximise the benefits that archaeologists bring to society. We are the authoritative and effective voice for archaeologists, bringing recognition and respect to our profession.

MEMBERSHIP
Student
Affiliate
Practitioner (PCIfA)
Associate (ACIfA)
Member (MCIfA)
Registered Organisation

ARCHITECTURE
Membership of Professional Institutions and Associations

ARCHITECTS REGISTRATION BOARD

8 Weymouth Street
London W1W 5BU
Tel: 020 7580 5861
Fax: 020 7436 5269
E-mail: info@arb.org.uk
Website: www.arb.org.uk

The ARB is the regulatory body for architects in the UK. Only individuals registered with the Board can use the title 'architect'. Applicants must have passed the recognized exams at a school of architecture in the UK (or have an equivalent non-UK professional qualification) and have at least 2 years' practical experience working under the supervision of an architect.

CHARTERED INSTITUTE OF ARCHITECTURAL TECHNOLOGISTS (CIAT)

397 City Road
London EC1V 1NH
Tel: 020 7278 2206
Fax: 020 7837 3194
E-mail: info@ciat.org.uk
Website: www.ciat.org.uk

CIAT represents professionals working and studying in the field of Architectural Technology. We are internationally recognised as the qualifying body for Chartered Architectural Technologists (MCIAT) and Architectural Technicians (TCIAT).

MEMBERSHIP
Student Member

Profile Candidate
Associate (ACIAT)
Architectural Technician (TCIAT)
Chartered Architectural Technologist (MCIAT)
Honorary Member (HonMCIAT)

DESIGNATORY LETTERS
ACIAT, TCIAT, MCIAT

ROYAL INSTITUTE OF BRITISH ARCHITECTS

66 Portland Place
London W1B 1AD
Tel: 020 7580 5533
E-mail: info@riba.org
Website: www.architecture.com

The Royal Institute of British Architects is the UK membership body for architecture and the architectural profession. We provide support for our 41,000 members worldwide in the form of training, technical services, publications and events, and set standards for the education of architects, both in the UK and overseas. We also work with government to improve the design quality of public buildings, new homes and new communities.

MEMBERSHIP
Student Member

Affiliate Member
Associate Member
Chartered Member
Fellow Member
Chartered Practice

QUALIFICATION/EXAMINATIONS
The RIBA Examination in Architecture for office-based candidates Part 1 and Part 2 (distance learning)

ART AND DESIGN

Membership of Professional Institutions and Associations

BRITISH ASSOCIATION OF ART THERAPISTS

Claremont
24–27 White Lion Street
London N1 9PD
Tel: 020 7686 4216
E-mail: info@baat.org
Website: www.baat.org

The BAAT is the professional organization for art therapists in the UK and has its own Code of Ethics of Professional Practice. We maintain a comprehensive directory of qualified art therapists and work to promote art therapy in the UK through 20 regional groups. We also have a European section and an international section.

MEMBERSHIP
Trainee Member
Associate Member
Full Member
Honorary Member
Fellow
Corporate Member

QUALIFICATION/EXAMINATIONS
The BAAT organizes a programme of CPD courses for Art Therapists. For details see the website.

D&AD

64 Cheshire Street
London E2 6EH
Tel: 020 7840 1111
Fax: 020 7840 0840
E-mail: info@dandad.co.uk
Website: www.dandad.org

Founded in 1962, D&AD is a professional association and educational charity with a membership of more than 2,000, working on behalf of the design and advertising communities. Our mission is to set creative standards, educate and inspire the next creative generation, and promote the importance of good design and advertising to business as a whole.

MEMBERSHIP
Awarded
Professional
Education Network

SOCIETY OF DESIGNER CRAFTSMEN (SDC)

24 Rivington Street
London EC2A 3DU
Tel: 020 7739 3663
E-mail: info@societyofdesignercraftsmen.org.uk
Website: www.societyofdesignercraftsmen.org.uk

The Society, which was founded in 1887 as the Arts and Crafts Exhibition Society, is the largest and oldest multi-craft society in the UK. Our aim is to emphasize designer-making where innovation, originality and quality are important; we provide promotional services and exhibiting opportunities to members.

MEMBERSHIP
Associate
Licentiate (LSDC)
Member (MSDC)
Fellow (FSDC)

QUALIFICATION/EXAMINATIONS
Membership is by direct application by an individual craftsman and assessment is on quality of craftsmanship and design.
New graduates can be assessed at New Designers or College degree show following graduation.
Application forms and criteria are on our website.

DESIGNATORY LETTERS
LSDC, MSDC, FSDC

THE BRITISH ASSOCIATION OF PAINTINGS CONSERVATOR-RESTORERS (BAPCR)

4 Caburn Crescent
Lewes
East Sussex BN7 1NR
Tel: 07989 559346
E-mail: BAPCRsecretary@gmail.com
Website: www.bapcr.org.uk

The British Association of Paintings Conservator-Restorers promotes and fosters the practice of paintings conservation in the United Kingdom and around the world.

Established in 1943, we are the oldest dedicated professional organisation for all conservator-restorers of paintings in the UK.

Our members are skilled professionals working in private practice or in established institutions.

MEMBERSHIP
Associate (Student)
Associate
Fellow

THE CHARTERED SOCIETY OF DESIGNERS

1 Cedar Court
Royal Oak Yard
Bermondsey Street
London SE1 3GA
Tel: 020 7357 8088
Fax: 020 7407 9878
E-mail: info@csd.org.uk
Website: www.csd.org.uk

The CSD, which was founded in 1930, is the professional body for designers and has more than 3,000 members. We promote sound principles of design in all areas in which design considerations apply, further design practice and encourage the study of design techniques for the benefit of the community.

MEMBERSHIP
Student Member
Associate (Assoc. CSD)
Member (MCSD)
Fellow (FCSD)

DESIGNATORY LETTERS
MCSD, FCSD

THE INDEX OF PROFESSIONAL MASTER DESIGNERS

Kensington House
33 Imperial Square
Cheltenham Spa
Gloucestershire GL50 1QZ
Tel: 08701 161823
Fax: 08702 626146
E-mail: masterdesigners@kensington-house.com

The Index was formed to provide a register of designers practising in all areas of design. Our objectives are to enable designers to achieve recognition and attain qualifications and also to accredit schools and training organizations offering suitable courses.

MEMBERSHIP
Student

Professional Designer (IPMD (DIP))
Master Designer (IPMD (MAS))

QUALIFICATION/EXAMINATIONS
Certificate of Excellence – Interior Design Students

DESIGNATORY LETTERS
IPMD (DIP), IPMD (MAS)

ASTRONOMY AND SPACE SCIENCE
Membership of Professional Institutions and Associations

THE BRITISH INTERPLANETARY SOCIETY

Arthur C Clarke House
27/29 South Lambeth Road
London SW8 1SZ
Tel: 020 7735 3160
Fax: 020 7582 7167
E-mail: info@bis-space.com
Website: www.bis-space.com

The BIS was formed in 1933 and has been at the forefront of actively promoting new ideas on space exploration at technical, educational and popular levels for 80 years. We serve the interests of those professionally involved with space, promote fundamental space research, technology and applications, encourage technical and scientific space studies, and undertake educational activities on space topics.

MEMBERSHIP
Member
Fellow (FBIS)

DESIGNATORY LETTERS
FBIS

AVIATION

Membership of Professional Institutions and Associations

THE GUILD OF AIR PILOTS AND AIR NAVIGATORS

Cobham House
9 Warwick Court
London WC1R 5DJ
Tel: 020 7404 4032
Fax: 020 7404 4035
E-mail: gapan@gapan.org
Website: www.gapan.org

The Guild, an active Livery Company of the City of London, represents pilot and navigator interests within all areas of aviation. Most of our members are, or have been, professional licence holders, or hold a private licence. Our aims include promoting the highest standards of air safety, liaising with all authorities connected with licensing, training and legislation, providing advice and facilitating exchange of information.

MEMBERSHIP
Associate
Freeman
Upper Freeman

QUALIFICATION/EXAMINATIONS
Master Air Pilot Certificate
Master Air Navigator Certificate
Master Rearcrew Certificate

THE GUILD OF AIR TRAFFIC CONTROL OFFICERS

Membership Services
4 St Mary's Road
Bingham
Nottingham
Nottinghamshire NG13 8DW
Tel: +44 (0)1949 876405
Fax: +44 (0) 1949 876405
E-mail: caf@gatco.org
Website: www.gatco.org

Founded in 1954, GATCO is an independent professional organization that exists to promote the highest standards in all aspects of Air Traffic Management. It is dedicated to the safety of all who travel by air.

MEMBERSHIP
Student Member
ATM Support Member
Non-Operational Member
Retired Member

FISO Member
ABM(W) Member
ATCO Abroad Member
ATCO UK Member
Corporate Member

QUALIFICATION/EXAMINATIONS
Qualifying criteria apply to all membership categories. Further information should be sought from GATCO Ltd, Membership Services.

AWARDS

Membership of Professional Institutions and Associations

CONFEDERATION OF PROFESSIONAL AWARDING BODIES (COPAB)

40 Archdale Road
East Dulwich
London SE22 9HJ
Tel: 0208 693 0555
Fax: 0208 693 0555
E-mail: secretary@copab.net; profblankson@snnp.org.uk
Website: www.copab.net

Confederation of Professional Awarding Bodies represents educational, vocational, technical and scientific fields world-wide. COPAB will works in partnership with colleges, universities, consultancies and all types of businesses to provide a coherent business and professional education to fulfil identified needs.

DESIGNATORY LETTERS
MCOPAB

BANKING

Membership of Professional Institutions and Associations

THE CHARTERED INSTITUTE OF BANKERS IN SCOTLAND

Drumsheugh House
38B Drumsheugh Gardens
Edinburgh EH3 7SW
Tel: 0131 473 7777
Fax: 0131 473 7788
E-mail: info@charteredbanker.com
Website: www.charteredbanker.com

The Chartered Institute of Bankers in Scotland provides world-class professional qualifications for both the UK and international markets. Our vision for the financial services industry is one of professionalism. We are the only organisation in the world entitled to award the designation 'Chartered Banker' to its members.

MEMBERSHIP
Student
Affiliate
Associate (ACIBS)
Member (MCIBS)
Fellow (FCIBS)

QUALIFICATION/EXAMINATIONS
Certificate
Diploma
Advanced Diploma
Chartered Banker

DESIGNATORY LETTERS
ACIBS, MCIBS, FCIBS

THE LONDON INSTITUTE OF BANKING & FINANCE

8th Floor
Peninsular House
36 Monument Street
London EC3R 8LJ
Tel: 0207 4447111
Fax: 0207 4447115
E-mail: customerservices@libf.ac.uk
Website: www.libf.ac.uk

We exist to advance banking and finance by providing outstanding education and thinking; equipping individuals with the knowledge to achieve what they want in their career.

And because we've been at the heart of the sector since 1879, we create connections and build partnerships that make banking and finance more accessible.

MEMBERSHIP
Member

Student Member
Associate
Fellow
Chartered Associate
Chartered Fellow

QUALIFICATION/EXAMINATIONS
Offering a wide range of qualifications for those employed or aspiring to a career in the financial services industry. For details see www.libf.ac.uk

BEAUTY THERAPY AND BEAUTY CULTURE
Membership of Professional Institutions and Associations

BRITISH ASSOCIATION OF BEAUTY THERAPY AND COSMETOLOGY LTD

BABTAC Limited
Ambrose House, Meteor Court
Barnett Way
Barnwood
Gloucester GL4 3GG
Tel: 0845 250 7277
Fax: 01452 611599
E-mail: info@babtac.com
Website: www.babtac.com

BABTAC was formed in 1977 and is a non-profit-making organization for beauticians and therapists in the UK. Members work to a rigorous code of ethics and good practice, both in terms of the treatments and therapies they offer and the way they conduct their relationships with their clients. CIBTAC, an international, educational awarding body that works closely with BABTAC, offers over 30 internationally recognized diplomas in beauty and complementary therapies to accredited colleges and students in the UK and abroad.

MEMBERSHIP
Student Member
Associate Member
Full Therapist Member
Full Hairdresser Member
Salon and Spa Member
International Member

QUALIFICATION/EXAMINATIONS
BABTAC offers a programme of short courses. For details see the BABTAC website. For CIBTAC diplomas see www.cibtac.com/courses_home.htm

BRITISH INSTITUTE AND ASSOCIATION OF ELECTROLYSIS LTD

40 Parkfield Road
Ickenham
Middlesex UB10 BLW
Tel: 08445 441373
E-mail: sec@electrolysis.co.uk
Website: www.electrolysis.co.uk

The BIAE is a non-profit-making organisation that demands a high standard of skill and ethical conduct from its members, who are spread throughout the UK and overseas. Candidate Electrolysists must complete the rigorous assessments, both theoretical and practical, of the BIAE Examining Board before being accepted onto the Register.

MEMBERSHIP
Member

QUALIFICATION/EXAMINATIONS
Certificate in Remedial Electrolysis (CRE)

FEDERATION OF HOLISTIC THERAPISTS

18 Shakespeare Business Centre
Hathaway Close
Eastleigh
Hampshire SO50 4SR
Tel: 023 8062 4350
Fax: 023 8062 4396
E-mail: info@fht.org.uk
Website: www.fht.org.uk

The FHT is the leading and largest professional beauty, sports and complementary therapist association in the UK, which has been representing the interests of holistic therapists since 1962. The FHT leads the industry by offering its members a Code of Conduct and Professional Practice, public liability insurance, access to regulation, a robust CPD programme with auditing, class-leading journal, local therapist network, and comprehensive business and public affairs updates.

MEMBERSHIP
Student

Affiliate
Associate
Member
Fellow
International

QUALIFICATION/EXAMINATIONS
Please see the FHT's website.

DESIGNATORY LETTERS
MFHT, FFHT, AFHT, AfFHT

ITEC

2nd Floor, Chiswick Gate
598–608 Chiswick High Road
London W4 5RT
Tel: 020 8994 4141
Fax: 020 8994 7880
E-mail: info@itecworld.co.uk
Website: www.itecworld.co.uk

ITEC is a leading international specialist examination board, providing high quality qualifications specialising in: Beauty & Spa Therapy, Hairdressing, Complementary Therapies, Sports & Fitness and Customer Service.

QUALIFICATION/EXAMINATIONS
Beauty & Spa Therapies
Hairdressing
Complementary Therapies
Sports & Fitness
Customer Service

BIOLOGICAL SCIENCES
Membership of Professional Institutions and Associations

INSTITUTE OF BIOMEDICAL SCIENCE

12 Coldbath Square
London EC1R 5HL
Tel: 020 7713 0214
Fax: 020 7837 9658
E-mail: mail@ibms.org
Website: www.ibms.org

The IBMS is the professional body for biomedical scientists in the UK. We aim to promote and develop the role of biomedical science within healthcare to deliver the best possible service for patient care and safety.

MEMBERSHIP
eStudent
Associate
Licentiate (LIBMS)
Member (MIBMS)
Fellow (FIBMS)
Company Member

QUALIFICATION/EXAMINATIONS
Certificate of Achievement Part I and II
Certificate of Competence (also required for registration with the Health and Care Professions Council (HCPC))
Specialist Diploma in:
Cellular Pathology, Clinical Biochemistry, Clinical Immunology, Cytopathology, Haematology & Transfusion Science, Histocompatibility & Immunogenetics (developed in conjunction with BSHI), Medical Microbiology, Transfusion Science, Virology
Diploma of Biomedical Science
Diploma of Specialist Practice
Higher Specialist Diploma in:
Cellular Pathology, Clinical Chemistry, Cytopathology, Haematology, Immunology, Histocompatibility & Immunogenetics (developed in conjunction with BSHI), Medical Microbiology, Transfusion Science, Virology
Diploma of Higher Specialist Practice
Complementary qualifications/examinations related to areas of scientific expertise (available to Members and/or Fellows)
Certificates and Diplomas of Expert Practice
Advanced Specialist Diplomas

DESIGNATORY LETTERS
LIBMS, MIBMS, FIBMS

ROYAL SOCIETY OF BIOLOGY

Charles Darwin House
12 Roger Street
London WC1N 2JU
E-mail: info@rsb.org.uk
Website: www.rsb.org.uk

The Royal Society of Biology is a single unified voice for biology: advising Government and influencing policy; advancing education and professional development; supporting our members, and engaging and encouraging public interest in the life sciences. The Society represents a diverse membership of individuals, learned societies and other organisations.

MEMBERSHIP
Associate Member (AMRSB)
Member (MRSB)
Fellow (FRSB)
Affiliate
Student

BioNet

QUALIFICATION/EXAMINATIONS
Chartered Biologist (CBiol)
Licenced by the Science Council to provide:
Registered Scientist (RSci)
Registered Science Technician (RSciTech)
Chartered Scientist (CSci)
Chartered Science Teacher (CSciTeach)

DESIGNATORY LETTERS
AMRSB, MRSB, FRSB, CBiol, CSci, CSciTeach, RSci, RSciTech

BREWING
Membership of Professional Institutions and Associations

INSTITUTE OF BREWING & DISTILLING

33 Clarges Street
Mayfair
London W1J 7EE
Tel: 020 7499 8144
Fax: 020 7499 1156
E-mail: enquiries@ibd.org.uk
Website: www.ibd.org.uk

The IBD is a members' organization dedicated to the education and training needs of brewers and distillers and those in related industries. We do this by offering a range of internationally recognized qualifications and the training to support them, through either direct instruction or distance learning.

MEMBERSHIP
Member
Honorary Member
Senior Member
Fellow (FIBD)
Honorary Fellow
Corporate Member
Student Member

Member in Retirement
Certificate Member

QUALIFICATION/EXAMINATIONS
Certificate in the Fundamentals of Brewing and Packaging of Beer (FBPB) (City & Guilds Level 2)
Certificate in the Fundamentals of Distilling (FD) (City & Guilds Level 2)
General Certificate in Brewing (GCB) (City & Guilds Level 3)
General Certificate in Distilling (GCD) (City & Guilds Level 3)
General Certificate in Packaging (GCP) (City & Guilds Level 3)

Diploma in Packaging (Dipl.Pack) (City & Guilds Level 4)

General Certificate in Spirits Packaging

General Certificate in Malting

Diploma in Brewing (Dipl.Brew) (City & Guilds Level 4)

Diploma in Distilling (Dipl.Distil) (City & Guilds Level 4)

Master Brewer (MBrew)

DESIGNATORY LETTERS

Dipl.Brew, Dipl.Distil, Dipl.Pack, MBrew, FIBD, Hon FIBD

BUILDING

Membership of Professional Institutions and Associations

INSTITUTE OF ASPHALT TECHNOLOGY

PO Box 15690
BATHGATE EH48 9BT
Tel: 01506 238397
E-mail: info@instituteofasphalt.org
Website: www.instituteofasphalt.org

The IAT is the UK's professional body for persons working in asphalt technology and those interested in aspects of the manufacture, placing, technology and uses of materials containing asphalt or bitumen. A fully audited CPD system for members has been available since 1994 and is now also offered in computerized format for ease of data entry and auditing, via members' own PCs.

MEMBERSHIP
Student

Technician (Tech.IAT)
Affiliate (AIAT)
Associate Member (AMIAT)
Member (MIAT)
Fellow (FIAT)
Honorary Fellow (Hon FIAT)

DESIGNATORY LETTERS
Tech.IAT, AIAT, AMIAT, MIAT, FIAT, Hon.FIAT

THE CHARTERED INSTITUTE OF BUILDING

Englemere
Kings Ride
Ascot
Berkshire SL5 7TB
Tel: 01344 630700
Fax: 01344 630777
E-mail: reception@ciob.org.uk
Website: www.ciob.org

The CIOB is the international voice of the construction industry. CIOB members are largely Construction Managers engaged in managing the development, conservation and improvement of the built environment, with a common commitment to achieving and maintaining the highest possible standards.

MEMBERSHIP
Student Member

Associate (ACIOB)
Incorporated (ICIOB)
Member (MCIOB)
Fellow (FCIOB)
Chartered Environmentalist (CENV)
Student in Employment
Educationalist
Concessionary

QUALIFICATION/EXAMINATIONS

The CIOB has routes to membership to suit a range of professionals from those with degrees or vocational qualifications to those with experience but no formal qualifications. All our members have a strong commitment to improve and develop themselves in a challenging and exciting career.

Chartered Member status is recognized internationally as the mark of a skilled professional in the construction industry. CIOB members are from a wide range of professions in the construction industry.

To find out more about our membership qualifications and joining the CIOB just visit our website www.ciob.org

The CIOB Awarding Body offers a suite of qualifications to enable site operatives to progress into management roles.

Level 3 Diploma in Site Supervisory Studies
Level 4 Certificate in Site Management
Level 4 Diploma in Site Management

The CIOB qualifications develop the skills and confidence to manage and coordinate all types of construction projects. The site management qualifications are nationally recognized and allow the learner to progress to higher education and National Vocational Qualifications (NVQs).

For more information on the Site Management Qualifications visit the website at www.ciob.org.uk/education/courseinfo/sitemanagement

DESIGNATORY LETTERS
ACIOB, ICIOB, MCIOB, FCIOB, CENV

THE INSTITUTE OF CARPENTERS

32 High Street
Wendover
Buckinghamshire HP22 6EA
Tel: 0844 879 7696
Fax: 01296 620981
E-mail: info@instituteofcarpenters.com
Website: www.instituteofcarpenters.com

The IOC was founded in 1890 to oversee training for carpenters and joiners and maintain high professional standards at a time when many feared that traditional skills were being lost. Today, while remaining committed to our original aims, we embrace many other wood craftsmen, such as shopfitters, furniture and cabinetmakers, boat builders (woodworking skills), structural post & beam carpenters (heavy structural timber framers), wheelwrights, wood carvers and wood turners, and offer professional status to those holding recognized qualifications.

MEMBERSHIP
Student
Mature Student
Affiliate
Licentiate (LIOC)
Member (MIOC)
Fellow (FIOC)
College Member
Corporate Member
Corporate Associate

QUALIFICATION/EXAMINATIONS
Foundation Examination
Intermediate Examination
Advanced Craft Examination
Fellowship Examination
Setting-Out Course

DESIGNATORY LETTERS
LIOC, MIOC, FIOC

THE INSTITUTE OF CLERKS OF WORKS AND CONSTRUCTION INSPECTORATE OF GREAT BRITAIN INC

28 Commerce Road
Lynch Wood
Peterborough PE2 6LR
Tel: 01733 405160
Fax: 01733 405161
E-mail: info@icwci.org
Website: www.icwci.org

The ICWCI is the professional body that supports quality construction through inspection. As a membership organization, we provide a support network of meeting centres, technical advice, publications and events to help keep our members up to date with the ever-changing construction industry.

MEMBERSHIP
Student

Licentiate (LICWCI)
Member (MICWCI)
Fellow (FICWCI)
Life Member
Honorary Member

DESIGNATORY LETTERS
LICWCI, MICWCI, FICWCI

BUSINESS STUDIES
Membership of Professional Institutions and Associations

ASSOCIATION OF BUSINESS RECOVERY PROFESSIONALS (R3)

8th Floor
120 Aldersgate Street
London EC1A 4JQ
Tel: 020 7566 4200
Fax: 020 7566 4224
E-mail: association@r3.org.uk
Website: www.r3.org.uk

The Association of Business Recovery Professionals (known by its brand name 'R3') is the leading professional association for insolvency, business recovery and turnaround specialists in the UK. A not-for-profit organization, it promotes best practice for professionals working with financially troubled individuals and businesses, and provides a forum for debate on key issues facing the profession.

MEMBERSHIP
New Professional (Student) Member

New Professional (Networking) Member
Associate Member (AABRP)
Full Member (MABRP)
Fellow (FABRP)

QUALIFICATION/EXAMINATIONS
R3 provides comprehensive Continuing Professional Education in the field of Insolvency and Restructuring. For details of courses see R3's website.

DESIGNATORY LETTERS
AABRP, MABRP, FABRP

INSTITUTE OF ASSESSORS AND INTERNAL VERIFIERS

PO Box 1138
Warrington WA4 9GS
Tel: 01925 485 786
E-mail: office@iavltd.co.uk
Website: www.iavltd.co.uk

The IAV is the professional organization representing assessors and internal verifiers in the UK in vocational training and assessment.

MEMBERSHIP
Affiliate Member
Associate Member
Licentiate Member

THE ACADEMY OF EXECUTIVES & ADMINISTRATORS

Office 13275
PO Box 4336
Manchester
United Kingdom M61 0BW
Tel: 01386 277973
E-mail: info@academyofexecutivesandadministrators.org.uk
Website: www.academyofexecutivesandadministrators.org.uk

The Academy of Executives & Administrators was founded in 2002 to give professional status and recognition to the knowledge and skills of executives and administrators. We encourage excellence and flexibility in the changing environment of executive and administrative roles, and support lifelong learning to help members fulfil their career ambitions.

MEMBERSHIP
Student Member (StudAEA)
Associate Member (AMAEA)
Member (MAEA)
Fellow (FAEA)

Companion (CAEA)

QUALIFICATION/EXAMINATIONS
Associate Diploma for Business Economists
Associate Diploma for Financial Managers
Associate Diploma for Assistant Accountants
Associate Diploma for Assistant Corporate Accountants
Associate Diploma for Trainers
Certified Administration Practitioner
Certified Executive Practitioner
Certified Budget and Planning Practitioner

THE ACADEMY OF MULTI-SKILLS

40 Pembroke Square
London
Middlesex W8 6PE
Tel: 02074605362
E-mail: jeffwooller@yahoo.co.uk
Website: www.academyofmulti-skillsuk.org

The Academy of Multi-Skills was founded in 1995 to give professional recognition to multi-skilled personnel, skilled trades, crafts and professions. The Academy encourages a positive and energetic attitude to the challenges of careers that require diversity, creativity and intellect, and recognizes the valuable contribution that these skills provide to society.

MEMBERSHIP
MEMBERSHIP
Student Member GBP 100 Stud AMS (Cert MS)
Associate GBP 200 AMAMS (Dip MS)
Full Member GBP 250 MAMS (Dip MS)
Fellow GBP 300 FAMS (Dip MS)
Doctorate Fellow GBP 3,000 DFAMS
Company GBP 500 COAMS

QUALIFICATION/EXAMINATIONS
Endorsed by TQUK – Professional Doctorate Diploma for Executives – Equivalent to Doctorate Degree (Level 8)

Level 7 Advanced Professional Diploma (Equivalent to Masters Degree)
Level 6 Professional Diploma (Equivalent to Bachelors Degree)

DESIGNATORY LETTERS
Stud AMS, AMAMS, MAMS, FAMS, DFAMS, COAMS

THE FACULTY OF SECRETARIES AND ADMINISTRATORS LIMITED

Brightstowe
Catteshall Lane
Godalming
Surrey GU7 1LL
Tel: 0871 288 6935
Fax: 0871 288 6935
E-mail: admin@facultyofsecretaries.org.uk
Website: www.facultyofsecretaries.co.uk

The Faculty is a professional body for corporate secretaries whose qualified designation is that of Certified Public or Corporate Secretary and since 1930 has led in promoting good, fair and liberal governance.

The Faculty kitemark embeds concepts of reasonableness and care for others in an organisation's operation and decision taking.

MEMBERSHIP
Membership Fellows (FFCS)
Associates (AFCS)
Member (MACS)
Ordinary Member
Student Member
Licentiate (LFCS)
Corporate

QUALIFICATION/EXAMINATIONS
Part 1 The Generic Business Assessment to ONC/D Level
Part 2 Professional Papers in Company Secretarial Practice, Company Law and Management, Secretarial and Administrative Practice, Commercial Law
Part 3 Professional Meetings Law and Procedure, Company Taxation, Accountancy and Finance, Company Law

Assessment of Senior Personnel for direct entry now involves a viva voce interview and rated questions on corporate secretaryship as well as exemptions based on an agreed list of qualifications and a declaration of working with the general ethos of the faculty.

Single subject examinations are available and a programme for the assessment of in-house courses for company secretaries, directors and trustees. The Faculty gives credit for approved attendance at Directory of Social Change, Institute of Directors and other recognised bodies', courses on governance, leadership and management where it is clear they are beneficial to the development of caring, fair and liberal governance. The Faculty supports the aims and objectives of 'The Commonwealth' and seeks to ensure a fit with the syllabi of related bodies in Commonwealth countries.

The Society of Teachers in Business Education monitors this interview process.

The Kitemark is an assessment which an organisation can go through to establish good and liberal governance and has formats for private, public and voluntary sector organisations.

The former designations of Certified Book-keeper and Certified Company Accountant at Licentiate Level or not now directly offered although records of equivalence and Licentiate graduation on these are kept and entry to the main qualification grades is done on an 'on-a-par' basis. The Faculty continues to support the promotion of English as a Foreign Language in conjunction with The Society of Teachers in Business Education and other national bodies and delivers courses as a body on the UK Register of training providers seeking to work with local bodies who are also so registered.

DESIGNATORY LETTERS
FFCS, AFCS, LFCS, MACS

THE INSTITUTE OF CHARTERED SECRETARIES AND ADMINISTRATORS

16 Park Crescent
London W1B 1AH
Tel: 020 7580 4741
Fax: 020 7323 1132
E-mail: studentsupport@icsaglobal.com
Website: www.icsaglobal.com

The Institute of Chartered Secretaries and Administrators is the international qualifying and membership body for the Chartered Secretary profession. With a global community of 37,000 members we provide Chartered Membership, training and a professional qualifying scheme to set you on the path to a diverse, challenging and rewarding career.

MEMBERSHIP
Affiliate
Graduate (GradICSA)
Associate (ACIS)
Fellow (FCIS)

QUALIFICATION/EXAMINATIONS
Chartered Secretaries Qualifying Scheme (CSQS)
Certificate in Offshore Finance and Administration
Diploma in Offshore Finance and Administration
Certificate in Company Secretarial Practice and Share Registration Practice
Certificate in Irish Company Secretarial Practice and Share Registration Practice
Certificate in Employee Share Plans
Postgraduate Certificate in Charity Management
ICSA Certificate in Further Education Governance

DESIGNATORY LETTERS
GradICSA, ACIS, FCIS

CATERING AND INSTITUTIONAL MANAGEMENT
Membership of Professional Institutions and Associations

BII

Wessex House
80 Park Street
Camberley
Surrey GU15 3PT
Tel: 01276 684449
E-mail: info@bii.org
Website: www.bii.org

Founded in 1981, BII is the professional body for the licensed retail sector with a remit to raise standards throughout the industry. BIIAB, the wholly owned awarding body of BII, does this through offering qualifications specifically tailored to, and designed in conjunction with, the industry.

MEMBERSHIP
There is a wide range of membership grades available, from those who have just started their careers in licensed retailing to those who have been in the industry for many years. The grade of membership awarded depends on both experience and qualifications and is determined by a points system.

Member of the Hotel Catering and Management Association, HCIMA.

QUALIFICATION/EXAMINATIONS
Qualifications for licensing
Award for Designated Premises Supervisors (Level 2)
Award for Licensing Practitioners (Alcohol) (Level 2)
Award for Personal Licence Holders (Level 2)
Award for Upskilling Door Supervisors (Level 2)
Award for Upskilling Door Supervisors (Scotland)
Award in Door Supervision (Level 2)
Award in Door Supervision (Scotland)
Award in Door Supervision (Northern Ireland)
Award in CCTV Operations (Public Space Surveillance) (Scotland)
Award in Crime Scene Preservation (Level 2)
Award in Drug Awareness for Licensed Hospitality Staff (Level 2)
Award in Fire Safety (Level 2)
Scottish Certificate for Licensees (Drugs Awareness)
Award in Isle of Man Licensing Law
Award in Jersey Licensing Law
Qualifications for new licensed retail managers
Award in Licensed Retailing (Level 2)
Award in Beer and Cellar Quality (Cask and Keg) (Level 2)
Award in Beer and Cellar Quality (Keg) (Level 2)
Scottish Certificate in Licensed Retailing

Qualifications for staff development
Award in Kitchen Management (Level 3)

Award in Introduction to Employment in the Hospitality Industry (Level 1)
Professional Barperson's Qualification
Award in Conflict Management for Licensed Premises Staff (Level 2)
Award in Customer Service Excellence (Licensed Hospitality)
Award in Food Safety in Catering (Level 2)
Award in Health and Safety in the Workplace (Level 2)
Isle of Man Security Staff Qualification

Qualifications for management development

Award in Licensed Hospitality Operations (Level 2)
Certificate in Licensed Hospitality Operations (Level 2)
Certificate in Licensed Hospitality Skills (Level 2)
Award in Hospitality Business Management (Level 3)
Certificate in Hospitality Business Management (Level 3)
Certificate in Multiple Licensed Premises Management (Level 4)
Qualifications for personal and social responsibility

Award in Alcohol Awareness (Level 1)
Award in Assessment of Licensed Premises (Social Responsibility) (Level 2)
Award in Assessment of Licensed Premises (Social Responsibility) (Scotland)

GUILD OF INTERNATIONAL PROFESSIONAL TOASTMASTERS

Life President: Ivor Spencer
22 Great Mead
Denmead
Waterlooville
Hampshire PO7 6HH
Tel: 07802 250477
E-mail: info@guildoftoastmasters.co.uk
Website: www.guildoftoastmasters.co.uk

The Guild of Professional Toastmasters was established over 30 years ago to improve standards in the profession and support its members. A 5-day course is offered to prospective members, who may apply for membership upon successful completion of the course. Applications are considered by the Fellows of the Guild.

MEMBERSHIP
Fellow (FGIntPT)

DESIGNATORY LETTERS
FGIntPT

INSTITUTE OF HOSPITALITY

Trinity Court
34 West Street
Sutton
Surrey SM1 1SH
Tel: 020 8661 4900
Fax: 020 8661 4901
E-mail: awardingbody@instituteofhospitality.org
Website: www.instituteofhospitality.org

The Institute of Hospitality is the international professional body for managers and leaders in hospitality, leisure and tourism. We offer professional qualifications, accredit academic programmes of study, endorse training courses providing professional development opportunities ranging from daily operational duties to board level strategy.

Uniting Professionals, Promoting Excellence, Facilitating Learning

MEMBERSHIP
Student Member
Affiliate
Associate (AIH)

Member (MIH)
Fellow (FIH)

QUALIFICATION/EXAMINATIONS
Institute of Hospitality Level 3 Diploma in Hospitality and Toursim Management (VRQ)
Institute of Hospitality Level 4 Diploma in Advanced Hospitality and Tourism Management (VRQ)
Institute of Hospitality Level 2 Award in Professional Cookery in Health and Social Care

DESIGNATORY LETTERS
AIH, MIH, FIH

CHEMISTRY
Membership of Professional Institutions and Associations

SOCIETY OF COSMETIC SCIENTISTS

Suite 5
Langham House West
Mill Street
Luton
Bedfordshire LU1 2NA
Tel: 01582 726661
Fax: 01582 405217
E-mail: gem.bektas@btconnect.com
Website: www.scs.org.uk

The main object of the Society, which was formed in 1948, is to advance the science of cosmetics. We endeavour to do this by attracting highly qualified scientists with both academic and industrial experience in cosmetics or a related science to our membership of around 900 members, and by means of our publications, educational programmes and scientific meetings.

MEMBERSHIP
Student
Affiliate
Associate Member
Member – B Grade
Member – A Grade
Honorary Member

QUALIFICATION/EXAMINATIONS
Certificate of Higher Education in Cosmetic Science

THE OIL AND COLOUR CHEMISTS' ASSOCIATION

4th Floor
Clayton House
59 Piccadilly
Manchester M1 2AQ
Tel: 0161 933 7280
E-mail: admin@occa.org.uk
Website: www.occa.org.uk

OCCA, founded in 1918, is a learned society comprising individual qualified persons employed in, or associated with, the worldwide surface coatings industries. Most of our members work in a technical capacity, but there are commercial and other senior personnel from throughout the surface coating industries. The word 'oil' in our title refers to vegetable oils, which once formed a major part of surface coatings' formulations.

MEMBERSHIP
Student Member
Ordinary Member
Honorary Member
Licentiate (LTSC)
Associate (ATSC)
Fellow (FTSC)

DESIGNATORY LETTERS
LTSC, ATSC, FTSC

THE ROYAL SOCIETY OF CHEMISTRY

Thomas Graham House
Science Park
Milton Road
Cambridge CB4 0WF
Tel: 01223 420066
Fax: 01223 423623
E-mail: membership@rsc.org
Website: www.rsc.org

The RSC is the UK professional body for chemical scientists and an international learned society for advancing the chemical sciences. With over 46,000 members worldwide and an internationally acclaimed publishing business, our activities span education and training, conferences, science policy and the promotion of the chemical sciences to the public.

MEMBERSHIP
Affiliate
Associate Member (AMRSC)
Member (MRSC)
Fellow (FRSC)

QUALIFICATION/EXAMINATIONS
NVQ Analytical Chemistry (Level 5)
Registered Scientist and Registered Science Technician
MSc in Chemical Technology and Management
Mastership in Chemical Analysis (MChemA)
Chartered Chemist (CChem)
Chartered Scientist (CSci)

DESIGNATORY LETTERS
AMRSC, MRSC, FRSC, CChem

CHIROPODY

Membership of Professional Institutions and Associations

BRITISH CHIROPODY AND PODIATRY ASSOCIATION

The New Hall
149 Bath Road
Maidenhead
Berkshire SL6 4LA
Tel: 01628 632440
Fax: 01628 674483
E-mail: membership@bcha-uk.org
Website: www.bcha-uk.org

The BChA, formed in 1959, is the largest professional organization in the UK representing the interests of independent private chiropodists / podiatrists. Since 2005 we have added foothealth practitioners to include our 7,000 members, most of whom work mainly in private practice. Those who are registered with the Health Professions Council may work in the NHS or in education.

MEMBERSHIP
Member (MSSCh & MBChA) – Podiatrists
Fellow (FSSCh) – Podiatrist

Associate members are foothealth practitioners trained by The SMAE Institute.

QUALIFICATION/EXAMINATIONS
Diploma in Podiatric Medicine (DipPodMed)
Foothealth practitioners carry the qualification – MAFHP

DESIGNATORY LETTERS
MSSCh, MBChA, FSSCh and MAFHP

THE INSTITUTE OF CHIROPODISTS AND PODIATRISTS

150 Lord Street
Southport
Merseyside PR9 0NP
Tel: 01704 546141
E-mail: secretary@iocp.org.uk
Website: www.iocp.org.uk

The Institute serves members throughout the whole of the profession of podiatry and podiatric medicine. Its members include chiropodists, podiatrists and podiatric surgeons, employed and self-employed at all levels of practice. The Institute certificate of membership is proof that members undertake to adhere to a strict code of ethics and professional conduct and that they have access to some of the UK's most innovative continuing professional development training.

The Institute is a democratic organisation with the election of officers both local and national being decided bi-annually by members. All members therefore play an active role in their own affairs. For more than 60 years the Institute has followed an independent line at the forefront of the profession it serves, for the progress and well-being of both the profession and the public.

The IOCP represents all levels of the profession and our CPD is open to both members and non-members, as by elevating professional standards we aim to improve public safety. We have branches throughout the UK and the Republic of Ireland, and members overseas, and hold lectures, seminars and workshops to enable members to keep up to date.

MEMBERSHIP
Full Member
Student
Associate

QUALIFICATION/EXAMINATIONS
MInstChP – Full Member
AInstFHP – Associate

THE SOCIETY OF CHIROPODISTS AND PODIATRISTS

Quartz House, 207 Providence Square
Mill Street
London SE1 2EW
Tel: 020 7234 8620
E-mail: reception@scpod.org
Website: www.scpod.org

The SCP is the professional body and trade union for registered podiatrists. Membership is restricted to those qualified for registration and the Society represents around 10,000 NHS podiatrists, private practitioners and students. We monitor standards of undergraduate education and provide opportunities for CPD for our members.

MEMBERSHIP
Member (MChS)
Associate

DESIGNATORY LETTERS
MChS

CHIROPRACTIC

Membership of Professional Institutions and Associations

MCTIMONEY CHIROPRACTIC ASSOCIATION

Crowmarsh Gifford
Wallingford
Oxfordshire OX10 8DJ
Tel: 01491 829211
E-mail: admin@mctimoney-chiropractic.org
Website: www.mctimoneychiropractic.org

The McTimoney Chiropractic Association is a professional association for Chiropractors, who in the UK are registered with the General Chiropractic Council.

MEMBERSHIP
Provisional Member

Full Member
Fellow

DESIGNATORY LETTERS
MMCA

SCOTTISH CHIROPRACTIC ASSOCIATION

1 Chisholm Avenue
Bishopton
Renfrewshire PA7 5JH
Tel: 0141 404 0260
E-mail: admin@sca-chiropractic.org
Website: www.sca-chiropractic.org

The SCA was formed in 1979 and now has more than 60 members practising in Scotland and over 120 associated members elsewhere in the UK and abroad. Our aims are to enhance the chiropractic profession in the UK, maintain high standards of professional practice, and provide advice and support to our members.

MEMBERSHIP
Member

UNITED CHIROPRACTIC ASSOCIATION

1st Floor
45 North Hill
Plymouth
Devon PL4 8EZ
Tel: 01752 658785
Fax: 01752 658786
E-mail: admin@united-chiropractic.org
Website: www.united-chiropractic.org

The UCA is a UK-based organization for qualified, professional, principal-based chiropractors, associates and students. Full membership is open to qualified, GCC-registered chiropractors from any recognized school of chiropractic.

MEMBERSHIP
Student
Associate

Affiliate
1st Year Graduate
2nd Year Graduate
Full Member
Overseas Member

THE CHURCHES
Membership of Professional Institutions and Associations

BAPTIST UNION OF SCOTLAND

48 Speirs Wharf
Glasgow G4 9TH
Tel: 0141 423 6169
Fax: 0141 424 1422
E-mail: admin@scottishbaptist.org.uk
Website: www.scottishbaptist.org.uk

The Baptist Union of Scotland was formed in 1869, when 51 churches with a total congregation of about 3,500 united. Today, with 162 churches and about 11,250 members, the Union strives for simplicity in organizational structure and promotes increasing contact between the local churches and the National Team, who function under the overall direction of the General Director.

QUALIFICATION/EXAMINATIONS
BD or BA in Theology
Graduate Diploma in Applied Theology through Work Based Learning
Graduate Diploma in Pastoral Studies
(awarded by the Scottish Baptist College, Paisley, and validated by the University of Paisley)

BRISTOL BAPTIST COLLEGE

The Promenade
Clifton Down
Clifton
Bristol BS8 3NJ
Tel: 0117 946 7050
Fax: 0117 946 7787
E-mail: reception@bristol-baptist.ac.uk
Website: www.bristol-baptist.ac.uk

The central aim of the College is to train men and women for ministry in the Church and in the world. We do this by enabling critical reflection upon the Bible and Christian theological tradition and on the contexts from which we come and within which we are placed.

QUALIFICATION/EXAMINATIONS
Certificate in Theological Studies
Diploma in Theological Studies
BA in Theological Studies
MA in Christian Theology
(all validated by the University of Bristol)

METHODIST CHURCH IN IRELAND

1 Fountainville Avenue
Belfast BT9 6AN
Tel: 028 9032 4554
Fax: 028 9023 9467
E-mail: secretary@irishmethodist.org
Website: www.irishmethodist.org

MEMBERSHIP
Candidates for training must normally have the standard of general education for university entrance. They must be accredited Local Preachers of the Methodist Church, and are examined by written papers in Biblical Studies and Theology and by oral aptitude and personality tests. After admission to training, candidates normally spend 3 years at Edgehill Theological College, Belfast, studying for a diploma or degree of Queen's University, Belfast, in New Testament Greek, Hebrew, the English Bible, Theology, Church History, Pastoral Psychology, or Homiletics. This is followed by 3 years as a probationer Minister working under a superintendent Minister. During probation the candidate continues study within a tutorial system and is examined by continuous assessment.

SCOTTISH EPISCOPAL INSTITUTE

Forbes House
21 Grosvenor Crescent
Edinburgh EH12 5EE
Tel: 0131 243 1347
E-mail: institute@scotland.anglican.org
Website: www.scotland.anglican.org

Candidates are trained for lay and ordained, stipendiary and non-stipendiary ministries in the Scottish Episcopal Church and the United Reformed Church.

The curriculum is delivered centrally through residential sessions and seminar teaching. The Diploma of Higher Education in Theology, Ministry and Mission and the BA in Theology, Ministry and Mission courses run by the Institute are validated by Common Awards/Durham University. Some students undertake degree programmes in parallel with their formation through Scottish Universities.

THE CHURCH IN WALES

St Michael's College
Llandaff
Cardiff CF5 2YJ
Tel: 029 205 63379
Fax: 029 208 38008
Website: www.stmichaels.ac.uk

The Church in Wales expects candidates for ordination and reader ministry to satisfy the requirements of recognized theological courses. University graduates usually spend at least 2 years full time (or its part time equivalent) at a theological college or course, and will be encouraged to study for a postgraduate degree.

Non-theological graduates are encouraged to study for a university degree, diploma or certificate in Theology, depending on their age and the ministry for which they are being trained. Non-graduate candidates must have at least 5 passes at GCSE and normally study for a university certificate or diploma in Theology or a degree in Theology if they have obtained the necessary grades at A level. These requirements may be modified in the case of older candidates.

THE CHURCH OF ENGLAND

Ministry Division of The Archbishops' Council
Church House
Great Smith Street
London SW1P 3AZ
Tel: 020 7898 1397
E-mail: keith.beech-gruneberg@churchofengland.org
Website: www.churchofengland.org/clergy-office-holders/ministry.aspx
www.aet-lambeth.org/

The Church of England's Ministry Division oversees training for ordination and licensed lay ministry/Reader ministry including the Common Awards created by the Church and validated by Durham University.

In addition, The Archbishop's Examination in Theology offers means of study at research degree level.

QUALIFICATION/EXAMINATIONS
Awards validated by Durham University:
Certificate of Higher Education in Theology, Ministry and Mission
Certificate of Higher Education in Christian Ministry and Mission (180 credits)

Diploma of Higher Education in Theology, Ministry and Mission
BA in Theology, Ministry and Mission
Graduate Certificate in Theology, Ministry and Mission
Graduate Diploma in Theology, Ministry and Mission
Postgraduate Certificate in Theology, Ministry and Mission
Postgraduate Diploma in Theology, Ministry and Mission
MA in Theology, Ministry and Mission
Archbishop's Examination:
Master of Philosophy
Doctor of Philosophy

THE CHURCH OF SCOTLAND

Church of Scotland Offices
121 George Street
Edinburgh EH2 4YN
Tel: 0131 225 5722
Website: www.churchofscotland.org.uk

The vision of The Church of Scotland is to be a church which seeks to inspire the people of Scotland and beyond with the Good News of Jesus Christ through enthusiastic worshipping, witnessing, nurturing and serving communities.

THE METHODIST CHURCH

Formation in Ministry Office (Initial Development of Ministries)
25 Marylebone Road
London NW1 5JR
Tel: 020 7486 5502
E-mail: helpdesk@methodistchurch.org.uk
Website: www.methodist.org.uk

Candidates for Diaconal or Presbyteral Ministry in the Methodist Church must have been members of the Methodist Church at least 2 years and are expected to offer at least 10 years of ministerial service. The first stage of preparation is Foundation Training, which requires 1 year (FT) or 2 years (PT) to complete, during which a person may apply to become a candidate for ordained ministry. The process of selection takes 6 months. To enter into training for Presbyteral Ministry, a candidate must be a trained Local Preacher, which involves taking the Methodist Local Preachers' Training Course, Faith & Worship. Deacons become members of the Methodist Diaconal and are not required to be preachers. Accepted candidates for either order receive 1 or 2 years of further theological training, which in most cases leads to a degree or diploma in Theology or Ministry. Upon completion of training, a candidate serves as a Methodist Minister for 2 years on probation before ordination. For Presbyters, the appointment may be to an itinerant appointment (stipendiary) or to a local appointment (usually non-stipendiary) or as licensed to minister in secular employment. Deacons are always itinerant.

THE MORAVIAN CHURCH IN GREAT BRITAIN AND IRELAND

Moravian Church House
5–7 Muswell Hill
London N10 3TJ
Tel: 020 8883 3409
Fax: 020 8365 3371
E-mail: office@moravian.org.uk
Website: www.moravian.org.uk

Candidates for Moravian Church Service must be members of the Moravian Church and would normally have completed the Lay Training Course and have the support of their local church committee. They should make an initial application to the Provincial Board of the Moravian Church. Their qualifications are examined by the Church Service Advisory Board, which reports on them to the Provincial Board, with whom the final decision rests. Normally the standard of education required for the work of the Ministry is a university Divinity degree or Certificate together with a thorough acquaintance with the history, principles and methods of the Moravian Church. Candidates receive guidance for the Ministry during a period of supervised service under the direction of experienced Ministers. A class of non-stipendiary Ministers has been established for those who wish to serve on a non-maintained basis. Training varies according to candidates' needs. In all cases applications should be made to the address given above.

THE PRESBYTERIAN CHURCH IN IRELAND

The Director of Ministerial Studies
Union Theological College
108 Botanic Avenue
Belfast BT7 1JT
Tel: 02890 205088
Fax: 02890 205099

Qualifications required: Under 30 – a non-theological degree; over 30 but under 40 (as reckoned on 1 October following application) – either a non-theological degree or 2 years, non-graduating Arts or 4 modules of PT BD study or 6 modules of PT study in Humanities acceptable to the Board of Studies; over 40 – not normally accepted, except in exceptional circumstances, where candidate is already possessed of good educational background and/or professional experience.

THE PRESBYTERIAN CHURCH OF WALES

Tabernacle Chapel
81 Merthyr Road
Whitchurch
Cardiff CF14 1DD
Tel: 02920 627465
Fax: 02920 616188
E-mail: swyddfa.office@ebcpcw.org.uk
Website: www.ebcpcw.org.uk

The Presbyterian Church of Wales (PCW) is a Protestant non-conformist denomination. Ordination is dependent on successful application through the local church and Presbytery to the Candidates and Training Department.

MEMBERSHIP
Ministers are ordained to the full-time, part-time or non-stipendiary ministry.

QUALIFICATION/EXAMINATIONS
Pastoral Studies course

THE ROMAN CATHOLIC CHURCH

Candidates for the priesthood in the RC Church attend a residential seminary course of at least 6 years. Among subjects studied are Philosophy, Psychology, Dogmatic and Moral Theology, Scripture, Church History, Canon Law, Liturgy, Catechetics, Communications and Pastoral Theology. Each college/seminary has its own arrangements for the university education of its students. Those who do not attend university take a final internal exam.

THE SALVATION ARMY

UK Headquarters
101 Newington Causeway
London SE1 6BN
Tel: 020 7367 4500
E-mail: info@salvationarmy.org.uk
Website: www.salvationarmy.org.uk

Salvation Army officers engaged in FT service are ordained ministers of religion, and are commissioned following a 2-year period of residential training at the William Booth College, Denmark Hill, London SE5 8BQ. This course – an HE Diploma in Salvation Army Officer Training – may now be undertaken by distance learning, or a mixture of residential and distance learning. Officers may be appointed to corps (church) work, to social services centres (for which additional professional qualifications are required) or to administrative posts.

THE SCOTTISH UNITED REFORMED AND CONGREGATIONAL COLLEGE

113 West Regent Street
Glasgow G2 2RU
Tel: 0141 248 5382
E-mail: Scottishcollege@urcscotland.org.uk
Website: www.scottishcollege.org.uk

The College is recognized as a resource centre for learning by the General Assembly of the United Reformed Church and is one of the institutions charged with responsibility for initial ministerial education.

QUALIFICATION/EXAMINATIONS
The College awards only its own certificate, which is part of the process of accreditation of ordinands as ministers of the United Reformed Church. Students, however, are normally concurrently matriculated for a degree, usually in Theology or Religious Studies, at a university.

THE UNITARIAN AND FREE CHRISTIAN CHURCHES

Essex Hall
London WC2R 3HY
Tel: 020 7240 2384
Fax: 020 7240 3089
E-mail: info@unitarian.org.uk
Website: www.unitarian.org.uk

Candidates accepted for training for the ministry in the Unitarian and Free Christian Churches take courses of training either at Manchester Academy & Harris College, Oxford (2 to 4 years' study for an Oxford degree in Theology/or Theology & Philosophy or an Oxford Certificate in Theology/Religious Studies), or at the Unitarian College (Luther King House, Brighton Grove, Rusholme, Manchester; an individually designed contextual theology course of the Partnership for Theological Education which may lead to a degree or other academic qualification validated by Chester or Manchester University). Alternative arrangements can be made for candidates wishing to study through the Welsh language. Placement work and Unitarian studies are also integral to ministerial preparation. Training normally takes 2 or more years.

THE UNITED REFORMED CHURCH

Church House
86 Tavistock Place
London WC1H 9RT
Tel: 020 7916 2020
Fax: 020 7916 2021
E-mail: urc@urc.org.uk
Website: www.urc.org.uk

Candidates for **Ministry of Word and Sacraments** must have been a member of the URC for at least 2 years. and complete a candidating process. Most then take a 3- or 4-year course of part-time or full-time academic study alongside a minimum of 800 hours of pastoral placements. The minimum required outcome is a Diploma of Higher Education, in Theology. **Church-related Community Workers** strengthen the local church's mission through community development. Candidates are required to obtain at least a Diploma in Theology and a Diploma in Community Work before being commissioned.
Lay Preacher's Certificate: The qualifying course for this takes 3 years in local groups, residential weekends, and practical work in churches.

THE WESLEYAN REFORM UNION

Church House
123 Queen Street
Sheffield S1 2DU
Tel: 0114 272 1938
E-mail: admin@thewru.co.uk
Website: www.thewru.com

The Wesleyan Reform Union has no training college of its own and encourages candidates for its Ministry to enter a Bible College for 2 or 3 years. All candidates are, however, under the personal supervision of a Union Tutor, who directs a Biblical Studies & Training Department offering fairly extensive courses. Candidates attend Headquarters once a year for an oral exam in Theology conducted by the Tutor in the presence of the Union Examination Committee; they also take written exams.

UNITED FREE CHURCH OF SCOTLAND

11 Newton Place
Glasgow G3 7PR
Tel: 01413 323435
E-mail: office@ufcos.org.uk
Website: www.ufcos.org.uk

The United Free Church of Scotland is a small presbyterian denomination which came into being in 1929. Those seeking to become candidates for the ministry should normally have been members of the denomination for at least a year. They will require to undertake a degree course in Theology.

CINEMA, FILM AND TELEVISION
Membership of Professional Institutions and Associations

INTERNATIONAL MOVING IMAGE SOCIETY (IMIS)

Pinewood Studios
Pinewood Road
Iver Heath
Buckinghamshire SL0 0NH
Tel: 01753 656656
E-mail: info@societyinmotion.com
Website: www.societyinmotion.com

The IMIS, formerly the BKSTS, was founded in 1931 to inspire, train, educate and connect all members of the media industry around the world. IMIS provides a series of lectures, training, and networking events as well as offering affordable membership rates.

MEMBERSHIP
Student Member
Associate Member
Full Member (MBKS)
Emeritus Member

Fellow (FBKS)

QUALIFICATION/EXAMINATIONS
For Full Membership:
Age 23 or over
5 years of experience in the industry
Submission of CV/Resume
(2) References

DESIGNATORY LETTERS
MBKS, FBKS

THE LONDON FILM SCHOOL

24 Shelton Street
Covent Garden
London WC2H 9UB
Tel: 020 7836 9642
Fax: 020 7497 3718
E-mail: info@lfs.org.uk
Website: www.lfs.org.uk

The LFS is one of the foremost independent film schools in Europe and is recognized by Skillset as a Centre of Excellence. It is a registered charity and a non-profit-making company, limited by guarantee. Since 1956 we have trained thousands of directors, cinematographers, editors and other film professionals from around the world.

QUALIFICATION/EXAMINATIONS
MA in Filmmaking (validated by London Metropolitan University)
MA in Screenwriting (validated by London Metropolitan University)
MA International Film Business
PhD Film by Practice

THE NATIONAL FILM AND TELEVISION SCHOOL

Beaconsfield Studios
Station Road
Beaconsfield
Buckinghamshire HP9 1LG
Tel: 01494 671234
Fax: 01494 674042
E-mail: info@nfts.co.uk
Website: www.nfts.co.uk

Creative Skillset Film Academy, the UK's leading film and television school, offers full-time MA and Diploma courses in all the key film and television disciplines, from Animation to VFX. Purpose-built studios include two film stages, a large television studio, and post-production facilities rivalling those of many professional companies.

QUALIFICATION/EXAMINATIONS
Diploma (in 1 of 8 disciplines)
MA in Film and Television (specializing in 1 of 13 disciplines)

CLEANING, LAUNDRY AND DRY CLEANING

Membership of Professional Institutions and Associations

BRITISH INSTITUTE OF CLEANING SCIENCE

9 Premier Court
Boarden Close
Moulton Park
Northampton
Northants NN3 6LF
Tel: 01604 678710
Fax: 01604 645988
E-mail: info@bics.org.uk
Website: www.bics.org.uk

The British Institute of Cleaning Science is the largest independent professional and educational body within the cleaning industry.

Our mission is to raise the standards of education and to build awareness of the cleaning industry, through professional standards and accredited training.

MEMBERSHIP
- **Student** – For individuals currently studying towards a cleaning related qualification e.g. an apprenticeship.
- **Practitioner Grade (PBICSc)** – For individuals who have achieved the Mandatory Units of the Cleaning Professional's Skills Suite (CPSS) and are awarded their Licence to Practice (PBICSc).
- **Competent Grade (CBICSc)** – For individuals who have achieved the three Mandatory Units plus a further three or more skills from the Cleaning Professional's Skills Suite (CPSS).
- **Licensed Assessor (LBICSc)** – For individuals who have achieved the three Mandatory Units plus a further seven or more skills from the Cleaning Professionals Skills Suite (CPSS) as well as the relevant training to become a Licensed Assessor.
- **Fellow of BICSc (FBICSc)** – BICSc may award the honour to individuals for exceptional service to the Institute, or to the cleaning industry as a whole.

QUALIFICATION/EXAMINATIONS
The Cleaning Professional's Skills Suite (CPSS)
Car Valeting Training
On Premises Laundry Training

Health and Safety Workshop
Train the Trainer Course
Other cleaning qualifications are also available

THE GUILD OF CLEANERS AND LAUNDERERS

56 Maple Drive
Larkhall
South Lanarkshire ML9 2AR
Tel: 01698 322669
E-mail: enquiries@gcl.org.uk
Website: www.gcl.org.uk

The Guild, formed in 1949, is a technical and professional society whose aim is to further knowledge and skill in all branches of the industry. We keep our members up to date through lectures, seminars and written reports, exchange information of mutual benefit with other organizations in the industry, and voice our opinion in relevant forums.

MEMBERSHIP
Young Guilder

Member
Associate (AGCL)
Advanced Member (AdGCL)
Licentiate (LGCL)
Fellow (FGCL)
Guild Plus Member

DESIGNATORY LETTERS
AGCL, AdGCL, LGCL, FGCL

COLOUR TECHNOLOGY
Membership of Professional Institutions and Associations

PAINTING AND DECORATING ASSOCIATION

32 Coton Road
Nuneaton
Warwickshire CV11 5TW
Tel: 024 7635 3776
Fax: 024 7635 4513
E-mail: info@paintingdecoratingassociation.co.uk
Website: www.paintingdecoratingassociation.co.uk

The PDA is a registered trade and employers' organization, catering exclusively for the needs of professional painting and decorating trade employers. The Association conducts no examinations, but all membership applications are scrutinized at branch level to ensure that only bona fide firms that agree to abide by our code of conduct are admitted.

MEMBERSHIP
Full Member
Associate

THE SOCIETY OF DYERS AND COLOURISTS

Perkin House
82 Grattan Road
Bradford BD1 2LU
Tel: 01274 725138
E-mail: members@sdc.org.uk
Website: www.sdc.org.uk

An educational charity, professional body and chartered society, serving globally all aspects of the coloration industries including the textile supply chain through the knowledgeable and enthusiastic involvement of its professional members and industry partners. Recognized as the authority for colour science and technology, delivering high-quality international qualifications and training programmes.

MEMBERSHIP
Individual Voting Member, Individual Non-voting Member, Individual Student Member, College Member, Company Member

QUALIFICATION/EXAMINATIONS
Fellowship (FSDC), Associateship (ASDC), Licentiateship (LSDC), Chartered Colourist (CCol), Textile Coloration Certificate, Foundation Textile Coloration Certificate.

DESIGNATORY LETTERS
FSDC, ASDC, LSDC, CCol

COMMUNICATIONS AND MEDIA
Membership of Professional Institutions and Associations

THE PICTURE RESEARCH ASSOCIATION

c/o 10 Marrick House
Mortimer Crescent
London NW6 5NY
Tel: 0771403017
E-mail: chair@picture-research.org.uk
Website: www.picture-research.org.uk

The PRA, founded in 1977, is a professional organization for picture researchers, picture editors and anyone specifically involved in the research, management and supply of visual material to the media industry. Our aims are to provide information and give support to our members, and to promote their interests and specific skills to potential employers.

MEMBERSHIP
Introductory Member
Full Member
Sponsors

QUALIFICATION/EXAMINATIONS
To qualify as a member of the Association you need a minimum of 2 years experience as a qualified picture researcher/picture editor, eg you were involved in the online search of images, working to a specific brief or project. You would have supplied both digital or analogue files for reproduction. You would also be required to have knowledge and experience of fee negotiations, clearances, copyright and licensing of photographic images from a selection of photographic sources and collections.
Sponsors: A full- or part-time employee of a picture library, picture agency or image archive who is directly involved in the supply of images to the media in general.

COMPUTING AND INFORMATION TECHNOLOGY
Membership of Professional Institutions and Associations

ASSOCIATION OF COMPUTER PROFESSIONALS

ACP
Chilverbridge House
Arlington
East Sussex BN26 6SB
Tel: 01323 871874
Fax: 01323 871875
E-mail: admin@acpexamboard.com
Website: www.acpexamboard.com

The ACP is an independent professional examining body, founded in 1984 to set and maintain standards of education that reflect the constantly changing requirements of the computer industry, both in the UK and overseas. We do so through the provision of course syllabuses and examinations to our carefully vetted training centres around the world.

MEMBERSHIP
Student
Practitioner
Graduate (GradACP)

Licentiate (LACP)
Associate (AACP)
Member (MACP)
Fellow (FACP)

QUALIFICATION/EXAMINATIONS
Please see the ACP's website for details of certificates and diplomas.

DESIGNATORY LETTERS
GradACP, LACP, AACP, MACP, FACP

BCS, THE CHARTERED INSTITUTE FOR IT

1st Floor, Block D
North Star House
North Star Avenue
Swindon
Wiltshire SN2 1FA
Tel: 01793 417417
Fax: 01793 417444
E-mail: customerservices@bcs.uk
Website: www.bcs.org

We promote wider social and economic progress through the advancement of information technology science and practice. We bring together industry, academics, practitioners and government to share knowledge, promote new thinking, inform the design of new curricula, shape public policy and inform the public.

Our vision is to be a world-class organisation for IT. Our 75,000 strong membership includes practitioners, businesses, academics and students in the UK and internationally. We deliver a range of professional development tools for practitioners and employees. A leading IT qualification body, we offer a range of widely recognised qualifications.

MEMBERSHIP
Memberships:
Associate Member (AMBCS)
Professional Member (MBCS)
Chartered IT Professional (CITP)
Fellowship (FBCS)
Student
Apprentice

Affiliate

QUALIFICATION/EXAMINATIONS
IT User Qualifications
- Computer and Online Basics – Understand the basics of how to use a computer
- Digital Skills – Develop skills for our digital world
- ECDL – Develop skills using office-based software
- e-safety – The online safety qualification for Schools
- ITQ – The flexible IT qualification – Create your own qualification, or use one of our tailor-made solutions

Higher Education Qualifications
- BCS Level 4 Certificate in IT/100/6190/2
- BCS Level 5 Diploma in IT/100/6190/3
- BCS Level 6 Professional Graduate Diploma in IT/100/6191/5

Professional Certification
- Business analysis
- Information security and CESG scheme
- Software testing

- IT service management (inc ITIL)
- Agile
- Project & programme management
- PRINCE2
- Solution development and architecture
- Consultancy
- Green IT
- Data centre management
- OpenStack software

Apprenticeships
- Cyber Intrusion Analyst
- Cyber Security Technologist
- Data Analyst
- Digital Marketer
- Infrastructure Technician
- Network Engineer
- Software Developer
- Software Tester
- Unified Communications Trouble Shooter

See the BCS website for details of other qualifications.

INSTITUTE FOR THE MANAGEMENT OF INFORMATION SYSTEMS

Suite A (Part) 2nd Floor
3 White Oak Square
London Road
Swanley
Kent BR8 7AG
Tel: 0845 850 0006
Fax: 0845 850 0007
E-mail: imis@bcs.org
Website: www.imis.org.uk

IMIS is one of the leading professional associations in the IT sector. A registered charity, it plays a prominent role in fostering greater understanding of IS management, in working to enhance the status of those engaged in the profession, and in promoting higher standards through better education and training worldwide.

MEMBERSHIP
Student Member
Practitioner Member
Licentiate Member (LIMIS)

Associate Member (AIMIS)
Full Member (MIMIS)
Fellow (FIMIS)

QUALIFICATION/EXAMINATIONS
Foundation
Diploma
Higher Diploma

DESIGNATORY LETTERS
LIMIS, AIMIS, MIMIS, FIMIS

INSTITUTION OF ANALYSTS AND PROGRAMMERS

Boundary House
Boston Road
London W7 2QE
Tel: 020 8434 3685
E-mail: admin@iap.org.uk
Website: www.iap.org.uk

The IAP is a professional organization for people who work in the development, installation and testing of business systems and computer software. Our aim is to promote high standards of competence and conduct among our members, to encourage them to develop their skills and progress their career, and to facilitate the advancement and spreading of knowledge within the profession.

MEMBERSHIP
Licentiate
Graduate (GradIAP)
Associate Member (AIAP)
Member (MIAP)
Fellow (FIAP)

DESIGNATORY LETTERS
GradIAP, AIAP, MIAP, FIAP

COUNSELLING
Membership of Professional Institutions and Associations

COUNSELLING LTD

Registered Office
5 Pear Tree Walk
Wakefield
West Yorkshire WF2 0HW
E-mail: via website
Website: www.counselling.ltd.uk

Counselling, a registered charity founded in 1998, is a membership organization for counsellors and psychotherapists in the UK that has established a network of about 2,700 affiliated CCC-registered counsellors, many of whom are able to provide occasional free or discounted face-to-face counselling with clients on low incomes.

MEMBERSHIP
Affiliate

CSCT COUNSELLING TRAINING

13 Coleshill Street
Sutton Coldfield
West Midlands B72 1SD
Tel: 0121 321 1396
Fax: 0121 355 5581
E-mail: info@counsellingtraining.com
Website: www.counsellingtraining.com

CSCT has been producing counselling training courses for over 25 years, during which time we have trained over 50,000 students. Our courses are offered PT via a network of colleges and private providers throughout the UK. Our training materials are written to the specifications of the appropriate awarding body and we provide 24-hour e-mail and telephone support from Client Services and the Academic Team.

QUALIFICATION/EXAMINATIONS
Please see the CSCT's website.

CREDIT MANAGEMENT
Membership of Professional Institutions and Associations

CHARTERED INSTITUTE OF CREDIT MANAGEMENT

The Water Mill
Station Road
South Luffenham
Oakham
Leicestershire LE15 8NB
Tel: 01780 722900
Fax: 01780 721333
E-mail: info@cicm.com
Website: www.cicm.com

CICM is the largest professional credit management organisation in Europe and the only one accredited by Ofqual as an awarding body. We represent the credit profession across trade, consumer and export credit, as well as in related activities such as collections, credit reporting, credit insurance and insolvency, promote excellence in credit management and raise awareness of its vital role in business and the community.

MEMBERSHIP
Affiliate
Associate Member (AICM)
Graduate Member (MICM(Grad))
Member (MICM)
Fellow (FICM)

Corporate Member

QUALIFICATION/EXAMINATIONS
Certificate in Credit Management
Level 3 Diploma in Credit Management
Level 5 Diploma in Credit Management
Certificate in Debt Collection
Diploma in Debt Collection
Certificate in Money and Debt Advice
Diploma in Money and Debt Advice
Certificate in High Court Enforcement (Level 4)
Diploma in High Court Enforcement (Level 4)
Diploma in High Court Enforcement (Level 5)

DESIGNATORY LETTERS
AICM, MICM (Grad), MICM, FIFA

DANCING
Membership of Professional Institutions and Associations

BRITISH BALLET ORGANIZATION

Woolborough House
39 Lonsdale Road
Barnes
London SW13 9JP
Tel: 020 8748 1241
Fax: 020 8748 1301
E-mail: info@bbo.org.uk
Website: www.bbo.org.uk

The BBO, founded in 1930, is an awarding body offering teacher training and examinations in classical ballet, tap, modern dance and jazz. We have schools throughout the UK and in several other countries.

MEMBERSHIP
Student Member
Senior Student Member
Affiliated Member
Student Teacher Member
Teacher Member

QUALIFICATION/EXAMINATIONS
Please see the BBO website for details.

IMPERIAL SOCIETY OF TEACHERS OF DANCING

Imperial House
22/26 Paul Street
London EC2A 4QE
Tel: +44 (0)20 7377 1577
Fax: +44 (0)20 7247 8829
E-mail: via website
Website: www.istd.org

The ISTD is a registered educational charity and examinations board. We aim to promote knowledge of dance, to maintain and improve teaching standards, and to qualify (by examination) teachers of dancing. Our dance techniques cover more than 12 different genres and are taught by more than 7,500 members by our members worldwide.

MEMBERSHIP
A range of 9 categories from Student to Life Membership.

QUALIFICATION/EXAMINATIONS
Please see our website www.istd.org or www.dance-teachers.org

DESIGNATORY LETTERS
ISTD

INTERNATIONAL DANCE TEACHERS' ASSOCIATION LIMITED

International House
76 Bennett Road
Brighton BN2 5JL
Tel: 01273 685652
Fax: 01273 674388
E-mail: via website
Website: www.idta.co.uk

The IDTA is one of the world's largest dance examination boards, with more than 7,000 members in 55 countries. Our aims are to promote knowledge and foster the art of dance in all its forms, to maintain and improve dancing standards, and to offer a comprehensive range of professional qualifications in all dance genres.

MEMBERSHIP
Associate (AIDTA)
Licentiate (LIDTA)
Fellow (FIDTA)

DESIGNATORY LETTERS
AIDTA, LIDTA, FIDTA

THE BENESH INSTITUTE

36 Battersea Square
London SW11 3RA
Tel: 020 7326 8035
E-mail: beneshinstitute@rad.org.uk
Website: www.benesh.org

The Benesh Institute is the international centre for Benesh Movement Notation (BMN) founded in 1962 to promote, develop and offer education in BMN. We also function as an examining body and professional centre, and are responsible for coordinating technical developments. Since 1997 The Benesh Institute has been incorporated within the Royal Academy of Dance.

QUALIFICATION/EXAMINATIONS
Certificate in Benesh Movement Notation (CBMN) (validated by the Royal Academy of Dance)
Diploma for Professional Benesh Movement Notators (DPBMN) (validated by the Royal Academy of Dance)
Associate of the Institute of Choreology (AI Chor)

DENTISTRY
Membership of Professional Institutions and Associations

BRITISH ASSOCIATION OF CLINICAL DENTAL TECHNOLOGY

44–46 Wollaton Road
Beeston
Nottingham N69 2NR
Tel: 0115 957 5370
Fax: 0115 925 4800
E-mail: info@bacdt.org.uk
Website: www.bacdt.org.uk

The CDTA provides political and educational representation for its members, who are registered with the General Dental Council and trained in designing, creating, constructing, repairing and rebasing

removable appliances to ensure optimal fit, maximum comfort and general wellbeing of patients. We
are committed to team dentistry and ensure that our
members work to the highest professional standards.

MEMBERSHIP
Full Membership
In training Membership
Practice Membership
Multi Practice Membership

BRITISH ASSOCIATION OF DENTAL NURSES

PO Box 4, Room 200
Hillhouse International Business Centre
Thornton-Cleveleys
Lancashire FY5 4QD
Tel: 01253 338360
E-mail: admin@badn.org.uk
Website: www.badn.org.uk

The BADN represents dental nurses, whether qualified or unqualified, working in general practice,
hospital, the community, the armed forces, industry,
practice management or reception, and has representation on the National Examining Board, the
Dental Nurses Standards and Training Advisory
Board and its Registration Committee, the Joint
Consultative Committee, and other bodies.

MEMBERSHIP
Associate Member
Full Member

BRITISH SOCIETY OF DENTAL HYGIENE AND THERAPY

First Floor
10-12 Albert Street
Rugby
Warwickshire CV21 2RS
Tel: 01788 575050
E-mail: enquiries@bsdht.org.uk
Website: www.bsdht.org.uk

The BSDHT is the only nationally recognised body
that represents dental hygienists. Join the UK's
largest professional body for practising dental hygienists, those dually qualified in dental hygiene and
therapy, and students of the profession. We represent
your interests, influence positive change for the
industry and provide information to the public. See
more at: www.bsdht.org.uk/#sthash.WHpbKNhV.dpuf. We have a membership of more than 3,500,
and look after their interests through liaising with the
Department of Health, General Dental Council,
British Dental Association and other organisations.

MEMBERSHIP
Member

DENTAL TECHNOLOGISTS ASSOCIATION

3 Kestral Court
Waterwells Drive
Waterwells Business Park
Gloucester GL2 2AT
Tel: 01452 886366
E-mail: via website
Website: www.dta-uk.org

The DTA is an organization that supports the development of the dental technology profession by encouraging and promoting education, including CPD, and for the exchange of views between dental technicians. We advise, develop and support dental technicians and maintain links with the government, other dental organizations, service providers and the public.

MEMBERSHIP
Member

GENERAL DENTAL COUNCIL

37 Wimpole Street
London W1G 8DQ
Tel: 0845 222 4141
E-mail: information@gdc-uk.org
Website: www.gdc-uk.org

The GDC regulates dental professionals in the UK. All dentists, clinical dental technicians, dental hygienists, dental nurses, dental technicians, dental therapists and orthodontic therapists must be registered with the GDC in order to work in the UK.

THE BRITISH DENTAL ASSOCIATION

64 Wimpole Street
London W1G 8YS
Tel: 020 7935 0875
Fax: 020 7487 5232
E-mail: enquiries@bda.org
Website: www.bda.org

The BDA, which was founded in 1880, is the professional association and trade union for dentists in the UK. Our aims are to advance the science, arts and ethics of dentistry, improve the UK's oral health, and promote the interests of our members. Membership, which is voluntary, stands at around 23,000, mostly in general practice.

MEMBERSHIP
Essential
Extra
Expert

DIETETICS
Membership of Professional Institutions and Associations

THE BRITISH DIETETIC ASSOCIATION

5th Floor
Charles House
148–49 Great Charles Street Queensway
Birmingham B3 3HT
Tel: 0121 200 8080
E-mail: info@bda.uk.com
Website: www.bda.uk.com

The BDA, established in 1936, is the UK's leading professional association and trade union for dietitians. Our aims are to advance the science and practice of dietetics and associated subjects, to promote education and training in the science and practice of dietetics and associated subjects, and to regulate relations between our 8,000+ members and their employers.

MEMBERSHIP
Full Member
Associate Member
Affiliate Member
Alliance Member
Student Member
International Member

DISTRIBUTION
Membership of Professional Institutions and Associations

THE CHARTERED INSTITUTE OF LOGISTICS AND TRANSPORT (UK)

Earlstrees Court
Earlstrees Road
Corby
Northamptonshire NN17 4AX
Tel: 01536 740104
Fax: 01536 740101
E-mail: membership@ciltuk.org.uk
Website: www.ciltuk.org.uk

The Chartered Institute of Logistics and Transport is the membership organisation for professionals involved in the movement of goods and people and their associated supply chains.
Members are involved in the management and design of infrastructure, systems, processes and information flows and in the management and development of effective organisations.

MEMBERSHIP
Learner
Full Time Student
Apprentice
e-Member

Affiliate
Member (MILT)
Chartered Member (CMILT)
Chartered Fellow (FCILT)

QUALIFICATION/EXAMINATIONS
Regulated qualifications cover areas within the Institute's nine Professional Sectors: Supply Chain, Transport Planning, Rail, Active Travel & Travel Planning, Bus & Coach, Ports Maritime & Waterways, Freight Forwarding, Aviation and Operations Management.
Regulated qualifications meet the regulatory requirements for the design, delivery, assessment and award

of units and qualifications, and are regulated by Ofqual and/or Qualifications Wales/CCEA Accreditation, if appropriate.

Level 1 – Award

Level 2 – Award, Certificate, Diploma

Level 3 – Award, Certificate

Level 4 – Certificate

Level 5 – Award, Certificate, Diploma, Professional Diploma

Level 6 – Advanced Diploma

Non-Regulated Programmes

Humanitarian Logistics (3 programmes)

Supply Chain Practitioner Award (Foundation, Professional and Master programmes)

Certificate of Customs Competency

Certified European Logistician (Junior, Senior, Master programmes)

Certified DOPsys (Delivery, Offload and Position System) (Technician, Team Leader, Project Manager)

DESIGNATORY LETTERS

MILT, CMILT, FCILT

DRAMATIC AND PERFORMING ARTS

Membership of Professional Institutions and Associations

DRAMA UK

Woburn House

20 Tavistock Square

London WC1H 9HB

Tel: 020 3393 6141

E-mail: info@dramauk.co.uk

Website: www.dramauk.co.uk

Drama UK was formed in 2012 following the merger of the National Council for Drama Training and the Conference of Drama Schools.

We act as an advocate for quality drama training; offer advice to students of all ages; and award a quality mark to the very best drama training available.

EQUITY

Guild House

Upper St Martins Lane

London WC2H 9EG

Tel: 020 7379 6000

E-mail: info@equity.org.uk

Website: www.equity.org.uk

Equity is the UK trade union representing professional performers and other creative workers from across the entertainment, creative and cultural industries. The main function of Equity is to negotiate minimum terms and conditions of employment for its members and to represent its members' interests to the government and other bodies.

MEMBERSHIP

Student Member

Graduate Member

Full Member

THE BRITISH (THEATRICAL) ARTS

12 Deveron Way
Rise Park
Romford
Essex RM1 4UL
Tel: 01708 756263
E-mail: sally.chennelle1@ntlworld.com
Website: www.britisharts.org

The British Arts is a non-profit-making organization dedicated to maintaining and where necessary raising the standard of the teaching of Performing Arts subjects. We work to encourage a strong technical foundation combined with an understanding of professional theatrical presentation and conduct exams in Dramatic Art, Classical & Stage Ballet, Mime, Tap, Musical Theatre and Modern Dance.

MEMBERSHIP
Student Member
Companion
Associate (Teaching and Non-teaching)
Member (Teaching and Non-teaching)
Advanced Teacher Member
Fellow

QUALIFICATION/EXAMINATIONS
Please see the British Arts website.

DRIVING INSTRUCTORS
Membership of Professional Institutions and Associations

REGISTER OF APPROVED DRIVING INSTRUCTORS

The Axis Building
112 Upper Parliament Street
Nottingham NG1 6LP
Tel: 0300 200 1122
E-mail: ADIReg@dvsa.gov.uk

The Register of Approved Driving Instructors (ADI) and the licensing scheme for trainee instructors (PDI) are administered under the provisions of the Road Traffic Act 1988 by the Department for Transport (DfT). It is an offence for anyone to give professional instruction (that is instruction paid for by or in respect of the pupil) in driving a motor car unless: (a) his or her name is on the Register of Approved Driving Instructors; or (b) he or she holds a 'trainee's licence to give instruction' issued by the Registrar.

QUALIFICATION/EXAMINATIONS
Please see the GOV.UK website (www.gov.uk/apply-to-become-a-driving-instructor) for details of the qualifying examinations.

EMBALMING

Membership of Professional Institutions and Associations

INTERNATIONAL EXAMINATIONS BOARD OF EMBALMERS

146 Alexandra Road
Great Wakering
Essex SS3 0GW
Tel: 01702 218907
E-mail: admin@iebe.co.uk

The Board examines candidates who wish to become qualified members of the British Institute of Embalmers (qv), which is not itself an examining body but can provide information packs (also available from the above address) that contain lists of approved schools and accredited tutors.

THE BRITISH INSTITUTE OF EMBALMERS

Anubis House
21c Station Road
Knowle
Solihull
West Midlands B93 0HL
Tel: 01564 778991
Fax: 01564 770812
E-mail: info@bioe.co.uk
Website: www.bioe.co.uk

The BIE, founded in 1927, is an organization for professional embalmers. Its objectives include supporting and protecting the status, character and interests of embalmers, promoting the efficient tuition of persons seeking to become embalmers, and encouraging the study and practice of improved methods of embalming.

MEMBERSHIP
Member (MBIE)
Fellow (FBIE)

DESIGNATORY LETTERS
MBIE, FBIE

EMPLOYMENT AND CAREERS SERVICES
Membership of Professional Institutions and Associations

CAREER DEVELOPMENT INSTITUTE

Ground Floor
Copthall House
1 New Road
Stourbridge
West Midlands DY8 1PH
Tel: 01384 376464
E-mail: hq@thecdi.net
Website: www.thecdi.net

The CDI is the largest UK-wide professional and membership body for career development professionals. Our aim is to support members and promote access to high-quality career development services, delivered by professionally qualified staff working within an appropriate ethical framework. Suitably qualified members can join the UK Register of Career Development Professionals.

MEMBERSHIP
Student Member
Full Member
Registered Member
Retired Member
Affiliate Organisation
School Affiliate

QUALIFICATION/EXAMINATIONS
Qualification in Career Development (QCD)
Qualification in Career Guidance (QCG)
Qualification in Career Guidance and Development (QCGD)
CDI Certificate in Career Guidance Theory (CCGT)
CDI Certificate in Careers Leadership (CCL)

RECRUITMENT AND EMPLOYMENT CONFEDERATION

Dorset House
First Floor
27–45 Stamford Street
London SE1 9NT
Tel: 020 7009 2100
E-mail: info@rec.uk.com
Website: www.rec.uk.com

The REC is the representative body for the UK's £27 billion private recruitment and staffing industry, with a membership of more than 8,000 Corporate Members comprising agencies and businesses from all sectors, and 6,000 members of the Institute of Recruitment Professionals (IRP) made up of recruitment consultants and other industry professionals.

MEMBERSHIP
Affiliate (AIRP)
Member (MIRP)
Fellow (FIRP)

QUALIFICATION/EXAMINATIONS
Certificate in Recruitment Practice (QCF)
Diploma in Recruitment Practice (QCF)
Diploma in Recruitment Management (QCF)

DESIGNATORY LETTERS
AIRP, MIRP, FIRP

ENGINEERING, AERONAUTICAL
Membership of Professional Institutions and Associations

ROYAL AERONAUTICAL SOCIETY

4 Hamilton Place
Hyde Park Corner
London W1J 7BQ
Tel: 020 7670 4300
Fax: 020 7670 4309
E-mail: raes@aerosociety.com
Website: www.aerosociety.com

The RAeS, founded in 1866 to further the science of aeronautics, is a multidisciplinary professional institution dedicated to the global aerospace community. We work on our members' behalf to promote the highest professional standards in all aerospace disciplines, to provide specialist information and act as a central forum for the exchange of ideas, and to play a leading role in influencing opinion on aviation matters.

MEMBERSHIP
Student Affiliate
Affiliate
Associate (ARAeS)
Associate Member (AMRAeS)
Member (MRAeS)
Companion (CRAeS)
Fellow (FRAeS)
Apprentice

ENGINEERING, AGRICULTURAL
Membership of Professional Institutions and Associations

BRITISH AGRICULTURAL AND GARDEN MACHINERY ASSOCIATION

Middleton House
2 Main Road
Middleton Cheney
Oxfordshire OX17 2TN
Tel: 01295 713344
Fax: 01295 711665
E-mail: info@bagma.com
Website: www.bagma.com

BAGMA is the trade association representing agricultural and garden machinery dealers in the UK. We have some 850 dealer members and 75 affiliated suppliers and allied industry companies. We offer a range of training and assessment courses through our online learning package and at approved Training and Assessment Centres.

QUALIFICATION/EXAMINATIONS
Please see the BAGMA website.

THE INSTITUTION OF AGRICULTURAL ENGINEERS

The Bullock Building (53)
University Way
Cranfield
Bedford
Bedfordshire MK43 0GH
Tel: 01234 750876
E-mail: secretary@iagre.org
Website: www.iagre.org

The Institution of Agricultural Engineers is the professional body for engineers, scientists, technologists and managers in agriculture and the environment, agri-technology and allied landbased industries, including forestry, food engineering and technology, amenity, renewable energy, horticulture and the environment. The IAgrE also administers the Landbased Engineering Technician Accreditation schemes (LTA) for industry.

MEMBERSHIP
Student
Affiliate (AIAgrE)
Technician (TIAgrE)

Associate Member (AMIAgrE)
Member (MIAgrE)
Fellow (FIAgrE)
Honorary Fellow

QUALIFICATION/EXAMINATIONS
Chartered Engineer (CEng), Chartered Environmentalist (CEnv), Incorporated Engineer (IEng), Engineering Technician (EngTech)

DESIGNATORY LETTERS
AIAgrE, AMIAgrE, TIAgrE, MIAgrE, FIAgrE

ENGINEERING, AUTOMOBILE
Membership of Professional Institutions and Associations

INSTITUTE OF AUTOMOTIVE ENGINEER ASSESSORS

The Firs
High Street
Whitchurch
Buckinghamshire HP22 4JU
Tel: 01296 642895
Fax: 01296 640044
E-mail: sally@theiaea.org
Website: www.iaea-online.org

The IAEA, a Professional Affiliate of the Engineering Council, was founded in 1932 and now represents more than 1,500 automotive engineer assessors responsible for activities such as vehicle damage assessment, accident reconstruction, investigation of mechanical failures, electrical failures and vehicle fires, providing expert witness testimony, repair assessment, car fleet surveys, and conciliation and arbitration.

MEMBERSHIP
Affiliate (AffInstAEA)
Associate (AInstAEA)
Member (MInstAEA)
Fellow (FInstAEA)

Honorary Fellow (HFInstAEA)

QUALIFICATION/EXAMINATIONS
Basic Principles of Maths & Physics Application to Accident Reconstruction
Motor Vehicle Legislation as related to Insurance Principles
Principles and Practice of Vehicle Damage Assessment
Motor Insurance
Automotive Technology

DESIGNATORY LETTERS
AffInstAEA, AInstAEA, MInstAEA, FInstAEA

THE INSTITUTE OF THE MOTOR INDUSTRY

Fanshaws
Brickendon
Hertford SG13 8PQ
Tel: 01992 511521
Fax: 01992 511548
E-mail: comms@theimi.org.uk
Website: www.motor.org.uk and www.automotivetechnician.org.uk

The IMI is the professional association for individuals working in the motor industry and exists to help individuals and employers improve professional standards and performance by qualifying, recognizing and developing people. We are the Sector Skills Council for the automotive retail industry, a Licensed Member of the Engineering Council and the governing body for Automotive Technician Accreditation (ATA) – the UK's first national voluntary assessment system for vehicle technicians.

MEMBERSHIP
Affiliate (AffIMI)

Licentiate (LIMI)
Associate (AMIMI)
Member (MIMI)
Fellow (FIMI)
For technicians only, there are two special IMI awards recognizing technical qualifications and experience:
AAE (Advanced Automotive Engineer)
CAE (Certificated Automotive Engineer)

DESIGNATORY LETTERS
AffIMI, LIMI, AMIMI, MIMI, FIMI, AAE, CAE

ENGINEERING, BUILDING SERVICES
Membership of Professional Institutions and Associations

THE CHARTERED INSTITUTION OF BUILDING SERVICES ENGINEERS

222 Balham High Road
London SW12 9BS
Tel: 020 8675 5211
Fax: 020 8675 5449
Website: www.cibse.org

CIBSE is the professional body for people involved in the design, construction, operation and maintenance of the engineering elements of a building other than its structure and enables it to operate efficiently by saving energy and contributing to a low carbon built environment. This includes heating, ventilation, air conditioning, electrical services, lighting etc.

MEMBERSHIP
Student Affiliate
Affiliate
Graduate
Companion
Licentiate (LCIBSE)
Associate (ACIBSE)
Member (MCIBSE)

Fellow (FCIBSE)
CIBSE is a licensed institution of the Engineering Council. This means that, as well as joining CIBSE, you will be Registered as a Chartered Engineer (CEng), Incorporated Engineer (IEng) or Engineering Technician (EngTech) when you have reached the appropriate level of qualification and professional skill.

QUALIFICATION/EXAMINATIONS
Please see the CIBSE website for more information www.cibse.org

DESIGNATORY LETTERS
LCIBSE, ACIBSE, MCIBSE, FCIBSE

ENGINEERING, CHEMICAL
Membership of Professional Institutions and Associations

THE INSTITUTION OF CHEMICAL ENGINEERS

Davis Building
Railway Terrace
Rugby
Warwickshire CV21 3HQ
Tel: 01788 578214
Fax: 01788 560833
E-mail: customerservices@icheme.org
Website: www.icheme.org

The IChemE, founded in 1922, is an international professional membership organization for chemical, biochemical and process engineers, and we have some 30,000 members in more than 113 countries. We promote competence and a commitment to sustainable development, advance the discipline for the benefit of society, and support the professional development of our members.

MEMBERSHIP
Student
Affiliate

Associate Member (AMIChemE)
Member (MIChemE)
Fellow (FIChemE)
Chartered Chemical Engineer (CEng MIChemE)
Chartered Engineer (CEng)
Chartered Scientist (CSci)
Chartered Environmentalist (CEnv)
Associate Fellow

DESIGNATORY LETTERS
AMIChemE, MIChemE, FIChemE, CEng MIChemE,
CEng, CSci, CEnv

ENGINEERING, CIVIL
Membership of Professional Institutions and Associations

INSTITUTION OF CIVIL ENGINEERS

1 Great George Street
Westminster
London SW1P 3AA
Tel: 020 7222 7722
E-mail: membership@ice.org.uk
Website: www.ice.org.uk

ICE is an international organization with over 90,000 members that promotes civil engineering around the world. Our purpose is to qualify professionals engaged in civil engineering, provide knowledge and best practice to all engaged in infrastructure, and advise policy makers on opportunites, issues and trends in the built environment.

MEMBERSHIP
Student
Graduate (GMICE)
Technician Member (MICE)
Member (MICE)
Associate Member (AMICE)
Fellow (FICE)

ENGINEERING, ELECTRICAL, ELECTRONIC AND MANUFACTURING
Membership of Professional Institutions and Associations

INSTITUTION OF LIGHTING PROFESSIONALS

Regent House
Regent Place
Rugby
Warwickshire CV21 2PN
Tel: 01788 576492
E-mail: info@theilp.org.uk
Website: www.theilp.org.uk

The ILP is a professional lighting association with about 2,000 members, including lighting designers, consultants and engineers. We are dedicated to excellence in lighting and to raising awareness about the important contribution of lighting in road safety, crime prevention and the environment. We support members by providing technical advice and encourage their CPD through our monthly journal and by holding a wide range of conferences, regional meetings, seminars and courses.

MEMBERSHIP
Apprentice
Student
Affiliate
Associate Member (AMILP)
Member (MILP)
Fellow (FILP)
Corporate Member
Premier Corporate Member
Engineering Technician (EngTech)
Incorporated Engineer (IEng)
Chartered Engineer (CEng)

QUALIFICATION/EXAMINATIONS
Exterior Lighting Diploma
LET Diploma in Lighting

DESIGNATORY LETTERS
AMILP, MILP, FILP, EngTech, IEng, CEng

THE INSTITUTION OF ENGINEERING AND TECHNOLOGY

Michael Faraday House
Stevenage
Hertfordshire SG1 2AY
Tel: 01438 313311
Fax: 01438 765526
E-mail: postmaster@theiet.org
Website: www.theiet.org

The IET is working to engineer a better world through our mission to inspire, inform and influence the global engineering community, supporting technology innovation to meet the needs of society. The IET has over 163,000 members in 127 countries, with offices in Europe, North America, South Asia and Asia-Pacific.

MEMBERSHIP
Student
Associate
Member (MIET)
Fellow (FIET)
Honorary Fellow
ICT Technician (ICTTech)
Engineering Technician (EngTech)
Incorporated Engineer (IEng)
Chartered Engineer (CEng)

DESIGNATORY LETTERS
FIET, ICTTech, EngTech, IEng, CEng, MIET

478

ENGINEERING, ENERGY
Membership of Professional Institutions and Associations

ENERGY INSTITUTE

61 New Cavendish Street
London W1G 7AR
Tel: 020 7467 7100
E-mail: info@energyinst.org
Website: www.energyinst.org

The EI is the chartered professional membership body for the energy industry, providing learning and networking opportunities, professional recognition and energy knowledge resources for individuals and companies worldwide. We offer professional qualifications including Chartered, Incorporated and Engineering Technician status for engineers, as well as Chartered Scientist, Chartered Energy Manager and Chartered Environmentalist.

MEMBERSHIP
Student Member
Graduate Member (GradEI)
Affiliate
Technician Member (TMEI)
Member (MEI)

Fellow (FEI)
Engineering Technician (EngTech)
Incorporated Engineer (IEng)
Chartered Engineer (CEng)
Chartered Scientist (CSci)
Chartered Environmentalist (CEnv)
Chartered Energy Manager (exclusive EI title)
Chartered Energy Engineer (exclusive EI title)
Chartered Petroleum Engineer (exclusive EI title)

DESIGNATORY LETTERS
GradEI, TMEI, MEI, FEI, EngTech, IEng, CEng, CEnv, CSci

ENGINEERING, ENVIRONMENTAL
Membership of Professional Institutions and Associations

INSTITUTE OF ENVIRONMENTAL MANAGEMENT AND ASSESSMENT

Saracen House
Lincoln LN6 7AS
Tel: 01522 540069
Fax: 01522 540090
E-mail: info@iema.net
Website: www.iema.net

The IEMA is a not-for-profit membership organization that provides recognition and support to environmental professionals and promotes sustainable development through improved environmental practice and performance. We have about 15,000 individual and corporate members in 87 countries, in the public, private and non-governmental sectors.

MEMBERSHIP
Student Member
Affiliate Member
Graduate Member
Associate (AIEMA)

Full Member (MIEMA)
Fellow (FIEMA)
Chartered Environmentalist (CEnv)
Corporate Member

QUALIFICATION/EXAMINATIONS
Foundation Certificate in Environmental Management
Associate Certificate in Environmental Management
Diploma

DESIGNATORY LETTERS
AIEMA, MIEMA, FIEMA, CEnv

THE CHARTERED INSTITUTION OF WATER AND ENVIRONMENTAL MANAGEMENT

15 John Street
London WC1N 2EB
Tel: 020 7831 3110
Fax: 020 7405 4967
E-mail: via website
Website: www.ciwem.org

Founded in 1895, CIWEM is an independent professional body and registered charity with 12,000 members that advances the science and practice of water and environmental management for a clean, green and sustainable world by promoting environmental excellence and professional development and training, supplying independent advice and evidence-based opinion, and providing a forum for debate through conferences, technical meetings and its publications.

MEMBERSHIP
Student

Associate ACIWEM
Graduate

Member MCIWEM C.WEM
Fellow FCIWEM C.WEM
Environmental Partner
Chartered Engineer (CEng)
Chartered Environmentalist (CEnv)
Chartered Scientist (CSci)

QUALIFICATION/EXAMINATIONS
Online training courses in partnership with Staffordshire University, accredited university courses at 12 leading institutions, CPD modules and Rural Environmental Management Programme

DESIGNATORY LETTERS
CEng, CEnv, CSi, C.WEM

THE SOCIETY OF ENVIRONMENTAL ENGINEERS

The Manor House
High Street
Buntingford
Hertfordshire SG9 9AB
Tel: 01763 271209
Fax: 01763 273255
E-mail: office@environmental.org.uk
Website: www.environmental.org.uk

The SEE, founded in 1959, is a professional society that promotes awareness of the discipline of environmental engineering (the measurement, modelling, control and simulation of all types of environment). We provide members with information, training and representation within this field and encourage communication and good practice in quality, reliability, and cost-effective product development and manufacture.

MEMBERSHIP
Student
Member
Corporate Member
Engineering Technician (EngTech)
Incorporated Engineer (IEng)
Chartered Engineer (CEng)

DESIGNATORY LETTERS
EngTech, IEng, CEng

ENGINEERING, FIRE
Membership of Professional Institutions and Associations

ASSOCIATION OF PRINCIPAL FIRE OFFICERS

9–11 Pebble Close
Amington
Tamworth
Staffordshire B77 4RD
Tel: 01827 302300
Fax: 01827 302399
E-mail: enquiries@apfo.org.uk
Website: www.apfo.org.uk

The APFO is the staff association of the most senior Fire Officers in the UK. Our objectives are: to represent and promote the interests of members in conditions of service and legal and employment matters; to negotiate and promote the settlement of disputes involving members; to provide assistance to members and their dependants in exceptional circumstances; and to provide support to members in matters concerning employment or a work-related injury.

MEMBERSHIP
Associate Member
Lifetime Past Member

CHIEF FIRE OFFICERS' ASSOCIATION

9–11 Pebble Close
Amington
Tamworth
Staffordshire B77 4RD
Tel: 01827 302300
Fax: 01827 302399
Website: www.cfoa.org.uk

The CFOA is a professional membership association of the most senior fire officers in the UK. We provide independent advice to the government, local authorities and others. Our aim is to reduce loss of life, personal injury and damage to property by improving the quality of fire fighting, rescue, fire protection and fire prevention in the UK.

MEMBERSHIP
Member

THE INSTITUTION OF FIRE ENGINEERS

IFE House
64–66 Cygnet Court
Timothy's Bridge Road
Stratford-upon-Avon CV37 9NW
Tel: 01789 261 463
Fax: 01789 296 426
E-mail: info@ife.org.uk
Website: www.ife.org.uk

The IFE, founded in 1918, is a non-profit-making professional body for fire professionals and has more than 12,000 members worldwide. Our aim is to encourage and improve the science and practice of fire extinction, fire prevention and fire engineering, to enhance technical networks, and to give advice and support to our members for the benefit of the community at large.

MEMBERSHIP
Student
Affiliate Member
Technician (TIFireE)
Graduate (GIFireE)
Associate (AIFireE)
Member (MIFireE)
Fellow (FIFireE)
Engineering Technician (EngTech)
Incorporated Engineer (IEng)
Chartered Engineer (CEng)
Affiliate Organization

QUALIFICATION/EXAMINATIONS
IFE Certificate in Fire Science, Operations and Safety (Level 2)
IFE Certificate in Fire Science, Operations, Fire Safety and Management (Level 3)
IFE Diploma in Fire Science and Fire Safety (Level 3)

DESIGNATORY LETTERS
TIFireE, GIFireE, AIFireE, MIFireE, FIFireE, EngTech, IEng, CEng

ENGINEERING, GAS
Membership of Professional Institutions and Associations

THE INSTITUTION OF GAS ENGINEERS AND MANAGERS

IGEM House
High Street
Kegworth
Derbyshire DE74 2DA
Tel: 0844 375 4436
Fax: 01509 678198
E-mail: general@igem.org.uk
Website: www.igem.org.uk

IGEM is licensed by EC(UK) and serves a wide range of professionals in the UK and international gas industry through membership and technical standards, having a diverse membership ranging from university students to qualified professionals. Anyone working or interested in the gas industry can form positive connections to enhance their career through IGEM.

MEMBERSHIP
Student Member
Associate (AIGEM)
Associate Member (AMIGEM)
Graduate Member (GradIGEM)
Member Manager (MIGEM)
Technician Member (Eng Tech (MIGEM))
Incorporated Member (I Eng (MIGEM))

Chartered Member (C Eng (MIGEM))
Fellow (C Eng (FIGEM))

DESIGNATORY LETTERS
MIGEM, Eng Tech (MIGEM), I Eng (MIGEM), C Eng
(MIGEM), C Eng (FIGEM)

ENGINEERING, GENERAL
Membership of Professional Institutions and Associations

ASSOCIATION OF COST ENGINEERS

Lea House
Sandbach
Cheshire CW11 1XL
Tel: 01270 764798
Fax: 01270 766180
E-mail: enquiries@acoste.org.uk
Website: www.acoste.org.uk

The ACostE represents the professional interests of those with responsibility for the prediction, planning and control of resources for engineering, manufacturing and construction. As a Professional Affiliate of The Engineering Council, we can propose suitably qualified members for the award of the titles of Chartered Engineer (CEng) and Incorporated Engineer (IEng).

Graduate (Grad A Cost E)
Member (MA Cost E)
Fellow (FA Cost E)
Honorary Fellow (Hon FA Cost E)
Certified Cost Engineer (CCE)
Engineering Technician (EngTech)
Incorporated Engineer (IEng)
Chartered Engineer (CEng)

MEMBERSHIP
Student
Associate (AA Cost E)
Companion (Companion A Cost E)

DESIGNATORY LETTERS
AA Cost E, Companion A Cost E, Grad A Cost E, MA Cost E, FA Cost E, CCE, EngTech, IEng, CEng

INSTITUTE OF MEASUREMENT AND CONTROL

87 Gower Street
London WC1E 6AF
Tel: 020 7387 4949
Fax: 020 7388 8431
E-mail: membership@instmc.org
Website: www.instmc.org

The IMC is a multidisciplinary body that brings together thinkers and practitioners from the many disciplines that have a common interest in measurement and control. Our object is to promote for the public benefit, by all available means, the general advancement of the science and practice of measurement and control technology and its application.

MEMBERSHIP
Student Member
Affiliate Member
Associate Member
Member (MemInstMC)
Fellow (FInstMC)
Honorary Fellow (HonFInstMC)

SEMTA – THE SECTOR SKILLS COUNCIL FOR SCIENCE, ENGINEERING AND MANUFACTURING TECHNOLOGIES

14 Upton Road
Watford
Hertfordshire WD18 0JT
Tel: 0845 643 9001
E-mail: via website
Website: www.semta.org.uk

Semta is part of the Skills for Business network of 25 employer-led Sector Skills Councils in the UK and works with employers in the aerospace, automotive, electrical, electronics, marine, mechanical, metals and science & bioscience sectors to ascertain their current and future skills needs and provide short- and long-term solutions to meet those needs.

THE ENGINEERING COUNCIL

2nd Floor
246 High Holborn
London WC1V 7EX
Tel: 020 3206 0500
Fax: 020 3206 0501
Website: www.engc.org.uk

The Engineering Council holds the national registers of Engineering Technicians (EngTech), Incorporated Engineers (IEng), Chartered Engineers (CEng) and Information and Communications Technology Technicians (ICTTech). We set and maintain internationally recognised standards of competence and ethics, ensuring that employers, government and society can have confidence in registrants' skills and commitment.

DESIGNATORY LETTERS
EngTech, IEng, CEng, ICTTech

WOMEN'S ENGINEERING SOCIETY

Michael Faraday House
Six Hills Way
Stevenage
Herts SG1 2AY
Tel: 01438 765506
E-mail: info@wes.org.uk
Website: www.wes.org.uk

The WES, founded in 1919, is a professional, not-for-profit network of women engineers, scientists and technologists, who offer inspiration, support and professional development. Working in partnership, we campaign to encourage women to participate and achieve as engineers, scientists and as leaders.

MEMBERSHIP
Student Member
Associate
Full Member (MWES)
Fellow
Company Member

DESIGNATORY LETTERS
WES

ENGINEERING, MARINE
Membership of Professional Institutions and Associations

THE INSTITUTE OF MARINE ENGINEERING, SCIENCE AND TECHNOLOGY

33 Aldgate High Street
London EC3N 1EN
Tel: +44 (0)20 7382 2600
Fax: +44 (0)20 7382 2670
E-mail: via website
Website: www.imarest.org

The IMarEST, established in 1889, is the leading international membership body and learned society for marine professionals and has more than 15,000 members worldwide. We have a strong international presence, with a network of 50 international branches, affiliations with major marine societies around the world, representation on the key marine technical committees and non-governmental status at the International Maritime Organization.

MEMBERSHIP
Membership Categories
IMarEST membership is open to everyone with an interest in the marine world across scientific, engineering and technological disciplines and applications.

Categories of membership are available to those who are seeking professional recognition, those who are currently studying or just starting out in their careers, or those who simply have a general interest in the IMarEST and its activities. There are no academic requirements for Non-corporate Membership of the IMarEST. However, professionals seeking Corporate Membership will require certain academic qualifications according to the type of membership being sought.
Corporate Membership Categories
Fellow (FIMarEST)
Fellows are those who qualify for the category of Member and have demonstrated to the satisfaction of Council a level of knowledge and understanding, competence and commitment involving superior responsibility for the conceptual design, management or the execution of important work in a marine related profession, and have given a commitment to abide by the Institute's Code of Professional Conduct.
Member (MIMarEST)
Members are those who qualify for the category of Associate Member and have demonstrated to the

satisfaction of Council that they have achieved a position of professional standing having normally been professionally engaged in the marine sector for a period of 5 years that includes significant responsibility and have given a commitment to abide by the Institute's Code of Professional Conduct.
Associate Member (AMIMarEST)
Associate Members are those demonstrating to the satisfaction of Council that they have achieved a position as a technician, or are professionally engaged in Initial Professional Development or occupy an occupational role in the marine sector, and have given a commitment to abide by the Institute's Code of Professional Conduct.
Non-corporate Membership Categories
Affiliate
Affiliates may either be those with an interest in, or who may contribute to, the activities of the Institute; or persons who, in the opinion of Council, can contribute to, or wish to have access to, the technical services of the Institute, being resident in a recognized overseas territory and also members of a professional society with which the Institute has a reciprocal arrangement.
Student (SIMarEST)
Student members are those enrolled on a programme of further or higher education accredited or recognized by the IMarEST.
Professional Registration
In addition to membership, the IMarEST is licensed to provide a range of registers covering the fields of engineering, science and technology. In addition, the IMarEST's Royal Charter empowers the Institute to offer registers designed to meet the specific needs of the marine profession. Corporate members can become registered (chartered) as follows:
Engineers
Chartered Engineer (CEng)
Chartered Marine Engineer (CMarEng)

Incorporated Engineer (IEng)
Incorporated Marine Engineer (IMarEng)
Engineering Technician (EngTech)
Marine Engineering Technician (MarEngTech)
Scientists
Chartered Scientist (CSci)
Chartered Marine Scientist (CMarSci)
Registered Marine Scientist (RMarSci)

Marine Technician (MarTech)
Technologists
Chartered Marine Technologist (CMarTech)
Registered Marine Technologist (RMarTech)
Marine Technician (MarTech)

DESIGNATORY LETTERS
SIMarEST, AMIMarEST, MIMarEST, FIMarEST

ENGINEERING, MECHANICAL
Membership of Professional Institutions and Associations

INSTITUTION OF MECHANICAL ENGINEERS

1 Birdcage Walk
Westminster
London SW1H 9JJ
Tel: 020 7222 7899
E-mail: enquiries@imeche.org
Website: www.imeche.org

The IMechE is a professional engineering body with about 80,000 members. Our aims are to promote sustainable energy and engineering sustainable supply, economic growth while mitigating and adapting to climate change and the depletion of natural resources, and safe, efficient transport systems to ensure less congestion and emissions, and to inspire, prepare and support tomorrow's engineers so we can respond to society's changes.

MEMBERSHIP
Affiliate

Associate Member (AMIMechE)
Member (MIMechE)
Fellow (FIMechE)
Engineering Technician (EngTech)
Incorporated Engineer (IEng)
Chartered Engineer (CEng)

DESIGNATORY LETTERS
AMIMechE, MIMechE, FIMechE, EngTech, IEng, CEng

ENGINEERING, MINING
Membership of Professional Institutions and Associations

INSTITUTE OF EXPLOSIVES ENGINEERS

Ground Floor, Unit 1
Greyfriars Business Park
Frank Foley Way
Stafford
Staffordshire ST16 2ST
Tel: 01785 594136
E-mail: vicki.hall@iexpe.org
Website: www.iexpe.org

The Institute of Explosives Engineers promotes the occupational competency, education and professional standing of those who work with explosives and provides consultative facilities for organizations and government departments within the explosives field.

MEMBERSHIP
Student
Associate (AIExpE)
Member (MIExpE)

Fellow (FIExpE)
Company
Company Affiliate

QUALIFICATION/EXAMINATIONS
CEng, IEng, Eng Tech

DESIGNATORY LETTERS
AIExpE, MIExpE, FIExpE

THE INSTITUTE OF MATERIALS, MINERALS AND MINING (IOM^3)

1 Carlton House Terrace
London SW1Y 5DB
Tel: 020 7451 7300
Fax: 020 7839 1702
E-mail: via website
Website: www.iom3.org

IOM^3 is a major UK engineering institution whose activities encompass the whole materials cycle, from exploration and extraction, through characterization, processing, forming, finishing and application, to product recycling and land reuse. We promote and develop all aspects of materials science and engineering, geology, mining and associated technologies, mineral and petroleum engineering and extraction metallurgy, as a leading authority in the worldwide materials and mining community.

MEMBERSHIP
Student
Graduate
Affiliate
Member (MIMMM)
Fellow (FIMMM)
Associate (AIMMM)
Technician (Eng Tech)

DESIGNATORY LETTERS
MIMMM, FIMMM, AIMMM, Eng Tech

THE INSTITUTE OF QUARRYING

McPherson House
8a Regan Way
Chetwynd Business Park
Chilwell
Nottingham NG9 6RZ
Tel: 0115 972 9995
E-mail: mail@quarrying.org
Website: www.quarrying.org

The Institute of Quarrying, which dates from 1917, is the international professional body for quarrying, construction materials and related extractive and processing industries, and has 6,000 members in some 50 countries. Our aim is to improve all aspects of operational performance through education and training at every level.

MEMBERSHIP
Student
Associate

Technical Member (TMIQ)
Member (MIQ)
Fellow (FIQ)

QUALIFICATION/EXAMINATIONS
Diploma in Quarry Technology
Professional Examination

DESIGNATORY LETTERS
TMIQ, MIQ, FIQ

ENGINEERING, NUCLEAR
Membership of Professional Institutions and Associations

THE NUCLEAR INSTITUTE

CK International House
1–6 Yarmouth Place
London WJ1 7BU
Tel: 020 3475 4701
E-mail: admin@nuclearinst.com
Website: www.nuclearinst.com

The NI (a Nominated Body of the UK Engineering and Science Councils) is the only professional membership body for the Nuclear Sector. We organize lectures, seminars and events at a regional and national level, have a vibrant young generation network and provide opportunities for career development and networking.

MEMBERSHIP
Student Member
Learned Member
Graduate Member
Technician Member (TNucI)
Associate Member (AMNucI)
Member (MNucI)
Fellow (FNucI)

New Structure from Jan 2016:
Affiliate (formerly Student)
Associate (formerly Learned and Graduate Members)
Member (MNucI)(incorporating Member, Associate Member and Technician Member)
Fellows (FNucI)
*Member and Fellow Grades require interview to assess competency and professional standards against The Nuclear Deltaxxx

QUALIFICATION/EXAMINATIONS
The Nuclear Deltaxxx

DESIGNATORY LETTERS
MNucI, FNucI

ENGINEERING, REFRACTORIES
Membership of Professional Institutions and Associations

INSTITUTE OF REFRACTORIES ENGINEERING

575 Trentham Road
Burton
Stoke on Trent
Staffs ST3 3BN
Tel: 01782 310 234
Fax: 01782 310 234
E-mail: secretary@ireng.org
Website: www.ireng.org

The IRE is a non-profit-making organization dedicated to fostering the science, technology and skills of refractories engineering and to serving the needs of refractories engineers worldwide. Our members have a background in R&D, design, engineering, manufacturing and installation contracting in the iron & steel, cement, non-ferrous, glass, chemical/petro-chemical incineration, power generation, ceramics/bricks and similar industries.

MEMBERSHIP
Student
Associate Member (AMI Ref Eng)
Member (MI Ref Eng)
Fellow (FI Ref Eng)

DESIGNATORY LETTERS
AMI Ref Eng, MI Ref Eng, FI Ref Eng

ENGINEERING, REFRIGERATION
Membership of Professional Institutions and Associations

THE INSTITUTE OF REFRIGERATION

Kelvin House
76 Mill Lane
Carshalton
Surrey SM5 2JR
Tel: 020 8647 7033
E-mail: ior@ior.org.uk
Website: www.ior.org.uk

The IOR is the professional body for the refrigeration, air conditioning and heat pump industries. It promotes the technical advancement and perfection of refrigeration, air conditioning and heat pumps, and the minimization of its effects on the environment, encourage the extension of refrigeration, air conditioning and heat pump services for the benefit of the community, and provides advice, CPD and support to interested individuals.

MEMBERSHIP
Student and Young Persons
Technician TMInstRAffiliate
Associate Member (AMInstR)
Fellow (FMInstR)Member (MInstR)
Service Engineering Section
Air Conditioning and Heat Pump Institute of the IOR

QUALIFICATION/EXAMINATIONS
REAL Zero CPD, REAL Skills Europe CPD, REAL Alternative
Engineering Council Registration

DESIGNATORY LETTERS
AMInstR, TMInstR, MInstR, FInstR

ENGINEERING, ROAD, RAIL AND TRANSPORT
Membership of Professional Institutions and Associations

INSTITUTE OF HIGHWAY ENGINEERS

De Morgan House
58 Russell Square
London WC1B 4HS
Tel: 020 7436 7487
Fax: 020 7436 7488
E-mail: secretary@theihe.org
Website: www.theihe.org

The IHE is the main professional body for highway and traffic professionals. We are run by engineers for engineers and technicians, and work to keep the standards of the profession high, to safeguard the interests of our members, and to ensure that their contribution is recognised.

MEMBERSHIP
Student Member
Apprentice Member (AppIHE)
Affiliate Member
Associate Member (AMIHE)
Member (MIHE)
Fellow (FIHE)
Engineering Technician (EngTech)
Incorporated Engineer (IEng)
Chartered Engineer (CEng)

QUALIFICATION/EXAMINATIONS
Prof Cert in Traffic Sign Design
Prof Cert in Traffic Signal Control
Prof Cert in Highway Development Management
Prof Cert in Highway Maintenance
Prof Cert for Winter Services Decision Makers and Managers
Prof Cert in Road Safety Engineering
Prof Cert in Cycling Infrastructure Design
Prof Cert in Public Realm
Prof Cert in Temporary Traffic Management
Prof Cert in Asset Management

DESIGNATORY LETTERS
AMIHE, MIHE, FIHE, EngTech, IEng, CEng

INSTITUTION OF RAILWAY SIGNAL ENGINEERS

4th Floor
1 Birdcage Walk
Westminster
London SW1H 9JJ
Tel: 020 7808 1180
Fax: 020 7808 1196
E-mail: hq@irse.org
Website: www.irse.org

The Institution of Railway Signal Engineers, known more usually as the IRSE, is an international organization, active throughout the world. It is the professional institution for all those engaged or interested in railway signalling and telecommunications and allied disciplines. Membership is open to anyone engaged or interested in the management, planning, design, installation, telecommunications or associated equipment.

MEMBERSHIP
Student
Associate
Accredited Technician
Associate Member
Member

Fellow
Companion

DESIGNATORY LETTERS
AMIRSE, MIRSE, FIRSE, CompIRSE

QUALIFICATION/EXAMINATIONS
Professional Examination

SOCIETY OF OPERATIONS ENGINEERS

22 Greencoat Place
London SW1P 1PR
Tel: 020 7630 1111
Fax: 020 7630 6677
E-mail: soe@soe.org.uk
Website: www.soe.org.uk

SOE is a professional membership organisation representing more than 16,000 individuals and companies in the engineering industry. It was formed in 2000 by the merger of the Institute of Road Transport Engineers (IRTE) and the Institution of Plant Engineers (IPlantE). The Society's third Professional Sector, the Bureau of Engineer Surveyors (BES), joined in 2004.

MEMBERSHIP
Associate Member (AMSOE)
Member (MSOE)
Fellow (FSOE)
Engineering Technician (EngTech)
Incorporated Engineer (IEng)
Chartered Engineer (CEng)

THE CHARTERED INSTITUTION OF HIGHWAYS AND TRANSPORTATION

119 Britannia Walk
London N1 7JE
Tel: 020 7336 1555
Fax: 020 7336 1556
E-mail: info@ciht.org.uk
Website: www.ciht.org.uk

The CIHT is a learned society and membership organization concerned with the planning, design, construction, maintenance and operation of land-based transport systems and infrastructure. CIHT provides professional development and networking opportunities to members, with routes to qualifications, cutting-edge technical conferences and exciting social events.

MEMBERSHIP
Student

Associate Member (AMCIHT)
Member (MCIHT)
Fellow (FCIHT)

QUALIFICATION/EXAMINATIONS
Transport Planning Professional (TPP) status (awarded jointly with the Transport Planning Society (TPS))

DESIGNATORY LETTERS
AMCIHT, MCIHT, FCIHT

ENGINEERING, SHEET METAL

Membership of Professional Institutions and Associations

INSTITUTE OF SHEET METAL ENGINEERING

102 Richmond Drive
Perton
Wolverhampton
West Midlands WV6 7UQ
Tel: 07891 499146
E-mail: ismesec@googlemail.com
Website: www.isme.org.uk

The ISME is a learned body with individual membership open to those employed in the sheet metal and associated industries and corporate membership open to relevant companies. Our aims are to promote the science of working and using sheet metal by providing opportunities for the exchange of ideas and information, and to encourage the professional development of our members.

MEMBERSHIP
Student Member
Member (MISME)
Fellow (FISME)
Corporate Member

DESIGNATORY LETTERS
MISME, FISME

ENGINEERING, STRUCTURAL

Membership of Professional Institutions and Associations

THE INSTITUTION OF STRUCTURAL ENGINEERS

47–58 Bastwick Street
London EC1V 3PS
Tel: 020 7235 4535
Fax: 020 7235 4294
E-mail: membership@istructe.org
Website: www.istructe.org

The Institution of Structural Engineers, founded in 1908, is the world's largest membership organization dedicated to the art and science of structural engineering. Our aims include: maintaining professional standards for structural engineering; ensuring continued technical excellence; advancing safety, creativity and innovation; and promoting a sustainable approach to both the structural engineering profession and the built environment.

MEMBERSHIP
Student

Graduate
Technician (TIStructE)
Associate Member (AMIStructE)
Associate (AIStructE)
Chartered Member (MIStructE)
Fellow (FIStructE)

DESIGNATORY LETTERS
TIStructE, AMIStructE, AIStructE, MIStructE, FIStructE

ENGINEERING, WATER

Membership of Professional Institutions and Associations

INSTITUTE OF WATER

4 Carlton Court
Team Valley
Gateshead
Tyne and Wear NE11 0AZ
Tel: 0191 422 0088
Fax: 0191 422 0087
E-mail: info@instituteofwater.org.uk
Website: www.instituteofwater.org.uk

The IW is the only institute concerned with the UK water industry. Our aim is to promote high standards of integrity, conduct and ethics, and to provide our members with an opportunity for CPD and growth through sharing knowledge, experience and networking opportunities.

MEMBERSHIP
Student Member
Associate Member
Full Member

Fellow
Honorary Member
Engineering Technician (EngTech)
Incorporated Engineer (IEng)
Chartered Engineer (CEng)
Chartered Environmentalist (CEnv)
Company Member

DESIGNATORY LETTERS
EngTech, IEng, CEng, CEnv

ENGINEERING DESIGN

Membership of Professional Institutions and Associations

THE INSTITUTION OF ENGINEERING DESIGNERS

Courtleigh
Westbury Leigh
Westbury
Wiltshire BA13 3TA
Tel: 01373 822801
Fax: 01373 858085
E-mail: via website
Website: www.ied.org.uk

Established in 1945, the IED represents 4,000 members worldwide working in engineering design, product design and CAD. Benefits include a bimonthly journal, access to an extensive library, legal advice helpline, local branch activities, and guidance and support to registration with the EC(UK) for suitably qualified members.

MEMBERSHIP
IED membership has two divisions: Engineering Design, and Product Design and Technology.
Each division has a range of membership grades: Student Member (StudIED), Graduate/Diplomate Member (GradIED/DipIED), Competent Draughting Associate (CDAIED), Associate (AIED), Member (MIED), Fellow (FIED), Affiliate

QUALIFICATION/EXAMINATIONS
Registration with EC(UK) for suitably qualified members

DESIGNATORY LETTERS
AIED, MIED, FIED

ENVIRONMENTAL SCIENCES
Membership of Professional Institutions and Associations

CHARTERED INSTITUTE OF ECOLOGY AND ENVIRONMENTAL MANAGEMENT

43 Southgate Street
Winchester
Hampshire SO23 9EH
Tel: 01962 868626
E-mail: enquiries@cieem.net
Website: https:// www.cieem.net/

Founded in 1991 to advance the science, technology and practice of ecology, environmental management and sustainable development to further conservation and the enhancement of biodiversity through education, training, study and research. CIEEM now has more than 5,000 members drawn from local authorities, government agencies, industry, environmental consultancy, teaching/research and NGOs.

MEMBERSHIP
Student Member
Qualifying Member
Graduate Member (Grad CIEEM)
Associate Member (ACIEEM)
Full Member (MCIEEM)
Fellow (FCIEEM)

DESIGNATORY LETTERS
Grad CIEEM, ACIEEM, MCIEEM, FCIEEM

EXPORT
Membership of Professional Institutions and Associations

THE INSTITUTE OF EXPORT

Export House
Minerva Business Park
Lynch Wood
Peterborough PE2 6FT
Tel: 01733 404400
E-mail: via website
Website: www.export.org.uk

Established since 1935 offering training and professional qualifications to those working within international trade. We are the only professional institute in the UK offering qualifications ranging from the new 14–19 Diploma up to a level 5 Diploma as well as standard and bespoke training courses for individuals and companies.

MEMBERSHIP
Affiliate
Student
Associate
Member MIEx (Grad)
Member MIEx
Fellow
Business

QUALIFICATION/EXAMINATIONS
Diploma in International Trade (DIT)
Certified International Trade Advisor (CIT)
Advanced Certificate in International Trade (ACIT)

Young International Trader (YIT)
Certificate in International Trade (CIT)
Foundation Degree (FdA)

FISHERIES MANAGEMENT
Membership of Professional Institutions and Associations

INSTITUTE OF FISHERIES MANAGEMENT

PO Box 679
Hull
East Yorkshire HU5 9AX
Tel: 0845 388 7012
E-mail: info@ifm.org.uk
Website: www.ifm.org.uk

The Institute of Fisheries Management is an international organization of persons sharing a common interest in the modern and sustainable management of recreational and commercial fisheries. It is a non-profit-making body and is a constituent body of the Society for the Environment.

MEMBERSHIP
Subscriber
Student Member
Associate Member (AMIFM)
Affiliate Member (AMIFM)
Registered Member (MIFM)

Fellow (FIFM)
Honorary Fellow (Hon FIFM)
Corporate Member
Honorary Member (Hon MIFM)

QUALIFICATION/EXAMINATIONS
Certificate
Diploma (accredited by The Open University)
Award
Short courses in a range of specialist subjects.

DESIGNATORY LETTERS
AMIFM, MIFM, FIFM, Hon FIFM, Hon MIFM

FLORISTRY
Membership of Professional Institutions and Associations

BRITISH FLORIST ASSOCIATION

PO Box 674
Wigan
Lancashire WN1 9LL
Tel: 0844 800 7299
E-mail: via website
Website: www.britishfloristassociation.org

The BFA, founded in 1951, is an awarding body that promotes the highest standards in professional floristry. We are responsible for preparing and setting the highest floristry qualifications and for designing programmes for the training of SOF judges and examiners. We provide help, advice and information to our more than 1,000 members, who include business owners, florists, training providers, and students.

MEMBERSHIP
Florist Individual

Student
Corporate
Associate

College Member
Honorary Member

FOOD SCIENCE AND NUTRITION
Membership of Professional Institutions and Associations

INSTITUTE OF FOOD SCIENCE AND TECHNOLOGY

5 Cambridge Court
210 Shepherd's Bush Road
London W6 7NJ
Tel: 020 7603 6316
E-mail: info@ifst.org
Website: www.ifst.org

IFST is the leading independent qualifying body for food professionals in Europe and the only professional body in the UK concerned with all aspects of food science and technology. As a registered charity we are independent of government, industry, lobby or special interest groups.

Member (MIFST)
Fellow (FIFST)
Chartered Scientist (CSci)
Registered Scientist (RSci)
Registered Science Technician (RSciTech)
Professional Food Sensory Group

MEMBERSHIP
Associate

DESIGNATORY LETTERS
MIFST, FIFST, CSci, RSci, RSciTech

FORESTRY AND ARBORICULTURE
Membership of Professional Institutions and Associations

INSTITUTE OF CHARTERED FORESTERS

59 George Street
Edinburgh EH2 2JG
Tel: 0131 240 1425
Fax: 0131 240 1424
E-mail: icf@charteredforesters.org
Website: www.charteredforesters.org

The ICF is the Royal Chartered body for foresters and arboriculturists in the UK. We have over 1,700 members, to whom we offer advice, guidance and support. We also strive to foster a greater public understanding and awareness of the profession, as the environment and its management become more relevant to everyone.

Supporter
Associate Member
Professional Member (MICFor)
Fellow (FICFor)

QUALIFICATION/EXAMINATIONS
Professional Membership Entry (PME) exam

MEMBERSHIP
Student Member

DESIGNATORY LETTERS
MICFor, FICFor

THE ARBORICULTURAL ASSOCIATION

The Malthouse
Stroud Green
Standish
Stonehouse
Gloucestershire GL10 3DL
Tel: 01242 522152
Fax: 01242 577766
E-mail: admin@trees.org.uk
Website: www.trees.org.uk

The Arboricultural Association, founded in 1964, is the leading body in the UK for the amenity tree care professional in either civic or commercial employment at craft, technical, supervisory, managerial or consultancy level. There are currently over 2,000 members of The Arboricultural Association in a variety of membership classes.

MEMBERSHIP
Student Member
Ordinary Member
Associate Member
Technician Member
Professional Member
Fellow
Fellow Retired
Corporate Member

QUALIFICATION/EXAMINATIONS
Arboricultural Association Approved Contractor
Arboricultural Association Registered Consultant

DESIGNATORY LETTERS
TechArborA, MArborA, FArborA

THE ROYAL FORESTRY SOCIETY

The Hay Barns
Home Farm Drive
Upton Estate
Banbury OX15 6HU
Tel: 01295 678588
Fax: 01295 670798
E-mail: rfshq@rfs.org.uk
Website: www.rfs.org.uk

The RFS was founded in 1882 and now has over 3,600 members. We are an educational charity dedicated to promoting the wise management of trees and woodlands, and to increasing understanding of forestry. We publish a popular journal, the *Quarterly Journal of Forestry*, arrange outdoor meetings, organize woodland study tours in the UK and overseas, run courses in forestry and arboriculture, and manage model woodlands.

MEMBERSHIP
Individual Member
Corporate Member
Student Member

QUALIFICATION/EXAMINATIONS
RFS Certificate in Arboriculture (Level 2)
RFS Certificate in Forestry (Level 2)
RFS Certificate in Silviculture (Level 3)

FOUNDRY TECHNOLOGY AND PATTERN MAKING
Membership of Professional Institutions and Associations

THE INSTITUTE OF CAST METALS ENGINEERS

National Metalforming Centre
47 Birmingham Road
West Bromwich
West Midlands B70 6PY
Tel: 01216 016979
Fax: 01216 016981
E-mail: info@icme.org.uk
Website: www.icme.org.uk

The ICME is the professional body for those in the castings and associated industry. It was formed in 1904, granted its first Royal Charter in 1921, a Third Supplemental Charter in 1994 and changed its name in 2001. The granting of the Third Supplemental Charter aligned its membership requirements with those of the EC(UK).

MEMBERSHIP
Student
Member (MICME)

Professional Member (Prof MICME)
Fellow (FICME)
Engineering Technician (EngTech)
Incorporated Engineer (IEng)
Chartered Engineer (CEng)
European Engineer (EurIng)

DESIGNATORY LETTERS
MICME, Prof MICME, FICME, EngTech, IEng, CEng, EurIng

FREIGHT FORWARDING
Membership of Professional Institutions and Associations

BRITISH INTERNATIONAL FREIGHT ASSOCIATION (BIFA)

Redfern House
Browells Lane
Feltham
Middlesex TW13 7EP
Tel: 020 8844 2266
E-mail: bifa@bifa.org
Website: www.bifa.org

BIFA is the principal trade association providing representation, training and support to British companies engaged in the international movement of freight to and from the UK by air, rail, road and sea. It is a not-for-profit organisation. Members are encouraged to contribute to the running of the Association.

MEMBERSHIP
Associate Member
Trade Member

FUNDRAISING
Membership of Professional Institutions and Associations

THE INSTITUTE OF FUNDRAISING

Institute of Fundraising
Charter House
13 – 15 Carteret Street
London SW1H 9DJ
Tel: 02078401000
E-mail: info@institute-of-fundraising.org.uk
Website: www.institute-of-fundraising.org.uk

The Institute of Fundraising is the professional body for fundraisers in the UK, representing over 6,000 individual fundraisers and 580 organisations. We provide professional support, act as a voice for fundraisers and promote best practice. We offer professional qualifications and training, and the annual three-day IoF Fundraising Convention is the largest fundraising conference of its type in Europe.

MEMBERSHIP
Associate
Full Member (MInstF)
Fully Certificated Member MInstF(Cert)
Diploma Qualified Member MInstF(Dip)
Advanced Diploma Qualified Member MInstF(AdvDip)
Organisational Member

QUALIFICATION/EXAMINATIONS
Certificate in Fundraising
Diploma in Fundraising
Advanced Diploma in Fundraising

DESIGNATORY LETTERS
MInstF, MInstF(Cert), MInstF(Dip), MinstF(AdvDip), FInstF, FInstF(Cert), FInstF(Dip), FInstF(AdvDip)

FUNERAL DIRECTING, BURIAL AND CREMATION ADMINISTRATION
Membership of Professional Institutions and Associations

NATIONAL ASSOCIATION OF FUNERAL DIRECTORS

618 Warwick Road
Solihull
West Midlands B91 1AA
Tel: 0845 230 1343
Fax: 0121 711 1351
E-mail: info@nafd.org.uk
Website: www.nafd.org.uk

The NAFD, founded in 1905, is an independent trade association whose members include more than 3,200 funeral homes throughout the UK, suppliers to the profession, and overseas funeral directing businesses. We provide support to our members and offer informed opinion to government.

MEMBERSHIP
Funeral Director (Category A) Member
Supplier (Category B) Member
Overseas Member

QUALIFICATION/EXAMINATIONS
Diploma in Funeral Arranging and Administration
(Dip.FAA)

Diploma in Funeral Directing (Dip.FD)

NATIONAL ASSOCIATION OF MEMORIAL MASONS

1 Castle Mews
Rugby
Warwickshire CV21 2AL
Tel: 01788 542264
Fax: 01788 542276
E-mail: enquiries@namm.org.uk
Website: www.namm.org.uk

The NAMM was formed in 1907 to promote excellence and craftsmanship within the memorial masonry trade. Our services to members include training, business advice, technical advice, promotion, a legal helpline, a conciliation and arbitration service, trade exhibitions and a conference. We protect members' interests through representation to the British Standards Institution (BSI) and the Burial & Cemeteries Advisory Group (BCAG).

MEMBERSHIP
Individual Associate Member
Affiliate Member
Full Retail and Wholesale Members
Company Associate Member
Corporate Associate Member
Overseas Member
Overseas Affiliate Member

THE INSTITUTE OF BURIAL AND CREMATION AUTHORITIES

ICCM National Office & Training Centre
City of London Cemetery
Aldersbrook Road
Manor Park
London E12 5DQ
Tel: 020 8989 4661
Fax: 020 8989 6112
E-mail: iccmjulie@gmail.com
Website: www.iccm-uk.com

Accredited education and training opportunities for those working in cemeteries and crematori.

Best practice guidance and policy for burial and cremation authorities.

MEMBERSHIP
Member (MICCM)
Associate Member (AICCM)
Fellow (FICCM)
Corporate
Associate Corporate

QUALIFICATION/EXAMINATIONS
Diploma – Fully Accredited NHC in Cemetery & Crematorium Management and the Management of Natural Burial Grounds
Cemetery Operatives Training Scheme – A comprehensive suite of City & Guilds accredited qualifications
Crematorium Technicians Training Scheme – BTEC accredited qualifications for crematory staff

DESIGNATORY LETTERS
MICCM, AICCM, FICCM

FURNISHING AND FURNITURE
Membership of Professional Institutions and Associations

FLOORING INDUSTRY TRAINING ASSOCIATION

4c St Marys Place
The Lace Market
Nottingham NG1 1PH
Tel: 0115 9506836
E-mail: info@fita.co.uk
Website: www.fita.co.uk

FITA was set up and is fully supported by the CFA and the NICF to provide training for the floor-covering industry. We have a fully equipped training centre at Loughborough, where the majority of our courses are run. We also offer tailor-made courses to suit individual specifications and requirements.

QUALIFICATION/EXAMINATIONS
FITA Training Courses
The Flooring Industry Flooring Association was set up by, and is fully supported by the CFA and NICF to provide training.

FITA has a fully equipped training centre at Loughborough in Leicestershire where the majority of our standard courses are run. FITA also offers tailor-made courses to suit your specifications and requirements, quotations on request.

FITA instructors have all passed assessments and knowledge exams and are supported on courses by technicians with specialist knowledge from the trade. FITA also enjoys the support of a considerable number of suppliers who freely donate materials, accessories and tools.

Fully trained staff are an asset to any company. The outlay for training courses far outweighs the initial cost.

Please be sure to book early to reserve your place on a course. Go to our Course Dates page for details of our latest courses and the training centres where they are being held.

Training courses considered suitable for Domestic Installers

Carpet Fitting – Basic
Carpet Fitting – Intermediate
Domestic Sheet Vinyl Fitting
Profitable Measuring and Quoting
Subfloor Preparation – Domestic
Training courses considered suitable for Commercial Installers
Commercial Vinyl Fitting – Advanced
Commercial Vinyl Fitting – Basic
Commercial Vinyl Fitting – Intermediate
Cost Effective Estimating and Planning
Linoleum Installation – Intermediate
Subfloor Preparation – Commercial
Training courses considered suitable for Domestic & Commercial Installers
Carpet Fitting – Advanced
Laminate and Wood Fitting – Basic
Linoleum Installation – Basic
Moisture – Preventing floor failures
Resilient / Luxury Vinyl Tile Fitting – Advanced
Resilient / Luxury Vinyl Tile Fitting – Basic
Wood Fitting – Advanced
Wood Fitting – Intermediate
Wood Sanding and Finishing

Assessments designed for FITA QA Accreditation
QA Card Adhered Carpet Assessment
QA Card Carpet Tile Assessment
QA Card Floating Timber Assessment
QA Card Resilient Sheet Assessment
QA Card Subfloor Preparation Assessment
QA Card Vinyl Tile Assessment

NATIONAL INSTITUTE OF CARPET AND FLOORLAYERS

4c St Marys Place
The Lace Market
Nottingham NG1 1PH
Tel: 0115 9583077
Fax: 0115 9412238
E-mail: info@nicfltd.org.uk
Website: www.nicfltd.org.uk

The NICF furthers the interests of its members by promoting excellence in the field of carpet and floorlaying and providing a range of benefits, products and services.

MEMBERSHIP
Master Fitter Member
Fitter Member
Trainee Fitter Member
Retailer Member
Associate Member
Patron Member

QUALIFICATION/EXAMINATIONS
Fitter qualification assessment
Master Fitter qualification assessment

GEMMOLOGY AND JEWELLERY
Membership of Professional Institutions and Associations

GEM-A

21 Ely Place
London EC1N 6TD
Tel: 020 7404 3334
Fax: 020 7404 8843
E-mail: information@gem-a.com
Website: www.gem-a.com

Gem-A, The Gemmological Association of Great Britain, is the world's longest established provider of gem and jewellery education. Our prestigious Gemmology and Diamond Diplomas are globally recognised as qualifications of the highest status. In addition to our educational programmes we also provide membership, including the world-famous FGA and DGA Memberships

MEMBERSHIP
Associate
Fellow (FGA)
Diamond Member (DGA)
Corporate Member
Gold Corporate Member

QUALIFICATION/EXAMINATIONS
Foundation Certificate in Gemmology
Diploma in Gemmology
Diamond Diploma

DESIGNATORY LETTERS
FGA, DGA

THE NATIONAL ASSOCIATION OF JEWELLERS

78A Luke Street
London EC2A 4XG
Tel: 020 7613 4445
E-mail: info@naj.co.uk
Website: www.naj.co.uk

The NAJ serves and supports the jewellery industry of Great Britain and Ireland. We promote high professional standards among our members, who must adhere to a code of professional practice. In return, we offer them advice, support and learning and development in the form of distance learning courses and short courses.

MEMBERSHIP
Alumni Member
Allied Member
Affiliate Member
Ordinary Member

QUALIFICATION/EXAMINATIONS
Professional Jewellers' Diploma (JET 1 Certificate)
Professional Jewellers' Diploma (JET 2 Diploma)
Professional Jewellers' Management Diploma
Professional Jewellers' Business Development Diploma
Certificate of Appraisal Theory (CAT)

GENEALOGY
Membership of Professional Institutions and Associations

SOCIETY OF GENEALOGISTS

14 Charterhouse Buildings
Goswell Road
London EC1M 7BA
Tel: 020 7251 8799
Fax: 020 7250 1800
E-mail: info@sog.org.uk
Website: www.sog.org.uk

The Society (founded 1911) is the National Family History Centre. A registered educational charity, it was founded to encourage and foster the study, science and knowledge of genealogy. This it does chiefly through its library, publications and extensive education programme of courses and events. It currently does not hold exams.

MEMBERSHIP
Member
Fellow (FSG)
Honorary Fellow (FSG Hon)

DESIGNATORY LETTERS
FSG, FSG Hon

THE HERALDRY SOCIETY

53 Hitchin Street
Baldock
Herts SG7 6AQ
Tel: 01462 892062
E-mail: memsecheraldrysociety@gmail.com
Website: www.theheraldrysociety.com

The Heraldry Society is a registered charity that aims to encourage interest in heraldry through publications, lectures, visits and related activities. Members receive *The Heraldry Gazette*, which contains heraldic news and comments, and Society information quarterly. We maintain contact with heraldic societies in many parts of the UK and abroad.

MEMBERSHIP
Associate Member
Ordinary Member

Fellow (FHS)
Honorary Fellow (Hon FHS)

QUALIFICATION/EXAMINATIONS
Elementary Certificate
Intermediate Certificate
Advanced Certificate
Diploma (DipHS)

DESIGNATORY LETTERS
FHS, Hon FHS

THE INSTITUTE OF HERALDIC AND GENEALOGICAL STUDIES

79–82 Northgate
Canterbury
Kent CT1 1BA
Tel: 01227 768664
Fax: 01227 765617
E-mail: registrar@ihgs.ac.uk
Website: www.ihgs.ac.uk

The IHGS, founded in 1961, is an independent educational charitable trust that offers a wide range of courses on family history, heraldry and related historical subjects, and has an extensive library, archive and research facilities. We also offer a genealogical and heraldic research service.

MEMBERSHIP
Associate Member
Graduate Member

QUALIFICATION/EXAMINATIONS
Correspondence Course in Genealogy

Correspondence Course in Heraldry
Online Course in Genealogy
Certificate in Genealogy
Higher Certificate in Genealogy
Diploma in Genealogy
Licentiateship in Heraldry and Genealogy
Online Course in Heraldry
Elementary online course in Genealogy

DESIGNATORY LETTERS
Dip Gen, LHG, FHG

GEOGRAPHY

Membership of Professional Institutions and Associations

ROYAL GEOGRAPHICAL SOCIETY (WITH THE INSTITUTE OF BRITISH GEOGRAPHERS)

1 Kensington Gore
London SW7 2AR
Tel: 020 7591 3000
Fax: 020 7591 3001
E-mail: via website
Website: www.rgs.org

The RGS-IBG is the learned society and professional body for geography. We aim to foster an understanding and informed enjoyment of our world: developing, supporting and promoting geographical research, expeditions and fieldwork, education, public engagement, and providing geography input to policy.

MEMBERSHIP
Young Geographer

Member
Postgraduate Fellow
Fellow
Chartered Geographer (CGeog)
Corporate Member

DESIGNATORY LETTERS
FRGS, CGeog

GEOLOGY

Membership of Professional Institutions and Associations

THE GEOLOGICAL SOCIETY

Burlington House
Piccadilly
London W1J 0BG
Tel: 020 7434 9944
Fax: 020 7439 8975
E-mail: enquiries@geolsoc.org.uk
Website: www.geolsoc.org.uk

The Geological Society, founded in 1807, is the UK's national organization for professional Earth scientists. The normal grade of membership is Fellow. Students may become Candidate Fellows. Members of the public not eligible for any other status may join as Friends.

MEMBERSHIP
Friend
Candidate Fellow
Fellow
Chartered Geologist

DESIGNATORY LETTERS
FGS, CGeol

GLASS TECHNOLOGY
Membership of Professional Institutions and Associations

BRITISH SOCIETY OF SCIENTIFIC GLASSBLOWERS

Glassblowing Department
S.U.E.R.C
Scottish Enterprise Technology Park Rankine Avenue
East Kilbride
Lanarkshire G75 0QF
Tel: 01355 270150
Fax: 01355 229898
E-mail: Robert.McLeod@glasgow.ac.uk
Website: www.bssg.co.uk

The Society was founded in 1960 for the benefit of those engaged in Scientific Glassblowing and its associated professions, and to uphold and further the status of Scientific Glassblowers. We welcome written submissions to our quarterly journal, which is circulated to members.

MEMBERSHIP
Associate
Student Member

Fellow
Full Member
Master
Honorary Member
Retired Member
Overseas Member

DESIGNATORY LETTERS
Master MBSSG, Fellow FBSSG

SOCIETY OF GLASS TECHNOLOGY

9 Churchill Way
Chapeltown
Sheffield
South Yorkshire S35 2PY
Tel: 0114 2634455
Fax: 0871 8754085
E-mail: info@sgt.org
Website: www.sgt.org

The objects of the Society of Glass Technology are to encourage and advance the study of the history, art, science, design, manufacture, after treatment, distribution and end use of glass of any and every kind.

MEMBERSHIP
Personal Member
Fellow (FSGT)
Fellow Emeritus
Honorary Fellow (HonFSGT)
Centenary Honorary Fellow (CentHonFSGT) only three and only in 2016, our centenary year.

Corporate Member

QUALIFICATION/EXAMINATIONS
Peer review by the Board of Fellows.
2016 was the SGT centenary and some Centenary Honorary Fellows will be created. These will be in addition to the limit of 12 for Honorary Fellows. Decided by the Board of Fellows as normal.

DESIGNATORY LETTERS
FSGT, HonFSGT

HAIRDRESSING
Membership of Professional Institutions and Associations

HABIA

Oxford House
Sixth Avenue
Sky Business Park, Robin Hood Airport
Doncaster
South Yorkshire DN9 3GG
Tel: 0845 6 123555
Fax: 01302 774949
E-mail: info@habia.org
Website: www.habia.org

Habia is the government-appointed standards-setting body for hair, beauty, nails, spa therapy, barbering and African-type hair, and creates the standards that form the basis of all qualifications, including NVQs, SVQs, apprenticeships, diplomas and foundation degrees, as well as industry codes of practice.

MEMBERSHIP
Habia offers a membership programme for training providers (Habia Members) and a wider, free membership for industry professionals and educators.

THE GUILD OF HAIRDRESSERS

Archway House
Barnsley S71 1AQ
Tel: 01226 786555
Fax: 01226 208300

The Guild of Hairdressers dates back to 1340, when it was part of the Guild of Barbers and Surgeons. Then in the late 16th century, when the surgeons split off, it became the Guild of Hairdressers, Wigmakers and Perfumers. Today it still exists for the benefit of its members, who adhere to a code of ethics and to whom it provides help and advice.

HEALTH AND HEALTH SERVICES
Membership of Professional Institutions and Associations

BRITISH OCCUPATIONAL HYGIENE SOCIETY (BOHS)

5/6 Melbourne Business Court
Millennium Way
Pride Park
Derby DE24 8LZ
Tel: 01332 298101
Fax: 01332 298099
E-mail: admin@bohs.org
Website: www.bohs.org

BOHS is the Chartered Society for Worker Health Protection – one of the largest occupational hygiene societies in Europe and the only professional society representing qualified occupational hygienists in the UK. BOHS provides internationally recognised qualifications, scientific conferences and membership services, and has almost 1,800 members in 56 countries.

MEMBERSHIP
Individual
Student
Affiliate (Corporate)
Retired
Associate (AFOH)
Licentiate (LFOH)
Chartered Member (CMFOH)
Specialist Member (MFOH(S))
Chartered Fellow (CFFOH)

QUALIFICATION/EXAMINATIONS
Since 1953, BOHS has been the only organisation dedicated to occupational hygiene, and to be awarded a Royal Charter – in recognition of its unique and pre-eminent role as the leading authority in occupational disease prevention. This also means that BOHS is the only occupational hygiene organisation to offer the opportunity to achieve 'Chartered Occupational Hygienist' status, via its professional development route: the BOHS Faculty of Occupational Hygiene sets, develops and maintains the professional standards of occupational hygienists. It is also an internationally recognised, and the only UK-based, examining board for qualifications in occupational hygiene. BOHS qualifications are widely regarded as the industry standard, and are recognised by HSE, UKAS and IOHA, and by national and international institutions, organisations and employers.

DESIGNATORY LETTERS
AFOH, LFOH, CMFOH, CFFOH

CHARTERED INSTITUTE OF ENVIRONMENTAL HEALTH

Chadwick Court
15 Hatfields
London SE1 8DJ
Tel: 020 7827 5800
Fax: 020 7806 0666
E-mail: via website
Website: www.cieh.org

The CIEH is an Awarding Organisation providing Ofqual regulated qualifications in Food Safety, Health & Safety, First Aid, Environmental Protection and Fire Safety.

MEMBERSHIP
Student Member
Associate
Accredited Associate
Graduate Member
Voting Member
Fellow

Chartered Environmental Health Practitioner

QUALIFICATION/EXAMINATIONS
The CIEH offers a range of Ofqual-regulated qualifications at four levels in health and safety, food safety, environmental protection, fire safety and education and training.

CHARTERED INSTITUTE OF ERGONOMICS & HUMAN FACTORS

Elms Court
Elms Grove
Loughborough
Leicestershire LE11 1RG
Tel: 07736 893350
E-mail: ciehf@ergonomics.org.uk
Website: www.ergonomics.org.uk

The Chartered Institute of Ergonomics & Human Factors, founded in 1949, is a UK-based professional society for ergonomists worldwide. We encourage and maintain high standards of professional practice through education, accreditation and development, promote the interests of our members across government, academia, business and industry, and raise awareness of ergonomics in general.

MEMBERSHIP
Student Member
Associate Member

Graduate Member
Registered Member
Fellow
Technical Member
Retired Member

QUALIFICATION/EXAMINATIONS
Chartered Ergonomist & Human Factors Specialist

DESIGNATORY LETTERS
C.ErgHF

INSTITUTE OF HEALTH PROMOTION AND EDUCATION

c/o Dawn Wills
20 Mardley Avenue
Welwyn
Hertfordshire AL6 0UD
Tel: c/o 01438 840040
E-mail: admin@ihpe.org.uk
Website: www.ihpe.org.uk

The IHPE was established 50 years ago to bring together professionals with a common interest in health education and promotion to share their experience, ideas and information. Our members come from a diverse range of backgrounds, including nursing, midwifery, health visiting, medicine, dentistry, public health, stress management, psychology and teaching.

MEMBERSHIP
Student Member
Associate Member (AIHPE)
Full Member (MIHPE)
Fellow (FIHPE)
Corporate Member

DESIGNATORY LETTERS
MIHPE, AIHPE, FIHPE

INSTITUTE OF HEALTH RECORDS AND INFORMATION MANAGEMENT

Marshall House
Heanor Gate Road
Heanor
Derbyshire DE75 7RG
Tel: 01773 713927
Fax: 01773 713927
E-mail: ihrim@zen.co.uk
Website: www.ihrim.co.uk

IHRIM was founded in 1948, primarily as an educational body, to provide qualifications as well as career and professional assistance to members. We encourage professionalism and high standards among our members who work in the fields of health records, information management, clinical coding and information governance.

MEMBERSHIP
Student
Affiliate
Licentiate
Certificated Member (CHRIM)
Accredited Clinical Coder (ACC)

Associate (AHRIM)
Fellow (FHRIM)
Corporate Affiliate

QUALIFICATION/EXAMINATIONS
Certificate of Technical Competence
Foundation exam
Certificate exam
Diploma exam
National Clinical Coding Qualification

DESIGNATORY LETTERS
CHRIM, ACC, AHRIM, FHRIM

INSTITUTE OF HEALTHCARE ENGINEERING AND ESTATE MANAGEMENT

2 Abingdon House
Cumberland Business Centre
Northumberland Road
Portsmouth PO5 1DS
Tel: 023 92 823186
Fax: 023 92 815927
E-mail: office@iheem.org.uk
Website: www.iheem.org.uk

The Institute of Healthcare Engineering and Estate Management (IHEEM) is a Professional Engineering Institute, a specialist institute for the Healthcare Estates Sector.

The Institute counts among its members employees of both public and private healthcare providers, as well as those employed in private sector engineering and consultancy firms and practices.

MEMBERSHIP
Graduate (GIHEEM)
Associate Member (AMIHEEM)
Technician (TIHEEM)
Member (MIHEEM)
Fellow (FIHEEM)

DESIGNATORY LETTERS
GIHEEM, AMIHEEM, TIHEEM, MIHEEM, FIHEEM

INSTITUTE OF HEALTHCARE MANAGEMENT

John Snow House
59 Mansell Street
London E1 8AN
Tel: 020 7265 7321
Fax: 020 7265 7301
E-mail: education@ihm.org.uk
Website: www.ihm.org.uk

The IHM is the professional organization for managers throughout healthcare, including the NHS, independent providers, healthcare consultants and the armed forces. Our focus is on improving patient/user care by publishing standards of management practice, promoting the IHM Code (which covers behavioural and ethical aspects of management practice) and establishing a CPD framework for our members.

MEMBERSHIP
Associate Member
Full Member (MIHM)

QUALIFICATION/EXAMINATIONS
Certificate in Health Management Studies (CertHMS)
Certificate in Health Services Management (CertHSM)
Certificate in Managing Health Services (CertMHS)
Certificate in Managing Health & Social Care (CertMHSC)
Diploma in Health Services Management (DipHSM)

DESIGNATORY LETTERS
MIHM, FIHM, CIHM

THE ROYAL SOCIETY FOR PUBLIC HEALTH

John Snow House
59 Mansell Street
London E1 8AN
Tel: 020 7265 7300
Fax: 020 7265 7301
E-mail: via website
Website: www.rsph.org.uk

The RSPH was formed in October 2008 by the merger of the Royal Society for the Promotion of Health (RSPH/RSH) and the Royal Institute of Public Health (RIPH). We offer a wide range of vocationally related qualifications in the fields of food safety and nutrition, hygiene, health and safety, pest control, health promotion and the built environment.

MEMBERSHIP
Associate (ARSPH)

Licentiate (LRSPH)
Member (MRSPH)
Fellow (FRSPH)
Student

QUALIFICATION/EXAMINATIONS
Please see the RSPH's website.

DESIGNATORY LETTERS
ARSPH, LRSPH, MRSPH, FRSPH

HORSES AND HORSE RIDING
Membership of Professional Institutions and Associations

EQUESTRIAN QUALIFICATIONS GB LTD

Equestrian Qualifications GB Ltd
Equestrian House
Abbey Park
Kenilworth
Warwickshire CV8 2XZ
Tel: 02476 840544
Fax: 02476 840501
E-mail: enquiries@eql.org.uk
Website: www.equestrian-qualifications.org.uk

EQL offers vocational and work-based qualifications for the Equestrian Industry. We work in partnership with a variety of organisations to develop and award qualifications for grooms, stable managers and coaches. Our qualifications include UKCC qualifications, British Horse Society qualifications, Work Based Diplomas, Scottish Vocational Qualifications and Equestrian Tourism Qualifications.

QUALIFICATION/EXAMINATIONS
Our Awards include:
Horse Knowledge and Care – Level 1 to Level 4
Riding Exams – Level 1 to Level 4

Coaching and Teaching – Level 2 to Level 5
UKCC Endorsed Certificates in Coaching (specialist routes) – Level 1 to Level 3
Work Based Diplomas
Scottish Vocational Qualifications

The BHS also offers higher level qualifications for BHS Instructor and Fellowship of the BHS, as well as those for the recreational horse owner.

EQL website: www.equestrian-qualifications.org.uk
BHS website: www.bhs.org.uk

HOUSING
Membership of Professional Institutions and Associations

THE CHARTERED INSTITUTE OF HOUSING

Octavia House
Westwood Way
Coventry CV4 8JP
Tel: 024 7685 1700
E-mail: membership.services@cih.org
Website: www.cih.org

The CIH is the professional body for people involved in housing and communities. We are a registered charity and not-for-profit organization. We have a diverse and growing membership of over 22,000 people – both in the public and private sectors – living and working in over 20 countries on five continents across the world.

MEMBERSHIP
Offering two grades of membership we look to support members at all stages of their career:
CIH Member
CIH Chartered Member
Visit www.cih.org/membership to find out more about CIH membership.

QUALIFICATION/EXAMINATIONS
Certificate Courses
The CIH offers a range of certificated courses at Levels 2, 3 and 4 delivered at various centres across the UK. They are also available by online learning.
Professional Qualifications
The CIH Professional Qualification can be achieved at either undergraduate or postgraduate level, FT or PT.

Please see the CIH's website for details.

DESIGNATORY LETTERS
CIH Members: CIH Member or CIHM, CIH Chartered Members: CIH Chartered Member or CIHCM (existing Fellows can continue to use FCIH and Honorary Members can use (Hon).

INDEXING
Membership of Professional Institutions and Associations

SOCIETY OF INDEXERS

Woodbourn Business Centre
10 Jessell Street
Sheffield S9 3HY
Tel: 01142 449561
E-mail: admin@indexers.org.uk
Website: www.indexers.org.uk

The Society of Indexers is the professional body for indexing in the UK and Ireland, and exists to promote indexing, the quality of indexes and the profession of indexing. We offer information to publishers and other organizations on commissioning indexes and our online directory 'Indexers Available' provides an up-to-date guide to indexers currently working in a wide range of fields.

MEMBERSHIP
Student Member
Member

Professional Member (MSocInd)
Advanced Professional Member (MSocInd(Adv))
Fellow (FSocInd)
Corporate Member

QUALIFICATION/EXAMINATIONS
Training in Indexing course
Advanced Test
Fellowship index submission

DESIGNATORY LETTERS
MSocInd, MSocInd(Adv), FSocInd

INDUSTRIAL SAFETY
Membership of Professional Institutions and Associations

BRITISH SAFETY COUNCIL

70 Chancellors Road
London W6 9RS
Tel: 020 8741 1231
Fax: 0844 583 4731
E-mail: info@britsafe.org
Website: www.britsafe.org

The BSC is one of the world's leading health and safety organizations. Our mission is to keep people healthy and safe at work. Our range of charitable initiatives, such as free health and safety qualifications for school children, is supported by a broad mix of commercial activities centred on membership, training, auditing and qualifications.

MEMBERSHIP
UK Member
International Member

QUALIFICATION/EXAMINATIONS
Award in COSHH Risk Assessment (Level 2)
Award in DSE Risk Assessment (Level 2)
Award in Fire Risk Assessment (Level 2)
Award in Manual Handling Risk Assessment (Level 2)
Award in Risk Assessment (Level 2)
Award in Supervising Staff Safely (Level 2)
Certificate in Occupational Health and Safety (Level 3)
Diploma in Occupational Health and Safety (Level 6)
International Certificate in Occupational Health and Safety
International Diploma in Occupational Health and Safety
Entry Level Award in Workplace Hazard Awareness
Award in Health and Safety at Work (Level 1)
Certificate in Fire Safety and Risk Management
National Certificate in Construction Health and Safety

HEALTH & SAFETY EXECUTIVE APPROVED MINING QUALIFICATIONS

Mining Qualifications, The Health & Safety Executive
2nd Floor, Foundry House
3 Millsands, Riverside Exchange
Sheffield
South Yorkshire S3 8NH
Tel: 0114 291 2394
Fax: 0114 291 2399
E-mail: sarah.johnson@hse.gsi.gov.uk
Website: www.hse.gov.uk/mining

The HSE issues First and Second Class Certificates of Qualification as required under the Management and Administration of Safety and Health at Mines Regulations (MASHAM) 1993 for the appointment of a manager and undermanager respectively, in mines of coal, shale and fireclay in the UK. It also issues certificates to Mining Mechanical and Mining Electrical Engineers, Mechanics and Electricians Class I and Class II, Mines Surveyor, and Mines Deputy. For details see: www.hse.gov.uk/mining

INTERNATIONAL INSTITUTE OF RISK AND SAFETY MANAGEMENT

Suite 7a
77 Fulham Palace Road
London W6 8JA
Tel: 020 8741 9100
Fax: 020 8741 1349
E-mail: info@iirsm.org
Website: www.iirsm.org

The IIRSM is a professional body for health & safety practitioners and specialists in associated professions. Our aim is to advance professional standards in accident prevention and occupational health throughout the world. We have more than 8,100 members, in the UK and over 70 other countries, to whom we provide support and offer advice via a technical helpline.

MEMBERSHIP
Student
Affiliate
Associate (AIIRSM)

Member (MIIRSM)
Specialist Member (SIIRSM)
Fellow (FIIRSM)
Specialist Fellow (SFIIRSM)

DESIGNATORY LETTERS
AIIRSM, MIIRSM, SIIRSM, FIIRSM, SFIIRSM

NEBOSH (THE NATIONAL EXAMINATION BOARD IN OCCUPATIONAL SAFETY AND HEALTH)

Dominus Way
Meridian Business Park
Leicester LE19 1QW
Tel: (+44) 116 263 4700
Fax: (+44) 116 282 4000
E-mail: info@nebosh.org.uk
Website: www.nebosh.org.uk

NEBOSH offers globally recognized qualifications designed to meet the health, safety, environmental and risk management needs of all places of work. Courses leading to NEBOSH qualifications attract over 50,000 candidates annually in over 120 countries around the world.

MEMBERSHIP
NEBOSH's National General Certificate, National Certificate in Fire Safety and Risk Management, National Certificate in Construction Health and Safety, and the International General Certificate are all accepted as meeting the academic requirements to apply for Technical Membership (Tech IOSH) of the Institution of Occupational Safety and Health (IOSH).

In partnership with the Association for Project Safety (APS) the NEBOSH National and International Certificates in Construction Health and Safety meet the headline entrance criteria requirements for Construction Safety Associate membership (AaPS).

In addition holders of either the NEBOSH National or International Diploma in Occupational Health and Safety and either the NEBOSH National or International Certificate in Construction Health and Safety meet the headline qualification entrance criteria requirements for Registered Construction Safety Practitioner (RMaPS).

NEBOSH environmental management qualifications are now being accepted by CIWEM (The Chartered Institution of Water and Environmental Management) as meeting its membership requirements.

The NEBOSH Certificate in Environmental Management will be accepted for its new Technician Membership grade entitling the use of post-nominal designation (TechCIWEM).

The NEBOSH National Diploma in Environmental Management fulfils the qualification requirements for non-chartered Member of CIWEM (MCIWEM). Progression on to chartered membership is a further opportunity.
The NEBOSH Certificate in Environmental Management meets the academic criteria to gain the globally recognised IEMA Associate (AIEMA) membership, whilst holders of the NEBOSH National Diploma in Environmental Management will be eligible to apply for IEMA Practitioner (PIEMA) level membership.
NEBOSH's National Diploma and International Diploma are accepted as meeting the requirements to apply for Graduate Membership (Grad IOSH) of the Institution of Occupational Safety and Health (IOSH).

A NEBOSH Diploma provides a sound basis for progression to MSc level: a number of UK universities offer MSc programmes that accept the National Diploma as a full or partial entry requirement.

The new Masters of Research (MRes) Degree is open to holders of a NEBOSH Diploma who wish to further their career in Health and Safety and/or Environment. It will be delivered by distance learning through research directly relevant to the candidate's own work.

QUALIFICATION/EXAMINATIONS

NEBOSH Environmental Awareness at Work Qualification

NEBOSH Health and Safety at Work Qualification

NEBOSH Health, Safety and Environment in the Process Industries Qualification

NEBOSH National Certificate in Construction Health and Safety

NEBOSH Certificate in Environmental Management

NEBOSH National Certificate in Fire Safety and Risk Management

NEBOSH National General Certificate in Occupational Health and Safety

NEBOSH International General Certificate in Occupational Health and Safety

NEBOSH International Technical Certificate in Oil and Gas Operational Safety

NEBOSH National Certificate in the Management of Health and Well-being at Work

NEBOSH International Certificate in Construction Health and Safety

NEBOSH International Certificate in Fire Safety and Risk Management

NEBOSH National Diploma in Environmental Management

NEBOSH National Diploma in Occupational Health and Safety

NEBOSH International Diploma in Occupational Health and Safety

Masters programmes in partnership with the University of Hull

MRes in Occupational Health and Safety Management

MRes in Occupational Health, Safety and Environmental Management

MRes in Environmental Management

MSc in Occupational Health and Safety Management

MSc in Occupational Health, Safety and Environmental Management

MSc in Environmental Management

NEBOSH Diploma in Regulatory Health and Safety – developed for the Health and Safety Executive for all new UK HSE Inspectors

DESIGNATORY LETTERS

DipNEBOSH, EnvDipNEBOSH

THE INSTITUTION OF OCCUPATIONAL SAFETY AND HEALTH

The Grange
Highfield Drive
Wigston
Leicestershire LE18 1NN
Tel: 0116 257 3100
Fax: 0116 257 3101
E-mail: membership@iosh.co.uk
Website: www.iosh.co.uk

Our membership totals over 46,000 – we are the focal point for health and safety professionals working in a diverse range of organisations.

Founded in 1945 IOSH is an independent, not-for-profit organization setting professional standards, supporting and developing members, and providing authoritative advice and guidance on health and safety issues.

MEMBERSHIP

Affiliate Member
Associate Member
Technical Member (Tech IOSH)
Graduate Member (Grad IOSH)
Chartered Member (CMIOSH)
Chartered Fellow (CFIOSH)

QUALIFICATION/EXAMINATIONS

For qualifications that meet our academic requirements for our designatory categories of membership please see the IOSH website: https:// www.iosh.co.uk/Membership/About-membership/Qualifications.aspx

DESIGNATORY LETTERS

AIOSH, Tech IOSH, Grad IOSH, CMIOSH, CFIOSH

INSURANCE AND ACTUARIAL WORK
Membership of Professional Institutions and Associations

ASSOCIATION OF AVERAGE ADJUSTERS

c/o RTI Ltd
2nd Floor, International House
1 St Katharine's Way
London E1W 1UN
Tel: 020 748 1250
E-mail: aaa@rtiForensics.com
Website: www.average-adjusters.com

The AAA was founded in 1869 to promote correct principles in the adjustment of marine insurance claims and general average, uniformity of practice among average adjusters and the maintenance of good professional conduct. It ensures the independence and impartiality of its members by imposing a strict code of conduct and has close links with other international associations and insurance markets.

MEMBERSHIP
Subscriber
Associate
Fellow

QUALIFICATION/EXAMINATIONS
The Association's examination consists of 6 modules. Passes in Modules A1 & A2 are required for Associateship, passes in Modules F3, F4, F5 and F6 for Fellowship. For details see the Association's website.

THE CHARTERED INSTITUTE OF LOSS ADJUSTERS

51–55 Gresham Street
London EC2V 7HQ
Tel: 020 7216 7580
E-mail: info@cila.co.uk
Website: www.cila.co.uk

The CILA, which was founded in 1941, is the professional body representing the claims specialists who investigate, negotiate and agree the conclusion of insurance and other claims on behalf of insurers and policyholders. We safeguard the interests of our members and maintain the high standards of the profession by requiring them to abide by our code of professional conduct.

MEMBERSHIP
Student Member
Ordinary Member
Certificate Member (Cert CILA)
Associate (ACILA)
Fellow (FCILA)
Honorary Member

QUALIFICATION/EXAMINATIONS
ACILA examination

DESIGNATORY LETTERS
Cert CILA, Dip CILA, ACILA, FCILA

THE CHARTERED INSURANCE INSTITUTE

42–48 High Road
South Woodford
London E18 2JP
Tel: 020 8989 8464
Fax: 020 8530 3052
E-mail: customer.serv@cii.co.uk
Website: www.cii.co.uk

The CII is the premier professional body for those working in the insurance and financial services industry. We are dedicated to promoting higher standards of competence and integrity through the provision of relevant qualifications for employees at all levels across all sectors of the industry.

MEMBERSHIP
Ordinary Member
Qualified Member
Associate Member (ACII)
Fellow (FCII)

QUALIFICATION/EXAMINATIONS
Award in Financial Planning
Certificate in Equity Release
Certificate in Financial Planning
Certificate in Insurance
Certificate in Life and Pensions
Certificate in Mortgage Advice
Diploma in Financial Planning
Diploma in Insurance
Advanced Diploma in Financial Planning

Advanced Diploma in Insurance
Award for the Foundation Insurance Test
Award in General Insurance
Award in London Market Insurance
Award in Customer Service Insurance
Award in Financial Administration
Award in Bancassurance
Award in Investment Planning
Certificate in Contract Wording
Certificate in Insurance and Financial Services
Certificate in London Market Insurance Specialisation
Certificate in Discretionary Investment Management
Certificate in Paraplanning
Certificate in Securities Advice and Dealing
Certificate in Investment Operations
Diploma in Regulated Financial Planning
MSc in Insurance and Risk Management
MSc in Wealth Management

DESIGNATORY LETTERS
ACII, FCII

THE FACULTY AND INSTITUTE OF ACTUARIES

Faculty of Actuaries
Maclaurin House
18 Dublin Street
Edinburgh EH1 3PP
Tel: 0131 240 1313
E-mail: faculty@actuaries.org.uk
Website: www.actuaries.org.uk

Institute of Actuaries
Staple Inn Hall
High Holborn
London WC1V 7QJ
Tel: 020 7632 2111
E-mail: institute@actuaries.org.uk

Napier House
4 Worcester Street
Oxford OX1 2AW
Tel: 01865 268211
E-mail: institute@actuaries.org.uk

Actuaries are experts in assessing the financial impact of tomorrow's uncertain events. They enable financial decisions to be made with more confidence by analysing the past, modelling the future, assessing the risks involved, and communicating what the results mean in financial terms.

MEMBERSHIP
Student Member
Affiliate Member

Associate (AFA or AIA)
Fellow (FFA or FIA)
Honorary Fellow

QUALIFICATION/EXAMINATIONS
Certificate in Financial Mathematics

DESIGNATORY LETTERS
AFA, AIA, FFA, FIA

JOURNALISM
Membership of Professional Institutions and Associations

NATIONAL COUNCIL FOR THE TRAINING OF JOURNALISTS

NCTJ Training Ltd
The New Granary
Newport
Saffron Walden
Essex CB11 3PL
Tel: 01799 544014
Fax: 01799 544015
E-mail: info@nctj.com
Website: www.nctj.com

The NCTJ provides a range of multimedia journalism training products and services in the UK, including: accredited courses; apprenticeships; qualifications and examinations; awards; careers information; distance learning; short courses and CPD; information and research; publications and events. We play an influential role in all areas of journalism education and training.

QUALIFICATION/EXAMINATIONS
Certificate in Foundation Journalism
Trailblazer Apprenticeship Standard for a Junior Journalist
Diploma in Journalism
National Qualification in Journalism (NQJ)

THE CHARTERED INSTITUTE OF JOURNALISTS

2 Dock Offices
Surrey Quays Road
London SE16 2XU
Tel: 020 7252 1187
Fax: 020 7232 2302
E-mail: memberservices@cioj.co.uk
Website: www.cioj.co.uk

The CIoJ, which dates back to 1884, is a professional body and trade union for journalists. We expect our members to uphold high standards in the way they work and to adhere to a strict code of conduct, and in return we champion journalistic freedom, protect their interests in the workplace and campaign for better working conditions.

MEMBERSHIP
Student Member
Affiliate Member
Trainee Member
Full Member
International Member

DESIGNATORY LETTERS
MCIJ – Member, FCIJ – Fellow

LAND AND PROPERTY
Membership of Professional Institutions and Associations

RICS (ROYAL INSTITUTION OF CHARTERED SURVEYORS)

Parliament Square
London SW1P 3AD
Tel: 024 7686 8555
Fax: 020 7334 3811
E-mail: contactrics@rics.org
Website: www.rics.org/careers

RICS, an independent, not-for-profit organization, has around 100,000 qualified members and more than 50,000 students and trainees in some 140 countries, and provides the world's leading professional qualification in land, property, construction and associated environmental issues. We accredit over 600 courses at leading universities worldwide and provide impartial, authoritative advice on key issues for business, society and governments.

MEMBERSHIP
Student
Associate (AssocRICS)
Member (MRICS)
Fellow (FRICS)

DESIGNATORY LETTERS
AssocRICS, MRICS, FRICS

THE COLLEGE OF ESTATE MANAGEMENT

Whiteknights
Reading
Berkshire RG6 6AW
Tel: 0118 921 4696
Fax: 0118 921 4620
E-mail: enquiries@cem.ac.uk
Website: www.cem.ac.uk

The College of Estate Management is the leading provider of supported distance learning for real estate and construction professionals. We have been playing a key role in the property world for over 90 years. At any one time we have over 4,000 students based all over the world.

QUALIFICATION/EXAMINATIONS
BCSC Diploma in Shopping Centre Management
BSc(Hons) Building Surveying
BSc(Hons) Construction Management
BSc(Hons) Estate Management
BSc(Hons) Property Management
BSc(Hons) Quantity Surveying
Postgraduate Diploma/MSc Conservation of the Historic Environment
Postgraduate Diploma/MSc Surveying
MBA Real Estate and Construction Management
Postgraduate Diploma/MSc Facilities Management
Postgraduate Diploma/MSc Property Investment
RICS Professional Membership Graduate Route – Adaptation 1

THE INSTITUTE OF REVENUES, RATING AND VALUATION

Northumberland House
5th Floor
303–306 High Holborn
London WC1V 7JZ
Tel: 020 7831 3505
Fax: 020 7831 2048
E-mail: education@irrv.org.uk
Website: www.irrv.org.uk

The Institute offers professional and technical qualifications for all those whose professional work is concerned with local authority revenues and benefits, valuation for rating, property taxation and the appeals procedure. Our qualifications are widely recognized throughout the profession.

MEMBERSHIP
Student Member
Affiliate Member
Graduate Member
Technician Member (Tech IRRV)
Corporate Member (IRRV)
Diploma Member (IRRV Dip)
Honours Member (IRRV Hons)
Honorary Member
Fellow (FIRRV)

QUALIFICATION/EXAMINATIONS
Level 3 Certificate in Local Taxation and Benefits
Level 3 Local Taxation & Benefits (RQF)
Professional Diploma in Local Taxation and Benefits
Honours

DESIGNATORY LETTERS
Tech IRRV, IRRV, IRRV (Dip), IRRV(Hons), FIRRV

THE NATIONAL FEDERATION OF PROPERTY PROFESSIONALS AWARDING BODY

Arbon House
6 Tournament Court
Edgehill Drive
Warwick CV34 6LG
Tel: 0845 250 6008
Fax: 01926 417789
E-mail: quals@nfopp.co.uk
Website: www.nfopp-awardingbody.co.uk

The **NFOPP Awarding Body** is committed to raising standards within agency through the provision of accredited, nationally recognized qualifications. We are recognized by the Qualifications and Examinations Regulator (Ofqual) and Welsh Government and we have to follow strict guidelines and maintain quality standards in the provision of all our qualifications.

MEMBERSHIP
For membership details of the following organizations please refer to the relevant website:
APIP: www.apip.co.uk
ARLA: www.arla.co.uk
ICBA: www.icba.uk.com
NAEA: www.naea.co.uk
NAVA: www.nava.org.uk

QUALIFICATION/EXAMINATIONS
NFoPP **Level 2 Award** in Introduction to Residential Property Management Practice (QCF)
NFoPP **Level 3 Technical Award** in Commercial Property Agency (QCF)
NFoPP **Level 3 Technical Award** in Real Property Auctioneering (QCF)
NFoPP **Level 3 Technical Award** in Residential Letting and Property Management (QCF)
NFoPP **Level 3 Technical Award** in Residential Letting and Property Management Northern Ireland (QCF)
NFoPP **Level 3 Technical Award** in Sale of Residential Property (QCF)
NFoPP **Level 3 Technical Award** in Chattels Auctioneering (QCF)
NFoPP **Level 3 Technical Award** in Residential Inventory Management & Practice (QCF)
NFoPP **Level 4 Certificate** in Residential Letting & Property Management (QCF)
NFoPP **Level 4 Certificate** in Sale of Residential Property (QCF)
NFoPP **Level 4 Certificate** in Commercial Property Agency (QCF)
NFoPP **Level 6 Technical Award** in Sale of Residential Property Scotland (SCQF)
NFoPP **Level 6 Technical Award** in Residential Letting & Property Management Scotland (SCQF)

THE PROPERTY CONSULTANTS SOCIETY

Basement Office
Surrey Court
1 Surrey Street
Arundel
West Sussex BN18 9DT
Tel: 01903 883787
E-mail: info@propertyconsultantssociety.org
Website: www.propertyconsultantssociety.org

The Property Consultants Society is a non-profit-making organization that offers advice to qualified surveyors, architects, valuers, auctioneers, land and estate agents, master builders, construction engineers, accountants and members of the legal profession to help them to undertake their property consultancy in a competent, legitimate and publicly acceptable way.

MEMBERSHIP
Student (SPCS)
Licentiate (LPCS)
Associate (APCS)
Fellow (FPCS)

Honorary Member

DESIGNATORY LETTERS
SPCS, LPCS, APCS, FPCS

LANDSCAPE ARCHITECTURE
Membership of Professional Institutions and Associations

LANDSCAPE INSTITUTE

Charles Darwin House
107 Gray's Inn Road
London WC1X 8TZ
Tel: 020 7685 2640
E-mail: membership@landscapeinstitute.org
Website: www.landscapeinstitute.org

The Landscape Institute (LI) is the chartered body for the landscape profession. It is an educational charity that promotes the art and science of landscape practice. The LI's aim, through the work of its members is to protect, conserve and enhance the natural and built environment for the public benefit.

The LI provides a professional home for all landscape practitioners including landscape scientists, landscape planners, landscape architects, landscape managers and urban designers, working across a variety of sectors both public and private.

MEMBERSHIP
Student Member

Affiliate Member
Licentiate Member
Chartered Member (CMLI)
Fellow (FLI)
Academic Member (AMLI)
Academic Fellow (AFLI)

QUALIFICATION/EXAMINATIONS
Pathway to Chartership oral examination conferring chartered professional status (CMLI)

DESIGNATORY LETTERS
CMLI, FLI

LANGUAGES, LINGUISTICS AND TRANSLATION
Membership of Professional Institutions and Associations

INSTITUTE OF TRANSLATION & INTERPRETING

Milton Keynes Business Centre
Foxhunter Drive
Linford Wood
Milton Keynes MK14 6GD
Tel: 01908 325250
Fax: 01908 325259
E-mail: info@iti.org.uk
Website: www.iti.org.uk

The Institute of Translation & Interpreting is one of the primary sources of information on these services to government, industry, the media and the general public. We promote the highest standards, providing guidance to those entering the profession and advice to those who offer language services and to their customers.

MEMBERSHIP
Associate (AITI)
Student

Qualified Member (MITI)
Corporate Member
Fellow

QUALIFICATION/EXAMINATIONS
Applicants for qualified membership must take an exam (translators) or attend an interview (interpreters).

THE CHARTERED INSTITUTE OF LINGUISTS

Saxon House
48 Southwark Street
London SE1 1UN
Tel: 020 7940 3100
Fax: 020 7940 3101
E-mail: info@iol.org.uk
Website: www.iol.org.uk

The Chartered Institute of Linguistics, founded in 1910, is a respected language assessment and accredited awarding body, with about 6,500 members. Our aims include promoting the learning and use of modern languages, improving the status of all professional linguistics, and ensuring the maintenance of high professional standards through adherence to our code of conduct.

MEMBERSHIP
Registered Student
Associate Member (ACIL)

Member (MCIL)
Fellow (FCIL)
Chartered Linguist (CL)

QUALIFICATION/EXAMINATIONS
Certificate in Bilingual Skills (CBS)
Diploma in Public Service Interpreting (DPSI)
International Diploma in Bilingual Translation (IDBT)
Diploma in Translation (DipTrans)

DESIGNATORY LETTERS
ACIL, MCIL, FCIL, CL

THE GREEK INSTITUTE

29 Onslow Gardens
London N21 1DY
Tel: 020 8360 7968
Fax: 020 8360 7968
E-mail: info@greekinstitute.co.uk
Website: www.greekinstitute.co.uk

The Greek Institute, which was founded in 1969, is a non-profit-making cultural organization that promotes Modern Greek studies and culture through lectures, publications, literary competitions, Greek cultural evenings and the award of Certificates and a Diploma which are recognized by many UK universities as equivalent to GCSE and GCE A level Modern Greek.

MEMBERSHIP
Member
Associate (AGI)
Fellow (FGI)

QUALIFICATION/EXAMINATIONS
Certificate in Greek Conversation – Basic Stage: Levels 1 and 2
Certificate in Greek Conversation – Intermediate Stage: Levels 3 and 4

Certificate in Greek Conversation – Higher Stage: Levels 5 and 6
Preliminary Certificate
Intermediate Certificate
Advanced Certificate

Diploma in Greek Translation (DipGrTrans)

DESIGNATORY LETTERS
AGI, FGI

LAW

ENGLAND AND WALES

MAGISTRATES

The President of the Courts of England and Wales, The Lord Chief Justice, is head of the Judiciary. He is responsible for the welfare, training and deployment of magistrates, for approving the names of the candidates recommended for appointment and for disciplinary action, short of removal. He also has responsibility for the protection of judicial independence and for working to ensure that the magistracy reflects the diversity of society as a whole.

There are key qualities that a magistrate must possess: good character, understanding and effective communication, social awareness, maturity and a sense of fairness, sound judgement, commitment and reliability. Magistrates do not sit exams nor do they have to be legally qualified.

Before sitting in court, magistrates must undertake some basic training, which includes structured observations in court. This covers practice and procedure in court, structured decision making, sentencing, and so on. New magistrates are assigned a mentor for the first year or so. Core training also involves visits to penal institutions to equip magistrates with the key knowledge they need. Consolidation training takes place at the end of the first year; this is designed to help magistrates plan for their ongoing development and prepare for their first appraisal which takes place about 12 to 18 months after appointment. Magistrates only sit in adult courts when first appointed. Having got that experience they may apply to sit in youth courts and family courts and have to undertake more training before they can sit.

Ongoing training and development includes appraisals which take place every three years, continuation training which takes place once every three years, usually before appraisals, update training on new legislation and procedures and threshold training which accompanies each development in a magistrate's role.

The Magistrates Association has more information about magistrates (www.magistrates-association.org.uk).

JUDGES

All judicial office holders are Her Majesty's Judges and as such all appointments are made by the Queen or her Ministers. All candidates for judicial appointment in England and Wales have been selected by the independent Judicial Appointments Commission (JAC, website: jac.judiciary.gov.uk), which passes its recommendations to the Lord Chancellor for approval. The key statutory responsibilities of the JAC are to select candidates solely on merit; to select only people of good character; to have regard to the need to encourage diversity in the range of people available for selection for appointments.

Once the JAC's selections have been received, the actual appointments are made in slightly different ways depending on the type of post. The Lord Chancellor appoints Deputy District Judges and most members of tribunals. The 30,000 unpaid magistrates who are selected by local Advisory Committees, not by the JAC, are also appointed by The Lord Chancellor. The Queen appoints High Court and Circuit Judges, Masters, Registrars and District Judges, District Judges (Magistrates Courts) and Recorders on the advice of the Lord Chancellor. A special panel convened by the JAC appoints the Lord Chief Justice. The Queen appoints Heads of Division, Court of Appeal judges and senior judges with lengthy judicial experience, on the recommendation of a selection panel convened by the JAC. Scotland and Northern Ireland have their own separate court systems, with their own arrangements for appointing members of the judiciary.

The Supreme Court (http://supremecourt.uk) has jurisdiction over the whole of the UK, so its Justices are not selected by the JAC, which is an England and Wales body. Rather, a special committee is set up, which is made up of the three judicial appointments bodies from around the UK (England and Wales,

Scotland and Northern Ireland), who recommend a name to Ministers. The Queen appoints the Justices on the basis of advice from the Prime Minister.

Candidates for appointment as Justices of the Supreme Court must have held high judicial office for two years or must have been practising barristers or solicitors of the senior courts for at least 15 years (www.supremecourt.uk/faqs.html#1d). More information about judges can be found at the Courts and Tribunals Judiciary website: www.judiciary.gov.uk

OFFICERS OF THE COURT

Officers of the Court include judicial and administrative staff; the former include Masters and Registrars, the latter secretaries and clerks to the judges and the staff who administer the court service. Details are given in *The English Legal System*, 17th edition, 2016–17 (Routledge). Qualifications for the judicial offices vary somewhat, but most appointments are limited to established barristers and solicitors.

THE LEGAL PROFESSION

The legal profession consists of two branches. Each performs distinct duties, although there is a degree of overlap in some aspects of their work.

Solicitors undertake all ordinary legal business for their clients (with whom they are in direct contact). They may also appear on behalf of a client in the magistrates and county courts and tribunals, and with specialist training are able to represent them in the higher courts (Crown Court, High Court and Court of Appeal). The website for the Law Society contains further information (www.lawsociety.org.uk).

Barristers (known collectively as the Bar and collectively and individually as Counsel) advise on legal problems submitted by solicitors and conduct cases in court when instructed by a solicitor; only barristers or qualified solicitor advocates may represent clients in the higher courts. More information on barristers can be found on The Bar Council website (www.barcouncil.org.uk).

LEGAL EXECUTIVES

Both graduates and non-graduates can work in a legal office with the option of qualifying as a solicitor through further vocational training. Chartered Legal Executive lawyers are 'authorised persons' undertaking 'reserved legal activities' alongside, for example, solicitors and barristers. As a general rule, a Chartered Legal Executive lawyer is able to

undertake all the same work that may be undertaken by a solicitor, with some conditions. The Chartered Institute of Legal Executives website has information on becoming a legal executive and the work they can undertake (www.cilex.org.uk).

CORONERS

Coroners must be barristers, solicitors or legally qualified medical practitioners of not less than five years standing. They are appointed by local authorities. There are approximately 95 coroner areas in England and Wales; each area is locally funded and resourced by local authorities. Coroners are independent judicial officers. When not engaged in coronal duties, coroners (apart from whole-time coroners) continue in their legal or medical practices. The Chief Coroner is head of the coroner system, assuming overall responsibility and providing national leadership for coroners in England and Wales. He oversees the implementation of the Coroner and Justice Act 2009. Further information from the Coroners Society of England and Wales, website: www.coronersociety.org.uk and the Crown Prosecution Service website: www.cps.gov.uk/legal/a_to_c/coroners/#a02.

BARRISTERS

Qualification as a barrister at the Bar of England and Wales

There are three stages that must be completed to qualify as a barrister. The academic stage consists of an undergraduate degree in law or in any other subject with a minimum of a 2:2. For those with an undergraduate degree in a subject other than law a one-year conversion course (CPE/GDL) must be completed.

Before commencing the vocational stage candidates must join one of the four Inns and then undertake the Bar Professional Training Course (BPTC), which is either one year full time or two years part time. The main skills taught on the BPTC are: casework skills, legal research, fact management, general written skills including opinion-writing (that is, giving written advice) and drafting, management and interpersonal skills including conference skills (interviewing clients), resolution of disputes out of court (ReDOC) and advocacy (court or tribunal appearances). The main areas of legal knowledge taught on the BPTC are: civil litigation, evidence and remedies, criminal litigation, evidence and sentencing, professional ethics, and two optional subjects or one double optional subject selected from a choice of at least six.

Three centralised assessments are set by a Central Examinations Board, which is comprised of experienced legal practitioners and academics appointed by the Bar Standards Board (BSB). The subjects that are centrally assessed are Civil Litigation, Evidence and Remedies, Criminal Litigation, Evidence and Sentencing and Professional Ethics. Applicants will also have to take the Bar Course Aptitude Test. It aims to test critical thinking and reasoning, but does not test legal knowledge. Practice tests are available on the BSB website. The Aptitude Test will ensure that those undertaking the BPTC have the required skills to succeed.

Once the BPCT has been successfully completed candidates are called to the Bar by their Inn. The Pupillage Stage consists of one year spent in an authorized pupillage training organization. Pupillage is divided into two parts: the non-practising six months (also known as the first six) and the practising six months (also known as the second six).

To find out more about all three stages of qualification as a barrister visit www.barcouncil.org.uk and www.barstandardsboard.org.uk

SOLICITORS

Qualification as a solicitor in England and Wales

To practise as a solicitor in England and Wales a person must have been admitted as a solicitor, his or her name having been entered on the Roll of Solicitors, and must hold a practising certificate issued by The Solicitors Regulation Authority (SRA) (Solicitors Regulation Authority, The Cube, 199 Wharfside Street, Birmingham B1 1RN; Tel: 0370 606 2555; www.sra.org.uk).

The SRA is the independent regulatory body of the Law Society of England and Wales. People will be admitted as solicitors only if they have passed the appropriate academic and vocational course and have completed a training contract and Professional Skills course, or have transferred from another jurisdiction or the Bar. The SRA controls the training of solicitors. Most solicitors become members of the Law Society, but membership is not compulsory. Intending solicitors other than Fellows of the Chartered Institute of Legal Executives (CILEx), Justices Clerk's Assistants and qualified lawyers from overseas, are required to serve a period of training with a practising solicitor after they have completed the legal practice course.

All new entrants to the profession are required to complete a Disclosure and Barring Service (DBS) standard disclosure prior to admission. Candidates wishing to start training must enrol as a student with the SRA and satisfy it that they have successfully completed the academic stage of training and there are no issues that may call their character and suitability into question.

It is not necessary for the first degree to be in law as about 20 per cent of solicitors qualify via the non-law graduate route. The key stages of this are:

- degree in any subject;
- Common Professional Examination/Graduate Diploma in Law;
- Legal Practice course;
- practice-based training incorporating the Professional Skills course;
- admission to the roll of solicitors.

THE COMMON PROFESSIONAL EXAMINATION (CPE) OR GRADUATE DIPLOMA IN LAW (GDL)

The seven taught modules are the foundation subjects prescribed by the Joint Academic Stage Board on behalf of the Law Society and General Council of the Bar: Criminal Law, Contract Law, the Law of Tort, Equity and Trusts, Public Law, European Union Law and Property Law. For an up-to-date list of course providers for the CPE, use the training provider search in the student section on the SRA website: www.sra.org.uk

THE LEGAL PRACTICE COURSE

Stage 1 covers core practice areas: Litigation, Property Law and Practice (PLP), Business Law and Practice (BLP); Course Skills: Research, Writing, Drafting, Interviewing and Advising, and Advocacy (these skills form an integral part of the compulsory and elective subjects) and also Professional Conduct and Regulation, Taxation and Wills and Administration of Estates. Stage 2 covers three vocational electives chosen from a range of corporate client or private client topics (the range of electives available can differ from institution to institution). An up-to-date list of course providers for the LPC is available using the training provider search in the student section on the SRA website: www.sra.org.uk

TRAINING CONTRACT

The training contract to be served by all intending solicitors, other than Fellows of the Institute of Legal Executives and Justices Clerk's Assistants, is usually two years full time or a part-time study training contract that normally lasts between three and four years. During this period the trainee works and is studying the last two years of a part-time qualifying law degree, the part-time Common Professional

Examination course and/or the part-time Legal Practice Course.

The law graduate who holds a qualifying law degree must complete the Legal Practice course at a recognized institution, and then serve under the training contract, usually for two years. The non-law graduate must first pass the Common Professional Exam (CPE) or the Postgraduate Diploma in Law, having attended either a one-year full-time or two-year part-time preparatory course. He or she may then serve under the training contract for two years after completion of a Legal Practice Course. A Professional Skills course must be attended and successfully completed during the training contract.

Fellows of the Institute of Chartered Legal Executives (CILEx) may obtain partial or full exemptions from the CPE and Justices Clerk's Assistants courses by virtue of similar subjects passed in their Fellowship exams or the Diploma in Magisterial Law. After passing or being exempted from the CPE, the Fellow/Justices Clerk's Assistant may be exempt from serving under a training contract following successful completion of a Legal Practice Course. A Professional Skills course must be taken prior to application for admission.

THE PROFESSIONAL SKILLS COURSE

The aim of the Professional Skills course is to build on the foundations laid in the Legal Practice Course so as to develop a trainee's professional skills. Providers of the course, trainees and their employers are encouraged to regard the course as the first stage of a trainee's lifetime professional development.

Built upon the Legal Practice Course, the course provides training in three subject areas: financial and business skills; advocacy and communication skills; client care and professional standards. Elective topics will also be chosen, which fall within one or more of these three core areas. All trainees have to complete all sections of the course satisfactorily before being admitted. The course consists of face-to-face instruction on the core subjects, for a minimum of 18 hours each for financial and business skills and advocacy and communication skills, and a minimum of 12 hours for client care and professional standards. The elective topics require a minimum total of 24 hours, of which a minimum of 12 hours must be face-to-face. The instruction must be completed during the training contract. The PSC is offered by accredited external course providers.

APPRENTICESHIPS

Legal apprenticeships have been introduced as alternative way to gain legal qualifications. While working for an employer, an apprentice can qualify as a solicitor, a legal executive or a paralegal. During the apprenticeship a combination of classroom and work-based learning is undertaken and the apprentice receives a salary. The minimum entry requirements can be found on the Law Society's website: www.lawsociety.org.uk. The apprenticeship lasts from five to six years. The apprentice is assessed by timed examination and a work-based assessment. The apprentice then takes a standardised practical legal exam in the last six months of the apprenticeship in order to qualify. Further information is available on the SRA's website and www.getingofar.gov.uk

QUALIFIED LAWYERS FROM OTHER JURISDICTIONS

Lawyers from certain foreign jurisdictions can apply for admission under the Qualified Lawyers Transfer Scheme Regulations 2011. They need to obtain a QLTS Certificate of Eligibility, but may be entitled to exemption from some or all of the QLTS assessments if they are:

- a lawyer qualified in the EEA/EU/Switzerland and seeking to qualify via Directive 2005/36/EC (recognition of professional qualifications)
- a lawyer qualified in Northern Ireland or Scotland
- a barrister who has qualified in England and Wales who has completed a pupillage.

The Solicitors Regulation Authority has appointed Kaplan QLTS as the assessment organization for the operation of the assessments (http://qlts.kaplan.co.uk) and the assessments are only available at Kaplan QLTS. The assessments are usually only available twice a year and take place in London. The email address for queries regarding eligibility is contact-centre@sra.org.uk.

EU, Northern Irish and Scottish lawyers and barristers qualified in England and Wales follow a different transfer process and should get in touch with the SRA Contact Centre for further information. SRA Contact Centre Tel: 0370 606 2555 (International callers: +44 (0)121 329 6800); Website: www.sra.org.uk/contact-us

All international applicants must satisfy the requirements and pass the QLTS Assessments. The Assessments are in two parts: Part 1 is a multiple choice test designed to test Part A of the SRA's Day One Outcomes, namely the knowledge of law expected of a newly qualified solicitor of England and Wales and consists of 180 questions; Part 2, is an Objective Structured Clinical Examination (OSCE). For the OSCE, candidates are examined in the skills of interviewing, advocacy/oral presentations, legal research, legal drafting and legal writing in business, civil and criminal litigation, property and probate.

EEA, Northern Irish and Scottish lawyers, and barristers qualified in England and Wales will be individually assessed against the Day One Outcomes. All transferees are required to prove their character and suitability to be a solicitor by taking the SRA Suitability Test. Candidates who have passed the LPC can get exemption from the Part 1 (MCT) assessment.

Prospective candidates wanting more information on QLTS can consult the website www.sra.org.uk/solicitors/qlts/key-features.page for guidance, or contact the SRA on 0370 606 2555 (International callers: +44(0)121 329 6800); Website: www.sra.org.uk/contact-us

SCOTLAND

The Court of Session, High Court of Justiciary, Sheriff Courts and Justice of the Peace Courts are administered by the Scottish Court service, an Executive Agency of the Scottish Government. For further information on Scottish Courts go to www.scotcourts.gov.uk

THE LEGAL PROFESSION

The profession consists of solicitors and advocates.

Qualification as a Solicitor in Scotland

Solicitors in Scotland have their names inserted in a Roll of Solicitors and are granted annual Certificates entitling them to practise by The Law Society of Scotland, contact details: Atria One, 144 Morrison Street, Edinburgh EH3 8EX; Tel: 0131 226 7411; e-mail: lawscot@lawscot.org.uk; website: www.lawscot.org.uk; Education and Careers e-mail: careers@lawscot.org.uk.

For any queries relating to qualifying as a solicitor in Scotland, including LLB/diploma providers, diploma validity, traineeships, admission as a solicitor, entrance certificates and training contracts, alternative routes to qualification and requalifying into Scotland, contact legaleduc@lawscot.org.uk.

A Certificate is granted to candidates who have passed approved exams, completed a term of practical training and been admitted as solicitors.

THE QUALIFYING EXAMINATIONS

The standard route to qualification is the LLB (the Ordinary degree is a three-year course, the Honours is four years) followed by the Diploma in Professional Legal Practice (Professional Education and Training Stage 1: PEAT 1) and then the traineeship, the period of paid in-office training working towards the standard of the qualified solicitor (Professional Education and Training Stage 2: PEAT 2). Outcomes in professionalism, professional ethics and standards, professional communication and business, commercial, financial and practice awareness apply across both PEAT 1 and 2, linking them and providing real clarity across the two stages.

All trainees are required to undertake Trainee Continuing Professional Development (TCPD). All solicitors are required to undertake CPD for a minimum of 20 hours each year. To support solicitors in their CPD activities, the Society provides basic templates, which can be completed online, to assist with identifying training needs, recording CPD undertaken and evaluating the outcome of the training. A wide range of activities are acceptable as CPD, including structured and formalized one-to-one training, coaching and online training.

An alternate route to qualifying as a solicitor in Scotland is by a combination of the Law Society's own examinations and three years pre-Diploma training. To be eligible to sit the Law Society's examinations, non-law graduates must find full-time employment as a pre-Diploma trainee with a qualified solicitor practising in Scotland. A pre-Diploma training contract lasts for three years. During the period of the training contract, a pre-Diploma trainee will study for the Law Society's examinations. The two routes to qualification (degree and Law Society exams) merge at this point as all intending solicitors are required to complete the Diploma in Professional Legal Practice. Upon successful completion of the Diploma the graduate will enter into a two-year post-Diploma training contract with a qualified solicitor practising in Scotland.

Transfer tests are in place for solicitors from England, Wales, Northern Ireland and other parts of the European Union who wish to requalify as Scottish solicitors.

Qualification as an advocate in Scotland

Barristers in Scotland are called Advocates. Scottish Advocates are not only members of the Faculty of Advocates but also members of the College of Justice and officers of the Court. The procedure for the admission of Intrants is subject in part to the control of the Court and in part to the control of the Faculty; the Court is responsible for most of the formal procedures and the Faculty for the exams and periods of professional training. To become an Intrant, applicants must produce evidence that they hold one of the following standard of degree: a degree with Honours, Second Class (Division 2) or above, in Scottish Law at a Scottish university, or a degree in Scottish Law at a Scottish university together with a degree with Honours, Second Class (Division 2) or above, in another subject at a UK university or an ordinary degree with distinction in Scottish Law at a Scottish university. A Diploma in Legal Practice from a Scottish University is also required, although in exceptional cases this requirement may be waived.

In order to go through the various stages of qualification and training, applicants must matriculate as intrants to the Faculty. Matriculation involves making an application to the Court of Session and to the Faculty.

An Intrant must also comply with the professional training required by the Faculty, which consists of a period of 21 months training in a solicitors office (although the Faculty recommends a traineeship of 24 months). Subject-for-subject exemptions are granted to Intrants who have passed exams at this standard in the course of a curriculum for a law degree at a Scottish university. Every Intrant must pass or be exempted from exams in the compulsory subjects and two optional subjects. In addition, and prior to the commencement of pupillage (also known as devilling) every Intrant must sit the Faculty's entrant examination in Evidence, Practice and Procedure. If successfully passed, the Intrant can then commence his or her pupillage.

During the first five or six weeks of pupillage pupils undertake the Foundation course. After about three months of work with their devil master, the pupils will participate in the February Skills course, comprising a series of performance workshops involving the use of documents in evidence, the conduct of a procedure roll discussion, workshops on judicial review, section 275 applications and working with expert evidence. Shortly before admission, the pupils attend the May Preparation for Practice course, covering workshops on vulnerable witnesses, longer motions, reclaiming motions, negotiation and mediation, as well as carrying out civil and criminal appeals before a serving judge.

Intrants who have passed all the necessary exams and undergone the necessary professional training as well as successfully completing their pupillage may apply to be admitted to membership of the Faculty and are admitted at a public meeting of the Faculty. Once admitted, Intrants are introduced to the Court by the Dean of Faculty, make a Declaration of Allegiance to the Sovereign in open Court and are then admitted by the Court to the public office of Advocate. For further information on becoming an advocate contact Faculty of Advocates, Parliament House, Edinburgh EH1 1RF; Tel: 0131 226 5071; e-mail: admissions@advocates.org.uk; website: www.advocates.org.uk

NORTHERN IRELAND

As in England and Wales, the superior courts are the Supreme Court, Court of Appeal, the High Court and the Crown Court. The latter is an exclusively criminal court. The Court of Appeal hears appeals on points of law in civil and criminal cases from all courts. Appeals lie from the Court of Appeal to the Supreme Court.

Inferior Courts: as in England and Wales, the county courts are principally civil courts, but in Northern Ireland they also hear appeals from conviction in the Magistrates Courts for summary offences.

Magistrates Courts: these deal principally with minor criminal offences (summary offences) and are presided over by Resident Magistrates (stipendiaries). Resident Magistrates are appointed by the Crown on the advice of the Lord Chancellor.

Coroners: coroners in Northern Ireland must be barristers or solicitors who have practised for not less than five years. They are appointed by the Lord Chancellor.

THE LEGAL PROFESSION

The legal profession in Northern Ireland consists of barristers and solicitors belonging to professional bodies organized on similar lines to those in England and Wales.

Qualification as a barrister in Northern Ireland

The path to becoming a barrister in Northern Ireland will differ depending on where you study, qualify and complete your pupillage training. There are different pathways for those who have trained as barristers in Northern Ireland, the Republic of Ireland or England and Wales. A different procedure exists for solicitors who wish to requalify as barristers or those who wish to transfer from European jurisdictions. Full information can be found at www.barofni.com/page/becoming-a-barrister

To qualify to practise as a barrister in Northern Ireland a candidate who has trained in Northern Ireland must have a recognized law degree of 2.1 honours standard or higher, or equivalent. The candidate must then complete the Bar Post-Graduate Diploma in Professional Legal Studies at the Institute of Professional Legal Studies, Queen's University, Belfast (IPLS). Finally the candidate must call to the Bar of Northern Ireland and complete a 12-month pupillage. Enquiries about the Bar can be made to the Bar Council Office, The Bar Library, 91 Chichester Street, Belfast BT1 3JQ; Tel: 028 9024 1523; website: www.barofni.com).

Qualification as a solicitor in Northern Ireland

The solicitors' professional body in Northern Ireland is the Law Society of Northern Ireland (Law Society House, 96 Victoria Street, Belfast BT1 3GN; Tel: 028 9023 1614; e-mail: enquiry@lawsoc-ni.org; website: www.lawsoc-ni.org). It has overall responsibility for education and admission to the profession.

Admission to training is generally dependent upon possession of a recognized law degree from a university. Law graduates must attend a two-year vocational apprenticeship course at the Institute of Professional Legal Studies, The Queen's University of Belfast, 10 Lennoxvale, Belfast, BT9 5BY; Tel: 028 9097 5567; e-mail: iplsenquiries@qub.ac.uk. On completion of the two-year apprenticeship newly qualified solicitors receive restricted practising certificates, which means that although they are fully qualified they cannot practise on their own account or in partnership for at least two more years.

Non-law graduates must satisfy the Society that they possess an acceptable degree in a discipline other than law and have attained a satisfactory level of legal knowledge in areas such as: Constitutional Law, Law of Tort, Law of Contract, Criminal Law, Equity, Land Law and Law of Evidence; that they have been offered a place in the Institute; and that they have obtained a Master (a solicitor with whom the applicant proposes to serve his or her apprenticeship).

Membership of Professional Institutions and Associations

CHARTERED INSTITUTE OF LEGAL EXECUTIVES (CILEX)

Kempston Manor
Kempston
Bedford MK42 7AB
Tel: 01234 841000
E-mail: membership@cilex.org.uk
Website: www.cilex.org.uk

The Chartered Institute of Legal Executives (CILEx) is the professional association which represents 20,000 Chartered Legal Executive lawyers, paralegals and other legal practitioners. Our role is to enhance the position and standing of Chartered Legal Executive lawyers in the legal profession. For more than 50 years, we have been offering unparalleled access to a flexible career in law. We work closely with Government and the Ministry of Justice and are recognised in England and Wales as one of the three core approved regulators of the legal profession alongside barristers and solicitors.

MEMBERSHIP
Student Member
Affiliate Member
Associate Member (ACILEx)
Graduate Member (GCILEx)
Chartered Legal Executive Lawyer (FCILEx)

QUALIFICATION/EXAMINATIONS
Level 1 Award/Certificate/Diploma in Legal Studies
Level 2 Award/Certificate/Diploma in Legal Studies
Level 2 Certificate/Diploma for Legal Secretaries
Level 3 Certificate/Diploma for Legal Secretaries
Level 3 Professional Diploma in Law and Practice
Level 3 Certificate in Law and Practice
Level 3 Certificate in Civil Litigation
Level 3 Certificate in Family Practice
Level 3 Certificate in Employment Practice
Level 3 Certificate in Private Client Practice
Level 3 Certificate in Property
Level 3 Diploma in Providing Legal Services

Level 4 Diploma in Commercial Litigation
Level 4 Diploma in Debt Recovery and Insolvency
Level 4 Diploma in Personal Injury Litigation
Level 4 Diploma in Providing Legal Services
Level 4 Extended Diploma in Personal Injury Litigation
Level 6 Certificate in Law
Level 6 Higher Diploma in Law and Practice
Graduate Fast-track Diploma (Level 6)

DESIGNATORY LETTERS
ACILEx, GCILEx, FCILEx

COUNCIL FOR LICENSED CONVEYANCERS

16 Glebe Road
Chelmsford
Essex CM1 1QG
Tel: 01245 349599
Fax: 01245 341300
E-mail: clc@clc-uk.org
Website: www.clc-uk.org

The CLC was established under the provisions of the Administration of Justice Act 1985 as the Regulatory Body for Licensed Conveyancers. Our purpose is to set entry standards and regulate the profession of Licensed Conveyancers effectively. CLC regulates Probate services provided by its licensed practitioners. CLC is an authorised regulator for ABS.

MEMBERSHIP
Student

Licensed Conveyancer
Probate Practitioner
ABS

QUALIFICATION/EXAMINATIONS
Foundation
Finals
Practical Training

THE ACADEMY OF EXPERTS

3 Gray's Inn Square
Gray's Inn
London WC1R 5AH
Tel: 020 7430 0333
Fax: 020 7430 0666
E-mail: admin@academy-experts.org
Website: www.academy-experts.org

The Academy of Experts, multidisciplinary body established in 1987 to establish and promote high objective standards for those acting as expert witnesses. We act as an accrediting and professional body, offering training, technical guidance and representation. In addition we promote cost-efficient dispute resolution, maintaining a register of qualified dispute resolvers.

MEMBERSHIP
Associate Member
Associate Member (AMAE)

Full Member (MAE)
Fellow (FAE)
Practising Corporate Member
Dispute Resolver Member

QUALIFICATION/EXAMINATIONS
There are examinations for upgrade.

DESIGNATORY LETTERS
AMAE, MAE, FAE, QDR

THE INSTITUTE OF LEGAL FINANCE AND MANAGEMENT (ILFM)

2nd Floor
Marlowe House
109 Station Road
Sidcup
Kent DA15 7ET
Tel: 020 8302 2867
Fax: 020 8302 7481
E-mail: kim.freeman@ilfm.org.uk
Website: www.ilfm.org.uk

The ILFM, which was founded in 1978, is a non-profit-making professional body dedicated to the education and support of specialist financial and administrative personnel working within the legal community. We encourage the development of our members' skills through educational courses, training workshops, seminars, conferences and our bimonthly magazine, *Legal Abacus*.

MEMBERSHIP
Ordinary Member
Diploma Member (ILFM (Dip))

Associate Member (AILFM)
Fellow Member (FILFM)
Affiliated Professional Member

QUALIFICATION/EXAMINATIONS
Diploma
Associate
Fellow

DESIGNATORY LETTERS
DILFM (Dip), AILFM, FILFM

THE LAW SOCIETY OF SCOTLAND

Atria One
144 Morrison Street
Edinburgh EH3 8EX
Tel: 0131 226 7411
Fax: 0131 225 2934
E-mail: lawscot@lawscot.org.uk
Website: www.lawscot.org.uk

The Law Society of Scotland is the membership organisation of Scottish solicitors. We promote the interests of the profession and of the public in relation to the profession. Our services include providing initial career advice, overseeing legal education in Scotland, handling admissions to the profession, monitoring trainees, providing post-qualifying legal education, and administering courses and examinations for the Society of Law Accountants in Scotland.

MEMBERSHIP
All practising solicitors in Scotland must be members of the Society and must hold a current Practising Certificate which is issued by the Society.
Students stuyding the LLB or Diploma can become Student Associates free of charge. Visit www.lawscot.org.uk/students for more information

QUALIFICATION/EXAMINATIONS
Please see the Law Society of Scotland's website.

LEISURE AND RECREATION MANAGEMENT
Membership of Professional Institutions and Associations

CHARTERED INSTITUTE FOR THE MANAGEMENT OF SPORT AND PHYSICAL ACTIVITY (CIMSPA)

Sportpark Loughborough University
3 Oakwood Drive
Loughborough
Leicestershire LE11 3QF
Tel: 01509 226474
Fax: 01509 226475
E-mail: info@cimspa.co.uk
Website: www.cimspa.co.uk

CIMSPA is the membership body for sport and physical activity professionals. We promote high standards and provide CPD as well as a wide range of training courses to our members in-house and at venues across the UK. We also work hard to influence government policy on behalf of our members.

MEMBERSHIP
Student Member
Affiliate Member
Associate Member
Member
Fellow
Companion
Chartered Member
Chartered Fellow
Retired Member

QUALIFICATION/EXAMINATIONS
National Pool Plant Operators Certificate
National Pool Plant Foundation Certificate
National Spa Pool Operators Certificate
Supervisory Management Certificate
Fitness Management Certificate
Health and Safety Management Certificate
Higher Professional Diploma in Sport and Recreation Management

Online Continuing Professional Development (CPD) (Entrance and Supervisory Level)
Online Continuing Professional Development (CPD) (Management Level)
Certificate in Leisure Operations (QCF) (1st4sport Level 2)
NVQ Award in Mechanical Ride Operation (QCF) (1st4sport Level 2)
NVQ Certificate in Active Leisure, Learning and Well-being Operational Services (QCF) (1st4sport Level 2)
Certificate in Leisure Management (QCF) (1st4sport Level 3)
NVQ Diploma in Leisure Management (QCF) (1st4sport Level 3)
NVQ Diploma in Sports Development (QCF) (1st4sport Level 3)
Award in Introductory Work in the Outdoors (QCF) (1st4sport Level 2)
NVQ Diploma in Outdoor Programmes (QCF) (1st4sport Level 3)
Award in Coordinating Sports Volunteers (QCF) (1st4sport Level 3)
Certificate in Managing Sports Volunteers (QCF) (1st4sport Level 3)

DESIGNATORY LETTERS
NPPO, RoPPPS, CPD, QCF

INSTITUTE OF GROUNDSMANSHIP

28 Stratford Office Village
Walker Avenue
Wolverton Mill East
Milton Keynes MK12 5TW
Tel: 01908 312511
Fax: 01908 311140
E-mail: iog@iog.org
Website: www.iog.org

The Institute of Groundsmanship is the only membership organisation supporting the whole of the grounds care industry. Serving the industry for more than 80 years, we provide a range of quality products, services and events including education, training and membership services, the national SALTEX exhibition, local information days, an annual conference and awards programme.

MEMBERSHIP
Student Member
Facility/Organisation Member
E-Member
Individual Member
Corporate and Corporate PLUS Member

QUALIFICATION/EXAMINATIONS
For details see: www.iog.org/training-training-courses.asp

LIBRARIANSHIP AND INFORMATION WORK
Membership of Professional Institutions and Associations

CHARTERED INSTITUTE OF LIBRARY AND INFORMATION PROFESSIONALS

7 Ridgmount Street
London WC1E 7AE
Tel: 020 7255 0500
Fax: 020 7255 0501
E-mail: memberservices@cilip.org.uk
Website: www.cilip.org.uk

CILIP is the leading voice for the information, knowledge management, and library profession. Our goal is to put information and library skills and professional values at the heart of a democratic, equal and prosperous society.

MEMBERSHIP
Ordinary Member, Certified Member (ACLIP), Chartered Member (MCLIP), Chartered Fellow (FCLIP), Revalidated Member or Fellow, Student Membership, Overseas Membership, Organisation Membership

QUALIFICATION/EXAMINATIONS
Application for levels of professional registration is through the submission of a portfolio of evidence meeting published criteria. Please contact the Institute for further information.

DESIGNATORY LETTERS
ACLIP, MCLIP, FCLIP

MANAGEMENT
Membership of Professional Institutions and Associations

ASSOCIATION FOR PROJECT MANAGEMENT

Ibis House
Regent Park
Summerleys Road
Princes Risborough
Buckinghamshire HP27 9LE
Tel: 0845 458 1944
E-mail: via website
Website: www.apm.org.uk

The association is a registered charity with over 19,500 individual and 500 corporate members making it the largest professional body of its kind in Europe. APM's mission statement is 'to develop and promote the professional disciplines of project and programme management for the public benefit'.

MEMBERSHIP
Student Member
Associate Member
Full Member (MAPM)
Fellow (FAPM)
Corporate Member
Honorary Member/ Fellow (HonFAPM)

QUALIFICATION/EXAMINATIONS
Introductory Certificate in Project Management (IC)
APMP
APMP for PRINCE2 Practitioners
Practitioner Qualification (PQ)
Risk level 1
Risk level 2
Pan sector standard:
Registered Project Professional (RPP)
Higher Apprenticeship:
Higher Apprenticeship in Project Management

DESIGNATORY LETTERS
MAPM, FAPM, HonFAPM, RPP

ASSOCIATION OF CERTIFIED COMMERCIAL DIPLOMATS (ACCD)

Commercial Diplomats Regulation Authority
ACCD Global Headquarters
Central Administration Office
PO Box 50561, Canary Wharf
London E16 3WY
Tel: +44(0)8445 864249
E-mail: enquiries@chartereddiplomats.org.uk
Website: www.commercialdiplomats.org.uk

Association of Certified Commercial Diplomats is the first independent accreditation and regulation authority, and extraterritorial global professional awarding body for commercial diplomats and diplomatic institutions. The umbrella of ACCD covers ambassadors, representatives of government, trade commissioners, advisors and negotiators, arbitrators, negotiators of IIAs, policy-makers & government officials, commercial judges, arbitrators, involved in trade, commercial and/or investment issues, commercial counsellors, IIA experts, academia, private sector & NGO representatives, officials in government ministries, parastatals, corporations, academic, public and private institutions worldwide. Its principal objectives are to provide accreditation and regulation, and to advance the interests of its members as qualified, certified and competent commercial diplomats. As the global voice, ACCD has overall responsibility, including the setting of policy and guidelines, as well as the qualification and accreditation procedures for the commercial diplomatic profession. ACCD is non-partisan, not-for-profit, independent of government, and uniquely the professional regulatory body for diplomatic institutions of higher learning providing advanced postgraduate, doctoral, and postdoctoral programmes on commercial judicial diplomatic affairs.

MEMBERSHIP
REGULATED MEMBERSHIP
Affiliate Professional
Associate
Member
Fellow

QUALIFICATION/EXAMINATIONS
ACCD REGULATED POSTGRADUATE AND POST QUALIFICATION EXAMINATIONS AND QUALIFICATIONS
Certificate of Competency
Advanced Certificate of Competency
Master Certificate of Competency
Advanced Master Certificate of Competency
ACCD REGULATED ACCREDITATIONS
Associate Expert (AE)
Qualified Advocate (QA)
Qualified Certified Diplomat (QCD)
Chartered Diplomat (C. Dipl)

DESIGNATORY LETTERS
ACDipl, MCD, MCDipl, M.Arb, DCD, DCDipl, FCDipl, QA, QCD, C. Dipl

AUA

AUA National Office
University of Manchester
Sackville Street Building
Manchester M60 1QD
Tel: 0161 275 2063
Fax: 0161 275 2036
E-mail: aua@aua.ac.uk
Website: www.aua.ac.uk

As a member-led organization with over 3,500 members, AUA promotes best practice in higher education management and exists to advance and promote professional recognition and development of those who work in higher and further education by encouraging and fostering sound methods of leadership, management and administration, through a range of professional development initiatives.

AUA members are individually and collectively committed to:
• the continuous development of their own and others' professional knowledge, skills and practices;
• actively championing equality of educational and professional opportunity;
• the advancement of higher education through the robust application of professional knowledge, skills and practices;
• the highest standards of fair, ethical and transparent professional behaviours.

AUA is at the forefront of professional development in higher education and has developed a sector-wide framework to support the development of professional services colleagues. Through continuing professional development, individuals, teams and institutions can foster skills and behaviours associated with the profession. AUA also holds the largest professional development annual conference in the UK higher education calendar.

MEMBERSHIP
Member (MAUA)
Accredited Member (AAUA)
Fellow (FAUA)
Honorary Member (FAUA)
Student Member (MAUA)

QUALIFICATION/EXAMINATIONS
Postgraduate Certificate in Professional Practice (PG Cert)
This programme is validated by The Open University and credits from the course can be used on a number of MA courses.

BRITISH INSTITUTE OF FACILITIES MANAGEMENT

Charringtons House (South)
The Causeway
Bishop's Stortford
Hertfordshire CM23 2ER
Tel: #44 (0)1279 712651
E-mail: qualifications@bifm.org.uk
Website: www.bifm.org.uk

The BIFM is the professional body for facilities management (FM). Founded in 1993, the Institute provides information, education, training and networking services for over 17,000 members – both individual professionals and employers. The BIFM is the professional body responsible for promoting excellence in facilities management for the benefit of practitioners, the economy and society.

MEMBERSHIP
Affiliate
Associate (ABIFM)
Member (MBIFM)
Certified Member (CBIFM)
Fellow (FBIFM)
Corporate Member

QUALIFICATION/EXAMINATIONS
BIFM Level 2 Certificate in Facilities Services
BIFM Level 2 Certificate in Facilities Services Principles
BIFM Level 3 Award in Facilities Management
BIFM Level 3 Certificate in Facilities Management
BIFM Level 3 Certificate in Facilities Management Practice
BIFM Level 3 Diploma in Facilities Management
BIFM Level 4 Award in Facilities Management
BIFM Level 4 Certificate in Facilities Management
BIFM Level 4 Diploma in Facilities Management
BIFM Level 5 Award in Facilities Management
BIFM Level 5 Certificate in Facilities Management
BIFM Level 5 Diploma in Facilities Management
BIFM Level 6 Award in Facilities Management
BIFM Level 6 Certificate in Facilities Management
BIFM Level 6 Extended Diploma in Facilities Management
BIFM Level 7 Certificate in Facilities Management
BIFM Level 7 Extended Diploma in Facilities Management

DESIGNATORY LETTERS
ABIFM, MBIFM, CBIFM, FBIFM

BUSINESS MANAGEMENT ASSOCIATION

2 Old College Court
29 Priory Street
Ware
Hertfordshire SG12 0DE
Tel: 03707369369
E-mail: enquiries@businessmanagement.org.uk
Website: www.businessmanagement.org.uk

The Business Management Association is a professional body for business owners and managers. We promote the aims and interests of the small business sector internationally, provide information and advice to our members, encourage networking between members, and seek to provide members with advanced knowledge, skill and qualifications in several aspects of management.

MEMBERSHIP
Affiliate (AffBMA)
Associate (ABMA)
Member (MBMA)
Fellow (FBMA)
Companion (CBMA)
Certified Manager (CertMgr)
Certified Master of Management (CMMgt)
Certified Master of Business Administration (CMBA)

Certified Doctor of Business Administration (CDBA)

QUALIFICATION/EXAMINATIONS
Entrepreneurs Award (EA)
Diploma In Business Management (DipBMA)

DESIGNATORY LETTERS
AffBMA, ABMA, MBMA, FBMA, CBMA, CertMgr, CMMgt, CMBA, CDBA, MCBMA, FCBMA

DIPLOMATIC ACADEMY OF EUROPE AND THE ATLANTIC

Institution for the Training of Commercial Diplomats
ACCD Global Headquarters
PO Box 50561, Canary Wharf
Greater London E16 3WY

Diplomatic Academy of Europe and the Atlantic is an authoritative knowledge-based international professional diplomatic institution whose activities include advanced research, training and development, provision of postgraduate and post-qualification commercial diplomatic education, and contribution to responsible commercial diplomatic practice and service. It is a key independent extraterritorial diplomatic organization established for the advancement and development of greater knowledge and skills in commercial diplomacy. DAEA offers a complete portfolio of specialized mandatory postgraduate programmes on commercial diplomacy.

MEMBERSHIP
Fellow of the Diplomatic Academy (FDA)

QUALIFICATION/EXAMINATIONS
MANDATORY EXAMINATIONS
Qualified Policy Advocate
Qualified Certified Diplomat
Chartered Diplomat
QUALIFICATIONS
Advanced Certificate of Competency
Master Certificate of Competency
Master of Commercial Diplomacy

DESIGNATORY LETTERS
ACDipl, MCDipl, DCD, FCD

FACULTY OF PROFESSIONAL BUSINESS AND TECHNICAL MANAGEMENT

Office 13275
PO Box 4336
Manchester
United Kingdom M61 0BW
Tel: 01386 277973
E-mail: info@pbtm.org.uk
Website: www.pbtm.org.uk

FPBTM was founded in 1983 to forge the link between business and technology. We give professional recognition to the knowledge and skills of managers in business and technology, supporting lifelong learning to help members fulfil their career ambitions and develop their potential.

MEMBERSHIP
Student Member (SFPBTM)
Technician Member (TMFPBTM)
Associate Member (AMFPBTM)
Member (MFPBTM)
Fellow (FFPBTM)
Companion (CFPBTM)

INSTITUTE OF ADMINISTRATIVE MANAGEMENT

Coppice House
Halesfield 7
Telford
Shropshire TF7 4NA
Tel: 01952 797396
E-mail: info@instam.org
Website: www.instam.org

The IAM is one of the oldest UK professional bodies, championing administration and management fields. It provides professional recognition, as well as professional development through CPD opportunities and qualifications. As part of the IQ group (IQ: Awarding Organisation & IQ Verify: UKAS Accredited Body), it is well equipped to aid businesses.

MEMBERSHIP
IAM Student
Non IAM Student
Affiliate
Associate (AInstAM)
Member (MInstAM)
Fellow (FInstAM)
Companion (CInstAM)

QUALIFICATION/EXAMINATIONS
IQ IAM Level 2 Diploma in Business Administration
IQ IAM Level 2 Diploma in Team Leading
IQ Level 2 Diploma in Customer Service
IQ IAM Level 3 Award in Professional PA and Administration Skills
IQ IAM Level 3 Certificate in Business and Administrative Management
IQ IAM Level 3 Diploma in Business and Administrative Management
IQ IAM Level 3 Diploma in Management
IQ Level 3 Award in Grant-funding Administration
IQ Level 3 Diploma in Customer Service
IQ IAM Level 4 Certificate in Office and Administration Management
IQ IAM Level 4 Certificate in Principles of Business Administration
IQ IAM Level 4 Diploma in Business and Administrative Management
IQ IAM Level 4 NVQ Diploma in Business Administration
IQ IAM Level 4 NVQ Diploma in Management
IQ IAM Level 5 Diploma in Business and Administrative Management

DESIGNATORY LETTERS
AInstAM, MInstAM, FInstAM, CInstAM

INSTITUTE OF CONSULTING

4th Floor
2 Savoy Court
Strand
London WC2R 0EZ
Tel: 020 7497 0580
Fax: 020 7497 0463
E-mail: welcome@ibconsulting.org.uk
Website: www.iconsulting.org.uk

The Institute of Consulting was formed in 2007 by the merger of the Institute of Business Advisers and the Institute of Management Consultancy, and we are the professional body for business consultants and advisers. Our aim is to raise the standards of professional practice in support of better business performance.

MEMBERSHIP
Student
Affiliate

Associate (AIBC)
Member (MIBC)
Fellow (FIBC)
Certified Business Advisor (CBA)
Certified Management Consultant (CMC)
Practice Member (corporate membership)

QUALIFICATION/EXAMINATIONS
Award in Professional Consulting (Level 5) (QCF)
Certificate in Professional Consulting (Level 5) (QCF)
Diploma in Professional Consulting (Level 5) (QCF)

Award in Business Support (Level 5) (QCF)
Certificate in Business Support (Level 5) (QCF)
Diploma in Business Support (Level 5) (QCF)
Award in Professional Consulting (Level 7) (QCF)
Certificate in Professional Consulting (Level 7) (QCF)
Diploma in Professional Consulting (Level 7) (QCF)
Certified Management Consultant Award (CMC)
Certified Business Advisor Award (CBA)

DESIGNATORY LETTERS
AIBC, MIBC, FIBC

INSTITUTE OF DIRECTORS

116 Pall Mall
London SW1Y 5ED
Tel: 020 7766 2601
E-mail: professionaldev@iod.com
Website: www.iod.com/development

The IoD represents professional leaders, with individual members ranging from entrepreneurs of start-up companies to CEOs of multinational organizations. The Institute's principal objectives are to advance the interests of its members as company directors, and to provide them with business facilities and a variety of services.

MEMBERSHIP
Student
Associate Member

Member (MIoD)
Fellow (FIoD)
Chartered Director (C Dir)

QUALIFICATION/EXAMINATIONS
Certificate in Company Direction (CertIoD)
Diploma in Company Direction (DipIoD)
Chartered Director (C Dir)

DESIGNATORY LETTERS
MIoD, FIoD, C Dir

INSTITUTE OF LEADERSHIP & MANAGEMENT

Stowe House
Netherstowe
Lichfield
Staffordshire WS13 6TJ
Tel: 01543 266867
Fax: 01543 266893
E-mail: customer@i-l-m.com
Website: www.i-l-m.com

The ILM supports, develops and informs leaders and managers at every stage of their career. With our broad range of industry-leading qualifications, membership services and learning resources, the ILM provides flexible development solutions that can be blended to meet the specific needs of employers and learners.

MEMBERSHIP
Studying Member
Professional Member

QUALIFICATION/EXAMINATIONS
Management
Principles of Team Leading including Foundation Award in Management Practice (Level 2)

Award, Certificate in Effective Team Member Skills (Level 2)

Award, Certificate in Leadership and Team Skills (Level 2)

NVQ Certificate in Team Leading (Level 2)

Certificate in Team Leading (Level 2)

NVQ Certificate in Management (Level 3)

Certificate in Effective Management (Level 3)

Certificate in Principles of Leadership and Management (Level 3)

Award, Certificate and Diploma in Leadership and Management (Level 4)

Diploma in Principles of Leadership and Management (Level 5)

NVQ Diploma in Management (Level 5)

Award in Management (Level 6)

NVQ Diploma in Management (Level 7)

Diploma in Strategic Leadership and Executive Management (Level 7)

Award, Certificate and Diploma in Executive Management (Level 7)

Leadership

Certificate in Leadership (Level 3)

Award in Leadership (Level 4)

Award, Certificate and Diploma in Strategic Leadership (Level 7)

Leadership and Management

Award, Certificate and Diploma in Leadership and Management (Level 3)

Award, Certificate and Diploma in Leadership and Management (Level 5)

Coaching and Mentoring

Certificate in Coaching and Mentoring (Level 3)

Certificate and Diploma in Coaching and Mentoring (Level 5)

Certificate and Diploma in Coaching Supervision (Level 7)

Certificate and Diploma in Executive Coaching and Leadership Mentoring (Level 7)

Specialist Management Qualifications

Environmental Management

Facilities Management

Equality and Diversity

Managing Volunteers

Sales Management

Waste Management

Business and Enterprise

Certificate in Enterprise (Level 2)

Award and Certificate in Enterprise and Entrepreneurship (Level 3)

Award in Management (Level 5)

Certificate and Diploma in Social Enterprise Support (Level 5)

Specialist Management Qualifications

Operational management

Service improvement

Waste management

Equality and diversity

Volunteer management

Management consultancy

Staff and organisational development

Quality improvement

Scottish Vocational Qualifications (SVQs)

SVQ 2 in Team Leading (Scottish Level 5)

SVQ 3 in Management (Scottish Level 7)

SVQ 4 in Management (Scottish Level 9)

SVQ 5 in Management (Scottish Level 11)

INSTITUTE OF MANAGEMENT SERVICES

Brooke House
24 Dam Street
Lichfield
Staffordshire WS13 6AA
Tel: 01543 266909
Fax: 01543 257848
E-mail: admin@ims-productivity.com
Website: www.ims-productivity.com

QUALIFICATION/EXAMINATIONS
IMS Certificate

DESIGNATORY LETTERS
AMS, MMS, FMS

INSTITUTE OF VALUE MANAGEMENT

PO Box 101
Ledbury
Herefordshire HR8 9JW
Tel: 01531 631444
E-mail: secretary@ivm.org.uk
Website: www.ivm.org.uk

The Institute aims to establish Value Management as an all-encompassing strategy for achieving value in every sector of the economy and to provide support in the innovative use of value management techniques.

MEMBERSHIP

Corporate – This grade is for organizations that use or promote value management and want to make a corporate statement to that effect. A Corporate Member may nominate up to 10 members of staff who will have full voting rights. Corporate members may use the designatory letters AIVM (or MIVM if they meet the requirements and make a successful application).

Student – This grade is for students studying full time for a UK qualification. Student members are not eligible to use any designatory letters.

Trainee – This grade is for individuals who have completed either an IVM accredited Foundation Course in Value Management in the previous 6 months or a Management of Value (MoV) Foundation Course in the previous 6 months. Trainee membership is limited to two years. Trainee Members are not eligible to use designatory letters.

Associate – This grade is open to individuals who have a demonstrable interest in Value Management and who either promote, use or are associated with Value Management. Associate Members may use the designatory letters AIVM.

Member – This grade is open to individuals who have considerable sector knowledge and skills in their profession and who meet at least one of the following requirements:
- Have successfully completed an IVM accredited VM2 Course
- Hold a QVA or CVA qualification
- Have successfully completed a Management of Value (MoV) Practitioner course
- Have a minimum of 3 years' experience working in a Value Management environment
- Hold a relevant professional qualification in Lean, Benefits or Project Management
Members may use the post nominals MIVM

Fellow – Fellowship of the Institute of Value Management is the most senior grade available and is reserved for those who have reached the highest echelons in their career. It is open to those who meet at least one of the following requirements:

- Have demonstrated significant experience or contribution to the field of Value Management
– Hold a current PVM qualification

Fellows may use the post nominals FIVM

QUALIFICATION/EXAMINATIONS

IVM Certification Board – The IVM's Certification Board is an independent body whose role is to implement and control the certification and training policies developed by the IVM and the European Governing Board (EGB), representing all the European value associations.

Certification Levels

There are three levels of recognised certification based on experience and knowledge:
- Qualified Value Associate (QVA) – (Europe)
- Professional in Value Management (PVM) – (Europe). This qualification signals competence to lead value studies in a variety of environments and contribute to the development of VM strategies.
- Trainer in Value Management (TVM) – (Europe). In order to develop competence to train to an appropriate standard, the qualification of Trainer in Value Management (TVM) has been introduced. This qualification is only available for PVMs with at least 2 years experience, who have completed an approved train the trainer course.

DESIGNATORY LETTERS
AIVM, MIVM, FIVM, HFIVM

INTERNATIONAL PROFESSIONAL MANAGERS ASSOCIATION

5 Starnes Court
Union Street
Maidstone
Kent ME14 1EB
Tel: 01622 672867
Fax: 01622 755149
E-mail: admin@ipma.co.uk
Website: www.ipma.co.uk

The IPMA is an international examining, licensing and regulatory professional body, which, through its qualifying examinations, enables practising managers to participate in and be part of the process of improving managerial performance and effectiveness in all areas of business, industry and public administration.

MEMBERSHIP
Student Member
Graduate Member (GRD PMA)
Licentiate Member (LMPMA)
Certified Associate (AMPMA)
Certified Member (MPMA)
Certified Fellow (FPMA)

QUALIFICATION/EXAMINATIONS
Certified International Professional Manager (CIPM) examinations
Foundation: Economics, Legal Environment of Business, Information Communication and Technology, Business Management, Statistical Methods for Business, Principles of Finance
Intermediate: Business Marketing, Entrepreneurship, Corporate Law, Management Accounting, Advanced Management Practice, Managing People
Professional Level 1: Human Resource Management, Management Decision Making, Organisational Behaviour, Information Systems Management, Operations Management
Professional Level 2: Business Policy and Strategic Management, Corporate Finance and Risk Management, Organisation Change and Development, Multinational Business Management, Case Study and a Project

DESIGNATORY LETTERS
GRD PMA, LMPMA, AMPMA, MPMA, FPMA, CIPM

THE ASSOCIATION OF BUSINESS EXECUTIVES

5th Floor, CI Tower
St Georges Square
New Malden
Surrey KT3 4TE
Tel: 020 8329 2930
Fax: 020 8329 2945
E-mail: info@abeuk.com
Website: www.abeuk.com

ABE is a professional membership body and examination board. We develop business and management qualifications at Levels 4, 5, 6 & 7 on the QCF framework. ABE's range of OFQUAL accredited qualifications provide progression routes to degree and Master's programmes worldwide.

MEMBERSHIP

MEMBERSHIP
Affiliate Member
Student Member
Associate Member (AMABE)
Member (MABE)
Fellow (FABE)

QUALIFICATION/EXAMINATIONS
Diploma Levels 4, 5 and 6 in:
Business Management
Management of Information Systems (Pathway)

Financial Management (Pathway)
Human Resource Management
Marketing Management
Travel, Tourism and Hospitality Management
Diploma in Business Development (Level 7)
Diploma in Business Start-Up and Entrepreneurship (Level 4)

DESIGNATORY LETTERS
AMABE, MABE, FABE

THE CHARTERED MANAGEMENT INSTITUTE

Customer Service Department
Management House
Cottingham Road
Corby
Northants NN17 1TT
Tel: 01536 204222
Fax: 01536 201651
E-mail: enquiries@managers.org.uk
Website: www.managers.org.uk

CMI is the only chartered professional body in the UK dedicated to promoting the highest standards of management and leadership excellence. With a member community of over 150,000, CMI gives managers and leaders, and their organisations, the skills they need to improve their performance and create an impact.

MEMBERSHIP
Affiliate
Associate (ACMI)
Member (MCMI)
Fellow (FCMI)
Chartered Member (CMgr MCMI)
Chartered Fellow (CMgr FCMI)
Companion (CCMI)
Chartered Companion (CMgr CCMI)

QUALIFICATION/EXAMINATIONS
The breadth and depth of our management and leadership qualification portfolio is unmatched. We have over 80 individual qualifications ranging from team leading, strategic management to coaching and mentoring to name a few.

To support your development we have a wide range of online and hardcopy resources and materials, including ManagementDirect and Pathways Workbooks. With CMI Membership you can also enjoy benefits of a Career Development Centre, mentoring and professional development.

We have a network of more than 500 Centres delivering our qualifications so you can always find somewhere to study that's convenient for you.

DESIGNATORY LETTERS
ACMI, MCMI, FCMI, CMgr MCMI, CMgr FCMI, CCMI, CMgr CCMI

THE INSTITUTE OF COMMERCIAL MANAGEMENT

ICM House
Yeoman Road
Ringwood
Hampshire BH24 3FA
Tel: 01202 490555
E-mail: info@icm.education
Website: www.icm.education

Established in 1975, the Institute is the leading professional body for Commercial and Business Development Managers. It provides examining and assessment services for those undertaking business and management studies and offers in excess of 200 programmes. The Institute works with public and private sector education and training providers in more than 100 countries.

MEMBERSHIP
Student Membership

QUALIFICATION/EXAMINATIONS
ICM Awards cover the following areas: Accounting & Finance; Business Studies; Commercial Management; Hospitality Management; Human Resource Development; Journalism; Legal Studies; Management Studies; Maritime Management; Marketing Management; Sales Management; Travel & Tourism

THE INSTITUTE OF MANAGEMENT SPECIALISTS

Office 13275
PO Box 4336
Manchester
United Kingdom M61 0BW
Tel: 01386 277973
E-mail: info@instituteofmanagementspecialists.org.uk
Website: www.instituteofmanagementspecialists.org.uk

The Institute of Management Specialists was founded in 1971 to give professional recognition to the knowledge and skills of managers and specialists. The Institute encourages management excellence and specialist expertise, and supports lifelong learning to help members fulfil their career ambitions.

Specialised Manager Awards are available in a range of specialised areas and IMS offers a CPD (Continuous Professional Development) programme leading to Certified Specialist Manager status.

MEMBERSHIP
Student Member (StudIMS)

Associate Member (AMIMS)
Member (MIMS)
Fellow (FIMS)
Companion (CompIMS)

QUALIFICATION/EXAMINATIONS
Diploma of Management and Leadership
Advanced Diploma of Management and Leadership
Professional Diploma of Management and Leadership
Executive Diploma of Management and Leadership

THE OXBRIDGE COLLEGE OF EDUCATION

Connaugh House
Benarth Road
Conwy
Wales
E-mail: admin@oxbridge-uk.org
Website: www.oxbridge-uk.org

The Oxbridge College of Education is a professional, autonomous, not-for-profit institution established to foster the concept of UK management education made available to all internationally. Oxbridge is built on the foundation of promoting state-of-the-art knowledge and expertise in all facets of management education, training and development for the global educational arena.

MEMBERSHIP
Associate Category (ACAM)
Member Category (MCAM)
Fellowship Category (FCAM)

QUALIFICATION/EXAMINATIONS
All programmes offered by Oxbridge College are accredited by Quality Assurance Commission UK. Programmes offered:
International Foundation Diploma

International Certificate in Restaurant & Catering Management
International Diploma in Business Management
International Diploma in Business (Restaurant & Catering Management)
International Diploma in Business (Tourism Management)
International Advanced Diploma in Business Management
International Advanced Diploma in Business (Restaurant & Catering Management)
International Advanced Diploma in Business (Tourism Management)
International Postgraduate Diploma in Hospitality Management
International Postgraduate Diploma in Business
International Postgraduate Diploma in Business with Specialization in: Marketing, Finance, Human Resource

THE SOCIETY OF BUSINESS PRACTITIONERS

PO Box 11
Sandbach
Cheshire CW11 3GE
Tel: 01270 526339
Fax: 01270 526339
E-mail: info@mamsasbp.org.uk
Website: www.mamsasbp.org.uk

SBP is an International Examination Board founded in 1956 by experienced educationalists and executives to fulfil a need to set standards in business practice achieved by examinations/assessments. Inexperienced and mature students should be able to follow careers in further education and/or be proficient in employment and receive the benefits of membership.

MEMBERSHIP
Student (StuSBP)
Member (MSBP)
Certified Professional Manager (CPMSBP)

Honorary Fellow
Professional Memberships *(Senior Professional Qualifications)*
Associateship (ASBP)
Licentiateship (LSBP)
Graduateship (GSBP)
Fellowship (FSBP)
These are certified competency-based Membership Awards open to persons occupied in business practice who are considered suitable by the Membership Committee.

CPD programmes are also offered for the Asia region.

QUALIFICATION/EXAMINATIONS
Diploma in Business Administration
Advanced Diploma in Business Administration
PGDip in Business Administration
PGDip in International Marketing
Diploma in Computer Studies
Advanced Diploma in Computer Studies

GradDip in IT & E-Commerce
GradDip in Entrepreneurship
Advanced Diploma in Accounting
Diploma & Advanced Diploma in Marketing Management (Joint Award with the Managing & Marketing Sales Association)

DESIGNATORY LETTERS
StuSBP, MSBP, CPMSBP, ASBP, LSBP, GSBP, FSBP

MANUFACTURING
Membership of Professional Institutions and Associations

THE INSTITUTE OF MANUFACTURING

OFFICE 13275
PO BOX 4336
MANCHESTER
United Kingdom M61 0BW
Tel: 01386 277973
E-mail: info@instituteofmanufacturing.org.uk
Website: www.instituteofmanufacturing.org.uk

The Institute of Manufacturing was founded in 1978 to give professional recognition to the knowledge and skills of people in all aspects of manufacturing. The Institute supports lifelong learning to help members fulfill their career ambitions and develop their potential.

Certified Manufacturing Practitioner award is available to recognise management knowledge with manufacturing experience.

MEMBERSHIP
Student Member (StudIManf)

Associate Member (AMIManf)
Member (MIManf)
Fellow (FIManf)
Companion (CompIManf)

QUALIFICATION/EXAMINATIONS
Diploma in Manufacturing Management
Advanced Diploma in Manufacturing Management
Professional Diploma Diploma in Manufacturing Management
Executive Diploma in Manufacturing Management
Certified Manufacturing Practitioner

MARKETING AND SALES

Membership of Professional Institutions and Associations

LONDON CENTRE OF MARKETING

Buckingham House West
Stanmore
London HA7 4EB
Tel: 020 8385 7766
Fax: 020 8385 7755
E-mail: info@lcmuk.com
Website: www.lcmuk.com

The London Centre of Marketing is an Ofqual accredited, non-political, Awarding Organisation based in London, which exists with the sole aim of providing internationally recognised professional qualifications in marketing and marketing management.

MEMBERSHIP
We offer three types of memberships:
1. Associate (ALCM)
2. Member (MLCM)
3. Fellow (FLCM)

QUALIFICATION/EXAMINATIONS
Diploma, Higher Diploma, Professional Diploma, Graduate Diploma and Postgraduate Dipolma in:
Business Management & Marketing
Human Resource Development & Marketing
Sales & Marketing Management
Travel & Tourism Marketing
Public Relations & Marketing
Entrepreneurship & Marketing

DESIGNATORY LETTERS
ALCM/MLCM/FLCM

MANAGING AND MARKETING SALES ASSOCIATION EXAMINATION BOARD

PO Box 11
Sandbach
Cheshire CW11 3GE
Tel: 01270 526339
Fax: 01270 526339
E-mail: info@mamsasbp.org.uk
Website: www.mamsasbp.org.uk

MAMSA is an international Examination Board offering qualifications in Sales, Marketing and Management and its senior specialist Diploma in Marketing Strategy. The importance of 'Customer Service' is emphasized throughout all the programmes.

MEMBERSHIP
Graduate (GradMAMSA)
Graduate Affiliate (GradAfMAMSA)
Professional (MMAMSA)
Fellow (FMAMSA)

QUALIFICATION/EXAMINATIONS
Standard Diploma in Salesmanship
Certificate in Sales Marketing
Higher Diploma in Marketing
Advanced Diploma in Sales Management
Certificate in Marketing Strategy
Diploma in Marketing Strategy & Management (Hypothesis/Thesis)
Diploma in Sales and Marketing Practices (Joint Award with the Society of Business Practitioners)
A CPD programme is also offered

MRS (THE MARKET RESEARCH SOCIETY)

The Old Trading House
15 Northburgh Street
London EC1V 0JR
Tel: 020 7490 4911
Fax: 020 7490 0608
E-mail: profdevelopment@mrs.org.uk
Website: www.mrs.org.uk

With members in more than 50 countries, MRS is the world's leading authority on research and business intelligence. For those who need, use, generate or interpret the evidence essential to making good decisions for commercial and public policy. MRS is an awarding body for vocationally related qualifications in research.

MEMBERSHIP
Student Member
Member (MMRS)
Certified Member (CMRS)

Fellow (FMRS)
Honorary Fellow (Hon. FMRS)

QUALIFICATION/EXAMINATIONS
MRS Certificate in Market and Social Research
MRS Certificate in Interviewing Skills
MRS Advanced Certificate in Market and Social Research Practice
MRS Diploma in Market and Social Research Practice

DESIGNATORY LETTERS
MMRS, CMRS, FMRS, Hon. FMRS

THE CHARTERED INSTITUTE OF MARKETING

Moor Hall
Maidenhead
Berkshire SL6 9QH
Tel: 01628 427120
Fax: 01628 427158
E-mail: qualifications@cim.co.uk
Website: www.cim.co.uk/learningzone

The Chartered Institute of Marketing is the leading international professional marketing body, with 47,000 members worldwide. We aim to improve the skills of marketing practitioners, enabling them to deliver exceptional results for their organization. Qualifications from Introductory to Chartered postgraduate level are offered to anyone wanting to develop their career in marketing.

MEMBERSHIP
Affiliate (Studying/Professional)
Associate (ACIM)
Member (MCIM)
Fellow (FCIM)

Chartered Marketer

QUALIFICATION/EXAMINATIONS
Professional Certificate in Marketing
Professional Diploma in Marketing
Chartered Postgraduate Diploma in Marketing
Diploma in Marketing Communications
Diploma in Digital Marketing
Professional Diploma in Marketing for Business Services and Solutions
Diploma in Digital Marketing (Mobile)
Diploma in Digital Marketing (Metrics and Analytics)
Diploma in Digital Marketing (Media and Branding)

Certificate in Professional Sales Practice

Advanced Certificate in Professional Sales Management Practice

Advanced Certificate in Account Management Practice

Intensive Diploma on Strategic Sales Practice

ACIM, MCIM, FCIM

THE INSTITUTE OF DIRECT AND DIGITAL MARKETING

DMA House
70 Margaret St
Fitzrovia
London W1W 8SS
Tel: 020 8614 0277
E-mail: ask@theidm.com
Website: www.theidm.com

For more than 30 years the IDM has existed to support, encourage and improve marketing performance from your first steps on the career ladder, right to the very top. We've become the trusted training partner for hundreds of leading brands from over 30 countries and have trained over 100,000 delegates. Now, as part of the DMA Group, we are the largest marketing association in Europe.

From foundation to advanced level, we have the cutting-edge content, world-class tutors and advanced delivery platforms that will help you prepare for your future.

MEMBERSHIP
Associate Member
Member
Fellow

QUALIFICATION/EXAMINATIONS
Professional Diploma in Digital Marketing
Professional Diploma in Digital Marketing with B2B
Professional Diploma in Direct and Digital
Professional Diploma in Direct and Digital Marketing with B2B
Postgraduate Diploma in Digital Marketing
Postgraduate Diploma in Digital Marketing with B2B
Postgraduate Diploma in Direct and Digital Marketing
Postgraduate Diploma in Direct and Digital Marketing with B2B
Professional Certificate in Social Media
Professional Certificate in Email Marketing
Professional Certificate in Search Marketing
Professional Certificate in Content Marketing
Award in Digital Copywriting
Award in Data Fundamentals
Award in Direct and Digital Marketing
Award in Digital Marketing
Award in General Data Protection Regulation (GDPR)
Award in Direct Mail

THE INSTITUTE OF SALES AND MARKETING MANAGEMENT (ISMM)

Basepoint Business & Innovation Centre
Unit 22A, 110 Butterfield
Great Marlings
Luton
Bedfordshire LU2 8DL
Tel: 01582 840001
E-mail: education@ismm.co.uk
Website: www.ismm.co.uk

Founded in 1911, the ISMM is the worldwide representative body for sales people. To help members improve their skills set the ISMM provide qualifications, approved by Ofqual, the UK Government's regulatory body for education. Written by qualified and experienced sales professionals they cover the salesperson's career right up to sales director level.

MEMBERSHIP
Affiliate
Associate (AInstSMM)
Member (MInstSMM)
Fellow (FInstSMM)
Companion (CInstSMM)

QUALIFICATION/EXAMINATIONS
Level 1 Award in Selling Lawfully and Ethically
Level 1 Award in Understanding the Sales Cycle
Level 1 Award in Understanding Marketing
Level 1 Award in Communication Skills in Sales
Level 1 Award in Sales and Marketing
Level 2 Award in Understanding Laws and Ethics of Selling
Level 2 Award in Understanding Marketing
Level 2 Award in Understanding Buyer Behaviour
Level 2 Award in Sales Targets
Level 2 Award in Selling to Customers
Level 2 Award in Understanding Selling to Customers
Level 2 Award in Telesales
Level 2 Certificate in Sales and Marketing
Level 3 Award in Preparing and Delivering a Sales Presentation
Level 3 Award in Handling Objections, Negotiating and Closing Deals
Level 3 Award in Understanding Influences on Buyer Behaviour
Level 3 Award in Understanding customer segmentation and profiling

Level 3 Award in Understanding sales and marketing in organisations
Level 3 Award in Using market information for sales
Level 3 Award in Time and territory management for sales people
Level 3 Award in Planning for professional development
Level 3 Award in Prospecting for new business
Level 3 Award in Sales pipeline management
Level 3 Certificate in Sales and Marketing
Level 3 Diploma in Sales and Marketing
Level 4 Award in Managing responsible selling
Level 4 Award in Understanding segmentation, targeting and positioning
Level 4 Award in Managing a sales team
Level 4 Award in Operational sales planning
Level 4 Award in Sales negotiations
Level 4 Award in Analysing the marketing environment
Level 4 Award in Finance for sales managers
Level 4 Award in Writing and delivering a sales proposal
Level 4 Certificate in Sales and Marketing Management
Level 4 Diploma in Sales and Marketing Management
Level 5 Award in Understanding and developing customer accounts
Level 5 Award in Understanding the integrated functions of sales and marketing
Level 5 Award in Sales forecasts and target setting
Level 5 Award in Leading a team
Level 5 Award in Motivation and compensation for sales teams
Level 5 Award in Coaching and mentoring
Level 5 Award in Designing, planning and managing sales territories
Level 5 Award in Analysing the financial potential and performance of customer accounts
Level 5 Award in Relationship management for account managers

Level 5 Award in Bid and tender management for account managers

Level 5 Award in Developing a product portfolio

Level 5 Certificate in Sales and Account Management

Level 5 Diploma in Sales and Account Management

Level 6 Award in Leading a culture for responsible selling

Level 6 Award in Leadership and management in sales

Level 6 Award in Planning and implementing sales and marketing strategy

Level 6 Award in Salesforce organisation

Level 6 Award in Sales forecasting and budgeting

Level 6 Award in Developing strategic relationships with major customers

Level 6 Award in Managing sales-related change

Level 6 Award in Developing and using customer insight

Level 6 Certificate in Strategic Sales Management

Level 6 Diploma in Strategic Sales Management

DESIGNATORY LETTERS
AInstSMM, MInstSMM, FInstSMM

MARTIAL ARTS
Membership of Professional Institutions and Associations

INSTITUTE OF MARTIAL ARTS AND SCIENCES

1 Henrietta Street
Bolton
Lancashire BL3 4HL
Tel: 07792 214993
E-mail: admin@instituteofmartialartsandsciences.com
Website: www.instituteofmartialartsandsciences.com

The IMAS is a professional institute for martial artists, dedicated to education and research in the martial arts and offering memberships, accredited training and qualifications, and university degrees in martial arts studies. IMAS publishes a quarterly, peer reviewed journal, and an annual yearbook containing its research articles.

MEMBERSHIP
Affiliate
Student
Associate (AIMAS)
Member (MIMAS)
Fellow (FIMAS)

QUALIFICATION/EXAMINATIONS
Accredited instructor training in partnership with the Teaching and Learning Academy
Specialist courses for police/security professionals
Higher Educational opportunities include: Graduate of the Institute of Martial Arts and Sciences (Grad. IMAS); BA(Hons); Masters by Research (MRes); Doctoral studies (PhD) available through our associated university in the UK

DESIGNATORY LETTERS
Grad.IMAS, BA(Hons), MRes, PhD

MASSAGE AND ALLIED THERAPIES
Membership of Professional Institutions and Associations

BRITISH MEDICAL ACUPUNCTURE SOCIETY

BMAS House
3 Winnington Court
Winnington Street
Northwich
Cheshire CW8 1AQ
Tel: 01606 786782
Fax: 01606 786783
E-mail: admin@medical-acupuncture.co.uk
Website: www.medical-acupuncture.co.uk

The BMAS was formed in 1980 as an association of medical practitioners interested in acupuncture and we now have a membership of more than 2,500 registered doctors and allied health professionals who practise acupuncture alongside more conventional techniques. We believe that acupuncture has an important role to play in healthcare and promote its use as a therapy following orthodox medical diagnosis by suitably trained practitioners. We run training programmes in the UK for doctors, dentists and other healthcare professionals.

MEMBERSHIP
Member
Accredited Member
Dental/Veterinary Member
Retired Member
Affiliated
Overseas Member

QUALIFICATION/EXAMINATIONS
Certificate of Basic Competence (CoBC)
Diploma of Medical Acupuncture (DipMedAc)

LCSP REGISTER OF REMEDIAL MASSEURS AND MANIPULATIVE THERAPISTS

38A High Street
Lowestoft
Suffolk NR32 1HY
Tel: 01502 563344
Fax: 01502 582220
E-mail: admin@lcsp.uk.com
Website: www.lcsp.uk.com

The Register accepts practitioners who currently work in Massage, Sports / Remedial Massage or Manipulative Therapy. Applicants must have completed a course of education at an establishment whose training meets or exceeds the National Occupational Standards. The Register offers heavily discounted comprehensive medical malpractice insurance, business support, regular communications and CPD.

MEMBERSHIP
Student Member
Associate Member (LCSP (Assoc))
Full Member (LCSP (Phys))
Affiliate
Fellow (FLCSP)
Honorary Member

DESIGNATORY LETTERS
LCSP (Assoc), LCSP (Phys), FLCSP

NORTHERN INSTITUTE OF MASSAGE LTD

14–16 St Mary's Place
Bury
Greater Manchester BL9 0DZ
Tel: 0161 797 1800
E-mail: information@nim.co.uk
Website: www.nim.co.uk

The NIM was founded in 1924 and offers professional training in Remedial Massage, Advanced Remedial Massage, and Manipulative Therapy. We also offer a number of CPD seminars and short courses to supplement our main training programme. Research is carried out mostly by therapists on patients from their own clinics or by students completing university courses.

QUALIFICATION/EXAMINATIONS
Advanced Remedial Massage Diploma
Manipulative Therapy Diploma

SOCIETY OF HOMEOPATHS

11 Brookfield Duncan Close
Moulton Park
Northampton NN3 6WL
Tel: 01604 817890
E-mail: info@homeopathy-soh.org
Website: www.homeopathy-soh.org

The Society of Homeopaths was established in 1978 and is now the largest organization registering professional homeopaths in Europe. Our vision is 'homeopathy for all' and we aim to achieve this both by supporting our members and by raising the profile of homeopathy in general.

MEMBERSHIP
Subscriber
Student Member
Student Clinical Member
Registered Member (RSHom)

DESIGNATORY LETTERS
RSHom

MATHEMATICS
Membership of Professional Institutions and Associations

EDINBURGH MATHEMATICAL SOCIETY

School of Mathematics, Edinburgh University
James Clerk Maxwell Building
Mayfield Road
Edinburgh EH9 3JZ
Tel: 01316 505060
Fax: 01316 506553
E-mail: queries@maths.ed.ac.uk
Website: www.maths.ed.ac.uk

The EMS, founded in 1883, is the principal mathematical society for the academic community in Scotland as well as mathematicians in industry and commerce. We organize meetings, publish a journal and support mathematical activities through various funds.

MEMBERSHIP
Ordinary Member

Reciprocal Member
Honorary Member

THE INSTITUTE OF MATHEMATICS AND ITS APPLICATIONS

Catherine Richards House
16 Nelson Street
Southend-on-Sea
Essex SS1 1EF
Tel: 01702 354020
Fax: 01702 354111
E-mail: post@ima.org.uk
Website: www.ima.org.uk

The IMA, founded in 1964, is the UK's learned society for mathematics and its applications. We promote mathematical research, education and careers, and the use of mathematics in business, industry and commerce. In 1990 the Institute was incorporated by Royal Charter and subsequently granted the right to award the status of Chartered Mathematician, Chartered Scientist and Chartered Mathematics Teacher.

MEMBERSHIP
Student

Affiliate
Associate Member (AMIMA)
Member (MIMA)
Fellow (FIMA)
Chartered Mathematician (CMath)
Chartered Mathematics Teacher (CMathTeach)
Chartered Scientist (CSci)

DESIGNATORY LETTERS
AMIMA, MIMA, FIMA, CMath, CMathTeach, CSci

THE MATHEMATICAL ASSOCIATION

259 London Road
Leicester LE2 3BE
Tel: 01162 210013
Fax: 01162 122835
E-mail: office@m-a.org.uk
Website: www.m-a.org.uk

The MA dates from 1871 and supports and improves the teaching and learning of mathematics and its applications, and provides opportunities for communication and collaboration between teachers and students of mathematics. We publish a number of books, journals and magazines, hold an annual conference and regional meetings, and organise

CPD events. We also confer with government re the curriculum and assessment.

MEMBERSHIP
Student Member
Personal Member
Institutional Member

MEDICAL HERBALISM
Membership of Professional Institutions and Associations

THE NATIONAL INSTITUTE OF MEDICAL HERBALISTS

Clover House
James Court
South Street
Exeter
Devon EX1 1EE
Tel: 01392 426022
Fax: 01392 498963
E-mail: info@nimh.org.uk
Website: www.nimh.org.uk

The NIMH is the UK's leading professional organization of qualified medical herbal practitioners. We maintain high standards of practice and patient care, and work to promote the benefits of western herbal medicine. We provide codes of conduct, ethics and practice, and represent the profession, patients and the public through participation in external processes.

MEMBERSHIP
Member (MNIMH) Membership is open to graduates holding a BSc(Hons) degree in Herbal Medicine from Lincoln College or University of Westminster. There is also a student affiliate membership scheme for those who are undergraduates of either of the above schools. We are also able to offer a distance learning course through Heartwood and a diploma in Herbal Medicine from the School of Herbal Medicine in Somerset. All the above courses allow memberhsip to the NIMH.

QUALIFICATION/EXAMINATIONS
The NIMH has historically managed its own accreditation process, with universities currently offering a BSc(Hons) degree in Herbal Medicine at Lincoln College and University of Westminster.
From 2011 accreditation of the above courses transferred to The European Herbal and Traditional Medicine Practitioners Association (EHTPA), as an umbrella body of Professional Herbal Medicine Associations, although graduates will continue to be eligible to apply for NIMH membership.

DESIGNATORY LETTERS
MNIMH, FNIMH

MEDICAL SECRETARIES
Membership of Professional Institutions and Associations

ASSOCIATION OF MEDICAL SECRETARIES, PRACTICE MANAGERS, ADMINISTRATORS AND RECEPTIONISTS

Tavistock House North
Tavistock Square
London WC1H 9LN
Tel: 020 7387 6005
Fax: 020 7388 2648
E-mail: info@amspar.co.uk
Website: www.amspar.com

AMSPAR is a professional membership and educational organization. We work with City & Guilds to provide non-clinical qualifications for health administration within the UK qualification frameworks. We aim to promote quality and coherence in the delivery of qualifications, and encourage and support standards of excellence in the pursuit of continuous professional development and lifelong learning.

MEMBERSHIP
Associate Member (AAMS)
Member (MAMS)
Fellow (FAMS)

QUALIFICATION/EXAMINATIONS
The Level 5 Diploma in Primary Care & Health Management
The Level 5 Certificate in Primary Care & Health Management
The Level 3 Diploma for Medical Secretaries
The Level 3 Certificate in Medical Administration
The Level 3 Certificate in Medical Terminology
The Level 3 Award in Legal Aspects of Medical Administration
The Level 3 Award in Medical Principles for the Administrator
The Level 3 Award in Medical Word Processing
The Level 3 Award in Production of Medical Documents from Recorded Speech
The Level 2 Diploma in Medical Administration
The Level 2 Certificate in Medical Administration
The Level 2 Award in Medical Terminology
The Level 2 Award in Working in the NHS
The Level 2 Award in Medical Word Processing
The Level 2 Award in Production of Medical Documents from Recorded Speech
The Level 3 Advanced Technical Diploma in Medical Administration
The Level 2 Technical Certificate in Medical Administrative Support

DESIGNATORY LETTERS
AAMS, MAMS, FAMS

MEDICINE

A student who wishes to qualify as a doctor in the UK must first obtain a primary qualification. Medical students in the UK typically study for five years to receive their medical degrees or for four years on a graduate-entry accelerated course. There are also courses offered for candidates with non-science subjects to offer at A level (or equivalent) that include the pre-medical year. The pre-medical year is a preliminary course in chemistry, physics and biology and lasts normally 30 weeks. Each medical school sets its own entry requirements, and may require applicants to complete clinical aptitude tests.

After graduation, a trainee doctor will enter the two-year Foundation Programme. There is a national application process for entry to the F1 year, but trainees successfully completing this year move into F2 without having to compete for a place. The trainee is provisionally registered with a licence to practise with the General Medical Council (GMC) while completing the first year and full registration is awarded upon completion of year one.

The F1 year aims to provide experience in a broad range of settings prior to full GMC registration. Regular work-based assessments take place, and trainees must maintain a national learning portfolio in order to progress.

The F2 year usually consists of four varied three-month placements giving trainees the opportunity to try a number of different specialities before making a decision about which specialty training programme they would like to pursue. More information can be found at www.nhscareers.nhs.uk

The GMC is charged with the responsibility under the Medical Act 1983 of keeping a register of all duly qualified medical practitioners. General Medical Council, Regent's Place, 350 Euston Road, London NW1 3JN; Tel: 0161 923 6602; e-mail: gmc@gmc-uk. org; website: www.gmc-uk.org. For information on how to apply to join the register, see www.gmc-uk. org/doctors/applications.asp

PRIMARY QUALIFICATIONS

The GMC decides which universities are entitled to issue medical degrees. Qualifying examinations are examinations held for the granting of one or more primary medical qualifications (PMQs) by any one of the bodies or combinations of bodies in the United Kingdom that are included in a list maintained by the GMC and published on the GMC's website (www. gmc-uk.org/education/undergraduate/awarding_bodies.asp).

LICENSING AND REVALIDATION

Doctors must be registered with a licence to practise with the General Medical Council (GMC) and hold a licence to practise medicine in the UK. The licence to practise gives a doctor the legal authority to undertake certain activities in the UK, for example prescribing, signing death or cremation certificates and holding certain medical posts (such as working as a doctor in the NHS). Any person whose fitness to practise is not impaired and who a) holds one or more primary United Kingdom qualifications and has satisfactorily completed an acceptable programme for provisionally registered doctors; or b) being a national of any relevant European State, holds one or more primary European qualifications, is entitled to be registered as a fully registered medical practitioner. Doctors who do not work in the UK, or who do not undertake any activities for which a licence is required, do not need to hold a licence to practise and can continue to be registered without a licence.

Revalidation ensures that all licensed doctors demonstrate on an ongoing basis that they are up to date and fit to practise in their chosen field and able to provide a good level of care. Licensed doctors have to revalidate, usually every five years, by having regular appraisals based on the GMC's core guidance for doctors, *Good Medical Practice*.

Membership of Professional Institutions and Associations

COLLEGE OF OPERATING DEPARTMENT PRACTITIONERS

130 Euston Road
London NW1 2AY
Tel: 0870 121 5414
E-mail: office@codp.org
Website: www.codp.org.uk

The CODP is the professional body for Operating Department Practitioners. It is a membership, not-for-profit organization that sets standards of education for the pre-registration aspect of the profession and promotes the enhancement of knowledge and skills, in the context of the multidisciplinary team, through regional, national and international networks.

MEMBERSHIP
Student Member
Association Member
Full College Member

ROYAL COLLEGE OF GENERAL PRACTITIONERS

30 Euston Square
London NW1 2FB
Tel: 020 3188 7400
Fax: 020 3188 7401
E-mail: info@rcgp.org.uk
Website: www.rcgp.org.uk

The aims of the College are to encourage, foster and maintain the highest possible standards in general medical practice. Full entry to the College is by MRCGP exam undertaken whilst in training for general practice, or by membership by assessment (MAP) in the case of qualified GPs.

MEMBERSHIP
Associate in Training
Associate
Member (MRCGP)
Fellow (FRCGP)

International Member (MRCGP[INT])
Undergraduate medical students and Foundation programme students may register with the College's Student Forum, which exposes the students to life in general practice.

QUALIFICATION/EXAMINATIONS
Assessment for Membership of the RCGP (MRCGP)

DESIGNATORY LETTERS
MRCGP, FRCGP

ROYAL COLLEGE OF OBSTETRICIANS AND GYNAECOLOGISTS

27 Sussex Place
London NW1 4RG
Tel: 020 7772 6200
E-mail: library@rcog.org.uk
Website: www.rcog.org.uk

The RCOG encourages the study and advancement of the science and practice of obstetrics and gynae-cology. We do this through postgraduate medical education and training development, and the pub-lication of clinical guidelines and reports on aspects of the specialty and service provision. The RCOG International Office works with other international organizations to help lower maternal morbidity and mortality in under-resourced countries.

MEMBERSHIP
Affiliate
Associate
Diplomate

Trainee – pre-membership
Member without Examination (MRCOG)
Member (MRCOG)
Fellow (FRCOG)
Fellow *honoris causa*
Fellow *ad eumdem* (FRCOG)
Honorary Fellow (FRCOG)

QUALIFICATION/EXAMINATIONS
MRCOG (Membership Exam)
FRCOG (Diploma)

DESIGNATORY LETTERS
MRCOG, FRCOG

ROYAL SOCIETY OF MEDICINE

1 Wimpole Street
London W1G 0AE
Tel: 020 7290 2900
Fax: 020 7290 2992
E-mail: membership@rsm.ac.uk
Website: www.rsm.ac.uk

The RSM, founded in 1805, is a medical charity that promotes the exchange of information and ideas in medical science. We provide a broad range of educational activities and opportunities for doctors, dentists, veterinary surgeons, students of these disciplines and allied healthcare professionals, organize conferences, and publish books and journals through our publishing division, RSM Press.

MEMBERSHIP
Student
Associate
Fellow
Corporate

QUALIFICATION/EXAMINATIONS
NONE

DESIGNATORY LETTERS
N/A

THE FEDERATION OF ROYAL COLLEGES OF PHYSICIANS OF THE UNITED KINGDOM

MRCP(UK)
11 St Andrews Place
Regent's Park
London NW1 4LE
Tel: +44 (0)20 3075 1248
E-mail: policy.officer@mrcpuk.org
Website: www.mrcpuk.org

The Federation is a partnership between the Royal College of Physicians of Edinburgh, the Royal College of Physicians and Surgeons of Glasgow and the Royal College of Physicians of London. Working together, the colleges develop and deliver membership and specialty examinations that are recognized around the world as quality benchmarks.

MEMBERSHIP
Membership of the Royal Colleges of Physicians (MRCP(UK)): Once candidates have successfully completed their final part of the examination they must then submit and complete the Form of Faith as a testimonial for election to membership.

QUALIFICATION/EXAMINATIONS
The Federation is responsible for a portfolio of examinations: MRCP(UK) Diploma (Membership of the Royal Colleges of Physicians of the United Kingdom): Candidates for the MRCP(UK) Diploma

may enter through the Royal College of Physicians of Edinburgh, the Royal College of Physicians and Surgeons of Glasgow, the Royal College of Physicians of London, or through the online application system. There are three components to the MRCP(UK) Diploma. The part 1 examination has a two-paper format. Each paper is 3 hours in duration and contains 100 multiple choice questions in one from five (best of five) format, where a candidate chooses the best answer from five possible answers. The part 2 written examination has a three-paper format. All papers in the MRCP(UK) part 2 written examination are 3 hours in duration and contain up to 100 multiple choice questions. The questions will usually have a clinical scenario, may include the results of investigations and may be illustrated. The part 2 clinical examination (PACES) consists of five clinical stations, each assessed by two independent examiners. Candidates will start at any one of the five stations, and then move round the carousel of stations at 20-minute intervals until they have completed the cycle. There is a 5-minute period between each station. Candidates may apply to sit the MRCP(UK) part 1 examination provided they graduated at least 12 months in advance of the examinations date (and have had at least 12 months' experience in medical employment). Candidates who have passed the part 1 examination can proceed to complete the remaining components. The MRCP(UK) Examination provides valid, reliable evidence of attainment in knowledge, clinical skills and behaviour, and is a mandatory component of assessment for Core Medical Training (CMT). The Specialty Certificate Examinations (SCEs): The Federation of Royal Colleges of Physicians of the UK, in association with Specialist Societies, has developed a programme to deliver Specialty Certificate Examinations within the new specialist training structure. The aim of these national assessments is to ensure that trainees have sufficient knowledge of their specialty to practise safely and competently as consultants. The Specialty Certificate Examination is delivered in computer-based format (referred to as CBT) at a Pearson VUE test centre. Each paper is based on the MRCP(UK) written paper format and contains 100 multiple choice questions in 'best of five' format. A Specialty Certificate Examination is a compulsory component of assessment for Certificate of Completion of Training (CCT) for all UK trainees whose specialist training began in or after August 2007 and is in one of the following specialties: Acute Medicine, Dermatology; Endocrinology and Diabetes; Gastroenterology; Geriatric Medicine; Infectious Diseases; Medical Oncology; Nephrology; Neurology; Palliative Medicine; Respiratory Medicine and Rheumatology.

DESIGNATORY LETTERS
MRCP(UK)

THE INSTITUTE OF CLINICAL RESEARCH

10 Cedar Court
Grove Park
White Waltham Road
Maidenhead
Tel: 0845 521 0056
E-mail: info@icr-global.org
Website: www.icr-global.org

The ICR was founded in 1978 and is now the largest professional clinical research body in Europe and India. Our aim is to promote knowledge and understanding by engaging with the healthcare community and the general public, to support and facilitate communication between our members, and to provide opportunities for learning and development to enhance professional competence.

MEMBERSHIP
Affiliate

Registered Member (RICR)
Professional Member (MICR)
Fellow (FICR)
Honorary Fellow (Hon FICR)

QUALIFICATION/EXAMINATIONS
Please see the ICR's website.

DESIGNATORY LETTERS
RICR, MICR, FICR, HonFICR

THE ROYAL COLLEGE OF ANAESTHETISTS

Churchill House
35 Red Lion Square
London WC1R 4SG
Tel: 020 7092 1500
Fax: 020 7092 1730
E-mail: info@rcoa.ac.uk
Website: www.rcoa.ac.uk

The RCoA, which dates from 1948, is the professional body responsible for the specialty of anaesthesia throughout the UK. Our principal responsibility is to ensure the quality of patient care through the maintenance of standards in anaesthesia, pain medicine and critical care. We set and run examinations, and provide CPD for all practising anaesthetists.

MEMBERSHIP
Trainee
Affiliate
Associate Member
Member (MRCA)
Associate Fellow
Fellow *ad eundem* (FRCA)
Fellow (FRCA)
Honorary Fellow (FRCA)

QUALIFICATION/EXAMINATIONS
FRCA Examinations (FRCA)

DESIGNATORY LETTERS
MRCA, FRCA

THE ROYAL COLLEGE OF PATHOLOGISTS

4th Floor, 21 Prescot Street
London E1 8BB
Tel: 020 7451 6700
E-mail: exams@rcpath.org
Website: www.rcpath.org

The College aims to advance the science and practice of pathology, to provide public education, to promote research in pathology and to disseminate the results.

MEMBERSHIP
Affiliate Member
Associate
Diplomate Member (DipRCPath)
Fellow (FRCPath)

QUALIFICATION/EXAMINATIONS
Training programmes are approved for all pathology specialities and sub-specialities. The exact examination arrangements vary for each speciality but they will all involve a Part 1 and a Part 2 which include, inter alia, written, practical and oral components. In addition the College offers a Diploma in Dermatopathology and a Diploma in Forensic Pathology and a Certificate in Autopsy, Cervical Cytology, Infection, and Medical Genetics. Further details may be obtained from the Examinations Department or the College's website.

DESIGNATORY LETTERS
DipRCPath, FRCPath

THE ROYAL COLLEGE OF PHYSICIANS AND SURGEONS OF GLASGOW

232–242 St Vincent Street
Glasgow G2 5RJ
Tel: 0141 2216072
Fax: 0141 2211804
E-mail: exams@rcpsg.ac.uk
Website: www.rcpsg.ac.uk

The Royal College of Physicians and Surgeons of Glasgow (RCPSG) welcomes professionals from a diverse range of disciplines. At present, our collegiate body includes Physicians, Surgeons, professionals in Dentistry, Travel Medicine, Podiatric Medicine and other professions allied to medicine. The College aims to provide career support to our membership through education, training, professional development, examinations and assessment, whilst acting as a charity and leading voice on health issues in order to set the highest standards of health care.

MEMBERSHIP
Fellow   FRCP(Glasg)/   FRCS(Glasg)/   FDS RCPS(Glasg)/   FFTM   RCPS(Glasg)/   FFPM RCPS(Glasg)
Member   MRCPS(Glasg)/   MFDS   RCPS(Glasg)/ MRCS(Glasg)/   MRCS(ENT)(Glasg)/   MFTM RCPS(Glasg)/ MFPM RCPS(Glasg)

Associate Member
Affiliate Member
Student Member

QUALIFICATION/EXAMINATIONS

Diploma in Otolaryngology – Head and Neck Surgery (DOHNS)
Diploma in Travel Medicine (DipTravMed)
Diploma in Expedition and Wilderness Medicine
Postgraduate Diploma in Clinical Education
Diploma of Membership of the Royal Colleges of Physicians of the United Kingdom (MRCP(UK))
Diploma of Membership of the Royal College of Surgeons (MRCS(Glasg))
Diploma of Membership of the Royal College of Surgeons (MRCS(ENT)(Glasg))
Diploma of Membership of the Faculty of Dental Surgery (MFDS RCPS(Glasg))
Diploma of Membership in (dental specialty) (M(dental specialty) RCPS(Glasg)
Diploma of Membership of the Faculty of Travel Medicine (MFTM RCPS(Glasg))
Diploma of Membership of the Faculty of Podiatric Medicine (MFPM RCPS(Glasg))
Diploma of Fellowship of the Royal College of Physicians and Surgeons of Glasgow in Ophthalmology (FRCS(Glasg))
Diploma of Fellowship of the Royal College of Physicians and Surgeons of Glasgow (FDS (dental specialty) RCPS(Glasg))
Diploma of Fellowship of the Royal College of Physicians and Surgeons of Glasgow (FRCSGlasg (surgical specialty))
Diploma of Fellowship of the Faculty of Travel Medicine (FFTM RCPS(Glasg))
Diploma of Fellowship of the Faculty of Podiatric Medicine (FFPM RCPS(Glasg))

DESIGNATORY LETTERS
MFDS   RCPS(Glasg),   MFTM   RCPS(Glasg), MRCP(UK),   MRCS(Glasg),   MRCS(ENT)(Glasg), MRCPS(Glasg), MFPM RCPS(Glasg), M(dental specialty)   RCPS(Glasg)/   FRCP(Glasg)/   FRCS(Glasg)/ FRCSGlasg(surgical specialty)/ FDS RCPS(Glasg)/ FRCS(Urol)(Glasg), FFTM RCPS(Glasg)

THE ROYAL COLLEGE OF PHYSICIANS OF EDINBURGH

9 Queen Street
Edinburgh EH2 1JQ
Tel: 01312 257324
E-mail: l.tedford@rcpe.ac.uk
Website: www.rcpe.ac.uk

The RCPE promotes the highest standards in internal medicine in the UK and internationally. Along with our sister Colleges in Glasgow and London we oversee the membership examination of the Royal Colleges of Physicians, MRCP(UK), enabling doctors to enter higher specialist training, leading eventually to a Certificate of Completion of Specialist Training (CCST).

MEMBERSHIP
Student + Foundation
Associate
Collegiate Member (MRCPE)
Fellow (FRCPE)

QUALIFICATION/EXAMINATIONS
MRCP(UK)
Specialty Certificate Examinations

DESIGNATORY LETTERS
MRCPE, FRCPE

THE ROYAL COLLEGE OF PHYSICIANS OF LONDON

11 St Andrews Place
Regent's Park
London NW1 4LE
Tel: +44 (0)20 3075 1649
E-mail: via website
Website: www.rcplondon.ac.uk

The Royal College of Physicians of London offers a Diploma in Geriatric Medicine (DGM) Examination and a Diploma in Tropical Medicine and Hygiene, run in conjunction with the London School of Tropical Medicine and Hygiene.

MEMBERSHIP
The Royal College of Physicians of London runs the MRCP(UK) Examination which is the MRCP(UK) membership examination. As the examination is run in conjunction with two other Royal Colleges of Physicians, this examination and the membership qualification MRCP(UK) are listed in this directory under *The Federation of Royal Colleges of Physicians.*

QUALIFICATION/EXAMINATIONS
Diploma in Geriatric Medicine The Diploma in Geriatric Medicine is designed to give recognition of competence in the provision of care of older people to General Practitioner vocational trainees, staff physicians and others working in non-consultant career posts in Departments of Geriatric Medicine, and other doctors with interests in or responsibilities for the care of older people.

The Diploma in Geriatric Medicine is available to all registered doctors. It is not primarily directed towards career geriatricians, but is generally to family doctors, psycho-geriatricians and indeed any doctor involved in the care of older people.

The Diploma in Geriatric Medicine is in two parts, the first of which is a written examination of multiple choice (best of 5) questions, lasting 2 hours and 30 minutes normally held twice a year at the Royal College of Physicians of London.

The second part is a Clinical Examination also held twice a year at various clinical centres in England and Wales. The clinical examination is a four-station standardized examination similar to an Objective Standard Clinical Examination (OSCE).

Diploma in Tropical Medicine and Hygiene The Diploma in Tropical Medicine and Hygiene is intended to test the knowledge required of physicians who wish to practise medicine effectively in developing countries.

Candidates for the Diploma in Tropical Medicine & Hygiene must hold a primary medical qualification recognized by the Royal College of Physicians of London.

The Royal College of Physicians of London will accept applications from candidates who are in the process of completing, or have completed within the last 5 years, the Tropical Medicine courses in London, Liverpool, Sheffield and Glasgow, which are recognized as appropriate training centres for the examination. The examination is held once a year over 2 days (unless required for a viva) and is conducted in the following sections: A **Practical Section** lasting 2 hours and 30 minutes consists of a mixture of microscopy specimens, including 20 'spot' questions that are set up on a microscope for identification. Other specimens require the candidate to use the microscopes themself. They are mainly parasitological and may include faecal, blood and haematological preparations together with some entomological specimens. A **Written Section** (3 hours and 20 minutes in total) consists of three papers. The **Clinical Paper** (1 hour) contains 18 compulsory questions. The first 16 are based on clinical pictures – usually of patients with abnormal physical signs; but occasionally laboratory slides, X-rays, or epidemiological data may be shown. There will be 2 or 3 questions on each, asking (for example) identification, diagnosis, further investigation, treatment etc. Each of these 16 questions is worth a maximum of 5 marks. The last 2 questions (17 and 18) are brief clinical cases, with 2 or 3 questions (again concentrating on diagnosis or differential diagnosis, investigation and treatment). The **Multiple Choice Question Paper** (1 hour and 20 minutes) consists of 40 multiple choice questions designed to test the knowledge of tropical medicine and hygiene over a wide area. The **Preventative Medicine Paper** (1 hour including 5 minutes reading time) consists of 10 questions of which the candidate must choose 5. Each question may have several parts, covering all aspects of preventative medicine and international community health in a tropical context.

There is also an **Oral ('Viva') Examination** for borderline candidates. The examination is conducted by two examiners. The first part of the examination (10 minutes) is a discussion of an illustrated clinical case history, which candidates are allowed to study for 10 minutes before the examination. The second part of the examination (10 minutes) consists of more general questions.

THE ROYAL COLLEGE OF PSYCHIATRISTS

21 Prescot Street
London E1 8BB
Tel: 020 7235 2351
Fax: 020 3701 2761
E-mail: reception@rcpsych.ac.uk
Website: www.rcpsych.ac.uk

The RCPsych is the professional and educational body for psychiatrists in the UK and Ireland. We are committed to improving the understanding of psychiatry and mental health, and are at the forefront in setting and achieving the highest standards through education, training and research. We actively promote psychiatry as a career, and provide guidance and support to our members and associates.

MEMBERSHIP
Pre-Membership Psychiatric Trainee
New Associate
Affiliate
Specialist Associate
Member (MRCPsych)
Fellow (FRCPsych)
Honorary Fellow
International Associate

QUALIFICATION/EXAMINATIONS
MRCPsych qualifying exams
Paper A – The Scientific and Theoretical Basis of Psychiatry
Paper B – Critical Review and the Clinical Topics in Psychiatry
CASC – Clinical Assessment of Skills and Competencies

DESIGNATORY LETTERS
MRCPsych, FRCPsych

THE ROYAL COLLEGE OF RADIOLOGISTS

63 Lincoln's Inn Fields
London WC2A 3JW
Tel: 020 7405 1282
E-mail: enquiries@rcr.ac.uk
Website: www.rcr.ac.uk

The Royal College of Radiologists (RCR) leads, supports and educates in medical imaging and cancer treatment. RCR sets and maintains the standards for entry to, and practice in, the specialties of clinical oncology and clinical radiology and shapes their future development for the benefit of patients. The College works to advance the science and practice of radiology and oncology. It furthers public awareness and education, and promotes study and research through setting professional standards of practice. It also sets the curriculum for the two specialties ensuring that high educational standards are met in the interests of safe and responsible practice.

MEMBERSHIP
Junior Member
Associate
Trainee
Member
Fellow (FRCR)
Honorary Member/Fellow (Hon MRCR/Hon FRCR)

QUALIFICATION/EXAMINATIONS
First FRCR Examination
Final FRCR Examination
Diploma in Dental and Maxillofacial Radiology (DDMFR)

DESIGNATORY LETTERS
FRCR, Hon MRCR, Hon FRCR

THE ROYAL COLLEGE OF SURGEONS OF EDINBURGH

Nicolson Street
Edinburgh EH8 9DW
Tel: 0131 527 1600
Fax: 0131 557 6406
E-mail: mail@rcsed.ac.uk
Website: www.rcsed.ac.uk

The Royal College of Surgeons of Edinburgh, which dates from 1505, is dedicated to the maintenance and promotion of the highest standards of surgical practice, through education, training and rigorous examination, and its liaison with external medical bodies. Today, with more than 20,000 Fellows and Members, we pride ourselves also on our innovation and adaptability.

MEMBERSHIP
Affiliate

Associate
Member (MRCSEd)
Fellow (FRCSEd)

QUALIFICATION/EXAMINATIONS
Please see the Royal College of Surgeons of Edinburgh website.

DESIGNATORY LETTERS
MRCSEd, FRCSEd

THE ROYAL COLLEGE OF SURGEONS OF ENGLAND

35–43 Lincoln's Inn Fields
London WC2A 3PE
Tel: 020 7405 3474
E-mail: membership@rcseng.ac.uk
Website: www.rcseng.ac.uk

The Royal College of Surgeons of England is committed to enabling surgeons to achieve and maintain the highest standards of surgical practice and patient care. We examine trainees, supervise the training of and provide support and advice for surgeons, promote and support surgical research in the UK, and liaise with the DoH, health authorities, Trusts and hospitals in the UK and other medical and academic organizations worldwide.

MEMBERSHIP
Affiliate
Associate
Fellow *ad eundem*
Membership *ad eundem*
Specialty Membership

QUALIFICATION/EXAMINATIONS
Please see the Royal College of Surgeons of England website.

THE WORSHIPFUL SOCIETY OF APOTHECARIES OF LONDON

Apothecaries' Hall
Black Friars Lane
London EC4V 6EJ
Tel: 020 7236 1180
Fax: 020 7329 3177
E-mail: via website
Website: www.apothecaries.org

The Society of Apothecaries of London was incorporated by Royal Charter in 1617 and allowed to prepare and sell drugs for medicinal purposes, laying the foundations of the British pharmaceutical industry. Later, apothecaries were permitted to prescribe and dispense medicines, becoming the forerunners of today's GPs. Now the Society is primarily an examining body.

QUALIFICATION/EXAMINATIONS
PGDip in Forensic Medical Sciences (DipFMS)
PGDip in Genitourinary Medicine (Dip GU Med)
PGDip in the History of Medicine (DHMSA)
PGDip in HIV Medicine (Dip HIV Med)
PGDip in the Medical Care of Catastrophes (DMCC)
PGDip in Medical Jurisprudence (Pathology) (DMJ[Path])
PGDip in the Philosophy of Medicine (DPMSA)

METALLURGY

Membership of Professional Institutions and Associations

INSTITUTE OF CORROSION

Barratt House
Kingsthorpe Road
Northampton NN2 6EZ
Tel: 01604 438222
E-mail: admin@icorr.org
Website: www.icorr.org

The Institute of Corrosion has since 1959 been serving the corrosion science, technology and engineering community in the fight against corrosion, which costs the UK around 4 per cent of GNP per annum. We promote the establishment and promotion of sound corrosion management practice, the advancement of cost-effective corrosion control measures, and a sustained effort to raise corrosion awareness at all stages of design, fabrication and operation.

MEMBERSHIP
Student Member
Ordinary Member
Technical Member (TICorr)
Professional Member (MICorr)
Fellow Member (FICorr)
Engineering Technician (EngTech)
Incorporated Engineer (IEng)
Chartered Engineer (CEng)
Chartered Scientist (CSci)

QUALIFICATION/EXAMINATIONS
Cathodic Protection Technician (Level 1)
Senior Cathodic Protection Technician (Level 2)
Senior Cathodic Protection Engineer (Level 3)
Painting Inspector (ICorr Levels 1, 2 and 3)
Coating Inspector (ICorr Levels 1, 2 and 3)
FireProofing Inspector Level 2
Insulation Inspector Level 2
Hot Dip Galvanizing Inspector Level 2

DESIGNATORY LETTERS
TICorr, MICorr, FICorr, EngTech, IEng, CEng

THE INSTITUTE OF METAL FINISHING

Exeter House
48 Holloway Head
Birmingham B1 1NQ
Tel: 01216 227387
Fax: 01216 666316
E-mail: exeterhouse@instituteofmetalfinishing.org
Website: www.uk-finishing.org.uk

The IMF, founded in 1925, provides a focus for surface engineering and finishing activities world-wide through the fulfilment of technical, educational and professional needs at all levels for individuals and companies involved in the coatings industry. We promote R&D within the industry and CPD for our members, cooperate with other institutes, and liaise with legislative bodies to influence decision making.

MEMBERSHIP
Student
Affiliate
Associate (AssocIMF)
Technician (TechIMF)
Licentiate (LIMF)
Member (MIMF)
Fellow (FIMF)
Engineering Technician (EngTech)
Sustaining Member (company)

QUALIFICATION/EXAMINATIONS
Foundation Certificate

Technician Certificate
Advanced Technician Certificate

DESIGNATORY LETTERS
AssocIMF, TechIMF, LIMF, MIMF, FIMF, EngTech

METEOROLOGY AND CLIMATOLOGY
Membership of Professional Institutions and Associations

MET OFFICE COLLEGE

Met Office
Fitzroy Road
Exeter
Devon EX1 3PB
Tel: 01392 885680
Fax: 01392 885681
E-mail: enquiries@metoffice.gov.uk
Website: www.metoffice.gov.uk

The Meteorological Office College is part of the Met Office and is located in Exeter, Devon. We provide meteorological training for our own staff and to meteorological services worldwide, as places become available on a fee-paying basis.

QUALIFICATION/EXAMINATIONS
Level 3 Diploma in Meteorological Observing (QCF)

Level 4 Certificate for a Meteorological Forecasting Technician (QCF)
Level 5 Diploma in Meteorological Forecasting (QCF)
Level 5 Award in Meteorological Briefing (QCF)
Level 5 Certificate in Meteorological Broadcasting (QCF)
Level 6 Diploma in Flood Forecasting (QCF)

ROYAL METEOROLOGICAL SOCIETY

104 Oxford Road
Reading RG1 7LL
Tel: 0118 956 8500
Fax: 0118 956 8571
E-mail: info@rmets.org
Website: www.rmets.org

The RMetS is the learned and professional society for anyone whose profession or interests are connected with weather and climate. It administers the NVQs of the profession and is the accreditation body for the status of Chartered Meteorologist. Its principal aim is the advancement of the understanding of weather and climate for the benefit of everyone.

MEMBERSHIP
Student

Associate Fellow
Fellow (FRMetS)
Honorary Member
Chartered Meteorologist (CMet)
School Member
Corporate Member

DESIGNATORY LETTERS
FRMetS, CMet

MICROSCOPY
Membership of Professional Institutions and Associations

THE ROYAL MICROSCOPICAL SOCIETY

37/38 St Clements
Oxford OX4 1AJ
Tel: 01865 254760
Fax: 01865 791237
E-mail: info@rms.org.uk
Website: www.rms.org.uk

The RMS, which dates from 1839, is an international scientific society dedicated to advancing the science of microscopy and the interests of its 1,400 members, who range from individuals interested in microscopy to scientists and company members representing manufacturers and suppliers of microscopes, other equipment and services.

MEMBERSHIP
Ordinary Member
Fellow (FRMS)
Corporate Member

DESIGNATORY LETTERS
FRMS

MUSEUM AND RELATED WORK
Membership of Professional Institutions and Associations

MUSEUMS ASSOCIATION

42 Clerkenwell Close
London EC1R 0AZ
Tel: 020 7566 7800
E-mail: info@museumsassociation.org
Website: www.museumsassociation.org

The MA is the oldest museums association in the world, set up in 1889 to guard the interests of museums and galleries. Today, we have 5,200 individual members, 600 institutional members and 250 corporate members. Our aim is to enhance the value of museums to society by sharing knowledge, developing skills, inspiring innovation and providing leadership.

MEMBERSHIP
Student
Volunteer
Professional Member
Associate (AMA)
Corporate Member
Institutional Member

DESIGNATORY LETTERS
AMA

MUSIC
Membership of Professional Institutions and Associations

ABRSM (ASSOCIATED BOARD OF THE ROYAL SCHOOLS OF MUSIC)

24 Portland Place
London W1B 1LU
Tel: 020 7636 5400
Fax: 020 7637 0234
E-mail: abrsm@abrsm.org
Website: www.abrsm.org

ABRSM's mission is to motivate musical achievement. We aim to support the development of learners and teachers in music education worldwide and to celebrate their achievements. We do this through authoritative and internationally recognized assessments, publications and professional development support for teachers, and through charitable donations.

MEMBERSHIP
Licentiate (LRSM)
Fellow (FRSM)

QUALIFICATION/EXAMINATIONS
Certificate of Teaching (CT ABRSM)
Diploma in Instrumental/Vocal Teaching (DipABRSM)
Diploma in Music Direction (DipABRSM)
Diploma in Music Performance (DipABRSM)

Please see the ABRSM website for details of other examinations and awards.

DESIGNATORY LETTERS
CT ABRSM, DipABRSM, LRSM, FRSM

INCORPORATED SOCIETY OF MUSICIANS

4–5 Inverness Mews
London W2 3JQ
Tel: 020 7221 3499
Fax: 020 7243 3437
E-mail: membership@ism.org
Website: www.ism.org

The Incorporated Society of Musicians (ISM) is the UK's professional body for musicians and a nationally recognised subject association for music. Since 1882 we have been promoting the importance of music and protecting the rights of those working within music. We are a wholly independent organisation supporting over 8,000 members.

MEMBERSHIP
Student Member
Full Member
Corporate Member
Graduate Member

MUSICAL INSTRUMENT TECHNOLOGY
Membership of Professional Institutions and Associations

PIANOFORTE TUNERS' ASSOCIATION

PO Box 230
Hailsham
East Sussex BN27 9EA
Tel: 0845 602 8796
E-mail: secretary@pianotuner.org.uk
Website: www.pianotuner.org.uk

The PTA is a professional body committed to improving standards, and applicants for membership must pass a theoretical and practical examination to prove their ability as a qualified piano tuner or technician. We publish a regular newsletter and hold an Annual Convention and General Meeting in different towns around Britain, to which members and aspiring non-members are invited.

MEMBERSHIP
Student
Patron
Associate
Technician Member
Member
Subscriber

THE INCORPORATED SOCIETY OF ORGAN BUILDERS

The Tower
7 Lower Port View
SALTASH
Cornwall PL12 4BY
Tel: 01752-842027
Fax: 01752-842027
E-mail: secretary@isob.co.uk
Website: www.isob.co.uk

The ISOB was founded in 1947 to advance the science and practice of organ building, to provide a central organization for organ builders, and to provide for the better definition and protection of the profession by a system of examinations and the issue of certificates and distinctions. We hold regular meetings and conferences around the UK and overseas.

MEMBERSHIP
Student Member

Ordinary Member (MISOB)
Associate Member (AISOB)
Fellow (FISOB)
Counsellor (CISOB)
Companion

DESIGNATORY LETTERS
MISOB, AISOB, FISOB, CISOB

NAVAL ARCHITECTURE
Membership of Professional Institutions and Associations

THE ROYAL INSTITUTION OF NAVAL ARCHITECTS

8–9 Northumberland Street
London WC2N 5DA
Tel: 020 7235 4622
Fax: 020 7259 5912
E-mail: membership@rina.org.uk
Website: www.rina.org.uk

The RINA is an internationally renowned professional institution whose members are involved at all levels in the design, construction, maintenance and operation of marine vessels and structures. Our members are widely represented in industry, universities and colleges, and maritime organizations in over 90 countries.

MEMBERSHIP
Student Member
Associate (AssocRINA)
Associate Member (AMRINA)
Member (MRINA)
Fellow (FRINA)

DESIGNATORY LETTERS
AssocRINA, AMRINA, MRINA, FRINA

NAVIGATION, SEAMANSHIP AND MARINE QUALIFICATIONS
Membership of Professional Institutions and Associations

THE NAUTICAL INSTITUTE

202 Lambeth Road
London SE1 7LQ
Tel: 020 7928 1351
Fax: 020 7401 2817
E-mail: sec@nautinst.org
Website: www.nautinst.org

The Nautical Institute is the international representative body for maritime professionals involved in the control of sea-going ships with an interest in nautical matters. It provides a wide range of services to enhance the professional standing and knowledge of members who are drawn from all sectors of the maritime world.

MEMBERSHIP
Honorary Fellow
Fellow (FNI)
Associate Fellow (AFNI)
Member (MNI)

Associate Member (AMNI)

QUALIFICATION/EXAMINATIONS
Harbour Master's Certificate
Pilotage Certificate
Command Diploma
International Sail Endorsement Scheme
Ice Navigator Scheme
Navigation Assessors Certificate

DESIGNATORY LETTERS
FNI, AFNI, MNI, AMNI

THE ROYAL INSTITUTE OF NAVIGATION

1 Kensington Gore
London SW7 2AT
Tel: 020 7591 3134
Fax: 020 7591 3131
E-mail: admin@rin.org.uk
Website: www.rin.org.uk

The RIN is a learned society with charitable status. Our aims are: to unite those with a professional or personal interest in any aspect of navigation in one unique body; to further the development of navigation in every sphere; and to increase public awareness of both the art and science of navigation, how it has shaped the past, how it impacts our world today, and how it will affect the future.

MEMBERSHIP
Junior Associate Member
Student

Associate
Member (MRIN)
Associate Fellow (AFRIN)
Fellow (FRIN)
Affiliate Club
Affiliate College or University
Corporate Member
Small Business

DESIGNATORY LETTERS
MRIN, AFRIN, FRIN

NON-DESTRUCTIVE TESTING
Membership of Professional Institutions and Associations

THE BRITISH INSTITUTE OF NON-DESTRUCTIVE TESTING

Midsummer House
Riverside Way
Bedford Road
Northampton NN1 5NX
Tel: 01604 438300
Fax: 01604 438301
E-mail: info@bindt.org
Website: www.bindt.org

The BINDT was formed in 1976 from the merger of the Society of Non-Destructive Examination (SONDE) and the Society of Industrial Radiology and Allied Methods of Non-Destructive Testing, later renamed the NDT Society of Great Britain (NDTS), both formed in 1954. Our aim is to promote and advance the science and practice of non-destructive testing, condition monitoring, diagnostic engineering and all other materials and quality testing disciplines.

MEMBERSHIP
Affiliate Member

Associate Member (AMInstNDT)
Member (MInstNDT)
Fellow (FInstNDT)
Engineering Technician (EngTech)
Incorporated Engineer (IEng)
Chartered Engineer (CEng)

Corporate Member (organisations)

DESIGNATORY LETTERS
AMInstNDT, MInstNDT, FInstNDT, EngTech, IEng, CEng

NURSERY NURSING
Membership of Professional Institutions and Associations

COUNCIL FOR AWARDS IN CHILDREN'S CARE AND EDUCATION

Apex House
81 Camp Road
St Albans
Hertfordshire AL1 5GB
Tel: 0845 347 2123
Fax: 01727 818618
E-mail: info@cache.org.uk
Website: www.cache.org.uk

CACHE is an Awarding Body that designs courses and qualifications in the care and education of children and young people. Our courses, which are widely available, range from entry level to advanced qualifications for sector professionals. We regularly lobby the government and other agencies to raise the quality and professionalism of child care.

QUALIFICATION/EXAMINATIONS
Please see the CACHE website.

THE SOCIETY OF NURSERY NURSING PRACTITIONERS

40 Archdale Road
East Dulwich
London SE22 9HJ
Tel: 0208 693 0555
Fax: 0208 693 0555
E-mail: info@snnp.org.uk
Website: www.snnp.org.uk

The Society is the only professional examining body in the field. Incorporated in 1991, it caters for the interests and aspirations of childminders, nursery nurses and all those who look after children and young people from birth to age 5. It also exists to raise the flagging professional image of nursery nurses.

MEMBERSHIP
Graduate (GSNNP)
Associate (ASNNP)
Fellow (FSNNP)

QUALIFICATION/EXAMINATIONS
The examinations in Early Childhood Studies are in three stages: Certificate, Advanced Certificate and Diploma. The subjects for all the examinations are the same but the questions are set and marked at the appropriate level. The subjects are:
Care of the sick child and special needs
Data investigation and interpretation
Early childhood play and learning
First aid and safety
Legal aspects of child care, health and community care
Management in the Early Years (Diploma level)
Managing self evaluation reflection
Observation, assessment and the young child
Overview of growth and development
Practice in service in child care
Pregnancy, birth and child development
Preparing for employment with young children
Protecting children from abuse
Social and psychological development
Working with parents and young children
Course work on a topic selected by the student

DESIGNATORY LETTERS
GSNNP, ASNNP, FSNNP

NURSING AND MIDWIFERY
Membership of Professional Institutions and Associations

THE NURSING & MIDWIFERY COUNCIL

23 Portland Place
London W1B 1PZ
Tel: 020 7333 9333
E-mail: UKenquiries@nmc-uk.org
Website: www.nmc-uk.org

We are the nursing and midwifery regulator for England, Wales, Scotland, Northern Ireland and the Islands. We exist to safeguard the health and well-being of the public.

OCCUPATIONAL THERAPY
Membership of Professional Institutions and Associations

ROYAL COLLEGE OF OCCUPATIONAL THERAPISTS

106–114 Borough High Street
Southwark
London SE1 1LB
Tel: 020 7357 6480
Fax: 020 7450 2299
E-mail: membership@cot.co.uk
Website: www.cot.org.uk

The Royal College of Occupational Therapists is the professional body for occupational therapy in the UK. The College has over 32,000 members and represents the profession nationally and internationally. COT accredits pre-registration occupational therapy degree programmes in 31 UK Universities.

MEMBERSHIP
Student Member
Associate
Discounted Associate
Professional Member
Discounted Professional Member
Self-employed Member
Retired Member
Overseas Member

QUALIFICATION/EXAMINATIONS
BA(Hons)
PG Dip
MSc

DESIGNATORY LETTERS
MRCOT

OPTICIANS (DISPENSING)

Dispensing opticians must be registered with the General Optical Council (GOC, 10 Old Bailey, London EC4M 7NG; Tel: 020 7580 3898; e-mail: goc@optical.org; website: www.optical.org). The GOC publishes registers of all optometrists, dispensing opticians, student opticians and optical businesses that are qualified and fit to practise, train or carry on business.

Qualification takes three years in total, and can be completed by combining a distance learning course or day release while working as a trainee under the supervision of a qualified and GOC-registered optician. Alternatively students can do a two-year full-time course followed by one year of supervised practice with a qualified and registered optician. The GOC has approved training courses in dispensing optics at the following institutions in the UK: Anglia Ruskin University, Association of British Dispensing Opticians (ABDO) College (Distance Learning Institute), Bradford College, City and Islington College, City University and Glasgow Caledonian University. All routes are assessed by final ABDO examinations. On successful completion of training you must register with the GOC in order to practise in the UK. Once qualified, you will need to undertake a minimum amount of continuing education and training to remain on the register. All registered dispensing opticians have to renew their registration each year: this is called 'retention'.

The approved training course for the contact lens specialty is run by ABDO College and City and Islington College. For further information contact the ABDO College (Tel: 01227 738 829 option 1; email: info@abdocollege.org.uk) or City and Islington College (Tel: 020 7700 9200; email: courseinfo@candi.ac. uk).

If you qualify as a dispensing optician and have worked in practice as a qualified dispensing optician for at least two years, the University of Bradford offers a career progression course that enables you to graduate with a degree in optometry by undertaking 6 months of distance-learning followed by 12 months of study at the University (Tel: 01274 236296; email: admissions-life@bradford. ac.uk).

Continuing education and training is a statutory requirement for all fully-qualified dispensing opticians. The CET scheme is a points-based scheme that runs over a three-year cycle. All full registrants must earn a minimum number of CET points by the end of each cycle to stay on the registers.

Nationals of EU/EEA countries who have gained optical quailfications in an EU/EEA country can apply to another EU/EEA country to have their qualifications recognised.

ENTRY REQUIREMENTS
Requirements vary according to the college or university, but typically five GCSEs at Grade C or above, to include Mathematics, English and Science and perhaps two or three A Levels at a minimum of a Grade D or equivalent are required. Relevant work experience will also be considered.

For further details contact the admissions tutor or check the website of the university you wish to apply to.

Membership of Professional Institutions and Associations

ASSOCIATION OF BRITISH DISPENSING OPTICIANS

199 Gloucester Terrace
London W2 6LD
Tel: 020 7298 5100
E-mail: general@abdolondon.org.uk
Website: www.abdo.org.uk

The ABDO is the qualifying body for dispensing opticians in the UK. Our aims are to advance the science and art of dispensing optics, to further the education and training of dispensing opticians, and to support and promote the interests of the profession.

MEMBERSHIP
Student Member
Associate Member
Full Member
Fellow (FBDO)

Elder

QUALIFICATION/EXAMINATIONS
Certificate in Contact Lens Practice (Level 6)
Diploma in The Assessment & Management of Low Vision (Level 6)
Diploma in Ophthalmic Dispensing (Level 6)
Diploma in Advanced Contact Lens Practice (Level 7)
Diploma in Spectacle Lens Design (Level 7)

DESIGNATORY LETTERS
FBDO

ASSOCIATION OF CONTACT LENS MANUFACTURERS

PO Box 735
Devizes
Wiltshire SN10 3TQ
Tel: 01380 860418
Fax: 01380 860863
E-mail: secgen@aclm.org.uk
Website: www.aclm.org.uk

The ACLM was founded in 1962 to publicize the work of UK contact lens manufacturers, to develop new products and to raise standards. Today we represent the manufacturers of the vast majority of prescription contact lenses and lens care products sold in the UK, and provide a cohesive voice for our members.

MEMBERSHIP
Member

OPTOMETRY

Careers in optometry are overseen by the General Optical Council (10 Old Bailey, London EC4M 7NG; Tel: 020 7580 3898; e-mail: goc@optical.org; website: www.optical.org). You can study for an undergraduate optometry degree from one of nine GOC-approved institutions in the UK: Anglia Ruskin University, Aston University, the University of Bradford, Cardiff University, City University, Glasgow Caledonian University, Plymouth University, the University of Manchester and the University of Ulster.

LENGTH OF COURSE
Usually four years in total (five in Scotland): a full-time three-year (four-year in Scotland) degree course, followed by one year's salaried pre-registration training with a practice under the guidance of a GOC-registered optometrist. This includes a series of assessments, set by the College of Optometry, or the University of Manchester, throughout the placement. Trainees must have gained a degree in Optometry at 2:2 or above and have a valid Certificate of Clinical Competency in order to enter a pre-registration placement. Trainees whose certificate has expired or who fail to achieve a 2:2 in their degree must successfully complete the GOC's Optometry Progression Scheme before entering a pre-registration placement.

ENTRY REQUIREMENTS
You will normally need five GCSEs (or equivalent) at grade C or above, one of which should be English; often maths and physics or double science are also required. You will normally be required to have three A Level passes/approximately 320 UCAS tariff points from the following subjects: physics, biology, chemistry or mathematics. Requirements vary between universities, so be sure to check the university's prospectus and/or consult the relevant admission tutors.

REGISTRATION
On successful completion of the pre-registration period of training, which includes work-based assessment and a final assessment on the Stage 2 core competencies for optometry, the qualified optometrist must register with the GOC in order to practise.

Nationals of EU/EEA countries who have gained optical qualifications in an EU/EEA country can apply to another EU/EEA country to have their qualifications recognised. For people who gained their qualification outside the EU/EEA the requirements for registration as an optometrist in the UK are detailed on the GOC website.

Membership of Professional Institutions and Associations

ASSOCIATION OF OPTOMETRISTS

2 Woodbridge Street
London EC1R 0DG
Tel: 020 7549 2000
Fax: 020 7251 8315
E-mail: postbox@aop.org.uk
Website: www.aop.org.uk

The AOP serves its members by promoting and protecting them, providing them with relevant services, representing and supporting them, enhancing their professional and business effectiveness, and expanding the role of optometry in primary and secondary eyecare.

MEMBERSHIP
Student Member
Honorary Member
Dispensing Associate
Full Member

ORTHOPTICS

Membership of Professional Institutions and Associations

BRITISH AND IRISH ORTHOPTIC SOCIETY

Salisbury House
Station Road
Cambridge CB1 2LA
Tel: 01353 66 55 41
E-mail: bios@orthoptics.org.uk
Website: www.orthoptics.org.uk

Orthoptists diagnose and treat problems with visual development and binocular vision (how the eyes work together as a pair), and eye movement disorders. They are experts in childhood vision screening. Most orthoptists in the UK work in the Ophthalmology Clinics of acute hospitals, treating patients with stroke, glaucoma, reading difficulties, neurological disorders, low vision and other conditions.

MEMBERSHIP
Student, Full, Associate

QUALIFICATION/EXAMINATIONS
Degrees in orthoptics are offered by Liverpool University (www.liv.ac.uk), Sheffield University (www.sheffield.ac.uk) and Glasgow Caledonian University (www.gcu.ac.uk)

OSTEOPATHY AND NATUROPATHY
Membership of Professional Institutions and Associations

BRITISH OSTEOPATHIC ASSOCIATION

3 Park Terrace
Manor Road
Luton
Bedfordshire LU1 3HN
Tel: 01582 488455
Fax: 01582 481533
E-mail: boa@osteopathy.org
Website: www.osteopathy.org

The BOA was formed in 1998 as a result of the merger of the British Osteopathic Association, the Osteopathic Association of Great Britain and the Guild of Osteopaths. We provide opportunities for individual and professional development in osteopathic practice and promote the highest standards of osteopathic education and research.

MEMBERSHIP
Student Member
1st/2nd/3rd/4th Year Graduate Member
Full Member
Overseas Member

PATENT AGENCY
Membership of Professional Institutions and Associations

THE CHARTERED INSTITUTE OF PATENT ATTORNEYS

95 Chancery Lane
London WC2A 1DT
Tel: 020 7405 9450
Fax: 020 7430 0471
E-mail: mail@cipa.org.uk
Website: www.cipa.org.uk

CIPA is the professional, training and examining body for patent attorneys in the UK. From 2010 the IP Regulation Board, an independent body within the CIPA, sets the standards for regulation of the profession. Trainees, all technical graduates, also study for the qualification to practise before the European Patent Office.

MEMBERSHIP
Student Member
Associate

Fellow
British Overseas Member
Foreign Member

QUALIFICATION/EXAMINATIONS
Qualifying examination for registration as a Patent Attorney

DESIGNATORY LETTERS
RPA, CPA

PENSION MANAGEMENT
Membership of Professional Institutions and Associations

THE PENSIONS MANAGEMENT INSTITUTE

PMI House
4–10 Artillery Lane
London E1 7LS
Tel: 020 7247 1452
Fax: 020 7375 0603
E-mail: via website
Website: www.pensions-pmi.org.uk

The Pensions Management Institute is the professional body that promotes standards of excellence and lifetime learning for pensions professionals and trustees through its qualifications, membership and ongoing support services. For further details please visit our website.

MEMBERSHIP
Student Membership
Certificate Membership
Diploma Membership
Associate Membership
Fellowship
Affiliate Membership
Trustee Group Membership

QUALIFICATION/EXAMINATIONS
Award in Pensions Essentials (APE)

Certificate in Pensions Essentials (CPE)
Certificate in Pension Calculations (CPC)
Certificate in Pensions Administration (CPA)
Diploma in Pensions Administration (DPA)
Retirement Provision Certificate (RPC)
Certificate in Pensions Automatic Enrolment (CPAE)
Diploma in Retirement Provision (DRP)
Diploma in Employee Benefits and Retirement Savings (DEBRS)
Diploma in International Employee Benefits (DipIEB)
Diploma in Regulated Retirement Advice (DRRA)
Advanced Diploma in Retirement Provision (ADRP)
Awards in Pensions Trusteeship (APT)

DESIGNATORY LETTERS
CertPMI, DipPMI, APMI, FPMI

PERSONNEL MANAGEMENT
Membership of Professional Institutions and Associations

CHARTERED INSTITUTE OF PERSONNEL AND DEVELOPMENT

151 The Broadway
Wimbledon
London SW19 1JQ
Tel: +44(0)20 8612 6208
Fax: +44(0)20 8612 6201
E-mail: membershipenquiry@cipd.co.uk
Website: www.cipd.co.uk

The CIPD is the world's largest Chartered HR and development professional body. With 135,000 members across 120 countries it supports and develops those responsible for the management and development of people within organisations.

MEMBERSHIP
Affiliate Member
Student Member
Associate Member (Assoc CIPD)
Chartered Member (MCIPD)

Chartered Fellow (FCIPD)
Academic Member
For further information see: www.cipd.co.uk/membership

QUALIFICATION/EXAMINATIONS
CIPD qualifications are available at three levels:
Level 3 Foundation
Level 5 Intermediate
Level 7 Advanced
In three different sizes:

Awards
Certificates
Diplomas
For more information and to find out where to study CIPD qualifications visit: www.cipd.co.uk/qualifications

DESIGNATORY LETTERS
Assoc CIPD, Chartered MCIPD, Chartered FCIPD, CCIPD

THE INSTITUTE OF CONTINUING PROFESSIONAL DEVELOPMENT

Royal Institute of Chartered Surveyors
Parliament Square
London SW1P 3AD
Tel: 020 7695 1673
E-mail: info@cpdinstitute.org
Website: www.cpdinstitute.org

The Institute of Continuing Professional Development is part of the Continuing Professional Development Foundation, an educational charitable trust providing high-quality and broad-ranging CPD since 1981. We serve the public interest by helping to raise the effectiveness of professionals through the promotion of CPD as an important and integral element of lifelong learning.

MEMBERSHIP
Member (MInstCPD)
Fellow (FInstCPD)

DESIGNATORY LETTERS
MInstCPD, FInstCPD

UK EMPLOYEE ASSISTANCE PROFESSIONALS ASSOCIATION

PO Box 7966
Wilson
Derby DE1 0XP
E-mail: info@eapa.org.uk
Website: www.eapa.org.uk

The UK Employee Assistance Professionals Association represents the interests of professionals concerned with employee assistance, psychological health and wellbeing in the UK. Members include external and internal EAP providers, purchasers, counsellors, consultants and trainers.

MEMBERSHIP
◆ Registered Internal Provider: £1,200 per annum

◆ Registered External Provider: £1,200 per annum
◆ Non Registered Provider: £500 per annum
◆ Consultant Associate Member: £300 per annum
◆ Associate Member: £150 per annum
◆ Individual Member: £50 per annum
◆ Student Member: £25 per annum

PHARMACY
Membership of Professional Institutions and Associations

GENERAL PHARMACEUTICAL COUNCIL

1 Lambeth High Street
London SE1 7JN
Tel: 020 7735 9141
Fax: 020 7735 7629
E-mail: enquiries@rpsgb.org
Website: www.pharmacyregulation.org

The RPSGB, which dates from 1841, is the professional body for pharmacists and pharmacy technicians in England, Scotland and Wales. Our primary objectives are to lead, regulate, develop and represent the profession. We promote advancement of the science and practice of pharmacy, and pharmaceutical education and knowledge, and liaise with government and other bodies in the interests of our members.

MEMBERSHIP
Pharmacy Technician
Pharmacist
Student

DESIGNATORY LETTERS
MRPharmS, FRPharmS

THE PHARMACEUTICAL SOCIETY OF NORTHERN IRELAND

73 University Street
Belfast BT7 1HL
Tel: 028 9032 6927
Fax: 028 9043 9919
E-mail: info@psni.org.uk
Website: www.psni.org.uk

The Pharmaceutical Society of Northern Ireland, founded in 1925, is the regulatory and professional body for pharmacists in Northern Ireland. It maintains a register of more than 2,000 pharmacists and over 500 pharmacy premises, and sets and promotes the standards for pharmacists' admission to and remaining on the register, thereby protecting public safety.

MEMBERSHIP
Trainee
Member

QUALIFICATION/EXAMINATIONS
Registration Examination

PHOTOGRAPHY

Membership of Professional Institutions and Associations

ASSOCIATION OF PHOTOGRAPHERS (AOP)

21 Downham Road
London N1 5AA
Tel: 020 7739 6669
E-mail: info@aophoto.co.uk
Website: www.the-aop.org

The AOP was founded in 1968 to promote the highest standards throughout the industry and to improve the rights of all professional photographers based in the UK. Our membership currently comprises 1,800 photographers and photographic assistants, and we are supported by photographers' agents, printers, and manufacturers and suppliers of photographic equipment.

MEMBERSHIP
Student Member
Assistant Member
Photographer (full) Member
Agent Member
College Member
Affiliated Company

BRITISH INSTITUTE OF PROFESSIONAL PHOTOGRAPHY

The Coach House
The Firs, High Street
Whitchurch
Aylesbury
Buckinghamshire HP22 4SJ
Tel: 01296 642020
Fax: 01296 641553
E-mail: info@bipp.com
Website: www.bipp.com

The BIPP is the qualifying body for professional photographers in the UK. We provide support, training and qualifications for photographers across all types of photography, and organize a number of regional activities and events. A not-for-profit organization, we ensure that professional standards are met and maintained.

MEMBERSHIP
Open to full- or part-time professional photographers. Join as a Provisional member (maximum of 1 year) and work towards gaining a professional qualification. Friends' & Student membership is also available.

QUALIFICATION/EXAMINATIONS
Three tiers of qualification:
Licentiateship (LBIPP)
Associateship (ABIPP)
Fellowship (FBIPP)
BIPP is also aligned with the BA Hons in Photography through the OCA. Full details of the qualifications criteria can be found at www.bipp.com

DESIGNATORY LETTERS
LBIPP, ABIPP, FBIPP

MASTER PHOTOGRAPHERS ASSOCIATION

Jubilee House
1 Chancery Lane
Darlington
Co Durham DL1 5QP
Tel: 01325 356555
Fax: 01325 357813
E-mail: general@mpauk.com
Website: www.mpauk.com

The MPA was founded in 1952 and is now the UK's only organization for FT, qualified professional photographers. We have more than 2,000 members, who enjoy a range of benefits, including education, qualifications, informative regional meetings, business building promotions and marketing support, and abide by the Association's Code of Conduct.

MEMBERSHIP
Licentiate (LMPA)
Associate (AMPA)
Fellow (FMPA)

QUALIFICATION/EXAMINATIONS
The Diploma in Photographic Practice (DipPP) is recognized by SkillSet, as a benchmark competence mapped to the Photo Imaging National Standards: it is available to all qualified members and is an assessment process of professional photographic business and personal skills.

DESIGNATORY LETTERS
LMPA, AMPA, FMPA, DipPP

THE ROYAL PHOTOGRAPHIC SOCIETY

Fenton House
122 Wells Road
Bath
Somerset BA2 3AH
Tel: 01225 325733
E-mail: reception@rps.org
Website: www.rps.org

The RPS was founded in 1853. It is an educational charity and membership organisaton with the aim of promoting photography and supporting photographers. It realises these through exhibitions, workshops and courses and a distinctions and qualifications programme. Membership is open to anyone. It acts as an advocate on behalf of photographers and photography with the media and government.

MEMBERSHIP
Member
Family
Student
65 and over
25 and under
Disabled
Overseas

QUALIFICATION/EXAMINATIONS
Licentiate (LRPS)
Associate (ARPS)
Fellowship (FRPS)
Qualified Imaging Scientist and Licentiate (QIS LRPS)
Graduate Imaging Scientist and Associate (GIS ARPS)
Accredited Imaging Scientist and Associate (AIS ARPS)
Accredited Senior Imaging Scientist and Fellow (ASIS FRPS)
Qualified in Imaging in the Creative Industries (QICI & LRPS)
Graduate in Imaging in the Creative Industries (GICI & ARPS)

Accredited in Imaging in the Creative Industries (AICI & ARPS)

Accredited Senior in Imaging in the Creative Industries (ASICI FRPS)

Creative Industries Qualification

DESIGNATORY LETTERS
LRPS, ARPS, FRPS

PHYSICS
Membership of Professional Institutions and Associations

INSTITUTE OF PHYSICS AND ENGINEERING IN MEDICINE

Fairmount House
230 Tadcaster Road
York YO24 1ES
Tel: 01904 610821
Fax: 01904 612279
E-mail: office@ipem.org.uk
Website: www.ipem.ac.uk

The IPEM is dedicated to bringing together physical science, engineering and clinical professionals in academia, healthcare services and industry to share knowledge, advance science and technology, and inform and educate the public, with the purpose of improving the understanding, detection and treatment of disease and the management of patients.

Affiliate
Associate
Medical Member (MedMIPEM)
Medical Fellow (MedFIPEM)
Corporate Member (MIPEM)
Fellow (FIPEM)
International

MEMBERSHIP
Student Member

DESIGNATORY LETTERS
MedMIPEM, MedFIPEM, IIPEM, MIPEM, FIPEM

THE INSTITUTE OF PHYSICS

76 Portland Place
London W1B 1NT
Tel: 020 7470 4800
Fax: 020 7470 4848
E-mail: physics@iop.org
Website: www.iop.org

The IOP is a scientific charity devoted to increasing the practice, understanding and application of physics. We have a worldwide membership of over 36,000 and are a leading communicator of physics-related science to all audiences, from specialists through to government and the general public. Our publishing company, IOP Publishing, is a world leader in scientific publishing and the electronic dissemination of physics.

MEMBERSHIP
Student Member
Affiliate
Associate Member (AMInstP)
Member (MInstP)
Fellow (FInstP)
Chartered Physicist (CPhys)
IOPi Member

DESIGNATORY LETTERS
AMInstP, MInstP, FInstP, CPhys

PHYSIOTHERAPY
Membership of Professional Institutions and Associations

THE CHARTERED SOCIETY OF PHYSIOTHERAPY

14 Bedford Row
London WC1R 4ED
Tel: 0207 306 6666
E-mail: via website
Website: www.csp.org.uk

The CSP is the professional, educational and trade union body for the UK's 52,000 chartered physiotherapists, physiotherapy students and assistants. In order to become a member of the CSP it is necessary to have undertaken a qualification recognized by the Health and Care Professions Council (HCPC) – see: www.hcpc-uk.org

MEMBERSHIP
Student Member
Associate
Member (MCSP)
Fellow (FCSP)

DESIGNATORY LETTERS
MCSP, FCSP

PLUMBING
Membership of Professional Institutions and Associations

CHARTERED INSTITUTE OF PLUMBING AND HEATING ENGINEERING

64 Station Lane
Hornchurch
Essex RM12 6NB
Tel: 01708 472791
Fax: 01708 448987
E-mail: info@ciphe.org.uk
Website: www.ciphe.org.uk

The CIPHE, founded in 1906, is the professional body for the UK plumbing and heating industry. Our membership of around 12,000 is made up of individuals from a wide range of backgrounds and includes consultants, specifiers, designers, public health engineers, lecturers, trainers, trainees and practitioners, as well as manufacturers and distributors.

MEMBERSHIP
Trainee
Affiliate
Companion (CompCIPHE)

Associate (ACIPHE)
Member (MCIPHE)
Fellow (FCIPHE)

QUALIFICATION/EXAMINATIONS
Apprentice, Journeyman and Master Plumber Certificate (awarded jointly with the Worshipful Company of Plumbers and the City & Guilds of London Institute)

DESIGNATORY LETTERS
CompCIPHE, ACIPHE, MCIPHE, FCIPHE

PRINTING

Membership of Professional Institutions and Associations

PROSKILLS UK

Unit 24 East Central
127 Olympic Avenue
Milton Park
Abingdon
Oxfordshire OX14 4SA
Tel: 01235 833844
E-mail: info@proskills.co.uk
Website: www.proskills.co.uk

Proskills UK is the bridge between employers and government on skills and training. Employer-led representing key industries including: Building Products, Coatings, Furniture, Furnishings & Interiors, Glass & Related Industries, Health and Safety Paper, Printing and Wood industries, which make up a third of the UK manufacturing sector. We help to raise the profile of the sector, set the skills standards and qualifications and ensure that the skills and funding system delivers against the current and future needs of the industries.

QUALIFICATION/EXAMINATIONS
Please see the Proskills UK website.

THE INSTITUTE OF PAPER, PRINTING AND PUBLISHING (IP3)

Claremont House
70–72 Alma Road
Windsor
Berks SL4 3EZ
Tel: 0870 330 8625
Fax: 0870 330 8615
E-mail: info@ip3.org.uk
Website: www.ip3.org.uk

IP3 is the professional body representing the interests of individuals within the paper, printing and publishing sector. It was formed in 2005 from the merger of the Institute of Paper, the Institute of Printing and the Institute of Publishing, and brought together more than 2,000 members and a wealth of knowledge.

MEMBERSHIP
Student

Associate (AIP3)
Member (MIP3)
Fellow (FIP3)

QUALIFICATION/EXAMINATIONS
Certificate

DESIGNATORY LETTERS
AIP3, MIP3, FIP3

PROFESSIONAL INVESTIGATION
Membership of Professional Institutions and Associations

THE INSTITUTE OF PROFESSIONAL INVESTIGATORS

Claremont House
70–72 Alma Road
Windsor
Berkshire SL4 3EZ
Tel: 0870 330 8622
Fax: 0870 330 8612
E-mail: admin@ipi.org.uk
Website: www.ipi.org.uk

The IPI was founded in 1976 as a professional body, catering primarily for the work and educational needs of professional investigators of all types and all specializations. We encourage members' CPD and require them to adhere to the Institute's strict code of ethics, and we promote the recognition of professional investigation as a profession by government, legislative bodies and the public.

MEMBERSHIP
Associate
Member (MIPI)
Student

Fellow (FIPI)

QUALIFICATION/EXAMINATIONS
The Institute provides an interactive online Foundation Course for students and others interested in becoming part of the investigative industry; this course also provides a refresher course for those who need to update their specialization and/or interest in other areas of investigative work.

DESIGNATORY LETTERS
MIPI, FIPI

PSYCHOANALYSIS
Membership of Professional Institutions and Associations

THE BRITISH PSYCHOANALYTICAL SOCIETY

Byron House
112a Shirland Road
London W9 2BT
Tel: 020 7563 5000
Fax: 020 7563 5001
E-mail: admin@iopa.org.uk
Website: www.psychoanalysis.org.uk

The British Psychoanalytical Society has c500 members and c60 candidates for membership. Our aims include: to support the development of psychoanalytical knowledge as a general theory of mind, to further the clinical and scientific standards of psychoanalysis, and to train high-quality psychoanalytical professionals in sufficient numbers to develop the profession.

MEMBERSHIP
Associate Member
Full Member
Fellow

PSYCHOLOGY
Membership of Professional Institutions and Associations

BRITISH PSYCHOLOGICAL SOCIETY

St Andrews House
48 Princess Road East
Leicester LE1 7DR
Tel: 0116 254 9568
Fax: 0116 227 1314
E-mail: enquiries@bps.org.uk
Website: www.bps.org.uk

Psychology is the scientific study of people, the mind and behaviour. The British Psychological Society is the representative body for psychology and psychologists in the UK. We are responsible for the development, promotion and application of psychology for the public good.

MEMBERSHIP
Student Member
Graduate Member (MBPsS)
Associate Fellow (AFBPsS)
Fellow (FBPsS)
Honorary Fellow (HonFBPsS)
Affiliate
Chartered Membership (CPsychol)
Subscriber
e-Subscriber

QUALIFICATION/EXAMINATIONS
Statement of Equivalence in Clinical Psychology (SoE)
Qualification in Educational Psychology (Scotland) (Stage 2)
Qualification in Forensic Psychology (Stage 2) (QFP)
Qualification in Clinical Neuropsychology (QiCN)
Qualification in Counselling Psychology (QCoP)
Qualification in Health Psychology (Stage 2)
Qualification in Occupational Psychology (QOccPsych)
Qualification in Sport & Exercise Psychology (QSEP)

DESIGNATORY LETTERS
MBPsS, AFBPsS, FBPsS, CPsychol, HonMBPsS, HonFBPsS, SoE

PSYCHOTHERAPY
Membership of Professional Institutions and Associations

ASSOCIATION OF CHILD PSYCHOTHERAPISTS

Unit 7, 19–23 Wedmore Street
London N19 4RU
Tel: 020 7281 8479
E-mail: admin@childpsychotherapy.org.uk
Website: www.childpsychotherapy.org.uk

The ACP is the main professional body for psychoanalytic child and adolescent psychotherapists in the UK. Our members work with children and young people as well as their parents, families and wider networks, treating a wide range of difficulties ranging from problems with sleeping and bed-wetting to eating disorders, self-harm, depression and anxiety.

MEMBERSHIP
Member

BRITISH ASSOCIATION FOR COUNSELLING AND PSYCHOTHERAPY

BACP House
15 St John's Business Park
Lutterworth
Leicestershire LE17 4HB
Tel: 01455 883300
Fax: 01455 550243
E-mail: bacp@bacp.co.uk
Website: www.bacp.co.uk

BACP is the largest and broadest body within the sector and participates in the development of counselling and psychotherapy at an international level. Our work with large and small organizations ranges from advising schools on how to set up a counselling service to assisting the NHS on service provision, working with voluntary agencies and supporting independent practitioners.

MEMBERSHIP
Individual Member
Registered Member (MBACP)
Senior Accredited Member (Snr Accred)
Student Member
Affiliate Member
Associate Member
Member (MBACP)
Accredited Member (MBACP Accred)
Fellow (FBACP)

QUALIFICATION/EXAMINATIONS
We run workshops for members and accredit individual counsellors/psychotherapists, supervisors, counselling services and training courses. For details see our website.

DESIGNATORY LETTERS
MBACP, MBACP (Accred), FBACP, Snr Accred

BRITISH ASSOCIATION FOR THE PERSON CENTRED APPROACH

BAPCA
PO Box 143
Ross-on-Wye
Herefordshire HR9 9AH
Tel: 01989 763863
E-mail: via website
Website: www.bapca.org.uk

The BAPCA was founded in 1989 as a non-religious, non-profit-making organization with the aim of advancing education in Client-Centred Psychotherapy and Counselling and the Person-Centred Approach through its publications and website, and cooperation with other national and international organizations with similar goals.

MEMBERSHIP
Individual Member
Joint Member
International Member
Institutional Member

BRITISH PSYCHOTHERAPY FOUNDATION

37 Mapesbury Road
London NW2 4HJ
Tel: 020 8452 9823
E-mail: mail@bap-psychotherapy.org
Website: www.bap-psychotherapy.org

The BAP is one of the longest established and largest independent providers of Jungian analytic and psychoanalytic psychotherapy for adults and children in the UK. We have been training psychoanalytic and Jungian psychotherapists for nearly 60 years, and our members work in the NHS, the corporate and voluntary sectors and as private practitioners.

MEMBERSHIP
Member

QUALIFICATION/EXAMINATIONS
Certificate/Diploma/MSc in Psychodynamics of Human Development (jointly with Birkbeck College, University of London)
DPsych in Child and Adolescent Psychotherapy (jointly with Birkbeck College, University of London)

CAMBRIDGE COLLEGE OF HYPNOTHERAPY

7 Bold Street
Warrington WA1 1DN
Tel: 01925 659303
E-mail: info@thecch.com
Website: www.hypnotherapytraining.org.uk

The CCH offers training to become a professional hypnotherapist. The course is accredited by the NCH, HA, APHP, NGH and NRAH. No formal qualifications are required to enrol on the course. What is required is a willingness to learn, a sense of humour and a genuine compassion and liking for people from all paths in life. This can be a very rewarding new or second career or a supplement to your current work / lifestyle. In addition to the College Diploma, it is possible to gain the HPD (Hypnotherapy Practitioner Diploma) which is awarded by ncfe and also possible to gain a Diploma awarded by the National Guild of Hypnotists in the USA. The HPD is at NVQ level 4/5 and has transferable credits of 45 for a first year degree with the Open University.

QUALIFICATION/EXAMINATIONS
Intermediate Practitioner Certificate
Diploma in Therapeutic Hypnosis (DipTHP)

DESIGNATORY LETTERS
DipTHP

NATIONAL COLLEGE OF HYPNOSIS AND PSYCHOTHERAPY

PO Box 5779
Loughborough
Leicestershire LE12 5ZF
Tel: 0845 257 8735
E-mail: enquiries@nchp.org.uk
Website: www.hypnotherapyuk.net

The NCHP is a not-for-profit organization founded in 1977 and now offers accredited hypnotherapy training, hypnosis training and psychotherapy training at weekends in Leicester, London, Manchester and Oxford. We also provide a programme of 1- and 2-day workshops and seminars, and (where appropriate) distance-learning courses.

MEMBERSHIP
United Kingdom Council for Psychotherapy
European Association for Psychotherapy
European Association for Hypno-Psychotherapy

QUALIFICATION/EXAMINATIONS
Foundation Course

Certificate in Hypno-Psychotherapy (CHP(NC))
Diploma in Hypno-Psychotherapy (DHP(NC))
Advanced Diploma in Hypno-Psychotherapy
(ADHP(NC))

NATIONAL COUNCIL OF PSYCHOTHERAPISTS

PO Box 541
Keighley BD21 9DS
Tel: 0800 170 1250
E-mail: info@thencp.org
Website: www.ncphq.co.uk

The National Council is a registering and accrediting body for psychotherapists, counsellors and coaches within the UK and also, through the International Council, the rest of the world.

Members can join the Council regardless of which discipline and where they completed their training.

MEMBERSHIP
Accredited Member (MNCP Accred)
Member (MNCP)
Fellow (FNCP)

DESIGNATORY LETTERS
ANCP, LNCP, MNCP, FNCP

THE FOUNDATION FOR PSYCHOTHERAPY AND COUNSELLING

5 Maidstone Buildings Mews
72–76 Borough High Street
London SE1 1GN
Tel: 0207 378 7392
E-mail: membership@thefpc.org.uk
Website: www.thefoundation-uk.org

The Foundation for Psychotherapy and Counselling was formed during the 1970s as the graduate body of WPF Therapy (the largest charitable provider of counselling and psychotherapy in England) and now has some 700 fully trained and qualified members, most of whom are in private practice.

MEMBERSHIP
Member

THE NATIONAL REGISTER OF HYPNOTHERAPISTS AND PSYCHOTHERAPISTS

Ground Floor
34 Altrincham Road
Wilmslow
Cheshire SK9 5ND
Tel: 0161 635 3530
E-mail: admin@nrhp.co.uk
Website: www.nrhp.co.uk

NRHP (est 1985) – a professional association of qualified hypno-psychotherapists who trained with a UKCP-accredited training organisation. Members are required to adhere to a code of ethics and carry appropriate insurance. We publish a Directory of Practitioners and offer a public referral service via our website and office. Member of the UKCP.

MEMBERSHIP
Student
Associate 1 (NRHP(Assoc 1))
Associate 2 (NRHP(Assoc 2))
Associate 3 (NRHP(Assoc 3))
Full Member (MNRHP)
Fellow (FNRHP)

DESIGNATORY LETTERS
NRHP(Assoc 1), NRHP(Assoc 2), NRHP(Assoc 3), MNRHP, FNRHP

UK COUNCIL FOR PSYCHOTHERAPY (UKCP)

2nd Floor Edward House
2 Wakley Street
London EC1V 7LT
Tel: 020 7014 9955
Fax: 020 7014 9977
E-mail: info@ukcp.org.uk
Website: www.psychotherapy.org.uk

UKCP is the leading professional body for the education, training, accreditation and regulation of psychotherapists and psychotherapeutic counsellors. Our register is accredited by the government's Professional Standards Authority. As part of our commitment to protecting the public, we work to improve access to psychotherapy, to support and disseminate research, to improve standards and to respond effectively to complaints against our members.

PURCHASING AND SUPPLY
Membership of Professional Institutions and Associations

THE CHARTERED INSTITUTE OF PROCUREMENT & SUPPLY

Easton House
Easton on the Hill
Stamford
Lincolnshire PE9 3NZ
Tel: 01780 756777
Fax: 01780 751610
E-mail: press@cips.org
Website: www.cips.org

The Chartered Institute of Procurement & Supply (CIPS) is the world's largest procurement and supply professional organisation. It is the worldwide centre of excellence on purchasing and supply management issues. CIPS has a global community of 120,000 in 150 different countries, including senior business people, high-ranking civil servants and leading academics. The activities of purchasing and supply chain professionals have a major impact on the profitability and efficiency of all types of organisation and CIPS offers corporate solutions packages to improve business profitability.

MEMBERSHIP
Student Member

Affiliate
Certificate Member
Diploma Member
Associate Member
Full Member (MCIPS)
Fellow (FCIPS)
Chartered Professional in Procurement and Supply

QUALIFICATION/EXAMINATIONS
Please see website: www.cips.org

DESIGNATORY LETTERS
MCIPS, FCIPS, Chartered Professional in procurement and supply

QUALITY ASSURANCE
Membership of Professional Institutions and Associations

THE CHARTERED QUALITY INSTITUTE

2nd Floor North
Chancery Exchange
10 Furnival Street
London EC4A 1AB
Tel: 020 7245 6722
Fax: 020 7245 6788
E-mail: membership@thecqi.org
Website: www.thecqi.org

The CQI is the chartered body for quality management professionals. Established in 1919, we gained a Royal Charter in 2006 and became the CQI shortly afterwards. Our vision is to place quality at the heart of every organization; we promote the benefits of quality management to industry, disseminate quality knowledge and resources, provide qualifications and training, and assess quality competence.

MEMBERSHIP
Student
Associate Member (ACQI)

Practitioner (PCQI)

Member, Chartered Quality Professional (MCQI, CQP)

Fellow, Chartered Quality Professional (FCQI, CQP)

QUALIFICATION/EXAMINATIONS

Level 3 Certificate in Quality Management (QCF)

Level 5 Certificate in Systems Management (QCF)

Level 5 Certificate in Assuring Service & Product Quality (QCF)

Level 5 Certificate in Managing Supply Chain Quality (QCF)

Level 5 Certificate in Quality Improvement for Business (QCF)

Level 5 Certificate in Quality Management Systems Audit (QCF)

Level 5 Diploma in Quality Management (QCF)

DESIGNATORY LETTERS

MCQI, CQP; FCQI, CQP

RADIOGRAPHY

Membership of Professional Institutions and Associations

THE SOCIETY OF RADIOGRAPHERS

207 Providence Square
Mill Street
London SE1 2EW
Tel: 020 7740 7200
Fax: 020 7740 7233
E-mail: via website
Website: www.sor.org

The Society of Radiographers, founded in 1920, represents diagnostic and therapeutic radiographers in the UK. Associated professionals working in medical imaging, radiation therapy and oncology are also welcome. It is responsible for their professional, educational, public and workplace interests. Together with the College of Radiographers, our charitable subsidiary, our efforts are directed towards education, research and other activities in support of the science and practice of radiography.

MEMBERSHIP

We have a range of membership options, including student, associate professional, healthcare support worker and assistant practitioner, retired and international membership options.

RETAIL

Membership of Professional Institutions and Associations

FOOD AND DRINK TRAINING AND EDUCATION COUNCIL LTD (FTC)

Icon Business Centre
4100 Park Approach
Leeds
West Yorkshire LS15 8GB
Tel: 0113 3970 398
E-mail: ftc@foodtraining.org.uk
Website: www.foodtraining.org.uk

Food and drink training and education council (ftc) formerly known as Meat Training Council (MTC). Ftc is a food industry skills-focused charity, dedicated to working collaboratively to build a world class food industry in the UK. We are involved in a range of practical and impactful charitable work to help support our industry in competing with the greatest nations in the world. We are the parent company of FDQ, a specialist food industry awarding organisation.

INSTITUTE OF MASTERS OF WINE

24 Fitzroy Square
London W1T 6EP
Tel: 020 7383 9130
Fax: 020 7383 9139
E-mail: peter@mastersofwine.org
Website: www.mastersofwine.org

The Institute of Masters of Wine is a membership body that represents the interests of its members (Masters of Wine), administers the MW Examination, and runs an education programme in preparation for the examination. We also hold a number of events throughout the year, including seminars and tastings, master classes, discussions and, every 4 years, a symposium, most of which are open to the public.

MEMBERSHIP
Master of Wine (MW)

QUALIFICATION/EXAMINATIONS
Master of Wine Examination

DESIGNATORY LETTERS
MW

THE BRITISH ANTIQUE DEALERS' ASSOCIATION

20 Rutland Gate
London SW7 1BD
Tel: 020 7589 4128
Fax: 020 7581 9083
E-mail: info@bada.org
Website: www.bada.org

BADA, which was founded in 1918, is the trade association for antique dealers in Britain. Our vetted members are elected for their high business standards and expertise, and adhere to a strict code of practice; we provide safeguards for members of the public who deal with our members, including independent arbitration if a dispute arises.

MEMBERSHIP
Member

THE GUILD OF ARCHITECTURAL IRONMONGERS

BPF House
6 Bath Place
Rivington Street
London EC2A 3JE
Tel: +44 (0)207 033 2480
E-mail: info@gai.org.uk
Website: www.gai.org.uk

The GAI represents the interests of architectural ironmongers and manufacturers of architectural ironmongery. We develop, promote and protect standards of integrity and excellence, and encourage academic study relating to the industry, operating an Institute for individual members to facilitate their continuous professional development. We liaise with various bodies on matters affecting the industry.

MEMBERSHIP
Affiliate Member
Associate Member
Full Member
Registered Architectural Ironmonger (Reg AI)

QUALIFICATION/EXAMINATIONS
The GAI provides a 3-year incremental training programme. Students are examined each year and must pass each stage in turn before progressing to the next. A Certificate is awarded to successful students each year, culminating in the GAI Diploma (Dip GAI) on successful completion of year 3.

DESIGNATORY LETTERS
Reg AI

THE INSTITUTE OF BUILDERS MERCHANTS

1180 Elliot Court
Coventry Business Park
Herald Avenue
Coventry CV5 6UB
Tel: 01767 650662
E-mail: admin@iobm.co.uk
Website: www.iobm.co.uk

To improve through seminars and website articles, the technical and general knowledge of persons engaged in builders' merchants; to verify management training courses with providers; to acknowledge personal achievements and award diplomas, certificates and other distinctions; to encourage the need for knowledge, integrity and efficiency in the builders' merchants industry.

MEMBERSHIP
Student
Associate
Member
Fellow
Corporate Supporter

QUALIFICATION/EXAMINATIONS
University Degree
The Institute of Builders Merchants Business Studies Course
The Builders Merchants Federation Diploma in Merchanting
Higher National Certificate (HNC) in Business Studies
Higher National Diploma (HND) in Business Studies
NVQ Level 4
Company management programmes as approved by the Board of Governors

THE SOCIETY OF SHOE FITTERS

c/o The Anchorage
28 Admirals Walk
Hingham
Norfolk NR9 4JL
Tel: 01953 851171
Fax: 01953 851190
E-mail: secretary@shoefitters-uk.org
Website: www.shoefitters-uk.org

The Society of Shoe Fitters, a non-profit organisation since 1959. Freely assists public and industry with footwear/fitting/foothealth enquiries via website, help line and leaflets. Teaches professional shoe fitting via five-month course, also instore training and application for experienced shoe fitters. Provides National Shoe Fitting Week and lobbies government for better health education.

MEMBERSHIP
Student Member
Associate Member
Member (MSSF)
Fellow (FSSF)
Associate Member (corporate membership)

QUALIFICATION/EXAMINATIONS
One-day on-site courses – certificate only

Five-month course leading to membership qualification
Entrance Examination and Entrance Application for experienced shoe fitters leading to qualification

DESIGNATORY LETTERS
MSSF, FSSF

SECURITY

Membership of Professional Institutions and Associations

THE SECURITY INSTITUTE

1 The Courtyard
Caldecote
Warwickshire CV10 0AS
E-mail: info@security-institute.org
Website: www.security-institute.org

The Security Institute promotes professionalism in the security world through its professional grades of membership, and encourages a proper understanding of the value of the security function by management. Membership can be an employment prerequisite, and successful students of the Certificate, Diploma and Advance Diploma enjoy enhanced credibility and automatic membership.

MEMBERSHIP
Affiliate/Student
Graduate
Associate (ASyI)

Member (MSyI)
Fellow (FSyI)
Chartered Security Professional (CSyP)

QUALIFICATION/EXAMINATIONS
Certificate in Security Management (Level 3)
Diploma in Security Management (Level 5)
Advanced Diploma in Security Management (Level 7)

DESIGNATORY LETTERS
ASyI, MSyI, FSyI, CSyP

SOCIAL WORK AND PROBATION

SOCIAL WORK
Social work is a career for people who like people and much of a social worker's time is spent working in the community, helping support and protect people who are vulnerable and at risk. They work with people who are experiencing social and emotional problems and their families if they are affected. They may help people who use services to claim benefits, plan budgets, obtain legal advice or deal with other local authority departments. Social workers undertake assessment in relation to childcare, mental health and criminal justice. Depending on individual needs, a social worker may arrange

services such as home care assistance or hospital treatment.

HEALTH AND CARE PROFESSIONS COUNCIL
The role of the Health and Care Professions Council (HCPC) is to protect the public. It does this by developing and monitoring strategy and policy for the HCPC, and ensuring that the organization fulfils its functions under the Health and Social Work Professions Order 2001. The Council has 12 members made up of 6 registrant and 6 lay members. The HCPC also runs committees to help the Council with its work. Four statutory committees have been set up to establish and monitor standards of education and

training and to deal with fitness to practise issues. In addition, the Council has established two non-statutory committees to provide it with advice and guidance on specific issues.

The HCPC is a regulator and keeps a register of health and care professionals who meet their standards for their training, professional skills, behaviour and health. It is an offence for someone to claim they are registered with the HCPC when they are not or to use a protected title they are not entitled to use. Each of the professions regulated by the HCPC have at least one professional title that must be registered.

The HCPC accredits universities that offer social work qualifications at both qualifying and post-qualifying levels, and quality-assures all social work courses.

EDUCATION AND TRAINING

Social workers need a breadth of skills, as they will act as an adviser, advocate, counsellor and listener. There are various routes to becoming a social worker, but you will need to gain a professional qualification in social work (usually at degree level) either on a full-time or part-time basis. This is offered at under-graduate and postgraduate masters level. It is also possible to take a degree course combining social work with mental health or learning disability nursing. To find HCPC-approved degree courses visit www.hcpc-uk.org/education/programmes/register

Students following a social work course may be eligible for a bursary from the Department of Health.

For further information visit the NHS Business Authority website: www.nhsbsa.nhs.uk/837.aspx and the Gov.UK website: www.gov.uk/social-work-bursaries

REGISTRATION

Social work regulation in the UK is covered by the HCPC in England, The Care Council for Wales in Wales, the Scottish Social Services Council (SSSC) in Scotland and the Northern Ireland Social Care Council (NISCC) in Northern Ireland. It is possible to register with more than one regulator.

For further details, contact The Health and Care Professions Council, Park House, 184 Kennington Park Road, London SE11 4BU; Tel: 0300 500 6184; Fax: 020 7820 9684; e-mail: registration@hcpc-uk.org; website: www.hcpc-uk.org

For information about social work training and registration in Scotland, contact Scottish Social Services Council, Compass House, 11 Riverside Drive, Dundee DD1 4NY; Tel: 0345 6030 891; website: www.sssc.uk.com (online contact form).

For information about social work training and registration in Wales, contact Care Council for Wales, South Gate House, Wood Street, Cardiff CF10 1EW; Tel: 0300 3033 444; e-mail: info@ccwales.org.uk; website: www.ccwales.org.uk

For information about social work training and registration in Northern Ireland, contact Northern Ireland Social Care Council, 7th Floor, Millennium House, 19--25 Great Victoria Street, Belfast BT2 7AQ; Tel: 028 9536 2600; e-mail: info@niscc.hscni.net; website: www.niscc.info

Membership of Professional Institutions and Associations

THE BRITISH ASSOCIATION OF SOCIAL WORKERS

16 Kent Street
Birmingham B5 6RD
Tel: 0121 6223911
Fax: 0121 6224860
E-mail: membership@basw.co.uk
Website: www.basw.co.uk

The BASW is the largest professional association representing social work and social workers in the UK. Whether you are qualified or not, experienced or just entering the profession, we are here to help, support, advise and campaign on your behalf.

MEMBERSHIP
Student Member
Affiliate
Member (4 categories)
Retired Member
Overseas Member

SOCIOLOGY
Membership of Professional Institutions and Associations

BRITISH SOCIOLOGICAL ASSOCIATION

Bailey Suite, Palatine House
Belmont Business Park
Belmont
Durham DH1 1TW
Tel: 0191 383 0839
Fax: 0191 383 0782
E-mail: enquiries@britsoc.org.uk
Website: www.britsoc.co.uk

The BSA was founded in 1951 to promote sociology in the UK. Our members include researchers, teachers, students and practitioners in a variety of fields. We provide a network of communication to all who are concerned with the promotion and use of sociology and sociological research.

SPEECH AND LANGUAGE THERAPY
Membership of Professional Institutions and Associations

ROYAL COLLEGE OF SPEECH AND LANGUAGE THERAPISTS

2 White Hart Yard
London SE1 1NX
Tel: 020 7378 1200
E-mail: info@rcslt.org
Website: www.rcslt.org

The RCSLT is the professional body for speech and language therapists and support workers. We set, promote and maintain high standards in education, clinical practice and ethical conduct. Our national campaigning work aims to improve services for people with speech, language, communication and swallowing needs and to influence health, education and social care policies.

MEMBERSHIP
Student Member
Newly Qualified Member
Full Member
Fellow (FRCSLT)
Honorary Fellow (Hon FRCSLT)

DESIGNATORY LETTERS
FRCSLT, Hon FRCSLT

SPORTS SCIENCE
Membership of Professional Institutions and Associations

LONDON SCHOOL OF SOFT TISSUE THERAPY

28 Station Parade
Willesden Green
London NW2 4NX
Tel: 020 8452 8855
Fax: 020 8452 4524
E-mail: via website
Website: www.lssm.com

.

MEMBERSHIP
Member

QUALIFICATION/EXAMINATIONS
Introductory Massage Workshop

Professional Diploma in Clinical Soft Tissue Therapy
(BTEC Level 5)

DESIGNATORY LETTERS
.

STATISTICS
Membership of Professional Institutions and Associations

THE ROYAL STATISTICAL SOCIETY

12 Errol Street
London EC1Y 8LX
Tel: 020 7638 8998
E-mail: rss@rss.org.uk
Website: www.rss.org.uk

The RSS is the learned society and professional body for statistics and statisticians in the UK. We have over 7,000 members worldwide, and are active in a wide range of areas both directly and indirectly relating to the study and application of statistics.

MEMBERSHIP
Student Member
Fellow

Affiliate
Graduate Statistician (GradStat)
Chartered Statistician (CStat)

QUALIFICATION/EXAMINATIONS
Ordinary Certificate in Statistics
Higher Certificate in Statistics
Graduate Diploma in Statistics

DESIGNATORY LETTERS
GradStat, CStat

STOCKBROKING AND SECURITIES
Membership of Professional Institutions and Associations

CFA SOCIETY OF THE UK

2nd Floor
135 Canon Street
London EC4N 5BP
Tel: 020 7280 9620
Fax: 020 7280 9636
E-mail: info@cfauk.org
Website: www.cfauk.org

The CFA Society of the UK was formerly the UK Society of Investment Professionals (UKSIP) and was renamed in 2007. Our aim is to promote the development of the investment profession in the UK through the promotion of the highest standards of ethical behaviour and the provision of education, professional development, information, career support and advocacy to our members.

MEMBERSHIP
IMC Member
Candidate Member
Affiliate Member
Regular Member

QUALIFICATION/EXAMINATIONS
Investment Management Certificate (IMC)

THE CHARTERED INSTITUTE FOR SECURITIES & INVESTMENT

8 Eastcheap
London EC3M 1AE
Tel: 020 7645 0600
E-mail: customersupport@cisi.org
Website: www.cisi.org.uk

The Chartered Institute for Securities & Investment is the largest professional body for practitioners in stockbroking, derivatives markets, investment management, corporate finance, operations and related activities, having over 44,000 members.

MEMBERSHIP
Student Member
Affiliate
Associate (ACSI)
Member (MCSI)
Chartered Member (Ch. MCSI)
Fellow (FCSI)
Chartered Fellow (Ch. FCSI)

QUALIFICATION/EXAMINATIONS
Introduction to Investment
Islamic Finance Qualification
IT in Investment Operations
Risk in Financial Services
Combating Financial Crime

Global Financial Compliance
Investment Operations Certificate (IOC) also known as Investment Administration Qualification (IAQ)
Certificate in Corporate Finance
Certificate in Investments
Certificate in Private Client Investment Advice & Management
International Certificate in Wealth Management
Investment Advice Diploma
Advanced Certificate in Global Securities Operations
Advanced Certificate in Operational Risk
Diploma in Investment Compliance
Diploma in Investment Operations
CISI Diploma
CISI Masters in Wealth Management
Fundamentals of Financial Services
International Introduction to Investment
Diploma in Finance, Risk & Investment
Certificate in Finance Risk & Decision Making

Certificate for Introduction to Securities & Investment
Level 3 Certificate in Investment Management
Level 3 International Certificate in Investment Management

Level 4 Certificate in Investment Management

DESIGNATORY LETTERS
ACSI, MCSI, Ch. MCSI, FCSI, Ch. FCSI

SURGICAL, DENTAL AND CARDIOLOGICAL TECHNICIANS
Membership of Professional Institutions and Associations

THE BRITISH INSTITUTE OF DENTAL AND SURGICAL TECHNOLOGISTS

4 Thompson Green
Shipley
West Yorkshire BD17 7PR
Tel: 0115 9683 182
E-mail: via website
Website: www.bidst.org

The BIDST has been established for over 70 years and exists to provide a vehicle for the continuing education of technicians within the spheres of dental and surgical technology. It is our aim to make membership of the Institute an aspiration for all technicians, raising standards and portraying an image of professionalism which professional technicians deserve.

MEMBERSHIP
Affiliate (Overseas)
Affiliate (DCP)
Affiliate (Student)
Associate
Member
Fellow
Corporate Member

DESIGNATORY LETTERS
LBIDST, FBIDST

SURVEYING
Membership of Professional Institutions and Associations

CHARTERED ASSOCIATION OF BUILDING ENGINEERS

Lutyens House
Billing Brook Road
Weston Favell
Northampton
Northamptonshire NN3 8NW
Tel: 44 (0)1604 404 121
E-mail: info@cbuilde.com
Website: www.cbuilde.com

The ABE is the professional body for those specializing in the technology of building and the management processes by which buildings are designed, constructed, renewed and maintained. Our objectives are to promote and advance the planning, design, construction, maintenance and repair of the built environment; to maintain a high standard of professional practice; and to encourage cooperation between professionals.

MEMBERSHIP
Student
Technician
Training Affiliate
Academic Affiliate
Associate Member (ABEng)
Graduate Member (GradBEng)
Corporate Member (MBEng)
Corporate Fellow (FBEng)
Honorary Fellow (HonFBEng)

QUALIFICATION/EXAMINATIONS
ABBE Level 3 NVQ Diploma in Town Planning Technical Support (QCF)
ABBE Level 3 NVQ Diploma in Conservation Technical Support (QCF)
ABBE Level 3 NVQ Diploma in Building Control Technical Support (QCF)
ABBE Level 6 NVQ Diploma in Building Control (QCF)

ABBE Level 6 NVQ Diploma in Town Planning (QCF)
Edexcel Level 3 NVQ Diploma in Construction Site Supervision (Construction) (QCF)
Edexcel Level 3 NVQ Diploma in Construction Contracting Operations (QCF)
Edexcel Level 6 NVQ Diploma in Construction Contracting Operations (QCF)
Edexcel Level 6 NVQ Diploma in Construction Site Management (Construction) (QCF)
Edexcel Level 6 NVQ Diploma in Senior Site Inspection (QCF)
Edexcel Level 6 NVQ Diploma in Built Environment Design Management (QCF)
Edexcel Level 7 NVQ Diploma in Built Environment Design and Consultancy Practice (QCF)
Edexcel Level 7 NVQ Diploma in Construction Senior Management (QCF)

DESIGNATORY LETTERS
ABEng, GradBEng, MBEng, FBEng

SWIMMING INSTRUCTION
Membership of Professional Institutions and Associations

THE SWIMMING TEACHERS' ASSOCIATION

Anchor House
Birch Street
Walsall
West Midlands WS2 8HZ
Tel: 01922 645097
Fax: 01922 720628
E-mail: sta@sta.co.uk
Website: www.sta.co.uk

The STA is dedicated to the preservation of human life by the teaching of swimming, lifesaving and survival techniques to as many people as possible, both in the UK and internationally. We offer a range of specialist training programmes and qualifications, which are used in more than 25 countries worldwide, and liaise with other organizations concerned with swimming teaching and water safety.

MEMBERSHIP
Junior Member
Associate Member (ASTA)
Qualified Member (MSTA)
Corporate Member

QUALIFICATION/EXAMINATIONS
STA Level 2 Award in Swimming Teaching (QCF)
STA Level 2 Certificate in Swimming Teaching (QCF)
STA Level 1 Award for Pool to Open Water Swimming Coaching (QCF)
STA Level 2 Award for Open Water Swimming Coaching (QCF)
STA Level 2 Award in Aquatic Teaching – People with Disabilities (QCF)
STA Level 2 Award in Aquatic Teaching – Baby & Pre-School (QCF)
STA Level 1 Award in Pool Emergency Procedures (QCF)
STA Level 2 Award for Pool Responder (QCF)
STA Level 2 Award for Pool Lifeguard (QCF)

STA Level 2 Award in Emergency First Aid at Work (QCF)

STA Level 2 Award in Paediatric First Aid (QCF)

STA Level 2 Award in Activity First Aid (QCF)

STA Level 2 Award in Swimming Pool Water Testing (QCF)

STA Level 2 Award in Swimming Pool Water Treatment (QCF)

STA Level 3 Award in Pool Plant Operations (QCF)

STA Level 3 Award in Preparing to Teach in the Lifelong Learning Sector (QCF)

STA Level 4 Award in Preparing to Teach in the Lifelong Learning Sector (QCF)

STA Professional Award in Teaching Swimming at SCQF Level 6

STA Professional Certificate in Teaching Swimming

STA Professional Award in Aquatic Teaching – Baby and Pre-School at SCQF Level 6

STA Professional Award in Pool Emergency Procedures at SCQF Level 6

STA Professional Award for Pool Responder at SCQF Level 7

STA Professional Award for Pool Lifeguard at SCQF Level 7

STA Award in Emergency First Aid at Work at SCQF Level 5

STA Award in First Aid at Work at SCQF Level 6

DESIGNATORY LETTERS
ASTA, MSTA

TAXATION
Membership of Professional Institutions and Associations

SOCIETY OF TRUST & ESTATE PRACTITIONERS

Artillery House (South)
11–19 Artillery Row
London SW1P 1RT
Tel: +44 (0)20 7340 0500
Fax: +44 (0)20 7340 0501
E-mail: step@step.org
Website: www.step.org

The Society of Trust and Estate Practitioners (STEP) is the worldwide professional association for practitioners dealing with family inheritance and succession planning. The Society helps to improve public understanding of the issues families face in this area and promotes education and high professional standards among its members.

MEMBERSHIP
Full members of STEP are the most experienced and senior practitioners in the field of trusts and estates.

QUALIFICATION/EXAMINATIONS
STEP Diplomas and Certificates are recognised as essential qualifications and TEPs are sought after by employers. A portfolio of courses has been designed to enhance your career, including the STEP Diploma for England & Wales (Trusts and Estates), STEP Diploma for Ireland, STEP Diploma for Scotland, STEP Diploma in International Trust Management and the STEP Diploma for Accountants & Tax Practitioners. The Certificate series includes the STEP Advanced Certificate in Family Business Advising, the STEP Certificate for Financial Services (Trusts and Estate Planning) and many more.

DESIGNATORY LETTERS
STEP

THE ASSOCIATION OF TAXATION TECHNICIANS

1st Floor
Artillery House
11–19 Artillery Row
London SW1P 1RT
Tel: 020 7340 0551
E-mail: info@att.org.uk
Website: www.att.org.uk

The ATT was founded in 1989 in recognition of the increasing demand for tax services and the development of tax practice as a professional activity in its own right. Our primary aim is to provide an appropriate qualification for individuals who undertake such work, and we now have more than 10,500 members, affiliates and registered students.

MEMBERSHIP
Member

QUALIFICATION/EXAMINATIONS
Certificate of Competency

DESIGNATORY LETTERS
ATT

THE CHARTERED INSTITUTE OF TAXATION

First Floor
11–19 Artillery Row
London SW1P 1RT
Tel: 020 7340 0550
E-mail: via website
Website: www.tax.org.uk

The CIOT, which dates from 1930, is the professional body for Chartered Tax Advisers and has 14,300 members. Our aims are to promote education in and the study of the administration and practice of taxation, and to achieve a better, more efficient, tax system for all affected by it – taxpayers, advisers and the authorities.

MEMBERSHIP
Member (CTA)

QUALIFICATION/EXAMINATIONS
Chartered Tax Adviser (CTA) examination
Advanced Diploma in International Taxation (ADIT)
VAT Compliance Diploma (VCD) (offered by the Institute of Indirect Taxation)

DESIGNATORY LETTERS
CTA, ATII, FTII

TAXI DRIVERS
Membership of Professional Institutions and Associations

TAXI DRIVERS (LONDON)

Cab drivers and cab proprietors in the Metropolitan Police District and City of London are licensed by an Assistant Commissioner of the Metropolitan Police, through the Public Carriage Office at 15 Penton Street, Islington N1 9PU. A cab driver's licence is valid for 3 years and a cab proprietor's licence for 1 year.

TEACHING/EDUCATION

Initial qualifications in the UK

Qualified Teacher Status

To obtain a teaching appointment as a qualified teacher in maintained schools and non-maintained special schools in England and Wales, it is necessary to have Qualified Teacher Status (QTS). To be qualified, teachers must have satisfactorily completed an approved course of initial teacher training (ITT), and to be able to teach in maintained schools in England must have successfully completed their induction period (there are similar arrangements for teaching in Scotland, Wales and Northern Ireland). The National College for Teaching and Leadership (NCTL), an executive agency of the Department for Education, is the awarding body for QTS.

Qualified Teacher Learning and Skills

Qualified Teacher Learning and Skills (QTLS) status is recognised in law as equal to QTS for teaching in schools. The Society for Education and Training (SET) provides QTLS which you can gain by successfully completing professional formation -- a process that enables you to demonstrate the ability to use effectively the skills and knowledge acquired whilst training to be a teacher and also the application of the occupational standards required of a teacher.

To apply for QTLS, you need an initial teacher training qualification at Level 5, for example, equivalent to the Diploma to Teach in the Lifelong Learning Sector (DTLLS) or Diploma in Education and Training (DET). You are also required to demonstrate numeracy and literacy qualifications at (or above) Level 2.

The Society for Education and Training also offers a recognition route to QTLS for members with substantial teaching experience but who do not hold a recognised teaching qualification. Visit the SET website for more information: https://set.etfoundation.co.uk. The Society for Education and Training, 157-197 Buckingham Palace Road, London, SW1W 9SP; telephone: 0800 093 9111 (free) or 020 3092 5001 (local call); email: membership.enquiries@etfoundation.co.uk.

Teacher training courses

Initial teacher training courses in England and Wales are provided by accredited training providers mainly through university departments of education. Courses available include Bachelor of Arts or Bachelor of Science with QTS, Bachelor of Education (BEd) for undergraduates, and Postgraduate Certificates of Education (PGCEs) for graduates.

Undergraduate training courses generally take three or four years full time, or four to six years part time. However, if you have undergraduate credits from previous study you may be able to complete a course in two years. A PGCE generally lasts one year full time, or up to two years part time.

There are also some employment-based routes into teaching. The School Direct Programme allows schools to recruit trainees with the expectation that they will go on to work in the school or group of schools in which they have been trained, though there is no guarantee of employment. There are more than 100 schools offering places. Courses generally last for one year full time.

School Direct offers two separate training options: the School Direct Training Programme and the School Direct Training Programme (salaried). The School Direct Training Programme (salaried) is open to graduates with three or more years' career experience (there may be exceptions for some subjects). Trainees will be employed as unqualified teachers with a salary subsidised by The National College for Teaching and Leadership. Trainees on a School Direct Training Programme will have to pay tuition fees to cover the cost of the course, but home and EU trainees will be eligible for a tuition fee loan to cover these costs and you might be eligible for funding through training bursaries or scholarships. For more information, see The National College for Teaching and Leadership, School Direct (https://www.gov.uk/government/organisations/national-college-for-teaching-and-leadership). With School Direct, you are selected for training by a school or group of schools in partnership with a university or SCITT.

School-centred initial teacher training (SCITT) is training in a school environment for those with a UK degree or an equivalent qualification. SCITT programmes are designed and delivered by groups of neighbouring schools and colleges; they are usually full time for one year. Taught by experienced, practising teachers, and often tailored towards local teaching needs, all SCITT courses lead to QTS. Many, though not all, will also award you a PGCE validated by a higher education institution. There are consortia of schools and colleges running SCITT courses all over England. These groups provide all kinds of SCITT, covering primary, middle years and the full range of secondary subjects. Application for SCITT courses is usually through UCAS (www.ucas.com/ ucas/teacher-training).

Teach First offers a two-year Leadership Development Programme for those interested in an employment-based route into teaching. Teach First enables graduates with a 2:1 or a First to spend two years working in secondary and primary schools in low income communities while earning a full-time salary. It offers the programme in different regions in the UK; during the application process you will be able to state your local area preference but they recommend that you be open minded about local area and understand that they will prioritise the needs of the schools and their children over the preferences of applicants. A PGCE is awarded on completion of the course. Candidates have to demonstrate a high proficiency in eight core competencies throughout this process to ensure they can achieve real impact for pupils: Humility, respect and empathy, interaction, leadership, planning and organising, problem solving, resilience, self-evaluation, and knowledge of Teach First and their academic subjects. Visit the Teach First website for further information: www.teachfirst.org.uk.

There are also other ways into teaching, including Troops to Teachers, Researchers in Schools and Assessment Only. Further details can be found at https://getintoteaching.education.gov.uk/explore-my-options/teacher-training-routes.

The qualification of Professional Graduate Diploma in Education (PGDE) is a one-year postgraduate degree course leading to registration as a primary or secondary school teacher in Scotland (see www.teachinscotland.org). Alternatively it is possible to undertake a four-year undergraduate degree course in education. In Scotland there are seven universities that offer teacher training courses: University of Aberdeen, University of Dundee, University of Edinburgh, University of Stirling, University of Glasgow, University of Strathclyde and University of the West of Scotland. For more information on how to apply for a teaching course in Scotland contact the Universities and Colleges Admissions System (UCAS), Tel: 0371 468 0469, www.ucas.com/ ucas/teacher-training. The General Teaching Council for Scotland is also a useful source of information: www.gtcs.org.uk.

The Education Workforce Council (EWC) is the independent regulator in Wales for teachers in maintained schools, Further Education teachers and learning support staff in both school and FE settings. Contact details: EWC 9th Floor Eastgate House, 35--

43 Newport Road, Cardiff, CF24 0AB; Tel: 029 20460099; Fax: 029 20475850; e-mail: information@ewc.wales; website: www.ewc.wales. EWC is responsible for administering the award of Qualified Teacher Status (QTS) in Wales, on behalf of the Welsh Government. The main ways to gain QTS in Wales are completion of a course of teacher training at an accredited institution in Wales (see www.teachertrainingcymru.org/home) or completion of employment-based training under the Graduate Teacher Programme (GTP). GTP programmes in Wales are managed and delivered by three regional centres of teacher training and education on behalf of the Welsh Government. Their contact details can be found at http://teachertrainingcymru.org/4

Initial Teacher Education (ITE) in Northern Ireland consists of the Postgraduate Certificate of Education course, approved by the Department of Education Northern Ireland, or a four-year BEd(Hons) course, which leads to recognition as a schoolteacher in Northern Ireland (see www.education-ni.gov.uk).

Qualifications for admission to training

Higher education institutions offering undergraduate ITT or ITE courses will set admissions criteria, typically two good A levels (or equivalent qualifications). Entrants to PGCE and other graduate training courses will require a relevant UK Bachelor's degree or a recognized equivalent and be expected to demonstrate a standard equivalent to GCSE grade C in English and mathematics (in Wales grade B, or equivalent is required), and additionally a standard equivalent to GCSE grade C in a science subject for those wishing to train to teach primary school children. Trainees who have undertaken their initial teacher training in England must pass professional skills tests in numeracy and literacy before starting the course. These tests cover core skills that teachers need in their jobs and QTS cannot be awarded until they are passed. If you are undertaking initial teacher training in Wales, you are not required to complete the skills tests in order to be awarded QTS.

There are various funding options available to support you throughout your teacher training. These include tax-free scholarships and bursaries. Your eligibility for financial support, and the amount you can expect to receive, generally depends on the subject you choose to teach, the class of your degree, and sometimes other qualifications and experience are taken into account too.

The National College for Teaching and Leadership
The National College for Teaching and Leadership is the executive agency of the Department for

Education (DfE). It is the body responsible for ITT in England and the award of QTS. It has two key aims: improving the quality of the education workforce; and helping schools to help each other to improve. NCTL works with schools to develop an education system supported locally by partnerships and led by the best head teachers. For information about the College, visit www.gov.uk/government/organisations/national-college-for-teaching-and-leadership.

General Teaching Councils

General Teaching Councils exist in Wales (EWC), Scotland (GTCS) and Northern Ireland (GTCNI). These councils hold registers of qualified teachers and also act as disciplinary bodies. You can find out more from their respective websites: EWC: www.ewc.wales; GTCS: www.gtcs.org.uk; GTCNI: www.gtcni.org.uk

Applications

Applications for undergraduate and postgraduate courses are made through UCAS. For courses in Northern Ireland visit the Department for Education on Northern Ireland's website (www.education-ni.gov.uk). You can find out more about training to teach from the following websites: UCAS: www.ucas.com; The National College for Teaching and Leadership: www.gov.uk/government/organisations/national-college-for-teaching-and-leadership and https://getintoteaching.education.gov.uk for queries relating to becoming a teacher, initial teacher training, recruitment opportunities or provision of relevant training.

Membership of Professional Institutions and Associations

TECHNICAL COMMUNICATIONS
Membership of Professional Institutions and Associations

THE INSTITUTE OF SCIENTIFIC AND TECHNICAL COMMUNICATORS (ISTC LTD)

Airport House
Purley Way
Croydon CR0 0XZ
Tel: 020 8253 4506
Fax: 020 8253 4510
E-mail: istc@istc.org.uk
Website: www.istc.org.uk

The ISTC is a non-profit-making organization and the largest UK body representing professional communicators and information designers. Our aims include improving standards of scientific and technical communication, promoting scientific and technical communication as a career, supporting our members, and consulting, cooperating and collaborating with other bodies that share our ideals.

MEMBERSHIP
Student
Associate
Junior
Member (MISTC)
Fellow (FISTC)
Business Affiliate

DESIGNATORY LETTERS
MISTC, FISTC

TEXTILES

Membership of Professional Institutions and Associations

THE TEXTILE INSTITUTE

8th Floor St James' Buildings
79 Oxford Street
Manchester M1 6FQ
Tel: 0161 2371188
Fax: 0161 2361991
E-mail: tiihq@textileinst.org.uk
Website: www.textileinstitute.org

The Textile Institute covers all disciplines – from technology and production to design, development and marketing – relating to fibres, fabrics, clothing, footwear, and interior and technical textiles.

MEMBERSHIP
Student
Individual
Licentiate (LTI)

Associate (CText ATI)
Fellow (CText FTI)
Companion
Honorary Fellow
Corporate

DESIGNATORY LETTERS
LTI, CText ATI, CText FTI

TIMBER TECHNOLOGY

Membership of Professional Institutions and Associations

WOOD TECHNOLOGY SOCIETY

The Boilerhouse
Springfield Business Park
Caunt Road
Grantham
Lincs NG31 7FZ
Tel: 01476 513880
Fax: 01476 513899
E-mail: emily.drury@iom3.org
Website: www.iom3.org/content/wood-technology

The Wood Technology Society (IWSc – a Division of the Institute of Materials, Minerals and Mining), formerly the Institute of Wood Science, is the professional body for the timber and allied industries. We promote and encourage a better understanding of timber, wood-based materials and associated timber processes, and are the UK examining body, awarding qualifications at Foundation, Certificate and Diploma level.

MEMBERSHIP
Student Member

Affiliate Member
Technician (EngTech)
Fellow (FIMMM)
Professional Member (MIMMM)
Graduate (Grad IMMM)
Corporate Member

QUALIFICATION/EXAMINATIONS
Level 2 Award in Timber and Panel Products (QCF)
Certificate
Diploma

DESIGNATORY LETTERS
TIWSc, LIWSc, MIWSc, FIWSc

TOWN AND COUNTRY PLANNING
Membership of Professional Institutions and Associations

ROYAL TOWN PLANNING INSTITUTE

41 Botolph Lane
London EC3R 8DL
Tel: 020 7929 9494
E-mail: education@rtpi.org.uk
Website: www.rtpi.org.uk

The RTPI is the largest professional institute for planners in Europe, with over 24,000 members. As well as promoting spatial planning, we develop and shape policy affecting the built environment, work to raise professional standards and support members through their education, training and career development.

MEMBERSHIP
Chartered Town Planner (MRTPI)
Fellow (FRTPI)
Associate Member (AssocRTPI)
Legal Associate (LARTPI)
Licentiate Member
Student Member
Retired Member
Affiliate
Honorary Member

QUALIFICATION/EXAMINATIONS
From January 2017 all routes to become a Chartered Town Planner are competency based and applicants must submit an Assessment of Professional Competence.
There are a range of educational pathways to Chartered Membership although the majority of applicants will have studied an accredited planning degree. Please see www.rtpi.org.uk/findacourse for a list of accredited training providers.

DESIGNATORY LETTERS
MRTPI, FRTPI, LARTPI, AssocRTPI

TRADING STANDARDS
Membership of Professional Institutions and Associations

THE CHARTERED TRADING STANDARDS INSTITUTE

1 Sylvan Court
Sylvan Way
Southfields Business Park
Basildon
Essex SS15 6TH
Tel: 01268 582200
Fax: 01268 582225
E-mail: institute@tsi.org.uk
Website: www.tradingstandards.uk

The CTSI, formed in 1881, is a not-for-profit membership association representing trading standards professionals in both the public and private sectors in the UK and overseas. CTSI encourages honest enterprise and business, and helps safeguard the economic, environmental, health and social well-being of consumers.

MEMBERSHIP
Student Member
Affiliate Member
Associate Member (ACTSI)
Full Member (MCTSI)
Chartered Trading Standards Practitioner (CTSP)
Fellow (FCTSI)
Corporate Affiliate
International

QUALIFICATION/EXAMINATIONS
The Trading Standards Qualifications Framework consists of:

Certificate of Competence
Core Skills in Consumer Affairs and Trading Standards
Module Certificate in Consumer Affairs and Trading Standards
Diploma in Consumer Affairs and Trading Standards
Higher Certificate in Consumer Affairs and Trading Standards
Higher Diploma in Consumer Affairs and Trading Standards

DESIGNATORY LETTERS
ACTSI, MCTSI, CTSP, FCTSI

TRANSPORT
Membership of Professional Institutions and Associations

INSTITUTE OF TRANSPORT ADMINISTRATION

The Old Studio
25 Greenfield Road
Westoning
Bedfordshire MK45 5JD
Tel: 01525 634940
Fax: 01525 750016
E-mail: director@iota.org.uk
Website: www.iota.org.uk

The primary aim of IoTA is to broaden and improve the knowledge, skills and experience of its members in the practice of efficient road, rail, air and sea transport. We are one of the few professional bodies still recognized within the terms of the Road Traffic 1968 (Statutory Instrument 78), wherein it is permitted to proffer qualified opinion as to the professional competence of its members. Established in 1944, the Institute continues to set new benchmark standards for the industry; promoting a policy of Experience Teaches.

MEMBERSHIP
Student (StInstTA)
Associate (AInstTA)
Honorary Member
Associate Member (AMInstTA)
Member (MInstTA)
Fellow (FInstTA)
Patron Scheme for Companies

DESIGNATORY LETTERS
StInstTA, AInstTA, AMInstTA, MInstTA, FInstTA

THE INSTITUTE OF TRAFFIC ACCIDENT INVESTIGATORS

Column House
London Road
Shrewsbury
Shropshire SY2 6NN
Tel: 08456 212066
E-mail: gensec@itai.org
Website: www.itai.org

The Institute provides a means of communication, education, representation and regulation in the field of Traffic Accident Investigation. Our main aim is to provide a forum for spreading knowledge and enhancing expertise among those engaged in the discipline. Members include police officers, lecturers in higher education and private practitioners.

MEMBERSHIP
Affiliate
Associate (AITAI)
Member (MITAI)

DESIGNATORY LETTERS
AITAI, MITAI

TRAVEL AND TOURISM
Membership of Professional Institutions and Associations

CONFEDERATION OF TOURISM AND HOSPITALITY

37 Duke Street
London W1U 1LN
Tel: 020 7258 9850
Fax: 020 7258 9869
E-mail: info@cthawards.com
Website: www.cthawards.com

The Confederation of Tourism and Hospitality is an awarding body approved by Ofqual, and registered on the QCA's National Qualifications Framework. We were established in 1982 to provide recognized standards of management and vocational training appropriate to the needs of the hotel and travel industries, via our syllabuses, examinations and awards.

MEMBERSHIP
Student Member
Professional Member (MCTH)
Honorary Fellow (FCTH)

QUALIFICATION/EXAMINATIONS
Level 2 Diploma in English Communication Skills (QCF)

Level 3 Diploma in Communication and Research Skills (QCF)
Level 3 Diploma in Tourism and Hospitality (QCF)
Level 4 Diploma in Hospitality Management (QCF)
Level 4 Diploma in Tourism Management (QCF)
Level 5 Diploma in Hospitality Management (QCF)
Level 5 Diploma in Tourism Management (QCF)
Level 6 Diploma in Hospitality and Tourism Management (QCF)
Level 7 Diploma in Hospitality and Tourism Management (QCF)

DESIGNATORY LETTERS
MCTH, FCTH

INSTITUTE OF TRAVEL AND TOURISM

PO Box 217
Ware
Hertfordshire SG12 8WY
Tel: 0844 4995 653
Fax: 0844 4995 654
E-mail: enquiries@itt.co.uk
Website: www.itt.co.uk

The ITT, founded in 1956, is a professional membership body for individuals employed in the travel and tourism industry. We provide support and guidance for our members throughout their career and offer them CPD and training to maintain standards for the benefit of the industry as a whole.

MEMBERSHIP
Student Member
Introductory Member
Affiliate Member
Member
Member (MInstTT)
Fellow
Fellow (FInstTT)
University/College Member
Group Member
Corporate Member
Retired Member

DESIGNATORY LETTERS
MInstTT, FInstTT

THE TOURISM MANAGEMENT INSTITUTE

c/o Hon Secretary, Dr Cathy Guthrie, FTMI, FTS
18 Cuninghill Avenue
Inverurie
Aberdeenshire AB51 3TZ
Tel: 01467 620769
E-mail: secretary@tmi.org.uk
Website: www.tmi.org.uk

TMI is the professional body for tourism destination managers. Its network of 250+ members shares information via website, conferences, e-mails and newsletters. The TMI CPD programme aims to support destination management professionals throughout their career. TMI HE Course Recognition gives students & lecturers assurance of industry engagement, relevance and employability.

MEMBERSHIP
Student
Associate (ATMI)
Member (MTMI)
Fellow (FTMI)

DESIGNATORY LETTERS
ATMI, MTMI, FTMI

THE TOURISM SOCIETY

Queens House
55–56 Lincoln's Inn Fields
London WC2A 3BH
Tel: 020 7269 9693
Fax: 020 7404 2465
E-mail: admin@tourismsociety.org
Website: www.tourismsociety.org

The Tourism Society, founded in 1977, is the professional membership body for people working in all sectors of tourism. We strive to drive up standards of professionalism and act as an advocate of tourism to the government and the public and private sectors, and liaise with other tourism professionals worldwide. We also provide advice, support and networking opportunities to our 1,200 or so members.

MEMBERSHIP
Student
Full Member (MTS)
Fellow (FTS)
Overseas/Retired Member
Group Member
Corporate Member
Graduate

DESIGNATORY LETTERS
MTS, FTS

VETERINARY SCIENCE
Membership of Professional Institutions and Associations

BRITISH VETERINARY ASSOCIATION

7 Mansfield Street
London W1G 9NQ
Tel: 020 7636 6541
Fax: 020 7908 6349
E-mail: bvahq@bva.co.uk
Website: www.bva.co.uk

The BVA is the representative body for the veterinary profession in the UK and has more than 11,500 members. We promote and support the interests of our members and the animals under their care, liaise with the government and are the leading provider of veterinary information to the media and general public.

MEMBERSHIP
Student Member
Associate Member
Full Member
Overseas Member

ROYAL COLLEGE OF VETERINARY SURGEONS

Belgravia House
62–64 Horseferry Road
London SW1P 2AF
Tel: 020 7222 2001
Fax: 020 7222 2004
E-mail: info@rcvs.org.uk
Website: www.rcvs.org.uk

The RCVS is the regulatory body for veterinary surgeons and veterinary nurses in the UK. We aim to enhance society through improved animal health and welfare. We do this by setting, upholding and advancing the educational, ethical and clinical standards of veterinary surgeons and veterinary nurses.

MEMBERSHIP
Member (MRCVS)

Fellow (FRCVS)
Registered veterinary nurse (RVN)

QUALIFICATION/EXAMINATIONS
Certificate in Advanced Veterinary Practice (CertAVP)
Diploma in Advanced Veterinary Nursing (DipAVN)

DESIGNATORY LETTERS
MRCVS, FRCVS, RVN

SOCIETY OF PRACTISING VETERINARY SURGEONS

The Governor's House
Cape Road
Warwick CV34 5DJ
Tel: 01926 410454
Fax: 01926 411350
E-mail: office@spvs.org.uk
Website: www.spvs.org.uk

The SPVS was founded in 1933 with the aim of promoting the interests of veterinary surgeons in private practice. We are a non-territorial division of the British Veterinary Association. Our remit is to advise on all aspects of managing the business of a clinical veterinary practice, and we hold one-day, weekend and week-long courses and an annual congress.

MEMBERSHIP
Student Member
Graduate Member
Practice Member
Retired Member

WASTES MANAGEMENT
Membership of Professional Institutions and Associations

CHARTERED INSTITUTION OF WASTES MANAGEMENT

9 Saxon Court
St Peter's Gardens
Marefair
Northampton NN1 1SX
Tel: 01604 620426
Fax: 01604 621339
E-mail: membership@ciwm.co.uk
Website: www.ciwm.co.uk

The CIWM represents more than 6,000 waste management professionals – predominantly in the UK but also overseas. We promote education, training and research in the scientific, technical and practical aspects of waste management for the safeguarding of the environment, and set and strive to maintain high standards for individuals working in the waste management industry.

MEMBERSHIP
Student Member
Technician Member (TechMCIWM)
Associate Member (AssocMCIWM)
Graduate Member (GradMCIWM)
Licentiate (LCIWM)
Member (MCIWM)
Fellow (FCIWM)
Affiliated Organization

QUALIFICATION/EXAMINATIONS
CIWM Training Services specializes in developing and providing waste management training for individuals and organizations. Each year we organize more than 70 courses. For details see the website.

DESIGNATORY LETTERS
TechMCIWM, AssocMCIWM, GradMCIWM, LCIWM, MCIWM, FCIWM

WATCH AND CLOCK MAKING AND REPAIRING
Membership of Professional Institutions and Associations

THE BRITISH HOROLOGICAL INSTITUTE LIMITED

Upton Hall
Upton
Newark
Nottinghamshire NG23 5TE
Tel: 01636 813795
Fax: 01636 812258
E-mail: via website
Website: www.bhi.co.uk

The BHI, which was formed in 1858 to promote horology, is a professional body with about 3,000 members worldwide. We provide education and specialist training, set recognized standards of excellence in workmanship and professional conduct, and support our members in their work, making, repairing and servicing clocks and watches.

MEMBERSHIP
Associate
Member (MBHI)
Fellow (FBHI)

QUALIFICATION/EXAMINATIONS
Diploma in Clock and Watch Servicing (Level 3)

Diploma in the Servicing and Repair of Clocks / Watches (Level 4)	*DESIGNATORY LETTERS*
	MBHI, FBHI
Diploma in the Repair, Restoration and Conservation of Clocks / Watches (Level 5)	

WELDING

Membership of Professional Institutions and Associations

THE WELDING INSTITUTE

Granta Park
Great Abington
Cambridge CB21 6AL
Tel: 01223 899000
E-mail: professional@twi.co.uk
Website: www.theweldinginstitute.com

The Welding Institute is the engineering institution for welding and joining professionals. We are committed to promoting the importance of welding/materials joining technology, given its importance as a key industrial technology governing the reliability and safety of many products, and to the advancement of education, training and CPD for our members.

MEMBERSHIP
Associate (AWeldI)

Technician (TechWeldI)
Member (MWeldI)
Fellow (FWeldI)
Engineering Technician (EngTech)
Incorporated Engineer (IEng)
Chartered Engineer (CEng)

DESIGNATORY LETTERS
AWeldI, TechWeldI, MWeldI, FWeldI, EngTech, IEng, CEng

WELFARE

Membership of Professional Institutions and Associations

INSTITUTE OF WELFARE

PO Box 5570
Stourbridge DY8 9BA
Tel: 0800 0 32 37 25
E-mail: info@instituteofwelfare.co.uk
Website: www.instituteofwelfare.co.uk

The Institute of Welfare was founded in 1945 and exists to promote the highest possible standards in the delivery of welfare to those who need it. We make representations to government, undertake research on welfare issues, encourage and facilitate the exchange of information, and provide opportunities for those engaged in welfare work to pursue CPD.

MEMBERSHIP
Affiliate Member
Member (MIW)
Fellow (FIW)
Companion (CIW)

DESIGNATORY LETTERS
MIW, FIW, CIW

Part 6

Bodies Accrediting
Independent Institutions

THE BRITISH ACCREDITATION COUNCIL FOR INDEPENDENT FURTHER AND HIGHER EDUCATION (BAC)

BAC is a registered charity that was established in 1984 to act as the national accrediting body for independent further and higher education. It is independent of both government and of the colleges it accredits.

A college that is accredited by BAC undergoes a thorough inspection every three or four years, with an interim visit in the middle of the accreditation cycle. BAC accreditation is not only available to colleges in the United Kingdom, there are now accredited colleges in 11 countries around the world. At present BAC accredits or approves 201 colleges in the United Kingdom and 25 overseas. Lists of accredited colleges are published each year; full details can be viewed on the BAC website (www.the-bac.org).

BAC has a close relationship with the accreditation scheme operated by Accreditation UK (in the field of English as a Foreign Language) and is a member of ENQA, the European Association for Quality Assurance in Higher Education. It maintains close links with The British Council, UK Council for International Student Affairs (UKCISA), UK NARIC, OFQUAL and the Federation of Awarding Bodies (FAB) and The Accreditation Body for Language Services (ABLS). In 2015 it was admitted onto the European Quality Assurance Register for Higher Education (EQAR).

Accreditation by BAC is recognized by the UK Visas and Immigration (UKVI) department of the Home Office as a qualifying requirement for institutions to enrol visa students.

Contact details for BAC are: BAC, Ground Floor, 14 Devonshire Square, London, EC2M 4YT; Tel: 0300 330 1400; Fax: 0300 330 1401; e-mail: info@the-bac.org; website: www.the-bac.org

THE BRITISH COUNCIL

The British Council runs the Accreditation UK scheme in partnership with English UK for the inspection and accreditation of organizations that provide courses in English as a Foreign Language (EFL) in Britain. The British Council aims to make quality language materials available to learners and teachers all over the world, and they offer over three million UK examinations worldwide, helping people gain access to trusted qualifications to support their career and study prospects.

Under the terms of the scheme, institutions are inspected rigorously every four years in the areas of management, resources and environment, teaching and learning, welfare and student services and care of under 18s. The scheme also includes a system of random spot-checking. The management and policy of the scheme are conducted by an independent board while a separate independent committee reviews inspectors' reports.

The majority of recognized schools are also members of English UK, which insists on British Council accreditation as a criterion for membership. In addition, all English UK members, of which there are around 450, are required to abide by the Association's Code of Practice and Regulations. English UK exists to raise the high standards of its members even further through conferences, training courses and publications. The association also represents the interests of members and students to government bodies, and promotes international student mobility.

Further information on the Accreditation UK scheme may be obtained from the Accreditation Unit, British Council, Bridgewater House, 58 Whitworth Street, Manchester M1 6BB;

Tel: 0161 957 7755; or use the online enquiry form at www.britishcouncil.org/contact; website: www.britishcouncil.org/education/accreditation

Further information on English UK may be obtained from English UK, 219 St John Street, London EC1V 4LY; Tel: 020 7608 7960; Fax: 020 7608 7961; e-mail: info@englishuk.com; website: www.englishuk.com

THE OPEN AND DISTANCE LEARNING QUALITY COUNCIL (ODLQC)

ODLQC was established in 1968 as the Council for the Accreditation of Correspondence Colleges, a joint initiative of the then Labour government and representatives of the sector. It is the principal accrediting body for a wide variety of providers of open and distance learning (ODL) in the UK, from commercial colleges to professional and public-sector institutions. Now independent, it nevertheless continues to have the informal support of government. ODLQC promotes quality by:

- establishing standards of education and training in ODL;
- recognizing good quality provision, wherever it occurs;
- supporting and protecting the interests of learners;
- encouraging the improvement of existing methods and the development of new ones;
- linking ODL with other forms of education and training;
- promoting wider recognition of the value of ODL.

Accreditation includes a rigorous assessment of educational provision, covering materials, tutorial support, publicity, contractual arrangements with learners and general administrative procedures, each of which is measured against the Council's published benchmark standards. If accredited, the provider is monitored on a regular basis and reassessed at least once every three years.

The Council promotes those colleges that it accredits, which are by definition quality providers of ODL, and acts as honest broker in matching accredited colleges to potential markets. A list of accredited providers is included on the Council's website: www.odlqc.org.uk. The Council also seeks to protect the interests of learners by promoting the importance of accreditation, and by offering advice and support directly to learners. At the same time, knowledge of good practice is disseminated more widely, and quality encouraged wherever ODL occurs.

The Council consists of members drawn from professional and public bodies involved in education, as well as representatives of accredited providers, and has strong links with other bodies in the sector, both in the UK and abroad.

All enquiries should be through the contact form on the website: www.odlqc.org.uk

THE COUNCIL FOR INDEPENDENT EDUCATION (CIFE)

CIFE was founded in 1973 to promote strict adherence by independent sixth-form and tutorial colleges to the highest standards of academic and professional integrity and to provide an inspection service for these colleges. All member colleges must be accredited by the British Accreditation Council for Independent Further and Higher Education (BAC), and/or the Independent Schools Inspectorate (ISI). CIFE colleges all undergo regular inspection by the Department for Education

They are also inspected either by the British Accreditation Council, the Independent Schools Inspectorate, or both. Ofsted (Office for Standards in Education) check college-provided accommodation and student welfare. Candidate membership is available for up to three years for colleges that are seeking BAC or ISI accreditation and otherwise satisfy CIFE's exacting membership criteria. All colleges must also abide by stringent codes of conduct and practice; the character and presentation of their published exam results are subject to regulation, and the accuracy of the information must be validated by BAC as academic auditor to CIFE. Full members are subject to reinspection by their accrediting bodies. There are 19 colleges in full or candidate membership of CIFE at present, spread throughout England but with concentrations in London and Oxford.

CIFE colleges offer a wide range of GCSE, A and AS level courses. In addition, some CIFE colleges offer English language tuition for students from overseas, and degree-level tuition. Most colleges also provide A level and GCSE revision courses during the Easter holidays. Further information on CIFE may be obtained from the CIFE website: www.cife.org.uk; Tel: 020 8767 8666; e-mail: enquiries@cife.org.uk

Part 7

Study Associations and the 'Learned Societies'

Study associations consist of people who wish to increase their knowledge of a particular subject or range of subjects; they may be professionals or amateurs. Some associations consist almost entirely of specialists (e.g. the Royal Statistical Society); others (e.g. the Royal Geographical Society and the Zoological Society of London) have a more general membership. The learned societies usually have two grades of membership: fellows and members. Some also admit group members (such as schools or libraries), known as corporate members, and junior associate, corresponding and overseas members, who pay lower subscriptions. Some also elect honorary fellows or members. The members of some societies may use designatory letters, but this does not mean that the holder is 'qualified' in the same sense as a doctor or a chartered accountant.

Membership of some learned societies is by election, and is commonly accepted as distinguishing the candidate by admission to an exclusive group. Candidates may be selected in respect of pre-eminence in their subject or in the public service. The chief associations of this type are the Royal Society (founded in 1660 and granted Royal Charters in 1662 and 1663), the Royal Academy of Arts (founded in 1768) and the British Academy (granted the Royal Charter in 1902).

The Royal Society (www.royalsociety.org)was established to improve 'natural knowledge' and is mainly concerned with pure and applied science and technology. Election to Fellowship (FRS) is regarded as one of the highest distinctions. The society elects Fellows, Foreign Members, Royal Fellows and Honorary Fellows. The Royal Academy (www.royalacademy.org.uk) was established to cultivate and improve the arts of painting, sculpture and architecture. There are two main grades of membership: Academicians (RAs) (including Senior Academicians) and the Honorary RAs, Honorary Fellows and Honorary Members. The British Academy (www.britac.ac.uk) is the UK's national academy for the humanities and the social sciences. It is the counterpart to the Royal Society that exists to serve the natural sciences. The Academy has Fellows (FBA), Corresponding Fellows and a small number of Honorary Fellows.

A list of learned societies and study associations can be found below.

OCCUPATIONAL ASSOCIATIONS

The occupational associations do not qualify practitioners but organize them. Some coordinate the activities of specialists and others promote the individual and collective interests of professionals working in a wider area. Both types also seek to safeguard the public interest and to offer an educational service to their members. The latter type of association is especially numerous among teachers (e.g. the National Union of Teachers (NUT), the Educational Institute of Scotland (EIS), NASWUT (the National Association of Schoolmasters/Union of Women Teachers) and the National Association of Head Teachers (NAHT)), and is represented in the medical profession by the British Medical Association.

LIST OF STUDY ASSOCIATIONS AND LEARNED SOCIETIES

This list largely excludes qualifying bodies, which are covered in Part 5. The date on the left is that of foundation or adoption of title.

Agriculture and related subjects

1926	Agricultural Economics Society (AES)	1839	Royal Agricultural Society of England
1952	British Agricultural History Society		(now part of Innovation for
1945	British Grassland Society		Agriculture)
1944	British Society of Animal Science	1882	Royal Forestry Society
	(BSAS)	1784	Royal Highland and Agricultural
1947	British Society of Soil Science		Society of Scotland (RHASS)
1921	Commonwealth Forestry Association	1804	Royal Horticultural Society (RHS)
	(CFA)	1854	Royal Scottish Forestry Society
1927	Herb Society of Great Britain	1904	Royal Welsh Agricultural Society
1925	Institute of Chartered Foresters (ICF)		(RWAS)
1938	Institution of Agricultural Engineers	1943	Society of Dairy Technology
	(IAgrE)	1945	The Soil Association
1947	International Fertiliser Society (IFS)		

Anthropology and related subjects

1963	African Studies Association of the UK	1972	Japan Foundation
	(ASAUK)	1891	Japan Society
1979	Association for the Study of Modern	1843	Royal Anthropological Institute of
	and Contemporary France		Great Britain and Ireland (the RAI)
1982	Association for the Study of Modern	1823	Royal Asiatic Society of Great Britain
	Italy		and Ireland
1946	Association of Social Anthropologists	1868	Royal Commonwealth Society (RCS)
	of the UK and Commonwealth	1901	Royal Society for Asian Affairs
1985	British Association for Irish Studies		(RSAA)
	(BAIS)	1936	Saltire Society
1974	British Association for Japanese	1977	Society for Caribbean Studies (SCS)
	Studies	1964	Society for Latin American Studies
1972	British Association for South Asian		(SLAS)
	Studies (BASAS)	1969	Society for Libyan Studies
1961	British Institute of Persian Studies	1983	Society for the Promotion of Byzantine
	(BIPS)		Studies
1973	British Society for Middle Eastern	1879	Society for the Promotion of Hellenic
	Studies (BRISMES)		Studies
1981	European Association for Jewish	1910	Society for the Promotion of Roman
	Studies (EAJS)		Studies
1878	Folklore Society	1969	University Association for
1943	Hispanic and Luso Brazilian Council		Contemporary European Studies
	(Canning House)		(UACES)
1974	International Association for the Study	1892	Viking Society for Northern Research
	of German Politics (IASGP)		

Archaeology and related subjects

1924	Ancient Monuments Society	1948	British Institute at Ankara (BIAA)
1979	Association for Environmental	1846	Cambrian Archaeological Association
	Archaeology (AEA)	1944	Council for British Archaeology
1843	British Archaeological Association	1838	Ecclesiological Society
	(BAA)	1882	Egypt Exploration Society
1996	British Epigraphy Society		

1855	London and Middlesex Archaeological Society (LAMAS)	1843	Royal Archaeological Institute
1865	Palestine Exploration Fund (PEF)	1967	Society for Post-Medieval Archaeology (SPMA)
1908	Prehistoric Society		

Art and Design

1974	Association of Art Historians (AAH)	1754	Royal Society for the Encouragement of Arts, Manufactures and Commerce (RSA)
1910	Contemporary Art Society		
1915	Design and Industries Association	1904	Royal Society of British Sculptors
1950	International Institute for Conservation of Historic and Artistic Works	1904	Royal Society of Marine Artists (RSMA)
		1895	Royal Society of Miniature Painters, Sculptors and Gravers
1888	National Society for Education in Art and Design (NSEAD)	1884	Royal Society of Painter-Printmakers
1898	Pastel Society	1891	Royal Society of Portrait Painters
1768	Royal Academy of Arts	1804	Royal Watercolour Society
1814	Royal Birmingham Society of Artists (RBSA)	1919	Society of Graphic Fine Art (SGFA)
		1952	Society of Portrait Sculptors
1883	Royal Institute of Oil-Painters (ROI)	1952	United Society of Artists
1831	Royal Institute of Painters in Watercolours	1955	William Morris Society
1826	Royal Scottish Academy of Art and Architecture		

Biology and related subjects

1936	Association for the Study of Animal Behaviour (ASAB)	1931	Society for Applied Microbiology (SfAM)
1904	Association of Applied Biologists (AAB)	1911	The Biochemical Society
		1913	The British Ecological Society (BES)
1968	Biomedical Engineering Society (BMES)	1896	The British Mycological Society
1836	Botanical Society of Scotland	1858	The British Ornithologists' Union (BOU)
1836	Botanical Society of the British Isles (BSBI)	1959	The British Society for Cell Biology (BSCB)
1896	British Bryological Society (BBS)	1933	The British Trust for Ornithology (BTO)
1929	Freshwater Biological Association (FBA)	1937	The Systematics Association
1889	Marine Biological Association (MBA)	1826	Zoological Society of London (ZSL)
1833	Royal Entomological Society		

Chemistry

1918	Oil and Colour Chemists' Association (OCCA)	1881	Society of Chemical Industry (SCI)
		1897	Society of Leather Technologists and Chemists (SLTC)
1980	Royal Society of Chemistry (RSC)		

Economics, Statistics and related subjects

1992	Chartered Association of Business Schools	1902	Royal Economic Society (RES)
1927	Economic History Society	1834	Royal Statistical Society (RSS)
1955	Institute of Economic Affairs (IEA)	1897	Scottish Economic Society (SES)

Engineering and related subjects

1997	Chartered Institute of Ergonomics and Human Factors	1866	Royal Aeronautical Society
1966	Concrete Society	1916	Royal Incorporation of Architects in Scotland (RIAS)
1946	Forum for the Built Environment (fbe) (formerly the Faculty of Building)	1860	Royal Institution of Naval Architects (RINA)
1997	Faculty of Party Wall Surveyors	1916	Society of Automotive Engineers (SAE)
1978	Institute of Concrete Technology (ICT)	1958	Society of Environmental Engineers
2006	Institution of Engineering and Technology (IET)	2003	The Energy Institute (EI)
1976	Royal Academy of Engineering (RAEng)	1899	Town and Country Planning Association (TCPA)

Geography, Geology and related subjects

1963	British Cartographic Society (BCS)	1971	Institution of Environmental Sciences (IES)
1949	British Geotechnical Society (BGA)	1876	Mineralogical Society of Great Britain and Ireland
1940	British Society of Rheology (BSR)		
1923	English Place-Name Society (EPNS) (University of Nottingham)	1847	Palaeontographical Society
1931	Gemmological Association of Great Britain (Gem-A)	1957	Paleontological Association
		1830	Royal Geographical Society (RGS)
1893	Geographical Association (GA)	1997	Royal Institute of Navigation (RIN)
1807	Geological Society of London	1884	Royal Scottish Geographical Society (RSGS)
1858	Geologists' Association (GA)		
1846	Hakluyt Society		

History and related subjects

1902	British Academy	1961	Institute of Heraldic and Genealogical Studies (IHGS)
1952	British Agricultural History Society (BAHS)	1921	Institute of Historical Research (IHR)
1888	British Record Society	1893	Jewish Historical Society of England
1932	British Records Association (BRA)	1964	London Record Society
1947	British Society for the History of Science (BSHS)	1920	Newcomen Society for the Study of the History of Engineering and Technology
1988	Centre for Metropolitan History (CMH)	1921	Oriental Ceramic Society (OCS)
1864	Early English Texts Society (EETS)	1868	Royal Historical Society (RHS)
1964	Furniture History Society (FHS)	1836	Royal Numismatic Society
1869	Harleian Society	1869	Royal Philatelic Society, London (RPSL)
1885	Huguenot Society of Great Britain and Ireland	1953	Scottish Genealogy Society
		1886	Scottish History Society

1897	Scottish Record Society	1707	Society of Antiquaries of London
1976	Social History Society	1780	Society of Antiquaries of Scotland
1921	Society for Army Historical Research	1956	Society of Architectural Historians in Great Britain (SAHGB)
1910	Society for Nautical Research		
1967	Society for Renaissance Studies	1911	Society of Genealogists
1970	Society for the Social History of Medicine (SSHM)	1906	The Historical Association
		1958	Victorian Society

Languages

1883	Alliance Française	1910	Chartered Institute of Linguists (CIOL)
1891	An Comunn Gaidhealach		
1981	Association for French Language Studies (AFLS)	1991	Instituto Cervantes
		1964	National Association for the Teaching of English (NATE)
1932	Association for German Studies in Great Britain and Ireland (AGS)		
		1993	University Council of Modern Languages (UCML)
1990	Association for Language Learning (ALL)		
		1988	Women in German Studies (WIGS)

Law

1958	British Institute of International and Comparative Law (BIICL)	1920	Royal Institute of International Affairs (Chatham House)
1972	Intellectual Property Bar Association	1965	Scottish Law Commission
1922	Law Society of Northern Ireland	1887	Selden Society (Queen Mary University)
1949	Law Society of Scotland		

Literature and Arts

1959	Yr Academi Gymreig (The Welsh Academy)	1904	Classical Association
		2009	Deans and Leaders of Arts, Social Sciences and Humanities (DASSH-UK)
1973	Alliance of Literary Societies (ALS)		
1969	Art Libraries Society (ARLIS/UK & Ireland)		
		1902	Dickens Fellowship
1970	Association for Scottish Literary Studies (ASLS)	1890	Edinburgh Bibliographical Society
		1906	English Association (University of Leicester)
1989	Association of Independent Libraries (AIL)		
		1886	Francis Bacon Society Inc
1892	Bibliographical Society	1960	H. G. Wells Society
1992	British Association for Information and Library Education and Research (BAILER)	1997	Historical Novel Society
		1973	Joseph Conrad Society
		1997	Leeds Philosophical and Literary Society
1975	British Comparative Literature Association (BCLA)		
		1906	Malone Society
1933	British Film Institute (BFI)	1781	Manchester Literary and Philosophical Society
1960	British Society of Aesthetics (BSA)		
1893	Bronte Society	1995	Philip Larkin Society
1949	Cambridge Bibliographical Society	1842	Philological Society
1935	Charles Lamb Society (CLB)		

1909	Poetry Society	2004	Society of College, National and
1820	Royal Society of Literature		University Libraries (SCONUL)
1884	Society of Authors	1968	Thomas Hardy Society

Management

1986	British Academy of Management (BAM)

Mathematics and Physics

1924	Astronomical Society of Edinburgh (ASE)	1927	British Institute of Radiology (BIR)
		1933	British Interplanetary Society (BIS)
1890	British Astronomical Association (BAA)	1871	Mathematical Association (MA)
		1820	Royal Astronomical Society (RAS)
1966	British Biophysical Society (BBS)	1850	Royal Meteorological Society (RMetS)

Medicine (including Psychology)

1887	Anatomical Society (AS)	1948	British Geriatrics Society (BGS)
1957	Association for Child and Adolescent Mental Health (ACAMH)	1832	British Medical Association (BMA)
		1950	British Neuropathological Society (BNS)
1957	Association for the Study of Medical Education (ASME)	1953	British Occupational Hygiene Society (BOHS)
1932	Association of Anaesthetists of GB and Ireland (AAGBI)	1965	British Orthodontic Society (BOS)
1933	Association of British Neurologists (ABN)	1918	British Orthopaedic Association (BOA)
1953	Association of Clinical Biochemistry and Laboratory Medicine (ACB)	1901	British Psychological Society (BPS)
		1948	British Society for Allergy and Clinical Immunology (BSACI)
1927	Association of Clinical Pathologists (ACP)	2011	British Association for Cytopathology (BAC)
1920	Association of Surgeons of GB and Ireland (ASGBI)	1937	British Society of Gastroenterology (BSG)
1971	BASO – The Association for Cancer Surgery	1960	British Society for Haematology (BSH)
1959	British Academy for Forensic Science (BAFS)	1947	British Society for Research on Ageing (BSRA)
2003	British Association for Sexual Health and HIV (BASHH)	1945	British Thoracic Society (BTS)
		2014	Chartered Institute of Ergonomics and Human Factors
1977	British Association of Clinical Anatomists (BACA)	1959	Chartered Society of Forensic Sciences
1950	British Association of Forensic Medicine (BAFM)	1934	Diabetes UK
		1946	Experimental Psychology Society (EPS)
1962	British Association of Oral Surgeons (BAOS)	1950	Faculty of Homeopathy
2008	British Association of Otohinolaryngology (ENT UK)	1819	Hunterian Society
		2014	Institute of Osteopathy (iO)
1954	British Association of Paediatric Surgeons (BAPS)	1924	Institute of Psychoanalysis
		1969	Institute of Occupational Medicine (IOM)
1945	British Association of Urological Surgeons (BAUS)		

1964	Institute of Pharmacy Management (IPM)	2008	Royal Society for Public Health (RSPH)
1773	Medical Society of London	1805	Royal Society of Medicine (RSM)
1901	Medico-Legal Society	1907	Royal Society of Tropical Medicine and Hygiene (RSTMH)
1941	Nutrition Society		
1906	Pathological Society of Great Britain and Ireland	1946	Society for Endocrinology
		1950	Society for Reproduction and Fertility (SRF)
1875	Royal Environmental Health Institute of Scotland (REHIS)	1884	Society for the Study of Addiction (SSA)
1734	Royal Medical Society		
1931	Royal Pharmaceutical Society of Great Britain (RPS)	1926	Society of British Neurological Surgeons

Music

1977	Alkan Society	1888	Plainsong and Medieval Music Society (PMMS)
1979	British Music Society		
1971	Chopin Society	1874	Royal Musical Association (RMA)
1932	English Folk Dance and Song Society (efdss)	1955	Welsh Music Guild
1882	Incorporated Society of Musicians (ISM)		

Philosophy

1880	Aristotelian Society	1781	Manchester Literary and Philosophical Society
1984	British Society for the History of Philosophy (BSHP)		
		1913	Philosophical Society of England
1819	Cambridge Philosophical Society	1925	Royal Institute of Philosophy
1990	Friedrich Nietzsche Society (FNS)	1802	Royal Philosophical Society of Glasgow
1979	Hegel Society of Great Britain (HSGB)		

Politics

1975	British International Studies Association (BISA)	1987	Institute of Welsh Affairs
		1974	International Association for the Study of German Politics (ISAGP)
1951	David Davies Memorial Institute of International Studies (Aberystwyth University)	1950	Political Studies Association (PSA)
		1868	Royal Commonwealth Society
1884	Electoral Reform Society (ERS)	1920	Royal Institute of International Affairs (Chatham House)
1945	Federal Trust for Education and Research		

Science general

1831	British Science Association (BSA)	1799	Royal Institution of Great Britain (Ri)
1947	British Society for the History of Science (BSHS)	1660	Royal Society
		1783	Royal Society of Edinburgh
1960	British Society for the Philosophy of Science (BSPS)		

Theology and Religious Studies

1908	Baptist Historical Society	1981	European Association for Jewish Studies (EAJS)
1954	British Association for the Study of Religions (BASR)	1903	Friends Historical Society
1904	Canterbury and York Society	1972	United Reformed Church History Society (Westminster College)
1904	Catholic Record Society		
1961	Ecclesiastical History Society (EHS)	1893	Wesley Historical Society

General Index

Note: In addition to the abbreviations listed at the beginning of the book, the following are used throughout the index; FE – Further Education; HE – Higher Education. Universities are listed under locations eg: Aberdeen, University of